D1188502

Handbook of Applied Behavior Analysis
Social and Instructional Processes

Handbook of Applied Behavior Analysis

Social and Instructional Processes

Edited by

A. Charles Catania
and
Thomas A. Brigham

IRVINGTON PUBLISHERS, INC., NEW YORK

Distributed by HALSTED PRESS, Division of
JOHN WILEY & SONS, INC.
NEW YORK   LONDON   TORONTO   SYDNEY

ELLSWORTH COMMUNITY COLLEGE
LEARNING RESOURCE CENTER
Iowa Falls, Iowa 50126

79-53 3 70   Accession No.

150.194
H191

Copyright © 1978 by Irvington Publishers, Inc.

All rights reserved. No part of this book may be reproduced in any manner whatever, including information storage or retrieval, in whole or in part (except for brief quotations in critical articles or reviews), without written permission from the publisher. For information, write to Irvington Publishers, Inc., 551 Fifth Avenue, New York, New York 10017.

Distributed by Halsted Press
A division of John Wiley & Sons, Inc., New York

Library of Congress Cataloging in Publication Data

Main entry under title:
Handbook of applied behavior analysis.

Includes bibliographical references and indexes.
1. Behaviorism. I. Catania, A. Charles.
II. Brigham, Thomas A.
BF 199.H35   150'.19'43   77-20991
ISBN 0-470-99347-2

Printed in the United States of America

The following are all copyrighted by the Society for the Experimental Analysis of Behavior, Inc. Reprinted by permission.

Chapter 3, Figure 1: Hall, R. V., Fox, R., Willard, D., Goldsmith, L., Emerson, M., Owen, M., Davis, F., & Porcia, E. The teacher as observer and experimenter in the modification of disputing and talking-out behaviors. *Journal of Applied Behavior Analysis,* 1971, 4, 142.
Chapter 3, Figure 2: Pierce, C. H., & Risley, T. R. Recreation as a reinforcer: Increasing membership and decreasing disruptions in an urban recreation center. *Journal of Applied Behavior Analysis,* 1974, 7, 409.
Chapter 3, Figure 3: Hall, R. V., Cristler, C., Cranston, S. S., & Tucker, B. Teachers and parents as researchers using multiple baselines. *Journal of Applied Behavior Analysis,* 1970, 3, 251.
Chapter 3, Figure 6: Dietz, S. M., & Repp, A. C. Decreasing classroom misbehavior through the use of DRL schedules of reinforcement. *Journal of Applied Behavior Analysis,* 1973, 6, 461.
Chapter 3, Figure 7: Hermann, J. A., de Montes, A. I., Dominguez, B., Montes, F., & Hopkins, B. L. Effects of bonuses for punctuality on the tardiness of industrial workers. *Journal of Applied Behavior Analysis,* 1973, 6, 567.
Chapter 3, Figure 4: Allen, G. J. Case study: Implementation of behavior modification techniques in summer camp settings. *Behavior Therapy,* 1973, 4, 573.
Chapter 3, Figure 5: McCullough, J. P., Cornell, J. E., McDaniel, M. H., & Mueller, R. K. Utilization of the simultaneous treatment design to improve student behavior in a first-grade classroom. *Journal of Consulting and Clinical Psychology,* 1974, 42, 291. Copyright © 1974 by the American Psychological Association. Reprinted by permission.

Since this page cannot accommodate all the copyright notices, the pages that follow constitute an extension of the copyright page.

Chapter 5, Figure 1:   Goldiamond, I. Perception, language and conceptualization rules. In B. Kleinmuntz (Ed.), *Problem solving: Research, method, and theory.* New York: Wiley, 1966, p. 190.
Chapter 5, Figure 2:   Whitehurst, G. J., & Novak, G. Modeling, imitation training, and the acquisition of sentence phrases. *Journal of Experimental Child Psychology,* 1973, **16**, 339.

Chapter 7, Figures 1-3:   Hake, D. F., & Vukelich, R. Analysis of the control exerted by a complex cooperation procedure. *Journal of the Experimental Analysis of Behavior,* 1973, **19**, 5, 8, 12.
Chapter 7, Figures 6-8 and Tables 2 and 3:   Hake, D. F., Vukelich, R. & Olvera, D. The measurement of sharing and cooperation as equity effects and some relationships between them. *Journal of the Experimental Analysis of Behavior,* 1975, **23**, 65, 67, 69, 71, 72.
Chapter 7, Figure 7:   Hake, D. F., Vukelich, R. & Olvera, D. The measurement of sharing and cooperation as equity effects and some relationship between them. *Journal of the Experimental Analysis of Behavior,* 1975, **23**, 67.

Chapter 8:   Rachlin, Howard, Self-control. *Behaviorism.* 1974, 2, 94-108, Fig. 1-3 and text material. Reprinted by permission, *Behaviorism,* Reno, Nevada.

Chapter 9, Figure 1:   Salzinger, K., Portnoy, S., & Feldman, R. S. The effect of approximation to the statistical structure of English on the emission of verbal responses, *Journal of Experimental Psychology,* 1962, **64**, 55, Fig. 2. Copyright © 1962 by the American Psychological Association. Reprinted by permission.
Chapter 9, Figure 2:   Salzinger, K., Portnoy, S., Pisoni, D. B., & Feldman, R. S. The immediacy hypothesis and response-produced stimuli in schizophrenic speech. *Journal of Abnormal Psychology,* 1970, **76**, Fig. 1. Copyright © 1970 by the American Psychological Association. Reprinted by permission.

The following in Chapter 10 are copyrighted by Science Research Associates, Inc. Used by permission of the publisher.

Chapter 10:   Becker, W. Englemann, S., & Thomas, D. The corrective reading program. In *Teaching 2: Cognitive Learning and Instruction.* Figure pages 64, 65, 68, 80, 143, 147 & 164.
Chapter 10:   Engelmann, S., Becker, W., Carnine, L., Meyers, L., Becker, J., Johnson, G. *Corrective Reading Program,* 184, text material.

Chapter 11, Figure 1:   Resnick, L. B., Wang, M. C., & Kaplan, J. Task analysis in curriculum design: A hierarchically sequenced introductory mathematics curriculum. *Journal of Applied Behavior Analysis,* 1973, **6**, 688. Copyright © 1973 by the Society for the Experimental Analysis of Behavior, Inc. Reprinted by permission.
Chapter 11, Figures 2 & 9:   Resnick, L. B., & Beck, I. L. Designing instruction in reading. In J. T. Guthrie (Ed.), *Aspects of reading acquisition.* Baltimore, Md.: John Hopkins University Press, 1077, in press, Figures 1 and 5.
Chapter 11, Figures 3 & 4:   Resnick, L. B., Woods, S. S., & Groen, G. J. An experimental test of five process models for subtraction. *Journal of Educational Psychology,* 1975, **67**(1), 19. Copyright © 1975 by American Psychological Association. Reprinted by permission.
Chapter 11, Figure 5:   Resnick, L. B. Task analysis in instructional design: Some cases for mathematics. In D. Klahr (Ed.), *Cognition and instruction.* Hillsdale, N.J.: Erlbaum Associates, 1976, Figure 8, 73.
Chapter 11, Figure 6:   Bruner, J. S. Some theorems of instruction illustrated with reference to mathematics. *NSSE Yearbook,* 1964, **63**(1), 324, 325.
Chapter 11, Figures 7 & 8:   Resnick, L. B., & Glaser, R. Problem solving and intelligence. In L. B. Resnick (Ed.), *The nature of intelligence.* Hillsdale, N.J.: Erlbaum Associates, 1976, pp. 212 and 218.

Chapter 12, Figures 1 & 3:   Liberman, A. M., *et al.* Perception of the speech code. *Psychological Review,* 1967, **74**, 436 & 432. Copyright © 1967 by the American Psychological Association.
Chapter 12, Figure 2:   Liberman, A. M. The grammars of speech and language. *Cognitive Psychology,* 1970, 1, 314. Copyright © 1970, Academic Press.

Chapter 13, Figure 1:   Barlow, John A. *Stimulus and response.* New York: Harper & Row, 1968, 55-56.

Chapter 14, Figure 1:   McMichael, J. S., & Corey, J. R. *Journal of Applied Behavior Analysis,* 1969, **2**, 81. Copyright © 1969 by the Society for the Experimental Analysis of Behavior, Inc. Reprinted by permission.

Chapter 14, Figure 2:   Lloyd, K. E., McMullin, W. E., & Fox, R. A. Rate of completing unit tests as a function of student-pacing and of instructor-pacing. In T. A. Brigham, R. Hawkins, J. Scott, & T. McLaughlin (Eds.), *Behavior analysis in education: Self-control and reading,* Dubuque, Iowa: Kendall/Hunt, 1976.

Chapter 14, Figure 3:   Johnston, J. M. & O'Neill, G. The analysis of performance criteria-defining course grades as a determinant of college student academic performance. *Journal of Applied Behavior Analysis,* 1973, **6**, 265. Copyright © 1973 by the Society for the Experimental Analysis of Behavior, Inc. Reprinted by permission.

Chapter 19, Figure 1:   Feallock, R., & Miller, L. K. The design and evaluation of a worksharing system for experimental group living. *Journal of Applied Behavior Analysis,* 1976, **9**, 282-284, Figure 1-3. Copyright © 1976 by the Society for the Experimental Analysis of Behavior, Inc. Reprinted by permission.

Table of Contents

Section III: Social and Educational Applications

Acknowledgments

The following publishers and journals have kindly granted permission to reproduce or adapt previously published figures, tables, and text material to which they hold the copyright:

Academic Press, one figure from *Behavior Therapy*; one figure from *Cognitive Psychology*; one figure from the *Journal of Experimental Child Psychology*.

American Psychological Association, one figure from the *Journal of Consulting and Clinical Psychology*; two figures from the *Journal of Educational Psychology*; one figure from *Psychological Review*.

Harper & Row Publishers, Inc., text material from *Stimulus and Response*, by John A. Barlow.

International Reading Association, text material from *Reading Research Quarterly*.

John Wiley & Sons, Inc., one figure from *Problem Solving: Research, Method, and Theory*, edited by B. Kleinmuntz.

Kendall/Hunt Publishing Company, one figure from *Behavior Analysis in Education: Self-Control and Reading*, edited by Tom A. Brigham, R. Hawkins, J. Scott, and T. F. McLaughlin.

Lawrence Erlbaum Associates, one figure from *Cognition and Instruction*, edited by D. Klahr; two figures from *The Nature of Intelligence*, edited by L. B. Resnick.

National Society for the Study of Education, two figures from *NSSE Yearbook*, 1964.

Science Research Associates, Inc., text material from *Corrective Reading Program*, by Siegfried Engelmann, Wesley Becker, Linda Carnine, Linda Meyers, Julie Becker, and Gary Johnson; text material from *Teaching 2 Cognitive Learning and Instruction*, by Wesley C. Becker, Siegfried Engelmann, and Don R. Thomas.

Society for the Experimental Analysis of Behavior, eight figures from the *Journal of Applied Behavior Analysis*; six figures and two tables from *Journal of the Experimental Analysis of Behavior*.

Willard F. Day, three figures and text material from *Behaviorism*.

Both editors were involved in all stages of the book from the initial selection of contributors to the final steps of proofreading; the order of listing is therefore necessarily arbitrary.

We particularly thank Ronald Cohen of Irvington Publishers for his professional handling of the various stages of production. We also thank the contributors for their patience and cooperation. Among others who have been involved in the book, we must especially acknowledge Jon S. Bailey, D. W. Carnine, and Brian Iwata. Special thanks to Judith Randolph, Jill Himmer and Geraldine Hansen for their expert secretarial skills and assistance. The list of those who contributed suggestions and help along the way ranges from our own families to individuals at many institutions across the country. Any list we could prepare would be bound to involve omission, and so we choose this sweeping note of appreciation. Any formal statement would in any case be inadequate in response to the enthusiasm, encouragement, and energy given by those who in various ways participated in this project. We hope the final product justifies the effort that so many have put into it.

Thomas A. Brigham   A. Charles Catania
Pullman, Washington   Columbia, Maryland

Contributors

Donald M. Baer (Chapter 1), Ph. D., University of Chicago, is Professor in the Department of Human Development at the University of Kansas. He has written numerous articles on the behavioral analysis of children's responses and co-authored with Sidney W. Bijou a series of important volumes on child development. His major professional interest continues to be the analysis of children's behavior.

Wesley C. Becker (Chapter 10), Ph.D., Stanford University, is Professor of Special Education at the University of Oregon. He spent fifteen years in psychology at the University of Illinois. In addition to research on classroom management, he has published two books for parents (*Parents Are Teachers* and *Successful Parenthood*) and three for teachers (*Teaching 1, Classroom Management; Teaching 2, Cognitive Learning and Instruction;* and *Teaching 3, Evaluation of Instruction*). With Engelmann, he co-directs the Direct Instruction Model, a Follow Through program for disadvantaged children in Kindergarten through third grade.

Thomas A. Brigham (Co-editor, Introduction, and Chapter 8), Ph.D., University of Kansas, is Associate Professor of Psychology and Director of the Center for Applied Behavioral Research at Washington State University. He has written extensively about applying operant procedures to problems of instruction in elementary schools. He has co-edited a conference volume, *Behavior analysis in education*, on self-control and reading, and has served on the Board of Editors of the *Journal of Applied Behavior Analysis*. His current interest is in teaching principles of behavior and self-control procedures to elementary school children.

Don Bushell, Jr. (Chapter 15), Ph.D., Sociology, Washington University, is Professor of Human Development at the University of Kansas. He is the former director of the Behavior Analysis Follow Through program and has written extensively on applying behavioral procedures in schools, including the book *Classroom behavior: A little book for teachers.*. His current professional interests are in a behaviorally engineered alternative school, the Century School, and development of a system to evaluate quality schools.

A. Charles Catania (Co-editor, Introduction), Ph.D., Harvard University, is Professor of Psychology at the University of Maryland Baltimore County. He has published articles on basic operant phenomena such as concurrent operants and schedule interactions. He is past Editor of the *Journal of the Experimental Analysis of Behavior* and has edited a volume on operant research, *Contemporary research in operant behavior*. His current professional interests include reinforcement schedules, the experimental and theoretical analysis of language, and self-control.

Siegfried Engelmann (Chapter 10) is Professor of Special Education at the University of Oregon. His work at the University of Illinois on teaching the disadvantaged led to the book, *Teaching the disadvantaged child in the preschool* (with Carl Berieter). Since 1968, with Becker, he has managed Follow Through programs for 10,000 disadvantaged children each year in twenty communities across the country. The instructional units in this program, called DISTAR, were designed by Engelmann. Engelmann has published a book for teachers, *Preventing failure in the primary grades*, and one on social action for parents, *Your child can succeed*, and has co-authored the series: *Teaching 1, Classroom Management; Teaching 2, Cognitive Learning and Instruction;* and *Teaching 3, Evaluation of Instruction*. His current research includes using a tactual-vocorder to teach the deaf.

James Filipczak (Chapter 16), M.S., Design-Science, Southern Illinois University, is Program Director of the PREP Project and Director of the Center for Education and Training, Institute for Behavioral Research, Inc. His professional interests are in application of principles of social learning theory and environmental design to development of social and academic skill in exceptional students. Specific research interests focus on developing and evaluating environmental and training program variables with highly disruptive and academically deficient adolescents.

Dean L. Fixsen (Chapter 18), Ph.D., University of Kansas, is a Research Fellow and Assistant to the Youth Care Director, The Boys Town Center for the Study of Youth Development, Father Flanagan's Boys' Home. He remains affiliated with the University of Kansas, is an Associate Editor of the *Journal of Applied Behavioral Analysis* and has written extensively on applied research with youths. His current professional interests are in developing and disseminating treatment programs for youths in trouble.

Wendy W. Ford (Chapter 11), B.A., Oberlin College, has worked at the Learning Research and Development Center, University of Pittsburgh, as a research assistant, writer, and editor.

Robert M. Friedman (Chapter 16), Ph.D., Florida State University, is a Research Associate, Co-Principal Investigator of the PREP Project, and Assistant to the President for Academic Affairs and Planning, Experimental College, Institute for Behavioral Research, Inc. His professional interests, research on the application of social learning principles to social and educational problems, include the development of behavior change programs within family and school contexts, with particular emphasis on problems of delinquency and child abuse.

Jacob L. Gewirtz (Chapter 4), Ph.D., The State University of Iowa, is a senior research scientist with the National Institute of Mental Health, Bethesda. He has taught at the University of Chicago and has been visiting professor at the Hebrew University of Jerusalem and the University of Hawaii. He is also adjunct Professor of Psychology at the University of Maryland Baltimore County. He has served on the editorial boards of *Child Development*, the *Journal of Applied Behavior Analysis*, the *Journal of Autism and Childhood Schizophrenia*, and *Youth and Society*. His interests include mechanisms of social learning and development, early experience, ethological contributions to learned behavior, observational and imitative learning, and the applications of learning conceptions to important life conditions.

Don F. Hake (Chapter 7), Ph.D., Southern Illinois University, is currently Professor and Coordinator of the Behavior Analysis Program in the Psychology Department at West Virginia University. Social behavior in children and energy conservation are his major research interests. A Fellow of the American Psychological Association, he has served as Associate Editor of *Journal of the Experimental Analysis of Behavior* and on the editorial board of the *Journal of Applied Behavior Analysis*.

Jay B. Heckler (Chapter 17), M.A., University of Florida, is a coordinator of laboratory operations at the Personalized Learning Center and a doctoral student in the experimental and applied analysis of behavior at the University of Florida. His research interests are in complex systems of concurrent schedules in higher education, and conditioned reinforcement in human affairs.

Alan E. Kazdin (Chapter 3), Ph.D., Northwestern University, is Associate Professor of Psychology at the Pennsylvania State University. He is Associate Editor for the *Journal of Applied Behavior Analysis* and *Behavior Therapy*. He has written extensively on token systems and on applied behavioral research in general and is the author of *Behavior Modification in Applied Settings*. He has conducted research on applying operant techniques in classroom and institutional settings, and on evaluating imagery-based behavior therapy techniques. Specific interests include token reinforcement, generalization and response maintenance techniques, vicarious reinforcement, response cost, assertion training, and covert modeling.

Alice Lies (Chapter 19), B.A., University of Kansas, is a doctoral student in the Department of Human Development and a research associate for the Experimental Living Project at the University of Kansas. In the Project, she has designed the food program; the instructional package training program for work inspectors; and the beginnings of a consumer evaluation instrument. Her professional interest is in developing a behaviorally engineered supportive community.

Kenneth E. Lloyd (Chapter 14), Ph.D., Ohio State University, is Professor and Chair of the Psychology Department at Drake University. A Fellow in the American Psychological Association and in the Psychology Section of the American Association of the Advancement of Science, he serves on the board of editors of several psychological journals. His professional interests and publications include behavioral analysis in higher education, energy conservation and deviant behavior. He has also published experimental analyses of schedule interactions with infrahuman behavior.

L. Keith Miller (Chapter 19), Ph.D., Sociology, University of Illinois, is Professor of Human Development at the University of Kansas. He met N. H. Azrin during his first teaching position in the Department of Sociology at Southern Illinois University. A six-month series of late-night arguments, all of which he lost, made him an enthusiast of operant psychology and its implications for sociology. After his teaching on the implications of operant psychology for sociology was not well received by the Department of Sociology at Washington University in St. Louis, he returned to work with N. H. Azrin at Anna State Hospital. In 1968, he joined the Department of Human Development at the University of Kansas. He has written on community self-help groups and personalized instruction, and is the author of *Principles of Everyday Behavior Analysis*. The Experimental Living Project, christened in January, 1972, in a house purchased by a non-profit corporation designed to provide low cost cooperative housing for University of Kansas students, has been entirely self-funded, receiving no grants.

K. Daniel O'Leary (Chapter 6), Ph.D., University of Illinois, is Professor of Psychology at the State University of New York at Stony Brook. He has conducted research on and written extensively about behavior analysis and behavior therapy with problem children. Co-author of *Behavior Therapy* and co-editor of *Classroom Management*, he is also Editor of the *Journal of Applied Behavior Analysis* and is on the editorial boards of several other journals. His current professional interests include self-management procedures for disruptive and hyperactive children and the behavioral analysis of children's behavior problems.

Dennis R. Olvera (Chapter 7), Ph.D., Southern Illinois University, is Staff Psychologist at W. A. Howe Developmental Center, Tinley Park, Illinois. His major professional interests are applied behavior analysis with special populations and behavior analysis of social interactions.

Henry S. Pennypacker (Chapter 17), Ph.D., Duke University, is Professor of Psychology at the University of Florida. He has led the development of personalized instructional systems at the university level, and has served on the editorial boards of the *Journal of Personalized Instruction, Journal of Applied Behavior Analysis* and *People Watching..* His areas of interest are experimental and applied analysis of cybernetic systems of service delivery, especially instruction, measurement of human behavior, and validation of educational practices.

Susanne F. Pennypacker (Chapter 17), B.A., University of Florida, is Director of the Personalized Learning Center, University of Florida. Her professional interests are cybernetic systems of instruction and administration in higher education, and the science of communication and control theory as applied to complex institutions.

Elery L. Phillips (Chapter 18), Ph.D., University of Kansas, is Director of Youth Care, Father Flanagan's Boys' Home. He is a member of the editorial board of the *Journal of Applied Behavior Analysis* and has written extensively on the development of the Achievement Place Program. He served as Chairman of the Board of Directors of Achievement Place from 1973 to 1975. His professional interests are developing and evaluating special environments for children and youths.

Howard Rachlin (Chapter 8), Ph.D., Harvard University, is Professor of Psychology at the State University of New York at Stony Brook. Consulting editor for *Behaviorism* and *Journal of Experimental Psychology* and former associate editor of *Journal of the Experimental Analysis of Behavior*, he has written *Introduction to Modern Behaviorism* and *Behavior and Learning.* His main areas of interest are self-control, experimental economics, behavioral contrast, and choice behavior.

Lauren Resnick (Chapter 11), Ed.D., Harvard University, is Associate Professor of Psychology, University of Pittsburgh. She joined the Learning Research and Development Center as Research Associate in 1966 and has been Associate Director since 1973. She has been a National Institute of Education Visiting Fellow and a Fellow at the Center for Advanced Studies in the Behavioral Sciences, Stanford. Her current professional interests are in experimental and developmental psychology, and specifically in applying behavioral science to educational policy and practice.

Paul Rozin (Chapter 12), Ph.D., Biology and Psychology, Harvard University, is Professor of Psychology at the University of Pennsylvania. His early research dealt with how rats select foods of nutritional value (specific hungers) and, later, how they avoid harmful foods. This work led to research on the problem of special types of learning, and the evolution of intelligence. His collaboration with Lila Gleitman, on the acquisition of reading, grew out of the conception of language learning as a specially adapted form of learning in the human species. The work with Lila Gleitman included experimental studies, theoretical papers, and the development of *Syllabary*, a reading curriculum. Most recently, he has returned to food selection and is now studying problems of human culinary practices; specifically, why people add characteristic flavorings to their food.

Kurt Salzinger (Chapter 9), Ph.D., Columbia University, is Principal Research Scientist and Head of the Section of Behavior Analysis and Modification at the New York State Psychiatric Institute, and Professor of Psychology at the Polytechnic Institute of New York. A Fellow of the American Psychological Association, the American Association for the Advancement of Science, and the New York Academy of Sciences, he is a recipient of the Stratton Award of the American Psychopathological Association. An active contributor to the research literature, he has authored or edited five books and over sixty papers. His major interests are in applying behavior theory to the analysis of language, abnormal phenomena, and such other areas as developmental psychology, problems in highway safety, and urban problems.

Robert E. Silverman (Chapter 13), Ph.D., Indiana University, is Professor of Psychology at New York University. He is interested in the psychology of learning, with particular emphasis on applications to education. This interest has involved him in consultantships with a variety of educational organizations here and abroad, including UNESCO. He is a member of several professional associations, and has authored journal articles, *How to write a program*, and an introductory text, *Psychology*.

Stephanie B. Stolz (Chapter 20), Ph.D., University of Washington, formerly Chief of the Small Grants Section, National Institute of Mental Health, is now Director of the Division of Alcohol, Drug Abuse and Mental Health, HEW Regional Office, Kansas City. She did post-doctoral work in behavior modification with Donald M. Baer and Montrose M. Wolf. A Fellow of the American Psychological Association, she was a member of the American Psychiatric Association Task Force on Behavior Therapy and the American Psychological Association Commission on Behavior Modification. She has served as Chair of the Board of Directors and President of the Society for the Experimental Analysis of Behavior, and as Secretary-Treasurer of the Association for Advancement of Behavior Therapy. Her professional interests are in the ethics of research and therapy, and more broadly in applied behavior analysis.

Grover J. Whitehurst (Chapter 5), Ph.D., University of Illinois, is Associate Professor of Psychology and Head of the Program in Developmental Psychology at the State University of New York at Stony Brook. He was Senior Lecturer in Psychology at the University of New South Wales during 1974-75. His research interests involve the relations between basic learning processes and the acquisition of complex skills such as language and conceptualization. He has published many technical articles and reviews, and is author (with R. Vasta) of *Child Behavior*. A member of the American Psychological Association and the Society for Research in Child Development, he has served on the editorial boards of the *Journal of Experimental Child Psychology* and the *Journal of Applied Behavior Analysis*.

Montrose M. Wolf (Chapter 18), Ph.D., Arizona State University, is Professor of Human Development at the University of Kansas. He is a past Editor of the *Journal of Applied Behavior Analysis* and currently is on the Board of Editors of that journal. He was a Review Committee member of the Center for the Study of Crime and Delinquency, and a Visiting Professor at the Menninger School of Psychiatry. He has written many articles and chapters on applied behavioral programs for troubled children. His continuing interest is in research with children with behavior problems.

Michael D. Zeiler (Chapter 2), Ph.D., New School for Social Research, is Professor of Psychology at Emory University. He has published extensively in child development as well as in the experimental analysis of behavior. He is current Editor of the *Journal of the Experimental Analysis of Behavior*. His major area of interest is in the experimental and theoretical analysis of reinforcement schedules.

THOMAS A. BRIGHAM and
A. CHARLES CATANIA

Introduction

The Behavior Analysis Technology

Many critics of modern science and technology have argued that the advances of the physical sciences have outstripped man's ability to deal with their products. As a consequence, there is a growing trend toward rejecting science and technology. An alternative view is that an equally effective social science must be developed. Skinner and others have championed this position over the years, some would say with dubious results. But if the physical sciences are used as a model, it becomes clear that it is not basic science but technology that makes large-scale contact with the public. Similarly, the solution of large social problems requires not a behavioral science per se but a behavioral technology. This book documents the beginnings of just such a technology: behavior analysis.

Technology is often viewed as something apart from science. It is possible, however, to analyze technology as the integration of basic research, applied research, and field application. The development of technology can be viewed as consisting of three stages: (1) the development of the foundation principles or basic science, (2) the development of procedures or demonstrations, and (3) the development of techniques of field application (Bushell & Brigham, 1971). Behavior analysis is progressing rapidly through these stages.

BEHAVIOR ANALYSIS: AN EMERGING TECHNOLOGY

The foundations of the behavior-analysis technology are the principles of operant theory, or the experimental analysis of behavior. The applied analysis of behavior developed out of experimental analysis as investigators attempted to apply laboratory procedures to the modification of human be-

1

havior. At first these efforts were designed to demonstrate that the principles of operant behavior applied to human behavior as well. But after a number of such demonstrations, emphasis shifted (Skinner, 1953a), and operant principles were used to analyze and modify important behavior. In 1965 Ayllon and Azrin published "The Measurement and Reinforcement of the Behavior of Psychotics." This paper exemplifies the development of applied behavior analysis. The investigators applied rigorous research methods to the field analysis of important human responses. At the same time, other researchers were conducting relevant studies (e.g., Birnbrauer, Wolf, Kidder, & Tague, 1965; H.L. Cohen, Filipczak, & Bis, 1968). These studies were powerful and exciting demonstrations that principles of behavior derived from basic research did operate in the real world, just as Skinner, Keller, Bijou, and others had predicted.

It is impossible to recapture the excitement that each new study generated as faculty and students rushed off to replicate and extend procedures to new populations or settings. Soon there were sufficient active investigators across the country generating applied behavioral research of high quality that the Society for the Experimental Analysis of Behavior decided to publish a new journal devoted exclusively to applied research. In the Spring of 1968 the new journal, *The Journal of Applied Behavior Analysis*, began publication. In the first issue the editorial policy of the journal was established as "the publication of original reports of experimental research involving applications of the analysis of behavior to problems of social importance." This policy was further elaborated by Baer, Wolf, and Risley (1968):

Thus, in summary, an applied behavior analysis will make obvious the importance of the behavior changed, its quantitative characteristics, the experimental manipulations which analyze with clarity what was responsible for the change, the technologically exact description of all procedures contributing to that change, the effectiveness of those procedures in making sufficient change for value, and the generality of that change [p. 97].

Many chapters in this volume continue to share these characteristics; in addition, however, there is something new that can be called programmatic replication. Programmatic replication is the essence of a well-developed technology in which integrated systems of procedures are replicated with large groups of people. This is the final step in the development of a technology of field application. For instance, the experimental operation of a token system in a laboratory classroom is an example of applied research, while the operation of token systems in classrooms around the country is an example of field application. The first requires knowledge of the basic science and the procedures of applied research; the second requires knowledge of the outcomes of applied research, the procedures of applied research, and the procedures of program delivery. Program delivery covers a wide range of procedures, essentially summarized as fitting the product to the needs of the consumer; i.e., the products of applied research must be taken to consumers in such a way that they can and will use it. For example, if a major business-machine company were to develop in one of its research programs a new typewriter keyboard that allowed trained typists to work more efficiently and comfortably, the company would still not be able to go out and sell it. First, the company would have to develop effective programs to teach people how to use it and to train its sales personnel to demonstrate it correctly, so that typists and their employers would find sufficient advantages to adopt it. Then the company would be able to deliver its new product. Behavioral procedures must be viewed in the same manner if the products of applied research are to be adopted by the general public. If behavior analysts believe they have better programs to teach children or university students, to correct delinquent behavior, or to build new communities, then they must apply their science to the problems of program delivery. The analysis of the problems of large-scale field application will complete the behavior-analysis technology.

EXPERIMENTAL FOUNDATIONS OF APPLIED BEHAVIOR ANALYSIS

This book attempts to survey the components of applied behavior research. It ranges from the experimental foundations of behavior analysis through prototype programs in field application. Baer (Chapter 1) discusses the relation between basic and applied research. The current status of basic research in the experimental analysis of behavior is examined by Zeiler (Chapter 2). Kazdin (Chapter 3) then surveys methodological issues in applied behavior research.

The next six chapters consider the current status of several experimental areas relevant to human social behavior. In a sense they constitute a behavioral social psychology. It is a sign of the growing sophistication of behavioral analysis that its methods and its conceptual framework have been able to encompass such issues as observational learning, cooperation, and language. The behaviorism of John B. Watson, built upon Pavlov's conditioning principles, viewed the organism as passively pushed and pulled by the environment. Contemporary behaviorism, as represented in this book, has a different view. Operant behavior is, by definition, behavior that changes the organism's world; it is behavior that *does* something. What position, therefore, could be more congenial with the view that what we do can make a difference in the world? Once we have come to understand some of the determinants of behavior, it does not follow that we must view the organism as passive: the behavioral point of view is completely compatible with a view of the organism as biological and active.

The consequences of an organism's behavior include the production or termination of particular stimulus events, as when a rat's lever press delivers a food pellet or turns off an electric shock. The relations between responses and their specific environmental consequences are called contingencies. But behavior can also alter the environment so that contingencies themselves are affected. The likelihood that a forager will find food in a meadow may depend a great deal upon whether the forager once planted seeds there; the forager who obtains sufficient control over that environment will eventually come to be called a farmer.

The reciprocal relation between organism and environment becomes even more complex in social situations. In any situation involving two people—parent and child, spouse and spouse, teacher and student, and so on—the responses of each individual are the stimuli for the other. Some of the issues addressed in Chapters 4 through 9 are concerned with the adequacy of contemporary behavioral accounts for dealing with such social interactions. Gewirtz (Chapter 4), for example, considers how various interactions between a mother's attention and an infant's crying may lead to different patterns of infant crying. Such concerns typically lead not only to an analysis of the empirical properties of behavioral interactions but also to an exploration of the language that serves to describe these phenomena. Thus, Gewirtz also goes on to examine how caregiver-child interactions may be related to traditional and more global concepts, such as attachment and dependency. A similar concern with the relation between behavioral phenomena and the language of behavior runs through the other chapters on the experimental foundations of human social interactions: Whitehurst (Chapter 5) on observational learning and imitation; O'Leary (Chapter 6) on token systems; Hake and Olvera (Chapter 7) on cooperation, sharing, competition and altruism; Rachlin and Brigham (Chapter 8; Parts I and II) on self-control; and Salzinger (Chapter 9) on language. The issues are sometimes controversial, but the phenomena considered provide the basis for the areas of application that are considered in subsequent chapters; thus the reader will wish to judge in each case whether the relevant behavior has been appropriately represented, whether any critical variables or phenomena have been left out, and whether the implications have been properly drawn.

THE TECHNOLOGY OF INSTRUCTION

Because the relation between student and teacher is one special case of social interaction, the next five chapters (Chapters 10-14) follow appropriately from those on the experimental foundations of human social behavior. In terms of orientations the chapters in this section are more wide-ranging than those that came before or those that come after. The reason is that the analysis of instruction has historically been explored in different ways by different types of psychologists. In some cases the differences have been primarily in language. In others, however, the specific problems have differed (Catania, 1973). The behaviorist, for example, tends to study problems of function, in which the issues are the effects of various relations among stimuli and responses; the cognitive psychologist, on the other hand, tends to be concerned with problems of structure, in which the issues are how environmental events and behavior are organized.

The different types of problems addressed by functional and structural approaches can be illustrated by examples from the teaching of reading. In a functional analysis the stimuli and responses of interest are typically held constant while the relations among them are altered; interactions between environmental events and behavior are studied in terms of contingency relations among discriminative stimuli, responses, and consequences. Using a simple case to illustrate: Methods for teaching letter names might be examined by varying the consequences of letter naming but not the teaching materials. For example, the effects of reinforcing correct responses might be compared with those of punishing errors. But contingencies can differ in ways more subtle than those distinguishing reinforcement from punishment. Thus, an analysis of the properties of illustrated children's readers might be concerned with relations between pictures and the sentences that they illustrate (cf. Harzem, Lee, & Miles, 1976). A problem of stimulus control exists if the pictures set the occasion for verbal descriptions corresponding sufficiently closely to the accompanying text that a teacher cannot reliably tell whether a child is responding to the picture, reading the text, or doing both in some combination. The problem can be addressed by manipulating relations among the child's verbal responses and their antecedent and consequent stimuli: The text might be presented alone, and the child's correct reading might be followed by a presentation of the picture as a consequence. A systematic study might then proceed to a functional analysis of how pictures and text, as antecedent and consequent stimuli, contribute to such responses as picking up books, turning pages, and uttering words. The functional analysis might show that pictures, as consequences, help maintain the child's picking up of books and turning of pages, but that as antecedent stimuli they compete with the text in occasioning the child's verbal behavior. Such an analysis might lead to a rationale for sequencing the relations among words and pictures in children's readers to maximize stimulus control by the words and reinforcing effects of the pictures.

A structural analysis proceeds differently: The relations among stimuli and responses are held constant while critical properties of one or the other are altered. In a simple case the properties of letter naming might be examined by varying the features of the letters to be learned while holding constant the contingencies in the learning situation. For example, the learning of uppercase could be compared with that of lowercase letters, and the relative difficulty of such critical lowercase features as up-down and left-right reversals could be assessed. But an account of the critical features of stimuli is not sufficient for an analysis of the organization of environmental events and behavior. Thus, an analysis of the structure of reading might proceed to a study of the hierarchical ordering of verbal stimuli and verbal responses. A problem of sequencing reading materials exists if the units of analysis on which the curriculum is based do not correspond sufficiently closely to the response units currently available in the learner's repertory. The problem could be addressed by manipulating the size and the sequencing of textual units: Reading materials might be presented in the form of letters, syllables, or whole words, and different directions of acquisition of the hierarchical structure of text might be compared (e.g., decomposing words into component letters or syllables, or synthesizing words from letters or syllables as minimal units). A structural analysis might show that different levels of hierarchical organization are appropriate at different stages of reading acquisition, and might lead to a rationale for arranging transitions from reading at one hierarchical level (e.g., letters or syllables) to reading at another (words or phrases). Throughout such an analysis, the correspondence between stimulus structure (e.g., in the properties of a text) and response structure (in the properties of the child's speech) would be a major concern.

With continued elaboration, the distinctions between functional and structural problems become less sharp than in the preceding exemplary cases, but that is to be expected. Function and structure are complementary and not mutually exclusive. Thus, there is no reason why structural concerns should not enter into a functional experiment, or vice versa. This section of the book, therefore, has been organized to illustrate how various approaches deal with the technology of instruction. It will be clear to the reader that not all contributors would call themselves behaviorists, and yet their convergence on common problems and issues is itself evidence of the progress each has made in grappling with the relevant issues in instruction.

Becker and Engelmann (Chapter 10) concern themselves with both the structure and the functions of behavior. They provide a systematic treatment of a behavioral approach to instruction, and illustrate its applications and accomplishments within the Follow Through Project. Resnick and Ford (Chapter 11) show how an approach in terms of information processing treats the analysis of instruction in both reading and arithmetic, and Rozin (Chapter 12) examines some implications of a cognitive approach to the nature of the alphabet and its significance for the teaching of reading. Systematic applications of behavioral principles to instruction are then considered by Silverman (Chapter 13) in a survey of various approaches to programmed instruction, and by Lloyd (Chapter 14) in a review of empirical findings from studies of self-paced university-level courses (Keller's Personalized System of Instruction or PSI). Whatever the reader's orientation, a comparison of the methods, assumptions, and results of these orientations toward the analysis of instruction is likely to be of interest.

PROGRAMMATIC APPLICATIONS OF BEHAVIOR TECHNOLOGY

The integration of basic and applied research with field applications and delivery represents a true technology, the application of an engineering approach to the solution of behavioral problems. Chapters 15 through 19 represent several attempts to develop such a behavioral technology. Bushell (Chapter 15) describes the Behavior Analysis Follow Through Project and its impact on the effectiveness of instruction in elementary schools in a variety of urban and rural settings. Filipczak and Friedman (Chapter 16) give an account of an applied program in secondary education, Project PREP, and examine the various ways in which parents, teachers, administrators, and the general community can interact with the development of such a program. Pennypacker, Heckler, and Pennypacker (Chapter 17) describe the establishment of the Personalized Learning Center, a university-wide system of individualized instruction. Fixsen, Phillips, and Wolf (Chapter 18) present the application of the Teaching Family Model to Achievement Place residences for delinquent juveniles. And Lies and Miller (Chapter 19) present a democratic community in the form of the Experimental Living Project. As these chapters testify, successful application requires the amalgamation of well-documented procedures into full-scale applied programs. Together, the chapters demonstrate the feasibility of behavior-analysis techniques for solving the problems of program delivery. Thus, these programs are models for the future development of behavior analysis as an engineering science.

The beginning of this introduction outlined the relations among basic and applied research and the problems of program delivery. The points bear repetition in the context of a specific case. Pennypacker, Heckler, and Pennypacker (Chapter 17), for example, provide the Personalized Learning Center as an illustration of how behavior-analysis technology can be applied to university instruction. Earlier, the basic principles of the science had been used to analyze problems of instruction and to design new procedures. These procedures were later tested in applied research settings (e.g., Keller, 1968), and soon other researchers were trying similar procedures in a variety of universities and in classes other than psychology. The result was a body of knowledge produced by applied behavior analysis on how to design and run a more effective university course (see Chapter 14). But if all of this knowledge was not to be restricted to a random course here or there in a university curriculum, then it was necessary to design and field-test an entire program of university-wide courses. This is exactly the challenge that Pennypacker and his associates accepted when they began to establish a university-wide system at the University of Florida. When applied researchers move beyond a single course in their own specialties (or out of an applied research setting in general), however, new problems are created. The researcher may know how to modify psychology curriculum materials to fit the format of a personalized system of instruction (PSI), but what about the economics, physics, history, zoology, and business administration instructors? Further, why should they participate at all? Similarly, what are the reinforcers that maintain the support of the university administration? How will the system be financed? With little effort, an interminable list of similar questions and problems could be generated. These are the problems

of program delivery. At this point, rather than abandoning their science/
technology and falling back on politics, as so often happens (e.g., Reppucci &
Saunders, 1974), Pennypacker et al. applied the principles of behavior
analysis to the problems of program delivery. Their analyses and solutions,
and those of the other contributors of these chapters, are now available for
use by others in solving similar problems. The future will undoubtedly bring
other programmatic applications.

ETHICS AND THE FUTURE OF BEHAVIOR ANALYSIS

A successful technology entails risks as well as benefits, and a behavioral technology in particular may be well-used or abused depending
upon the ends to which it is put. It is therefore fitting that the book closes
with an examination of the ethics of behavior analysis. Stolz (Chapter 20)
discusses not only how ethical considerations may modify applications of
behavioral research, but also how a behavioral analysis may bear in turn on
our understanding of ethical principles. Our parents saw the growth of
technologies based on the physical sciences, and we ourselves are observing
the contemporary impact of technologies based on the biological sciences.
Each of these has created new problems along with their solutions of old
ones. We have yet to see whether our society will be able to deal effectively
and ethically with such issues as energy conservation and environmental
pollution, overpopulation and the treatment of the aged. Our children will
see the impact of behavioral technologies. We must hope that these
technologies bring more new solutions than new problems, and that they
will also help to solve some of the problems that the earlier technologies
created. Let us therefore dedicate this book to both past and future: To our
parents for what has been done and to our children for what they may hope
to do.

SECTION I
FOUNDATIONS OF APPLIED BEHAVIOR RESEARCH

DONALD M. BAER

Chapter 1

On the Relation between Basic and Applied Research

No need to discuss relation
until you locate two parties.

A common stereotype of basic and applied research suggests that basic research discovers new knowledge, clarifies principles, and accomplishes carefully quantified statements of how much *A* results in how much *B*. Applied research then takes this knowledge and puts it to work in the service of society, solving practical problems and thereby maximizing happiness.

Another, less common stereotype asserts the opposite dependency: Applied research finds out what is possible and prevalent in the real world by solving problems that exist there. Basic research, thus informed of where the truth must lie, then proceeds to clarify it in laboratories, unconfounding whatever variables may have been packaged together in the real-life solutions, quantifying whatever functions may exist, and finally emerging with a language system that should explain why happiness is so maximal.

A third, very uncommon stereotype may prove to be more accurate and more valuable, and yet it is burdened by several disadvantages. One disadvantage is that this stereotype is not built on a distinction between basic and applied research. Since so much effort has been expended on arguing the relation between applied and basic research, simply abandoning both concepts may have too rueful a price. Another disadvantage is that this stereotype is not built on a duality or dichotomy of research styles; instead, it is based on a single concept which unfortunately is distributed along a continuum. Continua-based concepts are, it seems, always more difficult to explain than dichotomy-based concepts; hence they may prove correspondingly less likely to be adopted.

Finally, my guess is that the behavior of those scientists variously called basic and applied will not be changed much by so simple an operation as

11

pointing out to them that their supposedly distinct efforts are, after all, only modestly spaced points on a single underlying dimension. By the same token, my guess also is that the research-funding behavior of agencies committed to the single-minded facilitation of either basic or applied research will not be changed much either.

On the other hand, an argument so distressed by disadvantages can presumably do little harm, and the informed consent of readers should be correspondingly easy to secure. However, any group of readers usually has within it a subgroup composed of organisms in a state called "student." Students often are not yet locked into a research pattern, unlike the scientists and the agencies called basic and applied; because of this, they may be more susceptible to mere argument. Traditionally, students have been responsive to argument, even if not efficiently. If my argument should cause a few students to conduct their future research untroubled by whether it is basic or applied, it will have done as well as can be expected.

The argument necessarily begins a long time ago. A long time ago, there were experimental psychologists and clinical psychologists. The experimental psychologists were supposed to contribute to knowledge; the clinical psychologists were supposed to use that knowledge to do good. The clinical psychologists quickly discovered that too little knowledge was available to be used effectively to do good, and, quite naturally, they simply did good as well as they could in their own way.

Meanwhile, the experimental psychologists, undeterred by the need to solve social problems, continued to search for the great unified theory of behavior from which would derive all knowledge, including the solutions to the clinicians' problems. Consequently, their research was "basic," because it was meant to contribute only to the development of that theory. Naturally it took place in the laboratory: That was the most efficient place to prevent the action of unwanted variables that could affect the behavior under study, even though the variables were, unfortunately, irrelevant to the theory under study. Naturally, the experimental design most favored was the group-factorial design, which could undergo analysis of variance: That was the most efficient way to detect the function of the other, relevant variables under study, even if their function was weak, transitory, or inconsistent. After all, theory said that these variables should make a difference, on at least somebody, at least some of the time.

The result, apparently, was the proliferation of variables detected as sometimes functional. Because each such detection of a variable was the partial vindication of a theory that had posited the variable, there naturally resulted a corresponding proliferation of theories that had to be considered. Presumably, the experimental psychologists were working toward a single theory that would encompass the largest number of those variables that their exquisitely efficient experimental techniques had shown were at least sometimes functional and therefore had to be explained in any complete theory.

It was as if they were stocking the ark against the flood: No species was to be left out, but only a breeding pair of each was required. Hence reinforcers were awarded to any researcher who could detect yet another variable that would have to be accounted for (to be brought aboard); but no credit went to the researcher who displayed an already known variable. Thus, if tantrums were eliminated from an autistic child by intercepting their usual social consequences, that was considered unimportant: Reinforcement and extinction were already well understood, and no further demonstrations were needed. If the demonstration had been done in a research paradigm, then it might stand as "applied" research, but it was clear that, even so, it was no candidate for the ark (or even for the journal).

Of course, it would have been something the experimentalists could have shown to the clinicians—a bit of experimental psychology with which to do good better. The clinical psychologists, however, had already found that too much knowledge had accumulated now in experimental psychology to enable them to do good with it; and furthermore, the knowledge was too often about functions that must work for somebody other than their client of the moment. Thus the clinical psychologists perforce continued to do good as well as they could without experimental psychology.

In this context, a different approach to experimental psychology appeared, one termed the experimental analysis of behavior. For an experimental analysis, the problem was not to collect all the variables that could possibly be shown to affect some behavior in somebody at some time. Instead, the problem was to select behavior of interest, and then to discover the variables that could alter it dependably in any direction. The question was always posed for a single organism at a time. The powerful statistical tools of the earlier experimental psychologists were put aside in favor of producing effects that were so clear, consistent, and stable that they needed no statistical treatment to be seen: They were obvious in the data of the experiment if those data were simply summarized across their time course for the individual.

In short, the experimental analyst made two radical departures from the previous ways of the experimental psychologists. First, the experimental analyst was restricted to the discovery and use of only the powerful, always effective variables, rather than permitted the indiscriminate collecting of any variable that was ever functional to any degree. Second, the experimental analyst focused on behavior, rather than on theory. Paradoxically, these departures put the experimental analyst in an excellent position to stumble into a truly general behavior theory, for the experimental analyst would, of course, ask the obvious question about each successful analysis of successive behavior: Did the current analysis resemble any of the previous analyses? To the extent that the answer was "Yes," a unified behavior theory was beginning. It could be a theory built on the basic variables, those that were always effective, and it could be a theory that covered all behavior. It could be; the obvious question is, was it?

Experimental analysts, oriented to the criterion of generality, found again and again that reinforcement variables had analyzed a variety of behavior. That discovery did not preclude the possibility that other classes of variables might also analyze the same behavior. The consistency with which the reinforcement analysis emerged, however, suggested new and very forceful questions: Would a reinforcement analysis operate for any behavior? for all behavior? And so, to a considerable extent, experimental analysts became reinforcement theorists.

Reinforcement theory was, however, only a corollary of their basic logic, not the essence of it: If reinforcement variables proved to have limited generality, experimental analysts would no longer be nothing but reinforcement theorists. They would, though, continue analyzing one behavior after another in single organisms, noting what variables, if any did have generality across behavior, organisms, and settings. When some variables suggested themselves as general, experimental analysts would again become theorists, asking whether that class of variables always analyzed all behavior. These researchers, like the reinforcement theorists, would deserve the label "theorist," because dedication to establishing or denying the generality of a particular class of variables leads to highly selective, systematically disciplined research, rather than to the open-minded diverse curiosity characteristic of the natural scientist (or the experimental analyst not yet under the control of the generality question).

The pursuit of generality, whether of reinforcement variables or any other class of variables, inevitably will lead to research on social problems. This will happen for several reasons, and some of those reasons will allow a working label of "applied" to be invoked, but not in such a way as to create a fundamentally new category of research.

One reason for applying an experimental analysis to social problems is because they are among the most obvious candidates to be tried next in the test of generality. Quite a lot of barpresses, keypecks, switch closings, alley runs, and barrier leaps have already been analyzed and found amenable to reinforcement variables. A good deal of red and green, squares and triangles and other odd shapes, and myriad tones and buzzes have been discriminated under the press of a reinforcement contingency. Hardly anything else seems worth trying reinforcement on but language and social problems.

Another reason is that the individual-subject technique of experimental analysis may no longer prove a sufficient filter against the detection of minor variables. Laboratory techniques in this area have developed to such a degree of perfection that even weak variables are occasionally validated. Sidman (1960, p. 194) has suggested that applied scientists are those who must ask their questions with only minimal experimental control over the setting, while basic scientists are those who enjoy the ability to rule out many otherwise interfering factors. Consequently basic scientists are able to demonstrate a role for variables that could hardly be detected as functional in more loosely managed settings.

Without this natural check on the proliferation of minor variables that a general theory must account for, only the criterion of generality remains to keep experimental analysis from being overwhelmed by the multitude of its own unintegratable discoveries, as was its predecessor, experimental psychology. It is in exactly the loose, largely uncontrolled settings in which social problems are analyzed that screening for generality should occur. Generality will determine the basic importance of any variable, reinforcement-based or otherwise, for theory. To put it differently, what works on the social problems is what deserves to be counted among the most fundamental variables of a unified behavior theory. The conceptual promise of experimental analysis as a path toward a unified behavior theory may not be realized without those acid tests, whether it is reinforcement that passes the test or some other class of variables.

Still another reason for trying out experimental analysis on social problems is that many researchers never meant to validate a general behavior theory, advance the cause of science, or alleviate the conceptual problems of the graduate student approaching preliminary exams. They meant simply to solve the social problems. These researchers include, in principle if not in fact, the clinical psychologists who twice were rebuffed by experimental psychology (once because it knew too little and later because it knew too much). Here, they find—in an odd quirk of what used to be experimental psychology and is now experimental analysis—some knowledge that actually is useful in doing good, or at least in solving clients' problems.

Understandably, the clinical psychologists, who spent several generations doing good as well as they could without experimental psychology, now may show some resistance to being co-opted by the experimental analysts, who are hypothesizing a way to do good systematically well. But certainly they will be interested, even if negatively at first, because finally the contribution from research is relevant.

That research might even be said to be "applied," as a consequence. But to give it this label, and thereby consider it as something fundamentally different from the generality-testing research that preceded it, is unwarranted. Generality-testing research is no less generality-testing research simply because it is done by someone supremely uninterested in testing generality. The research still constitutes a test, even if the researcher will not report it that way.

Problem solvers may evade tests of generality, of course, by solving social problems in ways that are not even research, let alone applied research. But behavior analysis does not contain many completely prescribed solutions as yet. Rather, it contains some examples of solutions to related problems (usually simpler ones than our current problems), some principles and some rules of thumb. Therefore, the solution to our current problem, whatever that problem might be, usually requires innovation, improvisation, and variations on prior themes. If that is carried out in a way designed to prove to the inventor and to the audience that the resulting apparent solution is also the functional solution, then the endeavor is research. To call it applied research is to imply only that it will solve a social problem, or that it is part of the tooling-up necessary to mount a program that will solve a problem.

In the logic of experimental analysis, we should never dismiss a solution to a social problem as the mere application of a principle we already know. Rather, it is just such demonstrations that are the essence of what experimental analysis is about, for these demonstrations represent the testing of the generality of a principle in less controlled settings. Until principles are tested outside the carefully regulated confines of the laboratory, we will not know their robustness. Thus, in applying a known principle to a social problem, it is not the principle that is at issue, but the generality of the principle: its generality across settings, individuals, and problems.

The ultimate test of any principle of behavior lies in its ability to deal with social problems. If we have not used a principle to solve a particular social problem before, then we do not know if the generality of that principle extends that far, or if it is too delimited to apply to that problem. We need to know; the science needs to know. Our most basic question now is not the detection of principles, but the evaluation of the generality of the extremely numerous principles already in hand. Thus no research that solves a social problem is less than basic, even if it is applied as well.

MICHAEL D. ZEILER

Chapter 2

Principles of Behavioral Control[1]

De subjecto vetustissimo novissimam promovemus scientiam. From the oldest subject we bring the newest science—so Ebbinghaus described psychology in 1885. At that time philosophical speculation about the nature of the mind was being converted into an experimental analysis of conscious experience and psychological function. Now, almost a century later, psychology is turning another ancient concern into a scientific technology. How to teach is an old question, but a precise technology of effective teaching is new. It developed as an outgrowth of the science of behavior. When the principles of behavior revealed by refined experiments in the laboratory were found applicable outside the laboratory, an educational technology became possible. At this time, educators need to understand the apparently esoteric findings of the behavioral research laboratory, because increasingly sophisticated application poses an ongoing challenge to those concerned with optimizing the educational process.

Ideally, teachers instill knowledge and skills, develop and further creativity, have students learn to the utmost of their ability, and train students to work both independently and constructively with others. Over the years many students have approximated these ideals, although to what extent success is due to a true understanding of effective teaching or to individually talented teachers is debatable. To have an effective technology of teaching, it is necessary to isolate and understand the essential factors involved in good teaching, i.e., to know what it is that a teacher does that

1. Preparation of this chapter was facilitated by Research Grants HDO5752 from the National Institute of Child Health and Human Development and GB-25959 from the National Science Foundation. I would like to thank Eric Davis for his critical reading and many helpful suggestions on an earlier draft.

contributes to success or failure. One way of developing such understanding might be to observe teachers carefully to see how they interact with students, how they present material, and how they deal with particular situations as they arise. Then, by determining which students do and do not meet educational goals, it might be possible to relate success (or lack of it) to the particular teaching procedures. Such a plan could provide useful information, but has obvious drawbacks. For example, precise observation is difficult in classroom settings, the interactions between students and between student and teacher are often complex, and the observer is likely to be unaware of the effects of what other teachers are doing with the same students. In any event, the observation of experienced teachers by teachers in training has for years been incorporated into teacher education without developing a maximally effective educational system.

Another approach deals with education less directly by treating it as the technological offshoot of experimental psychology. Teaching involves the behavior of the teacher in relation to the student and vice versa. Teachers and students do things, i.e., they behave. The teacher can determine what the student knows only by observing behavior; conversely, the student can be affected only by what the teacher does or does not do. Even though both have private experiences and knowledge, neither is affected directly by the other's experience or knowledge but only by how the other acts. The point is that the teacher's concern is behavior, and the effectiveness of teaching is measured by changes in behavior. Education involves the acquisition of behavior, be it reading, performing operations on columns of numbers, making appropriate verbal responses, performing surgery or driving a car. To be truly effective, the desired behavior must be established and then maintained. At times it may be necessary to eliminate certain responses. For example, a disruptive child does not learn readily and may prevent others from doing so. To deal with the problem, the teacher must know how to eliminate inappropriate behavior. The student must also learn when one kind of behavior is appropriate and when it is not (the responses that are totally appropriate and desirable in a physical education class are not appropriate in a history class and vice versa). The general principles of behavior relate to exactly these issues: the development and maintenance of behavior; the elimination of behavior; and the occurrence of particular responses only under certain conditions. If the principles are understood, they can be used to accomplish the changes of concern to educators.

These principles have not been discovered in schools but in highly structured laboratory settings. The situations are artificial—just as the study of molecular movements in cloud chambers by physicists or the analysis of nucleic acids by biochemists are artificial—because they move the subject out of its normal environment and into the laboratory. But, as advances in engineering and medicine demonstrate, principles of great practical utility emerge. The same is true of the principles of behavior. Revealed in isolated form in highly contrived situations, often with species far removed from man, they are the basis of advances in education and psychotherapy. The other chapters of this book provide strong evidence for how the abstract principles of the laboratory make contact with the business of educators and of mankind in general.

This chapter explains the principles of behavior as they are now understood. As in any active field, new knowledge appears continually, so that many of the principles undoubtedly will be expanded or modified or supplemented in the future. Because the later chapters translate the general principles into specifics, no attempt will be made to do so here. The intention now is to describe basic research in behavior and to provide an overview of what that research has revealed.

THE EXPERIMENTAL ANALYSIS OF BEHAVIOR

The typical behavioral experiment is conducted with a small animal, most often a pigeon or a rat. These animals are easily and economically obtained and maintained. Fortunately the laws they reveal have proven essentially similar to those operating in humans, for otherwise practicality and convenience would not be a sufficient justification. Experiments are also conducted with humans, other primates and mammals, fish, and even insects; each has advantages for certain types of problems. This does not mean that researchers are building a pigeon psychology or a rat psychology or an animal psychology. An experimental subject is chosen for reasons of convenience and because there is sufficient basis for assuming generality of principles across species. Sometimes, particular effects are peculiar to a species or even to an age range within a species, but more often these restrictions are not encountered. The Darwinian thesis of continuity across species seems as applicable to the principles of behavior as to physical structure and function. The major difference emerging as the evolutionary ladder is ascended is, perhaps, increasing complexity in the repertoire of behavior possible.

The experimental environment usually is relatively barren. For pigeons, the experimental chamber is a small rectangular cubical that allows freedom of motion. This chamber is enclosed in a box with insulated walls, ceiling, and floor, thereby reducing the possibility of noise and completely eliminating extraneous visual stimuli from the experimental situation. A loudspeaker transmits a steady hissing sound that serves as a masking source to further preclude distracting noises. Ventilation is provided by exhaust fans and louvres. A dim light, known as a houselight, provides general illumination. The pigeon stands on a floor made of mesh or rods that allows waste matter to fall through into a tray. The front wall of the chamber contains a round plastic disk (the response key) about 1 in. (2.5 cm) in diameter and located 7–9 in. (18–23 cm) above the floor. The disk can be lit from the rear by different colors or geometric forms. When depressed, the disk activates a switch providing an electrical pulse to the controlling apparatus located outside the box (usually in a different room). A 2x2-in. (5x5-cm) square aperture below the key provides access to a tray of grain whenever a hopper is raised. The raising of the hopper is accompanied by the noise of its operation and by illumination of the aperture.

For rats, the apparatus usually has a lever located just above the floor instead of a key and a tray into which food pellets are discharged rather then the aperture-hopper combination. Also, there is often a loudspeaker which can transmit tones or other sounds. Visual stimuli usually are restricted to a lamp that can be turned on or off or to geometric forms. Stimuli differing in color are not used because rats are color blind. Different modifications are necessary for other species. Essentially, however, the apparatus for any subject is designed to have a response device, a way of presenting stimuli, and a method for presenting food or some other commodity that will maintain behavior.

Some experiments require advance preparation of the animal. For example, if food is to be presented during the experiment, it is necessary to ensure that it will be eaten. For this reason, animals are maintained on a regimen of food deprivation: The animal may gradually be reduced to 80% of its normal weight and be fed on a 24-hr. schedule. If not enough food is eaten during the experimental session to maintain the desired weight, a supplemental feeding is given afterward. Sessions usually occur from five to seven days per week. Supplemental feedings are given on any day that the experiment is not conducted.

Other experimental situations have examined running in an alley or making choices in a maze, but these are less prevalent now than in the past. In some experiments the animal may be restrained in a comfortably fitting device. For example, in the classical apparatus used by Pavlov (1927), dogs were restrained in harnesses during the experiment. All experimental procedures are designed to minimize distractions, and restraint may be necessary in some situations.

The experimenter arranges that certain events (stimuli) will occur and records the subject's responses. Usually only those responses that activate the key or lever are of interest, and no attention is paid to exactly how the activation occurred. Thus, it does not matter whether the key is activated by the pigeon's wing, beak, or tail; it is considered the same response (generally called keypecking). Responses are defined in terms of their effect on the environment (in this case, operations of the switch).

Some stimuli are presented independently of responses, and others appear as a consequence of responses. Certain stimuli may signal when responses have certain consequences, e.g., a red light may indicate that a keypeck will be followed by the presentation of food, and a green light may mean that food is not available. Red and green would then be referred to as antecedent stimuli, because they precede or set the occasion for a response. When the antecedent stimuli clearly exert control over responding (i.e., the bird pecks much more during red than during green), they are called discriminative stimuli. Food is a consequent stimulus because it follows the response. A consequent stimulus need not follow every response, but can occur according to many different plans or schedules. When a consequent stimulus is shown to maintain a response, it is known as a *reinforcer*, and the arrangement used to present it is known as the *schedule of reinforcement*. Discontinuing a previous reinforcer is referred to as *extinction*.

The experimenter prepares the subject and schedules stimuli. Everything else from the beginning to the end of the session is up to the subject. Each response is recorded (usually automatically). A cumulative record provides a detailed description of all of the behavior by showing responding at each moment in time, but often some single summary measure of behavior is desirable. Common summary measures are the number of responses occurring in a given condition and the time spent in a condition. Dividing the number of responses by time yields *response rate*, computing the mean time between successive responses gives average *interresponse time;* computing the mean time to the first response of a condition gives average *response latency*. Which measure is used varies with the requirements of particular experiments.

Some problems require systematic variations in stimuli, more than one response device, and other behavioral measures. These will be discussed as the need arises.

EXPERIMENTAL ARRANGEMENTS

An experimenter must specify what stimulus events will be displayed to a subject and what will be done with respect to certain responses. The various possibilities can be classified in terms of whether they involve stimuli alone or a conjunction of stimuli and responses. Three basic arrangements are of fundamental importance.

1. *The S-S Dependency.* Two stimuli can occur in certain temporal relations without reference to behavior. Such a relation is a stimulus-stimulus or S-S dependency. Behavior may change, but behavior is not a prerequisite for anything. The most familiar example of an effect of the S-S dependency is Pavlovian (classical, respondent) conditioning, in which two stimuli are paired without regard to responses. Conditioning is said to occur when a response resembling that originally elicited only by the second stimulus appears when the first is presented. Thus, when Pavlov (1927) rang a bell (S_1) and shortly thereafter presented food (S_2) to a dog, food followed the bell regardless of anything the dog did or did not do. After a number of pairings of the two stimuli, the dog came to salivate when the bell rang. The acquired response—salivating to the bell—arose from the stimulus pairing. Pavlovian conditioned responses are one of several effects of an S-S dependency.

2. *The R-S Dependency*. When a stimulus is presented only if a response occurs, this is a response-stimulus or R-S dependency. Behavior is an essential component of the arrangement because the experimenter's activities are dictated by what the subject does. For example, a child may be given a piece of candy (S) when he presses a lever (R). An effect of the R-S dependency may be to make the response occur more or less frequently; when it has such effects, instrumental or operant conditioning has occurred.

3. *The S-R-S Dependency*. A response may be followed by a stimulus only in the presence of some other stimulus. For example, a bar press may be followed by a piece of candy only if there is music playing. If there is no music, the press does not result in candy. When the response is affected by what stimulus is present, discriminative operant conditioning has occurred.

The three arrangements all involve stimuli, but differ in how the stimuli occur. In the S-S dependency, they are referred to as S_1 and S_2, in deference to their temporal order. In the R-S and S-R-S arrangements, a stimulus follows the response and can be referred to as the consequent stimulus. (The first stimulus in the S-R-S dependency is antecedent rather than consequent.) From the point of view of the dependencies arranged by the experimenter, the only additional arrangement involves the simple presentation of a single stimulus without reference either to responses or to other stimuli. For example, children might be given pieces of candy at any time no matter what they are doing or what stimulus is present. In such a case, the only antecedent would be time.

Stimuli can have a variety of effects. Some elicit a response (e.g., a blink of an eye to a puff of air is a reflexive reaction to the puff); stimuli that have such an effect are known as *eliciting stimuli* with respect to the particular response involved. A consequent stimulus (R-S and S-R-S procedures) may increase or decrease the frequency of the response that precedes it. If there is an increase, it is a *reinforcer;* (reinforcing stimulus). If there is a decrease, it is a *punisher* (punishing stimulus). The third potential of a stimulus is revealed in the discriminated operant (S-R-S) procedure. If a response increases or decreases in frequency when a certain antecedent stimulus is present, that stimulus is a *discriminative stimulus*.

REINFORCING STIMULI

The Nature of Reinforcing Stimuli

Psychologists have long been interested in specifying why certain stimuli are reinforcing. Thorndike (1911) identified reinforcers with satisfaction. When satisfaction followed a response, the tendency to make that response in the future increased; when discomfort followed a response, the tendency to make that response subsequently decreased. Thorndike defined satisfaction as a state that the organism strove to achieve and did nothing to avoid, i.e., a response that produced that state would recur in the future. But this definition produced total circularity: a response increases in strength because it produces satisfaction, and the state is identified as satisfying because the response increases in strength. Thorndike also attempted to explain reinforcement in terms of the readiness of neurons to function, but readiness too was identified with the change in behavior and so was equally circular. Postman (1947) provided an excellent account of the conceptual problems.

Hull (1943) eliminated circularity by identifying a reinforcing stimulus with the reduction of a physiological need or drive, thereby integrating a homeostatic view of motivation with reinforcement. However, even the staunchest and most sophisticated advocate of drive-reduction theory concluded that it probably was not a viable general account (Miller, N.E., 1963). Events that reduce biological needs (food to an organism deprived of food, water to a water-deprived animal, air, heat, etc.) are usually reinforcing, but all reinforcers do not seem to reduce needs.

Meehl (1950) offered the concept of trans-situationality as a solution to the circularity problem. Meehl hypothesized that a stimulus found reinforcing with respect to one response would reinforce all other responses as well. This, of course, was eminently open to experimental attack. Trans-situationality leads to the classification of some stimuli as intrinsically reinforcing and others as not reinforcing. Although it does not explain why a stimulus is reinforcing, it does avoid circularity and offers some generality and predictability. Trans-situationality has proven untenable, because stimuli do not have fixed properties. Food, a commonly used reinforcing stimulus, will not be effective after a large meal. Or, as Morse and Kelleher (1970) have shown, electric shock can serve as either a reinforcing or a punishing event depending on how it is scheduled to occur. A stimulus is reinforcing only under certain conditions; none is intrinsically reinforcing or punishing.

Another attempt at a general theory of reinforcement was offered by Premack (see Premack, 1965, for a review). Premack begins with the observation that reinforcing stimuli control responses, i.e., food controls eating, water controls drinking, etc. When these stimuli are effective reinforcers, it appears that they control responses having a very high probability of occurrence. Now, consider that the response to be reinforced (e.g., a lever press) has a lower probability for a food-deprived animal than eating when both lever and food are present. The Premack Principle is that the opportunity to engage in higher probability responses reinforces lower probability responses. Thus, the essential nature of a reinforcing stimulus is that it controls a response occurring with a higher probability than the response to be reinforced. Premack demonstrated his point by manipulating response probabilities and altering reinforcing potential. For example, the probability of drinking could be changed by varying water deprivation, and the probability of running in a wheel could be changed by varying the opportunity to run. If the opportunity to drink required running, running increased in frequency only if drinking had a higher probability than running. Conversely, if the opportunity to run required drinking, drinking increased if running had the higher probability. Thus, a given response (drinking or running) could either be reinforcing or not, depending on its relation to the other response.

In another experiment, children given the opportunity to eat candy and play a pinball machine differed in which activity was more likely to occur. Then, some had to operate the pinball machine to get candy, whereas others had to eat candy to have access to the machine. Candy reinforced pinball playing (increased its frequency) only for those children who originally had a higher likelihood of candy eating, and pinball reinforced candy eating for the others. Once again, the same event was or was not a reinforcer depending on relative response probabilities.

The Premack Principle has proven useful. An excellent example was provided by Homme, deBaca, Devine, Steinhorst, and Rickert (1963). When a teacher saw that active play was very likely to occur given an opportunity, access to such play was an effective reinforcer for other less likely responses, such as sitting quietly at a table and learning to read. The same activities may not have the highest likelihood for all children, and the hierarchies may even change for each individual. As a result, the teacher may have to change the activity made available after a response. In our current stage of knowledge, the Premack Principle is perhaps the most easily applied rule for identifying and selecting reinforcers.

Like drive-reduction theory, however, it is not the final statement on the essential nature of reinforcing events. Morse and Kelleher's demonstrations involving electric shock do not fit the hypothesis, because, under their conditions, shock is not responded to at a higher rate than are other stimuli. It has not been demonstrated that some highly probably response occurs in the presence of shock only when shock is positively reinforcing.

In summary, stimuli that reduce physiological needs and stimuli that control a high probability response typically are reinforcing. Despite exceptions to both rules, these are sufficiently safe generalizations to enable effective reinforcers to be discovered. At this time, though, there is no thoroughly adequate general theory of reinforcement. The general rules that emerge are that (1) no stimulus is intrinsically reinforcing; and (2) the effectiveness of a stimulus as a reinforcer depends on a complex of factors, including the organism's history, the particular nature of the current situation, and the way the stimulus occurs in relation to behavior.

How Reinforcing Stimuli Operate

In the R-S and S-R-S paradigms, the reinforcing stimulus depends on the response. What about this dependency is important? Research dealing with the presentation of reinforcing stimuli independent of responses indicates that the essential factor is the temporal relation between the response and the stimulus. As long as temporal relations are maintained, comparable effects occur whether or not the reinforcer presentation depends on a response.

Increases in response frequency with response-independent reinforcement were shown by Skinner's (1948a) superstitious pigeons. Food-deprived pigeons emitted ritualistic responses when food was presented at regular intervals independent of behavior. In this arrangement the stimulus (food) had no relation to any response or to any antecedent stimulus, but depended on elapsed time alone. A particular response apparently predominated if it happened to occur close in time to food presentation. When the response then increased in frequency, it became even more likely to be emitted in conjunction with the next food presentation, and the frequency increased still further. Thus the response was affected by its temporal contiguity to food in the absence of an R-S dependency. In an experiment with children (Zeiler, 1970), a reinforcer delivered dependent on not pressing a panel maintained whatever other response happened to precede it, whether it was pressing a different panel or crawling on the floor. In general close temporal contiguity between a response and a reinforcer will maintain the response whether the relation to the reinforcer is deliberate or accidental. The temporal relation is crucial in both.

Different schedules of reinforcement affect how responses are distributed in time (Ferster & Skinner, 1957). For example, if the first response occurring after 5 min. produces food, pigeons pause after each food presentation and then respond at either an increasing or a high steady rate. On the other hand, if food occurs for the first response emitted at irregular intervals averaging 5 min., the pause is much shorter and responses occur at a more consistent rate. Food can also be presented independent of responses and at either regular or irregular time periods. This also produces clear schedule effects. If food occurs at fixed times, a pause after food presentation is followed by an increasing rate of whatever response happened to precede the reinforcer (keypecking in this case); if food occurs at variable times, the response rate is more uniform (Zeiler, 1968). Not only does each type of response-independent reinforcement schedule exert characteristic effects on response patterning, but the patterns are similar to those of response-dependent reinforcement involving the same temporal regularity of reinforcement. Once again, common temporal relations produce common effects.

In the S-R-S dependency, responses come under the control of the antecedent stimulus in whose presence the responses produce the reinforcing stimulus. Morse and Skinner (1957) occasionally presented food dependent on a response while alternating two stimuli. The pigeons typically responded at a higher rate during one stimulus than during the other. It appeared that whatever stimulus happened to be present when the response was reinforced obtained control over behavior; response rates during that stimulus increased, while response rates during the other stimulus declined. Once that occurred, subsequent food presentations became even more likely in the presence of one stimulus, and the rate differential was enhanced. In this case, although there was only an R-S dependency, effects were like those of the S-R-S procedure. The relation between the prevailing antecedent stimulus and the reinforced response was entirely adventitious, and yet behavior came under the control of the stimulus just as if only that stimulus set the occasion for reinforcement. It was a superstitious discrimination. Again, the temporal relations appear responsible.

These observations imply that the R-S and S-R-S arrangements exert their effects simply because they guarantee close temporal relations and not because they are instances of cause and effect. What matters are the temporal relations between antecedent stimuli, responses, and reinforcing events. Detailed discussions of the implications of response-independent reinforcement further document the temporal nature of the response-reinforcer relation (Herrnstein, 1966; Zeiler, 1972).

Because whatever responses occur in close temporal proximity to the reinforcing event increase in frequency, a reinforcer typically affects several responses simultaneously. Several experiments show that when one response is required, others that happen to occur close in time to the reinforcer also are affected. For example, Catania and Cutts (1963) found that when either pigeons or humans were given a reinforcer for responding to one key or lever, responses to a second key or lever were also maintained at a substantial rate. These other responses were eliminated only if the procedure was changed so that they could not occur in close contiguity to the reinforcer. The maintenance of "other" responses seems to be a general property of response-dependent reinforcer presentation. It may even be that several responses, unrequired as well as required, are always maintained. A reinforcer operates on ongoing behavior (whatever it may be) to determine subsequent behavior; reinforcers do not discriminate between necessary and unnecessary behavior or between the intentions of the giver of the reinforcer (teacher, parent, etc.) and the responses that are reinforced because of temporal contiguity.

Eliciting Functions of Reinforcing Stimuli

Pavlovian conditioning. Reinforcing stimuli can have effects, either intentional or accidental, in addition to those of increasing or maintaining the frequency of responses. As Pavlov showed, a stimulus can elicit a response reflexively and the response will also occur to an antecedent stimulus. For example, a puff of air to the eye elicits a blink, and the blink will occur to a tone that precedes the puff. Since some of the most commonly used reinforcing stimuli (e.g., food, shock) have strong eliciting effects (e.g., salivation, withdrawal), it is not surprising that operant and Pavlovian conditioning and reflexive activities can and do occur simultaneously. M. M. Shapiro (1961) demonstrated these concurrent effects in dogs given food for barpressing. Barpressing increased in frequency, and the dogs also salivated copiously in the period just before and just after food delivery. It is likely that most reinforcing events elicit responses, and that these responses will also come to precede the reinforcer via Pavlovian conditioning. They will be manifested as anticipatory versions of the response first made only after the reinforcer appeared.

Previously Probable Responses. There are forms of elicitation in addition to reflexive control. R. L. Reid (1957) showed that a single presentation of a reinforcer would immediately reinstate a response that had been eliminated by extinction. Spradlin, Girardeau, and Hom (1966) found that once a response had been established by following it with a reinforcer, it then could be reduced in frequency by giving the reinforcer only when the response had not occurred for a while. However, even though the absence of the response was the requirement and the response decreased in frequency, the response was emitted immediately after receipt of the reinforcer, i.e., it was elicited. Such data indicate that a reinforcing stimulus sometimes elicits a response that previously had been involved with it in an R-S dependency,. Thus, reinforcers may elicit previously probable responses.

Aggression. Attack or aggressive behavior can be elicited. Azrin, Hutchinson, and Hake (1963) found that when a monkey was shocked, it attacked another monkey present in the same chamber. The monkeys fought so much immediately after each shock presentation that the experimenters had to intervene. In the absence of a history with shock, no fighting occurred. Ulrich and Azrin (1962) found fighting to be elicited by shock and other painful stimuli in different species as well.

Aggression is elicited by a period of nonreinforcement as well as by the presentation of a noxious stimulus. Azrin, Hutchinson, and Hake (1966) alternated periods of reinforced responding with periods during which reinforcers were not available, each signaled by a distinctive stimulus. Two pigeons were present in the apparatus, but only one could respond and receive the food; the other was restrained in a box that allowed its upper body and head to protrude. During the periods of nonreinforcement, the free pigeon attacked the other.

Kelly and Hake (1970) showed that extinction also elicits aggression in humans. They provided three response mechanisms: a knob operated by a pull of 3 lb (6.6 kg), a button requiring a push of 1.5 lb (3.3 kg), and a padded cushion that operated a switch when a force of at least 20 lb (44 kg) was exerted. Every 200 pulls of the knob produced money. Simultaneously, operation of either the button or the cushion avoided the presentation of a loud noise. The subjects were informed about the consequences of each response, i.e., that money was earned by knob-pulling and that noise was avoided or terminated by either of the other two responses. Both knob-pulling and an avoidance response were maintained, but at least 95% of the avoidance-escape responses were button presses. Then, the conditions were changed so that knob-pulls had no consequences (extinction). During the extinction period, all of the subjects emitted many responses to the cushion; given the force required, such responses amounted to vigorous punches. A control experiment showed that subjects would not simply emit some other avoidance-escape response when responses no longer earned money; the only one so affected was forceful punching of the cushion. The behavior closely resembled the attack of inanimate objects revealed during extinction in lower animals.

Certain schedules of food presentation can also elicit aggression. When food follows a fixed number of responses (fixed-ratio schedule) or follows the first response emitted after a constant period of time has elapsed (fixed-interval schedule), animals will attack another organism in the period just after food presentation (Gentry, 1968; Richards & Rilling, 1972).

The extensive literature on aggression shows a number of interesting relations. Attack can be reinforced as well as elicited. Azrin and Hutchinson (1967) gave pigeons food dependent on attacking another pigeon and found that the frequency of attack increased. Control conditions revealed that if the pigeons received food independent of their behavior, attack decreased. In addition to being reinforceable, the opportunity to attack can itself be reinforcing. Azrin, Hutchinson, and McLaughlin (1965) showed that if monkeys were being shocked, they would pull a chain if that response provided them with the opportunity to attack an inanimate object. In the absence of shock, they would not pull the chain. And, finally, shock-elicited aggression can be eliminated by delivering shock if attack occurs. Azrin (1970) found that shocks delivered independent of any response would elicit biting, but if bites then produced shock, the frequency of biting decreased. This is certainly a complex effect because a response was eliminated by presenting the stimulus that elicited it. Such data raise intriguing questions about the nature of elicitation: They suggest that a reflexive relation between a response and its eliciting stimulus may be modified by environmental consequences.

Species-Specific Approach Responses. Another type of behavior is elicited simply by pairing certain stimuli. When a stimulus appears briefly and occasionally and is followed by the presentation of food or the termination of shock, organisms will emit characteristic responses in the presence of the antecedent stimulus (Brown, P.L. & Jenkins, 1968; Rachlin, 1969). The particular response established is not arbitrary; on the contrary, it seems to be the one typically emitted by the species in interacting with salient events in the environment. Pigeons peck, rats paw or mouth, primates (including humans) touch the stimulus. The effect is reminiscent of Pavlovian conditioning in that an originally neutral stimulus comes to control a specific response because it reliably precedes a second stimulus. P. L. Brown and Jenkins (1968) referred to the effect as *autoshaping:* the particular response is shaped automatically via the pairing of stimuli.

The power of the S-S pairing in establishing conditioned approach responses is evident from other experiments. D. R. Williams and Williams (1969) presented a stimulus and followed it with food only if a pigeon did not peck; if a peck occurred, the stimulus terminated without food presentation (this differs from the autoshaping procedure in that pecking precluded food). Pecks occurred anyway. The approach response (pecking) was produced by this S-S relation and was not eliminated by the negative relation between the response and food. Whenever the pigeons pecked, the antecedent stimulus was not followed by food. The result was disruption of the S-S relation, and pecking disappeared. Then, however, the stimulus was once again paired with food, and pecking was reinstated. Apparently, species emit characteristic approach responses to stimuli that predict important events.

Summary. Reinforcing stimuli have numerous effects on behavior, and these effects can occur simultaneously. Reinforcers strengthen responses that are required to precede them; they strengthen responses that happen to precede them as well. In addition many reinforcers elicit certain responses that then come under the control of antecedent stimuli via Pavlovian conditioning. They also elicit a response previously but no longer probable. Also, certain stimuli elicit aggression: the stimuli having such an effect are not restricted to noxious events, even though these do reliably produce fighting. A positively reinforcing event is followed by aggressive behavior if the reinforcer appears according to certain schedules. Add to this that a stimulus preceding a reinforcing event will come to control species-specific approach responses, and the complexity of reinforcer presentation increases. A reinforcer delivery is a simply specified event that has multiple effects on behavior.

The sophisticated application of the principles of behavior requires sensitivity to the various properties of reinforcing stimuli, because only then is it possible to understand why a given type of behavior may be occurring. In the classroom, for example, children may fight or be disruptive because such behavior is followed by attention (an effective reinforcer for humans), or because some other response is no longer being reinforced (extinction-elicited aggression), or because it is elicited by the reinforcer used for some other response. Or, a child might bother an adult (approach near or touch an adult) not because that behavior is followed by a reinforcer but because that adult might often be correlated with the dispensation of reinforcers; this is a characteristic approach response of humans that comes under the control of an antecedent stimulus. Only careful observation and manipulation of the interactions between the child and salient features of the environment (including other people) will indicate why a given response is occurring and how it can be maintained or attenuated.

Conditioned Reinforcement

In human behavior reinforcing events often do not have direct biological significance. A plausible case can be made that whereas much infrahuman behavior is controlled by food, water, and other necessities, adult human activity is strongly influenced by stimuli that have no intrinsic significance. These stimuli develop their reinforcing ability through experience; they are known as *conditioned reinforcers*.

A stimulus paired with an unconditioned reinforcer (one that is reinforcing when first studied) will itself acquire reinforcing properties. For example, Kelleher (1961) showed that when responses produced a sound followed by food presentation, the sound alone could later support responding. However, the stimulus eventually loses its reinforcing properties if the pairing with an unconditioned reinforcer is abandoned permanently. This has its counterpart outside of the laboratory. Confederate money or the prewar German mark once were highly valued reinforcers but now have lost that property except to collectors.

Stimuli that continue to be at least occasionally correlated with an unconditioned reinforcer retain their reinforcing ability indefinitely. Consider a simple schedule of reinforcement in which a reinforcer follows the first response occurring after some regular time period has elapsed (fixed-interval schedule). Now suppose that the subject has to complete not one but three fixed intervals to produce food. Stimuli may be introduced into this situation in several ways. One is to have a different stimulus present during each successive fixed interval with food appearing when the third is completed. Or the same stimulus could be present during all three fixed intervals, but the completion of each produces a brief stimulus (e.g., a 0.5-sec. flash of light) with the third stimulus followed by food. These two arrangements can both maintain responding, and the stimuli used in either are durable conditioned reinforcers (Kelleher, 1966a,b; Marr, 1969, 1971).

Under certain conditions, responding will not be maintained. If a different stimulus is present for the duration of each component and more than three components must be completed before food presentation, responding may not be sustained. In contrast, responding will be maintained in numerous components if the only stimulus is the brief flash of light at the conclusion of each (Findley & Brady, 1965; Kelleher, 1966a; Lee & Gollub, 1971). Findley and Brady (1965) got chimpanzees to emit 120,000 responses per food presentation by breaking the total requirement into smaller sequences each followed by a brief stimulus, with only the last followed by food presentation. In human behavior, smiles or praise resemble brief stimuli, because they occur and disappear instead of being continuously present. They will therefore maintain much behavior.

The reason that brief stimulus presentations maintain extended sequences of behavior more effectively than do different distinctive stimuli correlated with each component involves the discriminative properties of the stimuli. With distinctive stimuli, the stimulus of the initial component is never correlated with the unconditioned reinforcer, and thereby indicates that the reinforcer is not presently available. This effect can be circumvented by having the stimuli appear in a random order (Kelleher & Fry, 1962), or by varying the number of components required (Findley, 1962), or by having the first stimulus recur in components after the first and also when the unconditioned reinforcer appears (Byrd, 1971).

In these ways the initial stimulus is at least occasionally correlated with the appearance of the unconditioned reinforcer. When a brief stimulus following each component is the only event preceding food presentation, no distinctive stimulus indicates which component is in effect, and therefore no cue indicates the availability of a reinforcer. The only potential source of discriminative control is the unconditioned reinforcer, because responses may never be reinforced right after reinforcement. Responding may be somewhat depressed, but the suppression is transitory.

It is essential to recognize the potential response-suppressing discriminative properties of reinforcing stimuli whenever it is deemed necessary to establish effective conditioned reinforcers. The effective use of a token economy requires sensitivity to this phenomenon. Kelleher (1958b) studied token reinforcement in chimpanzees. When 50 tokens were necessary to obtain food, responding was not well supported. Instead, there were very long pauses. If food required 100 tokens, however, but the animal was given 50 at the outset, responding was maintained even though 50 tokens still had to be earned. Having no tokens is readily discriminable from having 50, but apparently having 50 is not so well discriminated from having 100. In other words conditioned reinforcers operate most effectively when minimal observable stimuli differentiate the start from the end of an extended sequence.

Occasional pairing with an unconditioned reinforcer reliably establishes and maintains the effectiveness of a conditioned reinforcer. This does not mean, however, that pairing is absolutely necessary; in fact stimuli may acquire strong reinforcing ability even when they are never paired with an unconditioned reinforcer (Stubbs, 1971). A stimulus that clearly demarcates the completion of a response sequence may be reinforcing even if that particular stimulus never occurs in close temporal contiguity to the unconditioned reinforcer. The stimulus will not maintain its reinforcing ability, however, unless unconditioned reinforcers occur at least occasionally. Thus whether or not established by pairing with an unconditioned reinforcer, a stimulus that has become an effective reinforcer will not retain that ability indefinitely unless some more basic reinforcer continues to be available.

Stimuli that provide information about the prevailing conditions of unconditioned reinforcement may acquire reinforcing ability. Kelleher (1958c) made two telegraph keys available to chimpanzees. Irregular numbers of responses on one key resulted in food presentation (a variable-ratio schedule), but sometimes responses to that key had no effect (extinction). No stimulus indicated which schedule was in effect. Responses to the other key lit a window with a red lamp if the variable-ratio schedule operated and with a blue lamp if extinction was in effect. The chimpanzees pressed the second key, thereby obtaining information about the conditions of reinforcement. Responding to the stimulus-producing key was maintained by the lights, i.e., they were conditioned reinforcers. Subsequent work on this "observing response" procedure demonstrated that when a stimulus indicates the prevailing reinforcement conditions, it will acquire reinforcing ability. This operation, like pairing, will generate conditioned reinforcement.

The minimal necessary condition for establishing conditioned reinforcers is still uncertain. Pairing with unconditioned reinforcers is effective but not always essential, and providing information about prevailing reinforcement conditions is also effective. Whatever the ultimate explanation of conditioned reinforcement, a variety of procedures are available for converting a neutral to a reinforcing stimulus.

THE DEVELOPMENT AND MAINTENANCE OF BEHAVIOR

A given response has some frequency in the absence of any experimental treatment; this frequency is the *baseline or operant level*. It may vary with time of day (Premack & Bahwell, 1959) or deprivation of the opportunity to make the response (Kaye, H., 1967). Schoenfeld, Antonitis, and Bersh (1950) found that operant-level barpressing in rats decreased with successive tests as well as in successive periods of each test. A given operant level, therefore, is not a basic characteristic of either the response or the organism emitting it, but instead represents an interaction between a tendency to respond and environmental events.

The Development of Responses

Responses with a nonzero operant level often can be made more frequent by arranging that they be followed by a potent stimulus according to the R-S procedure. This, however, may not be the optimal procedure for making the response more probable, nor can it be effective if the operant level is zero. For example, one cannot teach a child to read by waiting for the appropriate response to be emitted spontaneously. Certain procedures for producing responses have already been discussed. If the response of interest can be elicited by a stimulus, it can be made to occur in a new situation via Pavlovian conditioning, by arranging that the stimulus occur in the situation. Once the response has been conditioned in this way, its frequency can be increased still further by arranging appropriate consequences for its occurrence. Siqueland and Lipsitt (1966) generated a high level of headturning in newborn infants by first eliciting turns with a stroke of the cheek, and then following such turns by the presentation of milk. Or, autoshaping can bring approach responses under the control of a stimulus. For the most part, though, the responses that can be manipulated in such ways are usually of lesser concern than are those not so easily related to an eliciting stimulus.

The problem is to generate the response. Among the methods for doing so are verbal instructions, modeling, guidance, and successive approximations.

1. *Instructions.* With humans it is often possible to produce a response by telling the person what to do or by asking him to do it. Once the response is emitted, it can then be reinforced. For example, Ayllon and Azrin (1964) wanted mental patients to pick up their eating utensils when going through a cafeteria line. Simply providing access to desirable items if the patients happened to pick up the utensils had little effect. When the patients were instructed to take utensils and then obtained the desirable items for doing so, the desired behavior occurred frequently. It is important to note that instructions alone resulted in some improvement, but a high level of behavior was obtained by initiating the response with instructions and then by following the response with a reinforcing stimulus.

Everyday experience testifies that instructions can generate a response. This procedure is effective, however, only if the organism has the readiness to respond to verbal stimuli and the ability to execute the response. This is not always the case with humans, nor is the ability to obey instructions likely to be more than minimally present in infrahumans without special training. If readiness to respond to instructions can be developed, it can be an excellent procedure, if not, some other technique is necessary.

2. *Modeling.* Another way of generating a response is by modeling it, i.e., by having the person imitate it. Children will imitate many responses if the imitation of even a few is followed by a reinforcing event. Baer and Sherman (1965) had nursery school children sit opposite a puppet that could nod its head, open and close its mouth, press a bar, and talk. The puppet verbally approved when the child imitated verbalizations, nods, and mouthings, and these responses were frequently imitated. In addition the child imitated barpresses, even though these imitations were never reinforced or provoked by instructions. Generalized imitation was established by explicit reinforcement of a few specific imitative responses.

As with instructions, modeling can be effective in generating the desired response. Imitation, however, is a learned response (see Chapter 5). Although it is an important method of learning in normal humans, it must itself be learned. It does not occur readily with lower organisms (e.g., Thorndike, 1911). Some other technique is necessary to develop imitation, but once it occurs it can be used to advantage in teaching new responses.

3. *Guidance*. Another procedure entails the manual guidance of the response by the teacher. For example, the teacher might raise a dog's paw or might clasp a child's hand to a spoon while using the spoon to feed him. Few published experiments have evaluated guidance procedures, but there is a good deal of laboratory lore and experience. A fine line separates guidance from coercion. When that line is crossed, there is so much resistance that the organism tries to escape the situation rather than be guided. Gentle handling can avoid this problem. Konorski (1967), who called the procedure "putting through," showed that guidance combined with reinforcement can be used effectively with lower animals. Foxx and Azrin (1973b) have provided a detailed description of how to guide humans effectively.

A highly effective procedure combines guidance, reinforcement, and the gradual withdrawal of manual support. In many cases an entire behavioral sequence can be guided and then assistance can be gradually withdrawn starting with the final response of the chain. This is known as *backward shaping* because it teaches the last segment of an entire response chain first. Backward shaping is illustrated in procedures used to teach a profoundly retarded girl to feed herself (Zeiler & Jervey, 1968). Initially, the girl's hand was clasped to a spoon while the spoon was loaded with food and brought to her mouth. Then her hand was released, and she placed the spoon in her mouth and ate. Training was conducted by releasing the spoon progressively earlier in the sequence. After 46 sessions, the girl was feeding herself without assistance. Before this training a variety of techniques had been used to try to get her to feed herself (modeling, instructions, teaching her the first part of the sequence first), but none had been successful. Backward shaping accomplished the goal.

In less than one hour, nursery school children have been taught to tie their own shoes by backward shaping (teach pulling the bows tight first, then work progressively backward) when other methods required weeks or were completely unsuccessful. Children have also been taught to write their names in the same way. First, their hands were guided in writing their entire names; then they were guided for all but the last part of the last letter; then for all but the last half of that letter; then for all but the last letter; then for parts of the next-to-last letter; and so forth until the entire name was written independently. Nursery school teachers reported this was the most effective teaching procedure they had ever used.

Backward shaping requires dividing the sequence into steps, each of which must be taught in reverse order. Step size is important; if the step is too large, the behavior may be lost, and it may be necessary to begin again. If the steps are too small, responding may become overly stereotyped and will not progress at optimal speed. If used properly, backward shaping is an excellent way to develop a unified sequence of responses.

Extended sequences must be established with care. Redd, Sidman, and Fletcher (1974) required monkeys to press keys in a certain sequence. New requirements were added to the first part of the sequence after smaller segments had been mastered. Incorrect responses resulted during a period of time in which no reinforcer was available. The monkeys responded correctly until there were seven or eight components. With larger requirements, they began to make errors and thereby terminated the sequence and the stimulus conditions correlated with it. Further analysis revealed that the termination of the sequence was itself reinforcing, i.e., the errors were actually being reinforced. Whenever the delivery of a reinforcer depends on the emission of a certain number of responses, early parts of the sequence are not themselves correlated with reinforcer delivery and may become aversive. Similar escape responses occur at the beginning of schedules of reinforcement that require the emission of a set number of responses (Azrin, 1961; Thompson, 1964). Such schedules and the behavioral sequences studied by Redd et al. share the property that reinforcers were never available just after another reinforcer had occurred, so that these time periods became discriminative stimuli correlated with extinction. This state of affairs may arise in classrooms or in any situation where the response requirement becomes too large.

Backward shaping draws its efficacy from conditioned reinforcement. It has long been known that when animals learn series of responses (e.g., running a multiple unit maze requiring a series of choices), the final choice point is learned first and then the others are mastered in a backward order. The reasons for this are complex. A correct choice at the final point is followed by food (or some other unconditioned reinforcer), so that the stimuli correlated with that point occur in a close relation to food. Stimuli paired with or correlated with an unconditioned reinforcer themselves take on reinforcing properties. Once that occurs, correct choices at the penultimate point are followed by the conditioned reinforcer (the final point) and thereby increase in probability. Now the stimuli correlated with the penultimate point become reinforcing, increase the probability of a correct response at the preceding point, and so forth until the entire maze is traversed correctly. In backward shaping, events are arranged so that the last response is emitted, is reinforced, and thereby the correlated stimuli become reinforcing and can establish the next earlier step in the sequence.

4. *Successive Approximations.* Successive approximations, or forward shaping, is the classic procedure for developing new responses. It

involves carefully observing ongoing behavior and picking out the response closest to the one desired, no matter how remote the correspondence may be. For example, if a mute child is to be taught to speak, the closest behavior to speaking might be occasional lip or mouth movements. By delivering a reinforcer following such movements, mouthing will become more prevalent and more extreme instances will occur. These can then be built into still more extreme movements, then into sounds, and finally into articulate speech. Skinner (1953a) has likened the process to sculpting: the artist knows the desired product but begins with an unformed piece of clay that is molded step by step until the product is attained.

Successive approximations can be laborious, and are probably not the method of choice if the response can be made to occur in some other way. It can be used when all else fails, however, because it draws on the fundamental properties of reinforcement and extinction in achieving its effects. Response differentiation indicates how and why forward shaping works.

Response Differentiation

Any response has a form, a location, and a duration; many have intensity as well. Form refers to how the response is executed (e.g., with hand, foot, mouth, etc.), location to spatial locus, duration to the temporal aspect of the response, and intensity to the force. Response shaping is often concerned with changing form although it may involve intensity and duration as well.

When a response is reinforced without respect to any of these properties, responding becomes stereotyped. (It is important to note that form, location, force, or duration are never completely unspecified because the response must always be emitted in some specific location, in some form, and must have some minimal force or duration to be registered.) Guthrie and Horton (1946) studied response form while giving cats food whenever they made contact with a pole. Although the precise way in which the pole was contacted was irrelevant, a given cat demonstrated stereotyped responding, i.e., it always hit the pole with the same paw or with the nose or with the hip, etc. Thus, even in the absence of specific requirements, the form of the response become constant. Similarly, Skinner (1938) found that when barpresses of any force or duration were followed by food only a restricted range of forces and durations came to predominate.

Extinction, like reinforcement, has characteristic effects. Skinner (1938) found three effects of extinction on barpressing: variability of forces and durations increased; presses became more forceful than when they had produced food; and responses eventually became less forceful with continued exposure to extinction. These general effects have been replicated often. For example, Antonitis (1951) observed them with respect to response locus, making the additional observation that with repeated cycles of reinforcement and extinction, the locus became increasingly stereotyped in each successive reconditioning phase.

When specific requirements are placed on a response property, behavior shifts in the direction of the requirement, whether the specification refers to force or to duration. Notterman and Mintz (1962) demonstrated the precision of control by presenting two stimuli to rats. In the presence of one, food was available for barpresses having forces between 5 and 10 g; in the presence of the other, forces had to be between 15 and 20 g. Probability distributions of emitted forces revealed peaks in the range appropriate for food presentation for each stimulus: during the first stimulus, the peak was between 5 and 10 g; during the other, it was between 15 and 20 g.

When a precise range of values of a property is specified, behavior may become increasingly stereotyped. For example, Herrick (1964) divided the distance through which a lever moved into eight sections. Food was given only if the bar was pressed to an intermediate area, and responses became concentrated at that point. Then, extinction was imposed. The effect was to increase the mean excursion of the bar, and to make the excursions more variable. Once again, reinforcement stereotyped the response and extinction made it both more variable and temporarily more intense.

These properties of reinforcement and extinction enable new behavior to develop and are the source of the effectiveness of successive approximations. Skinner (1938) obtained barpresses with forces of 100 g by progressively raising the force requirement. At each step food presentations established appropriate behavior. When the force requirement was increased, the initially emitted presses were not sufficiently intense to produce food, but nonreinforcement generated forces that met the new specification. These, then, came to predominate via reinforcement. The next change again resulted in nonreinforcement and in variability so that some responses met the new criterion, and force became stereotyped at the new level. Raising requirements in steps that are too large loses responding because the forces required are beyond the range produced by extinction at that time. If the specified behavior falls well outside of the range being emitted at the time the new criterion is imposed, responding may stop. For example, if a rat presses a bar with a range of forces never exceeding 30 g and the initial effects of extinction are to produce presses having forces no greater than 50 g, a requirement of 100 g will not come to control performance. Instead, there will be no reinforcers, and the response will return to its operant level. But if each requirement is imposed when the current performance encompasses the new value or if extinction will generate such a value, responding can be changed systematically.

Lower intensity responses can also be shaped, but more slowly. Weaker responses do not occur until the second phase of extinction, i.e., after the initial intensification. When the response finally becomes less forceful, it is followed by food presentation, becomes stereotyped, and thereby changes. Although this sort of downward shaping may take longer than the shaping of more forceful responses, large changes in requirements will not lose responding. The loudness of speech perhaps provides a good example. If an experimenter or a teacher requires very soft speech, many utterances will probably be emitted without reinforcement. At first the person is likely to speak more loudly, perhaps even to shout. As the probability of responding then weakens, shouting changes to muttering and grumbling, and finally the appropriate loudness occurs. So, where soft speech might be shaped without moving in small steps, durable loud talking would require a careful progression.

Thus, extinction is responsible for variability and the initial occurrence of a new response. Reinforcement stereotypes the behavior generated by extinction; it, in itself, will not generate novel behavior. The interplay of the two procedures is the essence of differential reinforcement by successive approximations, or shaping.

Schedules of Reinforcement

Once a response has been established, it can be maintained by delivering a reinforcing stimulus according to a variety of criteria. It is perhaps only rarely outside the laboratory that a reinforcer follows every response; more typically, reinforcers occur intermittently with respect to a particular response. Continuous reinforcement, or the delivery of a reinforcer for each response, is just one of numerous arrangements. The particular prescription (schedule) for the presentation of a reinforcer can involve time, responses, or a combination of both.

Schedules are classified in terms of the prerequisities they establish for reinforcer delivery. In *time schedules*, the stimulus appears whenever a certain period of time has elapsed, independent of responses. Successive time periods can be of constant duration, in which case the schedule is fixed time (FT); or, successive time periods can be of irregular duration, in which case the schedule is variable time (VT). Time schedules were discussed previously in the discussion of superstitious behavior: they increase the probability of whatever response happens to precede the reinforcer. In *ratio schedules*, the reinforcer appears following a certain number of responses. This number may be constant (fixed-ratio, or FR, schedule), or it may be irregular (variable-ratio, or VR, schedule). Continuous reinforcement, or an FR 1 schedule, describes the lower limit on ratio size. Ratio schedules establish characteristic performances in a variety of species, including humans. Typically, responses are emitted at a moderate to high rate, and often an integrated series of responses is preceded by a pause. [Ferster and Skinner (1957) show characteristics of ratio-schedule performance in pigeons; E. R. Long, Hammack, May, and Campbell (1958) show ratio performance in children. Among many studies, these are the most detailed single sources.] Pausing prior to responding is more characteristic of fixed than of variable-ratio schedules, and increases as ratio size is increased (Felton & Lyon, 1966).

All schedules other than ratio and time schedules involve combinations of responses and time. In *interval schedules*, the first response after a specified period of time has elapsed is followed by the reinforcing stimulus. If the time period is constant, it is a fixed-interval (FI) schedule; if the time is irregular, it is a variable-interval (VI) schedule. (Interval schedules differ from time schedules in requiring a response after the specified time has elapsed.) Under fixed-interval schedules with very short interval durations, infrahumans emit responses at a generally steady and moderate rate; as the durations are increased, responding is preceded by a pause (see Ferster and Skinner, 1957, for a survey of interval performance). Once responding begins, it continues until reinforcer presentation. Under variable-interval schedules, responses are emitted at a steadier rate with a tendency for rate to increase somewhat as time elapses. Fine-grained analyses indicate that the particular selection of inter-reinforcement intervals affects the constancy of response rate (Catania & Reynolds, 1968). Humans show behavior similar to other species on variable-interval schedules, but are less consistent with fixed-interval schedules. In the absence of explicit instructions, whether they pause after reinforcer presentation or respond throughout the interval depends on the particular response involved (Gonzalez & Waller, 1974; Holland, 1957). Whether the rate is high, moderate, or low is affected by previous history. If humans have been exposed earlier to ratio schedules, their rate under fixed-interval schedules is likely to be high or moderate; if they have been exposed to schedules producing low rates, responses are likely to be emitted slowly under fixed-interval schedules (DeCasper & Zeiler, 1972; Long, E. R., 1962; Weiner, 1969).

Other schedules (differentiation schedules) involve the delivery of a reinforcer dependent on some characteristic of performance. For example, the reinforcer may be presented whenever a response has not occurred for a period of time; this is a differential-reinforcement-of-not responding (DRO) schedule. It is also called an $\bar{R} > t$ schedule, where the bar over the R indicates the absence of the response, and t indicates the time that must elapse without the response before the reinforcer can be presented. Such a schedule will eliminate the criterion response. In another common differentiation schedule, the reinforcer is presented only when a specified period of time has elapsed without a response and then the response occurs. This is known as an $IRT > t$ (time between successive responses must be greater than time t) or a differential-reinforcement-of-low-rate (DRL) schedule. This schedule establishes a fairly steady response rate with longer time parameters producing lower rates (Malott & Cumming, 1964).

Reinforcement schedules are of central importance in behavior. Even the most easily specified schedule exerts its effects because it automatically brings into play a complex of controlling variables. Consider, for example, fixed-interval schedules. They specify only that the reinforcing event will follow the first response occurring after a certain time period: they require a single response after a fixed recurring time cycle. The result is either many responses emitted at a constant rate or a pause followed by a transition to either an accelerating or steady rate. An important characteristic is that the number of responses varies from one interval to the next (Dews, 1970). Also, large values of this schedule maintain many responses per reinforcer (with pigeons, a 40-min fixed-interval schedule of food presentation easily maintains an average of 1500 responses per interval). Fixed-interval performance is determined by the interaction of numerous variables. The determinants include factors imposed by the schedule as well as factors that arise through the performance generated. The number of responses emitted can be attributed to reinforcement plus a characteristic inherent in interval schedules. The number of responses per reinforcer delivery can vary widely. This variability is responsible for the ability of interval schedules to maintain a high average number of responses per reinforcer. Thus, interval schedules maintain many responses because they require only one. In contrast, ratio schedules requiring as many as 300 responses typically maintain responding poorly because the reinforcer cannot occur following fewer or more than the specified number of responses. Although the decrement in responding when more than one response is required is apparently paradoxical, the relation illustrates the subtlety involved in the control of behavior by reinforcing stimuli. The essential point is that each particular arrangement for delivering reinforcers exerts distinctive effects because it imposes a unique conjunction of variables.

In general, behavior is affected by requirements and by ongoing behavior itself. This becomes apparent in the study of reinforcement schedules, where one learns how controlling variables and ongoing behavior interact to govern performance. Schedules illustrate the sorts of variables that determine behavior and offer a setting for studying important interactions between behavior and environmental demands. An understanding of how human behavior is maintained and modified requires sensitivity to the factors brought into play by only superficially simple environmental arrangements. Behavior under specific schedules is less important than is the concept of schedule control—the understanding that particular prescriptions for reinforcer delivery mold behavior with precision because they arrange that particular sets of variables operate automatically.

An organism is said to be motivated to the extent that it works hard to achieve a given end. It has been the custom in the past to use motivation to explain changes in responding. But responses will be emitted eagerly (at a high rate) or apathetically (at a low rate) depending on the current schedule. Thus, the particular schedule determines motivation. The concept of motivation is a label that has proven unnecessary to the psychologist who understands schedule effects and the historical factors that operate to make a given stimulus an effective reinforcer; it is equally irrelevant to an individual committed to understanding behavior.

Negative Reinforcement (Escape)

When a response increases in probability because it terminates a stimulus, the procedure is known as *negative reinforcement*. A number of experiments have enabled comparisons of negative with positive reinforcement.

A major difference between negative and positive reinforcement is in the relation of the response to the reinforcing event. In the positive case the stimulus (e.g., food) is absent before and during the period of responding and occurs after the response. This means that unconditioned responses to the reinforcer are not occurring until after the response of interest. In negative reinforcement, however, the stimulus (e.g., electric shock) is present before and during the period of responding, and unconditioned responses to it can interfere with the behavior of interest. For example, the pigeons' response to moderate- or high-intensity shock is to pull its head back (Smith, R. F., Gustavson, & Gregor, 1972), and this is obviously incompatible with keypecking. As a result, it can be difficult to train a pigeon to peck to escape shock. Careful training procedures are necessary, such as presenting the shock at a low intensity that does not elicit head withdrawal before increasing it to a moderate or strong level (Hineline & Rachlin, 1969). Once the response has been established, it can then be maintained even with a high-intensity shock. One must always be sensitive to responses elicited by a stimulus when using escape training to modify behavior. To the extent that the stimulus elicits emotional behavior, aggression, withdrawal from the situation, or other competing behavior, the procedure is likely to be ineffective.

Even when effective, escape conditioning often results in the perseveration of inappropriate and ineffective responses. Rats will press a bar to escape from intense light or electric shock, but barpressing also occurs when the stimulus is absent (Keehn, 1967; Keller, 1941). The extent to which perseverance deriving from negative reinforcement underlies the behavior classified as obsessive-compulsive in the clinic has never been fully analyzed.

For the most part, negative reinforcement parallels positive reinforcement. The pattern of responding in time depends upon the current schedule of stimulus termination. There is a pause followed by a high rate if a fixed number of responses are required to terminate the stimulus (Hineline & Rachlin, 1969; Winograd, E., 1965), a pause followed by positive acceleration if the stimulus is terminated according to a fixed-interval schedule (Hineline & Rachlin, 1969), a steady rate if termination is according to a variable-interval schedule (Dinsmoor & Winograd, 1958), and a low, steady rate if termination is according to a DRL schedule (Cohen, P.S., 1970). These schedule effects closely resemble those of positive reinforcement. In addition a stimulus correlated with a negative reinforcer will take on conditioned reinforcing properties (e.g., Azrin, Holz, Hake, & Ayllon, 1963), and such stimuli can acquire discriminative control (Hineline & Rachlin, 1969; Morse & Kelleher, 1966).

Avoidance

In avoidance procedures, a response prevents the occurrence of a stimulus. The history and theoretical significance of avoidance conditioning has been reviewed by Herrnstein (1969). Without recapitulating that involved history here, it can be summarized by indicating that much of it deals with the problem of identifying the reinforcing event. How can the nonpresentation of a stimulus be a reinforcer? Nevertheless, despite the apparent insubstantiality of the reinforcer, it now seems that the reinforcer is indeed the reduction in the frequency of the stimulus.

Research with humans has documented how avoidance procedures establish and maintain a response. Schmitt and Marwell (1971b) showed that avoidance can determine whether humans will cooperate with each other (see Chapter 7 for a detailed analysis of cooperation). Two subjects were studied simultaneously; each had two ways of earning money by barpressing. One way was working independently; the other required cooperation. To indicate readiness to cooperate, one of the subjects had to operate a switch. Then, if the other person was also willing to cooperate, when one pressed the bar immediately after the other, both earned money. The amount of money that could be earned for each task was adjusted until cooperation occurred. Each person also could make an additional response during the periods of cooperation. This other response (a "take response") gave the taker a certain amount of the partner's money. If a take response could not be avoided, the subjects would not cooperate, thereby preventing takes from ever occurring. Schmitt and Marwell (1971a) arranged that a light come on for a brief time period when the partner made a take response. If the person could cancel the take response by switching to the individual task during the light period, cooperation was maintained. Once again the subjects avoided monetary loss.

Avoidance responses occur whether or not the stimulus event is signaled. If the absence of lever pressing results in occasional shocks, animals will press the lever even when there is no warning signal that shock is impending (Sidman, 1953). If there is a signal that shock is about to occur, responses occur when the signal appears (Sidman & Boren, 1957).

Responses that prevent the withdrawal of a positive reinforcer can also be maintained. The opportunity to view cartoons is an effective reinforcer for young children (Zeiler & Kelley, 1969). Baer (1960) allowed children to watch cartoons, but the cartoons were turned off whenever the children abstained from pressing a bar for a period of time. If each response added to viewing time, barpressing was maintained. Thus, the children avoided the termination of the movie. Lower organisms will also respond to avoid a time during which positive reinforcers are unavailable. If, however, responding is maintained by the avoidance of some stimulus, then the organism will escape from the avoidance situation into one in which no reinforcers at all are available (Verhave, 1962). Thus, whether a particular setting is escaped or avoided or maintains behavior depends on whether it is the presentation of a negative event or the termination of a positive event that is avoided. Avoidance appears to be important in the classroom. Given the paucity of positive reinforcers available in many schools, much behavior is probably maintained by the avoidance of unpleasantness. A response that produces escape from the situation, even into one in which nothing at all happens, may be maintained.

THE ELIMINATION OF BEHAVIOR

The discussion to this point dealt with the acquisition and maintenance of a response. It is also necessary to understand how responses are reduced in frequency or even eliminated from the organism's repertoire. Frequently the problem confronted by teachers and therapists is that of undesirable behavior, be it class disruption, neurotic compulsions, self-destruction, or whatever.

Extinction

Discontinuing a reinforcing stimulus (extinction) reduces the frequency of the previously established response in either the R-S or S-R-S arrangements. The speed of the ensuing decrement in responding depends on many factors.

The number of experiences with extinction is important. A series of transitions from reinforcement to extinction makes responding decline more rapidly with each successive exposure to extinction (Bullock, 1960). In fact if each response was previously reinforced, after several transitions the response will stop after one or two extinction trials (Dufort, Guttman, & Kimble, 1954). In contrast, in the first exposure to extinction, responding is not eliminated immediately. Skinner (1938) showed that even a single reinforcer would generate more than 50 barpresses in subsequent extinction. Neuringer (1970) found that three food presentations sustained responding in extinction for over 150 responses. Without a prior history with extinction, therefore, many responses occur, and a single reinforcer establishes far more responses than a single unreinforced response removes.

After a response has been eliminated via extinction, responding may recur simply as a function of time. This phenomenon is known as spontaneous recovery; it typifies operant as well as Pavlovian conditioning.

The prior history of reinforcement affects how quickly extinction operates. The more often the response is reinforced, the more resistant it is to extinction (Hearst, 1961). Another well-documented phenomenon is the relation of resistance-to-extinction to the previous intermittency of reinforcement. Humphreys (1939) reported that a response reinforced according to a VR 2 schedule (50% of the responses were followed by a reinforcer in a random order) was emitted more frequently in extinction than if every response was reinforced. This became known as the partial-reinforcement-extinction effect, and has been demonstrated in many experiments (Robbins, 1971). A relation between degree of intermittency and responding during extinction has also been demonstrated: the more intermittent the reinforcer presentations, the more responses occur in extinction (Hearst, 1961; Weinstock, 1958).

Instructions can influence responding in the absence of reinforcement. Weiner (1970) told one group that points equivalent to pennies could be earned by pressing a button, and that only 700 pennies could be acquired. A second group was given the same instructions, differing only in that they were told that the maximum number of pennies was 999. A third group was given no information about the maximum number. For all groups, every tenth response incremented the counter, and extinction was in force after 700 points were earned. Thus, Group 1 was given accurate instructions, Group 2 was misled, and Group 3 had no information beyond that provided by the absence of further point additions beyond 700. During extinction, Group 1 responded the least and Group 3 responded the most. Apparently, any instruction indicating that extinction was to occur facilitated the decrement in responding, and accurate instructions facilitated it maximally. It would seem that one way of increasing the effectiveness of extinction is to tell the subject truthfully that it will occur. Lying can maintain the response, but only temporarily. Habitual lying will result in the loss of control by instructions since there ceases to be a correspondence between instructions and the response-reinforcer relation. Any antecedent stimulus that loses its predictive ability soon stops being an effective discriminative stimulus for the availability of reinforcement, and thereby stops controlling responding.

Although extinction reduces the frequency of a previously reinforced response, a variety of variables influence how quickly the reduction occurs and how durable the response may be. But extinction has another effect as well: It often intensifies a response before eliminating it. This property of extinction was discussed previously as an inherent aspect of shaping, where its utility was stressed. In the context of response elimination, extinction should be expected to produce more frequent and extreme instances of the target behavior than occurred when the response was followed by a reinforcer. In deciding whether to use extinction, therefore, the teacher or therapist should consider whether more extreme instances of the undesirable behavior are even temporarily tolerable. It would not be the procedure of choice if one were concerned with eliminating self-destruction or aggression. The problem becomes still more complicated outside the laboratory when the teacher is not certain that the reinforcer has been correctly identified. If in fact the reinforcer has not been discontinued because the teacher has wrongly hypothesized what is maintaining the response, enhancement could be due to either the intensifying property of extinction or the maintained reinforcement.

Extinction raises other problems as well. As was discussed earlier, it may elicit aggression directed at other individuals or even at inanimate objects. In addition organisms respond to escape from or to avoid a situation involving extinction. These factors must all be weighed in considering extinction as a method for eliminating a response.

Punishment

Punishment, like reinforcement, describes an interaction between stimulus presentation and behavior: the reduction in the probability of a response when the response is followed by a stimulus. Thus, it is the opposite of positive reinforcement. In positive reinforcement the presentation of a stimulus increases response probability; in punishment, the presentation of a stimulus decreases the probability. The effects of punishment are symmetrical and opposite to those of positive reinforcement unless the stimulus has discriminative properties indicating the nonavailability of a reinforcer.

Discriminative properties develop if the presentation of the stimulus is correlated with discontinuing a positive reinforcer. For example, W. K. Estes (1944) first followed barpresses with food according to an FI 4-min schedule and then changed the schedule to extinction. For half of the rats, each response produced an electric shock; for the remainder, responses had no consequences. The rats receiving shock stopped barpressing more rapidly than did the others, but when the shock was discontinued, responding quickly returned to a high level. The loss of responding via punishment, therefore, was temporary. But since shock appeared when extinction was instituted, it served as a stimulus (response-produced) indicating the nonavailability of food. The removal of that stimulus restored responding by reinstating the conditions previously correlated with food presentations, i.e., the absence of shock following each response.

Holz and Azrin (1961) showed that response-produced shock could indeed have a discriminative function. They alternated sessions of extinction with sessions in which food was presented on a VI 2-min schedule. When the VI schedule was in effect, each response also produced a brief shock. Response rates were high throughout the VI sessions and low during extinction sessions. Since rates during the VI sessions were higher even before the first food delivery (after which the reinforcer could have indicated that a session involving food presentations was in effect), the shock was serving as a discriminative stimulus for the availability of food. Ayllon and Azrin (1966) provided humans with equal reinforcer presentations for each of two responses and maintained both equally. If one of the responses also produced a brief period of noise presentation, that response stopped. If, however, noise followed one response and only that one produced the reinforcer, only that response occurred. Once again, a potentially punishing event could operate as a discriminative stimulus for the current reinforcement conditions. When Holz and Azrin (1962) imposed an FI food schedule, they demonstrated that a response-produced shock could be used as a stimulus to indicate either the availability or nonavailability of food. If responses during the first three quarters of the interval produced shock and those in the final quarter did not, responding was depressed in the initial three quarters. Responses were controlled in the same way when only responses in the fourth quarter produced shocks. Thus, shock either suppressed or enhanced responding depending on whether it was correlated with food presentation or extinction.

If the schedule of positive reinforcement is not altered when shock is presented after each response, the shock does not acquire discriminative properties that override durable punishing effects. Under such conditions a response can be reduced effectively and even permanently. Schedule effects symmetrical to those of food presentation can be observed. Azrin (1956) provided food on a VI schedule and shock according to either an FI, VI, FT, or VT schedule. With the FI or FT schedules, response rate progressively decreased as the time of shock approached. This is the reverse of the rate increase over time when food is presented on an FI or FT schedule. With VI or VT shock, response rate was generally steady; once again, the patterning was similar to that with comparable food schedules. Furthermore, the interval schedules (FI and VI) reduced rate more than the time schedules (FT and VT). This is symmetrical to what occurs with food presentation, where interval schedules produce higher rates than time schedules.

Azrin and Holz (1966) and Rachlin and Herrnstein (1969) describe other ways in which punishment operates opposite to positive reinforcement. There is a parallel in the effects of varying the magnitude of reinforcers and punishers. Increasing the amount of food presented may increase response rate; increasing the shock intensity may decrease rate. Choices between alternative responses are influenced by the frequency of food presentation and by the frequency of shock presentation. As a general rule, Thorndike's position of 1911 that the Law of Effect is symmetrical was correct.

To be maximally effective, the punishing stimulus must be intense (Azrin & Holz, 1966; Rachlin, 1967). If the intensity is increased gradually, adaptation occurs and punishment may not be observed. This is probably why punishment is often not observed when parents try to eliminate undesirable responses of their children: they start with mild admonitions and then gradually progress to more intense stimuli. Adaptation occurs, and even the final stimulus (e.g., spanking) is ineffective in eliminating the behavior, even though it might have been effective had it been used from the outset. If the stimulus is intense and delivered promptly after undesired behavior, it will eliminate the response. These guidelines have been followed to control a variety of undesirable activities. Following a response with a noxious stimulus, when used correctly, is the most effective way to eliminate the behavior.

Because stimuli like shock, intense noise and other aversive events raise serious ethical problems, alternatives have been sought. Several investigators have arranged that undesired responses produce a period when positive reinforcers are temporarily unavailable (a time-out period). Baer (1962) allowed children to watch cartoons. If they sucked their thumbs, the movie was turned off for a time; the result was that thumbsucking occurred less often. McMillan (1967) showed that response-produced time-out could be approximately equivalent to response-produced shock in eliminating a response.

Time-out, being a period of extinction, may elicit aggression and other side effects. In applied settings, however, there is a problem not typically confronted in the laboratory: knowing what is reinforcing the unwanted behavior in the first place. If it is in fact teacher attention or some other positive aspect of the environment, following the response with time-out should be effective. But, as discussed earlier, if the response is occurring because it avoids or terminates an aversive stimulus (e.g., nagging), time-out will be reinforcing rather than punishing and the response preceding it will increase in frequency. In short, one must know what the time-out is from to anticipate its effects, and this may be difficult to ascertain.

Another procedure that may result in punishing effects is known as *response cost*. Weiner (1962) arranged that humans earn points according to variable-interval and fixed-interval schedules. Each reinforcer consisted of a 100-point increment. If one point was subtracted for each response, the rate of responding decreased substantially; in some cases, the rate did not recover even when responses later cost nothing. Subsequent research confirmed that responding can be reduced if reinforcers are subtracted by responses.

Another punishment procedure that shows significant promise is called *overcorrection* (Foxx and Azrin, 1973a). With this technique, undesired behavior has enduringly been reduced to a near-zero level. Overcorrection consists of having the person either intensively undertake acceptable versions of the response or intensively make reparations for his activity. An example of reparation was reported by Foxx and Azrin with two retarded girls who excessively mouthed either objects or their hands. Because mouthing introduces bacteria into the mouth, each mouthing was followed by having the girls brush their teeth (guided or enforced by the therapist). Undertaking acceptable versions of an undesired response is exemplified by a boy who repetitively clapped his hands. Each hand clap was followed by a period in which the teacher guided the boy's hands in purposive movements (i.e., in following specific instructions such as putting the hands in pockets, holding them over his head, etc.) In both cases, the undesired response was eliminated with no apparent side effects.

With overcorrection, just as with the response-dependent presentation of an aversive stimulus, the teacher need not be concerned with eliminating or identifying the reinforcer maintaining the undesirable behavior. Instead, the procedure can be used even when the behavior is reinforced at the same time. This is not the case with response cost, because that procedure requires that an effective reinforcer be reduced in amount by negative instances of behavior; it is also not the case with response-produced time-out, because that procedure requires that the ongoing reinforcer be identified and eliminated.

Premack (1971b) reported experiments that may elucidate the factors operating in overcorrection. In his experiments rats were required to perform a nonpreferred response (running in an activity wheel) when they emitted a preferred response (drinking). The result was a marked reduction in drinking. These data suggest that the essence of overcorrection may be not any intrinsic relation between the undesired response and the one following it, but rather the requirement to engage in nonpreferred behavior. More research is necessary to clarify what is involved in overcorrection; nevertheless, requiring and guaranteeing that an undesired response be followed by some other low-probability response has considerable promise as an effective technique for response elimination. To the extent that the required low-probability response can itself be beneficial, the procedure seems uniquely suited to the elimination of undesirable and the establishment of desirable responses.

Reinforcement Procedures

Three procedures for eliminating a response involve the presentation of a positive reinforcer. In one the stimulus is presented independent of responses, according to a time schedule. If a response is maintained by a positive reinforcer, the delivery of a reinforcing stimulus independent of any response typically reduces the frequency. For example, if keypecking is maintained by the delivery of food according to a fixed-interval schedule, changing the schedule to fixed time reduces the rate of keypecking (Herrnstein, 1966; Zeiler, 1968). The reasons for the decrement were discussed earlier in the context of superstitious behavior. Frequently, the response will be eliminated; at other times, it will be reduced in frequency but will persist at a low level.

Another reinforcement procedure entails the delivery of a reinforcer dependent on the nonoccurrence of the response. Such an arrangement is known as a differential-reinforcement-of-not-responding (DRO) schedule, or simply as an $\bar{R} > t$ schedule. This schedule reduces responding. It operates sometimes slower and sometimes faster than extinction (Uhl & Garcia, 1969;

Zeiler, 1971). If a response was previously reinforced and then reinforcer presentations are discontinued, the addition of a $\overline{R} > t$ schedule can have beneficial effects. In addition the $\overline{R} > t$ schedule may more durably eliminate the response. Uhl and Sherman (1971) found that it was more difficult to reestablish a response eliminated by the $\overline{R} > t$ schedule than one eliminated by extinction, and Zeiler (1971) reported that only extinction resulted in spontaneous recovery.

The effectiveness of the $\overline{R} > t$ schedule and time schedules involving a small range of equal time values has been compared. J. Davis and Bitterman (1971) first established barpressing by arranging food presentations according to a VI 30-sec schedule. Rats were paired on the basis of their response rates during this initial phase. A food pellet was delivered to one member of each pair whenever a press did not occur for 10 sec. The second member of the pair received a pellet at the same time, but without regard to its behavior. Thus, the second rat was on a variable-time schedule equivalent to the $\overline{R} > t$ 10-sec schedule in frequency of food presentation. The $\overline{R} > t$ 10-sec schedule eliminated responding more effectively than the variable-time schedule. Delivering a reinforcer dependent on not emitting a certain response therefore reduces the frequency of that response more readily than response-independent reinforcer presentations.

The $\overline{R} > t$ schedule specifies that the response of interest cannot occur in close conjunction with the reinforcer. It does not control what other response might be emitted close in time to the reinforcer. Whatever other behavior happens to be emitted at that time may increase in frequency and come to predominate (Harman, 1973; Zeiler, 1970). This aspect of the $\overline{R} > t$ schedule is most important for the person interested in using the schedule to eliminate an undesirable response. Although the schedule can abolish the target response, one cannot predict what other response will be established. It might be more or less desirable than the original, but the schedule leaves that open in specifying only that the target response cannot be followed by the reinforcing event.

Vukelich and Hake (1971) demonstrated that the $\overline{R} > t$ schedule might eliminate a response that was reinforced at the same time. The concern was with a severely retarded female who choked people. Paying attention to the patient during periods of nonaggression in conjunction with time-out for aggression reduced choking more than did time-out alone. Thus, an $\overline{R} > t$ schedule helped to control the choking. Note that whatever reinforced the choking in the first place probably still occurred. Because, as with many undesirable responses, the practitioner often cannot identify the reinforcer of the response, the procedure used to eliminate the behavior is imposed in the context of maintained reinforcement. Yet the $\overline{R} > t$ schedule appears able to eliminate a response even under such circumstances.

Another positive reinforcement procedure for eliminating a response involves specifying a competing response. Of course, the nonemission of a certain response specifies behavior that competes with that response, and thus the $\bar{R} > t$ schedule does specify competing behavior. It does not, however, prescribe the form that the competing behavior must assume, but states only that the target response must not occur. A response can also be eliminated by specifying that some specific other behavior be a prerequisite for the delivery of the reinforcer. Demonstrating the effectiveness of such a procedure in the laboratory is not difficult. If keypecking was to be eliminated in a pigeon, discontinuing the reinforcer for pecks at the key and presenting it for pecks at the opposite wall would be effective. Outside the laboratory, though, it is not always simple to institute extinction for the undesired response while presenting a reinforcer for another. As mentioned earlier, this would require identifying the reinforcer responsible for the inappropriate behavior. There are no direct laboratory analyses of the effectiveness of reinforcing competing behavior while the undesired target behavior also continues to be followed by a reinforcing stimulus. The closest parallels occur in experiments involving the availability of two or more responses, each correlated with some schedule of reinforcement. The effects of such arrangements will be dealt with subsequently in the section on choice and preference; these data indicate that both responses are likely to be maintained, with the frequency of each related to the consequences arranged by each schedule.

Foxx and Azrin (1973b) rapidly toilet trained profoundly retarded people. Their technique involved the elimination of soiling by combining overcorrection with reinforcement. When found soiled, the person was required to wash the living area with disinfectant several times, to clean himself or herself repeatedly, and to indulge in other nonpreferred behavior including practicing toileting. This is overcorrection. In addition, when periodic checks revealed that the person had been clean for a while, a reinforcer was given (reinforcement for not soiling). But that was not all. Correct toileting was also facilitated by a combination of guidance and reinforcer presentation. Here is a sophisticated procedure that draws on numerous principles for eliminating and producing responses simultaneously, and it does so in such a way that all work in combination to produce success. Toilet training was accomplished in a few days, while traditional procedures met with total failure.

Undesired behavior may also be reduced by indirect procedures. H.L. Cohen and Filipczak (1971) were interested in developing academic skills in juvenile delinquents residing in a reformatory. As might be expected, these boys had a history of behavior that competed with effective learning. When Cohen and Filipczak had potent reinforcers depend on academic grades, the boys studied and read before taking the tests. Also, they attended classes. Thus, much of what can be assumed to have been their previous disruptive behavior in school settings was changed. Ayllon and Roberts (1974) provided more direct data. Five children in a fifth-grade class were identified as the most disruptive of a virtually uncontrollable group. They left their seats without permission, talked at inappropriate times, and physically contacted other students during study periods. In the training program the students earned points based on the percentage of items correctly answered in workbooks. Points could be exchanged for a variety of privileges. Academic achievement increased and disruptive behavior decreased simultaneously. Discontinuing points for workbook performance reinstated the disruptive behavior and reduced academic achievement. Thus, undesirable behavior was attenuated indirectly. The reinforcement of behavior that accomplishes educational goals while eliminating disruption indirectly contributes to an optimal educational environment. Success in a particular environment may be a generally effective component in eliminating disruptive and counter-productive activities.

STIMULUS CONTROL

Stimulus control refers to situations in which behavior is determined by the prevailing antecedent stimulus; it arises in the S-R-S dependency. No behavior is appropriate or inappropriate per se; it is classified as one or the other depending upon when it occurs. Hitting oneself on the head is inappropriate under many conditions; on the other hand, it is appropriate if a mosquito is perched on the forehead. Undressing in public is inappropriate, but undressing under other conditions is totally appropriate. The analysis of stimulus control explains how behavior comes to be emitted only under certain stimuls conditions. It also deals with exactly what aspect of a stimulus is actually controlling the behavior and how it comes to assert that control.

Behavior is under stimulus control when responding varies depending on what stimulus is present. Discriminative and conditioned stimuli are similar in that both precede the response and are reliably followed by the response. They do differ, however. For example, often a conditioned stimulus is followed by a response closely resembling that elicited by an unconditioned stimulus, whereas a discriminative stimulus controls a response different in form from that elicited by the reinforcer. The simplest distinction is that a conditioned stimulus occurs in the S-S dependency whereas a discriminative stimulus is the antecedent event in the S-R-S arrangement.

The S-R-S arrangement contains both the R-S and S-S relations. Since the R-S dependency is known to increase responding, the S-S component may be responsible for bringing the response under stimulus control. Several experiments involving the separate application of each arrangement, followed by their combination suggests that this may be the case. W.K. Estes (1943) initially presented food to rats on a fixed-interval schedule involving barpressing (R-S). Then the lever was withdrawn, and a tone was paired with food independent of response (S-S). Afterward the lever was reintroduced, but responses had no effect. Presentations of the tone during this extinction period increased the frequency of barpressing, i.e., the rate of pressing varied depending on whether or not the tone was present. Thus, the tone, a stimulus never correlated with reinforced barpressing, resulted in stimulus control of barpressing. Several experiments varied this general theme (Bower & Kaufman, 1963; Morse & Skinner, 1958; Trapold & Overmier, 1972), and all showed that R-S and S-S arrangements applied separately combine to give stimulus control like that produced by the S-R-S dependency.

Combinations of S-S and R-S dependencies show how signals influence ongoing responding. The effects depend on numerous factors, including the schedule of reinforcement correlated with the response, the duration of the signal, and the type of stimulus signaled. In the reference experiment, W.K. Estes and Skinner (1941) correlated a fixed-interval schedule with barpressing. Occasionally, a tone appeared and terminated with the delivery of a brief electric shock. Even though the fixed-interval schedule continued during the tone, responding stopped. This phenomenon, which has become known as *conditioned suppression*, indicates that a warning signal for shock will suppress ongoing responding. Note that it consists of superimposing an S-S dependency (tone-shock) on an R-S dependency (barpress-food). The basic Estes-Skinner design (superimposing a warning signal for a response-independent event on an R-S baseline) has been studied with other signaled events. Responding is suppressed if the warning signal is for the delivery of a positive reinforcer (Azrin & Hake, 1969). On the other hand, if the baseline schedule is shock avoidance and the signal is for shock, responding is enhanced during the signal (Sidman, Herrnstein, & Conrad, 1957). Signaled schedule changes also have effects. Pliskoff (1963) showed that if a signal indicated a forthcoming change to one of two variable-interval schedules, response rate was suppressed during the signal for a high-valued schedule and enhanced during the signal for a low-valued schedule. In other words, warning signals can alter ongoing behavior, or, stated differently, R-S and S-S dependencies can interact.

Determinants of Stimulus Control

Several factors influence the development of stimulus control. One, of course, is the discriminability of the stimuli. For responding to depend on the presence or the absence of a given stimulus, the stimulus must be detectable; for one stimulus to control responding differently than another, the difference must be discriminable.

A second factor influencing stimulus control is the way the stimuli are presented. Given two stimuli, they can appear either simultaneously or successively. If the presentation is simultaneous, the organism must choose between them, unless it is possible to respond to both at the same time; if successive, the organism does or does not respond (or responds differently) in the presence of each.

A simultaneous discrimination is one of a class of arrangements known as *concurrent schedules.* In concurrent schedules two or more stimuli are presented simultaneously, and the organism is free to choose between them. Concurrent schedules may take several different forms (see Catania, 1966, for a review), but the essential effects are common to all. A successive discrimination is one type of *multiple schedule.* In multiple schedules, two or more stimuli are presented one at a time. The organism may or may not respond to each, but has no control over which is available. Simultaneous and successive discriminations therefore differ in how stimuli are presented; in both cases, the terms usually refer to cases in which responding to only one of the stimuli is correlated with reinforcer presentation.

    Concurrent Schedules. Findley (1958) pointed out that responding to one stimulus may be followed closely in time by a reinforcer delivered for responding to the other stimulus. Consider, for example, one stimulus correlated with a VI schedule, and the other correlated with extinction. Although only responses to the first stimulus are ever followed by the reinforcer, the subject might sometimes respond to the second stimulus. The longer the period of responding to that stimulus, the more likely it is that the reinforcer will be available for the next response to the VI stimulus. Hence, switching responses from one stimulus to the other are followed immediately by the reinforcer, and the response of switching is reinforced. Findley demonstrated that this in fact occurs. Reinforcement of switching is prevented when alternating responses to the two stimuli cannot be immediately followed by a reinforcer. This is accomplished by the changeover delay (COD) described by Herrnstein (1961). Each time the organism changes stimuli, a response to the new stimulus cannot produce a reinforcer for a specific time. So, in the concurrent variable-interval extinction schedule above, if the reinforcer should become available while the organism is responding to the extinction stimulus, the first response to the variable-interval stimulus is not followed by a reinforcer. Instead, the first response to that stimulus after the COD elapses is followed by the reinforcer. If the subject happens to return to the extinction stimulus during the COD period, the COD is reinitiated by the next response to the VI stimulus. The COD guarantees at least two successive responses to the VI stimulus before reinforcer presentation; it also ensures that alternating responding to both stimuli is separated from the reinforcer by at least the duration of the COD. Times as short as one-sec appear effective in reducing the effect of the reinforcer on switching.

    With a COD, preferences among the stimuli are controlled by the *frequency of reinforcement* correlated with each stimulus. Herrnstein (1961) calculated the proportion of the total reinforcers correlated with one of two stimuli and the proportion of the total responses to that stimulus. The two proportions, relative frequency of reinforcement and relative responding, approximately matched over a wide range of schedule values. Others replicated this matching function with a variety of concurrent schedules involving combinations of VI schedules. Responding in concurrent schedules is also proportional to the relative amount of reinforcement and relative delay of reinforcement correlated with each stimulus. (The literature is extensive: see Catania, 1966; Fantino, 1977; Herrnstein, 1970, for reviews, critiques, and discussions of theoretical implications and extensions.) The matching law relating responding to relative reinforcement frequency, magnitude, and delay (Herrnstein, 1970) has resulted in many experimental analyses, and has described responding in concurrent schedules.

Multiple Schedules. Quantitative analyses of responding in multiple schedules are more recent than such analyses of concurrent schedules. Lander and Irwin (1968) and Nevin (1974a) described relative response rates in each component of a multiple schedule when the stimuli alternate at fairly short intervals, and Nevin (1974b) analyzed changes in absolute rate in multiple schedules having longer components. Herrnstein (1970) hypothesized that the matching law can describe response rate in multiple as well as simple and concurrent schedules when uncontrolled responses and sources of reinforcement are taken into account. This generalized matching law lends itself to formal analysis and may prove an integrating theoretical principle (cf., Herrnstein, 1974).

Responding in each component of a multiple schedule can be affected by what goes on in other components. One such effect is that a reinforcer presentation correlated with one component can maintain responding in another. Morse (1955) found that responses were maintained in a stimulus correlated with extinction when they were followed closely by the appearance of another stimulus correlated with the availability of food. If two stimuli alternate either regularly or in a random pattern, responses in the presence of one can be followed almost immediately by a change to the other stimulus. Since stimuli paired with an unconditioned reinforcer typically acquire conditioned reinforcing properties, the response to one stimulus can be maintained by the appearance of the other, i.e., the conditioned reinforcer. Manipulations analogous to those used to eliminate the reinforcement of switching in concurrent schedules can prevent conditioned reinforcement from maintaining responding in a multiple schedule. Morse showed that responses in the presence of the extinction stimulus were attenuated when such responses could not be followed immediately by a stimulus change. If each response in extinction prolongs the period of extinction, these responses are eliminated.

Interactions occur when the schedule correlated with one stimulus is held constant while that correlated with the other stimulus is varied. Reynolds (1961a) described four interactions: (1) *positive contrast:* the response rate in the varied component decreases and that in the constant component increases; (2) *negative contrast:* the response rate in the varied component increases and that in the constant component decreases; (3) *positive induction:* the response rate increases in both components; (4) *negative induction:* the response rate decreases in both components. These four interactions show that what happens in the varied component influences behavior in the constant component; because the experimenter has not altered the schedule in the constant component, the changes in that behavior must be due to the alterations imposed in the varied component. The effects of changes in the conditions correlated with one stimulus on performance controlled by different stimuli has not been examined explicitly in applied research, even though the experimental data clearly indicate a high potential for important influences. Perhaps the changes produced deliberately in one kind of behavior regularly produce unsuspected changes in other responses.

In summary, whether discriminative stimuli are presented simultaneously in a concurrent schedule or successively in a multiple schedule, the reinforcement conditions correlated with one stimulus can influence behavior correlated with the other. Behavior comes under the control of each stimulus, while at the same time the specific performances can be the outcome of interactions among all of the stimuli.

Scheduling Factors in Stimulus Control

In successive discriminations, extinction is correlated with all but one stimulus (S+). Responding decreases during the stimuli correlated with extinction (S−) and may finally disappear altogether. Thus, stimulus control derives from the combination of reinforced responding during S+ and nonreinforced responding during S−. Terrace (1963) showed, however, that nonreinforced responding is not essential. When S− is presented at low intensity and for very short time periods, no responding occurs. It is then possible to increase the intensity and prolong the stimulus gradually without the organism ever responding. Finally, when S− appears at high intensity and for the same period as S+, still no responses occur, while responses continue at a high rate during S+. Terrace called this performance an *errorless discrimination*.

Research like Terrace's demonstrates that it is not necessary to make mistakes in order to learn and provides an experimental foundation for the development of programmed instruction (see Chapter 13). Sidman and Stoddard (1967) showed that errorless simultaneous discrimination performance could be developed in children. Furthermore, they found that discriminations that could not be learned using traditional trial-and-error procedures would be learned if the negative stimuli were introduced in progressive stages, so that errors did not occur. Stoddard and Sidman (1967) and Touchette (1968) showed that if discriminations were made progressively more difficult, children could make finer discriminations than were otherwise possible. These fading procedures, used to produce difficult discriminations, seem analogous to the shaping procedures used to generate responses.

This work demonstrates that the way stimulus presentations are arranged crucially influences stimulus control (see Chapters 10 and 11 for further analyses and applications). The way reinforcing stimuli are arranged also makes a difference. The particular schedule of reinforcement correlated with a particular stimulus will affect how well that stimulus controls behavior. For example, Hearst (1962) found that a stimulus correlated with a VI schedule controlled performance, but one correlated with a schedule of shock avoidance did not. Different schedules of food presentation have distinctive effects as well. Fixed-ratio and variable-interval schedules consistently produce more accurate discriminations than do IRT > t schedules, and sometimes produce sharper control than fixed-interval and variable-ratio schedules (Hearst, Koresko, & Poppen, 1964; Zeiler, 1969). In successive discriminations a fixed-ratio schedule in the presence of a particular stimulus will produce at least as good, and often better, control by that stimulus than will any other schedule. In simultaneous discriminations particular schedules seem to make less difference.

To summarize, stimulus control is determined by the discriminability of stimuli, by whether stimuli appear simultaneously or successively, by the way the stimuli are introduced, and by the schedule according to which responses are reinforced. Interactions among the components in discrimination situations show that while responding may differ depending on the current stimulus, the behavior is usually determined not only by the schedule correlated with that stimulus but by the entire context in which that stimulus appears.

The Controlling Stimulus

When a stimulus is controlling performance, what aspect of it is effective? What does it take to make one or another aspect salient for the organism? Answers to these questions are crucial for the teacher concerned with having students learn particular things about stimuli, and these answers are provided by research inquiring about controlling dimensions and alternative aspects of stimuli.

Dimensional Control

Dimensions refer to aspects of stimuli; they refer to the various continua along which stimuli can be ordered. For example, an auditory stimulus has a certain frequency and a certain intensity: frequency and intensity are separate aspects of the stimulus although both must exist for there to be a stimulus at all. The problem is that, because stimuli have several dimensions, it is not obvious which is effectively controlling responding. Suppose a pigeon responds in the presence of a green light and does not respond when the light is off. The bird could be controlled by the difference in color, by the difference in overall illumination, or by both. Any or all of the innumerable dimensions of stimuli may be critical in determining behavior and some may be totally irrelevant. A standard technique for determining whether or not a given dimension is significant consists of presenting other stimuli that differ in their value along the dimension of interest. If responding changes depending on the value, the dimension clearly is relevant. On the other hand, if responding is the same regardless of the stimulus presented, the dimension is irrelevant. The degree of change in response produced by changes along the stimulus dimension is referred to as a gradient. The slope of the gradient indicates the degree of control by the dimensions studied, because steeper slopes mean larger effects of change in value. A flat gradient means that responding is not affected by changes in the value along the dimension and that the dimension is not controlling behavior.

If responses are differentially reinforced with respect to two values on a dimension, that dimension will come to control responding (cf. Terrace, 1966). For example, if responding is reinforced in the presence of a vertical line and not in the presence of a horizontal line, responding will come under the control of line tilt.

A number of techniques are available for analyzing the gradients produced by S+ alone, by S− alone, and by the two stimuli in combination (see Hearst, Besley, and Farthing, 1970, for a review and methodological critique). In general if S+ and S− are not values along the same dimension (e.g., S+ as a line tilt and S− as a color), the gradient around S+ has its peak at S+ and declines as stimuli become progressively less similar to it; the gradient around S− has its low point at S− and rises with progressive stimulus changes. When S+ and S− are on the same dimension, their combined effects often yield a gradient having its peak not at S+ but at a stimulus displaced from S+ in a direction away from S−. Thus, if S+ is light with a wavelength of 550 nm (greenish yellow) and S− is a wavelength of 520 nm (green), the gradient may peak at around 580 nm (yellow). This phenomenon, *peak shift*, discovered by Hanson (1959), was predicted in 1937 by Spence from his theoretical analysis of how discriminations are formed.

When an organism is exposed only to one stimulus correlated with a simple reinforcement schedule, it is not entirely predictable whether any dimension of the stimulus will exert control. The data are complex. For example, pigeons may be controlled by color of a visual stimulus but not by properties of auditory stimuli (Guttman & Kalish, 1956; Jenkins, H.M., & Harrison, 1960), whereas rats may be controlled by auditory and not by visual stimuli. At this time the safest conclusion is that when an organism is exposed to only one stimulus, control depends on situational factors and innate or acquired predispositions, most of which probably have not yet been determined.

Given differential reinforcement with respect to two or more dimensions, the aspect that will control behavior is unknown. Reynolds (1961b), for example, presented two stimuli to pigeons according to a multiple schedule. One stimulus was a white triangle on a red background (S+), the other was a white circle on a green background (S−). Both pigeons responded differentially to the two stimuli, thereby indicating stimulus control. Subsequent tests showed that one of the birds was controlled by form (triangle *versus* circle) while the other was controlled by background color (red *versus* green). Thus, the source of control differed among pigeons. Many experiments have examined what variables are relevant in determining control by one or the other aspect of complex stimuli. Kamin (1969) indicated that a previous history with one aspect may prevent control by the other if the two are presented together later. This effect of prior training, known as *blocking*, illustrates that intensive experience with some property of the environment will preclude new stimuli from exerting control when they are imposed together with the old.

Another phenomenon is *overshadowing*. If an organism is trained initially with a compound stimulus and is then given one of the elements alone, control by that element is less than if the initial training had been only with one element. H.M. Jenkins and Sainsbury (1969) described still another relation among elements and compounds. If two displays are identical except for one distinguishing feature, it makes a difference whether the feature appears as part of S+ or S−. Stimulus control develops more readily when the distinguishing feature is part of S+; this is known as the *feature-positive effect*. Observations showed that pigeons responded to the distinguishing feature when it was on S+ and shifted away from it when it was on S−. This is referred to as *feature tracking*.

In summary, the way stimuli are presented and the organisms history play major roles in determining the aspect of a stimulus that controls performance. Stimulus control is selective: typically not all of the stimuli present at the moment of reinforcement will develop discriminative functions. Which ones do is determined by a complex of factors, and the explanation of selectivity is of considerable theoretical interest (cf. Rescorla & Wagner, 1972).

Alternative Stimulus Aspects

Consider the case of differential reinforcement with respect to two values on a dimension when the dimension clearly controls responding. The organism responds when only one of the values is present. Under such conditions responding is controlled by the dimension, but the source of the discrimination is not known. For example, if two tones differing in intensity (*A* and *B*) are presented and the organism responds only in the presence of *A*, either the specific intensities or the relation between them is important. If *A* is louder, the organism may be discriminating relative loudness (i.e., responding to the louder stimulus). A child who responds differently to two stimuli varying in area could be choosing on the basis of specific physical sizes or relational characteristics (larger or smaller) or perhaps something else. To discover the controlling aspect, *transposition* experiments are conducted in which a response is first brought under stimulus control, and then the organisms are given new sets of stimuli differing in the same dimension.

Their responses in the novel situations are determined by the property that was controlling responding originally.

In the long history of research on this question, experimenters typically have not tried to impose one or another kind of solution but have simply observed what occurs. Much research has focused on absolute *versus* relational stimulus control after organisms learn to choose among two or three stimuli varying on a single dimension (see Reese, 1968, for a review). The type of control depends on the number of stimuli, the particular dimensions, species, and developmental level. For example, with two stimuli differing in size, children below the age of four usually are controlled by specific sizes whereas older children are more likely to be influenced by relations. With three stimuli differing in size, children typically are controlled by the relation if S+ is the largest or smallest stimulus, but their behavior is less predictable if the stimulus is the middle-sized member of the set. Some are controlled by the middle-size relation, but others are controlled by the specific size of that stimulus. Adult humans are sensitive to both absolute and relational properties.

In *matching-to-sample* experiments, a common procedure is to provide an organism with three stimuli simultaneously arranged in a horizontal array. Only one of the two side stimuli (comparison stimuli) is the same as the center stimulus (standard stimulus). For example, each of three keys could be illuminated with either red (R), blue (B) or green (G) light. If the array is RRG or GRR or RRB or BRR, the red side key is correct (responses to that key are followed by a reinforcing stimulus); if the array is GGR, RGG, GGB, or BGG, the green side key is correct; if it is BRR, RBB, BBG, or GBB, the blue side key is correct. With three colors, each is correct and incorrect equally often and appears with each of the other colors the same number of times. Organisms come to make the correct response regardless of the stimulus display. Variables affecting the acquisition of the original discrimination include the schedule of reinforcement [FR reinforcement of correct responses produces the most accurate behavior (Ferster, 1960)], and the time interval separating the appearances of the standard and comparison stimuli [simultaneous presentation is best (cf. Blough, 1959)].

Tests often indicate that even though organisms are responding perfectly, performance is not controlled by the matching relation: when they are given new stimuli, they do not respond to the one that matches the sample. Instead, they seem to have learned a set of individual discriminations, i.e., they have learned which particular stimulus is correct in each individual case (Cumming & Berryman, 1965; Farthing & Opuda, 1974). No research has yet indicated the training necessary to produce control by the matching concept, or indeed what sort of training is necessary to get uniform control by any stimulus relation. Simply providing many different situations in which the same relationally defined member is always correlated with reinforcer presentation will not necessarily produce relational control. Research in progress indicates that in humans relational or absolute control can be obtained by combining verbal instructions with reinforcement consistently correlated with the particular characteristics.

But at least some relational characteristics can be learned without instructions. Herrnstein and Loveland (1964) showed slides to pigeons (each slide was presented only once), with food delivered only for responses emitted when the slide contained a person. Eventually, responding came under the control of the "people concept," and each new slide was responded to appropriately. Honig (1965) demonstrated that pigeons could learn the concepts of same and different. What appears necessary to generate control by concepts or relations is enough different individual problems to prevent each individual problem from being learned separately. If there are not a large number, even chimpanzees will learn the specific solutions to each problem (Kelleher, 1958a). The generality of this rule remains unclear. Despite the vast literature on concept formation and utilization in humans, few data indicate how and when humans are controlled by general concepts rather than by specific sets of individual solutions.

CONCLUSION

The preceding review presented the basic principles of behavior known at this time. A number of the principles are currently applied in the classroom and other settings; it can be anticipated that more applications will be forthcoming. The basic research laboratory has made available information on how behavior can be produced, maintained, and eliminated, but it has not always indicated exactly how these principles can be translated into practical use. Many of the following chapters can be viewed as providing such a translation.

ALAN E. KAZDIN

Chapter 3

Methodology of Applied Behavior Analysis

Research in applied behavior analysis has proliferated in recent years, as shown by the breadth of applications across settings, populations, and behavior (Kazdin, 1975a, 1975b; O'Leary, K.D., & Wilson, 1975; Ramp & Semb, 1975; Ulrich, Stachnik, & Mabry, 1970). Most interventions or treatment programs in applied behavior analysis derive from operant conditioning. Applied behavior analysis, however, refers to a particular therapeutic focus and methodological stance rather than to a conceptual position. The research is *applied* if it focuses upon clinically or socially significant behavior and attempts to achieve a behavior change of applied significance (Baer, Wolf, & Risley, 1968; Risley, 1970). Whether the research constitutes *behavior analysis* is determined by its methodological stance in implementing and evaluating treatment interventions: namely, the experimental analysis of behavior (Skinner, 1963). Thus, diverse interventions are encompassed by applied behavior analysis if they are conducted within the general methodological framework of the experimental analysis of behavior. This methodology is characterized by a distinct approach toward assessment, experimental design, and data evaluation and transcends a particular discipline or area of research (Kazdin, 1975c).

This chapter examines the methodology of applied behavior analysis. The topics include behavioral assessment, reliability of assessment, experimental design, and criteria for data evaluation. For each topic, the general approach is outlined, diverse methods, variations, and options are discussed, and specific limitations of alternative procedures are examined.

BEHAVIORAL ASSESSMENT

Specifying Responses and Controlling Conditions

Assessment in applied behavior analysis refers to the objective evaluation of overt responses. The evaluation focuses directly upon the target response—the response to be altered during the treatment intervention. Assessment of the target response accomplishes two related goals. First, it determines the frequency of the response before the intervention begins. This level of responding is the *baseline* or operant level. Second, assessment measures responding after the intervention has begun. Behavior change is assessed by comparing baseline performance with performance after the intervention.

In addition to the target response, antecedent and consequent events associated with the response are often assessed. Antecedent events (e.g., instructions, gestures, threats) and consequences (praise, reprimands) are manipulated to alter the target response. Often, responses of individuals who influence the client's behavior, such as parents, teachers, and peers, are the antecedent and consequent events that are manipulated.

The importance of assessing antecedent and consequent events cannot be overemphasized. The failure to observe events designed to alter the client's behavior can make the basis for behavior change unclear. For example, teacher praise is often used to alter students' study behavior. If teacher behavior is not assessed, the causes of change in studying may be ambiguous. It is not known whether the student's behavior changed in the intended direction because of the teacher's responses unless the teacher's behavior is observed. Moreover, the student's behavior may not change either because of the teacher's failure to implement the intended contingency or because of a failure of the correctly administered contingency to affect student behavior. Observation of the target response and the events manipulated to influence that response is essential to isolate the source of change.

Selecting the target response and the antecedent and consequent events to be observed requires preliminary observation. Before assessment, an investigator may observe the client informally to determine the range of the target response and to enumerate environmental events that might influence it. Descriptive notes may be taken to characterize the response and the antecedent and consequent events associated with it (Bijou, Peterson, & Ault, 1968). The notes may serve as a basis for a final response definition and method of assessment. Ultimately the target response must be defined precisely in behavioral terms.

Ideally a response definition has three characteristics: objectivity, clarity, and completeness (Hawkins & Dobes, 1976). To be *objective*, the definition should refer to observable characteristics of behavior or to environmental events. Definitions should not refer to inner states of the individual or to teleological terms that do not reflect properties of behavior itself. Thus, expressing anger, attempting to achieve a goal, and being hyperactive are not satisfactory "responses" for behavioral assessment. To be *clear*, the definition should be so unambiguous that it can be read, repeated, and paraphrased accurately. To be *complete*, the boundary conditions of the definition must be delineated, so that the responses to be included and excluded are enumerated. The completeness of the definition is a prerequisite to the objectivity of the response. If the range of responses included in the definition is not described carefully, observers have to infer or judge whether the response has occurred. For example, consider an objective and clear target response such as raising one's hand in a classroom. Observers might look at a child on a prearranged schedule to determine whether or not his or her hand is raised. In many instances (e.g., when the raised hand is fully extended), observers have no difficulty in agreeing that the hand is raised. Ambiguous instances, however, may require the observers' judgment. The child may rest a forearm on the top of the head while signaling the teacher, or keep an elbow on the desk while raising the forearm and the index finger of that hand in the teacher's direction. These latter responses are instances of handraising to teachers, who respond to them as such, and the response definition must specify whether or not these and related variations of handraising are to be included.

In practice, completeness of a definition derives from applying the definition on a preliminary basis and then making rules to handle ambiguous cases. For the relatively simple response of handraising, one would specify all the instances where the response is not obvious or requires judgment. For more complex responses, such as verbal interaction, cooperative tasks, compliance with instructions, and creative writing or speaking, the boundary conditions become increasingly complex and increasingly important to specify.

The extent to which a response definition is objective, clear, and complete determines, in part, the extent to which observers agree in scoring behavior. These conditions may also determine whether it is the subject's behavior or the observers' judgment that changes over the course of a project (Baer et al., 1968; Hawkins & Dotson, 1975). Precise criteria for a maximally objective, clear, and complete definition have not been specified. A rigorous test might provide a written description of the target response to two observers who are unfamiliar with the client, behavior, or setting. If, without communicating, these observers agree in scoring the response from the description alone, the definition has probably met the criteria adequately (cf. Hawkins & Dobes, 1976). But this test of the response definition must be tentative because, as discussed later, observers may agree in scoring for reasons independent of the precision of the response definition that it supposed to guide their behavior.

Methods of Assessment

The methods of assessment refer to how observed responses are scored and converted into data. Assessment of behavior of clients, or of individuals who influence the clients, can be achieved by different methods. The four strategies usually used in applied behavior analysis include frequency, interval, duration, and the number of individuals who perform a response.

Frequency Measure. Frequency, or the number of times that the response occurs in a given period, is extremely simple to use because the observer merely tallies response occurrences. A frequency measure is usually used when the target response is discrete and has a relatively constant duration. A discrete response has a clear beginning and end, so that a distinct instance can be counted (Skinner, 1966b). The response should consume a relatively constant amount of time, so that the tallied units are comparable. Ongoing behavior, such as smiling, talking, resting, and studying, usually is not easily recorded as a frequency because such responses are not sufficiently discrete or because their duration varies widely. For example, scoring talking with a frequency measure might be difficult because a given conversation may include long or short pauses in speech, interruptions of other individuals, whispers, etc. Also, a person may speak to one individual for 10 and to another individual continuously for 15 min. Because talking of this kind has no clear beginning or end unless precise definitions are given, and because talking episodes may vary in duration, frequency measures might be difficult to use.

Frequency measures have been used in applied behavior analysis across such behavior as correct academic responses (Harris, V.W., & Sherman, 1974), aggressive acts (Horton, 1970), words pronounced correctly (Bailey, J.S., Timbers, Phillips, & Wolf, 1972), self-abusive responses (Tanner & Zeiler, 1975), greeting responses (Kale, Kaye, Whelan, & Hopkins, 1968), and stealing episodes (Azrin & Wesolowski, 1974).

Frequency measures merely require noting response instances. Usually, behavior is observed for a constant time each day (or session), so that frequencies across days are directly comparable. Yet constant time periods across days are not essential because frequency is easily converted to rate of responding (by dividing response frequency by minutes of observation). Response rates are comparable across different durations of observation.

Frequency measures have several advantages. First, response frequency is easily recorded in naturalistic settings (e.g., by parents, teachers, ward attendants). Counting can be facilitated further by various devices, such as golf counters worn like wrist watches. Second, frequency measures readily reflect changes over time (Bijou et al., 1968). Response frequency or rate is sensitive to alterations of the contingencies of reinforcement. The principles of operant conditioning are based upon changes in response frequency, so it is desirable to observe frequency or rate directly (Skinner, 1953b, 1966b). Third, frequency expresses the amount of behavior, which is usually of concern in applied settings. Interventions are implemented to decrease or increase the number of times a certain response occurs, so frequency provides a direct measure of most program goals.

Interval Recording. Assessment is often based upon units of time rather than discrete responses. One time-based method is to record behavior during short intervals. Typically, interval recording samples behavior for a single block of time, such as 30 min. once a day. The block of time is divided into shorter intervals (e.g., 15 sec. intervals). During each interval, the target response is scored as having occurred or not occurred. If a discrete response such as hitting someone occurs one or more times in a single interval, the response is scored merely as having occurred; several responses within an interval are not counted separately. If the behavior is ongoing with an unclear beginning and end or occurs for a long period of time, it is scored in each interval in which it appears. Interval recording has been used for a variety of behavior, including appropriate mealtime responses (Barton, Guess, Garcia, & Baer, 1970), social responses (O'Conner, 1969), and uncooperative child behavior (Wahler, 1969b). Investigations in classroom settings have relied heavily upon interval recording to score whether students work on the classroom assignment, pay attention, sit in their seats, or engage in other appropriate classroom behavior (cf. Kazdin, 1975a; O'Leary, K.D., & O'Leary, 1972).

In one variation of interval recording, clients are observed at distinct periods throughout the day rather than continuously for a single time block. For example, whether individuals engage in the target response may be observed once an hour. This method, sometimes referred to as *time sampling*, involves observing at several separate moments in time. As with interval recording, behavior is classified as occurring or not occurring at a given time, but time sampling scores the behavior on the basis of performance at the *end* of an interval rather than on the basis of performance throughout the interval. Thus, the main differences between interval- and time-sampling methods are whether periods of observation occur in immediate succession or are separated in time, and whether the period is scored on the basis of performance during the interval or at the end of the interval.

Interval recording is probably the most frequent strategy in applied behavior analysis for three reasons. First, because it is flexible, any observable response can be recorded with it. Whether a response is discrete, varies in duration, is continuous, or sporadic, it can be classified as occurring or not occurring during a specific time interval. Second, several different responses can be scored simultaneously. During a given interval, an observer can score whether any of the several responses has or has not occurred (cf. Hart, Reynolds, Baer, Brawley, & Harris, 1968; Madsen, C.H., Becker, & Thomas, 1968). Third, the results of interval scoring are easily communicated to others. The proportion of intervals in which the target response occurs can be converted into a percentage that provides a simple measure of the amount of the response. Finally, interval recording is consistent with the goal of many programs that attempt to increase the time over which responses such as studying, exercising, or socializing occur. The percentage of intervals in which the response occurs reflects this goal directly.

Duration. Another time-based method of observation is response duration, used for a target response that is continuous (e.g., singing or whistling) rather than discrete or of exceedingly short time periods (e.g., hitting someone, making a gesture). Duration has been used for responses such as returning from school and errands (Phillips, E.L., 1968), working on classroom assignments (Surratt, Ulrich, & Hawkins, 1969), engaging in cooperative play (Redd, 1969), and responding socially (Whitman, Mercurio, & Caponigri, 1970).

Assessment of response duration merely requires starting and stopping a stopwatch or noting the times at which a response begins and ends. If the beginning and end of the response are not carefully defined, duration is difficult to measure. For example, crying may be assessed with a duration measure. Yet there may be ambiguity in scoring the response because a child may cry continuously for several minutes, whimper, whine, or moan for short periods, cease all noises for a few seconds, and begin intense crying again. To handle changes in the intensity of responses (crying to whining) and pauses (periods of silence), a decision has to be reached whether or not to include them in the response definition.

Response duration is appropriate when the goal is to increase or decrease the time a response lasts. In most programs the goal is to increase or decrease response frequency rather than its duration. When the goal is to alter response duration, interval recording is often selected because it is so flexible.

Number of Individuals. In some applied investigations the number of individuals who perform a given response is assessed. The measure does not analyze the individual client's response. Each individual is scored as having performed or not having performed the response, because the experimenter is interested in the number of individuals who meet a specific requirement. Counting individuals—a discrete measure that is easily recorded—has been used in situations with the goal of increasing the number of individuals who respond in a group situation. For example, investigators have assessed the number of individuals who come to class on time (Hall, R.V., Cristler, Cranston, & Tucker, 1970), complete their homework (Harris, V.W.,& Sherman, 1974), and participate in or attend various activities (Colman, A.D., & Boren, 1969; Miller, L.K., & Miller, 1970).

The number of individuals who perform a response may be a useful measure when the behavior of each individual is not of interest, as in large-scale social applications of operant techniques. For example, research that attempts to increase the use of mass transit rather than personal cars has used the number of individuals who board the bus to assess the effect of the intervention (Everett, Hayward, & Meyers, 1974). Generally, using the number of individuals as a measure of program effectiveness is not well suited to the careful analysis of individual behavior. As noted before, operant principles are directed at frequency of a given individual's responses. Performance of the individual, however, is lost when the number of individuals is used as a measure of behavior change. Whether to measure the number of individuals who engage in a response or not depends upon the goal of the program.

Summary. The method of assessment employed is dictated by such factors as the goals of the intervention, the specific responses observed, the rate of responding, the ease with which the response can be detected, and a variety of practical exigencies. While some responses appear to be more readily assessed by a particular method, alternative methods are usually available. For example, discrete responses such as self-injurious acts (headbanging) can be recorded either by frequency or by interval measures. A burst of self-injurious responses might be recorded by duration of responding.

Multiple Response Assessment

Assessment usually focuses on one or a few target responses. Naturally, the responses assessed are those focused upon directly as part of the intervention. Recent research suggests that altering a single target response may be associated with changes in diverse responses not focused upon directly and bearing no topographic relation to the target response. For example, reducing uncooperative child behavior in the home (not complying with commands, yelling, hitting, etc.) has been associated with a reduction in the frequency of bed-wetting and stuttering even though the latter were not focused upon directly (Nordquist, 1971; Wahler, Sperling, Thomas, Teeter, & Luper, 1970). Similarly, decreasing a boy's inappropriate talking at school was associated with increases in social behavior and disruptive behavior, and decreases in attentive behavior in a group situation and in the use of "girl's" toys (Sajwaj, Twardosz, & Burke, 1972, pp. 167-69). In addition, punishing self-stimulatory responses of children increased both the use of toys during free play and appropriate verbalizations (Epstein, Doke, Sajwaj, Sorrell, & Rimmer, 1974).

Recently, Wahler (1975) systematically examined responses that go together or cluster across settings and over time for a given individual. Analyses of response clusters are likely to provide theoretical and practical insights for designing interventions. Even though response covariation is not well understood, it may be valuable to assess multiple responses beyond that focused upon during the intervention. Altering one response is likely to have diverse side effects, including changes in "appropriate" and "inappropriate" responses (cf. Sajwaj et al., 1972).

In addition to response covariation for a given individual, an intervention may affect individuals other than the one for whom it was intended. A change in one individual's behavior may influence another individual's behavior as well. Providing praise, feedback, or tangible rewards to individuals for on-task performance in a classroom setting increases attentive behavior of individuals who are not exposed to the contingencies (Broden, Bruce,

Mitchell, Carter, & Hall, 1970; Christy, 1975; Drabman & Lahey, 1974; Kazdin, 1973b; Kazdin, Silverman, & Sittler, 1975; Kounin & Gump, 1958).

Because the effects of an intervention may spread, assessment of multiple responses of a single individual or several individuals beyond the focus of the intervention may be valuable. Perhaps the responses assessed should be dictated by examining areas commonly related to a client's adequate functioning, such as work or academic performance, social interaction, verbalizations, and so on. Although these responses might be topographically dissimilar from the response target, their assessment might demonstrate the breadth of changes produced by the intervention. Assessing behavior of individuals not included in the intervention also may have practical import. Even though it is not always feasible to apply a given intervention to many individuals, their responses may be affected by the intervention, and, if so, should be assessed.

RELIABILITY OF ASSESSMENT

In some applied investigations the target response is recorded automatically, so that human judgment is minimized or eliminated from data collection. A variety of automated devices has been used, such as a time clock to record tardiness of industrial workers (Hermann, de Montes, Dominguez, Montes, & Hopkins, 1973), a mechanical strain gage to record penile circumference to measure sexual arousal (Barlow, D.H., Becker, Leitenberg, & Agras, 1970), a sound-level meter to record noise level in a classroom (Schmidt & Ulrich, 1969), a counter in a cigarette case to record the frequency of opening the case to procure cigarettes (Powell, J., & Azrin, 1968), and a scale to weigh the amount of litter picked up or the amount of food eaten (Burgess, H., Clark, & Hendee, 1971; Madsen, C.H., Madsen, & Thompson, 1974), among others. The advantage of automated devices derives not only from their convenience but also from their precision. In the absence of human observers the consistency with which behavior is observed is maximized by automated data collection. Most applied investigations, however, rely upon human observers to record behavior. Typically, an observer scores a client's behavior according to a prespecified code. Scoring behavior requires that an observer make judgments about the occurrence of the response. The diversity of responses observed and the evaluation of behavior in naturalistic rather than laboratory settings usually precludes automated recording. Thus the extent to which behavior is observed consistently by observers is a major issue.

In applied behavior analysis the consistency of observation by two observers (interobserver agreement) has been referred to as *reliability*. Technically, this term should be avoided because of its general use in psychometric theory and its multiple specific meanings. Agreement between observers is not necessarily reliability if reliability refers to consistency in measuring behavior. As discussed elsewhere, observers can agree with each other although they observe behavior inconsistently. Despite the potential terminological problems, however, the term *reliability* will be retained here and used interchangeably with *interobserver agreement* to be consistent with established usage in applied behavior analysis.

Agreement between observers who independently record responses is central in assessing and evaluating behavior-change programs. Initially, agreement reflects the extent to which the target response is well defined. Lack of agreement can signify that the response definition is unclear or incomplete and that the behavior must be redefined. Thus the extent of agreement is, in part, a test of the adequacy of the response definition.

Interobserver agreement also assesses the accuracy with which the client's behavior is observed. With low agreement, the data may differ greatly depending upon who is scoring behavior. Variation in data due to the observer adds to any variability in client behavior and obscures actual performance. Evaluating the intervention depends, in part, upon data that are relatively stable. Measurement error contributes to variability and makes subsequent evaluation more difficult than would otherwise be the case. Indeed, if the variability due to assessment error is extremely large, establishing stable behavior and evaluating the intervention may be delayed. Sources of bias that may enter into assessment and increase variability will be treated separately later.

Methods of Calculating Reliability

Reliability provides an estimate of observers' agreement in scoring behavior. To estimate reliability, at least two observers are required who simultaneously score a given individual's behavior. Their scores are compared to determine the extent of agreement. Separate methods of calculating agreement may be distinguished depending in part on the assessment strategy used.

Total Frequency, Number of Individuals, and Duration. When a frequency measure, the number of individuals, or response duration is assessed, a comparison is usually made between the totals of the observations of each observer for an observation period. For a frequency measure (or a tally of the number of individuals), observer agreement is assessed by computing the extent to which observers agree on the total count for a given observation period. Often the two observers do not agree perfectly in the totals. Agreement is computed by dividing the smaller total by the larger total. The proportion usually is multiplied by 100 to form a percentage. For example, two hospital attendants might count the aggressive responses of a patient in a 1-hr period. One observer may obtain a total of 10 responses while the other might record 8 for the same time period. Dividing the smaller number (8) by the larger number (10) and multiplying by 100 yields

80% agreement on the total frequency. When the number of individuals who respond is counted, the same formula is applied.

Agreement on the total frequency does not indicate that observers agree a given percent of the time. The percentage is deceptive, in that it is possible for observers not to record the same response and yet have high total frequency agreement. Hence, the 8 responses recorded by one observer may not even have been included among the 10 responses recorded by the other. Together, the two observers scored 18 responses. It is unlikely in practice that observers would so exclusively score different responses, but the possibility reflects the general ambiguity of agreement on total frequency. Because there is no assurance that the observers agree on specific instances, high agreement on the total may be achieved without consistent agreement on specific instances.

Whether total frequency agreement should be used on a given occasion is controversial. The primary data in most investigations using frequency measures is the total frequency for a given session. Thus agreement on the total frequency may be important independent of moment-to-moment concurrence between observers. Yet when responses are of relatively high frequency, observers may show an extremely high percentage agreement on the total even if they infrequently agree on individual occurrences (cf. Johnson, S.M., & Bolstad, 1973).

Sometimes a more precise measure of agreement than total frequency can be used. In some cases, the frequency of correct responses (e.g., writing an academic assignment or complying with instructions) can be scored on the basis of discrete trials or opportunities for the response to occur. In these cases observers independently record the response on a specific trial. Subsequently, observers can be compared on a trial-by-trial basis. An agreement is counted when both observers record the response on a given trial. A disagreement is counted when one observer records the responses and the other does not. Reliability is calculated by dividing the number of agreements by the total number of agreements plus disagreements and multiplying by 100. The computation of response frequency on a trial-by-trial basis is relatively infrequent in the literature.

When response duration is assessed, calculation of agreement is similar to that with frequency assessment. Two observers record response duration in a given session. The shorter duration is divided by the longer duration and multiplied by 100 to form a percentage. Agreement so calculated refers to the total time (accumulated on a timer or stopwatch) rather than to identical scoring at any given moment in time. If duration is used for an ongoing response and the watch or timer is not repeatedly turned on and off, the likelihood of disagreement at any point in time is probably minimal.

Just as with frequency measures, agreement on response duration can sometimes be assessed on a trial-by-trial basis rather than by total time. For example, the duration of a teacher's contact with her students was timed in a classroom investigation (Scott, J.W., & Bushell, 1974). Each contact was timed separately, and agreement was counted if two observers scored within 1 sec of each other on the duration of a given contact. Reliability was computed using the trial-by-trial formula given for frequency. Percentage agreement reflects the trial-by-trial agreement for duration. But as with frequency measures, most investigations of response duration compute interobserver agreement on total response time, leaving ambiguous the agreement at any point in time.

Interval-by-Interval Agreement. Reliability of interval or time-sampling assessment strategies is calculated differently from that of total frequency. With interval assessment, the extent to which observers agree interval-by-interval can be calculated. Agreement is usually computed by determining the number of intervals within which two observers agree on the occurrence of the target response (Bijou et al., 1968). An agreement is counted if the two observers record the response as occurring in the same interval. Disagreement is counted for a given interval when one observer scores a response as occurring and the other does not. Reliability equals the number of agreements divided by the total number of agreements plus disagreements, multiplied by 100. For example, two observers who record study behavior for one hundred 10-sec intervals in a classroom situation may achieve 40 agreements and 10 disagreements. Reliability would be 40/(40 + 10) × 100 or 80% agreement. Agreement refers to the percent of intervals within which both observers scored the response.

Usually all observed intervals are not used to estimate interval-by-interval reliability. An interval is used only if at least one observer records the target response. Intervals in which observers agree that the response did not occur are usually omitted (Bijou et al., 1968). Agreement on nonoccurrences of the target response is excluded because observers may concur across many intervals in which the target response never occurred. If these intervals were counted as agreements, reliability estimates would be inflated over the level where occurrence alone is used (Hawkins & Dotson, 1975). Thus, in the above example, 50 intervals out of 100 were not included in the calculation of reliability. If included, these intervals would have counted as agreements. Counting these as agreements and using the above formula would raise the reliability to 90/(90 + 10) × 100 or 90%, which is higher than the previous level. At the extreme, assume that one observer recorded a response once in 50 intervals and a second observer also recorded one response, but in a different interval than the first observer. By the first method (computing reliability on response occurrences), their agreement is 0/2 × 100 or 0%, indicating that they had no agreement on the responses scored. But by the second method (computing reliability on occurrences and nonoccurrences), their agreement is 48/(48 + 2) × 100 or 96%, which is a percentage inconsistent with the observers' actual performance.

Calculating reliability based upon agreements of response occurrences rather than upon occurrences and nonoccurrences combined has problems of its own. The interpretation of percentage agreement is a function of the rate of responding. When responding is infrequent (i.e., the response is scored in relatively few intervals), the percentage of agreement can vary widely. Thus, if responding is scored in only one out of several intervals, agreement by the above formula would be either 0% or 100%. Of course, if responding is not recorded at all by two observers, agreement on occurrences alone could not be computed. In addition if the rate of responding is very high, it is likely that interobserver agreement would be high even if the observers disagreed in several instances.

The dependency of interval-by-interval agreement upon the rate of responding can be seen by examining the percentage agreement predicted on the basis of chance. Assume that two observers record the study behavior of a child for 100 intervals. If each observer records study behavior in 90 of 100 intervals, the expected reliability can be computed as the proportion of recorded study intervals for the first observer times the proportion for the second observer times 100. Thus, given the high frequency of target behavior, agreement on the basis of chance alone is $(0.90 \times 0.90) \times 100$ or 81%.[1] In contrast if study behavior is scored as occurring in only 20% of the intervals by each observer, the chance level of reliability by the same formula is substantially lower: $(0.20 \times 0.20) \times 100$ or 4%.

These calculations show that frequency of the assessed behavior can influence percentage agreement. Because interval-by-interval agreement depends upon response frequency, some investigators have suggested computing two different reliability percentages: one based upon agreements on occurrences and the other based upon agreements on nonoccurrences (Bijou, Peterson, Harris, Allen, & Johnston, 1969; Hawkins & Dotson, 1975). The value of this suggestion is that the relative frequency of occurrence and nonoccurrence of a target response is likely to change across experimental phases. Thus, the expected levels of reliability across phases in an experiment are subject to change. With frequent target responding, the expected level of reliability based on occurrences increases, but that based on nonoccurrences decreases. If both occurrence and nonoccurrence measures of agreement are provided, the precise pattern of observer agreement is more readily apparent.

1. The formulae for calculating the percentage of agreement expected by chance differ depending upon the definition of agreement. If agreements are restricted to intervals where both observers agree on the occurrence of the response, the formula is

$$(p_1 \times p_2) \times 100$$

where p_1 is the proportion of intervals of occurrence for observer 1, and p_2 is the proportion of intervals of occurrence for observer 2. If agreements are extended to include intervals where both observers agree on the nonoccurrence of the response as well, the formula becomes

$$[(p_1 \times p_2) + (q_1 \times q_2)] \times 100$$

where q_1 is the proportion of intervals of nonoccurrence for observer 1, and q_2 is the proportion of intervals of nonoccurrence for observer 2.

Correlation Coefficient. Interobserver agreement sometimes is expressed as a Pearson product-moment correlation, which can be used with any of the assessment strategies. Interobserver agreement is obtained by correlating the observers' totals for frequencies, intervals of agreement, durations, or numbers of individuals recorded across several sessions. Unfortunately, the problems of relying on totals to assess agreement are exacerbated with the correlation coefficient. The observations of two observers could correlate highly, or even perfectly, although the observers never agreed on a given occurrence of the response. Thus, correlation hides the moment-to-moment level of agreement. A related problem is that the totals may be extremely discrepant between observers without reducing the high correlation. A high correlation can be achieved between observers if there is a relatively constant amount of disagreement across sessions, and the observers tend to covary in the same direction. Because correlation coefficients allow an extremely large discrepancy between observers, it is used infrequently in calculating reliability in applied behavior analysis.

Level of Agreement

Agreement between observers has to reach an acceptable level before and throughout data collection. No single criterion for an acceptable level of agreement can be stated formally. The level required in a given project depends upon many factors, such as the variability of the observed behavior, the strength of the intervention, and the frequency of responding. An intervention that drastically changes behavior may be only partially obscured by fluctuations in the data from inconsistent observations. In contrast, weak effects of an intervention might be completely hidden by only moderately unreliable recording.

Although no universal criterion for agreement can be set, convention dictates that agreement should fall between 80 and 100%. Reliability lower than 80% suggests moderate error in recording that calls for training observers more thoroughly or clarifying the response definition. Although the majority of reliability estimates in the literature appear to fall within the above range, the actual consistency of observations probably is substantially lower. As discussed later, agreement between observers depends upon the conditions under which reliability is assessed. Many of these conditions inflate the reliability estimates.

Issues in Assessing Reliability

Reliability is assessed periodically to determine the consistency with which responses are observed throughout an experiment. Agreement between observers is assumed to reflect their consistency in applying the response definition. Recently this assumption has been questioned. Interobserver agreement is influenced by factors and sources of bias that are somewhat independent of consistency in applying the response definition.

Observer Awareness of Reliability Assessment. Reliability is checked only periodically on the assumption that observing occurs with similar consistency during periods not checked. Usually reliability checks include two observers who simultaneously record behavior. The observers are aware that reliability is being assessed, because they ordinarily do not observe behavior of the same client together. Research suggests that the observers' awareness that reliability is being checked influences their observations.

J. B. Reid (1970) evaluated the effects of observer awareness on reliability estimates. Observers rated videotapes of parent-child interaction under two conditions: in one they thought their observations were being compared to a standard (i.e., their reliability was being assessed), and in the other they thought there was no standard (i.e., their reliability was not being assessed). In fact, agreement with the standard was calculated for both sets of observations. Observers showed substantially higher reliability when they thought that reliability was being assessed. Indeed when they did not think reliability was being assessed, their agreement was approximately 25% lower. Other studies replicate the finding that when individuals are aware their reliability is being assessed, their agreement is higher than when they are unaware (Kent, R. N., Kanowitz, O'Leary, & Cheiken, 1977; Romanczyk, Kent, Diament, & O'Leary, 1973). In addition, awareness affects overall assessment of client performance. For example, observers recorded 20% less disruptive student behavior when they were unaware reliability was being assessed than when they were aware (Romanczyk et al., 1973).

Observer awareness may also vary when the reliability check is monitored by someone other than the observers. K. D. O'Leary and Kent (1973) reported that reliability tended to be lower when the experimenter was present during a reliability check. Thus, the observers may have communicated about their observations and inflated their reliability estimates when the experimenter was not monitoring their behavior. A related finding is that, given the raw data, reliability computed by observers tends to be higher than reliability computed by the experimenter (Kent, R. N., O'Leary, Diament, & Dietz, 1974).

Observer Drift. The consistent pairing of specific observers who conduct reliability checks may raise problems in interpreting reliability. Evidence suggests that observers who consistently work with each other and receive feedback on each other's performance develop idiosyncratic variations of the original response definition. In one report observers given the same behavioral codes modified these codes over time (O'Leary, K. D., & Kent, 1973). During training, observers met in small groups, completed observations, computed reliability, and discussed areas of disagreement with individuals in their group. Over time, individual subgroups modified the codes in different fashions. Thus, observers drifted from the original response definitions. Additional instances of observer drift are provided by R. N. Kent et al. (1974, 1977), who reported substantial differences among observer pairs.

Observer drift can distort data. Although observations within a subgroup of observers who work together and communicate about their observations may be reliable, their modifications of the codes may make their observations incompatible with those of observers with whom they do not work. If subgroups of observers differ across experimental conditions, as might be the case for observations in a between-group design across different schools, classrooms, or homes, comparisons of responses across groups may not even be meaningful, because the results may not reflect common behavioral definitions.

The problem of drift exists for within-subject comparisons as well. The data in one phase may not be directly comparable with data in earlier or later phases. If there is a differential drift across sets of observers, observations by one set of observers may not be comparable to those of another set either in any given phase or across phases.

The drift of behavioral codes among observers may be a function of the feedback that observers provide each other. Allowing subgroups of observers to discuss behavioral codes and to compute their own reliability may contribute to drift (O'Leary, K.D., & Kent, 1973). Even if observation patterns do not develop through communication among observers, drift may occur idiosyncratically for any given observer.

Information, Expectancies, and Feedback. Another source of bias in interobserver agreement is the observers' feedback, either from another observer (assessor) or from the experimenter. Romanczyk et al. (1973) determined that observer performance was influenced by knowing who the other observer was during a reliability check. Two assessors (reliability observers) were trained to differ slightly from a standard observational code in scoring behavior. In scoring the category "vocalization" for a child, one assessor scored the softest vocalization possible, whereas the other only scored loud vocalizations. Observers were trained by and communicated with each assessor, thereby learning their idiosyncratic patterns. After training, observers were checked with each assessor. The assessor used as the reliability standard markedly shifted the observer's criteria for scoring behavior. Interobserver agreement was a function of adjusting the definition to the assessor rather than of consistently observing behavior. Thus, the individual serving as the standard may influence the observer's definition of behavior.

Another two areas of bias are expectancies of the effect of the intervention and feedback from the experimenter. The effect of expectancies of client change on the performance of observers has been suggested in several studies (e.g., Azrin, Holz, Ulrich, & Goldiamond, 1961; Scott, Burton, & Yarrow, 1967). Kass and O'Leary (1970) told some observers that disruptive child behavior would increase and others that it would decrease during treatment. All individuals observed the same classroom videotapes, which in fact showed a decrease in disruptive behavior during treatment. In general those observers led to expect a decrease recorded a greater reduction in disruptive behavior than those led to expect an increase, although these results were not obtained for all responses scored. R. N. Kent et al. (1974) told some observers that disruptive behavior would decrease and others that it would not change from baseline. The data on videotape in fact showed no change in disruptive behavior across phases. Overall, expectancies did not influence observer recordings. But when observers were asked to characterize the effect of the program on a questionnaire, their evaluation reflected the expectancy of the experimenter.

During an investigation, experimenters may examine data and give observers feedback on how well the data fit with expectations. K. D. O'Leary, Kent, and Kanowitz (1975) gave observers an opportunity to score videotapes of children in a classroom. Observers were instructed that a token program (treatment) would alter disruptive behavior. Actually, tapes of baseline and treatment were matched for disruptive behavior and no treatment was given. The experimenter provided positive comments (approval) of the observers' data if a reduction in the target behavior was scored during the "treatment" phase, and negative comments (disappointment) if no change or an increase in the target behavior was scored. Instructions to expect change and feedback for scoring reductions in target behaviors biased the data. Interestingly, specific responses that observers were told would not change and for which no feedback was given were scored by the observers as not changing. These results suggest that expectancies and feedback about the effect of treatment influence observational data.

Recommendations for Assessing Reliability

Agreement does not simply reflect the adequacy of the response definition, because diverse conditions of reliability assessment dictate the level of agreement. Given the possibility of awareness of reliability assessment, of alteration of reliability estimates by observers, and of observer bias derived from expectancies and feedback, several recommendations for assessing reliability may be noted.

Awareness of reliability assessment might be handled in several ways. Initially, the conditions under which reliability is assessed should match the conditions under which observations are ordinarily made. If observers believe that their behavior is not being monitored, these conditions should be maintained during reliability checks. Thus, reliability checks should be unobtrusive or covert. One suggestion for conducting covert reliability assessment is to have individuals score the behavior of different target subjects simultaneously in a group of subjects. In some of the intervals, the same subjects might be observed, although this would not be divulged to the observers. Subsequently, comparisons of overlapping observations would provide an unobtrusive measure of reliability (O'Leary, K. D., & Kent, 1973). In practice these procedures may not be unobtrusive, due to interobserver communication or to events associated with the individual observed. Observers may realize that they are assessing behavior of the same individual simultaneously.

Another solution is to have an experimenter covertly assess reliability of observations throughout the program, as, for example, through a one-way mirror. This solution may assess reliability unobtrusively, but it could introduce other problems. For example, the experimenter might learn idiosyncratic codes of the observers and adjust observations accordingly.

Reliability assessment may be intentionally obtrusive. If reliability can be assessed daily (not a common practice), letting observers know that reliability is being assessed may have such desirable effects as maintaining high levels of agreement and decreasing cheating in computing reliability or communicating about observations (O'Leary, K. D., & Kent, 1973). In light of the literature comparing reliability computed by observers and experimenters, observers should not be involved in the actual computation of reliability (R. N. Kent et al., 1977; Rusch, Walker, & Greenwood, 1975).

Besides controlling the reactive effect of assessment and its by-products, observer drift must be prevented or at least assessed. One means of assessing observer drift during a project is periodically to bring in newly trained observers to assess reliability (cf. Skindrud, 1973). Comparison of newly trained observers with observers who are already participating can determine whether the codes change over time. Of course, differences between newly trained and experienced observers might reflect differential proficiency in applying the codes accurately rather than modifications per se. Yet any systematic alterations over time, including increases in proficiency, might also be reflected in observer drift.

A technique for controlling observer drift among subgroups of observers is to pair all observers with each other during training and reliability assessment so that differential drift does not develop. Observers should not be allowed to discuss their observations, compute their own reliabilities, and compare these computations with each other.

Drift can be assessed or controlled by videotaping the subject's behavior across sessions and by having observers score the tapes in random order. Any drift that develops would not differentially influence the observations in a particular phase if sessions were scored in random order. Usually, it is too time-consuming and expensive to tape all sessions and make observations at the end of a project. Also, data may be needed during the project to determine whether various phases of the intervention should be altered as a function of client behavior. Yet taped samples may be compared with the actual observations to assess drift over time.

Continually training observers as a group throughout the project may limit observer drift. Periodically, observers may meet as a group and rate behavior (perhaps on videotape) and receive immediate feedback on their observations. This procedure is likely to help prevent differential drift across observers. The group of observers might still drift eventually, although they continue training. The drift of the entire group may be prevented by conducting videotape training throughout the project with an agreed-upon performance standard.

Observer expectancies and feedback regarding client-behavior change may not be easily controlled. Often observers can readily detect an intervention, such as the use of tokens, and are alerted to the desired therapeutic effects. Observer expectancy effects might be controlled by bringing in new observers throughout the program who are unfamiliar with the reinforcement history of the client and the behavior change that has been achieved. Also, videotaping samples of performance throughout the project and subsequently rating these tapes in random order might help rule out the effect of differential expectancies across phases.

The utility of the recommendations cannot readily be determined. The problems of reactivity, drift, and bias in assessment in applied behavior analysis have only been revealed recently. Thus, whether any proposed solution will improve reliability assessment is unclear.

EXPERIMENTAL DESIGN

Assessment determines whether behavior changes over the course of the intervention. In the absence of objective assessment, behavior change is a matter of opinion and conjecture. Anecdotal estimates of behavior change are an inadequate substitute for objective and reliable assessment (cf. Kazdin, 1973d; Schnelle, 1974). Objective assessment of behavior can demonstrate change, but cannot reveal the cause or source of change when change occurs. Investigations attempt to demonstrate not only behavior change but the cause of the change as well. To accomplish these goals, behavior change and the intervention must be carefully evaluated.

Behavior may change systematically as a function of events other than the intervention. For example, an intervention might be carried out in the home to increase a child's compliance with parental instructions. The child may ignore or overtly resist his parents' instructions. The child's compliance with instructions ordinarily would be assessed for several days to determine baseline performance. After the baseline rate was determined, the intervention, such as praising the child for following instructions, would be introduced. Behavior may change with this intervention, but was the contingent delivery of praise responsible for the change? Alternative explanations of the change might be advanced. Initially, the introduction of praise in the home, whether or not its delivery was contingent upon behavior, may have led to change. Also, extraneous events associated with the intervention, such as illness, termination of an illness, events occurring at school, resolution or onset of parental conflict, or changes in the behavior of the childrens' peers or siblings, might have led to behavior change. Assessment of behavior cannot rule out the possibility that such extraneous events were responsible for behavior change.

The role of the intervention in behavior change can be demonstrated in many ways. The investigator who designs the program must structure the situation to demonstrate the specific contribution of the intervention. The plan of the program, referred to as the *experimental design*, determines what accounts for behavior change. The experimental design allows a causal inference to be made between behavior and the intervention by ruling out plausible rival interpretations (cf. Campbell & Stanley, 1963).

Different experimental designs in applied behavior analysis can be used to determine whether the intervention or the extraneous events altered behavior (Baer, 1975; Baer et al., 1968; Bijou et al., 1969; Gelfand & Hartmann, 1968; Hersen & Barlow, 1976; Kazdin, 1973c; 1975a; Leitenberg, 1973; Risley, 1970; Sidman, 1960). The following discussion details the ABAB, multiple-baseline, simultaneous-treatment, and changing-criterion designs, and problems attendant upon their use.

ABAB Design

The ABAB design examines the effect of an intervention by alternating the environmental contingencies over time. Typically, an intervention is implemented during some phases and withdrawn or altered in others. The absence of the intervention is usually referred to as the baseline (or A) phase, while the intervention is referred to as the experimental (or B) phase. The design is ABAB because A and B phases alternate.

An ABAB design assesses performance before implementing the intervention. The baseline phase is usually continued until responding stabilizes, or does not change systematically over time. It is assumed that performance would be similar in the future if no intervention were introduced, i.e., that baseline performance predicts the level of performance in the future without the intervention. After baseline stabilizes (several days are usually sufficient), the intervention is introduced. The intervention (e.g., reinforcement, punishment, or extinction contingencies) is continued until behavior stabilizes, usually at a level different from baseline performance. This demonstrates that the intervention is accompanied by behavior change, but the cause of the change cannot yet be determined. Because behavior change coincides with the intervention, it is likely that the program accounts for the change, but this cannot be determined at this point.

After behavior stabilizes, the intervention is withdrawn and the baseline condition is reinstated. A return to baseline conditions sometimes is referred to as a *reversal* phase because the experimental condition is withdrawn and behavior usually "reverses" (i.e., returns to or near the level of the original baseline). After behavior reverts to baseline levels, the intervention is reinstated.

The A and B conditions are not changed until performance during a given phase is stable or clearly different from the previous phase. When conditions are changed, the new level of behavior can be compared to the level predicted from the previous phase. Thus, performance during the intervention phase is compared to the projected level of performance in the previous baseline. When the intervention is withdrawn and baseline is reinstated, the accuracy of the level of performance predicted by the original baseline is assessed. Each phase of the ABAB design predicts the level of behavior that would result if no change were made in the contingencies. Returning to the conditions of a previous phase assesses whether the projected performance of that phase was accurate. In general, if performance changes in the experimental phase relative to the level predicted by baseline, reverts to baseline after the intervention is withdrawn, and then changes again when the intervention is reinstated, then the intervention is likely to have been responsible for change.

The ABAB design has frequently been referred to as a *reversal design* because of the reversal of experimental conditions and the tendency of behavior to reverse as a function of change in experimental conditions. Recently, the terminology has been altered to reduce confusion of the experimental procedures with behavior change (Hersen & Barlow, 1976). As discussed later, the term reversal design is sometimes reserved for a particular variation of the ABAB design (Leitenberg, 1973).

Investigations using ABAB designs are abundant (cf. Kazdin, 1975b). R. V. Hall, Fox, Willard, Goldsmith, Emerson, Owen, Davis, & Porcia (1971) evaluated the effect of teacher behavior on student deportment using an ABAB design. One experiment was conducted with a 15-yr old retarded male who frequently argued with the teacher and failed to comply with requests. The teacher ignored the boy whenever he disputed her requests or assignments and praised him whenever he began his assignment without arguing. As evident in Figure 3-1, disputes decreased with the intervention. When the intervention was withdrawn and the teacher attended to the disputes as she had during the original baseline, the response approached baseline levels. Finally, when the intervention was reinstated, behavior changed dramatically. Over a 2-week follow-up period after the investigation (post checks in Figure 3-1), disputes continued at a low level. The results unambiguously demonstrated the effect of the intervention.

Variations of the ABAB Design. The basic strategy of the ABAB design is to show that behavior is a function of the intervention. Three variations of the design demonstrate a functional relation. The variations differ according to what changes are made during the second A phase when the intervention is withdrawn.

In the first variation, as discussed in the previous example, the intervention is withdrawn completely during the second A phase so that baseline

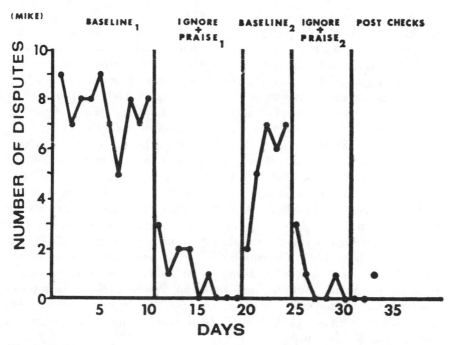

Fig. 3-1. Disputing behavior of a junior high school special-education student. Baseline₁—before the intervention. Ignore and Praise₁—ignoring disputes and praising compliance with assigned tasks. Baseline₂—attending to disputes. Ignore and Praise₂—return to ignoring disputes and praising compliance with assigned tasks. Post Checks—checks after the termination of the experiment. (From Hall, R.V., et al., 1971, p. 142).

conditions are reinstated. This version, which is most commonly used, has sometimes been referred to as the *withdrawal design* (Leitenberg, 1973).

In the second version the contingency between behavior and environmental consequences is removed in the second A phase. The consequences previously presented during the intervention phase continue to be delivered but are not contingent upon performance (cf. Hall, R. V., Lund, & Jackson, 1968). For example, if the child was praised for social interaction (playing with peers) during the intervention phase, the removal of the contingent relation between praise and behavior might consist of praising the child independently of performance. When the contingency between the performance and behavior is altered, behavior may revert to baseline or near baseline levels. This version of the ABAB design is used when the investigator wishes to show that the consequences per se do not control behavior except insofar as they are contingent upon particular responses.

The final version of the ABAB design also alters the contingency between consequences and behavior during the second A phase. In this phase, however, the contingency is reversed to demonstrate the effect of the intervention; all responses other than the original target response produce the consequences. If the intervention consisted of praising a child's social interaction, the second A phase might consist of reinforcing any behavior *except* social interaction. The events delivered during the intervention (praise) continue to be delivered during the second A phase, but they are delivered for nonperformance of the target response. The schedule in which every response except the target response is reinforced is referred to as differential reinforcement of other behavior. This schedule is designed to reverse the behavior rapidly from its intervention level (cf. Kale et al., 1968; Kazdin, 1973b; Surratt et al., 1969). Thus, with this schedule the child is likely to decrease social interaction. The term *reversal design* is sometimes reserved for this version of the ABAB design (Leitenberg, 1973).

Additional variations of the ABAB design include elaborations of the basic versions already outlined. In some versions several interventions are employed across phases before reinstating the second A phase. In other versions the design may begin with the intervention phase in a BABA fashion (Kazdin & Polster, 1973). The conditions used to return behavior to baseline levels do not change in these elaborations. Whether the second A phase is a return to the original baseline, noncontingent delivery of the consequences or differential reinforcement of other behavior, the purpose is to show that the contingency changes behavior. (For extensions of the ABAB design, see Hersen and Barlow, 1976.)

Limitations of the ABAB Design. The ABAB design demonstrates a functional relation by showing that behavior reverts to or approaches the original baseline level after the intervention is withdrawn or altered. The demonstration depends upon a reversal in behavior during the second A phase. Reliance upon a reversal in behavior introduces problems that may restrict the use of the design. One problem is that withdrawing the intervention to show a reversal in the rate of behavior does not always change behavior (Hewett, Taylor, & Artuso, 1969; Medland & Stachnik, 1972; Osborne, 1969); in such cases, whether the intervention or extraneous events changed behavior cannot be determined.

The irreversibility of behavior may occur for many reasons. First, when behavior does not approach baseline rates after the intervention is withdrawn, the intervention may not have been responsible for initial behavior change. Extraneous factors associated with the intervention may have changed. These factors may have remained in effect after the intervention was withdrawn. Second, the intervention may have been responsible for change, but other events may later have taken control over behavior (Baer, 1968). For example, praise may increase a child's social interaction. But once behavior increases, it may be maintained by peer attention rather than by teacher praise (cf. Jones, R. T., & Kazdin, 1975). Withdrawal of teacher praise may then have no effect. A third situation in which irreversibility may appear is with punishment. When the intervention completely suppresses or eliminates a response, withdrawal of the intervention may have no effect on behavior. If the behavior is virtually eliminated, the individual may never perform the target response and never encounter the change in the contingency. Several punishment studies have failed to find a reversal when the intervention is withdrawn (Azrin & Wesolowski, 1974; Foxx & Azrin, 1972, 1973a; Kazdin, 1971).

In these three circumstances, the irreversibility of behavior precludes showing that the intervention was responsible for behavior change. It is difficult to predict when another design should be used in place of the ABAB design because behavior will not reverse. Some investigators have suggested that once the intervention effects are apparent, the program should be withdrawn relatively quickly, thereby decreasing the likelihood of irreversibility and maintenance of behavior by external factors (Bijou et al., 1969).

A second restriction of the ABAB design is that reversing behavior to baseline levels is usually undesirable. For example, it would be undesirable to return behavior such as aggressive or self-injurious acts to baseline levels by withdrawing the program. In practice, parents, teachers, staff members, and investigators are sensitive about returning to baseline conditions that make the client worse. In some cases the intervention can be withdrawn for a very short period (e.g., a few days), thus minimizing the deleterious effects, but in other instances any withdrawal or alteration of the program may be undesirable.

Multiple-Baseline Designs

Multiple-baseline designs demonstrate the effect of an intervention by showing that behavior change accompanies introduction of the intervention at different points in time. Once the intervention is presented, it need not be withdrawn or altered to reverse behavior to baseline or near baseline levels. Thus, the multiple-baseline design is not limited by the two major restrictions of the ABAB design, the irreversibility of behavior or the undesirability of reversing behavior. Three versions of the multiple-baseline design are commonly used. In each version data are collected simultaneously across two or more baselines. The intervention is applied to different baselines at different points in time. The versions differ in the way the data are collected: across several responses, individuals, or situations.

Multiple-Baseline Design Across Responses. The multiple-baseline design across responses is used when one individual or a group of individuals has several responses to be changed. Baseline data are collected across two or more responses of a single individual or a group. After each baseline has stabilized, the intervention is applied to only one of the responses. Baseline conditions remain in effect for the other response(s). The initial response to which the intervention was applied is expected to change while other responses should remain at baseline levels. When rates are stable for all responses, the intervention is applied to the second response. Remaining responses continue under baseline conditions. Sequentially introducing the intervention across responses is continued until the intervention is applied to all responses for which baseline data were gathered. A causal relation between the intervention and behavior is clearly demonstrated if each response changes only when the intervention is introduced, and not before.

Pierce and Risley (1974, pp. 406-409) evaluated the effect of punishment in a community recreation center located in an economically deprived area. The participants in the center (400 over the course of the project) primarily included male teenagers. The problem in the center was a failure to maintain the facility, as evident by frequent littering of materials, misplaced equipment, and property damage. Rules were devised by the recreation director that, when violated, resulted in closing the facility early for a predetermined period of time. There was a 15-min loss for breaking Ping-Pong balls or paddles, and so on. Frequent checks of different violations were made so that the time would accumulate for early closing. Although the rules and consequences decreased violations, the director did not consistently enforce some of the rules.

Pierce and Risley evaluated the effect of consistent enforcement of the rules on three undesirable responses. Each of the three responses (littering in the game room, misplacing the pool rack, and littering in the hall) was assessed every day. During baseline, the director continued to enforce the rules occasionally or only when the violations appeared to be severe. The intervention consisted of enforcing the rules consistently, so that each infraction resulted in a time loss, as originally planned. The intervention was imposed on each response at a different time. As shown in Figure 3-2, each of the undesirable responses decreased when the intervention was introduced and not before. The causal relation between the intervention and behavior change is demonstrated by the specific effect of the contingency.

Multiple-Baseline Design Across Individuals. The multiple-baseline design across individuals is useful when a response has to be altered across several individuals in a group. Baseline data are collected for a particular response across two or more individuals. After the response of each individual has stabilized, the intervention is applied to only one of the individuals. Baseline conditions remain in effect for the other individuals. The response of the individual to whom the intervention is applied is likely to change while the response(s) of the other individuals is likely to remain at baseline levels. As behavior stabilizes for all individuals, the intervention is extended to another person. This procedure continues until the intervention is applied to all for whom baseline data were gathered. The effect of the intervention is clearly demonstrated if the behavior of each individual changes only when the intervention is introduced.

R. V. Hall et al. (1970) used this design with tenth-grade students who had been earning D and F grades on class quizzes. Baseline data were gathered on daily grades (A-F) for each student. After several days, the first student was told that whenever he earned a score of D or F on a quiz he

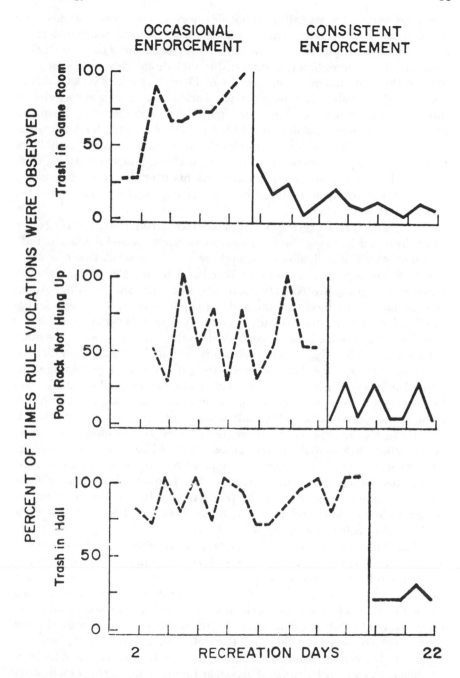

Fig. 3-2. Rule violations of male teenagers in a recreation center. Occasional Enforcement—only periodic enforcement of penalties for rule violation. Consistent Enforcement—enforcement of penalties for each violation. (From Pierce & Risley, 1974, p. 409.)

would be required to stay after school for tutoring. The other students were not exposed to the contingency, although baseline data continued to be collected for their quiz performance. When the behavior of the first student changed, the intervention was extended to include the second student. For each of the two students, quiz grades of D or F resulted in after-school tutoring. Eventually, the quiz behavior of the last student was included in the same contingency. As shown in Figure 3-3, the grades of each student improved only when the intervention (after-school tutoring for low grades) was introduced. This demonstrates that the intervention was responsible for behavior change. Extraneous events, such as changes in study habits, difficulty of the quizzes, or general improvements over time due to practice, could not adequately account for behavior change at the precise times the intervention was introduced.

   Multiple-Baseline Design across Situations, Settings, or Time. The multiple-baseline design across situations is useful when an individual or group of individuals responds or fails to respond across separate situations, settings, or time periods. Baseline data for a given response of an individual or group are collected across two or more situations or settings such as at home, in the classroom, and on the playground. After behavior has stabilized in each situation, the intervention is applied to behavior in the first situation. The baseline phase is continued for the same behavior in the other situation(s). Eventually, the intervention is extended to behavior in the next situation while baseline data continue to be gathered in the remaining situations. The intervention is extended to each situation until all situations have been included. A specific effect of the intervention is shown if behavior changes in a particular situation only when the intervention is introduced.

   Using this design, G. J. Allen (1973) attempted to eliminate bizarre verbalizations in a mentally brain-damaged 8-yr-old boy who was attending a summer camp. The boy engaged in frequent bizarre verbalizations that referred to fictitious pets and characters. His frequent discussion of these fantasies seemed to interfere with appropriate verbalizations and social interactions with adults and peers. Extinction was used to eliminate these verbalizations across a number of situations.

   Baseline data on these verbalizations were obtained across different settings in the camp. (See Figure 3-4.) The intervention was introduced in these different situations, starting with the one in which the boy's verbalizations were most frequent. The intervention consisted of ignoring the boy whenever he made a bizarre verbalization or asked a question that previously had led to such a verbalization. To extinguish these responses, the staff merely turned away from the boy. The staff attended to the boy, however, whenever his verbalizations were appropriate (e.g., discussions of feelings, the home, or camp activities). As shown in Figure 3-4, bizarre verbalizations tended to decline during the intervention in a given situation. The two final situations (cabin and educational settings), where the change associated with the intervention was negligible, are of interest because responding was very

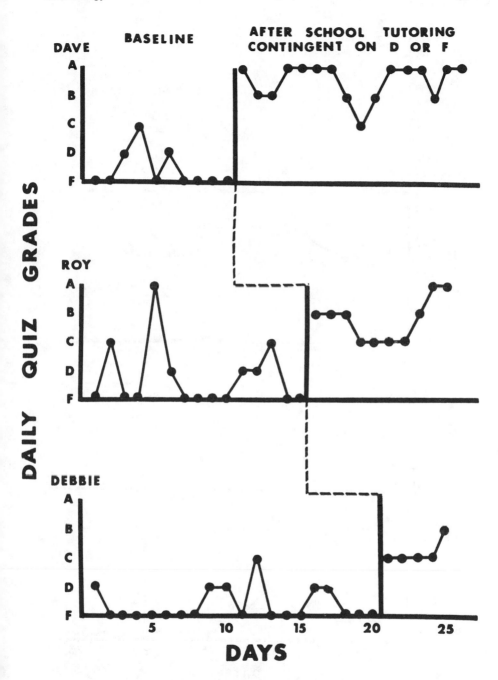

Fig. 3-3. Quiz grades for high-school students. Baseline—before the intervention. After-School Tutoring Contingent on D or F Grades—pupils required to stay after school if they scored a D or F on the daily quiz. (From Hall, R.V., et al., 1970, p. 251.)

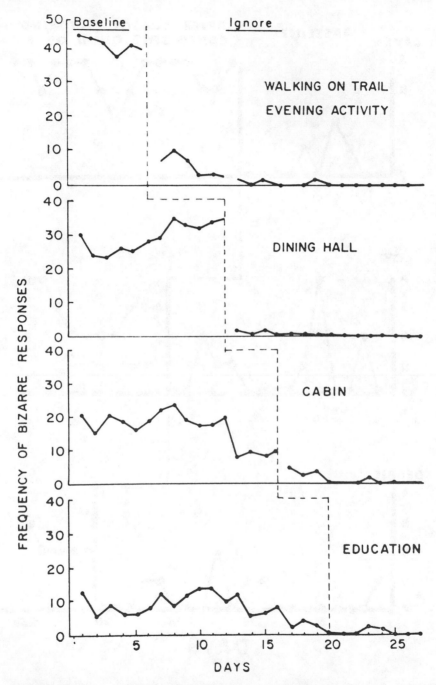

Fig. 3-4. Bizarre verbalizations of a "brain-damaged" boy at summer camp. Baseline—before the intervention. Ignore—turning away from the boy for bizarre verbalizations and attending to appropriate verbalizations. (From Allen, G.J., 1973, p. 573.)

low and declined slightly over time. The two initial baselines, however, suggest that the intervention exerted control over behavior.

Limitations of the Multiple-Baseline Design. Multiple-baseline designs demonstrate the effect of an intervention without a return to baseline conditions and temporary loss of some of the gains made during the intervention. Two considerations that determine whether or not the effect of the intervention can be inferred from the design include the number of baselines used and interdependence among the baselines (Kazdin & Kopel, 1975).

The precise number of baselines needed to demonstrate the effect of an intervention in the multiple-baseline design is not easily specified. While two baselines are minimum, more are usually desirable. As a general rule, the more baselines across which the effect of the intervention is demonstrated, the more convincing the causal relation. Some authors recommend three or more baselines (Barlow, D. H., & Hersen, 1973; Wolf & Risley, 1971), but whether an investigation provides a convincing demonstration across a given set of baselines is the function of such factors as the duration of baseline, the presence of trends or extensive variability in behavior during baseline, the rapidity of behavior change after the intervention, and the magnitude of behavior change. Depending upon these factors, few or many baselines might be needed to provide a convincing demonstration. Generally if baseline and intervention behaviors are stable and the intervention produces a rapid and marked effect, two or three baselines may be enough to demonstrate a causal relation. Because it is difficult to predict the magnitude of behavior change and the stability of behavior within phases, it is usually safer to select several baselines. Multiple-baseline designs have varied widely in number of baselines, with some experiments using the minimum of two (Milby, 1970) and others up to nine (Clark, H. B., Boyd, & Macrae, 1975).

The multiple-baseline design assumes that an intervention will affect all responses (or individuals or situations) similarly. In fact this assumption is not always tenable. If the effect of praise on classroom performance were evaluated in a multiple-baseline design across several individuals, praise might not be a reinforcer for everyone. Indeed, praise might even be an aversive stimulus for some (Levin, G., & Simmons, 1962). In this case the multiple-baseline design would not show a clear effect of the intervention across individuals.

The multiple-baseline design also depends upon selecting baselines that are independent, so that change in one baseline does not also change another. Yet the effects of the intervention may be general rather than specific (cf. Kazdin & Kopel, 1975). Demonstrating the effect of the intervention in the multiple-baseline design across behavior depends upon showing that behavior changes only when the intervention is introduced. Yet several studies report that altering one response is associated with changes in other responses not included in the intervention (Buell, Stoddard, Harris, &

Baer, 1968; Horton, 1970; Kazdin, 1973a; Maley, Feldman, & Ruskin, 1973; Nordquist, 1971; Wahler, 1975; Wahler et al., 1970). In situations where generalization across responses occurs, a multiple-baseline across responses might not unambiguously show the causal effect of the intervention.

In the multiple-baseline design across individuals, the demonstration depends upon showing that behavior of different individuals changes only when the intervention is introduced. Several studies have shown, however, that changing the behavior of one individual may alter the behavior of others for whom baseline conditions remain in effect (Broden et al., 1970; Christy, 1975; Drabman & Lahey, 1974; Kazdin, 1973b; Kazdin et al., 1975; Kounin & Gump, 1958). Thus, in situations in which the effects of the contingency extend beyond one individual, the multiple-baseline design across individuals may not show a causal effect of the intervention.

Similarly, in the multiple-baseline design across situations, an unambiguous demonstration depends upon changes in behavior only in those situations in which the intervention is in effect. Yet in some cases changing behavior in one situation may change behavior in other situations in which the intervention is not introduced (Bennett & Maley, 1973; Hunt & Zimmerman, 1969; Kazdin, 1973d). Thus, this version of the multiple-baseline design may not show a causal effect of the intervention if the situations are so similar that altering behavior in one situation changes behavior in another.

Each multiple-baseline design has the potential problem of the interdependence of the baselines from which the data were gathered. If the intervention is accompanied by generalized changes, behavior change cannot be unambiguously attributed to the intervention. It is difficult to predict in advance when the effects of an intervention will generalize across behavior, individuals, or situations. Generalized effects across different baselines currently appear to be exceptions rather than the rule.

Simultaneous-Treatment Design

The simultaneous-treatment design examines the effect of different interventions, each of which is implemented in the same phase of the program. The design is especially useful when the investigator is interested in determining which among two or more procedures is more effective. The design begins with baseline observation of a single response. After baseline is completed, two or more interventions are implemented to alter the response. The interventions are implemented in the same phase but under varied stimulus conditions. For example, two interventions would be compared by implementing both of them on a given day in the intervention phase. The interventions, however, are varied across periods of the day (morning and afternoon) and across individuals who administer the interventions (different staff members in an institution). The different interventions are balanced across all conditions so that their effects can be separated from these conditions. The intervention phase is continued, varying the conditions of administration, until responses stabilize under the separate interventions.

McCullough, Cornell, McDaniel, and Mueller (1974) used this design to increase cooperate play in a first-grade student. The child engaged in such uncooperative behavior as walking out of the room, sleeping, fighting, and playing at times when it was appropriate to complete classroom assignments. Two interventions were compared: praise for cooperative behavior and praise combined with time-out from reinforcement. Time-out consisted of removing the child from the classroom and placing him in an empty room for two min. The teacher and the teacher's aide administered the program. Each classroom day was divided into morning and afternoon periods.

After baseline observations across both morning and afternoon, the interventions were implemented. On a given day, each intervention was administered, but the individual who administered a particular intervention (teacher or teacher aide) and the time of day during which a particular intervention was administered (morning or afternoon) were balanced so that each intervention was administered an equal number of times by the teacher and teacher's aide across each period.

The results (Figure 3-5) show that praise alone (condition A) tended to be less effective than praise plus time-out (condition B). The experimenter implemented the more effective procedure for the third phase of the study. While this phase was not essential to the design, because the intervention effects were assessed in the second phase, it was implemented to demonstrate quickly the more effective intervention so that it could be applied during all periods.

Besides assessing the separate effects of two or more interventions, the differential effectiveness of staff members in altering client behavior also can be determined. Because each staff member administers the different contingencies, the separate effects can be determined for each staff member across all conditions.

Limitations of the Simultaneous-Treatment Design. The simultaneous-treatment design can examine any number of interventions during the intervention phase. But as more interventions are compared, the confounding effects of individuals who administer the specific intervention, of the time period in which each intervention is administered, or the combination of these factors, are increasingly difficult to remove. Difficulty derives from the large number of sessions required so that each intervention can be administered by a given individual and across time periods an equal number of times.

A potential limitation of the simultaneous-treatment design is the client's ability to discriminate the different contingencies. The client must discriminate that the staff members and time periods are not consistently correlated with a particular intervention, because the intervention varies across each of these dimensions. For relatively brief interventions, the dis-

A CASE STUDY

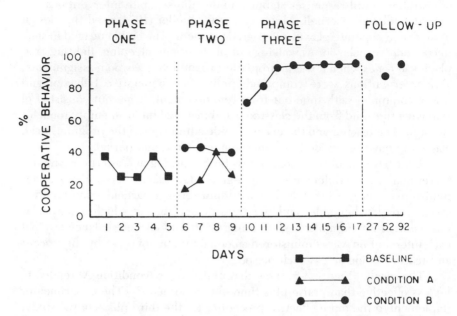

Fig. 3-5. Cooperative behavior of an elementary school student. Phase one (Baseline)—before the intervention. Phase two (Treatment)—two treatments administered concurrently (Treatment A: praise, Treatment B: praise plus time-out). Phase three (Treatment)—only one treatment administered (praise plus time-out). Follow-up—evaluation of behavior one week, one month, and two months after treatment was terminated. (From McCullough et al., 1973, p. 291.)

crimination may be especially difficult, and the interventions may not appear differentially effective. The client may change behavior during the intervention but fail to distinguish the different conditions because of the difficulty of the required discrimination.

A related concern is that the effects of administering each intervention in the same phase may differ from what they would be if the intervention were administered in separate phases. The effect of a given intervention sometimes is determined by other interventions administered in close temporal proximity (i.e., immediately before or concurrently). In one study time-out from reinforcement (isolation) was used to suppress such deviant behavior as aggressive acts and tantrums (White, G. D., Nielsen, & Johnson, 1972). Time-out durations (1, 15, and 30 min) were compared across 20 individuals, each receiving all three time-out durations. The effect of a given time-out duration was influenced in part by the duration previously administered. The shortest time-out was much more effective when it was the first duration administered than when it followed a longer duration. Thus, administering procedures in close proximity may produce different effects from those obtained by administering the procedures separately.

Changing-Criterion Design

In the changing-criterion design, the effect of the intervention is determined by showing that behavior changes as the criterion for contingent consequences changes. A causal relation between an intervention and behavior is demonstrated when behavior matches the criterion set for response consequences (Axelrod, Hall, Weis, & Rohrer, 1974).

The design begins with a baseline phase, after which the intervention is introduced. When the intervention is introduced, a specific level of performance is chosen as a criterion for the response consequences (e.g., token reinforcers). For example, a response may have to be performed at a certain rate, as specified by the investigator, to produce the reinforcer. When performance consistently meets the criterion, the criterion for reinforcement is changed (increased or made more stringent). A criterion is repeatedly changed throughout the intervention phase until the terminal goal of the program is achieved. The effect of the intervention is demonstrated if the behavior matches the criterion as the criterion is changed. If behavior changes with the new contingency, the intervention, rather than extraneous influences, probably changed behavior.

Dietz and Repp (1973) used a changing-criterion design to evaluate an intervention to decrease the rate that high-school students engaged in social rather than academic discussions. During an academic lesson, students frequently changed subjects and inappropriately talked about things other than their lesson. Because the goal was to eliminate undesirable talking, after baseline students were rewarded for *not* engaging in inappropriate verbalizations. The schedule of reinforcement was a variation of a differential-reinforcement-of-low-rates schedule; low rates of inappropriate talking were reinforced. The experimenters imposed different criteria for reinforcement during the intervention phase so that progressively fewer verbalizations were allowed. In the four intervention phases, the reinforcer-a free day (Friday) to be used as the students wished-was earned if verbalizations did not exceed the daily criterion (5, 3, 2, and 0) on the previous days.

Figure 3-6 shows that intervention-phase performance always equaled or surpassed the criterion (horizontal line). The last criterion was zero, which meant that the reinforcer was only earned if no inappropriate verbalizations were observed. Inappropriate talking followed the changing criterion. In the final phase of the experiment, the original baseline condition was reinstated, thus also making this an ABAB design. The last phase, of course, is not essential to the changing-criterion design.

Limitations of the Changing-Criterion Design. The changing-criterion design depends upon repeatedly changing the performance criterion and examining behavior relative to that new criterion. The design is especially well-suited to those terminal responses that are shaped gradually rather than those acquired in one or a few trials. To show that changes in the criterion account for reduction in behavior, behavior has to occur frequently

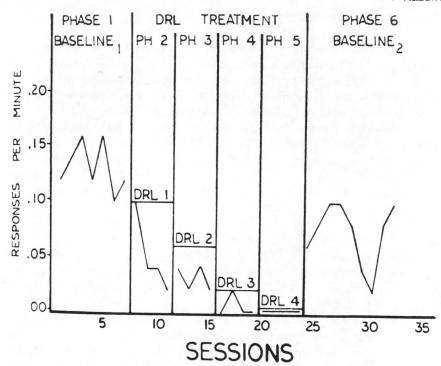

Fig. 3-6. Inappropriate verbalizations of a class of high-school students. Baseline₁—before the intervention. Treatment—separate phases (PH) in which a decreasingly lower rate of verbalizations was required to earn the reinforcer. The limit for the four phases was five or fewer responses during the session, three or fewer, two or fewer, or zero responses, respectively. Baseline₂—withdrawal of treatment. (From Dietz & Repp, 1973, p. 461.)

enough that several changes in a criterion can be made before the goal (response elimination) is achieved. If rapid changes occurred that surpassed the criterion for reinforcement, the specific effect of the contingency in altering behavior would be ambiguous. Thus, because of these requirements, the design is limited to demonstrating gradual rather than rapid changes.

In general the changing-criterion design may be less satisfactory than the designs previously discussed because the effects of extraneous events are not necessarily ruled out. The design depends upon showing a directional change in behavior over time. Yet extraneous events other than the intervention could result in directional changes. This design is strong only if performance matches the criterion very closely.

The changing-criterion design could be strengthened by making bidirectional changes in the criterion during the intervention phase; i.e., rather than simply making the criterion increasingly more stringent, making it more stringent at some points and less stringent at others. Essentially, during the intervention phase the criterion could be altered in different directions for brief periods that would be expected to increase or decrease performance. This variation rules out extraneous events in accounting for the results to a greater extent than the typical changing-criterion design, which examines unidirectional changes in behavior. Of course, the problems of irreversibility relevant to the ABAB design might affect the use of this variation.

Combined Intrasubject Designs

The description of the intrasubject designs implies that investigators select a particular design and complete the project without varying from this initial selection. While this is often the case, the description is deceptive. Investigators sometimes vary the design from their original plan as a function of the data. For example, the investigator may select a multiple-baseline design across a given individual's responses. Applying the intervention to the first response may alter all responses for which baseline data were gathered. Once the data show generalized effects, the experimenter may withdraw the intervention (i.e., return to baseline conditions) to demonstrate a causal relation between the intervention and behavior. The design becomes a combined version of multiple-baseline and ABAB designs. Because measurement in applied behavior analysis is continuous over time, the experimenter can react immediately to the data by altering the intervention or the experimental design as needed (cf. Skinner, 1963). New phases may be introduced to enhance therapeutic effects of the intervention or to demonstrate a causal relation between behavior and intervention.

Investigators often *initially* select combined designs. For example, an investigator may wish to show the specific effect of an intervention by using a changing criterion phase. To remove any ambiguity, a final phase may be added in which the intervention is withdrawn to see whether behavior returns to baseline levels (cf. Dietz & Repp, 1973).

Combined intrasubject designs are used frequently in applied behavior analysis. Design combinations are extremely useful because they can more firmly establish a causal relation. The adequacy of any demonstration is always a matter of degree. Combined designs can demonstrate the effect of the intervention in more than one fashion in a single investigation. As discussed later, intrasubject designs and between-group designs are often combined.

Traditional Between-Group Designs

Traditional research in psychology has emphasized group comparisons. In the basic design, a group that receives intervention is compared with one that does not. More typically, several groups are compared that differ in the specific interventions or parametric variations of a particular intervention. The effect of the intervention is measured by statistical comparisons of means between or among groups, to determine whether the obtained differences are likely to have occurred by chance. Traditional between-group designs and their variations have been described in numerous sources and will not be treated here (cf. Campbell & Stanley, 1963; Neale & Liebert, 1973; Underwood, 1957b; Underwood & Shaughnessy, 1975). It is important, however, to discuss traditional methodology briefly because it contrasts in many ways with the methodology of applied behavior analysis. In addition, features of between-group research have increasingly been combined with intrasubject designs (Kazdin, 1975b, 1975d).

Applied behavior analysis has relied primarily upon intrasubject-replication designs rather than between-group comparisons. Various features of between-group designs, in many cases not essential, are considered incompatible with a functional analysis of behavior (cf. Sidman, 1960). The goal of applied behavior research is to analyze behavior changes in relation to the environmental events of which they are a function. Yet several features of traditional experimentation often obscure the behavior change of individuals; these features are averaging the data across several subjects, emphasizing mean differences between groups, searching for statistical significance, and assessing behavior on relatively few occasions (e.g., pre- and postintervention assessment). Average performance of the group does not necessarily reflect what happens to individual subjects in an experiment. The issue has been referred to as the subject-generality problem, i.e., the extent to which the findings generalize from the group to the individual members (Sidman, 1960).

A goal of applied behavior analysis is to demonstrate behavior change by looking at behavior continuously over time and by examining performance of individual subjects rather than the group. Continuous assessment over time is important for conclusions about the effect of the intervention. In many cases, with assessment on only one or a few occasions, different conclusions about the intervention might be reached depending upon when the behavior was sampled after an intervention. For example, using extinction to alter behavior may or may not appear effective if behavior is assessed at only one point after treatment. Extinction is sometimes associated with a temporary increase in the extinguished behavior (e.g., extinction burst or spontaneous recovery). The absence of continuous assessment in most traditional experimentation precludes examining the course of behavior change.

Despite objections that might be leveled against traditional between-group designs, group comparisons can provide information not easily obtainable in intrasubject-replication designs. In many applied investigations, experimental questions are posed that can readily be handled by between-groups comparisons. Investigators increasingly have compared the effects of two interventions where both cannot be easily administered to the same

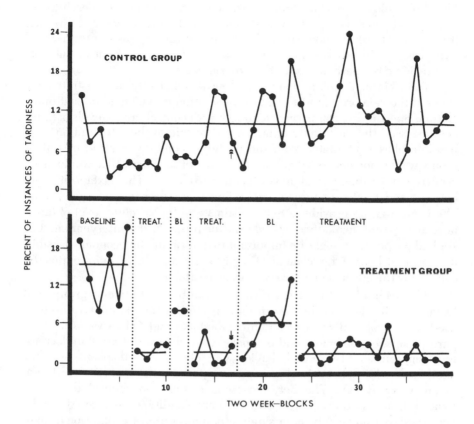

Fig. 3-7. Tardiness of industrial workers. Control group—no intervention throughout the study. Treatment group—Baseline (BL) in which no intervention was implemented and Treatment in which money was contingent upon punctuality. Horizontal lines represent the means for each condition. (From Hermann et al., 1973, p. 567.)

individual or group of individuals. Even in areas where treatments could be administered to the same group, it is sometimes undesirable to do this because, as noted earlier, the effect of one intervention may depend upon the previously administered intervention. Thus, comparisons between groups are especially useful to evaluate different treatments uninfluenced by other interventions (cf. Kazdin, 1973c).

An example of a combined between-group and intrasubject-replication design was provided by Hermann et al. (1973), who evaluated the efficacy of an incentive procedure to increase punctuality of workers in an industrial setting in Mexico. Of 12 individuals frequently tardy for work (1 or more min late), six were assigned to a treatment group and the other six to the control group. During the intervention, which was presented in an ABAB design, workers in the treatment group received a slip of paper daily for punctuality.

The slips could be exchanged for a maximum of 80¢ at the end of each week. The control group received no treatment over the experiment. The results (Figure 3-7, lower portion) showed that the treatment consistently reduced tardiness relative to baseline performance. In contrast control subjects slightly increased tardiness over the experiment.

The treatment group alone would have sufficiently demonstrated the effect of the reinforcer, but the control condition provided additional information. Specifically, comparing treatment with control-group levels of tardiness assessed the magnitude of improvement due to the intervention. The baseline phases alternated with the incentive condition for the treatment group would not necessarily show the level of tardiness that would have occurred if treatment had never been introduced. The juxtaposition of baseline and treatment periods can influence performance in each phase. The control group provides a better estimate of the absolute level of tardiness at any time for individuals who never received the intervention. For applied purposes, it might be important to determine the economic feasibility and cost-benefit for change of a given magnitude of intervention by comparing the effect of incentive versus no treatment.

The example illustrates a simple combined between-group and intrasubject-replication design. In various studies the combined design is used to evaluate different treatments. Kaufman and O'Leary (1972) compared token reinforcement and response cost (token withdrawal) in decreasing inappropriate classroom behavior. One class received tokens, whereas another class lost tokens. Each group was exposed to its respective treatment in an ABAB design. The between-group comparison allowed the investigators to assess the effect of two different conditions that could not be compared in a single-subject or single-group intrasubject-replication design. Various studies have compared two or more different treatments in an ABAB design (e.g., O'Leary, K.D., Becker, Evans, & Saudargas, 1969). Interventions administered in different phases, however, cannot be compared because of confounding sequence effects and history with the separate interventions (cf. Campbell & Stanley, 1963).

Increasingly, applied behavior analyses focus upon groups rather than individual subjects, thus making group comparisons somewhat more common. Interventions are implemented in settings where large numbers of individuals are involved (cf. Kazdin, 1975a, 1975b). For example, interventions have been designed to increase the number of individuals who help provide jobs for the unemployed (Jones, R.J., & Azrin, 1973, pp 348-351), to increase bus ridership (Everett et al., 1974), to control the behavior of individuals who use community recreational facilities (Pierce & Risley, 1974, pp 406-408), and to reduce littering in public places (Clark, R.N., Burgess, & Hendee, 1969).

In these studies behavior change of the individual is lost because the intervention focuses directly on the group. Indeed, the same individuals are not always observed over time in these projects. For example, in studies assessing the impact of interventions in social settings such as parks, campgrounds, and stores, the identity of individuals may not be known. In many applications the behavior of the individual per se may not always be of primary interest. For example, in decreasing consumption of fuel, contingency-management techniques might be imposed on a large group of individuals. The goal is to increase overall fuel consumption. A reduction for any individual may not be crucial as long as the overall level of change is achieved.

PROBLEMS IN DATA INTERPRETATION

Each of the designs discussed begins with a baseline phase. The intervention is evaluated by comparing performance during the intervention phase with performance projected from the preceding baseline phase. The evaluation is facilitated by having stable responding (Sidman, 1960). Stability refers to the absence of a trend in the data and to relatively small variability about a given level of performance. Trends and extensive variability during baseline or subsequent phases can interfere with evaluation of the intervention.

Trend in the Data

The stability of behavior is reflected in whether behavior systematically changes during the phase. Ideally, baseline data should show no trend before the intervention. Trends in baseline may pose problems for subsequent evaluation. Two trends are possible. First, behavior during baseline may change in the direction opposite from that to be achieved by the intervention. For example, a psychotic patient may show a reduction in rational statements in the hospital during baseline. The intervention, however, may be designed to increase rational statements. A trend in baseline showing reduction in the behavior subsequently to be increased is not likely to interfere with the subsequent conclusions about the intervention. On the basis of projecting baseline performance, the prediction would be that rational talk would cease unless an intervention was introduced. If the intervention is effective, it will alter both the trend and the level of rational speech. Thus, in cases where the intervention is designed to change behavior in a direction opposite from that of a trend in baseline, the trend is not problematic.

In contrast the baseline trend may be in the same direction as the change to be produced by the intervention. In these cases one might question whether to intervene at all. Often baseline improvement is sufficiently slow that some intervention is needed. For example, an autistic child engaging in frequent headbanging might gradually reduce the response during a baseline phase, but the reduction could be so gradual that serious physical injury might be inflicted unless the rate of change is accelerated. In a broader context, the crime rate in a given city might steadily decrease over several months, but the slow rate of change and the overall absolute level of crime might require an intervention to accelerate change. Thus, even when there is improvement in baseline, this change is sometimes not sufficient to obviate the need for intervening.

Despite the desirability of intervening in situations where baseline trends move in the direction of therapeutic change, evaluating the effect of the interventions may be difficult. The intervention has to produce marked changes to make conclusions about the data unambiguous. Because of the difficulty in evaluating the intervention with a systematic trend in the direction of therapeutic change in baseline, some authors recommend waiting for baseline to stabilize prior to intervening (e.g., Baer et al., 1968), but often this cannot be done for practical reasons.

When baseline improves, at least three alternative strategies exist. First, an ABAB design can be used, in which a procedure for changing behavior in the opposite direction can be repeatedly alternated with the intervention. Thus, the intervention could begin after baseline but, to overcome possible continued improvements when the intervention is withdrawn, behavior incompatible with the target response could be reinforced. Although this may be sufficient to reverse trends in behavior, there are problems associated with reversing significant behavior.

A second solution is to use a design in which the trend is less relevant to evaluate the intervention. For example, a trend in baseline is not especially problematic in the simultaneous-treatment design because the effect of two or more separate treatments on baseline behavior is the comparison of major interest. Thus, the interventions reveal the extent to which one procedure has more impact than the other on an existing trend.

A third solution is to use statistical techniques that can evaluate the effect of intervention relative to the baseline trend. Specific techniques, such as time-series analysis, can take into account the baseline trend and determine whether the trend or level of behavior is altered by the intervention (Glass, Willson, & Gottman, 1974; Gottman, 1973; Gottman, McFall, & Barnett, 1969; Jones, R.R., Vaught, & Reid, 1975; Kazdin, 1976). The statistical tests, however, are used infrequently in applied behavior analysis (cf. Schnelle & Frank, 1974; Schnelle, Kirchner, McNees, & Lawler, 1975).

Intrasubject Variability

Interpretability of data depends upon stable performance. Stability depends not only on whether there is a trend but also on variability of the data. As a general rule, the greater the variability, the greater the difficulty in demonstrating behavior change. In the extreme case, baseline performance for an individual may vary daily from 0 to 100% performance of the target behavior. The problem of such variability is determining whether any subsequent intervention alters performance. An intervention designed to increase behavior will be difficult to evaluate. Such baseline data usually cannot be used to predict the performance to be expected if the intervention was not implemented.

Extensive variability may result from different sources. If behavior is under the control of various stimuli, dramatically different performances may be evident in the presence of these stimuli (Redd, 1969). If different stimuli that control behavior are ignored, the behavior may appear more variable than it actually is under a given and constant stimulus condition.

Related to the above, cyclical events such as physiological cycles (e.g., circadian rhythms or menstrual cycles) or the effect of learned routines might account for variability. Behavior might show cyclical patterns within or across days or weeks (cf. Lindsley, 1960). A pattern of responding in the morning might be followed by a different pattern in the afternoon. Further, observers may add variability to the data by scoring behavior unreliably. The subject may perform the target response relatively consistently, but different observers changing the criteria for recording behavior or inconsistencies across a given observer over time may add to the variability.

Aside from these sources of variability, behavior may simply be quite variable across a given stimulus condition. Indeed, in some programs the goal may be to reduce the variability of a client's performance rather than merely to alter the level of performance. In any case large fluctuations in the data during baseline, for whatever reason, make evaluation of the intervention difficult. In some cases causes of the variability are revealed by carefully observing environmental events. Typically experimenters do not search for these sources of variability during baseline.

To facilitate evaluation of the intervention, investigators sometimes reduce the appearance of variability by averaging data points across consecutive days or sessions. The procedure consists of combining days (e.g., blocks of two or more days). By averaging performance across days or sessions, the fluctuations are reduced substantially and the data usually appear more stable. Of course, within-subject averaging of data distorts day-to-day behavior change. Yet such a procedure clarifies the level and trend of the performance relative to the day-to-day variability, so that various phases can be compared. Whenever possible, it is better to identify and to control the sources of variability than to reduce variability by averaging.

DATA EVALUATION

Experimental designs structure the situation so that the effect of the intervention can be distinguished from the effects of extraneous variables. Whether the intervention actually affects behavior has to be determined. Two criteria have been posed for evaluating research in applied behavior analysis: the experimental criterion and the therapeutic criterion (Risley, 1970).

The Experimental Criterion

The experimental criterion compares behavior during the intervention with what it would be like if the intervention had not been implemented. This criterion is not unique to applied research but is a characteristic of experimental research in general. In 'traditional between-group research, the criterion is met by comparing performance among groups and examining the differences statistically.

In applied behavior analysis the experimental criterion is met by replicating treatment effects over time. Baseline data are gathered to determine the present level of performance and to predict what behavior would be if no change were made in the contingencies. The intervention is evaluated by comparing the level of change to the projected level of baseline performance. Performance in each phase predicts the level of behavior in the next phase if no change in the contingency is made. Repeatedly showing that altering the contingency alters the level of performance in relation to the predicted levels fulfills the experimental criterion. For example, in the ABAB design the intervention effect is replicated over time for a single subject or group of subjects. Similarly, in a multiple-baseline design the intervention effect is replicated across the dimension for which multiple-baseline data have been gathered.

In practice the results clearly meet the experimental criterion in various ways. First, performance during the intervention phase may not overlap with performance during the baseline phase. The data points for baseline may not extend to the levels achieved by the data points during the intervention. If this pattern can be replicated over time with a given subject (ABAB design) or across responses, individuals, or situations (multiple-baseline designs), there is little doubt that the results are reliable and due to the intervention.

Second, a more typical criterion for experimental evaluation is related to the trends in each phase. The baseline phase is continued until a stable rate is achieved and there is no trend in the data, or there is a trend in the opposite direction from the anticipated effects of the intervention. When treatment is implemented, a definite trend is usually evident, indicating that behavior is changing from baseline. The intervention is continued until the trend departs from the projected trend of the baseline phase and stabilizes at a different level from baseline. When baseline conditions are reinstated, the trend is likely to change relative to the intervention. By alternating baseline and experimental phases, systematic changes in trend strongly argue for the experimental reliability of the effect. Thus the reliability of the effect is determined by the overall pattern of the data.

The Therapeutic Criterion

The second criterion for evaluating applied behavior analysis research is the therapeutic or applied criterion. This criterion refers to the applied value or importance of the change in behavior. Specifically it compares accomplished behavior change with the level of change required for the client's adequate functioning (Risley, 1970). Implicit in the criterion, of course, is that the behavior selected for modification is itself of clinical or social interest.

An applied criterion departs from traditional research that relies almost exclusively upon statistical significance. In applied behavior analysis, small changes in behavior of one or many individuals, even if experimentally reliable, often are not considered important. For example, reducing the self-destructive behavior of a psychotic child from 80% to 40% of the observed intervals per day probably would not be of applied significance. Even though the reduction is relatively large, the remaining level of behavior is far from the "normal social interaction" to which the individual might some day return. To be of clearly applied significance, the program would require a virtually complete elimination of all self-destructive behavior (cf. Lovaas & Simmons, 1969).

The precise criterion that makes the given change therapeutically significant is difficult to specify, because individuals in everyday life (parents, teachers, peers, friends) determine the levels of behavior that are deviant or acceptable. When behavior is altered, as evidenced by objective data, and when the individuals in contact with the client indicate that the original behavior goal has been satisfactorily achieved, the program has reached therapeutic significance. Ideally, applied interventions strive for changes that surpass statistical significance.

Statistical significance is ancillary to clinical value and is irrelevant for evaluating change to many investigators. The concern with therapeutic rather than statistical significance has led investigators to focus upon interventions that produce dramatic changes. Variables that have subtle influences on behavior are given lower priority. Of course, therapeutic results require gross rather than subtle changes in behavior in the majority of instances. While experimental manipulations with weak effects might be interesting of their own right and perhaps might prove eventually to have applied value, they would not solve the immediate problem of making a therapeutic change for a given client.

CONCLUSION

The discussion of the methodology of applied behavior analysis has covered such diverse topics as behavioral assessment, reliability, experimental design, and data evaluation. For each topic recent advances and refinements are evident. It is useful to review some of the more salient issues, advances, and trends to highlight the methodology of applied behavior analysis.

In assessment, investigators are increasingly using multiple-response assessment strategies. Changes effected in a single-target response are accompanied by diverse response changes in areas not included directly in the contingencies. Until relatively recently, multiple-response measures were rarely used. Yet as generalized effects became more evident, multiple-response assessment has been used more commonly in the literature.

In reliability, basic questions have been raised about calculating interobserver agreement. Although various formulae have been routinely used, the conditions under which they are appropriate only recently have been investigated. For example, topics such as the expected level of interobserver agreement for a given set of data and the dependence of reliability estimates on response rates have led to alternative means of specifying interobserver agreement (cf. Hawkins & Dobes, 1976; Hawkins & Dotson, 1975).

Recently artifacts that influence the assessment of interobserver agreement and problems with assessing reliability have been studied. Previous estimates of reliability have not taken into account such influences as observer awareness of reliability assessment, observer drift, observer expectancies for behavior change, and feedback from the experimenter.

In experimental design, reliance upon a single design is changing. The ABAB design and its variations have dominated applied behavior analysis, but the use of multiple-baseline, between-group, and combined designs is increasing (Kazdin, 1975b), and separate groups in the designs allow comparisons between treatments, or balance for different treatments varied within groups (Drabman, Spitalnik, & Spitalnik, 1974; White, G.D., et al., 1972).

In data evaluation, controversy exists over statistical evaluation (Hartmann, 1974; Keselman & Levanthal, 1974; Kratochwill, Alden, Demuth, Dawson, Panicucci, Arntson, McMurray, Hempstead, & Levin, 1974; Michael, 1974). Advances have been made in the statistical techniques available for single-subject research (Kazdin, 1976). In particular, time-series analysis is a potentially useful technique in applied behavior analysis. Despite the availability of statistical tests for single-subject research, the conditions under which such tests are desirable, appropriate, or relevant to data evaluation in applied behavior analysis remain controversial.

The advances, recent trends, and controversies suggest that methodology in applied behavior analysis is actively evolving. The advances provide more refined methodological tools to handle the technological advances and the extrapolation of applied behavior analysis to new situations. Thus the present chapter introduced rather than definitively treated the basic methodology of applied behavior analysis.

JACOB L. GEWIRTZ[1]

Chapter 4

Social Learning in Early Human Development

This chapter examines some mechanisms of human social learning and socialization, and attempts to cast the underlying phenomena into a consistent, operational and parsimonious framework. Wherever possible, simple conditioning concepts are used to order behavior in diverse settings, ranging from the simple responses of infants to the complex responses of adults. The issues dealt with are thought generic for all theories of social development, regardless of their orientation, heuristic flavor, or degree of formality. This operational approach to social learning employs the basic concepts of an operant-conditioning analysis, demonstrating their plausibility with examples from both research and life settings and applying them to a variety of substantive and practical issues. Further, some focal behavior systems in life settings are analyzed in a context where extant theories in the area have been characteristically informal or unsystematic and often posed in obscure cognitive or motivational terms.

Behavioral approaches to the social learning and socialization of the child commonly attempt to order, in terms of basic concepts and principles, many of the same phenomena and issues highlighted by clinical-developmental theories that have characteristically used less formal or explicit approaches to theory development and less systematic research procedures. Indeed the early behavioral social-learning approaches were inspired particularly by Freudian psychoanalytic theory, with its implicit emphasis on learning conceptions, its explicit emphasis on the importance of early experience in determining later behavior systems, and its treatment in the clinical literature of such specific issues as anxiety.

1. The author has prepared this chapter in his private capacity. No official support or endorsement by the Public Health Service is intended or should be inferred.

Several general conditioning approaches have set the tone for consideration of social learning in the past quarter century. In the 1940s and early 1950s, Hullian approaches, perhaps, did most to bridge the gap between the laboratory and the life setting (Dollard, Doob, Miller, Mowrer, & Sears, 1939; Dollard & Miller, 1950; Miller, N.E., 1959; Miller, N.E., & Dollard, 1941; Mowrer, 1950; Mowrer & Kluckhohn, 1944; Sears, 1951). From the late 1940s to the present, Skinner (1948b, 1953a) mounted attempts to extend his general conceptions to the social case, and was rapidly joined by researchers and theorists influenced by his theoretical approach (Bijou, 1955; Bijou & Baer, 1965; Ferster, 1961, 1963; Gewirtz, 1956, 1961b, 1969b). Their work has contributed much to the contemporary flavor of the field of social behavior and learning. In the last two decades, important technological advances have been made in the practical application of the concepts of acquired stimulus control over behavior and the contingencies (for the most part, social) maintaining that behavior. Stemming mainly from the utility of Skinner's (1938, 1953a, 1968) operational concepts, these advances were made particularly in the applied areas of behavior modification and education. The impact of this technology has also confirmed and broadened our understanding of generic stimulus-control issues in social-learning contexts (Baer, Peterson, & Sherman, 1967; Etzel & Gewirtz, 1967; Ferster, 1961; Gelfand, 1975; Gewirtz, 1977; Gewirtz & Boyd, 1977b). Attention has also been given to the conditions that can function as social reinforcers (Bijou & Baer, 1963; Bijou & Sturges, 1959; Gewirtz, 1956, 1961b, Stevenson, 1965) and to setting or context conditions that qualify the functioning of stimuli (in particular those from social sources) in their several roles (Gewirtz, 1969b, 1972e).

It is both reasonable and profitable to conceive of social behavior as following the general laws of behavior, but with the relevant stimuli mediated by the behavior of persons rather than by other environmental sources. On this basis, our study of human social behavior proceeds in the same way as learning-based studies of other behavior classes: by analysis of environmental variables, both past and present, that control the behavior. Such concepts provide a flexible model for ordering the complex developmental patterns characterizing the child's socialization, by detailing the changing conditions of environmental stimulation in family, school, and peer-group settings accompanying this development. The changing capacities of the child through developmental processes, such as those indexed in naturalistic approaches by the terms *organismic maturation, states, critical periods*, and the like (e.g., Piaget, 1951), might qualify this approach but would not change its essential features.

THE SOCIAL ENVIRONMENT AND ITS IMPLICATIONS

The social environment consists of those functional stimuli provided by people; and social behavior, whether in its acquisition, maintenance, or both, is behavior under the actual or potential control of such social stimuli. Except that stimuli occurring in natural settings are likely to be more variable than stimuli in contrived laboratory experiments, and that the term *social stimuli* usually denotes those occurring in natural settings, nothing is intrinsically special about stimuli provided by people or about social settings as contexts for learning. Thus, the term "social learning" simply defines a subcategory of learning that involves stimuli provided by people but that follows the same principles as nonsocial learning.

This does not imply that, because it has no special intrinsic qualities, social learning is not an important topic. Because of the nature of civilization, social learning, which is involved in and is the outcome of an individual's dealings with other human beings, is perhaps the most indispensable class of human learning and accounts for many of the distinctive behavioral qualities of humans. So much cueing and reinforcement in complex human-learning situations is social (e.g., discriminative settings for parental, teacher, or peer approval) that if social stimuli have not acquired strong discriminative and reinforcing value, a child's learning may not reach appropriate levels. Those who are greatly deficient in social learning are thus unable to fend for themselves in society; in some instances they are called *autistic*. For these reasons, the study of social stimuli (comprising the social environment) and social responses has a high priority. And this study must be carried out in the same way as the study of nonsocial learning: with careful analysis of stimulus-response processes.

The Definition of the Environment

The terms *environment* and *stimulation* occur often in everyday discourse and have been used more intuitively than precisely. Often characterized as "wholesome," "rich," or the like, these terms may be invoked as causes of certain patterns of behavioral development, and occasionally as labels for experimental or remedial treatments. Environment, stimulation, and their derivatives, such as "love" or "warmth," however, have neither universal definition nor consensually defined operational indices. Objects and events (including people and their behavior) in the child's presence have often been termed the child's "environment," whether or not those objects and events have actual or potential relevance for the child's behavior. Such a gross concept has but limited utility in a scientific approach. In a functional analysis, the term environment is a summary term for those events that actually or potentially function as "stimuli" directly to affect the individual's behavior. The aspects of behavior affected are termed *responses*. Under this functional conception, emphasis must be placed simultaneously on environment and behavior, with the units of analysis—stimuli and responses—assumed to be codetermined. At no analytic level is one concept meaningful without the other.

Responses here are characterized not topographically (in terms of their isolated characteristics as movements) but functionally (in terms of the cues and consequences that control the particular movements). Responses having the same topographic content often may serve entirely different ends (e.g., whistling a catchy tune versus whistling in the dark) and, conversely, those having manifestly different topographies may be functionally equivalent (e.g., whistling in the dark versus hiding under the covers). Thus, the functional approach requires the specification in parallel detail of both the responses to be fostered and their stimulus determinants. While conventional educational or psychological approaches have often been content to focus on the relation between demographic or other gross environmental variables (such as social class, gender, or chronological age) and equally rough indices of behavior (such as I.Q. or temperamental traits), a functional analysis examines the co-relation between observable responses and stimuli specified in equivalently grained units.

Given this definition of the functional environment, one can assess the "quality" of an environment. Thus, an abundance of events (physical objects, people, and their behavior) does not necessarily imply a "rich" environment unless it is known that *those* events are available and function as stimuli for child behavior. Increasing the number of available events, of course, provides more potential stimuli, but unless the events affect behavior, they are nonfunctional and have no qualitative value. For example, a jungle gym that a handicapped child cannot climb is only an ecological constraint, whereas play blocks that the child can manipulate provide functional stimuli for some ongoing behavior. Obviously, the quality of an environment may not be revealed by assessing only the availability or the abundance of events. Such assessment requires instead an analysis of the events and a determination of whether they actually interact with behavior.

Environmental Deficiency: Privation, Deprivation, and Shift Conditions

The environment-deficiency conceptions of *privation* and *deprivation* occupied a central role in formulations that attempted to relate deficiency conditions of stimulation in early childhood, as antecedents, to aberrations in later child-behavior patterns, as consequences (Bakwin, 1942, 1949; Bowlby, 1940, 1951, 1953; Goldfarb, 1945a, 1945b, 1955; Levy, 1937; Spitz, 1946a, 1946b, 1949, 1954; Yarrow, 1961).

Privation. Following our earlier analysis (Gewirtz, 1961a, 1961b), the term *stimulus privation* will be reserved for a paucity of all or particular classes of functional stimuli through lengthy time spans, usually during the early phases of a child's life, the very time when such stimuli would support basic learning. In some instances, abundant potential stimuli may be available but nonfunctional because of an absence of appropriate setting or context conditions or because of an inept mode of provision (e.g., noncontingent on behavior). For example, if social events are not made discriminative for behavior, they do not acquire cue or reinforcer value, and privation of social stimuli is said to have occurred. The child developing under these conditions may become generally responsive to nonsocial stimuli but unresponsive to social discriminative and reinforcing stimuli.

Deprivation. The term *stimulus deprivation* will refer to conditions involving gross shifts in maintaining environments, both long- and short-term, brought about by the removal or decreased availability of stimuli that had become functionally significant for key behavior systems of the child (such as those provided during routine interaction patterns with a significant figure, such as the mother). These conditions include (1) a reduction in the accustomed level of stimulation (2) changes in the quality or patterning of stimulation, (3) removal of contextual conditions that can enhance the efficacy of key stimuli, and/or (4) direct interference with responses controlled by such stimuli. Examples of such conditions include a child's separation from the principle caretaker or parent or that person's sudden and continuing rejection of the child. In such situations, the child may first behave as in the initial stages of experimental extinction, i.e., the response may initially increase compared to the rate exhibited under reinforcement conditions, and irrelevant emotional responses may further disrupt the response pattern and preclude the learning of new adaptive behavior.

The concept of stimulus deprivation emphasized in this section involved the unavailability of stimuli, mostly conditioned, in a setting in which these stimuli have been maintaining selected behavior systems, and differs from the usually short-term stimulus impoverishment sometimes termed *sensory deprivation* (as described, e.g., by Bevan, 1967).

The Deficiency-Motivation Conception. The assumed consequences of privation and deprivation have often been explained by a deficiency-motivation conception. Adherents of this conception have proposed that the short-term homeostatic drive model, generally used to order periodic requirements for appetitive stimuli (food and water), also can order long-term "hungers" or "needs" for such nonappetitive commodities as stimulation, affection, and love. The long-term deficiency model generally emphasizes a "need for stimuli" that can build up through time and, when unrequited, can produce aberrant behavior outcomes. Thus, if a child receives an inadequate supply of "essential" stimuli from his caregiving environment over a lengthy period, it is thought that systematic changes occur in some behavior related to the deprived stimulus commodities. Moreover, the "needs" that build up may result in the child's later exhibiting seemingly insatiable requirements for the earlier deficient stimulus commodities, as in extreme forms of dependence and attachment, or in total disinterest in social and nonsocial stimuli, as in developmental arrest, apathy, depression, and/or "shallowness of affect".

One implicit motivational analog of the deficiency model often used to explain the above outcomes is that of *hunger*. Spitz (1949), for example, wrote of "emotionally starved" children. The hunger model, however, cannot possibly order the reported conditions and results of regular, long-term deprivation: It operates only through hours, or at most a very few days; and it implies complete satiability after periodic deprivation, with no residual effects that could cumulate in time and manifest themselves in systematic changes in behavior maintained by the events of which the organism was earlier deprived. The deficiency model attempts to order through months and (more typically) years, not periodic and reversible but cumulating effects of recurring conditions of deprivation in the early life of the child, which result in systematic changes in behavior with reference to the withheld stimulus commodities. This model thus emphasizes a "need for stimuli" that can build up through time if unrequited, i.e., if less than some (unspecified) adequate level is supplied to the child over relatively many occasions through the longer term, either regularly or irregularly. The "need" that builds up in this way may lead later to the child's exhibiting apparently insatiable requirements for (and even the hoarding of) the stimulus commodities earlier provided in deficient supply, but sometimes it may lead to apathy or other aberrant behavior outcomes. In addition to the inherent difficulties of attempting to order long-term phenomena according to a short-term model, the drive concept inherent in these models is further limited by the irrelevant and even misleading excess meaning that derives from using the short-term homeostatic drive model in contexts quite different in their essential properties from those in which the term *childhood deprivation* has been applied.

Despite these arguments against the deficiency model for ordering long-term phenomena, the model is still often used implicitly or explicitly by theorists, therapists, and caretakers alike. Under the deficiency model, the solution for dealing with inadequate conditions is to provide a large number of stimuli without regard to their relation to the child's behavior. If this prescription were followed to the letter, the infrequent contingencies between responses and stimuli would minimally affect response acquisition, but could change the long-term maintenance level for stimulation in proportion to the rate of stimulus provision.

Actually, however, it is unlikely that a caretaker or therapist will ignore the child's behavior when providing stimuli. Rather, the caretaker is likely to provide the stimuli, if only inadvertently, in some functional relation to particular response classes of the child, and the response classes that are reinforced may vary from one caretaker to another. Thus, without a predetermined specification of the desired responses, many behavioral outcomes are possible. If the stimuli intended to constitute "sufficient" attention and love are provided contingent upon the child's disruptive or attention-seeking behavior, those responses will be strengthened and the result may be a response pattern that precludes the learning of more appropriate adaptive behavior. If, on the other hand, the caretaker provides those stimuli contingent upon more socially valued responses, such as those typical of the child's age group or oriented more toward autonomy and achievement, these responses will be strengthened and the outcome will be more favorable.

Ironically both of these behavior shifts can be used by advocates of the deficiency model to index the inadequacy of the previous setting. A high or increased incidence of attention-seeking behavior or disruptive emotional responses could be assumed to indicate that the child has a "hunger" for those stimuli believed to have been inadequately provided previously, and to require even more stimulation to satiate or reverse. The opposite outcome, the relative increase in appropriate behavior, may lead to the assumption that the new, more adequate environment has satisfied the child's hunger for the stimuli, because the child no longer appears to "need" as much attention and love and, therefore, appears more "secure"—a result also interpreted as validation for the deficiency model.

The routine use of a deficiency model, whether for appetitive or nonappetitive (including social) conditions, discourages close attention to environmental stimuli and behavior at the level of detail required by a differentiated learning analysis. In contrast, a conditioning analysis first specifies the conditions of stimulus control over responses existing before the removal of stimulus classes in deprivation, as well as the changed contingencies between the child's behavior and the stimuli in the new setting. Thus, the outcomes of environmental shifts are regarded in a learning analysis as reflecting an adjustment of the child's behavior to the changed conditions of stimulus provision in the new setting, which includes new learning by the child resulting from changed response-reinforcement contingencies. The basic assumption of a learning analysis overlooked by proponents of a deficiency conception is that, to understand the development of human social motivation under both normal and deficiency conditions of stimulation, it is not sufficient to focus simply on which or how many stimuli are provided to the child. Rather, one must take account of the circumstances under which stimuli are made available, and in particular whether these stimuli are functional and enter into effective contingencies with the child's behavior.

Environmental-Shift Conditions. A situation functionally identical to the preceding deficiency conditions can occur in the absence of any immediately obvious deprivation. For example, such a situation might be introduced by a shift in the stimulus conditions that maintain the child's behavior, as when a child enters nursery school. Because such shifts can change the stimuli controlling the child's behavior, they will often change the pattern of the child's responses. The greater the functional similarity between the stimuli provided in the former environment and the new one, in terms of caretaking routines and caretaker behavior, response definitions for reinforcement and reinforcement schedules, the easier it will be for the child to adjust to the new environment. Very likely the stimulus similarity between environments, including gender or facial features of caretakers, will also facilitate adjustment to the new setting.

On the other hand, if stimuli that had been maintaining much of the child's responses are not available in the new environment and functionally similar stimuli are not provided, the responses controlled by those stimuli may severely decline in frequency. It is axiomatic that a child will bring to a new environment those behavior systems maintained by the stimuli in the prior environment. The child's initial responses to stimuli in a new setting will be a function of the similarity between the new stimuli and those that controlled behavior in the earlier context. The rate at which some responses (e.g., "fear," avoidance) habituate to novel stimulus conditions (sometimes a slow process with disruptive effects when abundant startle and noxious stimuli are present) will also affect the child's initial behavior in the new setting. Thus when a child's environment shifts, previously stable behavior patterns may be disrupted, except in the unlikely event of a one-to-one correspondence between stimuli in old and new environments. The issue can be especially important when a child begins school, because this involves both a large-scale initial shift and routine smaller daily shifts from the family-home setting. Caregivers in the new setting should be made aware of the degree to which a child's behavior can rely on particular environmental stimuli, and of the difficulties that can occur when maintaining conditions are changed abruptly.

In essence a child's adjustment in a new environment will depend on (1) whether the new caregivers recognize the relevant discriminative and reinforcing stimuli controlling the child's responses and can provide them effectively; and (2) whether stimuli in the new setting acquire discriminative and reinforcing value to maintain appropriate responses and enable the learning of new response patterns. If caregivers in the new setting are not cognizant of these factors and are not flexibly responsive to the child, they may fail to shape behavior so that it is appropriate to the new setting. Thus the child may not acquire an acceptable response repertory there. Further a caretaker who does not consider the child's present level of functioning may respond purely in terms of expectations for children of that age group. A vicious cycle may result: the responses of the caretaker will not be appropriate to those of the child, and the child will drop farther behind in behavioral development. These conditions could eventually result in the child being labeled "unteachable." Another possible outcome is that nonreinforcement of formerly reinforced responses may lead to such emotional or other maladaptive behavior as tantrums. If the latter are reinforced by the caretaker's attention, they may increase in frequency in the new setting. Because they may be incompatible with new adaptive learning, another vicious cycle could then be set in motion that might result in the child's being labeled "untrainable," but this time due to "emotional disturbance."

Multiple Environments. A special case of changes in stimulus control involves independent but sometimes overlapping environmental settings that differ in their discriminative and reinforcing stimulus conditions for subsets of the child's responses, as in "multiple mothering." Each caregiver provides a different setting for the child, as defined by the unique discriminative and reinforcing stimuli presented to the child and the child response considered appropriate. Difficulties may arise initially when a certain response is considered appropriate by one caregiver but inappropriate by another. The child, however, usually learns readily to discriminate between the caregivers and caregiving roles of the functionally different environments, emitting responses appropriate to each. Such issues are important for the child in a residential institution, nursery school, or day-care center who is concurrently and/or sequentially in the charge of several persons. They are relevant also in understanding the child reared jointly by several persons in a household (e.g., parent, older sibling, grandparents, or maid).

As suggested elsewhere (Gewirtz, 1968a), infants in the care of busy or ambivalent caregivers, as in some institutional and family settings, might benefit from a program that strengthened those responses in their repertoires (e.g., eye contact, smiles, selected vocal responses) likely to provide potent reinforcers for the responses of caregivers. Such infants would be in a position to "compete" more effectively for the caregiver's limited attention, and a fertile basis could be established for the mutual acquisition of constructive interactions between child and caregiver responses.

The Interacting Caregiver-Child Environment. It is axiomatic that caregiver-child interactions provide many occasions for mutual stimulation and reinforcement. A corollary is that *both* interactors provide stimuli that can acquire control over the responses of the other. There has been too little emphasis on how the behavior of socializing agents adapts to that of their charges (for exceptions, see Bell, R.Q., 1968; Gewirtz, 1961b). Yet just as the caregiver can condition the child's behavior by providing reinforcing consequences, so also can the child's behavior mediate reinforcing stimuli that condition responses of the caregiver (Gewirtz & Boyd, 1977b). In this way the socializing environment is also socialized. Thus the child's smiling, vocalizing, reaching toward, eating well, ceasing to cry, or solving problems correctly can heavily reinforce many of the adult's responses (Gewirtz, 1968a). On this basis, "baby talk" or outlandish grimaces can enter the caregiver's response repertory as a function of differential reinforcement provided by an infant. And a caregiver may become "attached" to a charge on the same conditioning basis that is thought to underlie the child's attachment to a caregiver: Stimuli provided by the young child are associated with diverse potent reinforcers and thus become cues and conditioned reinforcers for the caregiver's responses.

The conditioning of caregiver behavior by an infant does not always have constructive implications, as illustrated by caregiver responses to high-rate instrumental crying. Because an infant's crying has strong aversive qualities, most adults will attempt to stop it in various ways (Gewirtz,

1961b). These attempts can sometimes have undesirable consequences, as when a caregiver interrupts some activity (such as the care of another infant in a day-care facility) to attend to the crier. Moreover, the successful caregiver response is reinforced and this increases the likelihood of attending to that child in the same way when the child cries again. Such attention can reinforce crying responses. Thus, although the caregiver attains momentary relief by attending to the crying, the long-range effect is to increase the very crying response that is so aversive to the caregiver. (Gewirtz, 1968b, has presented an analysis of the "vicious cycle" inherent in this mutual conditioning process. Related issues are considered in more detail later in the context of attachment indices.)

THE NATURE OF DEVELOPMENT

In a functional analysis the term *development* is an abstraction for systematic sequential changes in particular behavior patterns of interest. Under this orientation, environmental conditions could foster or retard child behavior, and their application is not limited by gross speculations such as innate "ability" or "potential." In contrast to a stimulus-deficiency conception, which emphasizes mere stimulus-availability or exposure independently of any contingent relations with behavior, a functional approach assumes that stimulus conditions can be manipulated throughout a child's history to produce varied outcomes, either early or late relative to chronological age or other group norms. By focusing on events that have a functional relation to behavior, namely discriminative and reinforcing stimuli, a functional approach indicates ways in which the environment can foster the child's changing capacities and thus maximize or optimize development in important behavior areas.

By providing a young organism with experience designed to foster a particular outcome, it is possible to facilitate the acquisition of response systems that ordinarily characterize much older organisms. Thus, 7-yr-old performance on a conceptual transfer task has been brought about in 3-yr-old children by subjecting them to a relatively rapid dimension-highlighting training procedure that compressed the relevant experience ordinarily received between ages three and seven (Caron, 1968). In this frame, even "advanced" children may be operating far below full potential in specified behavior realms (Gewirtz, 1969b). The opposite effect also can occur: Individuals may be provided with patterns of experience that retard the acquisition of behavior systems, so that their behavior is like that characteristic of younger-aged children.

Typically, developmental age norms for various responses (e.g, those of Bayley, 1969; Gesell & Amatruda, 1947; Terman & Merrill, 1937; Uzgiris & Hunt, 1967; Wechsler, 1958) have been collected in settings not designed to facilitate given behavior outcomes. Hence many such norms are unlikely to reflect the higher levels of development possible with a focused behavioral approach. A further limitation of these norms is that they are typically collected in terms of chronological age, which is in itself a questionable classification variable.

Problematic Variables in Analyses of Development

Maturation. When a systematic short-term change in behavior cannot be attributed routinely to learning or to some short-term performance operation (e.g., changes in some setting or ecological condition), it is often classified residually as due to "maturation." The term *maturation* is conventionally thought to apply in at least two behavior-change contexts: when topographically complete behavior suddenly appears in the child's repertory, either with or without an identified stimulus basis; or when a primitive approximation of a response suddenly appears in a child's repertory, with or without an identified stimulus that with monitored practice or simply the passage of time approaches the final topographic form of the response. An important implication of the maturation concept is that within the normal range of conditions the behavior change is essentially irreversible, in contrast to the corollary of reversibility inherent in the learning conception.

Thus, behavior that appears to enter the growing child's repertory suddenly is often attributed to maturation, the innately determined unfolding with age of a gradual plan of development independent of experience. But the sudden appearance of new behavior may often be due to a rapidly implemented learning procedure unnoticed by observers, other effects of experience not usually conceptualized as learning, or other factors underlying the behavior such as changes in stimulus threshold ("capacity") that may also be conceived as possible experiential-learning phenomena. The inability of a molar analysis, which emphasizes the impact of environmental stimuli on behavior, to specify plausibly the determinants of new behavior in terms of experience and learning effects may imply only that the currently available concepts and research techniques require improvement. It follows that the premature labeling of effects unexplainable under a given posture as due to either maturation or learning may be unwarranted, because it explains little and may obscure much. In such cases, the introduction of the maturation concept to account for behavior variations not readily explained, especially when unaccompanied by a systematic focus on the environmental events that may affect the behavior, may prematurely preclude the search for explanatory principles based upon specification of antecedent-consequent relations.

Chronological-Age Variables. Traditionally, behavioral development has been catalogued in terms of chronological age because of its presumed convenience in indexing successive changes in both physical structures and behavior systems of the organism. Age, however, is a pure index *only* of the passage of time in the physical world and not of the variables directly involved in development: the sequences of events experienced, the biological structures changed, or the resulting behavior systems. It is assumed here that the principles and functional relations characterizing behavior changes in early life are fundamentally similar to those in later life segments. By this analysis, age is an incidental (and possibly irrelevant) variable in behavioral development. Thus, a functional approach is concerned directly with the particular combinations and sequences of experience that are actually provided over time by environmental agencies, and with how these sequences can be manipulated. A behavioral approach is here advocated as being most efficient for optimizing behavioral development (Gewirtz, 1969b). If there is any benefit in grouping children homogeneously in settings by some criteria, the position would imply grouping by considerations other than age (e.g., by homogeneous behavioral characteristics). A further, albeit related, stratification might be in terms of behavior systems that are to be fostered.

Demographic-Setting Variables. Conditions for wholesome child development are not limited to family environments that include "natural" parents. Any environment that effectively implements conditions consonant with the initial evocation or shaping and subsequent support of consensually valued behavior is one fostering the development of that child. "Natural" intact families can be worse than some residential institutions or day-care centers insofar as they do not facilitate in the child wholesome behavior outcomes, or else produce unwholesome ones. Moreover, institutions can be engineered to provide relatively wholesome environments for children, while many families that provide relatively poor caregiving environments are not readily changed. Thus, there is no necessary correlation between institutional or foster-home residence and unwholesome behavior outcomes, or between natural family membership and wholesome outcomes. Other group-membership conditions, such as sibling-order status, culture group, and gender, are similarly crude independent variables and permit rather little leverage on the incidence of specific child-behavior outcome patterns (Gewirtz, 1969a).

Critical and Sensitive Period Concepts. The concepts of *critical* and *sensitive* periods have often been invoked to justify age-related training or intervention. *Critical period* refers to time spans in the individual's early life during which capacity to acquire certain behavior systems is assumed permanently lost if relevant experience is not provided. It has been assumed that during a *sensitive period* relatively large or rapidly occurring behavioral effects can be produced by *less* environmental stimulation than would be required to produce such effects at other time periods. These time spans are often specified imprecisely (e.g., "around 3 months") or broadly ("the last quarter of the first year," "during the second year of life"). An identified critical or sensitive period, however, may reflect merely the failure of researchers to note exceptions to their observations, i.e., the appearance of the behavior outside the age limits within which it earlier appeared. Thus, such age-linked notions depend on the samples of individuals and conditions that happen to be surveyed and may index merely sampling limitations.

Nevertheless, these age spans have often served as guideposts in practical application. For instance, the casually documented notions that infants cannot acquire attachments to an adult after "about" 9 months of life if they have not acquired one before, that they may not be able to transfer their attachment if they have acquired one, and/or that they display an "8-months' anxiety" (e.g., Spitz, 1950) have sometimes guided foster- and adoptive-home placement procedures. In such cases, more relevant and useful age-independent behavioral indices of the infant's capacity to adapt successfully to a new caretaker environment appear to be more or less neglected.

Any age-defined concept is limited in utility to the extent that it ignores the underlying processes. Research must focus on process, which requires a detailed analysis of the sequential features of environment-organism interaction. Once the processes through which cumulative experience affects behavior systems are examined, age-linked critical and sensitive periods lose even the modest precision their time limits might suggest. Specification of conditions that either prevent the acquisition of a behavior system or give it the appearance of irreversibility would further impeach the utility of a critical-period concept. For instance, if the acquisition of incompatible responses was the factor preventing or impeding the acquisition of a particular behavior system, then in principle techniques could be devised to eliminate these incompatible responses from the individual's repertoire. The sensitive-period concept of a unique time span of heightened or maximum susceptibility to particular environmental influences is similarly of questionable utility. The individual is changing continuously due to experience and organismic factors, and therefore the capacity to learn will vary throughout the life span. Further, even within a narrow segment of the life span, the probability of learning at any given moment may vary greatly as a function of diverse contextual setting conditions (Baer, 1970; Gewirtz, 1967, 1972e).

Development and Early Experience

Important systematic changes in the behavior systems of children can be indexed in several ways. The child's responses can increase in the number of sequences, their length, the smoothness of skill of their execution, or the number that can occur simultaneously. Changes can occur in the inhibition of certain responses and the occurrence of others in the presence of discriminative stimuli. In analyzing the sequential changes in the child's behavior, however, it would be an incomplete approach to focus on the response side of sequential behavioral units to the neglect of the stimulus side, as has often been the case. Behavior changes can often be accounted for by increased "responsivity" to stimuli, increasingly fine discriminations between stimuli (Bijou & Baer, 1963), and the increasing complexity of the stimulus patterns that acquire control over behavior. For example, upon hearing any auditory stimulus, an infant may initially orient its head in the direction in which its mother is usually found, but eventually will respond this way only to particular sounds appearing at certain times of day and in conjunction with a variety of other stimuli. Thus, the discriminative stimulus for head turning, insofar as it comes to involve a conditional discrimination, changes, while the single head-turning response it controls remains unchanged. Systematic increases in the complexity of an older child's behavior relative to that of a younger child's may be due primarily to systematic increases in the complexity of the stimuli provided by the controlling environment. Thus, the characteristics (some would term "developmental level") of a child's response systems could be determined by the range of functional stimuli experienced (cf., e.g., Vince, 1961). An analysis of changes in the controlling environment may explain more about the child's development than an analysis focused only on the child's behavior.

Further, as a child grows, some reinforcing stimuli may drop out functionally to be superseded by others, or their relative importance may change. Thus, food may decrease in reinforcing effectiveness relative to environmental change per se. It is also likely that the nature of the event patterns constituting the reinforcing property of certain stimuli changes as the child moves from one capacity "level" to a higher one. To illustrate, those stimulus changes that could be effected by rather gross movements of an infant's hands or fingers (e.g., interfering with light sources), originally produced by the most complex behavior of which the child was capable, might become increasingly less effective as reinforcing stimuli in the context of an increasingly complex response repertory. Thus also, the social reinforcing stimulus of attention may be superseded in importance by that of approval (to be attained from the caregiver-parent by successively more complex performances) in restricted settings in which the caregiver's approval mediates the delivery of most of the child's important reinforcing stimuli. A developmental analysis, as proposed here, would examine the origins and changes in reinforcing stimuli as functions of the roles they play in behavior important for the child in the context of changes in the child's receptor and effector capacity due to sequences of experience.

The emphasis upon experience is not meant to negate the effects of "heredity" upon the development of behavior systems. It is obvious that certain learnings are guided (i.e., facilitated or inhibited) by structural and constitutional factors. Thus, some responses that appear to be unlearned, perhaps because of the suddenness of their appearance, may be partially explained by the hereditarily determined growth of the receptor and/or effector systems that permit the rapid learning of behavior,

There are several reasons why early experience may significantly influence the development of behavior systems later in life. Some structural systems underlying behavior systems appear to require stimulus input to become or remain functional. For example, a physically developed eye may not be functional until it has been exposed to the light (Hinde, 1966). Second, many behavior systems of the organism depend directly upon the previous acquisition of component response systems. Thus, all forms of ambulatory behavior require the earlier acquisition of the ability to stand and maintain balance. Third, and perhaps most salient for our purposes, certain later behavior systems would appear to be more effectively established when supported by behavior systems that are usually learned early in life (such as eye contact, visual following, smiling, and vocalizing), and that can subsequently become the elements of diverse response complexes and sequences, including those directed at people.

These later behavior systems are often maintained by the same stimuli that maintained the earlier acquired responses, and on this basis, behavior systems acquired early in life may become pervasive and may often appear permanent and irreversible. Nevertheless, these systems would extinguish if the conditions maintaining them were removed (Gewirtz, 1961b). Thus, the strength of these behavior systems is often due *not* to their "irreversibility," but rather to the *locking in* of the behavior of the environment with the child's behavior, so that from earliest acquisition onward the maintaining contingencies might not even appear to be operating to the untrained observer. Further, in this locking-in process, the appearance of irreversibility of some behavior systems may result from the transfer of stimulus control from the initial sets of maintaining stimuli to different sets that, to the untrained observer, similarly might not appear to be operating (Etzel & Gewirtz, 1967). While strict elimination of reinforcement for such pervasive response classes is often unlikely to be implemented in life settings, it is possible in principle.

Assessing Development

The implementation of any new developmental program raises the question of how to assess the results. The answer depends in great part on the aims of the program. In the past, child training has tended to divide between two types of goals: (1) specific, discrete responses (e.g., counting, letter identification, color naming) and (2) global behavior traits (e.g., "intelligence," "creativity," "independence"). Each aim involves special assessment problems. With regard to discrete responses, one may be interested not only in the attainment of each skill in its narrowest sense, but in the extent to which training has generalized to new contexts, materials, or related behavior (e.g., from counting blocks to counting people or from counting to naming). In the case of general traits one is faced with the choice of measuring the overall trait or the specific responses subsumed under it. Also bearing consideration is the question of whether the trait concept itself, as an abstraction of behavior from many different discriminative contexts, is valid.

In an important sense, global attributes can be measured only in terms of specific discrete responses because the former can have little meaning without the identification of the specific responses subsumed under those global headings. A functional approach requires specifications of the responses to be trained and the discriminative contexts in which they are to be exhibited. This in turn determines what is to be tested and in what stimulus context and how the testing is to be done. In contrast, global assessment often represents a "buckshot" approach that attempts to sample response classes likely to be emitted by a child in diverse settings; yet it fails to specify what the responses are and takes little account of stimulus contexts in which the responses are differentially controlled. A functional approach, therefore, questions the potential utility and validity of assessment techniques designed to measure global attributes because the latter usually are not differentiated sufficiently and thus are only minimally useful. This is particularly true if they are used to assess the outcomes of focused programs designed to foster specific behavior systems, and no explicit logic relates what is tested to what was trained.

Conventional psychometric testing procedures do not always employ items to which each child has been exposed. The rationale for the inclusion of a particular test item is often based on the contribution an item will make to the "construct" or "predictive" validity of the test, with little regard for the probability that the item has occurred in the history of the individual for whom the test is intended. The justification for this procedure often invokes the concept of *generalization* or *induction* from specific behavior systems that some consider an important facet of program evaluation. From a learning conception of conditional responding, inductive generalization would derive from common elements in the conditional stimuli, the comparison stimuli that contain the discriminative stimulus, the relations among them, or even the broader contexts in which comparison and conditional stimulus classes appear. Thus, one may be interested in assessing whether the children can demonstrate responses slightly different from those involved in the original learning situation, and whether learned responses can occur in the presence of discriminative stimuli that vary from the training stimuli (in a remedial or day-care situation) or are embedded in larger stimulus complexes. For example, it may be relevant to determine whether the child, having been taught to copy a square, can copy a triangle; or whether the child, having learned to identify a square, can identify ("discriminate") it when it is embedded between two triangles. To this extent, one can justify the use of "test" items that involve discriminative stimuli and responses different from those emphasized in the treatment program.

The transfer of behavior from one context to another is often conceived to be a valued outcome that reflects the success of an enrichment treatment. Hence, additional comments about generalization are pertinent. When a response has come under the reinforcement control of stimuli in one context, it may occur in (generalize to) other contexts initially in proportion to their similarity to the context in which the behavior was first established. If there are no maintaining reinforcing contingencies for the response in the new context, the generalized response will rapidly drop out as the child "discriminates" the new from the original context. However, if the task is to produce a generalized response, then reinforcement contingencies must be present in those other settings (and in the presence of those stimuli) in which the (generalized) response is programmed to occur. In the same vein, discrimination can be effected by ensuring that reinforcement will be absent in all other settings (and in the presence of those stimuli) in which the response is programmed not to occur. In this conceptual context, it does not seem sensible to make a virtue of generalization of the response as the outcome of an enrichment program when (1) that generalization was not specifically programmed, and (2) what generalization occurs would depend entirely upon whether or not the treatment implemented happened to contain features that foster behavior transfer (which, in the typical case, would have been due only to adventitious selection considerations). Conversely, when generalization is specifically programmed, its occurrence would be weighted no differently than the occurrence of any other behavior pattern that was being fostered (Gewirtz, 1971c, 1972c).

To assure a meaningful testing situation, the discriminative and reinforcing stimuli as well as the contextual conditions must be compatible or continuous with the original training situation both before and during testing. In the usual interim period between training and psychometric testing, the behavior systems fostered in training may not be supported by environmental agencies, or may even be negated. Depending upon the intervening period and the stimuli to which the child is exposed, the behavior fostered under the training situation may disappear, either because stimuli functional for the fostered behavior are removed or because incompatible responses are reinforced. It is seldom realized that such interpolated activities can interfere with behavior specifically fostered during training. A learning analysis focused upon behavior and its maintaining conditions, however, enables such a prediction. These factors, often overlooked by traditional assessment, can affect test results and yet not reflect inadequacies in training procedures.

Potential disadvantages may also be included in the assessment situation itself. The testing procedures commonly used to evaluate behavior systems almost routinely change the context, and often the definition, of the behavior that the training procedures attempt to foster. What is tested is often remote from what was trained: A child may learn to count verbally, but be tested on written number identification. Further, the child's initial emotional responses to the unfamiliar tester and testing situation may not habituate before testing begins. These attenuating factors can be amplified by an assessment procedure that uses only a single test, as opposed to frequent or continuous behavior monitoring.

Under the behavioral model, training and testing are typically concurrent, interdependent processes. The effectiveness of a training procedure is assessed by continuous or repeated monitoring of target behavior change during application of a behavioral program. For example, in response shaping, the appropriateness of the reinforcer and the approximating steps chosen can be determined by the amount of behavior change. After each reinforcement, the child's behavior is observed to determine whether it is closer to the target behavior than before. The target response and not a hypothetical underlying entity is of primary interest and, through continuous monitoring, change in the attributes of the specified behavior can be identified. This approach has the advantages of (1) monitoring the rate of attaining various performance levels, (2) giving immediate feedback on the effectiveness of the training procedures, and (3) emphasizing performance criteria rather than time limits or trials to determine the length of training for any particular behavior.

Perhaps the best and most familiar example of the continuous interaction between training and testing is programmed instruction. The child reads a small amount of material and then is required to make a response that is immediately compared with the appropriate answer. The reading material specifically trains in a subject area and the response comparison tests this newly acquired knowledge. The test monitors the adequacy of the training and thus the behavior change produced by paced material. Results of the test automatically allow the child to (1) continue to the next block because the answers were correct, (2) correct the answers and then progress to the next block, or (3) return to passages read earlier to bring behavior up to criterion. Training and testing are an integral part of programmed instruction units and one aspect cannot proceed without the other. In like manner, in assessing the adequacy of any training setting in producing desired behavior changes, training and testing procedures must be built in as complementary processes. In the final analysis, the assessment of development and instructional procedures that contribute to it is the assessment of behavior.

THE ROLE OF LEARNING: CRYING AND ATTACHMENT AS ILLUSTRATIVE CASES

Functional behaviorism provides an advantageous system for heuristic analyses and for designing and working in new environmental settings. It affords a simple basis for handling phenomena by providing a ready means of focusing on both functional elements of the environment and the child behavior affected by them. Yet learning concepts are often misused in their application and misunderstood both by those who favor the behavioral heuristic and those who do not. This section summarizes some data and interpretations in a realm that has generated much controversy: early human infant crying. Basic learning concepts will be used to detail how the operant crying in the human infant's repertory can be maintained, modified, or eliminated; how it can come under discriminative control; and how, in the process of its differentiation, it can come in turn to control diverse concurrent maternal responses to the infant.

Further, crying in particular contexts, as upon signs of a mother's departure or a stranger's approach, has often served as a criterion index of attachment. Crying also often denotes physical distress or emotional reactions to some change in environmental conditions. Thus, an elucidation of crying as instrumental, as cued, and as elicited can serve as an exemplar of how behavioral concepts can be used to order the acquisition of diverse behavior systems by the young child in a period of life that many have called "formative" (Gewirtz, 1976).

Cued Instrumental Crying

The Anomalous Bell and Ainsworth Finding. In 1972, S. M. Bell and Ainsworth reported that maternal responding to infant crying interacted with that crying. From patterns of correlations across the four quarters of the first year of life derived from longitudinal observations of 26 mother-infant pairs, Bell and Ainsworth reported that consistent and prompt maternal responding to infant crying was associated with reduced frequency and duration of infant crying in later time quarters. S. M. Bell and Ainsworth (1972, pp. 1187-1188) referred this finding to the "popular belief" that, under the instrumental-learning paradigm, contingent maternal responding should reinforce (increase) infant crying and maternal failure to respond contingently should extinguish (decrease) that crying (see also Ainsworth, 1972, 1973). Thus, they concluded that ". . . the processes implicit in a decrease in crying must be more complex than these popular extrapolations from learning theory would suggest [p. 1188]," and accompanied this with the interpretation that contingent maternal responding did not promote those demanding and dependent behaviors that denote the "spoiled child" [p. 1187].

An implicit assumption in the child-care literature is that proper caregiving requires the caregiver to respond to the physical distress apparently underlying the types of crying termed *elicited*, *unconditioned*, or *expressive*, and that consistent caregiver responding to nonelicited infant crying could foster that very crying and thus "spoil" the child. A finding like the one highlighted by Bell and Ainsworth—that responding to infant crying actually reduces its incidence [p. 1171] —has obvious practical appeal to parents and other caregivers; but that report has also been conceptually provocative, apparently because many have assumed with Bell and Ainsworth that its conclusion contradicts standard expectations under the operant-learning paradigm. Thus, Sutton-Smith (1973) counterposed this finding to a demonstration by Etzel and Gewirtz (1967) that high-rate infant operant crying decreased systematically when caregivers ceased to respond to the crying and instead responded contingently to eye-contacting and smiling.

The Bell and Ainsworth conclusion also provided a more general basis for questioning operant-learning accounts of infant social learning beyond those involving crying (Bijou, 1974a; Bijou & Baer, 1965; Gewirtz, 1969b, 1971a, 1971b, 1972a, 1972c). In arguments over the differential adequacy of theoretical accounts, it has played a central role in the competition among conceptual and applied approaches to social development, both scientific and popular. Hence such theorists as Stone and Church (1973) interpreted the Bell and Ainsworth finding as indicating that ". . . responding to a baby's crying does not reinforce and so increase crying, but instead reduces it [p. 117]." Paraphrased as, ". . . the babies whose mothers always responded promptly cried less than the infants whose cries were often ignored," the conclusion was also the explicit basis of popularized pediatric advice given by a syndicated physician-columnist to newspaper-reading parents: "My advice to mothers is to respond to crying even when it's frequent. It is the infant's strongest language, and it expresses needs, not hostility or a demand to be spoiled [Kapel, 1974, p. 12A]." Based on the Bell and Ainsworth finding, Kapel's prescription assumed that there is no such thing as too much attention to a crying baby.

In this context, it becomes necessary to examine the bases for the Bell and Ainsworth conclusion, and to consider how a learning conception accounts for various infant-crying patterns that emerge from different patterns of caregiver responding to crying. The importance of this analysis stems not only from the need to understand the determinants of crying, but also from the fact that the arena of crying provides a testing ground for the adequacy of an operant-learning approach to human social development, given that caregiver responding constitutes a substantial portion of the environment (actual and potential) impinging upon the infant in early life.

Crying Attributes as Behavioral Units. A response and its reinforcing stimulus are defined functionally by systematic changes in some attributes of the response when the stimulus is presented contingent on it, compared to when the stimulus is not so presented. On this basis, potential operant classes of infant crying and of stimuli provided by maternal-response contingencies on that crying can be defined in great variety, including combinations of such crying attributes as latency, duration, intensity, and pattern. Thus, crying of short or long duration, or short but consistently intense crying, may comprise the response class on which reinforcing maternal behavior is consistently contingent. Alternatively, a mother may respond only to precursors of crying or to noncrying responses but never to crying itself. To simplify the exemplary cases that follow, it is assumed that a particular infant-crying response class constitutes a functional unit, that a mother will respond consistently and contingently to that class, and that the maternal response will provide a reinforcing stimulus for crying responses in that class.

One responsive mother may effectively shape her infant's loud, lengthy cries by ignoring both short, low-intensity precursors of crying and short, low-intensity cries and by responding expeditiously only to high-intensity, long-duration cries. A second responsive mother may shape the short, low-intensity cries of her infant by ignoring both the precursors of crying and lengthy, loud cries while responding rapidly and decisively only to short, low-intensity cries. A third responsive mother may foster behavior incompatible with her infant's crying—she may respond with dispatch only to short, low-intensity precursors of her infant's crying and/or to noncrying responses—to rear a child who cries rarely (and then mainly when physically painful events elicit crying). Each of these three interaction patterns (and various other patterns) could contribute to a positive correlation between infant crying and maternal ignoring of crying, much like the pattern S. M. Bell and Ainsworth (1972) reported.

Even in the best of circumstances, the goal of specifying causal relations from correlations is elusive (Gewirtz & Boyd, 1977a). But apart from this generic concern, the gross correlations of Bell and Ainsworth summarize configurations that omit the details required to determine the relevance of an operant-learning account. These details include the definition of the class of crying responses, whether that definition was used consistently, whether maternal responding was contingent, the latency distribution and consistency of that responding, and the like. Thus, the use of such remote data as Bell and Ainsworth's to test the value of an operant-learning account is not constructive.

The Conditioning of Crying. It is instructive to sketch how the elementary reinforcement schedule and latency conditions provided by maternal responding might determine infant-crying patterns. Conditions provided by infant crying might at the same time determine patterns of maternal responding. Highlighting a few routine variables that can affect the conditioning of infant-crying attributes in life settings may illustrate how to conduct a behavioral analysis, the range of outcomes for which that analysis might account, and its potential utility and power.

For simplicity, a particular class of infant-crying responses is assumed to constitute a functional unit. Further, it is assumed that a reinforcing agent who responds consistently and contingently to that class is present (e.g., a parent) and that the parent's responses, according to some schedule, will provide reinforcing stimuli for the crying responses. Again, a variety of potential definitions of response classes and of caregiver-response contingencies could include combinations of such crying attributes as latency, duration, intensity, and topography or pattern. Similarly, various classes of parental responses could be defined by combinations of these same attributes, together with content, and could provide discriminative or reinforcing stimuli to control infant-crying response classes. It is also conceivable that only certain kinds of contingent parental responding would provide reinforcing stimuli. For example, a parent picking up or briefly holding and rocking the infant but not the parent speaking quietly to the infant might reinforce some combination of attributes comprising a crying response class (Gewirtz, 1977).

Patterns of Maternal Responding to Infant Crying. Intermittent schedules of contingent stimulation,can produce higher and more stable rates of operant responding than can continuous schedules (Ferster & Skinner, 1957; Schoenfeld, 1970). For the Bell and Ainsworth case, it is conceivable that mothers who often ignored episodes of crying were maintaining certain classes of their infants' crying responses through intermittent schedules of reinforcement. Under a variety of fixed and variable ratio-based and time-based schedules of contingent maternal responding, an infant would be expected to show relatively high rates of these crying responses. If, in addition to responding contingently on an intermittent basis, some mothers tended to delay responding until crying episodes were intense and/or lengthy, stable crying patterns of high frequency and long duration might develop. Such training histories could produce operant crying that was relatively resistant to change. Hence efforts to ignore those responses (extinction) might not be readily successful, and the mothers involved might continue to respond intermittently to these crying responses.

The thesis is practical because it is readily possible to produce much behavior with little reinforcement or little behavior with much reinforcement, as long as some (relatively short) time is allowed for the environmental agency to move from the initial continuous reinforcement (probably typical of the original pattern of maternal responding to neonate crying) to the schedule chosen. Some simple exemplary schedules include variable interval (VI), variable ratio (VR), differential reinforcement of high or low rates of responding (DRH or DRL), and differential reinforcement of other (than crying) responses (DRO; cf. Chapter 2). In particular the DRO schedule may have special relevance to Bell and Ainsworth because it is a well-known technique for accomplishing the reported outcome.

Latency of Contingent Maternal Responding to Infant Crying. Immediacy of stimulus presentation contingent on a response is ordinarily critical in determining the reinforcing efficacy of the stimulus for that response. Thus, a social stimulus that immediately followed a vocal response of 3-month-old infants was an effective reinforcer of that response (Ramey & Ourth, 1971); and a nonsocial visual and auditory event contingent upon a hand-pull of 4- to 7-month-old infants was an effective reinforcer if it followed that response within 2 sec (Millar, 1972). But in both instances, if the event was delayed 3 or more sec it did not reinforce the response. As a response becomes established (stabilized) in a setting, the delay between it and its contingent consequence may be increased systematically without a change in its rate. As noted earlier, a mother who usually responds expeditiously to her infant's loud but short-lived crying and who responds rarely to precrying, lengthy crying, or low-intensity crying would be expected to produce an infant who characteristically emits short, loud crying responses. By the same token, the rapidity of mothers' contingent responding to their infants' protest-fuss precrying responses at one month of age would be expected to be correlated with the infants' fussing at 3 months of age, as reported by Moss (1974).

Given the latency criterion in initial conditioning, a maternal response that follows the offset of a crying episode by more than 2 sec may be nonfunctional for the infant's crying but functional for infant responses other than crying that either follow a crying episode or occur during episodic pauses in crying. Hence, delayed responding to an infant's crying may effectively place that response on a DRO schedule. The DRO schedule calls for reinforcement of any behavior other than the target behavior. To apply a DRO schedule to crying, a caregiver would reinforce any response other than crying only after a specified interval of noncrying. This schedule is often thought of as reinforcement of nontarget behavior (in this instance, reinforcement of noncrying). If it were used by a mother, observation would show much attention to baby and little crying by baby. Failure to observe the contingency represented by the DRO (or any other) schedule could lead the observer astray. This sketched possibility would represent a triumph of operant-conditioning logic rather than the reverse, and yet would produce the Bell and Ainsworth pattern used to impeach the operant-learning conception.

To flesh out this case further, it is conceivable that some mothers credited with frequent responding to crying episodes actually respond often or only to such responses as thumbsucking or orienting, evoked by unidentified stimuli or by the distal stimuli of maternal approach. Further, maternal-approach stimuli might acquire discriminative functions for attentive, noncrying infant responses that occasion the appearance of the smiling, soft-spoken mother. These maternal-approach responses in turn may be reinforced by the appearance of the quiet, attentive infant and also serve to cue further infant responses, thus maintaining an interchange of mutual discriminative and reinforcing stimuli for both mother and infant.

Some Likely Mutual-Conditioning Features of Infant Crying and Maternal Responding to That Crying. Parents the world over will give priority to their attempts to terminate the crying of their infants (Bowlby, 1958; Gewirtz, 1961b). In the natural course of events, a mother may respond conscientiously to her infant's cries. When contingent, this responding will often reinforce features of her infant's crying. At the same time, these maternal interventions may come under the control of the very infant crying they were intended to terminate, i.e., whose causes they were to alleviate. Thus, a mother's specific intervention response to her infant's crying may be reinforced by the intended consequence—the termination of the crying (Gewirtz, 1968a, 1969b). Concomitantly a mother's unsuccessful interventions, being unreinforced, could well cease occurring (unless closely accompanied by the successful techniques).

As a function of this differential reinforcement of her responding, that mother's interventions should come under the control of certain discriminative stimuli from her infant's appearance or behavior, whereas others of the mother's responses would likely come under the control of other cues from her baby's appearance and behavior (Gewirtz & Boyd, 1977b). If one employs criteria used to denote an infant's attachment to the mother, all or part of the pattern wherein a mother's responses come under the control of cues from her infant could denote that she had acquired an attachment to her infant.

If a mother is initially unresponsive to her infant's cries, she may not acquire readily a pattern of discriminative responding. A mother who fails to intervene effectively to quiet her infant may inadvertently shape lengthy or intense operant-crying episodes. This outcome could result also if a lengthy process is involved before a mother's responding to the infant's crying comes under the control of cues from its behavior. In addition, this process could involve increasingly lengthy unsuccessful interventions aversive to her. Her interventions would not be reinforced, nor in turn could they reinforce those of her infant's responses (e.g., eye contact, vocalization) incompatible with crying. The mother's dutiful intervention responses under conditions aversive to her might become locked in to maintain a pattern of long and loud crying episodes in her infant.

Attachment: Metaphor and Process

The present analysis attempts to blend concepts and phenomena from two disparate social-development literatures that involve different foci, levels of analysis, and data bases. The global *attachment* concept has been used variably, often as a metaphor, with few constraints, and has been denoted by diverse criterion indices. By contrast, maternal responding to infant crying has been considered mostly at the level of direct stimulus control over responses, where the functional relations may be referred to operant learning but not ordinarily to a superordinate global concept like attachment or mother love. Child-rearing values may enter to complicate the two conceptual foci, attachment and maternal responding to infant crying.

In this analysis the *attachment* metaphor is synonymous with "affectional bond," "tie," and "object relationship." In his evaluation of Freud's theory of object choice, Sears (1943) used the term *attachment* extensively for children's differential relations ("cathexes") to their parents. The attachment term, however, did not come into consensual use until after 1958, when Bowlby used it to characterize the child's "tie" to the mother, in the process blending concepts from psychoanalysis and animal ethology. In the present approach, *attachment* has stood as a convenient metaphor for aspects of the close reliance (often reciprocal) of one individual upon another, expressed in a variety of cued-response patterns (Gewirtz, 1961b, 1972a, 1977). This reliance may involve such pairs as mother and child, wife and husband, lover and loved one, child and child, person and animal, and, on rare occasions, even person and inanimate object or place.

In the literature of early human social development, attachment is a label for a complex of child-response patterns controlled by the discriminative and reinforcing stimulus characteristics of the *behavior* of an adult, usually the mother or main caregiver (the primary attachment "figure" or "object"). Thus, an attachment can be denoted by the occurrence of child responses under the control of stimuli from the attachment figure, and by the child's maintaining proximity to that person. The attachment metaphor has been used also to order concurrent reflections of that control process. Hence, it has been denoted by the child's differential responding favoring the attachment figure, or distress (e.g., crying) when separated from her or upon her preparations to depart, or even by an increase in the child's explorations of strange objects or places in her presence (Gewirtz, 1972d). In that same literature, *attachment* has also served occasionally to order adult response patterns under the control of a child's behavior (e.g., Gewirtz 1961b, 1972a; Klaus, Jerauld, Kreger, McAlpine, Steffa, & Kennell, 1972; Leifer, Leiderman, Barnett, & Williams, 1972). The stimulus-response functions ordinarily denoting attachment are pervasive. Upon disruption (e.g., by separation or rejection), these functions can become highly disorganized and often may be accompanied by intense emotional responding. Hence, increasingly the wide-ranging term *attachment* has become the focus of several approaches to social development in humans and animals (Bowlby, 1969, 1973; see also Gewirtz, 1972b, for a survey of five diverse approaches to attachment).

The dyadic functional relations labeled attachment in the present account are *not* limited to any developmental segment of life or to any particular interaction partners. Moreover, these dyadic functions may involve several figures concurrently and in any given time span. At the same time, the initiations these functions imply need not be reciprocated on each occasion by the attachment figure. Further, when a dyadic attachment pattern involving a parent, child, or mate is broken, such as by death or divorce, this conception encompasses the acquisition of new (replacement) functions with other partners (Gewirtz, 1961b, 1972a). The level of detail emphasized implies that the concept is entirely open with regard to such issues as whether a positive relation is expected between the formation of one or a few primary attachments in early life and the later capacity of the individual to enter close interpersonal relations (e.g., as Bowlby, 1969, has proposed). Little systematic information exists about the origins and courses of attachments, and even less about the reciprocal influences of one's partner's (e.g., a child's) characteristic behavior on the other partner's (e.g., an adult's) or about the relation between the formation of attachments in early life and adult capacity for developing close personal relations (Gewirtz, 1972a).

It follows that a specific attachment may be denoted by any one of a large variety of child-behavior patterns under the control of stimuli from the mother or some other person. But several writers have emphasized the attachment bond in contrast to attachment behavior. The focus has seemed to be on attachment as *entity* rather than as organizing concept or metaphor. Thus, Ainsworth (1972; Lamb, 1974) emphasized attachment as an *enduring* bond rather than as the specific behavior that "mediates" attachment and indicates its presence.

In the theoretical and research literatures, the concepts *attachment* and *dependence (dependency)* and the cued-response functions ordered by those terms have overlapped considerably (Gewirtz, 1972b; Maccoby & Masters, 1970). This overlap has been general, notwithstanding the fact that Bowlby (1969) and Ainsworth (1972), giving little consideration to the extensive literature generated under the aegis of dependence (e.g., Beller, 1955, 1959; Gewirtz, 1954, 1956; Sears, Whiting, Nowlis, & Sears, 1953), separated that term from attachment because of what they took to be its pejorative connotations. A heuristic distinction, determined by whether an individual's responses are under the control of stimuli from a *particular* person *(attachment)* or from any member of some *class* of persons *(dependence)* accounts for many of the behavioral phenomena in this literature, including those that have denoted dependence. The latter term would order responses under close social stimulus control, but not under the control of stimuli from a particular person (Gewirtz, 1972a).

Abstract terms like attachment and dependence may be useful on occasion. Such terms may have preliminary utility (1) in summarizing classes of stimulus-response functions within a wide range, especially when the relevant receptor and effector capacities of the child will undergo developmental changes; (2) in describing different phenotype stimulus-response functions (or their sequential changes in time) under the same process model; and/or (3) as a preliminary chapter heading. But even when useful, such abstract terms carry a burden of surplus meaning and may be unnecessary, particularly for describing straightforward demonstrations of acquired social stimulus control over instrumental responses.

Attachment Criteria. Constraints on the use of the conceptual metaphor of attachment have been few, and investigators have often differently emphasized sets of attachment indices. The level of analysis of such indices has often been so remote from the level characterizing the global attachment term that the need for such global terms at all has occasionally been questioned (e.g., Gewirtz, 1972a). Attachment theorists have emphasized the infant's behavior with reference to the mother (or other main caregiver), who is assumed typically to be the main attachment figure for the infant. In particular, attention has focused on the infant's behavior when the mother makes preparation to, or actually does, move away (ultimately remaining in view) or separate (ultimately disappearing from view). Thus, Bowlby (1969) proposed that an infant's attachment may be "activated" when the mother either moves away or disappears from view, and Ainsworth (1972) has been concerned with conditions (like distance from mother) that serve to "activate" attachment behavior. In these cases infant responses, particularly cries, to conditions of departure and separation have provided the basis for attachment indicators.

Crying (including fussing, whimpering, and whining) has been conceived of as stimulating a mother to come closer to her infant; and, like various other behavior, crying is said to become focused on an attachment figure (Bell, S. M., & Ainsworth, 1972; Bowlby, 1958, 1969). Hence crying in particular contexts [e.g., upon signs of a mother's departure (Schaffer & Emerson, 1964) or upon a stranger's approach (Ainsworth, 1967, 1972; Yarrow, 1967, 1972)] has often served as an attachment criterion (Gewirtz, 1972d). Indeed, crying on occasion has been the sole attachment index [e.g., when cued by separation (Schaffer & Emerson, 1964)]. It is therefore important for any theoretical conception to determine how any cues from caregivers could come to control responses (particularly crying) in the human infant's repertory, how they could be maintained, modified, or eliminated, and how they relate to the attachment metaphor. At the same time, crying can serve to exemplify how any attachment behavior cued by any attachment figure is acquired in any segment of the life span (Gewirtz, 1961b, 1972a, 1972d).

Attachment and the Conditioning of Crying to Departure or Separation Cues. The increasingly differentiated data base of operant learning in human infants (e.g., Hulsebus, 1973) has attested to the plausibility of conceiving that infant behavior within a wide range might come under the discriminative control of cues from the behavior or appearance of a particular other (the attachment figure), given appropriate contingent behavior from environmental agents. Insofar as contingent maternal responding provides positive reinforcing stimuli for infant protests and cries, those responses will come readily under the control of cues denoting the physical distance, departure, or absence of a parent. And when maternal behavior is no longer contingent on those cued infant responses, the cues should lose their control over those infant responses. In controlling infant responses, cues associated with parental distance, departure, or absence should function no differently from cues associated with the presence of such attachment figures. Hence, like cues from the presence of parents, ordinarily controlling such infant responses as orienting or smiling, cues from parental distance, departure, or absence controlling such responses as protesting or crying can also denote attachment in a functional account (Gewirtz, 1972a, 1972d). Such cued crying would no more need to connote affective states like those termed unhappiness, distress, or despair than such cued responses as smiles, orienting, approaching, or vocalizing would need to connote joy, satisfaction, or pleasure.

On the assumption that contingent maternal responding provides effective reinforcing stimuli for various infant responses, an infant's protests—or other cries that denote distress (Ainsworth & Wittig, 1969) —may become controlled by cues from the mother's preparations for departure (and by the ensuing short- or long-term separations) if the mother softens and responds, thereby delaying her departure, or otherwise hesitates or vacillates before departing. Similarly, particular types of cries may be shaped differentially under the control of cues denoting departure or absence (e.g., by a mother who responds only to her infant's plaintive cries). Likewise, an infant's cries may come under the control of cues from the mother's actual absence when those cries occasionally result in her return to the vicinity. In this case the infant's cries very likely would have to overcome physical and distance barriers, in addition to the mother's need to be away, to evoke a response from her. Those reinforced cries that come to be cued by that attachment figure's absence, therefore, may often be lengthy or intense.

For infants in the early weeks of life, crying is modifiable by caretaker attention, such as is provided by hovering over, talking to, and/or picking up the child (Etzel & Gewirtz, 1967). Diverse operant responses, which have also served occasionally as bases for attachment indices, can be affected by actual or simulated social-behavior contingencies in the first 3 months of life (well before the time some would expect that an attachment could have been acquired). The responses include eye contact, smiles, vocalizations, and cries (Hulsebus, 1973). If a single attachment index is used, therefore, a researcher working *outside* of a conditioning approach would do well to take account of the possibility that the attributes of the cued response on which it is based might reflect only a history in which the child's display of that behavior had been routinely reinforced in the same situation (e.g., crying cued by the mother's preparations to leave the child's vicinity). A nonlearning approach, therefore, would often find it necessary to address *directly* the issue of possibly-learned behavior systems serving as its criterion indices.

An argument for the present concern can be made with a widely cited report by Schaffer and Emerson (1964). They used several measures derived from what was essentially a single cued-response-based index of attachment. Those measures summarized the occurrence, intensity, and direction of infant protests (whimpers, fusses, and cries) after seven different types of separations from their mothers and others. On the basis of mothers' reports, Schaffer and Emerson concluded that the "intensity of attachment-to-mother at 18 months [p. 50]" (measured by the characteristic intensity of protests at separation) was a positive function of the frequency and speed with which a mother responded to her infant's crying.

One possible basis for these results is that the infants who protested/ cried most intensely at separation were largely those whose mothers attended immediately to their protests/cries, either directly or by hesitating or vacillating before departing. Thus, the contingent responding of those mothers might have reinforced protests/cries, so that cues provided by a mother's preparations for departure became discriminative for reinforcement of those responses. Schaffer and Emerson (1964, p. 51) raised this possibility in discussing the relation between attachment intensity and the frequency and speed of maternal responding to infant crying, but discounted it stating that cause and effect could not be disentangled in the context studied. At the same time, they suggested that the result could just as likely have reflected a mother's learning to give in to her infant's persistent crying. But this appears simply to be another way of saying the same thing, namely that contingent maternal responding can reinforce infant crying. Even so, an issue may still remain. The composite of the various measures of protests-in-separation situations used to index the child's attachment to the mother might have reflected only what the Schaffer and Emerson theory would take to be a limited fact: that, for this sample of children, mothers had systematically reinforced the protests/cries of their babies on some schedule, particularly when preparing to leave them (Gewirtz, 1976).

   Cued Responding and the Enduring Features of an Attachment. Stimulus control can account for much infant responding at separations and reunions and during absences. Hence, the marked decrease in responses denoting attachment in the absence of the attachment figure is due simply to the removal of the discriminative and reinforcing stimuli supporting those responses. When the controlling stimuli for orienting, smiling, and similar responses are again present after reunion, those responses should again be displayed to the attachment figure (Gewirtz, 1961b).

   Stimulus control accounts routinely for responses under close discriminative control not occurring in the absence of their controlling stimuli, but reoccurring when those controlling stimuli reappear. This concept also provides bases for understanding some types of delays occasionally noted at reunion after separation, before attachment responses are again exhibited to the reunited attachment figure: It may take some time before the controlling stimuli are presented effectively enough to be functional. A response under close stimulus control (like that denoting an attachment) will routinely diminish markedly in the absence of stimuli (like those from the attachment figure); just as routinely, it will increase markedly when the attachment figure providing the controlling stimuli reappears. Hence, it is axiomatic in an operant-learning framework that discriminated operants denoting attachment will endure undiminished in strength in the absence of an attachment figure, precluding the requirement to postulate an inner structure. Indeed, absence of the stimulus means that its function is unavailable for modification; thus its absence insulates its function, preserving its strength undiminished for controlling responses.

   In summary, therefore, patterns of crying cued by a mother's departures, separations, or absences might be understood as plausible outcomes of routine discriminated operant-conditioning procedures generated by the pattern of that mother's responding to her infant's crying. Such cued crying has been a common index of a baby's attachment to the mother and, on occasion, has been the only index. Using such a single index (or very few indices) under some attachment conceptions involves some risks. At the same time, the drastic diminution of cued responses denoting an attachment in the absence of the attachment figure and their equally marked reoccurrence upon the reappearance of that figure is explained by the concept of discriminated responding. In a functional framework, a concept of inner structure underlying attachment that endures in the absence of the attachment figure is gratuitous.

LEVELS OF ANALYSIS AND THE ROLES OF THEORY

The development and use of theories by psychological researchers has long been valued, and the past four decades have seen an increasingly self-conscious approach to theory generally, including that involved in the study of environmental impact on child social learning and development. This trend may have evolved in reaction to two quite different conditions: a nondisciplined empiricism coupled with the haphazard, almost atheoretical, way in which what were assumed to be implicitly valid "normative" data were collected in the last half century, and the sterility of purportedly articulate theories (like some variants of the psychoanalytic) that were subjected to the disciplinary requirements of neither conceptual consistency nor empirical verification.

The characteristic thinking has been that a theory generates research questions and then requires that the empirical answers be referred back to it to modify the theory as necessary. A good theory might be said to fit Piaget's (1951) assimilation-accommodation concept: derived from existing observational facts, it assimilates new empirical data as they are, but also accommodates to them when required to do so. And, given its utilitarian purpose, a theory must be discarded when it fails to accommodate to new empirical data. It is often said that only a theory, however preliminary, can point to the relations among important events and provide guidelines for identifying and controlling irrelevant factors. It is also recognized that it would be nearly impossible to gather data independent of a theory, however informal or preliminary or however difficult it may be for the investigator to articulate its assumptions.

In their understandable zeal to emphasize the utility of theory, however, many theorists of child-behavior development have seemed to ignore or minimize certain criteria for the efficiency of research, particularly prescriptions for the relations between theoretical assumptions and research operations. When a theoretical approach is sufficiently detailed, some of these mainly "metatheoretical" criteria are implied in the following questions for any research problem: What is the relative utility to the theory of each of the functional relations sought? Are there more appropriate relations to seek under the theory? Given the researcher's indicated or implied purpose, are the variables (indices) direct and immediately relevent to the functional relations highlighted by the theory or are they indirect and remote? Are they at the appropriate level of analysis for the researcher's approach? And are all of the variables at the same level of analysis? To the degree that such basic criteria are met, coordination between theoretical terms and empirical variables is greater, and it becomes possible routinely to modify the theory selectively for the purposes of consistency, increasing precision of concepts or greater parsimony within the framework of the theory.

Any empirical construct used to index environmental stimuli or the organism's behavior, as in parent-child interaction research, can be conceived to vary along a dimension of abstraction comprised of *levels of analysis*. Each level can be defined in terms of its position on a continuum, ranging from the macrolevel typical of sociological analyses to the microlevel typical of physiological and biochemical analyses. These levels are arbitrary in definition and number and might be conceived as flowing into one another. But no level of analysis should be conceived as more or less fundamental or adequate than another, as position on the continuum is not in itself a measure of its adequacy. The appropriateness of a level is determined entirely by the problem at hand, the purposes of the researcher (prediction, explanation, or implementation of change), and the particular set of circumstances.

Furthermore, as in Brunswik's (1939) analysis, a conceptual symmetry between dimensions may be conceived so that there is a level on one dimension that best corresponds to a level on the other. The continuum representing the receptor (environmental) system can be conceived as running parallel to that representing the effector (behavior) system. Thus, for every empirical concept that indexes the actions of the organism there will be a corresponding concept at an equivalent level of analysis to index the relevant stimulus aspects of the environment. No easy criterion exists, however, for selecting an environmental variable to correspond in terms of both level and measurement unit to a behavioral variable (and vice versa). At any analytic level, events might be grouped or combined in many ways to satisfy the requirements of a problem. Regardless of how informal the approach, the investigator must attempt to find the most parsimonious variable of the one type that will account for the variance in a given variable of the other type. Given the appropriateness of the index levels, the amount of variance in the performance variables accounted for by the input variables can serve as a separate criterion of the utility of the measures.

Relations between environmental and behavioral variables at the same level of analysis should account most efficiently for the relevant portion of variance in the behavior outcome data. The greater the difference between the levels of analysis of the input and output variables, the greater the resulting degree of inefficiency would be, whether or not a researcher's problem is defined to take this discrepancy into account. Thus, an increase in the residual, unexplained variance (reflecting inefficiency) can result when variables are selected at different levels of analysis because a variable at one level of analysis may have more than one correlate at other levels. Further, a variable selected at one level (e.g., a demographic, macrolevel, stimulus variable) may be relatively inefficient insofar as it correlates far less than perfectly with the unselected stimulus variable at the comparable level of analysis. Often the decision that the levels of the input and output variables correspond must be based on its plausibility with respect to the theory for which the relations are sought (Gewirtz, 1969a).

Abstractions in Analyses of Environment-Child Interaction

One-Sided and Two-Sided Summary or Index Variables. Most extant theories of parent-child interaction and socialization are process-oriented because they imply a focus on the sequential details of the interchange between the child and the caregiving environment, wherein stimuli provided by the appearance or behavior of the caregiver evoke or are consequences of the child's behavior. Each interchange unit is conceived to represent a point in a sequence and to contribute to the next point, within and across interchange episodes. Thus emphasis is on the interaction and on the systematic changes in both the child's and the caregiver's behavior resulting from recurring contingencies between them.

Yet upon examination of their coordinating definitions, many process-oriented theories of parent-child relations typically only implicitly relate empirical constructs to theoretical terms. Even more important, often neither their theoretical nor their empirical constructs are at a level optimally efficient for emphasizing process. Rather, the empirical constructs summarize through time spans (often lengthy ones) *either* the environmental events (e.g., *nurturance*) presumed to constitute the stimuli functional for the child's behavior *or* child behavior (e.g., dependence, attachment) —*not* the interchange features required to index the process of change. Indeed, even researches on the process and outcomes of parent-child interaction that lean heavily upon social-learning assumptions (Sears, Maccoby, & Levin, 1957; Sears et al., 1953) sometimes use mainly one-sided summary variables, which group information so as to give up features relevant under their theories. Because they tend to emphasize only the average response tendencies of the environment or of the child across situations, they are relatively insensitive to the sequential details of interactions.

One-sided variables used to summarize aspects of the *environment* that can have impact on particular child-behavior systems often have as their assumed indices such demographic classifications as: geographic area; culture group; residence and descent rules; institutional membership; social class; mother's and father's presence or absence; child's age, gender, and sibling-status pattern; mother's age, primiparity versus multiparity, and her employment outside the home; as well as help in the household, or the residence of several generations there. Sometimes the indices may be simply the institutional prescription for the role of the caregiver. Caretaking variables, which include nurturance, warmth, love, and acceptance (often qualified by consistency, frustration, or conflict), are another type of one-sided variable used to summarize those environmental details assumed to affect selected child behavior. One-sided variables summarizing the child's *responses* are most usually typified by "trait" concepts, which index response classes likely to be emitted in diverse stimulus settings. Some examples of trait-like concepts summarizing child-behavior systems are dependence, dominance, and hostility (sometimes also qualified by anxiety, consistency, frustration, or conflict).

Further, the use of one-sided variables can sometimes have unfortunate consequences when applied uncritically as labels in the life setting. In addition to minimizing the changing role of the stimuli that control a child's response class, the use of "trait" labels may be accompanied by the gratuitous assumption that the response class (whether innate or acquired) will persist throughout life in some form. (This usage of traits may be fundamentally identical to the assumption of "motives" for the child's behavior.) Such notions will often result in self-fulfilling prophecies. For example, a teacher who has been warned that a particular child is hostile would tend to expect hostile behavior from that child and might, therefore, interpret some behavior as reflecting the hostility she expects. If, as is often the case, her (negative) attention functions as a positive reinforcer for the child's hostile responses, she will inadvertently increase their emission. Similarly, if a teacher has been led to believe that a randomly-chosen child is intelligent or creative, she will very likely prime and reinforce those responses that conform to her notion of intelligence and creativity (Rosenthal & Jacobson, 1968). Such haphazard behavior outcomes would be less likely to occur if attention is focused not on gross one-sided summary variables or labels for behavior but rather on the sequential contingencies between relevant stimuli and responses.

The utility of one-sided variables often is reduced further by the inadequate methods by which they are measured. Indices for these variables often are derived from such sources as parent interviews or questionnaires, sometimes administered years after the occurrence of the parent-child interchanges being assessed, or from specific or global rating scales or projective tests. Even if these methods give reliable measures of verbal performance, it is questionable how well they actually reflect the stimuli or responses they are intended to assess. This is the case particularly when the gross indices directly reflect phenomena that are conceptually remote from the actual conditions impinging upon the child in parent-child interactions. Thus, the parental values or attitudes or child-rearing traits or personality organization or conflicts that many assessment devices have evolved may correlate only slightly, if at all, with the actual events impinging on the child that are relevant to a behavior system under study. Regardless of how they are assessed, the events that precede and follow members of a response class or the stimulus conditions that differentially control such responses are seldom determined or taken into account.

Thus, the limited value of a caretaker-role variable such as "love" or "warmth" is illustrated by the fact that the degree of love or warmth evidenced by the parent in interview or questionnaire data or projective tests and ordered in terms of global or specific rating scales may bear little direct relation to the functional stimuli that actually affect the child's behavior. To the young child with little or no appreciation of subtle verbal distinctions, qualities that many have termed "affection" or "love" can only be discriminated in the form of functional physical stimuli, e.g., visual and sound patterns, skin contact, etc. The infant or young child does not discriminate "attitudes" or "feelings," but may discriminate animated from expressionless faces, soothing from harsh sounds, gentle from hard squeezes, gradual from sudden movements, or one complex of these events from another. If the events implied by a gross term are not discriminated by the child (or the caregiver) and do not in any way affect behavior of theoretical interest, then those events are irrelevant to a social-learning analysis of the child's behavior system (and the caregiver's). As discriminative processes develop, the child may at a later age come to differentiate increasingly subtle indications of what many take to be "approval" and "love." Even so, as for the younger infant, these "indicators" must be discriminable physical events, and such stimuli (e.g., those provided through verbal statements) will have no relevance for the child's behavior if their value has not been conditioned by the functional discriminable stimulation at an earlier age (Gewirtz, 1961b, 1968a, 1968b, 1969b).

Of course, the utility of some of these global concepts for research can be improved by delimiting the functional relations they summarize. They may also be used in much the same way as such encompassing terms as learning or intelligence, i.e., as open-ended chapter headings for broad classes of functional relations rather than as tightly defined theoretical or empirical concepts. In principle either approach may be acceptable, but only as long as the assumptions underlying the approach and the concepts are clearly specified beforehand. For analyses of process, phenotypic and inexplicit abstract summary concepts tend to be inefficient, and the phenomena they summarize can best be dealt with if they are reduced to, and thereby replaced by, more explicit variables. Nonetheless, there may be research strategies for which the use of reasonably well-defined one-sided demographic or summary variables might be plausible, and even fruitful, at least at first. For example, apart from their utility for sociological or anthropological levels of analysis, demographic variables may be useful insofar as they may be gross indicators of environmental (even ecological) constraints on parent-child interaction. The gender of the adult, for example, determines behavior toward the child to some degree, and the gender of the child determines some of the stimuli received as well as behavior emitted.

Similarly, the birth order of a child may influence the child's environment because the experience of the mother in child rearing and the amount of attention and time she could devote to the child are affected (Gewirtz, J. L., & Gewirtz, 1965). Such indices, therefore, might be useful in (or a by-product of) the first stages of an empirical analysis that attempts to relate environment and behavior preparatory to mounting functional analyses.

Abstract Concepts and Cognitive Terms

A difficulty frequently encountered when inexplicit abstract concepts are used is that the ties between antecedent and consequent factors are often obscured. One result then is that a label for the behavior process at issue may come to serve as the "explanation" of that process (e.g., the concept of "schema"). Such concepts may also be used in theories that contain several terms with no specific referents and that therefore only appear to be comprehensive. While these ambiguous terms may facilitate the researcher's hunches about potentially interesting relations while operating within the prescientific context of discovery, it remains necessary to verify empirically the functional relations involved and to show through a sequence of discrete steps how theoretical terms definitively relate to empirical ones. The confusion of labels with explanation is especially evident in some cognitive approaches (e.g., Aronfreed's [1967, 1969a], Kohlberg's [1966], and Whiting's [1960; Burton & Whiting, 1961] approaches to identification, and perhaps also in Bandura [1969b]).

Thus, in attempting to explain the acquisition of identification behavior by children, Aronfreed assumed that children fairly rapidly form a "cognitive template" or "representational cognition" that serves for storage and retrieval of the model's behavior. However, he proposed no clear basis for the acquisition of a "cognitive template," except to imply that it depends (in an unspecified way) on the capacity to exert verbal control over behavior and that it may be acquired through a form of observational learning; nor does he tie this term to imitative-identificatory behaviors. Indeed, he provides no coordinating definitions between his theoretical terms and operations indexing environmental and behavioral phenomena. This "cognitive-template" concept, therefore, seems to offer an explanation for the acquisition of identification behavior only insofar as we are told that the acquisition of one is the basis for the acquisition of the other.

In a more general vein than Aronfreed's, Kohlberg (1966) has written of his theory being ". . . cognitive in that it stresses the active nature of the child's thought as he organizes his role perceptions and role learnings around his basic conceptions of his body and his world [p. 83]." Thus, Kohlberg stresses observational learning as ". . . cognitive in the sense that it is selective and internally organized by relational schemata rather than directly reflecting association in the outer world [p. 83]."

Cognitive-developmental approaches like these emphasize the metaphor of the "active organism." In such approaches, it appears that intrapsychic cognitive-act euphemisms, phrased in common-sense or immediate-experience language, are often used to characterize heuristically the bases for behavior in a given context. In such instances, however, it is often difficult to determine where the line is drawn that separates such heuristic variables from the required empirical ones. It is far from obvious whether the locus of such heuristic terms is meant to be the head of the subject or (the theory) of the scientist, or the immediate experience of the subject or that of the scientist as the subject. With this inexplicit usage, the distinction between the statement of a problem and its explanation can be obscured, and empirical questions can lose their importance or appear to be solved simply by the application of cognitive labels to them. A discussion of some differences in implication between theories that use an active-organism metaphor and those using a passive-organism metaphor can be found in Gewirtz and Boyd (1976) and Overton (1976).

Summary of Notes on Theory

Various ways have been considered to improve the study of environmental impact on child behavior. A more self-conscious use of theory by researchers has been urged so that the benefits of a theoretical approach to research could be exploited fully and some pitfalls of theory actively avoided. Efficient conceptual and research endeavors have been assumed to be those that avoid the costs that result from a lack of coordination between theoretical concepts and research operations, different levels of analytic abstraction among theoretical concepts, among empirical concepts, and/or among theoretical and empirical terms, inadequately defined variables and concepts, and ambiguous research purposes and procedures. Many investigations of parent-child relations seem limited by expansive concepts and variables and by unfocused research objectives, with one result being their frequent inability to define problems with precision in terms of any one set of variables. Some studies have tended to rely on the lore of psychology: using a finite number of variables that have become consensually valid more because of common research habits than because of their fruitfulness in providing meaningful functional relations, and ignoring many potential dependent variables that might otherwise have been used within the context of the events monitored. Other studies have tended to use many variables, at times seemingly without regard to their relation to the process under investigation. Indeed, some studies have appeared to collect data even before the focal research questions have been explicitly phrased. With the great differences between types of variables, the discrepancies in levels of analysis, and the definitional ambiguities of many studies, it is often difficult to ascertain whether some studies actually deal with similar subject matters, even when they purport to do so by using similar or identical labels for their theoretical and/or empirical concepts. Given the looseness of approach of such investigations (which must necessarily devote relatively more attention to their data analyses), it is not surprising that the outcome has often been a paucity of verifiable results.

A functional behavioral approach has been emphasized here because of its systematic focus upon the contexts and consequences of behavior and behavior-interchange sequences, its potency in organizing information, and its basis in well-established laws of behavior. While the advantages of a detailed learning approach in the search for functional relations have been stressed, no implication is intended that one level of analysis or level of conceptual complexity is always more "adequate" than another. A particular level of analysis, however, may be more efficient than others for a particular purpose or set of circumstances. Thus, the implication of levels of analysis for research is that when setting conditions are used to qualify molar studies of behavior processes like those termed learning or perception, it would be more efficient conceptually to use variables that fall near the stimulus-response variables characterizing a process than to use remote or reduced qualifying variables. A theory, however, must at least be sensitive to the relevance of data derived from other levels of analysis, while still remaining complete at its own level. Further, having a theory is itself not enough; to have continuing heuristic utility, a theory must be routinely scrutinized for internal consistency and for compatibility with accruing empirical data. And while researchers must routinely operate in both the prescientific context of discovery and the scientific context of verification, the formal results from the latter context provide a sound basis for scientific advances. Accordingly, sole emphasis on either conceptual issues or operational methodology is clearly inappropriate. It is hoped, therefore, that some of the arguments advanced here might have catalytic utility in environment-infant-interaction research.

GROVER J. WHITEHURST[1]

Chapter 5

Observational Learning

This chapter addresses a complex topic: a social exchange in which one person engages in an act that changes the behavior of someone observing that act and in which the behavior of the observer shares certain characteristics with that of the person observed.

The very vagueness of this description of what is usually called imitation or observational learning illustrates a problem central to this chapter: to bring some conceptual clarity to the phenomena of observational learning. Consider the following examples: (1) A child initially watches an adult sort clubs and hearts into one pile of cards and spades and diamonds into another. Continuing to select cards from the deck, the adult holds up a four of diamonds and a six of clubs. The adult asks, "Do these two go together?" The child says, "No." (2) An older child asks her younger brother, "Can you say, 'Peter Piper picked a peck of pickled peppers'?" The younger child successfully repeats the phrase. (3) Two friends stop at a candy-vending machine. One puts in a quarter, pushes the button for his selection, and nothing happens. He switches back and forth between the coin-return lever and the selection button several times without receiving the candy or his money. He steps aside to give his friend a turn. Though his friend has been waiting with money in hand, he now puts it back in his pocket rather than into the vending machine. (4) An experimenter in an imitation study tells a child to

1. Preparation of this chapter and some of the author's research reported herein were supported in part by funds from a Biomedical Science Support Grant (HEW #5505 RR 07067) awarded to the State University of New York at Stony Brook. Appreciation is expressed to Jacob L. Gewirtz, Robert M. Liebert, and Ross Vasta, who provided thoughtful comments on an earlier draft. The materials reviewed herein are largely limited to what was available when this chapter was first drafted.

"do this" while switching a light switch off and on with his thumb and forefinger. The child follows by switching the light with his elbow.

These examples point up the diversity of behavioral exchanges likely to be fit under the rubric of observational learning. Detailing similarities and differences among such examples will be necessary to lay the groundwork for an analysis of controlling variables. One issue raised by the preceding four examples concerns the role of behavioral similarity in observational learning or imitation. Only the second example included any topographical similarity between the behavior of the two members of the social unit. In the first example an adult created a stimulus distinction, determining a child's response completely unrelated to the form of the adult's response. The crux of the third example is that the second person was caused *not* to emit precisely the behavior engaged in by the first person. In the last example the child produced the same outcome as the adult modeling the act-outcome sequence, but the act itself—the behavior—was not topographically similar.

The issue of response similarity, among others, will not be dealt with at this point. Because observational learning has been actively studied for a considerable period, several theoretical approaches to the topic have been proposed and much research has been conducted. A new analysis depends on this previous effort and cannot be understood except in the context of what has come before. For this reason, the most important early research and theory will be reviewed first. The core of the chapter is a behavior-oriented analysis of observational learning. Within this framework, an effort will be made to outline a developmental theory of observational learning open to the systematic treatment of any and all functional relations occurring at the level of a psychological analysis.

HISTORICAL ROOTS

The Pre-Research Era

Plato spoke of the need for good models in the development of human conduct. Aristotle noted that "man is the most imitative of living creatures, and through imitation learns his earliest lessons." Of course, the gap between identifying a phenomenon and analyzing it scientifically is large. A first step beyond recognizing importance consists of describing the structure or manifestations of a phenomenon. As investigations of most topics proceed, these initial descriptions often lose their usefulness and are discarded or substantially modified. Surprisingly, this has not been the case with imitation and modeling. For example, the nineteenth-century French philosopher Tarde (1903) indicated that imitation, counterimitation, and nonimitation should be differentiated as theoretically significant response variations to the presentation of modeling stimuli. Current analyses are based on these same distinctions (cf. Liebert, Sobol, & Copeman, 1972).

In like manner the current debate concerning contiguity versus rein-forcement models of imitation (cf. Bandura, 1971a; Gewirtz, 1971a) post-dates similar theoretical concerns by 50 years. Humphreys (1921), along with Holt (1931) and Allport (1924), adopted a model of imitation based on conditioned-reflex and contiguity principles. Imitation of speech by young children provided an appropriate context for a presentation of the contiguity-reflexive view. Humphrey explained in the following manner the child who imitates the cries of other children: The unconditioned stimulus, pain, elicits an unconditioned response, crying. Crying is not only a re-sponse of the child's vocal apparatus; it is also an aural stimulus that the child hears. This stimulus, being paired with pain, becomes a conditioned stimulus. The sound of crying then elicits the response of crying. Because a child's own voice bears stimulus similarities to the voices of other children, the crying of peers elicits crying by a previously silent child. This analysis was also used to explain the iteration of the child's own cries. The first cry, elicited by pain, serves as the conditioned stimulus for the next cry, etc. Early analyses of imitative phenomena, as the previous example, were pre-sented without empirical support. Nonetheless, the notion of contiguity, albeit not in the context of the conditioned reflex, survives as the mechanism underlying imitation in the theoretical analyses of Bandura and Aronfreed.

Contingency models of imitation were also available at the same time as the contiguity-reflexive theories. Jersild (1933) suggested that if children were prompted to produce actions similar to the specific actions of their elders and received attention as a consequence, future actions of elders would be spontaneously imitated without need for further prompting. The continuity of this hypothesis with recent work is striking. For example, Gewirtz and Stingle's (1968) analysis of imitation as a functional matching-response class maintained by intermittent reinforcement includes the same interactions hypothesized by Jersild.

Although there are often pointed similarities between earlier theory and more recent work, pushing the parallels too far would be inappropriate. Early theorizing was filled with internal inconsistencies not presented here and not often found in modern analyses. But most important, the absence of research on issues raised by early theorists impeded further theoretical and empirical development. Though there was sophisticated casual observation, the study of modeling and imitation through the first third of this century stood at a prelaboratory stage.

Miller and Dollard

N. E. Miller and Dollard's *Social Learning and Imitation* (1941) pro-vided a significant advance by combining theorizing with experimentation. It is not surprising that Miller and Dollard's account, developed at Yale's Institute for Human Relations, bears the mark of Clark Hull: Drive, cue, response, and reward serve as the four theoretical parameters.

An example from *Social Learning and Imitation* provides an entry into their analysis. A younger child and his older brother are involved in a game with their father. Two pieces of candy are hidden and each boy is told he can eat the first piece he finds. On a signal from father, the boys begin to search. But the younger child, quite inappropriately, follows his older brother around and looks in those hiding places already searched. Eventually the older brother finds his piece of candy and stops looking. A this point, the younger child is unable to search by himself for the remaining piece and gives up. In explaining how this behavior develops, Miller and Dollard suggest the following. Before this particular game, the father often brought home candy for the two boys. The older brother discriminated the sound of father's footsteps on the stairs as a cue for father's arrival. Upon hearing this cue, he ran to be on hand when father entered the kitchen door, and thus was always given candy. On one occasion, the younger brother happened to be running behind his older brother toward the kitchen door. They both got a piece of candy as a result. On future occasions, whenever the younger brother saw the older brother running, he ran too. With this history, the younger brother imitated his older brother in a variety of situations, including the candy-finding game devised by the father.

Miller and Dollard identify this an as example of *matched-dependent imitation,* marked by the fact that (1) the imitator's response, running, was already in his repertoire and had to occur for other reasons before the imitative relation to the older brother's running could be rewarded; and (2) the actual similarities of the topographies of the two responses were not important and need not have been discriminated by the imitator. Thus, matched-dependent behavior consists of learning to match the outcomes of a model's behavior without any necessary similarity of response topography.

Miller & Dollard distinguished between matched-dependent behavior and *copying*. In copying the actual form of the model's behavior must be a functional stimulus for the observer. For example, in learning to sing, an imitator attempts to match actual stimulus characteristics of the notes provided by the voice teacher. Because the teacher in cases of copying provides differential feedback for closer and closer approximations to the modeled responses, new imitative behavior can be created. Also, according to Miller and Dollard, the stimulus of similarity becomes functional for the child whose copying is often rewarded. Thus, the child can come to monitor and change his own behavior toward closer approximations to the behavior of models.

Miller and Dollard's research with rats and children showed matched-dependent imitation could be learned and was a function of reinforcement. They also demonstrated matched-dependent behavior generalized to new situations. Further experiments showed that the control of imitative be-

havior by such "prestige" characteristics of the model as age was a straightforward result of the model's personal attributes becoming discriminative for
different probabilities of reinforcement for the observer's behavior. In a
chapter called "Imitation and Independent Learning," the subsequently
neglected topic of the transfer between control by the topography of a model's response and control by other stimuli was subjected to a thoughtful
analysis. Called learning-by-imitation, this was viewed as a process wherein
the observer initially imitates the model's response but eventually comes to
be controlled by the discriminative stimuli for the model's response. For
example, a teacher might sing notes from a piece of sheet music. The student, initially imitating the teacher's song though simultaneously viewing
the sheet music, may eventually be able to sing the song with no other
stimulus present than the sheet music.

Miller and Dollard's experiments on cue aspects of model prestige and
the analysis of learning-by-imitation are as cogent as anything subsequently
attempted. Their failures were tied in part to the Hullian theory within
which they were working, but more frequently were due to errors of omission. For example, the hypothesis that the stimulus dimension of similarity
could become an acquired drive (conditioned reinforcer) was never tested.
The phenomenon of copying topography was not subjected to experimentation. Other topics, such as imitation after a long delay and imitation of novel
behavior, were not analyzed. Bandura (1971a), for one, suggested these
deficiencies account for *Social Learning and Imitation* having little sustained
effect on research or theory after its publication. Another hypothesis attributes the absence of pervasive influence to World War Two and the general
turning from child research that occurred during that period (Stevenson,
1972). The latter explanation is more consistent with the contemporary relevance of many of the issues and hypotheses raised by Miller and Dollard, as
will be evident later.

MODERN APPROACHES

Cognitive Theories

Modern theories of modeling and imitation can be dichotomized on the
basis of whether hypothetical cognitive constructs are part of the explanatory
system. Fortunately much of the research can stand independently of the
theory from which it was generated.

Aronfreed and Mowrer. Mowrer (1960) and Aronfreed (1969)
concerned themselves with the motivation of imitation: Why does one person imitate another in the absence of immediate, external, and explicit reinforcement for so doing? Mowrer's contribution is the *autistic theory* of imitation, related to Freud's (1949) writing on *anaclitic identification*. In the first
stage of the hypothesized process, reinforcers to an observer are routinely
paired with certain responses of a model. Due to pairing, these responses

acquire positive value (become conditioned reinforcers) for the observer. Through stimulus generalization, observer's behavior similar to the model's also acquires positive value. In this way a reinforcement mechanism is produced whereby the production of behavior matched to the model increases in frequency.

In its basic form, much recommends the autistic theory as a tentative model for the processes underlying at least some types of imitative behavior. For example, infant speech over the first year changes systematically toward increasing similarity to the phonemic and prosodic characteristics of the speech community in which the child is reared. The culture-specific character of many of these developmental changes suggests a genetic model will be, at best, insufficient. And despite evidence that reinforcement contingencies can shape infant speech (Rheingold, Gewirtz, & Ross, 1959), parents do not apply differential reinforcement contingencies to prespeech vocalizations unless instructed to do so (Wahler, 1969a). The autistic hypothesis remains as the one clearly articulated and feasible speculation about the basis for imitation of adult linguistic characteristics by infants.

Aronfreed's (1969b) treatment of imitation is somewhat similar to Mowrer's, with the addition of an array of hypothetical cognitive constructs. According to Aronfreed, the observation of particular behavior or a behavior-contingency relation establishes a cognitive template of that observed event within the child. The fidelity with which this template represents the originally observed scene as well as the child's willingness to translate the template into an imitative action is determined in part by the level and type of affectivity present in the observational situation. Affectivity refers to operations such as delivery of positive reinforcers to the child or to the model as well as more subtle "positive" and "negative" qualities of the original situation in which behavior is modeled. According to Aronfreed, affectivity becomes coupled to the cognitive template formed during observation. Future behavioral reproduction of previously modeled behavior can then occur because "it strengthens or articulates the activity of its corresponding template and the affectivity which is coupled to that template [Aronfreed, 1969b]."

Bandura. The number of modeling and imitation papers increased ten-fold between 1950 and 1968. It would be fair to attribute much of the increase between 1960 and 1968 to Bandura and his associates. It is well, then, to examine Bandura's social-learning theory of modeling in some detail.

Bandura's theoretical approach has become more complex (Bandura, 1971a) since first presented (Bandura & Walters, 1963), but the basic aspects remain the same. Modeling, involving a behavioral episode performed by one person, the model, in the presence of another person, the observer, can have three effects on the observer's subsequent behavior. A behavior change in which the observer has never performed the behavior exemplified by the model but does so after the modeling episode is called *observational learning.* This "is demonstrated most clearly when models exhibit novel responses

which observers have not yet learned to make and which they later reproduce in substantially identical form [Bandura, 1971a, p. 6]." Bandura's pro-
totypic case comes from children's responses in the presence of a Bobo doll
after an adult model's aggressive behavior toward the doll. When the model
used novel words while pummeling the doll (e.g., lickitstikit), observing
children sometimes used the same words when given their chance to perform (Bandura, Ross, & Ross, 1963b).

Bandura's definition of observational learning presents real difficulties
because it depends on knowing whether an observer "knows how to make" a
response prior to modeling. In some cases this is merely a difficult measurement problem. In others it becomes a logical and epistemological issue. For
instance, if a child has produced all the syllables in *lickitstikit* in other
contexts before modeling, it could be argued that he "knows how to make
that word."

Modeling effects in the second category are identified as *inhibitory*. The
inhibitory phenomenon refers to a lowered probability of an observer's response after a similar response by the model. For example, aggressive responses in children have been lowered below baseline as a function of observing a model whose aggressive responses are punished (Bandura, 1965b).

Disinhibition and response facilitation refer to an increased probability
of an observer's response after observation of a similar response by a model.
The distinction made by Bandura (1971a) between disinhibition and response facilitation is somewhat unclear. The former apparently is used when
the response involved previously occurred infrequently because it was
phobic behavior but occurred with frequency after modeling. For example,
children who have been fearful of dogs will approach more readily after
observing a model whose approach to a dog is rewarded (Bandura, Grusec, &
Menlove, 1966). Response facilitation refers to such situations as clapping
when another claps, in which the model's behavior presumably signals the
appropriate time and place for the observer's behavior. Once again, one
must know the genesis of particular behavior before it can be categorized.

Bandura has chosen to emphasize what he calls observational learning as
more important than inhibition-disinhibition-facilitation effects because he
views the establishment of new behavior patterns as more theoretically and
practically significant than changes in the frequency or place of occurrence of
already occurring responses. It is doubtful, however, that different processes
are responsible for "novel" imitative behavior than are responsible for
changes in frequency of "old" behavior.

Reinforcement Theories

Generalized Imitation. The one detailed theoretical view of imitation from a reinforcement position offered since Miller and Dollard is due
to Gewirtz (1971a, 1971b; Gewirtz & Stingle, 1968). Earlier research, how-

ever, set the stage for this analysis. To a significant degree, research about the role of reinforcement in imitation has centered on the conditions that establish and maintain nonreinforced imitations. A study by Baer and Sherman (1964) first forayed into this area. Their procedure involved four responses modeled by a talking puppet. Three of the responses (nodding, mouthing, and nonsense statements) were preceded by the question, "Can you do this?" If the child imitated, the puppet reinforced the response verbally. The fourth response, barpressing, was modeled by the puppet at alternatively fast and slow rates. It was neither preceded by an instruction to copy nor followed by reinforcement for copying. For some subjects, imitating all four responses was a function of reinforcers delivered for three; barpressing increased as imitation of the other responses was reinforced, and it decreased as the previously reinforced responses were extinguished. When subjects barpressed, their response rates were alternatively fast or slow, consistent with the rates modeled by the puppet.

These results are somewhat surprising because an extinction procedure usually reduces responding. Yet barpressing, nominally extinguished, was maintained in strength. This finding produced a flurry of subsequent research and theory that will be considered later.

Gewirtz. Using generalized imitation as a base, Gewirtz and Stingle (1968) provided a theoretical account of identification processes in children. By *identification*, they referred to a child's adoption of a range of the behavior of an important caretaker, usually the same-sex parent. Gewirtz and Stingle viewed identification as the development of a generalized imitative repertoire. They proposed that the imitation of the diverse behavior of a same-sex parent, often in the absence of the model and after long delays, is a straightforward result of a previous history of extrinsic intermittent reinforcement of behavior matching adult performances. The concept of *response class* was drawn from Skinner's (1938) assertion that all responses equivalent in terms of their effects should be considered variants of the same class. For example, a rat's lever pressing with its nose on one occasion and with its paw on another are treated identically by the prevailing contingency. Gewirtz and Stingle suggested all matching behaviors are members of a response class because the prevailing contingencies define such a class. A further extension was to a response class under discriminative control. Just as the response class of lever pressing can become conditional upon the presence of a stimulus (e.g., a red light) correlated with the availability of reinforcement, so the response class of imitation can be focused on a particular individual (e.g., a same-sex parent) who sets the occasion for reinforcement of responses in the class. An imitative response in the absence of reinforcement occurs because the entire imitative class is maintained intermittently. Thus, many instances of imitative responses will not be reinforced directly. Imitative responses after delays and in the absence of the model were handled by noting that imitation always occurs after some delay and the child's imitative responses can be reinforced by the model or, in the model's absence, by other adults after considerable delays. These delays can be gradually lengthened. Identification becomes a by-product of instrumental learning in which responses matched to models and occurring in the presence of particular people or circumstances are reinforced intermittently. Our cultural patterns decree that imitation of the same-sex parent is predominantly reinforced, accounting for the particular behavioral pattern most often indexed as identification.

The theory proposed by Gewirtz and Stingle (1968) and Gewirtz (1969b, 1971a, 1971b) has much to recommend it. In their own words ". . . under a systematic learning approach . . . the relevant behaviors are potentially subject to acquisition, discrimination, facilitation, extinction, and other modifications according to well-established laws of behavior [Gewirtz & Stingle, 1968, p. 396]." However, this chapter is written at a time when the "laws of behavior" seem less well established than they did in the 1960s. At least boundary conditions, exceptions, and lacunae are being identified at a rate suggesting considerable and as yet unconsolidated complexity. The following treatment reflects these trends. No attempt is made to reduce observational learning to a small set of basic processes, though reductions are made when the data warrant. What follows is best described as an effort at definition and classification. What is observational learning and how is it to be analyzed? What are some questions that have been answered and what are some important issues remaining?

A BEHAVIORAL ANALYSIS OF OBSERVATIONAL LEARNING

Definition of Terms and Procedures

To this point, precise terminology has not been attempted. Researchers have adopted different vocabularies and their languages were required for a fair presentation of their views. In addition, observational learning is now so much a part of psychologists' common knowledge that issues may be discussed without particularly rigid wording. Nevertheless much can be gained by conceptual clarity, particularly in integrating data from various theories.

The terms *modeling, imitation, and observational learning* are often interchangeable in informal discourse, though there are important distinctions among them. In the present treatment *observational learning* will be an inclusive term for situations in which *the topography, functional outcome, and/or discriminative context of one organism's behavior controls a related characteristic of another's behavior.* The person whose behavior comes first in this functional relation will be called the *model*, and what the model does will be called *modeling*. The person whose behavior comes second will be called the *observer*, and what the observer does within the definition of observational learning will fall somewhere on an *imitative-counterimitative dimension*. The critical portions of this definition need to be examined individually. First is the assertion that three characteristics of a model's response can separately enter into observational-learning relations: the discriminative context, topography, and function.

Discriminative Context. Discriminative context refers to instances in which the stimuli preceding a model's response come to control the observer's responses. Other events are always temporally paired with a model's responses. In most cases these associated events will have been discriminative stimuli for the model, though the temporal association could be completely arbitrary. When the observer's responses come under the control of these associated stimuli, *observational discrimination* is said to have taken place.

The formation of an observational discrimination is demonstrated by an observer who, before modeling, uses the word "cup" in the presence of both cups and glasses. A model holds up a cup and says "cup" and then holds up a glass and says "glass". The observer's overall probability of saying "cup" does not change, but the circumstance under which he says it does. His response is subsequently controlled by the object, cup, rather than by both cups and glasses.

Another example is provided in Figure 5-1a: the model points out the stimulus that is his "favorite" from among an array of three stimuli, presents these stimuli individually to the observer, and asks him to indicate verbally which stimulus had been designated as the favorite. In this task, as in the prior example, there is no necessary relation between the form of the model's response and the observer's. The critical relation exists among the stimuli controlling their responses.

Topography. The topographical relation between model and observer responding has often been implicitly identified as observational learning or imitation. This is illustrated in Figure 5-1b by a model who produces a new word imitated by the observer. Another example is the reproduction by children of a puppet's lever pressing (Baer & Sherman, 1964). A final example is in the well-known studies by Bandura et al. (1963a, 1963b), in which children reproduced the topography of novel aggressive responses toward a Bobo doll.

Function. Just as the stimuli preceding a model's response and the topography of that response can control related facets of an observer's response, so too can the outcome or function of the model's response. In Figure 5-1c the painting of a fence is modeled for a young boy. The child imitates fence painting but uses a much more efficient method of responding. Here the function of the model's response—getting the fence painted—has its analog in the function of the observer's response—getting the fence painted. The responses themselves are not topographically related.

In some cases response topography can be completely separated from response outcome. When human models are completely absent and objects are made to move through a system of invisible wires, observing children are able to reproduce the sequence of events just as well as if a human had

Fig. 5-1. Examples of three types of observational-learning phenomena.

modeled the events for them (Dubanoski & Parton, 1971a, 1971b; Fouts & Parton, 1969; Parton & Geshuri, 1971). In this case the function of responding is reproduced; response topography is unnecessary.

    Abstraction. The definition of observational learning states that at least one of three characteristics of the model's behavior—discriminative context, topography, or function—controls a related characteristic of the observer's behavior. Earlier definitions of observational learning usually described the observer's behavior as *similar* to and controlled by the model's behavior. The present definition explicitly departs from the view that "similarity" is the *defining characteristic* of observational learning.

Building a definition of observational learning around similarity creates two problems. The first involves measurement. What is similarity and how are we to know when it has occurred? This issue has never been directly confronted, though virtually every work on observational learning or imitation since 1900 proceeded as if similarity and dissimilarity could be measured as a dichotomous variable. But in fact the decision whether a characteristic of one person's response is similar to that of another person's response is extraordinarily difficult, particularly when response topography is involved. Even in the most intuitively obvious examples of similarity, the model's behavior does not exactly match the observer's. For example, when mothers are asked to imitate speech sounds produced by their young children, they do so with confidence, but a spectographic analysis of the actual sound waves generated by the child and the imitating parent show vast differences (Lenneberg, 1964). The point is made by any other example of a topographically defined response. No response of one person is a point-to-point replication of the response of another. Even when observers are most likely to say that one person is "doing the same thing," as another, there still exist gross dissimilarities between the behaviors. As previously implied, this problem is less critical for the discriminative context or functional outcome aspects of observational learning. If a model opens a door and an observer follows by opening the same door, the consequences of the responses can be judged similar without serious ambiguity. Likewise, if a model pushes a lever in the presence of a red light and not in the presence of a green light and an observer subsequently says he "likes the red light best," there is no serious impediment to judging that the discriminative context of the two responses was similar.

The second problem with using similarity as the *sine qua non* of observational learning is that some phenomena related to observational learning do not involve response similarity, even in the lay use of that term. Such situations include those in which a model's behavior reduces the probability of such behavior from an observer. For example, black children viewing the aggressive behavior of white children become less aggressive (Thelen & Soltz, 1969). The most frequently mentioned example involves a model who touches a hot stove, yanks back his hand, and screams. Similar behavior by an observer is exceedingly unlikely. Other cases in addition to counterimitative behavior involve a systematic transformation between model and observer behavior. For example, if a preschool child faces an adult model who raises his right hand and says, "Do this," the child almost invariably will raise his left hand in response (Wapner & Cirillo, 1968).

If similarity is not to be the defining characteristic of observational learning, what is? *In observational learning there is a commonality, an abstraction, existing among the behaviors of the observer and the model that is produced by and functional for the observer.* Vast numbers of

abstractions are, of course, acquired by the developing child: "people,"
"animal," "noun," "airplane" are but a few examples of common stimulus
elements that come to control the child's appropriate response in a variety of
contexts. Each abstraction is important because each allows the child to
respond to new instances of the abstraction (e.g., a never-before-seen
airplane) with the appropriate response ("airplane") without further training.
The events of present concern are different from these other abstractions
because the commonality is defined across the behavior of two people, i.e.,
the abstraction is based on a commonality in a dyadic social relation.
Further, the common relation that is the basis of the abstraction must be
produced as well as discriminated by one member of the social unit, the
observer. The definitive outcome of other abstractions is that they allow a
common appropriate response to different stimuli, so that identification of
"novel" stimuli is possible. The abstraction of concern here allows *different*
responses appropriate to different stimuli, so that a novel response can be
made to a novel stimulus.

This abstraction has usually been called imitation, which in effect
suggests that the commonality involved is that of matching or similarity. But
we have already seen problems in equating similarity with observational
learning. By viewing imitation within the broader viewpoint of abstraction
(concept learning), a new conceptualization is possible. A brief diversion to
examine a match-to-sample problem is helpful in understanding the distinction that must be drawn. Goldiamond (1966) presents an abstraction problem
in which an arrow is presented as a sample along with several other arrows
serving as potential matches (see Figure 5-2). The correct choice on each
exposure is an arrow rotated 90 ° counterclockwise from that of the sample.
Match-to-sample differs from imitation in the important respect that the
matching stimulus is self-produced in imitation but selected in match-to-
sample. Nevertheless, important aspects of abstraction can be studied in a
match-to-sample paradigm: In Figure 5-2 the correct match could have been
an arrow of another rotational displacement from the sample and indeed any
degree of rotational change could arbitrarily be designated as correct and
could eventually serve as the basis for correct responding. To translate the
match-to-sample task into imitation, imagine the stimulus is an adult raising
his arm to a particular angle from the vertical and saying, "Do this" to an
observing child. Just as in the match-to-sample task, it should be possible to
teach the child to raise his own arm to the same angle, to an angle 90°
counterclockwise from that produced by the model, or to any other rotational deviation from the model's sample by manipulating contingencies.
The point is that an infinite number of possible function rules can relate the
model's behavior to the observer's behavior. As the rule relating the two
classes of behavior approaches a zero transformation, the process is labeled
imitation. As the transformation moves increasingly away from identity, the
process may come to be called *counterimitation*. To dichotomize the abstrac-

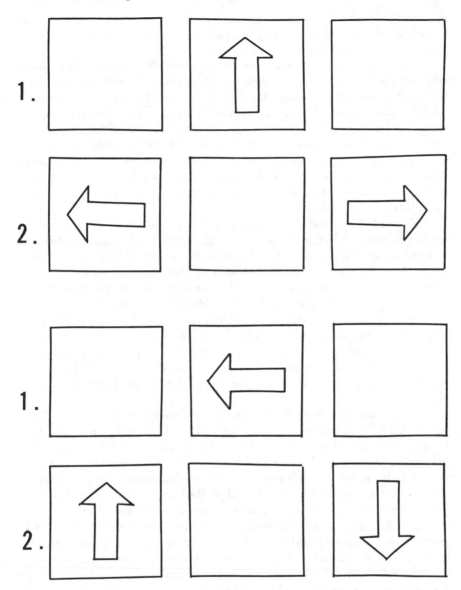

Fig. 5-2. A match-to-sample abstraction illustrating the arbitrary nature of the stimulus-response relation on the imitative-counterimitative dimension. (After Goldiamond, 1966, p. 191.)

tion relating the model's behavior to the observer's response into imitative and counterimitative classes based on the presence or absence of similarity is inappropriate. A continuum of variation can theoretically exist between a model's and an observer's response. An abstraction can be produced consisting of any range within that continuum. Imitation and counterimitation are merely labels applied to opposite ends of that continuum, and so cannot be more precisely defined in the general case.

The environment to which people are generally exposed will undoubtedly produce responses to models tending toward the imitation or counterimitation ends of the continuum. This is because the environment for the model and the observer will for the most part treat their behavior equivalently. Reinforcement or punishment, therefore, will tend to occur for behavior similar or dissimilar to that of the model. In the usual environment the type of behavior exemplified by the Goldiamond (1966) match-to-sample problem would not be reinforced. There is also a possibility, explored later, that the imitation end of the abstraction continuum has a primary reinforcement function for young children.

Figure 5-3 combines the imitation-counterimitation dimension with the three potentially functional stimulus characteristics of the model's behavior to produce an observational-learning space consisting of three polar dimensions. Any observer's response relevant to observational learning will fall somewhere in the response space. The positive poles of the three dimensions are the areas where the abstraction relating the model's behavior to the observer's behavior tends toward similarity and is called imitation. The negative ends of the dimensions involve an abstraction of dissimilarity and is called counterimitation. The center point of each dimension represents those cases in which there is no relation between the model's and the observer's behavior or in which the abstraction is not functional for the observer.

Two examples will show how the three dimensions in Figure 5-3 may order observational-learning interactions. (1) A child's father notices a loose board on the side of the garage. He obtains a hammer and a nail and, while his son watches, he nails the board back into place. In the father's absence the child hammers nails all over the side of the garage. Here neither the discriminative context (the loose board) or the functional outcome (the board nailed tight) of the father's response is imitated by the child. Only the response topography of hammering is imitated. This interaction would be positive on topography and neutral on the function and discriminative context dimensions. (2) Mary, driving a car with Tom as a passenger, is looking for a friend's house she knows to be on Main Street. When they reach the intersection of Main Street, Mary turns right and drives for several blocks without finding the house. As they circle back and approach the intersection of Main Street, Tom says, "Turn left this time." Mary does so, and the friend's house is soon found. In this example the discriminative context of Mary's response (the street sign for Main Street) exerts positive control on Tom's response. The topography of the model's response (turning the car wheel) is unrelated to the topography of the observer's response (saying "Turn left"). The functional outcome of the model's response (not finding the friend's house) is counterimitated by the observer. This interaction is posi-

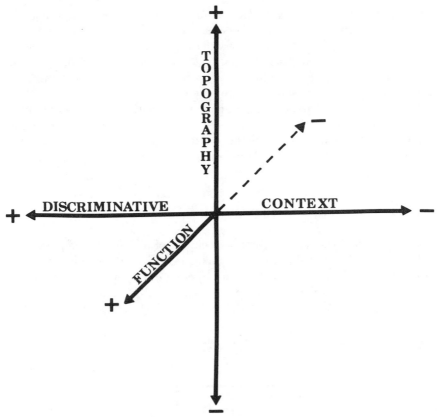

Fig. 5-3. The observational-learning response space. All responses by an observer relevant to observational learning will be related by a similarity-dissimilarity abstraction to the discriminative context, topography, and/or function of a model's behavior.

tive on discriminative context, neutral on topography, and negative on functional outcome.

Summary. The definitional model presented here offers several advantages over previous conceptualizations. By viewing imitation as referring to situations involving matching of discriminative context or functional outcome as well as response topography, a more inclusive approach to the study of observational learning should be possible. By recognizing that a critical characteristic of observational learning is a functional abstraction between model and observer behavior, the commonality in otherwise divergent examples of interpersonal influence will be evident. Further, research exploring the nature of this commonality, i.e., the nature of the abstraction process, should be possible on a systematic basis. Finally, the relativity of similarity or dissimilarity should allow the recognition of the importance of research on the fidelity of the relation between the observer's behavior and the model's behavior and the determinants of that fidelity.

The next section analyzes the major variables in the acquisition, maintenance, and modification of the three categories of observational learning
previously identified. To that end we will examine first the characteristics of
the complex of stimuli constituting a modeling episode. Second, attention
will be given to responses by the observer, both mediational and terminal.
Third, the effects of consequences for the observer's performance will be
analyzed. Fourth and finally, sequencing effects within the previous three
components of the observational-learning interaction will be viewed as im-
plying a developmental model of observational learning. These components
are pictured in Figure 5-4, which serves as a prospectus for the analysis that
follows.

The Modeling Stimulus Complex

The modeling stimulus complex consists of all events temporally associated with the model's behavior, including the model's behavior itself.
Our concern is with events that could *potentially* control the observer's
behavior. Whether any given event does control subsequent responding can
only be determined experimentally. As previously indicated, the model's

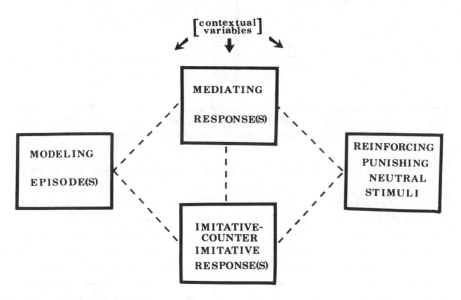

OBSERVATIONAL   LEARNING

Fig. 5-4. Components of the observational-learning process. Recycling possibilities
that are relevant to a developmental model exist among the components.

behavior illustrates the temporal relation involved in a three-term operant interaction. The model's behavior occurs in correlation with preceding events. The second component of the model's behavioral sequence is the response itself, and the third component is the functional outcome of the response.

The model's behavioral sequence can be distinguished from other stimulus variables present at the time of the model's actions but separate from his or her stimulus-response sequence. This second set of events will be called *contextual stimuli*. Like the components of the model's behavioral sequence, contextual stimuli potentially can be discriminative stimuli for the observer. They function to establish control by the components of the model's behavior. A contextual stimulus can be an explicit verbal instruction (e.g., "Do this" preceding the model's behavior). Or, at the other extreme, a contextual stimulus can be quite subtle [e.g., the model's manner of dress (Rosekrans, 1967)]. A contextual stimulus differs from the model's behavior in that it is not a part of the imitative-counterimitative relation that occurs. For example, if the way a model is dressed affects the probability that an observer will make the same choices as the model but the model's dress itself is not imitated, it is a contextual stimulus. We turn now to a more systematic presentation of the effects of the modeling sequence and contextual determinants.

Discriminative Context. The events that observational-learning teaching activities are often designed to make functional are the stimuli preceding the model's behavior. Of all the principal modeling theories, however, only N. E. Miller and Dollard's (1941) acknowledge the importance of the acquisition of control by these stimuli. Miller and Dollard deal with this phenomenon, in part, under the topic of *learning-by-imitation.* One of their examples follows:

A little boy, aged four and a half, is with his mother in a department store. While she is busy with other merchandise, he becomes fascinated by the BB guns on the adjoining counter. As soon as his mother is free, he drags her there, points to one of the guns, and asks, "What's that?" His mother answers, "a BB gun." He then repeats the word "BB" several times while looking at guns [p. 205].

The BB gun sets the occasion for the mother's labeling and the child's subsequent response. This situation illustrates both topographical imitation (the child had never said "BB" before) and the observational acquisition of a discrimination (the child's response, "BB," came partially under the stimulus control of the BB gun). Other theorists chose to focus on topographical imitation, as previously defined, to the exclusion of observational discrimination. For example, Bandura (1971a) speaks of place learning (imitation of a discrimination) as less frequent than response learning (imitation of topography). Baer and Sherman (1964) note that a child may be able to learn which of two cranks to turn to produce reinforcers by observing a model turning one crank and receiving nothing while turning the other crank and obtaining a reward. They suggest such phenomena (imitation of a discrimination) are of limited concern compared with situations in which similarity between the model's and the observer's behavior is an important dimension (imitation of topography).

The approach here treats acquisition of control by stimuli preceding the model's behavior equally with acquisition of control by the model's response. Observational discrimination is particularly relevant for language acquisition. The difference between a sophisticated 3-yr-old myna bird and a normal 3-yr-old child is not in the response topographies differentiated through imitation but in the discriminative control of those response elements. The child comes to talk about things, while the myna bird merely comes to talk. Some variables that may affect the likelihood of an observation discrimination are listed below. Little research has been conducted on this topic, so what follows constitutes tentative hypotheses.

1. Orienting Variables. Several conditions increase the probability that stimuli correlated with the model's response will acquire control. They may take the form of instructional cues, such as, "Look at this" uttered before presentation of the stimulus and the model's labeling response. Research on attentional behavior by Berlyne (1966) and others has emphasized stimulus change, incongruity, etc. as stimulus variables determining attentional responses. These principles are used implicitly in television advertisements and educational programs like Sesame Street. They should be examined systematically in the context of the formation of observational discriminations.

   In the opposite direction, procedures increasing the saliency of the model's response at the expense of that of the stimulus complex should lessen the likelihood nonresponse stimuli will gain control. Thus, while emphasizing a modeled utterance by increasing volume has a salutory effect on the probability of a child's subsequent imitation of response topography (Risley & Reynolds, 1970), it might have the opposite effect on the likelihood the child would learn to utter that verbalization under control of appropriate discriminative cues.

2. Contiguity Variables. The temporal and spatial contiguity between the stimuli preceding the model's behavior and the model's response, along with the regularity with which these stimuli are paired with the model's behavior, are important. Though not dealing with the model's behavior, Siegler and Liebert (1974) had elementary-school-aged children observe an experimenter placing a card into a "card-sorting machine" and the lighting of a bulb. Four conditions were obtained by crossing two conditions of regularity (low and high) with two conditions of temporal contiguity (low and high). The children in each condition were asked to judge whether they thought the card placement "caused the light to come on." For 8- and 9-yr-old children, both variables were effective and their effects were additive. The children were most likely to ascribe a relation between

the two events if they occurred together with high regularity and high contiguity. Mixed conditions (high contiguity-low regularity or high regularity-low contiguity) produced intermediate attributions of causality. Low regularity combined with low contiguity produced the lowest likelihood of assertions that the card placement and the light onset were related. For younger subjects (5- and 6-yr-old), regularity was a much weaker variable than contiguity.

This study may be strongly related to the typical observational-discrimination situation, in that the stimuli preceding the model's response may be analogous to card placement while the model's response may be analogous to light onset. If so, the closer together in time and the more regularly a model's response occurs in a particular discriminative context, the more likely is this discriminative context to acquire control over the observer's responding.

3. Transfer of Control Procedures. The basic parameters of the observational-discrimination paradigm are related to those encountered in errorless learning (Terrace, 1966). Of two stimuli, one (the model's behavior) is initially likely to control the observer's response while the other (the prior stimulus) is eventually likely to gain control. One would expect, therefore, that fading out the model's behavior would enhance the assumption of control by the other stimulus dimension. In fact this process has been used extensively in remedial language programs (Lovaas, 1967). For example, an exchange between a model-trainer and an observer-child might proceed as follows:

MODEL: What is this? (pause) A cup.
OBSERVER: A cup.
MODEL: Good.
MODEL: What is this? (pause) A cu___.
OBSERVER: ___p.
MODEL: Good.
MODEL: What is this? (pause) A c___.
OBSERVER: ___up.
MODEL: Good.
MODEL: What is this? (pause)
OBSERVER: A cup.
MODEL: Good.

The distinction between errorless learning and trial-and-error techniques is also relevant to observational discrimination procedures. A trial-and-error technique is exemplified in the following exchange:

MODEL: What is it?
OBSERVER: Pop goes the weasel.

MODEL: No, it is a cup.
MODEL: What is it?
OBSERVER: A cup.
MODEL: Good.

In frequently used procedures like these (Guess, Sailor, Rutherford, & Baer, 1968; Whitehurst, G.J., & Novak, 1973), errors are expected. When the child's responses come under the control of the proper objects or actions, they are reinforced. If the observation discrimination is not formed, he will be corrected. Maximization of reinforcement requires that the child's behavior comes to be controlled by the cues paired with the model's responses.

Variations on the trial-and-error method of establishing stimulus control deserve evaluation. These variations are assessed against the probability that the correct response will occur to new stimuli presented on unreinforced trials (probe trials). One important variable is the timing of the model's prompts. Modeling contingent on incorrect responses by the child appears more effective than modeling preceding every opportunity for the child's responses (Malouf & Dodd, 1972).

The Model's Response. The second part of the modeling stimulus complex is the model's response, defined either in topographical or functional terms. The focus of concern is an observer's ability to produce an infinite variety of behavior matched by some function rule to a similarly infinite variety of behavior produced by a model. For many children, this ability may grow out of a preliminary stage during which only copying of a discrete set of specific behavior is possible. The procedures leading from copying to observational learning have to do, in part, with the manner of presenting the model's behavior.

Schroeder and Baer (1972) compared serial with concurrent methods of presenting modeled vocal responses to be imitated by retarded children. In the serial method the observer was trained to mimic accurately one particular vocal item before the next was presented. In the concurrent method mimicry of three words was shaped simultaneously. Probe trials of unreinforced and untrained items were interspersed among the training trials. Although the total trials to attain accurate mimicry did not differ for the two procedures, the concurrent group was clearly superior on the probe trials. These data suggest that one factor in developing the child's ability to respond imitatively will be experiences that imply the equality of a variety of modeled behavior. Concurrent training in which several types of modeled behavior are interchanged seems more effective in creating an open-ended stimulus class of modeled events than serial training, in which each modeled behavior is presented in isolation.

It was noted that responses can be imitated on either topographical or functional dimensions. Parton and his associates (Dubanowski & Parton, 1971a, 1971b; Fouts & Parton, 1969; Parton & Geshuri, 1971) showed that response topography can be completely removed in some situations without reducing the observer's ability to reproduce sequences of environmental changes. There are classes of responses, however, where topography is intimately related to behavioral function. For example, no one would expect a football player to become proficient simply through observing football games. A naive observer, however, would behave more appropriately after observing an actual football game with players than he would after having watched the football make the same moves about the field with the players absent.

Other consequences of the form-function distinction may prove important. Baer, Peterson, and Sherman (1967), Bandura and Barab (1971), and Garcia, Baer, and Firestone (1971) showed that imitative responses may not occur across certain topographical dimensions with specific training directed toward such transfer. If this is the case within a topographical dimension, then a child should not be expected automatically to imitate functionally defined behavior if his training has only occurred on topographical respones, and vice versa.

Contextual Stimuli. Several components of the typical modeling episode may control the observer's subsequent behavior but are neither the model's behavior nor its discriminative antecedents. These stimulus variables are called contextual because they determine whether the modeling episode controls the observer's behavior and which aspects of the modeling sequence will be functional. Further, just as for verbal instructions under this rubric, the effectiveness of these variables will depend on a specific conditioning history.

The most explicit example of a contextual stimulus is the verbalization, "Do this", which often precedes the model's behavior in laboratory studies of imitation (Steinman, 1970a). While the function of "Do this" is partially to activate the observer's subsequent imitative performance, it serves the additional function paraphrased as, "Look at this." "Do this" is, of course, but one of many possible verbal statements by the model or some third person that can accompany a modeling episode. For example, attentional set was included as one variable along with modeling and reinforcement in a study of the usage of prepositional and passive sentence forms by elementary-school children (Bandura & Harris, 1966). The attentional set consisted of instructions to pay special attention to certain features of the modeling episode. This variable affected the observers' use of both prepositional and passive sentences. Appel, et al (1972) showed that "look" instructions have different effects on subsequent recall of a model's behavior than "remember" instructions. Redd and Winston (1973) demonstrated that less explicit verbal instructions can also strongly influence the likelihood that portions of a modeling episode will control the observer's behavior. While 4-yr-old children were observing a model responding on a two-choice discrimination game, either positive or negative statements were made about the model's choices:

e.g., "I like it, he pulled X" in one condition and "I don't like it, he pulled Y" in another condition. The child then had the opportunity to match the model's previous responses. In all cases the probability of responding correctly (e.g., choosing X) was greater after negative comments than after positive comments.

Other contextual stimuli are nonverbal and have to do with social characteristics of the model. For example, the model's race (Liebert et al., 1972), age (Miller, N.E., & Dollard, 1941), and sex (Hetherington & Frankie, 1967) have functional effects on observational learning. Even though a variable such as model's race differs radically in form from a verbal instruction such as, "Do this," both are contextual stimuli. In each of the examples, the variable determines the likelihood that aspects of the actual modeling episode will control the observer's behavior. Further, the function is clearly related to the past correlation of these stimuli with reinforcement contingencies.

A most important category of events viewed here as contextual stimuli has been labeled *vicarious consequences* by Bandura and others. The theoretical status of vicarious consequences has been the focus of considerable debate (cf. Bandura, 1971b; Gewirtz, 1971a). Bandura (1965a, 1965b, 1971b) argued that vicarious reinforcement or punishment has several effects, one of which is to serve as a basic process, analogous in its results to direct reinforcement delivered to the observer. Gewirtz (1971a, 1971b) proposed that consequences delivered to the model are functional for the observer to the extent they have served previously as discriminative stimuli for directly reinforced responses by the observer.

The advantage of Gewirtz's developmental position over Bandura's ahistorical approach is that a specific and testable hypothesis is offered to account for individual differences in observer's responsivity to vicarious reinforcement. It is unclear from Bandura's descriptions why there should be any systematic variation in the effectiveness of consequences to the model. Yet the function of vicarious consequences seems to fluctuate considerably. For example, Thelen and Soltz (1969) varied the race of children who served as observers of a white adult model whose aggressive behavior was reinforced or produced no consequences. As predicted from Bandura's theory (1971a), white children observing the reinforced aggression increased their aggressive responding compared with white children in the model-no consequences condition. However, black children actually decreased their aggressiveness compared with the model-no consequences control. Gewirtz's position suggests that the black children had a history in which imitation of the reinforced aggressive behavior of white models was likely to be punished. Though such an analysis is speculative, it is reasonable.

Intermittencies of reinforcement are one interesting source of data relating to the reinforcement-process versus discriminative-stimulus interpretations of vicarious reinforcement. If vicarious reinforcement is analogous to direct reinforcement in its effects, then similar manipulations of reinforcement schedules should produce similar effects. Bisese (1966) compared the effects of various ratios of direct and vicarious reinforcement on extinction of imitative behavior. Rather than having analogous effects, lower percentages of direct reinforcement led to increased responding in extinction, while lower percentages of vicarious reinforcement led to decreased responding in both acquisition and extinction. These results are consistent with a discriminative rather than a reinforcing function of consequences to the model.

In a review of vicarious reinforcement studies, Thelen and Rennie (1972) found that, relative to a control group, positive consequences increased the likelihood of observer's imitation in less than one half of the investigations surveyed. Model consequences were most likely to be functional when (1) an observer was present during the observer's opportunity to respond, (2) alternating modeling and response trials were used rather than one exposure to modeling and one opportunity to respond, (3) the observer was explicitly or implicitly told prior to modeling that he would have to perform, and (4) a high rather than a low percentage of the model's behavior produced consequences. Both the variability of results and the factors making vicarious reinforcement more likely are consistent with the discriminative-stimulus approach.

Liebert and Fernandez (1970) reconceptualized vicarious reinforcement in terms of an informational analysis. Bandura (1971a, 1972) also has appealed increasingly to an information vocabulary in discussing observational learning. An informational analysis of vicarious consequences suggests that from consequences delivered to the model, the observer derives potentially useful information about the importance of the model's behavior and the likely reaction of other people to behavior similar to the model's. Such an approach is roughly equivalent to the discriminative-stimulus hypothesis, but there are critical differences. The discriminative-stimulus hypothesis suggests specific histories that might result in a variety of vicarious-consequence effects. It is thus historical, developmental, and testable. The informational analysis, in contrast, has developed no means independent of the observer's response to assess the information that an observer derives from the vicarious consequences delivered to a model. Its predictive power derives solely from the observer and the experimenter having much the same culture and experiences. The experimenter predicts how the observer will perform by "putting himself in the place of" the observer.

Other contextual stimuli will be discussed under the rubric of responding by the observer, but, except for vicarious consequences, this whole category of variables has received practically no attention. Such inattention may have seemed justified by the possibility of relatively greater control by focusing on the direct reinforcement of imitative behavior. But technological goals warranting emphasis on one particular set of variables for a particular applied purpose are not often synonymous with the goal of isolating all sources of control that exist. Even within a technological perspective, the importance of contextual stimuli will increase as planners attempt to control behavior in circumstances in which direct contingencies are not feasible.

The Observer's Response

Mediating Responses. Neurological-chemical events within the skin of an observer mediate between a modeling episode and an observer's subsequent response. This assertion can be accepted without implications for the status of these neurochemical events in psychological theory. One approach, taken by physiological psychologists, is to explore directly the chain of neurochemical effects linking an observable stimulus to an observable response. The outcomes of such research are increasingly impressive. A second approach, taken by cognitive psychologists, is to construct models of what might mediate the control of external behavior by external stimuli and then to imbue them with explanatory functions. For example, it is said that a biologically transmitted language-acquisition device (LAD) acts upon the utterances that a child hears and formulates a set of rules determining how universal aspects of language are to be expressed in a particular culture. The LAD then determines the child's speech productions (McNeill, 1966). Never has a homunculus theory been more explicit. A third approach avoids the question of mediating events completely by asserting they are either unimportant to or not available for experimental analysis. The fourth approach, and the one favored here, abandons neurochemical mediators to biologists and physiologists but accepts the importance of mediating events at the level of a psychological analysis. Attention is focused on individual behavior and its determining context. These events can occur at the beginning and end of a causal chain and thus not be identified as mediators, or they can come between. Unfortunately, mediating behavior may often be private and thus difficult to manipulate and study. One approach is to develop a technology for the electronic amplification of such events (McGuigan & Schoonover, 1973); another is to study mediators when they occur at an observable level.

Coates and Hartup (1969) adopted the latter approach. Four- and seven-yr-old children observed a filmed sequence in which relatively novel motor behavior was displayed by a model. Children were told either to describe the model's behavior in their own words or to repeat an experimenter's description of the model's behavior, or they were given no instructions relating to verbalization. Among the 4-yr-olds, the induced-verbalization group reproduced the model's behavior better than the free-verbalization group, which was in turn superior to the no-instruction control. These differences were not present among the 7-yr-olds. Coding skills may be one factor that explains the older children's superior performance on observational-learning tasks; such differences between ages can be reduced by providing younger children with the appropriate mediating responses.

Verbalization was made overt so that the mediational activity was not hypothetical. As Day (1969) pointed out, there is no reason why a functional analysis should eschew private events. The appropriate criterion for a behavioral approach is that a process be ". . . directly observable, at least to *someone* [p. 326]."

Bandura and Jeffrey (1973) studied how complex sequences of modeled behavior were performed by college students after delays as a function of coding activities, repetition of coding activities (rehearsal), and practice of the modeled behavior. Coding combined with repetition of the codes increased the accuracy of reproducing the model's behavior after a week's delay. Practice of the actual behavior rather than the codes did not have a beneficial effect.

It is beyond the present scope to examine the development of mediational responding. But the suggestion that mediational activity, whether overt or covert, is no different than other responses implies that it will occur as a function of the same events controlling nonmediational responses.

Imitative-Counterimitative Responses. The discussion focuses first on the stimulus conditions activating the observer's observationally acquired responses, second on implications, if any, for a distinction between learning and performance, third on the importance of immediate imitative responding, and fourth on the nature of imitative responding.

1. Contextual Stimuli. Those discriminative stimuli that occur in the context of the modeling episode have been discussed. The interest here is in those stimuli occurring in the context of the observer's response.

Verbal instructions are an important category of contextual determinants of imitative responding. The most theoretically relevant verbal instructions involve *recall* versus *acceptance* statements (Liebert & Fernandez, 1970). Typically, a child in a recall condition observes a model making a series of choices on a stimulus selection series. The child is then shown the series again and asked to "Show the ones which [the model] liked best." In an acceptance condition the child is instructed to "Show the ones which *you* like best." These two types of verbal instructions lead the same child to match different choices after identical modeling episodes. For example, if the model's choices are verbally rewarded, the child in an acceptance condition will match those choices at above-chance level, whereas the child seeing the model's choices punished will show clear counterimitation. The child who observes no consequences to the model will perform at chance level. Under recall instructions, however, the child will match all of the model's choices with high accuracy (Liebert & Fernandez, 1970).

2. The Acquisition-Performance Distinction. Bandura (1965b, 1969a, 1971a) and others (Flanders, 1968; Liebert & Fernandez, 1970) suggested distinguishing between what the child learns in the original modeling episode and his subsequent performance because: (a) The observer's first overt response demonstrated to be a function of a modeling episode often does not occur until after a considerable delay. (b) The observer's performance can vary in the fidelity with which it matches the model's behavior owing to contextual cues that occur subsequent to the modeling episode. The previously cited research on *recall* versus *acceptance* instructions exemplifies the latter point.

On the other hand, as Gewirtz (1971a, 1971b) has convincingly argued, neither of these observations requires a distinction between learning and performance. A delay always occurs between a stimulus and a response, even if it is a short one. If special assumptions are not necessary for short delays, they should not be for long ones. The second observation also poses no difficulties, because behavior always has multiple determinants. A disparity among different dependent measures does not imply that some represent learning while others represent performance. All, in fact, are performance measures. [See the "awareness and learning" literature for treatment of a similar issue (Eriksen, 1960)].

Gewirtz's objections to an acquisition-performance distinction are well taken, but may be applicable only to approaches similar to Bandura's (1965b, 1969a, 1971a). In brief Bandura's position is that something is acquired at the time of modeling, stored centrally, and then activated when the occasion is propitious. The hypothetical central storage mechanisms constitute the problem with this theoretical approach. The emphasis of the theory inevitably becomes subject-versus-environment based. Thus one set of measures determines what the subject "knows," while another determines what the subject "wants to do." What the subject learns becomes a function of his "deployment of attentional strategies" as a function of his "expectations of reward," and so on. Statements like these indicate a turning away from an analysis of the conditions controlling behavior.

The position here, explicitly reflected in previous discussions, is that viewing acquisition and performance as separable though interrelated process *is* advantageous. This distinction has been made in the language of stimulus control. A stimulus, be it the model's behavioral topography or function, the stimuli preceding his behavior, or some relation among these events, can acquire a controlling function in the absence of an overt response by the observer. The exercise of this function and the form of the observer's behavior will depend on mediating responses and contextual stimuli. In a historical sequence the maintenance of processes that establish stimulus control may depend on overt responding and reinforcement of such responding. In other words stimulus control by an aspect of a modeling episode can be established in a particular instance without a response or reinforcement. But if stimulus control is to be established during other modeling episodes, then it may occasionally have to lead to responding and reinforcement. The establishment of stimulus control, though not overt, is conceived of as part of a chain of events that at least intermittently results in appropriately reinforced overt responding.

What advantages does this approach have over one that ignores any distinction between acquisition and performance? Differentiating events that determine whether the model's behavior acquires control from those determining how the observer performs and whether acquired stimulus control is maintained has many practical consequences. This distinction has not been important in many studies of discriminative control of operant responding because stimuli, responses, and reinforcers are repeated so frequently that no compelling reason exists to separate the establishment of stimulus control from responding. Often in observational learning, however, modeling of a response occurs only once and the occasion for a response demonstrating that the modeled behavior has become functional may never occur or may occur long after the modeling sequence. For example, I, as an observer, may be exposed to a model who says, "I would like you to meet Bob Young." I shake Bob's hand and say, "Glad to meet you." It may be days, weeks, or years before I see Bob Young again and am required to reproduce his name. If observational learning is to be produced in such situations, then variables primarily affecting acquisition as opposed to performance must be identified. This distinction is possible on temporal grounds. Those events occurring prior to or contiguous with the model's behavior will affect acquisition and place boundaries on the observer's future performance. Those events occurring after modeling will control the occurrence of the observer's response and the probability that stimulus control will be acquired on future occasions of modeling. These events include verbal instructions to the observer to recall the model's behavior, the presentation of stimuli that previously occurred in modeling (as in meeting Bob Young by chance a year after being introduced to him), and reinforcement of the observer's responding. In a historical analysis that takes into account many occurrences of modeling and observer responding, acquisition and performance and their associated independent variables will be interrelated.

   3. The Importance of Imitative Responding. One way to demonstrate the interrelatedness of acquisition and performance is to explore the function of imitative responding in the acquisition of behavior. G.J. Whitehurst and Novak (1973) demonstrated the importance of imitative responding on the acquisition of new grammatical response forms by preschool children. The procedure involved *probe* trials during which subjects without the benefit of modeling were presented pictures to "tell about," *modeling* trials during which a model used a sentence containing a targeted sentence-phrase type without allowing the subjects to imitate the utterance, and *training* trials which involved modeling and response reproduction by the observers if they did not produce the targeted phrase type themselves. In a multiple-baseline procedure, use of four sentence-phrase types (appositives, infinitives, prepositions, and participials) was determined on probe trials. Following baseline, *modeling* trials were interspersed among probe trials for a particular phrase type. If modeling did not produce the desired phrase on probe trials, training trials were substituted for modeling trials. This sequence occurred for each phrase type in turn.

   Figure 5-5 presents results from one representative subject. Modeling

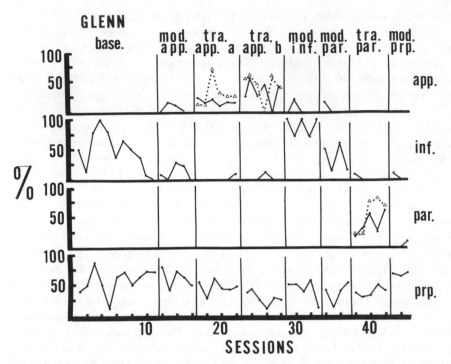

Fig. 5-5. A representative subject from G.J. Whitehurst and Novak (1973, p. 339). The solid lines represent the percent of probe trials on which sentences including one of the four phrase types (appositives—app., infinitives—inf., participials—par., and prepositions—prp.) occurred in each condition of the study. The dotted lines may be disregarded in the present context. The data demonstrate that immediate imitative responding (imitation training) may sometimes be necessary to produce generative usage of a modeled response form. (Modeling trials—mod., training trials—tra.)

alone was strongly effective only for some phrase types. Training, in contrast, produced the desired form in every case in which it was applied. Because the modeling and training trials differed primarily in the occurrence of an observer's immediate imitative response, the importance of such responding is shown. Nevertheless, immediate imitative responding is not always necessary, as evidenced by the strong influence of modeling of infinitives and the much weaker but reliable effect of modeling of appositives. Acquisition of stimulus control over responding can occur in the absence of immediate responding, but such responding does influence the control that emerges. In other cases that require elaborate coding behavior, however, immediate imitation may be detrimental to acquisition (Bandura & Jeffrey, 1973).

    4. Selective Imitation. What is the nature of imitative response? Does an observer attempt to copy all of the model's behavior or is imitation typically more discerning and *selective?* Jean Marc Itard (1962) noted the selectivity of some imitations in his classic work on the "wild boy" of Aveyron, first published in 1801:

I drew upon a blackboard two circles almost equal, one opposite myself and the other in front of Victor. I arranged upon six or eight points of the circumference of these circles six or eight letters of the alphabet and wrote the same letters within the circles but disposed them differently. Next I drew several lines in one of the circles leading to the letters placed in the circumferences. Victor did the same thing on the other circle. But because of the different arrangement of the letters, the most exact imitation nevertheless gave an entirely different figure from the one I had just offered as a model. Thence was to come the idea of a special kind of imitation which was not a matter of slavishly copying a given form but one of reproducing its spirit and manner without being held up by the apparent difference in the result [p. 84].

Selective imitation solves certain problems and raises others. In the area of language acquisition the role of imitation has often been minimized because much language is novel and, therefore, could not be imitated in the verbatim, slavish, parroting sense. The process of selective imitation, however, allows responses that are simultaneously imitative *and* novel and thereby solves the apparent logical contradiction between imitation and the facts of language acquisition (see Whitehurst, G.J., and Vasta, 1975, for a review).

The issue raised by selective imitation is what determines the target of selection. In language acquisition, which may be a special case, preliminary evidence suggests children imitate those words and grammatical structures they have begun to comprehend but are not proficient at producing (Bloom, D., Hood, & Lightbown, 1974; Whitehurst, G.J., & Vasta, 1975). This raises fascinating implications regarding the young child's ability to monitor his own inabilities and select models for imitation accordingly. This is what we do as adults when we pay a ski instructor for lessons, but the analogous process in a 3-yr-old is still somewhat surprising. At this point, knowledge of selective imitation is rudimentary. Good descriptive developmental data are needed followed by investigations of the mechanics of the process.

Reinforcement Contingencies

The role of reinforcement in establishing and maintaining imitative responding has been repeatedly demonstrated since the seminal research of N.E. Miller and Dollard (1941). Baer and Sherman (1964) were first to investigate the role of reinforcement in the occurrence of apparently nonreinforced imitations. When children's imitations of some of a model's responses were reinforced, the children also imitated other responses that were not reinforced. Several hypotheses have been advanced to account for this result, called *generalized imitation.*

Baer and Sherman's account may be called the *conditioned-*

reinforcement hypothesis. To explain their results, they appealed to a stimulus dimension of similarity. Because similarity must exist prior to reinforcement, it should become discriminative for reinforcement and hence a conditioned reinforcer. The subjects then match the model's responses to produce similarity, even in the absence of direct reinforcement of a given response. In support, J.A. Sherman, Saunders, and Brigham (1970) demonstrated that similarity is a functional stimulus dimension for children by alternatively reinforcing matching and mismatching responses on a match-to-sample task. Dimensional control by similarity was demonstrated by the maintenance of either matching or mismatching responses on nonreinforced probe trials depending on which category was being reinforced on training trials. In a similar vein Parton and Fouts (1969) showed that children maximized the matching response on a match-to-sample task in which they could produce either a matching or mismatching response. Parton and Priefert (1973) had adults imitate children. On some trials adults deliberately mismatched the child's behavior, while on others the child's behavior was copied. The colors of the objects (blocks) that the children manipulated were systematically correlated with whether the adult matched or mismatched. The children were later allowed to express a preference for the colors associated with matching or mismatching and systematically chose the former.

A logical argument against the conditioned-reinforcement hypothesis is that it does not explain why imitation is usually focused on particular individuals. In other words why should some types of similarity be reinforcing and others not? Another way to state this is to ask why individuals should ever stop imitating. But to criticize the conditioned-reinforcement hypothesis is not to suggest that similarity is not a functional stimulus dimension that plays an important role in imitation. For example, as the ability to imitate is first acquired, a child is unable to imitate new behavior though he can match those modeled actions that have been prompted and shaped previously. As experience is gained, however, new behavior can be imitated at the first opportunity without the need for shaping or prompting (Baer et al., 1967). The ability to do this is prima facie evidence that a dimension of similarity has become functional, because the ability to respond to new instances of a particular abstraction has always been taken as evidence of concept formation (Hull, 1920). In summary the role of similarity as a functional stimulus during imitation is supported, but the assertion that nonreinforced imitations are maintained by similarity as a conditioned reinforcer encounters logical and empirical difficulties.

The *discrimination-difficulty hypothesis*, advanced by Bandura (1969a), states children perform reinforced and nonreinforced imitations nondifferentially because they fail to discriminate the contingencies to which they are exposed. Bandura and Barab (1971) showed children are more likely to imitate nonreinforced behavior from the same topographical class as reinforced imitative behavior (motor-motor) than they are to imitate nonreinforced behavior from a different topographical class (motor-vocal). Garcia et al., (1971) found a similar effect. Assuming that ease of discrimination accounts for the topographical constraints on generalized imitation, these data support the discrimination hypothesis. Steinman (1970a, 1970b), however, demonstrated that nondifferential performance of reinforced and nonreinforced responses does not necesssarily mean the subject cannot discriminate the contingencies involved. In the Steinman studies, when reinforced and nonreinforced responses were modeled singly in a successive trial procedure ("Do this"), children imitated both responses at high levels. When the same subjects were presented the same responses in a choice procedure ("Do this . . . or do this."), however, they consistently performed those responses previously reinforced to the exclusion of the nonreinforced set. This also occurs within topographically narrow boundaries (Steinman & Boyce, 1971). Thus, something other than failure of discrimination is responsible for generalized imitation, at least within the experimental settings in which this research was conducted.

The *scheduling hypothesis* suggested by Gewirtz and Stingle (1968) advances the hypothesis that imitation is a functional response class maintained by intermittent reinforcement. This is, however, more a restatement of the problem than a hypothesis regarding its solution. While reinforcement is implicated as a key aspect of the phenomenon, the question still remains *why* both reinforced and nonreinforced imitations are maintained in strength. True, diverse responses producing the same outcome in the animal laboratory are maintained as a class by reinforcement. But the point is that all responses, e.g., pushing levers with nose or foot, are functional in *producing* reinforcement. If lever pushing with nose is extinguished, it stops. That an equivalent extinction effect often does not occur when an extinction operation is applied to imitative behavior is the crux of the problem. An appeal neither to response classes nor to contingent reinforcement explains generalized imitation, at least as it occurs in the laboratory.

The *social control hypothesis* (Peterson & Whitehurst, 1970; Steinman, 1970a, 1970b) implicates social stimuli acting as discriminative stimuli for compliance with direct or subtle instructions to perform. Peterson and Whitehurst found that a variety of extinction and reinforcement omission (DRO) procedures did not disrupt ongoing imitative behavior. But if the model left the room before the child had the opportunity to imitate, responding dropped to a low level. J. A. Martin (1971) showed that both imitative and nonimitative behavior, reinforced and nonreinforced, was maintained as long as "instruction following" was reinforced. Bandura and Barab (1971) administered a postexperimental interview to assess their subjects' explanations why they performed nonreinforced responses. Many subjects replied that they felt they were supposed to reproduce all modeled behavior. Waxler and Yarrow (1970) showed that nonreinforced imitations declined when instructions to imitate modeled behavior were not given. These studies suggest social cues, either explicit (e.g., instructions) or implicit (experimenter presence), are a controlling factor in maintaining nonreinforced behavior. Previous histories of reinforcement or punishment with respect to compliance with similar "demands" would be sufficient to maintain nonreinforced behavior over long periods. This would be particularly true if the compliance behavior had developed as avoidance responding, so that by complying the child avoided aversive consequences.

These experimental analyses of generalized imitation implicate several variables in the maintenance of nonreinforced imitations. Immediate reinforcement is important, particularly for retarded children (Baer et al., 1967). Control by the stimulus dimension of similarity between the observer's and model's responses is critical in novel imitations (Sherman, J. A. et al., 1970). Topographical characteristics of responses influence generalization beyond training stimuli (Garcia et al., 1971). Finally, social cues ultimately deriving their control from reinforcement contingencies are particularly important for normal preschool children (Peterson & Whitehurst, 1971).

Development of Imitation

Much research on observational learning has been ahistorical. In particular the social-learning tradition focused almost exclusively on normal children, studied in one or two brief experimental sessions. The limitations of such an approach have become increasingly obvious. Gewirtz and Stingle (1968) and Gewirtz (1969b, 1971a, 1971b) noted many interactions in normal preschool children that may derive from unobserved learning histories rather than from separate basic processes. Hartup and Coates (1972) have called for research on the imitative repertoire in children: "(1) as this repertoire changes over time and (2) as this repertoire varies according to the situational context [p. 64]."

Recognizing a need for developmental research is not the same as knowing how to proceed with such research. The Hartup and Coates (1972) statement is consistent with observations that changes in behavior are correlated with age and situation. Baer (1970) has characterized such an approach as *age psychology* and has argued instead for a *sequence-dependent* concept of development that is age-irrelevant. Sequence-dependent research aims at discovering how various sequences of events affect behavior and produce behavioral change. The choice here is for the sequence-dependent developmental research as opposed to age psychology.

Origins of Imitation. From a developmental perspective, a key issue concerns the necessary events for establishing an initial imitative repertoire. Several hypotheses bear on this issue. Research with retarded or autistic children (Baer et al., 1967; Lovaas, 1967; Sloane & MacAuley, 1968) demonstrates that an imitative repertoire can be established where there was none previously by initial prompting or "putting through" behavior in the presence of modeling cues followed by reinforcement and then eventually by fading prompts and thinning reinforcement. But more than one route to the same goal may exist, and it is of considerable theoretical and applied significance to know what other histories can produce observational learning.

One alternative is suggested by Hartup and Coates (1972), who hypothesize that children initally come to discriminate a matching relation not in the order model-response-reinforcement but in the sequence response-model-reinforcement. In other words, instead of the child matching an adult's response through accident or prompting it is the adult who initially imitates the child. Such a history, in which the child receives positive stimulation paired with a model-produced matching relation, might set the stage for self-production of matching.

Another possibility is that recycling the sequence—modeling-reinforcement—without the observer's responding is a sufficient condition for the later occurrence of responses matching the modeled behavior. This is the Mowrerian hypothesis, previously discussed.

A final hypothesis suggests that repeated presentation of modeling stimuli with opportunities for the observer's responding is solely sufficient to produce imitation without any external contingency imposed on the observer's response. Of all the relations that could occur between the model's behavior and the observer's, those that tend toward similarity are assumed to have a primary reinforcing function (Kaye, 1971; Parton & Priefert, 1973). This is similar to the hypothesis put forward by Baer and Sherman (1964), except that they viewed similarity as an acquired instead of a primary reinforcer.

Critical analysis of the role of reinforcement in initial imitations is difficult. By the time children have motor skills that allow testing of imitation, they could have a history of reinforcement for matching. Even if a contingent reinforcement history were completely ruled out, behavior consistent with the "similarity as reinforcer" hypothesis could also be produced by the Mowrerian process or the reversed imitation sequence suggested by Hartup and Coates (1972). Both processes involve reinforcement, but not as a direct consequence of imitating. Recognizing these limitations, it is still of interest to observe the course in young children of modeling-response opportunity sequences not involving reinforcement.

K. Kaye (1971) used a procedure with 7- to 10-month-old infants in which an adult repeated a pattern of phonemes (e.g., "ba-ba-ba-ba") for numerous trials followed by 5-sec opportunities for the infant to respond. To quote from Kaye, "In the first pauses the infant typically does no more than look at us; gradually, however, he smiles, vocalizes, repeats different phonemes with similar intonation ("ga-ga-ga"), and finally says "ba-ba-ba-ba." This may take as many as 70 repetitions by the model, followed by pauses [p. 4]." Kaye reported a similar procedure involving reaching around a transparent detour to obtain a toy. The study involved 6-month-old infants who did not reach around the screen to obtain the toy in a pretest; all repeatedly attempted to reach for the toy directly and were stopped by the screen. The training period involved an adult's repeated demonstrations of the reaching-around response followed by response opportunities for the infant. All the subjects were quickly successful in matching this response. This study demonstrated, if nothing else, the difficulty of controlling for reinforcement of imitation, because receipt of the object reached for could certainly function as a reinforcer for matching.

Beyond whether imitation occurs *initially* when consequences are neutral, what happens to the *course* of imitation in the absence of an external contingency? In unpublished research, Whitehurst, Bouzas, and Barrett-Goldfarb exposed a 16-month-old English-speaking child to a model's descriptions of objects in Spanish sentences. The child was brought to the laboratory and placed in a playpen. Periodically, the adult held up a toy and labeled it in Spanish (e.g., *"Estes es el caballo"*). The toy was then placed in the playpen for a fixed period of time. At intervals, the model picked up the toy and described it further (*"Tu puedes doblar el caballo"*) while pointing to or acting out the characteristic described. The same sequence of 42 Spanish sentences was repeated during each session. An observer recorded the child's vocalizations, which were later scored as Spanish, English, or mixed. No consequences were ever associated with the child's behavior. Figure 5-6 shows the cumulative Spanish and English utterances over sessions. Three facts are evident. First, a substantial amount of Spanish was produced by the subject without any contingency for such production. Seventy-six percent were immediately imitative in that they were taken wholly from the preceding model utterance and occurred within 20 sec of it. The remaining Spanish utterances virtually always occurred in the context in which they had been modeled but were more than 20 sec removed from the model's matching word or phrase. Second, a substantial amount of English was also produced in the absence of any immediate model or contingency. Finally, while English continued to occur at a constant rate, Spanish was initially infrequent, then occurred at a high rate, followed by a constantly decelerating rate until the study was terminated.

For reasons cited, it is impossible to say why imitative behavior initially occurred in the absence of a contingency. It is obvious, however, that in the absence of a reinforcement contingency the imitative behavior was not maintained. It is at least conceivable that initial imitations occur because similarity is a primary reinforcer or because it becomes a conditioned reinforcer through one of the other processes not involving direct reinforcement for matching. It seems likely, however, that matching must soon be embedded in a contingency or it will cease to occur.

Prior Behavioral Interactions. Developmental histories not directly involving the reinforcing or evoking stimuli of the modeling episode have demonstrable effects on observational learning. For example, Gelfand (1962) found the probability of imitation increased for subjects who had previously failed on a series of tasks. Similarly, interactions that have

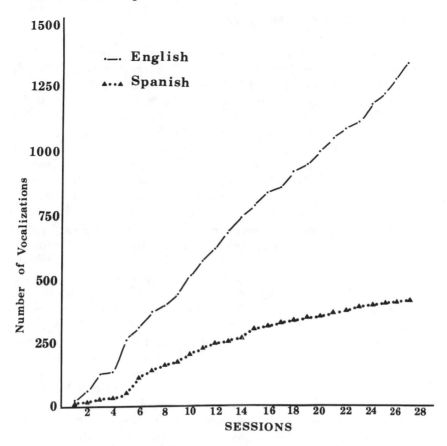

Fig. 5-6. Production of English and Spanish utterances by a young English-speaking child under conditions in which Spanish is modeled and no utterances are reinforced.

emotionalizing functions can change the likelihood of imitation (Bandura & Rosenthal, 1966).

Wahler and Nordquist (1973) studied the function of differential attention and time-out delivered by teachers or parents for compliance with commands that did not involve modeling or imitation. When the children's noncompliance produced time-out and differential attention was delivered for "good" behavior, rate of nonreinforced and noninstructed imitative behavior was very high. But when these disciplinary contingencies for opposition to adult commands were removed, imitative behavior decreased dramatically. This demonstrates that adult discipline is related directly to imitation and supports the earlier assertion that, for most children, imitative behavior is part of a larger response class consisting of responding appropriately to social cues and instructions.

SUMMARY AND FINAL WORD

Observational learning was conceptualized as a process in which the topography, functional outcome, and/or discriminative context of one organism's behavior controls a related characteristic of another's behavior. This definition differs from others in emphasizing the tripartite nature of the modeling stimulus and in characterizing the relation between model's behavior and observer's response as dimensional rather than as one of absolute similarity. Several problems are thereby avoided or solved. One need not know the genesis of behavior or whether it is "new" or "old" as one must in applying Bandura's (1971a) definitions. Seemingly unrelated types of imitation can be viewed as functions of control by different fragments of a modeling episode, e.g., matched-dependent behavior involves control by functional outcome and copying involves control by topography. Other topics like learning-by-imitation can be conceptualized in terms of the transfer of control between segments of the modeling episode, e.g., from topography to discriminative context in the case of observational learning of word meaning. In general this definition integrates several phenomena and allows the extension of theory and research on observational learning into areas where traditional definitions have caused difficulties (see Whitehurst, G. J., 1977).

Beyond definition, this chapter surveyed some of the more important variables affecting observational learning. Knowledge in some areas is relatively advanced. The role of reinforcement has been extensively researched, maintaining conditions for nonreinforced imitations are well catalogued, and vicarious reinforcement has been carefully analyzed. In other areas, however, knowledge is rudimentary or nonexistent. The origins of imitation are poorly understood, and good descriptive developmental studies have not been conducted; the process involved in acquisition of stimulus control by modeling stimuli as opposed to exercise of that control is still mysterious; and variables determining the targets of selective imitation are only beginning to be explored.

This discussion has been neutral with respect to whether observational learning is a basic process or a complex form of operant behavior. No doubt imitative behavior is sensitive to its consequences, but many relations between input and output will not be fully explicated by examining an individual's history of reinforcement. A behavior analytic approach, however, can successfully incorporate these variables without resorting to cognitive constructs. This chapter has been an attempt in this direction.

K. DANIEL O'LEARY[1]

Chapter 6

The Operant and Social Psychology of Token Systems

As any parent or educational observer knows, rewards for academic achievements and socially desired behavior in the classroom are not new. Prizes such as nuts, figs, and honey were used to reward academic achievement in the twelfth-century teaching of the Torah (O'Leary, K. D., & Drabman, 1971). Inducements such as nuts and figs were felt necessary because initially "the human spirit is narrow and while acquiring wisdom, hopes for material advantages." Later, however, students were admonished: "Do not be like servants who serve their master for the sake of receiving a reward, but rather be like those who serve their master without expecting a reward." Basically it was said that a student should initially learn the Torah by reward and punishment but that eventually he would "arrive at a stage of doing good for its own sake" (Birnbaum, 1962, pp. 330-331). This general philosophy, using tangible rewards to motivate students initially and having students learn to work for some higher good or less immediate reward, is essentially that of many psychologists who establish token reinforcement programs today. Although psychologists today might question whether students would continue to study and learn in the absence of some reward, they would certainly generally agree that the long-term goals of token programs would be to have students work for less tangible goals, such as mastery of material and fun in accomplishment, or longer-term goals, such as eventual recognition by peers and parents.

Historical examples of the use of rewards abound. For instance, in the sixteenth century Erasmus advocated the use of cherries and cakes to facili-

1. Support during the writing of this chapter was provided by NIMH Grant MH 21813 and U.S. Office of Education Grant OEG-0-71-28-72. The opinions expressed herein, however, do not necessarily reflect the position or policy of either agency. Special thanks is due Sharon Foster and David Santogrossi who critically evaluated earlier versions of this manuscript.

179

tate the teaching of Greek and Latin (Skinner, 1966a). Similarly in the early 1800s children in New York City schools were rewarded with praise, merit badges, and tickets that could be exchanged for toys. The reward and fine program was described as follows: (Ravitch, 1974, pp. 15-16):

The system of rewards . . . was based on currency of pasteboard tickets with a value of one-eighth of a penny. They could be redeemed for toys. Tickets were distributed daily to all of the monitors for performing their duties; the highest-ranking monitor, called the monitor general, received eight each day, while other monitors received fewer. Each day, the head boy of each draught was rewarded with a ticket. On promotion to a superior class, a scholar received twelve tickets. Each boy who attained the eighth class won fifty tickets. Each teacher had discretionary power over 1,000 tickets per month as special rewards for the deserving.

To discourage corporal punishment, which [was] strongly disapproved, students were fined tickets for various forms of misbehavior. The list of punishable offenses, like everything else, was explicit:

Offense	Fine in Tickets
Talking, playing, inattention, out of seats, etc.	4
Being disobedient or saucy to a monitor	4
Disobedience of inferior to superior monitor	8
Snatching books, slates, etc. from each other	4
Monitors reporting scholars without cause	6
Moving after the bell rings for silence	2
Stopping to play, or making a noise in the street on going home from school	4
Staring at persons who may come into the room	4
Blotting or soiling books	4
Monitors neglecting their duty	8
Having dirty face or hands (to be washed and fined)	4
Throwing stones	20
Calling ill names	20
Coming to school late, for every quarter of an hour	8
Playing truant, first time	20
Playing truant, second time	40
Fighting	50
Making a noise before school hours	4
Scratching or cutting the desks	20

Despite these sporadic uses of rewards and fines, the systematic use of rewards on a frequent basis in the classroom, hereafter called a token reinforcement program, is a recent phenomenon. The basic ingredients of a token reinforcement program include "(1) a set of instructions to the class about the behaviors that will be reinforced, (2) a means of making a potentially reinforcing stimulus—usually called a token—contingent upon behavior, and (3) a set of rules governing the exchange of tokens for back-up reinforcers such as prizes or opportunities to engage in special activities [O'Leary, K. D., & O'Leary, 1972, p. 259]." Generally, token reinforcement or reward programs have been used in special classroom settings to increase the academic and prosocial behavior of groups of emotionally disturbed or retarded children. Reports have been increasing, however, of token programs used in regular classrooms where a single "problem" child is the focus of the intervention (Patterson, G.R., 1974), and regular classes with nonproblem children also have become arenas for intervention with token programs. A survey of research published in the *Journal of Applied Behavior Analysis* from 1968 to 1973 reveals that both the number and proportion of publications on token reinforcement programs in classrooms have more than doubled (i.e., from three papers and 6% in 1968, to five and 14% in 1969, to 11 papers in both 1972 and 1973).[2] Only programs that included tokens in a form that could be accumulated or lost were counted. Motivational systems with no token medium of exchange but a direct relation between meeting a behavioral requirement and a reinforcer or between experimenter or teacher and one subject were not included in this survey (e.g., Dietz & Repp, 1973; Hopkins, Schutte, & Garton, 1971; Lovitt, Guppy, & Blattner, 1969; Osborne, 1969; Wilson & Hopkins, 1973). While actual figures on the use of token programs in schools are not currently available, it is likely that the aforementioned increase in research parallels a rise in the use of token programs in both public and private schools.

Before considering evaluations of token programs, consider the following vignette, which gives a flavor of the mechanics of one classroom's token reinforcement program:

Condon Elementary School is the oldest school in Eugene, Oregon. An experimental classroom for behavior problem children is located in one wing of the school. From 1966 to 1970, the classroom was part of the Engineered Learning Project (ELP), whose purpose was to develop methods of identifying and remediating the behavior problems of children in grades three through six. Children having disruptive behavior problems were referred to the classroom from local elementary schools. Children attended the classroom in groups of six for a 2-month period. After 2 months, they returned to the regular classroom from which they had been referred.

While in the classroom, the children received an intensive academic and behavioral program. Instruction was individualized for each child. The remedial program concentrated on improving basic skills in math,, reading, language, vocabulary, and spelling. The behavioral program focused on decreasing classroom behaviors that interfere with academic performance. Many of the children had very short attention spans. The first step was to lengthen attention spans so the children could take advantage of instruction [Walker, H. M., & Buckley, 1974, p. 5].

---

2. The author and Joan Fisher evaluated the *JABA* articles until perfect agreement was obtained.

A token system was established in which an 8½×11 point-record form divided into small squares was placed on each child's desk. Half of the squares were for social responses such as attending and following directions; the other half were for academic performance such as completion of assignments and high levels of accuracy (Walker, H. M., & Buckley, 1974, p. 176). Entries in the squares represented points that could be exchanged for a wide variety of back-up reinforcers (school supplies, chess sets, tutoring other children, listening to records, building models). Initially, points were awarded approximately every 10 min, and the points could be exchanged each day at 1 P.M. for backup reinforcers. The children were free to exchange their points for an inexpensive item or to accumulate them for a more expensive one.

Token programs such as this one offer many distinct advantages:

1. Responses to be reinforced are made explicit through a system of classroom rules and contingencies.
2. Feedback regarding academic and social behavior is frequent (in this case approximately every 10 min).
3. The token reinforcers (checks in the squares) are easily administered and are given less and less frequently as the child progresses academically and socially.
4. A wide variety of backup reinforcers makes it highly probable that, for any child at any time, at least one of the prizes or activities will be effective as a reinforcer.
5. The value of the teacher's supportive comments (praise and positive feedback) may be enhanced through a pairing of such comments with token and backup reinforcers.
6. The system encourages counting and saving of tokens, and as the reinforcers are made less frequent, greater frustration tolerance or delay of gratification is taught.

While the backup reinforcers are clearly important, many other factors are critical in implementing a successful token reinforcement program. Such factors are instruction, immediacy of token reinforcement, shaping or reinforcing gradual approximations to some terminal goal, ignoring or extinguishing minor disruptive behavior, and gradual changes in the schedule of token and backup reinforcement that require increasing academic productivity. Finally, some form of punisher is often required, such as infrequent reprimands or loss of points (response cost).

Six topics will be discussed in this chapter. First, the chapter will examine the specific effects of token programs on academic and social behavior. Second, the question of generalization of behavior change will be addressed both across situations and across behavior. Third, maintenance of behavior across time will be discussed. Factors long considered by social psychologists such as group atmosphere and attribution are addressed next, followed by an assessment of the current status of variables considered the domain of operant psychology, e.g., scheduling effects, secondary reinforcement, and response cost. Finally new trends and likely future applications of token reinforcement programs are explored.

The first section emphasizes two highly pragmatic questions: (1) What kinds of academic and social behavior can be changed with token programs? and (2) what is the extent of the change? The review here and throughout focuses primarily on the best controlled studies after 1970 (for a review of earlier studies, see O'Leary, K. D., and Drabman, 1971).

SPECIFIC EFFECTS OF TOKEN PROGRAMS

Academic Behavior

The immediate effects of rewarding specific academic behavior are clear. Better handwriting (Robin, O'Leary, & Armel, 1975), better English compositions (Brigham, Graubard, & Stans, 1972), increases in correctly completed math problems (Felixbrod, 1974; Felixbrod & O'Leary, 1973, 1974; Iwata & Bailey, 1974), increases in the reading units completed (Kaufman & O'Leary, 1972), increases in correctly read words during acquisition and retention trials (Lahey & Drabman, 1974), improved reading accuracy (Ayllon & Roberts, 1974), and increases in percent of assignments completed (McLaughlin & Malaby, 1972) have all been produced by token programs.

The effects of token programs as assessed by standardized academic tests are less clear than the immediate effects on specifically reinforced academic behavior. Frequent lack of careful matching or random assignment of subjects to experimental and control groups in experimental studies contributes to this lack of clarity. Hewett, Taylor, and Artuso (1969) used the California Achievement Test to evaluate the long-term effects of token programs on reading and arithmetic performance of emotionally disturbed children. The experimental classroom condition consisted of a token reinforcement program with tangible rewards and check marks. Children received check marks for being on time, following directions, and correctly completing assignments; the tangible rewards were candy, prizes, and extra time for arts and crafts. The control classroom condition consisted of "any classroom strategy" except the use of check marks and tangible rewards. The experimental and control classroom conditions remained in effect throughout the year. Two other classes began with the experimental condition and switched to the control condition at midyear. Finally two remaining classes began with the control condition and switched to the experimental condition at midyear. Reading and spelling gains were not influenced by the token program, but mathematics achievement was positively correlated with the token program. In a follow-up study, however, Hewett (1972) reported that educationally handicapped children in a token reinforcement program made significantly greater progress in reading and arithmetic than educationally handicapped students who were matched on the basis of age, sex, and I.Q. and who remained in the regular classroom.

H.L. Cohen and Filipczak (1971) used delinquent boys as student researchers who received money as a reward for academic achievement and exemplary social behavior in the classroom. A learning environment was developed in which students could work in private on self-contained, programmed instructional materials. The rate of gain per year as reflected on the Stanford Achievement Test (SAT) was reported as 1.5 or 2.0 depending upon the particular SAT series given. As Krumboltz (1973) emphasized, however, the evaluation of these academic gains is rendered uncertain for several reasons: (1) there was point payoff associated with the SAT testing, (2) no equivalent scores were presented for a control group, (3) only 32 of the 41 students had complete testing information available, and (4) results were based on estimates of anticipated gains for 1 yr extrapolated from actual grade changes over 8 months. In fact the actual mean grade-score change for 226 days was 1.22 or 0.93 depending upon whether the 1953 or 1963 SAT series was given. In the absence of control subjects it is difficult to evaluate such changes. Most state education departments define a school year as 180 days, and the average expected SAT gain in one academic year for average school pupils is 1 yr. Nonetheless, it is highly likely that delinquent students such as these would make much less than a 1 yr academic gain in 180 or 226 days, and therefore the gains reported by Cohen and Filipczak probably can be viewed as promising.

Significant improvements in academic behavior in remedial classes were noted by M. Clark, Lachowicz, and Wolf (1968) and Wolf, Giles, and Hall (1968). In the latter study 15 fifth- and sixth-grade children in an urban poverty area increased their SAT scores 1.5 yr as compared to a median gain of .8 for a control group ($n = 15$) that did not have a remedial program. Similarly Kaufman and O'Leary (1972) found Wide Range Achievement Test (WRAT) gains of .6 grade in 49 days of an after-school, remedial reading program in a psychiatric hospital school, whereas a control group lost .2 grade on the same test during an equivalent period of time. In a behaviorally oriented remedial reading program (Pelham, 1974) in which several variations of token programs were used (both material reinforcers and natural reinforcers, such as walks with the tutors, as backups) the average California Achievement Test gain was .64 yr for children with one semester or 30 hr of tutoring and 1.21 yr for children with two semesters, or 61 hr of tutoring. Based upon their previous testing, the average anticipated achievement test gain for these children before they entered the program was .26 for the first group and .40 for the second.

Impressive academic gains were recently reported by H. M. Walker and Buckley (1974) with eight classes of six children each who participated in a 2-month token reinforcement program in an experimental classroom for disruptive children. This token program was described earlier in the vignette of the engineered learning project. The mean gain in reading achievement (Gates-McKillop Reading Diagnostic Test) was .8 grade; the mean pretest score was 3.6 grades, and the mean posttest score was 4.4 grades. The mean gain in arithmetic was 1.0 grade. The mean pretest arithmetic score was 3.4, and the mean posttest score was 4.4. While there were no untreated control groups, the gains of .8 and 1.0 yr in 2 months are extremely impressive. The incentive system and educational materials are well delineated by Walker and Buckley in their book-length research report, and the promising results deserve replication by other investigators.

The effect of token systems has been further investigated through Project Follow-Through, a United States Office of Education project designed to improve the education of economically disadvantaged children from the time they enter kindergarten at the age of five through completion of grade four. In a Follow-Through program using an explicit token reinforcement system, Bushell (1974a) reported significantly greater gains on the Wide Range Achievement Tests in reading, spelling, and arithmetic for target than for control children in the same communities. Children received tokens for academic and social progress, which they could exchange for games, art projects, stories, and even the opportunity to do extra reading or arithmetic. Of particular interest was the suggestion that this Follow-Through program may have had a stabilizing influence on the neighborhoods it served. In 1969, in one sample, 50% of the control children moved to other schools during a 2-yr period, whereas only 23% of the Behavior Analysis Follow-Through children moved (see Chapter 15 for a more extensive discussion of this project).

In sum, token reinforcement programs clearly affect specific academic behavior such as writing responses, frames and reading units completed, and mathematics problems completed correctly. Although studies using standardized achievement tests have not always involved random assignments of subjects to conditions or careful subject matching, evidence is rapidly accumulating that token programs can improve performance on these tests.

Social Behavior

The effects of token programs on social behavior in a classroom have been clear for almost a decade. These effects were summarized by K. D. O'Leary and Drabman (1971) and need not be reviewed here. Two examples from these early studies, however, indicate the powerful influence of token programs on social behavior in a classroom. In a class of 17 children labeled emotionally disturbed, ratings exchangeable for backup reinforcers, such as school supplies and candy, were placed in a child's note pad every 20 min.

The ratings ranged from 1 to 10 and reflected the extent to which a child followed classroom rules. The introduction of the token program reduced average disruptive behavior (talking, noise, pushing, eating) from 76% in the base period to an average of 10% during the 2-month token period (O'Leary, K. D., & Becker, 1967). The effects of contingent and noncontingent special events on study behavior of 12 preschool children with above-average intelligence were evaluated by Bushell, Wrobel, and Michaelis (1968). Colored plastic washers served as tokens exchangeable for special events, such as short movies and a trip to a nearby park. The records of all 12 students indicated that noncontingent reinforcement was less effective in sustaining study behavior than contingent reinforcement. Since the review by K. D. O'Leary and Drabman (1971), several studies have further buttressed the large body of evidence documenting the effects of token programs on social behavior. V. W. Harris and Sherman (1973) used a group consequence procedure called the "Good Behavior Game" to reduce disruptive talking and out-of-seat behavior of fifth and sixth graders. The game involved having the teacher list rules, namely, that at certain times the children were not to be out of their seats or to talk to their classmates without permission. The class was divided into two teams and names for each team were written on the blackboard. If a team member talked or left his seat without permission, a mark was placed next to his team's name. At the end of the period, the team with fewer marks won the game and was allowed special privileges (e.g., wearing victory tags or being allowed to do special projects). Essentially the "Good Behavior Game" is a variation of a token program[3] involving (1) a set of instructions and specification of the undesired behavior, (2) check marks on the board contingent upon undesired behavior serving as tokens, and (3) a set of rules governing the exchange of tokens for backup reinforcers, viz., special privileges and projects. Drabman, Spitalnik, and Spitalnik (1974) found a significant decrease in disruptive behavior with four different token reinforcement programs in a "normal" first-grade classroom. The token reinforcement programs were as follows: "(1) individual reinforcement determined by individual performance; (2) group reinforcement determined by the behavior of the most disruptive child; (3) group reinforcement determined by the behavior of the least disruptive child; (4) group reinforcement determined by the behavior of a randomly chosen child." In a Latin-square design, all the children experienced 10 days in each of the four conditions. Although there were no differences in effectiveness of the four programs in reducing disruptive behavior, disruptive children were rated by their peers as more responsible when they were in a group reinforcement condition determined by the most disruptive child. Responsibility was assessed sociometrically by having children pick peers who "would be responsible

[3]As will become apparent in the "Response Cost" section, the procedures in the "Good Behavior Game" resemble a cost program, because undesired behavior immediately receives a check and large numbers of checks lose the game.

and who could help them do a very hard job." Ayllon and Roberts (1974) found that by reinforcing academic improvement of five fifth-grade boys, without placing any direct contingency on social behavior, classroom disruption declined drastically.

Parents' involvement in a token reinforcement program in school has been exemplified in a daily report-card system. The daily report-card system included dittoed notes saying, "Your child did very well in arithmetic" and parents rewarding their child's behavior. The parents were instructed to reward the child with special privileges only if they received a signed note from the teacher indicating that the child met his goal. Six of seven children showed clear improvement resulting from the application of this procedure (Hawkins, Sluyter, & Smith, 1972). Similar positive effects of home-based reinforcement programs with delinquents and children with learning disabilities were documented by J. S. Bailey, Wolf, and Phillips (1970), and McKenzie, Clark, Wolf, Kothera, and Benson (1968). More recently K. D. O'Leary, Pelham, Rosenbaum, and Price (1976) documented the effectiveness of a home-based token program with hyperactive children. In sum, token programs have successfully altered social behavior in classrooms in a host of studies.

GENERALIZATION

Generalization Across Situations

Generalization across situations refers to an effect produced in one situation and evident in another. Until recently, the preponderant evidence regarding generalization of appropriate behavior across situations has indicated that it does not occur in the absence of specific programming for it (Kuypers, Becker, & O'Leary, 1968; Meichenbaum, Bowers, & Ross, 1968; O'Leary, K. D., Becker, Evans, & Saudargas, 1969; Wolf, Giles, & Hall, 1968). In these studies the effects of a token program used in one lesson or at one time of day (e.g., A.M.) failed to generalize to another time of day (P.M.) when the system was not in effect. If one assumes that behavior is greatly influenced though not fully determined by the situation (Bowers, 1973), these results are not surprising. The cues indicating relatively large blocks of time in which token and backup reinforcers were or were not forthcoming were clear. On the other hand, Drabman, Spitalnik, and O'Leary (1973) and Turkewitz, O'Leary, and Ironsmith (1975) found that if a randomly selected 15-min period of a 1-hr tutorial class was designated as the nontoken period and the other three periods were token periods, generalization did occur. In addition, in the Turkewitz et al. study, when the percentage of token periods and the rewards themselves were gradually diminished, both generalization and maintenance of appropriate classroom behavior were evident.

Generalization across Behavior

Generalization across behavior refers to an effect on nonreinforced behavior that is associated with a change in reinforced behavior. Such an effect is seen when a teacher reinforces a child's response, "Thank you" but not "Please" and nonetheless finds increases in both, "Thank you" and "Please."

Ayllon and Roberts (1974) found that the classroom disruptive behavior of five fifth-grade boys in a regular class of 38 students dropped markedly when token reinforcement was applied to reading performance only. Systematic presentation of academic material and token reinforcement of math or reading almost completely eliminated disruptive behavior of four retarded boys, without any direct contingency placed on the disruptive behavior (Ayllon, Layman, & Burke, 1972). Alternatively, Hopps and Cobb (1973) found that reinforcement of group attending was associated with reading achievement test gains. Similarly, Iwata and Bailey (1974) found that reinforcing adherence to class rules (remaining seated, not disturbing neighbor, raising hand to get help from teacher, going to bathroom when nobody else was there) resulted in substantially increased problems completed. Ferritor, Buckholdt, Hamblin, and Smith (1972) found that if tokens were contingent upon attending to the task at hand, attending increased and disruptive behavior decreased, but no change was observed in percent or number of correct arithmetic problems completed. When correct solutions were directly rewarded, academic performance increased while attending showed no change and disruptions increased. When contingencies were simultaneously placed on attending, lack of disruption, and correct solutions, all three reflected change. The findings of Ferritor et al. (1972), unlike the results of other investigators discussed, failed to show generalization. But other investigators reinforced attending, on-task behavior, and even completion of homework assignments (not correctly completed assignments) with praise and free time and did not find generalization to academic productivity either (Harris, V. W., & Sherman, 1973; Hay, Hay, & Nelson, 1974). Given these results, the practitioner is best advised to reinforce both academic and social behavior but to emphasize the former.

A new area where generalization from token reinforcement programs has been found is in children's self-concepts. Using a pictorial self-concept scale based on statements of what children like and dislike about themselves, second- and fourth-grade children in an 8-week token program increased positive self-concept scores more than those who were not in a special class or token program (Parker, 1974). While the author admits that placement in a novel class with a lower teacher-student ratio may have been critical in producing the effect, the results suggest that the self-concept report, assumed to reflect covert behavior (thoughts), may be modified indirectly through the direct reinforcement of overt academic behavior.

MAINTENANCE

Until about 1972, investigators usually demonstrated effects by introducing, withdrawing and reintroducing token programs. These programs were relatively short (e.g., 2- to 3-week phases) and were not withdrawn gradually. When the programs were withdrawn the explanations given to the children were neither explicit nor designed to prevent strong protests. It was shown by using such designs that token reinforcement programs can have a dramatic, albeit often temporary, influence on children's behavior (Birnbrauer, Wolf, Kidder, & Tague, 1965; Bushell et al., 1968; Kaufman & O'Leary, 1972; Kuypers et al., 1968). Most studies indicated that the effects of token programs were not maintained in the absence of some form of continued reinforcement.

Recently, however, research on token programs used for extended periods has shown that their effects can be maintained. Dalton, Rubino, and Hislop (1973) reported an 8-week summer token reinforcement program that was more effective than verbal praise for correct responses in producing academic improvement of children with Down's syndrome. More important, 1 yr after the program ended the token group had significantly higher scores on academic tests than the nontoken group. Further, on the average the token group maintained the academic gains made during the summer, whereas the nontoken group showed a decline. Similarly a 10-yr follow-up of the retarded children in the Rainier School program (Birnbrauer et al., 1965) showed that they had achieved significantly better life adjustments than predicted from norms (Sulzbacher & Kidder, 1975). Turkewitz et al. (1975) gradually removed reinforcers during a 4-month token program in which children were taught to evaluate their own behavior. Basically the children first saw the teacher evaluate their behavior during a standard teacher-administered token program. Then the children were taught to evaluate their own behavior on the basis of how much work they thought they completed correctly and how well they behaved. They received bonus points for matching the teacher ratings, and they lost points for gross under- or over-evaluation. Disruptive behavior decreased and completion of academic work increased with the introduction of the token program, and during a 1-week period after the gradual withdrawal of back-up reinforcers, the children continued to display appropriate social behavior as well as high rates of task completion.

In an outcome study carried out with "conduct-disorder" children, R. N. Kent and O'Leary (1976) found that 9 months after a 20-25-week consultation program for parents and teachers, 16 treated children showed significantly greater academic gains on standardized tests and grades than 16 control students. Interestingly, while observational and rating measures between treated and control subjects differed significantly at termination, the two groups did not differ on grades or achievement tests at termination of treatment. A major thrust of the consultation program involved a home-based incentive program in which children received special privileges at home based on specific academic and behavioral improvements noted on a daily report card completed by the teacher. A teacher met with the children and their parents three times during the summer after the therapy program to encourage the parents to continue the tutorial work they began during treatment. Such encouragement plus continued parent tutorial effort during the summer after the therapy program and possibly into the next school year may have accounted for the differences in follow-up. Technically, such effects might not be called maintenance effects because grade and achievement tests were not significantly affected at termination of therapy. Nonetheless, the effects provide evidence that a behavioral program emphasizing home-based rewards can have long-range impact.

In a related study with two groups of elementary-school children referred for hyperactivity (Rosenbaum, O'Leary, & Jacob, 1975), a 4-week, daily, school-based reward program significantly decreased teacher-specified problem behavior and teacher ratings of hyperactivity. Both group and individual reward programs for each child's behavior were compared during a 4-week treatment and 4-week follow-up period. Each child was rated four times daily on individually determined target behavior. At the end of the school day, the child exchanged his cards for candy either for himself (individual reward) or for himself plus classmates (group reward). Standardized teacher ratings of hyperativity and weekly ratings of problem behavior were both significantly less in treatment than in baseline, although no differences were found between individual reward and group reward. The treatment effects were maintained during a 1-month follow-up period, but the groups did not differ in their maintenance effects.

H.M. Walker and Buckley (1972) analyzed different methods of reprogramming a child's environment after a 2-month experimental token program. Following the token program in a special class, children were placed in regular classrooms and assigned to one of four groups: (1) In "peer programming" the regular class was taught to support the target child's appropriate behavior and ignore disruptive behavior. Such reprogramming was accomplished by instituting a contingency in which the target child earned rewards such as parties, field trips, and cartoons, for the whole class. (2) The "equating stimulus" condition involved social reinforcement, token reinforcement, and aversive control in the form of a cost procedure and withdrawal from the class. This condition was intended to be as similar as possible to the initial 2-month program, except that the child was in his regular class. (3) "Teacher training" involved instruction in contingency management. (4) In the "control" condition no follow-up consultation was provided for the target child's teacher when he returned to the regular class. Walker and Buckley concluded that the "peer reprogramming" and "equating stimulus" conditions were significantly more effective in maintaining behavior than the no-treatment "control" condition, whereas the "teacher training" and "control" conditions were not significantly different. After reanalyzing their data considering the differential baseline levels of disruptive behavior, however, Cone (1973) questioned the differences among the three environmental reprogramming groups. Nonetheless, this study supports the notion that follow-up efforts are often needed to maintain behavior change. Unfortunately it provides no clear indication that the three types of follow-up efforts were differentially effective. Just as important, in the absence of a control group that neither participated in the original token program nor received any environmental reprogramming, it is not known whether the original token program was necessary to produce the "maintenance effects."

It is not always easy to determine what is behavioral maintenance (O'Leary, S. G., & O'Leary, 1977). For example, can one call behavior maintained if it is assessed in an environment that has been purposely reprogrammed? Can follow-up data from token reinforcement studies be used as evidence for maintenance if the teacher is continuing some aspect of the treatment? To be properly regarded as a maintenance effect, behavior change must be maintained with procedures that can be used readily by the teacher or child without outside assistance.

Treatment effectiveness is often judged by a child's posttreatment behavior, usually designated as follow-up. As Bijou (1974b) aptly remarked, however, follow-up findings "must be attributed to the consequences of the treatment program in interaction with the post-treatment history—unless we still believe in 'fixed' personality traits. A disadvantageous post-treatment history can make the most effective treatment program appear worthless; a favorable post-treatment history can cast a halo over a mediocre or even an inferior program." The essence of Bijou's message is clear: we need to expand our efforts to assess a child's posttreatment environment so that we can recognize when the child's posttreatment environment—not the treatment per se—may require alteration to produce maintenance. Even though we may be able to observe posttreatment environments, at some point our subjects must return to natural, unaltered, environments. Children in our programs will eventually meet teachers who have not been trained to deal with them in comparable ways. And, while we may be able to observe unaltered environments to which our charges move, we should begin to predict whether maintenance can be expected. Similarly, we should be able to begin specifically predicting the likelihood of maintenance in various types of unaltered environments. In making these predictions, the crucial role of environmental determinants of behavior must be recognized; no matter what success is evident in our treatment programs, many children will not continue to succeed without environmental support.

In summary, from a score of studies between 1965 and 1970, it is clear that brief token reinforcement programs did not lead to behavioral maintenance, i.e., extinction occurred (O'Leary, K.D., & Drabman, 1971). On the other hand, evidence is accumulating that token programs can produce maintenance effects when the program is longer than several weeks, when it is gradually withdrawn, when there is a transition from artificial to natural reinforcers after artificial reinforcers are used exclusively, and/or if the child's new environment is reprogrammed to facilitate maintenance. Careful observation of the environment in which maintenance is assessed may give us the kind of perspective needed to decide whether a child should be returned to an unaltered environment or whether environmental alteration is required.

SOCIAL PSYCHOLOGY OF TOKEN REINFORCEMENT PROGRAMS

This section includes topics, such as class atmosphere, attribution theory, and group effects, that have long been the domain of social psychologists. While it is possible to use an operant model to analyze phenomena in social psychology (McGinnies & Ferster, 1971), such efforts have been minimal, and very often such a language gap exists between operant and social psychologists that there is little chance of cross-fertilization between these two disciplines (but see Chapter 7). Thus, this section is couched in the language of social psychology, in the hope that certain phenomena investigated by social psychologists but with relevance to token programs will be evaluated as possible fruitful areas of further inquiry. Equally important, it is essential to review critically analog research in social psychology discussed both in the professional literature and public media (e.g., *Psychology Today*) as having major import for token programs in classrooms.

Group Atmosphere

Unfortunately, no analyses exist of the social atmosphere in which classroom token programs have flourished and been maintained (for an excellent discussion of social factors in an institution for delinquents, see Reppucci and Saunders, 1974). While token reinforcement programs have demonstrable effects in changing both social and academic behavior, a well-executed classroom token program requires considerable effort. Not only are analyses of the specific mutual reinforcement patterns between consultants and teachers necessary, but the more general teaching atmosphere deserves scrutiny; it would be worthwhile to analyze the effects of teacher (peer) support and administrative support for the particular program under investigation. Any special program, whether it be a perceptual training program, a program to teach social skills, or a tutorial program, requires continued administrative endorsement. Without such support one strong parental protest or one school board member's criticism can undo the efforts of a token reinforcement system (see Chapter 16).

Similarly, negative peer and parent attitudes can sabotage even the most valiant efforts to execute a token program. Finally, if some school-based consultative support is not available to teachers, a token program may well be simply a short-term experiment conducted by outsiders that terminates when the grant funds are spent.

Peer versus Teacher Control

An analysis of peer versus parent control has been well exemplified by Phillips, Bailey, and Wolf (1969), who reported on the successful use of an elected managership at Achievement Place, a home-style juvenile rehabilitation center. The most definitive comparison of teacher versus student administration of a classroom-based token program was completed by Drabman (1973). Using the Phillips et al. program as a prototype, Drabman had adolescent students in two psychiatric-hospital school classes elect class captains who administered points in a token program. The effectiveness of the elected captain system was compared with a standard teacher-administered token program in two other classes. The elected captains reduced disruptive behavior as much as the teachers. Following removal of backup reinforcers, when only ratings from the captain or teacher were given, the captain system was slightly more effective in maintaining appropriate behavior. Academic performance increased and cheating decreased through intermittent monitoring of student evaluations by either peers or teachers (Santogrossi, 1974). In sum, peers can be helpful in evaluating and monitoring student behavior in token programs. While the effects of peers and teachers in these regards have been approximately equal, it is too early to specify the conditions under which such effects can be obtained and the type of classroom control that can be transferred to students. In fact C. R. Greenwood, Sloane, and Baskin (1974) found that peer managers sometimes need very special training to dispense social and token reinforcers appropriately.

Group Processes

A variety of token reinforcement programs involve a group or a portion of a group. The common denominator of these group programs is a group consequence, i.e., an event that occurs for all members of the group. Such a consequence usually occurs following a determination of whether the stated contingency has been met by the target subject(s). For example, in an individual contingency-group consequence program (Patterson, G. R., 1965), the target child may have to complete 10 math problems per day to earn a piece of candy for himself and each class member. A group contingency program may require that every member of a class completes an assignment correctly before the class has recess. Many variations of token reinforcement programs involve consequences but do not always require all children to meet a stated contingency. In most programs, however, the class is aware that certain positive consequences (e.g., recess) may depend upon a person

or persons meeting a stated contingency. The knowledge that positive consequences for the class are determined by one or a few members may
prompt class members to pressure the target children to succeed. Unfortunately, we know very little about the nature of such pressure. For example,
do peer threats increase, as was found by Axelrod (1973), in a group contingency program? Can peer reminders to engage in appropriate work be
made in a fashion that is considered helpful and not aversive by the person
being prompted? If group consequence programs result in greater maintenance than individual contingency programs, as G. R. Patterson (1965) and
Rosenbaum et al. (1975) suggest, is such maintenance the result of peer
influence? If group consequence procedures are slightly more effective than
individually scheduled consequences, as several studies suggest (Hamblin,
Hathaway, & Wodarski, 1971; Herman & Tramontana, 1971; Long, J. D., &
Williams, 1973), are such procedures preferred by teachers who can judge
many aspects of the peer-influence process? Do group consequence programs make a target child better liked than if he or she were not in such a
program? Finally, how does the target child feel about being placed in a
group consequence program? In an exemplary study, V. W. Harris and
Sherman (1973) analyzed several components of a reinforcement program
involving groups. They found that division into teams and setting criteria for
winning the game were important variables in reducing disruptive behavior.
Although their study did not measure factors like peer pressure, it and a
study by C. H. Greenwood, Hopps, Delquadri, and Guild (1974) are the
only studies that evaluate systematically components of a program in a group
context. C. H. Greenwood et al. (1974) found that rules and feedback were
somewhat effective in increasing appropriate behavior, but the addition of
group and individual consequences resulted in even higher rates of appropriate behavior.

Attribution Theory Research

A recent burst of research in social psychology concerns the varied
effects of rewards. This research was spurred by the work of deCharms
(1968) and Deci (1971, 1972), who found that rewarding college students
with money for engaging in an "intrinsically interesting task" decreased their
interest in that task in the absence of such rewards. Basically, Deci's procedure consisted of asking college students to solve a number of interesting
puzzles during three experimental periods: (1) a baseline period in which the
subjects were requested to solve puzzles but received no pay following the
puzzle solving; (2) an experimental period in which subjects solved puzzles
and received pay for their participation in the study; and (3) a postexperimental session in which subjects were left alone to do whatever they wished,
including puzzle solving. During this last phase, subjects were observed
through a one-way mirror. A control group experienced all three conditions
but without reward in the experimental period. Deci found that subjects

who had been paid during the second session tended to decrease time spent working on puzzles from the first to third session more than subjects who had not been paid.

This topic was further explored with preschool children as subjects (Lepper & Greene, 1974; Lepper, Greene, & Nisbett, 1973). Those children who were told that they would receive rewards (certificates with a gold seal and ribbon) for engaging in play with magic markers spent less time playing with the magic markers after receiving the reward than those who did not receive it. But children who were not told they would receive a reward and yet received a "surprise" certificate after their play spent significantly more time playing with the magic markers in a posttest assessment than did those who had expected a reward and slightly more time than those who had not received a reward.

Lepper and Greene concluded: "A person's initial intrinsic interest in an activity may be effectively undermined by inducing that person to engage in the activity as an explicit means to some salient extrinsic goal [Lepper & Greene, 1974]." In other words, rewarding a child for engaging in a task may undermine the child's intrinsic interest in that task. Lepper and Greene have been cautious in their extrapolations to behavioral intervention programs, but others more hastily cite these data as having direct relevance for behavior modification research in the classroom. Levine and Fasnacht (1974) used the Deci and Lepper work as their springboard for criticizing the use of rewards in classroom management programs. They stated: "In our haste to demonstrate that learning can be increased, productivity raised, and manners improved, operantly oriented therapists may, in the long run, be decreasing the frequency of the very behaviors we wish to increase [p. 818]." A distinction between intrinsic and extrinsic motivation underlies the Deci and Lepper investigations. They used intrinsic motivation to refer to engaging in an activity for its own sake (in the absence of apparent external reward) and extrinsic motivation to refer to engaging in an activity to obtain a reward. Deci had hypothesized that those who earn rewards for engaging in formerly intrinsically motivated task will attribute the cause of their behavior to external factors (rewards) rather than internal factors ("I do this because I like it"). It was predicted that intrinsic motivation decreases when rewards are no longer available and thus children engage in the activity less often. Levine and Fasnacht failed to mention that a behavior intervention would be unnecessary if the child was already intrinsically motivated and engaged in the task at a high frequency. Behavior researchers rarely establish a token reinforcement program for children who already do their homework proficiently or behave well in the classroom. Rather, such programs are established for children who fail to do their homework or exhibit high rates of disruptive behavior in the classroom.

In addition to the inappropriate generalization from social psychology research to the problems addressed by behavior researchers who face children without high interest in their tasks, a second major analog problem is discussed by Reiss and Sushinsky (1975). They argue that criticisms of token reinforcement programs are inappropriately based on studies in which subjects expect rewards but in which rewards are not contingent upon their behavior across a series of days. Both Lepper's and Deci's studies were also based on a single trial rather than the usual multiple-trial procedures that characterize most operant research. Reiss and Sushinsky replicated previous findings that noncontingent, expected reward decreases interest in a task while also showing that a contingent multiple-trial procedure increases interest in the task. Furthermore, as mentioned previously, Felixbrod and O'Leary (1973, 1974) found that children who receive contingent rewards for correctly solved mathematics problems spend more time in mathematics activities after the rewards are discontinued than children who did not receive rewards. The most salient data contradicting the notion that a child rewarded for academic behavior later will spend less time engaging in that behavior have been obtained in the Behavior Analysis Follow-Through project (Chapter 15). Children who have graduated from this program involving a token reinforcement regime in grades 1-3 show greater academic achievement in grade 4 than their peers who were not in the program. More important, the gains of the Follow-Through children in grade 3 relative to the non-Follow-Through children were magnified in grade 4 when token programs were not in effect,[4] and when, according to Levine and Fasnacht, academic gain should have slowed considerably or even ceased.

OPERANT PSYCHOLOGY OF TOKEN REINFORCEMENT PROGRAMS

Scheduling Effects

Schedules of reinforcement have been a major hallmark of operant animal psychology (Ferster & Skinner, 1957). When barpressing is the dependent variable, patterns of human responding often resemble those of infrahumans. For example, a fixed-ratio schedule produces pauses after reinforcement followed by high terminal rates of responding. Variable-ratio and variable-interval schedules have similar effects on children and infrahumans: Variable-ratio schedules produce steady high rates of responding, while variable-interval schedules produce steady but lower rates. In contrast, simple fixed-interval schedules of reinforcement with humans do not always mimic schedule patterns of scalloping and pauses after reinforcement shown by rats (Long, E.R., Hammack, May, & Campbell, 1958; Orlando & Bijou, 1960; Weiner, 1969). Certain factors, however, will make it more likely that

4. Personal communication, Ann Ramsey, Behavior-Analysis Follow-Through, Lawrence, Kansas, October, 1974.

human responding maintained by fixed-interval schedules will resemble that of rats and pigeons: the availability of alternative reinforcement schedules (Poppen, 1972), histories of reinforcement for low rates of responding (Weiner, 1972), and response cost for high rates of responding (Weiner, 1972).

Although some similarities exist between humans and infrahumans in schedule control in laboratory studies, no direct extrapolation can be made from schedule control evidenced in an automated experimental chamber to a classroom setting because contingency operations in a classroom are usually far too complex and interdependent to meet classic scheduling definitions. For example, under a fixed-interval schedule, reinforcement is contingent upon the first response after a fixed interval of time has passed after a previous reinforcement. Responses before that time has passed are not reinforced. An example of a fixed-interval schedule in a token program was given by Sulzer and Mayer (1972), who described a teacher setting a timer for 5-min intervals and giving the child a token if the child were reading just after the timer rang. Obtaining the control necessary to analyze scheduling phenomena like the fixed-interval schedule just described is extremely difficult. Instead of interrupting the teaching pattern precisely every 5 min, the teacher may prefer to reinforce the child's reading at the end of a lesson that may vary from 15-30 min. If the teacher wished to reinforce every class member's reading on a fixed-interval schedule, observation of all children just after the timer rang would be required. Examples of the application of scheduling principles in applied settings are extremely difficult to find. Even Sulzer and Mayer's procedure does not accurately replicate fixed-interval scheduling as described by Ferster and Skinner (1957), because the reinforcer was not contingent upon the child's first response at any time after the 5-min interval; rather it depended on whether the child was working at exactly the end of the 5-min interval.

Even though strict analogs of experimental procedures cannot be conducted in a classroom, contingent reinforcement is clearly more effective than noncontingent reinforcement (Bushell et al., 1968). More important, since 1971, scheduling phenomena have been evaluated in several studies. McLaughlin and Malaby (1972) found suggestive evidence that a variable 4-day exchange of tokens for backup reinforcers was more effective than a fixed 5-day exchange. Unfortunately their design was confounded by an order effect, because the variable schedule occurred after the fixed schedule and the mean number of days between exchange in the variable condition was lower (4 days) than in the fixed-exchange condition (5 days). In a replication McLaughlin and Malaby (1975) kept the number of days between exchanges equal in the fixed and variable condition, but found only minimally suggestive evidence that a variable-exchange procedure produced more assignment completion than a fixed-exchange procedure.

Despite the apparent reliability of scheduling effects in the laboratory, few reinforcement schedules in the natural environment have been investigated parametrically. Fading of reinforcers is a very common practice, but its efficacy has not been compared to abrupt removal of reinforcers. Similarly, variable versus fixed schedules of reinforcement and assessment of the students' attitudes toward the classroom under various schedules of reinforcement await investigation. Furthermore, there have been no analyses of natural reinforcement schedules in classrooms or of the interaction between such schedules and stimulus control variables. Finally certain practical issues related to schedule control clearly deserve attention. For example, if children can obtain access to certain activities (e.g., playing on a climbing apparatus) after completing 15 math problems, it would be useful to know how long the children can spend on the climbing apparatus before such time spent playing interferes with academic productivity. Similarly, are there certain reinforcing activities (e.g., running around the room) that lead to more classroom disruption than if children had no opportunity to engage in them? Do evaluative reports or report cards have different impacts if they are given on a basis other than the usual four or five fixed times per year?

Reinforcing Teacher Behavior

One of the most interesting recent studies of classroom behavioral procedures involved a nontoken study that bears on all classroom management studies. Cossairt, Hall, and Hopkins (1973) used instructions, feedback, and feedback plus praise to three teachers for their appropriate use of praise in the classroom. In the instruction-only condition, teachers were instructed to praise students who attended to the teachers' instructions, and the teachers' instructions were then followed with a reminder that, "teacher praise for attending to instructions sometimes increases instruction-attending behavior." In the feedback condition the teachers were told how many praise comments they had made and how often the students attended to their instructions. The feedback and praise condition was composed of the same type of feedback plus intermittent praise from the experimenter. While instructions and feedback produced some increase in the teachers' praising of students, adding experimenter praise to instructions and feedback increased teachers' praising sharply. Concomitantly, in each of these conditions the children's appropriate behavior increased. The implication is clear. If consultants wish to change teacher behavior, they must practice what they preach. That is, to increase "appropriate" student behavior, the teachers must increase their praise for it, *and* the consultant must provide feedback and praise to teachers to maintain or increase their appropriate behavior.

Secondary Reinforcement

Conditioned or secondary reinforcement usually occupies a prominent place in operant conditioning texts (e.g., Reynolds, 1968). A conditioned or secondary reinforcer is a stimulus that is originally neutral but becomes a reinforcer because of its association with an unconditioned (primary) reinforcer or another conditioned reinforcer. For example, a word like "good" is initially meaningless to an infant, but after repeated pairings of the word "good" with pleasant events, such as hugs and eating candy, "good" becomes a word that may reinforce a variety of child behavior. Investigators have assumed that a teacher's positive comments to a child become reinforcing if they are paired with token and backup reinforcers. Although the teacher's positive comments in a token reinforcement program usually are not paired directly with a primary reinforcer, such as food, his or her comments are often paired with the presentation of a token (conditioned) reinforcer. But the assumption that pairing a teacher's praise with token and backup reinforcers increases the reinforcement value of praise over baseline levels has not been tested. Studies with "unresponsive" adult psychiatric patients (Stahl, Thomson, Leitenberg, & Hasazi, 1974) and autistic children (Lovaas, Freitag, Kinder, Rubenstein, Schaeffer, & Simmons, 1966) suggest that social stimuli such as the word "good" can acquire reinforcing properties by being paired with food. Presumably, reinforcing properties can be established more easily by pairing verbal stimuli with primary reinforcers than by pairing verbal stimuli with token reinforcers. Nonetheless, it is certainly theoretically possible that the usual pairing process in a token program could establish the teacher's verbal statements as conditioned (secondary) reinforcers.

Response Cost

The subtraction of previously earned tokens contingent upon particular behavior is known as response cost. As the name implies, certain undesired responses *cost* the individual tokens; more loosely, response cost is seen as loss of points or penalties. As indicated earlier, such response cost was used in nineteenth-century New York. The loss-of-point procedure was called fining and was used to avoid corporal punishment (Ravitch, 1974). For various reasons, however, both the token reinforcement programs and corporal punishment were eliminated later in the nineteenth century. The widespread use of token reinforcement programs is clearly a relatively recent phenomena, and most classroom token reinforcement programs of the past decade were limited to reinforcing good behavior. The general avoidance of cost procedures was probably influenced by Skinner's dictum that punishment only suppresses behavior and very often leads to undesirable side effects. In 1953 Skinner said, "In the long run, punishment, unlike reinforcement, works to the disadvantage of both the punished organism and the punishing agency [1953a, p. 183]." Despite the fact that laboratory evidence with animals indicated that punishment was effective and did not always involve side effects (Azrin & Holz, 1966; Solomon, 1964), investigators generally avoided punishment procedures in token programs. As Ayllon and Azrin (1968) noted, "The rationale for avoiding these noxious events was perhaps based more on ethical and moral considerations than on considerations of probable efficacy [p. 25]." The lack of practical means of coping with aggression and property damage probably prompted investigators working with adolescents to begin to use response cost procedures (Burchard, 1967; Phillips, E.L., 1968).

Kaufman and O'Leary (1972) compared reward alone with a cost program for hospitalized adolescent psychiatric patients in 2-hr-long after-school remedial reading classes. In the cost condition each of eight students received 10 poker chips that were placed in a jar at the beginning of every 15-min period. At the end of each 15-min period the students could lose tokens if they had not behaved well and worked hard. In the reward class the eight students began each 15-min period with no tokens, but at the end of the period they could earn from 1 to 10 tokens depending upon the teacher's evaluation of their behavior. The programs dramatically reduced disruptive behavior and were associated with gains in academic achievement but were not differentially effective. Bucher and Hawkins (1973) also found that reward and cost programs were equally effective for four academic under-achievers, and Iwata and Bailey (1974) found them equally effective with two groups ($n = 3$) of special-education students. Interestingly, neither Kaufman and O'Leary (1972) nor Bucher and Hawkins (1973) found differences between levels of disruptive behavior in the reward versus cost program in the intervals immediately following the addition or subtraction of points. Despite the absence of reward versus cost differences, both studies warn that a cost procedure may prompt a teacher to look for bad rather than good behavior and thus could inadvertently lead to increased use of threats, criticism, and reprimands. "In addition, timing of the subtraction of tokens may be critical. If a ward attendant or teacher took tokens away from adolescents *immediately* upon completion of the undesired behavior, more disruption might ensue than if the administration of point consequences occurred at fixed time intervals. For example, if tokens were taken away from an angry adolescent just after he was in a verbal battle with a classmate, the adolescent might be more likely to curse the teacher than if the token removal occurred 10 minutes after the altercation [O'Leary, S.G., & O'Leary, 1977, p. 487]." Another important factor in reward versus cost programs is whether or not the tokens subtracted were initially given freely or earned contingently (Iwata & Bailey, 1974). No classroom program has yet evaluted a response cost system in which the tokens removed were initially earned.

Many current token programs combine reward and cost factors with costs levied for a few types of very disruptive behavior, e.g., carrying knives and fighting. As exemplified by McLaughlin and Malaby (1972) and Kaufman (1971), when cost factors are a significant or even the sole consequence for behavior, the students evaluate the token program positively. Although the cost program developed by Kaufman (1971) and Kaufman and O'Leary (1972) functioned as a punishment procedure, it was *interpreted* by the students as if it were a reward program; when the students in the cost class were asked to describe the rules of their program to an independent evaluator, they said, "You lost some points if you misbehave—like you lose two points if you smoke, and you then get eight points to buy things at the store after dinner." These student evaluations point to the importance of the students' *perception* of a program. In this situation a response cost program that functioned as a punishment procedure was definitely interpreted as a positive rewarding intervention.

NEW DIRECTIONS AND APPLICATIONS

Teaching Self-Control

Regardless of theoretical orientation, it is generally agreed that a major goal of education is to teach self-management or self-control skills. Behavioral studies initially relied almost exclusively on external control of behavior by a change agent, such as a parent or a teacher. Faced with the problem of lack of maintenance and generalization, however, a number of investigators began to speculate that teaching self-management might increase the long-term effectiveness of treatment. Equally important, practicing clinical and educational psychologists found it frequently difficult to monitor children's or adolescents' behavior. For example, obtaining teacher evaluations of the behavior of a junior high-school student who has seven different teachers is sometimes impossible and at best is a cumbersome problem. Spurred by the problems facing the practicing clinician and the absence of generalization and maintenance, researchers began to investigate self-control procedures in clinical intervention. Self-control here refers to behavior initiated by the individual in the relative absence of external constraints (Thoresen & Mahoney, 1974).

Setting a Standard. It is common to hear teachers and parents approve of teaching children to set their own goals and standards. While the author shares that value, current research provides little evidence that self-determined standards operate differently from externally determined standards. In a series of three studies Felixbrod and O'Leary investigated the issue of externally determined versus self-determined standards (Felixbrod, 1974; Felixbrod & O'Leary, 1973, 1974). Children in one contingent reinforcement condition determined their own academic performance standards; in a second contingent reinforcement condition the same performance standards were externally imposed upon children whose performance standards were yoked to subjects in the first condition. Children in a nonreinforcement control condition performed in the absence of external reward. Points for correct answers were exchangeable for prizes at the end of the session. These studies and that of Glynn (1970) showed no difference between the two reward conditions in terms of time spent at the task or correct solutions during reward (acquisition) or extinction. Both the externally determined and self-determined reward subjects, however, had more correct solutions and spent more time at the task than did control subjects. While some unknown methodological problem may have precluded obtaining differences between externally imposed and self-imposed standards, with the exception of Lovitt and Curtiss (1969) other investigators generally have not obtained externally imposed and self-imposed differences (Bandura & Perloff, 1967).

In retrospect, it may be erroneous to think that behavior under *positive* control should be different when the contingencies (either externally determined or self-determined) are *identical*. It may, as an alternative, be more fruitful to pursue the explicit teaching of standard setting to establish generalized patterns that prompt varied classroom behavior in children. As children grow up, most parents hope that their child will independently set goals or standards for him- or herself. Parents and teachers also wish to avoid incessantly prompting or nagging a child to study or to complete his or her chores. Price and O'Leary (1974) found that arranging intermittent reinforcement for setting high standards resulted in high standards set by the children themselves. It is repeatedly found that children adopt performance standards modeled by adults in laboratory settings (Bandura, 1969a; Lepper, Sagotsky, & Mailer, 1975). It should be possible to combine modeling and direct reinforcement to teach children the kind of standard setting that could facilitate academic productivity as well as decreased dependence on adult supervision and direction in a classroom. It also should be noted that standard-setting studies have generally involved procedures in which an individual child sets a standard that is communicated to an investigator. Having children set their standards in a group might well result in greater productivity than if identical standards were imposed upon them. Variables such as public commitment, peer prompting, peer reinforcement, and competition would likely operate in favor of self-determined standard setting in a group context.

Self-Evaluation. Given the encouraging results of teaching self-evaluation to adolescents in psychiatric-hospital schools (Kaufman & O'Leary, 1972; Santogrossi, O'Leary, Romanczyk, & Kaufman, 1973), the teaching of self-evaluation in token reinforcement programs appears promising. For example, after reducing disruptive behavior in a standard teacher-administered token program, Drabman et al. (1973), following the suggestion of Santogrossi et al. (1973), taught children with severe behavior problems to evaluate their own behavior according to performance standards for academic and social behavior established by the teacher. If they evaluated their behavior in general or exact accord with the teacher's judgments, they earned bonus points in the token reinforcement program. To encourage as much student autonomy as possible and to reduce the necessity of constant teacher evaluation, the teacher gradually faded her checking of the students' self-ratings. In the final phase of treatment, the students evaluated their own behavior in the absence of teacher checking and continued to receive reinforcers awarded on the basis of their own evaluation. A control (nontoken) period assessed whether generalization to a period with no token or backup reinforcers occurred. This control period was randomly designated as one of four 15-min periods during the hour-long after-school remedial class. The results indicated that generalization to nontoken periods occurred and that the children continued to behave well when the teachers discontinued checking the students' behavior.

These results were replicated and extended by Turkewitz et al. (1975) who used a similar design to assess generalization but in addition assessed maintenance of appropriate behavior following removal of backup reinforcers and generalization to the regular classroom setting. While generalization and maintenance of appropriate classroom behavior were evident during the after-school class, appropriate behavior did not generalize to the students' regular class. The lack of generalization to the regular class underscores the need to teach children to use self-evaluation in a variety of settings, and not only the one in which the skill is taught. Such prompting coupled with some reinforcement from the regular classroom teacher during the initial stages of such a self-control program may be necessary to obtain generalization.

It should be emphasized that children and adolescents can readily evaluate their behavior in accord with teacher judgments (Drabman et al., 1973; Santogrossi et al., 1973; Turkewitz et al., 1975). Self-evaluation per se, however, was not effective in reducing disruptive behavior (Santogrossi et al., 1973; Turkewitz et al., 1975). Only after self-evaluation was used within a token program was self-evaluation alone associated with low rates of disruptive behavior.

The Token Economy as a Teaching Vehicle

Mr. Martin, a teacher in a local school district, gave a normal fifth-grade class a set of bottle caps that they used as legal tender while studying taxation. A king was overthrown; a new set of tax laws was established; and problems of inflation, supply and demand, and recession became rampant (Krasner & Krasner, 1973). The program was described as follows:

The behavior of the children was determined by the shifting directions of the economy as it progressed from a system of slavery to capitalism and then to socialism. The initial goal of this program, as determined by the teacher, was for the children to learn about and be more appreciative of historical and economic processes by reproducing them, to some extent, via the concept of a token economy. The children learned that prices and wages have a strong influence upon their behavior. The children then were able to control the program by introducing new and increasingly more complex relationships between "prices" and "wages" in much the same manner as in the world outside the classroom. This was evidenced by the spontaneous development of a welfare program to take care of those who didn't earn enough tokens to function in the economy. As a result of this program a considerable sophistication in economic functioning and human behavior developed on the part of the children [pp. 367-368].

A token economy thus may be used not only as a remediation procedure but also as a method of teaching in which one experiences economic changes brought about by fiat, vote, or a student economic planning board. With the classroom viewed as a microcosm of a nation, junior high- or even elementary-school students can probably learn and retain more principles of economics than they would from an introductory college economics course. The interaction between political, economic, and psychological principles could also be experienced and evaluated in a token economy in a regular classroom. For example, students' attitudes toward one another and feelings of competition and cooperation could easily be assessed in a social science unit in which a token economy serves as a major teaching vehicle.

Transmission of Interpersonal Influence Tactics

While some theorists have asserted that teachers and parents provide models of behavioral control for their children, there is little direct evidence that children adopt the disciplinary or control procedures that they themselves have experienced (Gelfand, Hartmann, Lamb, Smith, Mahon, & Paul, 1974). Nonetheless, there has been ambivalence toward token programs because of the concern that children will attempt to influence others by the use of material rewards and punishers (O'Leary, K.D., Poulos, & Devine, 1972). Gelfand et al. (1974) found that if 6 to 7-yr-old children are exposed to a marble dropping game in which an adult interacted with them using rewards and fines or acted nonresponsively, the children used similar teaching methods when playing with another child. Interestingly, children exposed to the unresponsive adult generally gave few consequences of any kind, but of those given, most were rewarding. In three different studies, children did not naturally impose aversive consequences on another child but did so after experiencing aversive consequences from adults. In brief such data should give one pause when building token programs that emphasize cost procedures, lest children or teenagers be unwittingly taught to control their peers by punishment. Fortunately these young children naturally had a positive and help-giving orientation toward the peer learner. Instructional efforts in the classroom should promote such a positive orientation. Children clearly attempt to influence one another in all avenues of endeavor, e.g., on the ball field, in the classroom, and in street-corner conversations. If the positive interpersonal influence in these situations can be encouraged, we can probably enhance the children's well-being. Thus, if as a function of exposure to a token program children occasionally adopt a strategy of offering a peer a material reward for helping them, such a change tactic is probably a better influence procedure than the coercive tactics they may currently use.

Choosing Novel Target Behavior

Choosing target behavior, i.e., the behavior to be changed, is an extremely complex problem that is not idiosyncratic to token programs. The choice of target behavior in token programs is especially important, however, because it now appears that almost any prosocial or academic behavior can be significantly altered with a token program. Winett and Winkler (1972) and K.D. O'Leary (1972) discussed the types of behavior most frequently changed in token programs and emphasized that behavior researchers should seriously question the changes they are being asked to make. Proponents can be found to support almost any change process imaginable, but as an anonymous reviewer of Winett and Winkler (1972) and K.D. O'Leary (1972) aptly noted, whether attending behavior or sitting in one's seat is later functional for a student is an empirical question. As indicated in the discussion of generalization, researchers have just begun analyzing the empirical relation among responses that occurs when one changes only certain responses. Furthermore, school-community dialogues regarding the types of skills, ideals, and affective experiences desired for our children are definitely needed. In fact in the author's community, Stony Brook, considerable useful dialogue is beginning among community members, the school board, and teachers regarding the types of classroom structure parents desire for their students. Such a dialogue has resulted in three choices of elementary classroom environments, and fortunately the system is designed so that almost all parents get their first choice. Unfortunately, in the absence of data regarding how one can reliably produce certain behavior in children, most individuals simply advocate the system most familiar to them and/or the one most compatible with their *present* educational philosophy.

Initially, classroom token reinforcement programs focused on changing prosocial behavior such as attending, being in seat, and raising one's hand, or academic products such as number correct, number completed, and quality of handwriting. It has now been shown that creative behavior can be changed. In one token program creative writing was increased (Brigham et al., 1972). In another creativity, as assessed by generating unusual uses for common items, was increased (LaGreca & Santogrossi, 1975). In another short stories were judged more creative when tokens were contingent on the students' use of different adjectives, verbs, and sentence beginnings (Maloney, K.B., & Hopkins, 1973). These studies have only begun the critical task of developing practical measures of the creativity that could be revealed in a classroom, and as yet almost no practical measures of creativity have been used at the high-school level. Nonetheless, they are important forays into areas largely ignored by behavioral psychologists.

Critical social problems such as racial tensions and hatred toward ethnic groups have received little attention from behavioral researchers. Hauserman, Walen, and Behling (1973) successfully used a token reinforcement program to promote integrated play in a first-grade class of five black and 20 white children. Reinforcing sitting with a new friend in a lunchroom led to playing together in the classroom. The authors noted that many people assume that social integration must begin first with an attitude change, which will then produce some generalized positive behavior change. Their data suggest that such assumptions about attitudes are unnecessary, at least with young children, but unfortunately no attitudinal or sociometric ratings were obtained in this study.

Choosing Educational Reinforcers

Free-time activities instead of material rewards are clearly increasing in token programs (O'Leary, S.G., & O'Leary, 1977), and studies have used academic activities as rewards for classroom performance (Brooks, R.B., & Snow, 1972; Cohen, H.L., & Filipczak, 1971; Levenkron, Santogrossi, & O'Leary, 1974). In these studies, however, the reinforcing effect of the academic activity was confounded with other free-time activities, monetary rewards, and/or other potential reinforcers, such as the opportunity to talk to a tutor. Taffel and O'Leary (1977) demonstrated the practicality of using special academic activities to reinforce academic performance. Basically, interesting math activities were used as reinforcers for completion of computational math problems. In practice it would be hoped that if such academic incentives were used to reinforce arithmetic behavior in classrooms for extended periods, the child would learn not only from the computational practice but also from the reinforcement period in which he or she engaged in novel math activities and games. Most important, there would be no need to withdraw such academic reinforcers; they would become an integral and lasting part of the learning environment.

SUMMARY

In 1971, K.D. O'Leary and Drabman stated that token reinforcement procedures have "demonstrated effectiveness in changing the academic and social behavior of very diverse child populations." Evidence supporting that statement continues to mount rapidly. Generalization across situations and across classes of behavior and maintenance of behavior after removal of token programs have been addressed, and some evidence has been presented that generalization and maintenance do occur. At present, however, the variables critical for producing generalization and maintenance are not clear. Reinforcing academic behavior appears to produce strong generalization to prosocial classroom behavior, whereas reinforcing prosocial classroom behavior alone produces only moderate (if any) generalization to academic behavior. Given current evidence, it is probably most desirable to reinforce *both* academic and prosocial classroom behavior, with an emphasis on the former. Generalization and maintenance occurred in studies in which various self-control strategies were taught, and self-evaluation combined with intermittent teacher checking offers considerable promise. Variables within the social psychology literature, such as group processes and peer influence, are seen as having as much import for token programs as operant principles of scheduling and secondary reinforcement. The choice of target behavior requires careful consideration, and a review of studies in which creativity and racical integration have been changed reflects researchers' attempts to alter more challenging and possibly more important behavior.

DON F. HAKE and DENNIS OLVERA[1]

Chapter 7

Cooperation, Competition, and Related Social Phenomena

"If people could only get along with each other " has been and is a common lament. To make matters worse, some things that could have been counted on to produce "getting-along behavior" just a few years ago—traditions, customs, religious practices and laws—are no longer as effective as they used to be. Zajonc (1966) suggested that these conditions, plus the realization that a science of social behavior promises new ways of predicting, understanding, and controlling how people get along, are responsible for the recent and rapid growth of social psychology. Without the discovery and dissemination of such knowledge by social psychologists, our bumper sticker—"Cooperate Now"—will probably not be very effective.

Although research in social psychology has provided great amounts of information, in many instances the clear and crisp answers required to solve even the simplest social problems have not been provided. One factor that may dampen the impact of social psychology is the seemingly diffuse nature of the effort within the field. Even subareas such as cooperation contain a vast array of procedures, effects, and approaches that differ so greatly it is surprising all of them are considered under the same topic. Social psychologists have also commented on this diffuseness. For example, "Let There Be Order, Please" was the title of a review of a new social psychology book that attempted to use a few basic principles to organize the area of

1. Work on this chapter began in 1973 while both authors were at Anna State Hospital and Southern Illinois University. The chapter was completed while Hake was at the Regional Institute for Children and Adolescents—Baltimore and Olvera was at the W. A. Howe Developmental Center, Tinley Park, Ill. Hake is now at West Virginia University. Thanks are due Dr. Ron Vukelich for his help during the initial planning phase.

social psychology. The reviewer stated, "Always a broad, heterogeneous, and somewhat disjointed subdiscipline . . . social psychology has become almost unmanageably complex . . . materials summarized by a single chapter are sometimes so varied and diffuse that they tax the human brain [Steiner, 1973, p. 14]."

Part of the diffuseness can be attributed to the fact that social psychology draws from a wide variety of analytical systems. In our opinion, however, a more important factor is the failure of research in social psychology always to produce precise definitions of the basic contingencies, principles, and phenomena. The importance attached to finding solutions to pressing social problems, such as racial conflict and television violence, has diverted attention from precise definition of the basic elements. The precise and consistent definition of basic elements is a prerequisite for the precise and consistent definition of more complicated phenomena. Hence, it is not surprising that the field appears diffuse.

Another approach to social psychology precisely defines basic principles by starting with the study of the behavior of the individual laboratory animal in simple, highly controlled situations. The basic principles for individual animals are then used to explain everyday human behavior, including social behavior. In this strategy the definitions are precise and consistent, but the drawbacks are the obvious differences between animals and humans and their situations, which make tenuous a direct translation of "single-animal" procedures to "human" or "human social" situations. The recent success in behavior analysis attests to the accuracy of the basic principles in applications to humans and human social problems. However, only some of the basic principles from animal research appear useful, and even these frequently have to be modified to fit the human situation.

Homans (1969) suggests the obvious solution in his criticism of the above approach: "One would have thought that a better strategy would have been to extend behavioral principles systematically to show their implications in the simpler social situations, such as interaction in small groups [p. 23]." This was, of course, the research strategy of Ogden Lindsley, who studied human behavior in controlled individual (Lindsley, 1964) and two-person situations (Lindsley, 1966) that allowed precise definition of contingencies and behavior. Some investigators followed the lead of Lindsley, but relative to the number working at the extremes (e.g., basic animal research or complicated social research), they are few.

The purpose of this chapter is to start with a human social situation that allows precise definitions. The definition of the most basic and common contingencies by which reinforcers are distributed in a controlled, two-person social situation hopefully will provide a sound basis for the analysis of cooperation and related social phenomena. Consistent with our emphasis upon the precise definition of basic human social behavior, the first question is not the common one indicated earlier, i.e., "What can we do to produce cooperation?"; rather it is, "What is cooperative behavior?"

DEFINITION OF COOPERATION

Minimal and Maximal Cooperation

A cooperative response is similar to nonsocial operant responses in that the delivery of a reinforcer depends on a response. It differs from nonsocial operants in that the reinforcer is delivered to another person. A cooperative response may also produce a reinforcer for the person making the response, but the defining characteristic is that it produces, either completely or partially, a reinforcer for someone else. Hence, if cooperative responses and nonsocial responses are differentiated in terms of the reinforcer's recipient, cooperative responses may be designated as "giving" responses and individual responses as "taking" responses. Altruism is another well-known social effect that involves giving responses and, for this reason, can be confused with cooperation.

The demonstration of a cooperation effect requires an increase in giving responses. A cooperation effect may be differentiated from an altruism effect by whether the responses of only one or of both persons increase: In pure altruism the giving responses of only one person increase, while in cooperation the giving responses of both persons increase. The cooperation contingency, therefore, must allow the reinforcers of both persons, not just one, to be at least in part dependent upon the responses of the other person.

As with nonsocial reinforcement contingencies, a cooperation effect requires the responses designated as cooperative to be under the control of the cooperation contingency rather than of some other contingency. One aspect of a cooperation contingency that could control responding is the reciprocal nature of the response-reinforcer dependency. The fact that the cooperative responses of both subjects increase, a requirement for any cooperation effect, usually indicates at least partial control by the reciprocal-reinforcement aspect of the cooperation contingency. Assuming that the cooperation contingency is the same or equal for each member of a pair, however, complete control by reciprocal reinforcement in cooperation means that the number of giving responses or the number of reinforcers of the two persons must be balanced or equal. Conversely, divergence of the reinforcers from equality indicates the extent to which cooperative responding is not completely under the control of the reciprocal-reinforcement dependency. The demonstration of control by reciprocal reinforcement requires both (1) an increase in giving responses for both persons and (2) an increase in the correspondence between the number of reinforcers and/or the number of giving responses of the two persons relative to a noncooperative control procedure or to the start of the cooperation contingency (Hake & Vukelich, 1973; Hake, Vukelich, & Olvera, 1975). If cooperation is to be considered a social response, correspondence should be calculated as the percent of one person's reinforcers or cooperative responses relative to the other person's, rather than relative to total trials or opportunities for cooperation (Hake et al., 1975). Simply, if cooperative behavior is social behavior, it should be under the control of the behavior of the other member of the pair (Keller and Schoenfeld, 1950). An increase in correspondence argues against control by altruism or by any other contingency that would produce a difference in the reinforcers delivered to each person. The mere increase in cooperative responses has been designated as the *minimal cooperation effect*, while the minimal effect plus increased correspondence has been designated as the *maximal cooperation effect* (Hake et al., 1975). Because both minimal and maximal effects result from the cooperation contingency, maximal cooperation is on the same dimension as minimal cooperation but is an extention of it or is simply an advanced type of cooperation.

In maximal cooperation, correspondence may increase in the distribution of reinforcers, responses, or both because equality may be possible on only one dimension if the distributions of reinforcers and responses can differ (e.g., if single responses can produce variable magnitudes of reinforcement). Except under unusual circumstances (e.g., a large and aversive response requirement) the reinforcement dimension would probably exert the most control.

Demonstration of maximal cooperation requires a cooperation contingency that allows deviations from equality as well as the possibility of reaching equality. Simply, if the procedure does not allow deviations from equality, correspondence between each person's reinforcers cannot increase. Hence, maximal cooperation cannot be assessed in the many cooperation procedures that either do not allow deviations from equality or allow deviations so small that no increase in correspondence can be demonstrated. Examples of the latter include Weingold and Webster (1964) and Hingten, Sanders, and DeMyer (1965), which required subjects to alternate single cooperative responses, thereby severely limiting deviations from equality.

Applied Advantages of Maximal Cooperation

From an applied point of view, minimal cooperation would seem the first step in shaping cooperation, but maximal cooperation would seem the ultimate goal. Maximal cooperation is more desirable than minimal cooperation for two major reasons. First, if the objective is to teach cooperation, maximal cooperation indicates a more complete learning of the cooperation contingency. Second, if the objective is to maintain cooperation, maximal cooperation is a more stable solution. When both persons provide reinforcers at about the same rate, the rate of reinforcement for each person will be more appropriate to the rate of cooperative responses than if there is a large deviation from correspondence, which ordinarily means that the person with the highest rate of response will receive the lowest rate of reinforcement. This latter point was nicely demonstrated by Boren's (1966) study in which each of two monkeys' daily food rations were completely dependent upon the cooperative responses of the other monkey. When the response rate of one monkey dropped very low relative to the rate of its coactor (the other monkey engaged in the same task), the coactor's responses were not reinforced sufficiently often to maintain their high rate. The cooperative responses of both monkeys eventually dropped to low levels that did not even produce a maintenance diet.

Examples of Minimal and Maximal Cooperation

Hake and Vukelich (1973) demonstrated both minimal and maximal effects with retardates who cooperated to work matching-to-sample problems. That study will be described in detail here because aspects will be used later to illustrate the basic dimensions of the cooperation situation.

For each person, reinforcers (money) depended upon correctly selecting the stimulus that matched a sample. Completing these problems required responses on each of two panels: (1) a matching panel for selecting the matching stimulus and (2) a sample panel for producing the sample stimulus. Figure 7-1 diagrams the matching-to-sample apparatus of each subject. The two subjects' matching panels were 6 m apart, but each subject's sample panel could be placed at different distances from his matching panel. For

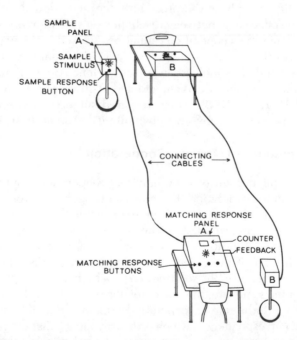

Fig. 7-1. Diagram of the matching-to-sample apparatus of each subject. Apparatus labeled A belongs to one subject and apparatus labeled B belongs to the other subject. (From Hake & Vukelich, 1973.)

each subject, either his own or his coactor's sample panel could be nearest his matching panel, so that less walking was required to reach one sample panel than to reach the other. Subjects could work either individually or cooperatively. If a subject worked individually, he first depressed his own sample-response button, which presented a red, green, or yellow sample stimulus for 1 sec on his sample panel. If he then pressed the button of the same color on his own matching panel, the response was reinforced. If his sample panel was at some distance from his matching panel, as in Figure 7-1, he had to get up from his seat and walk to his sample panel to produce his sample stimulus. When a subject worked cooperatively, he produced the sample stimulus for his coactor, who could remain seated and make the matching response. The subject then matched his own sample stimulus when his coactor produced it for him.

Initially, each subject's sample panel was next to his own matching panel, and he could produce his own sample stimulus and make his matching response while remaining seated. Figure 7-2 shows the individual (closed triangles) and cooperative (open circles) responses of each subject for each session as a function of the distance of the subject's sample panel from his matching panel. Each subject responded individually when his sample panel was next to his matching panel, and as it was gradually moved successively one quarter (1.5 m), one half (3 m), and three quarters (4.5 m) of the distance to his coactor's matching panel. But when each subject's sample panel was 6 m away from his own matching panel and next to his coactor's matching panel, as in Figure 7-1, cooperation emerged: Cooperative responses increased within the first or second session at this distance for four pairs, Subjects 1-8. The other two subjects did not cooperate in 15 sessions at the 6-m distance, and either never learned to cooperate (Subject 10), or cooperated (Subject 9) only after training with one of the other subjects. The cooperative pairs are those of interest for what follows. For these four pairs the minimal cooperation effect occurred throughout the sessions at 6 m and the subsequent sessions at 4.5 m. Most of the pairs returned to individual responding when their sample panels were at 3 m, and all returned to individual responding when their sample panels were again placed next to their matching panels. Subjects simply selected whichever solution involved the least amount of walking.

Because there were distances of the sample panel at which the subjects responded only individually or only cooperatively, the experiment also compared individual and cooperative sample-producing responses for each pair in terms of the degree of correspondence. These comparisons revealed a maximal cooperation effect: Correspondence between the subjects' responses was greater at those distances where the subjects responded cooperatively than at those distances where the subjects responded individually. The degree of correspondence in this experiment was calculated in terms of cooperative responses rather than reinforcers because there were large accuracy differences on the matching task for one pair (Subjects 3 and 4).

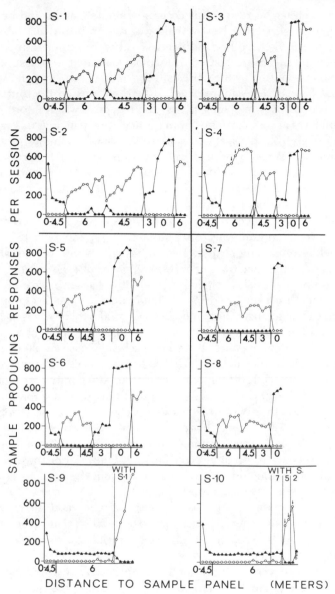

Fig. 7-2. Session-by-session plots of each subject's individual (closed triangles) and cooperative (open circles) responses as a function of the distance of his sample panel from his matching panel. Graphs of subjects who were tested together are placed above and below each other, except for Subjects 9 and 10, whose graphs are alongside each other. Determinations at 0 m are based on 8-min rather than 16-min sessions and have been multiplied by 2. The arrows above some points indicate that the subject was below chance accuracy on the matching task for that session. The extra panels on the graphs of Subjects 9 and 10 show the sessions these subjects were tested with other subjects who had learned to cooperate. (From Hake & Vukelich, 1973.)

TESTING FOR CONTROL BY THE COOPERATION CONTINGENCY

Responses That Have the Appearance of Cooperation but Are Controlled by Another Contingency

Moviegoers may be familiar with the stereotypical interrogator who asks his prisoner, "Why don't you cooperate so I can help you?" The audience's reaction to this line is generally one of mild amusement, and seems to be based on the common understanding that the instance mocks cooperation. But what aspects of the scene produce this reaction? Examining the definition of cooperation answers this question. A contingency is cooperative when the reinforcer for each person is at least partially dependent upon the other person's responses. Cooperative responses may be either negatively or positively reinforced for both persons, or positively reinforced for one person and negatively reinforced for the other. It follows then that the interrogator's use of the word "cooperate" cannot be faulted because the desired goal seems to be definable as cooperation, i.e., the prisoner's reinforcer (release or a reduced sentence) depends upon the interrogator's responses, and the interrogator's reinforcer (information) depends upon the prisoner's responses. The audience's amusement, however, follows from the understanding that other contingencies also may operate to produce the prisoner's "cooperative" behavior. More specifically, behavior that the interrogator designates as uncooperative would probably lead to aversive consequences by way of a thumbscrew, a rack, or other macabre apparatuses. The definition of cooperation specifies reinforcement for responding cooperatively; it does not specify other consequences for not responding cooperatively. In this example, the extraneous contingency is confounded with cooperation to such an extent that it makes the movie audience laugh. The prisoner's "cooperation" could be controlled as much by the contingency, "Give me information or you go to the rack" as by the cooperative exchange of information for a reduced sentence.

In this example the interrogator used the words "cooperation" and "help." If he wanted information, why did he not just say, "Give me information and I'll reduce your sentence"? The explanation may be that phrases such as "Let's cooperate" or "Let me help you" are similar to other stimuli: winks, using your first name, a salesman putting his arm around you. In situations with relatives or good friends these stimuli have been the occasion for reinforced responding often enough that they have become discriminative stimuli. It is therefore not surprising that some of the best interrogators and hucksters use such stimuli to create situations that seem to occasion reinforcement for the victim's appropriate response. Just as the interrogator example was not entirely cooperative, phrases such as "Let's cooperate" or "Let me do that for you" may prevent close examination of the actual contingencies in a situation. Or, stated from the victim's point of view, just as there is willingness to accept the "glitter" of iron pyrite as gold, there is an equal willingness to accept the "glitter" of words such as "help" and "cooperate" as signals for an equitable distribution of reinforcement. But all that glitters is not cooperation.

Calling behavior cooperative when it is really not controlled by the cooperation contingency also occurs in laboratory studies. The following sections identify three cooperation contingencies that should control behavior if that behavior is to be called cooperative (Hake & Vukelich, 1972). These sections also include methods for evaluating these three types of control. Although these evaluative methods are discussed in terms of laboratory research, they are equally relevant to applied situations, such as therapy. The discovery of a deviation from control by the cooperation contingency can tell the therapist when and how to intervene, and it can tell the man on the street when to beware and what he can do to make the situation more equitable.

Control by the Reinforcement Resulting from the Cooperation Contingency

Cooperative responding must be maintained by the reinforcement resulting from the cooperation contingency and not by any other source of reinforcement. This, of course, was the problem in the prisoner-interrogator example, where avoidance of the rack was an extra contingency that could have controlled the prisoner's behavior without any cooperation contingency. Consider also the child who earns an allowance for "cooperating" with his parents, i.e., he exchanges work for his parents' money. As in the prisoner-interrogator example, the child's behavior may be maintained solely by an extra contingency (parental scolding or spanking for no work) rather than by a cooperative exchange of reinforcers.

Similar difficulties may arise in cooperation research. For example, J. Taylor and Erspamer (1971) tied two rats together with a single wire that passed through holes in a partition at the back of the experimental chamber. The wire was long enough for one rat at a time to reach a food tray at the front of the chamber. The animals could cooperate by alternately going to the back of the chamber so that first one and then the other could move to the front of the chamber. Presumably, the cooperative response was maintained by food. However, the first rat might have "cooperated" because the second rat dragged it to the back of the chamber; further, the "cooperative" response of going to the back of the chamber could have been maintained by avoidance of the discomfort that resulted from the tension of the wire when the other rat pulled toward the food tray.

The demonstration of reinforcement control is even more crucial with humans, because humans can control behavior by instructions. Instructions can have two effects, the first of which does not interfere with control by the cooperation contingency. If one person explains the cooperation contingencies to a coactor, who then comes under the control of these contingencies, the instructions have simply speeded acquisition of the cooperative response. But if responding remains under the control of the partner's instructions and does not transfer to the cooperation contingencies, the resulting behavior could not be designated as cooperative. This could occur when the instructions include a threat of punishment for not cooperating, or when the other person can follow instructions but cannot learn the contingency. These latter types of instructional control may be common among young children or retarded persons.

The methods of evaluating reinforcer control in single-subject experiments may also be used in cooperation studies. The reinforcement specified in the cooperation contingency can be discontinued, as in extinction, or the cooperative response can produce a loss of reinforcers, as in response cost (Weiner, 1962). In both cases, cooperative responding would be expected to decrease. For example, in Hake and Vukelich (1973), response cost immediately reduced the cooperative responding of all but one of the four subjects. The fourth subject continued to respond even when his coactor was removed from the situation, thereby demonstrating that his responding could not be designated as cooperative.

Control by the Behavior of the Coactor

Cooperation ordinarily involves interactions between two persons. Complete control by such cooperation contingencies requires that each person has learned that another person is involved, or, simply, that the contingency is social. This control can be demonstrated by showing that the cooperative behavior of the coactor serves as a discriminative stimulus for the cooperative behavior of each participant. Azrin and Lindsley (1956) provides a good example of how one subject's responses can serve as discriminative stimuli for another subject's responses. The two subjects sat at a table opposite each other with three holes and a stylus in front of each of them. A subject had less than a second to place his stylus in the hole that corresponded to the hole in which his partner had placed his stylus. To meet the time requirement and to make the correct response, a subject had to watch where his partner placed his stylus.

Behavior that appears to be cooperative in a social situation may be entirely under the control of nonsocial contingencies. Consider, for example, the outwardly cooperative behavior of the person who sprays his neighbor's lawn against dandelions. The person's response may be maintained solely because it prevents dandelions from spreading to his own yard. If so, he would continue to spray the area even in the absence of cooperative behavior of the neighbor, or even if no one lived on the lot. Such observations would demonstrate that the "extra" spraying had nothing to do with cooperation; rather, it was under the control of a nonsocial contingency.

Even in studies of cooperation, what appears to be cooperative responding can sometimes be under the control of a nonsocial contingency. For example, consider Lindsley's (1966) procedure, in which cooperation consisted of a plunger-pulling response by one member of a pair followed within .5 sec by a plunger-pulling response from the other member. Under these contingencies, the behavior that was reinforced could have been under the control of the cooperative behavior of the coactor, i.e., one subject's behavior may have been a discriminative stimulus for the coactor's cooperative response. Behavior might also have been controlled by an individual high-rate contingency, i.e., a rate of about 120 responses per minute by both members of a pair would result in a high rate of reinforced responses. If cooperative behavior were under the control of the behavior of the coactor, most of a subject's responses would be within .5 sec of his coactor's responses while the number of individual responses, responses not meeting the .5 sec criterion, would be very low. On the other hand, a low percentage of cooperative responses relative to individual responses would indicate control by the nonsocial high-rate contingency. The latter type of control has been found for some subjects in the studies of Brotsky and Thomas (1967), Schmitt and Marwell (1968), and Vogler (1968). For example, in Brotsky and Thomas' study, which used a procedure similar to Lindsley's, only a quarter of the responses were cooperative. To show that the cooperative responses of both subjects were under the control of the coactor's behavior, the responses of Subject B could sometimes serve as the discriminative stimulus for the cooperative responses of Subject A and vice versa.

Cooperation procedures that do not require subjects to respond in strict alternation provide special problems. There are, however, other ways to demonstrate control by the behavior of the coactor. For example, maximal cooperation requires an increase in the degree of correspondence between the reinforcers and/or responses of the two persons; hence the demonstration of maximal cooperation would show that the cooperative responses of at least one of the persons was under the control of the reinforcers and/or responses of the coactor. Control by the mere presence of the coactor might also be considered an approximation to control by the behavior of the coactor. This type of social control was shown in Hake and Vukelich (1973). Figure 7-3 shows that the presence of the coactor was a stimulus for cooperative responding for five of six subjects because all responded cooperatively when the coactor was present, and all immediately switched to the noncooperative or individual solution as soon as their coactor was absent. The sixth subject made neither cooperative nor individual responses when her coactor was absent. Earlier in the experiment when her coactor had been present, however, she had made both cooperative and individual responses depending upon which had the lower response requirement for reinforcement. These findings suggest that her behavior was controlled by the instructions of her coactor rather than by the cooperation contingencies or the coactor's cooperative behavior.

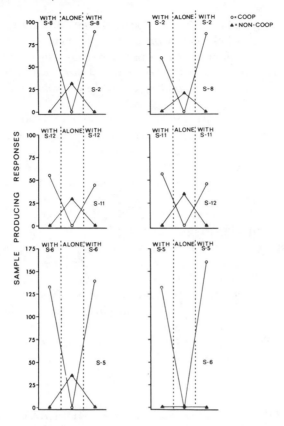

Fig. 7-3. Each subject's cooperative (open circles) and individual (closed triangles) responses as a function of the presence and absence of his partner. Each subject's sample panel was 6 m from his matching panel. (From Hake & Vukelich, 1973.)

Control by the Reciprocal Reinforcement Dependency

When the distribution of reinforcers or responses between the subjects can deviate from equality, control by the reciprocal-reinforcement aspect of the cooperation contingency can be demonstrated. Assuming that the contingency is the same for each member of the pair, this type of control is indicated by an increase in the correspondence between the number of reinforcers or cooperative responses between the participants as compared to a noncooperative control or to the start of the cooperation procedure. This is, of course, the maximal cooperation effect described earlier.

In some cases, control by the coactor's behavior can result in maximal cooperation, indicating control by reciprocal reinforcement, but maximal cooperation need not always be the result. Consider, for example, the case of a person who makes few cooperative responses relative to those of his partner but whose responses, when he does respond, are always under the control of his partner's behavior. In this example control by the partner's behavior does not result in maximal cooperation. In maximal cooperation not only are a subject's responses under the control of the coactor's behavior, but the number of the coactor's responses or reinforcers also serves as a discriminative stimulus.

As indicated earlier, most studies of cooperation have not demonstrated control by the reciprocal reinforcement dependency because they have measured only an increase in cooperative responses, the minimal effect. Even when maximal cooperation is measured, that effect may have been produced by only one of the persons. Determining whether each subject's cooperative responses are controlled by the number of reinforcers or cooperative responses of his partner first requires controlling the rate at which one subject and then the other makes cooperative responses or produces reinforcers. Whether each subject then adjusts his rate of cooperative responding or rate of producing reinforcers to his partner's can be determined. A within-session analysis can make all this unnecessary. For example, a maximal cooperation effect produced by both subjects would probably reveal some system of alternating reinforcers and several times within the session when the numbers of reinforcers were balanced. This maintenance of equality within sessions, first by one person and then by the other, would indicate that the responses of both persons produced the equality.

APPROACHES TO THE STUDY OF COOPERATION

Functional Analysis along Basic Dimensions of the Cooperation Situation

A functional analysis along the basic dimensions of the cooperation situation is the most obvious approach to studying cooperation. A functional analysis systematically varies the value of a given variable (e.g., the extent to which each person's reinforcers are dependent upon the other person's responses) while holding constant the value of other parameters. It yields a relation between the amount of cooperative responding and the values of the variable. Such functional relations tell us which variables can control cooperative responding and the values at which the largest changes can be expected.

Some of the basic dimensions of cooperation can be derived from existing literature, as evaluated in a recent review of cooperation research (Hake & Vukelich, 1972). That review concluded that much of the seemingly diffuse cooperation literature can be classified along the basic dimensions of the cooperation situation. Before considering that classification system, two factors responsible for the apparent diffuseness of the area of cooperation will be examined because these factors relate to the organization of the classification system.

There are two major reasons for the apparent diffuseness of the area of cooperation. First, the definition of cooperation, which states only that each person's reinforcers must depend at least in part upon the other's responses, includes several procedural dimensions, each of which has extremes that are vastly different. These extremes can be combined in ways that produce such idiosyncratic situations that either they do not appear to be related to cooperation or they appear to be special cases of cooperation. For this reason, the classification system of Hake and Vukelich (1972) defined the two extremes of each basic dimension, showed how to obtain intermediate points between the extremes, and illustrated how studies could be classified along each dimension.

A second source of the apparent diffuseness of the cooperation literature concerns the responses measured in cooperation studies. All cooperation research can be divided into two major categories: performance and choice procedures (Hake & Vukelich, 1972). In a performance procedure the rates of cooperative responding under the different values of a variable are compared by studying the values one at a time. A choice procedure, however, is analogous to a concurrent situation in which two or more values of a variable are studied at the same time by measuring the extent to which each value is chosen. Choice procedures can also be combined with performance by first requiring a choice and then making reinforcement depend upon a cooperative response (performance). Social psychology studies usually measure only choice, while most conditioning studies measure performance, either alone or in conjunction with choice. In many of the decision games of social psychology [e.g., the Prisoner's Dilemma game (Nemeth, 1970)] the choices or decisions have been between cooperation and competition, or at least that is the way the choices have been designated. These choices are relevant to an analysis of cooperation if the choices between cooperation and competition or the variables manipulated to affect choice represent values along a dimension of the cooperation situation. Both choice and performance procedures are important to the analysis of cooperation, but performance procedures are emphasized here because they show what is essential to produce and maintain cooperative behavior. For this reason, only studies that measure cooperation performance alone or both performance and choice in combination are used to illustrate the basic dimensions of the cooperation situation.

The classification system defines five dimensions along which cooperation situations can be classified. It also defines the extremes of each dimension and briefly describes a study or procedure at each extreme and at intermediate points. The five dimensions can be roughly classified in terms of whether they most closely describe (1) discriminative stimuli (e.g., the coactor as a discriminative stimulus), (2) the cooperative response (e.g., availability of alternative responses; deviations from reciprocity), or (3) the cooperation contingency (e.g., dependency upon coactor's responses for reinforcement; cost of the cooperative response). The order in which the dimensions are described, however, is based not upon this grouping of dimensions, but rather upon the dependence of the understanding of some dimensions upon prior descriptions of others.

   Dependency upon Coactor's Responses for Reinforcement: Interdependent and Dependent Cooperation Contingencies. According to the definition of cooperation, each person's reinforcers must depend, at least in part, upon the coactor's responses. The graphic presentation of

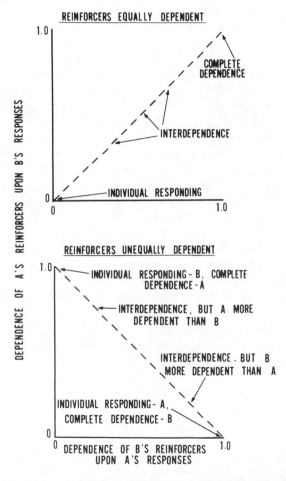

Fig. 7-4. The dependence dimension, when persons are equally dependent upon each other's responses for reinforcers (top) and when they are unequally dependent upon each other's responses for reinforcers (bottom). The *y*-axis shows the dependence of Person A's reinforcers upon B's responses, while the *x*-axis shows the dependence of Person B's reinforcers upon A's responses.

this dimension in Figure 7-4 shows that the extent of the dependency upon coactor's responses can vary. The dashed line in the top graph plots the points at which Persons A and B are equally dependent. Individual responding, where there is no dependency upon the coactor's responses, is at one extreme. Moving along the dashed line, cooperation begins when a person's reinforcers are largely dependent on his own responses and only slightly dependent on his partner's. Whenever the responses of both persons are involved in producing one person's reinforcers, regardless of the extent of the dependency, the cooperation procedure is designated as interdependent. The procedure of Hake and Vukelich (1973), described earlier, was interdependent: each subject produced the sample stimulus for his coactor, who then made his own matching response. Moving to the other end of this dimension, a person's reinforcers can largely or even entirely depend upon his coactor's responses. The extreme is, of course, the case in which a person's reinforcers depend entirely upon his partner's responses. Such a contingency is designated as dependent cooperation. An example of a dependent contingency is given in a study by Boren (1966), in which the only way each monkey could get a reinforcer was for its partner to press a lever 32 times. Rosenberg and Hall (1958) and Rosenberg (1959, 1960) are the only studies that have systematically studied values along the interdependent-dependent dimension.

Cooperation contingencies in everyday life can be more complicated, as when two persons each make different cooperative responses suited to their individual abilities or situation; consider, for example, a business partnership in which one person keeps the books and the other is in charge of sales. Also, the cooperation contingency does not have to be the same for both members of a partnership. For example, the reinforcers of one person can depend completely upon the partner's responses, while the partner's reinforcers can depend upon the responses of both. That situation may be called asymmetrical cooperation. The interdependence-dependence dimension with asymmetrical contingencies is illustrated in the bottom graph of Figure 7-4. At either extreme, both person's reinforcers depend entirely upon one person's responses. That person's responses would be described as a combination of individual and altruistic responses. Between the two extremes are interdependent contingencies with one or the other person's responses having a greater effect. Under asymmetrical contingencies, the persons might alternate who had the greatest responsibility for producing reinforcers. That might be called a mixed contingency.

Deviations from Reciprocity: Response Sharing and Response-Exchange Situations. Defining this dimension first requires definition of the basic unit of cooperation—a cooperation episode. A cooperation episode, the smallest unit of cooperative responding, refers to all of the responding, including at least one cooperative response, required for the delivery of one reinforcer. Whenever there has been enough responding, including at least one cooperative response, to produce a reinforcer, the basic unit has been completed (Hake & Vukelich, 1972, p. 333). An uninterrupted succession of cooperative episodes is designated a cooperation period (Hake & Vukelich, 1972).

Reciprocity refers to an equal number of responses and reinforcers for the two participants in a given cooperative episode or over an entire period of cooperation (Hake & Vukelich, 1972). The deviations from reciprocity allowed in cooperation situations can range from the extreme of reciprocity in each cooperative episode to the extreme of deviations from reciprocity in each episode. Situations that require reciprocity in each episode of cooperative responding are designated as response sharing. Reciprocity in each episode of cooperative responding can only occur in interdependent contingencies that require the same response from each person and deliver the same reinforcer to each person in each cooperative episode. For example, when two persons each receive the same reinforcer after they each pull their response plungers within .5 sec of one another (Lindsley, 1966), each episode results in reciprocity both in terms of the response requirement and the distribution of reinforcers, and the situation is designated as response sharing. An example from everyday life would be two workers mowing a large lawn. This is an interdependent cooperation contingency in which both workers make the same response and both receive the same reinforcers. Response sharing cannot occur in dependent contingencies because dependent contingencies require at least episodic deviations from reciprocity in responses and reinforcers.

At the other end of the dimension, response exchange does not require an equitable distribution of reinforcers during an episode of cooperative responding. Reciprocity is still possible, but responses and reinforcers are equalized over a cooperation period, rather than during a cooperative episode as in response sharing. Such situations are common, and one form might be characterized as, "I will do the work this time, you do it next." Thus, a man who mows his neighbor's lawn is probably not behaving altruistically; rather, he is probably responding as a result of a previous history in which he and his neighbor have occasionally exchanged the task of mowing each other's lawns. Hake and Vukelich (1973) provide an example of an interdependent cooperation contingency in which a given cooperative episode deviated from reciprocity both in response requirement (one subject produced the sample stimulus and the other made the matching response) and the distribution of reinforcers (only the matching response was reinforced). In that experiment, however, both responses and reinforcers could be and usually were equalized over the entire cooperation period. Because reciprocity is not required, response exchange situations can vary greatly: Unlike response sharing, they can be either dependent or interdependent; either one or both subjects can receive reinforcers during any given episode; and deviations from reciprocity can be in terms of response or reinforcers. Situations can also vary greatly in the extent of the deviations from reciprocity that they allow, but there have been no systematic studies along this dimension.

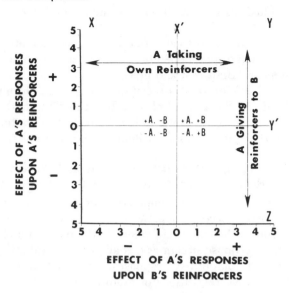

Fig. 7-5. The cost dimension for both individual *(X, X',* and *Y)* and cooperative *(Y, Y',* and *Z)* responses shown as the effect of A's responses upon his own *(y*-axis) and B's *(x*-axis) reinforcers.

Cost of the Cooperative Response: No-Cost and Cost Contingencies. Another dimension is the extent to which cooperative responses affect the reinforcers of the person making the cooperative response. At one end of the dimension, a person's cooperative responses increase his own as well as his coactor's reinforcers and, as a result, the contingency would be designated as "no cost." This would have to be the case for all response-sharing situations, (e.g., Lindsley, 1966) because there can only be a gain in reinforcers when each cooperative response produces the same reinforcers for each person. This endpoint of the cost dimension is illustrated at Y in Figure 7-5, which shows the cost dimension for Persons A and B as a function of both individual *(X, X', Y)* and cooperative *(Y, Y', Z)* responses of Person A. Free-operant situations with unlimited reinforcers (Hake & Vukelich, 1972) do not involve cost, because the reinforcers each subject can receive are limited only by the coactor's rate of cooperative responses and not his own. In other situations, however, the cooperative response may not result in any gain to the subject making the response, as at point *Y'* in Figure 25. And, further, in situations with a limited supply of reinforcers, such as trial procedures with a fixed number of trials, each cooperative response of one person (i.e., each reinforcer given to a coactor) subtracts from the total reinforcers the person might receive. This is illustrated at Z in Figure 7-5. Individual or noncooperative responses that occur in a social situation can also result in cost, as at *X* in Figure 7-5 where Person A's taking a reinforcer costs Person B. At *X'* the individual response of A does not cost B, and at Y

Person A's individual response is also cooperative, resulting in a gain for A and B.

Although cost reduces response rate in nonsocial situations (Weiner, 1962), to our knowledge no cooperation studies have compared cost and no-cost contingencies. Both cost and no-cost contingencies are common in the everyday world. We encounter social situations (e.g., piecework) where we are limited only by the amount of work we are willing to do, and situations (e.g., classes graded on a curve; athletic teams with a limited number of positions) where there is an enforced limit upon the number of available reinforcers.

Availability of Alternative Responses: Forced-Cooperation and Alternative-Response Situations. Cooperation situations that prevent alternative responses, either noncooperative or simply less cooperative, have been designated "forced" cooperation because the only alternative to cooperation is doing without the reinforcer. At the other end of the dimension are alternative-response situations that allow noncooperative responses, such as individual or competitive responses, that result in the same reinforcer as the cooperative response. For example, students frequently have the choice of working individually or working cooperatively with other students. Intermediate points on this dimension are choice situations that allow choices between several solutions that are all cooperative but differ in the degree to which they are cooperative. For example, the choices could vary in terms of the extent to which the cooperative responses produce the coactor's reinforcers (dependency dimension).

The Coactor as a Discriminative Stimulus: Nonsocial and Social Situations. Cooperative situations can also differ greatly in terms of the social nature of the situation. In nonsocial situations—one extreme of the dimension—subjects are prevented from learning that there is another subject in the experiment. For example, in some experiments of Sidowski and his colleagues (Sidowski, 1957; Sidowski, Wyckoff, & Tabory, 1956) the members of a pair were tested at the same time but in separate rooms, and were not told that they were in a social situation. The only sources of interaction were two buttons that each subject could use to give his coactor either points or shock. The purpose of these experiments was to determine the extent to which the laws of conditioning for individual subjects could control social behavior without the complex variables introduced by social interaction. These experiments showed that subjects could learn to cooperate (press the button that delivered points to their partner) regardless of whether they knew they had a partner. Sidowski concluded that the essential features of any social situation were: "(a) Two or more subjects have at their disposal responses which result in rewarding or punishing effects on the other subject. (b) The principal sources of reward and punishment for any subject depend on responses made by the other subject. (c) The responses controlling reward and punishment are subject to learning. It will be assumed that whatever else may be involved, at least the above features are present in any social situation [Sidowski, 1957, p. 318]." According to this reward-punishment analysis of the response interactions, whenever one of the subjects pressed the shock button, thereby punishing the other subject's previous response, the other subject switched to another button (either points or shock). Conversely, whenever one of the subjects pressed the point button, thereby reinforcing the other subject's previous response, the other subject repeated his previous response. Given the effects of reward and punishment upon the partner's subsequent responses, the only stable solution is cooperation, in which each subject produces points for his partner, because all other possibilities involve shock and thereby lead to a change in responding (a more detailed analysis is available in Kelley, Thibaut, Radloff, and Mundy, 1962; and Zajonc, 1966).

In social situations—the other end of the dimension—the subjects are tested in full view of one another, and they are either told about the social relation or they presumably learn it. This is considered important in most cooperation experiments because (1) cooperative behavior is observed under similar conditions in everyday life, (2) the situation allows evaluation of the extent to which the participants' responses are under the control of their coactor's responses, and (3) social stimuli may produce behavioral changes not easily produced under nonsocial situations or explained by the laws of conditioning for individual subjects (Hake & Vukelich, 1972). Behavioral changes attributable to the social nature of stimuli have been called "social emergents" (Lindsley, 1963, 1966) or "social-stimulus effects" (Hake, Vukelich, & Kaplan, 1973). For example, social facilitation (an increase in one person's responses as a result of the presence of another person) is a social stimulus effect. Studies have shown that some increases in responding can be produced by the social nature of the stimuli rather than by nonsocial mechanical stimuli (Hake & Laws, 1967; Hake, Powell, & Olsen, 1969). In these experiments, for example, a social facilitation effect was produced by the presence of another animal eating rather than by the mere activation of the other animal's food hopper. To demonstrate an effect of a social stimulus upon cooperative behavior, cooperative behavior under nonsocial and social situations must be compared. Few studies have isolated social stimulus effects well enough to evaluate their effect upon cooperative behavior. In his classic study, however, Lindsley (1966) found that learning was faster under social than nonsocial conditions and that the sight of the partner influenced the subjects' determination of who was to be the leader. Social-stimulus effects are discussed later in the context of a correlated-response approach to the study of cooperation.

Few studies other than those of Sidowski and Lindsley have examined more than one value along the nonsocial-social dimension. One reason is that intermediate values are difficult to produce: the subject either has a partner or he does not. There are, however, other possibilities. For example, the extent to which the coactor is accessible can be varied by systematically controlling the extent to which a coactor can be seen or heard

(Lindsley, 1966). Mechanical stimuli, such as lights and sounds previously associated with social stimuli, can also serve as intermediate conditions. We have used the term "quasisocial stimuli" to refer to stimuli that, due to previous experience or instructions, are associated with social stimuli (Hake & Vukelich, 1972). Some examples of quasisocial stimuli in everyday life are letters, pictures, porch lights, and cars.

Definition of Basic Dimensions: Conclusions

Definition of these basic dimensions of the cooperation situation suggests three major conclusions. First, cooperation situations that previously appeared so idiosyncratic as to be special cases of cooperation, or not cooperation at all, can usually be located at the extreme of one or more cooperation dimensions (e.g., nonsocial situations), and thereby fall within the cooperation literature. Second, few studies have systematically manipulated values along a particular dimension or even studied the two extremes of a dimension. Third, the classification system can also be used to discover combinations of dimensions that have not been studied, but that may be of practical or theoretical importance. Table 7-1 shows the possible combinations of the extremes of the five dimensions and a representative experiment for each combination that has been studied. Hake and Vukelich (1973) illustrate how the table can be used to arrive at a combination that may not have been studied but may be important. That study combined deviations from reciprocity with the availability of alternative responses because deviations from reciprocity during cooperative responding seemed to be an important factor affecting the choice of a noncooperative solution. It is surprising that many of the possible combinations have not been studied. Our perusal of about 50 studies revealed that over half were concerned with response sharing, even though response exchange allows a larger number of combinations (Table 7-1).

A Correlated-Response Approach to Cooperation

A number of different responses can ordinarily be observed when two persons cooperate. For example, cooperating persons frequently engage in the following responses: communication, which simply involves a person talking to his coactor; auditing, which involves one person checking his own and his coactor's scores or reinforcers; and, leadership, which involves one person's control of the distribution of work and/or reinforcement. These responses are neither cooperation itself nor are they a required part of cooperation. Rather, they are entirely optional responses that are often observed during cooperation. Because they are optional, and because they are often observed during cooperation, they have been designated as correlated responses.

Table 7-1
Possible Combinations of the Extremes of Five Dimensions of the Cooperation Situation and One Representative Study for Each Combination Studied.

(1)	(2)	(3)	(4)	(5)	Studies
Dimensions [a]					
INTERDEPENDENT	RESPONSE SHARING	No Cost	Forced	Nonsoc.	Lindsley (1966)
				Social	Lindsley (1966)
			Alt. Resp.	Nonsoc.	
				Social	Mithaug (1969)
	RESPONSE EXCHANGE	No Cost	Forced	Nonsoc.	
				Social	Boren (1966)
			Alt. Resp.	Nonsoc.	
				Social	Hake & Vukelich (1972)
		Cost	Forced	Nonsoc.	Rosenberg (1960)
				Social	Daniel (1942)
			Alt. Resp.	Nonsoc.	
				Social	
DEPENDENT	RESPONSE EXCHANGE	No Cost	Forced	Nonsoc.	Sidowski (1957)
				Social	Boren (1966)
			Alt. Resp.	Nonsoc.	
				Social	Hollis (1966)
		Cost	Forced	Nonsoc.	
				Social	
			Alt. Resp.	Nonsoc.	
				Social	Hake et al. (1975)

a The five dimensions are (1) dependency upon coactor's responses for reinforcement: interdependent and dependent cooperation contingencies, (2) deviations from reciprocity: response-sharing and response-exchange situations, (3) cost of the cooperative responses: no-cost and cost contingencies, (4) availability of alternative responses: forced-cooperation and alternative-response situations, (5) the coactor as a discriminative stimulus: nonsocial and social situations.

NOTE. Response sharing is not logically possible under dependent contingencies, and cost is not logically possible under response sharing.

Another approach to studying cooperation is to determine the effects of these correlated responses upon cooperation. The rationale is straightforward: When one response occurs along with another, the two responses may affect each other. The correlated-response approach systematically manipulates the extent to which correlated responses can occur for one or both persons and then evaluates the effect upon cooperation.

The correlated-response approach to the study of cooperation is the most purely social one, because correlated responses are usually at least in part under the control of social stimuli. The easiest way to evaluate the social nature of these responses is to vary the situation along the social-nonsocial dimension, and then to compare the extent to which these correlated responses occur in situations ranging from nonsocial to social. The extent to which the correlated response changes with social stimuli equals, by definition, the control of the correlated response by social as opposed to nonsocial stimuli. Behavioral changes that can be attributed to the social nature of stimuli have been referred to as *social emergents* (Lindsley, 1966) or *social stimulus effects* (Hake et al., 1973) and, as Lindsley (1966) pointed out, they make up the major subject matter of social psychology.

The purpose of this section is twofold. The first objective is to show the extent to which cooperation and related social phenomena generate correlated social responses. Auditing, one of the correlated social responses, will be examined in detail to illustrate this point. The second objective is to examine the possible effects upon cooperation of the most commonly observed correlated responses: auditing, communication, and leadership. It should be stressed that, because little research has been based on the approach, much of what follows is speculative.

I. Auditing. Hake et al. (1973) defined an audit response as one that is strengthened or maintained by allowing access to an existing . core. The score itself depends upon another response. An audit response that allows access to one's own score is designated as a self-audit. An audit response that allows access to a coactor's score is designated as a coactor audit. Audit responses are common in everyday life because humans make both self- and coactor audits in almost every social situation. Examples of common coactor audits include: "Let me see your report card."; "How long is your term paper?"; "How much money do you make?" Audit responses were noted by Hake and Vukelich (1973), when nearly all subjects often asked their partners how many points they had. In an apparent attempt to get a partner to work faster, a subject sometimes "underestimated" his own score when questioned by his coactor.

If audit responses were categorized in social psychology, they would fall under the topic of social comparisons (Festinger, 1954) because the two types of audit responses provide the essential information for a social comparison. The usual method of studying social comparisons has been to give a subject his score on a task relative to a group score on the same task, and then to determine the effect of the subject's relative position (e.g., high, low, middle) upon his subsequent performance. In these studies the scores have usually been provided either by the experimenter instead of by the subject, or by a response that produced other consequences besides providing information on scores; thus, this research says little about the rate of self- and coactor audit responses or the variables that affect them (Hake et al., 1973).

Hake et al. (1973) measured the rate of audit responses by making access to self- and coactor scores depend upon a button-press that illuminated the area behind a one-way glass that covered the scores. The basic apparatus is shown in Figure 7-6. Points exchangeable for money depended

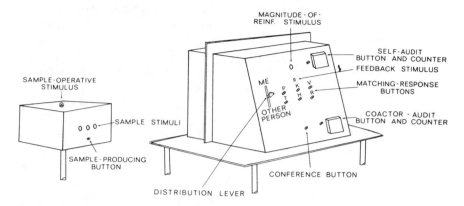

Fig. 7-6. Diagram of the sample panel (left) and the matching panel (right) of one subject. The self- and coactor audit buttons and counters are on the right side of the matching panel. (From Hake et al., 1975.)

upon the subject working matching-to-sample problems. Self- as well as coactor audits occurred at higher rates during social situations (cooperation and parallel work) than during nonsocial situations (no coactor), thereby indicating that at least some of both types of audits depend on social stimuli. The study also showed that the coactor's score was a critical social stimulus affecting self-audits: the rate of self-audits increased more relative to a non-social situation when the coactor was present and his score was accessible than when the coactor was present but his score was not accessible.

Auditing was a frequent response; subjects averaged about one self-audit and one coactor audit for every two problems. The frequent occurrence of a self- and a coactor audit within a brief time period (5 sec), which was designated as an interpersonal audit, indicated that having both scores at the same time was reinforcing. The interpersonal audits suggested that the difference between scores might also be a stimulus that affected the rate of audits. A later study (Vukelich & Hake, 1974), in which the distribution of matching-to-sample problems was arranged so that a given subject was consistently ahead, behind, or even with his coactor, revealed that subjects made more audits during even as opposed to ahead or behind conditions. The difference between scores as well as their absolute values were an effective feature of these stimuli. This finding in turn indicated the subjects were engaging in social comparisons because a difference stimulus necessarily requires a comparison of the two scores.

This objective audit system, as opposed to a subjective system that relies on verbal reports or no audit system at all, could affect cooperative behavior. Maximal cooperation is defined by the extent to which subjects obtained equal reinforcers; hence an objective audit system could increase cooperation by providing subjects with an accurate measure of the extent of their coactor's reciprocal responding, thereby allowing subjects to adjust their responding accordingly. Similar reasons are probably involved in the use of neutral countries or the United Nations as observers in international disputes: they provide an objective audit system. In contrast, a subjective audit system that relies on verbal report of the participants can be manipulated to advantage. For example, with no objective audit system (Hake & Vukelich, 1973), a subject may underestimate his own score to get his coactor to work faster. Such "underestimates" may have contributed to the correspondence of scores in that study being considerably less than 100%. Subsequent studies with an objective audit system produced correspondence levels of 95-100% (e.g., Hake et al., 1975). The extent to which an objective audit system affects cooperation could be assessed by systematically comparing the effects of (1) objective self and/or coactor audit scores, (2) a subjective audit system, and (3) no audit system.

2. *Leadership.* A leadership response during cooperation will be defined as one that determines (1) the responses to be made by each member of a pair, and/or (2) the reinforcers to be received by each member of the pair. Because the leadership response determines subsequent events, it ordinarily precedes other responding.

But not all leadership responses qualify as correlated responses. Consider a study by Lindsley (1966), in which subjects had to respond within .5 sec of each other to produce reinforcement. The initial response in each cooperative episode was designated as a leadership response because it determined when the other person had to respond. The person making the majority of these initial responses was designated as the leader. In that procedure, however, the leadership response was also a cooperative response. A leadership response is a correlated response only when it is optional. For example, consider a situation in which subjects have the options of (1) no leadership, with the distribution of responses and reinforcers left to individual decisions, joint decisions, chance, or the experimenter; or (2) leadership, with decisions concerning the distribution of reinforcers left to one of the subjects or some alternation between the two subjects. In this situation, leadership responses are optional and not part of the cooperative response. The choice between leadership and no-leadership conditions might be as casual as one person saying, "You do this and I'll do that," or the choice might be as explicit as a button-press that produced one of the two conditions in a concurrent schedule of reinforcement.

Leadership responses could be produced by increased density of reinforcement for one or both subjects or by other more social reinforcers such as "being in charge." Leadership resulting from the latter would probably qualify as a social-stimulus effect. As an example of the latter, consider Lindsley (1966), in which leadership responses did not alter the frequency or the distribution of reinforcers but subjects still displayed a preference for leadership.

Leadership could speed the acquisition of cooperative responding or efficient responding if one member of a pair learned an equitable or more efficient solution, i.e., leadership might set up new conditions under which more reinforcers were obtained than under previous conditions. In the natural environment the leader is expected to have the knowledge to guide followers to obtain the maximum amount of reinforcers for all. But just as leadership can increase equity, it can also have the reverse effect. If the leader has extensive control over the distribution of reinforcers while the followers have little or no control, inequity can result. The leader can give the followers a minimum but sufficient number of reinforcers to maintain cooperative responding, while taking the bulk of the reinforcers for himself. Political graft is an example.

The effects of leadership upon cooperation can be assessed by manipulating the presence and absence of the opportunity to make leadership responses. In addition to leadership choices, dependent variables could include the number of cooperative responses, the correspondence between reinforcers of the two persons, and the total reinforcers. Different forms of leadership, such as alternating leadership between persons, allowing persons to compete for leadership, or appointing one person as the leader, could also be compared with respect to their effects on cooperation. But discovering the kinds of contingencies that followers can place upon the behavior of the leader has always been and seems destined to remain the most important applied research topic (cf. Chapter 19).

Communication. Theoretically, cooperation contingencies should take effect regardless of whether subjects are allowed to communicate (Sidowski, 1957). Allowing communication, however, probably facilitates acquisition. Our studies monitored the content of communications, and measured the rate and length of communications by requiring the subjects to depress a "conference" button whenever they talked (Figure 7-6). The rate measures reveal that subjects do talk to each other, but at a decreasing rate over sessions. The content falls into two major categories: subjects do discuss potential solutions, including cooperation, particularly when there has been a change in the situation, but most of the conversations concern school or community-related events. Both types of communication may affect the development of cooperation. First, if one subject learns a cooperative solution, he could relate it to his coactor. The communicated knowledge would then reduce the time that would otherwise be required for the coactor to learn the solution by trial and error. In fact, in some cases, such as when one of the subjects is severely retarded, a solution might never be reached without communication. The second type of communication, which concerns school or community-related matters unrelated to the task, could also affect the development of cooperation because the communications may contain stimuli, either positive or negative, that could affect a subject's reaction to his coactor's requests or instructions. Simply, the exchange of reinforcers on one level, such as communication, may facilitate the exchange of reinforcers on another level, namely cooperation. Research on the effects of communication could evaluate the type of communication allowed as well as the mere presence or absence of communication.

RELATIONS BETWEEN MAXIMAL COOPERATION AND OTHER MAJOR EQUITY EFFECTS: MAXIMAL COOPERATION, ALTRUISM, SHARING, COMPETITION

Definition of an Equity Effect

Maximal cooperation can be described as an equity effect because, given that the members of a pair are working on equal contingencies, thedefinition of maximal cooperation requires a change toward equality in the numbers of reinforcers or cooperative responses of the coactors. A definition of an equity effect seems desirable because changes toward equal distributions can be reached in ways other than by cooperation. Further, a definition would allow a classification under which all equity effects could be categorized.

Our definition of an equity effect is similar to that of maximal cooperation, except that it does not specify the nature of the response by which equity is reached because equity can be reached through responses other than cooperative ones. An equity effect occurs when (1) there is an increase in the degree of correspondence between the reinforcers of the two persons, while (2) there is no change or an increase in total reinforcements. The second part of the definition ensures that an equity effect is not indicated when increased correspondence results from a decrease in reinforcement. For example, the extreme case of a change from 50 and 75 reinforcements for respective persons A and B to one reinforcement apiece would not be considered an equity effect. As with maximal cooperation, there are special cases in which equity may be calculated in terms of responses rather than reinforcements.

Sharing: The Other Major Equity Effect

One of our recent experiments (Hake et al., 1975) revealed a second major equity effect. That experiment resembled our previous ones in that a pair of subjects worked matching-to-sample problems for points exchangeable for money. The experiment differed in that it was a trial procedure with one problem per trial. Figure 7-6 is a diagram of one subject's apparatus. The subject who pressed his distribution lever first determined who was able to work and receive credit for the matching-to-sample problem. Not pressing the lever or pressing it second had no effect on the distribution of problems. If a subject pressed his distribution lever first, and he pushed it to a position labeled "other person," his coactor was able to work the problem. This was a cooperative response because the reinforcers the coactor received for working the problem were in part dependent upon the other subject's distributing the matching-to-sample problem to him. On the other hand, if a subject was the first to press his lever, and if he pressed it to a position labeled "me," he was able to work and receive credit for the problem. The responses by which a subject distributed problems to himself were designated "taking" responses, to distinguish them from the cooperative or "giving" responses by which he distributed problems to his coactor. The experiment revealed that subjects could reach equity through taking responses as well as through the cooperative or giving responses.

Equity solutions reached through taking responses are frequently observed in everyday life, and they are sometimes referred to as *sharing*. Consider two children who divide a box of cookies. The equal distributions are reached by the children each taking their share of the reinforcers, rather than giving reinforcers to each other as in cooperation. When equity is reached by taking responses rather than by giving responses, the phenomenon is designated as sharing (Hake et al., 1975).

Another defining feature of sharing is the absence of competitive responses. For example, because competitive responses are also taking responses, one might argue that an equitable distribution reached through taking responses was actually the result of competition between persons of equal ability rather than of sharing. But in competition both persons make taking responses for each reinforcer. Both subjects also make taking responses in sharing, but both do not make taking responses for each reinforcer (e.g., both children do not reach for every single cookie). Rather, in sharing there is only one taking response per reinforcer and such responses are usually alternated between persons in some consistent pattern (e.g., every other cookie or three cookies at a time). The combination of an equitable distribution of reinforcers and the absence of competitive taking responses rules out competition (Hake et al., 1975).

If the persons are not making competitive taking responses, are they not "letting" each other take reinforcers? In other words, does sharing not simply represent a failure to make the cooperative giving response observable and measurable? If so, does sharing really differ from cooperation? This was our first reaction. It is also probably because of such reasoning that sharing has not always been differentiated from cooperation in everyday situations or in the research literature (Hake et al., 1975). For example, sharing occurred in the experiments of A.G. Miller and Thomas (1972, Exp. II) and M.D. Madsen (1967, Exp. IV), but it was called cooperation. In these experiments, the reinforcer depended on pulling a string attached to a weighted pen and moving the pen to a target. Only one subject could receive a reinforcer on each trial. Because both subjects had strings attached to the pen and both could pull the pen to their respective targets, either subject could prevent the other from moving the pen to his target by pulling his string. The equitable solution was for each subject to let his coactor pull the pen to his target on alternate trials. This is what some subjects did, but the solution is defined here as sharing rather than cooperation. Why not make this "letting" response observable and measurable by requiring it to be overt? The reason is that by requiring an overt letting response, each person's reinforcers would then depend, in part, upon the letting responses of the other person, the contingency would be cooperative, and the letting responses would be the cooperative responses. Sharing becomes interdependent cooperation by requiring an observable letting response (Hake et al., 1975).

In summary, sharing is similar to maximal cooperation in that both are defined in terms of an increase in the correspondence of the two persons' reinforcers. Sharing differs from maximal cooperation in that the equitable distribution is reached by taking rather than giving responses. Sharing is similar to competition in that it involves taking responses, but it differs from competition in that only one subject makes a taking response per reinforcer.

Applied and Theoretical Reasons for Considering Sharing and Cooperation as Separate Phenomena

The importance of the distinction between cooperation and sharing is not limited to a mere difference in contingencies; the contingency differences appear to produce important behavioral differences as well. Hake et al. (1975) indicated that when subjects distribute reinforcers equitably, sharing rather than cooperation will be the method chosen most often. This finding is summarized in Table 7-2, which shows the response dimension and method of distribution by which each subject received most of his reinforcers. For 11 of the 14 subjects, most reinforcers were received through taking responses, and sharing was the predominant method of reinforcer distribution for nine of these 11 subjects. Only three subjects received most of their reinforcers through giving responses and cooperation.

There are three reasons why sharing might be chosen over cooperation (Hake et al., 1975). First, if competition were the initial method of responding, sharing would be an easier transition to an equitable method than cooperation because sharing is on the same response dimension as competition (taking) and would involve dropping only one taking response. A change to cooperation, however, would involve both dropping taking responses and switching to a new response dimension (giving). Second, sharing would be expected to be more stable behavior than cooperation because of a shorter delay of reinforcement. Reinforcement following a taking response is fairly immediate, but reinforcement and a giving response are separated by the potentially variable time until the coactor makes a giving response that presents a reinforcer to the subject. Third, from a developmental point of view, sharing would be expected to be more common with young children

Table 7-2

Response Dimension and Method of Reinforcer Distribution by Which Each Subject Received Most of His Reinforcers[a]

	Subject	Predominant Response Dimension	Predominant Method of Reinforcer Distribution
	1	Give	Cooperation
	2	Give	Cooperation
	3	Take	Sharing
Experiment I	4	Give	Cooperation
	5	Take	Sharing
	6	Take	Sharing
	7	Take	Sharing
	8	Take	Sharing
	9	Take	Sharing
	10	Take	Sharing
Experiment II	11	Take	Sharing
	12	Take	Sharing
	13	Take	Competition
	14	Take	Competition

[a]From Hake et al., 1975

because all species learn to take reinforcers before they learn to give them. Cooperation and giving responses would seem to develop later, perhaps after the development of verbal behavior, and after the child has learned to respond to requests such as, "Do this for me."

Making available a second equity solution such as sharing in addition to cooperation, or vice versa, should be another way of increasing the likelihood of reaching equity. For example, there may be situations in which one of the equity solutions might be easier or faster than the other. We have all heard the commonly voiced preference for sharing, "It's easier to do it myself." Similarly, we have all heard preferences for cooperation, such as, "Could you help me with mine?" Even if an additional solution is no easier, its availability may still increase the likelihood of equity because of history variables. For example, sharing might be preferred over cooperation when persons have had a previous disagreement: the persons might be able to let one another take reinforcers when they cannot give reinforcers to each other. Lindsley (1966), for example, described one subject who could lead but could not follow his partner.

Classification of Major Inequity Effects as Well as Major Equity Effects Along the Give and Take Response Dimensions

The biggest difference between maximal cooperation and sharing is that maximal cooperation involves giving responses while sharing involves taking responses. These two dimensions also include the basic responses involved in altruism and competition, the major inequity effects. An inequity effect is defined as a decrease in the correspondence of two persons' reinforcers. Altruism, like maximal cooperation, involves giving responses, but unlike cooperation, one person makes more giving responses than the other. Competition, like sharing, involves taking responses, but unlike sharing, both persons make taking responses for a single reinforcer. Classifying these four effects in terms both of giving and taking responses and of increased and decreased correspondence organizes the major equitable and inequitable methods of reinforcer distribution as shown in Table 7-3. Although there may be other methods of equitable and inequitable distribution, these seem the major ones.

Equity Effects Based on Mixed Response Patterns That Are Predominantly Competitive or Altruistic

Competition. Equity can be reached in two ways when competition is the predominant response pattern. First, equity can result when most of the responding is competitive if there is also a secondary response pattern of sharing or cooperation. The secondary patterns are characteristic of equity effects and usually occur near the end of the period of interaction. For example, in a school class, where grades are based upon relative performance, a student with high grades may choose to help another after he has completed his own work.

Second, equity can also result when competition is the only response

Table 7-3
Classification of Major Equity and Inequity Effects
Along Give and Take Response Dimensions[a]

	Equity Effects (Increased Correspondence)	Inequity Effects (Decreased Correspondence)
Take Responses	Sharing	Competition
Give Responses	Maximal Cooperation	Altruism

[a]From Hake et al., 1975.

pattern. A tied football game is a good example. In this case, however, the absence of secondary patterns of sharing or cooperative responses near the end of the game (e.g., throwing the game) indicates that the equitable distribution of scores was probably the result of the persons or teams responding with equal speed, force, or ability.

Altruism. An equitable distribution of reinforcers can also result from an altruistic distribution of the response requirements. This occurs when one person "takes charge" by giving half of the reinforcers to another person and taking half for himself, thereby making all of the responses himself but distributing the reinforcers equally. Such equitable altruism in everyday life is frequently signaled by the verbal statement, "I'll take care of everything."

Use of the Definitions to Distinguish Between the Various Equity and Inequity Effects

The data from Hake et al. (1975, pp. 67-72) illustrate that the definitions given previously can be used to name the various equity and inequity effects for pairs of persons (high-school students) who had several opportunities to distribute reinforcers between them. On each trial, a subject could (1) press his distribution lever down to give the matching-to-sample problem to his coactor (giving response), or (2) press his distribution lever up to take the problem for himself (taking response). The first pair member to respond determined the distribution of the problem. The values of the problems (1, 2, or 3 cents) were randomized, and whoever got to work the problem on a particular trial received the point value of the problem if he worked it correctly.

Distinguishing between Equity and Inequity. The correspondence of scores for each session was calculated by dividing the low score by the higher score. Figure 7-7 shows a session-by-session plot of the correspondence. The first and last panels show the correspondence for the baseline sessions, in which the problems and their point values were distributed automatically and randomly between the two pair members (random distribution). The random distribution provided a baseline for evaluating the changes in correspondence when the distribution of problems was made dependent upon responses (response-dependent distribution). An increase above baseline indicated an equity effect, while a decrease indicated an inequity effect. Figure 7-7 shows that correspondence increased for each pair when the distribution of problems was dependent upon the subjects' responses on the distribution lever. There was at least 95% correspondence for each of the last four sessions under the response-dependent condition. Three pairs attained this level within the first (Pair 3) or the second (Pairs 2 and 4) sessions of the response-dependent condition, while Pair 1 required five sessions. There were also some sessions with high correspondence dur-

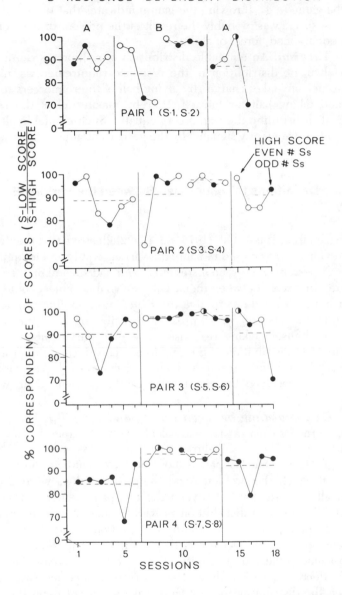

Fig. 7-7. Session-by-session plot of the correspondence of scores for each pair. Open circles indicate that the even-numbered subject had the higher number of points in the session; solid circles indicate that the odd-numbered subject had the higher number of points. Half-filled circles indicate 100% correspondence. The horizontal broken lines give the mean correspondence for each block of sessions under the baseline procedure, and for the first and last four sessions under the response-dependent procedure. (From Hake et al., 1975.)

ing baseline, but only Pair 3 had as many as three consecutive sessions with correspondence at or above 90%, and for no pair did the means under baseline (dashed lines) reach that of the last four sessions under the response-dependent condition.

Naming the Particular Equity or Inequity Effect. Although analysis of changes in correspondence did reveal equity effects, correspondence alone cannot reveal whether those effects were cooperation, sharing, or mixed. Similarly, correspondence alone cannot indicate whether the decreased correspondence during some of the early sessions was the result of altruism or competition.

Figure 7-8, which separates each subject's giving and taking responses, shows each pair's predominant method of distributing problems. The first two rows show the number of problems each subject gave or took for each session under the response-dependent condition. The last row, labeled "ineffective take responses," shows the number of taking responses each subject made after his coactor had already made a taking response and distributed

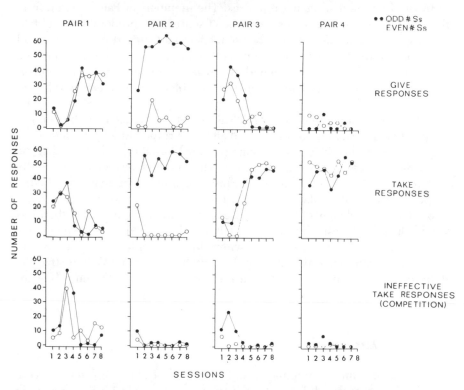

Fig. 7-8. Number of giving responses, taking responses, and ineffective taking responses for each session of the response-dependent procedure. Filled circles indicate response frequency for odd-numbered subjects and open circles indicate response frequency for even-numbered subjects. Half-filled circles indicate that members of a pair made the same number of responses. (From Hake et al., 1975.)

the problem to himself. Hence, the number of ineffective taking responses is the number of times both subjects emitted taking responses for the same problem (a taking response by one subject and an ineffective taking response by the other), and thereby indicates the number of competitive responses. The ineffective taking responses over sessions reveal that most pairs did compete initially, but that competition decreased to a low level by the last four sessions. Hence, the increased correspondence during the last four sessions (Figure 7-7) cannot be attributed to competition between subjects of nearly equal speed or a mixed but predominantly competitive effect.

The terminal method for the first pair was maximal cooperation, because the increased correspondence resulted from a predominance of giving responses (top row). Sharing was the terminal method for Pairs 3 and 4. Sharing was indicated by the predominance of taking responses (middle row), the absence of competition (bottom row), and the increased correspondence (Figure 7-7). For Pair 3, sharing was preceded by three sessions during which cooperation was predominant, as indicated by the higher number of giving than taking reponses. The members of Pair 4 shared from the start: the increased correspondence of scores, the predominance of taking responses, and the low number of ineffective taking responses were all evident from the first session. The pairs that shared simply alternated taking problems: for Pair 3, the person with the lowest score took the next problem, whereas the members of Pair 4 took alternate blocks of problems worth 5-20 points.

The terminal method for Pair 2 was mixed, involving a combination of cooperation and sharing. Subject 3 did all of the responding by giving part of the problems to his coactor and taking part for himself in such a way that the two subjects' scores were nearly equal. This method was a combination of maximal cooperation and sharing because the number of giving and taking responses (without a taking response from his coactor) were about equal. From the point of view of the response requirement alone, the method was predominantly altruistic because one pair member did all of the responding.

The major point here, as elsewhere in the chapter, has been in the precision of definition rather than in the empirical content. We hope that the definitions will be useful for classification no matter what the outcomes for any particular situation.

SUMMARY

In our initial examination of the area of social psychology, we were struck by its apparent diffuseness, which even extended to subareas such as cooperation. We suggested that one reason for this apparent diffuseness was the pressure put on social psychology to solve the world's many social problems. The rush to solve applied problems does not always allow the precise definitions necessary for solid and consistent foundations. The goal of this chapter was to provide some precise definitions in the area of cooperation through optimally controlled two-person experiments. Hence, our first question was not, "How do we produce cooperation?," but rather, "What is cooperation?."

What was achieved by our defintions? First, definitions of the cooperation contingency revealed two cooperation effects, minimal and maximal cooperation, that differed in the degree of control exerted by the cooperation contingency. The essential aspect of any cooperation contingency is that the reinforcers of each person depend at least in part upon the other person's responses. Minimal cooperation, the most common cooperation effect, was defined by the mere increase in both persons' cooperative responses. Maximal cooperation included minimal cooperation and an increase in the correspondence of the number of reinforcers obtained by the pair members. Minimal cooperation indicates control by the reinforcer resulting from the cooperation contingency, but maximal cooperation also indicates control by the reciprocal nature of the reinforcement contingency. Hence if complete learning is the goal, maximal cooperation is the target behavior.

Second, the definitions of cooperation suggested ways to test the extent to which responses are actually under the control of the contingency. In some cases, both in everyday life and in research, cooperative-like responses may not be cooperation. Real cooperative responding should pass the following tests: (a) Cooperative responses should be maintained by the reinforcer resulting from the cooperation contingency rather than by another reinforcer resulting from some other contingency. (b) If the cooperation situation is a social one, each person's responses should serve as a discriminative stimulus for the other person's responses so that the responses are under the control of social stimuli. (c) If the cooperative responding is under the control of the reciprocal nature of the cooperation contingency, cooperative responses should result in increased correspondence (maximal cooperation).

Third, the definition of the basic dimensions of the cooperation situation and the extremes of each dimension revealed that cooperation research is not as diffuse as our first glance suggested. The five basic dimensions can be loosely classified in terms of whether they most closely describe (a) discriminative stimuli (the coactor as a social stimulus), (b) the cooperative responses (availability of alternative responses, deviations from reciprocity), or (c) the cooperation contingency (dependency upon coactor's responses for reinforcement, cost of the cooperation response). The extremes of the basic dimensions differ greatly while still falling within the definition of cooperation. Classification of cooperation studies along basic dimensions revealed that studies that had previously appeared so idiosyncratic as to be special cases of cooperation or not related to cooperation at all were simply examples of studies at the extreme ends of the dimensions. For example, on the social dimension the extremes are social and nonsocial situations. Nonsocial situations are not as obviously related to cooperation as are social ones, but they are important in evaluating the extent to which cooperative responses are controlled by the contingency alone, uncomplicated by social stimuli. At the other end of the dimension, social situations are important because they are common in everyday life and because they show how social stimuli affect cooperative responses.

Fourth, the definitions of the basic dimensions of the cooperation situation and correlated social responses may offer suggestions for future research. For example, a functional analysis along a particular dimension of the cooperation situation is the most obvious approach to the study of cooperation; yet, classification of studies under the extremes of the five basic dimensions revealed few dimensions that had been completely explored. Also, correlated social responses, which were defined as responses that occur along with cooperation but are not required by the contingency, revealed another possible approach to the study of cooperation. The reasoning is that if correlated responses such as leadership and auditing occur along with cooperation, they may also affect it. This latter approach to the study of cooperation is the most social one because the occurrence of correlated social responses depends at least in part upon social stimuli.

Fifth, definition of the cooperation contingency can clarify the relations of cooperation to the other major methods of distributing reinforcers in social situations. For example, it is important to separate sharing from cooperation because sharing appears to be more common. The major difference between sharing and cooperation is that in cooperation each person's cooperative responses produce or give reinforcers to the coactor, while in sharing each person's responses produce or take reinforcers for himself. Simply, in cooperation subjects alternate giving reinforcers, while in sharing subjects alternate taking reinforcers. Both cooperation and sharing are defined by an increase in giving or taking responses, respectively, but more importantly both are defined by an increase in the correspondence of the pair members' scores. There are several reasons why sharing may be more common. For example, from a developmental point of view, persons learn to take before they learn to give. Sharing is also an easier resolution of competition than cooperation, because both sharing and competition involve taking responses.

Altruism and competition can also be classified in terms of giving and taking responses. Altruism, like cooperation, involves giving responses, but in altruism one person gives more than the other, resulting in decreased correspondence. Competition, like sharing, involves taking responses, but in competition both persons make taking responses for each reinforcer rather than alternating. Competition is usually associated with decreased correspondence. There are other methods of distributing reinforcers in social situations, but classification along the give and take dimension in terms of increased and decreased correspondence includes the major equitable and inequitable methods of reinforcer distribution and provides a means of distinguishing among them.

The goal has been to define precisely rather than to solve pressing social problems or even to show how to produce one equity effect or another. The rationale was that the definitions would help to organize the area and thereby provide a solid foundation for research into the more complicated issues of producing specific equity or inequity effects and solving pressing social problems. Although not explicitly stated until now, our hope has been that the definitions would be useful to social psychologists as well as to behavior analysts, and that the chapter would encourage more of the latter into the vital and important area of social behavior.

HOWARD RACHLIN[1]

Chapter 8

Self-Control: Part I

We ordinarily use the term *self-control* to describe decisions between alternatives arriving at different times. For instance, having a roast-beef sandwish for lunch provides a reward now; having cottage cheese instead can provide a reward tomorrow when I step on the scale. Take the temporal issue away and the issue of self-control goes away as well. If it were suddenly discovered that cottage cheese was just as fattening (and, therefore, had the same ultimate consequences for me) as a roast-beef sandwich and I still ate the cottage cheese, I would have to admit that I simply like the cottage cheese better. The decision, like one between blue and brown shirts, would become simply one of taste.

When the events chosen between are continuous, in the sense that they cannot be located in a brief temporal interval (e.g., working at a job and being paid at a certain rate), then self-control applies when the events differ in temporal extent. The primary rewards obtained by working at an unpleasant job must extend further in time than the job itself before we ascribe self-control to the worker when he works. If the unpleasantness and pleasantness are completely contemporaneous, self-control is not involved. We would see the worker as weighing the two factors and choosing to work only if the resultant was pleasant. Otherwise, why work? But let the worker's reward extend further in time (to providing for his family, enjoying luxuries, etc.), and working versus not working becomes a matter of self-control.

Psychologists studying self-control (Mischel, 1966; Rotter, 1954) have

1. Preparation of this chapter was supported by a grant from the National Science Foundation. For helpful comments on a previous draft, I thank G. Ainslie, W. Baum, E. Erwin, E. Fantino, R. J. Herrnstein, F. Levine, G. H. Whitehurst, and G. T. Wilson. This chapter is revised from an article that originally appeared in *Behaviorism*, 1974, 2, 94-108.

long noticed that self-control is a "now" versus "later" issue. Their subjects show self-control when they prefer larger rewards in the future to smaller rewards in the present or, symmetrically, when they avoid greater pain in the future in return for lesser pain in the present. In this context, visiting the dentist is showing self-control and not visiting shows lack of self-control. The hedonic picture looks something like that in Figure 8-1. The reason for indecision between two alternatives, one already assumed to be better than the other, is that the better alternative is only better in the long run. The worse alternative offers immediate benefit. The difference between someone who is controlling himself and someone who is not controlling himself is, thus, not in the spatial locus of control (from inside versus from outside his skin) as the term "self-control" seems to imply, but in the temporal locus: how far away from the present must we look to find the source of control. In establishing self-control, the question to ask is how control is shifted from immediate to distant consequences. Again, this is a temporal question, not a spatial one. As Skinner (1956b) has pointed out, however, psychologists have hesitated to ascribe causality to events temporally far apart. They have translated the action of distant events into present events and placed the present events inside the organism. Thus "ego strength," "internalization," "subjective probability," "resistance to frustration," and other cognitive or motivational terms have made their way into discussions of self-control. These terms refer to mediating mechanisms representing, in the present, a set of events that occurred in the past. The contention here is that these mediating

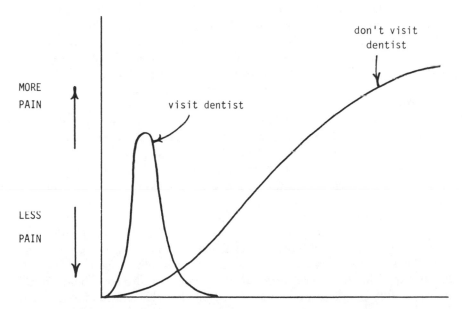

Fig. 8-1. Hypothetical diagram of the way pain would vary on visiting the dentist and without visiting the dentist.

mechanisms are not necessary to understand or empirically study self-control. They served the psychologist, as ether formerly served the physicist, as a way of bridging causes and their consequences when those causes and consequences were separated by an entity through which it was not believed that causality could act. In the case of physicists, this entity was unfilled space. In the case of psychologists, this entity is an unfilled temporal interval. As Staddon (1973) concluded in a recent analysis of causality in psychology, ". . . limitation of the causes of behavior to temporally contiguous stimuli is without justification."

WHAT CAN CAUSE BEHAVIOR?

Much recent psychological research has shown that a cause of behavior can be the relation between that behavior and events in the environment (Baum, 1973; Bloomfield, 1972; Herrnstein and Hineline, 1966; Maier, Seligman and Solomon, 1969). To take one example, Herrnstein and Hineline (1966) arranged a set of contingencies for a rat so that the rate of irregularly delivered brief electric shocks varied inversely with rate of barpressing. If the rats pressed faster, the shocks came slower; if they pressed slower, the shocks came faster. The rats learned to press the bar, although no single barpress avoided any single shock. The rate of barpresses and the rate of shocks were the critical variables. But the rate of a discrete event has no meaning at an instant of time. At any instant the event is either occurring (in which case its rate is infinite) or not occurring (in which case its rate is zero). Consider Figure 8-2. The pips represent shocks or barpresses in a hypothetical replication of the Herrnstein-Hineline experiment. It is generally true that the more barpresses, the fewer shocks. But if all the data were not available, an observer who saw just what was between M and N, O and P, or Q and R might conclude respectively that shocks were causing barpresses, that barpresses were causing shocks, or that the two were unrelated. Only an extended view of the temporal properties of barpresses and shocks allows us to see the true relation. Imagine a rat in the Herrnstein-Hineline experiment that presses the bar as in Figure 8-2. We can now ask, "What causes the barpresses?" In the light of the earlier discussion *the cause of the barpresses is the relation between barpresses and shocks as it has been experienced by the rat.*

Suppose that each barpress in the Herrnstein-Hineline experiment costs the rat something. We could imagine that the effort of pressing was increased or that a low-intensity shock followed each press. In that case, the immediate consequences of not pressing the bar would be painful (or effortful) but the long-term consequences of not pressing the bar would be still more painful. The picture would be something like that shown in Figure 8-1. Replace "visit dentist" by "press bar" and "don't visit dentist" by "don't press bar" and you have a fair picture of the rat's situation. Will rats press bars

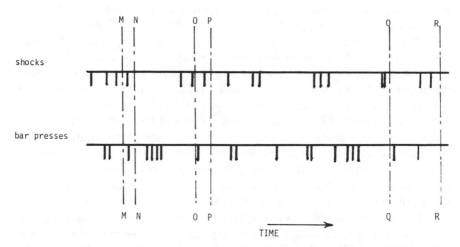

Fig. 8-2. Hypothetical pattern of shocks and responses in the Herrnstein-Hineline experiment. The pips on the top line stand for shocks and the pips on the bottom line stand for responses. The vertical dotted lines represent restricted periods of observation, M-N, O-P and Q-R.

under these conditions? In a more recent experiment, Lambert, Bersh, Hineline, and Smith (1973) arranged contingencies for a rat so that a press produced a single shock immediately but avoided several shocks of equal intensity later. The rats in the Lambert et al. experiment consistently pressed the bar. Can we say that the rats were exhibiting self-control? If the criterion for exhibiting self-control is choosing an alternative that involves a larger future good over a smaller present good, then these rats were exhibiting self-control; they avoided a more painful experience in the distant future in favor of a less painful experience in the immediate future.[2] If on the other hand, we insist that exertions of "ego-strength," "internalization," "expectancy," or other cognitive or motivational events must also go on somewhere within the rat, we shall have the difficult task of trying to verify their occurrence. But such explanatory efforts are unnecessary. The behavior itself is all the evidence we need that self-control is being exerted. What would we say if we discovered that the rat had the appropriate motivational or cognitive apparatus but did not press the bar? It would be pointless, then, to claim that the rat was controlling itself. It is the rat's behavior in relation to the contingencies imposed that comprises self-control.

Similar arguments apply as well to all human instances of self-control.

2. Fantino (1966) showed that pigeons could learn to show self-control in a symmetrical situation with positive reinforcement. The pigeons in Fantino's experiment could obtain an immediate reward (followed by a penalty) by pecking a red key or they could wait a few seconds until the key turned green and obtain a reward with no penalty. The pigeons initially pecked the red key, but after 6 months of training waited for the green key.

Human behavior is more complicated than a rat's behavior not because human behavior is controlled from inside while the rat's behavior is controlled from outside, but because the environmental events controlling human behavior probably occur over a wider temporal interval than those that control the behavior of the rat. When we refuse the third martini at a party (if we do refuse it), it is not because of an exercise of some force within us but part of a response to contingencies spread out widely in time. The wider contingencies involve events on the way home and the next morning, while the narrow contingencies involve only events at the party itself. Why we should act in accordance with wide contingencies rather than narrow ones that dictate acceptance of the drink is another question, which we shall try to deal with later. It suffices to say now that the question is answered no better by referring to internal events or states than it is without them.

Let us return to the rats in the Herrnstein-Hineline experiment. These rats were pressing the bar relatively rapidly and receiving relatively few shocks. We argue here that the contingency between the barpresses and the shocks is the cause of the barpressing. Traditional psychology would invoke the cognitive and motivational mediating mechanisms previously discussed. What is the purpose of those mechanisms? To avoid having an event at one time cause an event at another time, the concept of a state of the organism is introduced. Events at one time affect the state, and the state affects the behavior. The state in question may be motivational or cognitive. Past events are supposed to govern present events via the motivational or cognitive state. Herrnstein (1969), Bolles (1972), and Seligman and Johnston (1973) argued against motivational and for cognitive explanations of the barpressing of rats, but if we grant that temporally extended behavior is directly caused by events similarly extended, there is no need to refer to either kind of state. The notion that cognitive and motivational states mediate between past events and present behavior is not necessary. It obscures the search for the most direct causes of behavior because it tends to direct that search into the organism instead of into the organism's past.

To say that the origin of self-control is not in the self is not to say that the organism has no properties or has been subtracted from consideration. The biological properties of the organism determine which environmental events control which behavioral events. What has been subtracted are those psychological (as opposed to biological) properties of the organism, such as memory, expectancy, response strength, etc., that serve only to bridge temporal gaps. The remaining biological properties of the organism are those that serve for reaction to immediate as well as long-term contingencies. If a man is stabbed and he bleeds, no one will be tempted to talk about memory of the stabbing and response strength of the bleeding intervening between stabbing and bleeding, although the properties of his body determined that he would bleed when stabbed. But for temporally extended events such as dissatisfaction with a bad job, traditional psychological analysis will invoke memory, expectancy, and response strength to bring cause and effect into immediate temporal proximity. It is certainly something about the man that reacts to the long hours, low pay, hostile boss, etc., by complaining, going on strike, or quitting. But it is nevertheless these external temporally extended events that cause his behavior and not his immediate memories, expectations, and response strengths.

Often, widespread and narrow contingencies cause the same behavior. Working at a pleasant job provides rewards now and in the future. The relation previously experienced between these rewards and work, more directly than anything else, causes the work to be done. But often temporally extended events cause behavior in conflict with that caused by temporally constricted events. When such conflict arises, a choice has to be made between the constricted and extended consequences, the choice of extended consequences being self-control.

To say that the cause of action can be narrow or widespread in time is not to say that events have equal effects whenever they occur. There is often a greater weight attached to constricted than to widespread contingencies. The cognitive and motivational theorists invoke gradients of memory and certainty to explain the reduction in control by events far in the future. But given these gradients, they need not be applied first to the state of the organism and only then to its behavior. They can apply directly to behavior. Furthermore, many actions, and in the case of humans most of our significant actions, are unrelated to present causes. We move from one city to another, get married or divorced, get jobs or quit them, not because of anything that is happening at the very moment we perform these actions (even when the actions themselves are brief). It has proved difficult and fruitless, moreover, to trace chains of secondary reinforcers back from some presumably primary reinforcer just to bring the reinforcer in temporal proximity with the acts. If a man moves from Maine to Florida, he does not move because of the weather on the day he moves, although he may be moving because of the weather. The cognitive or motivational theorists will say that the weather in Maine causes a certain state in the man and the weather in Florida causes another state in the man and that moving is reinforced by a transition from one state to the other. But such states have been difficult to pin down. They are awkward, unparsimonious, and invite freewheeling theorizing that can explain anything. Their one convenience, of bringing causes and effects into temporal proximity, is simply not worth its price. The cause of a man's moving from Maine to Florida is most parsimoniously described in terms of the weather in Maine and the weather in Florida (in terms of mean temperatures and average snowfall, etc., i.e., nothing that could occur within a brief temporal interval).

Emphasizing the environment does not mean there are no individual differences in ability to exercise self-control. Like other abilities, self-control undoubtedly develops through some combination of genetic and environmental conditions. Heredity versus environment is not the main issue. What is at issue is whether the causes of behavior we label self-control are different in kind from the causes of behavior we label lack of self-control. Analysis reveals that the two causes differ in degree of temporal extent, and not in their place of origin.

TECHNIQUES OF SELF-CONTROL

The kind of self-control to which we have been referring might be called "brute-force" self-control. When the temptation is offered, it is simply refused. The martini is turned down at the party, the bakery is passed without a purchase, the dessert is pushed away, etc. The direct cause of such behavior is the long-term correlation between the behavior and its consequences.

It might be argued that the view espoused here applies well enough to brute-force self-control but not to more sophisticated techniques of self-control such as those developed by Weight Watchers or Alcoholics Anonymous, or the strategies we constantly invent in everyday life to manipulate our own behavior. Consider the following ways in which a student might get himself to study:

1. He simply studies despite the temptation to go to the movies instead.
2. He rewards himself for studying by going to the movies afterwards.
3. He has previously deposited a fairly large sum of money with a friend. He has instructed the friend to check every half hour during the evening to see that he is studying. If the friend does not find him studying, the friend is further instructed to send the money to a political party whose views are exactly contrary to those of the student.

So far we have discussed only the first alternative, and that only in theory. Let us reserve for the next section speculations on how self-control might be brought about, and turn now to the second and third alternatives. They are both forms of self-control because their object is to increase the likelihood that behavior will accord with its long-term consequences. They are fairly representative types of self-control often recommended by behavior therapists and might be called, respectively, *self-reinforcement* and *commitment*.

Let us consider self-reinforcement first. A little analysis reveals that reinforcers given to oneself do not support the behavior upon which they are contingent. Suppose for a moment that the student in our example increased his studying by going to the movies afterward. Now suppose that this self-reinforcement continued but external reinforcers, the good grades, the knowledge, the social approval to be gained from studying, were withdrawn. How long would studying continue without them? What would be the point of studying? Would going to the movies continue to "work" as a self-imposed reinforcer for studying? One does not have to experiment to answer these questions negatively.[3] In what sense, then, was the movie a reinforcer? This is a critical question because the test for a reinforcer must be whether it can support behavior. If we take away external reinforcers, leaving only self-reinforcement that supports no behavior other than that involved in its consumption,[4] then self-reinforcement loses its effectiveness.

It seems likely that self-reinforcement is a form of secondary reinforcement. Going to the movies might have increased studying not because of its reinforcing properties but because of its stimulus properties. This hypothesis could be tested by substituting neutral but strong stimuli for self-reinforcers. For instance, a student who rewards himself by eating a peanut after each 10 min of studying ought to study as well if, instead of eating it, he simply transfers the peanut from one dish to another as a way of counting 10-min study periods. The question is empirical, but in the research on self-reinforcement with humans or animals, it has rarely been addressed directly.[5]

A behavior therapist might ask his patient to institute a program of self-reinforcement for studying as sort of a cast or mold, but the therapist might not be satisfied until the cast was removed. The program might start with going to the movies as a self-reinforcer, switch to a more convenient and less time-consuming activity like eating peanuts after each 10 min of study, then switch to a program of record-keeping, and then nothing. Presumably by this time the contingency between studying and grades would be controlling studying directly. Relapses might be treated by returning to prior supports. The point is that the sequence from going to the movies to peanuts to record-keeping to nothing may not be a withdrawal of reinforcement but a withdrawal of stimuli.

Self-reinforcement may be like saying to oneself, "Yes, I did just do that," thereby performing the same function as the feedback click that tells the pigeon it has just pecked a key. If the correlation between events affects behavior, other things being equal, correlations between intense stimuli will

3. Yet self-reinforcement has emerged as an area of study with humans (Bandura 1971b) and even animals (Mahoney & Bandura, 1972). The design of these experiments has been criticized by Catania (1975). Catania argues, as I do here, that "self-reinforcement" is a misnomer. The situations in which self-reinforcement is studied, Catania says, are relevant to the concept of self-awareness.

4. The behavior involved in eating, chewing and swallowing, for instance, can be thought of as reinforced by the digestion of food. Restricted to such events, self-reinforcement is a valid and interesting concept. But the more common use of the term is in the sense of example number 2, where the behavior is not consummatory.

5. Bandura and Perloff (1967) had children set their own criterion for a task (turning a crank) and then reward themselves with tokens for reaching it. The children who set their own criterion turned as fast as those whose criterion was set for them (the latter group was also given tokens instead of rewarding themselves). The interesting part of this experiment is the setting of the criterion, which is a question of commitment (why didn't the children set the criterion as low as possible?), and not the self-reward. Once the criterion was set the children would have been disobeying the rules of the "game" (they were told that they were evaluating a game) had they rewarded themselves without reaching criterion.

affect behavior more than will correlations between weak stimuli. The feedback involved in self-reinforcement may well be more intense than the
normal proprioceptive and kinesthetic feedback of most behavior. Where
this is not the case, self-reinforcement should not work.

Occasionally the term self-reinforcement is used the way cognitive and
motivational internal mechanisms of self-control have been used, to bring
cause and effect into temporal contiguity. If, as the cognitive and motivational theorists assume, reinforcement must come immediately after the act
being reinforced but no immediate external reinforcer is observed, then one
has to be invented. Covert self-reinforcement is a likely candidate. It provides all the advantages of unobservable (hence, untestable) concepts while
preserving the flavor of behavioral terminology. But covert self-
reinforcement, rather than lending rigor to a basically vague underlying
concept, is in danger of lending vagueness to the basically rigorous behavioral terminology it borrows.

Now let us turn to the sorts of involved strategies exemplified by the
third alternative, where the student has made an agreement with his friend
to send his money to an opposing political party if he does not study. This
self-control involves a commitment. It is rather like the signing of a contract
specifying various kinds of performance in the future and setting forth penalties for failure to comply. Ainslie (described in Rachlin, 1970, pp. 185-189)
and Rachlin and Green (1972) argued that commitment of this kind follows
from the simple descriptions of choice advanced by Logan (1965) and
Herrnstein (1970). We showed that complicated internal mechanisms were
not necessary to explain commitment; rats and pigeons were capable of using
commitment strategies in stituations where the contingencies involved were
straightforward. Ainslie's argument and experiment differ in detail from
Green's and mine, but the main arguments are the same and will be summarized here.

Suppose that the long-term consequences of studying are valuable, but
occasionally the value of not studying rises above studying. The dilemma is
that, because of the short-term aversive consequences of studying, the time
in the presence of stimuli that make it possible to study (a quiet room with a
desk, a book, a pad, and sharpened pencils) is the very time that the value of
not studying rises above studying. As soon as those stimuli are removed, say,
while lying in bed in the morning, the value of studying assumes its usual
high place. This is where a commitment strategy is useful. The student is
offered the contract (the commitment outlined in the third alternative), and
it is accepted at a time when the value of studying is high. The commitment
reduces the student's choice; it compels him to study.

Figure 8-3 diagrams the commitment decision process in this case. Two
decisions are in question. Decision X takes place in the evening, when the
student is supposed to study. Decision Y takes place the morning before.
The decision at time X is between studying and not studying. But at time X

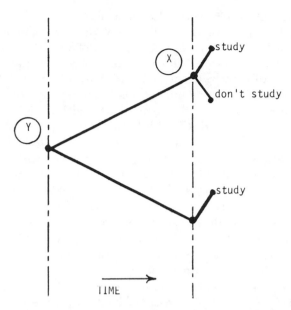

Fig. 8-3. Flow diagram of commitment to study. Choice at X is between studying and not studying. It is assumed that a student would not study at X. Choice at Y is between having a choice later (top arm) and being forced to study later (bottom arm). A student who would not study at X might nevertheless commit himself to study by choosing the bottom arm at Y.

the short-term consequences of not studying will determine the student's choice. Thus, not studying will be the invariable result. The other decision at time Y is whether to agree to the commitment. Assuming the commitment is effective (that the student absolutely will not tolerate sending his money to an opposing political party), instituting the commitment is equivalent to choosing the lower branch of Figure 8-3, to studying and experiencing the consequences thereof. But given the value structure as outlined, at time Y the value of studying is higher than that of not studying and the student must agree to the commitment.

Once the commitment is available and the contingencies are made effective, commitment behavior follows automatically. To emphasize that exercise of commitment was not dependent on ego strength, internalization, resistance to frustration, or other sophisticated cognitive or motivational apparatus, Ainslie showed with rats, and Green and Rachlin with pigeons, that relatively naive animals would exhibit commitment. The experiment Green and Rachlin did closely follows the schema of Figure 8-3. The choice at X for the pigeons was between a small immediate food reward (analogous to not studying in Figure 8-3) and a larger food reward delayed by several seconds (analogous to studying in Figure 8-3). The pigeons invariably chose the small immediate reward at X. But, at Y, several seconds before X, when they could choose to restrict subsequent alternatives, they chose not to have a choice; they chose the bottom branch of Figure 8-3 and obtained the larger (but delayed) reward. The values of the delays and amounts were determined by Herrnstein's (1970) model for choice, which predicts that preference varies directly with amount and inversely with delay.[6] The model further predicts that commitment will be more likely the greater the temporal separation between the choices at Y and X. This was also confirmed.

It is necessary to distinguish between two operations—the exercise of the commitment strategy and the invention of the strategy. While the exercise of commitment clearly has nothing to do with higher mental processes, the invention of commitment strategies is apparently another matter. The invention may be performed by the user (the student) or by another person (his friend or therapist), but inventing a commitment strategy is not exercising self-control. Neither does it take ego strength, internalization, etc. to invent a self-control strategy, any more than these qualities were needed for inventing the cotton gin. Self-control is the use of the strategy so that one's behavior will accord with its long-term consequences. And use of the strategy occurs automatically once an effective strategy is invented.

Invention of a complex strategy like that described previously (or Odysseus tying himself to the mast of his ship and plugging the ears of his crew with wax to sail past the sirens, hear their song, and still not sail his ship onto the rocks) may be a peculiarly human quality. Here contingencies are manipulated not between behavior and rewards directly, but between behavior and other complex contingencies. One might call the contingencies giving rise to such inventions *metacontingencies*. But metacontingencies of a relatively simple sort are to be found throughout behavioral research with animals. Compound schedules of reinforcement such as chained schedules involve behavior controlled not by reinforcement directly but by still another contingency between behavior and reinforcement.

To summarize, both self-reinforcement and commitment are related to self-control because they both increase the likelihood that behavior will be

6. According to Herrnstein's model, the relative value of two activities is:

$$\frac{V1}{V2} = \frac{A1}{A2} \cdot \frac{D2}{D1} ,$$

where A is amount and D is delay of reinforcement. In Green and Rachlin's experiment the first alternative was a small immediate reward and the second a larger delayed reward. $A1/A2$ always equalled .5, and $D2$ was always 4 sec greater than $D1$. Referring to Figure 8-3, at choice X,

$$\frac{V1}{V2} = .5\left(\frac{4}{0}\right) = \infty ,$$

predicting that the small immediate reward would be chosen. At choice Y, 10 sec earlier,

$$\frac{V1}{V2} = .5\left(\frac{4+10}{0+10}\right) = .7 ,$$

predicting that the large delayed reward would be chosen.

controlled by its long-term consequences. Self-reinforcement makes the relation between behavior and its consequences more vivid by providing stimuli correlated with those consequences. Commitment restricts choice so that behavior will automatically conform to long-term consequences.

TEACHING SELF-CONTROL

Unfortunately, we have little to say in this section. Most of the research on self-control has been on the personality correlates of people who are good at controlling themselves. The old, it seems, do it better than the young (Mischel, 1958), the sane better than the schizophrenic (Klein, 1967), the intelligent better than the unintelligent (Mischel & Metzner, 1962), the rich better than the poor (Maitland, 1976), etc. Obviously, self-control is a good thing. But environmental events that can generate self-control (i.e., shift the cause of behavior from short-term to long-term events) have not been systematically examined.

The preceding analysis would direct study to the following areas:

1. Does practice with long-term contingencies controlling one activity increase the likelihood that they will control other activities? The notion of "addictive personalities" implies that some people cannot or do not respond to long-term contingencies over a range of circumstances. Can they be taught to behave generally in accord with these contingencies? Perhaps a person who has learned not to overeat will have an easier time learning not to smoke. This implies that the way to begin curing harmful habits may be through control of other habits. For instance, alcoholics might first be trained to keep weight under control or to stop smoking. Control of eating an ice cream sundae by the next day's consequences might transfer to control of getting drunk by the next day's consequences.

2. The long-term antecedents and consequences of certain events might be isolated from those of other events by techniques to make them more vivid or salient. The subject is in pretty much the same state with respect to observation of events controlling his behavior as the observer is. The reason that we know better than anyone else what causes our behavior is not that we have access to our internal sources of control but simply that we have more behavioral data.

   Counting and timing events with mechanical or written aids and the techniques of self-reinforcement (and self-punishment) are, as we have indicated before, ways to increase the salience of the relation between behavior and its consequences. Simply counting calories has been found as effective in short-term weight reduction as self-reward, external monetary reward, aversive imagery in connection with food, and relaxation training (Romanczyk, Tracey, Wilson, & Thorpe, 1974). The reason may be that the reward for eating less is losing weight regardless of the subsidiary rewards inserted between the two events. These subsidiary rewards do no more than emphasize the relation between eating and losing weight, a function performed just as well by counting calories.

3. Finally, commitment strategies may be instituted. Like self-reinforcement strategies, they may be kept in force permanently. Behavior in accord with long-term contingencies is guaranteed as long as they are in force: If I habitually keep my alarm clock across the room from my bed, I will have to get out of bed every morning to turn it off. This technique of getting myself up in the morning is one that can conveniently be used every day. But often commitment strategies involve awkward or expensive apparatus, and because they are commitments they limit choice. Ironically in the ultimate long term, it may be better occasionally to behave according to short-term contingencies (i.e., to act impulsively). Rigid commitment does not allow such behavior and may be undesirable for that reason. Commitment strategies thus might often be instituted only to bring behavior initially into conformity with long-term consequences. Once these consequences are experienced, they may serve to maintain behavior by themselves. Recent experiments in Rachlin's laboratory with children show that some children over the course of several sessions (with a device like the one used with pigeons) came to rely less and less on commitment and more on brute-force self-control. Initially, when commitment was not available, those children who chose larger delayed rewards were less likely to use the commitment strategy when it was offered than the children who chose the smaller immediate reward. In other words there was a direct relation between impulsivity (choice of small immediate rewards) and use of commitment. As children became less impulsive, their need to restrict their choices in advance decreased as well.

It may be naive to expect that harmful habits with complex and varied etiologies should be curable by such straightforward techniques but, straightforward as the techniques may be, they have not yet been tried, perhaps because of a tendency to focus on the inner organism when faced with problems of self-control. If these techniques or similar ones work, it will be the best kind of evidence that such a focus is misplaced.

THOMAS A. BRIGHAM[1]

Self-Control: Part II

This chapter is not a literature review, nor is it a research critique, nor is it a how-to-do-it manual. Rather than reanalyzing specific aspects of self-control, an attempt will be made to examine and comment on the general area of self-control from an operant perspective. The term *self-control* has a variety of everyday meanings. Most commonly, self-control is assumed to be something possessed by an individual. As a corollary, it is also perceived as a characteristic or capacity that some individuals have and others do not. Consequently, it is not unusual to hear comments such as, "Bev has a great deal of self-control." What sort of behavior causes an observer to say that an individual possesses self-control? Typically, this honor is conferred for the following sorts of behavior: It is the middle of the semester. Sally is working on a term paper that is not due for another week when some friends come by and ask her to go to the latest movie with them. She considers and says she would like to go to the movie, but has to work on her term paper. Or, George is on the heavy side, but not really overweight. He and some friends have just finished dinner and it is time to order dessert. His friends all order lavish desserts while George declines and has only coffee, saying he has to watch his weight. These two, of course, are oversimplified examples, but they contain responses usually referred to as self-control: Each case involves an opportunity to engage in some desirable behavior (i.e., Sally enjoys having fun with her friends, and George likes rich desserts); also, in each instance the individual chooses an apparently less desirable alternative. Because the individual's behavior appears to contradict the observer's expectations, it calls for some sort of explanation.

1. The preparation of this chapter was supported in part by grant IROIMH26084-01 to the Center for Applied Behavioral Research, Washington State University from the applied branch of the National Institute of Mental Health.

Because the observer's disconfirmed expectation is based on a personal perception of the desirability of the alternative (e.g., going to the movie is more fun than writing a term paper), the observed behavior apparently cannot be explained in terms of the immediate environmental variables. Thus the observer, having eliminated the environment, has only one other place to look for the explanation of the behavior: within the individuals themselves. Consequently, it is not surprising that until recently, self-control was talked about in terms of such personality traits as character, will power, determination, etc.

In contrast to this traditional view, a growing body of literature suggests that such self-control can be systematically taught. This position developed from studying not those individuals who displayed a high degree of self-control but those who lacked it. Realistically it is more common to hear comments about George's lack of will power (e.g., "He can't seem to control his urge to eat") than possession of it. Similarly it is not the presence of self-control skills that brings the individual to a psychologist but their absence. Individuals complain that they cannot control their urges to smoke, drink, eat, engage in socially inappropriate responses, scream at their children, hit their wives or husbands, etc. On the other hand, such individuals cannot find the will power to study, complete projects, get to work on time, be nice to their families, make new friends. As long as will power or self-control is viewed as a personality characteristic, little help can be given to individuals with such problems. But as the problems are analyzed as kinds of behavior that may be learned, it becomes possible to develop programs to deal with them. In other words, if self-control responses are learned, then the absence of such responses can be remediated by simply teaching the appropriate responses.

The majority if not all of the situations where self-control is invoked appear to involve some difference between the immediate consequences of a response and its delayed consequences. Smoking is a good example of a response, the immediate consequences of which are positive for most smokers, but the accumulated delayed consequences of which are clearly negative. Smoking is further complicated because even when the delayed negative consequences occur, they are not easily discriminated by the individual. That is to say, not only are there no clear immediate aversive consequences, but the delayed consequences for each response (identified by medical research) are so small they cannot be discriminated by the individual. Later, when consequences such as coughing, sore throat, and shortness of breath do appear, smoking has been additionally strengthened by other behavioral processes to the point where the response is still difficult to eliminate when the consequences change. A process that contributes to self-control problems is antecedent stimulus control. In the case of smoking, the response is easy to emit concurrent or in conjunction with other responses in a wide variety of settings. As smoking occurs consistently in many situations, these stimuli set the occasion for subsequent smoking. For example, many people smoke while drinking coffee. Because the two responses occur together, engaging in one may become a cue for the other. Later, when the smoker attempts to quit, coffee provides powerful antecedent stimuli for smoking.

Another example of self-control based on a difference between immediate and delayed consequences involves going to the dentist. This instance appears to consist of immediate aversive stimuli and larger delayed aversive consequences. Here the individual may not go to the dentist because the response is followed by some pain or discomfort and is therefore punished. Such small immediate aversive consequences are apparently sufficient to reduce the likelihood of going to the dentist until the delayed consequences of not going are felt. The resulting painful stimulation then forces the person to visit the dentist to escape that pain. If the individual had simply gone to the dentist in the first place, the delayed aversive painful consequences could have been avoided. These two examples indicate that the difference between the immediate and delayed consequences is a major variable in self-control.

THE ROLE OF THE ENVIRONMENT

Are the phenomena of self-control behavioral phenomena? And if so, does the term self-control have any special meaning? The answer to both questions is yes. Self-control can be analyzed in terms of behavioral principles. But, in addition, self-control involves a special class of responses that has important implications for the analysis of behavior.

The authors of introductory psychology texts often begin the section on behaviorism and learning theory with the equation $B = f(E)$. The generally accepted translation of the equation is that behavior is a function of the environment. This, of course, is a difficult statement to argue with. It is also totally gratuitous because it does not specify how behavior is controlled by the environment. Most writers then go on to give examples from laboratory research of how the responses of an organism in an experimental chamber may be changed by manipulating aspects of the organism's environment. These instances of behavioral principles are extremely powerful, and by the end of the exposition the author has built a case for what may be called the controlling environment model of behavior. Greatly oversimplified, the major assumption of this model is that to change an individual's behavior you simply change that individual's environment. The student comes away with the impression that the environment is somehow a monolithic, immutable force that molds behavior irrespective of other factors.

The concept of the controlling environment is either explicitly or implicitly held by many psychologists both within and without operant psychology. What is wrong with this concept of the environment and behavior? Simply put, it is incorrect in its view of the environment. The usual criticism at this point is to say that the real environment is infinitely more complex than the laboratory one; that may be true, but it is not the critical error. The error is in how the typical laboratory environment is viewed and to a certain degree in how it operates. The laboratory environment is primarily a static one, in which the organism's responses have no direct effect on the basic contingencies that the experimenter has scheduled. This is by necessity: In order for an experimenter to evaluate the effects of a particular variable on behavior, an experimenter must carefully control that variable and others. But the environment is not impervious to the effects of the responding organism; it changes.

At this point the reader may object that the animal's behavior does interact with the experimenter's. The experimenter designs the environment, monitors the animal's responses in that environment, and changes the environment when appropriate. These activities of the experimenter represent a major advance in the methodology of the experimental analysis of behavior. This interaction of the investigator with the experimental organism is an important feature of inductive research (Sidman, 1960; Skinner, 1956a). Careful monitoring of the organism's responses allows the investigator to manipulate an independent variable and directly observe the effects on the animal's responding. Thus the laboratory environment does change in a systematic manner related to the organism's responses. But there are two differences between changes in the laboratory environment and those in the natural environment. The first is simply the immediacy of change. The relations between individual and environment are constantly and immediately changing in both small and large ways. This, of course, is mainly a difference of degree, but the importance of immediacy of a consequence contingent on a response is well documented. Similarly, it is likely that the immediacy of change plays an important role in the functioning of the natural environment.

The second difference is again one of degree and has to do with reciprocity. The relations between the organism and its environment are dynamic and reciprocal. The environment changes the organism's behavior, but it is changed by that behavior in turn. This is especially true for humans, where the important environment consists for the most part of other humans. In these situations the organism-environment distinction changes with perspective: one organism's responses can be another organism's stimuli.

There is, of course, a similar reciprocal relation between the experimenter's behavior and that of the experimental organism. But there is a form of insulation between the experimenter's responses and the changes in the organism's behavior; changes in the organism's behavior are systematically transformed, quantified, and analyzed, and, therefore, may have an impact on the experimenter's behavior only in remote and indirect ways. Although these processes may carry the weight of scientific method, they can lead to the view that changes in the environment are separate from changes in the experimenter's behavior. The conclusion is that the environment has changed the organism's behavior, but it ignores the complementary change in the environment (the experimenter's behavior) produced by the changes in the organism's responses.

Although this concept of the interaction between behavior and the environment is not a radical departure from current operant theory, the differences are important for the analysis of self-control. Skinner, in his analysis of operant behavior, has often focused on the effects of responses on the environment. One reason he selected the term operant was because the response operates on the environment. By implication to operate means to affect, to produce results, to change. Therefore, this informal definition of the operant implied that the response changes the environment (Skinner, 1953a). In his more formal discussions of the operant, however, Skinner chose to give a heavier weight to the role of the environment. Here it is the environment that affects the response, i.e., changes its frequency. Thus the operant becomes a response whose future probability of occurrence is a function of its stimulus consequences. But again, in his discussions of countercontrol (Skinner, 1948b, 1974) and self-control (Skinner, 1953a); he takes the position that the individual can change his or her own environment. But Skinner contends that in the ultimate the environment determines behavior:

If this is correct, little ultimate control remains with the individual. A man may spend a great deal of time designing his own life—he may choose the circumstances in which he is to live with great care, and he may manipulate his daily environment on an extensive scale. Such activity appears to exemplify a high order of self-determination. But it is also behavior, and we account for it in terms of other variables in the environment and history of the individual. It is these variables which provide the ultimate control [p 240].

What are we to make of these apparent inconsistencies in Skinner's position on the role of the environment? The problems are resolved by recognizing that these statements represent different levels of description in Skinner's analysis of behavior. As a consequence, it is possible to hold as a major theoretical assumption that in the ultimate it is the environment that controls behavior, but still to assert that in the day-to-day operation of the environment the individual can change the environment by behaving.

Unfortunately both critics and practitioners of the analysis of behavior too often focus on Skinner's statements about the environment as the ultimate source of control and ignore other aspects of his analysis of behavior. For the applied behavior researcher, however, Skinner's position on countercontrol and on the ability of the individual to change the environment is as important as his assumptions concerning the ultimate role of the environment in controlling behavior. To elaborate, when we teach someone a new skill, we do two things: We change that individual's behavior by an environmental manipulation, but we also make it possible for the individual to change the environment. For example, an extensive systematic environmental program may be required to teach a retarded child to speak. But the child who has once learned to speak has a whole new set of responses that can operate on and change his or her own environment. The child who can speak has a different environment from the child who cannot speak. True, it can be argued that the child changed because the environment changed, but we must not ignore the complementary changes in the child's ability to alter the environment. Augmenting an individual's ability to deal with the environment should be of more concern to the behavior analyst then changing behavior by manipulating the environment directly.

The controlling-environment position continues to be widely held because of its manipulative and explanatory power. When an experimenter places an organism in a particular environment arranged in a specific manner, it is an extremely powerful reinforcer for the experimenter if the organism's behavior conforms to a predicted outcome. Likewise, the application to human problems of those principles and procedures derived from the laboratory has been extremely successful in many instances. Numerous examples of such successes can be found in the *Journal of Applied Behavior Analysis, Behavior Therapy, Behavior Research and Therapy* and other journals. Also, there has been a very practical reason for the environmental emphasis in both laboratory and applied research: To date, it has been easier to manipulate the environment directly because more knowledge is currently available for isolating and manipulating environmental variables than for dealing with individual variables.

This position, however, appears to be reaching a point of diminishing returns as the sole basis for behavioral research and programs. An examination of many successful behavior modification research programs shows that they have involved powerful consequences in relatively constrained environments. For example, Lovaas's (1973) research with autistic children used powerful reinforcers and punishers in an extremely controlled environment. This in no way negates the achievements of Lovaas and his associates, but simply puts that research into the context of the controlling-environment model. Violating the constraints and assumptions of the model greatly reduces the applicability of behavior modification procedures if innovative corrections are not undertaken. Reppucci and Saunders (1974) found just these sorts of difficulties in their research at the Connecticut School for Boys. Their initial conception of the project was to design an environment that they would control to "shape up" the boys' behavior. In designing their programs, they appear to have assumed that their work with the boys represented a closed system, in that no one would interfere with their control of the boys' environment. Unfortunately the behavior of a variety of individuals, boys, administrators, politicians, etc., failed to match the investigator's expectations and impeded the operation of their controlled environment. Because they were unable to manipulate the environment as they had expected, they then concluded that the assumptions of the operant model about how to change behavior did not work and that what was needed was a new form of social psychology. Such an out-of-hand rejection of an operant approach appears inappropriate, because many programs, such as Achievement Place (Chapter 18), have overcome these difficulties. In the Achievement Place program, environmental changes are considered and adaptive self-control skills are taught. But as a consequence, this overall program and its procedures more closely fit the proposed model of the changing environment than that of the controlling one. Similarly, until the recent work on self-control procedures, the adult with minor to moderate adjustment problems who was still operating in the natural environment was generally outside the domain of behavior modification or behavior therapy. This was the case primarily because the assumptions about how to change behavior (i.e., making systematic changes in the environment) could not be made to operate in that individual's environment.

In general, because the model used in much behavior modification research has not adequately considered the interaction between the client and the modifier, the method for dealing with problems in a project has been to attempt to gain more control of the environment. This in turn has contributed greatly to the public's concern about behavior modification, as witnessed by the Erwin report (1974) and the Law Enforcement Assistance Agency's public statement of no longer supporting behavior modification projects (Law Enforcement Assistance Administration, 1974; see also Chapter 20 in this book).

Because of its emphasis on the reciprocal interactions between organism and environment, an analysis of the environment as proposed here makes it possible to anticipate these difficulties and to develop noncoercive procedures for dealing with them. For example, when the teacher is no longer considered an impervious controlling environment for the children in a class, we will teach the teacher in advance how to respond appropriately to the countercontrolling responses of the students, principal, and other teachers. Further, the notion of a changing environment and the corollary emphasis on the individual's ability to change the environment will make it possible to present the principles and procedures of applied behavioral research and behavior modification in a less threatening manner to the public (an important part of our environment).

Thus far, the arguments for a changing environment have rested on hypothetical examples and logical analyses. One has only to examine behavioral research from this new perspective, however, to discover many instances where this type of interaction occurs and plays a major role in the outcome. For example, watching a student in an introductory experimental psychology lab attempt to shape a rat's lever press illustrates the principles of a changing environment. By observing both organisms, it is difficult to tell which is the experimenter because the student's behavior changes in response to the rat's behavior; the rat by responding *changes* its environment, the student's behavior.

Another example occurred in a study of how hard children would work for the opportunity to choose their own reinforcers rather than having the experimenter choose them (Brigham & Stoerzinger, 1976). Basically, during

the initial stages of the study it was easy for the children to earn the opportunity to choose. Under these conditions all the children displayed a clear
preference for choosing. Next, it was made progressively more difficult to
earn this privilege. Although it was not anticipated in this study, this sort of
procedure in the laboratory sometimes produces aggressive responses that
are labeled *schedule-induced aggression* (Fantino, 1973). In the laboratory,
however, the aggression is directed at inanimate objects or other animals.
The experimenter counts these attacks and continues to manipulate the
environment to analyze what variables produce the aggression. Although our
procedures also produced aggression, there was an important difference:
Children did not direct their aggression at inanimate objects but at us and at
other children. As more children came into this condition, the area outside
the experimental chamber became totally chaotic, with children verbally and
physically attacking one another, refusing to participate in the study that
day, and threatening us with a variety of colorful fates. Needless to say, we
changed the procedures. Again the individual's behavior caused us to change
our behavior, and as a consequence the environment changed.

Another example of environmental change is provided by special-
education students who were taught to change their social and educational
environments (Graubard, Rosenberg, & Miller, 1974). Special-education
children often interact with a hostile environment that has labeled them
deviant and, therefore, as people who can be treated with less respect, subjected to more ridicule, given more negative comments, etc. Graubard et al.
taught a group of special-education children some simple reinforcement and
extinction techniques. They showed them how to reinforce the positive
comments of teachers and normal students. For example, the children were
taught to make the "uh huh" (I understand) response when a teacher carefully explained something to them, and to thank the teacher and praise the
teacher's efforts. On the other hand, the students broke eye contact after and
were generally unresponsive to the teacher's negative comments. Similar
procedures were used with other students in the school. Again these procedures involved the systematic manipulation of the environment to teach the
children the skills. But as their behavior was changed by the environment,
they in turn became more skillful in manipulating their environment. For
instance, when the special-education children used their new social skills,
there was an increase in positive comments, approaches etc. and a complementary decrease in negative ones by the teachers and "normal" students
toward the special-education children. The special-education students, by
changing their behavior, changed their environment and made further positive changes possible. In addition their changed behavior changed the
teacher's environment and that of other students, because the special-
education children were now a source of social reinforcers. Graubard et al.
(1974) appropriately labeled their approach an environmental or ecological
one.

What are the implications of this view of the environment for the area of self-control? First, self-control becomes a meaningful and accurate description of one's ability to control one's behavior by changing one's environment. A second implication follows from the observation that individuals currently vary in the extent that they have learned self-control behavior and consequently in their ability to change their own behavior and environment. The more self-control responses that individuals have learned, the more influence they will have on their own lives. Finally, it then follows that research in self-control offers tremendous potential for improving human society.

A BEHAVIOR ANALYSIS OF SELF-CONTROL

Given the proposition that self-control is a meaningful label for one's abilities to change the environment and one's own behavior, the next question is how these processes should be analyzed. Put another way, are the principles of behavior different when individuals apply them to the analysis and modification of their own behavior? From the experimental literature and anecdotal reports, it appears that the individual may be changed, but are the principles? For instance, as Sally learns to discriminate the social antecedents and consequences of her responses, she may become more sensitive and socially skilled. It is likely, however, that the principles of discrimination are the same as those involved when a rat in an experimental chamber learns to discriminate among complex stimuli. If the principles of behavior remain the same, then in the analysis of self-control we are studying the application of these principles and procedures by the individual to the analysis and modification of the individual's own behavior. This is not to suggest that individuals who do not understand the principles of behavior cannot exhibit self-control responses, but rather that the systematic development of self-control will be based on the application of these principles by the individual. Again, if the principles remain the same, then the same basic paradigms that organize those principles for the analysis of other phenomena may be used for the analysis of self-control. To date, however, attempts to analyze the phenomena associated with self-control have produced a variety of divergent theoretical formats and approaches. For example, Bandura (1971b) suggested that self-control may be analyzed in terms of three basic processes: self-monitoring, self-evaluation, and self-reinforcement. This formulation has been modified by breaking self-reinforcement into two distinct processes: self-determination of reinforcement and self-administration of reinforcers (Glynn, Thomas, & Shee, 1973). On the other hand, Kanfer and Karoly (1972) have attempted to apply an internal-external analysis to self-control phenomena. They suggest that any response situation may be analyzed in terms of alpha (external) and beta (internal) variables. The contribution of either of these variables to any response can vary between 0% and 100%. In self-control situations the beta variables predominate. They further argue that alpha variables may later function as beta variables. For example, signing a contract may initially involve alpha variables, but the contract and assorted cognitive responses may then become internalized (beta) variables affecting future responding. Also, in a recent analysis Kanfer, Cox, Greiner, and Karoly (1974) suggest that self-control responding involves two steps: first, the decision to control, and then the actual self-control responses. They further suggest that different variables affect responding at each step. Similarly, Premack (1970b), in his analysis of self-control, argued that individuals' perception of inconsistency in their behavior and their commitment to resolve that inconsistency is the most important component in the self-control process. In contrast, Skinner (1953a) and Rachlin (1974) focused their analyses on the specific controlled and controlling responses in the self-control situation.

Even this small sample of positions shows that research and speculation about self-control is producing divergent opinions. This sort of situation is a symptom of the fragmentation of an active research area. It would be most unfortunate if such a process were to occur in the area of self-control. Rather than more theories at this point, the analysis of self-control needs to focus on the two distinct sets of behavior involved: the problem responses and the corrective controlling responses. We shall first look at the defining characteristics of situations typically labeled self-control problems. As discussed earlier, the major casual variable in many problems of self-control is the difference between the immediate and delayed consequences of a response or a set of responses: There is some immediate consequence that has a controlling effect on the response while there are later consequences for the response or alternative incompatible responses that have opposite effects from the immediate consequences. For instance, the student who goes out to drink beer with his friends instead of finishing a term paper is emitting responses that have immediate positive consequences (e.g., drinking beer, talking to friends, escaping the term paper), but that may also have delayed aversive consequences (staying up all night to finish the paper, turning in a poor quality paper, not getting it in at all, and/or receiving a poor grade on the paper). Even though the student may swear he will never do that again (an apparent commitment response), it is likely that he will engage in similar responses in the future. If such behavior occurs often, we would say that this student has a self-control problem with studying. This particular example involves immediate positive consequences and delayed aversive consequences. Most problems of overconsumption (i.e., eating, drinking, smoking) appear to fit this particular set of contingencies. Both component contingencies must be present to produce self-control problems. If it were not for heart disease, lung cancer, emphysema, and the like, few people would worry about smoking. Thus, smoking would no longer be a self-control problem.

There are three other basic variations of these contingencies. A re-

Table 8-1
Responding (R_1) and not-responding (R_0) alternatives in self-control, and consequences for each alternative. The problem response is indicated by an asterisk (*).

Response	Example	Immediate consequence	Delayed consequence
*R_1	Smoking	Minor reinforcing event	Major aversive event
R_0	Not smoking	No reinforcing event	No aversive event
*R_1	Spending money	Minor reinforcing event	No reinforcing event
R_0	Not spending (saving)	No reinforcing event	Major reinforcing event
R_1	Going to dentist	Minor aversive event	No aversive event
*R_0	Not going to dentist	No aversive event	Major aversive event
R_1	Making new friends	Minor aversive event	Major reinforcing event
*R_0	Not meeting new people	No aversive event	No reinforcing event

sponse may have immediate aversive consequences but failure to make the response may have even larger delayed aversive consequences, as in the dental example. A similar set of contingencies is when an individual whose initial social interactions have been punished in the past is, as a consequence, less likely to make social advances. Here the reduction of important behavior by small immediate aversive consequences may lead to the long-range loss of greater positive social interactions with an increased sphere of friends and acquaintances, i.e., if the individual had emitted the approach responses, they may have led to the development of new friends and enjoyable activities. Finally, a response may produce a small immediate positive consequence, but not emitting that response and instead emitting an alternative response may produce a larger delayed positive consequence. Behavior such as saving money in small amounts may eventually result in the purchase of a large reinforcer while spending that same amount immediately might produce only small reinforcers.

Although behavioral psychologists have tried to avoid analyzing phenomena in terms of non-responding, non-responding appears to be an important component in analyzing self-control problems. In every self-control situation, the problem is a particular response that is either occurring or not occurring. As a consequence, it is important to examine the contingencies for both the occurrence and the non-occurrence of the target response. The four sets of immediate and delayed consequences for the target response are summarized in Table 8-1. The first two instances are situations where the self-control problem is the occurrence of the target response while in the second two it is the non-occurrence of a particular response that constitutes the problem. The contingencies in the table are identified in terms of both stimulus and operation; a response can affect either a reinforcing or an aversive stimulus.

An important feature of self-control is made explicit by these examples. The immediate contingencies involve small consequences, either positive or negative, while the delayed consequences are all major but potential. Cases are well documented of individuals who smoked two packs of cigarettes a day throughout their adult life, and who died of old age at 95 without any health problems related to smoking. Similarly, regular visits to the dentist will not guarantee the avoidance of serious dental problems.

A less obvious aspect of self-control problems follows from the nature of the consequences for the responses that need to be changed. The required direction of change is a function of the immediate consequences: when the immediate consequences are positive (e.g., smoking, or spending rather than saving), the target response needs to be decreased in frequency, and when the immediate consequences are negative (e.g., going to the dentist, or fighting shyness), the target response needs to be increased.

Most self-management studies, to date, have offered no theoretical framework for the analysis of self-control, but have simply attempted to manipulate the consequences associated with the problem response. On the other hand, theoretical approaches to the modification of problem responses focus on responses antecedent to the self-control problem response. To varying degrees, Premack (1970b), Kanfer and Karoly (1972), and Rachlin and Green (1972) can be seen as proponents of this position, by arguing that the antecedent response or responses somehow changes the value of the consequences for the problem response. Premack and Kanfer and Karoly concentrate on what might be called the decision to control. For example, Premack suggests that something happens that forces the individual to examine his or her behavior, and the behavior is found to be degrading. This in turn causes the individual to feel humiliation whenever the response occurs. As a consequence the person attempts to control the response to avoid the aversive stimuli associated with it. It is interesting to note that Skinner (1953a) similarly based his analysis of self-control on negative reinforcement. Skinner, however, does not suggest how this aversion develops, whereas Premack contends that the humiliation-decision sequence is necessary for self-control responding.

A different approach is taken by Rachlin and Green (1972; cf. Chapter 8: Part I in this book). They focus their analysis on what they label commitment responses. These responses commit the organism to engaging in a response that is incompatible with the problem response. In the standard situation the consequences for the two available responses will result in the organism emitting the problem response. But at an earlier time, the organism has an opportunity to emit the commitment response before the situation in which the problem response occurs. The commitment response is followed by a

different set of stimuli in the presence of which only the alternative response can occur (cf. Figure 8-3). The key to this interpretation is that preferences vary over time. The alcoholic, while sober, is more likely to make a commitment to abstain from drinking if the next opportunity to drink is sometime in the future than if the opportunity is immediately at hand. Thus, if the environment can be arranged appropriately, the organism will emit the commitment response and the desired response in turn. Rachlin and Green (1972) demonstrated these relations in an experiment in which pigeons when given the choice of responding for immediate 2-sec access to grain or delayed 4-sec access preferred the immediate consequence. From an analysis of the combined gradients of delay and magnitude, it was predicted that if the pigeons were forced to make the choice 10 sec in advance of the opportunity to earn an immediate or delayed reward, they would choose the larger but delayed reward. In general this prediction was confirmed. Rachlin and Green suggest that, when invented by an individual, the commitment-response paradigm may be used as one model for self-control.

Although there is much of value in the model, several problems make it impossible to extrapolate it directly to applied problems. First, in the laboratory setting, after making the commitment response the animal is left with the opportunity to emit only the alternative response; the problem response is made unavailable by the experimenters. Thus, as time passes the animal has no chance to emit the problem response. Unfortunately, one is hard pressed to come up with nonextreme commitment responses (we obviously must rule out responses with irreversible effects, such as cutting off one's hand or suicide) that make the problem response impossible. The locking cigarette case example (Azrin & Powell, 1968) cited by Rachlin and Green is a case in point. Despite ingenious behavioral engineering, the device proved to be a failure. It was reasoned that just after finishing a cigarette individuals would be willing to lock their cigarette cases for a period of time. This time interval would be gradually increased to the point at which the individuals would be smoking at an acceptable low level or would quit altogether. This arrangement appears to parallel the laboratory procedures of Rachlin and Green. Unfortunately the procedure did not work because, even though people were willing to lock the case, immediate cigarettes were freely available from other parts of the environment (e.g., other packs, friends, etc). Another difficulty with the model is that it relies solely on time to change the balance between the two competing consequences. The organism's preference is altered by introducing delays between commitment responses and opportunities to respond for the immediate consequences. This assumes that nothing will happen in the intervening time interval, but that is an extremely unlikely outcome. Because of these constraints on commitment response procedures, all of the procedures for changing behavior must be used in applied settings to deal with the sets of consequences in self-control problem situations.

These criticisms, however, do not negate the potential usefulness of the commitment response and the incompatible-response components of this paradigm. Even though commitment responses in the natural environment do not have the inevitability of those in the laboratory, they can help control behavior. Consider the person who attends Alcoholics Anonymous and makes a public statement admitting to alcoholism. This is a commitment response that changes the environment so that a group of peers who will reinforce not drinking now exists. It may, therefore, be useful to look at self-control as a two-part process, the first involving the commitment or decision response that makes the problem response more difficult to emit, and the second involving operations that change the consequences for the problem response. It is the ability to produce commitment responses, to analyze the environment, and to rearrange that environment that should be labeled self-control.

All of the basic contingency procedures of the analysis of behavior may be used to change the relations between the two consequences and produce the desired self-control response. The selection of the procedure should be based on an analysis of which of the basic sets of contingencies are operating. In a case where there is immediate reinforcement for the problem response but delayed aversive consequences, the most direct approach might be to provide some form of punishment to be delivered contingent on the problem response. On the other hand, if the problem response is followed by small aversive consequences, then some form of positive reinforcement should be used to increase the strength of the target response. For example, a person might schedule a dental appointment a month in advance. The appointment can be seen as a form of commitment response that makes the desired response more likely. As the appointment time nears, however, the person might call and cancel. To avoid this outcome, the person could arrange to have a friend or spouse reinforce keeping the appointment. This example involves both a commitment response and the manipulation of the consequences for the desired response. Other situations may involve these components to a greater or lesser degree. An example of manipulating consequences was involved in the case of a university colleague who was having difficulty getting to his office in the morning. After much discussion, he came up with the simple solution of having the departmental secretary call his office once every 15 min from 8:45 A.M. to 12:00 P.M. until he answered. If he answered by 9:30 A.M., she was to greet him warmly. On the other hand, if it was after 9:30 A.M. when he answered she was to be very formal and simply tell him what time it was. The secretary kept a record of the time he arrived each day and gave him the weekly record on Friday. With the assistance of his family, he was able to arrange for reinforcing events (e.g., favorite dinners, outings with sons, activities with his wife, etc.) if he had been at the office by 9:30 A.M. four of the five days. After a month of the program, he was in his office by 9:30 A.M. 90% of the time. Some might question this as an

example of self-control, but it meets the established criteria because the individual changed the environment to support the desired behavior.

Although manipulating the consequences of a response may be the most direct manner of changing that response, alternative techniques often may be desirable or required. An analysis of the problem response may show that it needs to be changed in topography rather than eliminated. Schaefer, Sobell, and Mills (1971) and Sobel, Schaefer, and Mills (1972) reported that alcohol abusers and alcoholics consistently emit drinking responses that are different from those of the social drinker. Problem drinkers typically order straight unmixed drinks, take large drinks (gulps), quickly reorder, and are unable to keep track of how much alcohol they have consumed. Finally, and not unexpectedly, they continue to drink long past the point at which social drinkers quit. Rather than trying to completely eliminate the drinking response, Sobel and Sobel (1973) developed a program to change the topography of the drinking response. The program consisted of three main components: teaching the subjects to order mixed drinks, to sip their drinks, and finally, to discriminate their blood alcohol levels and to stop or slow down when it reached a certain level (see Lovibond and Caddy, 1970, for a description of how to use a breathalyzer so that individuals may learn to estimate blood alcohol levels). Thus, it was possible to change aspects of these drinkers' behavior while maintaining most of the positive consequences associated with their drinking. Similarly, changing the topography and the pattern of eating responses is a major component of the Stuart and Davis (1972) program to control obesity.

A response analysis might also reveal that a self-control problem may exist because individuals do not have the required responses in their repertoires. In such cases, it would be necessary to identify the missing responses and develop a program to teach those responses. Again, little work has been done investigating this procedure as a self-management technique. The lack of interpersonal social skills appears to play an important role in depression. Again, the ability to discriminate and analyze such deficits is an important component of self-control.

SUMMARY

Much of the preceding discussion of self-control can be applied to the analysis of behavior in general. The phenomena associated with self-control simply make it easier to point out the reciprocal involvement of the organism with the environment. This sort of organism-environment interaction occurs to varying degrees in all responding. The concept that the individual can manipulate his or her environment is embodied in the notion of countercontrol. In his discussions of countercontrol, Skinner has most often referred to punishment and negative reinforcement as countercontrol measures. He has emphasized, however, that the individual and society as a whole would benefit greatly if we would learn to use positive reinforcement to control behavior. As individuals learn more self-control skills, they will become capable of manipulating their environment in positive ways. As a consequence, the development of systematic courses in self-control (realistically a point in time still distant) holds the potential for improving not only the ability of individuals to deal with their problems but society as well.

KURT SALZINGER[1]

Chapter 9

Language Behavior

Amidst the furor that constitutes the learned debate of how best to study language, this chapter will try to show, by sketching out a systematic approach and by citing supporting empirical evidence, that viewing language as behavior constitutes a viable approach to its elucidation. The reader interested in looking at some of the competing approaches is advised to read Reber (1973), who sees three different currents in the study of language: behavioral (which will be explicated here), generativist [which is no doubt most responsible for the renewed interest in language in psychology today (Chomsky, 1965, 1972)], and what Reber deems the compromise between the two approaches: the cognitive approach (perhaps best exemplified by Neisser, 1967, whose book has become the springboard for such research).

THE STUDY OF LANGUAGE

Behaviorists have responded to these varying approaches in differing ways. The cognitivist approach has been largely ignored by them, with two exceptions. K. Salzinger (1973b) reviewed Neisser (1967) and showed that while the theoretical approach taken by the cognitivists was unsatisfactory, the kinds of problems that they attack are important and well within the ability of the behavioral approach to solve. Segal (1977), on the other hand, takes the view that even some of the cognitive concepts should be used as part of the behavioral approach. As to the generativist approach, K. Salzinger (1967, 1970, 1973c, 1975; Salzinger, K., & Eckerman, 1967; Sal-

1. The author gratefully acknowledges the comments on this chapter by Richard S. Feldman and Erica Garcia.

275

zinger, K., & Feldman, 1973, see especially the introduction) has rejected it entirely, while Catania (1972) is willing to leave to the followers of Chomsky what interests them—structure—while retaining control over what interests behaviorists—function.

Even though the generative approach is still important in psychology and linguistics, we must point out that it is being attacked, not only by psychologists but also by other linguists. Lakoff (1969) as far back as 1969 objected to the absence of meaning in Chomsky's system; in fact he even added the meaning component as critical to judgments of grammaticality.

Diver's Approach to the Study of Language

Perhaps most interesting among linguists who disagree with Chomsky are William Diver (1969) and his colleagues and students (Garcia, 1975, Zubin, 1972). They go much further with respect to meaning and grammar and, more important, reject entirely the notion that one can do any analysis of language without taking into account extralinguistic factors. Just to give some basic examples, this approach to linguistics denies the generativist notions of surface versus deep structure and competence versus performance. The basic assumption, that linguistics ought to concern itself with communication and to relate morphological aspects of language to how speakers communicate, makes this particular approach to language behavior most congenial to the behavioral view discussed here.

Essentially, Diver sees the linguist's task as that of correlating the non-random distribution of the observable phenomena of language with the message that is being communicated. In the cited paper, Diver (1969) tried to relate inflectional elements of Greek to the intended message. If we translate this into behavioral terminology, we can say that he is interested in determining what variables control these inflectional elements. For example, in English, the inflectional ending signifying the plural might tell us that the speaker's emission of that ending is controlled by a reinforcement contingency including the presence of more than one object; the absence of that ending would presumably tell us that the emission of the word without the ending is controlled by a reinforcement contingency involving one object. By concentrating on the determinants of inflectional elements, Diver is able to relate them to controlling variables by examining the contexts in which they occur. If they occur in contexts indicating more than one object, then one can make certain by empirical verification of numbers of such instances.

Although some of the determining variables, such as singular versus plural or past versus nonpast, are already known, other controlling variables, such as what he calls the relevance of the verb forms, are not. To present only one example of Diver's analysis of the Homeric verb, we find that the more central an action is to a narrative, the more likely the verb is to be in one form, and the less central an action (as, e.g., in the mention of an activity that did not take place), the more likely the verb is to be in a different form. While grammarians often characterize the choice of various forms as happenstance or as somehow indicating defectiveness in the grammatical system, Diver has shown lawfulness in the use of the forms.

The Current State of Psycholinguistics

Despite the current weakening of the generativist approach to language, the recent awakening of a general interest in language in psychology is to be ascribed to that approach as preached to psychologists, mainly by George Miller (1962). Since he introduced generativist linguistics into psychology, research into language in psychology increased greatly, as demonstrated by the many journals that have begun publishing and the many books and conferences on a world-wide basis that have continued to argue about the finer points of linguistic structures. One hopeful sign from the point of view of the behaviorist is that Miller himself seems already to have left grammar for semantics. Nevertheless, a recent review starts by saying: "The fundamental problem in psycholinguistics is simple to formulate: what happens when we understand sentences [Johnson-Laird, 1974, p. 135]."

The approach here will be quite different. Although the sentence may well turn out to be a unit of response, we should not start out with this assumption. Other units of verbal behavior clearly exist (Salzinger, K., 1973c), and any analysis that begins by limiting itself to one unit is bound to find limited generalizations; in addition, constructed verbal utterances, as opposed to those actually emitted by speakers under given conditions, place another limit on how much we can learn from the analysis of those utterances. The cognitive psychologists and the generative grammarians have abandoned language as behavior, first by focusing their interest on the mental events assumed to underlie it, and second by restricting much of their study of language to artificially constructed samples. With actually emitted behavior, one can discover the variables that control the emission of the behavior, whereas with artificial constructions that source of information is simply not available.

What we have described so far then is the current setting in psychology in which language behavior is studied. As even a selective review will show, many of the experiments fail to provide the kind of information essential for a behavioral analysis. Nevertheless, behaviorists must not ignore the empirical research that is available in abundance, and, for that reason, we shall report it here.

The Behavioral Approach

There remains the question of why the behavioral approach has lain dormant for so long. Skinner's work in animal learning, education, and ab-

normal psychology blossomed, while his systematic treatment of verbal behavior (Skinner, 1957) almost died on the vine. Historians of science will
have to provide the full explanation, but certainly one reason for the failure
of Skinner's book to stimulate research lay in the fact that it presented
essentially no data. Another reason was, ironically enough, the data that
other psychologists such as J.J. Jenkins and Palermo (1964) did collect under
the behaviorist banner. The basic problem with their work, as with Braine's
(1963), was that neither paid any attention either to discriminative (except
some limited verbal ones) or to reinforcing stimuli. The consequence was
that they placed all their explanatory eggs in the intraverbal basket; one
aspect of the response had to explain another—a little like having the characteristics of one pecking response explain the characteristics of others.

This misplaced emphasis by some investigators using the behavioral
approach led sociolinguists, who ought to be sympathetic to the behavioral
approach, to reject it. Slama-Cazacu (1973), in an otherwise cogent discussion of what she calls "socio-psycholinguistics," states that the behaviorist
tradition does not allow for social variables. It will be part of the burden of
this chapter to show that the behaviorist point of view is particularly suited to
include the social, cultural, and physical environmental variables in the
study of language.

Animal Language

The third reason for the lack of impact of the behavioral approach upon
the study of language stemmed from unsuccessful attempts to teach nonhuman primates to communicate. Thus the Kelloggs (1933) and K.J. Hayes and
Nissen (1971) seemed to show that nonhuman primates are incapable of
learning language. Because they failed to teach language, various physiological barriers were postulated. Some spoke of a kind of aphasia as responsible
for the ape's failure; some blamed it on too little lateralization of the brain;
and no further research on the problem took place for the next couple of
decades. As it turns out, however, lateralization is to be found even in the
lowly bird (Nottebohm, 1970). Furthermore, Lieberman, Klatt, and Wilson
(1969) discovered that the basic problem the Kelloggs and K.J. Hayes and
Nissen faced was not in the brain but in the vocal tract. And, of course, by
this time everybody knows that the Gardners (Gardner, B.T., & Gardner,
1971, 1975; Gardner, R.A., & Gardner, 1969) have taught sign language to a
chimpanzee, that Premack (1970a, 1971a) has taught his chimpanzee a plastic
kind of language, and that most recently, Rumbaugh and Gill (1976) and
Rumbaugh, Gill, and von Glasersfeld (1973) have taught their chimpanzee
reading and sentence completion by using a computer. The fascinating findings in animal communication show, if we still need to be convinced of it, the
great flexibility of the functioning of many animals (Salzinger, K., 1973a).
Additional evidence convinces us of the wisdom of using current nonhuman

primates to inform us about the origin of language in human beings (Hill, 1972; Lieberman, P., 1973). B.B. Beck (1973) demonstrated the cooperative use of tools by captive Hamadryas baboons. Because baboons may be conceived of as more primitive than chimpanzees (the animals generally used for demonstrating language), this study provides some evidence for how tool using was probably instrumental in hominization and, therefore, in the learning of speech. It is of particular interest that cooperative-tool use was not produced by a special experimenter-training procedure but rather developed in the face of an environmental requirement.

Why so much discussion of animal language? Because, as behaviorists, we are trying to show the continuity between the behavior of animals and human beings. This continuity justifies our extrapolation from the experimental results obtained with animals to human beings. Extrapolation is, of course, not new; neither is it based exclusively on the recent results showing that one can teach chimpanzees to communicate. Rather it is based on the simple and straightforward scientific view that one should not invoke new concepts and new theories unless and until they are clearly needed.

Unfortunately, there is no agreement on this issue. Thus Chomsky (1972) views language as being generated by a special device somewhere in the brain that can both produce and understand entirely new expressions. It is this property of language that Chomsky claims makes the "acquisition of even its barest rudiments . . . quite beyond the capacities of an otherwise intelligent ape [Chomsky, 1972, p. 66]." When Chomsky made this statement, he was apparently unaware of the work of the Gardners, Premack, or Rumbaugh's group. Nevertheless, this author has no reason to believe that he now has a different view. R. Brown (1973) questions whether Chomsky's strictures, that there must be a surface structure of language that directs the way in which sounds are arranged when spoken and a deeper structure that determines meaning, even apply to children's language behavior. Nevertheless, Brown creates his own strictures to ensure that human language remains quite clearly different from the communication processes of lower animals. He demands that animals be capable of a language that has the properties of semanticity (communicating some information about the environment), productivity (being able to emit new, "original" sentences and to understand them as well) and displacement (talking about things not there).

These properties of language, as they come from Hockett's (1960) classification, are certainly all within the scope of the behavior of many animals (Salzinger, K., 1973a). Semanticity, the control exerted by the environment, is demonstrated whenever a psychologist does an experiment in which discriminative control is exerted; productivity is demonstrated whenever an animal emits members of a response class that were not specifically reinforced or responds to a new stimulus similar to a discriminative stimulus to which responses had been reinforced; finally, the property of displacement is actually a misnomer, for even human beings must have a stimulus to which they respond. It is naive to believe that when I speak of "ancient Rome," I have somehow displaced the stimulus, "ancient Rome," that controls that utterance. In point of fact, we have never seen or otherwise sensed many of the referents of words that we respond with, thus clearly requiring some other stimulus, namely the word itself, to evoke our responses. Without having to agree that chimpanzees can learn complicated repertoires of language behavior, we are forced to admit that their behavior in other situations reflects the properties posited to underlie it. Nevertheless, Brown concludes that the chimpanzees have learned only some very simple kinds of language; he is particularly suspicious of Premack's chimpanzee, feeling that some kind of artifact might have crept into those experiments through the experimenter's direct handling of the animal. Rumbaugh et al.'s experiments using the computer to intervene between experimenter and subject would seem even more clearly to obviate this, but Brown was apparently not aware of those experiments when he wrote his book. At any rate, the evidence now leads us to believe that our understanding of human language will profit from the theory and techniques found useful in the study of lower animals. In addition, this chapter will demonstrate that very important direct applications of behavior theory to human language behavior have already occurred.

THE BEHAVIORAL APPROACH TO LANGUAGE

No monolithic behavioral theory of psychology exists. We shall argue that the systematic view presented by Skinner (1938, 1953a, 1974) and used to describe psychology in general (Salzinger, K., 1969b), but not necessarily Skinner's (1957) detailed view of verbal behavior, however seminal, is the best behavioral view to embrace for the sake of solving the problems of language behavior. This implies a great deal of similarity to the theories of Staats (1967, 1968), which are, of course, derived from Skinner, and the sharing of some of the principles of what is referred to as association theory. We will not go into the differences among behaviorism, neobehaviorism, partial behaviorism, and radical behaviorism. The major point in favor of the systematic Skinnerian (radical behaviorism) approach is that it is all-encompassing. In true Skinnerian fashion, we will use both operant (instrumental) and respondent (classical) conditioning in elucidating language as stimulus and language as response. When we speak of behavior theory, we will be referring to the Skinnerian framework.

Reinforcement Contingency and a Definition of Language

The most important contribution that Skinner made to behavior theory is the concept of reinforcement contingency. That concept is a statement about control. Essentially, it states that when members of response classes are emitted on certain occasions (discriminative stimuli), they are reinforced by certain consequences (reinforcing stimuli). This basic relation can be stated symbolically by $S^D \ldots R{\to}S^R$ where S^D is a discriminative stimulus in the presence of which any member of a particular response class (R) is followed by a particular reinforcing stimulus (S^R). In this basic paradigm the reader should note that we are talking about *classes* of discriminative stimuli, *classes* of responses (Salzinger, K., 1967), and *classes* of reinforcing stimuli. Furthermore, the reinforcing stimulus is to be interpreted in the most general way as a strengthening stimulus. Thus the reinforcer may strenthen behavior by following it, as a positive reinforcer, or by being eliminated or prevented or postponed by the response, as a negative reinforcer. Our concern will not be whether the reinforcer controls one way or another, but only that consequences of behavior do control the behavior.

Very important in this paradigm is that most of the reinforcement process is mediated by another person. Not all, however. Problem-solving verbal behavior may directly produce immediate consequences in much the same way as does a nonverbal response. The delay in time caused by the mediation of the actor's own verbal response to the correct nonverbal response is not as uncertain as is the mediation by another individual, whose reliability may vary. Thus the definition of verbal behavior as behavior whose reinforcement is mediated by another individual—even with the additional proviso that Skinner (1957) makes, namely, that the reinforcing behavior itself is a learned response—is not quite complete if it omits the factor of verbal behavior's regulatory control of one's own verbal and nonverbal behavior. Nevertheless, it is true that the regulatory verbal behavior that people emit must be learned in the context of having another person reinforce it appropriately. In the equation that represents the reinforcement contingency, the reinforcer is only sometimes the explicit external type of event that it typically is in animal experiments. Recalling a line of poetry by subvocalizing preceding lines is reinforced by the emission (subvocally) of that line. At least that is the most immediate consequence, with later consequences—such as being able to recite the line in public—coming after a considerably longer period of time. Another special property of verbal behavior is that it is much more likely than nonverbal behavior to be intermittently reinforced, with the consequence of greater resistance to extinction than other behavior. We must add to this the ease with which verbal behavior can be emitted, particularly subvocally, since it requires no operandum in any special environment. These properties make verbal behavior admirably suited for thinking. People can present themselves at any time with verbal discriminative stimuli and thus with the conditions that lead to reinforcement. What are some of the verbal responses that constitute these discriminative stimuli? Recalling a name that does not immediately come to mind; figuring out all the pleasant things that will happen to one; counting one's money or other blessings; figuring out how many days or hours to some positively reinforcing event.

Interestingly enough one can also torture oneself by the same method: possibly here we are talking about the mechanism of depression, in which individuals present to themselves the kinds of verbal statements that produce the "feelings" of depression. This raises the question of why statements that are clearly aversive continue to be emitted by the depressed invididual. Among normal individuals, such statements usually cease and the more positive statements continue because of their positively reinforcing value. Part of the answer no doubt relates to the reinforcers of sympathy that such statements evoke; part relates to the avoidance of aversive stimuli that such statements make possible. In any case it must be obvious that subvocal responses are more common than, say, subwalking, although presumably that is in part due to the societal contingencies on the two different kinds of behavior. This higher frequency of subverbal versus subnonverbal behavior can be attributed to the fact that subverbal responses are more plentiful, take less effort, and, as indicated, require less environmental support (cf. Skinner, 1974).

The Competence-Performance Distinction

Psycholinguists make much of the competence-performance distinction. They maintain that the distinction allows them to handle such problems as how people understand sentences they never heard before and produce sentences they never said before. The behavior theorist, however, can appeal to such concepts as stimulus generalization and response generalization to explain the responses. Furthermore, that speakers do not always perform equally well each time they speak is not to be explained by the same underlying competence obscured by "trivial" environmental factors. The behavioral view uses the reinforcement-contingency concept and puts this problem in empirical perspective. Since all responses are conditioned in the presence of particular discriminative stimuli, on a later occasion some responses might be absent merely because the appropriate discriminative stimulus has not been presented; in other cases the absence of the response might be accounted for by the fact that the subject has not been trained or at least has not yet learned the response; in still another case the response might not be emitted because it has been extinguished or because the event used earlier as a reinforcer no longer acts as such (e.g., due to satiation or discontinued pairing of the conditioned reinforcer with other reinforcers); the response might not be emitted because of too weak a discriminative stimulus or because only part of the stimulus complex is being presented.

Specifying these reasons for the lack of a response seems preferable to saying that the performance does not always reflect the competence. Competence cannot be assessed except through performance. Thus the concept seems to be a value judgment only, because presumably no psycholinguist would be willing to say that an individual was competent to say something who only repeated what another said. But how about reading? And how about reading parts and being prompted for the other parts? And how about saying it "spontaneously" in part (spontaneous is, of course, not accurate because under such circumstances the other verbal responses act as discriminative stimuli) and being prompted in part? The concept of competence does not help in understanding language behavior; on the contrary, it obscures the conditions under which the speaker will emit any given responses (also see Salzinger, K., 1975).

The Concept of Rule

Psycholinguists use the mental concept of *rule* to explain the complexity of language. Reber (1973) justifies the validity of this concept on the basis of the close correspondence between the rules constructed by psycholinguists and the verbal behavior related to them. He gives the example of the conditions under which one will admit that a child has a rule system, namely that the child's speech is regular, that the regularity is extended to new instances, and that the child is able to detect deviations from this regularity. The question, however, is why one needs rules at all, if they are only shorthand notations for the conditions of the behavior. The concept that better explains the emission of speech in children is that of reinforcement contingency.

How will we use the reinforcement contingency in elucidating language behavior? First we will view language as stimulus, for both other verbal behavior and nonverbal behavior. Then we will view language as response, under the control both of nonverbal stimuli and of social and cultural variables. Finally, we will speak of the acquisition of language as a conditioning procedure.

LANGUAGE AS STIMULUS

The Effect of Language Stimuli on Verbal Behavior

We emit much of our verbal behavior in direct response to the verbal behavior of others. Language as stimulus occurs in conversation, lectures, written texts, questions, or directions. In our society the importance of the language-language relation is attested to by how easy it is to get into trouble or to attain fame by verbal behavior alone. The critical stimulus is verbal when we instruct a student to write an essay about "an adventure you had" or the perennial "how you spent your summer." The instructor commonly believes that the writer is being asked to generate verbal behavior out of whole cloth or without benefit of stimulus, but in fact the material is generated by verbal responses initiated by the teacher's directions. That the environment in which the instructions are rendered also has important discriminative stimulus properties is often ignored under these conditions; in many cases those properties account for the different essays written when the same directions are given by the same teacher in different classrooms, when weather conditions are different, etc. But we will take up these physical stimuli later.

How do verbal stimuli evoke responses? Skinner (1957) has defined a number of verbal response classes in terms of their relations to the verbal stimuli. He calls the first class echoic. Echoic behavior consists of vocal responses that match the sound pattern of a verbal stimulus just presented.

The second class of verbal behavior, describing a relation between verbal stimulus and verbal response, is textual behavior. Textual behavior consists of vocal responses to nonauditory verbal stimuli such as letters arranged as words, hieroglyphs, and even pictographs. Like echoic behavior, textual behavior entails a formal correspondence between stimulus and response, but unlike echoic behavior, the correspondence for textual behavior is between different dimensions: auditory effects produced by the verbal behavior and visual (or tactile, as in Braille) effects produced by the stimuli. Textual behavior is involved in the process of reading.

The third class of verbal behavior is intraverbal behavior. Intraverbal behavior consists of verbal (vocal or written) responses controlled by verbal stimuli generated by the speaker's own prior verbal responses or those of another speaker, without a point-to-point correspondence to the stimuli that evoke them. The control of stimulus over response is generally less exact (less predictable) than in the case of repetition (echoic responses) and reading (textual behavior); nevertheless, in some cases the control is still very precise, as in arithmetic, the scientific definition of terms, and the labeling of people by means of proper nouns; in other cases the stimulus-response relations at least appear to have more freedom of variation. In adults the "free" associations evoked by the instruction to, "give the first word that comes to mind," in addition to being thematically related to the stimulus word, largely consists of responses of the same part of speech as the stimulus word. In children, the response words, although also thematically related to the stimulus words, are very often a different part of speech than the stimulus word. The former has been called paradigmatic and the latter syntagmatic (see Salzinger, S., 1973, for an experimental comparison of these two response classes).

The final class of verbal responses under the control of verbal stimuli is autoclitic behavior. It addresses the problem that verbal behavior depends on other verbal behavior emitted by the speaker; it consists of verbal responses such as qualifying, quantifying, grammar, and syntax, i.e., verbal responses dependent on other verbal behavior of the speaker. As such, this classification system has not engendered much experimental work. Some notable exceptions are Horner and Gussow (1972) and K. W. Estes (1945), whose dissertation was apparently done while Skinner was formulating his system.

An Application of "Rodential" Behavior Theory

Some twelve years after the publication of Skinner's *Verbal Behavior*, a professor of English (Zoellner, 1969) published "Talk-Write: A Behavioral Pedagogy for Composition" based solely on what he called Skinner's rodential behavior theory. His treatise presents a survey of behavior theory and many of its applications. In trying to improve the lot of the freshman English student and at the same time eliminate the feelings of depression that follow upon marking themes, Zoellner proposes a form of teaching writing (as opposed to thinking about writing, or planning to write, or reading about writing, or realizing the errors of one's ways) that makes use of behavior theory in as sophisticated a way as anyone could hope for from a well-versed behavior technologist. He first correctly charges that the present form of teaching writing concentrates not on the act of writing but on the product. He recognizes that the present attitude toward its teaching is fed by the medical model. Bad writing is viewed by current English teachers as merely a symptom of bad thinking. Bad thinking cannot be dealt with directly if you assume that it is an entirely internal process. The consequence of this model is that one can merely point out the many errors that students typically make on their themes and hope that somehow this procedure will improve their thinking and thus their writing.

Zoellner proposes a plan to improve the teaching of writing, based on his insightful observation that the student who seems entirely incapable of writing a single clear, understandable sentence is nevertheless quite ready, when asked to explain what he meant by it, to express it vocally. To begin with, Zoellner includes in his program what he calls "vocal-to-scribal dialogue' between teacher and student. Furthermore, he redesigns the classroom to contain several blackboards and oversized pads on which the students may write their sentences. Rather than writing alone, they write in public, watching others write and engaging in imitation learning. Furthermore, the teacher walks around immediately reinforcing the writing of small bits of verbal behavior; under these circumstances the teacher is also able to reinforce ever closer approximations to the good English sentence that is the ultimate goal. The fact that erasers and many sheets of paper abound makes much more likely the response of rewriting, a bit of behavior usually very difficult to instill in college students.

This classroom is envisioned very much like an art studio, in which the teacher walks around commenting on the work, making suggestions, reinforcing good approximations, etc. Because the talk regularly preceding the writing constitutes only what Zoellner calls protoscribal behavior, the students will also explicitly learn what changes they must make to transfer vocal to written behavior; in this way they learn how one translates from the conversational, paralinguistic (gesture, intonation, and hesitation in speech) to the written form by means of punctuation, additional words, and special word orders. Without apparently being aware of Keller's teaching method, Zoellner included it in his scheme for teaching writing. Finally, alternately talking and writing, the students learn to improve not only their writing but also their talking, certainly a worthy goal.

Some empirical studies have compared vocal and written verbal behavior under well-controlled conditions. Nerbonne and Hipskind (1973) found that written and vocal vocabularies differ primarily in that the written material is less repetitive and uses longer words as measured by number of syllables. Although Portnoy (1973), who fully reviews other studies comparing oral to written verbal behavior, found that only the longest words significantly differed between the two types of verbal behavior, she replicated the finding that the written material had more different words (less repetition) than the oral material.

Communicability of Verbal Behavior

More relevant to Zoellner's program, however, are the differences in communicability or comprehensibility. This property of verbal behavior is measured by what the originator (Taylor, W. L., 1953) called the cloze procedure, a technique devised to measure readability. He took samples from several authors' writings and deleted every fifth word. He then submitted typewritten versions of these mutilated texts to groups of undergraduates and asked them to guess the missing words. The more correct restorations of the exact words deleted from each passage, the more readable he considered the passage.

In our laboratory studies of schizophrenia, a disorder said to be characterized by a deficit in communication, we showed quantitatively that schizophrenics are harder to understand, according to this measure, than normals (Salzinger, K., Portnoy, & Feldman, 1964, 1966; Salzinger, K., Portnoy, Pisoni, & Feldman, 1970) and that their degree of communication deficit predicts the duration of their mental-hospital stay. The more communicable their speech at the time of hospitalization, the shorter their stay.

Portnoy (1973) compared oral and written verbal behavior with the cloze procedure. All subjects both wrote and spoke. Subjects differed significantly. Some communicated more effectively when they spoke and others when they wrote. Those subjects whose communicability was greater when they wrote than when they spoke used longer words both in their oral samples and in their written samples. The best speakers were those whose speech was more communicable than their writing; the best writers were those whose writing was more communicable than their speech. The subjects were college undergraduates and thus the population that Zoellner was talking about. Perhaps if they had gone through the kind of course that he envisioned they would have communicated equally well in the two verbal modalities. In any case the cloze procedure might provide a reasonable, objective measure of the success of a writing course.

Intraverbal Response Strength Among Short Bits of Language

Measures like the cloze procedure, its derivatives, and its antecedents, are particularly useful for measuring intraverbal response strength in continuous verbal behavior. Properties of single words or other short stimulus bits of verbal material (e.g., nonsense syllables) have been measured in psychology for a much longer time and still constitute a principal interest of verbal-learning psychologists. We will not review this literature because books have been written (e.g., Hall, J.F., 1971) and significant articles in the area have been collected (Kausler, 1966; Postman & Keppel, 1969; Slamecka, 1967). But even here, the isolated nonsense syllable has given way to the nonsense syllable in relation to external variables. Berko (1958) related it to number of objects (or "creatures"). A nonsense figure was presented, with the explanation that this peculiar creature is called a "wug"; two creatures were then shown, and children were asked to complete the sentence, "There are two ———." The results led her to conclude that children (preschoolers and first graders) "possessed" morphological rules. Four- to 7-yr-olds supplied plural endings in a "consistent and orderly manner." Plurality, as indicated by pictures of two things, evoked well-controlled responses from these children. Here, we submit that the "rules" inhere in the analyst, not in the child; the child demonstrated discriminative control, i.e., the bound morpheme showing plurality of nouns as indicated by the letter s was controlled by number of objects in the picture.

K. Salzinger and Eckerman (1967) inserted the isolated nonsense syllable into sentences differing in grammatical complexity as defined by Chomsky's (1957) generative grammar. Taking Chomsky at his word concerning the independence of meaning and grammar, they constructed both simple declarative sentences in the active mood (the simple structure) and negative questions in the passive mood (the complex structure) in a nonsense-syllable-with-function-words-controlled jabberwocky. Examples of such sentences are, declarative: "And the piqy kews were beboving the nazer zumaps dygly;" passive negative: "Weren't the nazer zumaps dygly beboved by the piqy kews?" Although generative grammar predicted that the grammatically more complex sentences would not be recalled as well as the simple sentences, no such difference was found, thus calling into question the validity of the independence of grammar and meaning and of the definition of sentence complexity.

Motor Theory of Speech Perception

Psycholinguists have been studying verbal stimuli even shorter than the nonsense syllable, and these studies have been critical in the theories of language developed over the years. The research, conducted in large part at the Haskins Laboratory, has given birth to the motor theory of speech perception. Essentially, this theory seeks to explain the perception of speech sounds. To gain better control over those sounds, an instrument that converts hand-painted spectrograms back into sound stimuli has been employed. Because these sound stimuli can be varied, they allow the experimenter to determine how much the physical characteristics of the sound stimulus can change before the subject hears a different sound. This experiment and others like it have consistently shown (Liberman, A. M., Harris, Hoffman, & Griffith, 1957) that the labeling of the sound stimuli changes in a typically abrupt manner, unlike the gradual change when we present other physical stimuli.

The Haskins group concluded that because the acoustic cues (painted spectrographs) did not by themselves act as the independent variable for speech perception, and because the perception of the sounds (phonemes) appears to be categorical (particular sound stimuli receive a particular label close to either 100% or 0% of the time), speech perception takes place by synthesis. Essentially this means that subjects listening to speech sounds recognize them by matching them to the way they would produce those sounds. Exactly what is assumed to be matched has changed over the years; at first the actual articulators were thought to be involved; the speed necessary for the kind of understanding we are capable of, however, made it obvious that the articulators were too slow; the Haskins group then retreated to the position that synthesis took place by way of the neuromotor commands that usually preceded the hearer's production of those sounds when the hearer acted as a speaker.

Many investigators have found fault with this theory. Lane (1965, 1967) produced categorical perception merely by using a procedure in which two stimuli chosen from a physical continuum were discriminative stimuli for two different responses. Kopp and Udin (1969) replicated Lane's findings. On the other hand, Studdert-Kennedy, Liberman, Harris, and Cooper (1970) were unable to produce categorical perception merely by conditioning; they asserted that the speech sounds were special, i.e., innately determined, and not merely to be produced so easily by a short conditioning session. Pisoni (1971) tried conditioning and concluded that its effectiveness varied with the subject. We do not seem to have definitive data, therefore, on this question.

When Eimas, Siqueland, Jusczyk, and Vigorito (1971) reported that 1- and 4-month-old infants also discriminate artificial sounds in a categorical manner, the conditioning explanation seemed much in doubt. The motor theory of perception, however, was also questioned because such young infants do not yet produce the consonant sounds they seem capable of discriminating. Furthermore, the Eimas et al. work has not been unanimously replicated (Doty, 1974); in addition, some investigators raised questions about specification of the infants' response and others about the high rate of subject loss in testing. Thus once again we are forced to conclude "not proved."

The motor theory of perception is also criticized on the grounds that it would take some 17,000 different motor commands to emit the phonemes because they differ not only in terms of their identity in isolation but also as a function of the phonemes that precede and follow them (MacNeilage, 1970). It therefore seems safe to conclude that if verbal stimuli differ from others, they do not do so in having to be produced to be understood. A difficulty inherent in any perception-by-production theory becomes obvious when one considers the perception of music or art. Although art works are certainly complex as stimuli and no doubt can be categorized by composer or artist, period of composition, style, etc., no one would insist that one sound like a symphony orchestra or even give the neuromotor commands to approximate such sounds in order to be able to recognize the music of Mozart or discriminate it from rock-and-roll (for more extended criticism of perception by synthesis, see Salzinger, K., 1973b; cf. Chapter 12 in this book).

Intraverbal Response Strength of the Single Word

As already indicated, research psychologists in language studied the single word, or, the more adventurous, the single word embedded in a context of other words or in association with them. We now know that verbal units, like nonverbal units, vary in size because they gain their significance from their function, not from their topography (Salzinger, K., 1973c). Word associations precede the beginning of psychology proper, when philosophers talked of the association of ideas. As early as 1910, however, Kent and Rosanoff quantified verbal behavior by constructing a table of associations. Normal individuals were consistent in the classes and even the identities of words they emitted when given "free" word-association instructions. Galton and Cattell had already worked on reaction times in the word association test. Word associations show much lawfulness: They are high-frequency responses according to English word counts based on continuous text (Howes, 1957; Johnson, D.M., 1956) and therefore reflect continuous language behavior; the greater the agreement among different subjects in the associations they give to a particular word, the faster each subject emits them (Lattal, 1955; Schlosberg & Heineman, 1950); the stronger a particular response to a stimulus word, the earlier in a sequence of responses it occurs (Bousfield & Barclay, 1950); the larger the number of stimulus-related words preceding the stimulus word, the greater the number of related words evoked (Howes and Osgood, 1954; Salzinger, S., 1973); etc. The literature is replete with examples of the relations in word association data, and we shall not belabor the point that, given a well-controlled situation, verbal behavior follows predictable paths.

Another approach to verbal stimuli has extracted "meaning" by the semantic differential (Osgood, C. E., Suci, & Tannenbaum, 1957; Snider & Osgood, 1969), a form of controlled word association in which the subject is required to emit a judgment on a 7-point bipolar scale rather than by "any word that comes to mind." The scales are arranged in accordance with three basic factors: evaluation (how good a word seems to the respondent), activity (how active the word seems), and potency (how strong the word seems). Osgood viewed these measures and their factor analysis as providing a measure of meaning. Meaning is thus defined operationally by the controlled associations that constitute Osgood's rating scales. But this is just another demonstration of the lawfulness of verbal behavior. The semantic differential produces clusters of words whose coherence can be verified by determining whether such words are a response class, i.e., whether when some members of the class are reinforced, other members also increase in frequency (Portnoy & Salzinger, 1964). G. A. Miller (1969) had subjects sort words into as many groups as they wished and then performed an hierarchical cluster analysis of meaning, and Deese (1962) studied meaning by essentially measuring the degree to which the word associations of different words overlapped. Finally, to take but one other method of measuring the meaning of single words in terms of their relation to other words, Fillenbaum and Rapoport (1971) had subjects judge the similarity of various sets of words directly.

Of all these methods, Osgood's semantic differential is perhaps the most practical to apply, whereas Deese's analysis, based directly on word associations, may well turn out to be most practical for predicting people's reactions in applied situations. This kind of information should, for example, be useful in creating thematic prompts for a program so that the learner acquires material efficiently. By knowing which words are more likely to evoke other words, the programmer may well benefit practically from these theoretical studies.

At least in Osgood's case, theory and practice are very much interrelated. Osgood views the semantic differential as an index of a mediation process inherent in language. One part of the mediation process is r_m, an unobservable, response-like event that takes place inside the organism and is itself a response to the external "sign" or verbal stimulus; r_m evokes an unobservable stimulus-like event, s_m, also inside the organism; it, in turn, gives rise to the observable mediated response, presumably but not necessarily verbal. Finally, the total observable response to the significate, that is, the *object*, also evokes the r_m because the significate is paired with the sign. The mediation process, the $r_m \rightarrow s_m$ relation, is what, according to Osgood, distinguishes his theory from the simpler, one-stage Skinnerian theory. C. E. Osgood (1968) maintains that r_m differs from Skinner's hypothesized subvocal responses because the latter must be a replica of the response to the sign, while Osgood's r_m need only be a *part* of the total response an individual makes to a significate. It is not clear what is gained by positing that subvocal, or subresponses in general, always mediate between an observable stimulus and observable response; much, if not all, of "meaning" can be fully explicated by observable stimuli and observable responses, and the multiplicity of the different responses for each stimulus along with the mechanism of respondent conditioning ought to suffice to explain the variety of meanings that the semantic differential suggests.

Staats and Staats (1963) showed that emitting some words while viewing others changed the meaning of the words viewed, when meaning was defined by Osgood's semantic differential. Staats (1967) interprets the words viewed (e.g., names of nationalities) as conditional stimuli, and the words that the subject hears and repeats while viewing the conditional stimuli (e.g., laudatory expressions) as unconditional stimuli. Eventually the conditioned stimulus elicits a meaning response similar to that elicited by the unconditioned stimulus. It is also possible, however, to describe the procedure in terms of operant conditioning: The verbal stimulus viewed is the discriminative stimulus and the word that the subject hears and emits is the operant response. The semantic differential judgment may then be attributed to the recently learned subvocal response acting as a discriminative stimulus for the semantic differential judgment. Nevertheless, Staats does point out that one should take into account both respondent and operant conditioning in discussing language behavior, and in this we totally agree. Presumably respondent and operant conditioning always take place together and it thus only becomes a question of how important each type of conditioning is in a particular situation. Because the semantic differential attempts to get at connotative meaning, i.e., emotional meaning (where the autonomic nervous system provides the stimuli for the verbal responses), Staats has argued that the respondent conditioning model is important in his procedure.

What are we to make of these experiments on meaning? Meaning, as already indicated, is defined operationally in terms of some controlled association procedure and thus refers essentially to verbal responses controlled by verbal stimuli.

Intraverbal Response Strength in Longer Language Segments

Having discussed several ways in which psychologists have studied verbal behavior through small verbal units, we now turn to longer segments. Carroll (1972) reviews different methods of analysis of longer segments of verbal behavior in his introductory chapter to Carroll and Freedle (1972). In discussing comprehension, he speaks of exposing subjects to verbal material either in whole or in degraded form and then asking them to respond to it. In tests of memory the ultimate degradation consists of asking the subject to reproduce the heard or read material; the discriminative stimulus for recall is quite general. In some cases the memory test consists of supplying the subject with only "true" key words as discriminative stimuli for recall; in other cases the experimenter presents other discriminative stimuli; they have various relations to the original material presented but because they are not *the* original material, the discriminative stimuli may be considered "false." Other memory tests have the subject answer questions about a passage just read; again of great importance is the form and content of the question determining the degree to which it contains discriminative stimuli for the correct answer.

Many investigators have criticized memory tests as indices of comprehensibility or of the complexity of grammatical structures (Fillenbaum, 1970). When the time between stimulus presentation and recall test is too short, the subject may simply give an answer by rote, whereas if the time period is too long, then the answer may reflect only or primarily the subject's ability to remember; in either case it is a matter of specifying very precisely the relevant discriminative stimuli and the responses required. In the former (too short) case, the subject's responses may not require an association different from mere repetition. If we mean by comprehension, however, that the subject must be able to reproduce the material later after being exposed to other material, then we must have the subject paraphrase (emit associations other than repetition) the material because that leads to optimal recall. Better recall on paraphrasing is probably because the subject can use familiar words and word sequences, whereas reconstruction by rote involves both words and sequences of words not in the subject's repertory of paraphrasing. When the period between original presentation and subsequent recall is too long, the recall itself will probably depend too much on the particular words used as discriminative stimuli rather than on the original comprehension.

Carroll lists other types of comprehensibility tests. Subjective judgments of understanding, as Carroll himself points out, are not valid in a competitive testing situation. Also, even when the subject is not in such a situation, some of the discriminative stimuli would evoke an answer of "I understand" when others would not. Specifying these discriminative stimuli might well be impossible. Other tests of comprehensibility consist of matching tasks, viz. sentences to pictures, or instructions for nonverbal responses. These two types of tests might well measure different kinds of comprehensibility. The final kind of degraded stimulus material that Carroll proposes is based on the cloze procedure, to which we now return.

The Cloze Procedure

Various forms of the cloze procedure have been used for many years. Shannon (1951) invented what has come to be called the Shannon guessing game. Subjects are required to guess a message letter by letter until they have guessed the entire message. The number of guesses at each position is then used to calculate how redundant that sample of text is. Several investigators have applied a similar technique to words (Freedle, 1973; Goldman-Eisler, 1967, 1968; Schoenfeld & Cumming, 1973a). Freedle also investigated serial guessing effects. Since organisms do not emit responses (including verbal ones) at random, the question arises as to how much bias such guessing exerts on estimating the redundancy of the language. To test for this bias, Freedle compared guesses with a random sample of sentences selected from various texts. He sorted the guesses into various response classes in terms of their frequency of occurrence in the English language or their length. Serial effects were greatest when the guesser was given no context word and decreased rapidly when the experimenter supplied one or more context stimuli. The guesser required four context words before being able to match the word-class distributions in the text. Procedures such as the Shannon guessing game might thus not necessarily reflect the intraverbal contingencies that pertain to written text.

The statistical approximations to English by G. A. Miller and Selfridge (1950) constitute another approach to language as stimulus. Successive subjects have the task of including groups of words in sentences. Thus, for second-order approximation to English, the experimenter presents a common word such as *the* and asks the subject to use it in a sentence. Then the experimenter takes the first word that the subject used after *the*, and gives it to the next subject to use in a new sentence; the third subject is given the new word of the second subject, and so on, until the required number of words have been collected. For fourth-order approximation, the experimenter gives each successive subject three words; for each subject the experimenter drops off the earliest word in the original sequence and presents the most recent three words. Simply, each approximation is constructed by having a subject speak a sentence using the number-of-the-approximation-minus-one words and then using the next word that the subject gives, dropping off the first, in the construction of the next sentence. Miller and Selfridge used the passages generated in this way as material to be memorized. They found that the higher the approximation to English (they used text as the highest), the larger the percentage of words correctly recalled.

K. Salzinger, Portnoy, and Feldman (1962) applied the cloze procedure to approximations to English to measure comprehensibility of material already explored by memory techniques. Using the data obtained by Selfridge (1949), they plotted the recall data against the statistical order spaced according to the comprehensibility of the passages as revealed by the cloze procedure (Figure 9-1). The improvement of recall was much greater as a function of the introduction of the first- and second-order dependency among words than Miller and Selfridge's graphing in accordance with the simple ordinality of the passages would lead one to assume. Furthermore the text material that Miller and Selfridge happened to choose was near fifth-order approximation to English. Although recall and comprehensibility data agree in general-rank ordering of the passages, the low orders of intraverbal dependency make a proportionately larger contribution to good recall than do higher orders of approximation. Thus immediate recall is most sensitive to the shortest relation spans.

Short-span relations were the subject of another study. Comparing

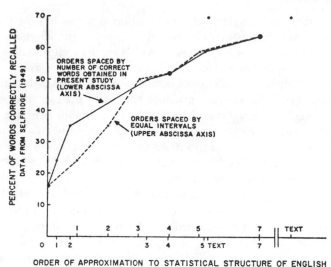

ORDER OF APPROXIMATION TO STATISTICAL STRUCTURE OF ENGLISH

Fig. 9-1. Percentage of words correctly recalled (Selfridge, 1949) as a function of order of approximation to English, with an equal-interval scale for orders (dashed line), and with the intervals determined by the average number of words guessed correctly in the study (solid line). (From K. Salzinger et al., 1962.)

normal to schizophrenic speech with a modified cloze procedure, K. Salzinger et al. (1970) found that an increase in context increased correctly guessing the words that the original speaker had emitted. Compared to normal speech, the gaps in schizophrenic speech were clozed generally less accurately with large amounts of context, but more accurately with less context (Figure 9-2). The words selected for this task were taken from normal and schizophrenic monologues, with pairs of subjects matched with respect to sex, age, education, and speech community. The words in this study had been blanks in previous cloze procedure studies (Salzinger, K., et. al., 1964, 1966). In this study these blanks were matched in terms of part of speech (lexical words, i.e., noun, verb, adjective, or adverb, versus function words, i.e., articles, conjunctions, and prepositions) and the magnitude of predictability in the cloze procedure. Thus a difference under these conditions shows this technique to be very sensitive to contextual effects.

Figure 9-2 shows that from 16 words of bilateral context on, additional words do not improve performance. A final point about these results concerns the different parts of speech. The schizophrenic function words that were low in predictability under the full cloze procedure conditions (but matched to the normal ones) consistently evoked fewer correct responses than the normal low-predictability function words.

Schoenfeld and Cumming (1973a) examined the relation between the boundaries established by subjects who partitioned a prose passage into "idea units" and subjects' sequential guessing of the passage word by word.

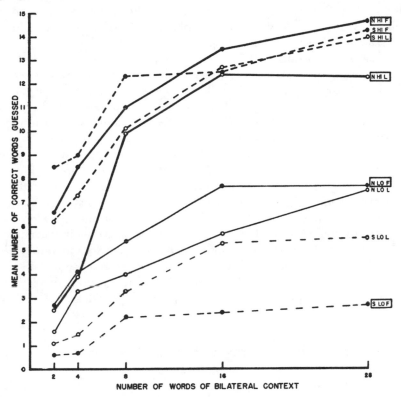

Fig. 9-2. Mean number of correct words guessed in schizophrenic and normal speech segments by 230 clozers as a function of number of words of bilateral context, with type of word as a parameter. (The boxed word types designate statistically significant trends (p < .05) over increasing degrees of bilateral context. S, Schizophrenic; N, Normal; Hi, High Context; Lo, Low Context; F, function words; L, lexical words.) (From K. Salzinger et al., 1970.)

These boundaries are not always followed by an increase in uncertainty, or by an increase in disagreement among subjects as to which word comes next. Goldman-Eisler (1967, 1968), on the other hand, found more uncertainty for words uttered after pauses in speech than for words uttered fluently. Presumably the speaker, during the pauses, emits subvocal responses whose absence in overt speech removes relevant discriminative stimuli and therefore makes it more difficult for the hearer to guess the missing word.

Other cloze variants used sentence frames with various words or bound morphemes in certain positions of the sentences (Feldman, 1973; Schoenfeld & Cumming, 1973b). These sentence frames were constructed to gauge the effect of certain words and various parts of speech, and the sentence positions these words occupied, on the kinds of sentences that subjects produced. Agreement on the words placed in each position was also measured.

Although the findings are complicated, they show that sentence position itself, as well as single words or morphemes placed in sentence frames, constrain the subjects' sentence responses.

Finally, S. Salzinger (1973) directly compared speech evoked by two different sets of instructions: she told one group of subjects to speak continuously on any topic they wished until told to stop; she told another group to, "Give words one at a time that are *not* in sentences." The first speech samples were called syntagmatic because they can be described in part by the rules of syntax; the second series of verbal responses were called paradigmatic because they cannot be described by the rules of syntax; moreover, words in this class when uttered in sequence are typically the same part of speech. Selective deletion of different words showed that the syntagmatic sequences act like chains of responses in that each word is a discriminative stimulus for the succeding word in the sequence, whereas the paradigmatic sequences act like members of a response class in that any word in the paradigmatic group is a discriminative stimulus for any other. There are too many other variants of the cloze procedure to describe. [See Salzinger, K., and Feldman (1973) for a review of the various types of communicability or comprehensibility measures that can be derived by different forms of deletions of given verbal material.]

The Effect of Language Stimuli on Nonverbal Behavior

Past research has most characteristically tried to remain entirely within language behavior to explain it. Both generative grammar and verbal learning experiments with nonsense syllables or even with words have tried to explain meaning, understanding, comprehensibility, grammar, and acquisition of language in terms of the effect of language on other verbal responses, whether these were judgments on a scale, answers to questions, paraphrasing, or even filling in deleted words in the cloze procedure. Obviously, such an approach is not enough. To understand language behavior, we also need to know what control it exerts over nonverbal behavior.

Respondent Conditioning

Much research has been directed at finding a surer index of meaning than the flimsy verbal behavior of another individual. This research has faithfully followed respondent conditioning procedures. The subject is exposed to an unconditional stimulus (US) such as food in the mouth for salivary conditioning or an electric shock or a loud noise for galvanic skin-response conditioning. The subject is also exposed to a verbal stimulus, either visually or aurally. The verbal stimulus is the conditional stimulus (CS). Sometimes the experiment is complicated by having both CS+'s and CS-'s. The former is the stimulus that is always paired with the US, while the latter is always presented alone. The final step in this kind of conditioning consists of testing for what is called semantic generalization. The experimenter presents the subject, whose response has been conditioned, with stimuli that resemble the CS in varying ways.

The master and pioneer in semantic generalization was, of course, Gregory Razran (1961, 1971, to take but two references in which the reader can find examples of his many ingenious experiments). He found more generalization to words related semantically to the CS than to those related phonetographically or by sound alone. Razran's (1936) experiment, in which he used himself as the sole subject because he needed one who spoke a number of languages, showed that the magnitude of salivation to the word "saliva," presented in the various languages that he spoke, increased as his familiarity with each particular language increased.

Staats and Hammond (1972) followed up that experiment by testing salivation to food-related words as opposed to nonfood words. Subjects deprived of food for approximately 16 hr showed a greater differential between food- and nonfood-word responses than did subjects deprived of food for only 3 hr. These findings attest to conditioning in the course of living; the mere presence of certain words while food is ingested appears enough for conditioning to take place. That the relation is accentuated when the subject is food-deprived is particularly important in that it follows the findings of respondent conditioning in nonverbal experiments. Although this conditioning is commonly done with single words, Razran used sentences as conditional stimuli many years ago. He showed that subjects respond to the overall meaning of sentences rather than to particular words only. A great many methodological and theoretical problems persist (see, for example, Feather, 1965; Grant, 1972), but we need merely note that enough data exist now to suggest that the respondent is a good candidate for the position of meaning mediator that Osgood postulated.

Operant Conditioning

Operant behavior is of greater interest to social and educational psychologists, and we turn our attention to it now. The question is to what extent an individual's nonverbal behavior is controlled by verbal behavior. The difficulty of answering this question is particularly obvious in very young children and constitutes an area of research with some controversy related to the competence-performance distinction.

Fraser, Bellugi, and Brown (1963) investigated this problem by using three different methods. They studied comprehension by having the child point to the picture that corresponded to each of two contrasting sentences. They studied production in two ways: (1) by imitation (the child merely had to repeat the sentences) and (2) by production (the child had to say the sentences that corresponded to each of the pictures). To take an example, the child might be shown pictures of two sheep; in one picture only one sheep is jumping and in the other both are jumping. The correct sentence for the first picture would then be, "The sheep is jumping," while for the second picture the correct sentence would be, "The sheep are jumping." The children's imitation is superior to their understanding in that they are able to imitate sentences that they do not correctly ascribe to pictures by pointing to them; this was interpreted as meaning that they essentially imitate by rote. These same children, however, did not emit correct sentences corresponding to each of the pictures with the same level of accuracy as they were able to point to the correct picture.

The latter finding has been used by psycholinguists as proof that, because the child is capable of understanding before speaking, one cannot explain the learning of language by the reinforcement of correct utterances; its essential nature (read "rules") is learned before there is any opportunity for the reinforcement process to take place. This argument is, of course, flawed by the gratuitous assumption made by many psycholinguists that responding to language must be the same as speaking it; a stimulus need not be produced to control behavior. This study can be discounted on other grounds as well, however, namely on the basis of a scoring artifact. Fernald (1972) showed that a rescoring of the Fraser et al. data eliminated the understanding-production difference; in fact a slightly larger number of correct responses occurred in production than in comprehension. The problem was that the comprehension task required the subjects merely to make one of two choices, i.e., to indicate which of two pictures referred to each sentence; with respect to the production task, however, where the subjects had to say each sentence, they could be wrong merely by emitting a novel or unrelated sentence, or with respect to the noun alone or the verb alone, or both, etc. Clearly the comprehension task had a statistical advantage over the production task. When Fernald removed this advantage, he also removed the superiority of comprehension over production. This suggests that, at least for 3-yr-olds, language behavior and language as stimulus are at approximately the same level. For children, certainly under normal circumstances, responding appropriately to verbal stimuli is reinforced just as is responding appropriately verbally. (We shall come back to exactly what is reinforced in the child's speech.)

Shipley, Smith, and Gleitman (1969) were also interested in competence, in what children "know" about the language they hear and speak. Their experiment tried to determine the parts of verbal stimuli that control children's behavior. Two-yr-old children were given commands in well-formed sentences and in sentences without function words, a form not unlike their own speech (what Brown, R., 1973, has called telegraphic speech). The older of these children responded with greater accuracy to the well-formed sentences than to the telegraphic speech they themselves used. R. Brown (1973) disagreed with the conclusion that the children's competence exceeded their verbal productions. He explained the results not by the child's better understanding of the included function words, but rather by the apparent peculiarity (to the child) of the mother's speech when she uses telegraphic speech.

We fortunately have a replication of the original experiment. Kramer (1973) repeated the Shipley et al. experiment with some improvements. She excluded the nonsense words but included sentences that were semantically peculiar. Her stimulus material included well-formed sentences, such as "Sit in the chair;" well-formed but telegraphic sentences, such as "Sit chair;" nonwell-formed lengthened sentences, such as "Chair the in sit;" nonwell-formed telegraphic sentences, such as "Chair sit;" semantically peculiar (anomalous) well-formed and lengthened sentences, such as "Throw me the chair;" anomalous telegraphic sentences, such as "Throw chair;" anomalous nonwell-formed lengthened sentences, such as "Chair the me throw;" and finally, anomalous nonwell-formed telegraphic sentences, such as "Chair throw." The anomalous sentences were used to determine whether the child understood *both* the noun and the verb of each sentence. If children sat on the chair when instructed to throw it, their following the instruction in the nonanomalous case was presumably a function of their previously reinforced behavior in relation to chairs rather than of a current understanding of the entire sentence. The children did just as well when given the telegraphic sentences as when given the well-formed ones, but did considerably worse when given the anomalous sentences than when given the nonanomalous ones. When children heard the anomalous sentences, they often disregarded the anomalous verb by doing what one usually does with the particular noun. An example was when a child, instructed to sit on the telephone, instead talked on the telephone. Thus, the correct interpretation of the Shipley et al. study is that the children simply responded to the nouns in both well-formed and telegraphic speech. Once again, understanding does not precede performance.

When one talks of the control of verbal stimuli over nonverbal behavior, one cannot leave out the great Russian psychologist, Luria (1967, 1969). By using a simple bulbpressing task, he demonstrated that children of different ages show varying degrees of control by verbal stimuli, apparently at first responding only to the intonation patterns, and later to the semantic aspects of the verbal stimulus. In this country we might mention the work of Lovaas (1961, 1964) and Hekmat and Vanian (1971). The latter were influenced by Staats' work in their use of semantic desensitization. Lovaas showed the effect of the operant conditioning of food words on eating behavior (Lovaas, 1961) and the effect of such verbal conditioning on aggressive behavior (Lovaas, 1964) in children.

LANGUAGE AS RESPONSE

Much research on language as stimulus has necessarily required our talking of language as response as well. Thus the cloze studies and their variants could be viewed as either language-as-stimulus or language-as-response studies. When we talk about sociolinguistics, we will also be viewing language as response.

We must point out the problems of response unit (Salzinger, K., 1973c) and response class (Salzinger, K., 1967). The unit is that amount of verbal behavior that functions in a cohesive fashion; what we count as a unit of verbal behavior at any given time must change with our particular area of interest; it must of course be determined by our empirical findings of lawfulness. In other words, we can only make educated guesses about what will constitute a reasonable unit in each study (e.g., whether it be a word, syllable, sentence, etc.); our data will then tell us whether or not we were right. The same holds for response class. A response class has as members all responses that are a function of the same variable. It is also probably true that the unit size increases with age and with repetition of the verbal behavior. We might thus imagine that a candidate running for office could acquire an entire speech as a response unit. Furthermore the various speeches, and also the short statements to the press, might be considered members of the same response class. The truth of this supposition would depend only on whether empirical examination yielded lawful variation in these units and response classes as a function of some reasonable independent variables.

Language Behavior under the Control of Nonverbal Stimuli

Since it is easier to vary the verbal environment or verbal stimuli than the nonverbal environment or nonverbal stimuli, most experiments in verbal learning have investigated the variation in verbal behavior only as a function of other verbal behavior. Yet it is manifestly true that we speak differently in different environments. Skinner (1957) defined verbal responses under the control of the nonverbal environment as tacts.

That discriminative stimulus control is not always obvious has led some people to invest the speaker with the stimuli controlling the emission of the responses. Some investigators continue to speak of intentions being critical to an understanding of what the speaker "wanted" to say; although this does present a certain intuitive sense of rightness or at least common sense, we are thereby merely placing the site of control beyond scientific scrutiny.

The problem of "what happened to the stimulus" seems to be particularly difficult when a subject emits a verbal response in the absence of the supposedly sole controlling stimulus. In one study by Goldiamond and Hawkins (1958) each subject was exposed to a series of verbal stimuli a different number of times. Then they were asked to report which of these stimuli appeared in a tachistoscope. They emitted their responses in proportion to the number of times they saw and rehearsed saying them before the experiment. The subjects were in fact shown none of the verbal stimuli in the tachistoscope. What then was the discriminative stimulus for their response? The answer obviously lies in the other discriminative stimuli: the rest of the environment, the experimenters, the experimental room, the experimenters' instructions indicating that those stimuli would be exposed for brief periods of time, and finally the differing numbers of pre-experimental exposures to those verbal stimuli.

Although not commonly considered part of the verbal-behavior literature, psychophysics often relies on the degree to which verbal responses are controlled by physical stimuli. Most of the time they are considered a nuisance because the investigators' interest does not lie in the response but in the stimulus value that the subject senses. Nonetheless, the response class chosen does affect discrimination ability. S. Salzinger, Salzinger, and Patenaude (1970) investigated judgments of length in 3- to 6-yr-olds. Half the children were told to identify the various stimuli by color names, and the other half were told to identify the same stimuli by the numbers 1, 2, 3, and 4. When the investigators introduced an anchor stimulus (a stimulus of extreme value on the dimension judged and one that commonly causes a shift in judgment), the children who had learned to label the lines ordinally, with numbers, resisted the anchor more effectively than those who had learned to label the stimuli nominally, with colors. We have here an example of how different verbal response classes controlled by the same physical stimuli can be differently affected. The ordinal-scale responses that focus the subjects' attention on relating one stimulus to another helped the subjects keep their judgments constant in the face of the anchor stimulus. Thus, verbal responses are controlled by physical stimuli, but that control depends at least in part on the relation of each response to other members of the response class.

Although ability to name objects is of great interest to neurologists, who study this function in aphasic patients, it has not, by and large, captured the imagination of today's psycholinguists. There are exceptions. Oldfield and Wingfield (1964) found that line drawings of objects evoked their names in proportion to the general frequency of the name in the English language (Thorndike & Lorge, 1944). Petrinovich and Hardyck (1970) compared responses to word stimuli and those to corresponding picture stimuli. Stimuli generalized from picture to word more than vice versa. It is also interesting that subjects recall paired associates better when they are responses to pictures than when they are responses to other words (Snodgrass, Volvovitz, & Walfish, 1972).

The currently favored interpretation is that pictures evoke images (Paivio, 1971), which are then more easily "available" than the related word might be. This raises the question of private events, whose existence behaviorists do not doubt (Skinner, 1957) but whose measurement presents a difficult problem. The question is whether the subjects exposed to a picture later "present themselves with an image" when they recall the verbal response. Presumably one can ask a similar question about what the subjects do in the Goldiamond-Hawkins experiment; do they conjure up a view of the word they report seeing? We need some ingenious experimentation to answer these questions. In one sense, however, it seems obvious that one can present oneself with a visual stimulus, or image, as when one tries to remember without looking where a particular book is on the bookshelf. But to return to the findings about pictures: They show that physical stimuli cannot be ignored, because nonverbal stimuli often control verbal behavior with greater strength than do verbal stimuli.

Another line of research comes' closer to the everyday problem of speech in a complex environment. Underwood (1957a) demonstrated that the more verbal lists a subject has learned, the poorer the recall of the next list. This phenomenon is known in verbal learning as proactive interference. Dallett and Wilcox (1968) demonstrated that when they changed the environment radically from that in which the previous lists were learned, the new list was recalled with fewer errors than when learned in the same environment as the other lists. Thus the classical phenomenon of proactive interference is related to the environment in which the list is learned. Similar effects have been established for retroactive interference (Bilodeau & Schlosberg 1951; Greenspoon & Ranyard, 1957). There is simply no way of ignoring the environment; it exists, and because it does, it exerts an influence over the responses that organisms emit, be the organisms rats, pigeons, goldfish, or human beings and be the responses barpresses, pecks, nonsense syllables, or conversations.

Reading. Reading is still another form of stimulus control over verbal responses. The cloze procedure, discussed previously, relates to one aspect of reading, namely, the intraverbal stimulus control exerted over good readers when they rapidly scan a page. In the initial learning of reading, however, the physical stimuli that we call letters exert the primary control over the verbal responses. The controversy about how to teach reading continues to be with us, apparently independently of new findings. The arguments seem invariant. Should the child learn by whole words or by sounding out? No doubt the basic problem is that our educational system is forever forced to mete out one method of teaching to all children, whereas different children require different methods. The few children who seem to learn easily before systematic teaching clearly need only some help in sounding out particularly hard or unfamiliar words (Torrey, 1969). Other children may have difficulty because their pronunciation, understanding, or familiarity with the words or word combinations are sufficiently different from those of the teacher or book they are trying to decipher; they do not have the advantage accruing to those whose pronunciation and word orderings agree with the material they are reading. Other children may have difficulty in learning to read because their responses are not appropriately reinforced, at home or at school. Given all these difficulties, plus some not mentioned, it should not be surprising that the reading problem has not abated (cf. Chapters 10-12).

From the point of view of behavior theory, reading demonstrates all the problems of learning to speak plus others, because the relevant characteristics of written stimuli are not easily discriminable. Furthermore, because the same letter evokes different verbal responses in different contexts of letters and words, the reader is in conflict with respect to which sound is correct. Finally, the combinations of the sounds the reading student produces are often not recognizable to him or her (cf. Staats, 1968).

One fact about reading difficulty ought to be surprising. Because we have already shown that pictures (nonverbal stimuli) control verbal behavior even more effectively than verbal stimuli, why does the child not learn to read easily? The answer may well lie in the lack of detail or individuality of the letter pictures. Rozin, Poritsky, and Sotsky (1971), using 30 different Chinese characters to represent 30 English words, were able to teach so-called nonreaders to read sentences and short stories within 2-6 hr. While the faster learning might also be ascribed to the whole-word method as opposed to the more abstract phonetic method, the use of stimuli other than English letters is interesting.

Another method of dealing practically with inadequacies of the orthodox alphabet is the i.t.a. method (the initial teaching alphabet, Downing, 1964). Because traditional orthography presents serious difficulties to a child learning to read, an alphabet slightly different from the common one in appearance (i.t.a.) but that makes it relatively easy to transfer to the traditional alphabet once it has been learned largely eliminates conflict of stimuli. It has 43 different characters, more than the traditional alphabet, but in contrast to the traditional alphabet each character has only one sound no matter in what context it is presented.

The problem of sound combination when using sounding out was solved by a rather ingenious technique. Homme, deBaca, Cottingham, and Homme (1968) determined that the child's peculiar combination of sounds does not act as a discriminative stimulus for recognizing the word. The experimenters therefore presented sounded-out pronunciations of various words the children were likely to produce in their own reading until they learned the correct pronunciations of these words. The investigators trained the children so that their concatenated pronunciations of the words were stimuli for correct pronunciations. Thus, "kuh-a-tuh" would then be the discriminative stimulus for "cat."

The Cloze Procedure and Nonverbal Discriminative Stimuli. Before leaving language as response to nonverbal discriminative stimuli, we return to the cloze procedure. R. A. Clark, Williams, and Tannenbaum (1965) presented cloze forms of the texts of the verbal behavior of people asked either to describe or interpret the meaning of abstract paintings. Half of the clozers were shown the painting and half were not. Furthermore half the blanks in the texts were function words and the other half lexical words. Clozers did not differ in ability to fill in the blanks containing function words over any of the conditions. On the other hand correct guessing of the lexical words was greater when the clozers had the picture in front of them, whether the verbal behavior described or interpreted the painting. In addition the communicability of the interpretation passage was no worse than that of the description passage. Thus we have an example of how a technique particularly sensitive to intraverbal relations is nevertheless influenced by the nonverbal stimulus present when the speaker spoke.

Goldman-Eisler (1967, 1968) did similar studies by having subjects either describe or interpret cartoons. Interpretive speech produced more pausing and was more difficult to guess than descriptive speech. Perhaps explaining why a cartoon is funny involves more subvocal behavior than interpreting a painting, thereby eliminating only for cartoon interpretations some of the discriminative stimuli from which the clozer might guess the missing word. Clearly, more research is needed to determine how discriminative stimuli affect both producing and understanding verbal behavior.

Language Behavior under the Control of Social and Cultural Variables

We have already alluded to the importance of this aspect of language behavior. Behavior theory deals with sociolinguistics through the audience variable as a major discriminative stimulus determining verbal behavior, and through the cultural reinforcement history acquired by the individual. Each person learns to emit certain classes of verbal and nonverbal responses under the control of certain verbal and nonverbal classes of discriminative stimuli. The exact content of these classes of stimuli and responses is determined by the culture, consisting of both small (family, friends) and large (ethnic, national) groups. Research in this area requires combined knowledge from anthropology, sociology, and psychology. Any such combination is by definition not simple. We refer the reader to these different points of view (Ervin-Tripp, 1968, 1972; Fishman, 1970; Giglioli, 1972; Hymes, 1974; Robinson, 1972).

One other general point must be made about sociolinguistics. By its very nature it contradicts Chomsky's generative grammar approach. Labov (1972) is perhaps most explicit. The generative grammar model states that such self-embedded structures as, "The man that the girl that I used to go with married just got drafted." are grammatical. It is not in fact clear that everybody, including nonlinguists, accepts this as grammatical, but let us assume it for the sake of argument. Labov argues that because use or comprehension of such structures is not evident in natural conversation, the generative model does not "rest on a solid foundation." Chomsky's theory maintains that language behavior is basically homogeneous and that one can treat the variations merely as mistakes recognizable by the speaker, thus showing that the rules are known. Labov, on the other hand, points out that variation of language (structure, if you will), not homogeneity, is the rule;

heterogeneity of language is, according to Labov, "the natural result of basic linguistic factors." In other words, any linguistic theory must concern itself with this variation. According to Labov (and other sociolinguists), any theory that does not is not a reasonable linguistic theory, because the study of language outside the social context is not the study of linguistics at all. A behavioral account also agrees that language behavior is multiply determined.

The effect of society and culture on language is not made simpler merely by citing them as variables, and the psychologist interested in such variables still has the job of defining them both conceptually and operationally. Once that is done, however, the researcher can measure language by any of the techniques already discussed. Osser and Endler (1970), for example, examined the particular vocabularies of different social classes in Ontario, Canada. Subjects were required to select from two words the one they used most frequently. If they used both equally often, they were required to so indicate; if they used another word more frequently than either of the two listed, then they were asked to write that word down. The two lists of words were response classes defined to be British or American in origin. The example the subjects were given was: "He put some_____ on his toast. □ A. jam □ B. preserves." Upper socioeconomic class subjects chose words of American and English origin about equally often, but lower-class subjects chose American words more than three times as often as British words. The choice of response class suggests something about cultural identification, if we mean by the latter that subjects inclined to use the words of one culture are also inclined to have the values (find reinforcing the same kinds of things and activities) of that culture. Such a study begs for a check in a free-response situation in which subjects are merely exposed to the situational variables that might evoke the kinds of words presented in the forced-choice situation. Also of interest would be the transmission of the different vocabularies; is it through the material subjects read (books, newspapers, textbooks) or the language they are exposed to in conversations with relatives (especially parents), teachers, peers? Or, finally, is it a function of the kind of vocabulary forced by co-members of their socio-economic group?

Robinson (1972) reviewed comparisons of the language behavior of middle and lower socioeconomic class (or, as he prefers to call them, working-class) children. B. Bernstein's theory (1970) states that lower-class children have a restricted code in their language behavior, whereas the middle-class children have both restricted and elaborated language behavior. The restricted code consists of short, grammatically simple sentences that are often unfinished and makes limited use of adjectives and adverbs. The elaborated code language is much more accurate in grammar, includes adjectives and adverbs in a discriminating fashion, and uses prepositions indicating both logical relations and temporal and spatial contiguity. These language studies (Williams, F., 1970) show the deficit inherent in the speaker (in this case, the poor and minority groups) and suggest compensatory education to improve these children's language to the point where they could take better advantage of the language of textbooks and teachers than they now can.

One can examine differences in language behavior from another point of view, however: as a difference in the frequency of different language responses. Labov (1970) represents this position. The difference position (Williams, F., 1970) states that the teacher and the school cannot deal with the child's different language because the languages are mismatched. Evidence for such a mismatch was adduced by Peisach (1965) and Deutsch, Levinson, Brown, and Peisach (1967) by the cloze procedure. It is hazardous to use loaded words such as "restricted" and "elaborated" (cf. Leacock, 1972, on abstract versus concrete speech) to define behavioral differences; if one stays close to operationally defined terms, then what is being discussed becomes more obvious to the consumer of the research information, and which way to proceed is also more obvious to the researcher who wishes to analyze the situation further. Even when one has taken social and cultural variables into account by systematically varying them to determine differences in language behavior, other variables must still also be manipulated to find the conditions under which the child will use adjectives and adverbs in large number or infrequently, the conditions under which the referent will be clearly marked (the verbal response will be clearly under the stimulus control of some particular aspect of the environment), and those under which the referent will be vague (stimulus control unclear).

B. Bernstein (1970) pointed out family conditions that might account for differences between the social classes; he also (Bernstein, B., 1972) stated that when he calls a child's language code "restricted," he does not mean that the child is incapable of emitting elaborated speech in all contexts, but only that fewer such contexts evoke it. The moral is that we must state our generalizations in terms of the well-known reinforcement contingency formula (the occasion of the response, the response in question, and the consequence of that response), rather than in more global but vaguer terms. Cazden (1970) reviewed studies that varied either the audience or the general speech situation of children and found tremendous variation in language behavior, both in quantity and in quality. Notably absent is any explicit reference to reinforcement, although the situations described presumably differ greatly in this respect as well.

Sociolinguistics and Behavior Theory. In a study explicitly based on Skinner's behavior theory but also sociolinguistic in approach (Horner & Gussow, 1972), the complete verbal exchanges of two 3-yr-old black children were tape-recorded for two days in their respective, very poor, homes. Using Skinner's (1957) classes of mands (verbal responses that specify the reinforcer as in, "Gimme a cookie" or "Leave me alone") and tacts (verbal responses essentially controlled by the environment, by discriminative stimuli), they showed that mothers mand about twice as often as they tact to these children, whereas the children mand approximately as often as they tact to their mothers. Unfortunately the data are limited to two children, but the methodology and categories of analysis could profitably be extended to additional children.

The finding of more mands from mothers than from children has a counterpart in letters exchanged by emotionally disturbed preadolescents and their parents (Salzinger, K., 1958). The latter clearly manded more than the children, even though the parents' mands consisted of advice about the children's behavior while the smaller number of children's mands were concerned with concrete objects.

Language Behavior and Indices of Socioeconomic Class. Let us return once more to the cloze procedure, because it is obviously suited to studying social-class variables. Robinson (1965) found that working-class boys tended to agree more among themselves in filling in the blanks of written-language samples of both middle- and working-class boys than did middle-class boys confronted with the same task. Because the working-class boys were not significantly different from the middle-class boys in intelligence, Robinson attributed the greater agreement among the former to their greater tendency to conform. As in the case of *restricted* language codes, we must question the term *conformity*, because it too has surplus meaning with educational implications unwarranted by the research.

Heider (1971) examined language in problem solving. She asked a group of 10-yr-olds (equally divided among middle-class white, lower-class white, and lower-class black children) to describe six abstract and six face stimuli so that another child could pick out each item in turn. These descriptions were then actually given to children and their accuracy of item selection gauged. Although middle-class children gave descriptions that yielded greater accuracy in guessing the item and did better in selecting a given item from a description, the language style that produced the most correct selections was also the style most often used by each socioeconomic class. There were no consistent differences between black and white children. We have here evidence for differences in language behavior, in the context of a specific task, between members of different socioeconomic classes.

Language Behavior and Social Contact Patterns. In these studies of sociolinguistics we have talked of specifying social variables by indices, which is what one does when referring to socioeconomic classes. Now we describe a study dealing more directly with the effect of a social variable, social contact, as a determining factor in language. Because the cloze procedure yields a general index of communicability, it can be related to the social distance between individuals. K. Salzinger, Hammer, Portnoy, and Polgar (1970) had each subject write three 500-word stories: one about the writer's own experience, one about a friend's experience, and one about a character's experience in a book or a movie. The stories were then converted into cloze form and each writer was required to guess the missing words. Each writer was also asked which of the other writers in the group he or she knew. Of the three types of stories, those about a friend were more accurately restored when the clozer knew who the author of the story was. This was not true for the other two types of stories.

In a more detailed study (Hammer, Polgar, & Salzinger, 1969; Salzinger, K., et al., 1970) on social networks among people who frequented a coffee and doughnut shop, observation of their conversations allowed a number of predictions about their verbal behavior. The more often an individual spoke or was spoken to by others, the better his or her speech sample (collected at another time) was predicted in cloze form. Furthermore, people predict better cloze samples from those who talk to them frequently than from those who talk to them less frequently. The cloze procedure identifies the conditions that determine how well one person communicates with another. As such, this technique seems to be the best available for the study of social and cultural variables.

OPERANT CONDITIONING AND THE ACQUISITION OF LANGUAGE

Even the psychologist most innocent of current psycholinguistics must by this time realize that a behavioral approach is definitely not the most popular one. In fact most works in this area still begin by reiterating what they consider to be the final word on the irrelevance of behavior theory, namely Chomsky's (1959) review of Skinner's (1957) *Verbal Behavior*. In addition, some vague statement is often made about the "fact" that behavior theory cannot, in principle, deal with language and that the generative grammatical approach is therefore the only one of any value.

Learning versus Development

Schlesinger (1971), in a paper titled "Learning Grammar," felt he must begin by explaining why he clings "to the old-fashioned view that grammar can be learnt." He also argued that the generative grammarians, aside from assuming that some part of the process is innate, do not explain how children convert the surface structure of the sentences they hear to deep structure, a conversion which, according to Chomsky (1965), is the only way children can understand the sentence. Schlesinger, accepting that a deep structure is necessary to understand and speak, nevertheless rejects its relation to grammar; instead he views deep structure as related to the intentions of the speaker and hearer; the intentions are a summary of what the speaker wants to say and the hearer believes the speaker wants to say. Then Schlesinger posits realization rules as a substitute for Chomsky's transformation rules. The realization rules permit the speaker to convert the intention to the utterance by taking into account the rules of grammar. What is learned, according to Schlesinger, are the rules of grammar necessary to put the intentions into sounds, words, and sentences. Understanding consists of reversing the process by converting the heard utterance into the original intention. Although Schlesinger uses the notion of rules, he does one thing that brings him closer to a behavioral account of the acquisition of language: he takes into account, as a primary factor, the meaning (the nongrammatical determinants) of speech and understanding. He points out that students of children's language must accompany their transcripts of children's speech with the events taking place (some of the nongrammatical determinants of speech) at the time the child is talking. This kind of description would allow the experimenter to guess what was controlling the speech of the child. L. Bloom (1970) also stressed recording what takes place during speech. The only real objection one can have to Schlesinger's theory (besides the use of terms such as rules) is the notion that the child must manipulate something inside (wherever that is) to emit language.

Although R. Brown (1973) credits Schlesinger (1971) and L. Bloom (1970) with rediscovering nonverbal stimuli, he still ignores Schlesinger's statements about learning. McNeill (1966), perhaps the strongest proponent of innateness in language acquisition, rejects learning on the basis of such examples as the following exchange between a mother and child, in which the mother tries valiantly to correct the child's double negative by asking him to imitate what she is saying.

CHILD: Nobody don't like me.
MOTHER: No, say "Nobody likes me."
CHILD: Nobody don't like me.
— (eight repetitions of this dialogue)
MOTHER: No, now listen carefully; say, *"Nobody likes me."*
CHILD: Oh! Nobody don't likes me. [p. 69].

According to McNeill, the exchange "demonstrates the relative impenetrability of the child's grammar to adult models, even under the instruction (given by the mother's 'no') to change."

One is tempted to ask many questions about this interaction. Because many psycholinguists maintain that parents do not as a rule correct children's grammatical practices, it is puzzling that the mother should have chosen to correct the *grammar* of this particular abnegating statement. Second, the situation looks very much as if the child were playing a game with the mother, in which the positive reinforcer might well be the mother's repetition of the sentence. Of course, we would have to have other information to establish that it was functioning as a reinforcer; from the information presented, however, that is exactly what was happening. If it turned out that the child for the most part holds the mother's attention with these kinds of interchanges and at other times she pays no attention, then we would be much surer that we have here only another example of control by a reinforcer. Third, any behavior modifier faced with such a situation would not use the kind of repetition that this mother illustrated. If one were really interested in establishing that the child cannot possibly use the adult form of the statement, one would first have to test a gradual shaping procedure, in which the child learned to repeat parts of the required sentence with elements gradually added only as the child became ready for them. Under these circumstances even many speech-deficient children acquire language behavior, and one would therefore expect this (presumably normal) child to acquire it also. Fourth, the expected learning under these circumstances suffered from the absence of supporting environmental stimuli. Normally language is learned in the presence of the objects that control the verbal responses. The discriminative stimulus for the sentence, "Nobody likes me" in that conversation is rather remote.

Discriminative Stimuli in Language Acquisition

Although Chomsky led many psycholinguists to believe that the objects controlling the semantic aspects of the verbal response are the least important aspect of language, some experimental evidence is to the contrary. Moeser and Bregman (1972, 1973) taught subjects a miniature artificial language under different conditions. The learning of the artificial language (specifically, knowing the relations between words, and how to combine them by rules made to simulate the phrase-structure rules posited for natural languages) took place only when the language behavior was learned in reference to a picture. This difference in learning between the picture-present and picture-absent conditions was not eliminated even when the number of sentence presentations was as large as 3200. But once the subjects had learned the rules of the miniature language system through the pairing of sentences with pictures, then they could learn the class membership of new words through verbal context alone. With respect to McNeill's (1966) example of "relative impenetrability" to adult models, we must conclude: not demonstrated.

Reinforcement in Language Acquisition

R. Brown and Hanlon (1970) asked how children change their grammatical structure from the telegraphic to the well-formed kind that characterizes adult speech. Their first test evaluated communication pressure. Examining those times when grammatical form changes, they inspected all interlocutor's (e.g., mother's) responses to the child's questions. Because the questions all called for answers, the responses could be classified into "sequiturs" (answers which clearly convey that the question is understood, as in the answer, "We ate them all" to the question, "Where Christmas cookies?") and "nonsequiturs" (answers consisting of irrelevancies or no response, as in the answer, "Your spoon?" to the question, "Where my spoon?"). The child's utterances were classified into those that were well formed and those that were not; the percentage of sequiturs to the not-well-formed utterances and to the well-formed utterances was the same: 45%. As for nonsequiturs, 47% followed the not-well-formed utterances and 42% followed the well-formed ones, apparently a not statistically significant difference. As for individual children and individual types of questions, the sequiturs sometimes predominantly follow well-formed utterances but not always. The authors concluded that the data present no evidence favoring communication pressure for well-formed utterances.

From the behavioral view, one would expect communication pressure to constitute an important aspect of verbal behavior. A mother's response signifying comprehension of the child's question (sequitur) ought to act as a reinforcer. The question, however, is how much the comprehending response (as defined by Brown, R., and Hanlon, 1970) affects the child's behavior under different circumstances. It may be correct to consider the response that there are no more cookies when a child asks for them as demonstrating the parent's comprehension; it must be obvious, however, that the child would in this instance, as in many others, have much preferred the cookies to the comprehension. From the child's point of view, that parent's response constitutes an aversive stimulus indicating the absence of further positive reinforcers. In animals such a stimulus controls unwanted responses to great effect.

On the other side of the interlocutor's response-class definition problem are such responses as partial repetition of what the child has said, as in "Your spoon?" (which Brown, R., and Hanlon, 1970, classify as nonsequiturs) in response to "Where my spoon?" Even by the comprehensibility criterion, one could argue that repeating part of a question at least sometimes indicates comprehension; it is also a discriminative stimulus for repeating the question. The authors pay no attention to the substantive nature of the question, whether the parent is willing or able to yield to the child the asked-for object or privilege. It seems that reinforcement of the proper grammatical structure would, under normal circumstances, come only as a by-product of the reinforcement of proper substantive questions (i.e., those that make sense semantically to the interlocutor). Also left out of this classification is the reinforcing quality of word play: When a parent says something irrelevant, it may still be reinforcing. Because the classification includes among the nonsequiturs positive reinforcers and discriminative stimuli for more speech of the same kind and among the sequiturs stimuli indicating absence of further reinforcers, such as refusing a child something on the basis of a question, we therefore conclude that Brown and Hanlon did not in fact test the relevance of communication pressure to the acquisition of language behavior.

R. Brown and Hanlon (1970) examined the relevance of reinforcement to language acquisition by monitoring contingent approval. To test contingent approval, they isolated all the instances they could find, in the speech of three children at two stages of language development, in which the parent responded in such ways as, "That's right," "Correct," "Very good," and "Yes," and contrasted them with the speech followed by such disapprovals as, "That's wrong," "That's not right," or "No." They characterized the syntactic correctness of children's utterances that preceded approval or disapproval. Few utterances were followed by such explicit approval or disapproval; nevertheless, the parent did not tend to approve syntactically intact sentences more frequently than nonintact ones. Brown and Hanlon give examples such as

CHILD: Draw a boot paper.
MOTHER: That's right. Draw a boot on paper.
CHILD: Mama isn't boy, he a girl.
MOTHER: That's right.
CHILD: There's the animal farmhouse.
MOTHER: No, that's a lighthouse.

What can we make of this? To begin with, this kind of analysis does not include all or even the significant reinforcers. Obviously cookies are much more important for the young child than being told, "That's right." Neither the method of measuring communication pressure nor of following up contingent approval and disapproval accurately or completely counts positive or negative reinforcers. Second, at different times parents reinforce different kinds of behavior. Thus, if the child has to learn that a particular building is a lighthouse, the wise parent will reinforce the semantic accuracy rather than the grammatical form of the statement. The mother trying to persuade her child to draw a boot on paper will reinforce the expression of willingness to do so rather than the correct grammatical structure of that utterance. Besides, even though the mother says, "That's right," in the previous example, she also repeats the phrase in its corrected form. We are forced to conclude that the Brown-Hanlon studies do not adequately test the role of behavioral variables in the interchange between mother and child and between other interlocutors and child.

By way of contrast let us recall the analysis provided by Horner and Gussow (1972), who tape-recorded two complete days of interchange for each of two slum children. In both cases the experimenters were not present during recording, thus providing a better sample of child-other interactions than the Brown-Hanlon samples collected with the experimenter present (even though he or she had become familiar to the child over a long period of time). Mary emitted five times as many mands for attention than did the people in her environment toward her, while John had a ratio of only two to one for the same category. Why was there this difference? To begin with, Mary's speech was less intelligible than John's. As a result, people around her kept manding repetition and she did the same by way of imitation. In addition her own speech was generally repetitious. The authors point out that this child's repetitiousness, evident even in imaginary play, was also produced by the inattentiveness of her environment. Mary was *never* manded to continue talking, while John was so manded 7% of the time. In addition Mary's audience did not usually respond positively to her verbally stated mands. As a consequence she spent much of her time manding attention, both verbally and by whining and screaming.

The richness of the interactions between a child and the environment, which consists of inanimate factors and of other people and how they behave, cannot be measured by some simple count of the number of "yes's" emitted by the mother. The nature of reinforcement is not formally marked in that manner. Furthermore, discriminative stimuli are presented by both the animate and the inanimate environment; different response classes are reinforced at different times and places and at different ages of the child. What we need is not another experiment testing whether reinforcement works. Rather, we need to learn exactly how reinforcement functions to produce the well-known regularities that everyone (including cognitive psychologists) measures.

This is not to say that discussions of language acquisition make much mention of the operant-conditioning literature. Such discussions (e.g., Brown, R., 1973; Vetter & Howell, 1971) typically lack *experimental* citation almost completely in the testing of how language behavior is actually acquired, as opposed to the many studies informing us how much has been acquired at any given time or stage. Psycholinguists have not generally experimented on language acquisition because they almost completely accept the notion that language develops like any other biological function, such as walking (Lenneberg, 1967); given that assumption, the learning problem seems rather trivial and is ignored.

Nevertheless, rediscovery of the environment and how it controls the language of children, along with the increasing number of children studied, has shown that the same grammar does not describe all the children's early verbal behavior. The erstwhile basic notion of the pivot grammar has given way to examination of semantic properties of language behavior. Bloom (1970) says: ". . . this study would cast some doubt on the view of language development as the same innately preprogrammed behavior for all children [p. 227]." Bowerman (1973) also concluded that grammar without meaning is not enough to understand the acquisition of language. Studying children's acquisition of Finnish, she concludes "the kinds of concepts children use in generating their earliest two- and three-word constructions may be primarily semantic [p. 227]." She goes on to suggest that, to take but one example, what might have the semantic function of agent (person who does something) at first might be represented by the grammatical concept of "sentence subject" at a later age.

The Operant Conditioning of Verbal Behavior

The operant conditioning of verbal behavior was given much impetus by Greenspoon's (1955) experiment. Subjects increased saying plural nouns when the experimenter uttered the sound "mm-hm" following each such word. This finding, along with most subjects' unawareness of the reinforcement contingency, made the procedure particularly appropriate as an analog for what Dollard and Miller (1950) contended takes place in psychotherapy.

Greenspoon's experiment provoked an outpouring of verbal conditioning experiments, some using the same response class as his. K. Salzinger, Portnoy, Zlotogura, and Keisner (1963) were concerned with precise response-class definition. Because a plural noun in English can also be a third-person singular verb, these investigators reinforced plural nouns in the appropriate context only, i.e., when emitted in sentences, a form that left no ambiguity with respect to class membership. Subjects were instructed to speak on any topic as long as they spoke in time to a metronome beat set to evoke one word per second. This allowed the experimenters to evaluate each word as it came and thus to reinforce each plural noun without undue delay. The proportion of plural nouns increased from an operant level through successive conditioning periods and gradually decreased through successive extinction periods. A further analysis of the subclasses of plural nouns into those words ending in an "/s/" sound, as in desks, as opposed to those ending in a "/z/" sound, as in days, showed that only the latter increased significantly. On the other hand, all words (nouns, verbs, etc.) ending in "/z/" did not change significantly over the experiment; the responce class was not a larger class defined simply by sound. Dixon and Hammond (1970), apparently unaware of this experiment, compared the conditionability of plural nouns ending in "/z/" and "/s/." Although both sound-defined response classes could be conditioned when the criterion of conditioning was comparison to a control group, the plural nouns ending in "/z/" increased more than those ending in "/s/," thus partially replicating the K. Salzinger et al. study (1963).

Many experiments unfortunately used a research design that essentially produced the "awareness" controversy. Subjects read "sentences" in which their task was to join one of three pronouns to a verb. "Awareness" constituted a more important variable in studies of this type than in Greenspoon's, and investigators repeatedly asked whether people could be conditioned without being aware of it (Krasner, 1967). The basic problem, however, was elsewhere. The conditioning sessions were set up as problems for the sophomore students to solve, and the students spent their time generating hypotheses to explain what was happening. Furthermore the simplicity of the response and the small size of the response class (Salzinger, K., 1967) made the subjects aware of the reinforcement contingency; They simply noted such relations as those between their use of the pronoun "he" and the experimenter's "mm-hm" or "good." The fact that the student was able to observe, "Whenever I say 'he,' the experimenter says 'good,' " is not at all surprising, nor is the fact that this kind of self-instruction should radically alter behavior. We already know that children learn fairly early to control their problem-solving behavior by means of their language behavior; we would expect no less from a college student. But the most important point is that when humans control their own behavior by means of verbal responses, it does not constitute an argument against the reality of operant conditioning but rather points out the significance of the verbal response as a discriminative stimulus.

On the other hand, not all behavior conditioned or controlled by reinforcers and/or discriminative stimuli is controlled by *verbal* responses generated by the subject. If we had to make verbal responses to produce each and every next response and if we had to respond verbally to each and every reinforcer, we would have no time left to make those "next" responses. Experiments with both normal and schizophrenic subjects (Salzinger, K., & Pisoni, 1958, 1960, to take but two examples among many) have shown that one can condition such response classes as statements of self-referred affect (I hate, I love, I'm happy, I'm sad, etc.) without the subjects realizing that they are responding to reinforcement or even that they are participating in an experiment. These studies showed that interviewers trying to find out something about another person while using only general questions may manipulate the very response classes for which they are searching. The implications for the clinician studying personality are obvious. Also of interest is the inversion of this relation: the interviewer is not only an independent variable in influencing the interviewee but a dependent variable influenced by the interviewee. K. Salzinger and Pisoni (1961) showed that subjects differ sufficiently in acquisition to produce differences in how many reinforcers could be delivered to a given subject. It follows that in a relatively short period of interview assessment, interviewer influence will vary with the acquisition of behavior as well as with the interviewer's tendency to reinforce.

The interviewee effect on the interviewer was directly studied by Rosenfeld and Baer (1969). They essentially made the interviewer believe that he was the experimenter; in fact, the interviewee was the experimenter. The interviewer considered it his job to reinforce the interviewee's chin rubs; in fact, these chin rubs constituted the reinforcers for the interviewer's verbal behavior, consisting of the words "yeah" in some cases and "mm-hm" in others. The interviewer's verbal behavior varied as the contingency of reinforcement was changed by the interviewee. Furthermore the interviewer showed no awareness at all that these responses were being reinforced.

Rosenfeld and Baer (1970) did a second experiment using an experimenter-subject paradigm, in which the "experimenter" was actually the subject and the "subject" actually the experimenter. The response reinforced was specified by the form in which the "experimenter" asked the "subject" to make the next response. The "experimenter" had been told to reduce the subject's disfluencies of speech by giving the "subject" points whenever she spoke fluently. In fact, the disfluencies and fluencies (presented on tape so that the "experimenter" believed she was hearing a live speaker) were made contingent on the "experimenter's" emission of such responses as "next word" or "O.K." Two "experimenters" showed the expected changes with the changes in reinforcement contingency, but showed no awareness even though their behavior was definitely manipulated.

We mention only one more experiment on verbal conditioning. Weiss, Lombardo, Warren, and Kelley (1971) showed that the opportunity to reply to a person who disagrees with one constitutes a reinforcer in a conversation. There is no need to describe all the experiments in the literature; many reviews are available (Holz & Azrin, 1966; Kanfer, 1968; Krasner, 1958; Salzinger, K., 1959, 1969a).

Operant Conditioning of Children's Verbal Behavior

While many investigators spent time working with the reinforcement of adult verbal behavior, some pursued the acquisition of verbal behavior in children directly. Rather than arguing about whether verbal behavior is or is not acquired through learning and rather than trying to find the answer in the complicated multivariable situation of the natural interaction of mother and child, they decided to work with the effect of reinforcement on the sound production of very young children. Rheingold, Gewirtz, and Ross (1959) used the following three acts as reinforcers: the experimenter smiled, emitted three "tsk" sounds, and lightly touched the infant's abdomen with thumb and fingers. The reinforcer was contingent on all the 3-month-old infants' vocalizations except for straining sounds, coughs, whistles, squeaks, and cries of protest. Vocalizations increased significantly from baseline to conditioning and decreased during extinction. Arguments aside about whether these babblings constitute the forerunners of speech, vocalizations were definitely controllable by reinforcement contingencies of the kind that might occur in a natural social situation.

Weisberg (1963) repeated the original experiment including a nonsocial reinforcer as well as a social one. Simply introducing an unresponding adult after the child had been alone did not increase vocalization; nor did the noncontingent delivery of the social reinforcer; nor did the contingent delivery of nonsocial reinforcers (chimes). Only the contingent delivery of the social reinforcer increased vocalization. Todd and Palmer (1968) repeated the experiment with the same age infants using a tape-recorded female voice saying such things as, "Hello baby, pretty baby" as a reinforcer. Conditioning was more successful when an adult was present during the delivery of the reinforcers, but both cases showed substantial conditioning.

Haugan and McIntire (1972) compared vocal imitation, tactile stimulation, and food as reinforcers for vocalization of 3- to 6-month-old infants. All three were effective reinforcers, but imitation was the most effective. Reinforcers were equally effective for all ages of infants studied, except that the 6-month-olds had higher rates of vocalization during extinction. Finally, Routh (1969), using infants from 2- to 7-months-old, increased vocalization with the same kind of contingent reinforcer as Rheingold et al. (1959). Even more interesting, the contingent reinforcer for vowel as opposed to consonant sounds (in which the vocal passage is constricted in some way) produced the appropriate kind of sound in the infant. Even at this early age, response differentiation of an infant's verbal (or, at least, vocal) behavior by a reinforcement contingency is possible.

Using children from 15- to 20-months old, Hursh and Sherman (1973) demonstrated that parents could increase the emission of particular syllables. They manipulated such syllables as, "dee," "bah," or "bee," already in the child's repertory but not with high frequency. The experimenters had the parents model the sounds chosen, e.g., "Tommy, can you say, 'dee'?" and then praise any repetition by saying "That's good, Tommy, you said 'dee'!". The model was presented both before and after the correct response. Both the modeling and praise increased specific sounds made by these children. Thus we have more evidence for a behavioral mechanism of language acquisition in children. The fact that the conditioning procedure was carried out by parents using social reinforcers makes the evidence more convincing. This experiment bridges the work on very young children and on the older children whose language behavior we discuss later.

The application of conditioning procedures to still older children has also proved successful. S. Salzinger, Salzinger, Portnoy, Eckman, Bacon, Deutsch, and Zubin (1962) conditioned the speech of preschool and first-grade children by means of a device called Happy the Clown. After telling the children a story about the clown who is happy only when children talk to him, these investigators used the lighting of the clown's nose as the reinforcer; the children were also told that the happier the clown gets, the more often he flashes his nose on and off; if he is "very very happy" he also delivers a present at the end of the game (experiment). Speech increased with nose flashes (reinforcers) contingent on speech and decreased or remained the same when the reinforcer was omitted. Furthermore those children whose self-referred statements were reinforced increased not only that response class but also the frequency of speech in general. In children of this age, general speech is largely composed of self-references.

Operant Conditioning of Language in Speech-Deficient Children

Much research on operant conditioning and language acquisition is done on children who have difficulty in developing it "naturally." Research on retarded children, autistic children, stutterers, clutterers, and aphasics is summarized in papers by Lahey (1973b) and Sloane and MacAulay (1968). The other kind of language problem derives from different language communities (Lahey, 1973a). Lahey argues that one must be careful to keep intact the child's cultural heritage; on the other hand, all children ought to learn some language responses to take advantage of school and the world outside school. In this context immediate feedback of the kind described in Zoellner's (1969) talk-write program should improve the writing of fifth graders. By making points contingent first on the total number of words, then on the number of different words, and finally on the number of new words, Brigham, Graubard, and Stans (1972) sought to improve the quantity and quality of the writing of these youngsters. Although the contingency was not explicit with respect to the quality of the composition, the quality improved, as shown by the children's improved ideas in their compositions. Apparently because language consists of connected responses, the reinforcement of sheer quantity improves quality as well. Further, association of reinforcement with writing increased the joy of writing and thus probably contributed to the quality of the compositions.

An early application of operant conditioning to instating speech was attempted by K. Salzinger, Feldman, Cowan, and Salzinger (1965). Using candy as reinforcers, the experimenters conditioned speech in two speech-deficient children. One, a 4-yr old, was completely deficient, although he emitted a great variety of vocalizations not under any apparent discriminative control; the other, also 4-yr old, had a repertory of a few words. The two children also had many other problems: temper tantrums, no toilet training, etc. The experimenters therefore had to work with the children not only on the speech-deficit problem but also on other behavior. Furthermore one of the peculiarities surrounding such children, even when they are among trained ward personnel, is that nobody speaks to them. In contrast most mothers of normal children talk to them even when they are not yet able to speak back. Being surrounded by silence and being pushed around rather than being asked to do things is not conducive to learning to speak. One aspect of the conditioning program, therefore, was to talk to the children about everything that was happening, so that if they had any tendency to repeat they would have the opportunity to do so. The imitation procedure was important in the conditioning. The experimenter began by giving the children candy merely for approaching, then for coming to the room in which the experimenter wanted to work, and finally for emitting sounds. The first child's utterances, which did not include words, were initially reinforced on a continuous basis, then on increasingly greater ratio schedules.

Discrimination training along with the conditioning of imitation was instituted with the first child by giving him a book of pictures and some stuffed animals; the experimenter pointed at a particular picture or object, said the word repeatedly, and then waited for the child to repeat it, making the reinforcer contingent on some approximation to the correct word. As for reception of language, the child was also trained to bring the experimenter the particular object that he or she named. This procedure enabled the child to acquire a small vocabulary that was sometimes under discriminative control. Although the child improved his receptive communication in being able to follow at least familiar instructions and learned to emit some words, in the 9 months available to the experimenters, he never learned to combine words. He might not have learned even with more time because fairly definite signs of neurological deficit were found.

The second child had some words initially in his repertory. The words that could be clearly identified were "no" and "key," both used in correct contexts as far as the experimenters could determine. The experimenter used both candy and his own speech as reinforcers, i.e., in the experimental setting he answered the child with a remark as long as the child's own remark. Not only the candy but apparently even the speech of the experimenter had by this time become a reinforcer causing an increase in response rate. Further evidence for the increasing importance of social reinforcement is that while in later sessions the child seemed as eager as before to have the experimenter give him candy, he often delayed eating it and occasionally even made a game out of returning it after asking for it.

After the child's general rate of verbal response increased, he was given a sentence frame; the experimenter said, "Say, 'Give me *candy.*'" The child's utterance was reinforced with candy; thereafter saying the word "candy" alone was never reinforced. The child not only learned to utter this simple sentence but also generalized this frame in much the same way as claimed by psycholinguists for the pivot construction. In that construction the child learns to combine words in such a way that one (the pivot) is used frequently and others (used less frequently) are placed before or after it, but not both. As already mentioned, the grammatical explanation for this construction has by this time been rejected by those same psycholinguists. In this case, where the acquisition of language was slow and where the process was controlled at least in part by the experimenters, it is even more obvious that the frame works as a mand, in which whatever word the child places in the frame is specifically reinforced. As a consequence, the child learned to say such things as, "Gimme *pick it up*" (meaning that someone else should pick it up) as well as such poetic expressions as, "Gimme no more cloudy again" (meaning that he wanted better weather so that he could be taken outdoors). This stage of his language acquisition demonstrated a rather efficient use of the sentence frame. Whatever he wanted, he placed into the "Gimme _____" frame, unfettered by the limitations of adult grammar. This child has been followed up for many years and now speaks fluently.

Operant conditioning has been greatly extended in instating speech. Lovaas (1973), in his program with autistic children, found it necessary to start by suppressing self-destructive behavior before initiating language learning. The program is quite extensive and films are available showing how it is done. The child is taught to tact (Skinner's term) or to name objects in the environment, to construct sentences, to ask questions, to describe things happening currently and things in the past, and even to talk "spontaneously." All this behavior is taught by shaping procedures and by fading stimuli that were originally necessary to evoke the responses; as the original stimulus is faded out, the appropriate stimulus is faded in to complete the transfer. To take but one example, imitation includes a fading out of the experimenter's stimulus; the experimenter supplies the same response less loudly and less completely until eventually the more appropriate stimulus is faded in, so that it takes over control of the response. B. Gray and Ryan (1973) recently presented a detailed language conditioning program so that others may make use of the technique. They include evaluation instruments so that the language conditioner can gauge the progress made by an objective criterion.

The operant approach to language is empirical, and therefore it should not be surprising that imitation learning, or what has come to be called modeling or observational learning (techniques used rarely with animals), has been accepted as a major technique for instating language behavior. Some research has been summarized by Zimmerman and Rosenthal (1974). Although these writers speak of "rule-governed" behavior, it is easy to translate their word *rule* into the more familiar behavioral term *reinforcement contingency*. The term *rule* does not mean that speakers instruct themselves or that anyone else does. The term, when explicitly stated, describes regularities in behavior. It is such regularities that the term reinforcement contingency refers to and it is this aspect of *rule* that can be easily translated. Perhaps the most important point that Zimmerman and Rosenthal make is that imitation must not be confused with mimicry. The matching of responses need not be an exact topographical matching any more than any response member of a given class matches exactly the other members of that class.

Since verbal conditioning began its recent revival with the conditioning of plural nouns, it is instructive to follow this response class in situations where the learner is still acquiring plural endings. Guess, Sailor, Rutherford, and Baer (1968) worked with a severely retarded girl. They taught her to emit singular or plural nouns in response to objects shown. The girl learned to use the plural form appropriately even for words that had not been specifically reinforced, thus showing the kind of generalization that linguists call productivity but which, of course, merely demonstrates the power of plurality as a stimulus (more than one object of a particular class).

An interesting finding in this study led to the experiment by Sailor (1971). The original study found that the plural-noun class actually consisted of two subclasses, nouns ending in the "/s/" sound and nouns ending in the "/z/" sound. This finding replicates studies by K. Salzinger et al. (1963) and Dixon and Hammond (1970) with normal college students. Sailor (1971) examined the integrity of the plural response class by reinforcing one of the subclasses and measuring generalization to the other. By reinforcing words whose correct ending is "/z/," as in dogs, planes, and screws, he was able to examine whether the retarded children would generalize this ending to such words as cups, hats, and blocks that take the "/s/" ending. The results indicated that the children generalized the learned "/z/" sound for plurality to all nouns regardless of the correct English rule, thus supporting the integrity of the sound-defined response class.

Guess and Baer (1973) investigated generalization from one modality to another in retarded children. Training plurality in the receptive (or productive) modality for the ending of "s," they at the same time trained plurality in the productive (or receptive) modality for the ending "es." Little generalization occurred from one to the other modality, suggesting that even when the training is done concurrently, the kind of generalization that psycholinguists often assume is not necessary. Nevertheless, this lack of generalization may be related to the retardation of the children; on the other hand, it should be checked with normal children. The extension of the plural to inclusion in sentences was accomplished by Garcia, Guess, and Byrnes (1973). A retarded girl who had no sentences in her repertory was trained through imitation and reinforcement to emit sentences including plurality. She also learned to emit new items in the appropriate form (singular versus plural).

Other examples of the instatement of various grammatical response classes are in Lahey (1971), who trained Head Start children to emit more descriptive adjectives by modeling such descriptions without explicit reinforcement. Schumaker and Sherman (1970) trained three retarded children to emit verbs in appropriate present and past forms. They also found generalization to verbs not specifically trained. Rubin and Stolz (1974) showed that pronouns of self-reference could be increased in a severely retarded adolescent and with appropriate explicit programming generalized to other occasions in so-called spontaneous speech. Finally, telegraphic speech in language-disordered children can be converted into sentence form (Fygetakis & Gray, 1970; Wheeler & Sulzer, 1970). Again we find evidence for generalization from specifically trained stimuli to novel stimuli.

CONCLUSIONS

The author hopes that by this time the reader, if not yet fully convinced, will at least begin to share his evident faith in being able to apply the behavior-theory approach to language. All of us, operant conditioners and psycholinguists alike, agree that language behavior is complex. The question to be answered, and answered empirically, is whether the complexity of behavior theory is sufficient to cope with the complexity of language. A few years ago, this author wrote of the complexity of behavior with respect to the application of operant conditioning to disordered behavior (Salzinger, K., 1968). These statements apply equally to language behavior. Here we shall only list the complexities referred to in that paper: response class and the related concept of response generalization, imitation learning, variable response unit size, response-produced stimulus control including the generation or suppression of other responses, and the operant/respondent conditioning overlap. This chapter illustrated how each of these complexities may operate in language behavior.

SECTION II

INSTRUCTIONAL SYSTEMS AND ANALYSES

WESLEY C. BECKER and SIEGFRIED ENGELMANN

Chapter 10

Systems for Basic Instruction: Theory and Applications[1,2]

This chapter specifies principles that provide a rationale for designing, selecting, and sequencing tasks for basic instructional programs. We then describe one instructional system using programs developed from these principles.

PART 1. PROGRAMMING PROCEDURES

The major goal of instructional programs is to teach competencies extending beyond the specific tasks used in instruction. The goal is to teach a *general case*. A general case has been taught when, after instruction on some tasks in a particular class, any task in that class can be performed correctly. When a general case has been taught with respect to a class of stimuli, we say a *concept* has been taught. A concept is defined by the stimulus properties uniquely common to a set of stimulus instances. Note that this implies that the definition of a concept ("what is *uniquely* common") may change as the set of concepts to be discriminated from each other changes. When a general case has been taught with respect to a class of responses, we say an *operation*, a *response class*, or a *discriminated operant*

1. Parts of this chapter are adapted from materials published in Becker, Engelmann, and Thomas, *Teaching 2: Cognitive Learning and Instruction.* Palo Alto, SRA, 1975b, and are reprinted here with permission of the copyright holder SRA. No parts of this chapter may be reproduced without permission of SRA and the authors.
2. The University of Oregon Follow Through Project was supported by funds from the U.S. Office of Education, Department of School Systems, Division of Compensatory Education, Follow Through Branch, under Grant No. OEG-070-4257 (286).

has been taught (Baer, Peterson, & Sherman, 1967; Garcia, Guess, & Byrnes, 1973; Sherman, J. A., Saunders, & Brigham, 1970; Skinner, 1938). An operation is defined by the common effects of a set of responses under stimulus control.

The use of the term operation to refer generally to discriminated operants or response classes may be a potential source of confusion for the reader. In the operant literature *experimental operation* is a term reserved for the experimenter's behavior (and/or his equipment's) rather than the subject's. But the mental operations of Piaget, the construction operations of a carpenter, the operations performed by an experimenter, and discriminated operant responses share fundamental properties. By using the term *operation* instead of *discriminated operant*, we hope to foster a conceptual convergence between cognitive and operant psychology and to avoid the common tendency of those in education to treat operants as specific responses.

As we shall see, teaching a general case requires teaching a sequence of tasks, i.e., a program. Programming theory is concerned with principles for selecting, modifying, and ordering tasks in a program.

PROGRAMMING IMPLICATIONS FOR THE STUDY OF DIS-CRIMINATION LEARNING

Concept learning is a special case of the stimulus control of operant behavior. When a person can respond one way to instances of a concept and another way to not-instances, we say the concept has been learned. The basic procedure for establishing stimulus control is, of course, *differential reinforcement*. Correct responses are reinforced and incorrect responses are not. The process involved is called discrimination learning. To show what is involved in concept teaching, we will examine four different procedures for establishing stimulus control. (See Chapter 2 for a discussion of basic research in stimulus control.)

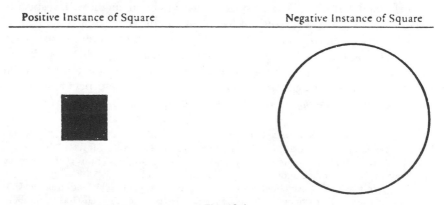

| Positive Instance of Square | Negative Instance of Square |

Fig. 10-1.

Procedure 1

The simplest stimulus control procedure uses two stimulus instances or examples. A particular response is reinforced in the presence of one stimulus and not the other. For example, in Figure 10-1 the square and circle are presented repeatedly until the student says "square" to the square and "not-square" to the circle. Now suppose we test to see what has been learned using other squares and circles. We present a black circle and it is called "square." Or perhaps a small circle is called "square." Our training has failed to establish the desired concept.

Implications. If a discrimination can be made between instances and not-instances of a concept on the basis of stimulus properties other than those to be taught, a discrimination may be learned in terms of those other properties (Lashley, 1938; Reynolds, 1961b).

Procedure 2

Suppose we use the preceding example, but now control for irrelevant stimuli by making them the same for our instance and not-instance of square. For example, in Figure 10-2 the square and circle differ only in shape, not size or color. Again we train until the discrimination is learned. When we now test with examples differing markedly in size, color, or pattern from the training examples, we find the discrimination is no longer made.

Implications. When irrelevant stimulus properties are held constant in training, the more the new cases differ from the training examples in irrelevant properties, the less likely the discrimination will be made in the new case.

Procedure 3

Suppose now that we present a series of instances and not-instances of square with varying irrelevant properties. We might present them as pairs or singly. Figure 10-3 shows pairs for which the task is "Point to the square."

| Positive Instance of Square | Negative Instance of Square |

Fig. 10-2.

Stimulus Pair   Figure Chosen

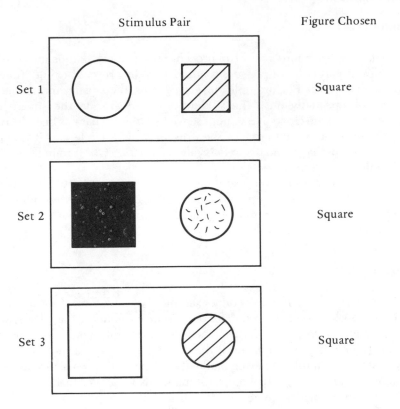

Set 1   Square

Set 2   Square

Set 3   Square

Fig. 10-3.   Pairs of instances and not-instances of square with varying irrelevant properties.

With an adequate number of examples, a perfect performance is found on test trials with "new" examples.

Harlow (1959; Moon and Harlow, 1955) has shown that a procedure like this can be used to teach monkeys concepts such as *oddity* ("Choose the one that is different"). When irrelevant stimulus properties (e.g., form, position) are varied, they can no longer be consistently associated with reinforcement. They therefore will not control responding. Reinforcement is maximized only by responding to properties correlated with reinforcement (e.g., the property of oddity, which pertains to the stimulus that is not the same as the other two). The oddity example shows that relevant properties are not restricted to simple physical properties of individual stimuli; they may also include properties of the relations among several different stimuli. In a Harlow experiment a monkey might be given four trials on each of a series of problems like those shown in Figure 10-4. After about 250 problems, it responds correctly on the first trial with a new set about 90% of the time. For the concept *oddity*, form and position are irrelevant. When form and position are varied from trial to trial (or every four trials), monkeys learn to

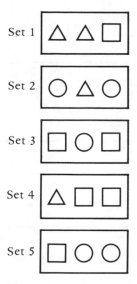

Fig. 10-4. Examples of oddity problems.

choose the one not like the other two and not to respond to either of the two objects that are the same.

Ferster and Hammer (1966) also demonstrated the importance of this procedure. In teaching arithmetic concepts to chimpanzees, they found it necessary to vary all stimuli not related to the reinforcement contingency (all stimuli irrelevant to the concept being taught). Chimpanzees did not attend to the *number* of items in an example if responding to color, position, shape, size, or some other irrelevant cue was consistently reinforced.

Implications. By presenting many instances and not-instances in which irrelevant stimulus properties are varied, it is possible to teach a discrimination that will be maintained when new instances involving the varied irrelevant properties are presented. A general case can be taught. But how general is it?

Another look at Procedure 2

Suppose in procedure 2, where irrelevant properties were kept constant, we had tested with these figures, keeping irrelevant properties constant but using new not-instances (Figure 10-5). On this test the responses imply that the child was responding to corners and/or straight sides in discriminating square from circle, but 90° angles and equal sides were not responded to as essential properties. We would infer that it is because these stimulus properties were not discriminated that rectangles and triangles were called "square."

Similarly Harlow's monkeys would likely have responded incorrectly if

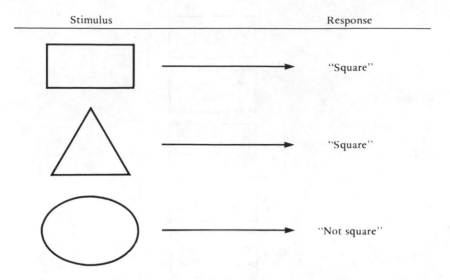

| Stimulus | Response |

Fig. 10-5. A test involving new not-instances.

they had been presented with test problems of the sort shown in Figure 10-6. *Oddity* in Harlow's experiments was "Choose the one of three objects that is different from both of the others." Because the monkeys were not taught how to respond to sets where no object was odd (by the Harlow definition), there was a good chance that responses would occur to some irrelevant characteristics.

   Implications. If two concepts differ in many ways, one can learn to discriminate between them by attending to any essential difference. However, if new concepts (sharing some properties) are added to the teaching set, it will be necessary to teach additional essential properties for previously taught concepts.

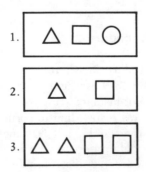

Fig. 10-6. New not-instance for oddity problem.

Procedure 4. Teaching Discriminations among a Set of Related Concepts

Figure 10-7 shows five instances of concepts from the set of closed geometric figures. The figure illustrates a set of related concepts, sets of essential properties of concepts (e.g., *a, b, c, d* for square), and the discriminations to be learned if the set of concepts is to be learned. The number of possible discriminations is indicated by the numbers on the lines connecting pairs of figures. The essential properties given in Figure 10-7 are sufficient to permit discrimination of the members of the set. Alternative sets of properties could also be defined (e.g., for a square, four equal straight sides and equal angles).

Two fundamentally different procedures can be followed in teaching discriminations among a set of related concepts.

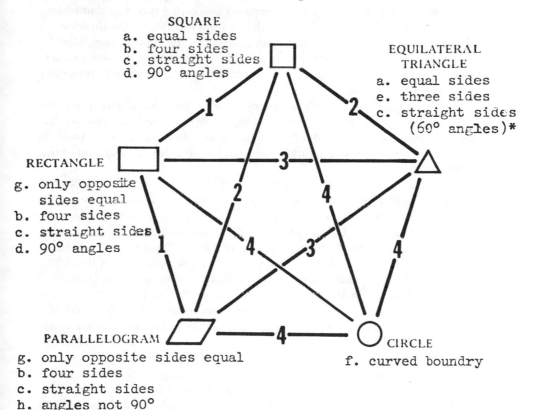

* This property or equal sides is redundant, but both can be a basis for discrimination.

Fig. 10-7. A set of related concepts and their essential properties. Numbers on connecting lines indicate the number of ways in which two concepts can be discriminated.

Procedure 4a. Teaching Successive Pairs of Discriminations

First, responding to square and circle is taught to a criterion of perfect performance. Then responding to square and rectangle is brought to criterion. Then rectangle and circle, etc., until all 10 pairs of discriminations have been taught.

Procedure 4b. Cumulatively Adding to the Concepts Discriminated from Each Other

Teach the discrimination of square from circle. Then add equilateral triangle and bring all three to criterion when presented randomly. Then add parallelogram to make a set of four concepts discriminated from each other. Finally, add rectangle to make a set of five.

Ferster and Hammer (1966) compared successive-pair and cumulative programming procedures for teaching number-symbol identification to chimpanzees. After the successive-pair procedure, the chimpanzees failed to respond above chance to randomly presented members of the number set. With cumulative programming, the discrimination of randomly presented numbers was accurate.

Implications of Procedures 4a and 4b. Cumulative programming is essential to teaching naive learners sets of related concepts so that they can respond correctly to randomly presented instances of the set (old or new). Cumulative programming is essential to the inductive teaching of the general case.

The reason cumulative programming is so important can be illustrated from Figure 10-7. Square can be discriminated from circle on the basis of the difference between any property, a or b or c or d, and property e. Suppose responding to square and circle is brought to criterion and the property of square used in the discrimination is c (straight sides). Next suppose we teach the discrimination of rectangle from circle. Again straight sides is the relevant property. Next, we teach the discrimination of square from rectangle. Straight sides are no longer an essential property. Suppose the new discrimination is made on the basis of four equal sides versus only opposite sides equal. We go on like this, a pair at a time. With this procedure, it is not necessary to learn the conjunctive rule that square is *a plus b plus c plus d* in the set of closed geometric figures. Partial rules are learned that become inadequate when new pairs are added to the set. This problem will arise with any multiple-attribute concept sharing properties with related concepts. Cumulative programming, in which the current teaching set is brought to criterion before a new member is added, overcomes this problem. A theory of programming should provide rational procedures for cumulative programming.

Concept Learning as a Multiple Discrimination Problem

We learn about concepts because we are taught to respond one way to instances of a concept and another way to not-instances. The alternative procedures for establishing stimulus control over responding, illustrated in the preceding section, point to *two* important sets of discriminations critical to learning concepts:

1. *Within instances or not-instances, it is necessary to discriminate relevant stimulus properties from irrelevant properties.* For example, an instance of "red" might be shaped like a truck (irrelevant), be made of wood (irrelevant), and be sitting on a table (irrelevant). Colors have to be discriminated from shapes, materials, and positions. Within a not-instance of "red" (say, a blue rubber ball) the relevant property of the not-instance (blueness) must also be discriminated from the irrelevant properties (ball shape, rubber material, held in the hand).
2. *Between instances and not-instances, it is necessary to discriminate between relevant properties of the instances and not-instances.* For example, to learn about red it is necessary to learn to discriminate not-red by learning to respond to blue, orange, yellow, green, etc., as the "not-red set."

The two aspects of this multiple discrimination problem are illustrated in Figure 10-8. If $S+$ stands for the relevant properties of instances of a concept, $S-$ stands for the relevant properties of not-instances of a concept, and S_i refers to irrelevant properties of instances or not-instances, then the problem is learning to discriminate *within* instances, $S+$ from S_i, or $S-$ from

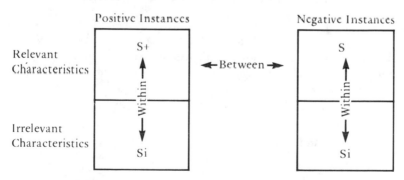

Note: S+, S−, and Si may be a single characteristic or a
        set of characteristics.

Fig. 10-8. Concept learning as a multiple discrimination problem.

S_i, and to discriminate *between* instances, $S+$ from $S-$. $S+$ and $S-$ are used as procedural concepts when planning instruction, e.g., "Instances of red will be $S+$ in this program." $S+$ and $S-$ are functional concepts when testing for the effects of instruction, e.g., "Johnny called all the red objects 'red.'" He learned to discriminate redness.

SUMMARY OF PROGRAMMING IMPLICATIONS

Given that the teaching of concepts requires differential reinforcement of discriminations within and between instances used to teach concepts, and that related concepts must be taught as sets, an efficient teaching program for naive learners must meet the following requirements:

1. The program must include a *set* of instances and not-instances. A single instance and not-instance will not do.
2. The set of instances should be selected so that *all* instances possess *all* relevant concept characteristics, and *all* not-instances possess only *some* or *none* of these characteristics. Do not choose the set so that wrong responses can be reinforced.
3. Irrelevant properties *within* instances and not-instances must be varied. If this is not done, a misrule may be taught. The student may learn to call trucks "red" if all instances of red used in teaching are shaped like trucks.
4. The program must be cumulative, so that the critical discriminations in the *enlarging set* of concepts are taught.

For the experienced learner, deductive teaching from rules can also be used. For more details, see W. C. Becker, Engelmann, and Thomas (1975b).

THE ANALYSIS OF STIMULUS PROPERTIES

A little arithmetic will quickly show that if *all* possible discriminations among the properties of *all* possible concepts had to be taught, the job would be impossible. The number of pairs in a set of n things is $n(n - 1)/2$. Assuming *only one* relevant property in the discrimination of each pair of concepts (and there are usually more), it would require the teaching of 325 discriminations to teach the 26 capital letters of the alphabet. A concept

Positive Instances   Negative Instances

| S + |
| Sc |
| Si |

| S - |
| Sc |
| Si |

Fig. 10-9. The analysis of stimulus instances into three groups of properties.

vocabulary of 20,000 words would require mastery of 200 million discriminations, again assuming only one discrimination per pair. Fortunately, knowledge of where errors occur in discrimination learning and the logical analysis of the similarities and differences among concepts can be used to simplify the teaching process. The product of this analysis provides additional principles for a theory of programming.

Stimulus Properties Common to Two or More Concepts (Sc)

Examples used to teach concepts can be analyzed for three kinds of stimulus properties. In Figure 10-9, $S+$ and $S-$ are the relevant properties of instances and not-instances, respectively. S_i properties are irrelevant stimulus properties. The S_c symbol refers to stimulus properties common to the instances of two or more concepts. S_c properties are the bases for forming higher-order concepts. They describe the structure of relations among concepts.

Whether a property common to instances of several concepts is treated as S_c or $S+$ depends on the set of concepts being analyzed. For example, in a set of concepts that includes only *mammals*, instances of the concepts *horse* and *person* have in common the properties of being warm-blooded, having mammary glands, etc. These are S_c properties. These properties would not distinguish *horse* from *person* (would not be $S+$) in a set that included only mammals, but in a set including all *animals* they could be $S+$ for discriminating mammals from reptiles.

The role played by the type of analysis defining S_c and $S+$ can be further illustrated by returning to Figure 10-7. In this example, *equal sides* is common to *squares* and *equilateral triangles*. If there were only two concepts in the analysis, *equal sides* would be S_c. It is common to both concepts and not useful in discriminating between them. In the total set of concepts to be discriminated, however, *equal sides* is essential $(S+)$ to both *square* and *equilateral triangle* and is needed to discriminate these concepts from other closed geometric figures.

Discrimination Failures (Errors)

A person has learned a discrimination when he responds differentially to two or more classes of stimuli. Suppose a child is taught to say "red" to instances of the color red within a specified range of red colors, and to say "not red" to instances of blue, white, and black. Very likely the child, if presented with instances of orange, would call them red. When someone responds to a new stimulus in the same way as to a previously taught stimulus having some of the same properties, the event is called *stimulus generalization*.

Stimulus generalization implies a failure to discriminate. If the teacher or programmer can predict when stimulus generalization is likely to occur, difficulties can be anticipated and possibly prevented. Three factors control stimulus generalization, or the likelihood of responding to new concept instances as if they were members of a previously learned class:

1. The *number of identical stimulus properties* (S_c) shared by the instances of two concepts.
2. The *number and magnitude of the differences in concept properties between two concepts* ($S+$ - $S-$ differences).
3. The degree of *prior discrimination training* with respect to concept differences.

In the example of red and orange above, all three factors entered into the prediction that orange would be responded to in the same way as red. First, red and orange share the property of being colors (reflected or emitted light). Second, red and orange are more similar (differ less) in spectral composition than orange and blue, orange and white, or orange and black. Third, the training history did not provide training that orange was *not* red.

It is commonplace in psychology to say that stimulus generalization is a function of *stimulus similarity*. The notion of stimulus similarity is imprecise, failing to recognize that similarity involves all three factors listed above: identical shared properties, number and sizes of differences, and prior training in the discriminations involved. With this analysis the teacher and programmer can use several approaches to reduce or prevent errors in designing teaching sequences.

Consider the letters *a* and *d*. These letters share the characteristics (S_c) of being letters and being formed in the same manner. They differ only in the length of the stem. If the difference in the stem length is small (*d d*), a greater difficulty in discriminating *a* from *d* is likely than if the difference in length is large (*a d*). Also, one can predict that these two letters are more likely to be generalized (or confused) than either would be with *s* (cf. Gibson, 1965). A programmer could reduce the possibility of stimulus generalization by exaggerating the difference in stem length. He could also make *a* and *d* more discriminable by making *a* this way: a ; and *d* this way: d. If this is done, some of the common properties (S_c) are eliminated.

Another approach to the problem of confusing *a* and *d* would be not to change the stimulus to reduce similarity but to focus training directly on the difference in stem length. The program could give much practice on this discrimination to ensure that *a* and *d* are not confused.

Two Types of Concept Analysis Used in Programming

Concept *pair analysis* is used to analyze sets of related concepts to determine which are most alike and which are most different. Concept *structure analysis* is used to determine the sets of related concepts. The programmer must give special attention to highly similar concept pairs in sequencing them and teaching essential discriminations. To illustrate, we can classify the 10 possible pairs of different concepts in Figure 10-7 into groups based on how many properties are different. For example, rectangle and square differ in one way, while rectangle and circle differ in four ways.

Pairs of concepts differ in the number of ways in which they are the same (S_c) or different ($S+$ versus $S-$). When concepts differ in many ways, only a sampling of ways in which they differ need be taught. The student need only learn to respond to one of the differences to be right. When there are few differences, each of the differences must be taught. In the set given in Figure 10-7 programming would focus extensively on the two pairs with only one difference, moderately on those with two differences, and briefly on those with three or four differences. The programmer might also consider the relative difficulty of each difference if evidence were available.

The number of common properties can vary independently of the number of differences. For example, *dog* and *horse* have many more common properties than *dog* and *tree*. When there are many common properties, more instruction is likely to be needed, just as when there are few differences. Actually, one might work with a ratio of common properties to differences in judging the difficulty of a discrimination (independent of knowledge of the learning history).

Another kind of concept analysis used in programming is concerned with the structuring of concepts. For example, concepts can be ordered into domains based on matter, space, and time by considering the increasing number of concepts assumed in providing a teaching demonstration of new concepts from each domain. W.C. Becker et al. (1975b, p. 146) list five domains as follows:

1. Concepts about *objects*: e.g., living things, man-made things, cars, fish, plants.
2. Concepts about *object properties*: e.g., mass, heat, state, structure, parts, shape, size, surface properties, and color.
3. Concepts about *object relations* (in space): e.g., order, location, direction, relative position, relative size, number, family relations, arbitrary relations.
4. Concepts about *events in time and space*: e.g., conservation of mass or movement, changes in energy, changes in group composition (such as addition), and changes in government.
5. Concepts about *relations among events in time and space* (cause and effect): e.g., "For every action, there is an equal and opposite reaction"; "Responses followed by reinforcement are strengthened."

Objects are stimulus instances that can be pointed to, moved, or touched. The whole stimulus instance is involved: "This is a *ball*. This is not a ball." Object concepts provide the simplest demonstrations for concept teaching. Once objects can be named, the next simplest step is to talk about their properties. "This ball *is red*. This ball is not red." The next step in complexity is to require comparisons of object properties (relation concepts). "This ball *is larger* than that one." "This tree *is closer* than that tree." The next step in complexity adds a temporal dimension to the comparison (event concepts). "The ball *got larger* when he pumped it up." "The ice cream *melted*." "He *ran* home." Finally, we can look at relations among events (causal concepts). "The heat from the sun melted the ice cream." The teaching of causal concepts requires the prior understanding of temporal relations, events such as getting hot or melting, and object properties of hot and cold, solid and liquid, and the objects sun and ice cream. We have speculated elsewhere (Becker et al., 1975b) that it is this *logical* dependence of concepts from the higher-numbered domains on concepts from the lower-numbered domains that underlies the empirical evidence for developmental stages in the work of Piaget. Mental stages appear to occur just because it is easier to learn some concepts before others. The goal in programming is to teach one thing at a time. By attending to this logical structure among domains, it is possible to approach this goal.

The programmer can use information about domains to help order the sequence in which concepts are taught, and can also facilitate discriminations among major types of concepts by using a common format for concepts within a domain. For example, the following format is typically used for teaching object concepts: "This is a (an) ———. What is this?" The common format teaches that the task involves identifying an object by saying its name. All tasks of the same format involve the same operations. When teaching object properties, a new format should be used. Instead of saying, "This is red. . ." (the format for objects, which might lead the child to respond with *red* as another name for *truck*), this format is used: "This *(object)* is *(attribute)*. What *(attribute class)* is this?" In the case of the red truck, the format is filled in as follows: "This *truck* is *red*. What *color* is this *truck*?" This format teaches that the task involves identifying an object property of the class given and naming it. With repeated examples, the child learns how to do problems of a given type more efficiently. The child learns how to learn by learning to follow verbal directions that are useful in learning a large group of concepts. (See Becker, W. C., et al., 1975b.)

Polars are a subgrouping of object properties that have an additional structure of their own. The logic of the structure of polars is this: "If it is not A, it is B." "If it is not wet, it is dry." "If it is not hard, it is soft." Polars are a two-member group, so if you know it is one, you also know it is not the other (and vice versa). The use of a common format can teach this logic of two-member classes.

Similarly, to teach about action concepts the program should first ensure that the action can be identified and then use a distinctive format, such as: "Point to the *man*. What is the *man doing*?"

In programming concepts that are ordered in hierarchies with the goal of teaching the hierarchy itself, the programmer should include concepts from two levels at the same time. (See Figure 10-10.) To teach about varieties of mammals, first distinguish mammals from not-mammals, and then teach the subgroupings of mammals. "This mammal is an elephant." To teach varieties of dogs, first be sure the concept of dog is established, and then teach subclasses such as Collie, St. Bernard, and Basset. This approach permits a direct teaching of the ways in which concepts are related to each other, i.e., it teaches about concept hierarchies; it also teaches that an instance of one concept can also be an instance of another concept; and, it focuses instruction on the groups of concepts and their instances that share the most properties and must be carefully discriminated from each other.

The primary goal in the analysis of concept structure is to determine groups of concepts whose members have common properties (S_c) and to identify groups that are independent of each other. Independent groupings can sometimes be taught concurrently as separate lesson tracks. Interrelated groupings are analyzed for hierarchical structuring, with the higher-order structures given priority in setting up teaching formats.

PROGRAMMING IMPLICATIONS FROM THE STUDY OF RESPONSE LEARNING

Operations

Operations (or discriminated operants, if you prefer) are related to specific responses just as concepts are related to specific stimuli. An opera-

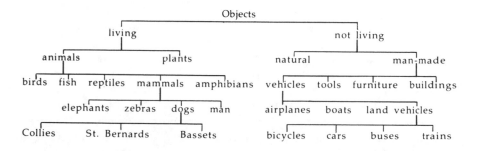

Fig. 10-10. A concept hierarchy based on objects.

tion is defined by the common effects of a set of responses under the control of a discriminative stimulus. For example, a lever-pressing operation may be inferred from any number of specific responses that depress a lever far enough to actuate some consequence. The observer (or teacher), however, could only infer that the lever press is an instance of a more general operation if it occurs on signal (or in a particular setting). Random lever pressing provides no evidence for a *class of responses having a common effect*. The teacher cannot *know* an operation has been learned unless it occurs to some discriminative stimulus.

In behavioral development the nature of the stimulus control over units of behavior may shift as larger functional units are formed from the chaining of smaller units. For example, early in learning to read by a phonic method, verbal responses are controlled by separate letters (or special groups), not words. Later the verbal responding may be controlled by words, not letters. The student may or may not still be able to say the sounds one at a time. This can be tested by presenting the appropriate discriminative stimuli.

An important consideration in programming operations is the fact that most operations can be analyzed into components. For example, opening a lock can be analyzed into the components of *inserting* the key and *turning* the key. Because behavior takes time, it can "always" be subdivided into parts. However, the term *component operations* is used only if each part is under the control of a separate discriminative stimulus and there is a common effect of the components. When analyzing operations, the programmer seeks the minimum number of functional units of behavior that can be used as building blocks in the maximum number of response sequences when appropriately cued. For example, in teaching oral language concepts, *words* are the useful functional units. In teaching beginning reading by a phonic method (e.g., DISTAR), individual letters (or special groups such as -ing) controlling a sound are the basic units. In spelling programs the letter names are the functional units, although letter sounds can be used for words whose sounds are regular.

Response Sequences

Component operations can be used to build three kinds of response sequences: longer operants that are functional units (these have traditionally been called "habits"), rule chains, and creative sequences.

Habits. In the functional unit we call a habit, the stimulus produced in making one response is the cue for the next response, and there are no alternative responses. Saying the letters of the alphabet forward is an example. The learning of this sequence forward will do little to help you say it backward, or to start with a particular letter and go backward. In teaching a habit sequence, the component operations are typically taught first and then the sequence is taught using prompts. It is important to recognize that what is called "habit learning" is based on the same building blocks as so-called "intelligent learning," discussed later.

Rule Chains. Rule chains are procedures used to solve sets of problems with known solutions. Each step in the chain produces information (stimuli) needed to carry out the next step. For example, in DISTAR I Arithmetic, the student is taught to solve addition problems of the form $A + B = \square$ with these rules:

1. Place as many lines under the first number (A) as are in the set the number stands for.
2. Place as many lines under the second number (B) as the number stands for.
3. Count all the lines to find the total of the two numbers.
4. Place the total in the box.

The result would be $4 + 3 = \boxed{7}$

After prompted practice with five or six examples of problems using these rules, any problem of this type (within the taught range of numbers) could be solved. The set of rules teaches a problem-solving strategy appropriate to a particular class of problems. What is learned is a sequence of rules controlling a variety of responses that can produce solutions to problems not solved before. Most problems of fact that can be put into general classes have rule-chain solutions. Some construction problems also have acceptable rule-chain solutions. Examples might be a recipe for making a cake or a plan for building a dog house.

Creative Designs. The response sequencing involved in solving design problems also depends upon component operations. In man's most creative work—the design of new art, new literature, new buildings, and new methods of transportation—we again deal with response sequences. In this case, however, there are no fixed rules and there is no clear ordering of steps. Criteria for a solution may be specified so that different end results can be evaluated as better or worse. The task requires logically or behaviorally tracing the implication of alternative decisions from one decision point to future decision points. The possible multiple alternatives available after each step is made must be considered to find optimal solutions. The distinction between using rule chains to solve problems of fact and using creative sequences to solve design problems parallels Guilford's (1965) distinction between convergent and divergent thinking.

Concepts about Operations

For every possible operation, there exists a possible concept about that operation. It is important to distinguish between the two. In learning an operation, the student learns how to do something that is an instance of a more general case. In learning a concept, the student learns to respond to stimulus events as members of a common class. When a student learns to add, he is learning an operation. However, when the student observes examples of adding and not-adding presented by the teacher, he or she is observing instances and not-instances of the *concept* of addition. What is an example of an operation for the *doer* is an example of a concept for the *observer*. Any verb that applies to human action, while referring to behavior, necessarily implies a concept of that behavior.

Teaching Requirements

The response requirements of a *given* task are taught by using prompts, reinforcing appropriate responses, and not reinforcing inappropriate responses. Physical prompting and modeling are the most commonly used prompts. However, to teach an operation requires a sequence of tasks involving the operation and those not-operations that might be confused with it. For example, to teach a young child to throw on cue, the first step is to specify other hand-movements that might be confused with throwing, such as placing, pushing, holding, and lifting. Then, a general task format is devised to encompass the possible different tasks. A series of tasks can then be generated.

Starting with two operations, a new one is added to the set as the first two are mastered, and so on to build the set. The tasks might be of the following form, in which the teacher makes the statement and the student is to complete the action:

"*Throw* the ball *to* me."
"*Put* the ball *on* the table."
"*Throw* the ball *at* the wall."
"*Throw* the balloon *to* me."
"*Put* the spoon *on* the table."
"*Lift* the spoon *up to* your mouth."

Correct responses are reinforced and errors are corrected. If a number of tasks involving the operation are taught while the irrelevant response requirements are varied, a point will be reached where new tasks involving that operation are performed correctly on the first presentation. This means that a discriminated operant or an operation has been taught. Recent research on generalized imitation (Baer et al., 1967) and generative language (Garcia et al., 1973; Guess, Sailor, Rutherford, & Baer, 1968; Sailor, 1971; Twardosz & Baer, 1973) support the effectiveness of these procedures.

To teach chains of operations, component operations are taught first and then sequenced in complex tasks. When the chain is to be learned as a habit, the same ordering is used each time. When flexible sequencing of components is required in the future (as in reading words by sounds or saying sentences), irrelevant properties are systematically varied to prevent teaching misrules.

BASIC STEPS IN BUILDING A PROGRAM

Given the requirements for teaching concepts and operations, and procedures for linking these together into problem-solving sequences, we are ready to outline eight steps to take in building a program.

1. *Specify the program objectives as sets of related tasks, any one of which the student can perform.* In reading, for example, an objective might be saying aloud (decoding) any of the 10,000 most frequent English words in print.
2. *Analyze each of the terminal objectives into component skills that involve related sets of concepts and operations.* In the case of both concepts and operations, the goal is to minimize the number of different teaching strategies (formats) used in the program. When many things can be taught with a common set of directions, the learning of later members of the set is faster than earlier ones (Harlow, 1959). Thus, larger sets promise a more rapid learning rate per member.

   The analysis of concepts looks for higher-order structurings of related sets of concepts. The following example illustrates the placing of a series of tasks into a common format (rule chain) to teach concepts needed in the analysis of fractions. In the traditional teaching of fractions, the first examples presented usually have 1 as the numerator (½, ¼, etc.). Problems arise later, however, when the children encounter examples of fractions that do not have 1 as the numerator. Some of the children will have learned a misrule, which is that the top number of the fraction is irrelevant.

   A more efficient approach is to examine the full range of fraction operations and devise a method of analysis (a rule chain) that will allow the students to analyze and represent any fraction, less than one or greater than one.

   One method of analysis is to train the children to (a) start with the bottom number of the fraction, (b) make a statement about how many parts are in each group (each whole) based on the bottom number, and (c) refer to the top number as indicating "how many parts we have" (Engelmann & Carnine, 1971).

   For example, the fraction ¾ would be taught as follows: "There are four parts in each group." (We do not know how many groups there are, but we know that each group we make must have four parts.)

"And we *have* three parts" (which we can show by coloring three parts). Through this analysis we can now deal with the question of whether fractions are more than one whole or less than one whole. "If there are four parts in each group, how many parts would you need to *have* to end up with one group?" ("Four.") "And if you *have* less than four parts, you have less than a group; if you have more than four parts, you have more than a group." Not only is the general case taught; it is taught in such·a way that the initial exercises lead directly to the more advanced exercises (those that involve reducing fractions, algebraic formats, etc.).

The analysis of operations seeks the minimum number of component operations that can be used for the largest number of complex response sequences. The analysis process is repeated until component tasks are identified that involve a single teaching strategy. An example of the component analysis focusing on operations can be taken from decoding in reading First, decoding of *regular* and *irregular words* require different teaching procedures. Regular word reading can be analyzed into the components of *reading sounds* and *blending sounds* into words. Blending sounds requires different procedures for *stop sounds* ("t," "b") and *continuous sounds* ("aaa," "mmm"). Irregular words form two classes, those falling into *sight words* and *irregular-word families* (e.g., tame, fine, tone contrasted with tam, fin, and ton).

3. *Specify the general-case task formats for each of the groups identified in step 2.* A task format is a general framework that can be filled in to provide examples of many related concepts and operations. For example, in decoding sounds this format might be followed: Teacher: (Point to the word.) "Read this word by sounds." Student: "mmmaaannn." Teacher: "Say it fast." Student: "man."

Here is a format for the family of irregular words (vowel conversions): Present a short-vowel stem word (e.g., *tap, tin, ton, pet*) and have the students read the word. Then say, "Here's a rule." (Point to the vowel.) "If I put an *e* on the end of a word, you say the name of this letter when you say the word. What's the name of this letter?" Go back and forth between long-vowel and short-vowel form. *(Note:* the prompts in a format, such as the rule about *e,* are faded over time.) Figure 10-11 illustrates some language formats from DISTAR Language I (Engelmann, Osborn, & Engelmann, 1969).

4. *Analyze the task formats for prerequisite skills.* Prerequisite skills are determined by a component analysis of the formats specified in step 3. This analysis is used to specify program entry skills or to develop programs to teach preskills that are absent. For example, reading individual sounds has as prerequisite skills discriminating letters, imitating sounds, and following the directions *look* and *say* when the teacher says "Read this sound." The "Say it fast" task in sounding out

CATEGORIES

47

Praise the children for correct responses. Correct mistakes immediately.

Task 1   Vehicles
Group Activity

a. **Point to the motorboat.** This is a vehicle.
Is this vehicle a car? *No.*
Is this vehicle a bus? *No.*
Is this vehicle a boat? *Yes.*
This vehicle is a boat. Say the whole thing.
This vehicle is a boat.

This vehicle is a boat. This boat is a motorboat.
b. **Point to the rowboat.** Is this vehicle a boat? *Yes.*
Is this vehicle a bus? *No.*
Is this vehicle a train? *No.*
This vehicle is a boat. What kind of vehicle is this?
Say the whole thing. *This vehicle is a boat.*
This vehicle is a boat. This boat is a rowboat.

Individual Activity

c. Point to a picture and ask: Is this vehicle a car?
What kind of vehicle is this? **Require full responses.**

Task 2   Vehicles
Fooler Game

a. I'm going to name some vehicles and see if I can trick you.
What am I going to talk about? *Vehicles.*
When I name something that's not a vehicle, you say "stop."
Listen now. What am I going to name? *Vehicles.*
Here we go: airplane, truck, boat, **apple,** bicycle.
Stop. You said "apple."
What's wrong with apple? Can an apple take you places? *No.*
Is an apple a vehicle? *No.* Say the whole thing.
An apple is not a vehicle.
That's right. An apple is not a vehicle. I couldn't fool you.
● **To correct: If the children don't catch the mistake, act amused.**
I said "apple." I fooled you. Is an apple a vehicle?
Can an apple take you places? *No,* that's silly.
An apple can't take you places, so it's not a vehicle.
You should have stopped me when I said "apple."

b. **Repeat the game. Use only a few examples if the children have trouble.**
Let's see if I can fool you this time: truck, boat, **snake,** bicycle.
Stop. You said "snake."
What's wrong with snake? Can a snake take you places? *No.*
Is a snake a vehicle? *No.* Say the whole thing.
A snake is not a vehicle.
That's right. A snake is not a vehicle.

Fig. 10-11.   Examples of formats from the DISTAR Language I program.

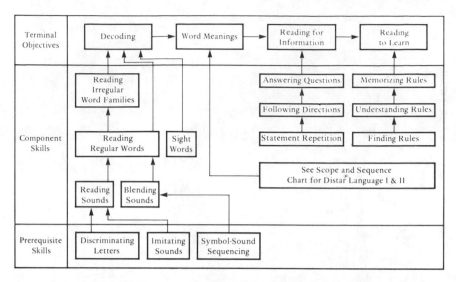

Fig. 10-12. Program sequence chart for reading comprehension. Arrows show dependent relations among terminal objectives, component skills, and prerequisite skills.

and reading words has as prerequisites saying the sounds for each written symbol (without pausing between sounds), and then speeding this up when given the signal "Say it fast." "mmmmaaaannnn" becomes "mmaann" or, better, "man."

5. *Use the information derived so far to construct a program-sequence chart for the terminal objectives, component skills, and prerequisite skills.* The chart should show the dependencies and independencies among the objectives, components, and prerequisites. Component tasks are always taught before more complex chains involving those components. The goal in good programming is to try to teach just one new thing at a time. Figure 10-12 shows a partial analysis of the major objectives of reading with comprehension (Becker, W. C., et al., 1975b, p. 167).

6. *Within sets of terminal, component, and prerequisite tasks sharing a common task format, determine by analysis which pairs of concepts and/or operations lead to tasks that are more alike or are more difficult because of their length.* In reading individual sounds "m" and "n" have more visually in common than "m" and "a." Auditorily, "p" and "b" have more in common than "p" and "a." The responses in making an "e" (as in *egg)* and an "i" (as in *is)* have more in common than do "e" and "k" (as in *kit).* The analysis has to go far enough to identify those pairs most likely to be confused with each other. In reading words, *not* and *note, his* and *this, rober* and *robber* have more in common than *not* and *his, note* and *this,* or *not* and *robber.*

7. *Modify initial teaching concepts (operations, rules) as needed to re-*

duce shared characteristics or to simplify them. In DISTAR Reading I, for example, the letters are made as in Figure 10-13. The letters *a* and *d* are not confused with each other because they are not drawn as sticks and circles as in some beginning reading programs. The long vowels are identified by bars over them. When two letters make one sound, they are connected.

8. *Sequence the order of introduction of concepts or operations within a common format, and select and sequence tasks in ways that meet the*

Fig. 10-13. Sounds from revised DISTAR Reading I.

requirements for teaching concepts and operations. In sequencing *concepts* within related sets, the programmer needs to keep these principles in mind:

    a. Begin with one pair of concepts and add new members to the set one at a time, always bringing the set to criterion before going on.

    b. Where concepts have many shared characteristics and few or small differences, more teaching is required or the initial teaching concepts must be modified.

    c. Concepts easier to discriminate from each other should be taught before those more difficult to discriminate. Pairs of concepts likely to be confused with each other should be separated from each other in the program.

In selecting examples to teach specific concepts, the programmer should keep these principles in mind:

    a. A set of instances and not-instances is required.

    b. The set should be designed so that all instances possess all relevant properties, and all not-instances possess only some or none of them.

    c. Irrelevant properties within instances and not-instances must be varied to avoid teaching misrules.

Additional programming principles for selecting and sequencing tasks consider the values a concept property can take on. When a concept property can take on more than one value, it is said to have *range.* When a concept property has only one value, it is said to be *fixed.* The values of $S+$ and $S-$ together form a set of values that are the instances of a higher-order concept. For example, if instances of red are $S+$, and instances of blue, green, and so forth are $S-$, together the $S+$ and $S-$ instances are $S+$ for the higher-order concept "color." If the higher-order concept is all numbers under 100 and $S+$ is 4, $S-$ is all other numbers 0 to 99. If $S+$ is "larger than," $S-$ must be "same as" and "smaller than." Together $S+$ and $S-$ define the set *relative size* (of two things). The values of S_i properties are one whole set by themselves. Irrelevant properties (S_i) are instances of concepts that are independent of the concept being taught. If $S+$ and $S-$ involve all numbers under 100, color is an S_i. The numbers should be presented in any color.

    d. The principle of *focus* is to focus attention on critical discriminations by changing one thing at a time. Four subrules operationalize the focus principle: (i) If there is more than one essential property, focus programming first on the property that will lead to the greatest reduction in alternative possibilities. (ii) To teach a fixed property, switch from an instance to a not-instance, changing only the fixed property. (iii) To teach the range of $S+$ or $S-$, present a series of instances (or not-instances) in which nothing changes but the value of $S+$ or $S-$. (iv) To teach the range of an irrelevant property, present a series of instances or not-instances in which only the values of the irrelevant property change.

e. The principle of *interpolation* applies when teaching a property that has a range of values. Sample the range with at least three instances, but do not be exhaustive. The student is taught the logical rule: "The range shown is a sample. Interpolate."

f. The principle of *extrapolation* also applies when teaching a property that has a range of values. Sample the range of instances and show the boundary starting the range of not-instances. The student is taught the logical rule: "Any not-instance more different than those demonstrated must also be a not-instance."

g. The principle of *comparison* facilitates the ready comparison of instances and not-instances (Clark, D.C., 1971). This can be accomplished by (i) changing one thing at a time, as in the focus procedures; (ii) using simultaneous rather than successive presentation; and/or (iii) presenting carefully chosen pairs of instances and not-instances.

When the target of the programming is teaching operations rather than concepts, the key teaching procedures involve prompting, differential reinforcement, and fading of prompts. It is important to build sets of tasks involving related operations to be differentiated from each other and to vary irrelevant response properties by the way in which examples are chosen.

The choice of prompts and how they are faded starts with "good guesses" that must then be empirically tested. If, when a prompt is faded, errors occur that are not easily eliminated, then smaller steps in removing the prompt should be considered.

Another major consideration in sequencing tasks to teach operations is the difficulty of specific tasks. Tasks may be more difficult because the response is longer or because shared properties lead to confusions with other tasks. For example, consider this task: $2 + 9 =$ ▯ . The student says "two" and then counts the lines under 9 until "eleven" is reached. With this procedure, $2 + 9 =$ ▯ is a harder problem than $9 + 2 =$ ▯ . Thus, $9 + 2$ should come first because there is a greater response requirement for $2 + 9$. In solving $2 + 5 =$ ▯ the student encounters "five" on the way to "seven." Since the student is also learning to make the response "five" (and stop) when he sees the numeral 5, this task could be more confusing than $5 + 2 = \square$ //

9. *The final step is to evaluate the program.* There are five considerations in evaluating a program.

    a. Are the teaching demonstrations of new concepts consistent with only one interpretation?

    b. Are the skills sequenced so that all component skills are taught before a complex skill is introduced? A simple test is to see if any error students make can be corrected by using a variation of what has already been taught.

    c. Are error rates consistent with efficient prompting and fading?

    d. Does the program teach what it sets out to teach? Is student behavior consistent with stated objectives? Is it successful compared with other programs?

    e. Are the teaching skills required by the program readily trained? This can be tested by trying to train teachers to use the program. If there is consistent difficulty in learning to present some tasks, the tasks need to be either specified more clearly or changed to make them easier to present.

SUMMARY OF PART 1

Programming is a problem in creative design. There are some logical and empirical principles to be followed, but the pieces can be put together in many ways. Programs are not right or wrong, but good or poor. In this chapter we have looked at some components of a theory of programming for basic instruction of naive learners. Many of the analyses would also be appropriate in programming for the experienced learner, but the method used would be less inductive and the number of discriminations needed to be taught for a given concept would likely be fewer. In fact comparisons of programming methods as a function of the experience of the learner are needed.

An examination of the requirements for teaching concepts to naive learners indicated that concept learning is a multiple discrimination problem. Within instances or not-instances of concepts, it is necessary to discriminate relevant stimulus properties from irrelevant properties ($S+$ from S_i, and $S-$ from S_i). Between instances and not-instances, it is necessary to discriminate between relevant properties of the instances and relevant properties of the not-instances ($S+$ from $S-$).

Four procedures for establishing stimulus control over operant behavior were examined for their implications for teaching a general case. This examination indicated that a concept cannot be taught with a single instance and not-instance. A set of instances is required to isolate essential concept properties. In this set, all instances should possess all relevant concept properties and not-instances only some or none of them. Within instances and not-instances, irrelevant properties must be varied to avoid teaching misrules and to isolate essential properties. When concepts fall into sets of related concepts that can easily be confused with each other, it is important to teach the set through a cumulative addition of new members to the set. Each time a new member is added, the set is brought to criterion. This procedure will ensure that all essential discriminations will be learned and the members of the concept set will not be confused with (mistaken for) each other.

Decisions on which of the thousands of possible discriminations to teach in building a program involve knowledge of where errors are likely to occur. In proposing one answer to this question, we introduced the idea of common properties (S_c). These are stimulus properties common to a set of concepts under analysis. Errors are likely to occur when stimulus generalization occurs. Stimulus generalization will occur more often when the number of identical stimulus properties (S_c) shared by instances of two or more concepts is high, when the number and magnitude of the differences between concepts $(S+ - S-)$ is low, and when prior discrimination training with respect to the differences is low. With knowledge of these factors, the programmer can reduce shared properties in the early stages of instruction, magnify small differences, or explicitly teach a critical discrimination.

Two types of concept analysis are important in programming. In the analysis of concept structure, the programmer looks for interrelated groups of concepts and independent groupings. Interrelated groupings have common characteristics and are analyzed for hierarchical structuring, with the higher-order structures given priority in designing teaching formats. Once related groups of concepts have been identified, one focuses on analyzing pairs of concepts within a related set to be taught with a common format. In analyzing pairs of concepts, one looks for the concepts most likely to be confused with each other, i.e., concepts most likely to show stimulus generalization from one to the other.

An operation is defined by the common effect produced by a class of responses under stimulus control. Behavior always has a temporal dimension. It is therefore usually possible to break behavior down into smaller units. From the point of view of the teacher and programmer, the critical question is "What units?" The answer is, "No smaller than the smallest functional unit required to build behavior sequences." In naming things, the functional unit is the name word. In reading by sounds, the functional unit is the sound. Operations are functional units of behavior. The analysis of responses in programming seeks the minimum number of functional units of behavior that can be used as building blocks in the maximum number of response sequences when appropriately cued.

Component operations can be built into habits and rule chains. They can also be used in the most creative human activities. In a habit the stimuli

produced in making one response are the cues for the next response. In a
rule chain each step in the chain provides the stimuli needed to carry out the
next steps, but these stimuli will differ from problem to problem.

Prompting and differential reinforcement are the basic procedures for
teaching the response requirements of a task. Beyond that, a sequence of
tasks (a program) is required that will isolate the essential properties of the
operations from nonessential properties and will differentiate a given operation from related operations. Cumulative programming is used to teach a set
of related operations. To teach response sequences, component operations
are taught first and then put together. If behavior sequences are to be used
in a variety of orders (as in language), then it is important to vary the order
when teaching sequences. Otherwise, habits will be learned.

Part 1 concluded by describing the major steps in building a program.

PART 2. APPLICATIONS TO A SYSTEM OF INSTRUCTION

The function of an instructional system is to maximize the probability that desired learning will occur for all persons going through the system.
Instructional systems may be designed in an infinite variety of ways. However, restraints are placed on design by behavior change procedures known
to be effective, by the structure of what is to be taught, and by the prior
learning of the student. These restraints lead to certain common features in
Bushell's Behavior Analysis Model, or the Engelmann-Becker Direct-
Instruction Model. The common features are

1. Devices for assessment of entry skills.
2. A medium (media) for presentation of stimulus events.
3. A program that controls the sequences of presentation of stimulus
   events (including branching).
4. Procedures for installing the system.
5. Procedures for maintaining quality control over both student and
   teacher performance.

We will attempt to piece together some of the more important features
of instructional systems that efficiently teach concepts and operations. We
will draw on seven years of field work in teaching disadvantaged students
in Project Follow Through. Our initial goal was to design a system that would
teach economically-deprived students the basic skills needed to function in
most schools (reading, language, and arithmetic skills). Our outcome evaluations indicate that we are achieving this objective. We are now beginning
experimentally to factor out some components of the system that may be
crucial to this outcome.

Our premise has been that the first objective of research in an applied study should be to demonstrate the effectiveness of the program. Once effectiveness is demonstrated, the next objective should be to analyze the role of the program components. Because we are only now moving into this second stage of field research, the main goals of this report are to describe the program design and its rationale and to present current outcome evaluations.

PROJECT FOLLOW THROUGH

Project Follow Through was initiated when it appeared that gains made in some effective Head Start programs were being washed out in the early school grades. Originally planned as an operational program, it was converted to a planned variation experiment when the initial funding level was cut from $120 million to $15 million. While authorized under the Economic Opportunity Act, the program was administered by the Office of Education from the start. A pilot program was started in 1967-1968 in 40 school districts. During this year, the decision to find out what worked was made, and program sponsors were sought. Each Follow Through community was asked to select from a set of predeveloped approaches the one with which it would like to work.

Consideration was given to the possibility of combining some sponsors into consortia. For example, the University of Oregon Direct-Instruction Model, the University of Pittsburgh Individualized Early-Learning Model, and the University of Kansas Behavior Analysis Model relied on modern behaviorism for basic principles. But the differences between approaches were considerable. Pittsburgh and Oregon were developing their own materials. One used individualized instruction and the other small-group instruction as the main vehicle. Kansas relied almost entirely on published materials. Thus, the idea of consortia was abandoned.

After preliminary discussions, 18 sponsoring groups were invited to present proposals to Follow-Through communities for consideration. Formally sponsored programs were begun in the summer of 1969. Eventually, 165 school districts and 22 sponsors were involved (Egbert, 1973).

By 1970, we at Oregon were working with 20 school districts, starting at the beginning level and adding a grade a year until the students were in third grade. A new group of beginning level students has been added to the study each year since 1968. In a given year, more than 9000 students are in the Oregon-sponsored program.

The Follow-Through guidelines call for a program of comprehensive services including health care, social and psychological services, community involvement, and an educational program. Sponsors could be responsible for any or all of these services. In most cases, however, the communities assumed responsibility for health and nutrition programs. The focus in what follows is on the system built to install and operate the educational program.

THE OREGON DIRECT-INSTRUCTION MODEL

The direct-instruction model built by Engelmann and Becker was based on the initial assumption that disadvantaged students learn more only if they are taught more. The task, therefore, was viewed as one of devising a *system* that would get more teaching into the classroom.

Basic Components

Our Follow-Through instructional system was developed with these components:

1. *Increased Manpower in the Classroom.* Two aides (usually parents of the students) were added in grades K, 1, and 2. One aide was added in grade 3.
2. *Structured Daily Programs.* Manpower by itself does not ensure that more teaching goes on in the classroom. Organization of the school day, a good program, and training are needed to use the added manpower effectively. The classrooms were set up so that the teachers and aides worked in booths (for sound control) with groups of 4 to 7 students. The teachers and aides became specialists in one of the three basic programs (Reading, Language, and Arithmetic) and a schedule was devised, fitting each school's timetable, that rotated the students through teaching groups and through activities where the students worked on their own. Small-group instruction lasted approximately 30 min in each subject area at Level I and II. At Level III, 15 min of instruction was followed by 30 min of self-directed practice in workbooks. The planning also included the structuring of large-group instructional activities.
3. *Programmed Lessons.* The programs in Reading, Arithmetic, and Language, now published as DISTAR, were built to meet the requirements of effective small-group instruction.
4. *An Efficient Teaching Method.* A variety of procedures (discussed below) were devised to allow the teacher in small-group instruction to function as effectively as a teacher in a one-on-one situation.
5. *Training and Supervision.* A new system requires new skills, and new skills call for training. Complex systems also require supervision to ensure that the parts keep working together.
6. *Monitoring.* Feedback is required in any system to show whether it is working or not. Feedback was built into our model to continually assess teacher performance and student mastery of program skills.

Points 3 through 6 are discussed in more detail later.

Teaching Procedures

In our program we emphasize the use of small-group instruction. Both advantages and disadvantages are associated with this form of instruction. One advantage is the potential for providing good models. Most students learn readily from models. Students can be taught a great deal about instruction when shown correct examples of what to do. A second advantage is the potential for providing numerous needed repetitions in a positive way. The teacher can transform drill into a sing-along that is actually fun. It is harder to build some types of enthusiasm while working with an individual student. For example, it may require a Spanish-speaking student 500 corrected repetitions to produce some of the more basic English statements, such as "The ball is under the box." To provide these repetitions in a one-on-one situation can be indeed painful, both to teacher and student. In the group the students can be challenged and the presentation paced so that drill becomes a game. A third advantage is the potential for getting the timid student to respond more easily in a group than in an individual situation. Suppose the group is saying in cadence: "Four plus one equals five . . . Four plus two equals six . . . ." Seeing the models and the fun that others are having can prompt the timid student to join in. In a one-on-one situation, the teacher often resorts to coaxing the student and thereby reinforcing not responding.

Some of the disadvantages or dangers in small-group instruction are that (1) the teacher wastes a lot of time individually correcting different errors by different students; (2) the teacher fails to hold attention of the group and to use procedures that can teach every student; and (3) the teacher tends to reinforce some students' inadequate performances.

These disadvantages can be overcome by carefully designing instructional procedures and by providing training in their use. In the Engelmann-Becker small-group instructional model, these problems were met in three ways:

1. *Corrections.* When traditional instructional programs are used in the group situation, the teacher is frequently confronted with the awkward choice of spending much of the period working with different individual students on problems that often do not affect the other members of the group, ignoring many mistakes and "pretending" that they did not happen, and/or keying on several students in the group (usually the highest performers) and responding only to their responses.

   These problems can be solved by carefully preparing the program ahead of time to buttress against mistakes made by any student capable of entering the program. For example, we know empirically that a percentage of beginning readers will leave off the beginning sound of many words. They might call *mat* "at," *fan* 'an," or *run* "un." Knowing this, we preteach skills that buttress against the mistake and allow for a simple correction. After teaching a few sounds, we teach the students a particular type of rhyming format before they begin decoding simple words. In that format we present different beginning sounds and different endings. For example, the teacher writes *m* on the board. The teacher says, "We're going to rhyme with 'at.' What are we rhyming with? . . . Rhymes with 'at.' " The teacher touches the *m* and the student produces the sound "mmm." As the teacher signals, the student completes the word *mat*. After working on hundreds of similar tasks, with different endings and different beginnings, the student has mastered rhyming, a skill that can help in beginning reading. We have buttressed against the mistake and have made the correction simple. If the student now makes the mistake of saying "at" when decoding the word *mat* (a possibility, even after the preteaching), the correction is simple. The teacher touches the *m* in *mat* and says, "Rhymes with 'at,' " then signals by moving her hand under the word. "Mat," the student says. The correction requires only a few seconds. Similarly careful programming will buttress against possible mistakes by appropriate preteaching.

One might argue that such programming would be a waste of time for more skillful students. In our experience this has not usually been the case when teaching beginning skills. With more capable students, some parts of the program simply test for the presence of skills. If they are present, the teacher goes on. In our testing program, however, we have found that most students need some instruction on most tasks. What varies is the number of repetitions or corrections required for mastery.

2. *Maintaining Attention and Teaching Every Student.* When working in a one-on-one situation, attention can be maintained more easily because attending is socially reinforced more consistently. To achieve the same attention in the group situation, the teacher should seat the students so that he or she can reach out and touch every student. Our experience shows that (within limits) the closer the teacher sits to the students, the more uniformly they attend. The teacher also needs to learn to attend to and respond to the responses of each student in the group. This skill must be practiced under supervision to be learned. A number of procedures are involved: (a) seating the students so that the lowest performers are directly in front of the teacher, (b) testing these students individually more frequently than others in the group, and (c) teaching to the lowest performer in the group with the understanding that if the lowest performer has mastered a task, the other students in the group will also have mastered it.

Another technique that can be introduced to maintain attention and ensure that every student is taught is responding to *signals*. In a one-on-one situation, the teacher does not have to control the timing of the student's responses. The teacher asks a question and the student answers it. In the small-group instructional setting, however, a serious problem may result if the teacher merely asks the group questions and allows the students to respond more or less when they feel like it. The problem is that some students will initiate the response and others will merely copy the responses of the initiators. When the teacher asks, "What kind of animal is this?," two students immediately respond, "Fish." The rest respond a moment later. The teacher praises the students, but some were not responding to the stimulus, "What kind of animal is this?" They were responding to the other students' answer, "Fish." The teacher therefore may be teaching these students a serious misrule about instruction. The teacher taught them that copying answers is reinforced, not listening to questions or attending to the stimuli presented in the task.

This problem can be solved by requiring students to respond on signal. If all of the students are required to respond in this way, the teacher can quickly identify those students who copy responses. They answer late. Also, the teacher can use quick individual turns to check out any questionable responses (those that may be late). The individual turns provide students with a demonstration that they are accountable for the skills presented to the group.

3. *Effective Reinforcement Skills.* The way in which the teacher uses praise is an important variable in the student's achievement. Let us say that there are eight students in a group. On a series of tasks six students perform adequately, initiating correct responses, while the other two students respond erratically. At the end of the series the teacher tells the students, "You did a good job." The teacher may even give the students some tangible reinforcer, such as a piece of candy or points. In tasks that have right and wrong answers this kind of praise is dangerous. The teacher may justify the procedure by arguing that this is "shaping" the responses of the two students who did not respond correctly. But this is not shaping; this is telling them that they did it the right way. In later tasks, these students will understandably do what they have done in the past. It may be some time before they discover that the responses that they have learned to produce are wrong. The teacher must guard against this situation by (a) making the task objectives attainable, and (b) *carefully* reinforcing only correct responses when dealing with tasks that have right and wrong answers (e.g., discrimination tasks).

Summary of Teaching Procedures. Small-group instruction was selected in our model because it can be designed to be as effective as that in the one-on-one format. For small-group instruction to realize its potential, however, instructional programs must be modified. The program must provide for preteaching of all necessary skills. Furthermore, the program must allow students to master each of the skills presented. A number of other techniques must be introduced to the small-group format to ensure that the *function* of the instruction is retained. These include sitting close to the group, teaching to the lowest performer, using signals to coordinate respond-ing, and being careful to reinforce right responses. As a result, small-group instruction will look quite different from one-on-one instruction. Function-ally, however, it can achieve effects at least as strong as those obtained one-on-one, and do so more economically.

A final reason for selecting small-group direct instruction has to do with a broader policy related to instruction. About 80% of the cost of instruction is represented by teachers. They are an important investment made by school systems. To protect this investment, training should be geared to making teachers more effective in producing the desired results with students. In the teacher-directed small group, there is a great potential for effective instruction. It becomes possible to teach teachers the precise skills required for effective instruction, skills that will generalize across content areas. This model gives the teacher a significant and central role within a workable setting.

Instructional Programs[3]

The core of the instructional program consists of programmed teacher presentation materials in reading, arithmetic, and language at three levels, published by Science Research Associates under the trade name DISTAR (*D*irect *I*nstructional *S*ystems for *T*eaching *A*nd *R*emediation). The programs provide the teacher with examples of concepts that are clearly presented. They indicate in detail how to present tasks, questions, and directions so that they are clear. They sequence the skills to be taught, so the students proceed a step at a time. They teach the "general case" so that students master generalized concepts and operations than can be applied to many situations; they use cumulative programming, and in many other ways exemplify the procedures described in Part 1.

DISTAR Reading I and II. The Reading I and II programs teach decoding and comprehension skills. After sounds and prereading skills such as rhyming and blending are presented, the students are taught to read words. First they are taught regular words, such as *sam*, where each symbol is named by a single sound and each sound is continuous. The next set of words has a stop sound first (a sound that cannot be held), which makes blending more difficult: *hat, can, tan*. All words up to this point can be sounded out, blended, and said. Irregular words cannot be approached in this way. If the word *was* were spelled by sounds, it would be *wuz*. The

[3]The DISTAR Level I and II programs are now available in revised editions. The programs described are from the first edition.

students are taught that there are many exceptions in reading. These words are taught as special cases and the students are taught to recognize them by sight. The final decoding skill taught is the special sound that letter combinations make. These are also irregular, because they cannot be decoded by sounding out each letter. The sounds of *ou* are very different when they appear in the word *cloud* than when *o* and *u* do not appear together. Sentence Reading comes next. First the students read the sentence with a signal for each word; then they read the entire sentence from one signal. The teacher asks comprehension questions about several of the sentences and about the story. The story's content is usually novel: animal characters, exaggerations, and surprises. More advanced comprehension skills are taught in Read the Items. For example, the students read item 4. "When the teacher says, 'stand up,' read item 6." Item 6 says, "Hold up three yellow cards." The students must read each word carefully, or they will not be able to follow the instruction (Engelmann & Bruner, 1968, 1969, 1974).

DISTAR Reading III. In Reading III students are taught to read to learn new information. The program is intended to teach students to read textbooks on their own and answer concept questions. Some of the stories are historical. In some cases the event is retold; in other cases two characters travel through time and experience life as it was lived in earlier times. Most of the stories are science related. The students read about scientific laws and then apply what they have read to exercises that follow the story. They use what they have just read to figure out problems. Topics such as astronomy, muscles, measurement, speed, and the atom are presented (Engelmann & Stearns, 1972).

DISTAR Arithmetic I. The DISTAR Arithmetic programs are designed to teach the usual problem-solving operations. The students are taught arithmetic facts after they can perform the operations. Finally, they learn the several fundamental laws or rules of mathematics. *Arithmetic I* teaches problem-solving operations based on counting by one. In addition they count forward to the number they start with and count forward by one for each number that is added. In 7 + 3 the student counts 7 and then counts three more times for the plus three: 8, 9, 10. In subtraction they count forward to the number they start with and count backward by one for each number that is subtracted. In 7 − 3 the student counts 7 and then counts backward three times for minus three: 6, 5, 4. Algebraic variations of addition are also taught. The students work problems by making lines and using a fact-deviation strategy. They use both methods to solve story problems. The equality rule gives the students a problem-solving strategy that they use with both addition and subtraction. The rule is: "You must end up with the same number on this side and on the other side." It is a general operation for testing equality in an equation. After figuring out which side they count on first in a problem and whether they add or subtract, the students are ready to solve the problem. The students are expected to memorize 30 facts during Arithmetic I (Engelmann & Carnine, 1970).

DISTAR Arithmetic II. In Arithmetic II the students are taught new counting operations; in multiplication they count by numbers other than one and in fractions they count parts, numbers less than one. They work regular multiplication problems (2 x 4, which is originally read as "count by 2, four times") and algebra problems (2 x ? = 8). In fractions they learn to decode the fraction (in the fraction 2/3 the bottom number tells us that there are three parts in each group and the top number tells us that we have two parts); to tell whether a fraction is less than one, equal to one, or more than one; and to multiply fractions, reducing their answer if it reduces to a whole number. The main rule taught in Level II is an extension of the equality rule. The *revaluing rule* provides a general operation for changing the form of equations. The rule states: "Whatever you do to revalue one side of an equation you must do to revalue the other side of the equation." If you have 4 = 4 and you change one side (e.g., 4 = 4 + 2), the equation is no longer true. You must also revalue the other side to 4 + 2 = 4 + 2, or 4 + 1 + 1 = 4 + 2. Now the sides are equal again. Using this rule, the teacher can show why the associative, commutative, and distributive laws hold. Before presenting the remaining addition facts, the teacher shows how the facts fit together, i.e., how they are a related set of statements. Analogies teach that sets of numbers follow rules. Fact derivation is a method for figuring out an unknown fact working from a known fact. if the students do not know what 2 + 5 equals, but they know that 2 + 2 equals 4, they count

$$2 + 2 = 4$$
$$2 + 3 = 5$$
$$2 + 4 = 6$$
$$2 + 5 = 7$$

Then the students are taught to memorize a few facts each day (Engelmann & Carnine, 1971).

DISTAR Arithmetic III. In Arithmetic III the students are taught three new operations: algebra, factoring, and division, and the traditional arithmetic operations are extended. *Algebra* uses the revaluing rule: for example, $a + 7 = 9$. To solve for a, you must change + 7 into zero; you must minus seven on the right: $a = 9 - 7$. *Factoring* is the beginning of division. The students count by different numbers in order to find pairs of factors for a number. They use the same algebra multiplication counting operation they were taught in Level II. The number is 12. When you count by 3 you hit 12, so 3 is a factor of 12. When you count by 3 to 12, you count 4 times, so 4 is the other factor. The children are taught to work problems such as

$$\begin{array}{r} 329 \\ 1412 \\ +706 \\ \hline \end{array} \qquad \begin{array}{r} 473 \\ -129 \\ \hline \end{array} \qquad \begin{array}{r} 623 \\ \times\ 4 \\ \hline \end{array} \qquad 4\overline{)137} \qquad 6 - 3\ \text{x}\ 2 + 1 =$$

$$\frac{6}{3} - \frac{1}{3} = \qquad\qquad \frac{4}{3} + \frac{2}{3} = \qquad\qquad \frac{3}{2} \text{ x } \frac{1}{4} =$$

The students also use these operations in solving story problems.

The students are taught to use a rule or equation to relate a set of instances to a set of answers. In *substitution* the students are given the rule and a set of instances. They derive the set of answers. If the rule were $a + 6 = ?$ and $a = 2$, then $a + 6 = 8$; if $a = 3$, then $a + 6 = 9$. In *analogies* the students are given a set of instances (n) and the set of answers. They derive the rule

Instances (n)	Answers
3	4
7	8
4	5

"What is the rule?" $(n + 1 = ?)$. Before subtraction facts are taught, the relation between addition and subtraction facts is taught. If $9 + 3 = 12$, then $9 = 12 - 3$ and $3 = 12 - 9$. Then the subtraction and multiplication facts are taught (Engelmann & Carnine, 1972).

DISTAR Language I. In Language I the students are taught object names, object properties, and relations among objects. They are also given practice in making a wide variety of statements. Some of the object properties taught are color, shape, pattern, parts, use, and location. The relations include quality—comparisons such as bigger; quantity—only, all, some, and none; space—prepositions; time—before-after and first-then; conditionality—if-then and and-or; causality—why; and multiple attributes—talking about two properties or relations at once. A picture shows three balls, one small and yellow, one large and blue, and one small and blue. When the teacher says, "Show me a small blue ball," the student must listen to both the comparison small and the color blue. If the student just attends to small, he may pick the small *yellow* ball. The student who just attends to blue may pick the *large* blue ball (Engelmann et al., 1969).

DISTAR Language II. (The Language II program teaches new object properties, object relations, new information (e.g., measurement and the calendar), and the creative use of prior information (e.g., thinking up new functions for objects based on the student's knowledge of the properties of the object). The emphasis in Level II is on new ways of talking about objects and of using words to talk about other words. The first new way of talking about objects is an extension of multiple attributes. Description tasks teach the students to identify many properties or relations that they see in certain objects or events. In some tasks the object described is referred to by a nonsense name. The students must attend to the properties of an object so that they can figure out the object's name. In classification the students group different objects or events according to common shared characteristics. Things that we can eat are food. Man-made things that take us places are vehicles. Definition tasks set one object off from all the other objects considered. The object is placed in the smallest possible class, and then characteristics are identified that set the object off from other members of the class. A car is a vehicle (the smallest class) that drives down the road (sets car off from other vehicles such as ship or airplane) and has a trunk (sets car off from other vehicles that drive down the road such as a truck or bus). To teach questioning skills, the teacher thinks of an object. The students ask questions such as: "What class is it in? Where do you find it? What parts does it have? How do you use it? What is it made of?" By asking these questions the students can identify the object. More difficult tasks use words to talk about other words. Synonyms and opposites are rules for relating one word to another word. The synonym for "hard" is "difficult." Some of the analogy rules that relate words to each other are: "A word is to its synonym"; "An object is to a part of that object"; "An object is to how that object is used"; "An object is to what that object is made of"; "An object is to where you find that object [Engelmann & Osborn, 1971]."

   DISTAR *Language III*. In Language III the students work from statements in a problem-solving situation. In the statement, "The boy is smiling," you know what the boy is doing, but you do not know why he is smiling or what he is wearing. After the students can state what information is given, they determine whether the information is redundant, whether the information is relevant, and whether deductions based on the information are true, false, or doubtful. For example,

Goal: A boy wants to eat cereal and milk.
Statements: The boy had cereal but he could not find any milk. (relevant)
He wore a red shirt.   (irrelevant)
He could not find any milk.   (redundant)
Deductions: He can have milk and cereal now.   (false)
He will never eat milk and cereal.   (doubtful)
He must obtain some milk if he wants to eat milk and cereal now.   (true)

   A second goal of Language III is to teach grammar: e.g., to discriminate between sentences and fragments; to identify subjects, verbs, and predicates; to make subjects and verbs agree; to discriminate among and punctuate statements, questions, and commands; to identify adjectives and adverbs; to use proper verb tenses; and to use punctuation, capitals, commas, quotation marks, contractions, and abbreviations. Throughout Language III the students' writing skills are developed. The students use written statements to answer questions, make up stories, and describe events or objects (Engelmann & Osborn, 1973).

   These programs are supplemented by programs in writing, spelling, music, art, etc. Provisions are also made for preparing the students to graduate into a more typical fourth grade.

Procedures for Installing the Program

Contracting. In Follow Through a sponsor is required to sit down with representatives of a school district and a project officer from the Office of Education and negotiate an agreement specifying mutual responsibilities. The basis for an agreement is essentially this: "We have a program that can successfully teach academic skills. These are the minimal conditions required if the program is to succeed." The conditions include specification of budgetary requirements for staff, materials, and facilities; specification of job functions for aides, teachers, principals, supervisors, and others; specification of preservice and in-service training requirements; specification of evaluation procedures; specification of monitoring procedures; and specification of a method for dealing with contract violations.

We were initially naive and trusting, and sometimes failed to get the right conditions into an agreement. The forces operating to resist change in educational practices are very strong, and can only be countered by strong and explicit sanctions when an agreement is not kept. The strongest sanction we had for some time was threatening to withdraw as sponsor if changes were not implemented to keep the agreements made initially. Because parents were actively involved in the program from the start, the sponsor could also take grievances to the parent group. Often this led to political action by parents that produced the changes needed from the school administration.

If we were to write new contracts today, we would insist that no changes be made in key personnel, such as program directors and principals, without their prior understanding and acceptance of the initial agreement. Some of our major problems in maintaining effective programs occurred when such changes led to conflicts in "philosophy" of instruction.

Training and Supervision. The goal of training is to provide the teacher with the skills required to teach within a small-group direct-instruction model. This training has generally been accomplished in a one- or two-week preservice workshop, through continuing in-service sessions of about 2 hr a week, and through classroom supervision. Detailed procedural manuals have been prepared for trainers and participants in training. The key is to know what the teachers should be able to do and to devise procedures to teach the required skills. Precision in specifying and training essential teaching skills is only possible within a structured teaching system.

Our preservice workshops focus on teaching the general requirements for teaching any task. This is accomplished through exercises that analyze a task into its components and through demonstration and practice with a variety of key tasks from each program. The use of signals, precise presentation of tasks, reinforcement, and corrections are emphasized. The procedure is not unlike that used by an actor learning a new role in a play. The participants work mostly in small groups with a supervisor serving as a coach. Checkouts for proficiency are required periodically throughout the workshop. Time is also devoted to planning classroom schedules and to continuous testing for monitoring of progress and regrouping of students.

A video-tape library, illustrating how to teach key tasks, is provided for in-service training. While preservice training focuses on general requirements for teaching and the key formats for the first 30 to 60 days of the program, in-service training focuses mainly on preparing teachers for new formats coming up in their programs. The procedure is still basically the same: practice, critique, practice, checkout. The video-tape library allows teachers to practice new formats on their own. Video tapes of classroom teaching are also used in training. Some of these tapes are sent to the model sponsor at the University of Oregon for review and critique.

Another phase of in-service training involves a programmed course in behavior modification and the teaching principles underlying the model (Becker, W. C., Engelmann, & Thomas, 1975a). This is conducted on site and course credit is provided through the University of Oregon.

Classroom supervision is provided by consultants trained by the sponsor. Many of these are former teachers from the local site. There is approximately one local supervisor for every 200 students in the program. In working with teachers and aides, the supervisor observes performance and provides a critique. The supervisor may actually stop a teacher presentation and give a demonstration to the teacher using his or her group. Assignments may be given on a specific skill to be checked on the supervisor's next visit. Teacher supervisors are also required to make periodic video tapes of their supervision procedures that are reviewed by the project managers.

Our project managers are experienced in teaching as well as in supervision. They know the classroom operation of the program thoroughly and assume responsibility for all phases of it. It is the manager's job to adapt instructional and training schedules to local needs, to stay abreast of site problems based on first-hand observation, reports from the site, and progress reports on the students, and to work out solutions to local problems. Unlike most professionals in educational management, our managers are able to go into the classroom and teach students to demonstrate correct procedures. Also, they spend most of their time in the classroom, in viewing tapes of teaching, or in training sessions with teachers and aides, rather than behind a desk.

Monitoring of Student Progress

The managers and supervisors provide the first line of quality control on teacher performance. The information obtained permits guidance of continuing in-service training. The next line of quality control comes through biweekly reports of teaching activities and continuous-progress testing. Built into the programs are teacher-given tests to check each new skill as it is taught. To monitor student progress independently of the teacher, paraprofessionals give continuous-progress tests in each area each six weeks. Every two weeks test results in one area are summarized by students on four-copy IBM forms (with names and numbers preprinted by group). These biweekly reports also show absences for the two-week period and show where each group is in each program. Copies of the report go to the teacher, the supervisor, the Follow Through Director, and our data analysis center. The reports can be used locally to regroup the students or to provide special remediation or acceleration. They also provide a basis for summary analyses of progress for management by the sponsor. Trouble spots can be determined and worked on.

The Arithmetic I Continuous Progress Test will be used as an example for all of the tests. The test consists of several tracks that cover the major skills in the program. The student record form is illustrated in Figure 10-14. The abbreviations across the top stand for the track names, such as Object Counting (OC) or Algebra Addition (AA). The testing begins according to the student's current lesson placement in the program. For example, if a student were on Lesson 100, testing would begin with those items in the row identifying the 94-103 lesson range (items 7, 15, etc.). The tester goes ahead to the next item in a track if the first is passed, and moves back if it is failed. Since each item (which is actually a set of tasks) is selected to reflect 10 days of progress in the track, the scores can be directly interpreted in relation to lesson placement in the program. If a student is two items ahead of where the teacher has him, he is 20 lessons ahead. If a student is two items behind, he is 20 lessons behind. To make the tests useful diagnostically, a key is provided, so that for any item missed the teacher has a direct reference to the tasks that must be taught.

Management reports are produced by computer from the bi-weekly reports. These reports keep track of group gains in lesson days and on the Continuous Progress Tests. Projections are made and compared with target goals for each group for the year. When projections fall behind goals, adjustments in the program can be made at the site to attempt to reach the goals before it is too late to do anything about it. Management reports also keep track of school calendars and absences, so that it is possible to base projections for each site on local conditions that affect teaching days available.

SOME ILLUSTRATIVE RESULTS

Since the fall of 1968, six entering-level groups of students (called cohorts) have completed at least two years of the program. Except for the first year, we attempted to test every child at entry on the Wide Range Achievement Test (WRAT). This can be given orally to young children and is

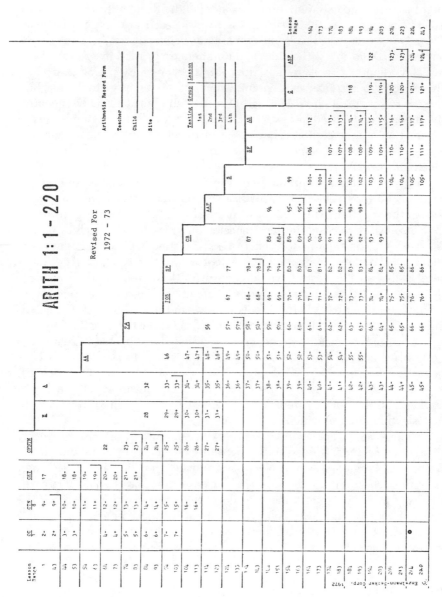

Fig. 10-4. Continuous-Test Record Form for Arithmetic I.

useful in long-term follow up. Starting in the spring of 1972, the Metropolitan Achievement Test (MAT) was added to the test schedule at the ends of grades 1, 2, and 3. The MAT provides measures of reading comprehension, more extensive testing of spelling and arithmetic skills, and a test of language usage. In the fifth and sixth grade follow-up studies, the MAT also provides a test on science. The Primary I (Form F) was used at the end of the first grade, Primary II (Form F) at the end of the second, the Elementary Level (Form F) at the end of the third, and the Intermediate Level in the fifth and sixth grades. Testing was carried out under the supervision of the Oregon field staff by local teachers and aides. Careful training for and monitoring of testing followed.

The data discussed are based on the 11,487 low-income (poor) students who started at the beginning level and had more than one test record in our files. They entered the program between September 1968 and September 1973. Of these 11,487 students, a little more than half are from K-starting sites and the rest are from first-starting sites. Not all of these students had tests at each test period; this is especially true at the Pre-K or Pre-first levels. For most test scores the actual Ns are approximately as follows, for K-starting and first-starting sites, respectively:

Pre-K	Post-K	Post-1	Post-2	Post-3
2435	5181	4810	3302	1988;

	Pre-1	Post-1	Post-2	Post-3
	2412	5160	4665	3629.

The Ns at the end of the third grade are smaller because two groups (cohorts) that started in K and one group that started in first had not yet finished at the time of testing. The entry level testing is low because the first cohort was not pretested at all, and only about half of the next two cohorts were pretested.

The analysis excludes students entering the program beyond the first level. Students who left the program early are included for the years they were full-time Follow Through students. This approach provides the maximum N for the analysis of program impact. To check for selective biases in the outcomes because of changes in the students, we also analyzed year-to-year gains and full-term pre- to post-gains (K-3 or 1-3) on the same students. These analyses do not materially change any conclusions except to make the actual gains about two-tenths of a grade level higher. When Non-low-income children are added to the analysis (20% of the sample), there is another slight increment in the level of performance. Children who entered the program late perform a year lower on the average. This would be expected if the program were important.

Norm-Referenced Gains

A major goal of the Direct-Instruction Model has been to get low-income Follow Through students on a par with national norms by the end of the third grade. Figure 10-15 shows the degree to which this goal has been

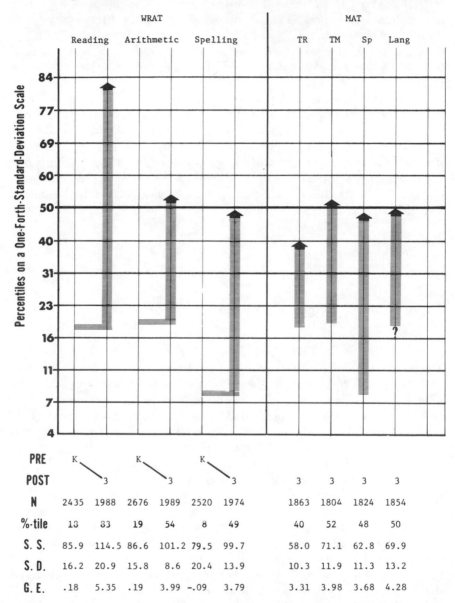

Fig. 10-15. Norm-referenced gains on the WRAT and MAT from kindergarten through third grade for K-starting low-income, Engelmann-Becker Follow Through students.

achieved for students starting the program in kindergarten. With the entry-level performances on the WRAT as baselines for both WRAT and MAT performances, substantial gains against the norms are present for all measures. These gains are displayed in Figure 10-15 as percentiles on a one-fourth standard-deviation scale. This method of plotting permits the easy interpretation provided by percentiles as well as showing the magnitude of effects in standard score units. Figure 10-15 also provides Ns, percentiles (%-tile), standard scores (S.S.), standard deviations of the standard scores (S.D.), and mean grade equivalent scores (G.E.). Standard scores for the WRAT have a mean of 100 and a standard deviation of 15. Standard scores for the MAT increase about 10 points with each grade level but keep a standard deviation of about 10.

Figure 10-15 shows that the gain against the norm group on WRAT Reading (decoding) is about 1¾ standard deviation units. These low-income students are close to *a standard deviation above the norm* in this important reading skill at the end of the third grade. On MAT Total Reading (TR), which measures reading comprehension, the students fall slightly below the national norm. On both WRAT Arithmetic and MAT Total Math (TM), our low-income Follow Through students are at the national norm. On both spelling tests (Sp), they gained but still fall a little short of the norm group median. On the MAT Language test (Lang), they are once again above the norm group median. An analysis of the effects by year of entry groups (cohorts) shows progressive improvements for later K-starting cohorts (Becker, W.C., & Engelmann, 1976).

How do these results compare to the national Follow-Through results for other approaches? Abt Associates, who are in charge of the data analysis for the national evaluation, provided the average scores for low-income students working with 13 Follow Through (FT) sponsors (Abt Associates, 1977). They also provided the means for the Non-Follow Through (NFT) control groups. The NFT groups are more advantaged than the FT groups on most socioeconomic measures, and, as shown in Figure 10-16, do better on MAT measures than FT students. Figure 10-16 shows that Direct-Instruction-Model (E-B) students test one-half standard deviation above the average for 13 Follow Through sponsors on MAT Reading. On MAT Total Math, the Direct-Instruction (E-B) group exceeds the national Follow-Through average by one full standard deviation. The E-B group also exceeds the Non-Follow Through control group by nearly as much. On MAT Spelling, which we did not emphasize early in the program, the Direct-Instruction (E-B) students are one-quarter standard deviation above the national average of Follow Through sponsors, but only equal to the NFT group. On MAT Language, the Direct-Instruction (E-B) group has clearly been taught grammatical usage better than the Follow-Through average. (We do not have the NFT mean for Language.) Figure 10-16 also provides Ns, percentiles (%-tile), standard scores (S.S.) standard deviations of standard scores (S.D.), and mean grade equivalent scores (G.E.).

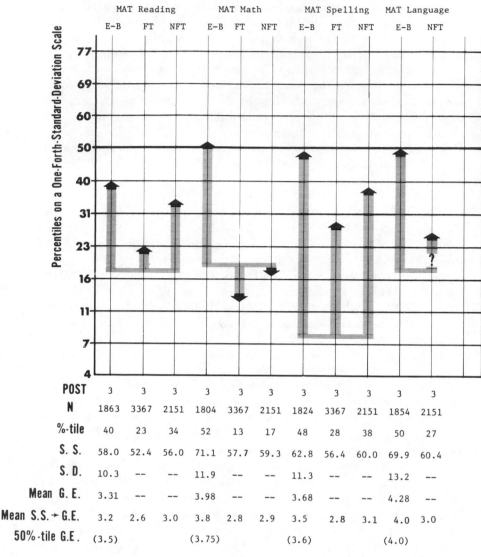

Fig. 10-16. MAT scores at the end of third grade for K-starting low-income students in the E-B program, in programs sponsored by 13 Follow Through Sponsors (FT), and in the control groups for the 13 Follow Through Sponsors (NFT). FT and NFT data are from the national evaluation of students entering kindergarten in 1970. (Abt Associates, 1973.)

The data from first-starting sites show a narrowing of the gap with national norms, but with one less year to teach, the effects across the board are about *one-quarter standard deviation below* those shown for K-sites in Figure 10-15. There is a significant advantage in a compensatory catch-up program of having one year more to teach when that time is used efficiently.

A Controlled Within-Project Comparison

In 1970 we started the program in the BIA school in Cherokee, North Carolina. Because this is the only school on the reservation, the constancy in student population and staffing provides a rather clear-cut indication of program impact. The program was started in kindergarten, first grade, and second grade at the same time—providing a basis for comparing the performance of all the children in these grades as they progressively felt the impact of the model. Since 1970 we also have data on three additional cohorts that permit further assessment of the progressive effects of better implementation (two of these cohorts had not yet finished third grade at the time of testing).

The results from this analysis at the end of the third grade are given in Table 10-1 (a fuller report may be found in Becker, W.C., and Engelmann, 1976).

For each measure, Table 10-1 shows progressive improvement with more years of the program or longer implementation of the program. Not shown in Table 10-1 are the even further improvements shown by the next cohort at the end of kindergarten, first, and second grades. For the WRAT, separate significance tests were computed for the combined four-year groups (E4) against each of the control groups (C2 and C3) using standard scores. Only one comparison is not significant. On the MAT all comparisons of the combined four-year groups are significantly better than the three-year group. An examination of the percentiles for the combined four-year groups shows all but spelling (45th percentile) to be at norm (50th percentile) or above.

Fifth and Sixth Grade Follow Up

Approximately 700 Follow Through fifth and sixth graders and 700 Non-Follow Through comparison students were tested in seven sites at the end of the fifth or sixth grade. The WRAT (Levels 1 and 2) and the MAT (Intermediate level), were given in most cases. The comparison groups were from schools having students with similar backgrounds. With samples of 35 to 100, however, student variations in important background characteristics are to be expected. For this reason, a covariance analysis was used to adjust mean differences on outcome measures for differences in student sex, father's education, mother's education, number of siblings, income status, and white-nonwhite status. Four comparisons were made for most sites on the WRAT (Reading and Arithmetic using both levels of the test) and ten comparisons were made on the MAT (Word Knowledge, Reading, Total Reading, Language, Spelling, Math Computation, Math Concepts, Math Problem Solving, Total Math, and Science). The results showed 53 significant differences out of a possible 149 at the .05 level using a one-tailed test.

Table 10-1
End of Third-Grade Results for Cherokee Groups Having Two (C2), Three (C3), and Four (E4) Years of Program

| | | | WRAT | | | | | | | MAT | | | | | | | | | | | |
| | | | Reading | | | Arithmetic | | | | Total reading | | | Total math | | | Language | | | Spelling | | |
Group	Start of program	N	G.E.	S.S.	S.D.	G.E.	S.S.	S.D.	N	G.E.	S.S.	S.D.	G.E.	S.S.	S.D.	G.E.	S.S.	S.D.	G.E.	S.S.	S.D.
C2	2nd-70	99	3.7	98	15.2	3.2	94	6.8	109	3.2	56.9	10.2	3.8	69.7	9.8	3.7	65.8	10.7	3.3	59.0	11.2
C3	1st-70	114	5.0	112	23.1	3.6	98	9.2	102	3.5	60.3	9.9	4.3	74.3	11.5	5.0	75.7	11.0	3.6	61.4	12.8
E4	K-70	103	5.0	112	21.6	4.0	102	8.6	83	3.7	61.5	11.8	4.5	76.0	13.0	5.0	75.7	13.4	3.7	63.4	11.6
E4	K-71	85	5.3	115	20.5	4.1	103	8.6													
Significance of differences for Standard scores																					
	C2-E4		.001			.001				.01			.001			.001			.5		
	C3-E4		N.S.			.001															
Percentiles for combined E(4) groups			82nd			58th				50th			66th			66th			45th		

C = Control
E = Experimental
N = Number of Cases

G.E. = Grade Equivalent Means
S.S. = Standard Score Means
S.D. = Standard Deviation of Standard Score

Of these, 50 favored Follow Through and 3 favored Non-Follow Through groups. WRAT Reading measures showed highly significant differences in favor of Follow Through in 14 of the 20 comparisons. Two other comparisons reached the .07 level. WRAT Arithmetic showed significant comparisons favoring Follow Through in 4 of the 20 measures. Two more were close (.07). MAT Reading measures showed 11 out of 39 comparisons were significant in favoring Follow Through and 3 more were close ($p < 0.10$). MAT Math favored Follow Through significantly for 12 of 40 comparisons; Science for 3 of 10; Language for 2 of 10; and Spelling 4 of 10. One negative finding was found for WRAT Level 1 Arithmetic. In this case the Level 2 Arithmetic was almost significant in the opposite direction. The other two negative findings were on the MAT Spelling test. Spelling was not a strong point of the program in the early years.

Overall, the results strongly support an effect of the model that is persisting (in the absence of special programs) two and three years later. The results in reading (both MAT and WRAT) are especially encouraging.

In math there is a strong trend for MAT Math Problem Solving to show significant or nearly significant effects even when other measures of math number facts are going against Follow Through. This suggests that the problem-solving approach taught in DISTAR Arithmetic has long-term implications. We would expect even stronger results to show when the students get to algebra, because the DISTAR approach focused on row functions prepares the students well for algebra. The findings in Science can be attributed to the DISTAR Reading III program, which uses a science content base to teach students to learn new rules and apply them in their reading tasks.

The magnitude of student gains in the years after Follow Through were in many cases disappointing. There were considerable losses against national norms from third to fifth or third to sixth grade. Losses were especially great on math measures, and then reading comprehension. Reading decoding skills were maintained, and apparently some schools taught spelling effectively in the intervening years. There is a clear implication that compensatory programs cannot be expected to maintain gains after the programs are stopped unless all schools are prepared to provide effective teaching for every child. This is certainly not the case today.

Achievement of Students with Low IQs

One of our concerns is the development of procedures for teaching the hard-to-teach student. A large group of such children can be defined by their low IQs. We have examined the academic gains for our students with IQs below 80. Figure 10-17 shows comparisons of WRAT Reading gains for low-IQ children and all of our disadvantaged Follow Through children. Our kindergarten sample size is low for the Post-K—Post-3 comparisons ($N = 40$) because two cohorts have not yet finished third grade. The data show that

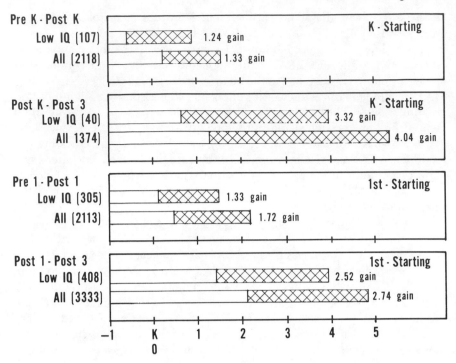

Fig. 10-17. Reading gains of low IQ disadvantaged children. (Shaded area indicates gain for the time period shown to the left of the chart. *N*s in parentheses.) Low IQ = IQ of 80 or less in Engelmann-Becker Follow Through Program. All = All children in Engelmann-Becker Follow Through Program.

low IQ children (mean 73 at pretest and ranging as low as 50) gain more than a year on WRAT Reading for each year of instruction. On the average, they gain approximately 1.2 grade levels each year, while the gain for the total group averages 1.35 grade levels each year.

Gains in WRAT Arithmetic produce very similar results. The low IQ students' average gain over four years (K-starting) is .95 G.E., while the All group averages 1.00. For first-starting children, the average gain for the low IQ group is 1.04 and the All group 1.07.

Examining the number of lessons taught each year to the various groups shows that low IQ children receive about 30 fewer DISTAR lessons in kindergarten and 25 fewer in first grade. After that, the differential drops to less than 15. There is an implication that what a child can learn and how much can be learned is less a function of IQ and more a function of method of instruction.

Table 10-2 shows the IQ gains by groups used in the analysis. Statistical regression effects would make the Pre-K to Post-K and Pre-1 to Post-1 gains for the low IQ groups greater than the true gains. The amount of regression would not likely exceed 1 to 2 times the standard error of measurement, or 4

Table 10-2
Slosson IQ GAINS for Low IQ and All Groups

Pre K-Post K	Pre	Post	Gain	S.D. Gain	N
Low IQ	73.0	93.8	*20.8*	12.1	142
ALL	103.3	112.8	*9.5*	14.2	2270
Post K-Post 3	Pre	Post	Gain	S.D. Gain	N
Low IQ	80.3	87.8	*7.5*	15.0	38
ALL	109.3	107.9	*−1.4*	14.0	1305
Pre 1-Post 1	Pre	Post	Gain	S.D. Gain	N
Low IQ	72.5	85.5	*13.0*	10.8	319
ALL	94.7	100.1	*5.5*	12.0	2113
Post 1-Post 3	Pre	Post	Gain	S.D. Gain	N
Low IQ	78.7	83.4	*4.7*	12.9	387
ALL	99.2	101.6	*2.5*	13.4	3081

to 6 IQ points. The K-starting and first-starting All groups both show net IQ gains Pre-K to Post-3 of about 8 points. No regression effects influence these gains. Thus, we would estimate the true gains for the Low IQ students to be somewhere between 8 and 14 points.

National Evaluation Report

A report of the national evaluation of Follow Through (Abt Associates 1977) covering comparisons for cohort 2 and 3 supports our own conclusions about the effectiveness of the Direct-Instruction Model. They found that the E-B model was specific in stating that children participating in the FT program are expected to, on the average, perform at the same level as their middle-class peers by the end of third grade. Their overall conclusion was that this goal has largely been achieved (Abt Associates, 1977).

PROCESS STUDIES

With the demonstration that a program works comes concern as to why it works. A number of studies have been carried out or are still in process under the direction of Douglas Carnine of the College of Education, University of Oregon, to demonstrate various functional components of the program, including the principles used in programming, specific teaching behaviors, and training procedures for installing the program. Studies of teaching techniques have investigated the effects of pacing, use of corrections, reinforcement, feedback, and signals for group responding. For example, rapid pacing results in more correct responses and fewer off-task responses than slow pacing in DISTAR instruction. When the teacher asked about 12 questions per minute, the children answered correctly about 80% of the time and were off-task only 10% of the time. When the teacher asked four questions per minute, the children answered correctly about 30% of the time and were off-task about 70% of the time.

Initial studies of teacher training focused on whether training makes a difference. It does. Current studies are aimed at using the teaching techniques that have been shown to make a difference in student performance and determining what it takes to train teachers in their use.

The studies of programming principles lead to such procedural statements as these:

1. Students will learn a concept's critical attributes more quickly if the examples and not-examples are presented in *pairs* rather than singly.
2. Students will learn a concept's critical attributes more quickly if the examples differ from the not-examples in terms of a *single* critical attribute.
3. Students will learn to name examples of different concepts more quickly if examples that are either visually or acoustically similar are *separated* from each other in the order of introduction.

SUMMARY OF PART 2

We have described the design, rationale, and some findings for an instructional system to teach basic cognitive skills to students who have a high probability of school failure. The system we built used added manpower, planned use of time, daily programmed lessons, and a face-to-face small-group method of instruction.

Small-group instruction was used in the system because it is more economical than one-on-one instruction, it can provide individual evaluation of oral responding, it can provide individual corrections for the naive learner, and it can be made as effective as one-on-one instruction with the use of effective program materials, signals, choral responding, etc.

The instructional programs provide for three years of instruction in reading, arithmetic, and language. They use the programming principles discussed in Part 1 and aim at effectively teaching the general case.

Our instructional system contains a number of procedures for installing and maintaining these programs. Contracts are required to spell out mutual obligations. Training and supervision programs are designed to ensure that appropriate teaching skills are learned. Student progress is monitored through biweekly reports on the number of lessons taught and the results of continuous progress testing. Management reports by computer from the biweekly reports help to spot problems before it is too late. The analysis of six cohorts of data on Follow Through students show excellent progress of the students. There is clearly an implication that poor students do not have to be school failures if instructional methods are improved. A number of studies of process variables have been completed or are in progress that help to pinpoint critical features of the model.

LAUREN B. RESNICK with WENDY W. FORD[1]

Chapter 11

The Analysis of Tasks for Instruction: An Information-Processing Approach

A psychology of instruction requires strategies for linking scientific knowledge and constructs with practical tasks of education. Among the links required is a means of describing the subject matter, the material to be learned, in psychological terms. Such descriptions are the first step in applying existing psychological knowledge to instructional problems. They also reveal gaps in existing knowledge, suggest new questions for research closely linked to instructional concerns, and thus serve to keep basic and applied psychology in fruitful interaction. This chapter takes as its general theme the actual and potential role of task analysis as a strategy for applying psychological constructs to instruction. We mean by *task analysis* the study of performance on complex tasks, such as those encountered in school, to reveal the psychological processes involved. These analyses translate subject-matter descriptions into psychological descriptions of behavior and suggest underlying organizations of skills and knowledge capable of leading to or producing skilled performance. They are, thus, critical in bringing the constructs of psychology to bear on instructional design.

1. Preparation of this chapter was supported by the Learning Research and Development Center, assisted in part by funds from the National Institute of Education (NIE), U.S. Department of Health, Education, and Welfare. The opinions expressed do not necessarily reflect the position or policy of NIE, and no official endorsement should be inferred. Major sections of this chapter are adapted from L.B. Resnick, "Task Analysis in Instructional Design: Some Cases from Mathematics" which appears in D. Klahr (Ed.), *Cognition and Instruction* (Hillsdale, N.J.: Erlbaum Associates, 1976). The sections on early reading and reading comprehension are adapted from L.B. Resnick and I.L. Beck, "Designing Instruction in Reading: Interaction of Theory and Practice," which appears in J.T. Guthrie (Ed.), *Aspects of Reading Acquisition* (Baltimore, Md.: Johns Hopkins Press, 1976). Permission of the editors and publishers of these volumes is gratefully acknowledged.

Task analyses are performed, although not usually under that name, in virtually all psychological investigations of cognitive activity. Whenever performances are analyzed into components—for experimental, interpretive, or theoretical purposes—task analysis of some kind is involved. Task analyses for instructional purposes, however, have some special characteristics that should be mentioned at the outset. First, they must be analyses of relatively complex tasks, because the tasks we are interested in teaching are usually more complex than the laboratory tasks that traditionally occupy experimental psychologists. Second, instructional task analyses must yield descriptions of tasks in terms of processes or basic units recognized by the psychological research community. Thus, while the starting point for instructional task analyses is prescribed by social decisions about what is important to teach, the outcomes of such analyses, psychological descriptions of complex performances, must be determined by the state of theory and knowledge in psychology. It is not always easy to fulfill both these criteria at once; instructional relevance is often defined in terms different from those that psychologists use in building their theories. Third, instructionally oriented task analyses must reveal elements of the task that lend themselves to teaching. The function of task analysis is to examine complex performances and display in them a substructure teachable either through direct instruction in the components or through practice in tasks that call upon the same or related processes. Finally, instructional task analyses must attempt to account for differences between early and later forms of competence. Analyses for instructional purposes cannot *just* describe the expert's performance (although such description will almost always be a part of such analyses). They must also describe performance characteristics of novices and attempt to discover or point to key differences between novices and experts, thereby suggesting ways of arranging experiences that will help novices become experts. Instructional task analyses, in other words, should elucidate the relation between activity *during* learning and competence *resulting from* learning. It should suggest a way of organizing knowledge to assist in its acquisition, recognizing that this organization may differ from those that are most efficient for expert use of that knowledge.

Although the study of complex cognitive tasks has never dominated empirical psychology, significant occasions exist in which psychologists have turned their attention to such tasks. Not all have been instructional in intent, but several important attempts bear examination because they have substantially influenced instructional theory or practice, or because, considered with instructional questions in mind, they offer insight into the possible nature of a theory of instruction based on cognitive psychology. This chapter will focus largely on information-processing approaches to task analysis. Information processing is the label used by the growing number of psychologists concerned with intellectual behavior or "cognition." As is often the case with an emerging branch of study, it is easier to point to examples of information-processing research than to give a complete or consensual definition of it. Nevertheless, psychologists working in this area tend to share certain assumptions and research strategies.

Information-processing studies attempt to account for performance on cognitive tasks in terms of temporally ordered actions (internal or external). Frequently, but not universally, information-processing models for cognitive tasks are expressed as "programs" for performance of particular tasks. These are often formalized as computer programs, whose theoretical validity is judged by their ability to simulate actual human performance.

Most information-processing theories and models characterize the human mind in terms of memory, i.e., the way information is stored, accessed, and operated upon. Distinctions are made among different kinds or "levels" of memory. While the details and the labels vary, most theories distinguish between a sensory intake register through which information from the environment enters the system, a working memory (sometimes called short-term or intermediate-term memory) in which the actual processing work goes on, and a long-term (semantic) memory in which everything one knows is stored, probably permanently. Research shows that the sensory register has limited capacity, both in the length of time material can be held (perhaps half a second) and in the amount of material that can be registered at one time. At the other extreme, long-term memory is conceived to be virtually unlimited in capacity. Any number of items can enter it; and once entered, an item is not forgotten or lost, although it may become difficult to access if it is not well related to other items in memory or to cues in the external environment.

Within this general structure, working memory is pivotal: Only by being processed in working memory can material from the external environment enter the individual's long-term store of knowledge, and only by entering working memory can information from the long-term store be accessed and used in the course of thinking. Processing in working memory is usually assumed to be serial—one action at a time. Further, working memory is considered to have a limited number of "slots" that can be filled, so that it is only by rehearsing or by "chunking" material into larger units (so that a body of interrelated information takes up a single slot) that loss of information from working memory can be avoided.

In characterizing information-processing analyses of complex tasks, it is useful to distinguish between rational and empirical task analyses. *Rational task analyses* describe "idealized" performances, i.e., those that succeed in responding to task demands, often in highly efficient ways, but not necessarily in ways in which humans actually perform the tasks. Work in artificial or machine intelligence is a form of rational task analysis today being applied to increasingly complex kinds of tasks. So are some much less ambitious analyses of simple tasks, some of which are discussed below. *Empirical task analyses* interpret data from human performances of tasks (errors, latencies, self-reports, eye or hand movements, etc.) and describe (model) the processes that account for such data. In practice rational and empirical analyses are rarely sharply separated. Rational analyses, for example, may provide the starting point for empirical data collection and lead to an iterative process in which successively closer matches to human-performance models are made. Nevertheless, the distinction is a useful one in considering the kind of information-processing analysis that will be most valuable for instruction.

Before proceeding to a full discussion of information-processing analyses and their instructional uses, we will briefly describe some past efforts to analyze intellectual competence in psychological terms. Rather than giving an exhaustive history of task analysis, we highlight certain accounts that have considerably influenced psychology or instruction, or both, and that form landmarks in the history and current status of this branch of instructional psychology.

A SELECTIVE HISTORY OF TASK ANALYSIS

The three major predecessors of modern information-processing task analysis were the associationist/behaviorist tradition (Thorndike, Gagné), the Gestalt school (especially Max Wertheimer), and Piagetian analyses. The approaches of these groups to task analysis reflected both substantive and methodological differences in their theoretical positions, differences that in turn affected the kinds of contributions each made to instruction.

The Associationist-Behaviorist Tradition

Early in this century, when experimental and educational psychology were closely allied, Edward L. Thorndike attempted to translate the associationist "laws of effect," which he himself was active in developing, into a set of prescriptions for teaching arithmetic (Thorndike, 1922). Thorndike analyzed arithmetic tasks in terms of specific connections, or bonds, between sets of stimuli and responses (e.g., the bond between "2 + 2" and "4" in the expression "2 + 2 = 4") are proposed that instruction be organized to maximize learning of both individual bonds and relations among them.

For Thorndike, the laws of learning, and thus of pedagogy, were those dealing with such drill and practice as would strengthen the bonds. Questions about under- and over-learning and about amount and distribution of practice were considered. These topics continue to occupy psychologists— although rarely directly in the context of school instruction—and they heavily, though indirectly, influence instructional practice even now. What is important about Thorndike's work, however, is that he was concerned not only with the laws of learning in general, but also with the laws of learning as applied to a particular discipline, arithmetic. He left the laboratory to engage in applied research, but brought with him the theory and, to a large extent, the methodology of the experimental laboratory. He thus began a tradition of experimental work in instruction by psychologists.

Thorndike recognized the need for careful sequencing in presenting the elements of arithmetic. But he proposed no systematic theory or method of analysis to guide this sequencing. In the decades following Thorndike's work mathematics educators and educational psychologists (e.g., Brownell & Stretch, 1931; Hydle & Clapp, 1927) studied, with varying degrees of care and precision, the relative difficulty of different kinds of mathematical problems. They thus empirically, if not theoretically, extended Thorndike's work in instructional analysis. The implication was that arranging tasks according to their order of difficulty would optimize learning, especially of the more difficult tasks. Skinner's (1953a) prescription for the use of "successive approximations" in instruction represented a refinement of this basic idea. But neither Skinner nor his immediate interpreters proposed a systematic strategy for generating the order of successive approximations, i.e., the sequence of tasks in instruction. Not until the 1960s and Gagné's work on hierarchies of learning (Gagné, 1962, 1968) did any organized theory of sequencing for instructional purposes appear within the behaviorist tradition.

Learning hierarchies are nested sets of tasks in which positive transfer from simpler to more complex tasks is expected. The "simpler" tasks in a hierarchy are not just easier to learn; they are included in or are components of the more complex ones. Acquiring a complex capability, then, is a matter of cumulating capabilities through successive levels of complexity. Transfer occurs because the simpler tasks are included in the more complex. Thus learning hierarchies embody a special version of a "common elements" theory of transfer.

Widespread use of hierarchy analysis has begun among instructional designers, particularly in mathematics and science (see White, 1973). For the most part, the analyses have been of the kind Gagné originally described. Thus, hierarchies for instruction for any task are typically generated by answering the question, "What kind of capability would an individual have to possess to be able to perform this task successfully, were we to give only instructions?" One or more subordinate tasks are specified in response to this question, and the question is then applied to the subordinate tasks. Presumably, to answer the question that generates subordinate tasks, one must have some idea of what kinds of operations—mental or otherwise—an individual engages in when performing the complex task. But this model of performance is left implicit in Gagné's work.

Gestalt Psychology and the Analysis of Mathematical Tasks

Gestalt psychology was an immigrant in America. In its first generation it spoke a language so unlike the rest of American psychology that it was barely listened to. Now, in a period when we speak easily of cognition and mental operations, the gestalt formulations take on more interest. Gestalt theory was fundamentally concerned with perception and, particularly, the apprehension of "structure." With respect to the complex processes of thinking, the concepts of structure led to a concern with "understanding" or "insight," often accompanied by a visual representation of some kind. Several gestalt psychologists, particularly Wertheimer (1959) and his students (Katona, 1940; Luchins & Luchins, 1970), attempted to apply the basic principles of gestalt interpretations to problems of instruction and, in particular, to the teaching of mathematics. Wertheimer's *Productive Thinking* (1959) discussed work on several mathematics problems (e.g., finding the area of a parallelogram, proving the equality of angles, Gauss's formula for the sum of a series, etc.). Wertheimer's analyses of these tasks consisted of displaying the structure on which solutions are based, rather than analyzing actual performance. Thus, for example, the problem of finding the area of a parallelogram was seen as a problem of "gap fitting"—too much on one side, too little on the other. Once the gap was filled and a rectangle formed, a general principle for finding area could be applied. Recognizing the nature of the problem—the possibility of transforming the parallelogram into a rectangle—constituted for Wertheimer "understanding" or "insight."

Though Wertheimer talked little about general schemes for instruction, he implied the necessity of analyzing tasks in perceptual and structural terms. Just how the understanding of these structures and the relation of separate elements to the whole problem were to be taught was not made clear. Wertheimer suggested introducing exercises to focus students' attention on certain aspects of the problem structure, thereby increasing the likelihood of insight. He also spoke of operations involved in thinking—grouping, reorganizing, structuring—for which ways of teaching might be devised.

Piagetian Analyses

A discussion of Piagetian task analysis must consider two quite distinct bodies of literature in succession: (1) Piaget's own work (and that of others in Geneva), and (2) attempts, largely by Americans and British psychologists, to isolate the specific concepts and processes underlying performance on Piagetian tasks.

Piaget's own work seeks to characterize cognitive development as a succession of logical structures commanded by individuals over time (see, e.g., Piaget, 1970a, 1970b). Piaget's "clinical method" of research yields great quantities of raw process data: protocols of children's responses to various tasks and questions. The protocols are interpreted in terms of the child's "having" or "not having" structures of different kinds. Explanation of a task performance for Piaget consists of descriptions of the logical structures that underlie it and of the structures that ontogenetically preceded and therefore "gave birth" to the current ones.

Piaget's tasks are chosen to exemplify logical structures assumed to be universal. Many turn out to involve mathematics, but not, by and large, the mathematics taught in school. One result has been considerable debate over whether the Piagetian tasks should become the basis of the school curriculum, whether they are teachable at all, and whether they set limits on what other mathematical content can be taught. (For differing points of view on this matter, see Furth, 1970; Kamii, 1972; Kohlberg, 1968; Rohwer, 1971b.) Piaget's most important contribution to task analysis for instructional purposes is probably his pointing out in compelling fashion the important differences in the ways children and adults approach certain tasks, the knowledge they bring to them, and the logical structures they have available. But his particular form of logical analysis does not go far enough in elucidating the *psychological* aspects of behavior on these tasks, i.e., what people actually do. Certainly for psychologists accustomed to the explicit detail of information-processing analysis, Piaget's leaps from observations to inferences about logical structure are often difficult to follow.

Much English-language research on Piagetian tasks has focused on locating specific concepts or component processes underlying the ability to perform well on particular tasks. Conservation tasks have been most heavily studied, classification tasks probably next most heavily, with relatively little study of tasks characteristic of the formal rather than concrete stage(s) of operational thinking. Two basic strategies can be distinguished: one is to vary the task in small ways to allow inferences about the kinds of cognitive processes used (Smedslund, 1964, 1967a, 1967b); the second is to instruct children in a concept or process hypothesized to underlie performance on some Piagetian task, and then to see whether they become able to perform the task (e.g., Bearison, 1969; Gelman, 1969). A review of studies involving instruction in Piagetian tasks (Glaser & Resnick, 1972) suggests that Piagetian concepts are indeed instructable or at least lend themselves to analysis into certain prerequisite skills that may be instructable. These studies, however, also suggest how delicate the process of task analysis and instruction is for tasks of any psychological complexity. For the most part, these neo-Piagetian studies investigate single or closely related groups of tasks and look for competence versus incompetence rather than for stages or transformations of competence. There are a few exceptions, largely in recent attempts to interpret changes in performance on Piagetian tasks in terms of information-processing constructs (see Klahr, 1976). These investigations attempt to analyze sequences of Piagetian tasks so that adding one or two simple processes to an individual's repertoire or modifying extant processes can be shown to account for successively more complex performances on the Piagetian tasks. This work, which makes heavy use of computer-simulation strategies, provides a convenient point of return to our presentation of information-processing approaches to task analysis.

The remainder of this chapter considers information-processing analyses of several kinds. We describe first some work in rational analysis explicitly concerned with instructional design requirements in the areas of beginning reading and mathematics. Next we describe some empirical analyses of relatively simple mathematics tasks. We then consider the relation between rational and empirical analysis for instructional purposes. A final section considers the problem of more complex tasks—namely, problem solving and reading comprehension, and what the role of formal simulations and empirically studied information-processing models might be in such domains.

RATIONAL TASK ANALYSIS FOR CURRICULUM DESIGN

Rational task analysis can be defined as an attempt to specify processes or procedures that would be used in highly efficient performance of some task. The result is a detailed description of an "idealized" performance: one that solves the problem in minimal moves, does little backtracking, and makes few or no errors. Typically, a rational task analysis is derived from the structure of the subject matter and makes few explicit assumptions about the limitations of human-memory capacity or perceptual encoding processes. Even without extensive empirical study, informal rational task analysis can serve in many cases as a way of prescribing what to teach (i.e., teach children to perform the processes laid out in the analysis), and the effectiveness of this instruction serves as a partial validation of the analysis. To convey the flavor and intent of rational task analysis as applied to instruction, some studies conducted by Resnick and others on simple arithmetic tasks are presented briefly, followed by a more detailed task analysis for early reading.

Analysis of Arithmetic Tasks

The arithmetic work initially grew out of an attempt to apply learning hierarchy theory to the problem of designing a preschool and kindergarten mathematics curriculum. To secure agreement among the development staff on the probable ordering of tasks, it was necessary to introduce a method in which the processes hypothesized to be involved in performing a particular task were explicitly laid out (Resnick, Wang, & Kaplan, 1973). Figure 11-1 is an example of the analyses that resulted. The topmost box shows the task being analyzed, the entry above the line describing the presented stimulus and the entry below the line the expected response. Thus, Box Ia is read "Given a fixed ordered set of objects, the child can count the objects." The second row of boxes in the figure shows a hypothesized sequence of behavior engaged in as the presented task is performed. Arrows indicate a temporally organized procedure or routine. The lower portions of the chart identify capabilities thought to be either necessary to performance of (prerequisite to) or helpful in learning (propaedeutic to) the main task. The identified prerequisite and propaedeutic tasks were used to build hierarchies of objectives that formed the basis of a curriculum.

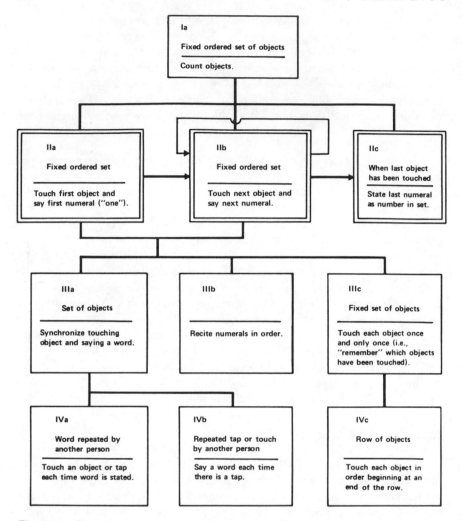

Fig. 11-1. Analysis of an early mathematics task. (From Resnick et al., 1973, p. 688.)

At the outset, the process analyses functioned as aids in developing prescriptions for instruction. The kind of research that seemed most directly relevant to that prescriptive function was carried out, i.e., research that examined the extent to which the analyses generated valid task sequences that aided learning of the most complex tasks in the set. Two research strategies were involved. The first was to conduct scaling studies. In these studies, tests on several tasks were given to a sample of children prior to instruction, and the results were evaluated for the extent to which the tests formed a Guttman scale in accord with the predicted prerequisite relations (e.g., Wang, M.C., 1973; Wang, M.C., Resnick, & Boozer, 1971). A good approximation to a Guttman scale implied strong prerequisite relations among the tasks, relations that specified optimal teaching orders. A second set of studies (Caruso & Resnick, 1971; Resnick, Siegel, & Kresh, 1971) more directly assessed transfer relations among small sets of tasks. Tasks in a small hierarchy were taught in simple-to-complex and complex-to-simple orders, and transfer effects were examined on trials to criterion and related measures. These studies showed that teaching in hierarchical sequence was the best way of assuring that all or most of the children in a group learned all the objectives. For the minority who were capable of learning the more complex objectives without intervening instruction, however, skipping prerequisites was a faster way to learn. What these children apparently did was to acquire prerequisite behavior in the course of learning the most complex tasks.

An important instructional question raised by these results is whether we can match instructional strategies to individuals' relative ability to learn on their own, i.e., without going through direct instruction in all the steps of a hierarchy. Before we can answer that question, however, we will probably need more systematic theories than are now available of how learning occurs with minimal instruction (Resnick & Glaser, 1976).

The kind of task analysis used in these studies described performance in temporally organized sequences and identified general information-processing abilities, such as perceptual ordering [Figure 11-1 (IV c)], memory (III c), and temporal synchrony (III a), that are called on in performing a specific complex task. As formal information-processing models, however, these analyses were incomplete, because they did not specify every step (e.g., stop rules were not typically specified where recursive loops occurred) nor did they explicitly deal with overall control mechanisms or total memory load. In addition, they were not empirically verified as process analyses. Although many observations of performance were made, there was no attempt to match predicted or "ideal" performance with actual performances. The hierarchy tests confirmed the validity of the instructional sequencing decisions made on the basis of the analyses, but did not necessarily confirm the details of the analyses. Performance strategies different from those in these analyses might have produced similar sequences of acquisition or transfer effects. Thus, while the scaling and transfer studies met instructional needs quite well, they did not constitute validations of the models' details. The strategies of empirical task analysis, described later, are more useful for that purpose.

Analyses of Beginning Reading Skills

As part of the development of a reading program for the primary grades, Resnick and Beck (1976) engaged in some rather extensive rational analysis of the process of decoding. They adopted an approach to decoding that requires the child to sound out separate phonemes and then assemble them into words through "blending." This approach seemed sensible because it directs the child's attention to the letters as they are sounded, and thus directly helps children to learn the print-to-sound relations of the language. Furthermore, a natural feedback system is inherent in the process: As they blend the sounds together, children can test what they said against what "sounds right." An often cited objection to this approach to decoding is the difficulty many children have in learning to blend sounds together into a word. It was therefore desirable to find a way of simplifying and making more explicit the process of putting sounds together. For this purpose, Resnick and Beck began with an analysis of two possible strategies of blending, one commonly used in initial reading and one developed while working with children who were having difficulty in learning to read.

Figure 11-2 shows the general structure of the two blending routines. In each case, the routine is capable of decoding single-syllable, regularly spelled words, the typical vocabulary of a beginning phonics program. Part *a* depicts a procedure in which the sound of each grapheme is given and stored, the synthesis occurring only after the final phoneme has been pronounced. This is called final blending, because blending is postponed until the very last step; Part *b* shows a procedure for successive blending. As soon as two sounds are produced, they are blended, and successive phonemes are incorporated in the blend as they are pronounced.

The final and successive blending routines can be thought of as different "executive programs" calling upon the same set of decisions and actions: finding graphemes in sequence (component A), pronouncing identified graphemes (component B), storing (remembering) pronounced sounds (component C), deciding whether more graphemes remain to be sounded (components D and E), blending (component F); and, finally, in each case testing the produced word against one's linguistic knowledge to determine whether it is an acceptable decoding. The two routines differ only in the organization of these components, a difference that appears to have important consequences for the ease of learning and performing the decoding act.

To illustrate the differences between the two blending routines, consider the word *cats* as an example. The child who uses the final blending routine would proceed as follows: "/k/ /a/ /t/ /s/ *cats*." The child who uses successive blending routine would proceed thus: "/k/ /a/ /ka/ /t/ /kat/ /s/ /kats/ *cats*." As this example shows, the routines differ in two respects: (1) the maximum number of sound units to be held in memory during the course of decoding, and (2) the maximum number of units to be blended during a given attempt. The final blending routine requires remembering all of the separate units that the reader identifies as graphemes and blending them in a single operation. The successive blending routine never requires remembering or blending more than two units.

It would seem at first glance that while the two routines might produce very different levels of difficulty for pronouncing long or complex words, they would be of approximately equal difficulty for pronouncing the shorter words (no more than three or four graphemes) that compose the beginning

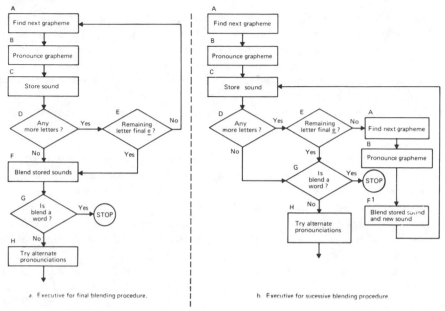

Fig. 11-2. Executive routines for synthetic decoding. (From Resnick & Beck, 1976.)

reading vocabulary of any phonically oriented instruction. After all, first-grade children normally have a memory span that can easily encompass three elements. The digit-span test of the Stanford-Binet, for example, expects memory of three digits at age three and five digits at age seven.

Tests such as the digit span, however, require only that items be held in memory. Items need not be generated, and no competing processing interferes with retention. This, however, is not the case during decoding. A substantial amount of other processing must occur simultaneously with the retention of the phoneme elements. Assuming a limited working memory, as is common in virtually all current information-processing theories, this additional processing is likely to interfere with remembering the sounds; or, rehearsal of the sounds may interfere with other processing (Baddeley & Hitch, 1974; Posner & Rossman, 1965). In either case, decoding may not succeed.

The complexity of the competing processing tasks can best be appreciated by considering one of the subroutines involved in the two blending procedures. The subroutine for Find Next Grapheme (A in Figure 11-2) is required because of a small but significant number of cases in which graphemes consist of pairs of letters that carry one single sound. Such graphemes are digraphs (e.g., <ch>, <ea>) or diphthongs (e.g., <oy>). If the reader neglects to "look ahead" to detect the presence of a digraph or a diphthong, then the word cannot be correctly decoded. The first step is to find the leftmost letter not yet sounded and then, if more letters remain, to find the next letter after that. Having focused upon two successive letters, the reader must decide whether they form a single digraph or diphthong. This decision assumes that the individual has in long-term memory a list of digraphs and diphthongs with which the current letter sequence is matched. Presumably, this list is gradually compiled during the course of learning to read and becomes longer and longer as reading ability increases. If two letters form a digraph or diphthong, they are classified jointly as a grapheme; if the two letters do not form a single grapheme, attention is returned to the first letter identified in the subroutine, and that letter is classified as a grapheme.

Embedded in these simple acts is a complex set of requirements for maintaining left-to-right encoding and keeping track spatially of one's position within a word and within a line of text. This spatial information must be retained despite the interruptions of sounding. Thus simply identifying a grapheme may place considerable demands upon a beginning reader, demands that compete for processing space with retention of the sounded-out phonemes.

The foregoing example shows how task analysis may be used in designing instruction. In deciding between two possible methods of teaching blending, detailed rational task analyses were used to pinpoint the differences, similarities, and relative advantages of the two options. This comparison of the final and successive blending procedures strongly suggests the advantages of the successive procedure. The advantage lies essentially in the reduction of memory load, which for many children may make the difference between a learnable and an unlearnable word attack routine. For this reason, the successive blending routine is systematically taught in the reading program developed on the basis of those analyses.[2]

EMPIRICAL ANALYSES OF SPECIFIC TASKS

Rational analyses of mathematics and reading skills have been useful in clarifying the subject-matter structures of the skills to be taught, and have suggested that certain sequences and procedures might be preferred over others in designing instruction. What can empirical task analyses suggest about teaching specific skills? An obvious possibility is to use process models of proficient performance as direct specifications of what to teach. Models of skilled performance are often powerful as descriptions of an ultimate goal of instruction. They do not take into account, however, the capabilities of the learners as they enter the instructional situation. We describe here some experiments on simple mathematics and classification

---

2. The program is designed to teach primary grades reading in a school environment committed to adapting to individual differences. The program is being used in trial versions with several hundred kindergarten and primary grade children. The program is complex and uses multiple resources such as teacher- and cassette-led instruction, self-instructional materials, games, and free reading activities (Beck, I.L., 1977; Beck, I.L., & Mitroff, 1972; and Resnick & Beck, 1976).

tasks that suggest a special kind of link between what is taught and how skilled performance proceeds. The experiments suggest that what we teach children to do and how they perform a relatively short time after instruction are not identical, but neither are they unrelated. They suggest that children seek simplifying procedures that lead them to construct, or "invent," efficient routines that might be very difficult to teach directly. Two of the studies were conducted by Resnick and Groen and their students; the third was conducted by J.G. Wallace at Warwick University in England.

Subtraction

One study (Woods, Resnick, & Groen, 1975) examined simple subtraction processes (e.g., $5 - 4 = ?$) in second and fourth graders. The method was borrowed from Groen and others' work on simple addition processes (Groen & Parkman, 1972) and open-sentence equations (Groen & Poll, 1973). The experimenters gave children a set of subtraction problems and collected response latencies. Five possible models for performing subtraction problems (of the form $m - n = ?$; with $0 < m \leqslant 9$, $0 < n \leqslant 9$) were hypothesized, and predicted response latencies for each problem for each performance model were worked out based on the number of steps required according to the model. Regression analysis was then used to fit observed to predicted latency functions and thus select the model an individual child was using.

Of the five models tested, two accounted for the performance of all but a few subjects:

Decrementing Model: Set a counter to m, decrease it n times, then "read" the counter. For this model, latencies should rise as a function of the value of n, and the slope of the regression line should reflect the speed of each decrementing operation. This function is shown in Figure 11-3.

Choice Model: Depending on which has fewer steps, perform either the decrementing routine (previously described) or another in which a counter is set to n and is then *incremented* until the counter reading matches m. The number of increments is then read as the answer. For this model, it is necessary to assume a process of choosing whether to "increment up" or "decrement down." Assuming that this choice process takes the same amount of time regardless of the values of m and n, latencies should rise as a function of whichever is smaller, n or $(m - n)$. This function is shown in Figure 11-4.

Individual data were analyzed first and a best-fit model selected for each child. Then children were grouped according to the model they fit, and the pooled data were analyzed. All fourth graders and most second graders were best fit by the choice model. It seems unlikely that the children had been directly taught the choice model for solving subtraction problems during

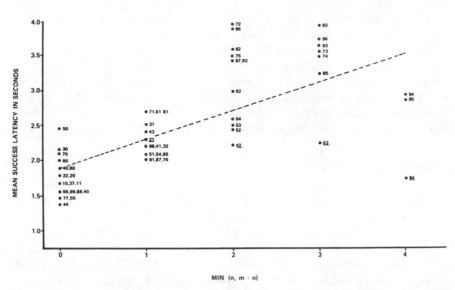

Fig. 11-3. Plot of reaction times for second graders solving subtraction problems of the form $m - n = ?$: Decrementing Model. Numbers beside solid dots denote actual problems (e.g., ● 54, 65 signifies that problems 5 − 4 and 6 − 5 both had a mean success latency specified by the ●). Underlined problems were omitted in the regression analysis. (From Woods et al., 1975, p. 19.)

their arithmetic training. The procedure would be difficult to communicate to 6- and 7-yr-olds and might confuse rather than enlighten children at their first exposure to subtraction. Most probably, the children had been taught initially to construct the m set (increment the counter m times), count out the n set (decrement n times), and then count ("read out") the remainder. This algorithm is close to the one described as the decrementing model. The decrementing model is, in fact, derivable from the algorithm we assume is typically taught by simply dropping the steps of constructing the m set and counting the remainder. Thus, it seems reasonable that a child would develop the decrementing model quite quickly. The choice model, however, cannot be derived from the teaching algorithm in so direct a way. Instead, an invention (the possibility of counting up from n) must be made. This invention is probably based on observation of the relations between numbers in addition and subtraction over a large number of instances. Yet the invention appears to have been made as early as the end of second grade by most of the children.

Addition

In another study, Groen and Resnick (1977) looked more directly at the relation between the algorithm taught and later performance. In the subtraction study one could only guess at what children had been taught,

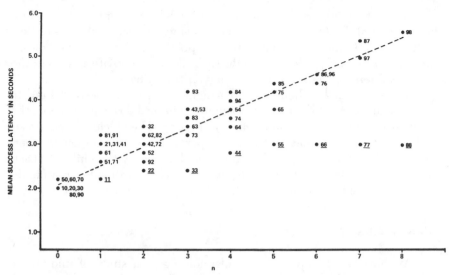

Fig. 11-4. Plot of reaction times for second graders solving subtraction problems: Choice Model. Min (n, m − n) reads "the smaller of n and m − n)." (From Woods et al., 1975, p. 20.)

based on a general knowledge of elementary school practice. In this addition study, the experimenters controlled the teaching by doing it themselves. They taught 4-yr-olds to solve single-digit addition problems of the form $m + n = ?$ (where m and n ranged from 0 to 5 by using the following algorithm: (1) count out m blocks, (2) count out n blocks; (3) combine the subsets, and (4) count the combined set. The children were then given about two practice sessions a week for many weeks. As soon as each child was performing the addition algorithm smoothly using blocks, the blocks were taken away and the children were asked to give their answers on a device that allowed latency data to be collected. The children's typical response when blocks were removed was to begin counting out sets on their fingers. Eventually, however, most shifted to internal processing.

Suppes and Groen (1967) had earlier shown that by the end of the first grade, most children added using a choice-type model in which they set a counter to m or n, whichever was larger, and then incremented by the smaller of the two numbers. This is known as the *min* (minimum) model because the latencies fit min (m, n). A few children used the procedure of incrementing m times, then incrementing n more times, and then reading the counter. This can be termed the *sum* model (latencies fit $[m + n]$). The sum model is derivable from the procedure taught in the previously de-scribed addition study by simply dropping steps (3) and (4) of that algorithm, and it requires no choice. The *min* model, however, requires an invention based on recognizing that sums are the same regardless of the order in which numbers are added and that it is faster to increment by the smaller quantity. For five of the six children whose data have been analyzed thus far, it is clear that by the final two test sessions the *min* model gave significant and "best" fit. In general the trend over blocks of trials was for subjects' data to be fit well by the *min* model as soon as they stopped counting overtly on most of the trials. It is as if these children discovered commutativity as soon as they were confident enough to stop counting on their fingers.

In these studies children were taught one routine derived from the subject matter. After some practice but no additional direct instruction, they performed a different and more efficient routine. The efficiency was a result of fewer steps (not, apparently, faster performance of component operations), which in turn required a choice or decision by the child. A strictly algorithmic routine, in other words, was converted into another routine that solved the problem more efficiently.

Class Inclusion

Wallace (1972) reported a similar finding in a study of information-processing models of class inclusion. After training in the prerequisite skills as hypothesized on the basis of an information-processing analysis, subjects were presented a typical class inclusion task in which they were asked to tell, for example, "Which is more, the red ones or the triangles?" They had been taught to pass through the object array twice, each time quantifying the objects on one of the value dimensions (color, shape) and then comparing them to determine which was more. At the posttest administered immediately after training, some of the children were able to perform more efficiently by quantifying on the first pass objects having only one of the dimensions named by the experimenter. For example, Wallace presented a subject with eight triangles, seven of which were red and one green. Asked, "Which is more, the red ones or the triangles?," one subject answered, "There's one green triangle and that makes it more triangles." Because the set having only one of the named dimensions in the class inclusion task is usually the minor subset, this procedure quickly yields the answer. It seems likely that a phenomenon of this kind (the transformation of algorithms by the learner) is more general than we have thought up to now. At least some process data that appear difficult to interpret when averaged over time may show interpretable regularity when earlier and later phases of performance are examined separately.

Implications for Instruction

What do these findings imply for instruction? On the face of it, it would seem we ought to abandon the algorithmic routines suggested by rational task analysis in favor of directly teaching the more environmentally responsive processes that appear to characterize even semi-skilled performance. In other words we ought to conclude that the initial rational analyses are wrong because they do not match skilled performance, and, therefore, they should not be used in instruction. Rather, we should perform detailed empirical analyses of skilled performance on all the tasks a curriculum comprises, and directly teach the routines uncovered in the course of such analysis.

Such a conclusion, we believe, would be mistaken. It rests on the assumption that efficient instruction is *necessarily* direct instruction in skilled performance strategies, rather than instruction in routines that put learners in a good position to discover or invent efficient strategies for themselves. That is what the children did in the studies just reported. They learned the routine taught but then invented a more efficient routine for themselves. It seems reasonable to suppose (although empirical tests comparing different instructional strategies are needed to draw a strong conclusion) that the teaching routines were good ones, because they taught the specific skills in a way that called upon children's discovery and invention abilities. These empirical analyses thus provide the foundation of a conceptual scheme for choosing instructional routines.

CONSTRUCTING TEACHING ROUTINES

As the preceding sections have shown, tasks can be described in terms of their structures: how they relate to the subject matter of which they are a part, the information they call on, and their logical aspects. Piaget's task analyses were concerned with these structures, and so were Gestalt analyses. Tasks can also be described in terms of performance, i.e., what people do when they perform tasks. These performances are what most of today's information-processing psychologists seek to model. Neither structural analyses nor performance models directly prescribe what to teach, however. The studies just described suggest that when instruction is our concern, we must construct special routines for teaching, routines that link the task's structure to what is known about skilled performance of the task. These teaching routines are not induced directly from either the task structure or the analysis of skilled performance. They are, rather, *constructions* by the instructor designed to help people *become* skilled performers.

A Conceptual Scheme

To put the case in its most general form, it seems useful to think of a "triangulation" between the structure of a task as defined by the subject matter, the performance of skilled individuals on the task, and a teaching or acquisition routine that helps novices learn the task. All three terms in this conceptualization must stand in strong relation to each of the others; thus the image of triangulation schematized in Figure 11-5. Most empirical information-processing analyses have been concerned with the relation between the elements defining the base of the triangle, i.e., with the relation

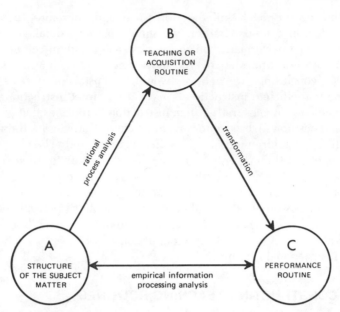

Fig. 11-5. Relations between teaching routines, performance routines, and structure of subject matter. (From Resnick, 1976.)

between the structure of the subject matter, or "task environment" (A), and performance (C). Thus, most empirical task analyses are state theories describing performance on a given kind of task at a given point in learning or development, but not attempting to account for acquisition of performance. Earlier, we described rational task analyses of early reading and mathematics skills that were developed in the course of instructional work (Resnick & Beck, 1976; Resnick, Wang, & Kaplan, 1973). These were primarily concerned with the structure of the task (A) and an idealized routine that represents the subject matter well and thus suggests a good teaching routine (B). The validation studies in mathematics (Wang, M.C., 1973; Wang, M.C., Resnick, & Boozer, 1971) were, in effect, tests of the extent to which the teaching routines and sequences derived through these analyses succeeded in conveying the subject matter to learners. The success of the reading program in teaching simple decoding validates the reading analyses in much the same way.

The teaching routine, once acquired, must also put the learner in a position to move to more skilled or fluent performance. It is this relation between teaching routines (B) and performance routines (C) that the empirical analyses of subtraction and addition began to clarify. Gaining understanding of the "transformation" processes that link these two routines is a necessary step in completing the triangulation that brings information-processing theory into clear relation with instructional design.

This triangulation of relations suggests that a good teaching routine: (1)

must adequately display the underlying structure of the subject matter, (2) must be easy to demonstrate or teach, and (3) must be capable of transformation into an efficient performance routine. The teaching routine is designed to facilitate acquisition. It provides the connecting link between the structure of the subject matter and skilled performance. Thus, teaching routines must be constructed specifically to meet these criteria. This may require considerable artistry, and not all routines will successfully meet all the criteria. Let us consider some examples.

Evaluation of Some Existing Teaching Routines

The addition routine Groen and Resnick (1977) taught embodies the union-of-sets definition of addition. Thus, it is a mathematically correct procedure and represents the subject-matter structure clearly. The routine is also easy to demonstrate and to learn. Their 4-yr-old subjects (who knew only how to count objects when they began the experiment) were performing addition virtually perfectly, using the blocks, after about a half hour of practice. The routine the children were taught is awkward and slow to perform, however. None of us would like to use it in our daily activities, and neither, apparently, did the 4-yr-olds. Nevertheless, the data show that the routine is transformable—by a series of steps we can imagine but cannot for the moment document empirically—to the more efficient performance routine of the *min* model. Further, this performance routine exemplifies another aspect of the subject-matter structure, commutativity. Thus, the proposed triangulation is completed. A teaching routine derived by rational task analysis of the subject-matter structure is transformed to a performance routine that reflects a more sophisticated definition of the subject matter. This skilled performance reflects the structure of the subject matter but at a different level; it includes efficiencies based on elimination of redundant steps, the use of larger units of information, etc. The case is similar for the subtraction study (Woods, Resnick, & Groen, 1975). The routine presumed to have been taught in school exemplifies a partitioning-of-sets definition of subtraction. The performance routine derived by the children is not only more efficient, but also reflects a more sophisticated aspect of the subject-matter structure, namely, the complementary relation between addition and subtraction operations.

The decoding routines described for reading (Resnick & Beck, 1976) also appear to meet the triangulation requirements. The rational analyses represent the subject matter of grapheme-phoneme correspondences in the form of an idealized performance. The routines include a representation of the grapheme structure, as opposed to single-letter structure, of English (as in the Find Next Grapheme subroutine). The successive blending procedure was selected as a teaching routine because the analyses suggested it would be learned more easily, thus meeting the teachability criterion.

With respect to transformability, skilled readers do not often go through a decoding process as detailed as the one we have shown. They do not usually read in single grapheme units. In fact, the speed at which normal skilled reading occurs suggests that for much reading there may not be a full intervening translation into an auditory form. Even when they encounter difficult words, skilled readers are likely to analyze the words in terms of syllabic or morphemic units rather than graphemes. Although the units change, it seems reasonable to suggest that the basic flow of generating and combining sounds is probably the same for more advanced as for beginning readers (Cf. Chapter 12). The material in Figure 11-2, for example, could be rewritten substituting the more general term *unit* for *grapheme* or *letter*. Thus, subroutine A would read, "Find next unit"; B, "Pronounce unit"; D, "Any more units?" (subroutine E, the check for final *e*, would perhaps drop out). Storing sounds, blending them, and testing them against aural vocabulary would proceed much as shown in Figure 11-2. Thus, the routines taught appear to meet the transformability requirement, although accumulating evidence suggests that some children may need explicit help in making the transition to larger units of processing.

Many teaching routines fail to meet the criteria enumerated above. Some are awkward to teach; such would be the case, for example, were one to undertake to teach 4-yr-olds the *min* model for addition. Others fail to display the subject-matter structure in a way that is transparent to children. For example, traditional algorithmic methods of teaching carrying and borrowing do not display the underlying structure (base arithmetic and its notation) from which the routines are derived.

Sometimes instructional routines are developed to display the subject-matter structure but do not meet the transformability criterion, i.e., they are not easily mapped onto a performance routine that is efficient and direct. An example of a performance routine that fails on the criterion of transformability is one proposed by Bruner (1964) for teaching factoring of quadratic expressions. Bruner succeeded in teaching third graders to factor by creating a "model" of the expression using blocks. As shown in Figure 11-6(a), the large square is x units long and x wide, thus x^2. The rod is x units long and one unit wide, thus x. The small cube is 1×1, thus 1. As in Part b children can arrange these three elements in squares that have equal factors—e.g., $(x + 1)(x + 1)$, $(x + 2)(x + 2)$—and that can also be expressed as quadratics—e.g., $(x^2 + 2x + 1)$, $(x^2 + 4x + 4)$. Allowing children to manipulate the blocks may be excellent for displaying and promoting insight into the structure of the subject matter, but there appears no way to transform the square-arrangement routine to a factoring procedure without the blocks.

Certain other teaching routines in early mathematics do meet the transformability criterion while still representing the mathematical structure. For example, measurement can be taught as a process of dividing into equal units. Wertheimer (1959) did this when he used division of a figure into

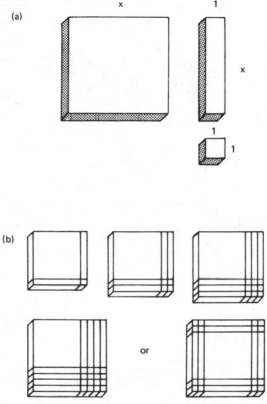

Fig. 11-6. (a) Three components for quadratic construction. (b) Squares of ever-increasing size constructed with components. (From Bruner, 1964, p. 324 & 325.)

squares as a means of finding its area. Bearison (1969), in a less widely known experiment, induced a generalized conservation concept by showing children how to count the number of 30-ml beakers of liquid that were poured into beakers of different sizes and by then demonstrating the principle of conservation by pouring equal quantities of liquid into containers of different shapes. This generalized principle of measurement, exemplified in the liquid measurement procedure, produced conservation responses in tests of number, mass, length, and continuous and discontinuous area and quantity that lasted at least 6 months. Similarly, the number base system (including carrying and borrowing) can be taught using blocks in sizes of one, ten, and one hundred, placed in units, tens, and hundreds columns as in Figure 11-7 (Dienes, 1966, 1967). With these blocks, carrying can be represented by trading or exchanging extra (i.e., more than nine) blocks in a column for a larger block that is placed in the next column. Such an exchange would be necessary for the bottom display in Figure 11-7 before the block display could be notated. A reverse exchange operation can be used to represent

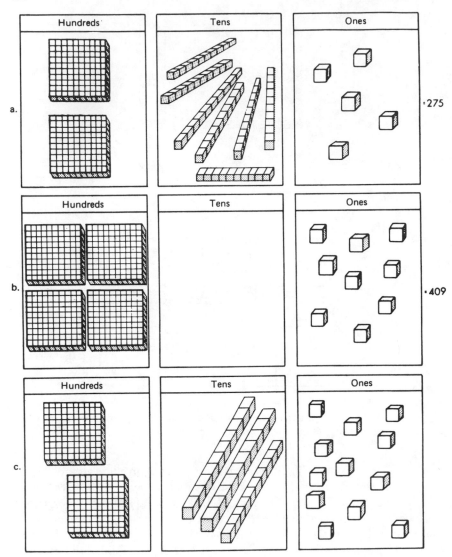

Fig. 11-7. Block displays for notation problem. (From Resnick & Glaser, 1976.)

subtraction. In each of these cases, as the physical representation is drop-ped, a performance routine can be constructed that initially performs "as if" the representation were present, and then gradually becomes more abstracted from it. This is what we believe occurred in the Groen and Resnick (1977) addition teaching experiment.

These observations suggest that most people, even quite young chil-dren, use environmental feedback to simplify performance routines. They invent variations even when we teach them strict algorithms. One implication is that the traditional line between algorithmic and inventive teaching disappears. We are faced not so much with a choice between teaching by rote or teaching by discovery as with a problem of finding teaching rules that will enhance the probability of discovery, rules that somehow invite simplification or combination with other rules. This way of thinking also draws attention to the extent to which we presently depend, in our normal instructional practices, on this kind of invention and discovery by learners. Our instruction is rarely complete; and rather than taking care to point out the simplifying and organizing principles that underlie what we teach, we often not only choose less than elegant instances, but also expect learners to find the underlying principles for themselves. This suggests that differences in learning ability, often expressed as intelligence or aptitude, may in fact be differences in the amount of support individuals require in making the simplifying and organizing inventions that produce skilled performance. Some individuals will seek and find order in the most disordered presentations; most will do well if the presentations (the teaching routines) are good representations of underlying structures; still others may need explicit help in finding efficient strategies for performance.

ANALYZING AND TEACHING GENERALIZED "LEARNING TO LEARN" ABILITIES

The preceding suggests that the transition from acquisition to skilled performance of a task often demands the invention of new or simplifying routines. People apparently invent even within the confines of algorithmic instruction. We also know that individuals differ substantially in how facile they are at inventing. Thus one appropriate concern for instruction is the possibility of teaching general strategies for invention and discovery, strategies that will help learners be less dependent on the instructor's elegance in presenting particular tasks. An interest in teaching such general "learning to learn" abilities, as they are often called, has been widely expressed by educators and psychologists. But few successes have been reported, and there is little scientific basis at the present time for such instruction. As in the instruction of any other ability, the first step in teaching general abilities is developing a psychological description—a task analysis—of the competence sought. Such analyses are only now beginning to become available.

Problem-Solving Skills

A growing number of information-processing analyses of different problem-solving tasks provide a potential basis for instruction. Without further testing and experimentation, however, it is by no means evident that

analysis of skilled performance on complex problems can be directly translated into instructional interventions. One test of this possibility was carried
out recently by Holzman (Holzman, Glaser, & Pellegrino, 1976). In an effort
to determine the instructability of a generalized pattern-detection skill, this
study used an analysis of behavior on series completion tasks that had been
carried out earlier by Kotovsky and Simon (1973). The Kotovsky-Simon
analysis identified three principal subroutines for discovering the pattern in
letter series completion tasks similar to those used on many intelligence
tests. These were (1) detecting the "period" of the pattern, i.e., the repeating units of a certain number of letters, such as three in the pattern
abmcdmefm . . . or four in the pattern *defgefghfg* . . ., (2) determining the
rule that generates each symbol in the period, and (3) testing the inferred
rule to see if it holds for all the letters that have been presented. These
subroutines in turn were shown to be dependent upon recognizing three
basic relations between items in the series presented: *identity* (e.g., *f* to *f*),
next in the alphabet (e.g., *f* to *g*), or *backward next* (e.g., *h* to *g*). These three
relations exhaust those found in the Thurstone letter series completion task
(Thurstone & Thurstone, 1941) that Kotovsky and Simon used as a basis,
although a much more extended and complex list of relations could of course
be used in generating series completion problems.

Based on the Kotovsky-Simon analysis, Holzman taught children from
first through sixth grade the three basic relations and strategies for finding
periods. Instruction in finding periods was done in such a way as to prevent
extrapolation to other subroutines. Children trained in these relations and
periodicity subroutines improved significantly on the letter series completion task from pre- to posttest. They also improved significantly more than
control children who simply took the pre- and posttest and did not practice
the series completion task. Comparisons of particular types of errors for the
training and control groups showed that the trained children improved significantly more than the controls where there were more difficult relations
(e.g., *next* as opposed to *identity*) and on the generally more difficult problems. Control children showed a practice effect, due to experience with the
test itself, limited largely to improvement on the most easily detectable
relation (i.e., *identity*). This study suggests the possibility of using formal
simulations as the basis for designing instructional programs. The particular
suggestion is that as information-processing analyses succeed in identifying
the processes underlying problem solution, these processes, or at least some
of them, can be taught directly.

What possibilities exist for analyses of problem-solving abilities that are
even more general than those Holzman found, and what might these yield as
a basis for instruction that would truly generate learning to learn abilities?
This question is considered by Resnick and Glaser (1976) in a report on
several studies of invention behavior in mathematics and related tasks.
There it is argued that the processes involved in problem solving of certain
kinds are probably the same ones involved in learning in the absence of

direct or complete instruction, and that instruction in those processes might constitute a means of increasing an individual's intelligence.

Using current information-processing constructs, Resnick and Glaser characterize problem-solving invention as the process of encoding a problem (i.e., building a representation in working memory) and then searching

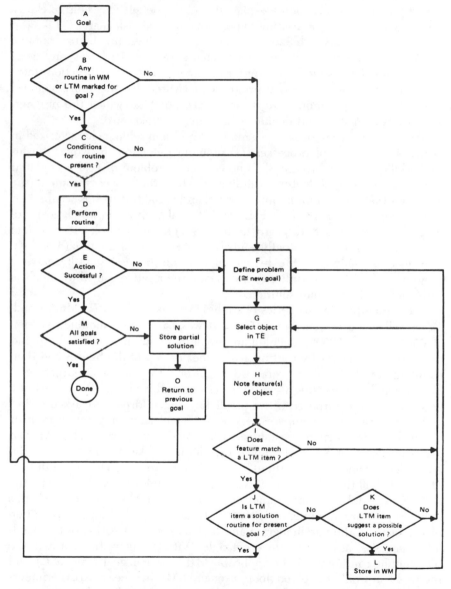

Fig. 11-8. A model for solving invention problems. WM: working memory; LTM: long-term memory. (From Resnick & Glaser, 1976.)

long-term memory for a stored routine (whole or partial) relevant to the problem formulated. If a routine that works under present conditions of the task environment is not found, further features of the task environment may be noted or the immediate goal of problem-solving activity redefined so that routines not previously recognized as relevant or usable may become so. Figure 11-8 represents a model developed to study and validate this conception of problem solving. Some explanation of the details may help to clarify how it represents the processing hypothesized in the task analysis. Like the earlier flow diagrams of blending processes in reading, this figure contains two kinds of statements: direction statements (rectangular boxes) and decisions (diamonds). Using the computer program analogy, the direction statements can be considered subprograms activated by the more general problem-solving program. The decisions are points at which the program assesses its own state and decides what move to make next.

This task analysis embodies a model of problem solving characterized in terms of three sets of processes: (1) problem detection, in which the inapplicability of "usual routines" is noted and a problem or goal formulated (Figure 11-8, A-E), (2) feature scanning, in which the task environment (the external situation, including both physical and social features) is scanned for cues to appropriate responses (F-L), and (3) goal analysis, in which goals are successively reformulated, partly on the basis of external task cues, to yield soluble subgoals that eventually contribute to solution of the task (A and F). This model, made possible by an information-processing task analysis, suggested a number of studies to investigate the relative contribution of the three aspects to problem solution.

For example, in one series of studies (Morris, L.L., 1975; Mulholland, 1974; Pellegrino & Schadler, 1974) that was based on a modified version of Wertheimer's (1959) parallelogram problem, children were taught to find the area of rectangles by putting 1-in. cubes on top of the figures and then counting the blocks. They were also taught how to transform nonrectangles into rectangles by cutting them with scissors and replacing the pieces in a new way. Next, confronted with a parallelogram, children were asked to find how big it was or to compare its size to that of another parallelogram or rectangle. This instruction established the initial goal (Figure 11-8, A). The problem could not be solved, however, simply by placing the blocks on the parallelogram and counting them (the "no" route from C). The blocks did not fit, they fell off the edges, etc. It was hoped the children would redefine the goal (F) as, "Make this into something I *can* use the blocks with." With this new goal, feature-scanning activities (G, H, and I) would lead to recognition of the "gap" in the parallelogram and thus to a transformation of the parallelogram ("yes" at I and J) into a rectangle. With the figure transformed, the block-fitting routine would be applicable to the original goal ("yes" at C), and the problem would be solved (loop through D-M). In successive experiments the conditions were varied to learn the effect of problem detection, goal analysis, and feature detection on problem solving.

With respect to problem detection, these studies showed that if people do not notice they are confronting a problem, in that their usual routines do not apply in the situation, they not only plunge ahead into errors, but also have a difficult time using subsequent information that might have aided them in discovering their mistake. For example, once children started putting blocks on the untransformed parallelogram, they found it hard to stop and think about a new way to solve the problem. On the other hand, when children were taught to detect the problem (ask themselves whether their usual routine was applicable), their likelihood of solving the problem increased markedly. To examine the influence of the task environment on problem solving, the condition was varied to make it as different as possible from conditions during training of the component routines. This increased the children's likelihood of noticing features conducive to transformation.

The most important aspect of problem solving, according to these experiments, proved to be goal analysis. In any problem-solving situation, which routines are accessed from long-term memory, and even which features in the environment are noticed, depend very heavily on how the problem is presented. The goal accepted by the individual affects cueing and retrieval of the relevant information. Pellegrino and Schadler (1974) varied the parallelogram problem by asking the children what they thought their problem was and how their proposed actions would help solve it before permitting them overt moves toward solutions. The children were thus forced to verbalize a goal (representation) of the problem. By looking ahead and evaluating their goals and plans for solution, these children were apparently spared many wrong moves; 14 out of 16 readily solved the parallelogram problem compared to only 6 out of 16 who were not asked to look ahead.

Thus, it appears that verbalizing goals and strategies before attempting to solve a problem greatly enhances the likelihood of solution. It seems possible that individuals could also be taught to be conscious of the role of environmental cues in problem solving. Instruction in strategies of feature scanning and goal analysis might enhance the probability of their noticing cues that prompt effective actions while recognizing and somehow "deactivating" those that prompt ineffective actions. Extending this general argument of self-regulation as a major characteristic of successful learning and problem solving, similar instruction in self-questioning and self-monitoring strategies might be an effective way of enhancing other generalized abilities, such as those involved in reading comprehension.

Reading Comprehension

When people read printed material, they are engaging in very complex behavior. Not only must they decode individual words, but they must group words and then sentences to extract their meaning, a task that involves several levels of processing. How does one go about describing these processes, especially for the purpose of designing instruction in comprehension skills? Several researchers have attempted to analyze various components of reading comprehension. Such work includes artificial intelligence efforts on sentence processing (Winograd, 1972) and story comprehension (Charniak, 1972), simulation models of the understanding of verbal instructions (Hayes & Simon, 1974), and increasing empirical work on natural language and text processing. Although many of these models are highly suggestive, none are as yet explicitly directed toward instructional concerns. As a guideline for thinking about instructional research, Resnick and Beck (1976) have developed a general map of reading comprehension processes. This map is not a formal model, but rather a description that directs attention to some of the most important psychological and instructional issues that need to be addressed.

Figure 11-9 represents the hypothesized flow of behavior for an effective reader reading a moderately difficult text. The top line of the figure describes the flow of processing and self-monitoring for a reader who encounters no difficulties in the course of reading. Of course, most readers will be interrupted occasionally when they encounter difficulty in recognizing words or in interpreting meaning. These difficulties require readers to search for further information, as described in quite general terms by the sequences shown below decisions 1 through 4.

An ongoing text processing activity is assumed (the "process text" boxes in the top line). This processing activity is interrupted by occasions on which the reader decides he or she has inadequate information and initiates a search for just enough information to satisfy the demand for an adequate level of comprehension. The first such interruption is for an unrecognized word (decision 1). It is important to note that a skilled reader will probably not interrupt reading for every unrecognized word, nor even attend to every separate word in the text (Goodman, 1970). However, a certain "adequate" level of word recognition is required, and even skilled readers will occasionally encounter unrecognized words significant to the general meaning of the text and requiring word attack skills to "decode" the word. A second type of interruption occurs when a word is found that has an unclear meaning and appears important enough to comprehension to warrant further information search (decision 2). At decision 3, processing is interrupted by awareness of a sentence or clause whose meaning is not completely clear.

We come finally, at decision 4, to a situation in which an entire section (paragraph, chapter, or whatever) is seen as unclear. An expanded discussion of this processing sequence is presented here to show how the diagram attempts to describe human performance. When the reader recognizes that the section has not been understood, the first likely act is to reread it (4A). Unclear words (4C) or unclear sentences (4D) may be the source of difficulty. If so, the reader returns to the word-meaning or sentence-meaning strands (under decisions 1 and 2). If neither of these seems to be the cause of

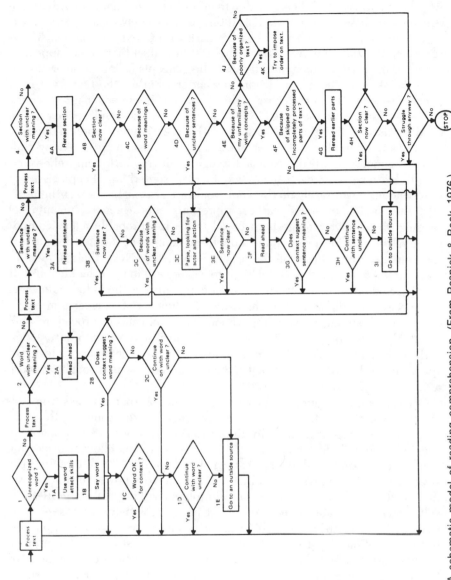

Fig. 11-9. A schematic model of reading comprehension. (From Resnick & Beck, 1976.)

difficulty, a set of further tests may occur. The reader may try to decide whether the present difficulty is due to his or her own unfamiliarity with the concepts discussed in the text (4E). If this seems a likely cause, perhaps it is due to incomplete processing of earlier parts of the text (4F), in which case rereading the earlier parts (4G) may help. If the difficulties do not appear to reside in the reader's unfamiliarity with the concepts (a "no" answer at 4E), then the skilled reader may begin to wonder whether the text itself is so poorly written that it is the cause of the problem (4J). He or she may then try to impose order on the text (4K). If all of these tests and actions fail to produce clarification (the "no" answer at 4J and 4H), a fundamental decision must finally be made whether or not to struggle ahead anyway. Many children in school probably do struggle through, with very little comprehension, simply because they have been told to read something. People reading independently will rarely do this, nor would we reasonably expect them to.

This model, as stated earlier, represents only a general mapping of reading processes. It suggests in broad terms the probable major components of the reading process and how these components might interact; it does not attempt to describe the processes in detail. Nevertheless, even in this simplified outline the model helps to maker certain important features of reading evident. Perhaps the most important feature is the indeterminacy of the process, its trial-and-error character. Reading is not an algorithmic process in which straightforward application of a set of rules or procedures will invariably yield comprehension of a text. Rather, it is a kind of interaction with a text, an interaction in which information is sought at various levels of specificity and in which a gradual reduction in unknowns is sought as more and more of the text is processed.

One general suggestion for reading instruction that emerges from this characterization is that readers be explicitly taught some of the self-monitoring strategies implied by the model. Even if we are still unable to specify the details for some of the processes, it seems likely that alerting readers to the kinds of difficulty that may be encountered and to some broad strategies for dealing with the difficulties may be very powerful. Earlier, we discussed recent work in mathematical problem solving that suggested that self-consciousness about goals and overt planning activity increase success (see also Greeno, 1973). Some of the same principles are probably applicable to reading. What the present model outlines is some strategies for interacting with a text, and it shows the strategies to be heuristic, i.e., to depend on the reader's judgment along the way concerning how well he or she is gathering and interpreting the necessary information.

The model also suggests that reading is a very context-bound activity; the characteristics of the text will have a great effect upon what constitutes an effective reading strategy. Thus, there is no single way to read well. Even the most skilled readers will sometimes encounter texts that are not processed without considerable search activity. Further, success in reading depends partly upon the knowledge the reader brings to the text. Unfamiliarity with the language and concepts of the subject matter is often a cause of difficulty in comprehension, unless the text is explicitly designed to introduce the reader to some new topic. The instructional implication of this is that reading comprehension may best be taught in the context of other subject matters rather than as a separate discipline to allow the acquisition of a broad range of knowledge as the basis for effective reading.

SOME GENERAL CONCLUSIONS

The specific suggestions that can now be offered for instruction of generalized learning abilities are limited, because relatively little has been done thus far on developing task analyses that characterize these general processes in instructable terms. Rational analysis seems less likely to yield good suggestions for generalized abilities than for specific tasks; thus empirical task analyses seem to be called for. Further, the rigor of formal models seems especially important where the processes are little understood, as in reading comprehension, and where task environments are loosely structured, as is often the case where problem solving and discovery are called for. Thus, to design instruction in these important generalized skills, it will probably be necessary to engage in the most costly and extended forms of task analysis: those that are formally stated and empirically validated. To the extent that the analyses identify instructable processes, instructional experiments can serve as one of the major forms of empirical validation of the performance models proposed. A mutual interaction between scientific and instructional concerns can thus be envisaged. It is with respect to these general abilities in learning, comprehension, and problem solving that information-processing analysis may have the most to offer instruction, just as instructional efforts may have the most to offer psychological knowledge.

PAUL ROZIN[1]

Chapter 12

The Acquisition of Basic Alphabetic Principles: A Structural Approach

Every normal American comes to speak English in the first years of life. This regular unfolding of speech and language occurs in a rather orderly way, across wide ranges of intelligence and cultural environments, and without explicit instruction. In contrast, many otherwise normal Americans never achieve competence in reading so that they can efficiently extract meaning from print. This failure occurs in spite of extensive, explicit instruction in reading.

The reading-speaking disparity is paradoxical because, at first glance, language acquisition seems a much more formidable challenge than reading acquisition. If fluency in English is attained, with all the complex semantic syntactic and phonological competences it implies, learning a new code of some 26 items based on the already-learned speech system should be embarrassingly simple.

The apparent conceptual simplicity of acquiring fluency in reading English must be misleading in some way. The mismatch between intuition or common sense and the facts of acquisition suggests that some important, presently undescribed principles of learning or education might be at work. Study of this problem is also imperative because of the serious social consequences of reading failure in a society where understanding the printed

1. This chapter is, in large part, a condensed and modified version of two long chapters written by the author in collaboration with Lila R. Gleitman (Gleitman & Rozin, 1977; Rozin & Gleitman, 1977a, 1977b). The basic analysis of the reading task and the curriculum described were full collaborative efforts with Lila Gleitman, so that the editorial "we" in this chapter is a literal "we." I thank Lila Gleitman and Elizabeth Rozin for their comments on this manuscript, and Henry Gleitman for many valuable comments on many of the ideas expressed here. See footnotes 3 and 4 for other acknowledgments.

word is an absolutely fundamental prerequisite to success. For these reasons, we address here the problem of early reading acquisition.

In the first section we take a basically common-sense approach to analyzing the reading process, with the view that understanding must precede any attempt to organize an instructional program of an ordered sequence of learnable units. One cannot decide what activities to motivate or reinforce without a structural analysis of the task. We approach early reading instruction by narrowing down from a very broad perspective, beginning with the most distant constraints on acquisition: the information potentially available in English orthography. We then ask how much of this information is actually used by adult readers, and how they use it. With the target performance thus defined, we ask what must actually be taught to children. In particular, we acknowledge the possibility that they must be taught some things that adult readers do not do, as transitional aids to acquisition. We then move on to isolate the focus for instruction by considering what children know before they begin reading instruction and what they will learn later without explicit instruction. The residue, which we believe is in large part related to the nature of the alphabetic representation of speech, is what must be taught.

In the second section we ask why the alphabetic principle forms a substantial barrier to reading acquisition. We discuss in some detail the background material in speech production and perception that forms a basis for understanding this problem. We claim that all speakers must perform, in the course of listening and speaking, the very same phonological segmentation processes that form the basis for the alphabetic orthography and that constitute a formidable conceptual barrier to reading acquisition. The problem for educators is to make learners *aware* of, or give them *access* to, their own mental processes. We believe that the problem of gaining access to knowledge already in the head poses a major general challenge for the psychology of learning and education.

In the third section of the paper we apply the common-sense and structural analysis of the first part and the theoretical issues raised in the second part to the actual teaching of reading. Here, functional considerations such as motivation and appropriate form of presentation merge with the prior structural considerations (see Catania, 1973, for a discussion of the complementarity of the structural and functional approaches). We outline a curriculum designed to teach the basic concepts of the alphabetic writing system by retracing the history or evolution of writing.

We cite the vast and sometimes highly technical research literature only sparingly, and refer the reader to two papers that provide much greater detail (Gleitman & Rozin, 1977; Rozin & Gleitman, 1977a; see also Gibson & Levin, 1975; Kavanagh and Mattingly, 1972; Levin, H., & Williams, 1970; Reber and Scarborough, 1977, for other discussions of issues raised here). We believe, however, that the fundamental issues can be described adequately without too much technical information. In fact common sense seems an

excellent guide in most areas of reading: when it is at variance with sophisticated laboratory results, there is every reason to suspect the laboratory
results. In one critical area, however, common sense and adult intuition go
awry, and this concerns the segmentation of speech into "phoneme" units.
We believe this issue is at the heart of the reading "problem," and explains
the unusual difficulty often experienced in early reading acquisition. For this
reason, we include some technical material in our discussion of this issue.

A COMMON SENSE ANALYSIS OF READING ACQUISITION

The Stimulus: What Information Is Available in Written English?

In interactions with print, a reader is ultimately constrained by the
information available on the page. A brief discussion of our writing system is
therefore in order, as a first step in understanding reading. For better or
worse, we are wedded to a specific alphabetic writing system. At its core, it
is obviously a system for representing the sequential sounds of speech on
paper. All written words in English contain some information about their
pronunciation. Indeed, a literate person who does not understand English
can sound out written English well enough that English speakers can understand it.

The letter units of the alphabet correspond, more or less, to elementary
phonological units called phonemes, which are blended together to form
words. For words like *bag, hint, carpet, hospital, vindicate* and many thousands of others, the relation between orthography and pronunciation is
straightforward. On the other hand, English is famous for its "irregularities."
Cough, thought, and *though,* for example, provide much less than adequate
information to allow a naive reader to generate an accurate pronunciation.
Many departures from "regularity" are informative, however, in that they
provide syntactic or semantic information. For example, alternative spellings
for homonyms (e.g., *ate* and *eight; know* and *no*) allow the reader to determine the different meanings of words indistinguishable in speech. These
semantic differences between the homonyms are respected in other uses.
Thus the semantic differences between *fair* and *fare* is represented in the
words *fairly* and *carfare.*

Sometimes, variants of words with common meanings but somewhat
different pronunciations share common spellings. Thus, *telegraph* and *telegraphy* (where *telegraphy* sounds like it should be spelled tuhlegraphy) or
Canada and Canadian (where Canadian sounds like it should be spelled
Cuhnadian) preserve semantic relations at the expense of apparent
phonological "compromises."[2]

2. The examples given here, and many others, may be considered "regular" spellings, in that

Some small amount of English writing is "extra-alphabetic," and provides no pronunciation information. Most prominent here are the numerals, and commonly used signs such as $ and &. Furthermore, certain features of the orthography, like the spaces between words, are more clearly related to the underlying organization of speech and language than to the sound of speech. The words in spoken sentences merge together without consistent pauses between them, in contrast to the written representation of these same sentences.

In summary, English orthography is in large part a phonological transcription of speech, but nonphonological information is also available in writing in many forms. Ours is a mixed orthography that represents language at many levels.

The Target Performance: How Do Adult Readers Process Written English?

Our purpose in discussing what the adult reader actually does during reading is twofold. First, the discussion will clarify what the final target should be: what do we want the aspiring reader to be like as an adult? Although the best learning path to this goal might be indirect, it will surely serve us well to know the endpoint. Second, some have used their views of what adult readers do to infer proper methods of reading instruction. We do not believe it is advisable to make such jumps without great caution, but since the jumps have been made, we propose to give some attention to the adult.

Let us select the average American adult reader as our target. Such a person, reading at 200-300 words per minute (Harris, A. J., 1970), is an effective user of print; such rates are high enough to encourage reading of newspapers, street signs, magazines and books, and to make the route to meaning through print about as efficient as the route through speech and ear. If all people could read as well as the present average reader, there would be no reading problem. (We are aware that many people read at rates substantially above 200-300 words per minute; for such people, the following arguments are less applicable, but still relevant.)

The naive adult reader's view of the reading process, the common-sense view, seems like a good point of departure. This view is that reading involves going through text letter by letter, and converting each letter to a sound representation. Thus, letter by letter and word by word, the message in the print is built up in the form of "inner speech." Meaning comes from the interpretation of this inner speech. In other words, the common-sense view

they contain the information providing a correct pronunciation. There appears to be a phonological rule in English that requires that any short vowel in an unaccented syllable be pronounced as "uh." A speaker presumably knows this rule implicitly, and so can render correct pronunciations of words like *Canadian*. (see Chomsky & Halle, 1968, or Gleitman & Rozin, 1977).

is that the adult reader does just what the stumbling child reader does in sounding out, but does it very rapidly and smoothly. We refer to this description of the adult reader as a "plodder through print."

A contrasting view, held primarily by some sophisticated professionals, sees the adult reader more as an "explorer of the printed page" (Smith, F., 1971). In this view, the reader does not go through a phonological intermediary but moves directly from print to meaning. And, like an explorer, the reader is thought of as judiciously *sampling* information from the page, presumably in the same way the visual world is sampled (Hochberg, 1970). The explorer view does not center on the letter as the unit of reading: syllables, words, or phrases might be apprehended as wholes, without dissection into their component letters. More critically, the reader is thought of as actively extracting meaning from the page: building up expectations based on contextual clues, material already read, etc., and sampling from various parts of the page to confirm or disconfirm these expectations. This process has been described as a "psycholinguistic guessing game" (Goodman, 1969).

Neither of these extreme models is advanced enough to be an adequate model of the adult reader. In fact at present no adequate model of adult reading exists. We are confident that normal adult readers use both types of strategies in different degrees, depending on reading skill and the nature of the materials read. Also, plodder and explorer processes could occur simultaneously.

It is easy to see that adult humans are *capable* of operating in both plodder and explorer modes. People often guess individual words or phrases that are blurred or deleted in printed text, and sometimes explicitly sample from the printed page when scanning material. Evidence for the feasibility of other explorer tendencies comes from the existence of hundreds of millions of literate Chinese: These people read a writing system that does not segment words into their component sounds, but rather has individual characters that stand for the meanings of individual words. Plodding is clearly at work when an adult generates a pronunciation for an entirely unfamiliar printed word, or in the "reading" of unfamiliar foreign languages. This often happens in Hebrew schools in the United States, and also among some Ethiopian children, who learn to "decode" religious texts in a church language they do not understand before they learn to read their native language (Ferguson, 1971).

None of these feasibility determinations indicates what the adult reader normally does in reading relatively familiar material. The literature is controversial and relates to the great controversy in reading education between decoding and whole-word approaches. While admitting that abundant data support both positions, and recognizing that the two positions are not necessarily incompatible, we shall emphasize evidence favoring a fundamental role for plodding or decoding. This is because the dispute over whether an important decoding component exists in adult reading has been a central part of the debate over whether alphabetic principles should be taught.

There are two broad arguments against the significant use of the decoding or plodding strategies by the average adult reader. One is that many average adults do not appear to sound out words, and claim they do not. Of course, many other average adults *do* claim they sound out words in their head. The important issue, however, is that the whole point of reading practice is to arrive at a stage where decoding of print is highly automatized. And this means that it can be done without direct awareness or attention. The second broad argument is that plodding takes too long, and is not consistent with normal reading rates. This argument is patently false. The average reader reads at 200-300 words per minute. Some people, without specific training, can read out loud at rates well above 200 words per minute (Huey, 1968). Presumably they could "sound-out" faster in their heads, without taking time out for breathing. People also understand speech speeded up to rates of about 275 words per minute at normal levels of comprehension (Foulke & Sticht, 1969). Hence, far from destroying the plodder notion average reading rates support it, because they fairly closely match the maximal rates of reading out loud or comprehending speech.

Turning now to the normal performance of the adult reader, research evidence exists for both plodder and explorer tendencies. The explorer view is plausible because the printed page is initially processed visually, and, in general, perception of the visual world is often described with terms like "sampling" and "active construction." On the other hand, many studies of human cognition have shown that human subjects preferentially convert visual-verbal material into an auditory-speech mode, as for example in remembering printed words (Neisser, 1967; Posner, 1969). This general support for both views is buttressed by specific experimental results. For example, word-perception errors in reading include both phonological (decoding) and semantic (explorer) errors. One rather clear-cut finding is that shapes of whole words are not critical features used by readers in normal reading. Readers show almost normal word-recognition abilities and almost normal reading rates when faced with materials in which the orthography severely distorts the normal shape of words [e.g., lower and uppercase alternation, as in *rEaCh* (Smith, F., et al., 1969; McClelland, 1977)].

Most recent studies converge on the notion that the adult reader takes advantage of both explicit and implicit knowledge of English orthographic rules in constructing representations of perceived words (see Baron, 1978; Brooks, L., 1977; McClelland, 1977; Rozin & Gleitman, 1977a). These rules account for the acceptability of *glip* but not *glpi* as regular English spellings. Included are such well-known rules as, "*U* always following *q*." Although the set of English orthographic rules is far from fully describable at this time, it is presumed that there is such a set and that it generates all acceptable letter strings in English and no unacceptable strings. It is believe that the orthographic rules facilitate the perception of and memory for English words, or pseudowords constructed from the rules. Of course, using the rules implies perceiving individual letters.

Although it is possible that humans learn these rules purely on the basis of the visual regularities in the letter strings (Brooks, L., 1977; Reber, 1967), the obvious relation of English letter strings to English pronunciation suggests a role for phonology. That fluent adults can read phonologically regular forms of well-learned words more rapidly than equally familiar, irregularly spelled homonyms (won versus one) suggests active phonological processing (Baron and Strawson, 1977; see L. Brooks, 1977, for additional evidence). But even if the adult reader relies primarily on orthographic rules in perceiving, processing, and remembering printed words, the decoding skills related to these rules would provide, at the least, a mnemonic device for acquiring them. The predictability of English letter strings and their relation to well-learned auditory representations presumably account for the substantial difference between the reading vocabularies of literate Chinese (a few thousand words) and English (about 50,000 words).

We conclude that adult readers typically perceive letters in reading, and actively use implicitly learned relations among letter strings in dealing with print. They often, but not always, convert letter strings into an auditory verbal form, and characteristically superimpose on these plodding activities higher level skills such as text sampling and inference from context. In short, and not surprisingly, the reader approaches a text that represents language at many different levels with strategies that take advantage of this diversity of information. This is not always apparent because sampling and decoding are highly practiced skills and go on more or less automatically. In this way, the reader can focus attention on getting the meaning from the printed page.

The Focus of Instruction: What Aspects of Adult Reading Must Be Taught?

Fluent readers must be familiar with the language they are to read, including its semantic, syntactic, and phonological aspects. They must recognize the letters of the alphabet and their sounds, and must understand the relation between print, meaning, and the sounds of language. They must be highly skilled at rendering meaning from print, either by direct decoding through the sound equivalent of the printed letters, or possibly, for familiar words, by direct access from letter strings to meaning. They must be able to do this well enough to concentrate on the meaning of what is being read. And they must be able to make educated guesses using contextual cues, sample judiciously from the text, and construct the meaning of the printed passage. Which of these many skills are most critical for early reading acquisition? Which are already within the competence of the preliterate child, and which will be acquired without specific instruction? A critical subgroup of skills may remain, which have to be explicitly taught. In this section an attempt will be made to identify these critical skills.

It should be clear at the outset that what must be taught need not be the most fundamental aspects of the task. An accomplished driver might fail at driving a particular car by not finding the ignition switch or by not properly engaging the safety belt. In these cases this rather trivial knowledge has to be taught rather than the already mastered skills of driving. Similarly, in teaching a child to ride a bicycle, one must realize that as a tricycle rider the child has already learned certain skills: pedaling, steering, and the like. A few new critical skills, like balance, must be taught. And other skills, such as smooth turning and fine control of the bicycle, need not be taught because bicycle riders with modest skills, if they do enough riding, will improve through general experience. They will get to the point where very little effort need be spent on balancing or turning, so more can be spent on looking around for cars or at the scenery. We maintain that the case is much the same for reading.

Before turning to an analysis of what aspects of adult performance must be explicitly taught, we must consider the possibility that the aspiring reader may have to learn some additional, transitional skills that are not apparent in adult performance but that may help in reaching the goal of adult performance.

The Teaching of Temporarily Useful Skills: Is the Alphabet Useful as a Crutch? Uncertainty about the nature of adult reading has left open the possibility that decoding is only used in special circumstances, such as in reading new words. We believe this view ignores much of the evidence. It requires the interpretation that what appears to be smoothly automatized decoding in the adults is not decoding at all. It fails to recognize the probably important role of phonology and alphabetic principles in orthographic regularity. But because some researchers in the field make this assumption (e.g., Goodman, 1973), it is worth entertaining the possibility of a minimal role for the alphabet in skilled adult reading. Such an assumption can also be seen as justifying whole-word teaching methods. Under this assumption, the teaching of alphabetic principles to beginning readers would have to be justified as a "crutch," with all the negative connotations that this word has in education.

There is great danger in jumping from an adult task analysis to a program for teaching the components of adult performance. Transitional devices or crutches are often used in skill learning, as when one holds the side of the swimming pool while learning to kick, or when a child uses a spoon to eat foods that will later be eaten with a fork. Another example is teaching "snow plowing" to novice skiers. This skill is useful to the novice in maintaining balance, but is not normally used by experienced skiers. For motivational or functional reasons, a transitional system may be taught to ease progress in early stages of skill learning even though it will be discarded later. Surely one would be doing ill service to the building trades by forbidding scaffolds because they are not part of the final building.

It would seem that the alphabet is, at an absolute minimum, an extremely useful mnemonic device that helps young readers deal with many words they will see in print by providing a reference to the already well-learned spoken word equivalents. Each day beginning readers encounter for the first time in print a great many familiar spoken words. In an analysis of an Australian elementary reading series, 41% of the 2747 different words in the books occurred only once and 73% oocurred less than five times (Firth, 1972). Yet average Australian children handle this material; so an Australian (or American) second grader can recognize about as many words as a Chinese adult. The fact is that once children gain modest fluency in decoding, usually in the first few years of school, reading becomes easier and easier and finally becomes self-motivating. Mastery of our writing system is especially difficult at the beginning but gets easier, whereas for Chinese, with its tens of thousands of relatively arbitrary characters, the basic concepts are easy but reading gets more and more difficult as the memory load increases.

A reader can only take advantage of the visual similarity of *mouse* and *house* by reference to pronunciation. We claim that it is this relation, with its mnemonic advantages, that accounts for the vast differences in written word recognition between Chinese and Americans. On visual grounds alone, the Chinese orthography is surely more distinctive and easier to learn. The phonological mnemonic also provides both the motivation and structural basis for learning the orthographic rules that ultimately seem to assume central importance in adult reading.

Accepting the importance of learning alphabetic principles, other issues of transitional learning can be raised. Early reading acquisition, when basic alphabetic principles have been more or less mastered but the process of decoding is painfully slow, is usually a period of frustration. Under these circumstances, children often spend so much effort generating a pronunciation that they fail to grasp the meaning of a passage. Because the meaning constitutes a large part of the motivation, it is important to maintain the child's interest in the task so that practice will continue. Practice will lead to fluent decoding. Some children develop ways to improve their performance, such as following the line of text with a finger. Activities like the traveling finger, while surely not a part of adult performance, may facilitate acquisition because the improved performance maintains the motivation for practice.

One might also wish to discourage certain adult performance in the beginning reader, just as one would discourage learning diving before swimming. Beginning readers are much inclined to use contextual clues when tackling print. They often use the picture in a text to avoid decoding some of the words. If one were commited to a decoding approach this activity might reasonably be discouraged by removing the pictures, even though adults regularly use contextual clues. The relevant skills may well reappear spontaneously when the contextual material is reintroduced after a certain amount of decoding mastery.

Assuming a tight linkage between adult performance and a prescription for what must be taught is not justifiable. The assumption is particularly dangerous when the adult task is not well understood, and yet the assumption is repeatedly made. It is evident not only in the design and selection of curricula but also in theoretical positions on reading acquisition (Goodman, 1973). The dangers of making this assumption are so great that we illustrate them in the following parable (Gleitman & Rozin, 1973a):

Driving for Destination

No wonder so many people never learn to drive these days! We try to teach the prospective driver to turn the steering wheel, step on pedals, and shift gears. But how many learners are turned off by repetitive drills in such inherently uninteresting tasks? These methods ignore the very purpose of driving: *destinations!*

Our teaching methods must always focus upon this central goal of all driving. The fluid driver obviously concentrates upon *where* he is going and is typically unaware of such minor details as shifting gears and turning wheels. After all, adults drive much too fast to proceed gear by gear, turn by turn.

We must encourage and build upon the student's ability to extract destinations directly from the automobile. To do this, we emphasize at all times *where* the student is going. In initial training, the learner is provided with *realistic destination contexts:* he might be placed in a car on the New Jersey Turnpike, moving at 50 mph, and told to "Drive for Philadelphia!" (Careless practitioners have sometimes set overextended destination goals such as *Destination: Los Angeles* for a novice driver starting from New York.)

Although methods research has not yet clearly demonstrated an advantage to the whole-destination method (samples are unaccountably small), we know that as a consequence of so-called "synthetic" teaching techniques, our driving schools today are filled with people who can turn wheels and shift gears all day long, but without having the faintest notion *where* they are going or *why*.

No method that ignores the ultimate purpose of driving can ever hope to succeed [pp. 500-501].

What the Preliterate Child Already Knows. The most complex prerequisite to successful reading is acquaintance with the language. There is no reason to believe that this ordinarily presents a problem and thus must be taught. The preliterate 4-, 5- or 6-yr-old has substantial command of his native language. A casual conversation with a 4-yr-old, or a 7-yr-old reading failure for that matter, settles this issue. Of particular relevance to early decoding skills: the average child of 3 or 4 already makes most of the critical phonological distinctions needed to deal fully with his language (Moskowitz, 1970, 1971). From the point of view of semantics and syntax, it should be obvious that virtually no 5- or 6-yr-old has any trouble comprehending by ear the highly simplified material necessarily used in early reading curricula: "Run, Spot, Run" or "See the Bee" do not tax the 5-yr-old's comprehension.

Just as preliterate children are competent users of language, they are also competent perceivers of the visual world. As competent perceivers, at least according to current theory, they are constantly sampling and actively constructing representations of the world. They do not know to apply these skills meaningfully to the printed page, but the skills are available in the context of normal vision. In a sense then, preliterate children already possess, in some contexts, the most complex skills and abilities that the process of reading will call upon.

At a more mundane level, reading the alphabet requires the knowledge or discrimination of the letter shapes and of the names or sounds of these letters. Such abilities are surely within the capacities of almost all first graders (Calfee, Chapman, & Venezky, 1972), but often have to be taught explicitly (see Gibson, 1965, 1970, for a general discussion of this issue). Although many children have difficulty learning letter names or sounds, their problems with this auditory-visual mapping cannot result from the absence of appropriate general capacities or experience. After all, the preliterate child has a vocabulary of many concrete nouns that refer to visually defined objects. Rather, the problem must lie either in the stimulus characteristics, perhaps the abstractness, of the letters and/or their names and sounds, or in the way these pairings are experienced or taught in schools.

What the Child Will Acquire without Explicit Teaching. Again, isolation of "spontaneously" acquired skills simplifies reading instruction because instruction can be oriented most effectively toward skills that must be taught. The explorer skills of sampling from text, constructing meaning, and the like are surely an important part of fluent reading, but we question whether they must be *taught*. They are not usually taught, except in speed-reading courses. Yet fluent adults regularly use these skills because sampling from the visual world and constructing meanings from partial information are part of the normal and natural process of looking at (or listening to) the world and making sense of it. The explorer components of reading involve getting the child to look at the printed page as he already looks at the world. As decoding fluency develops, these natural skills come to the fore. Indeed a serious problem in teaching early decoding skills is that children find ways of using context, pictures, and other information to infer meanings, without decoding individual words.

Automatizing basic decoding is fundamental to ultimate success in reading. It is not clear, however, that it can be taught, because we do not understand the process of automatization. It just seems to occur with extensive practice. If beginning readers are getting enough satisfaction (e.g., meaning) from reading, they are likely to continue at it and get the requisite experience. Some sort of guidance (e.g., in working out the pronunciation of longer words or particularly difficult letter combinations) is important, especially in the earlier stages of reading acquisition. The basic strategy, however, is to establish reading as a self-maintaining task, from which automatization will follow.

What Must Be Taught

We indicated, in discussing what the child already knows, that some instruction in letter recognition and letter sounds and names is usually required. In early reading acquisition, however, we believe that the major skills and capacities demanding instruction involve the relation between writing, meaning, and speech: the basic idea of writing, and the specific skills involved in converting written material into parallel speech representations (decoding). We now ask which aspects of "breaking" the alphabetic code present the greatest challenges to teachers and students.

We believe that the most natural analysis and ordering of the components involved in understanding the alphabet comes from the history of writing itself. Man's sequential discoveries or inventions leading to the alphabet are used here as a framework to explore the sources of particular difficulty for the aspiring reader. [The basic stages in this process are outlined in Figure 12-1. See the studies by Gelb (1952) and Gleitman and Rozin (1977) for a more detailed treatment.]

The earliest stage of writing, *semasiography* or picture writing, is illustrated by cave paintings, and involves the direct representation of meanings in visual form, with no explicit reference to speech. It is a formalization of what people do all the time in making sense out of the visual world, and in visually communicating with one another. Its virtue is that it is direct and extremely easy to decipher. Its shortcomings are the difficulty of representing many meanings pictorially and the artistic demands made on the writer (Figure 12-1A).

The search for a writing system more capable of transmitting a wider variety of meanings led, some thousands of years before Christ, to the invention of systems that included conventional symbols essentially representing words. These *logographies* could then represent language, as speech, by arranging word symbols (logographs) to correspond to the ordered words of speech (Figure 12-1B). In this type of system, when a simple iconic character could not be devised (as for abstract concepts such as *pity*), visual representations related to the concept were used, or arbitrary visual forms were invented. Modern Chinese has many of the properties of logographic systems, in that each Chinese character stands for a meaningful word (Figure 12-2). Logographies include many arbitrary visual elements, and require from the reader some ability to segment speech into words. They are, however, rather easy to learn because the characters are related to their meanings and children find it relatively easy to divide speech into word units (Holden & Macginitie, 1972; Rosner, 1972, 1974). That many preschool children do not understand the *idea* of reading, getting meaning by looking at squiggles on the page, suggests that the requirements at this level are not utterly trivial (Downing, 1970). For early acquisition, however, logographies do not offer great problems. This is clear from the absence of reports of difficulty in the *early stages* of learning to read Chinese or the logographic portion of

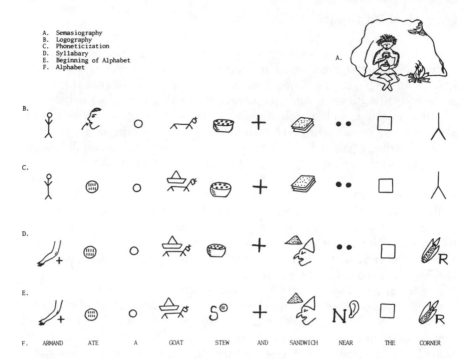

A. Semasiography
B. Logography
C. Phoneticization
D. Syllabary
E. Beginning of Alphabet
F. Alphabet

F.   ARMAND   ATE   A   GOAT   STEW   AND   SANDWICH   NEAR   THE   CORNER

Fig. 12-1.   A schematic and simplified outline of the history of writing. The somewhat contrived sentence or thought: "Armand ate a goat stew and sandwich near the corner" is conveyed on paper in successively more abstract representations, in keeping with the general course of the history of writing. The first representation (A), illustrates semasiography, or the direct representation of the thought in pictorial form. In the second representation, logography (B), the sentence is represented word-by-word, with symbols meaningfully related, wherever possible, to the words they represent. Limits on our artistic ability and imagination, and similar limitations on early man, leave room for much ambiguity here. Also note the necessarily arbitrary symbols for *a* and *the*, and the highly abstract meaningful relation between the symbol and word for *and* and *near*. In the third stage, phoneticization (C), some ambiguity is reduced for two of the items. The symbol for *ate* is replaced by the less ambiguous symbol for its homonym, *eight*. Also, the animal picture that is supposed to stand for *goat* is disambiguated with a phonetic complement: *boat*. This symbol should then be read "Looks like animal, sounds like *boat*." The fourth stage, syllabary (D), completely represents the sentence in terms of its component syllables, and thus can be considered to be a pure phonography, although many of the single-syllable symbols retain logographic characteristics. In this sentence the ambiguous stick-man symbol standing for *armand* is rewritten in terms of its two component syllables: *arm* and *and*. Similarly, *sandwich* is rewritten as the syllables *sand* and *witch*. And finally, *corner* is rewritten in terms of its two component syllables, *corn* and *er*. An arbitrary symbol had to be used for the "er" sound, and we conveniently selected *r*. The fifth version of the sentence, an early alphabetic version (E), represents the beginning of alphabetic orthography. The word *stew* is rewritten as an initial *s* followed by a picturable subcomponent of this syllable, *two*. Similarly, *near* is rewritten as *n* and *ear*. Further extension of the alphabetic principle eventually leads to the familiar alphabetic representation shown in the last (F) row.

Japanese. More persuasive is that in 3 to 6 hrs of tutoring, second-grade inner-city American children who had failed to learn the basic elements of reading learned to read meaningful English material represented logographically as 30 Chinese characters (Figure 12-2; Rozin, Poritsky, & Sotsky, 1971). This should not be too surprising: after all, every five-yr-old can provide names for many familiar faces, cars, buildings, etc. Why should there be a problem learning names for 30 distinctive Chinese characters and then stringing them together to form recognizable sentences?

We conclude that the conceptual issues raised by logographies can be rather easily mastered by almost all children. The problem with logographies comes later, as the reader must master thousands of symbols, each related to a particular meaning. By American standards all Chinese might be considered to have a reading problem, because their reading vocabulary is much smaller than their speaking vocabulary.

Very early in the history of writing, humans realized they could more easily convey meaning in writing by taking advantage of sound relations in their language. This process, called *phoneticization*, appeared in ancient (and modern) scripts in a variety of ways. A major impetus was probably reduction of the memory load, because visual symbols represented concepts that al-

Fig. 12-2. Logographic writing: a few sentences in modern Chinese. These three sentences were among those read by second-grade subjects in an experiment by Rozin, et al., (1971). Note the one-to-one mapping of English words to unitary Chinese characters (words in the translation not directly represented by Chinese characters are included in parentheses). The principle of a phonetic complement is illustrated by the sign for *red* in part C. This character is a compound of two characters: the element on the left signifies *silk,* and the element on the right, which looks like I, is pronounced *ung.* The pronunciation of the word *red* in Mandarin Chinese is *hung.* Thus, *ung* is a phonetic clue for the proper reading of this character.

ready had a spoken version in virtually all cases. Phoneticization was particularly useful in the visual representation of proper names.

One means of simplication was the rebus. A written symbol with a clean-cut reference was also used to represent a word of different meaning but similar sound. Words could be represented by their homonyms. Thus a picture of a saw could be used to represent the past tense of "see" (Figure 12-1C). Supplementary symbols were also introduced as clues to the pronunciation of a logograph. For example, the Chinese word, *ma,* meaning "ant," written as 𧉟蚂 , is made up of two characters, one meaning insect, 虫, and the other meaning horse, 马 but pronounced *ma* (Wang, W. S.-Y., 1973). Such a symbol would be read, "Means an insect, sounds like *ma*" (see also Figure 12-1C and the legend of Figure 12-2). Some form of phoneticization occurs in almost all known and deciphered scripts of the past or present.

Phoneticization is a rather sophisticated concept. During the first five or six years of life, children learn to characterize things visually on the basis of their experience: by and large, things with similar appearances have similar meanings or functions. Suddenly when the child is faced with the alphabet, the tables are turned. *Car* and *far* look alike but have no meaning in common, whereas *car* and *automobile* look very different but have similar meanings. The idea that sound may mediate between print and meaning may not come easily.

In its extreme form phoneticization results in scripts that directly represent the sounds of speech rather than meanings. In such scripts, like our alphabet, written length of words corresponds to spoken length. This simple relation, which is at the heart of phoneticization, is not appreciated by many prereaders. School children were shown pairs of short and long written words (e.g., *mow* and *motorcycle*) and asked, "Which one was *mow* (or *motorcycle*)?" On a series of items of this sort, only 10% of inner-city kindergarteners performed well, in contrast to 48% of inner-city first graders, 43% of suburban kindergarteners, and virtually all suburban first graders (Rozin, Bressman, & Taft, 1974). It would appear that some teaching was in order: surely the concepts involved are fundamental to understanding the alphabet.

As phoneticization permeated further and further into logographies, there came a point for many scripts where the logographic elements virtually disappeared, so that writing directly represented the sounds of speech. In the early forms of sound-stream based writing, syllables were the fundamental speech units corresponding to written elements. Such scripts were called *syllabaries* (e.g., Mesopotamian cuneiform). Writing represented the stream of syllables in an utterance: the word *monkey* could be written as two syllables *mon* and *key* (Figure 12-1D). In the linguistic communities that used syllabaries, it was possible to represent all speech utterances in written form. The reader-writer had only to memorize a rather small set of syllable elements, ranging from forty to a few hundred (if English were written as a syllabary, the number would be a few thousand, because our consonant clusters result in a greater number of syllables). The marked reduction in memory load apparently outbalanced the somewhat greater conceptual demands made in learning a syllabary, because syllabaries were independently invented many times and widely disseminated (Gelb, 1952). Syllabaries require a syllabic segmentation of speech; this is undoubtedly more difficult than segmentation into words (Rosner 1972, 1974) but still quite manageable. As we shall report later, first graders who have difficulty with alphabetic concepts can master a syllabary without much difficulty, but it certainly must be taught.

The final stage of the evolution of writing was the alphabet. As far as is known, it was only invented once (Gelb, 1952) but it spread around the world from its Mediterranean origins. The principles involved are identical to those in a syllabary: segmentation of speech into units smaller than whole words, and construction of all words in the language by recombining these elements. The difference in the alphabet is that the unit is more molecular: roughly, the "phoneme." This unit, as we shall point out in some detail later, is much more abstract than the syllable. At the outset, progress with the alphabet depends on an ability to segment speech into phonemic units: the child must be able to hear that *car* has three "sounds," that it can be generated by blending three sound elements, and that *car*, *cat,* and *cog* all start with the same sound element. All of these tasks are difficult for children (Rosner, 1972, 1974; Liberman et al., 1974). Because children have trouble in becoming aware of those elements of speech on which the alphabet is based, it is not surprising that extensive teaching is usually required to produce basic alphabetic competence (Calfee et al., 1972; Gleitman & Rozin, 1973b; Liberman, I. Y., Shankweiler, Fischer, & Carter, 1974; Rosner & Simon, 1971; Rozin & Gleitman, 1977a; and the section on Syllabary in this chapter).

Many children, especially in American inner cities, are unable to read simple, regularly spelled "words" like *nug* or *mip* by the end of the first or second grade. This cannot be attributed to the great and confusing "irregularity" in many English spellings, because many curricula focus on the regular spellings and deemphasize the exceptions in the first year.

Alas, it is not the case that some of the basic insights of the alphabetic system are achieved all at once and lead to rapid success in terms of decoding fluency. Reading teachers are well aware that a dull and often painful and long period intervenes between achievement of some of the basic ideas and reading fluent enough to be enjoyable. A great many children in the first few years of elementary school and beyond have the basic idea of decoding, but do it in such a stumbling way that it interferes with their reading comprehension and pleasure.

The alphabet presumably spread, in spite of all of these difficulties in acquisition, because it reduced the number of basic written elements that had to be learned, and also in some cases represented the sounds of speech less ambiguously than some of the systems antedating it (e.g., some syllabaries used a single symbol to represent a set of different syllables, such as *ke, ka, ko, ki*).

This brief review of the history of writing and the conceptual problems produced at each stage reveals several fundamental trends. Writing systems consistently evolved toward fewer and more abstract symbols and more reliance on mapping the sounds of speech. The elements became visually more abstract as they showed less and less iconic similarity to their referents, and phonologically more abstract as they referred to more and more molecular components of the soundstream of speech. These advances eased the total acquisition of the writing system by lightening the memory load for elements. This great advantage to the aspiring reader who had attained a basic conceptual grasp of the system had another side: each advance made the system conceptually more difficult and abstract, and therefore harder to learn in the early stages. In general, writing systems became easier and easier to master completely but harder for the beginner. In a sense the alphabet was invented *by* adults *for* adults.

We argued that lack of insight into the nature of the alphabet and fluency in reading alphabetic materials present substantial difficulties to many children. The most potent reason for believing such difficulties are in large part responsible for reading failures is simply the *centrality* of alphabetic competence in both reading acquisition and fluent adult performance. Need one cite evidence that inability to swim will produce problems in playing water polo? Failure to master the most basic alphabetic concepts is likely to lead to a pattern of spiraling failure. In practice the poor decoder finds reading a chore, and is not likely to be motivated to practice. Early differences among children in understanding the alphabet would thus tend to become exaggerated. Competent earlier readers will read more and will attack new words confident that they will be able to pronounce and comprehend them.

We hesitate to buttress the strong common-sense argument with correlational data because an enormous variety of skills, capacities, and personal or socioeconomic characteristics have been linked to reading success or failure (e.g., Harris, A.J., 1970). But we overcome our hesitation enough to cite two studies that show, with impressive data, that phonological decoding abilities (e.g., as measured by ability to read nonsense words) are excellent predictors of ability to read and comprehend meaningful materials (Firth, 1972; Shankweiler & Liberman, 1972). The greater success of reading curricula that explicitly teach the alphabetic code also supports this point (Chall, 1967).

We conclude that both common sense and much research evidence support the need for early teaching of alphabetic concepts and for encouraging facility in decoding. The rest of this chapter concerns theoretical and practical implications of this conclusion, with particular emphasis on learning and teaching the basic nature of the alphabetic system.

UNDERSTANDING THE ALPHABET AND THE PROBLEM OF ACCESS TO LINGUISTIC KNOWLEDGE: SOME GENERAL ISSUES IN PSYCHOLOGY AND EDUCATION

In this section we argue that the difficulty in achieving understanding of the alphabet is directly related to the abstractness of the representation of speech in alphabetic writing. We try to show why the preliterate child has trouble comprehending alphabetic units even though they correspond to the very units used by that child in speech production and perception. We then confront the general problem of how to increase the accessibility of linguistic or other knowledge already in the head. This issue extends well beyond the domain of the reading acquisition problem.

The Cognitive-Linguistic Basis of the Alphabet: Phonological Segmentation

The alphabet represents speech as a series of discrete symbols. The sound patterns represented are in fact continous, and change gradually over time (Figure 12-3). The tracking of a continuous stimulus by a discrete set of elements is at the heart of the alphabetic problem, especially because the continuous soundstream cannot be physically decomposed into separately identifiable discrete acoustic components. This is not to say, however, that there is no relation between the alphabet and the sounds of speech: rather, it appears that the relation is abstract. The alphabet represents what goes on in the head during speech more faithfully than it represents the actual sounds of speech. We propose to outline the relation among the three critical representations related to reading: the organization of phonology in the head, the soundstream of speech, and the alphabetic writing system. This account essentially describes fundamental recent work in linguistics and psychology (Chomsky, 1965; Chomsky & Halle, 1968; Liberman, A. M., Cooper, Shankweiler, & Studdert-Kennedy, 1967; Stevens, 1972; and see Gleitman and Rozin, 1977 or Fodor, Bever, and Garrett, 1974, for more detailed statements).

We begin by describing the current view of the relation between the representation of speech in the head and the actual soundstream as it leaves the mouth. Speech is conceived as represented in the head by abstract units called systematic phonemes. These are discrete elements or concepts, which correspond very roughly to our alphabetic symbols. In generating speech these discrete representations undergo two transformations: the first from systematic phonemes to phones (bundles of articulatory commands), and the second from these phones to the continuous soundstream of speech.

The first transformation is of minimal interest for our purposes. Discrete abstract representations (systematic phonemes) are converted into discrete sets of articulatory commands (phones); each phone is conceived as a set of

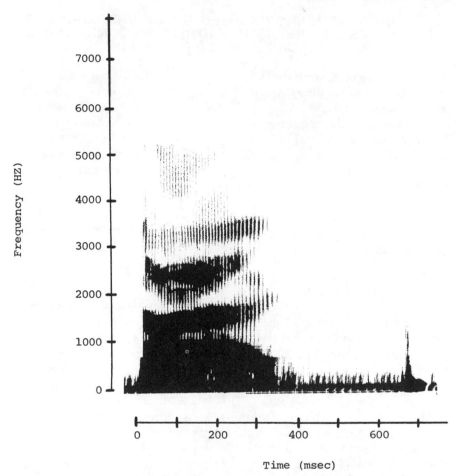

Fig. 12-3. Sound spectrogram of the spoken word *bag.* The darker an area or point, the more acoustic energy is present at that frequency and time. The bands of energy that are relatively consistent over time are called formants. The lower two formants are sufficient to produce the perception of *bag.* The computer-generated sound spectrogram of *bag* at the bottom of Figure 12-4 represents only the two lowest formants.

instructions to the articulatory apparatus, specifying the shape of the vocal tract, lip position, activity of the vocal chords, etc.

The second transformation, from articulatory commands to the sound-stream, is critical in accounting for the difficulty of the alphabetic insight because here the discrete representation becomes continuous. Articulatory commands corresponding to each of the phones in an utterance are presumably sent from the brain to the articulatory apparatus in sequence. Thus, for the word *bag,* it is presumed that commands for "b", "a" and "g" pass down the appropriate cranial nerves in order (Figure 12-4: Liberman, A. M., et al., 1967). The problem of transformation arises in the conversion of nerve

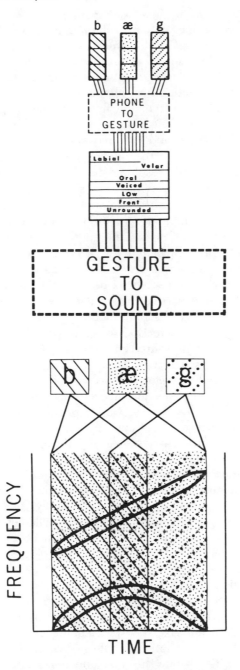

Fig. 12-4. Schematic model of speech production as formulated by the Haskins Group. The figure shows production of the word *bag* in two stages: a conversion from phone to articulatory gesture, and from articulatory gesture to sound. (From Liberman, 1970, p. 314.)

impulses to muscular events in the vocal apparatus. The muscles of articulation respond much more sluggishly than the nerve signals. Thus, when the "g" command for *bag* arrives at the muscles they are just beginning to respond to the earlier "b" and "a" commands. As a result, the commands overlap significantly, producing a smoothly varying, continuous change in the musculature and obliterating neat phone boundaries.

A further consequence is that the final articulatory position for any particular phone may not be reached, because the muscle movements it programs interact with earlier and later movements. Other interactions in the vocal appartus further cloud the relation between the discrete sets of articulatory commands and the resulting sound. Each command arrives at the vocal apparatus in the context of prior and subsequent commands. Thus, the actual position of the various articulators when a command arrives depends on what particular commands (phones) preceded it. If, for example, a particular command includes touching the middle (as opposed to the tip or the back) of the tongue to the palate (e.g., "k"), the actual execution would depend on where the tongue was before the arrival of this command. Indeed, the production of speech seems to be better described as a series of commands directed toward particular articulatory targets (e.g., tongue at midpalate) than as specific muscle movements (Stevens, 1972).

As a result of these characteristics of speech production: (1) discrete systematic phonemes are represented continuously (Figures 12-3 and 12-4) and in such a way that the sound wave at any point in time includes information about several different phonemes; (2) because of the overlap and interaction, the soundstream cannot be decomposed into the discrete units that underly it; and (3) any individual systematic phoneme or phone may be represented physically in a variety of ways, depending on context. Thus, the physical representation of the initial consonant "d" depends on the following vowel (Figure 12-5). A certain amount of articulatory invariance is common to all these "d's" because the initial "d" commands produce a specific configuration of the articulatory apparatus; but the command for the following vowel modifies this configuration almost immediately. In fact there is no audible pure "d" sound. All the audible sounds of syllables beginning with "d" reflect interaction of the "d" with the subsequent vowel. The initial sound waves actually mark the transition from the "d" position to the subsequent vowel position (Figure 12-5).

Figure 12-5 is instructive for another reason. It represents a simplified, computer-generated sound spectrogram, which has the essential features of the corresponding speech sounds. These patterns are heard as the indicated sounds when played to humans. The overlapping or shingling of phone representations can be demonstrated with these stimuli, or with tapes of real speech, by attempting to separate the two components (e.g., by splicing the tape). With "du," for example, the listener hears "du's" with shorter and shorter "u's" as the tape is sliced off from the "u" end. Suddenly, at some point, a peculiar noise that does not sound at all like speech is heard. With-

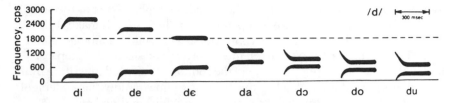

Fig. 12-5. Synthetic, computer-generated sound spectrograms sufficient to produce perceptions of various "d" plus vowel syllables. (From Liberman, Cooper, Shankweiler, & Studdert-Kennedy, 1967, p. 436.)

out the "u," the remaining sound is nothing like a "d." There is no way of isolating the "d": in the absence of context, a pure "d" cannot be heard or produced. This is why, in pronouncing "d" for beginning readers, we must say "duh," appending a weak vowel in order to pronounce the consonant.

Phones vary in the degree to which they interact with their neighbors and in the degree to which they can be isolated from the soundstream. The stop consonants ("d," "t," "k," "g," "p," "b") cannot be produced in isolation. At the other extreme, the vowel sounds can be produced easily in isolation, and have a more identifiable and invariant sound pattern. The remaining consonants lie between these extremes.

Fortunately for us as listeners as well as speakers, our ears and auditory system can handle and decode the highly encoded soundstream of speech and, possibly through processes complementing those of production, arrive at a systematic phoneme interpretation of what is heard. At least, it is clear that adults and children have no trouble understanding speech. There is much evidence that the human auditory system is specialized for the phonological analysis of speech signals (Liberman, A. M., et al., 1967).

The relation of these aspects of speech production and perception to problems in learning the alphabet should be clear. In general there is considerable "distance" between the alphabetic script and the soundstream. The reader's job is to get back to the underlying representation of the soundstream, where the alphabetic correspondence is good, because the letters of the alphabet correspond rather well on a one-to-one mapping with the phones or systematic phonemes.

Two essential features of speech encoding are clearly represented in the problem of teaching the alphabet. One concerns blending and segmentation (e.g., hearing that *bag* has three sounds). We argued that *bag* really does have three sounds, represented most concretely as three distinct and ordered sets of articulatory commands, but that these discrete sounds are not recoverable from the sound itself. It is doubtful if a physicist would ever come to the conclusion that *bag* had three sounds just by examining its sound pattern along with the pattern of other words. Some reference to the underlying basis in the head would seem necessary. Corresponding to the problem of segmenting speech into phonemic units is the problem of synthesizing speech by blending the elements. The shingling of phonemes in the sound-stream of speech and the context dependence of these sounds makes this task difficult, especially for the stop consonants. The child cannot be given a concrete example of the sound element corresponding to the stop consonants: "duh" is not a representation of the sound represented in writing by *d*. And "duh-i-guh" does not make "dig" no matter how rapidly these elements are spoken, simply because "dig" contains no "duh" and no "guh."

A second problem in reading acquisition is getting children to hear common elements in different utterances: learning, for example, that *big*, *bag*, and *bug* all start with the same sound. As we pointed out, especially for stop consonants, the similarity or invariance inheres weakly in the sound pattern and strongly in the common articulatory targets corresponding to the beginning of each syllable. Again, just as in blending and segmentation, the teacher cannot point to the physical referent of at least some of the alphabetic units.

We cannot overemphasize that, according to our analysis, the fundamental early problem in mastering the alphabet has nothing directly to do with reading and writing, but rather with awareness of speech processes. A child who comes to understand phonemic segmentation of speech has the key to making sense out of discrete alphabetic writing even before ever having seen it [the centrality of phonological awareness in early reading acquisition has been supported and discussed by Gleitman and Rozin (1973b), Liberman, I. Y., et al. (1974), Mattingly (1972), Rozin and Gleitman (1977a) and Savin (1972)].

THE PROBLEM OF PHONOLOGICAL AWARENESS: GAINING ACCESS TO PHONOLOGICAL PROCESSES IN THE HEAD

We began by noting that learning to read alphabets seems easier than learning to speak but yet leads to more failures. A more careful comparison of the reading-writing and speaking-listening processes illuminates this paradox.

Speaking is essentially a universal characteristic of mankind; reading is far from universal. Speaking develops without explicit instruction; reading almost always involves explicit and specific instruction. Speaking develops in a regular sequence, orderly in time (Lenneberg, 1967); reading appears at widely different ages and the component skills do not reliably appear in the same order across children. These comparisons suggest that speaking is a natural act for which we are built. It is the result of tens of thousands of years of evolutionary selection. Reading of alphabets, by contrast, is a new event, surely no more than a few thousand years old. This is not a long time by evolutionary standards. Thus, alphabetic reading is a new cultural acquisition tied into an old, highly specialized biological system. The difference between reading and speaking is clear in linguistic usage: we talk about the *invention* of the alphabet, but surely not about the *invention* of the phoneme.

Human language can be conceived as a highly specialized and adapted system, with speech as its natural output and hearing as its natural input channel. Many features of the human auditory system seem designed for speech reception (Liberman, A. M., et al., 1967) as many features of the oro-pharynx are clearly designed for articulatory purposes (Lieberman, 1975). We now know that normally one human cerebral hemisphere is specialized to do the greater part of language and speech processing (Gazzaniga, 1970). Furthermore, the brain circuitry performing essential linguistic functions is localized in the tissue surrounding the sylvian fissure. The physical reality of a language processor in the head is demonstrated by a patient who suffered severe brain damage to the tissue surrounding these language areas. The result was a "talking machine": the patient could repeat spoken utterances, thus doing complicated decoding of speech and re-encoding into articulatory commands, but showed no signs of any comprehension, or any type of contact between the linguistic input or output and the rest of the brain (Geschwind, Quadfasel, & Segarra, 1968). In this case we can see the isolation, and hence the reality, of the language-speech circuitry.

This phonological encoding and decoding machinery is already present and functioning in the head of every preliterate child (Eimas et al., 1971). The sounds of speech are naturally fed into this machinery through the ear. The preliterate child's ear and the parts of the brain subserving language functions are sensitive to all the distinctions necessary for speech perception and for understanding the alphabet. Preliterate children do not normally confuse spoken words differing in one phoneme, like *bat* and *rat*, or *bag* and *rag*. At some level the preliterate child recognizes that *dig* and *dog* start with the same sound and that both have three sounds. The "part" of the preliterate child that is involved with speaking and listening "knows" these things. The rest does not.

This is illustrated clearly by Blank (1968). She found, like others, that children with reading disability performed rather poorly on the Wepman (1958) test, in which they indicated whether pairs of heard words were the same or different. Pairs that were different differed in only one phoneme (e.g., *pat*, *bat*). Children who performed poorly (e.g., by saying that different pairs were the same) in fact distinguished between members of these pairs in speech. When asked to repeat each member of the pair after it was spoken, they made the appropriate responses (e.g., *bat* and *pat*). The problem was not in hearing but in understanding what same and different meant in reference to the sound patterns. In short, the problem was in talking about sound differences, or phonological awareness. Along the same lines, kindergarteners readily learn to indicate in which position (first, second, or third) two written trigrams differ (e.g., *mit* and *mat*), but have great difficulty in learning to indicate in which position two spoken trigrams differ ("mit" and "mat") (Smith, J. A., 1974).

The distinction between linguistic capacities and awareness of the operation of these capacities has been explored by Gleitman and her colleagues (Gleitman, Gleitman, & Shipley, 1973; Rozin & Gleitman, 1977a). These works indicate a gradual unfolding of the child's "metalinguistic" abilities and suggest that awareness of phonological aspects of language may normally develop later than awareness of semantic or syntactic aspects.

In summary, the highly specialized phonological processor in the brain is "tightly wired" into the mouth output and the ear input and is not easily accessible from other inputs or outputs. Alphabetic writing, a relatively new invention, is based upon some fundamental features of this system. There has been little time to evolve special connections or "access" to this system from visual or other inputs, so that it is usually difficult to use it in contexts other than the one for which it evolved. The problem for education is to give children some insight into what they are doing in decoding or encoding speech, or to teach them what they already "know," deep in their brain, in another context.

The Problem of Accessibility and Its Implications for the Psychology of Learning and Education

We believe that a significant portion of human learning can be described, along with the alphabetic insight, as gaining access to knowledge already in the head (see Rozin, 1976, for a more general discussion of this issue). Many useful "programs" in the head evolved in connection with particular functions or systems, and remained relatively tightly wired into these original systems. The complex processing that goes on in the visual system, resulting in a coherent interpretation of a visual scene (e.g., the phenomena of motion or space perception) is an example of an inaccessible but highly sophisticated system. We *learn* to draw using laws of perspective that are in many ways the same as the operating principles of depth perception in our visual system. We *learn* mnemonic devices that depend on features like organization, which seem a fundamental part of our normal memory processing. We *learn* textbook grammar, which on the face of it is a rather unsatisfactory attempt to describe the syntactic rules operative in all our heads. In all these areas the human ability to *use* these programs in their natural context predates by tens of thousands of years the human ability to *talk about* them, apply them to other situations, or teach them. It should be worth exploring what happens when access is gained to one of these programs, and how this happens. Achieving access may bring a particular program to consciousness, in which case it can often be verbally described and applied in a wide variety of contexts. It is also conceivable that a program would become accessible to a few systems without reaching consciousness (Rozin, 1976).

The concept of access could be described in terms of a computer analogy. A program can exist in a specific application, but not be available (e.g., not on the right tape or not coded in the proper way) for use in another routine. The problem with the computer is simply to establish some sort of connection between the program and a new system. The concept of access implied here, and applied to humans, can be interpreted as gaining real contact with the appropriate circuitry in the head.

We argued elsewhere that the evolution and development of intelligence can be described, in part, as increasing the access to programs already in the head (Rozin, 1976). Most relevant is the idea that some aspects of cognitive development can be described as increased accessibility. Piaget's concept of décalage (Flavell, 1963; Piaget, 1955) describes a sequence in which particular programs (e.g., those responsible for "conservation") appear initially in narrow contexts (originally only numbers are conserved) and gradually extend through other domains (weight, volume, etc.) over a period of years, until eventually the general principle of conservation appears and can be stated abstractly. This process could be described as increasing accessibility of a program already in the head, for it must have been somewhere in the head at the time that number conservation appeared. The Piagetian example suggests that access may be increased through normal experience and interaction with the world, and/or through the normal process of maturation of the nervous system. Similar factors could be responsible for the gradual awareness of different aspects of language (Gleitman et al., 1973). Unfortunately these descriptive examples give us little insight into the *process* of gaining access.

Attaining the alphabetic insight may provide the best example of increasing access. As we pointed out, the process through which this occurs is obscure. Apparently extensive exposure to the principle is a central factor. Access may also be attainable in some systems (but not too effectively with the alphabet), by simply stating the principle in the head. But the peculiar thing about the alphabetic insight, unlike some of the other examples, is that when it is attained it seems completely obvious. It is as if contact *is* established with a representation deep in the head, and the "match" is compelling. Literate adults are often puzzled that children cannot hear the obvious fact that *bag* has three sounds. We do not know whether the type of learning described here differs in significant ways from more traditional learning, as when two external events are related. In the case of reading the alphabet, the problem for one who is behavioristically inclined is that it is almost impossible to manipulate conceptual categories, and that is unfortunately what the referent for the alphabet letter is.

As is so often the case, the pedagogy of early reading must rely heavily on common sense. Common sense says to isolate the problem (which we believe we did in the first section of this chapter), and then try to approximate it as closely as possible in instruction, i.e., teach what is closest to what you cannot teach, and try to orient the learner to the critical dimensions. Somehow, experience with reading the alphabet and sounding out does lead most children eventually to understand the system.

We have couched the early reading problem in terms of *gaining* access to what is already in the speech system. Ironically, the acquisition of reading also provides a clear example of another fascinating puzzle for the psychology of learning and education. This could be described as *loss* of access, but is usually described as automatization. Somehow, after extensive practice the initially laborious decoding task comes to be performed effortlessly and with minimal attention. Surely the skilled reader pays attention to meaning and not to deciphering letter strings (with or without a phonological intermediary). This type of performance might be describable in terms of forming larger processing chunks or handling a process at a lower level of function in the nervous system. Fluent readers often appear unaware of performing any molecular analysis, although data from reading and word perception suggest that they do. We know virtually nothing about the type of learning that goes on here. Strikingly, it is the highly automatized and practiced skills that are most resistant to disturbance and are most likely to survive brain insults or the degeneration of senility. We do not know what it means to automatize something. About all we can say is that practice makes perfect, and automatic.

There is yet one more instructive feature of reading. We mentioned earlier that readers learn about the orthographic rules of English (Baron, 1978; Brooks, L., 1977; McClelland, 1977; Rozin and Gleitman, 1977a). Readers, however, are typically unaware of the very rules they appear to use in processing words thousands of times each day. Unlike phonological rules, there is presumably no strong predisposition to handle this type of new material. Rather, in some poorly understood way, exposure to large amounts of regular orthographic material leads to some sort of induction of the underlying rules. This type of apparently implicit learning has been demonstrated for invented and arbitrary orthographic rules as well as for rules based on English phonology (Brooks, L., 1977; Reber, 1967). Subjects show evidence of learning some of the underlying rules used to generate symbol strings they are exposed to, even when their only task is to memorize the strings and there is no indication that a set of rules generated the strings. At least some subjects are unaware of this after the experiment, even though they give evidence of actually using the rules. This appears yet another example of a sort of inaccessible learning, which makes its way into behavior but not into consciousness. Once again, the study of reading points to an important and underappreciated aspect of the psychology of learning.

We are left with a series of open questions about learning processes and levels of assessibility. In particular we raised the question whether the learning process is different when the material to be learned is already in the learner's repertory but in a tightly wired adapted system. It is not clear whether principles such as generalization and transfer apply to this type of learning. We try next to apply our analysis of reading and the problem of accessibility to the actual teaching of initial alphabetic skills.

TEACHING THE ALPHABET

This section deals with a restrictive instructional goal: teaching the alphabetic principle. It is an exercise in curriculum development that attempts to combine a structural analysis of reading with the general biological framework implied by the concept of accessibility. Appropriately, it takes an historical-evolutionary approach to teaching the alphabetic principle.

General Problems in the Design and Evaluation of Curricula

Any curriculum must, of necessity, take into account both structural and functional considerations. The analysis of the reading process and the beginning reader's knowledge and capacities leads to the selection of natural units and a conceptually appropriate sequence of ideas and materials. A structural analysis alone, however, is not sufficient. Functional concerns must enter because the conceptual content of a curriculum is only effective if it is assimilated by the learner. The form of materials, rate of conceptual movement, and total motivational plan of the curriculum is essential to success. Function without structure might lead, for example, to reinforcement of reading components that were not meaningful parts of the reading task, or use of a building block or unit too molecular or too molar (e.g., the whole-word) for introductory stages. On the other hand, a well-thought-out concept of early reading instruction could easily fail as a curriculum because of inattention to maintaining the interest and involvement of the student. This is especially clear in gaining fluency in decoding, where extended practice, in any of a variety of forms, is probably adequate to produce fluency. Once the basic insight is attained, the task in many ways is to motivate a child to work through sounding out thousands of words without "turning off." Even at the level of the alphabetic insight, hearing "buh-a-tuh, bat" and the like thousands of times may produce the desired results. The problem is in part getting the student to sit and listen to dull stuff like this over and over again. Television programs such as the Electric Company may have solved part of this problem.

Before delving into curriculum design, a sour note must be sounded. The past record and prognosis for progress in reading acquisition through curriculum change is bleak. What more need be said than that a Midwestern school district now reports great success in teaching reading with the McGuffey readers of the last century. And why not, since lots of children 100 years ago learned to read English with the curricula available in those days (possibly, "Trot, James, Trot")? The sad fact is that the history of reading curricula has involved cycles or fads, having to do with such things (Fries, 1963) as whole-word or soundstream-oriented approaches, or the nature of the content material in readers. Despite the wide variety of reading methods, no one curriculum or group of curricula has attained preeminence. Only through a massive and careful survey was it even possible to conclude that soundstream-oriented approaches have an advantage over whole-word approaches (Chall, 1967). Most children learn to read no matter what curriculum is used, and some do not learn with any available curriculum. Careful research in education has indicated that practically nothing matters in predicting the success of students other than their own knowledge, intelligence, capacities, or attitudes at the onset of any particular curriculum (e.g. Coleman, J. S., et al., 1966). And it is probable that after the enormous contribution of individual differences among children, the next best predictors have to do with intelligence or related capacities of peers, quality of teacher, school, and home environment. The curriculum sits rather low among the determiners of success.

In light of these considerations it is surprising that virtually all existent reading curricula based on teaching the alphabetic principle start out almost immediately with alphabetic concepts. Beginning with these concepts can produce confusion because the prior principles may be obscured by failure to understand the alphabetic-phonemic unit. This may explain, for example, the failure of many inner-city kindergarteners and first graders to understand that longer written words take longer to say (Rozin et al., 1974).

Common sense says a curriculum should have some effect and there are probably better and worse ways to teach English reading. Data suggest it is worth making sure that children learn what the alphabet is about (Chall, 1967; Firth, 1972; Shankweiler & Liberman, 1972). It is quite possible that significant curricular effects have been masked in the past by an incredible amount of uncontrolled variability virtually inherent in the school situation. We maintain that a reading curriculum that would actually reduce the amount of reading disability by 10-20%, a feat of enormous social significance, could probably not be shown to be effective in the real world. This is simply because it would be embedded in a complex matrix of forces, many of which would be more powerful determiners of reading performance and would vary randomly or nonrandomly across "control" and "experimental" classes, children, or school districts. Teachers, children, schools, and home environments cannot really be equated. Even if they could, these and the nature of the particular curriculum would interact. The teacher's style interacts with the curriculum, and surely the teacher's enthusiasm for the curriculum is likely to affect its success. Some teachers (or schools or school systems) resist new curricula and are suspicious of them, while others applaud innovation, enthusiastically support new curricula and give an extra effort that may result in transient success. This has been the story for many widely heralded educational innovations.

Curriculum comparison is also plagued by the problem of measurement. How does one compare different curricula that teach different skills in different orders? Ultimately the only fair test is final reading comprehension skill, say in the fourth grade. But this requires successive years of consistent exposure to the same experimental curriculum, a feat hard to achieve in a real world that wants to see progress on at least a yearly basis.

These factors obscuring curricular effects are in principle controllable with large enough samples, careful procedures, and massive expenditure of research funds. Of course, the better a curriculum is the more likely its effects will emerge above the noise. A truly superb curriculum would need little testing. It would be appreciated and adopted by almost any teacher who tried it or heard about it.

These sobering considerations lead one to question the procedures to be used in validating a curriculum. We see three alternatives:

1. Massive curriculum testing in the real world, in classrooms with classroom teachers, and the best possible controls. This approach clearly has the greatest face validity, but the least chance of showing results.
2. Small controlled experiments, in laboratories or special classrooms, showing that under very well defined circumstances, curricula (or, more properly components of curricula) are relatively effective in achieving their goals.
3. Reliance on common sense and current understanding of reading acquisition to devise a conceptually sound curriculum, and using this basis rather than results from probably inadequate testing as the justification for curriculum use. This alternative would be more satisfying if there were better theoretical formulations of reading acquisition.

In light of the history of evaluating curricula we lean toward the last alternative. For our own curriculum, we naively hoped that the first alternative, real-world testing, would work. We now know better. But, we rush to point out that a reasonable curriculum cannot be devised without feedback from real children, preferably in real classrooms. Here again, functional considerations come to the fore: It is hard to know in advance what materials will engage children and what concepts require more or less practice and exposure.

An Historical Approach to Early Reading Acquisition

Our analysis of early reading acquisition naturally leads to the history of writing as a guide for a reading curriculum. The history of writing, current knowledge in linguistics and psychology, and common sense suggest that the early reader of the alphabet must comprehend all of the following:

In reading one gets meaning from things on the page (semasiography).

The things separated by spaces on the page correspond to words in the language, and are strung along in the order of words in speech (logography).

What is actually represented by the marks on the page is the sounds of speech: words that look alike sound alike (phoneticization).

The speech representation is based on subword units of speech, which can be combined and recombined to represent different words (syllabary).

The letter, the particular unit used in the alphabet, corresponds to the systematic phoneme (alphabet).

As we pointed out, this sequence moves from direct representation of meaning on paper (or rock) to more and more abstract representations. We argued above, based largely on experience with the acquisition of different types of writing systems (Gleitman & Rozin, 1973b; Rozin, Poritsky, & Sotsky, 1971; Sakamoto & Makita, 1973), that the historical sequence also moves steadily from easy to difficult. Because it does not appear very difficult to teach any of these components of reading other than the alphabetic concept itself, it makes sense to teach the earlier forms first. For both motivation and conceptual clarity, why not teach what we know how to teach and what children can easily learn, and at least isolate the problem of greatest difficulty? We presume that it is better to introduce the alphabetic concept to a child who is already motivated to read and who understands that the writing system tracks the sounds of speech in terms of sound units.

In light of these considerations it is surprising that virtually all existent reading curricula based on teaching the alphabetic principle start out almost immediately with alphabetic concepts. Beginning with these concepts can produce confusion because the prior principles may be obscured by failure to understand the alphabetic-phonemic unit. This may explain, for example, the failure of many inner-city kindergarteners and first graders to understand that longer written words take longer to say (Rozin et al., 1974).

The Syllable as a Transitional Unit in Reading Instruction

In our historical approach to reading, the syllable assumes center stage as a unit of writing. This is because syllabaries incorporate all of the basic concepts of reading and writing except the alphabetic unit. There are both empirical and theoretical reasons for using the syllable as a fundamental unit.

Historically the alphabet was preceded by syllabaries and evolved from a syllabary (Gelb, 1952). Syllabaries were independently invented many times and complete syllabaries or mixtures of syllabic and logographic systems were widespread, especially in the Middle and Near East, for thousands of years before the appearance of the alphabet (Diringer, 1962;

Gelb, 1952). The alphabet arose, so far as is known, only once. Thus, it would appear that it is much easier for humans to invent a syllabary.

Cross-cultural evidence indicates that syllabaries are easy to learn. The Cherokee in the last century represented their language as a syllabary and had a 90% literacy rate in 1830 (Walker, W., 1969). Modern Japanese is written partly in syllabic form (the Kana scripts). Thus the word pronounced *katakana* in Japanese is represented by a sequence of four symbols standing for, *ka-ta-ka-na*. Japanese investigators report that early acquisition of this system goes easily and rapidly. Many children learn to read the approximately 47 elements in the syllabary and blend them into words before formal instruction in schools (Sakamoto & Makita, 1973). Furthermore, there is virtually no *early* reading problem in Japan. Acquisition and use of the syllabic component of Japanese writing is almost universal.

Much evidence suggests that syllables are easier to comprehend and manipulate than phonemes. Young children are better at segmenting speech into syllabic than phonemic components (Elkonin, 1973; Liberman, I. Y., et al., 1974). They are better at recognizing spoken words that are segmented syllabically (e.g., "pa-per") than phonemically (e.g., "puh-aper") (Allen, M. W., Rozin, & Gleitman, 1972), and better at blending syllables than phonemes (Brown, D. L., 1971). They are more proficient at deleting syllables from words (e.g., take "car" out of "carpet") than at deleting phonemes from words [e.g., take "d" out of "dog" (Rosner & Simon, 1971)].

It is reassuring that all this evidence for ease of learning segmentation at the syllabic level is supported by facts at the level of speech production and perception. The work of the Haskins group (Liberman, A. M., et al., 1967) indicates that *syllables are the smallest coherent units of speech*. Spoken syllables are *discrete* units rather directly linked with their underlying discrete phonological representations in the head. The complex conversion of discrete phonemes to shingled continuous sound patterns does not apply to syllables. Thus, although rapid playing of tapes of "buh" and "ag" will never sound the same as "bag," tapes of "car" and "pet" played in sequence will produce "carpet." Syllables can be rather neatly extracted intact from the soundstream, explaining the greater ease in a whole variety of syllable manipulation tasks. It is possible to instruct a child precisely about syllables, because they can be pronounced in isolation. Syllables have corresponding superficial and deep representations in the language system, and therefore it is not surprising that they were used first by the ancients and can be appreciated earlier by children. Syllables also appear to function in *adults* as meaningful units of speech perception (Savin & Bever, 1970) and as appropriate units for decoding difficult, unfamiliar words (Rozin & Gleitman, 1977a).

Syllabary—An Historically Oriented Introduction to Reading

This section summarizes a curriculum developed over the last five years by the author in collaboration with Lila R. Gleitman (Rozin & Gleitman, 1974, 1977b), and with the aid and advice of several colleagues, teachers, and students.[3] This version is a mixture of the latest modification and a 1973-1974 edition that was subjected to an in-school evaluation. After describing the curriculum, we comment on several difficult decisions and problems that arose in going from an idea to its concrete realization in a curriculum.

Syllabary got its name because the major part of the curriculum involves mastery of 60-70 English syllables, which are used to represent about 200 English multisyllabic words. The curriculum has five stages, associated with the five stages described in the history of writing (see the curriculum outline in Figure 12-6). Basically, the time devoted to each stage is related to the difficulty of the concepts for kindergarteners or first graders. The materials for each section are designed so that they can be used and built upon in later sections. Physically the curriculum consists of a series of games, a pack of cards with syllable elements on them, a set of workbooks, and a set of graded readers. The curriculum proceeds through the following sequence.

Semasiography–Reading for Meaning through Pictures. Children are first exposed to the notion that meaning can be extracted from many kinds of visual displays and real objects. The teacher reads to them. They try to figure out the message in pictures that "tell a story." In doing this they experience both the ease and directness of semasiographies, and their limitations and ambiguities. They play communication games in which one player must convey information to others without speaking, using only paper and pencil or chalk and blackboard (Figure 12-6).

Logography–Reading Words Represented as Visual Symbols. Children are introduced to the idea that a row of visual symbols can track the words of a sentence. They play with cards showing pictures of objects, actions, or relations that correspond to English words. Teachers and pupils try to construct sentences with these cards (e.g., "man hit bee:" Figure 12-7) and discuss their meanings. At this point the child is "writing" as well as reading, constructing messages by placing cards in sequence. Neither the semasiographic nor the logographic section of the curriculum presented any significant learning problem for any population we studied, including inner-city kindergarteners.

Phoneticization–Representation of the Soundstream of Speech in Writing. Phoneticization is the first component of the program at which some difficulty may be experienced. Its purpose is to get the child to

3. The development of this curriculum would not have been possible without the participation of a number of dedicated students, research associates, and teachers. We would like to particularly acknowledge major contributions by Margaret Allen, Barbara Chaddock, Judy Buchanan, Muffy Siegel, and Beth Bressman for the early versions, and Ivy Kuhn and Muffy Siegel for the more recent versions. The more recent versions (1973-1975) have been supported by Curriculum Development Associates; Dr. Morton Botel provided valuable advice and Lisa Esser provided excellent artistic support. The early versions of the curriculum (1973 and before) were in part supported by NIH Grant MH 20041 to Lila Gleitman and NAF Grant GB 8013 to Paul Rozin.

CONCEPTUAL OUTLINE OF THE SYLLABARY CURRICULUM

	SEMASIOGRAPHY	LOGOGRAPHY	PHONETICIZATION	SYLLABARY	INTRODUCTION TO THE ALPHABET
DESCRIPTION	Reading for meaning through pictures	Mapping between spoken words and visual symbols	Focusing on sound rather than meaning by developing awareness of sound segmentation	Constructing and segmenting meaningful words and sentences in terms of syllables	Segmenting and blending initial consonant sounds
ACTIVITIES	Interpretation of pictures	Reading material of the form: bee, hit, can, pen, in, hand	"Speaking slowly" game; Nonsense noise game: goo la la goo; Rebus homonyms: man can saw can; Concrete blends: rainbow	Basic blends of meaningful syllables: sand witch = sandwich; Addition of meaningless syllables (e.g., terminal y, er, ing): long|er; Partial fading of segmentation cues: be•ing	Blends using initial consonant sounds: s•ing; s•and

Fig. 12-6. Conceptual outline of the syllabary curriculum. (After Rozin & Gleitman, 1974, 1977b.)

attend to the soundstream of speech and to become aware that speech can be divided into segments that can be represented visually. Awareness of segmentation is encouraged in a "speaking slowly" game, in which the teacher and later the children pronounce familiar polysyllabic words with explicit breaks at syllable boundaries (e.g., "ti-ger"). The listener is to guess the word by "blending" the syllables back together. A "nonsense noise" game introduces the idea that any sound can be represented visually. Children invent noises and a nonsense figure is assigned by mutual consent to each noise. The figures are then written out in rows on the blackboard and read off in quick sequence, leading to an entertaining symphony of noises (Figure 12-6). Not surprisingly, while syllable blending and segmentation require some drill for some learners, the nonsense sequences are extremely easy to read.

From this point on, the curriculum is pervaded by attention to the sounds of speech and to the manipulation of these sounds or the syllable cards representing them. Syllable element cards (Figure 12-7) serve as a substitute for writing. Through all but the first stage (semasiography), the cards are constantly used to construct sentences.

We next introduce the rebus, which involves using homographs (same writing) for homonyms (same sounds). For example, the *can* card (meaning and picturing a tin can), in Figure 12-6, introduced during the logographic section of the curriculum, is now also used to represent the auxiliary verb *can* (e.g., "man can saw can")." This conceptual leap seems to require little or

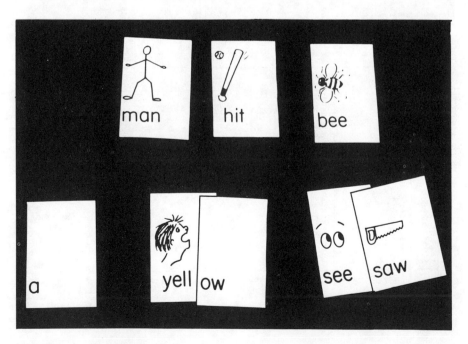

Fig. 12-7. Syllable cards in use.

no explicit teaching; children grasp it almost immediately and often read rebus sentences without even commenting on it (Gleitman & Rozin, 1973b). The rebus represents the child's first explicit clue that orthography maps sound and does not map meaning directly.

The pictorial representation on the cards serves several purposes. First, if a picture of a can represents both the meaning referred to by the picture and also the meaningfully unrelated auxiliary verb, then it is the sound, not the meaning, of these two words that links them orthographically. This is essential for reading any soundstream-oriented script. Second, the pictorial hint is a useful mnemonic for acquiring the English orthographic form printed directly below it. Third, the pictorial representation of word meanings makes reading sentences easy by speeding up the identification of individual items. This same pictorial approach to introducing reading has been used with some success in another program (The Peabody Rebus Reading Program by Woodcock, 1968; Woodcock, Clark, & Davies, 1968). The picture clue enables children to present to themselves, without teacher aid, the required paired associate (the sound suggested by the picture and the written form).

In this stage (and at the beginning of the syllabary stage), children also play a game in which they combine pictures representing one-syllable words (e.g., *sand* and *witch; rain* and *bow*) to make new words *sandwich; rainbow:* Figure 12-6). In these combinations the pictures are used for their sound value. There is no sand in *sandwich* (beach parties excepted).

Syllabary–Reading Syllable Sequences. We then extend this blending exercise by introducing more syllables written in English orthography and accompanied by a picture clue (Figures 12-6 to 12-8). In traditional programs blending is introduced at the phone level ("buh-a-tuh"), where it has least physical reality. Our aim is to get the blending concept across first in terms of the concrete, physically discrete, syllabic segments. Sixty to eighty syllables are taught, most with supplementary pictorial representations. Children learn to read these and then to combine them with previously learned elements to form new words and sentences, especially by manipulating syllable cards (Figure 12-7). Graded readers and workbooks support these activities (Figures 12-8 and 12-9). Most of the syllables introduced early have a word meaning (e.g., *man, bee*), while less concrete or meaningful syllables like *ing* and *er* are introduced later. Most of the meaningful syllables are written with a pictorial hint above them. The format is such that the pictures can be covered with a strip of paper while the English orthography is exposed. In this manner the reader can consult the pictures only when necessary (Figures 12-7 to 12-9). Some of the pictorial hints are rather abstract, such as ▣ for *side* (Figure 12-8). (In some versions of the program, the pictorial hints were gradually faded out a few at a time at later stages of training. Specific exercises in matching pictorial hints with the corresponding word were provided.) The convention for blending (i.e., for representing bisyllabic words) is continuity of the pair of syllable cards (Figure

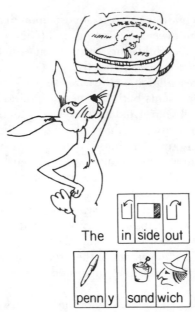

The | in | side | out

penn | y | sand | wich

Fig. 12-8. A page from one of the first books of the syllabary curriculum, corresponding to the early part of the syllabary stage. (From Rozin & Gleitman, . . . 1974.)

12-7), or, on the printed page, immediately adjoined boxes (Figure 12-8).
Later in training, a less obtrusive "dot" replaces the boxed syllables (Figure
12-9). Enough material is provided in the syllabary stage to produce rather
fluent handling of this type of material. There is enough vocabulary so that
engaging books can be written using only the prescribed syllable elements
(Figure 12-9).

   Alphabet. The introduction of alphabetic concepts actually begins
during the syllabary stage. Included among the later syllabary elements are
two syllables (*er*, as in runner; *le* as in *little*) that lose their syllabic integrity
in some words, becoming more like single phonemes (e.g., *beer* and *whale*).
We also introduce into the syllabary some common spelling patterns and
word families (e.g., *and, hand, sand*).

   Our belief that phonemic segmentation is a critical stumbling block in
early reading acquisition led us to approach the alphabet through a series of
approximations. We introduced initial *s* as the first letter, because *s* is a
relatively context insensitive phoneme that can be pronounced rather well in
isolation and is relatively easy to blend (Brown, D. L., 1971). It is introduced
as an initial sound blended onto already learned syllables (e.g., *it, am*; Figure 12-6), and is used in games, exercises, and story books. Thus we begin
with an easy blend and incorporate it immediately into a meaningful text. All
the other material in the text was previously learned. The most recent
curriculum stops with initial *s*. The 1973-1974 curriculum continued through
initial *f, r* and *b*, and terminal *s*.

"Sill•y   Mon•go,   a   key   will

not   o•pen   the   sand ,   and   no

litt•le   sea•le   is   in•side ."

Fig. 12-9. A page from an intermediate level reader in the syllabary curriculum. Segmentation cues have shifted from boxes to dots. The page also illustrates the rebus fading procedure. The word *sand* was originally introduced with a pictorial hint, which has been eliminated by this stage. (From Rozin & Gleitman, 1974.)

DECISIONS IN SHAPING A CURRICULUM: SOME FUNCTIONAL CONSIDERATIONS

The general conception of the curriculum hardly constrains the form it might take. We faced hundreds of decisions as to format or content and could not possibly test all alternatives. Rather, we relied on common sense, our experience, and the experience of the colleagues, students, and teachers associated with this project. Some possibilities were checked out in quick tryouts in the classroom; others were incorporated in the curriculum for 1 yr and then dropped in the next version.

Experience in the classroom led to our decision to devote most curricular material and teaching time to mastery of a syllabary. We felt that these concepts were of particular importance and of significant difficulty. We also felt that the syllabary would serve the reader well as a base for learning the alphabet. We limited the alphabet section because a great many adequately or imaginatively designed curricula begin at this level. Our major goal was to introduce the alphabetic insight.

We felt that it was particularly important for children to become actively engaged in the reading process, and for this reason, introduced the syllabary cards. Writing with the rebuses would have been difficult. But furthermore, writing is often painfully slow at this age and we did not wish it to interfere with progress in reading. The syllable cards represent a compromise on this point.

The rebus representation is the most salient feature of the curriculum. We used it from the first because of its historical validity and its mnemonic value. It has lived up to all expectations. Words with rebus pictures were learned much more rapidly than others; the rebus representations allowed the children to read for meaning very early in the curriculum. Words like *get* and *the*, presented without pictures (about two thirds of the elements are pictured), were not well learned by many children. For many, mastery of such words was the limiting factor on their progress in the curriculum. They could blend syllables well, but stumbled over these words. We found, somewhat to our surprise, that even picture aids with rather abstract relation to their referents (e.g., ☐ for SIDE or ⟷ for LONG) had mnemonic value, and thus facilitated learning. This must be due, in large part, to the greater visual distinctiveness and coherence of these representations (Brooks, L., 1977), and possibly also to some semantic-iconic resemblance between symbol and meaning in some cases.

We relied on rebus aids with some hesitation. We saw their motivational value, but also realized that they might deflect attention from the letter sequences that would have to be learned eventually and that might serve as clues to deciphering alphabetic writing. For example, by attending only to the rebuses, a child might not notice the fundamental relation between *sand* and *hand* in the orthography. For these reasons, in the 1973-1974 version of the curriculum we introduced specific matching exercises in which the child learned to associate the English orthographic form of a word with its rebus. This was done for 30 of the 51 pictured items. Eventually, for these 30, the pictures were dropped out of the printed material (Figure 12-9). We used a multiple-choice test to evaluate word-recognition skills of children in seven first-grade inner-city classes who had used the curriculum during the school year (Figure 12-10A). They scored 82% correct (25% was chance) on the faded-out items. We included a few test items for rebus elements that were not faded-out or drilled in class. Surprisingly children did rather well on these too (63% correct), suggesting incidental learning and encouraging us to eliminate the drills in later versions of the curriculum.

In general given the basic orientation of the curriculum, we opted for versions and approaches that would minimize memory load and encourage reading of print for meaning, so that motivation for reading would remain high. Our selection of syllables was strongly influenced by functional consid-

Fig. 12-10. Sample items from the test of competence with the syllabic components of the "syllabary" curriculum. Items of type A test recognition of the meaning of a particular syllable. The child's task is to select the pictorial hint that has actually been used with the syllable in the curriculum. Children must select one of the four choices, all of which are pictorial representations used in the syllabary. Items of type B test for the ability to recognize syllable blends already taught in the curriculum. Note that the negative choices were made as difficult as possible: one shares a common first syllable with the target word *(bull)* and another shares a common last syllable *(et)*. The items of type C test the ability to read blends involving a new syllable element. Because the new element *(crack,* in this example) was taught just a moment before this item was presented, we can be confident that the child had not encountered *cracker* before. Again the incorrect choices have some phonological resemblance to *cracker.*

erations. We selected as many elements as possible that could be represented with rebuses, and also introduced elements (e.g., *the, it*) that would be useful in writing sentences and stories. Structural considerations entered too, however. We introduced syllables that would combine with others in many ways (e.g., *long* in *longer, along, belong*) and would represent basic English spelling patterns and rhymes *(hand, sand; can, man; up, pup)*. In short, curriculum development involved close interaction of structural (cognitive) and functional (motivational) considerations, with a lot of guessing and common sense to estimate the effects of the great variety of alternatives.

Evaluation

Syllabary has been used for 4 yr in a wide range of regular kindergarten and first-grade classrooms, in both the inner city and suburbs. This sample included two inner-city classrooms with a particularly poor prognosis for reading success. They were the bottom two of six first-grade classes in a school where the entire third grade scored at the twenty-fourth percentile on national reading achievement tests. Syllabary was used as the only first-year reading curriculum in about 20 classes over the 4-yr period and was taught entirely by the regular classroom teachers. Teacher evaluation of the curriculum has varied from dedicated enthusiasm to slight negativity.

The general results of the classroom trials are that virtually all children readily learn to read semasiographies and logographies and learn the idea of phoneticization. Some skill at reading the syllabary was achieved by all children and fluency by most, so that most children could successfully read a new two-syllable word (Figure 12-10c). Even the lowest class showed progress on this point. Many children moved smoothly to the alphabetic stage and ultimately into more traditional curricula. Quite a few of the children with the poorest prognosis for reading success, however, experienced a great deal of trouble with alphabetic concepts. Students in all classes, including the two lowest, showed a capability to blend an initial consonant sound onto a known syllable (e.g., $r + ing$) even when they encountered a particular blend for the first time, but some students in the slowest classes could not do this well. Completion of the curriculum took a few weeks to a full school year, depending primarily on the general reading readiness of the classes at the beginning of the first grade. The lowest two classes did not advance to the alphabetic stage in the curriculum in the first year, even though some of the students showed some ability with alphabetic blending by the end of the year (see Rozin and Gleitman, 1977a, for more details).

A "controlled" evaluation of the curriculum was carried out in 1973-1974, with seven inner-city first-grade Syllabary classes and 10 comparable control classes exposed to traditional soundstream-oriented reading curricula.[4] At the end of the year, there was no difference between pairs of children from these groups, matched for reading readiness at the beginning of the year, on standard reading achievement tests administered by the school system. This can be taken as an encouraging result, because control children were explicitly taught the types of material on these tests whereas syllabary children spent little or, in some cases, virtually no time on the alphabetic skills tested.

Although the major impetus for the syllabary curriculum was structural, the main effects may have been functional. Children rapidly get to the point where they can read simple books. This results in high motivation to read. Children frequently took the books home, and often read syllabary materials in class outside of the formal reading lesson. Most teachers felt that the curriculum produced children who liked to read. Thus, at a minimum, chil-

4. We thank many members of the school systems of Philadelphia and Lower Merion Township, from district superintendents to principals and teachers, for their cooperation in making the development and testing of this curriculum possible.

dren who pass through *Syllabary* have learned all the basic concepts of reading but one, and have a positive attitude toward reading.

At this point, the best argument in favor of syllabary instruction is based on common sense rather than data from evaluation. We are convinced of the soundness of the structure of our approach, but are far from certain that we have found the right vehicle for realizing the concepts and skills we wish to teach. Perhaps it would be better to teach segmentation in a purely auditory way, without the mediation of visual symbols (Elkonin, 1973; Rosner, 1972, 1974; Rosner & Simon, 1971). Rosner (1972, 1974) had some success in teaching phonological segmentation by beginning with segmentation of noises (e.g., a series of claps) and other concrete elements, and then moving gradually to more difficult units, from words to syllables to phonemes. His approach differs from ours in that it deals with speech segmentation without written representations, but shares with Syllabary the approach to the problem through successive approximation, moving from concrete to abstract.

In summary the most clear-cut result of the use of Syllabary is to confirm the analysis made earlier in this chapter. Of all the concepts involved in early reading acquisition, the alphabetic principle is by far the most difficult to learn and teach.

CONCLUSIONS

We attempted to address directly the problem of teaching initial reading skills. We discovered that to define what should be taught we had to perform a structural analysis of reading. This indicated that information exists about many levels of language in English writing and that the adult reader appropriately deals with print at many levels. We argued that alphabetic processes, including letter recognition and direct or indirect use of phonological segmentation principles, are fundamental to adult reading. We claimed that adult word perception and reading are based in large part on something like a speeded up and highly automatized version of what young children do when they sound out words, except that orthographic rules dealing with letter strings may replace the phonological ("sounding-out") rules on which they were originally based. Analysis of the preliterate child and young reader suggests that basic alphabetic skills are what must be taught. These skills are rarely acquired spontaneously and are of essential importance for progress in reading. They have enormous mnemonic value in allowing the child to bring his extensive knowledge of words in speech to bear on the reading task. We find all of these conclusions comforting, because they show that thousands of years of the evolution of writing have not been in vain. This evolution has been a steady movement toward greater representation of the sounds of speech and toward the use of more and more molecular units, culminating in the alphabet.

Actually, most of what is needed to be a fluent reader is already possessed by the preliterate child. Adult reading is a fascinating blend of the *natural* ability to decode and encode speech and comprehend language, and the *natural* ability to look at the world and construct a useful model of it. The wedding of these two natural capacities requires the alphabetic insight. Until the mapping from speech into writing is appreciated and fluency is obtained with it, the essential form of visual-information representation in our writing system cannot be properly used.

We claim that this is the critical step in early reading acquisition, and that it is an extremely difficult step to take. It involves an understanding that speech can be segmented into phonemiç units that correspond to alphabetic units. This is not true of the speech sounds themselves, but only of their underlying representation in the head. The problem for aspiring readers is to develop awareness of how their own auditory system and "language brain" segments speech. Even though preliterate children already know about phonological segmentation at the level of speech, it is very difficult for them to gain access to this knowledge. We suggest that this may be a type of learning different from the types described in the psychology of learning. Our assertion is that the fundamental problem in alphabetic acquisition is phonological and is not in itself necessarily related to the writing system. The big problem is in realizing that the spoken word "car" has three sounds. This awareness of phonemic segmentation makes understanding the alphabet not as easy as ABC.

The structural analysis of reading leads to the design of a curriculum in which the concepts necessary for alphabetic understanding are arrayed in a cognitively and historically valid sequence. We believe that structural analysis is prerequisite to a sensible approach to reading instruction, but that it must be combined with functional considerations to result in effective teaching. This is especially true because we do not know how to teach the alphabetic principle, but we do know that extensive exposure to the sounds and segmentation of speech, and their relation to written words, works in most cases. Because "practice makes perfect" remains as one of the most certain laws of learning, we need both the structural knowledge to suggest what to practice and functional principles to guarantee that it will be practiced.

Our own curricular attempts confirm the importance of combined structural and functional approaches and the particular difficulty of attaining the last stage in the history of writing: the mapping between the letters of the alphabet and phonemes. We still do not know how to teach this mapping. We wish that our society would not impose such a tight schedule on progress in reading, since some maturational processes may be involved in gaining access to phonology. There is nothing more tragic than a young child who has been "turned off" from a natural interest in reading because of frustration in the early stages of decoding. The important issue is that reading be reasonably well mastered by the time of young adulthood and it does not really matter whether this happens at five, eight, or even twelve.

There is neither a well worked-out theoretical model to account for the alphabetic insight nor a universally effective method for teaching it. A type of learning may be involved that has not been explored yet in basic research. We can only be thankful that millions of little children learn to use the alphabet every year. It remains a mystery.

ROBERT E. SILVERMAN

Chapter 13

Programmed Instruction

The publication of B. F. Skinner's "The Science of Learning and the Art of Teaching" (1954) and "Teaching Machines" (1958) heralded the beginning of a new era in psychology's relation to education. The psychology of learning seemed at last about to have an increased impact on educational practices. The idea of teaching machines and the concept of programmed instruction generated considerable enthusiam and equal controversy. What began as a proposal took on the trappings of a movement, and some felt we were on the threshold of a revolution in education.

Programmed instruction refers to a wide variety of systems and materials, but in its early period of development was defined by four features: (1) The instructional material requires the learner to be an active participant. The material ensures that the student reads carefully and responds to questions within the program. (2) The student is informed with minimal delay whether a response is correct or incorrect. (3) The student proceeds at his or her own pace. (4) The material is revised until all properly qualified students can reach the stated objectives of the program.

From its early promise to its present status within psychology and education, programmed instruction has found itself on the obstacle-strewn path of educational innovation. It has been oversold, misunderstood, trivialized, and poorly developed. It is all things to all observers, and like many new ideas in education it has been relegated to the status of "tool." But it is alive, and it still retains some of its initial promise if not its vigor.

A BRIEF HISTORY OF PROGRAMMED INSTRUCTION

The recent history of programmed instruction began with Skinner's 1954 and 1958 papers, but many observers mark the early papers of Sidney

L. Pressey (1926, 1927) as the origin of the teaching-machine idea and as a forerunner of programmed instruction. Pressey's initial interest was in creating a labor-saving device to administer and score multiple-choice examinations. He built a simple apparatus that enabled a student to read a question presented in an aperture and then to select an answer from among four alternatives by pressing a key. If the student was correct, a new question appeared; if wrong, the original question remained in view. In the course of experimenting with his machine, Pressey found that it aided learning.

Encouraged by his initial experience with his device, Pressey went on to examine its possible benefits in light of what was known about learning. In 1927 he wrote:

. . . the law of recency operates to establish the correct answer in the mind of the learner, since always the last answer chosen is the right answer. The correct response must almost inevitably be the most frequent, since the correct response is the only response by which the learner can go on to the next question; and since whenever a wrong response is made, it must be compensated for by a further correct reaction. The "law of exercise" is thus automatically made to function to establish the right response. Since the learner can progress only by making the right reaction, is penalized every time he makes a wrong answer by being required to answer the question one more time and is rewarded for two consecutive right reponses by the elimination of that question, the "law of effect" is constantly operating to further learning [p. 551].

Pressey's work did not cause much stir in either psychology or education. Perhaps the zeitgeist was not right, because at that time there was little or no ferment about the need to modify educational practice. The lack of any sustained interest in Pressey's device was probably also due to the absence of an established system of learning and fundamental data. Pressey's reference to the laws of recency, exercise, and effect did not constitute a basis for the emergence of a technology. The laws themselves did not represent a paradigm that could support or stimulate a program of research and application.

No real movement toward an applied science of instruction began until the publication of Skinner's 1954 and 1958 papers. Reasoning from his successful applications of operant conditioning in the laboratory, Skinner outlined how a mechanical device could be used to present academic subject matter and also control response-reinforcement contingencies. Skinner's devices differed from Pressey's; the Skinner machines had students emitting responses rather than choosing among multiple-choice alternatives. The response was followed by the presentation of the correct response, with confirmation serving as a reinforcer. Some of the Skinner devices were designed so that the student could not proceed to the next item until the correct response was made to the item at hand.

The most important difference between Pressey's machine and Skinner's was Skinner's emphasis on programming. In his 1958 paper Skinner stated:

The success of such a machine depends on the material used in it. The task of programming a given subject is at first sight rather formidable. Many helpful techniques can be derived from a general analysis of the relevant behavioral processes, verbal and non-verbal. Specific forms of behavior are to be evoked and, through differential reinforcement, brought under the control of specific stimuli [p. 140].

Skinner's attention to the task of programming shifted emphasis from devices as such to the material to be taught. Machines were useful in presenting material in a controlled sequence and in confirming responses, but it became obvious that these functions could be accomplished by means of books. Glaser, Homme, and Evans (1959) designed a "programmed textbook" as a means of presenting programs. Machines became less popular and questions about how to present programs were replaced by questions about systems of programming.

Skinner advocated a system of programming ostensibly based on the operant-conditioning paradigm. The emphasis is on reinforcing successive approximations to the correct response. The student proceeds step by step through a sequence designed to maximize the probability of a correct response in the presence of the appropriate stimuli. Each step is designed with the specific objectives of the program in mind. The precise specification of objectives is an important feature of programming based on the operant paradigm. Even more crucial is the analysis of the specific behavior required to reach the objectives. The programmer must decide what responses are relevant and what responses are most important. The responses determine what will be learned, and getting the correct responses to occur is a fundamental problem in such programming.

In the early days of programmed instruction, Norman Crowder (1959) proposed a system of "intrinsic programming" that was less response oriented then Skinner's approach. Crowder's model was the tutor-student system in which the program (book or device) presents information, requires answers to questions based on the information, and provides feedback based on the student's answers. If the answer is correct, the program allows the student to move on to the next item; if incorrect, the student is required to go back to a review sequence or on into a remedial branch.

Crowder's technique, often referred to as the branching method, led to the publication of the so-called scrambled books. In such books the student reads some material, usually a page or less in length, and then answers a multiple-choice question. The student makes a choice and is then directed to a page depending on the choice. If the choice is correct, the next item tells the student so and presents new information. If the choice is incorrect, the item tells that he or she is wrong and usually tells why. The student then returns to the original item or in some cases may continue for a few items in a remedial sequence. Crowder's orientation (1962) is, in part, described as follows:

Intrinsic programming assumes that the basic learning takes place during the student's exposure to the new material. The multiple-choice question is asked to find out whether the student has learned; it is not necessarily regarded as playing an active part in the primary learning process. The view of the learning process itself is essentially naturalistic, or, if you will, naive. We do not pretend to know in any very useful detail exactly why students are able to learn from exposure to symbolic material, but we postulate with great confidence that such learning does occur [p. 8].

Another approach to programming, originated by T. F. Gilbert (1962), evolved from a modification of Skinner's position. Gilbert advocated making use of the largest feasible response units that result in a discriminable environmental effect. His method, called "mathetics," entailed an analysis of the student's "operant span," the largest set of responses within the subject matter that the student can manage at one time. He asserts that one should not fractionate subject matter "into steps that make no sense [Gilbert, 1962]." Sequences should be constructed that enable the student to make as comprehensive a class of responses as possible. In learning the classical conditioning paradigm, for example, the student may be required to learn the functions and roles of the unconditioned stimulus, unconditioned response, conditioned stimulus, and conditioned response at one time rather than as separate responses.

According to Gilbert, the matheticist seeks to identify the minimum number of stimulus-response units and also to find possible sources of interfering stimuli. A lesson plan involves preparing a set of procedures for teaching each link in the chain of responses that lead to mastery of the material. Lesson plans are constructed so that the student proceeds from the last response in the chain to the first, a procedure sometimes referred to as backward chaining. In this way the student makes the terminal or goal response each time a unit of the chain is learned. The lesson plan is implemented by demonstrating each response to the student, then prompting the responses and then providing an opportunity for the response without benefit of the prompts.

THE VARIOUS POSITIONS

The history of programmed instruction reflects a potpourri of influences and interests. Laboratory scientists and educational practitioners have had a hand in its development, and within each group there has been a wide range of attitudes and approaches. However, four categories or sources of influence can be identified. Of these four, two involve behavioral psychology, one is derived from research in training methods, and one stems from cognitive psychology. The two behavioral positions emphasize either the principle of reinforcement or the classical conditioning or contiguity paradigm. A third position, the tutor-student model, is based on the view that the teaching-learning relation is essentially a process of communication. The fourth position, represented by cognitive psychology, concerns itself with perceptual processes and their role in learning.

The Behavioral Position: Reinforcement

The behavioral position is, in general, response oriented. The basic principle is that the learner's responses determine what is learned. Learning depends on what the learner does. The emphasis is on the responses that the student makes in the presence of instructional material rather than on the information contained in the material. It is not assumed that exposure to the material will ensure that it will be learned (Skinner, 1961). Although the behavioral position is response centered, it does not ignore stimulus variables. Its main concern is in seeing that the appropriate responses occur in the presence of the appropriate stimuli.

The behavioral reinforcement paradigm represents learning in terms of the changes in response rate or response probability that occur when reinforcement is contingent upon the emission of particular responses. Holland (1960) described this position succinctly in stating, "Behavior is learned only when it is emitted and reinforced." The basic units of analysis are responses, reinforcers, and stimuli.

In applying the behavioral reinforcement paradigm to the construction of programs, the material is arranged to ensure that the appropriate responses are emitted in the presence of the proper stimuli and that such responses are reinforced. The responses to be learned must first be identified, and then provision must be made to see that the responses are emitted. According to Markle (1969), there are three basic principles:

1. For learning to occur, the learner must make the responses to be learned. The student learns what the program leads him to do.
2. Incorrect responses or errors should be minimized. The program should control the learner's behavior; if the learner makes errors, the program is at fault.
3. Immediate knowledge of the correctness of a response serves to maintain that response. In other words confirmation is reinforcing.

These principles require additional discussion because controversy surrounds the application of each case to programmed instruction.

The Principle of Responding. In dealing with the principle of responding, overt and covert responses must be distinguished. Because learning does occur in the absence of overt responses, it would be naive to limit the concept of responding to overt responses only. Programmers quickly recognize, however, that observable responses are easier to teach, because their progress can be monitored.

The problem of how to deal with covert responses tends to be treated pragmatically. Programmers who adopt the reinforcement position try to arrange the conditions of learning and the materials to be learned so that the learner's overt responses are relevant to the specific objectives. By having the learner use Ohm's law, for example, a programmer can show that learning is occurring. The learner may be making many covert responses at or before the moment he writes $E = IR$, but his writing the formula stands as a relevant response in its own right.

The entire question of overt responding has been the subject of considerable research (Tobias, 1973). The results of this research, however, are at best equivocal. Some early studies reviewed by Anderson (1967) indicated that programs requiring overt responses did not lead to more learning than those that did not require them. Holland (1967; Holland & Kemp, 1965; Kemp & Holland, 1966) sought to reconcile his results with the position that overt responding is important. He used a "blackout ratio" to rate the quality of programs in which overt responding was not more effective than no overt responding. The blackout ratio is the proportion of words in the program that can be deleted without increasing the percentage of student errors within a program. A high blackout ratio indicates, according to Holland, that the program may contain much nonprogrammed material. If the student can answer correctly without having to read a large proportion of the material (the blacked-out material), then his answers do not depend on that material. Such programs, according to Kemp and Holland (1966), contain too many overprompted items. An example of "blacked-out" material is shown in Figure 13-1.

Kemp and Holland (1966) reported that, among the programs they

Normal Frames	**Blacked Out Frames**
22. A B - - - of Exchange (Draft) is convenient for the payment of debts.	22. A B - - - of Exchange (Draft)■
23. The seller of merchandise by sending a Bill of E - - - - - - - drawn on the buyer and attaching the shipping documents to a bank for collection can be assured that the merchandise will not be delivered to the buyer until the buyer pays for it.	23. Bill of E - - - - - - -

Fig. 13-1. A sample of two "blacked-out" frames. The B_____ represents a formal prompt for the word bill and the E_____ a formal prompt for the word exchange. (From Holland & Kemp, 1965, p. 268.)

examined, those that did not favor overt responding had higher blackout ratios than those favoring overt responding. According to their analysis, excessive prompting seen in the high blackout ratios tends to minimize the benefits of programming and of overt responding. In such programs, many of the responses may be trivial and thus not require overt responding.

The blackout ratio suggests a method for analyzing and comparing programs, but the technique lacks sufficient precision to support the assertions of Holland and his associates. A very wordy program may have a high blackout ratio but still be relatively free of excessive prompting or trivial responses. Wordiness alone does not mean a program is excessively prompted. Furthermore, Kemp and Holland's contention about the relation between blackout ratios and overt responding needs support with data on the effects of blacking out material on achievement. Holland (1967) provided some indirect support in a retrospective analysis of some of his earlier research. He reported that a program containing irrelevant responses yielded poorer posttest performance than the same program containing only relevant responses. Karis, Kent, and Gilbert (1970) found, however, that adding irrelevant material had no significant effect on either program errors or retention-test performance. They also found no evidence of an interaction involving response mode (overt versus covert) and the amount of irrelevant content.

Tobias (1969, 1973; Tobias & Abramson, 1971) examined the relation between the familiarity of material to be learned and the effects of overt responding. He reported that when the material to be learned is unfamiliar, programs requiring overt responses of the constructed type generally produce higher learning scores than programs requiring multiple-choice responses or no overt responses. He suggested that the responses for familiar material may already be in the student's repertoire and, unlike unfamiliar material, the student does not need to make the responses to learn them. When new responses are required, overt responding may be needed. Tobias's analysis resembles that of Lumsdaine and May (1965), who predicted that overt responding "will be especially important where response learning is required rather than merely association between a new stimulus and an already learned response."

   Errors. That programs should minimize student errors stems from the principle that the learner's responses determine what is learned. If the student makes an incorrect response, that response may be learned. Even reading the wrong choice in a multiple-choice question can have undesirable effects. Skinner (1961) argues, "Neither the vigorous correction of wrong choices nor the confirmation of the right choice will free the student of the verbal and non-verbal associations generated by reading the wrong items [p. 63]."

   The error issue is part of the folklore of education, and discussions about the role of errors are often accompanied by anecdotal evidence and interpretation-laden conclusions. Crowder (1961), for example, argued, ". . . I have never been an advocate of questions so easy that the learner rarely, if ever, makes an error . . . and I think experience is accumulating that shows that if the questions asked are too easy, the student loses motivation after a while [p. 25]."

Pressey (1963b) took a similar position when he stated, "The writer has seen no satisfactory evidence that any unfortunate results follow from a wrong choice in an autoinstructional item dealing with meaningful matter, if the wrong is at once shown to be wrong and the right to be correct. Instead, the presence of wrong choices can clarify meanings [p. 6]."

Elovson (1971) provides some data supporting the view that errors do not necessarily impair learning. Using a paired-associate task, she found that errors only tend to be repeated if the error does not lead to information about the correct response. Errors followed by information about the correct response resulted in as many or more correct responses on subsequent trials as did reward or confirmation.

Some data, however, suggest that the principle of minimal errors is correct. Kaess and Zeaman (1960), using a punchboard device of Pressey's, found that the opportunity to make errors in multiple-choice items was positively correlated with the persistence of errors. Subjects who learned a list of 30 psychological terms in a series of trials in which the items on the first trial consisted of two or more choices made more errors on subsequent trials than did those whose first trial consisted of only one choice (the correct one). The opportunity to make errors increased the probability that the errors would be repeated. These results conflict with Elovson's, but the Elovson study emphasized that errors do not persist if corrective information follows upon them.

Silverman and Summers (1964) found that learning binary arithmetic was more efficient with a low-error program than with a high-error program. The efficiency score consisted of achievement divided by time to complete the program. This study also examined the relation between the possible motivating effect of errors and the effect of confirmation. No evidence was found to support the position espoused by Pressey (1964) that errors increase motivation and thus make confirmation more reinforcing.

O'Day (1971) found that learner errors in programmed instruction are negatively correlated with achievement test scores. In a program requiring overt responses, the correlation between errors during the program and achievement test scores was $-.77$ ($N = 112$); for a program of the Pressey type (1963b, 1964), the correlation was $-.69$. The lowest correlations between errors and test scores were for programs administered with machine-presented feedback. The correlations ranged from $-.51$ to $-.32$.

The Role of Confirmation. The function of confirmation is interpreted in two ways. One view emphasizes the information provided by confirmation, and the other sees confirmation as a form of positive reinforcement that increases the probability of responses leading to it. The reinforcement view tends also to expand the possible range of events that may reinforce. Cook and Mechner (1961), for example, suggested that allowing the learner to advance to the next frame may be used as a reinforcer. Silberman (1965) suggested that deriving meaning from interesting test material is probably reinforcing. Berman (1967) used a point system as a form of reinforcement, with the points having monetary value. A learner earns points by completing a unit in an allotted time and/or by making no more than a predefined number of errors. And, of course, there are a wide variety of other possible reinforcers, such as those used in traditional educational practice.

The role of confirmation as a reinforcer is controversial, because the data do not clearly show that confirmation is either necessary or effective. Krumboltz and Weisman (1962) found that a nonconfirmation group learned as well as a group receiving continuous confirmation; O.K. Moore (1962) reported that student achievement in a programmed learning task was not significantly affected by response confirmation; and Ripple (1962) found no support for the view that response confirmation improves learning in a programmed lesson. More recently, O'Day (1971) also reported that response confirmation does not seem to contribute much to programmed learning.

Studies such as those cited, however, are difficult to interpret because they do not control the behavior of peeking. Little or no attempt is made to ensure that students cannot peek at the correct response before they make their own response. In the absence of such controls, meaningful comparisons between confirmation and nonconfirmation cannot be made. In one study that controlled peeking Anderson, Kulhavy, and Andre (1971) found that confirmation did assist programmed learning. Students who responded and then received confirmation learned more than those who received no confirmation or those who could peek at the correct response before they responded. A second study by the same authors (1972), however, failed to find a significant advantage for confirmation over no confirmation. Karis, et al. (1970) also controlled peeking and failed to find any evidence to support confirmation.

Another difficulty in interpreting the confirmation studies comes from the lack of information about possible implicit confirmation provided by the sequential development of the material. In carefully sequenced material it is often possible for the learner to confirm his previous responses by reading the items that follow. In a good program the sequence of frames can be a source of confirmation because the learner recognizes that his response is correct when he finds the meaning in frame 2 as a consequence of his having read and correctly answered frame 1. The learner's response to frame 2 is confirmed in his reading of frame 3, etc.

One programmer has skillfully capitalized on the sequential development of programs by using an approach he calls "conversational chaining" (Barlow, 1960). With this technique, the answer to each frame is embedded in the frame that follows. An example of this system is shown in Figure 13-2.

If confirmation is regarded as a form of reinforcement, what happens when confirmation is provided intermittently, as if on a partial reinforcement

B.F. Skinner calls the kind of responses that operate upon a situation as well as respond to the situation (38) _____ (operants or respondents, which would you guess?).

Operants operate upon a situation and sometimes seem to be uncaused—that is, they do not seem to be elicited by any specific (39)_____

Operants sometimes do not seem to be elicited by any specific stimulus. Operants appear to be emitted (meaning "sent out") by the (40)_____ himself.

Fig. 13-2. An example of "conversational chaining" (From Barlow, 1968, pp. 55-56.)

schedule? Krumboltz and Keisler (1965) considered the question and concluded that it may not be appropriate to speak of partial reinforcement in connection with programmed instruction. They point out that all the sources of reinforcement cannot be controlled, especially in using "complex cognitive material with accomplished students." In other words, the intermittency of confirmation per se does not guarantee that the student is not getting continuous confirmation within the materials by means of the sequence or other cues. Krumboltz and Keisler did attempt, however, to see if some regularities might emerge under different schedules of confirmation. Their initial results showed some relation between errors on an immediate posttest and what they refer to as the "degree of reinforcement." Students whose correct responses were confirmed continuously did slightly better (fewer errors) than those who received confirmation on every fifth frame or every tenth frame. But a second posttest 2 months later showed no differences among the various conditions.

The cited studies dealing with the role of confirmation confound the information aspect of confirmation with its reinforcing properties. It is difficult to separate the two functions; and if one accepts the information-hypothesis view of conditioned reinforcement (D'Amato, 1974), the two functions should be regarded as inseparable. The information hypothesis is based on the position that a conditioned reinforcer has acquired reinforcing properties because it has been associated with rewards following it. Being correct is a conditioned reinforcer, not because it was simply associated with rewards, but because it announces that rewards occur after correct responses have been made and confirmed as correct (Longstreth, 1971). The student does not continue to make correct responses because being correct has been paired with praise or tangible rewards. He makes correct responses because in finding they are correct he also learns to expect and receive rewards for being correct.

Although the information-hypothesis approach lacks firm empirical support, the research to date does not preclude further study (D'Amato, 1974); the hypothesis has potentially useful implications for programmers. If the hypothesis were supported, it would suggest that confirmation should lead to other, perhaps more tangible, rewards.

The Behavioral Position: S-R Contiguity

The stimulus-response contiguity position also emphasizes responses, but unlike the reinforcement position, it represents learning solely in terms of the association of stimuli and responses. Learning takes place when a stimulus and response occur together. As a result of this association, the stimulus is likely to elicit the response at another time (Guthrie, 1935). The basic units of analysis are stimulus, response, and association. Little use is made of the concept of reinforcement. Confirmation is regarded as a source of information, as a means of telling the learner what to do.

The contiguity position stresses the technique of getting responses to occur. To teach a learner something, you must arrange the conditions that elicit the appropriate responses. The emphasis is on identifying stimuli that will get out the desired responses. Lumsdaine (1962), a champion of the contiguity position, has stated:

Nevertheless, I am very much dissatisfied with reinforcement concepts as a guide to the instructional programmer; my dissatisfaction reflects in large part the fact that manipulation of reinforcement contingencies does not seem to be what even the most ardently Skinnerian programmers actually *do* when they start writing the frames of a program for an academic or technical subject. It is true that they try to select response patterns that they believe should be reinforced (in the sense of being strengthened or made more probable at least) and to get relevant responses elicited in an appropriate context. But I think that what preoccupies the programmer's attention—and I believe rightly so—is the manipulation of prompting cues, not the manipulation of reward schedules [p. 143].

Lumsdaine's analysis is not incompatible with the reinforcement position taken by Bushell (1973), who describes operant conditioning as a three-component operation involving prompting, responding, and reinforcing (see Chapter 15).

Lumsdaine (1962) cites three studies that support his emphasis on prompting. Using paired-associate learning, Cook and Kendler (1956) and Cook (1958) found that response prompting produced faster learning than did response confirmation. The prompting technique consisted of prompting the response member of the pair before the student had made a response. Angell and Lumsdaine (1961) found that in a paired-associates task "adequate prompting" can attenuate the effects of variations in confirmation. These paired-associates studies may not be directly applicable to programmed instruction, but O'Day (1971) provides some support for Lumsdaine's argument. O'Day found that in programmed learning prompting was more effective than confirmation, particularly in the early stages of learning.

Lumsdaine (1961) suggests that reinforcement may be essential in situations in which it is necessary to shape the desired response because the response cannot be readily elicited. As examples of difficult-to-elicit responses, he suggests the articulation of new phonemes in second-language learning, motor-coordination responses, and "various forms of socially important behavior." For much academic learning, however, the appropriate responses are readily elicited by guidance or demonstration. In such learning the major problem is one of establishing appropriate stimulus control. Appropriate stimulus control is established by a process of prompting and the gradual fading or vanishing of the prompts. The prompt elicits the response in association with the relevant stimuli. As the prompt is withdrawn (faded) the relevant stimuli take over the response-eliciting function.

The literature on prompting is extensive, although much of it is didactic rather than analytical. All of the "How To" books pay considerable attention to the art of prompting. Skinner (1958) helped set the stage for the practice. He also distinguished between priming and prompting (1968). A prime shows and/or tells the student what to do. For example, in teaching a youngster to print a letter, the teacher may prime by printing the letter and instructing the child to copy his printing. In subsequent trials the teacher may print only part of the letter and have the child complete the printing. The partial letter serves as a prompt, a supplementary or auxiliary stimulus that helps the student to make the correct response. A prompt differs from a prime in that a prompt makes the appropriate response more probable, but it does not guarantee its occurrence. A distinction is also made between formal prompts and thematic prompts. A formal prompt indicates the form of the response, such as the first letter of a word, number of letters, key letter, or sound. A thematic prompt makes use of the student's prior learning, his verbal habits and generalizations. The use of an analogy is a typical thematic prompt.

The difference between the reinforcement and contiguity positions is highlighted by Lumsdaine's assertion (1962):

The reason for the importance of the manipulation of cues is simply that for a very wide range of responses appropriate for academic subject matters we already have at the outset of a program sequence an adequate unconditional stimulus (UCS); that is, we have an adequate way to elicit most of the desired responses whenever required—for example, if need be, by simply having the learner copy any given verbal response. The problem is not to identify the right response or to get it to occur, but to attach it to the right stimulus context. This attachment is brought about by causing the response (through suitable prompting) to occur in the desired context and by subsequently vanishing out the prompts [pp. 138-139].

Skinner (1968) on the other hand, sees teaching as more than a system of eliciting certain responses in the presence of certain stimuli. He warns about the excessive use of primes and prompts:

Those who believe that a student learns mainly by executing behavior are often puzzled by techniques of prompting and vanishing prompts. If the student cannot respond, why should he not be given maximal help? . . . A distinction must be made between two kinds of help. The teacher helps the student respond on a given occasion and he helps him so that he will respond on similar occasions in the future. He must often give him the first kind of help, but he is teaching only when he gives him the second. Unfortunately the two are incompatible. To help a student learn, the teacher must so far as possible refrain from helping him respond [pp. 215-216].

Although the reinforcement and contiguity positions need not be regarded as in opposition, disagreement in emphasis is sufficient to suggest that their differences be explored further. Both positions agree that the learner must make appropriate responses, and both agree that the responses must be under appropriate stimulus control. But the contiguity position argues that techniques of informing the learner what to do and when and where to do it take precedence over the identification and manipulation of reinforcers. W. K. Estes (1972) suggests that in human learning it is useful to pay special attention to the information the learner receives about the probability of the response-reinforcement relations that obtain during learning. W. K. Estes (1972) argues:

. . . that in the case of a normal human learner a reward does not necessarily strengthen, nor a punishment weaken, the response which produces it. In order to predict the effects in either case we need to take account not only of the relation between the stimulus to which the individual responds and the reinforcing event which ensues but also of any other information available to the learner bearing upon the probability that the same relationship will prevail on future occasions [pp. 728-729].

The Tutor-Student Model

The tutor-student model in programmed instruction, associated with the "intrinsic" programming of Crowder (1959), is based on the idea of tutor and student interaction, in which each responds to the other. This model represents a different kind and level of analysis than is found in the behavioral models. The teaching-learning relation is seen as a process of communication. Learning takes place during the student's exposure to the material; questions are asked to determine whether the student understands what he has been exposed to; and remedial material is presented to deal with poorly understood material.

Crowder's method tries to include three essential features of the tutor-student situation: (1) the tutor presents new information to the student; (2) the student is required to use the information, usually by answering questions; (3) the tutor is responsive to the student, either providing new information if the student has been correct, or reviewing the original information, or introducing remedial information if the student has been incorrect. According to Walther and Crowder (1965), a properly designed question within a unit of information should serve to:

1. Determine whether the student has learned the material just presented;

2. Select appropriate corrective material if the student has not learned;

3. Provide desirable practice with the concept involved;

4. Keep the student actively working at the material, and

5. Presumably, if the student gets the question right, serve a desirable motivational purpose [p. 40].

The characteristic features of intrinsic programs come, in large part, from training situations. Such features do not pretend to have the same functions as principles derived from laboratory studies of learning. But Crowder and his co-workers attempt to bring into their system some principles from psychology. Walther and Crowder (1965) state:

Field theory is applied through the effective organization of the material, the step size, the level of difficulty of the questions, and the information provided on the wrong-answer pages. The individual's psychological field is increased only by relating new experience and new information through experiences, concepts, ideas and information already within the field. In intrinsic programming, this is done by moving from the familiar to the unfamiliar. At points where communication breaks down because the information is outside the student's psychological field, wrong-answer pages are provided which explain the concept in other terms that can be related to the student's past experience. As each step or concept is incorporated into the student's psychological field, the field becomes extended in this subject area. The program then capitalizes upon this expanded field to develop further expansion [p. 36].

They go on to consider the concept of closure:

Gestalt closure is achieved through skillful review and use of lesson tests. In various fields of endeavor, individuals successfully achieve both short range and intermediate goals. Achievement results, in a sense of completion known as closure. In intrinsic programming, the successful answer to a multiple-choice question provides an immediate and limited closure. Confirmation of the right answer accomplishes the same function in the frames of a linear program. However, an endless succession of immediate closures loses its effectiveness in learning situations. To combat this, periodic intermediate closures must also be provided; lesson review and testing can accomplish this end only when they are expertly prepared. A high failure rate on a test fails to achieve closure on the part of the student and a very easy test fails to maintain the student's level of aspiration [p. 37].

Pressey's "auto-elucidative" programming (Pressey & Kinzer, 1964) may be considered as an example of the tutor-student model. In this form of programming the student reads a segment of text and then responds to multiple-choice questions that provide immediate confirmation. If the learner's first response (choice) to a question is incorrect, he continues to respond until he is correct. Pressey and Kinzer claim that the technique is more effective than linear programs based on the stimulus-response position. O'Day (1971) failed, however, to find support for the auto-elucidative method. It turned out to be among the least effective procedures he studied.

The Cognitive Approach

Cognitive psychology concerns itself with the processes that intervene between stimulus and response. The approach views the learner as doing more than responding to stimuli; he is seen as processing incoming stimuli, with his responses being determined by the processing. For the cognitive psychologist, education is the process of reorganizing experience. Learning involves changes in processing, or more specifically in perceiving. In studying learning one tries to discover how perceptions can be changed. The cognitive psychologist is interested in the dynamics of perceptual organization and in the processes that enable the learner to develop new perceptions. He is interested in strategies of learning (Bruner, 1961), in the structural properties of the material to be learned (Bruner, 1966), and in the attentional processes that are necessary for learning to occur (Anderson, 1970). The underlying processes are stressed, rather than the responses to be learned. Hilgard (1964), for example, states: "Thus the response at the end, what it is that fills in the blank, is merely a marker of some sort to show that the essential responses have been made, or, to put it into cognitive terms, that the essential relationships have been understood [p. 136]." The cognitive psychologist is less concerned about distinguishing between overt and covert responses. The understanding of relations is important, and specific overt responses may or may not be signs of such understanding.

Klaus (1965) pointed out that the cognitive approach (he refers to it as the "stimulus-centered" aproach) stresses configurations and principles. The way the material is presented, in terms of its organization and structure, is emphasized. Klaus suggested that programmers with a cognitive orientation would be concerned about ways to avoid fragmenting the material into chunks that lose the main idea.

Few cognitive psychologists would argue that their approach forms the basis for programmed instruction. But many would stress that their position has much to offer the technology, particularly in calling attention to processes that set the stage for effective learning. Rothkopf's (1970) concept of "mathemagenic" activities, for example, identifies such processes as set, attention, information processing, and rehearsal; and calls attention to their possible roles in learning. Rothkopf (1966, 1968) showed that questions interspersed at intervals following a segment of text affect the way students read the text. Such questions can facilitate retention of what was read because they lead students to be careful and precise in their reading. Frase (1968) found that frequent prequestions (questions asked prior to reading) decreased retention and that frequent postquestions increased retention.

The cognitive approach and the tutor-student approach have much in common, although the cognitive approach is more systematic and more experimentally oriented. Pressey (1963b), representing an aspect of the tutor-student position, argued that "silent assimilative reading" is a basic tool of learning and that the "emerged capacities" of man, particularly language, make a cognitive approach more useful than a learning-theory approach. He suggested that programs include questions to "enhance the clarity and stability of cognitive structure [p. 3]."

Both the cognitive and the tutor-student approaches emphasize the stimulus properties of the material. Both approaches take the position that material organized within some cognitive structure will be more easily grasped and learned. In support of this position, Gagné (1969) showed that retention is improved when the material is organized by means of a superordinate arrangement involving introductory general topic sentences. Ausubel and Fitzgerald (1961) suggested that "advanced introductory material at a high level of abstraction, generality and inclusiveness" influences cognitive structure; and in support of this view, D. J. Allen (1970) reported that such "advance organizers" improve the long-term retention of prose material for high-ability students.

THE TREATMENT OF INDIVIDUAL DIFFERENCES

In discussions of the applications of psychology to education, no topic generates more heat than that of individual differences. For some psychologists, individual differences constitute a major reason for psychology's involvement in education. Other psychologists regard individual differences as a class of variables to be reckoned with but not a matter of central interest. And in programmed instruction there is the position that good programs, because of their effectiveness, will reduce the range of individual differences in achievement (Hilgard & Bower, 1966). But as Skinner (1961) suggests, the fact that programs may help to "solve many of the problems raised by differences among students" does not mean that all students will be reduced to a single pattern. Walther and Crowder (1965) view individual differences as the reason to write programs. They assert, ". . . thus, the intrinsically programmed portions of the course adapt to the individual differences among the students and allow the programmer to achieve the desired educational objectives with students of heterogeneous backgrounds [p. 36]."

In spite of the references made to individual differences, little attention has been paid to them in studies of programmed instruction. In Lumsdaine and May's (1965) review of research in the area of educational media, including programmed instruction, learner characteristics are regarded simply as "modifying or sorting variables;" and little further mention is made of them. The research done tends to use gross estimates of individual differences in terms of IQ scores or aptitude test scores and such means of classification shed almost no light on the variables responsible for individual differences.

It has been suggested that the customary methods for measuring individual differences may not be useful because these measures arise out of a psychometric tradition more concerned with classification than with the identification of variables affecting learning (Glaser & Resnick, 1972). Sawiris (1966) considered the view that it may be more useful to pay attention to the entering behaviors of the learners than to measures of so-called basic abilities. Davis, Marzocco, and Denny (1970) further support those who oppose psychometric classification as a means of studying individual differences. They found that, with one exception, a wide variety of psychometric measures (English placement, arithmetic placement, an attitude scale, a memory test, and others) failed to identify the best programmed-instruction mode for given students. A reading test, however, did show some slight correlation with the instructional modes.

In place of the traditional psychometric approach, what seems needed is the type of approach described by Rohwer (1971a). Rohwer identified a class of variables he labels "mental elaborations." He found that 4-yr-old children perform better in a paired-associates task when instructed to use verbal elaborations (making up a statement containing the word-pair) or visual elaborations (imagining the objects represented by the words). Training children to use such elaborations improved their ability to learn paired associates. Glaser and Resnick (1972) pointed out that Rohwer's approach suggests that the problem of individual differences may be dealt with by attempting to identify the kinds of cognitive processes required by different tasks and then by determining the extent to which these processes occur in individual learners. As applied to programmed instruction, one might consider the functions of attention, language, discrimination ability, etc.

Individual differences in responsiveness to various reinforcers is another neglected area. Every reinforcer, including confirmation, is not equally effective for every student. Several investigators using conditioning tasks have reported that confirmation, praise, and tangible reinforcers have different effects on different children. Zigler and Kanzer (1962) found that praise was more effective with lower- than with middle-class children, but confirmation in the form of words such as "right" or "correct" was more effective with middle- than with lower-class children. Cradler and Goodwin (1971) reported that material reward (M&M candies) was more effective with lower- than with middle-class children, while symbolic reinforcement (plus marks) or social reinforcement was more effective with middle- than with lower-class children. Cradler and Goodwin also noted that older children were more responsive to social or symbolic reinforcement. The implications of these studies are generally overlooked by programmers, who, for the most part, continue to regard confirmation as reinforcing and who do not worry about individual differences in its reinforcing effectiveness.

PROGRAMMED INSTRUCTION AND APPLIED BEHAVIOR ANALYSIS

Baer, Wolf, and Risley (1968) have identified seven criteria to be used in evaluating studies that purport to involve applied behavior analysis.

They state, ". . . the study must be applied, behavioral and analytic; in addition it should be technological, conceptually systematic, and effective [p. 10]." These criteria also appear useful for examining and evaluating programmed instruction. Since programmed instruction is obviously an applied discipline, that criterion needs little discussion. Each of the other criteria, however, does warrant consideration.

Behavioral Aspects of Programmed Instruction

Programmed instruction is of necessity behavioral, because programmers must deal with responses. Whatever a programmer's frame of reference, he must identify what the student is to learn, and he must do so in terms of specific responses. Furthermore, he needs to determine by what means the student will come to make the responses required to meet the objectives he has identified.

The issue of defining objectives has produced an extensive literature. The early writings were primarily hortatory. Mager's (1961) excellent little book urged programmers to avoid vaguely worded statements of objectives. Mager admonished his readers to avoid such words as "know," "understand," and "appreciate." Such words do not precisely describe what the learner will be able to do. Mager advised that objectives should describe what the learner's behavior will be. For example, a good objective might state, "He will be able to solve the following types of equations: $AX^2 + B - X + Y = O$." or, "He will be able to explain what the symbols on a weather map mean."

As programmed instruction developed, more attention was paid to systems for writing objectives. Many of these systems are derived from the writings of B. S. Bloom and his associates (1956). Bloom's approach is more content oriented than analytical or behavioral. He and his associates were primarily concerned with developing a standardized terminology that would serve the following functions (1956):

1. To help clarify and tighten language for educational objectives;
2. To provide a convenient system for describing and ordering test items, examination techniques, and evaluation instruments;
3. To provide a framework for comparing and studying educational programs;
4. To describe some of the principles of ordering human-learning outcomes . . . that a useful theory of learning must be able to explain.

The literature dealing with objectives indicates that the content-oriented approach is more influential than the behavioral approach. Unfortunately, even more apparent is the failure of content-oriented approaches to deal with systems of identifying and describing behavioral change. While there has been much discussion of "entering behavior" and "terminal behavior," specific responses that may be or should be considered are seldom identified. Little attention is given to the question of competing responses or to the probability of particular responses. Too often the term behavior is used generally and not in reference to a specific behavioral event.

Some observers have recognized the need for behavior analysis and for precision in the description of objectives. Hively (1961) pointed out that programming requires specifying the behaviors that comprise the so-called terminal behaviors (the objectives). To describe what a student has learned, we also need to identify the responses the student made on route to the terminal behavior. Resnick (1963) referred to these en-route behaviors as "component behaviors." She suggested that the identification of components may be necessary in identifying the terminal behavior, and that individual differences may be viewed in terms of different component behaviors among students.

Gagné (1970) took cognizance of behavior analysis when he described a method for identifying objectives by working back from the terminal objective. He suggested that once the terminal objective has been defined, one works back to identify a "subordinate set of subtopics." This end-to-beginning analysis continues from topic to topic until the analysis comes to a stopping point, the point where the student has the prerequisite behavior. Each subtopic is subjected to analysis in order to specify a learning hierarchy. The hierarchy consists of what the learner is able to do and it proceeds upward to what he should be able to do if the learning is successful.

Analytic Aspects of Programmed Instruction

Research in programmed instruction attempts to be analytic when it seeks to identify key variables. Studies of the role of confirmation are analytic, for example, when they examine the extent to which confirmation plays a part in programmed learning. That much of this research has produced equivocal findings is largely the result of methodological flaws in the research. It was indicated previously, for example, that most confirmation studies failed to separate individual response confirmation from the confirmation produced by the program sequence itself. Most analyses suffered from a "shotgun" research approach. They did not give sufficient attention to breaking down the variables into their effective components to determine which variables play a part in programmed-instruction behavior control.

Very little research in programmed instruction has demonstrated reliable control over behavior. Neither the "reversal" technique nor the multiple-baseline method (Baer, Wolf, & Risley, 1968) is found in studies of programming variables. These techniques are often difficult to apply in instructional research, but the state of the research done leads directly to the conclusion that these techniques should be tried.

Technological Aspects of Programmed Instruction

Programmed instruction is or should be a technology, but it only super-ficially meets Baer, Wolf, and Risley's criteria of having techniques that are "completely identified and described." New programmers can be trained to replicate the procedures of other programmers, but very often the older, established programmers insist that their "experience" adds a dimension to their skill. In training programmers, seldom are the salient variables in programming so explicitly described that the newly trained programmer has a set of principles and practices that he can (or should) follow to the letter. The "How To" texts such as Markle (1969) and Silverman (1970) are useful, but in no sense do they pretend to technology in the same way that a manual designed to train electricians would.

Conceptual Systems in Programmed Instruction

Baer, Wolf, and Risley (1968) take the position that "the field of applied behavior analysis will probably advance best if the published descriptions of its procedures are not only precisely technological, but also strive for rele-vance to principle (p. 14)." Programmed instruction falls short of meeting this criterion, because it is difficult to argue that programmed instruction has striven for relevance to principle. On the contrary, it more and more resem-bles a discipline based on a collection of unrelated principles, opinions, intuitions, and unsystematic efforts at innovation. Many of its advocates appear to be prouder of their eclecticism than of their interest in a unifying set of principles.

Some will argue that any new discipline must be ready to use whatever seems to work; it cannot exclude concepts or methods because they fail to fit a predetermined system. Such arguments have a sensible and virtuous ring to them, but their virtue and common sense often belie their failure to recognize the need for a technology to be firmly based on principles, even when the principles appear to be constraining.

Conant (1961) voiced concern over the fact that, ". . . the use of a strong theoretical component from psychology has not yet attained anything like a prominent place in educational research [p. 18]." A strong theoretical com-ponent from psychology is involved, to some extent, in programmed instruc-tion, but there is evidence that the influence of systematic psychology is continually being eroded. There is even some question as to how closely related programmed instruction is to the general psychology of learning. One reads that the student who has learned to respond with "Paris" to the question, "What is the capital of France?" has "not necessarily" learned the answer to the question, "Paris is the capital of what country? (Markle, 1969, p. 5)." Such an assertion at best minimizes and at worst ignores the body of data in paired-associates learning. Subjects do learn the reverse relation, albeit the reversal may be less efficiently learned than the forward associates (Deese & Hulse, 1967). Furthermore, with highly available stimulus and response words, associations in either direction are highly probable (Ekstrand, 1966).

Effectiveness of Programmed Instruction

The claims that programmed instruction is effective are too numerous and varied to document. Programs do work in that they show teaching effects. As of 1973, 3500 programmed units or texts in 167 subject-matter areas were available for use (Hendershot, 1973), and the numbers continue to grow. Many of these programs are accompanied by some form of validation data, such as field tests or reports of small-sample tryouts.

The critics of programmed instruction seldom argue that it does not teach, but they do argue that it is impersonal, destructive of creativity and student initiative, oversimplified, etc. The advocates range from those who insist that any and all subject matter can be taught this way to those who claim that it is only a tool, best used as an adjunct to traditional instruction.

In view of the many claims and counterclaims, it is apparent that the research is not extensive or conclusive enough to speak for itself. We still need to determine the effects of programming in specific areas of learning. Test scores are not sufficient indices of behavior change because they do not provide much information about changes in responses.

Generality of Programmed Instruction

The durability and generality of programmed instruction effects remain an open question in much the same way that the durability of most instruction is open to question. Long-range studies are hard to find in all areas of educational application. Durability and generality are most often a function of conditions that extend beyond the immediate learning situation. Few psychologists should doubt that the durability of learning can be controlled if attention is paid to schedules of reinforcement. And few would disagree with the premise that generality is also manageable, at least in part, through the deliberate extension of stimulus control.

PROSPECTS

Programmed instruction has had an influence on other educational technologies, such as individually prescribed instruction and computer-assisted instruction. Individually prescribed instruction did not originate as a result of the development of programmed instruction, but the programming concept has helped to show how individualization may be accomplished. The growing interest in ways to individualize teaching bodes well for the further development of programmed instruction. Individualization requires an interest in the same variables that contribute to the design and use of programs.

Computer-assisted instruction is a movement within its own right. While there is a relation between programmed instruction and computer-assisted instruction, they are not interdependent approaches. Perhaps they should be more closely associated; the work of Suppes (1966) and Atkinson (1968) suggests that both systems will benefit from a productive relation between them. It is becoming increasingly clear that the computer can be a powerful means of implementing and extending the techniques of programmed instruction. Computers permit a variety of ways to present material, to confirm responses, to be responsive to the individual learner (by means of branching), and to process data dealing with the learner's progress (Feurzig, 1968). Techniques of computer graphics, whereby pictorial information can be stored, processed, and retrieved by a computer, extend the range of stimulus, response, and reinforcement possibilities. With the aid of computers, programs need not be limited, as they usually are, to verbal symbols. Furthermore, animation makes it possible to develop exercises dealing with complex mathematical and physical relations in very effective ways.

While programmed instruction's prospects within individually prescribed instruction and computer-assisted instruction are good, the basic technology has not realized its earlier promise. It has not had a noticeable impact on general educational practice. Some observers are not surprised, for they predicted at the outset that the idea would find its place on the shelf with other "tools" or "teaching aids." But others had more ambitious expectations, seeing programming as the beginning of a new understanding of the teaching-learning process and as the beginning of a new applied science of teaching.

It is apparent that programmed instruction has been too limited in its outlook. Programmers have been primarily interested in the programming of specific subject matters and have been confined by the restrictions imposed by the subject matters. Furthermore, many research-oriented programmers have dwelt on the techniques of frame writing and program construction and have paid too little attention to the behavior of learning. Programmed instruction's potential value for teaching some of the basic skills of learning has largely been overlooked.

Some programmers do try to analyze and identify relevant behavior, but their analysis frequently takes for granted many prerequisite learning skills. For example, it is usually assumed that the student can discriminate whether his responses match or even approximate the confirmation material. Furthermore, it is assumed that the student's standards of matching resemble the programmer's standards. Both assumptions are unjustified; many students have difficulty matching their responses to the criterion material. And the matching standards of students are frequently lower than the programmer's standards.

The matching-to-criterion problem can be effectively dealt with by programming. Discriminating correct matches as well as establishing standards of evaluating the match can be shaped. The frames shown in Figure 13-3 provide a partial illustration of what such shaping may look like in programmed form.

1. John drew a house that looked like this.
   His teacher had wanted him to draw this house.
   Was John's drawing correct?

   Ans.   No.

2. If John had drawn this house   , would it be
   pretty close to the one that the teacher wanted?

   Ans. Yes. But something is missing.

3. What is missing in John's drawing in frame 2?

   Ans. The chimney and the smoke

4. If now John's teacher asks him to draw a design like this
   and John draws this   , is John correct?

   Ans. No. John is close, but his
   drawing is not the same as
   his teacher's.

5. Which one of the following designs matches this one?

   a.   b.   c.   d.

   Ans.   d

Fig. 13.3   A sample part of a matching-to-criterion sequence.

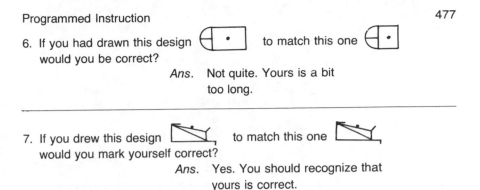

6. If you had drawn this design ⊟• to match this one ⊟•
   would you be correct?

   Ans. Not quite. Yours is a bit
   too long.

7. If you drew this design ⊿ to match this one ⊿
   would you mark yourself correct?

   Ans. Yes. You should recognize that
   yours is correct.

Fig. 13.3 (continued)

Shaping the discrimination of correct matches between responses and confirmation also contains pitfalls. The student might become too dependent upon the authority of the program and become unable to judge for himself whether he is performing correctly. The student might become too passive and learn to await signs from others that he is doing what he should. Such passive behavior may be acceptable in the beginning, but it is clearly counterproductive in later, more advanced forms of learning.

Programming can, however, be used to wean students away from exclusive reliance on externally imposed criteria. Some, but unfortunately very few, programmers take the opportunity to shape independence. Markle's program in vocabulary development (1962) and her "Good Frames and Bad" (1969) let the student know that his ideas and opinions have value and should be expressed. She occasionally uses the device of having the student express his own opinion. Questions asking "Would you call this a ————?" provide a means for the student to give his view. Responses to such questions cannot be called incorrect.

The five frames shown in Figure 13-4 partially illustrate a sequence designed to foster student initiative and independence.

Most teachers are aware that merely telling a child to "pay attention" seldom results in persistent attending. Furthermore, many children fail to discriminate the relevant stimuli. They do not know what they should be paying attention to, and they do not see much connection between their paying attention and any favorable consequences. But attention, like other behavior, can be shaped and placed under stimulus control. The systematic use of prompting and fading of prompts in programs can be an effective means of controlling attention. Programs also permit arranging contingencies in which searching for and attending to relevant stimuli is reinforced.

Good students usually acquire the skill of pacing themselves. They learn to study at the pace best suited to the material and to their own learning abilities. This skill is not a "knack;" it is learned and it can be taught. Because

1. Here are 6 objects

Here they are arranged into 2 groups

(1)   (2)

You can see that group 1 has the tall objects and group 2 the short ones.

We could also have arranged them this way

(1)   (2)

Here group 1 has the lined objects and group 2 the unlined ones. The presence of lines is the principle we used to group the objects.

There is at least one other principle we could have used for grouping the objects. We could have put the four-sided objects into one group and the three-sided objects into the other group.

---

2. Here are some symbols   ‖ ⦀ ⧘ ⧘ ⦀ ⧘ ⧘ ‖
Arrange them into 2 groups according to some principle or idea

(1) _____ (2) _____

                     Ans.   You could have made these 2 groups

                  (1)   ‖ ⧘ ⦀ ⧘   (2)   ⦀ ⧘ ⧘ ‖

                  according to the principle of size

        or   You might have noticed that some of the symbols contained 2 vertical lines and some 3. You could use the principle of number and arrange them this way

                  (1)   ‖ ⧘ ⧘ ‖   (2)   ⦀ ⧘ ⦀ ⧘

Fig. 13-4. Sample of a programmed sequence designed to foster student initiative and independence.

or You could have arranged them according to the principle that some have a horizontal line and some do not. They could be arranged this way

(1)  ‖ ⦀ ⦀‖ (2)  ₶ ₶ ₶ ₶

Any of these arrangements is correct, just as long as there is some principle involved.

---

3. Arrange these letters into 2 groups, any 2 that you prefer.

a X d u B e O z

Ans. You could have made these 2 groups

(1) *a O B X* (2) *d u e z*

according to the principle or capital and small letters

or these (1) *a O e u* (2) *B X d z*

according to the principle of vowels and consonants

or these (1) *a u d z* (2) *O B X e*

according to whether they are printed or written

or perhaps you found some other principle not described here. There are other principles that could be used.

Fig. 13-4 (continued)

4. Try arranging the following words into 2 groups according to some principle. You do not have to put the same number of words into each group.

cow, mule, salmon, ant, rat, chicken, lobster, lamb, alligator, elephant, duck, donkey

Ans.   There are a number of possible arrangements.
State the principle that you used to
arrange the words.

---

5. You might have stated that you arranged the words in frame 4
according to where the animals lived (land or water).
(1) duck, frog, salmon, lobster, alligator
(2) cow, mule, ant, rat, chicken, donkey, elephant,
or you might have used the size of the animals
(1) rat, duck, ant, chicken, frog, salmon, lobster
(2) cow, alligator, elephant, donkey, mule
or you might have arranged them according to whether or not
they are ordinarily eaten by people.
(1) cow, duck, frog, chicken, salmon, lobster
(2) mule, rat, ant, elephant, alligator, donkey,
or maybe you found another way of grouping the words. Your
way will be correct if it is based on some principle. Is it?

Fig. 13-4 (continued)

self-pacing is one ingredient of programmed instruction, programs can be useful in teaching students how to pace themselves. Programmed units can be designed to blend accuracy and speed requirements to progressively shape self-pacing. Too often programs are constructed in which the time factor is ignored. Such programs offer little opportunity for a student to acquire pacing skills.

Students' ability to cope with failure differ widely. Some children are overwhelmed by a failure and seek ways to escape or avoid situations in which a failure may occur. In the classroom, such escape or avoidance is often disasterous. When it is observed in students it is regarded as a special problem, somehow separate from the problem of teaching and learning. The clinician refers to "anxiety," or "fear of failure," or "low achievement motivation," etc.; and where possible attempts to deal with such problems by means of therapy.

Programmed instruction may offer a more direct and possible more effective means of dealing with the escape or avoidance patterns seen in children who withdraw from any failure. Programs can be constructed that include a mixture of success and failure in ways that allow fairly precise control of the ratio of success to failure. Furthermore such programs can provide sequences in which successes follow failures in ways that reinforce persistence. Progressive shifting of the success-failure ratios can be used to wean the student from artificial sequences to more standard programmed materials.

Programmed instruction may offer a more direct and possibly more learners that is generally not possible with conventional instructional methods. Learning difficulties or even disabilities can be identified in a careful analysis of the responses that students make to programmed materials. Failures in discrimination or generalization or in combining principles or in classifying or in remembering and so on can be observed within special programmed units.

A behavioral approach to the identification and analysis of learning difficulties suggests that observation of the behavior in question is the best source of information. Programs permit such observation, and they can be designed to seek out particular forms of difficulty. For example, special units dealing with discrimination and generalization could be used to uncover difficulties in conceptual behavior. Analysis and synthesis sequences could be constructed to observe the tactics a student uses (or fails to use) in dealing with problem-solving tasks. Furthermore, the use of programs for diagnostic purposes is closely related to their use as remedial teaching tools.

It seems clear that programmed instruction has much more to offer applied behavioral science than has been witnessed thus far. The limitations seen by its critics have little to do with its potential. It is a discipline that can have a real impact on educational practices. It should become an example (or a model) of the applied analysis of behavior in educational settings. If programmed instruction is to develop into an effective instrument, bridging the gap between laboratory and classroom, its advocates would do well to take seriously its origins in behavior science. Unless this is done, the kind of healthy interaction between technology and basic science described by Glaser (1973) cannot take place. The interaction position is tenable only if the technology maintains direct links to the science. A set of techniques that unsystematically picks and chooses its principles does not receive the benefits of applied behavior analysis and is not likely to serve or be served by basic science.

KENNETH E. LLOYD [1]

Chapter 14

Behavior Analysis and Technology in Higher Education

Much of the research and thought about classroom management presented here was outlined half a century ago by Thorndike (1913, 1923). Thorndike's empirical investigation of the relations between responses and consequent stimuli led to his statement of the law of effect (Thorndike, 1911). Later he directed his attention to educational psychology and other applied problems.

After Thorndike and for about 40 years, most experimental psychologists interested in learning engaged in laboratory studies of the learning process, tested hypotheses about concepts and theories of learning, and formulated explanations not simply in terms of independent and dependent variables but of intervening variables as well (Ausubel & Robinson, 1969). In a symposium entitled, "Can the Laws of Learning Be Applied in the Classroom," Spence (1959) summed up this orientation by stating, ". . . the phenomena that the experimental psychologist interested in the problem of learning has taken as the object of his studies, and about which he has attempted to formulate his theories, have little or nothing to do with learning in real life situations, including even the kinds of learning that are supposed to go on in the classroom [p. 84]."

For Spence (1959), the basic and applied work of Thorndike confused the educational psychologist into thinking that "all studies of animal learning must have been undertaken with a view to finding principles of use to educational psychology and other areas of practical application [p. 86]."

The intervening years substantiated Spence's position. The learning

[1]The author wishes to express appreciation to James M. Johnston, Georgia State University; David G. Born, University of Utah; and Ruth G. Wylie, Drake University for their critical reading of a draft of this manuscript and for their many helpful comments.

theories of the 1930's, 1940's, and 1950's had little or nothing to do with learning in real life. Despite the hope that theories of learning would eventually "lead to the discovery of general laws and the formulation of systematic theories of a comprehensive nature [Spence, 1959, p. 87]" a much more theoretically modest system led to comprehensive applications of principles of behavior to human problems (Skinner, 1938). Skinner published in the 1930's as well, but not until the 1950's did an extensive experimental analysis of behavior appear (Ferster & Skinner, 1957; Honig, 1966; *Journal of the Experimental Analysis of Benavior*, 1958-present). A short time later the now widespread applied analysis of behavior began in nursery schools and institutions for the psychotic and the retarded (Ullman & Krasner, 1965). Today we are closer to the Thorndikian thinking of 1913 than to the thinking of the learning theorists who occupied the years in between.

For example, more emphasis is placed upon an empirical law of effect than upon a theoretical law of effect. Thorndike (1913) was well aware of the empirical nature of the law of effect:

"The reader will understand that the approval and disapproval which are thus satisfying and annoying to the natural man are far from identical, in either case, with the behavior which proceeds from cultivated moral approbation and condemnation. The sickly frown of a Sunday School teacher at her scholar's mischief may be prepotently an attention to him rather than the others, may contain a semi-envious recognition of him as a force to be reckoned with, and may even reveal a lurking admiration for his deviltry. It then will be instinctively accepted as approval [p. 89].

Just how one goes about applying principles of behavior in socially significant settings is not immediately obvious. Although psychologists have long been employed in applied settings, this need not indicate that they have been applying experimentally established principles of behavior in those settings. Such psychologists followed a medical model more often than a psychological model (Ullman & Krasner, 1965). An intermediate area between purely experimental research and directly applied technology is required. Current writers, concerned with applying the psychology of learning to social problems, agree on the need for applied research that comes between basic research and actual application of a principle in a classroom (Baer, Wolf, & Risley, 1968; Bugelski, 1964, pp. 21-32; Bushell & Brigham, 1971; Hilgard & Bower, 1966, pp. 541-584). The classroom manager must know more than that the principle of reinforcement operates in educational situations. It is not enough to know that reinforcement is defined functionally in terms of both procedures and effects upon behavior. In addition to knowing the principle, a body of literature must also exist showing how specific stimulus events (extra recess time, permission to clean the fish bowl, etc.), when contingent upon responses (sitting quietly and facing forward, correctly answering 15 problems, etc.) can increase the future occurrence of those responses. This literature must also explicate observing procedures, reliability measures, baseline data, intervention techniques, and continuous assessment in terms of both behavior change and cost effectiveness. Experimental psychologists are uninterested in developing this literature, and the potential consumers of psychological data—teachers, educational psychologists, counselors, psychiatric staff workers, etc.—have so far been unable to do so. The consumer will contact an applied research literature and not a basic research literature (Bijou, 1970).

COMMENTS ON CONTEMPORARY EDUCATIONAL PSYCHOLOGY

Educational psychologists are disappointed with the psychology of learning. Learning studies using simple tasks, nonhuman subjects, and theoretically oriented problems are neither seemingly nor actually relevant (Ausubel & Robinson, 1969; Glock, 1971, p. 72). Although educational psychology textbooks usually include summaries of the learning theories in one chapter, the contents are seldom related to other chapters (Bernard, 1972; Eson, 1972; Garry & Kingsley, 1970; Mathis, Cotton, & Sechrest, 1970; Pittenger & Gooding, 1971; Powell, M., & Magnum, 1971). For example, Bernard (1972) devotes 2.5 pages to Pavlov, 6.5 pages to Thorndike, 2.5 to Guthrie, Skinner, and Mowrer combined, 3.5 to field theory, and 1.5 to phenomenology and humanistic psychology. Later chapters include lists of suggestions, neither referenced or related to these theorists, for teaching both slow learners and gifted learners. It might be difficult to find references for some suggestions, e.g., "Blame and censure will be more effective with the gifted child than with the slow learner—though this should not be interpreted as a blanket recommendation (Bernard, 1972, p. 328)." A recent text by Anderson and Faust (1973), unlike most educational psychology texts, acknowledges learning principles throughout the book. Most of the references however, are not directly concerned with college or university education (see Fox, 1962, and McKeachie, 1963, for exceptions).

The irrelevance of the experimental psychologists' literature to the educational psychologist emphasizes the need for a transition stage in which experimental data are translated into effective social action. Perhaps because direct application of experimental psychology to socially significant problems has been lacking, eductional psychologists have turned to more readily assimilated points of view. Kolesnik (1970) states:

The human being . . . cannot be understood in terms of measureable, observable behavior alone. He is a unique, unified person, a purposeful individual . . . in search of values that can and will give his existence meaning. . . . he is motivated by a desire to live the richest, fullest, most rewarding life that he is capable of, and it is the function of his teachers to help him do so [p. vii].

Educators have shown a preference for the "inside story" [Skinner,

1969, p. 269], to explain behavior with unobservable entities inside the skin of the student rather than in terms of observable factors in the student's environment.

THE KELLER METHOD: PERSONALIZED SYSTEM OF INSTRUCTION (PSI)

The beginning of an applied analysis of behavior in the college classroom may be credited to Keller (1965, 1966, 1967, 1968, 1969), who first outlined the characteristics of a course organized around certain principles of behavior and who presented the first data from students enrolled in such a course. His work stimulated a series of papers describing similar courses and presenting additional data from students (Born & Zlutnick, 1972; Burnstein, 1971; Cheney & Powers, 1971; Collier & Smith, 1971; Cooper, 1973; Ferster, 1968; Gallup, 1969, 1970, 1974; Hartley, 1972; Lloyd & Knutzen, 1969; Malott & Svinicki, 1969; Michael, 1971; Minke & Carlson, 1972; Sherman, J.G., 1974a, 1974b, 1974d; Sullivan, 1972). Keller's original methods, and some later courses that differed in various ways from the original, are described in detail. Then the behavior of enrolled students is examined.

Distinctive Features of PSI

In the course prospectus given to students at the beginning of the term, Keller listed five features of the personalized system of instruction: self-pacing, unit mastery, a minimum of lectures, a stress on written assignments, and the use of undergraduate proctors. Keller-type courses embody other characteristics that further distinguish them from "traditional university courses." The notion of a traditional university course is admittedly vague [although Cooper (1973) has identified some traditional course characteristics]. Nevertheless, the term will be useful in pointing out procedural differences between Keller courses and methods frequently encountered in university courses.

Self-Pacing Self-pacing or student-pacing meant that the student decided when to complete course assignments. The assignments were divided into relatively small units of homework. The student prepared for a test on each unit by studying during class time or on his or her own time. The student could take the first unit test during the first week of the term or during the tenth week. The instructor imposed no direct rewards for rapid work or direct penalties for slow work. Presumably the student-pacing feature allowed for individual differences in the rate at which students worked, permitting students individually to compensate for the competing activities indigenous to a college campus.

Unit Mastery Unit perfection or unit mastery specified that the student could proceed to new course material only after demonstrating mastery of the prior assignment. Mastery referred to perfect performance on a written unit test that consisted of 10 fill-in questions and one short-answer essay question. The student who missed one or two items on a unit test was required to study material for at least 30 min before attempting a retest. The student who failed more than four items received no credit for items successfully answered and was required to retake the entire test. The student who missed no items would have been asked to discuss one or two of them orally anyway. Unit mastery meant studying, or restudying if necessary, assigned material until a test could be passed at some specified criterion level, which for Keller was perfect performance. All students were assumed to be capable of performing the work at criterion level. Some students passed the unit test the first time it was attempted; others required two or three attempts. Thirty unit tests were assigned in the Keller course; some covered reading assignments and some covered laboratory exercises.

In traditional university courses, the instructor typically tests all students at specified times (i.e., testing is instructor paced) and students are permitted only one opportunity to take a test; their first test score is their final test score. After one test, all students are permitted to proceed to the material for the second test regardless of how they performed on the first. Tests tend to be infrequent (e.g., two or three per term). Testing in a traditional course is used to differentiate among students; testing in the Keller method measures whether a student is ready to proceed to the next part of the course. In a traditional course a student who answers, say 60% of the test items correctly may receive a C; in a Keller course that same student would be required to restudy the material until correctly answering 100% of the test items. At the end of a Keller course students differ in how many unit tests they have completed; they do not differ in how well they have performed on those units they passed.

The unit mastery notion follows directly from laboratory and elementary classroom criteria for an acceptable response. If a pigeon's pecks on a key in a laboratory experiment are reinforced with 4-sec access to grain when the force of the peck exceeds .9 newtons, a peck with a force of .45 newtons is not reinforced with 2-sec access to grain. Similarly a first-grade pupil's correctly printing "A" may be reinforced, but if he printed "Λ", he would be asked to try again. At the university level, however, students may pass a course with far less than complete mastery. A student may receive a final grade of C if he correctly answers 60% of the multiple-choice items on a midterm and a final examination. That the student answered 40% of the items incorrectly is ignored. Similarly, on a specific test item worth two points a partial definition of a term might receive one point. The instructor could later prompt the complete definition, but the student would not be asked to reproduce the definition correctly.

Lectures   Lectures and demonstrations in a Keller-type course were not viewed as imparting information to students. Instead, only students who had already completed specified units of work were permitted to attend lectures and demonstrations. No examinations were based on the lectures. The intent was to provide lectures to those students who had demonstrated their readiness to appreciate them. Attending a lecture would not provide students with information helpful for the next test, but would provide students with information which they presumably could better appreciate because they had completed related assignments.

Teacher-Student Communication Emphasis shifts in teacher-student communication, from the student as passive recipient of the teacher's lectures to one in which the student is actively reading, studying, and writing on his own while the teacher acts as planner, coordinator, manager, and occasional lecturer. The common classroom problem of attempting to induce attention to a lecture was circumvented by arranging an environment in which the students themselves produced those responses that an instructor ordinarily emitted during a lecture. Rather than allowing the instructor to recite the material for the nth time in a lecture, the student was asked to produce it at least once at a high level of mastery during a unit test.

The student was aided in his original reading of the material by a set of approximately 30 questions comprising a study guide for each unit. The student answered these study questions while reading. Answering study-guide questions presumably prepared him for passing the unit test.

Undergraduate Proctors Testing and retesting from 50-100 students individually on 30-50 unit tests requires more hours than instructors and assistants together typically invest in a course. To provide individual testing, Keller (1968) expanded the size of his teaching staff by using undergraduate proctors, a procedure "which permits repeated testing, immediate scoring, almost unavoidable tutoring, and a marked enhancement of the personal-social aspect of the educational process [p. 83]." A typical undergraduate proctor had passed the course with an A grade and received 2 or 3 hours of course credit for proctoring. Keller assigned 10 students to each proctor. They maintained regular office hours in an assigned room and met weekly with the instructor to discuss the course organization (see also Etters, 1967).

In addition to completing the 30 unit tests students took a final examination covering the term's work and consisting of questions that, in large part, had been answered before. The students' score on the final exam accounted for 25% of their final grade; the number of completed unit tests accounted for 75% of their final grade.

The Keller method bore many similarities to the more familiar programmed instruction from which the system developed (Sherman, J.G. 1974b, 1974c). The two approaches share a careful task analysis, a concern for terminal performance, and an opportunity for individual progress. They differ in the size of response units. Programmed instruction is more concerned with molecular units; personalized instruction is concerned with constructing a molar environment for modifying student behavior. Specifying this environment can provide a more precise measure of student behavior than has been attempted at the university level.

Variations of the Keller Method among Contingency Management Systems

After Keller's early reports, other course descriptions were published. None were identical replications but all were designed in the same spirit of educational change. Despite an expressed concern about changing Keller's original procedures (Green, 1971a; Sherman, J.G., 1974a, pp. 4-5) variation has occurred (cf. the comparison studies described later and Wodarski and Buckholdt, 1975) and is empirically desirable (Kazdin, 1973c, p. 532). These variations lead to such phrases as *behavioral systems and contingency management systems* in addition to the original label, *personalized system of instruction* and its abbreviation, PSI. The word *contingency*, in *contingency management system*, refers to a rule relating antecedent and consequent stimuli to a response. Contingency management systems specify the arrangement of new contingencies or the rearrangement of existing contingencies in order to change behavior. Three variations of PSI will be described in detail. One replaced written unit tests with oral interviews (Ferster, 1968), the second permitted students to decide how much material would be included in a unit test (Born, Gledhill, & Davis, 1972), and the third increased the complexity of assignments as students progressed through the course (Lloyd & Knutzen, 1969).

Ferster (1968) described an individualized introductory psychology course in which 91 students enrolled. He assigned 17-18 students to each of five proctors. One lecture was given during the term. Students spent the remainder of the class time (4-5 hr per week) preparing for or taking tests. The major departure from the Keller method was Ferster's use of oral interviews during unit tests. A student who had prepared for a unit test approached a proctor in the classroom to request an interview. The proctor would either interview the student or request another student in the class who had already passed this unit's interview to conduct the interview. This interview system imposed a double contingency on the student: before attempting to pass the second unit interview a student not only had to pass the interview for the first unit but also had to interview another student on the first unit: "Each student is required to listen once for each time he speaks [Ferster, 1968, p. 521]."

The interviews, like Keller's written unit tests, were a prepared set of questions given to the interviewer by the teaching staff. As before, the student could challenge questions and the interviewer could reword questions. During an interview the student was permitted to refer to textbook, notes, or outlines. The intent again was to determine whether the student had mastered the material. Passing an interview meant 100% mastery of the interviewer's questions. Ferster assumed that both taking and administering an interview helped to establish this behavior in the student's repertory. The teaching staff (instructor, graduate assistants, and undergraduate proctors) conducted approximately 10% of each student's interviews. Ferster argued that the course material was cumulative (i.e., the fifth unit depended on the material in the preceding four). Thus, a staff member conducting an interview on a later unit could detect inadequacies in prior interviews conducted by students in the class. A subsequent textbook (Ferster & Perrott, 1968) included study questions that could be used for interviews.

The use of interviews to replace written answers would not seem to violate Keller's original purpose in using many unit tests to induce active student responding. In addition to passing the interviews students were required to pass written exercises administered after the completion of three to five interviews. A final exam was also given.

In a second modified Keller method (Born et al., 1972) two groups of students studying the psychology of learning took unit tests that differed in the amount of material covered by each test. Students in the Keller section were given 16 unit tests. Students in the modified Keller section were permitted to decide the size of the unit over which they wished to be tested. Because the total material to be learned was the same in both sections, the amount of material in any one unit test was inversely related to the total number of tests to be taken. Thus, this was an additional procedure by which students could pace their responding. Keller (1968, p. 84) considered high frequency of testing to be an advantage of his system; The Born et al. (1972) modification could either decrease or increase test frequency. In this case, the possible range was from three tests (students had to pass all the prior) unit tests before taking two midterms and one final examination) to probably 57 tests (the number of sections in the textbook). The two sections also differed in that students in the modified Keller section could obtain extra points contributing to their final grade by performing small experiments, by reading and writing reports in areas of special interest, etc.

Permitting students to perform different kinds of activities rather than only asking them repeatedly to pass unit tests was a major feature of the third variation of the Keller Method (Lloyd & Knutzen, 1969). Students were encouraged to engage in a wide variety of activities so that they would perform many of the activities of psychologists (see complete assignment lists in Lloyd, 1971, p. 19; and in Lloyd and Knutzen, 1969, p. 126). Within broad limits students could choose which and how many of these activities to complete. Activities were assigned a maximum and a minimum point value. If necessary, the student reworked the assignment until at least the minimum points were obtained; these points were accumulated and were the basis for the final course grade. Final letter grades were given point values at the beginning of the term. From the start, students could decide the grade toward which they wished to work.

The activities for which points could be earned varied from attending a class meeting (2 points), to going on a field trip (65 points), to writing a term paper (100 points). Originally the assignment of point values to activities was arbitrary (Lloyd & Knutzen, 1969), but later the point values were adjusted (Lloyd, 1971) based on suggestions from both teaching staff and students. Although the activities differed for the different letter grades, sequences of assignments became progessively more complicated for the different letter grades. For example, the A assignment of a term paper was divided into components at the lower grades. Writing a term paper was judged to involve at least the following: reading and abstracting journal articles (a 10-point D activity), combining similar kinds of articles into an organized discussion (a 25-point C activity), and showing how apparently unrelated articles could be related to the term-paper topic (a 40-point B activity). Finally, putting these different activities together constituted a term paper and an A activity.

These changes in course format led to several departures from the Keller method. As assignments became more complicated (i.e., a term paper versus a 10-item unit test), they were not graded immediately in the presence of students. Instead, papers were turned in for grading and returned later. Students were not assigned to one particular member of the teaching staff. Instead, they could consult with any proctor, teaching assistant, or instructor.

No final or midterm examinations were given in the Lloyd courses. Keller, Ferster, and Born et al., all gave final exams with grade weightings of 25% to 50%. Although these authors did not explicitly say so, it is apparent that a student could not retake the final or midterm to improve his score. The first score was the final score, and cut-off scores for letter grades were not computed until these final scores were obtained (see especially Born et al., 1972, and a discussion in Johnston and O'Neill, 1973, p. 262). Thus, a student always operated during the course with some uncertainty about his final grade. Undoubtedly the uncertainty about final grades was considerably reduced in these courses compared to traditional university courses. These courses not only removed uncertainty about final grade cut-off scores, but also removed aspects of relative grading. A student's performance was always compared with the original grade criteria, and never with the performance of other students in the course.

Contingency Management Systems in Disciplines Other than Psychology

A final variation concerns the content or subject matter of the course itself. The courses previously described were in introductory psychology, psychology of learning, and the experimental analysis of behavior. Some involved laboratory work and others did not. Similar procedures have been used in courses in elementary statistics (Myers, 1970) and in child development (Semb, 1974, 1975). From the many papers read at professional meetings (e.g., Michael, 1971), from newsletters (e.g., *Personalized System of Instruction Newsletter*, 1971) and from personal communications, it appears that almost every course in the psychology curriculum has been organized according to the Keller plan at some university. To those intimately involved in developing the system, the range of content areas to which the method has been applied will come as no surprise, because the procedures presumably deal primarily with the behavior of students and teaching staff and should be independent of course content. Nonetheless, it has been argued that the Keller method is more appropriate for engineering courses than for courses in the "soft" sciences (Koen, 1970a, 1970b; Philippas & Sommerfeldt, 1972). The broadest perspective on course content can be obtained by examining some Keller-type courses in fields other than psychology.

The biological sciences were among the first to develop similar systems employing audiotutorial techniques and minicourses (Postlethwait, Novak, & Murray, 1969; Postlethwait & Russell, 1971). Courses in genetics (Becker & Shumway, 1972) and in plant morphology (Hoshaw, Kurtz, & Ferko, 1969) were described. Student pacing of assignments, unit perfection or learning for mastery (Block, 1971), and individualized study environments were used. Lectures were replaced by short assignments completed in a "learning center" located in the departmental offices. One feature of the Keller method missing was the use of undergraduate proctors (Moore, J.W., Mahan, & Ritts, 1969). The biologist authors of these articles claimed as much instructor and student enthusiasm for the method as did the psychologists.

Some degree of student pacing of repeatable tests and a "learning center" for test taking staffed by undergraduate teaching assistants were reported by Hammer and Henderson (1972a, 1972b; Hammer, Henderson, & Johnston, 1972) in business-administration courses. An innovation was the use of photographs on student identification cards with demographic data added to the student's photograph. The instructor used the cards during class meetings for rapid recognition of students. The Keller method has been described (Calvin, 1970) and successfully used (Roop, 1973) in the economics literature. Keller-course descriptions are also found in anthropology (Witters & Kent, 1972), education (Alba & Pennypacker, 1972), several subdisciplines of engineering (Hoberock, 1971, 1972; Hoberock, Koen, Roth, & Wagner, 1972; Koen, 1970a, 1970b, 1971, 1973; Koen & Keller, 1971), foreign languages (Bailey, 1975), library science (Knightly & Sayre, 1972), philosophy (Moore, Mahan, & Ritts, 1969), physics (D'Arruda, 1973); Friedman, C.P., 1972; Green, 1971a, 1971b, 1973; Philippas & Sommerfeldt, 1972) and political science (Hobart, Goldman, & Fishel, 1973). Still other references are available through the *Personalized System of Instruction Newsletter* (1971).

The wide variety of course content to which the Keller method has been applied is suggestive of its future growth. But wide acceptance and future growth of an educational technique need not be positively correlated with research evidence supporting its value. A technique may be accepted on the basis of vivid descriptive adjectives with or without the empirical data to recommend its use. Simply describing differences in course formats omits the distinguishing feature of a behavioral analysis: the demonstration that procedural differences actually produce reliable, observable differences in students' behavior (Baer et al., 1968; Kazdin, 1973c). The preceding course descriptions in no way indicate that the procedures were an improvement over typical university classroom procedures. For example, a course description does not prove that interviews produce different performances than written unit tests, or that size of study unit is a relevant variable, or that performing D, C, and B activities will improve term papers. A behavioral analysis of contingency management systems in university courses must eventually document the relative effectiveness of different procedures. Research articles are now accumulating that permit a first approximation to an empirical evaluation. Thus, the following sections of this chapter examine how university students respond when confronted with contingency management systems.

COMPARISONS OF PSI WITH TRADITIONAL COURSES

At least 29 comparisons of performance of one or more sections of a Keller class with a traditional class on a common criterion measure (a final examination or a combination of one or more midterm exams plus a final exam) have been reported. Seventeen studies indicated higher criterion scores for the Keller method based upon a statistical analysis, four obtained results partially showing higher scores for the Keller section, and eight reported no statistical differences between the classes. No comparisons indicated a superiority for the traditional method. At least eight other articles reported comparisons of final letter grades favoring the Keller section (Bailey, L. G., 1975; Hoberock, 1971, 1972; Keller, 1968; Koen, 1970a, 1971; Protopappas, 1974; Sullivan, 1972). Insufficiently described criteria for the grades however, prohibited critical comparisons (Kulik, Kulik, & Carmicheal, 1974). The comparison studies are discussed in relation to experimental design, class activities, and criterion measures. The 29 comparisons are included in 25 references cited in this section.

Experimental Design

In the most often used experimental design, two or more sections of the same course were taught by two or more different methods and then student performance on a common criterion was compared statistically. The design is simple and familiar but has not been noted for its success (Dubin & Taveggia, 1968; Shoemaker, 1972). Important design issues are the number of students in each section, the manner in which students were assigned to a particular section, tests of section equivalence before the courses began, and techniques for ensuring objectivity in constructing and scoring the criterion tests. The class size varied from Keller sections of five (Roop, 1973) and seven (Born et al., 1972), to a traditional section of 204 (Corey, Valente, & Shamow, 1974). Class sizes in the same comparison were usually similar, e.g., 36 and 40 (Alba & Pennypacker, 1972), 45 and 42 (Cooper & Greiner, 1971). The median class size was 40 for traditional sections and 39 for Keller sections.

Assignment of students to one or both sections was random (Witters & Kent, 1972), haphazard as students registered for the courses (Born, Davis, Whelan, & Jackson, 1972), or determined by university procedures (Sheppard & McDermott, 1970). Students were sometimes pretested for equivalence on dependent measures hypothesized to be correlated with the criterion.

Twenty-three comparisons controlled section assignment and/or demonstrated initial equivalence based on entering mean grade-point average. Cooper and Greiner (1971), C.J. Morris and Kimbrell (1972) and Stalling (1971) further established initial equivalence of attitudes, prior psychology courses, and aptitudes.

Wodarski and Buckholdt (1975) and Kulik et al. (1974) questioned the adequacy of these procedures for assigning students to groups and for testing initial equivalence. The absence of between-group differences in mean grade-point averages does not answer the more basic question of whether grade-point average is a relevant matching variable. Arbitrarily labeling one section of students as a control group does not mean that a truly functional control group has been established; this group may not differ from the experimental group solely in terms of the independent variable.

One characteristic of the comparison studies that was a part of both experimental design and class activities was the teaching staff in the two sections. The Keller sections would be expected to have larger teaching staffs and they did, although in one case nine instructors were involved in teaching two large traditional sections (Stalling, 1971). Either the same instructor taught both sections (Sheppard & McDermott, 1970), or two instructors alternated between sections (Philippas & Sommerfeldt, 1972; Stalling, Ward, & Dunlop, 1972). Sometimes the sections were taught by different instructors in different years (Muir, 1972; Roop, 1973). The size and distribution of the teaching staff, important as it is, may be less critical than the staff's knowledge that one class is experimental and the other a control (Wodarski & Buckholdt, 1975). Such knowledge may be difficult to conceal, but procedures to ensure objectivity in grading criterion tests were used in nine studies. They included blind grading by a disinterested person (Alba & Pennypacker, 1972), independent grading and subsequent correlation by the teaching staff (Born et al., 1972; Born, Davis, Whelan, & Jackson, 1972; Johnston & Pennypacker, 1971; Sheppard & McDermott, 1970), construction of items by a disinterested person (Stalling, 1971; Stalling et al, 1972), and spot checking (Corey et al., 1974; McMichael & Corey, 1969). Cooper and Greiner (1971) rechecked unit tests originally graded by students but did not report rechecking the criterion measure. Although it may seem trite to question the reliability of scoring multiple-choice answer sheets, the author has seldom if ever returned a set of exams to a class without having at least one or two students report grading errors. Midterm exams are often checked by the students themselves. That final exams are usually not so checked emphasizes the need for reliability measures.

None of the studies maximized all five design features, i.e., Keller-type class size greater than 40, standard class size greater than 40, controlled section assignment of students, demonstrations of initial equivalence, and reliability of scoring tests. Six studies included four of the features (Born, Davis, Whelan, & Jackson, 1972; Johnston & Pennypacker, 1971; Philippas & Sommerfeldt, 1972; Sheppard & McDermott, 1970; Stalling, 1971; Witters & Kent, 1972) and six included only one feature (Hapkiewicz, 1972; Moore, J.W., et al., 1969; Morris, C.J., & Kimbrell, 1972; Muir, 1972; Roop, 1973; Rosati, 1975).

Class Activities: The Independent Variable Package

In 27 comparisons, class time for the traditional sections was devoted to lectures by one or more instructors. Instead of lectures, Alba and Pennypacker (1972) and Sheppard and McDermott (1970) used a variety of classroom activities intended to equate the behavior (but not the contingencies on the behavior) of the students in the two groups. In the Keller sections 19 studies permitted self-pacing, 11 required 100% mastery, 14 offered optional lectures, 29 included unit tests (or interviews), and 17 used undergraduate proctors. The use of unit tests was the only feature common to all comparison studies. The five characteristics of the Keller method were included in six studies (Billings, 1972; Born et al., 1972; Born, Davis, Whelan, & Jackson, 1972; Corey et al., 1974; McMichael & Corey, 1969; Philippas & Sommerfeldt, 1972). Four characteristics were included in four studies (Alba & Pennypacker, 1972; Hapkiewicz, 1972; Morris, C.J., & Kimbrell, 1972; Sheppard & McDermott, 1970). Stalling (1971) included only one, and 11 comparisons included only two (Cooper & Greiner, 1971; Johnston & Pennypacker, 1971; Moore, J.W., & Gagné, 1973; Moore, J.W., Hauck, & Gagné, 1973; Roop, 1973; Stalling et al., 1972; Witters & Kent, 1972).

Evaluation of the Experimental Designs and the Independent Variable Package

Most studies in some fashion controlled student assignment to sections and/or tested for initial equivalence of the sections on some covariant, but only nine studies reported an objective system for scoring the criterion test. Although almost all studies organized the traditional section on a lecture basis, 19 comparisons included only three or fewer of the five characteristics identifying the Keller method in their experimental class. Future studies need to measure the reliability of scoring the dependent variable and to include more characteristics of the teaching method evaluated. In essence the 29 studies compared a traditional lecture section of students taking one or two relatively long tests with an experimental section taking a large number of short unit tests. When this chapter later takes up length of assignment per unit test, size of unit and frequency of testing are discussed as confounded variables. This same confounding occurred in the comparison studies.

The comparison studies are not unlike other applied analyses of behavior in which "investigators usually introduce multi-variable packages to see whether the whole thing has any effect," and often "the role of the individual components is trivial [Kazdin, 1973c, p. 532]." Some individual components of the comparison studies may be trivial and others may not. It is not necessary at the moment to investigate each of the five Keller components separately, but any comparison study should minimally include the entire multivariable package of the Keller method. Eventually the teaching package might prove reducible to one variable, frequency of testing.

Common Criterion Measure: The Dependent Variable

Because frequency of testing was an important feature of the comparison studies it is important to examine the test items themselves. Unit tests contained short-answer essay items (Born, Davis, Whelan, & Jackson, 1972; Johnston & Pennypacker, 1971), fill-in-the-blank items (Corey et al., 1974; McMichael & Corey, 1969), and/or multiple-choice items (Cooper & Greiner, 1971; Stalling et al., 1972). Some criterion tests also contained short-answer essay items (Johnston & Pennypacker, 1971), or fill-in items (Born et al., 1972), but most (24) contained multiple-choice items. Although not necessarily a basic characteristic, fill-in or essay items are compatible with Keller's concern for active student participation. Multiple-choice items on criterion tests are consistent with many traditional courses. Apparently almost all authors were willing to challenge the traditional method with its own criterion.

Ten comparisons used fill-in items or interviews in unit tests and compared groups on a criterion test consisting of multiple-choice items. Four obtained statistically reliable between-class differences (Corey et al., 1974; McMichael & Corey, 1969; Roop, 1973; Sheppard and McDermott, 1970) and six did not (Alba & Pennypacker, 1972; Born et al., 1972; Born, Davis, Whelan, & Jackson 1972; Cole, Martin, & Vincent, 1975; Hapkiewicz, 1972; Muir, 1972). Twelve comparisons used multiple-choice items in unit tests and compared groups on a criterion test consisting of multiple-choice items only. Ten of these comparisons obtained reliable differences (Cooper & Greiner, 1971; Moore, J.W., & Gagné, 1973; Moore, J.W., et al., 1973; Moore, J.W., et al., 1969; Stalling, 1971; Witters & Kent, 1972) and two did not (Philippas & Sommerfeldt, 1972; Stalling et al., 1972). Multiple-choice items on both unit and criterion tests seem to increase the chances of obtaining statistically significant group differences. The remaining seven comparisons either did not analyze their results by item type or did not use multiple-choice items in their criterion. Three reported statistically reliable differences (Clark, S.G., 1975; Morris & Kimbrell, 1972; Rosati, 1975) and four reported no differences between sections (Becker & Shumway, 1972; Billings, 1972; Johnston & Pennypacker, 1971; Moore, J.W., & Gagné, 1973). Given these relations, subsequent comparison studies would do well to justify the kind of item used on unit tests in relation to that used in criterion tests (see Wodarski and Buckholdt, 1975, for a similar discussion).

Ten studies included four or five of the Keller method characteristics in their experimental sections. Seven demonstrated significant group differences and three did not for all criterion-item combinations. If only multiple-choice criterion items are considered, then three studies demonstrated a difference (Corey et al., 1974; McMichael & Corey, 1969; Sheppard & McDermott, 1970), and five did not [Alba & Pennypacker, 1972 (note actual error scores in their Table 1, p. 123); Born et al., 1972; Born, Davis, Whelan, & Jackson, 1972; Hapkiewicz, 1972; Philippas & Sommerfeldt, 1972]. The remaining two studies (Billings, 1972; Morris, C.J., & Kimbrell, 1972) did not specify multiple-choice items in their criterion tests. It would be folly to conclude that the comparison studies demonstrated the advantages of the Keller method so well as "to make further collection of data redundant [Nelson & Scott, 1972, p. 294]."

Evaluation of the Dependent Variable

The consumers of a behavioral change ultimately decide its fate. In this case students overwhelmingly favor the Keller method (see Consumer Report section). College deans, department heads, and faculty members who are also consumers remain to be convinced despite the widespread use of the method. Statistically significant differences on a multiple-choice final examination are not likely to be the most convincing evidence to bring about social change. Slightly more than 1000 students were enrolled in the courses reporting positive results. The mean absolute difference in criterion scores between groups was approximately seven multiple-choice items. No one would seriously argue that seven multiple-choice items should be the basis for reorganizing a university system. Part of the problem stems from experimental designs using indirect, discrete response measures averaged across many subjects. Instead of conducting studies with group designs to prove an hypothesis, one can successively examine effects on a direct, continuous response measure of the presence or absence of specific environmental conditions.

Most authors did not analyze the possible relation between the responses presumably reinforced during the course and the responses required during the criterion measure (see Born et al., 1972, for an exception). Instead, they chose most often the response that instructors have used in traditional courses, viz., multiple-choice items. If the desired terminal behavior is an increase in the multiple-choice items correctly answered, then proctors would do well to reinforce responding to multiple-choice items during the course. This is not done because responses to multiple-choice items are not the terminal behavior of concern (cf., e.g., Bostow and O'Connor, 1973, p. 606). The fact is Keller courses seek to develop specific behavioral repertoires, while traditional university courses aim at developing less identifiable phenomena like understanding, appreciation, insight, and knowledge. As Kulik et al. (1974) have pointed out, Keller courses and traditional courses have different outlooks on learning and testing.

Negative results in a few published studies always raise the question of how many other negative results are unpublished. Negative and positive results of studies presumably testing the same hypotheses are usually most readily interpretable when investigators cease asking whether Method A is superior to Method B and begin to ask more specific questions about the conditions under which Method A is likely to be superior to Method B or vice versa. Answering more specific questions requires that at least some of the individual characteristics of the entire multivariable Keller package be examined.

An alternative criterion for comparison might be a test known to be sensitive to changes in student responses during the term. Such a test has been constructed using a multiple-baseline design (Baer et al., 1968; Kazdin, 1973c; Miller, L.K., & Weaver, 1972, 1975). The course was divided into four content areas successively made available to students. Students mastered (90% level) 26 unit tests derived from one-word-answer study guides. Proctors answered questions about the text but not about study guides. A 48-item generalization test with four subtests (each with 12 entirely new items) covering each of the four content areas was administered each week for 13 weeks. The four subtests defined four different baselines. During the first week all four subtests were in baseline; during the second and third weeks, the content for the first subtest was being trained while the other three remained in baseline; from the fourth through sixth week the content for the second subtest was being trained, the content for the first subtest moved to a posttreatment condition, and the final two subtests remained in baseline. This procedure continued until the thirteenth week when all subtests were in a posttreatment condition. Mean correct responses on each subtest were low during baseline and rose during those semester weeks when their content area was being trained. All subtest scores remained high during the posttreatment condition. Given an independent measure of the test's items (such as agreement among judges that the items measured responses to stimuli along a generalization continuum), then different teaching methods could be evaluated on a criterion known to be sensitive to changes in student behavior.

Additional Bases For Comparison

Four studies retested students after elapsed intervals of 2 months (Cole et al., 1975), five months (Cooper & Greiner, 1971), nine months (Corey et al., 1974) or fifteen months (Moore, J.W., et al., 1973). Considerably reduced numbers of students were tested at the follow-up exams. (e.g., from 204 to 18 in Corey et al., 1974). All studies reported statistically significant differences favoring Keller classes. Because the two classes already differed at the end of the course, however, these "retention" differences could merely reflect differences in original learning and not differences in the loss of course material (Lloyd, 1960).

In addition to measuring retention, J.W. Moore et al. (1973) and J.W. Moore and Gagné (1973) compared the mean grade-point averages of experimental and control students in the next course of the same subject matter in which they enrolled. This measure of the transfer effects from one course to another indicated a significant effect in the next physics course (Moore, J.W., et al., 1973) but not in subsequent courses in religion, psychology, or biology (Moore, J.W.& Gagné, 1973).

Hursh, Wildgen, Minkin, Minkin, Sherman, and Wolf (1975) compared pretest and posttest scores of two groups of 17 students on broad, general questions regarding behavior modification (e.g., how to toilet train a child) not specifically covered in the course. Between the pre and posttests both groups were enrolled in personalized courses, one in behavior modification and one in nutrition. The pretest means were 7.9 and 7.8 respectively. The posttest means were 11.5 and 7.4, respectively. The general questions were used to demonstrate that students acquired a general as well as a specific repertory in these courses.

Mean differences between traditional and Keller sections are not the only changes of concern. Most authors also report some measure of student-to-student variability within a section, either graphically or statistically (e.g., standard deviations). In Figure 14-1 (McMichael & Corey, 1969), the frequency distribution for the Keller (experimental) section was skewed toward the lower scores and the range was restricted. Both of these features seem desirable outcomes.

McMichael and Corey (1969) compared three traditional (control) sections to their Keller section. This design feature permitted the authors to demonstrate that similar teaching methods did not whereas different teaching methods did produce statistically different results. Six other studies used

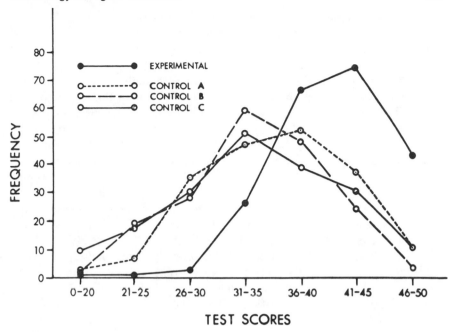

Fig. 14-1. Distribution of test scores for the three control classes and the experimental class. The mean score for the experimental class was 40; for Control A, 35; Control B, 34; and Control C, 34. (McMichael & Corey, 1969, Figure 1, p. 81.)

either multiple Keller sections (Born et al., 1972; Stalling et al., 1972), multiple traditional sections (Stalling, 1971), or both (Johnston & Pennypacker, 1971; Moore, J.W., & Gagné, 1973; Moore, J.W., et al., 1969; Roop, 1973; Witters & Kent, 1972). In all but Moore and Gagné, similar results were obtained with similar methods and different results were obtained with different methods.

Reliability of Dependent and Independent Variables

Because grading assignments in contingency management systems often involves a large teaching staff (instructor, graduate teaching assistants, undergraduate proctors) intergrader agreement must be very high. Staff members regraded a sample of assignments without knowledge of the original grading (Burgess, Epling, Lloyd, & Morrow, 1971; Lloyd, McMullin, & Fox, 1976). The number of tests both the original and repeating grader scored as passing plus the number both scored as failing was divided by the total number of tests scored. This reliability ratio was computed for different semester weeks and for different teaching staff combinations (e.g., instructor versus teaching assistant, teaching assistant versus proctor, etc.). Teaching staff members regraded some tests for which they had also been the original grader.

In one course the instructor, the teaching assistant, and one of two proctors regraded 192 short-answer unit tests originally graded by the students in the class. Reliability ratios were .98 ($N = 65$) for the instructor, .95 ($N = 60$) for the teaching assistant, and .93 ($N = 67$) for the proctors. In another course a sample of unit tests, originally graded by the teaching staff, was regraded. Pearson Product-Moment correlations and reliability ratios for eight pairs of original and repeat graders averaged higher than .90. Agreement was highest when the same individual was both original and repeat grader. For all grader pairs, agreement was generally higher for fill-in items than for short-answer items. This difference may have been because the fill-in items were pretested (McMichael & Corey, 1971a, 1971b) while the short-answer essay items were not.

Generally, reliability ratios were higher than correlations. Neither, however, were sufficiently discrepant to warrant students' concern about who graded their tests. From a students' point of view a reliability ratio is more relevant than a correlation. The reliability ratios were based on whether a unit test was passed or failed. The correlations were based on the actual points obtained. To pass a test required 17 of 20 possible points (85% mastery). Whether a student received 17, 18, 19, or 20 points was relatively inconsequential compared to passing or failing a test.

The correlations just reported are equivalent to those from other authors (Born et al., 1972; Johnston & Pennypacker, 1971; Quigley, 1975; Semb, 1974, 1975; Semb, Conyers, Spencer, & Sosa, 1975; Semb, Hopkins, & Hursh, 1973). Correlational data are reassuring but lack the conviction of an experimental analysis of grading procedures. If different grading procedures used successively by the same graders in an ABA reversal design (Baer et al., 1968; Kazdin, 1973c) produced different reliability scores, then some basis for identifying effective procedures would be available.

Studies directly observing student preparation for unit tests in a study hall, (Burt, 1975; Mawhinney, Bostow, Laws, Blumenfeld, & Hopkins, 1971) obtained similar reliability coefficients for test scoring. Sometimes interobserver disagreements may simply be eliminated. In Lloyd, Garlington, Lowry, Burgess, Euler, and Knowlton (1972) several observers simultaneously took attendance in a large auditorium. If a disagreement occurred, recounts continued until agreement was reached.

The above studies were concerned with the reliability of the dependent variable (unit test scores, final examination scores, time spent studying, or classroom attendance). When complex independent variables are used, interobserver agreement regarding the application of the variables is as important as agreement on the dependent variable. For example, one final examination consisted of two kinds of items: "those that required (students) to recognize instances of a concept or principle, and those that required (students) to recall and/or apply concepts and principles to novel situations" (Morris & Kimbrell, 1972). The criteria used to determine whether a given item would be categorized as a "Recognition Item" or as a "Recall and Application Item" were not described. These two kinds of items constituted independent variables. Evidence that independent observers can agree on categorizing these items would be necessary before repeating their study (cf. Kissler & Lloyd, 1973, p. 188; Miller, L.K., & Weaver, 1975; Semb, 1974, 1975; Semb et al., 1973, 1975).

Farmer, Lachter, Blaustein, and Cole (1972) examined the effects of the presence or absence of proctors during unit tests, but did not specify how they checked whether the proctors were actually present or absent. Quigley (1975) provided a set of behavioral definitions for a proctor's Reliability Report. Tape recordings were made of a sample of student-proctor testing sessions. Second observers, who rescored the student and the proctor by listening to the tape recordings, reached a mean agreement of 96%. Proctor behavior is likely to be studied more frequently in the future (Hursh et al., 1975; Johnston & Pennypacker, 1971, p. 235), and reliable specifications of how proctors interact with students will be needed to reproduce the research.

Responses of Students to the Components of Contingency Management

Prior studies compared terminal performance of groups of students experiencing different course contingencies. The following studies examined some individual features of contingency management systems. The effects of different features were sometimes assessed in terms of a terminal criterion and sometimes in terms of a continuous response measure throughout the course. The studies are ordered somewhat in the sequence in which a student enrolled in a course would encounter the different contingencies.

Completing Assignments

Several investigators reported cumulative number of assignments completed as a function of time intervals during the course (Burgess et al., 1971; Burt, 1975; Ferster, 1968; Johnston & O'Neill, 1973; Johnston & Pennypacker, 1971; Lloyd, 1971; Lloyd & Knutzen, 1969; Lloyd et al., 1976; Mawhinney et al., 1971; Sutterer & Holloway, 1975). These response rate curves are measures more compatible with an applied analysis of behavior than are the indirect, discrete response measures of the comparison studies.

Cumulative response curves of individual students operating under self-pacing contingencies indicate that students complete few assignments early in the semester and complete many assignments late in the semester: they cram (Cheney & Powers, 1971, p. 166; Green, 1971b, p. 770; Minke &

Carlson, 1972, pp. 15-16). Even though the instructor may not impose time contingencies during the semester, the university environment often does so in the form of midterm grades, vacations (Sutterer & Holloway, 1975), the end of the semester, or reverting grades of incomplete to a failure if not completed within some time period. Responding under a fixed temporal contingency is often characterized by few responses early in the interval and many responses later in the interval (Ferster & Skinner, 1957), and students' behavior fits this pattern (Mawhinney et al., 1971). In effect, self-pacing in the Keller system allows the rate at which students complete course requirements to be determined by variables other than those controlled by the instructor (Bostow & O'Connor, 1973).

The semester week during which students began to turn in assignments was positively correlated with the final grade they received even though a grade of incomplete was freely available (Lloyd, 1971; Lloyd & Knutzen, 1969; Sheppard & McDermott, 1970). Sutterer and Holloway (1975) did not replicate this correlation, however. Studies that directly observed students' studying (as contrasted to noting when assignments were submitted) also reported pause and run responding (Burt, 1975; Mawhinney et al., 1971).

Pacing Contingencies

Altering course contingencies can change these study patterns. All assignments may be paced by the instructor (Malott & Svinicki, 1969). Giving bonus points (which counted toward the final grade) for completing assignments early, or raising and lowering point requirements for the final letter grades (cf. Sutterer and Holloway, 1975) changed response rates during the semester but not final grade distributions (Lloyd, 1971).

Three groups of students (randomly assigned) who received different numbers of points per unit test during different thirds of the semester were compared on rate of completing unit tests, on extra work completed, and on final examination performance (Bitgood & Segrave, 1975). The increasing point group (8 points per unit test during the first third of term, 10 during the middle, and 12 during the final third) took more unit tests in each successive third. The constant point group (10 points per unit test each third of the term) also increased but less than the increasing point group. The decreasing point group (12, 10, 8 points) took many tests during the first two thirds of the semester and then took fewest tests during the last third. The decreasing point group completed the most extra work while the increasing point group completed the least. The three groups did not differ on final exam performance.

In another group design study (Semb et al., 1975), some groups were given extra points for working fast and others lost points for working slowly. Students' rates of completing unit tests and criterion tests were compared with a linear rate throughout the semester. Students whose daily rate departed from this linear rate received or lost extra points depending upon the experimental rules that operated in their group. The students in groups with contingencies for receiving extra points or losing points began working sooner than students in a control group that was self-paced. Once again the groups did not differ on exams.

The effect of different pacing contingencies was investigated in two kinds of within-subject designs as well as the between-group designs previously described. In the first within-subject design, unit tests were instructor-paced early in the term, student paced in the middle of the term, and then instructor paced at the end. Students consistently completed more unit tests during the instructor-paced contingencies (Lloyd et al., 1976; Miller, L.K., Weaver, & Semb, 1974).

In the second design, two different pacing contingencies were placed on two different categories of assignments (Lloyd, 1971). The two cumulative response curves for each student were very different. The form and content of the two categories of assignments also differed. In a repetition of this design (Lloyd et al., 1976) 70 students were given two study guides identical in form each week for eight weeks. Questions on each study guide covered the same assignment. One study guide in each pair covered a student-paced unit test which could be completed (85% mastery) any time during weeks 2-15 of the semester. The other study guide covered an instructor-paced unit test administered during class time each week for weeks 2-9.

Individual cumulative curves for 27 students are presented in Figure 14-2. The y-axes for each are cumulative number of tests passed. Two curves from the same origin (end of week 2) are plotted at one-week intervals for each student. The smooth curves indicate the rate of passing the instructor-paced unit tests (classroom tests). The curves with solid circles indicate the rate of passing the student-paced unit tests (office-hour tests). Students who obtained final grades of A, B, and C are plotted in separate rows. Within each row students are ranked according to when they passed the eight student-paced tests. For example, Student 1A (who performed optimally) passed the paired unit tests each week. Student 14A passed one instructor-paced test each week, but waited until week 3 to pass the first student-paced test, until week 7 to pass the second and third, and, finally, until week 10 to pass the eighth student-paced test. Student 17C passed three instructor-paced tests in weeks 1-3, was absent on Week 5, and then passed the remaining four tests. This same student waited until Week 15 before completing any student-paced tests.

The course described by Lloyd (1971) approximated a common university situation in which a student enrolls concurrently in several courses whose assignments differ in content and in pacing. In contrast the course in Figure 14-2 maximized the similarity of instructor-paced and student-paced unit tests. A student preparing for an instructor-paced test read the same material required for the paired student-paced test. The student might most economically have taken both quizzes the same week; only students 1A, 3A,

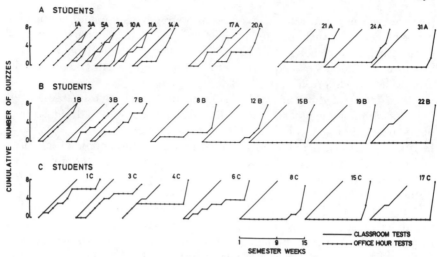

Fig. 14-2. Pairs of individual cumulative curves for 27 students from Course A. The three ordinates indicate number of tests passed by A, B, and C students. The data are plotted at one week intervals on the abscissa. Number and letter on each pair of curves indicate the students' rank within each grade category. Rate of passing Instructor-Paced (Classroom) Tests is shown by the line curves; rate of passing Student-Paced (Office Hours) Tests is shown by curves with filled circles.

5A, 7A, 10A, 11A, and 4C responded optimally some or all of the time.

A presumed advantage of student pacing of assignments is shared by students and staff (Keller, 1968; Kulik et al., 1974; Whitehurst, G.J., 1972). In a student-paced course, work could be distributed in time so as not to interfere with assignments in other, concurrent, and probably instructor-paced, courses. Most work in other courses would be due near the middle and end of the semester. The above data, however, did not indicate that students optimally distributed their time on student-paced tests. In fact most students delayed tests until late in the semester when other courses likely demanded greater efforts.

Student pacing should permit work rates commensurate with study skills and other factors. If anything, student pacing resulted in students working considerably slower than they could have. Over 90% of the students performed acceptably week after week on the instructor-paced assignments, yet most performed at much lower rates on the student-paced work.

Although self pacing increased differences among students, whether this operated to the advantage or disadvantage of students depended on other factors. For example, in Figure 14-2 all students eventually completed 15 tests by week 15 and, according to the course contingencies, all received at least a C grade; the rate at which they completed the unit tests was inconsequential. As Figure 14-2 shows, all eight student-paced tests could be completed in one week (see Students 22B and 17C). In the Lloyd (1971) course, the other assignments could not be completed in one week; they were too complex. In that course, starting early enabled a student to continue working toward a higher grade; starting late precluded further work.

Other authors included some instructor-pacing contingencies. Born et al., (1972) and Witters and Kent (1972) administered midterm examinations at fixed times. To be eligible to take a midterm exam, students had to have previously completed all unit tests related to that midterm. Bostow and O'Connor (1973), Cooper and Greiner (1971), Roop (1973), Stalling (1971), and Stalling et al. (1972) administered unit tests in class each week.

Most instructor-pacing contingencies designed to maintain steady rates of responding by students were probably aversive, although instructor pacing could be based on positive reinforcing contingencies. Bonus points can be given for work turned in early (Bitgood & Kuch, 1971). A reinforcement menu (Addison & Homme, 1966) based on a preference list of assignments (Lloyd & Knutzen, 1969) can be constructed. An early final can be scheduled for students who complete unit tests quickly (Born, 1975).

All of these studies emphasized that pacing contingencies change student response rates during a semester. None showed any effect on a criterion test. Instructors offering a wholly student-paced course quickly recognize the logistical problem of adequately testing all the students who confront the proctors in the last two weeks of the semester. As Sutterer and Holloway (1975) appropriately pointed out, however, instructor pacing should be justified on the basis of improved student performance and not merely as a logistical convenience.

Withdrawing from the Course

Completing a Keller course is like completing a chain of responses, i.e., passing each unit has both reinforcing and discriminative properties. The passing score not only reinforces prior responding (studying) but also signals that it is permissible to proceed to the next unit. Faced with a long chain of responses, subjects often pause (Kelleher, 1966a); they may also escape. Born et al. (1972), Born and Whelan (1973), Keller (1968), Philippas and Sommerfeldt (1972), and Sheppard and McDermott (1970) amply documented that more students withdrew from Keller courses than from traditional courses. Frequency distributions plotting percent of students against letter grades varying from A through F to withdrawal are U-shaped (Keller, 1968).

If poorer students withdraw from Keller sections, then the superiority of Keller classes on final examinations could be due to variables other than those considered essential to personalized instruction. This probably was not the case with the comparison studies, although Kulik et al. (1974), concluded that withdrawals did bias the results. Thirteen comparison studies specified the number of students withdrawing from their courses. Six did not observe differential withdrawals (Alba & Pennypacker, 1972; Cooper & Greiner, 1971; McMichael & Corey, 1969; Moore, J.W., et al., 1973; Moore, J.W., et al., 1969; Stalling, 1971). Of seven studies noting differential withdrawals, three had very few withdrawals (Born et al., 1972; Morris, C.J., & Kimbrell, 1972; Rosati, 1975); one failed to find a difference favoring the Keller method (Philippas & Sommerfeldt, 1972); one reported no difference in mean grade-point averages for students who withdrew and those who stayed (Sheppard & McDermott, 1970); and two reported more withdrawals from the traditional section (Cole et al., 1975; Moore, J.W., & Gagné, 1973).

But other studies reported considerable differences in withdrawals. In seven courses examined by Born and Whelan (1973), withdrawals from Keller sections were three to five times greater than from traditional sections and students who withdrew had lower grade-point averages. The latter was also true for the smaller number of students withdrawing from traditional courses. Students did not seem to withdraw due to failure, because 80% had passed the last unit test attempted (see also Sutterer and Holloway, 1975). But 96% of the withdrawing students had waited longer than nonwithdrawing students before beginning to take tests. Wood and Wylie (1975) replicated these results and found close agreement of mean grade-point average and mean American College Test percentile rank with letter grades (A-F and withdraw). Personalized instruction courses may encourage the withdrawal of poorer students instead of helping them complete the course.

Final grade distributions for Keller courses frequently reveal that most students receive A's and B's. If students with lower grade-point averages withdraw, then students who would normally receive a C apparently receive a B or A, but students who would normally receive an F or D withdraw. Subsequent research should identify conditions that will induce potentially withdrawing students to remain and work.

Preparation for Unit Tests

The data on pacing contingencies indicate when students completed unit tests. This need not reflect when and how they studied. Two measures of studying have been reported: one is a direct, continuous measure of studying in a special classroom (Mawhinney et al., 1971) and the other is a self-report form which is turned in when a unit test is attempted (Johnston, Roberts & O'Neill, 1972). Consistent study patterns emerged but no relation to criterion measures has been demonstrated. In one report, all studying by 20 students who had volunteered to participate was observed through a one-way mirror that looked on a special room in which all study materials were kept (Mawhinney et al., 1971). Observers recorded the time students sat at a study table with study materials open on the table. The independent variable was the testing schedule. Tests were administered each day or each week in one experiment and each day or every three weeks in a second experiment. Students studied daily when tested daily. As the intertest interval increased, daily absences from the study room increased early in the interval and study time increased later in the interval. The courses were conducted over nine- and ten-week terms and each condition was repeated in an ABAB order. This design permitted a replication of conditions within each study. In experiment II, daily testing occurred during weeks 1 and 2 and weeks 6 and 7; three-week testing occurred during weeks 3-5 and 8-10. This was the first published study to use a reversal design within a university course.

Although this experiment described studying in detail, it did not present test scores as a function of intertest interval. Burt (1975) used both response measures as a function of concurrent assignment schedules. From an introductory psychology class of approximately 300 students, 45 volunteered for this special class. Of these, 24 with different grade-point averages were selected; four students later withdrew. All studying was conducted in a room with an adjoining observation room. Reading materials and study guides were cut from published materials. All identification titles and names were removed. The reading materials had not been used in other courses taught at the university. Local book stores did not stock the materials.

Twenty pairs of assignments, judged equal in difficulty on the basis of number of pages, questions, and concepts, were prepared. Points toward final grades depended upon completing the 40 study guides and taking four midterm exams plus a final exam. The midterm exams occurred every three weeks (weeks 4, 7, 10, and 13). Weeks 14 and 15 served as review before the final exam during week 16. For one of each pair of assignments, study guides could be completed at any time during a three-week interval and the student received points for correct responses. For the other of each pair of assignments, points were given only if one study guide was completed within four days of completing the last study guide.

The two pacing contingencies produced clearly differentiated study patterns. More assignments were completed on the four-day than on the three-week pacing contingency. Scores on the midterm or final exams did not differ as a function of pacing. Half the materials from each pacing condition were available for review before the final exam; reviewing increased performance considerably. The study patterns confirmed those of Mawhinney et al. (1971), but whether study patterns affect performance has not been demonstrated.

Born, Davis, Whelan, and Jackson (1972) also restricted course reading and study materials to a monitored study center. Observers recorded when students entered and left. A Keller section was compared with a traditional lecture section. Students in the Keller section spent more hours (mean was = 46 hr) in the study center than students in the traditional section (mean was = 30 hr). Keller students could attend only occasional lectures; students in the traditional section could attend three lectures per week. The mean attendance at these lectures was 19 hr which, if added to the 30 hr these students spent in the study center, removed any section difference in course preparation time.

In the second method of measuring studying, students were trained to fill out a study report form for each unit test (Johnston, Walters, O'Neill, & Rasheed, 1975). The form covered such information as time spent reading the assignment, underlining, rereading, using visual aids, etc. The correspondence between actual and reported preparation was assessed by varying the number of pages assigned to different units of work. For seven successive unit tests covering reading assignments of 60, 90, 30, 90, 60, 30, and 60 pages, the mean reported first-reading times in minutes were approximately 130, 160, 90, 180, 100, 105, and 130, respectively. Assignment length and reported reading times corresponded closely. In a similar study, the total reported mean study times of approximately 400, 525, 350, 375, 650, 375 and 450 min varied directly with the successive unit reading assignments of 30, 60, 30, 60, 90, 60, and 90 pages. The mean reported percent of time spent reading the text for the first time varied directly with unit assignment length. The mean reported percent of time spent rereading the text, summarizing the text, and writing terms, names, and definitions varied inversely with assignment length (O'Neill, Johnston, Walters, & Rasheed, 1975).

Additional validity for the study report form was obtained by noting, for example: that rereading assignments or rereading written aids was not reported until after reading the assignment for the first time or after preparing the written aids had been reported; that students, constructing their own unit tests while studying, reported writing the same kind of items as would appear on the unit test; that rereading or transcribing lecture notes was not reported during periods when no lectures were presented; and that responses such as underlining or taking notes were most frequently reported as occurring during the first reading. The goal of this research was to relate study behavior to teaching methods and to performance on criterion measures. Johnston et al. (1975), argued that the study report form could provide more and different response measures than observers in a separate study room could record. Because so little information about studying is available, both direct observation and self-reporting procedures need to be continued.

Study Guides

Unit tests often consist of fill-in or short-answer essay items. Students are usually required to answer all or almost all the items correctly before trying the next unit. Instructors typically provide students with study questions covering the reading assignment for each unit test. The purpose has been to alert the student to the most important parts of the assignment. Unit tests have been constructed from items identical to those on the study guides or from entirely different items or from a combination of both.

In investigating the effect of study guides on criterion tests and unit tests, three criterion tests during the term contained four kinds of items (Semb et al., 1973): new items, items appearing on a prior unit test but not in a study guide, items appearing in a study guide but not on a prior unit test; and items appearing both in prior study guides and on prior unit tests. Student performance on the three criterion tests increased directly with prior exposure to items either on unit tests or in study guides. In a second experiment students took unit tests containing ten short-answer essay items. Four items appeared in a prior study guide along with their answers; four items appeared with no answer provided; and two items had not previously been seen by the students. The mean percent correct responses on 16 unit tests were 96% for items with answers, 92% for unanswered items, and 74% for new items. The data supported the facilitative effect of giving students questions covering the material on the unit tests.

Given that study guides are important factors determining performance on unit tests, the effect of unit tests on final exams has been investigated (Semb, 1975). In a counterbalanced ABAB design students either turned in answers to study questions without taking unit tests or took unit tests. In either condition proctors required 100% mastery of 10 items. When grading a study guide, proctors only examined those answers that would have appeared on a unit test had one been administered. One half of the students turned in answers for the first four units of the course while the other half took unit tests on these same four units. During the next four units the conditions were reversed for the two groups. The presence or absence of unit tests had no effect on final exam scores.

Similar negative results appeared in comparing performances of four groups of students on weekly Wednesday exams as a function of the tests they had to take on Mondays and Tuesdays (Williams, R.L., 1975). One group was tested on study guides each Monday and Tuesday, one group took both study guide and lecture tests, and the last group took no tests. Students taking both tests scored more points on Wednesday tests, but the difference was not statistically significant. In both studies students had access to study guides. Some were tested on the study guides and some were not. The critical variable may be the study guides rather than the unit tests on the study guides. Because the only consistency among the comparison studies was the presence of unit tests in the Keller sections, it is important to determine conclusively whether unit tests or simply study guides are the critical independent variables.

In addition to various combinations of study-guide items and unit-test items, midterm exams may be required. In a counterbalanced ABAB reversal design, Semb (1975) either did or did not require students to pass (100% mastery) a midterm exam after passing four unit tests. Under condition A students in one group were only required to pass four unit tests. Under condition B these same students passed four unit tests plus an hour exam.

Students in the other group were exposed to the conditions in a BABA order. The presence or absence of midterm exams had no effect on final exam scores.

The effect of written answers to study-guide questions was compared in two other procedures (Whitehurst, G.J., 1972). Unit tests were given every Friday for eight weeks. On Wednesdays, students were required to submit written answers to a study guide, to be interviewed by a proctor who asked questions from the study guide, or to attend group discussions based on the study guide. Students completed each of the three procedures twice in a counterbalanced order over six of eight weeks. They were not required to attend on Wednesdays for the remaining two weeks. The mean number of incorrect answers (on 25-item multiple-choice unit tests administered on Fridays) was 1.56 for written answers, 1.65 for tutorials, 1.88 for discussion groups, and 1.90 for no attendnace on Wednesdays. Written answers to study guides resulted in fewest errors.

These same students were asked which Wednesday procedure they found most helpful in preparing for unit tests: 44% chose group discussion, 34% chose tutorial, and 22% chose written answers. Their preference for each procedure was the same when asked which they enjoyed. This direct reversal of test performance and verbal preference for the three procedures is undoubtedly a function of many variables. G.J. Whitehurst (1972) treated the Wednesday procedures as preparation time. How the students actually prepared on, say, Thursday evenings is not known, but could have controlled their verbal performance. If a future study were to observe all preparation by students (cf. Burt, 1975; Mawhinney et al., 1971), then verbal preference and perparation in and out of the classroom could be compared.

Degrees of Mastery

Whether a student passes a unit test depends not only upon his own preparation but also upon the level of mastery set by the instructor. Performance improves with higher mastery requirements (Bostow & Blumfeld, 1972; Bostow & O'Connor, 1973; Johnston & O'Neill, 1973; Semb, 1974). The effect of mastery requirements can be measured on at least three dependent variables: unit tests and review tests, number of test retakes, and criterion tests. Johnston and O'Neill (1973) compared performance on unit tests when mastery criteria for passing were absent (a traditional course control), low (60% correct), medium (75%), and high (90%). Four groups of students were tested. Group I performed throughout the nine-week term with no mastery criteria; their final grades were determined by a distribution of their scores at the end of the term. Groups II, III, and IV were shifted from one mastery level to another in three different serial orders in an ABCA counterbalanced reversal design. Conditions were shifted on an individual basis as student performance stabilized. The dependent variable was a rate measure (Johnston & Pennypacker, 1971): the proctor timed the testing session and then counted the items answered correctly and incorrectly. Next the proctor calculated the rate of reading and answering items correctly and incorrectly (number of items divided by elapsed time) over about 10 min.

Figure 14-3 (Johnston & O'Neill, 1973) shows the mean responses per minute of the final performance on unit tests under each criterion for groups I-IV. The response rates for group I were approximately equal to those for the low criterion condition of groups II-IV. The response rates in groups II-IV varied directly with the criterion rates regardless of the serial order in which the rates were encountered. The final performance on a given criterion never equaled the initial performance (e.g., in group II rates under the initial high criterion were higher than under the final high criterion). The initial rate of responding was too high; the final rate was always closer to the actual criterion. The mean number of attempts required to pass a unit test increased as the criterion increased.

Using mastery levels of 100% and 60% in an ABA counterbalanced design, Semb (1974) compared the percentage of correct responses on unit tests, review tests of recall items (items in prior study guides), and new items. The percentage of correct responses on first attempts was greater

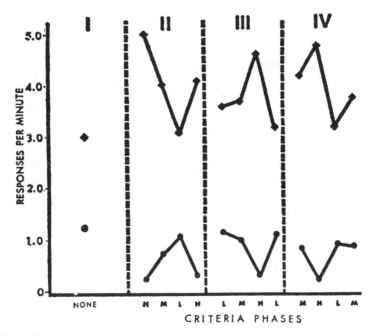

Fig. 14-3. Mean of final performances on units completed under each set of criteria for Experiments I to IV. Diamonds represent correct responses and circles represent incorrect responses, H = high, M = medium, and L = low criteria. (Johnston & O'Neill, 1973, Figure 2, p. 265.)

under the 100% mastery than under the 60% mastery condition for both unit tests and review tests and for both recall and new items. The percentage of correct new items was always less than that of recall items. The total attempts required to pass either unit or review tests increased as the criterion increased.

In addition to these two dependent measures, Semb also obtained five successive response measures on an achievement test containing entirely new items (Miller, L.K., & Weaver, 1972). The achievement test items covered the entire course. This test was administered the first day of class and after each successive fourth of the course. Gain scores (later tests minus pretest percentage of correct responses) increased or decreased depending upon whether 100% or 60% mastery was required. The results of both studies agree with Johnston and O'Neill's (1973), conclusion that "with respect to criteria the teacher should start high and go higher" [p. 268].

Bostow and Blumfeld (1972) and Bostow and O'Connor (1973) examined a different procedure involving mastery criteria. Students took an instructor-paced unit test in class, received their scores on it the next day, and then, if not satisfied with this first score, could take a second unit test. The mastery level set by the instructor was zero; the student was simply given a chance to improve the initial score (Cooper & Greiner, 1971; Stalling, 1971). The experiment was concerned with inducing more students to try to improve their initial score by varying the weightings used to score the first test.

The independent variable was employed in a within-subject counterbalanced ABAB design in one study and in a between-subject randomly assigned group design in two studies. In one condition students either could choose to accept their first test score (Bostow & Blumfeld, 1972) or were required to accept it (Bostow & O'Connor, 1973). In the other condition students whose first unit test scores were less than 80% mastery essentially received zero credit unless they took the second test. Students in this latter condition took more Friday tests (Bostow & Blumfeld, 1972), had higher mean initial test scores (Bostow & Blumfeld, 1972), and statistically outperformed ($P < .05$) students in the former condition on the final exam (Bostow & Blumfeld, 1972; Bostow & O'Connor, 1973).

Final letter grades made available to students set a different level of mastery. Offering students only an A or F alternative follows directly from the arguments for 100% mastery of unit tests (Malott & Svinicki, 1969). If students must obtain 100% mastery of each unit test to pass it, then they should likewise be required to complete all unit tests available, and doing so would be equivalent to an A grade. C. Whitehurst and Whitehurst (1975) compared final grade distributions of three groups of students enrolled in different sections of the same course. One group could obtain seven final grades: A, B+, B, C+, C, D, or F; the other group could obtain two final grades; A or F. There were more A's and more F's in the latter group. Differences between groups for number of A's were statistically significant.

No statistical analyses were reported for the F grades. The groups did not differ on a pretest-posttest criterion measure or on a course evaluation.

At the end of the course students were distributed into all seven grade categories. This has been the author's experience when, in different courses, different combinations of final grades (e.g., no D's, no B's or D's, etc.) have been offered. Whenever a grade has been offered some students have accepted (sic) it. If a given letter grade was not offered, then it remains unclear whether students who would have received it actually obtained higher or lower grades. The C. Whitehurst and Whitehurst data (1975) suggest that both happen (although they did not make this interpretation). The author has frequently asked students at the beginning of courses which grade they intended to obtain. Of hundreds of students, none ever listed a D; the author no longer offers D grades.

Size of Unit (or Frequency of Testing)

Keller (1968), advocating many short unit tests, gave 30 in his course; subsequent investigators used fewer unit tests. In an ABA design performance on review tests and achievement tests of short assignments (unit tests plus review tests) was compared with long assignments (only review tests), Semb (1974) found that the percentage of correct responses was greater with short assignments. The long assignment condition required more test retakes. These data are not conclusive. It would not be necessary for the short assignment condition to include a review test, as was the case here. Second, Semb (1974, Figure 3) indicates that the third review test was particularly difficult. This test was also the review test for the long assignment condition.

In another study (Born, 1975) one group had to pass 18 unit tests of essay items; a second group had to pass nine tests (two units per test) and the last group had to pass six tests (three units per test). Performance on the final exam (40 new multiple-choice items and 60 new short-answer essay items) did not differ as a function of the size of the unit tests. The groups' progress through the course was very similar. Semb (194) and Born (1975) varied size of unit in slightly different ways. Semb compared performance on review tests; Born compared performance on a final exam. Although their results are different, these procedural differences make them noncontradictory.

The independent variable, size of unit, could as well be labeled frequency of testing. Frequency and size have been confounded in the aforementioned comparisons. One experiment avoided this confounding by holding number of unit tests constant while varying the number of pages of text assigned to each unit (O'Neill et al., 1975). The mean percentage of correct answers on the first attempt to pass a unit test and the mean number of attempts necessary to reach the 90% mastery criterion varied directly with unit size. The mean percentage of correct answers on the final attempt to pass a unit test did not vary as a function of unit size; on their final attempts students scored close to the required 90% mastery level regardless of the size of the unit assignment. No criterion tests (midterms or final exams) were used.

Experimental designs for assessing assignment length are essentially identical to some experimental designs used by the comparison studies to test an entirely different hypothesis. For example, Witters and Kent (1972) administered 5 or 6 one-hour exams (in different comparisons) to traditional and Keller classes; the summed scores on these tests constituted the dependent variable. Students in the Keller classes completed several unit tests prior to each hour exam; students in the traditional classes did not do so (cf. also Dustin, 1971; Hapkiewicz, 1972; Keys, 1934, for similar designs). Witters and Kent (1972) and Born (1975) used a between-group design and students could not retake hour exams. Semb used a within-subject design and students had to retake review tests until they reached 100% mastery. Nonetheless, assignment length as defined (namely, the presence of different numbers, including zero, of unit tests before a criterion test) operated in all the comparison studies. All the comparison studies used unit tests in their Keller classes and not in their traditional classes. Stated still another way, the size of unit in the Keller classes was small, whereas that in the traditional classes was very large.

Lectures as Consequences as Well as Prompts

Keller (1968) suggested that lectures and demonstrations should occasionally be available to those students who completed a certain number of unit tests. Lectures were viewed as reinforcers for completing prior tests rather than as means of imparting information about forthcoming tests. Broudy's (1963) characterization of the lecture as the "core of scholastic instruction" pointed to its value "when books were scarce." Then it was a "reading of a book by the master (who) might embellish the reading with commentaries and explanations [p. 18]." After the Scholastics the printing press eliminated the scarcity of books but not lectures. In another context, Fischer (1970) envisioned a college in which students inserted one dollar into a turnstile that permitted them access to the lecture of their choice; the number of dollars in the turnstile determined the lecturer's salary.

Thorndike, (1923) questioned the traditional use of class time:

The actual facts, principles and applications given in a college course of ninety hours can often be printed in a book that a capable reader could get through in nine hours. The extra eighty hours must have a value equal to eighty hours of such study, experiment, problem solving and the like as could be guided by printed directions if it is to be justifiable. One reason why children seem to learn so much better from personal teaching than from books is that many of them spend much time in class meetings and little time upon books [p. 162].

The lecture and demonstration methods represent an approach to a limiting extreme in which the teacher lets the pupil find out nothing which he could possibly be told or shown. They frankly present the student with conclusions, trusting that he will use them to earn more. They ask of him only that he will attend to and do his best to understand, questions which he did not himself frame and answers which he did not himself work out. They try to give him an educational fortune as one bequeaths property by will [p. 188].

Some authors set up rules resembling Keller's but did not enforce the contingency (e.g., McMichael & Corey, 1969). Lloyd et al. (1972) using ABA reversal designs reported data on lecture attendance as a function of three separate contingencies in three courses. Following a baseline of noncontingent lectures students received points worth one unit test for attending lectures in one course, or received information relevant to questions on future unit tests during lectures in another course. At the end of baseline approximately 40% of the students were attending weekly lectures. The contingencies for the two courses increased attendance to 90%; removing these contingencies decreased attendance to baseline. Following baseline in a third course attendance was made contingent upon completing certain assignments. Attendance, which had been slowly declining during baseline, dropped rapidly during the contingency and remained low (5%) after the contingency was removed. Lectures in the first two courses were given by the two instructors responsible for each course. As a control for instructor behavior several different instructors were used in the third course. As measured by attendance, no evidence for the reinforcing properties of lectures was found.

In Lloyd et al. (1972), course attendance decreased throughout baseline. Similar decreases in attendance at lectures in Keller courses have been reported by Born and Herbert (1971), Ferster (1968), Gallup (1969), and G.J. Whitehurst (1972). Using an AB design, G.J. Whitehurst (1972) reported a rapid decrease in attendance at group discussions after attendance was no longer required.

That lectures do not serve as reinforcing events need not eliminate all usefulness in meeting with the entire class from time to time. Short lectures can be followed by one or two item tests with point value and make it worthwhile for the student to attend (Williams, R.L., 1975). The author and an assistant have offered concurrent lectures for a single class; no systematic data are available but student response appeared favorable. From many personal communications and personal experiences weekly or bi-weekly class meetings seem of value, although the lack of empirical data prevents any recommendation.

Group Contingencies

In the previously described studies points or final grades were awarded on the basis of each student's performance. Points or grades could be awarded on the basis of some measure of the performance of the entire class. Group contingencies in classrooms with persons younger than university students have been effective in reducing classroom noise level (Schmidt & Ulrich, 1969), in changing gestures (Sulzbacher & Houser, 1968), and in increasing attendance (Packard, 1970). Performance under one form of group contingency was compared with performance under an individual contingency (Burgess et al., 1971) in a counterbalanced ABA reversal design.

Eight groups of approximately 22 students each completed assignments during weeks 2-4 and weeks 8-10 under individual contingencies; all received whatever points they had earned. During weeks 5-7 and weeks 11-13, they completed assignments under a group contingency. Every student in the group received the mean number of points earned by the three students in the group with the lowest point total for that three-week period. Eight other groups of students began the course under group contingencies and ended under individual contingencies.

The dependent variable was the mean number of points actually earned by each student within a condition (even though the number received may have been less than the number actually earned under the group contingency). The median actual points for the groups beginning on individual contingencies were: 30 for individual contingency, 20 for group contingency, 67 for individual, and 55 for group for the four conditions. The median actual points for the groups beginning on group contingencies were 20 for group contingency, 37 for individual contingency, 35 for group, and 100 for individual. Performance under the individual contingency was always superior to performance under the adjacent group contingency. The superiority occurred early in the semester when few points were earned as well as late in the semester when many more points were earned. This particular group contingency was relatively severe and ineffective. Other kinds of group contingencies in groups of varying sizes must be studied before any general conclusions are possible.

Student Behavior as a Function of Proctor Behavior

The value of proctors has never been understated in the literature of the Keller method. They provide personal contact with students in a large class—contact a single instructor could not provide. They can answer questions a student is embarrassed to ask the professor. They can provide immediate feedback to responses on unit tests. Collectively, they can operate a testing center 40 hr a week. They are fresh, young, and eager.

The percentage of unit tests at which a proctor was present (0%, 25%, 50%, 75%, 100%) was manipulated by Farmer et al. (1972). For the students who never encountered a proctor the number of retests was greatest and the final performance was lowest. The other groups did not differ statistically from each other. No data on group variability (e.g., standard deviations) were presented. The authors did not specify the behavior their proctors were assumed to emit while interacting with a student nor were any direct observations of proctor responding reported. The authors recommended intermittent proctoring. It is not clear from their data exactly which unit tests were proctored in the 25% group. There were 20 units tests in all. The five proctored ones could have been the first five, the middle five, the last five, etc. If a subsequent study introduced proctoring during the middle-unit tests only, then a reversal design could be accomplished with one group of subjects and the data could be analyzed in terms of individual proctors.

The percentages of correct responses on initial attempts at unit tests and of retakes of unit tests as a function of whether or not proctors discussed incorrect answers with students were compared (Hursh et al., 1975). For half the students proctors discussed errors on the first five unit tests and not on the second five; the order was reversed for the other half of the students. The percentage of correct responses on initial attempts at unit tests was 98% with discussion and 94% without discussion. The percentage of required retakes was 3% with discussion and 18% without discussion. During the discussion the proctor prompted, discussed relevant information, or asked leading questions until the student could respond correctly. Without this correction process provided by the proctor, 35% of the initial attempts on tests would have been scored as failures. Thus students who took tests with a proctor discussing their errors actually came to the test less well prepared than students who were not proctored. For the final five unit tests students could choose to have errors discussed or not discussed; in 237 of 238 choices students opted for discussion of incorrect responses with a proctor. Research on proctor interaction will contribute to the development of an experimental analysis of social behavior (McGinnies & Ferster, 1971). The present data, however, do not permit clear conclusions.

Proctor Behavior as a Function of Having Proctored

Proctoring is assumed to benefit not only the student but also the proctor (Gallup, 1970; Green, 1971a; Keller, 1968; Koen, 1971; Sherman, J.G., 1974a). No data have been published to document this point even though proctors often receive university credit for their work. It is insufficient simply to cite the familiar adage that the best way to learn material is to teach it (Sherman, J.G., 1974b). Many issues involved in presenting social prompts and social reinforcers to university students are common to all areas of the applied analysis of behavior. It is recognized that elementary-school teachers (Becker, Engelmann, & Thomas, 1971) and psychiatric ward personnel (Kazdin & Bootkin, 1972) can benefit from training in social interactions. Similar investigations of interactions between proctors, graduate assistants, tenured full professors, and undergraduate students should be initiated.

At the very least it should be possible to demonstrate that proctors learn some course content while proctoring. Unpublished data from two courses taught by the author and William E. McMullin document an improvement in proctor performance under certain conditions and a lack of improvement under other conditions. The dependent measures were identical 60-item multiple-choice pretests and posttests administered to undergraduate proctors at week 1 and week 10 of the semester during which they proctored introductory psychology courses. In one course 23 proctors (first through fourth year undergraduates) obtained 27 mean correct responses on the pretest and 38 on the posttest. In this course the unit tests administered by the proctors covered the major textbook in the course (Kendler & Kendler, 1971). The multiple-choice items on the pre- and posttests also came from this textbook.

In a second course two groups of 11 second-semester first-year undergraduate proctors obtained 43% and 48% mean correct responses on the pretest. The group scoring 43% were then informed that they would not begin proctoring until after week 10, when more students would be taking unit tests. The other 11 proctors began proctoring immediately. On the week 10 posttest the nonworking proctors obtained 48% mean correct responses and the working proctors obtained 50% mean correct responses. Two sets of unit tests were used in this course. One set was derived from Kendler and Kendler (1971) and the other from Atkinson (1971). The instructor and the graduate assistants administered unit tests from Kendler and Kendler while working proctors administered unit tests from Atkinson only. Several Kendler and Kendler textbooks were always in the proctor room. Students taking unit tests from Atkinson were concurrently taking unit tests from Kendler and Kendler. All the multiple-choice items on the criterion pretest and posttest came from Kendler and Kendler. Despite the many opportunities to become familiar with the Kendler and Kendler text, the 11 working proctors failed to improve their performance on the posttest either in comparision with their own pretest or with nonworking proctors. These are clearly preliminary data, presented here in a cautionary vein to suggest some limits on the changes in proctor behavior to be anticipated.

Consumer Reports

Having completed a PSI course, students are in a position to evaluate it. Generally, students overwhelmingly prefer the Keller method to traditional courses; they often think the course is difficult, and that the self-pacing feature is the most desirable aspect of the course (Kulik et al., 1974). The reader interested in greater detail should especially consult Born and Herbert (1971), Cooper and Greiner (1971), Gallup (1969), Linder and Whitehurst (1973), Lloyd and Knutzen (1969) and Witters and Kent (1972). Student evaluations are themselves responses that should change as the course contingencies change. No one has shown that students would change their course evaluations if successively exposed to different contingencies in a counterbalanced ABA reversal design.

The inverse relation between test performance and verbal evaluation reported by G.J. Whitehurst (1972) suggested that the independent variables controlling a subject's verbal responses to a questionnaire and those controlling the responses to the actual situation described in the questionnaire are different. Psychologists have often opted to measure the verbal report and to assume some kind of positive correlation (see Kutner, Wilkins, and Yarrow, 1952, for an early assessment of this correlation) between the two response classes. In theory (Skinner, 1957) and in practice (Risley & Hart, 1968), the correlation may be positive, negative, or zero depending upon prior reinforcement histories of one or both of the response classes.

An alternative, although not necessarily a substitute, is a direct measure of the response of interest. Four studies have given students a choice of alternative classroom conditions. The Hursh et al. (1975) data indicated an overwhelming choice for discussion of incorrect responses with a proctor. In another study students could choose the type of item to be included on a unit test (Lockhart, Sexton, & Lea, 1975). The item pool for unit tests consisted of 40 fill-in items and 40 multiple-choice items matched for course content. Unit tests consisted of 40 items; the first contained both kinds of items in blocks of ten in counterbalanced orders. In subsequent unit tests students could choose the item type for the next 10 items. If they chose the same item type for two blocks of ten items, they were forced to switch to the other type. Considering only free choices, students chose multiple-choice items over fill-in items by a mean difference of 37%. Students chose multiple-choice items regardless of whether they had just completed a block of multiple-choice items or of fill-in items. Response accuracy on unit tests did not vary as a function of item type. Students were not requested to indicate their choice of items verbally.

An almost 100% choice for the Keller method over a traditional lecture method was demonstrated during a 15-week term in which students were exposed to a traditional lecture method for weeks 1-3 and 7-9 and to a Keller method for weeks 4-6 and 10-12 (Lloyd, McMullin, Fox, Rinke, & Duncan, 1974). During weeks 13-15, when they were offered an actual choice of either method, 176 of the 178 students chose the Keller method. Similar results were obtained by Born (unpublished). After completing half the course under the Keller method, students could choose to finish the course in a Keller section, in a lecture section, or by just taking the final examination. Of 63 students, 62 chose the Keller section.

Actual choices validate some of the verbal behavior in student-evaluation questionnaires, but they do not indicate the basis for the choice. The basis could be established by directly manipulating consequences for one or both choices. In a study of such correspondence (Risley & Hart, 1968), the responses of interest were the hours students planned to study,

the hours actually studied, and the degree of correspondence between planning and actual studying (Nielson, Lloyd, & Lloyd, 1974). University students with low high-school grade-point averages reported each noon the
times and places where they planned to study during the following 24-hr
period for any of their courses. Direct observations of their studying were
made at half-hour intervals. Students were given points toward a final course
grade for simply submitting their plans, for increasing their actual study
time, for planning to study more time, or for correspondence between planned and actual studying. The latter condition produced the greatest agreement between verbal report and actual behavior. Giving points only for
planning resulted in the last correspondence.

SUMMARY

In a review of university courses Lloyd (1971) listed several decisions an instructor would have to make before beginning a course. The same
decisions still have to be made, but now more evidence is available to
determine some of the choices.

The first decision concerned which terminal behavior was to be established at the end of the course and which assignments would be more likely
to lead to that terminal behavior. No research has been devoted to this
problem. The second decision concerned the number and difficulty of assignments to be associated with whatever final letter grades are to be used.
The studies on degree of mastery of unit tests strongly argue for high standards. The third decision involved selecting a reinforcer. Lectures appear to
be ineffective as reinforcers. Potential reinforcers on a university campus
beyond the immediate grades or points in a course have not been explored.
The fourth decision was whether to reply on student pacing or instructor
pacing. Although no data are available to show that pacing affects performance on a criterion test, considerable data show that student pacing leads
to substantial test taking at the end of the term.

Lloyd (1971) also cited five questions that potential users of behavioral
systems frequently ask and offered tentative answers. Subsequent research
has provided some evidence bearing on three of these questions: Does the
system reinforce quantity at the expense of quality? (Again see the research
on level of mastery.); Do students understand the material or are they just
doing the work? (see Hursh et al., 1975; L. K. Miller & Weaver, 1972, 1975);
and, Do students do any better in these courses than in lecture courses? (See
the comparison studies.) No systematic data are available to answer a fourth
question, Would the system work for a graduate course as well as an undergraduate course? The remaining question, Is the meaning of a grade changing?, has not been researched but has stimulated many faculty discussions.

It is also possible to take a second look at Keller's (1968) original five
course characteristics. The subsequent research strongly supports unit tests

and/or study guides and an insistence upon 100% mastery of unit tests. The research also supports, although less strongly, undergraduate proctors and a large number of unit tests. Lectures do not serve as reinforcers, according to the available data. Student pacing, although a hazard in terms of instructor logistics, has yet to be shown a detriment to criterion test performance.

To date the research emphasis has derived largely from the university classroom as traditionally structured. Response measures, for example, have been geared to three-semester-hour courses and final examinations. Response measures could be much smaller or larger (Greenspoon, 1974; McKean, Newman, & Purtle, 1974). Another example of the control on research exerted by the traditional classroom has been the reliance on grades as convenient behavioral consequences. The problems in high education have not been consistently viewed in terms of fundamental principles of behavior, although Keller's writings have been a tremendous step in this direction. The research has not been systematically concerned with reinforcing stimuli, with discriminative stimuli, or with component and terminal responses.

No work has evaluated or identified assignments or contingencies that most effectively produce specific student responses (e.g., those conditions that result in students working independently, or with peers, or that increase or decrease cheating, etc.).

An early section cautioned the reader against an overly eager acceptance of the Keller method. It was pointed out that changes in educational practices have not historically been correlated with empirical evidence supporting the changes. There are, in short, fads in education. It was hoped that such would not be the case with Keller's suggestions for organizing university courses. Although the comparison studies leave much to be desired, an analysis of higher education has begun. Many college instructors are now following the old graduate school cliché that admonishes the new Ph.D. to "combine teaching and research." An empirically oriented outlook toward instructional practices cannot help but modify the behavior of the instructor in directions supported by objective information.

SECTION III
SOCIAL AND EDUCATIONAL APPLICATIONS

DON BUSHELL, JR.[1]

Chapter 15

An Engineering Approach to The Elementary Classroom: The Behavior Analysis Follow-Through Project

A distinction must be drawn between applied behavior analysis as a clinical procedure and applied behavior as an engineering technique. Implicitly or explicitly, every problem in applied behavior analysis is shaped by the analyst's decision to emphasize one of two approaches: (1) to adapt the individual's behavior to the existing environment (clinical approach), or (2) to design a new or altered environment (engineering approach).

THE CLINICAL APPROACH

Until recently, behavior analysts have been trained in traditional graduate psychology programs. That may help to explain why most research

1 Although singly authored, the content of this chapter represents the contributions of many students and colleagues in the Department of Human Development at the University of Kansas, and several at other universities. Thomas A. Brigham, Co-editor of the present volume, and Joan Jacobson Brigham were the author's collaborators in the original design of the Behavior Analysis program for Follow Through. In the years since, a large number of talented people have developed and refined the program, which is now a tangible expression of our collective conviction that applied behavior analysis is capable of making valuable contributions to education in general, and to the education of poor children in particular. The Behavior Analysis program is now under the capable direction of Eugene A. Ramp, with Ann K. Branden, Donald A. Jackson, and Lynn C. Weis as Associate Directors. It is also a pleasure to acknowledge the thoughtfulness of Joel Levin of The University of Wisconsin, and of Arthur E. Wise, a Visiting Scholar at The Education Policy Research Institute, Washington, D.C., who were kind enough to offer a critique of an earlier version of this chapter. The preparation of this chapter was supported in part by a Grant from the U.S. Office of Education, OEG-0-8-522422-4433.

literature has been devoted to improving the undesirable or maladaptive behavior of *individual* clients or patients. The typical research question has followed Baer, Wolf, and Risley (1968) in asking how "to get an individual to do something effectively" in a given environment. Operationally, the question is approached with a teaching sequence designed to bring the behavior of an individual under the appropriate control of "natural" contingencies in that environment.

By definition, natural contingencies are adequate to maintain the appropriate behavior of most people, but for various reasons they may not be functional for a particular individual. Consequently the clinical problem is implicitly defined according to normative criteria. A problem exists when normal conditions of the environment do not have normal effects on the behavior of an individual. Therapy consists of *temporarily* adjusting the environment to secure behavioral control, and then fading that control toward the natural environmental conditions; or of shaping new responses that bring the individual into contact with natural contingencies previously out of reach. For the most part, the clinical approach takes the environment as a given.

THE ENGINEERING APPROACH

When the same or similar problems are evident over and over again, it may be appropriate to search for deficiencies in the design of the environment rather than in the behavioral repertories of individuals. Traffic engineers, for example, when observing a high accident rate at a particular intersection, are expected to redesign that intersection with a new left-turn lane or modified signal lights. The engineers could of course try to teach each individual driver the particular skill needed to avoid the unique dangers of that intersection and not alter the environment at all. They could but probably would not, because they are trained to look at traffic control as a problem of environmental design (an engineering problem) rather than as a problem of individual driver capabilities (a clinical problem). For the most part, the engineering approach takes the environment not as a given, but as the thing to be changed and managed. The engineered change is meant to be enduring, in contrast to the transitory environmental modification of the clinical approach.

Failing to distinguish clearly between the objectives of clinical and engineering applications seems the root of a recent debate. In a stimulating discussion in the *Journal of Applied Behavior Analysis*, Winett and Winkler (1972) chided behavior modifiers for teaching children to "be still, be quiet, be docile." K.D. O'Leary's (1972) rejoinder initially rejected the assertion as empirically unsupported, then tacitly accepted it by entertaining the possibility that it may be adaptive for school children to "be still, be quiet, be docile." The issue was then further confused by editorial comments that tended to ignore the original indictment and focused instead on the need to ask experimental rather than philosophical questions.

The apparent disagreement can be reconceptualized by observing that Winett and Winkler were actually criticizing the absence of engineering applications more than they were attacking the clinical applications that have helped individual teachers and children. If a teacher asks for help in controlling an unruly class, clinical support to correct that particular problem seems entirely appropriate. Urging more work to engineer a new environment so that children's tolerance of intolerable classrooms is not shaped also seems entirely appropriate, but different.

While clinical applications tend to be individual, normally initiated by the client, and conducted in a relatively private or out-patient arrangement, engineering applications are designed for groups and conducted in institutional settings (normally public-supported institutions). Indeed the genesis of an engineering problem is almost invariably institutional in nature. Social institutions, according to sociology, are conventional and patterned ways in which society attempts to deal with recurrent social problems. Family relations, socialization (child rearing and education), occupational training, deviance, illness, and death are recurrent problems for any social group, and all societies have developed institutionalized ways of dealing with them. The problem is that social institutions seldom function as well as might be hoped.

Many familiar examples show that the behavior problems of the inmate or patient frequently become worse rather than better as a result of institutional practices. The criminal becomes "hardened" rather than rehabilitated by prison experience; the psychiatric patient develops more problems in the ward than were present on admission; hospitalization sees a decline in patient vitality resulting from the ward environment; and children are more handicapped educationally the longer they attend ghetto schools. Each of these is an example of an institution aggravating the problems it is intended to alleviate; each illustrates institutional practices in need of engineered modification.

Even though the *Journal of Applied Behavior Analysis* has been devoted almost exclusively to the experimental verification of clinical procedures, many significant advances in the field of applied behavior analysis arose from projects attempting to design or actually implement new institutional environments. The grand paradigm, of course, is provided by the engineered community described by Skinner in *Walden Two* (1948b). Subsequently, Birnbrauer, Wolf, Kidder, and Tague (1965) designed and operated a classroom program for institutionalized retarded children at the Rainier School in Washington. McKee (1964) used behavioral techniques to design an educational system in the Draper Prison Project in Alabama. After designing an innovative system for high-risk college entrants at Southern Illinois University (Cohen, H.L., Kibler, & Miles, 1964), Cohen went on to build the Case Project (Cohen, H.L., Filipczak, & Bis, 1967) at the National Training School for Boys in Washington, D.C. Ayllon and Azrin (1965) transformed a psychiatric ward from a custodial environment to an educational setting at the Anna State Hospital in Illinois. Burchard (1967) described the design of a programmed environment for retarded delinquents at the Murdock Center in North Carolina. Rule and Salzberg used behavioral techniques to design and operate a community elementary school in Colorado Springs (Salzberg, 1972). The Engelmann-Becker model for Project Follow Through established a new design for primary-level classroom education in hundreds of classrooms throughout the country (see Chapter 10). Ulrich (1975) is working to establish an experimental community near Kalamazoo, Michigan. Miller and Feallock (1975) have established a successful group-living system for college students in Lawrence, Kansas (see Chapter 19). The outstanding example of behavior analysis as an engineering technique is provided by the Achievement-Place Program described in Chapter 18.

Each of these programs exemplifies how behavior analysis can, and does, take an engineering approach to designing and operating more effective social institutions. Although many techniques and procedures in these systems are identical to those in clinical applications, the engineering task begins with a different set of assumptions and a unique set of requirements.

Characteristics of the Engineering Approach

The instances of successful programs are still too few to assure that the requirements for designing an effective social institution are fully understood. Nevertheless, some approximate guidelines are evident, and their statement here should provide a basis for further development as well as a framework for describing an engineering project known as the Behavior Analysis Follow Through Project.

Program Description. A program description is the handbook or manual that guides action, much as a set of blueprints or working drawings guides a builder. When the environment is social rather than phsycial, however, the description emphasizes procedures and detailed role prescriptions. The program description is not as technical as the methods section of a research report because it is not intended to stand alone as a complete set of prescriptions for every situation. It does, however, explain the objectives and procedures of the program sufficiently that potential clients may evaluate the relevance of the approach for their situation.

A demonstration project provides the best possible program description. A single attractive demonstration of effect speaks more clearly than volumes of printed material. The fact that the new system is successful is the best possible indication that it can be successful in other settings.

Training: The Delivery System. Potential clients who read a compelling program description or see a convincing demonstration project next want to know how to replicate the program in their own situation. The answer is provided by a description of the training procedures. Training can be considered in a series of levels ranging from the easiest and cheapest (read a manual and follow its instructions) to a complex and protracted sequence of consultations, workshops, and practicum experiences that, in some cases, approximates graduate education. The objective of training is to give the trainee (teacher, teaching parent, ward attendant, supervisor, etc.) the skills needed to implement the program accurately and completely. The obvious rule is to use the cheapest procedure that works. Less obvious rules are discussed later.

Quality Control: The Maintenance System. The essence of the engineered environment is that it is replicable. The components and procedures of its design are sufficiently detailed that it can be reproduced within acceptable limits in varied settings. Like McDonald's restaurants or Mobil stations, the procedures and their products need to be predictable independent of locale. That kind of replicability can only result from highly refined quality-control procedures. Three elements comprise a quality-control system: (1) a recording and reporting system that provides repeated measures of effect (current status), (2) a feedback system responsive to the measures of effect, and (3) a system of differential consequences tied to the measures of effect.

The three requirements (description, training, and quality control) are interdependent; none stands alone. Although it is not within the scope of this chapter, it would be possible to demonstrate that the reason most of the aforementioned engineering programs were never replicated beyond the original demonstration project was the lack of well-developed training systems and quality-control procedures.

BEHAVIOR ANALYSIS IN EDUCATION

It was asserted at the outset that behavior analysts shape the problems they confront by viewing them as either clinical or engineering problems. Most behavior analysts who worked in classroom situations took the clinical approach at the invitation of a teacher or a principal (client) who sought help with a specific problem. Most of those problems were in the area of classroom management, and so, as Winett and Winkler (1972) observed, the preponderance of published reports focused on the elimination of student behavior the teacher considered disruptive. Behavior analysis in education has, in fact, been highly correlated with procedures to make children "be still, be quiet, be docile." Happily, however, correlation is *not* cause, and the existence of a pattern does not establish the necessity of that pattern.

The ubiquity of behavior problems can be taken as the clearest possible indication that the problem is the school environment and not the disposition or capability of individual students or teachers. In the extreme, this view sees the contemporary institution of the public elementary school as a social problem itself. To apply powerful clinical techniques to help a few individuals adjust to a poorly designed environment may be a disservice to society if it delays the design of an improved school environment for educators and students.

The design described and discussed in the following pages attempted to take an engineering rather than a clinical approach to the problems of the elementary classroom. It is a program that arose from a particular set of social and economic circumstances. Consequently the special circumstances of its inception and development need to be kept in mind.

The Problem in Education

In the middle 1960's the initiation of federally supported compensatory education programs explicitly recognized that the problems of poverty and ethnic minorities are interlocked with the problems of the schools (see Hughes & Hughes, 1972). The Economic Opportunity Act of 1964, closely followed by the Elementary and Secondary Education Act of 1965 (especially Title I of ESEA), combined to illuminate the magnification of the problems of education in schools serving the urban and rural poor.

Educational policymakers have commonly assumed that the achievement gains of poor children are less than those of middle-class children. Because we do not test all school children each year in this country, the data supporting the assumption range from observers' impressions to local data from the testing programs of individual school districts. Nevertheless, the regularity of the findings led Charters to observe that the correlation between social class and success in school "has been so consistently confirmed by research that it now can be regarded as an empirical law [Charters, 1963, pp. 739-740]." The Coleman Report, published in 1966, added some specificity to the problem description. Coleman found that the test scores of minority children fell further behind those of majority children each year they were in school. Minority children who had not dropped out of school by grade 12 were 3.3 yr behind their majority counterparts (Coleman, J.S., 1966). Obviously the deficiency would be even greater if the achievement levels of the dropouts were included.

An oversimplified portrait of the problem is presented in Figure 15-1, which graphically represents the cumulative loss predicted for poor children. While middle-class children gain a year in achievement each year they are enrolled in school, poor children gain roughly two thirds of a year in achievement for each year of enrollment.

The Head Start Solution

The initiation of Head Start in the summer of 1965 attempted to break the cycle of poverty by enhancing the preschool development of poor chil-

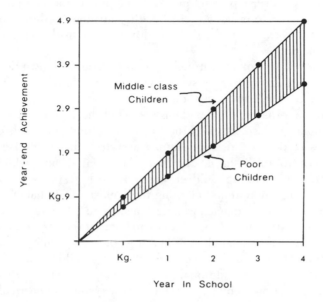

Fig. 15-1. Differential rates of academic progress for middle-class and poor children. The upper line represents the rate of academic gain of 1 yr per school year that is expected of middle-class children. The lower line represents the two-thirds of a year per school year rate of gain expected of poor children in conventional school programs. The shaded area describes the progressive deficit accumulated by poor children. (Kg is kindergarten.)

dren. The first (and undoubtedly premature) evaluation of that initial eight-week summer program (Wolff & Stein, 1966) failed to find any advantage at the end of kindergarten for the children with Head Start experience. The director of the Office of Economic Opportunity, Sargent Shriver, responded by claiming that the improved readiness of Head Start children had been quashed by the public schools; and in January 1967 President Johnson asked Congress to support a program to follow up the gains of Head Start. The resulting program is called Follow Through.

The Follow Through Solution

Because of limited funding, Follow Through has operated as a research program for some rather than as a service program for all children who graduate from Head Start each year. After a pilot year (1967-1968), Follow

Through pursued a research strategy known as *planned variation*. Under the planned variation strategy, the same general problem is attacked differently by each of 22 intervention agents called program sponsors. Sponsors work with as few as one and as many as 21 projects located in communities throughout the country. Each project is required to provide for the direct participation of children's parents in the development and operation of the program; and each is to provide such "health, nutritional, education, social, and other services as . . . will aid the children to attain their full potential [Egbert, 1973, p. 5]."

At the outset, all Follow Through sponsors made their own determination of how the traditional school system was deficient in meeting the needs of poor children. The nature of their diagnoses determined the design of their proposed alternative system. Those who felt the schools were middle-class institutions, unresponsive to the particular ethnic, cultural, or social circumstances of poor children, designed a system that shifted more administrative control to the local community of parents. Those who felt that the free development of the children was blocked by repressive classroom management designed systems releasing the children from harsh and arbitrary rules of conduct and encouraging teachers to respond more to the children and to control them less. Those who felt that the racism inherent in the schools systematically taught the children they were inferior designed systems intended to enhance the self-concept of the children and their parents. Those who felt that traditional instructional practices were inappropriate to the needs of poor children designed new systems of curriculum and instruction.

Every sponsor had the same charge: "Describe a program that will solve the educational problems of poor children. Then, be prepared to work with any community that elects to use its Follow Through funds to implement the new educational program you have described in kindergarten through third grade. The effects of your approach will ultimately be evaluated in comparison with the effects achieved by all other sponsors."

THE BEHAVIOR ANALYSIS DESIGN FOR FOLLOW THROUGH

The design of a new system must always extend beyond currently available data. By 1968 applied behavior analysis had produced a few score clinical demonstrations of its effectiveness. Even though the *Journal of Applied Behavior Analysis* had not yet begun publication, the field's rapidly growing bibliography of accomplishment had served notice of its beneficial implications for education. The test posed by Follow Through, however, was whether this approach, or any approach, could produce its benefits in the midst of an ongoing public-school system. There were no data on this question in 1968.

Program Scope

Follow Through was designed to be implemented gradually, one grade level at a time, beginning with the entering year (usually kindergarten) and expanding to the next higher grade each year until it was operating as a full kindergarten through third-grade program. The enabling legislation made no provision for grades above third. Consequently *Behavior Analysis* began as a small program for 746 children in 28 kindergarten classrooms in five school districts: the Hopi Day Schools in northern Arizona; Portageville, in the Missouri boot-heel; Philadelphia, Pa.; Trenton, N.J.; and the upper edge of the south Bronx, N.Y.

The children in these classes were black, white, Puerto Rican, and Indian; their teachers ranged from first-year people with provisional certificates to those with 18 yr of classroom experience; the settings were both urban and rural; and the buildings were both new and very old. About the only consistent factor across all the sites is that the children were poor.

New communities were awarded Follow Through grants the following year, 1969. Seven of these new communities elected to adopt the Behavior Analysis model and so joined the original group of five in the process of implementing the program. The new projects were in Pittsfield, in the Berkshire mountains of Massachusetts; Louisville, Ky.; Indianapolis, Ind.; Waukegan, in northern Illinois; Meridian County, at the southern tip of Illinois; Kansas City, Mo.; and the Northern Cheyenne Tribe in southeastern Montana. These new sites brought the second-year enrollment in Behavior Analysis classes to 2800. From the fourth year (1971-1972) to the present, the program has annually served over 7000 kindergarten through third-grade children in approximately 300 classrooms of 15 separate projects.

Goals

The basic ground rules of behavior analysis make it difficult to deal with those diagnoses of school problems that have vague or ambiguous physical referents. Still, there is a kind of subjective validity to the frequently cited concerns over what sociologists describe as the alienation of the community from the school. Behaviorally, it is more appropriate to observe that the school is too often avoided by parents, who know it only as the place that calls when their children are behavior problems, learning problems, truant, tardy, or ill. For inner-city children, aggression, hustling, conning, and being cool are all likely to be reinforced outside the school. Inside the classroom, the demonstration of those skills is likely to be punished. For a child whose existing skills are extinguished or worse, and who lacks skills to bring his behavior into contact with approved reinforcers in the school environment, the results seem predictable. School in a poor neighborhood is a highly visible institution that is frequently a source of punishers for parents and children and infrequently a source of reinforcers. From this kind of initial analysis, the basic objectives of the Behavior Analysis program were developed.

The first objective was to help classroom teachers (including permanent and parent aides) to become more effective behavior modifiers with particular skill in the uses of approval and token reinforcement. Because it was all too prevalent in the classrooms we encountered, special emphasis was given to eliminating all forms of punishment.

The second objective was to take advantage of the Head Start background of the children by introducing formal instruction in reading, handwriting, and mathematics at the kindergarten level. This meant replacing the whole-class presentations of the traditional kindergarten with intensive small-group and individual instruction.

The third basic objective was to introduce parents into the classroom as instructional agents. As paid members of the school staff working cooperatively with certified personnel, the parents might then find the school a new source of social and financial reinforcers.

These basic objectives were sought in situations where teachers did not volunteer but were assigned to the program by local supervisors, and where the obvious forms of differential reinforcement for teachers' behavior (such as merit pay) are prohibited by law, unions, or local politics.

Program Characteristics

Only rather general objectives were reflected in the description of the model in the fall of 1968, but by the end of that first year, the program took on a basic form it retained ever since. Specific procedures were developed, added, modified, revised, and abandoned in subsequent years, but the greatest changes were in the procedures for training school district personnel, and in providing useful feedback to projects. The general pattern of classroom operations has been relatively standard through the years.

Classroom Staff. Many considerations contributed to the staffing pattern developed for Behavior Analysis classrooms. First, because effective shaping requires lots of consequences for lots of behavior, it seemed desirable to provide for small-group instruction and individual tutoring by adding more teachers. Second, the active involvement of the parents in the program was considered essential in the federal guidelines of the program.

Politically it was clear from the outset that the informed support of the children's parents was to be vital. Because Follow Through was funded out of Title II (the community action title) of the Economic Opportunity Act, a parent group known as the Policy Advisory Committee (PAC) had an important advise-and-consent function in program affairs.

The form of parent participation adopted in the Behavior Analysis model, however, was influenced as much by educational as by political considerations. Before 1968, a form of the Behavior Analysis program had been applied in the Juniper Gardens Parent Cooperative Preschool, a Head Start Research and Demonstration Project in Kansas City, Kans. The co-op program was singular in that it was staffed and operated by the parents of the children who attended. The success of that project demonstrated that parents could be very effective teachers, and also offered encouragement that the program's impact may have been expanded because the parents extended their classroom use of contingent praise into the home.

For these reasons, the Behavior Analysis program created two positions for the parent teaching aides in each classroom. The specific objectives of this procedure were (1) to develop a clientele that was well informed about the program by virtue of direct classroom participation in it, (2) to make the teachers more responsive and accountable to the community by bringing them into a direct working association with the parents, (3) to provide needed teaching positions within the economic limits of the program, and (4) to provide needed additional income for the parents.

The parent aides are first hired for a six- to eight-week period during the year their child is in kindergarten. These are considered training positions and they are filled in a sequence that brings 11 parents into each kindergarten classroom during the first year. The next year some of these parents return to work for a longer period in the first grade. And so it continues each year. As the children progress and the curriculum becomes more sophisticated, the teaching skills of the parents improve with experience and training. Many of the parents who have gone through this sequence have now been hired by their school district as full-time teacher aides. Because Follow Through schools are also Title I (ESEA) target schools, a classroom aide position is provided by Title I funds in the primary grades. Consequently a Behavior Analysis classroom in Follow Through contains a certified lead teacher, paid with district funds; a permanent aide, paid with Title I funds; and two parent aides, paid with Follow Through funds.

Curriculum. Following the assumption of Staats and Butterfield (1965) that children gain access to a school's reinforcers as a function of their academic performances, the Behavior Analysis curriculum emphasizes the core subjects of reading, arithmetic, handwriting, and spelling. Although there are variations, the usual pattern is for the certified teacher to be responsible for reading instruction, the permanent aide for arithmetic, and the parent aides for handwriting and spelling. The ideal selection criteria, described in detail elsewhere (Bushell, 1973, Chapter 4), can be summarized briefly. The criteria conform to the requirements of shaping and they define the desirable qualities of any instructional sequence, including published curriculum materials. The ideal curriculum:

1. Describes the behavior of which the student will be capable at the end of the sequence.

2. Measures the student's entering skills.
3. Requires frequent responding by the student.
4. Contains clear criteria for a correct response.
5. Provides for periodic testing of progress.
6. Allows for individual rates of progress.

The faithful use of these criteria was tempered by the realities of availability, cost, and training requirements. A curriculum meeting all six criteria that existed only in someone's laboratory school could not be selected for practical as well as political reasons. As a practical matter, the materials had to be readily available in sufficient quantity to meet the immediate needs of thousands of children in projects throughout the country. The political issue is a consequence of the fact that many school districts purchase all supplies from "approved lists," and it can be difficult to get new materials on the list. These two factors, combined with a profound reluctance to get involved in curriculum development, recommended the use of commercially available materials. The only exceptions were primers for handwriting and reading where no appropriate commercial materials could be found. In these two instances it was necessary to develop, publish, and distribute the needed materials.

Unreasonably high cost eliminated at least one commercially available curriculum that scored rather well on the basic selection criteria. Finally, in those situations where several curricula were rated comparable on the selection criteria, the one chosen required least training for its effective use by paraprofessionals.

As a result of all these considerations, the Behavior Analysis curriculum for Follow Through is:

Reading
   Behavior Analysis Phonics Primer, Behavior Analysis Sponsor. Lawrence: University of Kansas. Then *Programmed Reading*, Buchanan and Sullivan Associates. St. Louis: McGraw-Hill (Webster). Then *Reading Laboratory Series*. Chicago: Science Research Associates, Inc.
Mathematics
   Sets and Numbers, Suppes and others. N.Y.: Random House (Singer).
Language Arts
   Behavior Analysis Handwriting Primer, Behavior-Analysis Sponsor. Lawrence: University of Kansas. Then *Handwriting with Write & See*, Skinner and Krakower. Chicago: Lyons and Carnahan. Or, *Kittle's Penmanship*. N.Y.: American Book Company. Then *Basic Goals in Spelling*, Kottmeyer and Claus. St Louis: McGraw-Hill (Webster). Or *Words and Patterns*, Day and Lightbody. Chicago: Science Research Associates, Inc.

Motivational System. Token reinforcement procedures have a variety of benefits that are much better documented now than they were in

1968 (Kazdin & Bootzin, 1972; Chapter 6 in this book). Beyond their effects for children, however, tokens provide many discriminative stimuli for teachers (Mandelker, Brigham, & Bushell, 1970). A pocket full of tokens to be dispensed during an instructional period is a constant jingling reminder for the teacher to be alert for the good responses and improved approximations of the children. The child who lacks enough tokens to participate in an exchange period clearly and immediately indicates a problem. The lack of tokens may signal that this child was inadvertently ignored during the instruction period, or was confronted with an assignment beyond his ability, or was uninterested in the activities for which the tokens could be exchanged. Whatever the problem, its acute and immediate visibility greatly improves the probability that it will be quickly corrected.

Tokens are also an invaluable aid to teacher training. It is relatively easy to train a teacher to praise children for their good work and improving performance, but to maintain that desirable teaching behavior in the absence of direct and continuous supervision can be difficult. A rule stating that tokens are always to be delivered with descriptive praise (praise that explicitly describes the behavior the teacher likes) sets a clear training objective. In the initial implementation of the Behavior Analysis program, the tokens provided a substantive body of technique and procedure that was unfamiliar to the teachers. This unfamiliarity gave us (the intruding would-be innovators) a specifically identifiable area of competence and expertise that lent needed credibility to our activities. Our training could be explicit. Tokens leave a frozen record of the rate and distribution of a teacher's approving contacts with children during an instructional period. Consequently their use preempts the possibility of differing interpretations by teacher and trainer of the type illustrated by such statements as, "No, I'm sure I gave him as much attention as I gave her." The tokens provide a running public record of the performance of both the teacher and the student. Because the effects of token procedures on children's behavior are well described elsewhere (Chapter 6), it is only necessary to describe how they are used in Behavior Analysis classrooms.

During an instructional period, the class is arranged into four small groups of six to eight children with each group working on a different academic subject under the direction of a teaching adult. As the children work with their materials, the teacher moves from one child to another being careful not to follow a predictable pattern and only initiating contacts with children who appear to be working. At each contact the child's written work is checked and the child is asked for an oral recitation of current work. A token, along with descriptive praise, is delivered contingent on correct *vocal* behavior (there are too many inappropriate ways to get correct marks on paper); the child is encouraged to continue the good work, and the teacher moves to contact another child in the group who appears to be working.

At the end of the instructional period (its length varies from 10 min at the beginning of kindergarten to 60 min by the end of third grade) the children have the opportunity to exchange their accumulated tokens for one of several activities. Each exchange period offers at least six different activities, and each activity requires a different number of tokens in proportion to its attractiveness. The menu of activities changes from period to period and from day to day in order to keep things new and interesting. The activities are of the sort intrinsic to a regular primary level classroom (e.g., games, arts and crafts projects, dancing, stories, singing, time in the gym or playground, and the opportunity to work on extra reading or arithmetic). This no-cost practical system arranges the classroom environment so that a child who is more productive during an instructional period has a greater range of choices during the following exchange period. The appropriately differential consequence is relatively immediate and is provided several times each day.

Measurement Procedures. The effective allocation of training and support resources depends on the ability to monitor local program procedures and the progress of the children. A functional monitoring system must provide ongoing feedback that can be used to adjust and refine program operations. In a laboratory class observational measures are both helpful and practical. With many classrooms separated by hundreds of miles, however, continuous direct observation is not practical. The requirement is for a limited number of reliable measures that can be obtained with very little effort in a standard form that permits rapid analysis and feedback.

Experience has winnowed our focus to three critical variables: the week to week placement of the children in the curricula (rate of progress), the children's performance on embedded tests (accuracy), and the amount of time devoted to instruction each day.

Following the last instructional period each week, the teacher records the book and page number on which each child is working in each curriculum on that day. The recording is done on a preprinted class roster form called the Weekly Individual Progress Record (WIPR). A child's absences during the week, if any, are also recorded on the form. Week-to-week comparisons of placement describe a child's progress through the curricula and, at any time, provide a clear prediction of year-end placement. When the rate of progress is deficient, corrective procedures can be instituted quickly; and when progress is adequate to achieve year-end objectives, compliments are in order for both the teacher and student.

Information on progress describes acquisition only if it is coupled with information on accuracy. Although some Behavior Analysis teachers maintain daily records on the accuracy of written and oral work, most do not. They consider the effort too great in proportion to the benefits. Instead, a simple convention is employed whereby a student must pass each embedded test with 80% accuracy before moving on to new material. Failure to reach the 80% level results in immediate remediation (usually by tutoring), concentrating on the specific areas of difficulty rather than reviewing the entire unit. All of the curriculum materials in the program have frequent embedded tests that safeguard against moving on to material beyond a child's current ability, or that provide a cue that the child might be skipped ahead in the curriculum.

Information on how the teacher allocates each day's available time is provided by a Daily Schedule Form (DSF). Unlike the traditional lesson plan calling for a prediction about what will be done, the DSF is an after-the-fact log of what actually occurred. The teacher records the beginning and ending time of each activity during the day on the DSF. A collection of these reports from any class describes the time devoted to (1) instruction, (2) exchanges, and (3) all other activities (e.g., lunch, bathroom breaks, field trips, assemblies, etc.). When, for example, the reading progress of a class is deficient, information from the DSF's provides the basis for precise practical recommendations on how to increase reading time. Without this information, consultants and trainers are left in the awkward position of having to offer platitudes like, "Better try and improve the reading." Teachers do not appreciate that kind of help.

How these three measures are combined into a functional monitoring and feedback system is described in the discussion of the Behavior Analysis quality-control system.

INITIAL TRAINING: THE DELIVERY SYSTEM

For the most part, experimental data on the effects of behavior analysis in education have come from relatively well-controlled classroom settings convenient to the experimenter. The challenge of Follow Through is that it requires the replication of the basic program model in remote sites that are remarkably inconvenient and regularly beset by teachers' strikes and other misfortunes. Experience has taught us that clear descriptions of method and procedure are necessary but not sufficient to achieve comparable effects in Massachusetts and in Arizona. Consequently even though the basic elements of a Behavior Analysis classroom have been the same since 1968, our training and support procedures have changed and developed continuously. In this area, our approach to a difficult engineering problem has most evidenced trial-and-error procedures (and too often error).

Some Un-recommendations

Even though it is not customary to publish unsuccessful procedures, it may help others to know something of the training and delivery strategies we abandoned, and why.

Perhaps reflecting our own academic backgrounds, our first training attempt was in an intensive summer institute for new teachers and aides. Held at the University of Kansas in 1968, the institute was successful in teaching the trainees an impressive array of verbal skills about the literature and principles of applied behavior analysis. The institute was also successful in helping staff and trainees become good friends. The data collected during the fall semester, however, made it clear that the institute had not altered the teaching behavior of the trainees when they returned to the familiar environment of their own classrooms. We have held no more academic institutes.

Midway through the first year, desperation prompted us to conduct an in-class workshop on the site of one of the projects. For three days we modeled the procedures of a Behavior Analysis class and systematically put teachers, aides, and parents through the process of conducting brief lesson segments with small groups of children under close supervision. The beneficial changes in classroom operations were immediate, substantial, and endured for the balance of the year.

Encouraged by the success of the local workshop procedure, we opened the next program year with a series of regional and local workshops that began in the western states in August and concluded in the northeast eight weeks later. After repeating the sequence again in the middle of that year, it became evident that even though it continued to be effective, the procedure was far too costly in time, energy, and money. The traveling teams of trainers were simply worn out by the combined demands of extended travel and intense training.

The next year two regional training centers were established, one in Lawrence, Kans. and the other in Philadelphia, Pa. Each center contained four operating classrooms with the normal complement of teachers and aides. For the next 2 yr, trainees traveled from their home districts to one of the centers for a one-week practicum sequence. The program of the week could be somewhat tailored to the individual trainee, but generally began with academic training and ended with the trainees conducting the demonstration class as they would their own. Because small groups of trainees came to the centers throughout the year, it took longer to make the first training contact with teachers new to the program, but the added personal attention seemed worth it. The centers were as effective as local workshops and spared the training staff exhausting travel. Still, however, they were too costly, and they set the occasion for several trainees to observe, "This is all very well, but the children in my room are different."

Current Training Procedures

The training centers no longer operate, and the present delivery system for Behavior Analysis consists of four components. Two of these (district advisors and staff trainers) have been part of the delivery system since the beginning of the program. The other two (local training classes with demonstrations and training manuals) replaced the functions of the former institutes, workshops, and training centers.

Each Behavior Analysis project is the direct and personal responsibility of a behavior analyst designated as the district advisor. The district advisor uses the telephone, the mail, and monthly visits to see that the local project staff receives appropriate in-service support and technical training. Initially, when a project is small, the advisor may provide classroom training personally, but as the project grows these functions are assumed by local training specialists, called staff trainers, who are themselves trained by the district advisor.

The second component of the training system consists of two training positions for every 10 classes. These two trainers, one who concentrates on the needs of lead teachers and permanent aides and the other who concentrates on supporting the teaching parents, continually work in the classroom to improve the performance and refine the teaching techniques of the entire project staff. With practice and continued support from the district advisor, many of these trainers have become extremely skilled behavior modifiers.

Third, each project is responsible for the operation of its own training and demonstration classes. These local training classrooms have replaced the former workshops and training centers, and provide intensive individualized practicum experience for the teachers, aides, and parents. These settings provide the opportunity to rehearse observation and recording techniques, specific curriculum strategies, planning, and management techniques with the help of the demonstration teacher and the staff trainer. These classrooms are always available to train teaching teams from other district classrooms, and they avoid the "My children are different" complaint. Even though this procedure means that a teacher may not receive initial training until many weeks after the start of a school year, the end result, over a 2-yr period, is a much higher level of program implementation.

Fourth, the basics of the Behavior Analysis approach to classroom behavior management and the teaching of each curriculum are specified in a series of training manuals that describe program characteristics (Bushell & Ramp, 1974), token procedures (Bushell, 1974b), beginning reading instruction (Becker, J., & Jackson, 1974), instruction in other core curricula (Jackson, 1974), and training procedures (Jackson & Minnis Hazel, 1974). That a program begun in 1968 has training manuals dated 1974 testifies that it took a long time for the teachers with whom we work to shape our behavior to the point at which they were satisfied. The lack of a sensitive feedback system from the teachers to us was a flaw in the original design of the program that persisted too long. How that problem is being alleviated is part of the description of the quality-control system.

QUALITY CONTROL: THE MAINTENANCE AND SUPPORT SYSTEM

The history of educational intervention has been a sequence of laments over the fact that promising new practices turn out to be transitory deviations rather than enduring alterations in school procedures (see, e.g., Rogers, 1968; C.E. Silberman, 1970; Ford Foundation, 1972). Once the original innovators leave the scene, the novel practices they introduced fade into conformity with convention and tradition. The Follow Through experience strongly suggested that the impermanence of institutional modifications results from deficiencies in training and in quality control, but particularly in quality control.

The functions of traditional role relations and incentive systems within an institution are not abruptly set aside by an innovative program. Innovation is a gradual shaping process that needs to establish new social relations and new incentive systems if it is going to achieve genuine institutional change. Teachers, principals, and curriculum supervisors can only respond to the performance of the demonstration teacher according to traditional criteria (i.e., with disapproval for deviance) until their praise and approval come to be controlled by new and different discriminative stimuli—new and different kinds of data. It is a long process, and does not happen automatically. The principle of extinction makes it evident that a teacher will not continue to strain to improve children's rates of academic progress if progress is never mentioned in the teachers' lounge and peer approval is only exchanged for advances in teaching deportment. Consequently a quality-control system has both monitoring and support functions.

As previously noted, the three parts of a quality-control system are recording and reporting procedures, feedback procedures, and consequences. Panyan, Boozer, and Morris (1970) provided an experimental demonstration of the value of the first two elements, and even suggested that feedback itself is a reinforcing consequence. The way in which the Behavior Analysis Follow Through Project attempts to provide adequate quality control derives from the program's goal of accelerating the academic progress of the children it serves.

Recording and Reporting

The most fundamental data on each Behavior Analysis classroom are provided by the Weekly Individual Progress Records (WIPR) that report each child's placement in reading, arithmetic, handwriting, and spelling. Each curriculum series in use in these subjects can be represented by a chart similar to that in Figure 15-2. Each vertical step on the chart represents a number of pages. The steps have been constructed so that each requires about the same time to complete. The horizontal axis of the chart indicates the 40 weeks of the school year. Entering the number of children working on each step every week creates an informative record of class progress.

Figure 15-2 shows 25 weeks of progress in reading by a class of kindergarten children. The heavy line was added to locate the median child each

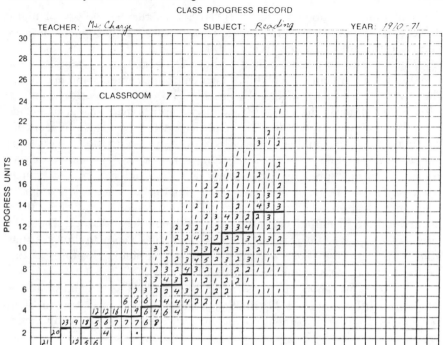

Fig. 15-2. Sample weekly class progress record of the progress in reading of a class of kindergarten children. The progress units are successive groups of pages in the reading curriculum. The entries on the chart record the number of students working in each unit each week.

week. Simple inspection of these records provides information on the rate of general progress, the degree of individualization, the placement range, and any difficulty with the materials (e.g., as indicated by the slow progress through step 4). As a monitoring device, these charts are invaluable. For all their virtues, however, they have a few problems. First, it is a tedious accounting task for a teacher to transform placement information into entries on these charts. Second, useful information is lost when the individual data of the WIPR's are aggregated on the charts. Third, because these are after-the-fact data, they do not provide all the help needed to use WIPR data as a basis for prescribing procedural changes.

Feedback

The rapid feedback of prescriptive recommendations based on WIPR data is made possible by a new system called BANCS (Behavior Analysis

National Communication System). BANCS uses the technology of high-speed data communications to provide closer, more timely support for each Behavior Analysis classroom (Weis, 1974).

Each classroom teacher initiates the BANCS system by completing a weekly roster containing each child's curriculum placements and absences. These rosters are then collected by an aide who translates each placement into a series of marks that can be "read" by an optical mark reader manufactured by OpScan Corporation. The OpScan machine reads the placement information on each child and transmits it by telephone to the University of Kansas Computation Center. The computer analysis evaluates current placement against previous placements and then determines how much progress needs to be made by each child during the coming week in order to reach individual preset year-end targets. This new target information is then automatically transmitted back to a teletype in the local district. The aide returns the report to the classroom teacher and gives a copy to the local staff trainer. The process takes less than 18 hr to complete. The form of the feedback report is illustrated in Figure 15-3.

The fictitious report indicates that Bailey, T., was reading on p. 127 of *Programmed Reading Book 14* (Buchanan and Sullivan Associates, 1973) on September 26. The placement corresponds to Step 44 in the reading cur-

```
BEHAVIOR ANALYSIS REPORT TO:    CASEBIER      WOODLAWN    TRENTON
REPORT NO.   2, VERSION - H      CODE - 050413160          3RD          0925
MESSAGES -

              READING                         :            MATH
                                              :
       STUDENT     09/26    SUCCESS    10/01  :TRG:   09/24     SUCCESS    10/01
       ID NAME  ABS BK-PG STEP W*RATIO*Y TARGET :OPT:  BK-PG STEP W*RATIO*Y TARGET

  01BAILEY, T   1 14,127 44  - 14/ 39-  15, 23  C:A   3,162 43  + 10/  7+   3,170
  02BREECH, C     21, 25 57  + 24/ 23+  21, 48  A:A   3,160 42  + 10/ 10+   3,170
  03BINION, T   1 18, 73 52  -  5/ 21-  18, 95  A:A   3,163 43  +  8/  7+   3,171
  04BRITTAIN,   4 19,  1 53  +  5/  5-  19, 26  A:A   3,163 43  -  2/  3-   4,171
  05DAVIS, RO     18, 62 51  + 24/ 24+  18, 86  A:A   3,150 42  + 12/ 11+   3,161
  06GLADNEY,      20,142 56  + 12/ 10+  21,  7  A:B   3,180 43  + 16/ 13+   3,192
  07JOHNSON,    1 19, 56 53  - 19/ 20+  19, 80  A:B   3,200 44  + 12/ 11-   3,211
  08KENNY, JU     23,144 62  NO TARGET SPECS    A:A   4,  1 51  -  4/  5+   4,106
  09PORTER, R     17,132 50  + 25/ 65+  18, 53  B:A   3,141 42  + 11/ 11+   3,152
  10POWERS, T   1    121     MISSING BOOK #     A:A   3,150 42  + 12/  9+   3,159

  11RUSSELL,      21, 21 57  - 18/ 23+  21, 44  A:A   3,      CONFLICTING PAGE#'S
  12WALKER, R     18,130 52  + 21/ 21+  19,  7  A:A   3,151 42  +  9/  9+   3.160
  13CROSS, MA     17,130 52  + 26/ 25+  18, 11  A:A   3,180 43  + 10/  8+   3,188
  14FOWLKES,    1 20, 21 55  -  5/ 11-  20, 33  A:A   4,  5 51  +  5/  4+   4,110
  15GAILLIARD      6,100 27  +  8/  8-   6,109  F:C   3, 20 35  + 10/ 10-   3, 30
  16MORRIS, L     20, 18 55  + 12/ 11+  20, 29  A:A   4, 12 51  -  1/  5+   4, 13
  17HARRIS, O     19, 44 53  + 24/ 20-  19, 60  A:A   3,131 41  + 13/ 12+   3,143
  18JONES, AN     21,130 57  --21/ 10-  21,144  A:A   3,167 43  + 13/  8+   3,174
  19LEACHMAN,   1 18,  1 51  UPDATED PLACEMENT   A:A   3,182 44  UPDATED PLACEMENT
  20REVENGE,    2 20, 31 55  UPDATED PLACEMENT   A:A   3,190 44  UPDATED PLACEMENT
  21WRIGHT,     1 19,122 54  UPDATED PLACEMENT   A:A   3,180 43  UPDATED PLACEMENT
```

Fig. 15-3. Fictitious sample of a BANCS weekly feedback report to a third-grade teacher named Casebier in Woodlawn School, Trenton, N.J. For each student in the class, reading placements and prescriptions are shown on the left half of the report, arithmetic placements and prescriptions are on the right.

riculum. Under the heading "Success Ratio," the entry "—14/39—" indicates that Bailey advanced only 14 pages during the previous week which
was less than the 39 pages targeted. Hence, the minus next to the 14.
Further, the "—" following "39" indicates that if he continues to progress at
the rate of only 14 pages per week Bailey will end the year below his present
individual year-end target. To prevent this, his target for October 1 is set at
page 23 of *Book 15*—a 40-page target.

With this information, Bailey's teacher is able to adjust his instructional
schedule appropriately to get him back on target toward his year-end objective. In this case that adjustment might consist of increasing Bailey's reading
instruction by shortening his math period, because the report indicated that
he is progressing well above his target rate in math.

The local staff trainer who monitors these reports can move to assist in
specific and timely ways rather than simply dropping into a classroom to ask,
"How's it going?" Further, when a class report begins to show an increasing
proportion of minus signs in the "Success Ratio" columns, indicating that too
many children are falling behind targets, intensive training and support can
be mobilized to correct the problem. On the other hand, when the proportion of plusses indicate increasing numbers of children are exceeding targets,
the trainer can tell the principal about an outstanding teaching team.

These basic data, in summary form, are also fed back to district personnel in the form of semiannual status reports that include key descriptive
information for every Behavior Analysis classroom in the country. Because
the descriptors in these reports are the same for the Hopi program as for the
Bronx, everyone can assess the progress of each classroom relative to all
others.

Consequences

The obvious and direct forms of differential reward (merit pay, contingent bonuses, etc.) are not acceptable to teacher organizations. Consequently the Behavior Analysis program attempted to link desirable performance to traditional reward systems. Most recently, emphasis is being
given to recognizing certificates given to teachers and aides for criterion
teaching performance.

The Performance Certificate for Behavior Analysis Teachers.
Whatever the training and support procedures of the program have been,
they have always been more effective with some teachers than others. The
performance certificate is one rather concrete way of publicly recognizing
proficiency and simultaneously making the proficiency criteria explicit. In
contrast to several earlier versions that proved cumbersome to manage, the
current performance criteria for certification seem both parsimonious and
relevant. The procedure has not been in use long enough to permit its
complete evaluation, but reactions from teachers and staff trainers thus far

have been uniformly positive. The process can be managed entirely by the local staff trainer, and allows teachers and aides to earn certificates in as little as four weeks if all goes well. Three sets of criteria are considered in the procedure.

   Instructional Teaching Criteria for the Performance Certificate. When a teacher wishes to earn a certificate, he or she invites the staff trainer to conduct a formal observation during a small-group instruction period. The 10-min observation yields data on teaching interactions (contacts). If these data support a "yes" answer to each of the following items, the first set of performance criteria has been met.

1. 80% of the children are on-task.
2. 100% of the teacher's contacts are to on-task children.
3. 100% of the teacher's contacts contain praise.
4. 100% of tokens are delivered with praise.
5. 90% of the teacher's contacts that include prompts also contain descriptive praise and a token.
6. 0% of the teacher's contacts contain disapproval.
7. 80% accuracy demonstrated by four children (picked at random and checked by trainer).
8. Time-out, if needed, is applied appropriately (as specified, in training materials).

   Exchange Teaching Criteria for the Performance Certificate. A second evaluation, also conducted at the invitation of the teacher, follows the same general routine, but the behavior of interest is different. These criteria specify the operation of the motivational system, and the trainer's observation determines that: the backup (exchange) activities are planned and prepared beforehand; the content and prices (number of tokens) of the backups vary at the two exchanges observed on the same day; prices are set independently by each instructional group, but are the same for all children in a single group; each child is allowed to choose any activity for which enough tokens are presented; children who elect not to exchange or who do not have enough tokens sit quietly during the exchange period; the first child ready to exchange is allowed to do so without having to wait for others; at least one backup contributes to academic-skills development; the adults participate in the backup activities; adults praise appropriate interaction during the exchange; and, at the end of the exchange period, instruction begins with the first child who comes to the table.

   Student Progress Criterion for the Performance Certificate. The final performance criterion for certification requires that, for a period of four weeks, 80% of the children in the teacher's own instructional groups be reported on target by the computer feedback. This can be four weeks each of which are at 80% or better, or an average of 80% for four weeks combined.

The total procedure requires a criterion teaching performance and a criterion exchange performance on each of two occasions at least four weeks apart. These observations, plus four weeks of criterion progress by the children, complete the procedure. If any performance drops below criterion, staff trainers can make specific recommendations on how to correct problems and follow up with assistance and additional feedback on improvements.

Although the certificate is delivered in recognition of excellent performance, it may be most important because the three sets of criteria serve as excellent training objectives. In their present form, these objectives are clearly understood by the teachers, and they precisely define the training tasks that must be met by the local staff trainer. The Behavior Analysis Specialist Certificate must be earned annually. It is not a license for anything, nor is it backed up by other rewards. The certificate is documentary recognition of achievement that enables the district advisor to send the teacher a complimentary letter with a copy for the personnel file in the Superintendent's office and a copy to the building principal.

The Project Management Team. Another way of linking program objectives to local reward systems is provided by a group called a Project Management Team. The design of this team was initially fashioned by the program staff in Philadelphia to include the central office Follow Through coordinator, building principals, staff trainers, Policy Advisory Committee chairs, and other specialists invited in on an ad hoc basis when their expertise can contribute to the agenda. The team meets monthly to discuss program procedures, to work out ways of solving specific local problems, and to ensure that program procedures articulate well with district regulations and the provisions of the union contract. The team is singularly effective as a device for making the Behavior Analysis program a legitimate activity within the district. Because parents, project staff, and central office administrators are all active participants, program recommendations are accepted as indigenous to the system by classroom staffs rather than as unwelcome intrusions from Kansas.

Client Satisfaction. Quality control works both ways. Our performance as a sponsoring organization needs to be effectively controlled by the parents and educators we serve. Separate questionnaire forms are given to administrators, teachers, trainers, aides, and parents to gather information about the local acceptance of our performance and to indicate areas where the Behavior Analysis program needs further modification and refinement. The questionnaires are brief rating scales allowing each respondent to indicate his or her approval or disapproval of program practices, and also provide the opportunity to make specific recommendations. It is difficult to overemphasize the importance and utility of this simple evaluation strategy. It is not merely cosmetic. It is extremely functional in pointing up potential problems before they become serious items of contention or debilitating controvery. A more complete discussion of client satisfaction is provided in Chapter 18 by Fixsen, Phillips, and Wolf, whose work in this area pointed the way for the Behavior Analysis program.

ACADEMIC EFFECTS OF BEHAVIOR ANALYSIS, 1968-1975

Descriptions of the outcomes of the Behavior Analysis Follow Through project, no matter how drawn, are bound to appear flawed or incomplete to some. In the years since 1968 most of the program's effects have gone undocumented. Depending on one's perspective, the important effects have been economic, organizational, political, or educational. Even though the intent of the enabling legislation for Follow Through was broad enough to span all of these perspectives, the realities of the national evaluation program have emphasized only some of these and ignored others.

Willems (1974) has enjoined behaviorists to collect a variety of measures over long periods of time to describe program outcomes more completely. It is a useful injunction only to the extent that Willems is able to recommend solutions to the problem of limited resources of manpower and money. The resources of the Behavior Analysis program and those of the national Follow Through program have been limited. Those limitations tended to give evaluation priority to those effects that could be measured with relative ease and economy. It is a set of outcome priorities that is legitimately criticized by most educators as narrow and incomplete, but until measurement technology and financial support are both greatly expanded, the situation is not likely to change.

The goals of the Behavior Analysis program are to improve the basic academic skills of children in kindergarten through third grade and to involve their parents directly in the process. Fortunately, the program's goals for the children can be evaluated by the type of measure emphasized in the national evaluation scheme: the standardized test of academic achievement. By testing the children in the program at the end of each year as they progress through their first 4 yr (K-3) of elementary school, it is possible to construct several comparisons describing the relative success of the program in meeting its academic objectives. For the methodological purist, the available group comparisons fall short of the explanatory power inherent in reversal designs, but the elegance of an experimental reversal of effect is completely lost on the parents and educators who are the clients of the Behavior Analysis program.

Comparisons With Expected Performance

As already noted, on an actuarial basis poor children fall behind their middle-class counterparts about one third of a year each year they attend school. Consequently the most direct, and in many ways the most powerful, evaluation of the Behavior Analysis program is found in the extent to which it helps children break that predicted performance loss. Given the well-accepted correlation between poverty and academic deficiency, a program that eliminated that correlation would constitute a successful intervention.

The Trenton Study. The contract for the national Follow Through evaluation was competitively won by the Stanford Research Institute (SRI) in 1968. SRI was to collect data from a variety of Follow Through sites around the nation to document, among other things, the performance of children in different sponsored approaches. Not all Follow Through sites were included in this national evaluation. Among the five Behavior Analysis sites that first year, only Trenton, N.J. was not included in the national sample. Anticipating the need to present evaluation data to the Trenton Board of Education, the Follow Through staff in Trenton and the sponsor's staff at the University of Kansas cooperatively developed a limited evaluation design. That design called for a comparison of the year-end performance of two groups of children on the Wide Range Achievement Test (WRAT). A Behavior Analysis group was made up of every other child on the kindergarten roster of two different classes in two different schools. A comparison group was similarly composed of every other child from two kindergarten classes in two additional schools that were judged to be comparable in every way, but did not have a Behavior Analysis program. All four schools were Title I target schools; all served children of similar neighborhoods; the children in both groups had similar Head Start experience; and the local district had originally thought that all four schools would be Follow Through schools.

That fortuitous comparison, stimulated by Trenton's omission from the national evaluation, provided the first pair of data points in a longitudinal analysis that still continues. Following these two groups of children through successive years provided information about the academic effects of Behavior Analysis and about the actual performance gains of poor children not enrolled in the program. In one city, at least, it has been possible to evaluate the accuracy of the generalization that the rate of achievement gain for poor children is about two thirds of a year per school year.

Figure 15-4 describes the progress in reading achievement of these two groups of children through the end of fifth grade in the spring of 1974. The zero point in the spring of 1968 represents the assumption of comparability in these two groups as they completed Head Start. By the end of kindergarten the 30 Behavior Analysis children averaged 1.3 (first grade, third month) on the reading portion of the WRAT and the 20 comparison children averaged K.5 (kindergarten, fifth month). At this point, the comparison children were 4 months below the middle-class norm of K.9 (kindergarten, ninth month), while the Behavior Analysis children were six months above expected performance levels for poor children and 4 months above the expected level for middle-class children. Throughout the next 3 yr, the Behavior Analysis children continued to expand their gains over the comparison group. At the completion of their 4 yr of Follow Through in 1972, the original 30

Mean Year-end Achievement
Reading[1]

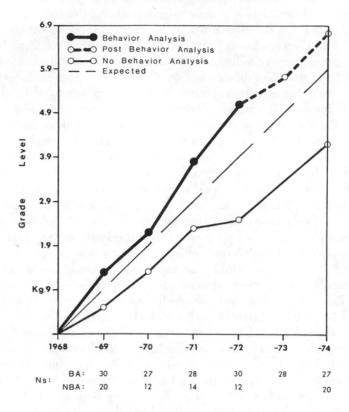

1. Wide Range Achievement Test

Fig. 15-4. A longitudinal comparison of the reading achievement scores of two comparable groups of children in Trenton, N.J. The Behavior-Analysis Follow-Through children (BA) achieved above the middle-class norm (shown by the dashed line) through 4 yr of the program and two follow-up postchecks. The comparable group of children with no Behavior Analysis experience (NBA) fell progressively behind the norm through their first 6 yr of school.

Behavior Analysis children averaged 5.1 in reading (1.2 yr ahead of the test norm of 3.9 and 2.6 yr ahead of the comparison group).

Two yr of follow-up data are provided by the postchecks of 1973 and 1974. The children of the Behavior Analysis group continued to perform above grade level (reading at 6.7 at the end of fifth grade); and the original 20 comparison children continued to fall behind (reading at 4.2 at the end of fifth grade). Unfortunately, the comparison children were not tested at the end of fourth grade in 1973. Special effort by the local project staff to locate and test all of the children of both groups in the spring of 1974, however, provided the most complete data on both cohorts since the spring of 1969. Over the total 6-yr period, the Behavior Analysis children gained at the rate of 1.1 yr per school year and the comparison children gained at the rate of .7. While supporting the efficacy of the Behavior Analysis program, these data also support the prediction that poor children in conventional school programs fall progressively behind test norms at the rate of about 3 months per school year.

Comparisons with Test Norms

However encouraging the results of the Trenton data, they are incomplete in several ways. First, they describe the progress of only the first cohort of children enrolled in the Behavior Analysis program. Considerable preceding discussion established that the training and support procedures of the program changed considerably over the years. Every year the children in this first cohort were taught by teachers attempting the Behavior Analysis program for the first time.

Further, Trenton is only one of 15 Behavior Analysis projects in 12 different communities throughout the country. The single instance of encouragement immediately calls for more comprehensive information on program effects across all project sites. Those data are presented in Figure 15-5, which traces the reading progress of children in all Behavior Analysis projects from the spring of 1969 (the end of the first program year) through the spring of 1975. The children represented are *cohort* children.

A cohort is defined as those children continously enrolled in Behavior Analysis from entering kindergarten to the completion of third grade. Consequently the cohort population of an entering class is permanently defined only when that class completes third grade. For classes that have not yet completed third grade, the cohort group consists of the children continuously enrolled since entering kindergarten through the last grade completed by the class.

In Figure 15-5, final cohorts have been identified for the classes that entered in 1968 through 1971. The fourth- and fifth-grade scores provide 1- and 2-yr postchecks on the performance of cohort groups that have "graduated" from the program.

Because it was initially thought that SRI would provide achievement data for all programs, our evaluations were rather limited in scope during the early years. Not until the spring of 1972 was a systematic program of year-end testing established in an effort to obtain data on the largest possible proportion of Behavior Analysis children. For this reason, the percentage of each cohort tested (the number in parentheses below each box) is much lower in the first 3 yr than in the last 4.

Several conclusions seem appropriate from these data. First, the reltive stability of the means of a given grade level from year to year indicate

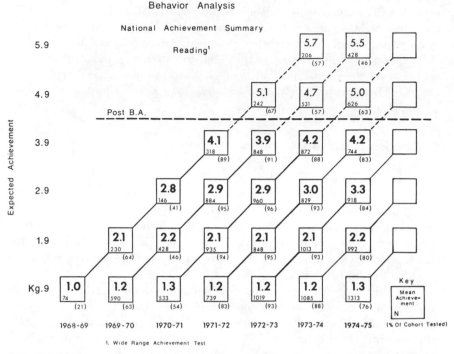

Fig. 15-5. Mean reading achievement score, expressed in grade equivalents, for all cohort children tested each year in all Behavior Analysis projects, year ending 1969 through 1975. The diagnals trace the progress of each cohort group through the 4 yr of the program and for two successive annual postchecks. The number of children tested is reported in the lower left corner of each box, and the percent of the cohort group tested is reported in the parentheses outside each box.

the successful replication of program effects with seven successive cohorts. This stability suggests that the several changes in training procedures over the years improved the efficiency and economy of training, but the effects remained relatively constant. Second, the children in Behavior Analysis programs consistently scored at or above the expected grade-level norms of the Wide Range Achievement Test in reading. The single exception among the 22 data points is at the end of second grade, when the first cohort group scored 2.8 rather than 2.9. By the end of third grade, however, the cohort average is again above grade level at 4.2.

Observing the consistently high performance of these children across a variety of community settings and across 7 yr, some have asked if the outcomes might be attributed to special attention, as in some kind of Hawthorne effect (but cf. Parsons, 1974). There is no satisfactory way to dismiss such a possibility, but neither does it diminish the results. Those who prefer to infer the existence of mediating variables such as the Hawthorne effect will be pleased to learn that Behavior Analysis has a set of procedures that sustains the benefits of that effect in the 15 projects of 12 communities for 7 years

It should also be noted that the fourth- and fifth-grade postchecks indicate that the rate of year-to-year gain is diminished when the children leave the Behavior Analysis program and return to the conventional, single-teacher, self-contained classroom. While enrolled in the Behavior Analysis program, the children gained nearly 1.1 yr per school year. After leaving the program, they gained at the rate of .8 yr per year. Those educators and policymakers who seek a single one-shot intervention as the ameliorative for all educational problems of poor children in conventional school programs will be tempted to use this 3-month decline in the rate of annual progress to depreciate the efficacy of Behavior Analysis. Those educators and policymakers who understand better the nature of the relation between student performance and the characteristics of the instructional environment will find the effects of the Behavior Analysis program a basis for altering the instructional practices in fourth and fifth grades.

Finally, one additional perspective on these data is helpful in dismissing the possibility that the effects of the Behavior Analysis program are restricted to a few communities so that the national aggregate masks the lacks of effect in several sites.

Figure 15-6 displays (community by community and grade by grade) the mean grade-level score in reading for all cohort children tested in the spring of 1975. By examining each vertical column of figures, it is possible to see the contribution that the children of a particular grade in a specific community make to the national mean score for that grade. Of the 36 entries, kindergarten through third grade, only three are below the expected grade level for middle-class children.

Comparisons with Similar Groups

It was not until the spring of 1973 that we began to collect data on many comparison children in Behavior Analysis communities throughout the nation. By this time it had become evident that the scope and complexity of the national evaluation made it impossible for SRI to provide timely reports on the progress of the planned variation experiment. With the help of local school district personnel, comparison schools that closely matched the Follow Through schools with which we were working were identified. Like the Behavior Analysis children, the comparison children attended schools receiving Title I funds, and their neighborhoods and family situations were similar. In a few districts the comparison children tended to have higher family incomes because the lowest income children were enrolled in Follow Through. The comparison schools were more heavily sampled at the higher grade levels (fourth and fifth) to provide a sharper picture of the post-Behavior Analysis effects in the middle grades.

BEHAVIOR ANALYSIS
POSTTEST SCORES 1975 [1]
READING

	KG.9	1.9	2.9	3.9	4.9	5.9
BRONX	1.2 111	1.9 75	3.9 63	4.2 56	5.9 37	7.0 21
HOPI	1.2 12	1.9 24	3.3 22	4.8 2	4.7 16	8.1 5
INDIANAPOLIS	1.3 40	2.1 35	3.1 30	3.1 41	6.8 24	7.5 21
KANSAS CITY	1.3 122	2.2 88	3.1 78	4.4 78	5.0 58	7.5 7
LOUISVILLE	1.3 177	2.1 145	3.0 130	3.6 106	4.2 70	4.5 66
MERIDIAN	1.2 91	2.5 62	4.5 58	6.3 58	5.9 64	–
NO. CHEYENNE	1.0 68	1.8 52	2.9 45	4.5 35	4.8 10	–
PHILADELPHIA	1.2 241	2.1 195	3.0 183	4.1 151	4.7 140	5.1 130
PITTSFIELD	1.2 47	2.8 31	2.9 28	4.5 17	4.5 20	5.3 23
PORTAGEVILLE	1.5 83	2.3 68	3.8 61	4.7 37	6.1 32	7.8 40
TRENTON	1.2 183	2.2 113	3.1 131	4.1 101	4.5 93	4.8 71
WAUKEGAN	1.4 138	2.4 104	3.1 89	4.7 62	5.0 62	5.7 44
TOTAL PROJECT	1.3 1313	2.2 992	3.3 918	4.2 744	5.0 626	5.5 428

1. Wide Range Achievement Test (8/9)

Fig. 15-6. Mean reading achievement scores, expressed in grade equivalents, for all cohort children tested at each grade level in every Behavior-Analysis community, spring, 1975. The lighter numerals of the last two columns report postchecks on program graduates. The small numerals just below each mean grade equivalent score report the number of children tested. The Total Project means in the bottom row correspond to the means in the right-hand column of Figure 15-5.

The data in Figure 15-7 compare the 1975 year-end reading scores of about 5000 Behavior Analysis children with those of about 2400 comparison children who had no Behavior Analysis experience. These children were drawn from five urban communities with comparable children (Bronx, N.Y., Kansas City, Mo., Louisville, Ky., Trenton, N.J., and Waukegan, Ill). Consequently it cannot be asserted that the group is representative of rural and Indian projects for which no appropriate comparisons were available. It is possible to observe, however, that the general pattern of these scores conforms to the previously discussed expectation of cumulative deficiency

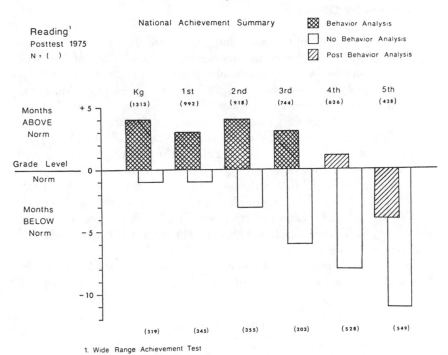

Fig. 15-7. Comparison of the mean reading achievement scores (spring, 1975) of Behavior Analysis cohort children with a similar group of non-Behavior-Analysis children aggregated from five urban school districts.

for poor children in conventional school programs. The fifth-grade children in this group were 11 months below grade level. The fifth graders who had completed the Behavior Analysis program (2 yr earlier) were 4 months below grade level.

The mean data in the preceding figures were computed conservatively. The nature of this instrument (like all standardized achievement tests) is such that while grade equivalent scores (1.2, 3.4, etc.) are equal interval, the raw scores (points awarded for each correct response) are not. As the response requirement increases for more advanced items, fewer raw-score points are needed to advance one grade-equivalent unit. The liberal analyst may elect to average grade-equivalent scores; the conservative will average raw scores and then convert to a grade equivalent. In Fig. 15-5, for example, 744 third graders are shown to average 4.2 in reading. Their raw scores were averaged and then converted to a grade equivalent. If each child's score had first been converted to a grade equivalent and these then averaged, the group mean would have been 3 or 4 months higher. The psychometric rules for determining the preferred method are sufficiently debatable that the conservative route seems advisable in the present instance.

Comparisons by Others

The data presented in the preceding figures are the product of evaluation programs conducted by, or in cooperation with, the sponsor organization. It is reasonable for the cautious observer to seek the evaluation of a disinterested analyst to test the credibility of sponsor claims. Since the initiation of Follow Through as a planned variation experiment, SRI has carried the responsibility for gathering program data on the entire national program. The current design of the national evaluation calls for a longitudinal analysis of the year-to-year gains of Follow Through children compared with those of many non-Follow-Through children. The first "official" evaluation cohort consists of children who entered kindergarten in the fall of 1971. This is the cohort most heavily sampled, and whose performance has been evaluated with a battery of test instruments adopted as the primary metric for describing the effects of Follow Through. The battery is heavily weighted by standardized achievement tests.

The end-of-kindergarten data on children entering in 1971 obtained by SRI testers were turned over to another evaluation agency, Abt Associates,

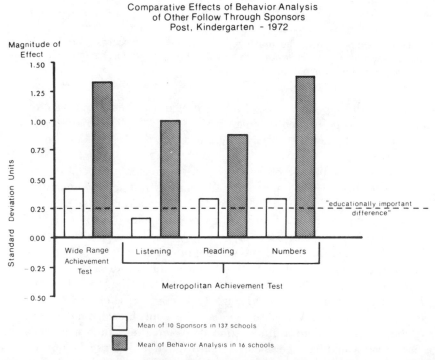

Fig. 15-8. Comparison of standardized achievement test scores of Behavior Analysis kindergarten children with Follow Through children in other sponsored programs.

for analysis and reporting. In 1973 an Abt Associates' technical report presented the comparative analysis of Follow Through effects based on the first-year performance of the 1971 entering group. The complete longitudinal analysis of this cohort will be available in 1977. The first data point of a 4 yr longitudinal analysis is not to be construed as a complete evaluation. Nevertheless, it does provide a kind of reliability check on the other data considered.

The data in Figure 15-8 are taken from the 1973 Abt report, and compare the results reported for the Behavior Analysis program with those of all Follow Through sponsors evaluated (including Behavior Analysis). The total Follow Through effects (open bars) describe the adjusted outcomes of kindergarten children in 137 Follow Through schools served by 10 different sponsors. The results are given in standard deviation units to provide a comparable metric across all evaluation instruments and an estimate of the practical importance of the outcomes. The Abt report used a mean difference between Follow Through and comparison groups of .25 standard deviations as being *educationally* important. Consequently any bar that rises .25 or higher represents a year-end difference favoring Follow Through that is more than statistically significant; it is considered by Abt Associates to be educationally important. On this graph, any difference favoring the non-Follow Through comparison group would be represented by a bar extending down from the zero axis. The "Wide Range Achievement Test" column shows aggregated outcomes on its three parts (reading, spelling, arithmetic); the "Metropolitan Achievement Test" columns show outcomes on listening, reading, and numbers.

ON REDESIGNING THE SCHOOLS

Follow Through, as a part of the War on Poverty, was designed and implemented out of a working assumption that the poverty cycle could be broken by better school programs for poor children. It is an assumption with much face validity, but it has some problems. Even if vigorously pursued, it could take a couple of generations to test the premise that educational change will redistribute the national wealth. There is little possibility that policymakers will defer judgment that long to wait for data. It is far more likely that policy statements and positions will continue to be based on deductions from logic and correlation.

Jencks, Smith, Acland, Bane, Cohen, Gintis, Heyns, and Michelson (1972), for example, evaluated several correlations and came to the conclusion that, "Economic success seems to depend on varieties of luck and on-the-job competence that are only moderately related to family background, schooling, or scores on standardized tests [p. 8]." It is a contention quite contrary to the assumptions behind the educational intervention programs of the middle 1960's, and will undoubtedly be used by many to argue against the utility of redesigning school programs. Jencks et al., however, while rejecting the connection between poor education and poverty, support educational reform on the pragmatic ground that, because children spend a fifth of their lives in school, it should be a pleasant and rewarding experience in itself, whether or not it leads to a better life. Interestingly although the reasons behind recommendations for educational reform vary to the point of direct opposition, a strong consensus supports the need for institutional change.

Can the Schools be Changed?

Yes, the schools can be changed. Follow Through is probably the largest federally sponsored program of educational change undertaken since the Morrill Acts of 1862 and 1890 redesigned American higher education by granting public lands to states for colleges that would offer courses in agriculture and engineering. Because the Morrill Acts had focused objectives and big reinforcers they reformed the classic institution of the college and gave it a utilitarian emphasis that remains distinctively American. The early results from Follow Through indicate that it too is capable of achieving planned change in the institutional practices of elementary schools. Follow Through is by no means a large program in dollar terms. The annual Follow Through budget is approximately $60 million, while Title I of ESEA is a $2 billion program. Yet the blunt assessment of the effects of Title I by John Hughes (Hughes & Hughes, 1972), its original administrator, is that, ". . . it didn't work, [p. 134]."

The final and conclusive evaluation of the Behavior Analysis approach to Follow Through may never be written. Complex social problems are seldom resolved by decisive experiments. Nevertheless, the data now accumulating indicate that it can work and is working. Applied behavior analysis can be used as an engineering strategy to achieve institutional change. A small demonstration that Behavior Analysis *can* reform education does not, however, justify the assumption that it *will* reform education. Good design capability is not the same as actual engineering accomplishment.

Our experience in the public schools since 1968 has provided several lessons that ought to be shared. Other behavior analysts who choose to work with the public schools will individually elect to adopt either a clinical or an engineering approach. The following observations are addressed to those who take the engineer's view.

Lessons for the Engineer

The characteristics of an engineering approach were discussed in a general way at the beginning of this chapter. The components of an engineering strategy (design, delivery system, and quality-control system) provide terminal criteria, but the process of implementing these components is a task accomplished in a long series of approximations. As with most educational programs, small approximations are better than large.

Begin Small. A great wisdom of Follow Through was that it began as a program for entering (usually kindergarten) children. The next year, as the first-year children advanced, the program was expanded with them. It took 4 yr to reach full kindergarten through third-grade implementation. During those years of gradual expansion we were socialized to the local circumstances of each school district and the districts grew accustomed to our presence. Although each district has unique circumstances and customs, elementary schools throughout the nation are more alike than they are different. Much of that similarity stems from the practice of funding schools according to their average daily attendance. It is not appropriate to develop the implications of that practice here, but the financing of schools contingent on attendance without regard for any measure of performance may be the most fundamental handicap of the institution.

Local Is Best. Local training is the most effective. This is a premise not likely to surprise any behaviorist, but we kept forgetting it. From the trainers' point of view, the short-run economy and convenience of bringing trainees to the trainers is very attractive. The extra effort and expense of sending trainers into the trainees' work setting, however, has been more cost-effective in the long run. To the extent that our experience in this regard has general relevance to teacher trainers, it raises some tough ques/ tions about the traditional practices of teachers' colleges and summer institute programs.

As presently organized, teacher-training institutions are not directly or functionally related to operating school programs. In that respect they make the same error we made during the early years of the program. It is possible to imagine the dramatic changes that could result if teacher-training institutions developed strong in-service training programs providing day-to-day support for practicing teachers as they work in their own classrooms.

For the Behavior Analysis program the key actor in the training program is the local staff trainer. The trainers are local teachers, part of the local system, trained by the sponsor to provide continuing training support to a group of their fellow teachers. Ignoring the cautions of the Peter Principle, these trainers are promoted out of their classrooms by virtue of their excellent performance and placed in a new training and support role. Because they are intimately familiar with local circumstances (styles of individual teachers, students, building procedures, and district policy), they are able to provide individualized and highly responsive support to classroom teams in a way that is both timely and practical. To the extent that their suggestions are initially effective, they acquire a role supportive to teachers rather than one that is supervisory and punitive.

Teachers Need Tenderness. Teachers respond well to practical suggestions and poorly to theoretical presentations. Our suggestions became more helpful and our presence more welcome as we learned to talk less about concepts such as differential reinforcement, thinning the schedule, lowering the response cost, and tightening the contingency. Instead, we have learned how to concentrate on concrete suggestions in the form of specific procedures. For the teacher who wants to learn more about our orientation and principles of behavior, several districts have arranged for graduate-level introductory courses. Classroom training is procedural, and is conducted in plain English, not jargon.

The conventional elementary classroom teacher works in unusual isolation from his or her peers. Each classroom in a building is filled with children but is seldom entered by other members of the staff. The professional behavior of the teacher, whether excellent or deficient, rarely attracts any form of collegial approval or disapproval. The nature of the school social organization is such that regular strategies for recognizing and reinforcing exemplary teaching behavior are far too limited. The instances of approval, when they do occur, tend to be apart from pedagogy. Building principals give approval to teachers largely for maintaining order and being cooperative. Raises and promotions are given for supporting the system rather than serving the clients (children and parents); and conventional psychological procedures encourage referring difficult problems out of the classroom rather than dealing with them *in situ.*

Principals, school psychologists, helping teachers, and consultants need to learn how to be an appreciative audience for the instructional skills of classroom teachers. New systems need to be devised similar to BANCS that can set the occasion for all the support personnel of a building to appreciate and approve effective instruction. Data on class progress can serve this function when they are handled in a way that avoids big-brotherism and potentially damaging surveillance. A new kind of training for principals and other specialists could teach them how to use such data to enrich the presently lean reinforcement schedules of teachers.

Parents. Parent participation is a charming bit of rhetoric that means very little in the operation of most schools. The contemporary school has not developed a functional role for parents that has an obvious and direct connection to student progress. True, many schools have some sort of program for parent volunteers, but these tend to be more of a burden on both school and volunteer than a stable and dependable asset. The usual notion is that parents lack the professional training needed to be truly helpful in classroom instruction. Our experience has taught us quite the contrary. With proper specification of their tasks and adequate training, parents are excellent small-group instructors and tutors.

The resistance of teachers to the intrusion of parents into their classroom is temporary. As the teacher learns that the help of a parent aide makes it possible to do better those things the teacher is uniquely trained to do, the parent becomes a valued colleague. Parents who are informed about classroom practices, as a result of their own experience, provide enormous amounts of social approval for good teacher behavior. Most parents have an intense interest in the academic progress of their children. That interest is a resource the schools must learn how to tap with a little patience, a little training, and a little money. A small investment in planning useful roles for parents that carry very modest honoraria can return important educational benefits and lead to a new level of community support for schools as institutions, and for school personnel as individuals.

Curriculum Practices. Unfortunately many assume that a new curriculum series will solve learning problems. Nothing in our experience supports that assumption. Some published materials come quite close to meeting the requirements of excellence discussed in the Curriculum Section, but even these have little effect if they are poorly used, or used too little. Similarly, poorly constructed materials can be quite effective in the hands of a teacher who can restructure them to meet the requirements of a good shaping sequence. The critical factor is pedagogy, not materials. Obviously they are not completely independent factors, but we have been taught to emphasize how the materials are used (pedagogy) rather than to emphasize what the materials are (curriculum).

Two additional points deserve consideration. First, because of the assumption that learning problems result from curriculum deficiencies, curricula are changed too often and for the wrong reasons. Most of the standard curriculum series in reading and math are built around a particular unifying concept held by the authors. Some are more linear and lean toward a pattern of achieving mastery over one skill and then moving on to the next related skill in the sequence. Others follow a spiral pattern that introduces lots of skills and subsequently loops back on those same skills time and time again to augment and refine them. Even though learning principles might favor the more linear approach, either approach can be effective if it is left intact and consistently used. Too often, however, a child has one particular curriculum for 2 or 3 yr, and is then shifted to another. The coherence of the initial approach is destroyed; new teaching strategies need to be developed (a slow process); and the result is more rather than fewer problems.

Our experience strongly recommends that curriculum changes be made carefully and deliberately between, rather than within, generations of students. If a school district wishes to accept the rhetoric of book salesmen or the incentives of federal funds as a basis for changing from one curriculum to another, the new series should be introduced at its lowest level so that children who begin with it stay with it. Children who begin in a particular series should not be shifted out of it except in very unusual circumstances.

The second point to consider is, perhaps, the most important. Children's academic progress is primarily a function of the amount of instruction they receive. Differences accounted for by comparisions of curriculum A versus curriculum B are insignificant beside the differences accounted for by comparisons of 10 min versus 60 min of daily instruction. In spite of this self-evident maxim, teachers are not taught how to manage instructional time.

The Rule of Relevance.   Ayllon and Azrin (1968) formulated an extension of the principle of extinction called the "Relevance of Behavior Rule: Teach only those behaviors that will continue to be reinforced after training." There is little danger that the children will unlearn the skills they have developed as Follow Through students. For them, Behavior Analysis adhered to the rule of relevance and taught them behavior that will continue to be reinforced in the school environment. The schedule of reinforcement may be lean and unsystematic, but reading, handling the basic language of mathematics and writing coherent sentences are not likely to be extinguished or punished.

For the teachers, parents, and administrators in the program, however, the prospects seem less encouraging. Working as a team, educators and parents have learned to accelerate the achievements of poor children so they are indistinguishable from the achievements of nonpoor children. By using well-structured curricula in small groups with the motivational support of a token reinforcement system, they have learned to operate an alternative system of primary education. The system is demonstrably effective and, to a surprising degree, has met the original goals and objectives set in 1968. The pervasive national problem addressed by Follow Through is soluble. Whether or not the solutions developed by Follow Through conform to the rule of relevance, however, depends on national priorities. The social and political climate that supported the War on Poverty in the mid-1960's provided lots of reinforcement for an engineering approach to social problem solving. Like all wars, the War on Poverty was expensive, and, because our society's priorities have shifted, the funds for its prosecution are no longer available. This may leave a lot of parents, teachers, and administrators with sophisticated skills for which there is no market.

By some standards, Follow Through is expensive. A typical project has been funded at the rate of about $725 per child per year—$725 over and above the support normally provided by local and state funds. Less than half that amount is for the educational program; the remainder provides comprehensive services (e.g., medical and dental care, a nutritional program, and social services). An additional $60 to $70 per child has been granted to the sponsors for the development and delivery of their program models. Whether Follow Through is adding a lot of money or a little depends in part on where it is spent. Northern urban school districts often have budgets in excess of $1200 per child per school year. For them, Follow Through increases the money available for some children by 62%. In some rural southern districts, Follow Through represents nearly a 200% increase over the annual amount of $400 provided locally for each child.

If educational programs like Follow Through are not able to compete for scarce federal dollars as they could in the past, the rule of relevance may have been broken. On the other hand, if we continue to extend and refine the engineering approach in applied behavior analysis, the problem of cost is also soluble. Prototypes are always expensive. The existence of the prototype, however, permits the engineering emphasis to shift from development toward the problem of economical production. We have learned that it can be done. Now we need to learn how to do it on a much larger scale at a much lower cost per child. The record to date offers the best possible indication that the engineering capability of applied behavior analysis is equal to the task.

JAMES FILIPCZAK and ROBERT M. FRIEDMAN[1]

Chapter 16

Some Controls on Applied Research in a Public Secondary School: Project PREP

Increasingly during the last 20 years, experimental and clinical programs of behavioral control have been viewed with what Goldiamond (1965) termed "justified and unjustified alarm." Diverse communities of the humanistic and scientific world have raised both legitimate and ill-founded criticism of the motives, ethics, objectives, analytic strategies, and procedures of the behavioral researcher. Even a cursory review of the lay and professional literature on behavior change (e.g., Heller & Kiraly, 1974; Hilts, 1974; Kazdin, 1975a; Schwitzgebel, 1971; Winett & Winkler, 1972) reveals that questionable procedures may be practiced by apparently responsible and accredited professionals. Questions about the behavioral researcher's activities arise in the public media (Oelsner, 1974), and attempts are made to formalize societal countercontrol by legislation or administrative action (Trotter & Warren, 1974).

As such evidence indicates, the halcyon days of behavioral intervention may be over. No longer is the behavioral researcher granted unconditional welcome to the schools or other natural settings to operate in a self-defined manner (Ulrich, Wolfe, & Bluhm, 1970). Now the researcher experiences extreme social pressure both before and while conducting his programs in

1. The activities described here were supported principally by research grants (MH14443 and MH21950) through the Center for Studies on Crime and Delinquency of the National Institute of Mental Health, awarded to the Institute for Behavioral Research, Silver Spring, Maryland. Other support was derived from cooperating school systems and school staff who provided both the effort and experience that made the program work. We thank them here anonymously to protect the privacy of all participants. The views expressed here are those of the authors and do not necessarily represent views on any agency named or alluded to.

public settings (Reppucci & Saunders, 1974), and is forced to work as much politically as experimentally.

This chapter presumes (because of direct evidence) that the consumer (client and/or subject) currently exerts considerable formal and informal control over practices such as behavior modification in the public (or natural) setting. These natural safeguards form the sustaining bulwark without which the more professional or peer controls would soon prove ineffective.

The description here documents a range of effective natural safeguards found to exist in a large-scale research and demonstration project named PREP (Preparation through Responsive Educational Programs). From initial conception and objectives statement to operation and evaluation, these controls guarded against inappropriate practice. Yet they contributed significantly to the work load of the staff, inhibited even innocuous nonconsented change (thereby restricting the flexibility of the program), and decreased the opportunity to apply behavioral procedures of "proven" effectiveness.

These differing needs and requirements may form the base of the problem for behavioral researchers interested in extending such procedures on a relatively large scale to the natural environment. Their behavior is punished by natural consequences, as it should be, if they wield their behavior wands without thoroughly responding to a network of formal and informal controls that may protect the client. Their behavior is punished by different (but still natural) consequences if the series of controls exercised by people directly and indirectly involved in the program weakens their research or therapeutic performances.

Unfortunately, it may be impossible for behavioral researchers to have the best of both worlds: maximally rigorous safeguards for the client, and the control in research or therapy needed to achieve optimal results. They must determine how to achieve the best balance between these in their efforts. Similarly, on a societal level it is equally necessary for an optimal balance point to be identified between the need to adequately protect our citizens and the need to encourage the research that has the potential for furthering knowledge in significant practical spheres.

The description of PREP indicates that despite great caution in providing maximal safeguards to all project participants, conflicts developed at times that shifted the balance away from the actual research. It is hoped that this account will instruct and reveal the forces in the natural environment that can alter potent research tactics.

Many problems and examples here are not unique to behavioral research and may be familiar to all applied researchers, regardless of their theoretical orientation and research procedures. While this may be the case, research that uses behavior modification techniques may be particularly susceptible to the types of controls discussed, because the very label "behavior modification" elicits strong emotional responses from many lay and professional people.

PROGRAM DESCRIPTION

The PREP project is a federally funded program of research and demonstration mounted in public-school settings, focusing on academic- and social-skills learning for large numbers of poorly performing adolescents and their families. The program is based on both cognitive and behavioral learning principles. The school staff is trained to conduct these procedures and work closely with the community. Although PREP has often been viewed by its designers, their peers, and the public as a "behavior modification" project, its focus has been broader than this label suggests.

PREP is not unique in dealing with these problem areas within an educational setting. Academic-skills training has long concerned the behaviorist (Lovitt, Guppy, & Blattner, 1969), and social skills have received similar but often independent emphasis (Burchard, 1971). Public-school personnel have been trained to conduct behavioral programs in schools (Hall, R.V., Panyan, Rabon, & Broden, 1968), and research with parents of school children has been reported often (e.g., Patterson, McNeal, Hawkins, & Phelps, 1967). While most behavioral efforts within public schools involved small numbers of students, programs have used large groups (Clark, H.B., 1972), including some with disruptive, noninstitutionalized adolescents (Nolen, Kunzelman W., & Haring, 1967). Although behavioral researchers have controlled classroom behavior primarily through the manipulation of consequent conditions, research has also focused on antecedent variables, such as curriculum (Corey & Shamow, 1972). It is possible to find reports of programs that incorporate all but a few of the elements noted previously (see Cohen, H.L., Keyworth, Kleiner, and Libert, 1971, as one example). PREP is one of the few efforts to integrate into one program all elements: academic- and social-skills training; teacher training; research and training with parents; work with large groups of disruptive and academically deficient, noninstitutionalized adolescents; development and evaluation of antecedent stimuli, such as curriculum; and assessment of effects of consequences.

Objectives and Procedures

The primary goals of PREP demanded learning materials and teaching strategies that would permit public-school teachers to conduct effective academic- and social-skills development programs without directly involving the professional psychologist. PREP's antecedents were programs for institutionalized adolescents (Cohen, H.L., Filipczak & Bis, 1968), where different problems of institutional change exist. PREP made the transition from a nonpublic-school laboratory setting (using its own staff as trainers), through an in-school program mounted by its own staff and supported by teachers, to the management of the entire spectrum of training programs by the teachers themselves. This succession of steps was PREP's acknowledgment of the need to conduct its research and development efforts in the natural setting where its final value would be assessed (Cohen, H.L., Filipczak, Boren, Goding, Storm, Bishop, & Breiling, 1974). PREP's training program included four distinct but interrelated components:

- academic training in reading, English language, and mathematics that permitted rapid and thorough skill development;
- social or interpersonal training that provided immediate and generalizable behavioral skill development concerning both in-school and out-of-school problems;
- family liaison and skills training that prompted increased parental involvement in school activities, and the development of reasonable programs of family management within the home; and
- teacher and other staff training intended to help them conduct all phases of this program.

Students (between 60 and 120 per school, per year) have been selected for participation in PREP on the basis of strong evidence of academic and/or social problems: failing grades, many disciplinary referrals, chronic absenteeism, frequent tardiness or suspension, poor performance on standardized tests or teacher observations of poor classroom performance, contacts with police or other juvenile-problem agencies, etc. Wherever possible, students have been randomly assigned to experimental and control groups to permit overall assessment of program effects. PREP's training objectives were aimed at an improvement of skills at least double that shown by control students.

In a program as broad as PREP, each involved professional ascribes motives or objectives to the project that reflect personal perceptions or interests. For example, in most instances administrators of the school and the school board perceived *educational gain* as the most important (or, even the *only*) general objective. Contrarily, the funding agency viewed *stopping or preventing maladaptive social behavior in the community* as the most important general objective. While PREP staff shared the funding agency's point of view, developing an effective and viable model for improving in-school performance was viewed as an important goal in itself. Consequently, three different perceptions existed among influential administrators as to the relative importance of various objectives. This resulted in different focuses for accountability and required clear specification of research criteria and job duties to ensure that all objectives were accomplished. No matter how precisely such objectives were stated, however, and regardless of how clearly various administrators understood each other's priorities, PREP staff found that the differences in overall objectives debilitated their efforts. This problem is not unusual when trying to achieve change in two settings (school and community) but working in only one (school).

Experimentally the training components have been given singly or in

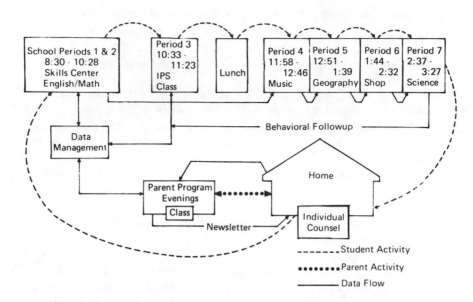

Fig. 16-1. Activity and data flow for a normal project day.

various combinations during PREP's history. For example, Figure 16-1 describes the first year's daily in-school program, in which experimental students received all components of student-focused training simultaneously. PREP students participated in two periods of English (including reading) and/or math work in the Skills Center, and one period of the IPS (Interpersonal Skills) class per day. During these periods, the PREP students worked only with students similarly selected and enrolled in the project. Thereafter, they joined the remainder of their grade-level classmates in a range of other subject classes. As a result, PREP students were not isolated from the rest of the school population. Yet they were required to carry to each non-PREP class a behavior follow-up form on which their non-PREP teachers could rate their academic and social performance. This information, along with other data from the PREP classes, was fed back to the parents on daily, weekly, and grading period bases. Families could also participate in training programs held at the school in the evenings. Further, families could meet with graduate-student workers at home to plan personal-behavior-development programs.

Most learning activities in which the students participated were based on individualized instructional procedures. Group activities were used as needed to help build skills related to such settings. Positive-reinforcement-based incentive programs were incorporated into each program component. This basic program model was used in each of the steps PREP made developmentally since the first year.

Results

During its first 2 years in a public school (1971-1972 and 1972-1973), the program operated in a junior high school in a suburban county in the Washington-Baltimore area. For the next two years (1973-1974 and 1974-1975), the program functioned in a middle school in a semirural community and in an urban junior high school in the same general area. A total of 331 students participated in PREP during these years. The results of the project are reported elsewhere (e.g., Cohen, H.L. et al., 1974; Filipczak, 1973) but are summarized here.

Throughout the project, standardized norm-referenced achievement tests were used as one measure of student academic-skills progress. Students taking the PREP academic classes consistently out-performed students randomly assigned to other groups. Over the past 4 yr, significant differences in favor of PREP academic students were found at the .05 level or greater on 11 of 19 subtests, while no significant differences were found in favor of nonacademic students. The gain was greater than 1.5 yr on seven of 19 subtests, and greater than 1 yr on 14 of 19 occasions. In 14 of 19 comparisons, the gains of PREP academic students exceeded control students by at least a half a year, and on five of these comparisons the difference was greater than a full year of progress. The magnitude of academic gains by the PREP students, measured by progress within the individualized curricula in the program, was between 1 and 3 yr in every case.

Consistent improvement in grades was also achieved by academic students in comparison to other students. This improvement occurred in each of the 4 years in PREP and non-PREP classes. This generalization of the effects of the academic program has been particularly encouraging.

Pre- and post comparisons and comparisons with matched subjects suggest that PREP students make progress in reducing frequency of suspension and frequency of disciplinary referrals in comparison to non-PREP students. During the past year, significant gains were also made in attendance by PREP students in comparison with matched control students.

While the results of the program were consistently favorable over the past 4 yr, an important part of the program evaluation remains to be conducted. This will entail a follow-up evaluation to determine the long-term effects of the program on the in-school behavior of the students and, as important, on their behavior in the community. This evaluation is presently in its early stages.

TYPES OF CONTROLS

During each year PREP worked in the public schools, a wide-ranging set of controls was exerted over its operation by nonproject staff and subjects. These controls became effective before any student enrolled in the project and continued through every student's term of stay. Examples of the more explicit controls over the operations of PREP are described briefly in the following sections to identify useful natural safeguards that may be used in other projects of similar intent.

Nonuser Peer and Professional Controls

Federally funded projects such as PREP are subject to control over the extent, breadth, and type of behavior management or modification activity from inception. Although many readers recognize and may have themselves experienced such controls, descriptions may prove either instructive or confirmatory. Each control is required for adequately formulating a proposal and each is a hurdle to be surmounted before a project award statement is received.

The first type of subject protection built into such a program is based on the ethical, methodological, and experimental considerations of the principal investigator. The choices made in these areas are a product of ethical and technical training and relevant professional experiences. The initial steps in developing a project problem statement must be made by the investigator, but these decisions are influenced by close associates or others involved in such efforts. The investigator's efforts are subject to advice, correction, and reinforcement variables applied by others. In PREP's case (as with many projects funded by the federal government), there is at least an implication that cooperating agencies and prospective subjects will also participate in the formulation of program design and procedures. Recommendations or demands of either group can profoundly affect the development of a proposal. A statement of agreement to collaborate in the described effort by the cooperating agency must be included in the submitted proposal.

Thus, PREP was required to subject the proposal to review by three groups of staff of the grantee institution. A Human Subjects Review Committee received the project after it had been through client and participant review procedures. The majority of the committee consisted of lay or professional persons who served voluntarily (and without pay) and who were not members of the institutional research community. Strict guidelines were applied to the review of all proposals concerning human subjects. Only the principal staff of the project could present such an application to this committee, and they were required to give positive and concrete evidence of compliance with high ethical standards for informed consent, confidentiality and security of information, and a low ratio of risk to benefit.

Further review of the proposed project was obtained through the management and staff structure of the institution. Here, both the supervisors and the peers of the investigator were permitted to contribute to the review process. Financial and procedural questions predominated, but these groups were still able to provide additional commentary to the benefit of the program and its participants before the proposal was submitted to the funding agency.

The review by the specified grantor agency is the most time consuming and potentially the most detailed. The final proposal submitted for the project undergoes specific review by appropriate agency staff that pertains to all elements of the proposal (finances, compliance with the agency's mission, merit, practicality, ethics of procedures, etc.). If accepted, the proposal is reviewed further for its merit by groups such as a standing agency review committee, site visit teams (in the case of new or questionable proposals), agency councils, and staff teams. At any step in this process, the project may be denied, its priority lowered, its direction changed, the financial-funding potential reduced, etc. Such a review provides initial assurance to subjects that their interests will be protected. The entire process demands clear, well-formulated, high quality, subject-appropriate programs of research or training. The review constitutes the first formal line of defense against the charlatan and the unethical practitioner, but not the last.

Local Professional and Leader Controls

Two other distinct types of control were exerted over the PREP project after submission of the proposal, but before the initiation of the project in the public schools. First, the project (in its totality—each phase, element, and component) was more formally reviewed and approved by administrative officials of the school jurisdiction. Second, a comparable review was undertaken by leadership groups of the community. In both cases, these reviews were extensions of efforts begun before the proposal was submitted to the funding agency.

Such review, critique, and administrative action by the local school jurisdiction can be both exhaustive and time consuming. As indicated in Figure 16-2, this procedure incorporated (in one jurisdiction) a total of 11 distinct steps within the school structure (excluding the final informed consent of parents for their children's participation).

This county school organization administers nearly 150 schools that serve over 120,000 students in a county with over 500,000 population. For a project such as PREP to be permitted operation in one of these schools, it is necessary to secure the formal approval of the:

- School Staff
- Principal
- Area Director (an assistant superintendent)
- Department of Administration
- Department of Instructional and Pupil Services (including curriculum development, program appraisal, and pupil services offices)
- Department of Research

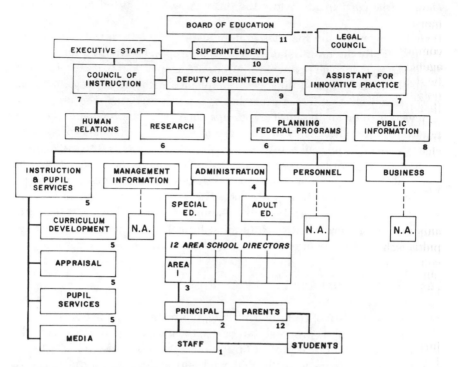

Fig. 16-2. School administrative organization.

- Council of Instruction
- Deputy Superintendent
- Superintendent
- Board of Education

In addition, information must be passed to and advice secured from the Federal Programs Office, the Public Information Office, and the Assistant for Innovative Practice. At each of these steps, the project could be required to review, extend, subtract from, or otherwise modify its proposed activities.

PREP did not follow this sequence exactly as specified when it attempted to secure the original enabling mandate for operation in this school jurisdiction. Responsible school staff recommended (and helped PREP negotiate) a series of steps that excluded important liaison with agencies such as the Department of Research, the Deputy Superintendent, the Council of Instruction, and the school board. Despite the failure to make all necessary stops along the way, PREP staff spent approximately 5 months of part-time effort completing negotiations with the county to start the program.

Because PREP failed to secure the required set of approvals, it became subject to intense criticism from a small number of local organizations opposed to behavior modification and underwent a critical media blitz that radically affected program operations during one school year. These charges and news reports coincided with a heated school-board election, illustrating that local political issues can have substantial impact on such a program.

In the second project setting, the same general type of school administrative regulations had to be observed, but another requirement was added. This particular school draws from a highly diverse socioeconomic population, who live within a geographically large school jurisdiction. To provide cohesion within this school, the principal established a standing committee termed the Principal's Advisory Council (PAC), drawing members from all segments of the community. The PAC is empowered to comment on or supervise on-going activities of the school, having the right to initiate its own plans and regulate other efforts. PREP presented its proposed set of activities to this group for advice and consent. The socioeconomic divergence, coupled with the specific background of the group's membership (including a minister, housewives, an engineer, a trailer-court owner, etc.), promoted wide-ranging sentiment on specific elements of the proposal. In each case, it was necessary to accommodate the actual intentions of PREP with those strong positions held by the group's membership. Another nearly 5 months was spent securing the required approvals for PREP's work in this second school.

Although no specific documentation was retained on the actual number of changes PREP was required to make to its plans (as approved by both grantor and grantee staff or consultants), these two sets of additional review procedures had a profound impact on the final set of procedures that PREP would use. Yet in both cases, to disregard such directed respecification could well have promoted a community situation that would not tolerate the project.

The divergent requirements and aspirations of the professional researcher, the professional educator, the lay educational leaders, political groups of the community, etc., can create a maze of objectives and standards that is frustrating to all involved. All persons view their requirements as the most important or meaningful, to the casual disregard of most others. In practice, however, all these requirements impinge on the researcher who hopes to mount a program in the schools, who may ask, as did PREP staff, "Is the limited research I'm able to do in the natural environment worth the effort I have to expend getting and keeping my foot in the door?"

Parent Controls

Parents of enrolled students usually have infrequent direct contact with the daily operations of the PREP project. They meet with training staff (PREP and/or teachers) far less often during the year than do their children. They spend the least time of any type of participant learning new skills from the staff. The participation (when it occurs in such a free situation) is often tangential. Yet they exercise formidable control over the behavior-modification efforts of the staff.

First, the policy of the grantee institution (and that of the National Institute of Mental Health) requires truly informed consent from both parents and children who participate in PREP's activities. The procedure for deriving this informed consent is detailed, lengthy, and of great effort for the staff. Figure 16-3 describes the sequence of selection procedures used by PREP during the second of its school-based years. This sequence may be appropriately modified to accommodate different entrance testing and experimental and control-group placement processes.

In this procedure, the parent and/or child have five distinct opportunities to say "No" to participation in PREP. The first two steps in the selection procedure are beyond the parent's control while initial decisions are made on the eligibility of the student for placement in PREP. Between steps 3 and 4, the first choice is whether or not this described activity meets the parent's and the child's criteria for appropriateness. Again, between steps 5 and 6, and 6 and 7, the subjects are asked to make informed choices about their potential participation. By this stage in the process (which usually covers about 2 summer months), the participants have received three descriptions of PREP's goals and procedures (in increasing detail and sophistication). They are then asked in step 7 formally to sign an agreement form that summarizes the program's operational details, clearly spells out their unreserved rights to other in-school training options, and describes how they may withdraw from participation at *any* later time with no retribution. Recent files of PREP show that (from a total of 343 children so recommended to

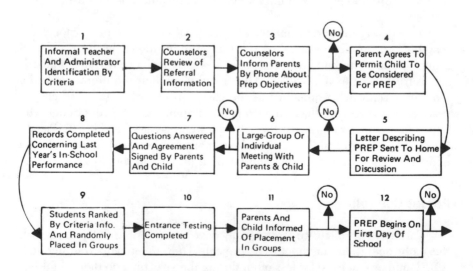

Fig. 16-3. Sequence of selection procedures.

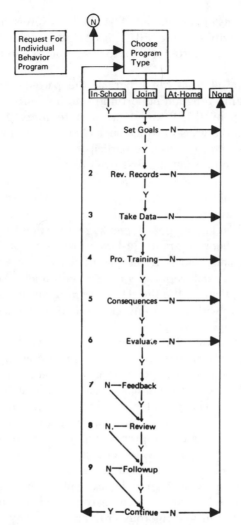

Fig. 16-4. Individual behavior program control.

PREP in its first 4 yr) nine were withdrawn from the selection procedure after step 3 and three were withdrawn after step 6—a withdrawal rate before initiation of involvement with any project procedure of 3.5%.

From the remaining total of 331 children (70 of whom were involved for a 2 yr period), 46 terminated their participation in PREP after the program began. Of these 46 terminating students, 21 were forced to leave for reasons of family household relocation, while another nine were transferred to a different school. Only 16 sets of parents (4.8%) chose to terminate their child's participation in PREP after it began. In ten of these 16 instances, the child completed 1 yr of a planned 2-yr program before being withdrawn.

This means that 28 sets of parents out of 343 (8.2%) exercised the maximum control over the activities of the PREP investigators with their children: Participation was not permitted either to begin or to extend through its planned term.

Beyond withdrawal from the program, the parents were afforded a range of specific within-program opportunities to influence and control the activities undertaken by PREP investigators or teachers. Figure 16-4 describes in brief form the ways in which such choices were made by parents after they permitted their children to participate in the overall activities of PREP (specifically used during the first two project years).

Students in the experimental group(s) may need (in the view of PREP staff, teachers, or administrators) training services beyond those included in the routine PREP activities. Parents and students are permitted to choose among three special program types, depending on the need expressed by the staff or parent: in-school programs, at-home programs, or joint programs between the home and school. If the parent decides that no program is needed or desired, the staff request is terminated (unless the behavior becomes more severe). If any of the three types of program are accepted by the parent, staff negotiate with the parent and student on ground rules for the specific individual behavior program.

The first six elements of the program (setting goals, reviewing past PREP and other records, taking baseline data, providing appropriate training, providing appropriate consequences, and evaluating the program) are all mandatory. If the parent does not agree to each of these steps, the program is not begun. The parent may then select any one or all of the subsequent elements (7-9) for inclusion in the program, but none is mandatory. A contractual and negotiation process applied to developing individual behavior programs resulted in a wide-ranging and flexible opportunity for both the staff and teachers to contribute to the solution of most problems. Over the course of one school year, for example, a total of 18 behavior problems were referred by staff to this parent/child negotiation process. Four of these resulted in less rigorous programs than envisioned by staff, three were made more stringent by students and parents, eight paralleled those originally conceived by the staff, and three were rejected in total. In addition, one started program was terminated by request of the parent. Operated in this manner, a behavioral program in a public setting cannot escape stringent controls by those parents who choose to apply them.

Teacher Controls

PREP operates its program with children through a number of intermediaries: teachers, counselors, and administrators of the cooperating school. Consequently, any training tactic or objective evaluative effort originally perceived as important by the PREP staff (either for the program in general or for any student in particular) can undergo mild or substantial change when managed by school staff. The degree to which such change occurs varies with the extent of overlap in the goals, skills, operating contingencies, and experience of school and project staff. Such overlap is extended through skill-development training of school staff and reinforcement of their approximating efforts. Yet the project staff learns as much (through the same means) as do the teachers and counselors. Each different school setting in which PREP works requires a change in focus on issues of student-training objectives, applicable reinforcers, etc. This process of interchange among project staff (who know the project's objectives), the teachers (who know the characteristics of their school), and the students and parents (who often know precisely what they want) routinely influences the daily and long-term operations of the project. Because the teachers are "middlemen," their involvement always has important impact. Only one such example is given here.

One teacher indicated during the pre-school training period that she was unlikely to be able to provide high-level verbal reinforcers to students in her class. She said that she would try her best, but that her teaching strengths simply did not lie in this area. With her assistance, PREP staff designed a training program that (eventually) included provisions for mild desensitization to student misbehavior, extensive modeling processes, clearly defined behavioral performances, explicit behavior prompts (in the form of charts, directive posters, daily floor-plan guides, etc.), simple self and observer counting procedures, several positive reinforcement techniques (including contingent student praise, staff praise, staff help for other work, data posting, administrative comments, written letters of commendation, visits from supervisors, etc.), and daily or less frequent feedback and review sessions.

Independent observers made baseline counts for this teacher that indicated her verbal behavior toward students included an average of 5% "praise" comments, 45% "neutral" (or instructive) comments, and 50% "misbehavior-attending" (e.g., "sit down," "be quiet,"and "start your work now") comments, usually delivered with a disapproving tone of voice. Modeling, direct instructions in class, praise by staff, observer recording, and daily feedback were used first in an attempt to change this behavior to an eventual target of 10% misbehavior-attending and 50% praise comments. Within seven sessions, the misbehavior-attending comments had dropped to 12% and praise comments had increased to 22% of all comments. This change resulted in intense praise from PREP staff, administration, and supervisors (including letters of commendation for her personnel file and the opportunity to act as subject-team leader). PREP observers were withdrawn as the recording controls were slowly faded from staff to the teacher. Praise comments fell to near-baseline levels (5% of all comments). When the observers were reintroduced, the praise ratio climbed to 25% of total comments. Even though all other measures planned for this program were tried, there was no increment in this percent of praise comments over the term of the school year. As could be expected, the rate of student work in this class was the lowest of any class PREP worked with during this year.

As this example indicates, the behavior of PREP teachers has major impact on the everyday operations of the project, despite the intentions and training regimen devised by the staff. This is inevitably the case in projects that depend on existing staff to mediate the ultimate behavior change.

Student Controls

Of all the forms of control that can be exerted over the behavior controller in the school setting, the one discussed least often is the countercontrol directed by the student. When such student controls are exercised effectively, they can be viewed as "the failures" in the program. Clearly, PREP's individual behavior-development efforts are based on the premise that the student and parent will work with the teachers to define a set of goals for appropriate behavior satisfactory to all parties. PREP staff acted to ensure that the goals were objective and measurable and that the necessary implements (such as recording forms, reporting forms, etc.) and liaison mechanisms (telephones, meeting offices, etc.) were available. After appropriate objectives were established, PREP became a means of facilitating their achievement.

In this situation the student most typically has a major hand in defining the program, either by specifying the reinforcers applicable for improving performance or by helping state desired target behavior, or both. In such instances the student-based control over the behavior controller is direct, frequent, interactive, and distinctly reinforcing to the behavior controller. Each learns what the other has as objectives, and programs may be readily framed on such a base. The extent of this control appears to be more pervasive with adolescents than with younger children.

One example of such positive control became the delight of many teachers who worked with PREP. Colin was enrolled in PREP's academic-training component. His records indicated an above-average intelligence; average academic grades; achievement test scores more than 2 yr lower than his grade placement; and frequent referrals from teachers for disruptive, aggressive, and vulgar verbal behavior. An individual program was undertaken by his teachers to improve his slow rate of work in class, resulting in an improvement from zero assignments completed per week in the first month to more than five completed per week for the next month and a half.

Colin and his teachers were both pleased with these positive changes. Yet Colin also was found by independent observers to demonstrate inappropriate verbal behavior toward his math teacher. The teacher felt compelled to require more appropriate behavior from Colin in this class. Arrangements were made with Colin and his parents to set up an individualized behavior program focusing on this verbal performance. The parents agreed that such an effort was needed and expressed a willingness to provide any backup support needed for the program's design, conduct, or reinforcement.

Colin and the teacher sat down to discuss the situation. Colin agreed with the teacher that his comments in class were demeaning to her and indicated that he was willing to attempt a change in his performance. They discussed some simple methods of record keeping and established a rather traditional teacher-directed reinforcement program. PREP staff and the teacher concluded that the program could be easily managed and that there was a strong likelihood of success. Yet, over a two-week period, Colin's rate of inappropriate verbal behavior toward the teacher was maintained, despite frequent contingent praise and earned extra recreational time. As Colin and the teacher reviewed this lack of progress, Colin expressed intrigue with a different form of record keeping used in another class. This procedure featured recording by both the teacher and the student. The teacher recorded instances of appropriate and inappropriate behavior of the student (along with the moment-to-moment instances of reinforcement points awarded). The student, in turn, recorded each instance of contact by the teacher and the reinforcement points awarded. This procedure permitted the teacher and the student to monitor and reinforce each other's behavior. The student felt that the control he thereby had over the teacher "was great," as he was able to feed back her contacts with him to prompt or reinforce her efforts. Results obtained by both were validated at the end of each class period with the other party. Using this procedure, Colin's inappropriate verbal behavior with the teacher decreased to half the prior rate (although never to zero) and remained at this level for 2 months until the end of the year. Yet, Colin was able to direct the teacher to a procedure that better fit his perception of what was proper in this situation. This example serves to illustrate the reciprocal control exerted by the teacher and student (Bandura, 1974).

Control by Nonusers

As indicated earlier, projects such as PREP are continually subject to critique, evaluation, or simple review by agencies outside the project's operations. These may be independent evaluators selected by the client, the funding agency, or the grantee institution itself. Most project directors understand the need for such evaluation, the procedures such agents undertake, and the consequences of their efforts. PREP has undergone such evaluations, and the staff recognizes the help evaluations can give. Another kind of independent evaluator however, made a more profound impact on daily operations than could any professional team. The press came to PREP. These activities had an impact on project operations controlling planned efforts in a major way for more than 2 months.

A reporter from a major Washington, D.C., newspaper visited the project six weeks after the start of the school year. The reporter was convinced that PREP had been both operating illegally in the school and performing unethically with parents and children. The resulting newspaper report (Bauer, 1972) was followed by a deluge of requests to visit from local reporters from newspapers, radio, and television. School officials, parents, national magazine reporters, and personnel of other projects descended on PREP for observation of its operations. These intense demands for observation and inspection had two principal effects.

The first was on the time of the principal project staff. For example, before publication of the newspaper article the project director spent an average of 2½ hrs per week meeting with project visitors through the first six weeks of the year. Figure 16-5 presents the number of hours spent by the director in such "public-relations" meetings over the school year. The asterisk at week 7 indicates the publication of the newspaper article.

These data are simple and clear. For 11 subsequent weeks, the director spent a minimum of three times as much time in public liaison as in the earlier six weeks. For six of these 11 weeks, over 10 hrs were spent in public meetings. In addition, the preparation time for these meetings consumed at least as much time as the meetings themselves. Understandably, the director spent little time on issues concerning practical operations of the project. Whether intended or not, this intensive demand on the time of the director (and other staff as well) prevented a wide range of behavior development with the students that year.

The second effect concerned the activities of the students in the project. In prior years, PREP found that students' work on learning materials accelerated during the first three weeks (after the diagnostic testing) and stabilized over the year at approximately 23 work units (an empirically based measure) per hour. Figure 16-6 shows the record of work units in one class (others

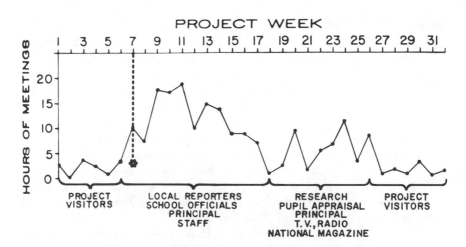

Fig. 16-5 Project director's time spent in public-relations meetings.

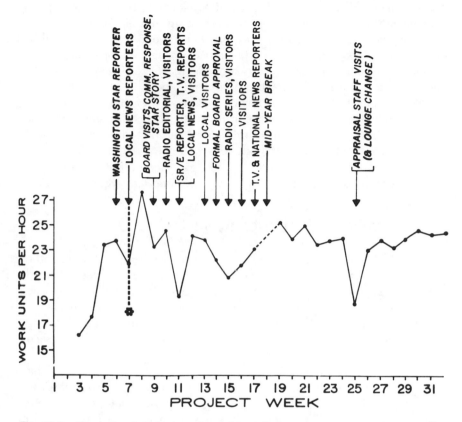

Fig. 16-6. Example of student work rate by project week.

were similar) over the year's term. Again, the asterisk indicates publication of the newspaper story.

By week 5, student work units had reached the level found in prior years. Normally, this rate would continue, with minor variations, through the year. Yet in week 7, as the original newspaper story was published and the furor began, the work units of students began to fluctuate markedly. The high point in week 8 (that the students attributed to "wanting to show those reporters how hard we can work") and the lows during weeks 11, 15, and 25 were simply at odd variance to prior performances. As the major influx of visitors slowed after week 17, the rate of student work resumed a near stable level. Only week 25 (associated with a major change in reinforcing activities in the students' lounge) showed a sharp difference from those rates after week 17.

Despite the improvement in student performance noted throughout the year, this operation while under close scrutiny appeared to have an impact in yet another way. During the end-of-the-year testing in late May, several students behaved more poorly than usual. Students chatted, marked random answers on their prepared answer sheets, got up to walk around the room, etc. Many of these students were experimental group participants and had shown high work output and participation throughout the year. County school-system personnel who were supervising the testing were appalled. They questioned a number of these students about the reasons for their behavior. Some students noted they did not know why they had "acted that way." Most noted that they had been tested twice already that school year (pretest in September and midtest in January) and that they "were through" being asked to perform for everybody who wanted to see the "guinea pigs" of PREP (their words). Achievement test score gains for all students during that year were depressed in relation to both earlier and later years.

SUMMARY AND CONCLUSIONS

PREP found that the degree of control over its operations by others is formidable indeed. For nearly one third of a school year, forces outside the project (and quite incidental to its initiation, operation, or scientific evaluation) controlled the project's activities in a most direct and (in the staff and parents' view) detrimental manner. Yet this is only the most flagrant example in PREP of control exerted over the behavior controller in the public secondary school.

The more important issue is the degree to which such control on a routine basis is *pervasive* for the behavioral researcher in the natural setting. Prior to initiating the proposal, ethical, procedural, scientific, and other considerations affect the conceptualizations on which the project will be built. Controls exerted by peers in the researcher's own institution, in the public agency that funds the research, and in the school administration that will house the project significantly extend, detract from, or otherwise modify the proposed effort. Others who will play a vital role in the project (such as parents, school leaders, and vocal community groups) have as much impact, but usually in different areas of concern. And this all occurs before the program begins operation. Once it starts, the issue of control over the behavior controller reduces to "more of the same," with important additions. To the controls exerted by the school administration, parents, and community groups, one finds important additional contributions made by the teachers who actually conduct the training, the children who participate in the research program, and (because of the school's unique relation to the larger social system) almost anybody else.

With many projects, the long-term implications for such control may be more than the collective behavior controllers yet imagine. Vast outlays of time, effort, and money may be (and probably are) devoted by these investigators to negotiating each of the controls detailed here. Only crude estimates from personal experience demonstrate that diversion of such time, effort, and money for these issues detracts from researcher and/or demonstration activities. The behavior of the behavioral research who disregards these attempts at control by others will be punished, and the likelihood of aversive consequences is as strong if effort is diverted from research or demonstration activities. Applied behavioral researchers must choose how much they are willing to allow these controls to influence the research effort. Even more basically, they must decide whether they are willing to pay the price and bring their skills and knowledge into the social arena or remain in more sterilized (and maybe more sterile) laboratory settings.

But the picture is not all negative. As London (1974) notes, "A decent society regulates all technology that is powerful enough to affect the general welfare, at once restricting the technicians as little as possible and as much as necessary." The contracts (whether expressed or implied) between behavioral researcher and subjects must be formulated just as any other contract between professional and client. To the extent that such contracts eventually benefit society, society will regulate the behavioral researcher's efforts "as little as possible." To the extent such benefit is not derived, the converse applies.

The remaining constraints that impinge on the behavioral researcher's programs in a public institution are generally of the practical programmatic or political types. In certain cases, as stated by Reppucci and Saunders (1974), theoretical perspective on such practical issues may be afforded by disciplines outside that which forms the program's major elements. In other instances, sophisticated theoretical understanding is required less than a straightforward application of common sense about means of dealing with individuals and institutions. Rather reasonable, clear-cut, and natural contingencies of reinforcement appear to be in effect for the behavioral researcher's programs. Most behavioral researchers should welcome such direct application of the theory they promote.

H. S. PENNYPACKER, J. B.
PENNYPACKER

Chapter 17

A University-Wide System of Personalized Instruction: The Personalized Learning Center

Since the pioneering efforts by B.F. Skinner in the late 1950's to apply the principles of a natural science of behavior to the problem of individualizing college instruction, a new discipline has emerged that possesses a vast literature descriptive of a rapidly expanding technology. The contributions of Keller (1966, 1968), Malott and Svinicki (1969), McMichael and Corey (1969), Sheppard and McDermott (1970), Born and Herbert (1971), and Johnston and Pennypacker (1971) are among the most generally cited anchors for published reports of attempts to develop and apply an empirically sound technology of behavior change in the college classroom (see Chapter 14 for a more detailed description of major genera of these problems). With a handful of exceptions (e.g., Elkins, 1975; Toft, 1975), these efforts have been directed at one or a few classes, usually in Psychology or Education, although by now virtually every academic discipline has been touched somewhere by the technology (Johnston, 1974, 1975; Vargas & Fraley, 1975). Although the technology has been shown applicable across disciplines, the extension to a systematic, campus-wide instructional technology envisioned by Vargas and Fraley (1975) has generally failed to occur except in the case of two highly innovative, small colleges (Elkins, 1975; Toft, 1975). We are aware of but a single exception to this generality—the University of Florida—and the circumstances surrounding this exception merit some attention and analysis.

It is no doubt true that the complex of behavior involved in any educational innovation has multiple determinants. Nevertheless, some combination of positive and negative reinforcers is probably responsible for shaping and maintaining approximations to an effective innovation; the academy is not known to punish perseverance in traditional teaching practices and thereby force variation that would lead to innovation. Such consequences as happier students, reduced uneasiness about the dubious cost benefit of traditional instruction, and the opportunity to promulgate a philosophy of behavior by repeatedly demonstrating its technological benefits in a real-life situation have all been cited as reinforcers for the early innovators. None of these consequences are especially reinforcing for the deans or vice-presidents of a large state university, however, and some, such as the philosophy of behaviorism or public remonstration concerning the traditionally low correlation between tuition and educational benefit measured by change in behavior, are known to be mildly aversive. Happier students provide reinforcers to administrators to the extent that they less frequently engage in organized destructive or disruptive activities or that they eventually bestow resources upon the institution in their future roles as alumni. Most administrators do not have sufficient contact with students to experience the reinforcers attendant to a student publicly reordering the priorities of his/her life as a result of a singular educational experience that an instructor arranged.

It is not surprising, then, that extensions of an effective educational innovation to domains beyond the administrative purview of the individual innovator are rare, if not altogether nonexistent. Reinforcers for appropriate initiating or supportive behavior on the part of higher officials have not been arranged, or even specified. Moreover, it would ordinarily be beyond the capability of the innovator to arrange such reinforcers, even if able to designate them.

In the early 1970's at the University of Florida, a combination of circumstances prevailed which constituted an exception to this rule and thereby led to the general statement of the rule. These were (1) The presence of a large group of students in whose academic success the institution had a conspicuous financial and political commitment and who, as a group, were dropping out at a disturbingly high rate; (2) Local availability of an innovative technology and a cadre of trained personnel to administer it; and (3) A dean who was willing to gamble that (2) could reduce the aversiveness of (1) by engendering a higher success rate in that student population without diluting the institution's academic standards.

Briefly, in response to organized pressure from various minority groups, the university sought, beginning in 1968, to make available to all citizens of the state the resources of its oldest and largest institution of higher education. For a variety of reasons, this meant waiving for the majority of special cases certain traditional entrance requirements. It was also seen to mean providing special programs, both financial and educational, for the benefit of those participants who would need either or both kinds of assistance to enjoy a reasonable chance of success. Over a 4-yr span the educational program, a somewhat typical mixture of individualized tutoring and humanistic counseling, managed to stabilize the drop-out rate at approximately 40%. This performance was unacceptable to the newly appointed dean of the college responsible for the program's administration, particularly in view of the financial and humanitarian loss it represented. Accordingly, in 1972 he sought advice and assistance in developing an extension of the general technology developed earlier at the institution (Johnston & Pennypacker, 1971) to meet the academic needs of this population of students. This unique concatenation of circumstances set the occasion for the evolution of what has become a campus-wide system of personalized instruction—a system whose structure, function, and current status is described in this chapter.

BASIC CONSIDERATIONS IN THE DESIGN OF AN INSTRUCTIONAL SYSTEM

It is commonly agreed that education at any level involves arranging environments to engender change in the behavior of people called learners or students. Although disputes continue as to the nature of the various independent processes responsible for such change, there can be no gainsaying that change must be in the direction of some objective and that assessment is ultimately made in terms of what learners *do*. Any instructional technology, therefore, must provide for a system of measurement by which the behavior and behavior change of the learners can be described.

The behavior of any organism is a continuous transactional process between that organism and its environment. The instructional technologist cannot directly alter the learner, and so must concentrate upon various details of the learner's environment. Moreover, because the learner-environment interaction is continuous, effective instruction should at least approach continuity, lest uncontrolled environmental variables undo the effects of sporadic instructional endeavors. Accordingly an effective instructional technology is one that contacts the learner as often as possible.

Finally, an effective instructional technology must be maximally adaptable to the changing needs of the learner. For this to occur, sensitive feedback apparatus must be designed so that all concerned with the instructional process can make informed adjustments in each learner's environment as the need arises, and then monitor the effects of each adjustment for further possible corrective action.

This role played by measurement in any effective instructional technology is clearly paramount. In developing the basic behavioral technology of college teaching (Johnston & Pennypacker, 1971) primary emphasis was placed on continuous, direct measurement of student behavior using rate and/or frequency as the basic datum (Skinner, 1938). We discovered early that without such a maximally sensitive measurement system to continuously monitor each student's performance over time the term *individualized instruction* becomes rather hollow. Although mastery learning in terms of a percentage of items correctly answered was easily achieved using a modified proctor system, such measurement is grossly insensitive to the actual changes in student behavior that must be detected if an efficient system is to be developed. A group of students can all achieve, say, 75% correct on their initial attempt at the materials of a unit. Tactics for moving each student to 95% correct will, if truly individualized, depend upon decisions made from other measured aspects of each student's performance. With a fully sensitive measurement system, Keller's (1968) well-known dictum, "The student is always right" occupies the same level of strategic importance that the behavior of individual infrahuman organisms did in the development of the parent science (Skinner, 1938).

Extension of the technology from a single, senior-level course to several freshman-level courses cutting across disciplines presupposed retaining the basic measurement strategy that permitted creation of the technology in the first place. Developing optimal procedures and administrative structures for their delivery becomes a natural, orderly process if one adheres to the basic engineering principle, "Form follows function and function is determined by measurement." Our basic strategy, then, was to continue using the principles of direct behavioral measurement to support the development of a system whose elements are defined by end points in a series of cybernetic loops, each characterized by a bi-directional flow of information. Such elements only attain formal status within the structure when it has been demonstrated that their operation is functional, as defined by a measured effect on the final product: behavior change of students. It is therefore instructive to pause and consider in some detail the nature and rationale of our system of direct behavioral measurement.

OVERVIEW OF THE MEASUREMENT SYSTEM

The importance of Skinner's (1938, 1950, 1953a) designation of frequency (number of occurrences per unit time) as the basic unit of behavioral measurement has not been fully appreciated by many exporters of behavioral technology into various domains of education. In a situation such as ours, however, the overriding need for an absolute, universal measure of behavior leaves little room for choice. The vast array of stimulus materials, response topographies, and interacting contingencies that arise when multiple courses are offered to students and must be monitored simultaneously demands a unit of measurement at once maximally sensitive and maximally general. Frequency satisfies this requirement. Moreover, unlike most psychological measures, it is absolute; its application to the single case is fully meaningful without reference to a normative or standardization sample or tabled values of a density function.

The first derivative of frequency with respect to time (called *celeration* by Lindsley) provides, as Skinner (1938) also pointed out, an equally universal and sensitive measure of behavior change. Because of the wide range of behavior frequencies encountered across students and across courses, we

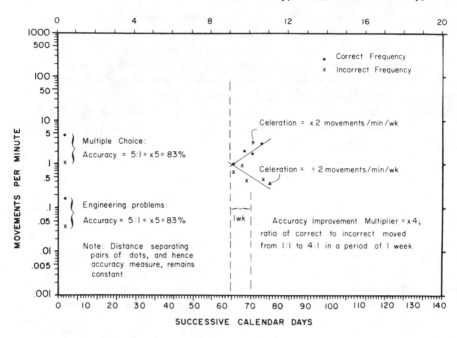

Fig. Fig. 17-1. Facsimile of the Standard Behavior Chart, showing measures of frequency, accuracy, celeration, and accuracy improvement.

found it desirable to adopt Lindsley's semilogarithmic Standard Behavior Chart, shown in Figure 17-1, as our vehicle for all visual display and analysis of behavioral data (Pennypacker, Koenig, & Lindsley, 1972). This chart combines a six-cycle logarithmic scale of frequencies on the y-axis with continuous units of calendar time on the x-axis and thus affords a single, standard format easily recognized and interpreted by all concerned, from individual students to top administrators.

Table 17-1 summarizes the basic and derived measures of behavior and behavior change that are currently in use. Essentially these measures are all combinations of various elementary counting and timing operations. Accuracy is an algebraic combination of the frequencies of correct and incorrect responding into a ratio that appears as a constant linear distance on the chart, regardless of the basic frequency. An accuracy ratio of 5 correct for every incorrect, for example, will always appear as the same distance separating the two frequencies, regardless of whether the frequencies are 10 correct and 2 incorrect per hour, as may happen with engineering problems, or 5 correct and 1 incorrect per minute, as often occurs on multiple-choice tests. Thus, we are able by inspection alone to compare accuracy change measures across students or across courses or both without losing the information inherent in the time parameter of the frequency unit. A simple percent correct measure clearly lacks this sensitivity.

The measures summarized in Table 17-1 can be readily obtained from a student's chart and are thus immediately available for description at the single-course, single-student level of analysis. Because of the standard nature of these measures, it is meaningful to collect them and, with the aid of the computer, prepare summaries across any number of program parameters. Thus, at the level where analysis of groups of individual charts becomes impractical, descriptive and analytic continuity is afforded by the computer, which, as we shall see, has become an indispensable management tool. Enlisting the aid of the computer in this fashion does no violence to the basic integrity of the measurement system; no new measures are created or derived, and the data are always immediately reducible to direct measures of the performance of individual students.

STRUCTURE AND OPERATIONAL FUNCTION OF THE PERSONALIZED LEARNING CENTER

Let us turn now to a fairly detailed description of the various functions of the Personalized Learning Center and, in so doing, examine the

Table 17-1
Basic Behavioral Measures Used in Academic Measurement

Term	Symbol	Definition
Frequency of Correct Responding	F_c	$\dfrac{\text{Number of Correct Responses}}{\text{Time of Session}}$
Frequency of Incorrect Responding	F_i	$\dfrac{\text{Number of Incorrect Responses}}{\text{Time of Session}}$
Accuracy (A)	$\dfrac{F_c}{F_i}$	Ratio of Correct to Incorrect Frequency[a]
Celeration	$\left(\dfrac{F\text{ ending}}{F\text{ beginning}}\right)^{1/t}$	Rate of Change in Frequency per Unit Time
Effectiveness (E)	$\dfrac{A\text{ ending}}{A\text{ beginning}}$	Total Change in Accuracy
Accuracy Improvement Multiplier (AIM)	$E^{1/t}$	Rate of Change in Accuracy per Unit Time
Average AIM	$\left[\prod\limits_{i=1}^{k}(E_i)\right]^{\frac{1}{\Sigma t_k}}$	Geometric Mean Effectiveness across k Units, Students, Instructors, Courses, etc.

[a] If either response count is zero, .9 is substituted on the assumption that the true frequency is not zero, only some value less than 1 / time of session.

interrelation among the structures that have evolved to expedite these functions.

The most basic functional element of this instructional system is known as the *performance session*. It is during the performance session that the student emits samples of the behavior, usually verbal, that is to be modified. As in most other systems of individualized instruction, this behavior is immediately measured and feedback concerning both accuracy and improvement is delivered promptly to the student. In the Personalized Learning Center, this function is performed by *peer advisors*—specially trained, somewhat advanced students who receive course credit for their services.

Because volume increases greatly, compared with a single-course application, when as many as 20 different courses are simultaneously managed in the same facility, we inserted an additional level of management personnel immediately above the peer advisor. These individuals are known as *advisor coordinators* and are responsible for directly supervising the peer advisors as well as monitoring and managing the flow of paper produced by the performance samples. In addition, advisor coordinators serve as quality-control technicians; they collect and maintain continuous frequency records on such things as peer advisor grading accuracy, peer advisor attendance, availability and consumption of appointment times for student performance sessions, and any special operational problems that arise. Advisor coordinators are responsible for routine reduction, display, and analysis of all resulting data and are given considerable latitude in suggesting and implementing procedural improvements, subject, of course, to immediate measured validation.

Currently, approximately 1000 student course enrollments are processed by the center each quarter. This requires from 125-150 peer advisors and 20-25 advisor coordinators. In addition a full-time, nonstudent *performance clerk*, on duty at all times, is responsible for maintaining security of all materials, maintaining all student records and ensuring their availability as needed by the peer advisors and advisor coordinators, and coordinating the flow of test and evaluation materials through the center. The relations among these several functions are diagrammed in Figure 17-2.

Advisor coordinators are recruited from varied sources, including the Department of Psychology and the College of Education, as well as the ranks of successful and enthusiastic peer advisors. Almost without exception, they have formal training in the experimental analysis of behavior and frequently go on to graduate school in that discipline. Whenever possible, they receive a small stipend for their services, making them paraprofessionals in the best sense of the term.

An illustration of the contribution of the advisor coordinators is furnished by a recent study conducted to establish effective pacing contingencies for maintaining student attendance. While there are reports in the literature of successful application of grade benefits in the form of bonus points, we found that our student population, lacking as it does a rich history

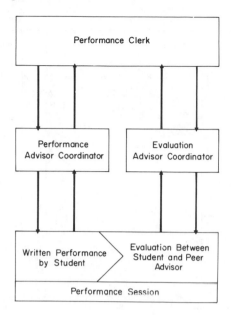

Fig. 17-2. Immediate support structure for the performance-session function.

of academic behavior maintained by grade reinforcers, is generally insensitive to promises of what are probably nonfunctional future consequences. Accordingly, a limited-hold procedure was established in several courses whereby performance had to occur by a specified deadline for any credit to accrue. This contingency is more readily contacted when expiration of the deadline produces an immediate withdrawal of the materials; the effects of subsequent attendance can be immediately noted and corresponding educational gain demonstrated for the balance of the term.

Gathering the data for this study was a primary responsibility of the advisor coordinators. Each day for each course, they monitored the frequency of available appointments and the frequency of appointments used. The effects of the limited hold on daily appointment-use frequency are shown in panel A of Figure 17-3. The pattern of accelerating appointment use as the deadline approached is as expected if the announced contingency is functional. In contrast panel B shows the attendance results in a course in which the limited hold had been announced but in which students discovered that the instructor was granting extensions and exemptions, thus rendering the announced contingency nonfunctional. Visual inspection of these data convinced the instructor that announced contingencies must be contacted to be effective, and the consistency of his subsequent behavior has improved accordingly. Thus, a major function of the advisor coordinators is the collection of quality-control data that serve as a discriminative stimulus for subsequent alteration of instructor behavior. In this way, relatively naive

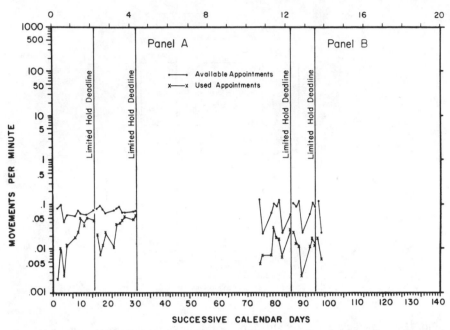

Fig. 17-3. Illustration of data collected by advisor coordinators showing effects of functional and announced-only limited-hold contingencies on patterns of attendance.

instructors are contacting the same consequences that shaped the behavior of the innovators.

Figure 17-4 diagrammatically illustrates the relations of the performance-session structures to additional support and service functions of the center. For example, the center has a limited student-advisement service that advises students with special academic needs and coordinates the enrollment in center courses with the registrar's office. Further, this unit assumes primary responsibility for assisting students in removing "incomplete" or "hold" grades and ensuring that their records are changed accordingly.

The appointment coordinator supervises and participates in the actual scheduling of student appointments for performance sessions. The scheduling of appointment availability requires matching the schedules of the 125 peer advisors with the requisite number of 20-min time blocks required for each course each day, and then allocating these across the times of day to equalize traffic density in the limited space. Computer programs have been written to assist in this function so that the main duty of the appointment coordinator is to ensure that students make and keep appointments in accordance with their individual needs. Typically, up to 500 appointments may be made daily.

The curriculum production unit has two main functions: creation and distribution. First, it receives from participating faculty all test items, grouped according to units of course material, to which the students will be responding in performance sessions. This material is then stored in the IBM 370, master lists are proofed and edited, and programs activated to produce individualized random samples of questions, together with separable answer keys, which are batch printed on a daily basis. These materials are then delivered to the performance lab in the quantities indicated by the projected appointment data. A major responsibility of the curriculum production personnel depends on their relations with the participating faculty; ensuring availability of sufficient materials with adequate lead time for production and delivery requires both tact and persistence in the extreme. Procrastinating instructors promptly encounter the natural contingencies generated by irate students who resist disruptions in the unit-by-unit pacing inherent in the system. Once received from instructors, turn-around time for curriculum delivery to the students has been reduced to a matter of a few days or, with special priority computer execution, a few hours.

In addition to the service personnel already described, the center employs a cadre of tutors who offer intensive, specialized instruction in the major academic areas represented: mathematics, social studies, physical science, biological science, and the humanities. Access to this service may be obtained by a student at any time, but is mandatory following a series of performances in which minimal criteria of mastery or improvement are not observed. Renewal of opportunity to participate in performance sessions is contingent upon presentation of written evidence of a tutorial session. Tutor effectiveness is monitored, of course, in terms of measured improvement on the student's performance chart. Tutors whose efforts fail to produce such evidence are not retained.

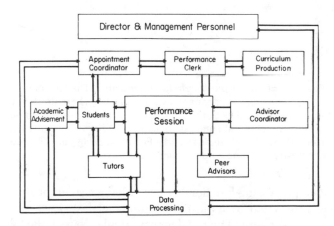

Fig. 17-4. Diagram of cybernetic connections of all elements internal to the center, from the performance session outward. See text for explanation of function of each element.

```
QUARTER: FA75    TIME PERIOD: 920 - 1203
COURSE: MS 301   SECTION: 5473   INSTRUCTOR: YOON          UNITS: 6   CREDITS: 5
```

	NAME	S S NUMBER	TOTAL APPOINTMT	CURRENT UNIT	TOTAL APPOINTMT	AVERAGE MAX PERCENT
1:	STUDENT S NAME	261-21-8140	/ 9	3 /	9	73.3
2:	STUDENT S NAME	264-29-6623	/ 1	4 /	1	75.0
3:	STUDENT S NAME	262-17-3534	/ 7	4 /	7	74.5
4:	STUDENT S NAME	263-39-7179	/ 7	4 /	7	81.5
5:	STUDENT S NAME	361-48-1625	/ 3	3 /	3	76.3
6:	STUDENT S NAME	049-48-8218	/ 7	3 /	7	70.7
7:	STUDENT S NAME	330-50-6129	/ 2	2 /	2	54.0
8:	STUDENT S NAME	119-48-5762	/ 8	5 /	8	79.5
9:	STUDENT S NAME	261-11-4991	/ 0	* /	*	0.0
10:	STUDENT S NAME	262-33-6439	/ 5	3 /	5	58.5
11:	STUDENT S NAME	263-21-8594	/ 1	1 /	1	0.0
12:	STUDENT S NAME	261-27-1400	/ 4	3 /	4	59.3
13:	STUDENT S NAME	388-48-8262	/ 0	* /	*	0.0
14:	STUDENT S NAME	200-36-1685	/ 2	1 /	2	65.0
15:	STUDENT S NAME	267-11-6776	/ 4	3 /	4	71.3
16:	STUDENT S NAME	264-13-6652	/ 0	* /	*	0.0
17:	STUDENT S NAME	261-27-1266	/ 0	* /	*	0.0
18:	STUDENT S NAME	254-74-8453	/ 1	1 /	1	40.0
19:	STUDENT S NAME	266-33-4295	/ 6	4 /	6	90.5
20:	STUDENT S NAME	264-13-3267	/ 5	2 /	5	54.0

```
                                 72       1- 5      4.5        64.0
                                TOTAL     RANGE      MEAN       MEAN
```

	UNIT # 1			UNIT # 2			UNIT # 3			UNIT # 4			UNIT # 5		
	# A	MX P CRCT PT	BN P	# A	MX P CRCT PT	BN P	# A	MX P CRCT PT	BN P	# A	MX P CRCT PT	BN P	# A	MX P CRCT PT	BN P
1:	3	80.0		3	80.0	*	3	60.0							
2:										1	75.0	*			
3:	1	35.0		2	86.0	*	2	98.0	*	2	79.0	*			
4:	2	64.0	*	3	74.0	*	1	89.0	*	1	90.0	*			
5:	1	70.0	*	1	79.0	*	1	80.0	*						
6:	2	45.0		3	92.0	*	2	75.0	*						
7:				2	54.0										
8:	2	70.0	*	2	100.0	*	1	92.0	*	2	92.0	*	1	43.5	
10:	1	17.5		2	76.0	*	2	82.0	*						
11:	1														
12:	1	10.0		2	95.0	*	1	73.0	*						
14:	2	65.0													
15:	1	50.0		2	92.0	*	1	72.0	*						
18:	1	40.0													
19:	3	100.0		1	87.0	*	1	90.0	*	1	85.0	*			
20:	2	43.0		3	65.0										

Fig. 17-5. Example of weekly printout to faculty member. The time period is selectable by the operator; in this case, it spans the whole quarter. There are two total appointment columns, one for the time period specified and one for the entire quarter in case they are not identical. The unit summary headers are: Number of Attempts, Maximum Percent Correct, Bonus Points (if any), and a Pass-Fail designator. The numbers in the left column correspond to the student numbers above.

The data processing function has expanded considerably in the last year and is now supervised by a full-time systems analyst. Each time a student performs on a given unit of material for a particular course, the following data are recorded: name, social security number, date, course number, unit number, number of items answered correctly, number of items answered incorrectly, number of minutes spent answering items, number of minutes spent discussing performance with the peer advisor, whether or not criterion was met, bonus points awarded (if any), and any referrals or special actions. These data are immediately displayed on the student's chart and serve as the basis for prompt evaluation and feedback. Each evening, the same data are collected for all performances of the day and are fed by remote typewriter terminal into the IBM 370. An extensive package of APL interactive software permits these data to be sorted, summarized, and retrieved in various formats appropriate to the needs of various groups and individuals. For example, participating faculty members receive a weekly printout updating the performance records of the students in their section(s). Program directors receive a similar printout for all students in their program, and anyone can retrieve the data for a particular student at any time, such as when special advisement is occurring. Figures 17-5, 17-6, and 17-7 illustrate these printouts. The formats were designed by the recipients themselves on the theory that they would be more likely to make use of data they requested if it were in a form they requested rather than one we found appealing.

Currently the data-processing personnel are concerning themselves with problems of long-range follow up and evaluation in coordination with the central record-keeping facilities of the university. Additionally the enormous volume of performance data generated quarterly has created storage problems for the APL package, and ways of off-line storage that incorporate rapid accessibility are being sought. This problem will reach acute dimensions as the center continues to grow and expands the availability of its services to a larger segment of the campus community. Using the computer

```
FOLLOWING ARE THE STUDENTS THAT HAVE A PROGRAM STATUS OF: 090000000
QUARTER: FA75    ENDING DATE: 1203
                                                 TOTAL    AVERAGE  INST  TUTOR
                NAME        S S NUMBER   COURSES  APPOINTMT MAX PCT  REF   REF
               ==========  ==========  =======  ========= ======= ====  =====
    1:  STUDENT S NAME  134-48-4156   CMS 11X      6       45.2      1     1
    2:  STUDENT S NAME  267-29-6076   CPS 13Z      -
    3:  STUDENT S NAME  261-29-5956   CPS 13Z      7       66.3      3     1
                                      SSC 221      6       55.0      1     3
    4:  STUDENT S NAME  300-54-4392   CPS 13Z      7       65.8      1     1
                                      SSC 221      7       65.0      2     2


                    UNIT # 1      UNIT # 2      UNIT # 3      UNIT # 4
                  ============  ============  ============  ============
                  #  MX P BN    #  MX P BN    #  MX P BN    #  MX P BN
        COURSES   A  CRCT PT P  A  CRCT PT P  A  CRCT PT P  A  CRCT PT P
        -------   -  ----- -- - -  ----- -- - -  ----- -- - -  ----- -- -
    1:  CMS 11X   4  53.3      1  75.0      *  1   7.1
    3:  CPS 13Z   4  67.5      3  65.0
    3:  SSC 221   3  50.0      3  60.0
    4:  CPS 13Z   2  77.5   *  3  67.5         2  52.5
    4:  SSC 221   3  55.0      4  75.0      *
```

Fig. 17-6. Printout for all students having the designated program status indicator. There are 9^9 possible designators allowing for retrieval against virtually any combination of student characteristics.

```
QUARTER: FA75    ENDING DATE: 1203
                                                        TOTAL    AVERAGE   INST  TUTOR
            NAME           S S NUMBER    COURSES     APPOINTMT  MAX PCT   REF    REF
      ================     ===========   =======     =========  =======  ====  =====
   1:  STUDENT S NAME      266-31-0956   CPS 13Z         9        70.0      2      2
                                         HUM 21X         6        92.4
                                         CPS 21X         5        59.0


                  UNIT # 1           UNIT # 2           UNIT # 3           UNIT # 4
                ============       ============       ============       ============
                #  MX P BN         #  MX P BN         #  MX P BN         #  MX P BN
        COURSES A  CRCT PT P       A  CRCT PT P       A  CPCT PT P       A  CRCT PT P
        ------- -  ----- -- -      -  ----- -- -      -  ----- -- -      -  ----- -- -
   1: CPS 13Z   1  80.0     *      3  55.0            3  67.5            2  77.5     *
   1: HUM 21X   2  85.0     *      1  82.0     *      1 100.0     *      1  95.0     *
   1: CBS 21X   2  38.0            3  80.0     *


                  UNIT # 5           UNIT # 6           UNIT # 7           UNIT # 8
                ============       ============       ============       ============
                #  MX P BN         #  MX P BN         #  MX P BN         #  MX P BN
        COURSES A  CRCT PT P       A  CRCT PT P       A  CRCT PT P       A  CRCT PT P
        ------- -  ----- -- -      -  ----- -- -      -  ----- -- -      -  ----- -- -
   1: HUM 21X   1 100.0     *
```

Fig. 17-7. Printout for a single student.

as a management tool in large-scale systems of personalized instruction is an obvious necessity if the system is effectively data based, but the problems posed even for a large university computer are not negligible and should be anticipated.

Before discussing the interface of the center with other major units of the campus, a hard-won note of caution should be sounded to potential replicators or adopters of this system. Creation of a sensitive system of cybernetic interchanges between traditional campus structures and a highly empirical, innovative instructional technology provides the conditions for magnifying the effects of any lack of imaginative administration within the peripheral structure. Administrators who construe their duty to be primarily regulatory have not, in our experience, been receptive to the demands for imaginative leadership posed by a nearly continuous flow of data. It therefore becomes necessary, on occasion, to redirect the flow of data away from a structure the place of which within the formal organization might seem ideal, and instead attempt to formalize a working functional relation with some other structure that may initially seem remote from the overall instructional objective. Many of the relations displayed in Figure 17-8 evolved from this strategy and some presently displayed there may dissolve as a result of changes in administrative personnel that occur for reasons other than the best educational interests of the students.

The current place and function of the Personalized Learning Center with respect to other administrative units on campus is diagrammed in Figure 17-8. Each participating or supporting structure is shown relating to the center by means of arrows intended to indicate the cybernetic character of information flow in both directions. At this writing, the center is a fully integrated structure within the delivery apparatus for the instructional service of the institution. Further, it is funded almost entirely by "hard" money generated, as the diagram shows, by units whose mission is primarily instructional.

As shown in Figure 17-8 the center is under the direct administrative aegis of the Office of Instructional Resources, which in turn reports directly to the institution's chief academic administrative officer. This arrangement highlights the instructional function of the institution and relieves the largely ceremonial character that an agency like Office of Instructional Resources typically manifests in the traditional structure. By ensuring that the credit for solution to the problems of special students (minority students and student athletes) redounds principally to the Office of Instructional Resources, an arrangement has been created whereby that structure gains leverage to carry out the type of integrated instructional function envisioned by several educational theorists (e.g., Vargas and Fraley, 1975). This outcome is predicated, of course, on demonstrated effectiveness of the center's activities and it is to this issue that we now direct our attention.

PRELIMINARY EVALUATION OF THE EFFECTIVENESS OF THE PERSONALIZED LEARNING CENTER

The system of direct behavioral measurement that we described and illustrated earlier may be extended readily to a system of cost-benefit

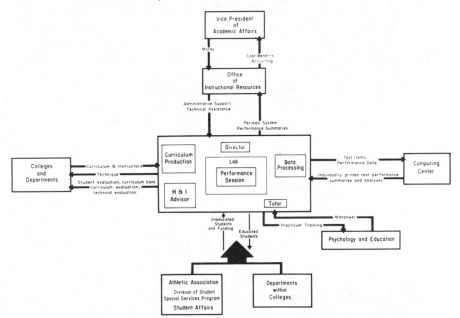

Fig. 17-8. Diagram showing cybernetic relations of the center to other campus structures.

accounting wherein effectiveness and benefit are defined in terms of objectively measured behavior change (Pennypacker, Koenig, & Seaver, 1974). Reluctantly, we concluded that relying exclusively on this practice is premature, although to be sure analyses of this type are in continuous use as an internal management tool. The fact is that no one asked for these data and, unfortunately, the preconceptions and contingencies that prevail throughout all levels of the educational establishment are as yet incompatible with a need for information of this type. Only gradually will society come to accept the notion that behavior change per dollar or per unit of time furnishes the only legitimate basis for accounting the activities of enterprises whose function is educational, broadly defined. Until that time it is prudent to evaluate the activities of such entities as the Personalized Learning Center in terms of the prevailing academic currency, always seeking to add precision and direct measurement in response to occasional expressions of dissatisfaction, voiced either by consumers or administrators, with the vagueness of that currency.

The prevailing academic currency combines grade points, credit hours, and binary measures of terminal success furnished by head counts at graduation with rather precise dollar figures allocated to structures, not functions. An entity such as the Personalized Learning Center must justify its claim to continued existence by providing competitive and satisfying data in these terms, for these are the primitives of the language of the budget and policy makers.

In the first two years of the center's existence, the drop-out rate for that important segment of our student clientele whose problems occasioned our initial ventures was reduced from 40% to less than 6%. In other words, the probability now exceeds .94 that a student entering this program will successfully complete the first 2 yr at the university. Data are just now becoming available to support the contention that such a student will have approximately a .90 probability of receiving an earned baccalaureate degree from the institution. Further, at this writing, no participating student athlete is in danger of being declared ineligible for NCAA competition for academic reasons.

Table 17-2 is a summary of the past year's academic output, listed quarter by quarter for purposes of assessing growth. The benefit measures presented in Table 17-2 are grade distributions; no similar distributions are available before 1972 because the exact data are irretrievable. Assuming, however, that a reasonable description of prior outcomes would be furnished by a unimodal, symmetric distribution, the statistical significance of the change shown in Table 17-2 exceeds published tabled values. More pertinent from the point of view of the present discussion, however, is the fact that the additional cost to the institution for one student to take one course through the center was approximately $43.75. Assuming the student eventually receives one of the five letter grades, the numerical grade expectancy is 3.07, or a high B. This represents a sizeable benefit for those students not

Table 17-2
Output Summary for the Personalized Learning Center:
1974-1975 Academic Year

Quarter	Courses	Student-Course Enrollments	Performance Sessions	Performance (Minutes)	Discussion (Minutes)	GRADES					
						A	B	C	D	E	Other
Summer '74	15	431	4.288	104,043	34,935	83	160	85	2	3	98
Fall '74	23	766	6,293	136,882	51,925	194	188	145	22	24	193
Winter '75	19	813	5,586	106,76⁻	43,778	352	188	63	6	15	189
Spring '75	18	732	6,204	134,330	52,270	304	155	38	16	32	187
Totals	75	2,742	22,371	478,016	182,908	933	691	331	46	74	667
						34%	25%	12%	2%	3%	24%

expected to succeed at all at a cost roughly equivalent to that incurred by adding a lab section to a basic science course.

A slightly longer-range indicator of the effectiveness of the center's program was obtained in a recent study that compared the performance of two groups in an intermediate chemistry course. One group ($n = 49$) took the introductory chemistry course through the center; the other ($n = 50$) took the course in a more traditional format involving large lecture and discussion groups. Both groups responded to the same sets of test questions. The performances of the two groups in the intermediate chemistry course offered in traditional format the next quarter did not differ significantly, although the mean of the group that had been through the center was slightly higher. Both groups showed a reduction in performance in the second course, but the reduction showed by the control group (mean difference = 85.0 points) clearly exceeded that of the PLC group (mean difference = 51.8), suggesting that somewhat greater retention was operating in the PLC group. Moreover, the correlation between total point scores earned in both courses was .45 for the PLC group and only .17 for the control group. While neither value indicates the operation of a high level of experimental control, it is reassuring to see that performance in a prerequisite course offered through the center is a better predictor of subsequent performance in a noncenter course than is performance in the same prerequisite offered traditionally. Although this finding must sustain several replications before it can effect policy, its implications for screening courses like chemistry are profound. In principle, application of a sound behavioral technology should not only maximize the achievement of all students in the course, but should either increase their likelihood of success in future courses or provide predictive evidence that a prompt reassessment of their academic goals may be in order. In either case, the overall efficiency of the educational process is enhanced.

STRATEGIES FOR THE FUTURE

In its few short years of existence, the Personalized Learning Center displayed relatively rapid growth and achieved functional stabilization within the complex of structures that define the institution. It now exists as a publicized, permanent alternative to traditional instruction, available to any academic unit interested in participating in the service and willing to bear a portion of the cost. Further, its support arises almost entirely from indigenous sources; a deliberate effort was made to resist the temptation to secure outside funding because to do so would have placed the center's survival under an artificial set of contingencies not directly related to its demonstrated and perceived local effectiveness. The back alleys of educational innovation are strewn with the rusting remains of highly successful prototypes that everyone applauded but no one supported after the grant dried up, and we had no desire to add to this academic blight. The center's very existence and its regulated growth demonstrate directly that it has provided, and is continuing to provide, a service perceived as valuable by those responsible for allocating the institution's resources. If the center is to continue to grow and retain its character as an innovative, dynamic, and rather unpredictable entity, we must continue to adhere rigidly to the dictum that, "form follows function and function is determined by measurement." Let us illustrate the application of this strategy in approaching the solution of two perpetual problems: space and quality control.

As with many appended functions, the center was and is housed in a temporary barracks that is both overcrowded and unattractive. This situation provided strong temptation to begin agitation for larger, permanent quarters. Projecting the established growth pattern of the center over the next 5 yr, however, immediately reveals that success in such efforts would, in the long run, be fatal. The growth potential of the center would appear to require a structure approaching the size of the football stadium which, even if it were feasible, would represent such an outlay of resources that further functional variation would be impeded by a heavily capitalized, rigid physical and spatial structure. Figure 17-8 suggests a more dynamic alternative—physical decentralization with greater reliance on communication technology to maintain the functional cybernetic connections among elements. Accordingly we are now beginning to develop the satellite Performance Laboratories, using space available in the engineering, nursing, and psychology departments but maintaining cybernetic coherence with the aid of telephones, small motorized vehicles, and the computer. Following the strategy successfully innovated by banks who opened branches in suburbs as the population density dissolved within the central city, we aim to deliver the service efficiently where it is needed, making use of the facilities already occupied by the academic units who are our "customers." Needless to say, the reduction in consumer response cost implied by such a delivery concept overcomes a substantial portion of the initial resistance of many potential customers. Further, the presence of a variety of mini-centers ensures continuing variation—the precious requisite of any evolutionary process— from which further technological advances may emerge and be validated. A central monolithic structure could easily lead to homogenization of practice; stagnation and eventual decay are then but a matter of time.

A central problem in maintaining quality-control is selecting, training, and retaining the peer advisors. Presently, these individuals are recruited from various sources with the only requirements being a B average, at least a B in the course in which the peer-advisement function is to be performed, and a willingness to participate and register for the training course. This course is offered for variable credit and may be repeated up to a maximum of eight credits. Consequently the turnover in peer advisors, while not total each quarter, is quite high, averaging between 50% and 75%.

The availability of a standardized, continuous, and direct system of measurement of student progress provides the basis for a potentially innovative solution to this problem. Peer-advisor productivity, measured in terms of a combination of student accuracy and celeration, can readily be retrieved from the computer. Standards for a productivity index are now being empirically established, preparatory to installing a pro-rata system of tuition rebates for successful peer advisors. Basically, a certain quantity of student performance will be exchangable for a certain amount of tuition-exempt registration, the exact ratios now being experimentally determined. These rebates will replace the current credit-hour consequence and will not limit frequency like the credit-hour procedure. As a result, good peer advisors will not only be able to participate as often as they want, but they will also be financing a part of their education in the process. This proposal has the tentative approval of the university administration because it involves no additional disbursements (albeit a small loss in revenue), offers a valid and fully accountable form of work-study, and appears capable of maintaining virtually any desired level of effectiveness and productivity in this crucial element of the operating structure.

Obviously in the absence of a highly sensitive, objective, and universal measurement technology such a system would be totally unworkable and subject to unremitting abuse, especially in economically difficult times. The achievements of the parent science, however, depended heavily on such a measurement strategy, and we are confident that our technological application will continue to enjoy similar success to the extent that we remain loyal to that strategy. Any educational system must have as its principle objective the production and documentation of desired changes in the behavior of its clients, the students. Full accountability becomes not the end, but the means by which such systems are allowed to evolve, and the validity of any accountability practice cannot exceed the validity of the measurement system that defines it. From the natural science of behavior we borrowed a measurement system the validity of which is demonstrably without peer; from our principal beneficiaries—our students—we hope we have gained the wisdom to use it wisely and humanely.

DEAN L. FIXSEN, ELERY L. PHILLIPS, and MONTROSE M.
WOLF[1]

Chapter 18

Mission-Oriented Behavior Research: The Teaching-Family Model

The *Teaching Family model* of group home treatment for youths in trouble has been evolving at Achievement Place in Lawrence, Kans. since 1967. The primary objectives of the Achievement Place research program have been to develop a community-based, family-style, behavior modification group-home treatment model for delinquent and predelinquent youths that is effective, economical, satisfactory to its consumers, and replicable in other communities.

The failure and substantial cost of institutional treatment programs for deviant children and their often inhumane and debilitating conditions have been documented by many authors (Goffman, 1961; James, 1971; Stuart 1970; Wolfensberger, 1970), as well as by the President's Commission on Law Enforcement and Administration of Justice (1967). These and others have emphasized the importance of developing community-based alterna-

1. The development of the Teaching Family model has been supported by grants MH 16609, MH 20030, and MH 13644 from the National Institute of Mental Health (Center for Studies of Crime and Delinquency) to the Bureau of Child Research and Department of Human Development at the University of Kansas. We would like to express our appreciation to Frances D. Horowitz and Richard L. Schiefelbusch for their consistent administrative support and to the many students and colleagues who provided the effort and intellectual climate that made the project possible: Debbie Allen, Jenny and Hector Ayala, Jon Bailey, Curt Braukmann, Linda and Willie Brown, Ronda and Mike Davis, Stan Eitzen, Joan Fixsen, Margaret and Dennis Ford, Deena and Terry Harper, Robert Kifer, Kathi Kirigin, Karen and Dennis Maloney, Bonnie and Neil Minkin, Elaine Phillips, Sharon and Dave Russell, Barbara and Gary Timbers, Alan Willner, Sandra Wolf, and the courageous couples who agreed to become the first teaching-parents in a developing program. The section on evaluation of the overall Achievement Place program was taken from an unpublished paper by Kathryn A. Kirigin, Elery L. Phillips, Dean L. Fixsen, Jay Atwater, Mitchel Taubman and Montrose M. Wolf.

tives for youths in danger of institutionalization. One direction of the community-based treatment movement has been the development of group homes designed to provide services for those youths who may not need institutionalization but who do seem to need more than probation services (Empey, 1967; Keller & Alper, 1970). Many states, including Florida, Massachusetts, California, North Carolina, Connecticut, Washington, and Kansas, have begun to deinstitutionalize their correctional programs for delinquents, and are establishing group homes as one alternative. The need to develop effective, practical, humane, and replicable group-home treatment models is apparent.

During the past 7 yr we have attempted to develop *Achievement Place* as one model of group-home treatment. Achievement Place is a community-based, family-style, behavior modification, group-home treatment program for six to eight delinquent or predelinquent youths from 12- through 15-yr old. The program is directed by a board of directors made up of members of the community. The board is responsible for the financial, personnel, and policy aspects of the program.

The treatment program is administered by a couple that we refer to as *teaching-parents*. The title teaching-parents is given to distinguish them from more traditional, untrained, custodial house parents or foster parents. In the Achievement Place model the teaching-parents are given a year's professional training that includes classroom instruction, supervised practicum experience, and formal evaluation by the social-services agencies in their community, as well as by a community board of directors, the court, the schools, the youths, and the parents of the youths.

The function of the Achievement Place program is to help youths in danger of institutionalization remain in their communities. Our assumption is that these youths are at risk because of the reaction to the youths' disturbing behavior by the parents, schools, court, and social-welfare personnel. Thus, the role of the teaching-parents is twofold: (1) to teach the youths the behavioral skills that will make it more likely that they will be reacted to positively by their community and (2) to assume responsibility for the youths and become their advocate in the community.

The *behavioral-skills training* component is based on a behavior deficiency model of deviant behavior. The youths' behavior problems are viewed as due to their lack of essential skills. These behavioral deficiencies are considered a result of inadequate histories of reinforcement and instruction rather than internal psychopathology. The goal of the behavioral-treatment program, therefore, is to establish through reinforcement and instruction the important behavioral competencies in social, academic, prevocational, and self-care skills that the youths have not acquired. The assumption is that after learning these skills the youths will be more successful in their homes and schools, the natural reinforcement from this success will maintain the new appropriate behavior, and this will lead to greater acceptance by the parents and the community.

The Achievement Place behavioral-skills training program has four main elements: a motivation system (token economy), a self-government system, a comprehensive behavioral-skills training curriculum, and the development of a reciprocally reinforcing relationship between the youths and the teaching parents (such a relationship enhances the reinforcing effect of the teaching-parents' social interaction and allows them to fade out the more artificial token reinforcement).

The *advocacy* role of the teaching-parents is carried out in the community and is on an individual basis. That is, when a particular youth is brought to the attention of the court, police, welfare, or school officials because of something done, the teaching-parents intervene on behalf of the youth to keep the youth out of an institution and in the community or in school. If the agency personnel and the parents of the youth have a strong relationship with the teaching-parents, they are likely to invite the teaching-parents' participation in decisions about the youth and, in any case, they are likely to be responsive to their suggestions concerning the youth. Once the teaching-parents help to secure a decision in favor of a youth they must then help the youth be successful in the community or school for the following weeks to assure the agency personnel that the group home can handle the youth's problems. This is very important because the agency personnel may feel that they are "taking a chance" by letting a youth return to the group home after having committed some offense in the community. If the youth commits further offenses in the next few days or weeks, the agency personnel probably will be less likely to listen to the teaching-parents in the future.

For example, one youth was being considered by the court for placement in an institution, but the teaching-parents had an opening in their home and convinced the judge that the group home could handle the youth's problems. However, at the disposition hearing the youth looked at the floor, did not respond to questions, and finally became very emotional, cursed the judge and the lawyers, toppled a few chairs, and tried to leave the court room. The judge called a short recess during which he informed the teaching-parents that he had changed his mind and would send the youth to an institution because of her severe emotional problems. The teaching-parents asked for a one-week delay of the disposition hearing and asked to have temporary custody of the youth during that week; the judge agreed. For the next week the teaching-parents worked with the youth to teach her how to be responsive to the questions that were asked by the judge and the lawyers, how to maintain eye contact, how to take negative feedback without becoming emotional, and how to act during the hearing. The teaching-parents also frequently talked with the judge to assure him that the youth was adjusting well to the group home and was making progress. At the final disposition hearing the judge was impressed with her "new attitude" and with the teaching-parents' ability to handle her problems, and he assigned her to the group home and not to the institution.

In this case the relation the teaching-parents had with the judge helped them perform their advocacy roles in initially convincing the judge not to send the youth to an institution and in later convincing the judge to wait a week before making a decision. The teaching-parents reinforced the judge's "taking a chance" by helping the youth learn new skills to present herself more favorably at the second disposition hearing.

By developing positive relationships with the court, police, and school personnel the teaching-parents can almost assure that when the parents or a member of these agencies has a complaint about a youth in a Teaching Family group home, they will contact the teaching-parents and give them an opportunity to solve the problem. This is a diversionary function in that the parents and agency personnel who have the services of a teaching-parent are less dependent upon the formal juvenile justice system. Thus, when a problem arises, the parents and agency personnel can simply call the teaching-parents because they know the teaching-parents will take the responsibility for solving the problem without further involving the youth in the juvenile justice system.

A DISSEMINATION MODEL

National dissemination of social-service programs is not new. Community mental health centers, the war on poverty, the work incentive program, the new math teaching packages, and performance contracting in education are only a few recent examples. In these cases, economists, social scientists, and educators attempted to solve the pressing social problems of deviant behavior, poverty, unemployment, and illiteracy. Such large-scale dissemination is often based on a model program or simply on the hopeful application of "basic social-science principles." Once such large-scale programs are approved and funded by legislation or bureaucratic resolve they are implemented on a national scale within a year or two. The technical problems of implementing the programs, improving the programs to serve the public needs, and providing adequate quality control are left to program administrators at various levels. Thus, on a national level the programs have to be developed and implemented at the same time. Occasionally national programs are evaluated to determine whether they are producing the desired effects, but often measures of the effects of the social services are not attempted. The result is that large and expensive programs come and go and little is learned. One possible explanation is that the political contingencies for bureaucrats and politicians make the *introduction* of new programs more important than their effects.

This style of national-program implementation without careful initial research, development, and evaluation makes no sense. It is similar to an aircraft company developing the blueprints of an innovative aircraft design, mass producing the new airplanes directly from the blueprints, and selling the airplanes to commercial airlines without first building, troubleshooting, and evaluating prototype models. Chances are that railroads would be more popular today if airplanes were designed this way.

An alternative process for developing and disseminating social-service models has been proposed by Shah and Lalley (1973), who suggested five stages through which a program must progress. In the first stage, *model development and testing*, a prototype program is begun to develop effective, efficient, and practical procedures. Also, the financing and costs of the program, types of clients served, community reaction to the program, etc., can be assessed. Another critical element is the replication of the prototype model to further test its feasibility. This first stage may require 3 to 6 yr, depending upon the knowledge in the field and the technological problems encountered. The second stage, *project evaluation*, may require an additional 2 or 3 yr. In this stage follow-up data are collected to determine whether the overall project is successful in ameliorating the social problem it was designed to affect. This stage may also include an independent evaluation by professionals from another discipline, to determine whether the effects of the program are general or confined to the specific measures developed by the original investigators. The data from this stage must demonstrate the value and significance of the program before the other stages are attempted.

In the third stage, *user-oriented information dissemination*, the investigators continue to refine and evaluate the model and to disseminate technical research reports to their professional colleagues but they also begin to prepare special materials for program administrators, policy makers, and other potential users of the program model. This information is designed to encourage use of the model and to stimulate requests for technical assistance in establishing similar programs. After user interest and demand for the model have been established, the fourth stage is added. In this *model-related training stage*, further research and planning develop a training program to prepare the staff to operate the model on a broad scale. This stage immediately leads to the fifth and final stage of *model replication and evaluation*. As more staff are trained to operate the model, the model will be used by a variety of agencies who do not have the same experience, funds, or technical background as the original investigators. To disseminate the model, procedures must be developed to assist users technically, to control the quality of the procedures, and, in general, assure proper use of the model. Follow-up data are also collected on these general replications of the model.

At each stage the research findings provide feedback on the practicality of the program and on the effectiveness of the services delivered. The data from training and evaluation of project replications provide feedback to the investigators, who continue to refine and improve the model. As improvements are made, revisions of the staff-training program are made generally available through the user-oriented information-dissemination program. The concurrent activities in each of the five stages, therefore, interact with every other stage, and all five stages are necessary for national dissemination of model treatment programs.

It may require 10-12 yr to develop a model treatment program that can be disseminated on a national scale. While this represents a substantial investment of energy and funds, it also represents a patient, organized research and planning effort that has as its mission the practical solution of a national social problem. Often many of the basic principles and procedures needed to design a mission-oriented project are available in the literature but the organization and technology to apply those basic principles to a social problem must be developed. That is, when problems are encountered or when choices among procedures must be made, research is conducted to find solutions to these practical problems. Perhaps as applied researchers conduct more mission-oriented research, they will discover more efficient ways to develop disseminable programs (Baer, 1975), and perhaps more of our social-service programs will succeed.

CHARACTERISTICS OF ACHIEVEMENT PLACE YOUTHS

The youths who come to Achievement Place typically have had difficulty at home, at school, and in the community. Of the first 41 youths admitted to Achievement Place, 26 had spent time in jail, 22 had been in some type of residential treatment, and 40 had received nonresidential treatment such as probation services or psychological services. The youths had missed an average of 44 days out of a possible 180 days of school during the year before entering Achievement Place, and 29 youths were suspended from school at the time of admission to the program. On the average, the youths were in the seventh grade when they entered Achievement Place, but their achievement test scores placed them at the fifth-grade level. Before entering the program, 12 youths were in special-education classes, 23 youths had failed one or more grades, and the average grade achieved in their classes for 1 yr was a D− (.6 on a 4.0 scale).

The 41 youths admitted to Achievement Place ranged in age from 10- to 16-yr old and averaged 13.8-yr old. Twenty-four of the boys were white, 12 were black, 4 were American-Indian, and 1 was Mexican-American. Twenty-seven of the youths came from family situations in which only one or neither of the parents were living in the natural home. One came from a family situation in which the annual income exceeded $7000, while 28 came from families that had an annual income of $4000 or less (22 of these families were on welfare).

All 41 of the youths had been adjudicated by the juvenile court (i.e., a court hearing was held to assess the evidence pertaining to the youth and the judge recommended that the youth be placed in Achievement Place). Twenty-three youths had been involved in at least one delinquent (felony-type) act, 16 had been charged with drug abuse, and 37 had been involved in a variety of other antisocial acts. The average number of police and court contacts was about three per youth. The youths' first police contact occurred at an average age of 12.6 yr and their first adjudication occurred at an average age of 13.7 yr.

The youths had been given many labels by professionals with whom they had come into contact. These labels included cultural deprivation, adolescent adjustment reaction, unsocialized aggression, childhood schizophrenia, psychopathic personality, retardation, psychotic, sexual deviation, pyromania, suicidal tendency, and autism. The school system had labeled the youths as behavior problems, emotionally disturbed, slow learners and retarded (cf. Chapter 4).

AN OVERVIEW OF THE TREATMENT PROGRAM

Family-Style Living

A Teaching Family program offers family-style but professional treatment. In the original Achievement Place, and in other programs based on the Teaching Family model, professional teaching-parents live in the facility 24 hr a day with a "family" of six to eight adolescent youths. Having a small group allows the teaching-parents to interact extensively with each youth, to develop a reciprocally reinforcing relationship with him, and to produce much change in a short time. The teaching-parents and the youths come to know each other well, and there is ample opportunity for social behavior that occurs only in small family groups. One further advantage of a family-style treatment program is that it can be used by communities of any size. Small rural communities may require only one treatment facility. Urban settings may require facilities scattered throughout the community. In larger communities, some treatment facilities may "specialize" and take boys or girls with a specific type of difficulty in school or in the community. Even in larger communities, however, each facility should be controlled by the citizens of the immediate area. This ensures community cooperation and accountability.

Professional Teaching-Parents

Each Teaching Family group-home treatment program is directed by a pair of professional teaching-parents (a married couple) who are the primary staff of the group home. The teaching-parents have wide-ranging duties and responsibilities. They design and carry out treatment procedures to correct problem behavior and to teach alternative appropriate behavior to the youths; they supervise the youths' activities at home, in school, in the community, and at the group home; they establish and maintain good working relations with the juvenile court, the welfare department, the schools, the local mental-health services, parents, community civic groups, etc. Thus, the teaching-parents direct the treatment program, live with the youth, carry out the treatment procedures, and act as administrators by generating community support for the program and by using community resources to benefit the youths.

The teaching-parents' responsibilities for developing mutually reinforcing relationships with their youths and for teaching appropriate behavior are carried out using a variety of procedures that either have been or are being evaluated. For example, teaching appropriate behavior involves combining social reinforcement, token reinforcement, instruction, demonstration, and practice, each of which is fairly well understood. On the other hand, the procedures for establishing a reinforcing relation are much less well developed. Even so, the youths have described several elements that are very important to them. Thus, the teaching-parents are encouraged to use humor, affection, sympathy, concern, respect, fun, and flexibility in their moment-by-moment interactions with the youths. The goal is to understand exactly what behavior is involved so that it can be more easily taught to teaching-parents and result in a more positive relationship with the youths.

Systematic Treatment Program

The Teaching Family model emphasizes *individual* behavioral treatment in a group setting, because no two youths have identical backgrounds or problems. The treatment program and specific behavioral goals for the youths are based on behavior that members of their families, schools, community, the youths themselves, and the teaching-parents decide should be taught. The motivation system (token economy) is uniquely suited to changing the behaviors of delinquent, disturbed, or dependent-neglected youths.

Community Responsibility for the Program

A Teaching Family treatment program is community-controlled and is thus responsive to the unique characteristics of the community or neighborhood it serves. This responsiveness is ensured by placing the responsibility for the program, physical facility, and financial matters in the hands of a local Board of Directors. The Board of Directors, in cooperation with the teaching-parents, local school officials, Juvenile Court officials, representatives of local church groups, and other interested citizens, determine the goals of the treatment program and evaluate the program in terms of those goals. The Board of Directors is represented on the Candidate Selection Committee. The committee also includes a school official, a Juvenile Court official, a social worker from the welfare department, and the teaching-parents. This committee selects candidates who are most in need of treatment: youths who are the greatest threat to their community, schools, homes, and selves. Thus, through the Board of Directors the community has control of (and responsibility for) the entire program.

Community-Based Program

A Teaching Family group home is community-based, which means that the program serves youths from the neighborhood or county in which the group home is located. Having a community-based program allows the youths to attend their own schools and frequently visit their natural homes on weekends and holidays. This is very important because it provides an opportunity for the teaching-parents, in cooperation with the youths' parents and teachers, to help the youths solve their problems in school and at home. If the problems of the youths can be solved in their own community, in their own schools and homes, and with their own peer groups, then the chances for their eventual success are greatly enhanced. A community-based group home also allows the teaching-parents to follow closely the progress of the youths after they leave the treatment program and to assist further if needed.

Furthermore, a Teaching Family provides a new peer group for the youths. Each youth who enters the program comes under the influence of a peer group already working toward the goals of the program. Thus, both the peers and the teaching-parents serve as examples of appropriate behavior. Even after the youths leave the program they can remain members of the Teaching Family peer group and continue to visit the home, eat an occasional meal there, or spend the night. The continuing support the youths receive from their peers is an important aspect of the Teaching Family program. Another advantage of having a community-based program is that persons in the community can see the changes in behavior. This often leads to further improvements in behavior because persons who were once critical begin to accept the youths.

RESEARCH ON THE TREATMENT PROGRAM

The Teaching Family treatment program consists of motivational and instructional procedures designed to teach social, academic, vocational and self-care behavior. Several of these procedures have been evaluated.

Social Skills

The boys that come to Achievement Place usually lack many of the interpersonal skills necessary for successful family and community living. They are often described by parents, teachers, and peers as defiant, uncooperative, argumentative, dishonest, cruel, aggressive, moody, disruptive, and assaultive. Our assumption is that by learning more appropriate social skills for solving interpersonal problems, the youths' opportunities for interpersonal rewards should greatly increase not only at Achievement Place but in their natural homes, schools, and jobs as well.

Three basic social skills are probably the most important behavioral goals of the Achievement Place treatment program. In our opinion, mastery of these three social skills can mean that a youth with few other skills may still be accepted. Without these critical skills success or even survival in the family, school, and community is unlikely. The three basic social skills are (1) democratic decision making and problem solving, (2) appropriate responses to criticism from an adult or peer, and (3) appropriate responses to routine instructions from an adult or peer.

Self-Government.   A self-government system designed to teach the youths many of the social skills involved in democratic decision making and problem solving has been established and evaluated.. The youths are taught to establish democratically many of their own rules of behavior, to monitor their peers' violations of the rules, and to determine a rule violator's guilt or innocence and the consequences for the violator. Two experiments (Fixsen, Phillips, and Wolf, 1973b) evaluated the effects of some of the procedures on the boys' participation in the self-government system. Experiment I showed that more boys participated in the discussion of consequences for a rule violation when they had complete responsibility for setting the consequence during trials than when the teaching-parents set the consequence for each rule violation before the trial. An analysis of the rule violations in this experiment indicated that the boys reported more of the rule violations that resulted in trials than the teaching-parents, school personnel, or parents. The boys reported rule violations that occurred in the community and at school as well as at Achievement Place, including more of the serious rule violations than came to the attention of the teaching-parents. In Experiment II, more trials were called when the teaching-parents were responsible for calling trials on rule violations reported by the peers than when the boys were responsible for calling trials. When the youths earned points for calling trials, the average number of trials per day increased, but more trivial rule violations were reported. Thus, aspects of the democratic decision-making process in a small group can be studied and variables that affect participation can be identified and evaluated.

Responses to Criticism.   Inappropriate responses to routine criticism from adults and peers frequently seems to have led to serious trouble for these youths. Timbers, Timbers, Fixsen, Phillips, and Wolf (1973) found that point consequences combined with teaching appropriate alternative behavior effectively reduced the youths' arguing, pouting, and tantrum behavior that occurred in response to criticism or negative feedback. The youths were taught the following appropriate responses to criticism: (1) *maintaining eye contact*; (2) *acknowledging the criticism* by saying something like "OK;" (3) *refraining from inappropriate behavior* such as frowning, saying something unintelligible under the breath, cursing, complaining, threatening, or looking angry; and (4) *controlling their immediate emotional reaction* by *delaying* any attempt to present a grievance until they had recovered from their emotional reaction. Presenting *any* complaint during the evening self-government meeting rather than immediately after a criticism is established by instruction and maintained by reinforcement. Fines are often reduced if complaints are brought up in the self-government session. The treatment procedure includes instructing the youths about appropriate behavior by having them role play the behavior during demonstration and practice sessions, presenting point consequences and praise for appropriate behavior, and administering fines if the behavior is not appropriate. On the average, the youths responded appropriately to criticism 83% of the time following treatment as compared to only 7% of the time before treatment.

Responses to Instructions. The third critical social skill involves the appropriate response to routine instructions. Many of the youths who come to Achievement Place have not learned to follow simple basic instructions from adults or peers. Frequently these youths will respond in a negative and defiant manner when given an instruction to do a routine minor task. These youths must learn how to respond to routine instructions not only because this skill is important in school, at home, and on the job, but also because the treatment program at Achievement Place is really an educational program and is dependent upon the youths being able to learn a wide variety of skills through instruction. The teaching-parents begin teaching a new youth appropriate instruction-following behavior using very small, easy tasks that they are sure the youth will complete successfully. For example, a teaching parent may begin by asking the new youth to come with him to see how he should lock the back door at night or by asking the youth to go out to the kitchen and have a snack. Gradually the teaching-parents progress to more demanding instructions at a rate that allows the youth to continue to be successful. Literally hundreds of instructions are given the first few days that a youth is in the home. As the instructions become more difficult, token reinforcement and praise are appropriately increased. In an experiment by E.L. Phillips, Phillips, Fixsen, and Wolf (1971), a youth given this training followed about 10-25% of the instructions during baseline conditions and about 100% of the instructions while the training and point conditions were in effect. A correlated effect of the treatment was an increase in on-task behavior and a decrease in complaints.

Other Social Behavior. Similar procedures have been used to teach other social skills. Phillips (1968, Experiment V) found that point consequences and a correction procedure that consisted of suggesting an appropriate alternative were effective in eliminating "ain't" from one youth's behavior. In another study J.S. Bailey, Timbers, Phillips, and Wolf (1972) modified the articulation errors of two of the boys by using the boys' peers as trainers. In their first experiment, using a multiple-baseline design, error words involving the "/1/," "/r/," "/th/," and "/ting/" sounds were successfully treated by both a group of peers and by individual peers. Also, generalization occurred to words that were not trained. The speech-correction procedure used by peers involved several variables including modeling, peer approval, contingent points, and feedback. Peers could function as speech therapists without instructions, feedback, or the presence of an adult, and payment of points to peers for detecting correct articulations produced closer agreement with the experimenter than when they were paid points for finding incorrect articulations. The results were replicated with another subject who had similar articulation errors. In addition, the second experiment showed that peer speech-correction procedures generalized to the correct use of target words in sentences and to significant improvements on standard tests of articulation.

Maloney, Harper, Braukmann, Fixsen, Phillips, and Wolf (1976) extended these procedures to conversation skills. In this experiment youths were taught to give more complete responses to questions that were commonly asked by visitors to the group home. During baseline, the youths gave complete responses to only about 40% of the questions, but after training and point consequences were made available according to a multiple-baseline design, the youths responded appropriately to about 100% of the questions. Also, distracting conversation (e.g., saying "huh," talking too fast) was reduced by making a small point fine contingent on each occurrence of the behavior, and appropriate conversational behavior (e.g., eye contact, voice level) was increased by contingent points (Phillips, E.L., Phillips, Fixsen, & Wolf, 1973).

The motivation system also has been used to improve the youths' introduction skills (Phillips, E.A., et al., 1973. Experiment II) and greeting skills (Timbers et al., 1973, Experiment II) from a 0-25% level before training of each skill to 75-100% after training. Similarly, promptness in returning from errands (Phillips, E.L., 1968, Experiment III) and at meal time (Phillips, E.L., Phillips, Fixsen, and Wolf, 1971, Experiment I) was improved when a small point fine was contingent on each minute youths were late. Also Phillips (1968, Experiment I) found that a small point fine was sufficient to reduce aggressive statements by the youths to zero. Aggressive statements were much higher under a baseline condition or a correction procedure (where the youths were asked to "Stop that kind of talk") than when a point loss was contingent on the behavior.

The social skills taught at Achievement Place are also encouraged in the natural home by a *remote reinforcement system.* Each time a youth goes home for a holiday or a weekend the teaching-parents send a behavior checklist ("homenote") for the parents to fill out before the youth returns. The youth then earns or loses points at Achievement Place depending upon how the parents mark the homenote. The effectiveness of this remote reinforcement system was recently evaluated by Turnbough, Brown, Fixsen, Phillips, and Wolf (1973). In this experiment the parents of a youth about to enter Achievement Place, were asked to list about 10 classes of behavior they would like their son to change (some were appropriate behavior they wanted to increase and others were inappropriate behavior they wanted to decrease). Several days of baseline data were taken (using the parent's list as a behavior checklist) before the youth entered Achievement Place. After the youth entered Achievement Place, the teaching-parents began teaching the youth new social skills and implemented the regular homenote-feedback system with the parents. Data continued to be collected with the parent's list as a behavior checklist. The youth's inappropriate behavior in his natural home was reduced from about 50-60% during baseline to about 10-20% after entering Achievement Place. For one youth, the homenote was then discontinued for several weeks, and the youth's inappropriate behavior at home increased to about 40%. When the homenote was again used the inappropriate behavior dropped to about 10%. After the youth had been in Achievement Place for several months, the homenote was again discontinued and this time there was no appreciable change in the youth's home behavior. These data suggest that the homenote was effective in controlling the youth's behavior at home and that, after continued use, the appropriate behavior was maintained in the home.

Academic Skills

The youths placed in Achievement Place had relatively long histories of problems in school. Teachers, principals, and parents reported many social and academic difficulties in the classroom, and the school records indicated that most of the youths had failed classes and had been suspended from school. Because of these difficulties, school-related behavior has continued as an area of investigation.

To develop a *remote reinforcement procedure* to improve the youths' behavior in the public-school classroom, J.S. Bailey, Wolf, and Phillips (1970) carried out three experiments. In Experiment I, five youths from Achievement Place attended a special summer-school math class where study behavior and rule violations were measured daily for each youth. The youths were required to take a "report card" for the teacher to mark. The teacher simply marked "yes" or "no" whether a youth had studied the whole period and obeyed the class rules. All "yes's" earned privileges in the home that day but a "no" lost some of the privileges. Privileges dispensed remotely (at Achievement Place) significantly improved classroom performance. In Experiments II and III, home-based reinforcement also improved study behavior of two youths in public-school classrooms. In addition, Experiment III suggested that the daily feedback and reinforcement could be faded without much loss in study behavior. The remote reinforcement procedure was thus an effective and practical technique. Kirigin, Bailey, Phillips, Fixsen, and Wolf (unpublished manuscript) systematically replicated the remote reinforcement study and extended the analysis to academic output.

The results replicated the previously reported effectiveness of remote reinforcement procedures for the modification of study and disruptive classroom behavior of the youths. Consequences for academic output alone, however, were sufficient neither to increase output nor to eliminate disruptive classroom behavior.

Kirigin, Phillips, Timbers, Fixsen and Wolf (1977) studied two youths who had records of failing grades and poor academic performance in the public school. The youths received points for completing daily homework assignments, for handing in the assignments to their teachers, and for weekly grades. The youths were required to carry a daily homenote card to math class and to write in their assigned homework. The public-school teachers were asked to check whether the youths had properly recorded the assignments, to mark (yes or no) whether the previous day's assignments had been turned in, and to sign the cards. Using a reversal design to evaluate the effectiveness of the procedure, all consequences for homework behavior and grades were introduced, withdrawn, and reinstated. With point consequences, the youths consistently handed in 100% of their homework assignments each week and averaged grades of C or better; when consequences were withdrawn, both youths showed a decrease of assignments completed and handed in to less than 50% with a corresponding drop in grades.

Phillips (1968, Experiment IV) compared the effects of several consequences on the youths' preparation of homework assignments. Money, weekly free time, and daily free time produced only small improvements in the youths' preparation of homework assignments but point consequences resulted in nearly 100% completion of the assignments. Similarly, E.L. Phillips et al., (1971, Experiment IV) found that point consequences contingent on the number of correct answers on a news quiz increased the percentage of youths who watched the news on TV and, to a lesser extent, increased the percentage of correct answers for the youths who watched the news.

In another study Kirigin, Timbers, Ayala, Fixsen, Phillips, and Wolf (1973) attempted to increase the independent reading of two youths. Various strategies consisting of point consequences for reading, point consequences plus tutoring, and a tutoring-avoidance condition were implemented, and their effects on independent reading were monitored. Point consequences alone or combined with tutoring were not sufficient to increase independent reading. Independent reading was established only when the avoidance contingency was introduced. The results indicate that tutoring, for some individuals, is an aversive event that can be used to motivate increased levels of reading.

Vocational Skills

Training in basic vocational skills has been a goal of the treatment program at Achievement Place. Three experiments by Braukmann, Maloney, Fixsen, Phillips, and Wolf (1974) analyzed the effectiveness of an "instructional package" (a set of specific materials and procedures) in teaching job-interview skills to six youths. All three experiments demonstrated the effectiveness of the instructional package in modifying each youth's personal appearance, social behavior, volunteering of information, posture, and looking at the interviewer in a simulated interview situation. Experiment I also demonstrated that three untrained college-student trainers could use the instructional package effectively to teach the interview skills.

Ayala, Minkin, Phillips, Fixsen, and Wolf (1977) developed a set of training and feedback procedures that produced appropriate performance on a Saturday morning job of cleaning the restrooms at three service stations. In two experiments the effects of training and feedback upon the restroom-cleaning behavior of four youths were assessed. These experiments indicated that (1) the level of cleaning improved from about 25% during baseline to about 75% during treatment in those service stations where the treatment and feedback components were instituted, (2) initially the effects of the treatment component were specific to the particular service station in which the treatment was given, (3) generalization of the effects of training and feedback occurred after the treatment package was systematically withdrawn from the initial service station and later instituted in one of the remaining untreated settings. In addition the service-station operators rated the youths' performance as better than that of a commercial cleaning firm that had previously contracted to clean the restrooms.

Self-Care Skills

Self-care skills are routinely taught to the youths and a few of these have been investigated. Self-care skills also have been dependent variables in studies of self-recording (a self-control procedure) and of the elected manager procedure, in our attempt to develop practical and effective systems for administering routine self-care tasks.

Some behavioral researchers have suggested that self-recording (the recording of one's own behavior) is an effective behavioral procedure. The effects and reliability of the boys' recording their own room-cleaning behavior and that of their peers were measured in two experiments (Fixsen, Phillips and Wolf, 1972). These experiments indicated that (1) the boys were not "naturally" reliable observers, (2) the reliability of peer reporting could be improved by providing training on the behavioral definitions and by making points contingent on agreement between each boy's peer report and an independent adult observer's report, (3) the reliability of self-reporting could be improved by making points contingent on agreement between the self-report and the trained peer's report, and (4) self-reports and peer reports did not produce a systematic effect on the youths' room-cleaning behavior as measured by an independent observer. Although these experiments showed that the youths could be taught to be reliable observers, the training and maintenance procedures did not appear practical.

A more practical procedure seemed to be a manager system where one youth had responsibility for supervising his peers on various tasks. In a series of experiments (Phillips, E.L., Phillips, Wolf, and Fixsen, 1973) several arrangements for assigning routine tasks and for providing point consequences for task performance were compared for their *effectiveness* in accomplishing the tasks and for their *preference* by the youths. The independent variables studied included: (1) individually assigned tasks versus group assigned tasks; (2) consequences for individual performance versus consequences for group performance; (3) a peer managership that could be earned by the highest bidder versus a peer managership that could be determined democratically by the peers. The results suggested that among those systems studied the system that best met the criteria of effectiveness and preference involved a *democratically elected peer manager* who had the authority to give and to take away points for his peers' performance.

In earlier research on self-care skills, E.L. Phillips (1968, Experiment II) found that bathroom cleaning was improved from a baseline level of 25% to a level of 75% when a peer manager was given the responsibility for organizing the youths to clean the bathroom and for giving or taking away points based on their performance. When all youths were given the responsibility for cleaning the bathrooms with no peer manager, the level of cleanliness fell to about 25%. E.L. Phillips et al. (1971, Experiment II) found that the youths' room-cleaning behavior was maintained at about a 90% level when point consequences were made available for room cleaning. When the points were withdrawn, the cleanliness fell to less than 50%. In the final condition the behavior increased to about 90% when points were again given for room cleaning, and the behavior was maintained for over 6 months after the point consequences were faded to only 8% of the days. Apparently the youths' room-cleaning behavior could be maintained with only infrequent consequences for room cleaning.

E.L. Phillips et al. (1971, Experiment III) found that the youths saved considerable amounts of money when point consequences were available for deposit but saved little money when no points were available. Later, when points were given only for deposits occurring on specific days, the youths deposited their money almost exclusively on those days. These results indicate that saving money never became independent of the point consequences. In order to promote saving money, it seems to be necessary to pay the youths "interest" on their deposits.

EVALUATION OF THE OVERALL ACHIEVEMENT PLACE PROGRAM

Our primary objective has been to develop a community-based group-home program that would provide an alternative for youths in danger of being institutionalized and that would help the youths acquire skills that would enhance the likelihood of success in their community. Accordingly our primary comparison of the Achievement Place youths should be with youths who have been treated in an institutional treatment program. Unique problems, however, are inherent in evaluating a group-home program by comparing it with the effects of an institutional treatment program. Random assignment is the ideal manner of assigning subjects to the treatment programs that are compared. But it is not usually feasible to assign youths randomly to a group home and to an institutional treatment program. Because these programs are vastly different in terms of their restrictiveness on the freedom of the individual, it is ethically questionable whether a youth, who normally would be considered eligible for treatment in his community in a group home, should be placed in an institution solely for purposes of evaluating the group-home program. On the other hand, when the decision to randomly assign youths produces less restriction of the youths, then random assignment is a defensible procedure. An example would be when a state agency administering both institutional and community treatment programs randomly assigns to community placement some youths who would normally be institutionalized (see Palmer, 1974).

The local agencies, however, consider the Achievement Place program a service agency in a continuum of treatment services from a family-counseling program in the community mental-health center to actual institutionalization. Thus, a youth referred to Achievement Place is considered one *in danger* of institutionalization but one who has the right to attempt to succeed with a less restrictive form of treatment.

In addition, proper evaluation of the effects of a treatment program requires a substantial sample size. Unfortunately, a group home, unlike a large institution, only deals with a few youths each year. Thus, it will be necessary to continue to evaluate Achievement Place youths during the next few years and track the youths admitted to the replications before an acceptable sample size will exist.

Youths

Candidates were selected for the program by a selection committee made up of personnel from the court, welfare, and school, as well as one of the teaching-parents. Their selection criteria were:

Inclusion
1. Age: The youth usually must be between 12 and 16 yr old (specified by the licensing requirements.)
2. IQ: The youth should have an IQ of at least 70.
3. Locale: The youth must reside within the county.
4. Presenting Problem: The youth's behavior problems and status with court, school, and family are such that, in the opinion of the Selection Committee, the youth is in danger of institutionalization.

5. Court Adjudication: The youth's problems are so serious that the court has or is about to adjudicate the youth.
6. Failure of Less Restrictive or Structured Forms of Intervention: The youth typically has failed to respond favorably to probation or counseling services available in the community.
7. Family: The youth must have a family in the community (parents, relatives, or foster parents) to return to with the assistance of the program staff.

Exclusion
1. Certain Violent Offenses: A youth who has committed murder, forcible rape, or armed robbery would be excluded from consideration as a candidate for the program. The rationale is that the community often is not willing to tolerate the continued presence in the community of a youth who had committed such a serious offense.
2. Drug Addiction: A youth who shows serious physiological dependence on dangerous narcotics (e.g., heroin or barbituates) as judged by a physician, would be temporarily excluded because of the lack of appropriate medical supervision in the Achievement Place facility.
3. Serious physical disabilities: A youth with a major physical handicap (e.g., blindness or confinement to a wheel chair) that would not permit normal mobility within the group home, school, or community would be excluded.

We gathered data on 26 youths who have been in the Achievement Place program and 37 seemingly comparable youths who have not been in the Achievement Place program. The comparison youths were either treated in an institutional program or considered by the selection committee to be in danger of institutionalization. Both groups include two subgroups. The first set of subgroups consists of the first 18 youths in the Achievement Place program and 19 comparision youths who attended the state Boys School. This subgroup of comparison youths was determined by the probation officer, who identified 19 youths from the community who were potential candidates for Achievement Place.

The second set of subgroups originated by *random selection*. There are typically more candidates eligible for admission in the Achievement Place program than there are available openings. When this occurs random selection provides a fair way to determine who among the eligible candidates will enter the program. In addition random selection reduces the likelihood of a biased selection based on a youth's "bad reputation," race, or other personal characteristics. If out of several referrals three meet the selection criteria, one of the youths is selected randomly. The other two youths, *randomly not selected*, are placed in the randomly determined comparison group. These youths are, of course, considered for treatment by the other agencies that work with youths. A youth in the randomly determined comparison group who later is reprocessed by the court and again becomes a candidate for the program would again be included in the selection pool, but again the choice of the youth for admission would be made on a random basis. Thus far, data have been gathered for 2 yr following selection for eight youths randomly selected to attend Achievement Place and 18 comparison youths randomly not selected.

Achievement Place as an Alternative to Institutionalization

Some preliminary information was collected about the role of Achievement Place as an alternative to institutionalization. The cumulative percentage of youths institutionalized 1 yr and 2 yr after they were randomly either selected or not selected to enter Achievement Place showed that, of the eight youths who went to Achievement Place, one youth (12%) was institutionalized during the first year following selection. No additional youths were institutionalized during the second year. Of the 18 youths randomly not selected, eight (44%) were institutionalized during the first year following selection. During the second year post-selection, the youths institutionalized rose by two, to 56%.

Thus, these data tentatively suggest that the majority of youths considered for admission to Achievement Place are genuinely in danger of institutionalization, and that Achievement Place does act as an alternative to institutionalization for these youths.

The average age of the randomly selected youths admitted to Achievement Place was 14 yr, 7 months. The randomly determined comparison group youths were 15-yr old on the average, at the time of selection. The comparison youths who were institutionalized following selection were an average of 15-yr, 3-months old when they were admitted to an institution.

In addition to the comparability of age at the time of selection for both the randomly selected Achievement Place group and the randomly determined comparison group, the median police and court contacts during the year preceding selection provided another indication of comparability. The median contacts with the police and court prior to selection was 3.48 for the comparison group and 3.00 for the Achievement Place youths.

Posttreatment Institutionalization

What proportion of the youths who enter the Achievement Place program are later institutionalized? The posttreatment institutionalization rate of the first 18 youths who entered Achievement Place was compared with the reinstitutionalization rate of the 19 comparison youths placed in the state Boys School. (There are no posttreatment reinstitutionalization data for the random group due to the small number of those institutionalized who completed the institutional program.) Approximately twice as many youths who went to the Boys School were institutionalized after their treatment than were youths who participated in the Achievement Place program. By the end of the first year posttreatment, 37% of the Boys School youths had been reinstitutionalized and 17% of the Achievement Place youths had been institutionalized. These figures indicate the in-program failures for both programs. During the second year the cumulative percentage of youths institutionalized after their original treatment program increased to 47% for the Boys School Group and to 22% for the Achievement Place group. Thus, approximately twice as many youths from the Boys School group were receiving further institutional treatment after having completed their original treatment program.

Police and Court Contacts

We collected data on the police and court contacts before, during, and after treatment for the nonrandom Achievement Place and Boys School youths. The youths in each group had a similar number of contacts with the police and court before treatment, with each youth averaging about three contacts. During treatment the Achievement Place youths improved markedly, averaging less than one contact per youth, even though they were still in the community and still available to commit further offenses. Nevertheless, 2 yr after treatment, each group averaged about one and one-half contacts with no appreciable difference between the groups.

This finding seems to indicate that the program needs to be further refined to improve the youths' behavior after they leave the program. Perhaps this could be done by improving the system for monitoring and assisting the youths after they leave the program or by further refining the procedures for working with parents during the time the youths are in the group home. Even with additional support, however, the natural or foster homes to which many of the youths return after leaving Achievement Place may not be capable of providing the care, supervision, and instruction needed for the youths to be successful and to stay out of trouble with the police and court. Thus, another possibility would be to develop group foster-care homes that would be semipermanent residences for the youths through high school.

The finding of no difference after treatment may also be confounded by the differential postrelease institutionalization of the two groups. In a previous section we noted that more than twice as many Boys School youths were institutionalized after treatment. It is possible that in both groups, the youths institutionalized after treatment were those who would have been most likely to commit further offenses in the community. Thus, the current postrelease police and court contact data may be biased in favor of the Boys

School because they had more youths in the institutions during the time the police and court data were collected. This possibility will be further assessed by continuing to collect follow-up data on the youths over the next several years.

Independent Evaluation

An independent evaluation of the Achievement Place program was reported by Eitzen (1975). Eitzen stated that

The dependent variable for behavior modifiers has been limited to overt behavior. As long as the behavior of a delinquent becomes more socially acceptable, for example, it matters little to them if there is a concomitant shift in attitudes. Whether there is a change in attitudes is an important question, however, for at least two reasons: (1) an attitude change corresponding with a change in behavior will increase the probability of a lasting effect; and (2) such a demonstration will make the case for behavior modification more compelling to community agencies contemplating which direction to take in their efforts to attack a particular social problem. The primary research question for the study reported here is: does exposure to the rehabilitation techniques of behavior modification change the attitudes of delinquents so that they more closely approximate the norms of the community? (p. 295)

Eitzen devised a questionnaire that included scales of achievement orientation, internal-external attitudes, Machiavellianism, self-esteem, and feelings about various authority figures. The questionnaire was administered to each boy in Achievement Place during his first 3 months in the home, again between 4 and 8 months, sometime after 9 months, and again at the completion of his stay. To assess whether the Achievement Place experience brought the attitudes of the youths in line with average boys, all eighth-grade boys from a Lawrence, Kans, junior-high school were given the same questionnaire. The junior-high school chosen was in the school district in which most families of Achievement Place youths live. In summarizing the results, Eitzen stated:

The findings reported here are impressive in their support of the Achievement Place experience. Accompanying the behavioral changes of these delinquent boys are positive shifts in attitudes. The greatest shifts in attitudes were from poor to good self-esteem and from externality to internality. Not only were these changes more favorable over time, but they were dramatic—from much more negative than the comparison group at the beginning to much more favorable than the comparison group at the post-test.

No support was found for a behavior modification milieu making youngsters more Machiavellian. This "no difference" finding is in fact a favorable one for this technique, since it negates the criticism often charged that the objects of behavior modification will become more manipulative in their social relationships as a consequence of their being manipulated. (p. 298)

Consumer Evaluation

As another part of the overall program evaluation, a "consumer" evaluation is carried out annually. Questionnaires are sent to all individuals and
agencies that have contact with the program to have them rate the effectiveness of the teaching parents in dealing with the problems of the youths and
the cooperativeness of the teaching parents in their interactions with each
individual or agency. Questionnaires are sent to the judge and probation
officers in the Juvenile Court, the director and social workers in the Department of Social Welfare, the principals and teachers in the schools the
youths attend, the members of the Board of Directors, and the parents of the
youths. A professional teaching-parent or a member of the training staff also
makes an on-site visit to evaluate the professional skills of the teaching-
parents and to give a questionnaire to the youths to have them rate the
fairness, concern, and pleasantness of the teaching-parents and the degree to
which they feel the program has helped them get along better with their
parents, teachers, and friends. The annual evaluation is summarized and
sent to the teaching-parents, the Board of Directors, and each agency in the
community that has direct contact with the program. The annual consumer
evaluation of each program ensures the accountability of the teaching-parents to the community and provides detailed feedback to the teaching-
parents concerning the strengths and weaknesses of their program. A group
home that does not carry out an annual consumer evaluation is not usually
considered a Teaching Family program.

Cost Evaluation

The cost of purchasing, renovating, and furnishing a large, older home
for Achievement Place was about $6000 per bed for an eight-bed group
home. This compares with a cost of about $25,000 per bed for construction of
an institution. The total cost of operating Achievement Place is about $5500
per youth per year. This compares with a cost of about $12,000 per youth per
year for institutions in Kansas.

INFORMATION DISSEMINATION

Published research articles provide information on specific aspects
of the program that have been experimentally developed and evaluated. But
not all aspects of the treatment model have been evaluated or described in
these reports. To provide a more complete description, two books, a film,
and four chapters have been written.

One book, *The Teaching-Family Handbook* (Phillips, E.L., Phillips,
Fixsen, & Wolf, 1974), provides a detailed, technical description of all as-

pects of the treatment program. The handbook was written as a textbook for the teaching-parent training program and as a complete description for those interested in using the Teaching Family model. The other book, *Achievement Place: A Novel* (Allen, J.D., Phillips, Phillips, Fixsen, & Wolf, 1972), provides a fictionalized account of one boy's stay at Achievement Place. The story is told from a boy's point of view, and was designed to interest community groups and individuals in starting group-home programs and to recruit teaching-parent trainees. A 30-min, black and white film entitled "Achievement Place" (Phillips, E.L, Phillips, Bailey, Fixsen, & Wolf, 1970) was produced to describe the program to professional and student audiences, such as juvenile-court personnel, lawyers, police, psychologists, social workers, college students, behavioral scientists, and special educators.

Four chapters for edited books provide general descriptions of the program, usually emphasizing some aspect of the program. One chapter is mostly concerned with the self-government system (Wolf, Phillips, & Fixsen, 1972), one provides more detailed information on the point system (Fixsen, Wolf, & Phillips, 1973), a third emphasizes evaluation and outcome data (Fixsen, Phillips, & Wolf, 1973a), and a fourth describes the training program for teaching-parents (Braukmann, Fixsen, Kirigin, Phillips, Phillips & Wolf, 1975).

In addition to the written materials, dissemination conferences have provided information to decision makers. About 20 to 30 participants in responsible state and local government positions are invited to attend a two-day conference. During each conference the treatment program, outcome data, cost data, and training program for the teaching-parents are explained, and questions raised by the participants are answered. These conferences are held to attempt to affect state and local policy concerning community-based group homes.

The availability of the written materials has generated many requests for technical assistance and information about the program. Recently a study (Turnbough, Fixsen, Phillips, & Wolf, 1973) was carried out to determine which materials generate the most interest in the Achievement Place program and to indicate how well the various materials answer questions about the program. For this study, 90 requests for general information were randomly divided into four groups. One group was sent a set of three reprints describing research conducted at Achievement Place, a second group was sent a brochure describing the general Achievement Place program, a third group was sent a copy of the *Teaching-Family Handbook*, which gives a detailed description of the program, and a fourth group was sent a copy of *Achievement Place: A Novel*. Each of the 90 people was also sent a form containing questions about the usefulness of the information and listing several other types of information about the program that could be obtained by checking a box next to each listing.

Based on an 80% return of the forms, the reprints were most often requested for additional information, followed by the handbook, brochure, and novel. Apparently the people who requested information about the program saw the more technical descriptions of the program as more useful.

PROGRAM TO TRAIN TEACHING PARENTS

One aim of the Achievement Place program has been to develop a training program for teaching-parents that can replicate the Achievement Place model and provide trained teaching-parents for communities that request this kind of resource for their youths. During the last 3 yr we established the foundations of a 1-yr teaching-parent training program. If the trainees choose, they may earn graduate credit for their training and work toward an M.A. degree in the Department of Human Development at the University of Kansas.

The teaching-parents who have been trained have usually had a B.A. degree in the behavioral sciences (psychology, sociology, social work, education) before receiving specific training to prepare them as teaching-parents. The special training for teaching-parents consists of a five-part sequence: (1) a one-week workshop (about 50 hr of instruction) at the University of Kansas that provides the teaching-parents with the basic knowledge and skills required to establish and operate a treatment program; (2) a 3-month practicum and consultation period when the teaching-parents begin working in residential treatment settings where they receive frequent (several times a week) telephone consultation from the training staff; (3) an evaluation of the treatment program at the end of the third month by the training staff and by each of the consumers of the program (including the Juvenile Court, the department of social welfare, the schools, the youths, and their parents); (4) a second one-week workshop at the University of Kansas that provides the teaching-parents with more detailed information on maintaining a successful treatment program and on evaluating their own programs; and (5) further evaluations of the treatment program by the training staff after 6 months of operation and again after 12 months of operation, with continued intermittent telephone consultation with the teaching-parent trainees.

The evaluations of the treatment program after 3 months and 6 months provide private feedback to the teaching-parent trainees to indicate where their treatment program is strongest and where additional effort may be required. The results of the evaluation at the end of 12 months are made available to the Board of Directors of the residential setting and the agencies that refer the youths to the program as well as to the teaching-parent trainees. The Board of Directors is firmly urged to continue to carry out evaluations of their program at least once a year.

If a set of teaching-parent trainees is not effective in some areas as measured by the 3-month evaluation, they receive further training during the second workshop and continued consultation from the training staff after the workshop. Their effectiveness is again evaluated at the end of 6 months and further training, consultation, and technical assistance are given as required. In most cases, the teaching-parent trainees are reasonably effective at the end of 3-months and continue to improve during their year of training. At the end of the year the first Annual Evaluation is carried out, and most couples are then certified as teaching-parents on the basis of their evaluated effectiveness and successful completion of the training sequence.

Kirigin, Ayala, Braukmann, Brown, Phillips, Fixsen, and Wolf (1975) evaluated the first workshop in the training sequence. The workshop consists of a week of intensive instruction, demonstrations, video-taped sequences, role-playing situations, and practicum experience in the basic skills required to set up and manage a Teaching Family group-home treatment program. In this experiment four couples participated in the workshop and two other couples did not receive training. All the couples were pretested in five role-playing situations involving typical interactions between a teaching-parent and a youth. The youth role was played by a graduate-student member of the training staff. The couples were tested over the same situations midway through the workshop and again on the final day. An analysis of the specific behavior components that constituted the style of teaching interaction taught in the workshop indicated that those couples participating in the workshop doubled their use of teaching interaction components, while untrained couples maintained about their pretest level of performance. The results suggest that the training procedures were effective in teaching the measured skills.

Teaching-Parent Tenure

Staff turnover is a problem in most child-caring programs, and teaching-parents are no exception. So far we find that 85-90% of the teaching-parents stay on the job for 15 months and only 10-15% longer than 18 months. We suspect that two issues are related to teaching-parent tenure. One issue is the skills of the teaching-parents in dealing with the youths. The teaching-parents who leave during the first year usually quit after only a few months because they did not realize how difficult it would be to live with a group of six to eight adolescents and be responsive to the youths' parents and teachers and to community agencies. Another issue is the working conditions for the teaching-parents. This includes adequate time off on weekends, during the week, and on vacations; adequate private living space for the teaching-parents and their children; and salary. We found great variability in this category among different group homes. We recently began helping teaching-parents hire alternates who work full or half-time under the direction of the teaching parents so they can have more time off. We also began convincing the Boards of Directors to build a private apartment for the teaching-parents onto their group homes. And we began advocating a minimum salary of

$15,000 per year per couple (which is only $7500 each plus free room and board).

We are also encouraging teaching-parents to buy their own group homes. We suspect that this entrepreneur model would increase the investment of teaching-parents in the program and would hold more long-term reinforcers for them. Many couples who are excellent teaching-parents complain that they do not feel they have the same financial and professional advantages of other professionals in the community (e.g., they do not own their own home, they are not free to travel to meetings). Perhaps the entrepreneur model would improve these conditions sufficiently to increase the tenure of teaching-parents.

The tenure of teaching-parents is an extremely important issue to us because it may be related to the lack of maintenance of low rates of police and court contacts after the youths leave the program. It may be that the teaching-parents will need to maintain a strong, continuing relationship with their youths until they finish high school to maintain low rates of police and court contacts. Thus, in this complex behavioral system we are trying to develop, it seems that the reinforcers for the child-care staff are as important as those for the youths.

CONCLUSION

After 7 years, the Teaching Family model has progressed through the first four stages of the development and dissemination plan proposed by Shah and Lalley: the model has been developed and research on treatment procedures has continued, the overall evaluation of the program has been initiated and additional follow-up data continue to be collected, user-oriented information has been prepared and some has been evaluated, model-related training has been initiated and research on training continues. We are just entering the model replication and evaluation stage. In this stage we expect to encounter new problems that will require further research and planning before practical solutions are found. By continuing to follow where the data lead we expect to solve these problems, and in the next 5 years we hope to have a replicable model that can be used on a national scale.

ALICE LIES and L. KEITH MILLER

Chapter 19

A Behaviorally Engineered Democratic Community: The Experimental Living Project

It has been argued that methods of unparalleled effectiveness for helping individuals with a wide range of behavioral problems have been developed by the field of applied behavior analysis (Ullman & Krasner, 1965). Methods have been developed that improve the lives of mental patients (Ayllon & Azrin, 1968; Patterson & Teigen, 1973), increase academic behavior in public-education classrooms (Semb, 1972), treat severely disturbed children (Lovaas, Koegel, Simmons, & Long, 1973), and remediate a wide variety of other behavior problems (Franks & Wilson, 1973). Behavioral technologies offer effective and humane solutions to these social problems.

Despite this success, social practice has not been widely modified by the existence of these technologies. Only a tiny fraction of all public-school classrooms, mental-hospital wards, and programs for severely disturbed children use behavior analysis. It may be that contingencies now embedded in American institutions will prevent the widespread adoption of our technology. It is not hard to imagine that vested interests among businessmen, corruption in government, and featherbedding by unions could so distort the decision-making process that humane and effective methods for solving social problems would go unnoticed.

It may be necessary for behavior analysts to regard overcoming these impediments to social change as part of their task. One approach is to analyze the contingencies relating to a specific treatment and then to design a behaviorally engineered dissemination system (Risley, Clark, & Cataldo, 1976). Of course, given the complex interlocking of modern society, this may not be possible in all or even most cases. A radical restructuring of society may be necessary to create an "experimental society" that constantly seeks empirically more effective and more desired ways of doing things. While creating an experimental society may be beyond our reach, we may be able to create healthy communities supportive of experimentation.

It may be possible to use existing behavioral technologies to design a program for a small community that promotes a harmonious life-style for its citizens through behavioral experimentation. Before the advent of behavioral technology, Skinner in *Walden Two* suggested the use of a labor credit system to organize the basic work of such a community. He also envisioned using positive social reinforcement to foster positive interactions between marital partners and between parents and children. Skinner labeled his proposed social innovations the "Good Life." He has since argued that such "Good-Life" communities may be the only practical way to produce the large-scale change implied by the accomplishments of applied behavior analysis (Skinner, 1976). Such a community will not be easy to build because there are few models to imitate. If done systematically, however, it may be possible to build a multifamily community that does foster the "Good Life."

This chapter describes *The Experimental Living Project*, a behaviorally engineered living environment for 30 unmarried students at the University of Kansas. This small community was selected as a starting point for building community development technology because complex problems inherent in marital relations and in child-rearing do not occur. The goal has been to create a technology for solving problems that occur when people live together.

THE UNIVERSITY OF KANSAS EXPERIMENTAL LIVING PROJECT

Thirty University of Kansas students live in The Experimental Living Project at Lawrence, Kans. At any one time, approximately 29% of the members are graduate students and the rest are undergraduates. Of the undergraduates, 66% are juniors or seniors. On the average, 36% of the members are female; this approximates the university percentage of 43%. Member's fields of study include business, psychology, behavior modification, social work, chemistry, and fine arts. Most of the members come from Kansas and Missouri; a few come from as far away as New York or California, and several come from other countries. Overall, the members seem to represent a cross section of the university population.

The Experimental Living Project is housed in a large three-story frame house that contains 30 private sleeping rooms, a lounge, an institutional kitchen, a snack kitchen, a dining-meeting room, a laundry room with a washer and dryer, a TV room, a pool room, an exercise room, storage rooms, and a shop. Each student has a room with ample space for a desk, bed, and personal belongings. Students who do their share of the work pay an average of $43 per month for rent and $22 per month for food, which pays for one main meal a day six days a week.

The purpose of The Experimental Living Project has been to engineer behaviorally a positive, workable group-living situation for single university students. The goals of the project have been to solve three problems that have caused other groups to disband. These three goals are: (1) to establish an equitable worksharing system, (2) to create an egalitarian and democratic leadership system, and (3) to design a system for the transmission of an adaptable culture through generations of members. These goals are in various stages of development, and the following three sections discuss the progress made toward their attainment. Each section first presents a behavioral rationale for a goal, and then describes a behaviorally engineered system designed to attain that goal, along with a description of experimental analyses of its effectiveness. The last section of the chapter presents a description of future directions for The Experimental Living Project.

GOAL ONE: AN EQUITABLE WORKSHARING SYSTEM

Behavioral rationale

Probably the most fundamental problem of any group-living situation is how to get the group to share equitably in the work. As a simple matter of survival, a group needs at least to provide its members with a well-maintained and clean environment. This is particularly true of a group whose members come from America's middle class, where such services are taken for granted. Many communes have tried to do without a structured system for getting the routine work done. Accounts of such communes make frequent reference to the breakdown of the sharing of the routine work (Lanes, 1971) and the unpleasant consequences that follow.

Failure to equitably share routine work has severe ramifications for the group. Negative interpersonal behavior may increase between group members. Working members may try to get others to work by nagging, complaining, or coercing. If successful, their rate of nagging, complaining, or coercing will increase. Conversely, nonworking members may be able to stop such behavior by punishing it. Whichever occurs, it would be unpleasant to live in such a group.

Groups that succeed in staying together frequently end up with one or more strong leaders or "managers" who ensure that the routine housework gets done. Yet avoidance of such an unequal sharing of authority is a major reason for forming experimental living groups. An egalitarian, efficient worksharing system would ensure that everyone does a fair share of the routine housework without anyone having an unequal amount of authority.

Behaviorally Engineered Solution

A behavioral worksharing system that provides positive consequences for working was designed to ensure the equal participation of all members in the completion of routine work. The three components of this worksharing system are (1) a behavioral specification of all the common chores in the project, (2) a mechanism for determining whether these chores have been completed, and (3) a system for providing positive consequences for members who do their share of the work. A description of each of the three major components of the worksharing system follows.

Worksharing Component 1: Behavioral Specification: Each of the 100 common chores in the project has been specified in an *inspection checklist*, which is a list of tasks essential to the completion of that chore. An example of an inspection checklist for the chore of cleaning the lounge is as follows: pick up trash, sweep up dirt, vacuum or shake out rug, empty and clean out ash trays, empty trashbasket, mop floor, and return items to proper place. Each task on the checklist has a definition that specifies what the outcome must be for that task to be judged completed. For example, an empty trashbasket must be no more than half full and must have a plastic liner in it so that garbage cannot fall directly into the basket. The inspection checklists and task definitions ensure that members know exactly what each chore will entail before they do it.

Worksharing Component 2: Accountability: The second component of the worksharing system is accountability. One positive result of the behavioral specifications of the chores is that it makes possible a mechanism for determining whether these jobs have been done properly. Each night an inspector checks the routine jobs for that day according to the standard inspection checklists and task definitions. Hence, the Project has quality control on work completion by holding members accountable for the work they agree to do. This inspection requires about one-half hr per day.

Worksharing Component 3: Positive Consequences: The third component of the worksharing system is to provide positive consequences for members who do their share of the work. Members are awarded credits for each job completed. Before moving in, members agree to earn 100 credits a week in return for a $40 rent reduction.

This rent reduction is provided contingently. The mechanics for this are: Members pay a $40 work deposit before moving in; then for each month they complete the specified work they receive a $40 rent reduction the following month. The member who fails to do part of the specified work loses a proportional amount of rent reduction.

The reduction is possible because the project does not need to hire maids, cooks, or janitors. The remaining $43 in rent that a member does pay is used for unavoidable expenses (e.g., taxes, repairs, and utilities). The fact that members earn 98% of their possible rent reduction indicates the effectiveness of this contingency.

These three components (behavioral specifications, accountability, and positive consequences) form the basis of the worksharing system. The system works in the following way. About 100 regular common chores, such as cleaning bathrooms or preparing a meal, must be done in the project each week. In addition, monthly cleaning jobs or repair jobs need to be done. A list of these jobs and when they are to be completed is posted once a week. Members then sign up for the jobs they will do the following week. The sign-up system allows the members flexibility in what they do and when. They may do their work all in one day or spread it out across the week. They may do all cleaning jobs or they may do cleaning, cooking, and repair jobs. Members have a great deal of freedom in task selection.

Members must earn 100 credits per week, which approximates 5-6 hr of work. Each of the regular jobs was timed and assigned 15 credits for each hour it took. These credit values were then adjusted according to the desirability of the job. For example, almost everyone likes to cook, so cooking is paid at the rate of 15 credits per hour; not as many people like to dishwash, so dishwashing is paid at a rate of 25 credits per hour; and few people like to clean a greasy stove, so that job is paid at the rate of 30 credits per hour. Adjustments of credits upward or downward are made by majority vote of the project with one restriction. Any adjustments to increase credits must be counterbalanced by an equal decrease in credits for another job. This prevents the credit economy from becoming inflated. Because each member earns 100 credits per week, the project has a stable credit economy of 3000 credits or 200 work hours per week.

The credit system is flexible. A member who earns over 100 credits a week can save them for another week or give them to a friend. A member who earns less than 100 credits a week can borrow from past savings or from a friend. The member who does neither loses a small part of the rent reduction. Past records of average credit weeks show that approximately 51% of the members earn all their 100 credits in one week, 37% have some credits saved, 7% have credits transferred to them, and 5% lose a small part of their rent reduction (Miller, L.K., Lies, Petersen, & Feallock, 1976). Members need not do all their work each week; they can save up so that they can take time off or they can borrow from a friend during hard times.

There is one other important contingency in the worksharing system; a member who signs up for a job and fails to complete as least 70% of that job loses $2 of the rent reduction. This contingency ensures that a member with savings will not miss a job signed up for simply because of not needing the credits.

Experimental Analysis of the Worksharing System

Three major experiments have been done to determine the effectiveness of different aspects of the worksharing system. Inspections, the credit

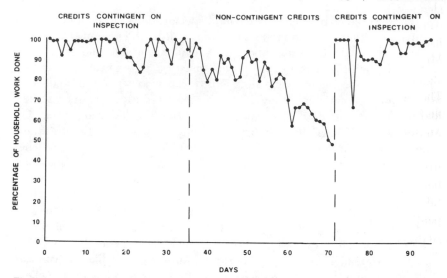

Fig. 19-1. Percentage of housework done across three conditions: credits contingent on inspection, noncontingent credits, and credits contigent on inspection. The vertical dashed lines indicate the points at which the conditions were changed.

system, and rent reduction were all analyzed using single-subject designs. In all three experiments the percentage of household work done was a major dependent variable. The following is a brief description of each experiment (details have been presented in Feallock and Miller, 1976).

Worksharing Experiment 1:   The first experiment analyzed the need for an inspection system. It is possible that people would do their share of the housework without being held accountable for it. A reversal design with three conditions analyzed whether it was necessary for credits to be contingent upon inspection. Housework performance was analyzed when credits for it were contingent upon inspection, when such credits were noncontingent, and again when they were contingent.

Figure 19-1 shows the effect of contingent credits upon members' housework performance. When credits were contingent upon inspection, a mean of 96% of all housework tasks passed inspection. When credits were awarded noncontingently, this average dropped to 77%. When the condition was returned to contingent credits, the average rose to 95%. These data show that credits contingent upon inspection are necessary for the functioning of the worksharing system.

Worksharing Experiment 2.   The second experiment examined the necessity of credits. It could be that posting results of an accurate inspection would be enough to maintain work behavior. A simple reversal design examined the role of credits in maintaining the completion of housework and the amount of painting done on the outside of the project. The percentages

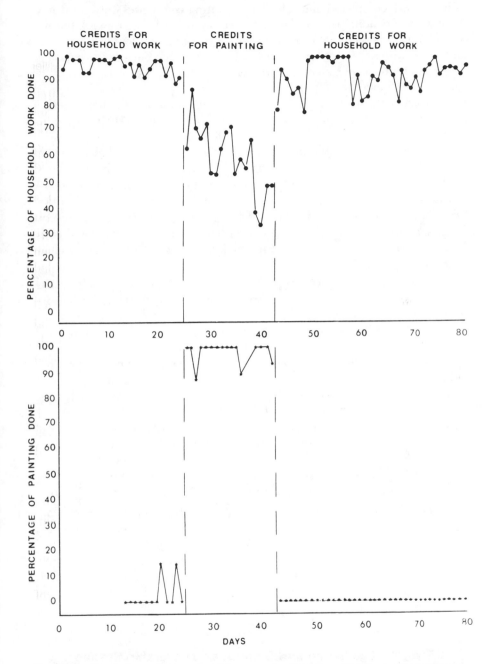

Fig. 19-2. Percentage of houseword done across three conditions: credits for housework, credits for painting but not for housework, and credits for housework. The vertical dashed lines indicate the points at which the conditions were changed.

of housework completed and scheduled painting completed were measured during three conditions: when credits were awarded for housework but not for painting; when credits were awarded for painting but not for housework; and again when credits were awarded for housework but not for painting. Throughout the experiment, members were required to earn credits for their rent reduction.

Figure 19-2 shows that when credits were awarded for housework a mean of 96% of the housework tasks passed inspection. When no credits were awarded for housework, this mean fell to 60%. When credits were again awarded for housework, this mean increased to 93%. Likewise, when no credits were awarded for painting, only a mean of 3% of the scheduled painting was done. When credits were awarded for painting, a mean of 99% of the scheduled painting was done. Again, when no credits were awarded for painting, no painting was done. An interesting note is that the second condition, credits for painting but not for housework, was terminated early because members wanted the credits back so that they could have a clean house again.

Worksharing Experiment 3.   The third experiment analyzed the necessity of the backup rent reduction. For this experiment, housework performance was analyzed when reductions were awarded contingent upon earning 100 credits per week, when reductions were noncontingent, and again when reductions were contingent.

Figure 19-3 shows the effect of the rent reduction upon housework behavior. During the weeks when rent reductions were contingent upon earning 100 credits, a mean of 94% of the housework tasks passed inspection. When rent reductions were given noncontingently, the percentage of housework tasks that passed inspection gradually decreased to an average of 67% during the last four weeks of this condition. When the condition was reversed and rent reductions were again contingent, an average of 94% of the housework tasks passed inspection. Thus, for the group as a whole, contingent rent reductions were necessary to maintain housework behavior.

These three experiments demonstrate that high percentages of work done in the worksharing system are maintained when the members are held accountable and provided positive consequences for their work. They further show that the three components of the worksharing system (inspection, credits, and rent reductions) are all functional. These three experiments empirically illustrate the functionality of the behaviorally designed worksharing system.

Goal Two: An Egalitarian and Democratic Leadership System

Behavioral Rationale.   All of the common chores are organized within the worksharing system, and most members can perform these chores

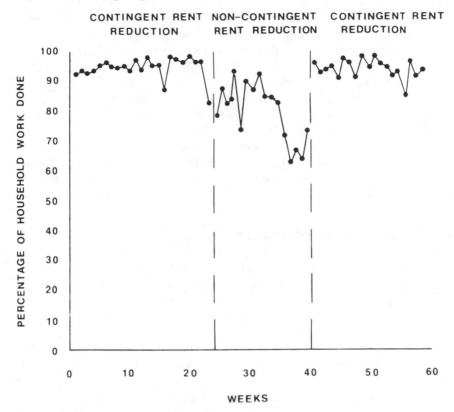

Fig. 19-3. Percentage of housework done across three conditions: contingent rent reduction, noncontingent rent reduction, and contingent rent reduction. The vertical dashed lines indicate the points at which the conditions were changed.

with a minimal amount of explanation. In fact most tasks can be done directly from the inspection checklist. Some jobs in the project, however, require expertise or special skills. For example, very few members move into the project with prior knowledge of how to budget income for a group. Each group, to survive, must have at least one person who has these skills.

Typically a leader who does have expertise emerges within most communes. Observers of communes report that contemporary communes are increasingly organized around a leader, because anarchistic communes fail to survive (Gardner, 1973). The price of success for experimental communities seems to be the acceptance of some form of leadership (Roberts, 1971). Thus, developing leadership is an important problem for any experimental community.

Unfortunately, leadership and power may go hand in hand. The role of a leader can be so abused that the communal society becomes no more than a dictatorial society. This can occur for at least three reasons. First, it is

difficult to hold a leader accountable because much of what the leader does is
not routine. Two, leadership jobs usually involve responsibility for valued
objects, such as money or food, or involve managing the behavior of other
individuals. This puts a leader in the position to perform favors for other
group members, such as letting a member pay rent late. This member is
then in debt to the leader and must return the favor in order to have a chance
for future favors. This type of power can eventually lead to the corruption of
the entire system. Third, leadership jobs often require rare skills, so that the
leader can threaten to leave unless other members follow the leader's
wishes. The group has no bargaining power when dealing with such a leader.
These three features taken together make the corruption of leadership positions too likely.

Behaviorally Engineered Solution

The work of The Experimental Living Project is administered within
eight separate programs called a coordinating system. These programs are (1)
cleaning, (2) food, (3) repair, (4) inspection, (5) rental, (6) financial, (7) educational, and (8) supervisory. All work in these programs is part of the worksharing system.

Some of the jobs within each of these programs require special skills.
These jobs are *contract* jobs. Each job has been carefully specified so that all
members can be trained to do each of the contract jobs, and so that contract
job holders can be held accountable by the group for their work.

Each program in the coordinating system is described below in terms of
the work done in it and its most important standard procedure. This is
followed by a description of the necessary components of the entire coordinating system.

1. *The Cleaning Program.* The cleaning program is designed to keep all the
   public areas in the project clean and neat so that members can comfortably use them. Most of this cleaning is done routinely through the worksharing system described earlier. One member of the project, the cleaning coordinator, sees to it that cleaning supplies are always available for
   the routine work. In addition this member specifies all nonroutine cleaning that must be done, such as washing down the bathroom walls.
2. *The Food Program.* The food program is designed to provide members
   with one main evening meal a day six days a week. The monthly food bill
   is $22 a month for approximately 27 meals (averaging 81¢ per meal). The
   food program has a standard semester menu in which each meal has a
   main dish, a vegetable, rice or potatoes, and a fruit or a dessert. Generally within a week there are three or four hamburger dishes, one chicken
   dish, one or more expensive meat dishes, and one or two meatless or fish
   meals. This menu provides the member with a variety of inexpensive

good food. In addition the recipes in the menu are carefully specified so that any member can cook them, regardless of past cooking experience. Since men do about 50% of the everyday cooking, shopping, and cleanup, sexual stereotyping has virtually been eliminated from this program. Also the food program is so specified that the food coordinator's only job is to check the work of others and to keep an inventory of items to be bought wholesale.

3. *The Repair Program.* The repair program is currently being developed. The purpose of this program is to have members do as many needed repairs as possible. One component of the program is a set of detailed inspection sheets which aid in the location of needed repairs. Another component is a set of detailed job descriptions for the 100 most commonly recurring jobs and for the 20 most frequently used repair skills. These job descriptions will be tested until most house members can use them. In addition a special program has been developed to teach members with repair skills how to write and test new job descriptions. This program is now being thoroughly tested. The development of these procedures permits the project to move gradually from reliance on experienced handymen to reliance on its own members. It is hoped also that this will eliminate any sexual stereotyping associated with repair jobs. Women now do repair jobs but they do not do as large a proportion as men. This is being corrected, however, and at present the repair coordinator is a woman. Her job is to check what work needs to be done, post it, and inspect the repair when it has been completed.

4. *The Inspection System.* The inspection system is a mechanism for checking whether the routine jobs in the project have been completed. This mechanism relies on a group of members who hold the contract job of inspector. Each night at 8:00 P.M., an inspector checks the routine jobs according to the task definitions for that job. After inspecting each job, the inspector marks down on the inspection checklist which tasks in that job have been completed and which have not. Regular daily inspection provides two benefits. First, the ratings give the project consistent feedback on how the routine work of the project is completed; and second, they are essential for keeping the worksharing system fair, because they provide the information necessary for providing consequences for each member's work.

One component of the inspection system is a reliability inspector. This inspector examines the jobs done in the project according to a random schedule. The agreements between the reliability inspector and the regular inspector are computed with the number of credits awarded each of them depending on how well they agree. Thus, the project is protected from inspectors who might abuse their positions. The reliability for the first 50 weeks of the inspection system averaged 95%.

5. *Rental Program.* One member in the project holds the contract job of renter. The renter is responsible for admitting and interviewing new

members. This involves showing prospective members around the project, explaining the worksharing system, and specifying the rules by which the project is governed. A prospective member is also shown a contract, which specifies a rent-payment schedule, and *The Experimental Living Project Handbook*, which contains all the governing rules of the project. Besides renting rooms, the renter has several additional duties described later.

6. *The Financial System.* The goal of the financial system is to have all monies handled by members while maintaining a sound financial base for the project. A system of checks and balances has been designed to ensure the proper handling of these monies. This system involves the interlocking work of several contract job holders. The treasurer is responsible for budgeting the rent and paying the bills. The comptroller provides a check on the treasurer by keeping a separate record of what bills need to be paid. The comptroller also collects the rent and deposits it. The renter checks to make sure that the right amount has been collected from each member by comparing a copy of each rent receipt with his record of what should have been collected. Finally the treasurer ensures that the comptroller has deposited the money by checking the bank-deposit slips against a copy of the renter's records. This system protects the project from any member's private pocketing of project funds. Further, it reduces the misuse of funds because the cooperation of the renter, comptroller, and treasurer would be required. This is unlikely. A further check on this system is described in "The Supervisory Program" section.

At present, a minimum of $1800 is collected each month. This money is allocated to various categories according to an established budget. As shown by the budgeting categories in Table 19-1, money is set aside for future expenses. For example, $300 is set aside each month to pay insurance and taxes, which are once-a-year expenses. Hence the project maintains a sound financial base by budgeting its monies and by having a system of checks and balances to ensure that money is used according to that budget.

7. *The Educational Program.* This program is designed to develop an understanding of behavioral principles among the members of the project and to transmit the community culture from one generation to the next. This program is described in more detail in the section, "The Transmission of an Adaptable Culture through Generations."

8. *The Supervisory Program.* Jobs in this program involve the overseeing of all work in the project. There are two contract jobs in this program. The member who holds the contract job of credit recorder tallies up each member's credit balance at the end of each week according to credits saved, credits earned, and credits transferred. Credits are awarded for each job on a percentage basis according to the inspection ratings. If 90/ of the tasks within a job have passed inspection, a member receives full

Table 19-1
The Experimental Living Project Budget 1975-1976

Category	Monthly Allocation	Minimum Balance
Utilities	$ 310	$ 500
Small Repairs	70	150
Major Repairs	120	1500
Cleaning Supplies	50	25
Equipment	25	100
Insurance and Taxes	120	300
Loan Repayment	300	0
Miscellaneous	25	25
Reserves	60	500
Food	a	200
House Improvements	b	0
Total	$ 1080c	$ 3300

a All food payments.
b All income in excess of $1080 (except food payments).
c Plus House Improvements and food payments.

credit for having completed that job. But if only 80-89/ of the tasks passed, the member receives only 80/ of the credits awarded for that job, etc. If 70/ or less of the tasks passed inspection, no credits are awarded and the member who signed up for the job loses $2.

The other job in the supervisory program is the auditor. The auditor iis responsible for checking the work of all contract job holders. All contract job holders fill out a weekly self-report form for the auditor. The auditor directly inspects some portion of each contract work and compares this to the self report form.

The coordinating system has six main components, some of which have already been described. They are (a) specific job descriptions, (b) auditing of job performance, (c) consequences, (d) limited term, (e) maximum of half a member's credits to be earned as a coordinator, and (f) training programs for each job. The specific job descriptions, the auditing of job performance, and the consequences arranged for job performance have already been described. The coordinating system is part of the worksharing system and all jobs, skilled or unskilled, are treated in the same way. Routine work, like coordinating jobs, is specified according to task definitions, and is checked by an inspector; coordinating jobs are checked by the auditor. Consequences are arranged for member's performance on routine work just as they are for the performance on contract jobs. Because of the power involved, several additional restrictions are placed on the holding of a contract job.

A contract job holder may have a particular job for only a limited time (5 months). At the end of this term the job must be assumed by another member. This prevents any one member from maintaining a monopoly on a job, and also helps ensure that the office is not subverted in subtle and unanticipated ways.

By limiting the number of credits a person can earn by being a coordinator, the project has ensured that no one member can hold more than one contract job. This means that any leader must do a substantial amount of routine work in the project. And the coordinators are in constant contact with the effects of their leadership decisions. Also, this prevents a member accumulating too much power by holding many contract jobs at the same time. Within the project, there are 10 contract jobs distributed among 30 members, which is a substantial distribution of power throughout the membership.

The key component of the coordinating system is the training program for each contract job. As noted earlier, not all members have the special skills necessary to do each of the contract jobs such as budgeting.

A major innovation has been the development of instructional packages for the training of each coordinating job. An instructional package outlines each task in a coordinating job. The instructional packages provide hypothetical examples on which a member training for a job can practice the tasks for that job. These examples give the trainee some practical experience with actual job duties before taking over the responsibilities of that job. At present, over 100 of these instructional packages are in the final stages of development. Each package covers one of the duties of a coordinator. They are now being tested and revised until they successfully train the average house member in that specific duty.

The effectiveness of the instructional packages for the renter's job has been analyzed (Petersen, D.L., & Miller, 1976). For this analysis, a simulated situation called a *mastery test* was developed. This mastery test consisted of a series of hypothetical situations that covered all of the activities that a renter could possibly engage in within one month. The test permitted the repeated measurement of a person's ability to perform the renter's tasks.

A multiple-baseline design was used to analyze the training effectiveness of the instructional packages for the renter's job. For this experiment, two students volunteered to serve as trainees for the job. Trainees' performance on the mastery test was measured for three sessions during each of the following conditions: (1) baseline, when each trainee was given a list of rules for the renter, (2) training of the first trainee while the second still used the rules, and (3) training of the second trainee. The percentage of renter's tasks performed correctly by trainees increased after the introduction of the instructional packages from 38.5% before training to 97.7% after training.

Thus, the instructional packages for the renter's job were effective training tools.

Instructional packages have been effective in training public-speaking skills (Fawcett & Miller, 1975), canvassing skills for a low-income service center (Fawcett, Miller & Braukmann, 1977), student-proctoring skills for a university course (Weaver & Miller, 1975), and job skills for infant and toddler day-care centers (Risley et al., 1976). For The Experimental Living Project, the use of such packages means that many people with a wide variety of backgrounds can be effectively trained to perform complex tasks. This permits all members of the group to share in leadership responsibilities.

GOAL THREE: THE TRANSMISSION OF AN ADAPTABLE CULTURE THROUGH GENERATIONS

Behavioral Rationale

Most individuals who move into experimental communities are interested in having a voice and a vote in how that community is run. But unless all individuals in that group are thoroughly knowledgeable in the group-living system of that community and the rationale for that system, they can inadvertently bring about its collapse. This possibility results from the tendency of most people to act under short-term consequences rather than long-term consequences. Their actions can have serious ramifications throughout the network of the whole system without their being aware of it until the system finally collapses. For example, suppose that a member is short of money and asks for a reduction in the food bill. If most people in the group do not understand how the project is financed, they may grant the exception to be "nice." This and decisions like it may result in a major deficit in the food budget. The group might then decide to take money from the repair fund to pay for the food bill. If a furnace were then to break down or a pipe to burst, the members of the project would either have to pay for the repair out of their own pockets, or not get the furnace or the pipe fixed. This could have serious long-range ramifications for the project, because members would not want to pay the bill out of their own pockets nor would they want to go without the heating or the plumbing services. A quarrel could break out that could result in members leaving, and then there would be even less rent money for the following month. This could eventually lead to the breakup of the project. Obviously no one incident could do this much damage, but a series of them could. Hence, in a successful community each member must be aware of the long-term consequences of decisions.

Members also need to be able to change the system as necessary. To do this, they must understand the entire system and the consequences of their actions. For example, fuel prices are increasing and more money must be set aside each month for utilities. Members need to understand the finance system in order to set aside more money for utilities while allowing for other unavoidable expenses. The ability to adapt to changing conditions is a necessary component of a culture that is to survive.

Another problem is passing on the culture from one generation of members to the next. Most of the worksharing experiments were completed within the first 2 yr of the project. If there were no cultural transmission system, future generations of members would not be able to draw on these data when making decisions. These experiments would have to be done over and over again simply because one generation did not tell the next what it had done. Also, if the coodinating jobs were not transmitted from one generation to the next, the group would disband, or the work of organization would be done all over again, or an authoritarian leader would emerge.

A Behavioral Solution

Several strategies have been developed for handling these problems (1) A handbook has been written that specifies the rules of the project, the worksharing system, and the coordinating system; (2) a course on behavioral principles has been developed; (3) instructional packages for each coordinating job are being written and tested; and (4) a manual on how to write instructional packages has been written and tested. All of these strategies have been developed with an eye toward creating a culture that can be adapted and transmitted through generations of members.

Transmission Strategy 1: Handbook. The handbook contains the rules that members agree to live by. In it are self-governance rules, social rules, descriptions of the worksharing and coordinating systems along with rationales for these two systems. In the handbook any major changes in the project are recorded for future generations. The worksharing and coordinating systems have already been described. The following describes the rules for the project.

Two kinds of rules are in the handbook: self-governance rules and social rules. The rules for self-government provide the mechanism for members to change or to add to the present system. One provision is that any change in the system requires a 75% majority vote; this ensures that a strong majority of the members are in favor of the change. These votes take place at a weekly meeting for which members are paid 15 credits for attending. Members, therefore, have access to the decision-making process and are paid for participating in it. The social rules are those general rules that members agree to abide by. For example, one rule is, "Any stealing in the project, from the project or from another member, is grounds for immediate eviction." Overall, the social rules are designed to promote a harmonious and pleasant house.

Transmission Strategy 2: Course on Behavioral Principles.

An introductory textbook called *Principles of Everyday Behavior Analysis* (Miller, 1975) is the text that is used for this course. In this book students are taught to identify basic behavioral principles in short fictional examples of everyday situations. A detailed description of the programming procedure (called "concept programming") is available elsewhere (Miller & Weaver, 1976). Research has shown that students who master this program can correctly answer questions about novel examples with a mean of 75% compared to a mean of 15% before mastering the program.

This course is taught by the education coordinator using a personalized system of instruction (Keller, 1968). For the course, members read a short lesson, answer programmed study-guide questions about it, and then take a quiz graded by the education coordinator. At present, about half the membership has gone through this text. None of the behavioral systems for worksharing or the coordinating system has been voted out.

Transmission Strategy 3: Instructional Packages. The purpose of the instructional packages is to facilitate the turnover of a coordinator job from one member to the next. D.L. Petersen and Miller (1976) analyzed whether the renter instructional packages were more effective in facilitating job turnover than an oral training procedure was. Their analysis compared two groups of five subjects. One group used an oral training procedure. For this group, the first member was trained by means of the renter instructional packages. This newly trained renter then explained the renter's task to a successor, who in turn trained a successor, etc. A second group used the same sequence, except that each newly trained renter used the written instructional packages to train a successor. The renter's job was turned over four times in each group. The oral training procedure produced an average decrement of 15% on mastery test performance per turnover, going from 98% to 38%. For the instructional-package training group, however, performance across turnovers was stable and high, with an average performance of 93% for all members.

Transmission Strategy 4: Manual on How To Write Instructional Packages. A manual has been developed called *How To Write Instructional Programs* (Thomas & Miller, 1975). The purpose of this manual is to train project members in the skill of writing instructional packages. It provides a mechanism whereby the project can add or change coordinators' jobs as necessary. Without this manual, the project would either depend on a trained researcher to change the instructional packages or revert to an oral training procedure for the changes.

The effectiveness of this manual for training members to write instructional packages was analyzed. One part of the analysis had two subjects write an instructional package before and after training based on the manual. Each subject wrote packages on two different credit-recorder tasks, package A and package B. Before training, subject 1 wrote package A and subject 2 wrote package B. After training, subject 1 wrote package B and subject 2 wrote package A. This counterbalanced design controlled for package difficulty.

The mean percentage of correct program writing behavior increased from a mean of 6.4% before training to a mean of 95.4% after training. Thus, the training manual was effective in training the two subjects to write instructional packages.

Summary.   These four strategies taken together solve some of the problems confronting groups in developing and adapting their culture. A detailed handbook and a course on behavioral principles provide project members with the information they need to assess some of the ramifications of their votes. Rules of self-governance ensure that the project as a whole will move in directions that have been decided upon by a majority of the membership. Instructional packages provide a mechanism for the turnover of coordinating jobs from one member to the next. A manual on how to write instructional packages provides the project with the mechanism for adapting the coordinators' jobs to changing conditions. In conclusion, these four strategies provide a mechanism for the transmission of an adaptable culture through generations.

CONCLUSIONS

The Experimental Living Project to date has worked toward three main goals. The first goal is to develop an equitable worksharing system. This is important because such a system is needed to provide the project with food, shelter, and a clean environment. A worksharing system was described that is designed to accomplish this goal. This system involves specifying each chore in the project, keeping members accountable for their work by an inspection system, and providing consequences for members' work through a credit system and rent reduction. An experimental analysis demonstrated that each of these components was necessary in the worksharing system.

The second goal is developing an egalitarian and democratic leadership system. This is important because leadership offices are easily corruptible. A coordinating system was described that is designed to accomplish this goal. In this system, each leadership job is specified, checked by an auditor, and provided consequences through the credit economy. Rules limiting the power of leaders have been formulated. They state that: no members can hold a job for over 5 months, earn more than half their credits doing that job, or hold more than one contract job at a time. A key component of this system is the training programs for each coordinating job, which permit many members to be effectively trained for complex leadership tasks. These technologies have permitted the project to decentralize and hold accountable the power required to run it.

The third goal is the development of a system for developing and transmitting an adaptable culture. This is necessary for the continued growth of the project. A detailed handbook and a course on behavioral principles may provide members with some skills to assess the ramifications of their votes. Rules of self-governance ensure that the project as a whole will move in directions that have been decided upon by a majority of the membership. Instructional packages provide a mechanism for the turnover of coordinating jobs from one member to the next. A manual on how to write instructional packages provides the project with a mechanism for adapting coordinators' jobs to changing conditions. These components provide the first step toward a mechanism for developing an adaptable culture.

EVALUATION

This chapter outlined a behavioral approach to creating a community devoted to experimentation. The Experimental Living Project has experimentally analyzed components of three community self-management systems. It has been shown empirically that credits contingent upon inspections with backup reinforcers of contingent rent reductions are necessary for the functioning of the worksharing system. It has also been shown that instructional packages are effective in training coordinating positions in the project, and that these packages facilitate job turnover from one member to the next. Finally, it has been shown that a manual on how to write instructional packages is effective in training people to write instructional packages for the coordinating system. Thus the effectiveness of all the components has been shown empirically.

One premise of the project is that a community must empirically evaluate the effectiveness of its programs. Part of this evaluation must be determining how much a program will cost in time and money. A complete cost-effectiveness analysis would compare the cost and effectiveness of a program with those of other programs with similar goals. This is especially important if the community is trying to create a model for other communities. Effective programs have less chance of being adopted if they are considerably more expensive than other programs. Hence, one goal of such a community must be to design programs that are either as effective as existing programs at less cost or are more effective than existing programs at the same cost.

A partial cost-effectiveness analysis of The Experimental Living Project has been completed. Costs to residents for The Experimental Living Project were compared to those for dormitories and scholarship halls at the University of Kansas. Rent for a private room in the project costs an average of $43 per month. Rent in the dormitory for the same type of room costs $78 per month. Rent in a scholarship hall costs an average of $49.85 per month, but the facilities are not comparable because there is always more than one occupant per room. Food costs at the project are $22 per month for six evening meals per week, or about 81¢ per meal. In a dormitory, the cost for the same number of evening meals is $47.69, or $1.76 per meal; this includes the cost of hiring cooks, janitors, and dishwashers. Food costs were not available for the scholarship halls. Members of the project spend approximately 5.8 hr per week working for the project. Scholarship-hall residents spend 5.5 hr while dormitory residents report spending 1.2 hr. In terms of costs to residents, The Experimental Living Project compares favorably to both dormitories and scholarship halls.

Another part of an empirical evaluation should be *social validation.* Social validation involves obtaining a quantifiable sample of the verbal behavior of the relevant judges (cf. Chapter 18, pp. 618-624). For example, a behavioral system that effectively produces cooking behavior that results in bad-tasting food is not acceptable. One way to find out how well residents like a food program is to ask them to rate it on a seven-point Likert scale. Their rating the food good is evidence that the food program is adequate; whereas their rating the food bad is evidence that the program needs to be redesigned. Social validation is important when the social significance of targeted behavior is not known. It is particularly important in a community whose members have to live under any programs that are adopted.

As part of the validation process, members of The Experimental Living Project were asked the question, "Overall, how much do you enjoy living here, compared to a dorm?" Members rated this question on a seven-point scale where "1" meant they enjoyed living in the project less than in a dormitory, and "7" meant that they enjoyed living in the project more than a dormitory. The average rating for this question was 5.7, indicating that members enjoyed living in the project much more than they enjoyed living in a dormitory. On similar questions using seven-point scales, members said: the project was as clean as a dorm (average rating of 4.1); they liked the food better (average rating of 6.3), repairs were done as rapidly in the project as in a dormitory (average rating of 4.0), and their rent money was spent in ways that benefited them more in the project than it had in a dormitory (average rating of 5.9). These data indicate that the project compares favorably to a dormitory, and that residents like the project better than they liked the dormitory.

In a survey, residents of dormitories, scholarship halls, sororities, fraternities and The Experimental Living Project were asked to rate their residences on 23 dimensions. To summarize the data, residents of the project reported being as satisfied as residents of dormitories and scholarship halls were, but were not quite as satisfied as residents of sororities and fraternities.

Another measure of how well people like living in the project is how long they stay. Figure 19-4 shows the mean number of months in the project per member (cf. Miller and Feallock, 1975) for the first 4 yr of the project's existence. The mean number of months in the project per member has been steadily increasing. For the first year of operation, the overall mean number of months in the Project per member was 3.4 months. For the second year,

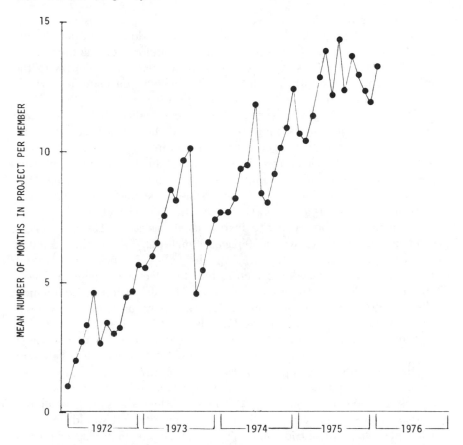

Fig. 19-4. The mean number of months in the project per member was computed for each month of the project's existence. This figure was derived by adding the cumulative number of months each member had been there and dividing that sum by the number of members in the project that month.

this increased to 7.2 months. For the third year, it was 11.4 months. Finally, for the fourth year of operation, it was 12.4 months. These social-validation data as a whole suggest that project residents are satisfied with the outcomes of the behaviorally engineered systems.

FUTURE DIRECTIONS

The development of the three major technologies described permits other projects to be considered: One future direction is the dissemination of the project to other settings. This may be possible because the behavioral systems for the project have been developed with a heavy reliance on written forms. These forms serve a dual purpose: (1) they provide a mechanism for recording how well the work in the project is being completed; and (2) they specify the work that needs to be done. For example, the inspection checklists not only provide a mechanism for checking the routine work of project members, but they also specify each of the tasks in the routine chores. These forms, coupled with other written materials already developed, outline the basic functions of the project.

The basics of the worksharing system are specified in the inspection checklists, the routine-work sign-up sheets, and the credit balance sheets. The coordinating system is specified in the auditor check sheets for each coordinating job, the cleaning-supply inventory sheets, the cookbook, the repair inventory sheets, the equipment-supply inventory sheets, and the financial record books. The transmission system is specified in the handbook, *The Principles of Everyday Behavior Analysis*, the instructional packages, and the manual on how to write instructional packages. These materials taken together constitute over 2000 pages of material. They outline in detail most of the transactions in the project. The only procedures they do not outline are start-up procedures such as how to select and finance a house. They may well form a strong foundation for a totally written dissemination package that would teach potential residents of a new community how to set up and operate a replication of The Experimental Living Project.

A totally written dissemination package could make the dissemination of the project economically feasible in three ways. First, it may be possible for potential residents to set up a replication of the project with little direct intervention by a trained researcher or an experienced member of the original project. Second, members of the new residence would have all the materials necessary for carrying on their community and would not have frequent recourse to outside help. Third, since the materials contain a mechanism for change, these potential residents might be able to adapt the program to meet their own needs without hiring a professional staff. The written training materials may furnish an inexpensive mechanism for exporting the program to other settings.

Another challenging direction that The Experimental Living Project can now actively pursue is the building of a behavioral culture that promotes a harmonious lifestyle for its members. It may now be possible to undertake this task, because most of the negative interactions between members over work and power has been eliminated by the basic systems described in this chapter. On this foundation, members now have the opportunity to build a "Good-Life" community.

What the components of a "Good-Life" community will be is speculative. Most likely one component will be designed to train members in positive social interactions. Although no one has yet designed such an ambitious training procedure, there is evidence that such social skills can be trained (Minkin, Braukmann, Minkin, Timbers, Timbers, Fixsen, Phillips, & Wolf, 1976; Kifer, Lewis, Green, & Phillips, 1974; and McFall & Twentymen,

1974). Another component may be to train members in self-modification skills that will enable them to grow as individuals. Again, there is some evidence that this may be possible (Budzynski & Stoyva, 1969; Jacobsen, 1962; Mahoney & Thoresen, 1974). There will be other components to this "Good-Life" community not yet envisioned. Surely, it will be exciting to be part of a culture that fosters harmonious relation between its members and that promotes individual growth.

A long-term future direction of The Experimental Living Project may be to systematically develop a multifamily community. Present thinking is to approach this in four stages. The basis of this strategy is to add only one level of major complexity at a time. This reduces the probability of failure because it does not needlessly endanger such delicate relations as those between marital partners and between parents and children. Rather, a sound foundation can be built at each stage so that the next stage can devote its energies to dealing with one additional complexity.

The Experimental Living Project has been selected as a starting point. Because it is a group of single students, no permanent relations are involved. In the project, basic worksharing, leadership, and transmission systems have been developed. It may also be possible to begin to build a culture that fosters harmonious relations between members and that promotes individual growth. Such information will be needed for the next three stages of development where permanent relations will be involved.

The second stage of development could be the design of a community for married couples. Sexual and social jealousy may be major problems in any community that has married people. It will be necessary to develop behavioral technologies for making average marriages strong enough to withstand the problems of community living. It may be possible to use the existing behavioral technology for marriage counseling (Azrin, Naster, & Jones, 1973; Stuart, 1969).

The third stage of development could be the expansion of the community to include families with children. Extensive work has already been done on family therapy (Mash, Hamerlynck, & Handy, 1976; Patterson, G.R., 1971) and on the education of children (Semb, 1972). These technologies may lay the groundwork for the design of systematic child-rearing practices.

Finally, the fourth stage could be the design of a comprehensive multifamily community. Such a community could be partially self-sustaining and provide such services as an effective educational system. Such a community would permit better assessment of whether behavioral principles can be used to intentionally design a "Good-Life" community.

The Experimental Living Project may afford the unique opportunity to systematically explore the use of behavior modification in the development of a community supportive of experimentation. Its mistakes and its successes, if empirically and systematically validated, may provide necessary information for the building of a "Good-Life" community.

STEPHANIE B. STOLZ[1]

Chapter 20

Ethics of Social and Educational Interventions: Historical Context and a Behavioral Analysis

Much concern has been expressed about the ethics of behavior control, and especially about psychosurgery and behavior modification (Heldman, 1973; Shapiro, M.H., 1974; U.S. Congress, 1974a, 1974b; Winett & Winkler, 1972). Critics voice fears of "mind control," and charge that behavior modification tends to dehumanize man (Carrera & Adams, 1970); they also raise legitimate questions about protecting the rights of participants in attempts to influence behavior (Wexler, 1973). At the same time, other writers declare that behavior therapists have been in the forefront of those offering protection for their clients' rights (Davison & Stuart, 1975), and that because of the effectiveness of their interventions, those using behavioral methods have been more concerned about the ethics of social control than other professionals (London, 1964).

Because behavioral interventions are usually nonintrusive and reversible, behavior modification would seem to pose relatively minor ethical issues compared to many aspects of medical research and practice where interventions may be intrusive or may produce irreversible changes. Drugs may induce psychoses, and operations like psychosurgery are irreversible. Accepted societal practices also cause profound behavior change: Life-long imprisonment markedly affects an individual's behavior, and even a short

1. This chapter was written by the author in her private capacity. No official support or endorsement by the ADAMHA is intended or should be inferred.

I thank A.C. Catania for persistent encouragement when my ratios were especially strained, T.A. Brigham, Ms. M.W. Harvey, and most particularly D.M. Baer for their helpful suggestions on earlier versions of this chapter.

period of incarceration is highly aversive. On the other hand, some critics of behavior modification evaluate these same comparisons quite differently. Spece (1972) suggests that some may feel that behavior modification is more of a threat than drug therapy, for example, because although "the effects of drugs wear off . . . behavior modification may produce significant, long-lasting changes [p. 657]."

The extent to which the practice of behavior modification actually involves ethical problems and potential abuses is impossible to assess validly and objectively because of the value issues involved. One empirical analysis of evaluations of the ethics of therapy (Stolz, 1975) suggests that ethical problems in research on therapy are not concentrated in behavior-therapy projects. This study examined reports of one government review committee's discussions of grant applications for psychotherapy and behavior-therapy research, and found that roughly the same proportion of psychotherapy and behavior-therapy projects was criticized for their ethics. In the absence of any other data, evaluation of the relative riskiness of behavior modification or of the care taken by behavioral professionals is reduced to prejudice and polemic.

Consideration of these issues, however, is unquestionably important. Speaking about medicine, Braceland (1969) presents a caution equally applicable in behavior modification. He says that unless the practitioner "is well-guided in ethical concepts, the temptation may be great to handle" the treatment problem "expeditiously and without concern [p. 234]" for its long range ethical implications.

In this chapter, ethical concepts relevant to social and educational interventions based on behavior-modification technology are analyzed to see how they might be restated in the terms of applied behavior analysis. First, however, ethical problems that have been raised in connection with applied behavior analysis will be set in the context of broader concerns for the rights of patients and research subjects.

THE HISTORICAL CONTEXT

At the end of World War II, the atrocities committed by the scientists working for the Nazis were discovered. Since then, scientists, physicians, and others whose activities involve human subjects have come under increasing control and regulation. The civil-rights movement and, more recently, a continuing series of court cases concerned with issues such as the right to privacy, the right to effective treatment, and the right to protection from harm have further focused attention on individuals' rights and on scientific and therapeutic activities involving humans. Concurrently, the rights of human participants in research have been expanded and clarified.

International Codes

Initial regulations applied only to medical research. Following the exposure at the Nuremberg trials of the Nazi experiments, the United States
Military Tribunal (cf. Bernstein, J.E., 1975) rendered a decision that formulated rules of conduct for performing medical experiments. These rules of
conduct underlie the ethics codes of medical professions in many countries.
Briefly, the Nuremberg code states that the subject should voluntarily consent; the experiment should produce results for the good of society; human
research should be based on animal studies; unnecessary suffering and injury
should be avoided; studies in which the procedures have a risk of death or
disabling injury should not be conducted unless the researchers serve as
subjects; risks should not outweigh benefits; the subject should be protected
against even remote risk of injury or death; the researchers should be scientifically qualified; the subjects should know that they are free to withdraw at
any time; and the scientist should terminate the study at any time that
continuation of it entails a risk of injury or death to the subject (Bernstein,
J.E., 1975).

The Declaration of Helsinki (World Medical Association, 1964), a statement by the World Medical Association on clinical research with humans, is
the only other major international statement of protection for the subjects of
medical experiments. The basic principles of this declaration, quite similar
to the Nuremberg Code, state that clinical research with humans should be
based on animal experiments; clinical research should be conducted only by
scientifically qualified persons, supervised by qualified physicians; the benefits of clinical research should outweigh the risks; and special caution
should be exercised when the personality of the subject is liable to be altered
by the experimental procedures. In addition, the Declaration of Helsinki
stated that patients and subjects in clinical research should freely give written, informed consent, and should be free to withdraw from the study at any
time.

Both the Declaration of Helsinki and a statement by the British Medical
Research Council (Medical Research Council, 1964) issued at the same time
distinguished between treatment-related research and nontherapeutic clinical research. The former involves use of a new therapeutic measure on a
patient population expected to benefit from it; the latter involves study of
procedures solely for scientific purposes, in which the subjects are not expected to benefit from their participation. Both codes describe this distinction as fundamental and note that treatment-related research is subject to
the usual standards of professional conduct of medical practice, while non-
beneficial interventions fall under research-related rules, including stricter
requirements for obtaining consent. This distinction is maintained in more
recent sets of regulations.

U.S. Government Regulations

Since the early 1960's, the Department of Health, Education, and Welfare (DHEW) has been developing regulations for medical experimentation with humans, and, more recently, for psychological experimentation and any other activity with humans that receives federal support. Most of these extensions of protection to patients and subjects have followed public exposure of some flagrant abuse.

The first federal agency to develop regulations for the protection of human subjects was the Food and Drug Administration (FDA), in response to congressional investigation and legislation, and in reaction to experiences with the drug Thalidomide, which deformed the fetus when taken by pregnant women. The 1962 FDA regulations stated that investigators of new drugs should obtain the consent of the persons to whom the drug is to be administered or their representatives, except where obtaining such consent would not be feasible or would be contrary to the best interests of the subjects. The regulations were also concerned with drug efficacy and advertising.

Later modifications of the FDA regulations are reviewed in detail by Curran (1969). Briefly, following the adoption of the regulations after the enactment of the Drug Amendments Act of 1962, the regulations were not clarified until another dramatic abuse came to light, this time the cancer-cell implant case at the Jewish Chronic Disease Hospital in Brooklyn, where patients had been used as subjects in a study of rejection of live cancer cells. The issue here was that the patients had not been told that the cells were cancerous when their consent to participation in research had been obtained. The 1967 FDA policy was the product of many factors, including extensive public concern about this case (Curran, 1969). The 1967 policy revised the consent requirement so that patients had to give knowledgeable consent; the ambiguities in the exceptions regarding consent in the 1962 law were also clarified, and subjects had to be told if they might be in the control group. In 1971, FDA regulations were further revised to require a review committee to screen and approve protocols involving investigational new drugs when the experimentation was to be done with institutionalized subjects, and in most other investigational new-drug research as well.

The National Institutes of Health (NIH) had had formal guidelines for intramural research since 1953. Beginning in the mid-1960's, the NIH developed an extensive set of regulations for the protection of human subjects in extramural research, and an elaborate clearance process involving review committees at the investigator's institution and further review at the national level. The first step in the development of these regulations was a statement by the Surgeon General of the Public Health Service (PHS) in 1966, requiring grantee institutions to establish committees to review studies proposing clinical research with humans, to consider subjects' rights, to ensure that consent was appropriately obtained, and to evaluate the risks and potential benefits of proposed studies. These requirements, initially applicable only to clinical research and research training grants, were soon extended to all PHS grants, including those for research in behavioral and social science (Curran, 1969). In 1971, a detailed policy statement (Department of Health, Education, and Welfare, 1971) supplemented the 1966 policy; this statement covered all research grants and contracts, and also development and demonstration activities. The evolution of the PHS guidelines is reviewed in detail by Curran (1969) and Gray (1975).

Under the current DHEW system, responsibility for the protection of human subjects is shared by the Institutional Review Board at the investigator's institution, the peer review committee of nonfederal experts that evaluates the application, the staff of the funding agency, and the staff of the Office for Protection from Research Risks, DHEW. Basic regulations (Chapter 45, Code of Federal Regulations, Subtitle A, Part 46) governing the protection of human subjects involved in research, development, and related activities supported or conducted by DHEW through grants and contracts were published in 1974;[2] regulations providing additional protection for human fetuses, pregnant women, and human *in vitro* fertilization were published in 1975.[3] Regulations are planned for other persons who may have diminished capacity to provide informed consent, such as prisoners, children, and the institutionalized mentally disabled.

The Professional Associations' Involvement

The American Psychological Association (APA) developed its first formal code of ethics in 1953. As recently as 1963, this was still apparently the only functioning code that had been officially adopted by a scientific organization (Cranberg, 1963), although the Nuremberg Code or variants of it had been adopted by several medical associations (Wolfensberger, 1967). The APA code has been revised several times since 1953. The 1973 version (Ad Hoc Committee on Ethical Standards in Psychological Research, 1973) was empirically based, with principles deriving from a consideration of "critical incidents" submitted in response to a systematic survey of the membership. The current APA code was published in 1977 (American Psychological Association, 1977).

In 1968, the American Psychiatric Association initiated the appointment of a series of task forces charged with reporting to the membership on new and controversial procedures within psychiatry. The task forces considered the available research evidence on the efficacy of the new methods, as well as

2. 39 Federal Register 18914 (May 30, 1974), with minor technical amendments in 40 Federal Register 11854 (March 13, 1975).
    3. 40 Federal Register 33526 (August 8, 1975).

their ethical implications. The first of their reports, on encounter groups, was published in 1970 (Yalom, Fidler, Frank, Mann, Sata, Parloff, & Seashore, 1970).

The Professional Associations and Behavior Modification. The American Psychiatric Association's fifth task force was the Task Force on Behavior Therapy. This group, appointed in 1971, was composed of four psychiatrists, a psychiatric resident, four psychologists, and a social worker; both dynamic psychiatrists and behavior therapists were included. The report of the task force concluded, "Behavior therapy and behavioral principles employed in the analysis of clinical phenomena have reached a stage of development where they now unquestionably have much to offer informed clinicians in the service of modern clinical and social psychiatry" [Birk, Stolz, Brady, Brady, Lazarus, Lynch, Rosenthal, Skelton, Stevens, & Thomas, 1973, p. 64].

The Association for Advancement of Behavior Therapy (AABT) is a national organization of several thousand professionals, including psychologists, psychiatrists, and social workers, who are active in behavior therapy and behavior modification. The AABT in 1974 developed a system of consultative committees coordinated by the president of the association. Persons who are concerned about present or proposed behavior-therapy programs or procedures, especially in institutions, can ask the AABT president to appoint a committee to go to the site, investigate, and make an advisory report. These reports are compiled into a casebook of standards of practice.

In 1974, the then-president of the American Psychological Association, Albert Bandura, responding to a request from the APA's Board of Social and Ethical Responsibility, appointed a committee charged with focusing on the area of applied behavior analysis in research and practice, in order to recommend effective courses of action to deal with the legal, ethical, and professional issues raised by behavior-influencing procedures. The membership of the APA Commission on Behavior Modification included six psychologists, one psychiatrist, two attorneys active in mental-health law, and a philosopher. As with the American Psychiatric Association Task Force on Behavior Therapy, a wide range of viewpoints was represented. The commission's report was completed in 1977 (Stolz & Associates, 1978).

Societal Concerns

Since the late 1960's, private organizations and foundations have been increasingly involved in programs dealing with the ethics of behavioral interventions, and have called numerous conferences to explore the issues. For example, the Institute of Society, Ethics, and the Life Sciences of the Hastings Center (Hastings-on-Hudson, New York), founded in 1969, held a series of meetings between 1971 and 1973 in which leaders in mental-health research, practice, and public policy explored the problems of behavior control by drugs, the media, and physical manipulation of the brain, and discussed issues relating to the use of behavior control in education and in total institutions such as prisons and mental hospitals. The institute also established an experimental teaching program on medical ethics at Columbia University, and has a professional staff with a continuing interest in ethical issues. The Behavioral Law Center of the Institute for Behavioral Research (Silver Spring, Maryland) held a conference in 1975, directed explicitly to the ethics of behavior modification as used in closed institutions; the proceedings of that conference are published in the *Arizona Law Review* (1975, Issue 1).

Since the early 1970's, court decisions having direct or indirect implications for the practice of behavior modification have been increasingly frequent. Many of these cases involved attorneys from two organizations created in 1972, the Mental Health Law Project and the National Prison Project of the American Civil Liberties Union Foundation.

The developing mental health case law reflects societal concern about accountability, civil liberties, and the rights of all disadvantaged groups, including prisoners, mental patients, and the mentally retarded. Reviews of mental health law, as it relates to behavior modification, can be found in papers by Begelman (1975), P.R. Friedman (1975), Kassirer (1974a, 1974b), R. Martin (1975), Stolz, Wienckowski, and Brown (1975), and Wexler (1973). A continuing source of thoughtful commentary on this body of law is the *Journal of Psychiatry and Law*, which began publication in 1973.

  Congressional Involvement. In addition to the activities of the courts, congressmen have criticized behavioral technology and expressed concern about the treatment of research subjects and infringements on freedoms in therapy and research in general and in behavior modification in particular. The initial congressional interest in a behavioral technology grew out of publicity surrounding the Neuro-Research Foundation's research project on brain disease and violent behavior, funded jointly from 1971-1973 by the Law Enforcement Assistance Administration (LEAA) of the Department of Justice and by the Department of Health, Education, and Welfare. These projects planned to use psychosurgery and chemical interventions in experimental attempts to understand and control violent and destructive human behavior presumed to be a direct result of brain dysfunction.

Responding to congressional concern, the National Institute of Mental Health (NIMH) and the National Institute of Neurological and Communicative Disorders and Stroke (NINCDS) established an Inter-Institute Work Group on Brain and Behavior to examine a variety of aspects of the issue of psychosurgery. Also, NIMH published a detailed study of the merits and implications of psychosurgery (Brown, B.S., Wienckowski, & Bivens, 1973), and NINCDS sponsored four workshops on aggressive behavior. NINCDS also published a report on aggressive and violent behavior (U.S. Congress, 1974b) reviewing the present state of research on those topics, and recommending that any further research be conducted with careful protection for the rights of subjects involved in those studies.

Another area about which Congress has expressed considerable concern is the use of behavioral technology in prisons. Much interest has centered on a program at the Medical Center for Federal Prisoners, Springfield, Mo., called the Special Treatment and Rehabilitative Training Program, and given the acronym START. This program, supported by the Federal Bureau of Prisons, "had several ingredients of a behavior modification system [Friedman, P.R., 1975, p. 93]." It was designed for prisoners who had chronically failed to adjust to the environment of federal prisons; such prisoners, transferred to Missouri, were to be taught behavior necessary for prison life. The START program used a "level system," in which advancement to higher levels depended on the prisoner's cooperation with the routine. The initial level involved rather severe deprivations, which were supposed to enhance the reinforcing value of the program's consequences (Kassirer, 1974a, 1974b; Opton, 1974).

Hearings were held by the House of Representatives on the use of behavior modification in the START program (U.S. Congress, 1974a), and a suit was filed by the American Civil Liberties Union challenging the program on a variety of constitutional grounds.[4] The program was terminated by the Bureau of Prisons, which said that it was uneconomical because too few prisoners were involved for the expenses; as a result, the case was not decided on constitutional grounds. The court did rule, however, that prisoners transferred to such programs had minimal rights of due process, rights that had been violated in this instance (see Footnote 4).

The Senate Subcommittee on Constitutional Rights, and especially Senator Sam J. Ervin, Jr., also expressed concern about issues involving constitutional rights of prisoners, in the context of a general concern for constitutional rights of research subjects and institutionalized persons. Senator Ervin pressed the Law Enforcement Assistance Administration especially concerning the behavior-modification projects that it was supporting in prisons. In February 1974, the administrator of the LEAA announced that he had banned the use of LEAA funds for "psychosurgery, medical research, behavior modification—including aversion therapy—and chemotherapy [U.S. Congress, 1974b, p. 420]." The use of LEAA funds for behavior modification was banned "because there are no technical and professional skills on the LEAA staff to screen, evaluate or monitor such projects [p. 420]."

The termination of the programs was criticized by the American Psychological Association as an injustice to the public and to prison inmates. An APA news release (Feb. 15, 1974) said that the LEAA decision would tend to "stifle the development of humane forms of treatment that provide the of-

4. Clonce v. Richardson, 379 F. Supp. 338 (W.D.Mo. 1974).

fender the opportunity to fully realize his or her potential as a contributing member of society." As events turned out, however, the LEAA guidelines, when they became available, were written to permit research in areas that did not involve physical or psychological risk to the prisoners, and it seems that all behavior-modification programs, except those using aversive control, are considered not to involve such risks (cf. U.S. Congress, 1974b).

Completing its 3-year investigation of behavior modification, the Subcommittee on Constitutional Rights of the Committee of the Judiciary published a report of over 600 pages on the federal role in behavior modification and the implications of behavior-modification technology for individual rights (U.S. Congress, 1974b). This report documents in detail the extent of federal support for research on behavior modification, criticizes the government's involvement in such projects, and calls for "continuing legislative oversight . . . to ensure that constitutional rights and privacy are well protected [p. 45]" when behavior modification is used.

Another report generated in part by congressional concern about behavior-modification programs was by the National Institute of Mental Health (Brown, B.S., Wienckowski, & Stolz, 1975). This policy statement reviewed what is known about the efficacy of behavior modification and dealt with some of the relevant social concerns. The report concluded:

Professional evaluation of [behavior modification] techniques and public discussion of them can help prevent abuses in the use of behavior modification procedures, as well as foster public understanding and acceptance of beneficial procedures. . . . Both continued monitoring of behavior modification by the public and further research on this important technology are needed to serve society and the individuals who make it up [p. 24].

In 1974, Congress passed the National Research Act (PL 93-348), which, among other things, established the National Commission for the Protection of Human Subjects of Biomedical and Behavioral Research. The act also provides for the establishment of a permanent National Advisory Council for the Protection of Human Subjects, within the Department of Health, Education, and Welfare.

The establishment of the national commission followed exposure of several scandals involving research subjects, including the Tuskeegee, Alabama, syphilis experiments, in which subjects with syphilis were denied known effective treatments for many years because of their participation in the study; the research on violence and the brain, discussed previously, and research on a possible genetic basis for violence, the so-called XYY studies.

The life of the national commission was originally from 1974-1976, and was later extended. It was charged with developing regulations for research on human fetuses and with investigating several issues, including the implications for the protection of subjects of research advances such as behavior modification and the problems of obtaining informed consent from children, prisoners, and any institutionalized mentally infirm asked to participate in experiments. The national commission also has had a continuing concern with psychosurgery. It has been asked to determine the need for a mechanism extending the DHEW regulations for the protection of human subjects beyond DHEW-funded research activities to all activities with human subjects, including research and health services.

The national commission reports and makes recommendations to the Secretary of the Department of Health, Education, and Welfare; the National Research Act requires the Secretary to publish any recommendations that the commission makes and either to accept them or explain publicly why any changes have been made. The commission's first report (see Footnote 3) dealing with research on human fetuses, pregnant women, and human *in vitro* fertilization led to DHEW regulations in those areas (See Footnote 3).

Conclusion

Since World War II, control of those who do research with human subjects has been extended by professional and scientific organizations' codes, by litigation, and by legislation. The trend to increasingly close regulation has not yet come to an end; new regulations are currently being formulated. Although behavior-modification research and practice have been to some extent a stimulus for the regulations and rulings, by far the largest part of the concern has been with respect to medical research. Behavior-modification research and practice are, however, subject to the regulations that have been formulated, as well as to emerging legal rulings.

The court decisions, regulations, and codes are important steps in defining the rights of subjects, patients, and clients more clearly. Although behavior-modification research and service programs may have to adapt their procedures so that participants' rights are appropriately recognized, human rights have gained from the recent changes.

AN ANALYSIS OF ETHICAL CONCEPTS

In philosophy, ethics is, of course, not a collection of statements about what is right and wrong, but rather is the study of the nature of value concepts and of the general principles that justify the application of value judgments to human actions. What is ethics in the terminology of applied behavior analysis?

According to Skinner's (1971) analysis of ethical concepts, values refer to reinforcing consequences, and morals and ethics to the customs of groups or cultures. All these concepts have to do with the more remote consequences of our behavior, in Skinner's view. Making a value judgment, calling something good or bad, is a way of classifying the thing in terms of long-range reinforcing effects. In Skinner's example,

"You should (you ought to) tell the truth" is a value judgment to the extent that it refers to reinforcing contingencies. We might translate it as follows: "If you are reinforced by the approval of your fellow men, you will be reinforced when you tell the truth." The value is to be found in the social contingencies maintained for purposes of control. It is an ethical or moral judgment in the sense that ethos and mores refer to the customary practices of a group [pp. 112-113].

In this view, positively valued things are those that are reinforcing to us, and ethical or prescriptive statements ("You should tell the truth") are indirect references to controlling contingencies ("If you tell the truth, society, will generally reinforce your behavior"), including the contingencies that reinforce the behavior of the speaker ("If you tell the truth, that will reinforce my behavior").

Skinner (1971) contends that calling behavior "good" or "ethical" is a way of mediating otherwise long-term societal contingencies. In the long run, behavior that we identify as good or ethical will lead to reinforcement for the person behaving; identifying the cultural norm by labeling the behavior as good or ethical is an additional, more immediate consequence that functions to maintain the behavior. The ethical norm itself is, in this analysis, a statement of the social contingencies. Ethical behavior results when short-run personal reinforcers are congruent with long-run societal reinforcers; ethical conflicts reflect conflicts between reinforcement contingencies. For example, when behavioral researchers and civil libertarians differ on the ethical acceptability of an application of behavioral technology (Stolz, 1975), this disagreement could be seen as the result of the differing conditions of which the behavior of each group is a function.

Begelman (1973, 1975) contends that Skinner's naturalistic view of ethics incorrectly tries to reduce ethical issues simply to questions of fact. He argues that knowledge of the contingencies on the behavior of the various actors in a situation is an empirical matter only somewhat related to values, and would not in itself resolve an ethical dispute. Further, in his view, the behavioral approach to ethics should not be seen as a final means of solving these dilemmas.

A behavioral analysis may not be a final means of resolving ethical dilemmas. Nevertheless, analysis of the relevant short- and long-term contingencies can provide important insights into critical aspects of the behavior of those involved in environmental interventions. The rest of this chapter takes just such an approach to the discussion of the ethics of behavior modification.

Contingencies of Social and Educational Interventions

Researchers, clinicians, and other professionals using behavioral methods have been highly sensitive to the role of the contingencies of reinforcement in their interventions. Applied behavior analysis, as described in all the other chapters in this book, hinges on establishing new relations between the individual's behavior and the environment or on changing the existing relations.

When ethics is the topic, however, contingency analysis is ignored, and behaviorists fall back on notions of "autonomous man" (Skinner, 1971). Further, when behavioral professionals design procedures to protect the rights of participants in behavioral programs, the regulations and guidelines fail to consider the social contingencies affecting the behavior of those involved. For example, B.S. Brown et al. (1975) suggested the following procedures:

Ethical responsibility demands that members of the client population or their representatives be seriously consulted about both the means and the goals of programs, before the programs are introduced to change behavior. The persons planning the program need to evaluate the extent to which the members of the target population can give truly informed consent to the program. . . . The client himself, or the advisory committee, together with the mental health worker, should weigh the potential benefits to the client of the change that is expected to result from the proposed behavior modification program, against an evaluation of possible risks from using the program. . . .In many cases, the individual whose behavior is to be changed will be able to negotiate the proposed means and goals directly with the professional personnel. . . . However, when the program concerns individuals who have been shown to be incapable of making their own decision, it will be necessary for the mental health worker to deal with a representative or surrogate for the specific persons who would participate in the proposed program. . . . When the mental health worker is not directly accountable to his client, an advisory committee should be established that would cooperate with the mental health professional in choosing the methods and goals of the behavior modification program [pp. 20-21].

What classes of behavior are referred to in this passage? In the order in which they would occur in practice, they include the professional determining whether clients can give informed consent to the goals and means of the proposed program, deciding to consult representatives of the clients if the clients are not competent, preparing the consent form, weighing the risks and benefits together with clients or their representatives, and contracting with the clients or their representatives on goals and means.

This passage and the immediately subsequent paragraphs in that source do discuss possible consequences for various parts of this behavior chain. The reinforcers for the behavior involved in the decision to conduct an environmental intervention in a particular way with a particular goal have not, however, been adequately considered in most discussions of guidelines and regulations. Further, no empirical analysis of this decision-making sequence has been conducted. Rather, most attention in writings on the ethics of behavior modification has been directed toward the contingencies involved in the intervention, those contingencies explicitly manipulated in the course of doing research or delivering services.

The contingencies involved in deciding whether to intervene, which responses to modify, and how to modify them are no less important, even though they may be less obvious. Skinner (1971) has suggested: "We are likely to single out the conspicuous examples of control, because in their abruptness and clarity of effect, they seem to start something, but it is a great mistake to ignore the inconspicuous forms [pp. 168-169]." The remainder of this chapter is concerned with an analysis of these less conspicuous reinforcement contingencies.

Decision-Making in Behavioral Programs

The preceding paragraphs identified a few steps in the behavioral sequence that come before an intervention is initiated. Here is a more complete list of the relevant classes of behavior:
  - determining who the client is;
  - determining that some form of intervention is needed;
  - selecting possible goals for the program;
  - selecting alternative means of reaching those goals;
  - determining whether the target population can give informed consent to the goals and means of the program; if not, selecting representatives for them;
  - preparing a description of alternative goals and means;
  - weighing the risks and benefits, and contracting on the goals and means to be used.

The discussion will consider each of these classes of behavior in turn and attempt to identify sources of reinforcement for the behavior of the individuals involved. Although the technology of behavior modification may be ethically neutral (Skinner, 1971), every step of the sequence, from the determination of who the client is to the implementation of the intervention, involves behavior subject to immediate and long-term reinforcement: each step involves values.

  Who Is the Client? In each setting where interventions are made, for each type of individual found in those settings, professionals must decide who their client is, i.e., who the person or group is that controls the professionals' reinforcers. Typically, the client is the source of the professionals' salary or fee; ideally, the client is the person whose behavior is being modified.

In an out-patient setting, when clients' fees represent all or most of a therapist's reimbursement, the ostensible client is the actual one. In many instances, however, behavioral professionals receive their fees, salary, and employment from agencies or institutions not directly involved in the environmental intervention. The professional's client is then the agency, but the target of modification is a patient, prisoner, or student.

Holland (1977) pointed out that the mental health worker's client is always the person or institution who is paying the bills, the one who has hired the professional; behavioral professionals working for a school system, mental hospital, or prison cannot, in Holland's view, avoid having that institution as their client, regardless of the extent to which the pupil, prisoner, or inmate may be involved in decisions about the goals and means of the intervention. Fees, salaries, and employment are powerful immediate contingencies. Mental health workers have to avoid exceeding the limits of tolerance of their employer in order to avoid the loss of what may be their major source of income. As a result, when the long-term societal contingencies on their behavior, their values, conflict with their employer's goals, the short-run consequences are likely to compete successfully with the long-term ones. The mental health worker will resolve the ethical dilemma in a way that reflects the goals of the person or institution in control of the more powerful immediate contingencies.

Krasner and Ullmann (1965) made this point explicit: "If a person is being supported by society (as in a psychiatric hospital), then it is appropriate for an authorized agent of society to alter his behavior. On the other hand, behavior modification is inappropriate if the person is a self-supporting, contributing member of society [p. 363]." In other words, only when individuals are in control of the contingencies on their therapist are those individuals the appropriate ones to determine the goals for their own behavior; when those individuals are not paying the bills, but rather society (the hospital) has hired the professional, then, according to Krasner and Ullmann, it is up to society (the hospital personnel) and the professional to determine the course of the intervention. This approach is put into practice at the Huntsville-Madison County Mental Health Center, where goals for the clients are determined by the staff (who are paid chiefly by local funds), or, when the staff cannot decide on how to deal with a particular client, by community advisory boards who hold the final power in that center (Heldman, 1973).

In many of the settings in which behavioral technology is used, such as those described in the preceding chapters, the client may be different from the person whose behavior is to be changed. When significant short-run reinforcers are in the control of someone other than the target individual, professionals will tend to minimize the probability of losing those reinforcers by designing programs for the convenience of the true client (cf. Halleck, 1971; Szasz, 1970). Although the interests of the client may well coincide with those of the target individual, they also may not.

The distinction between the true client, who is the source of immediate reinforcers for the professional, and the individual who is the target of the

behavioral program is important especially in regard to the efficacy of countercontrol. Countercontrol—the influence on the behavior of the professional by the person who is the target of the behavioral program—is pervasive in behavior-change efforts. The behavior-influence process is always a
reciprocal one: One person may attempt to shape the behavior of another
through changing the consequences of that person's behavior, but at the
same time, the first person's behavior is shaped by the other's response.

When the professional's and client's values are congruent, countercontrol can be an important source of feedback to the mental-health worker,
providing information on the success of the intervention. On the other hand,
when professionals and clients do not share the same values, the clients'
influence on the professionals' behavior may be their only means of restrain-
ing attempts to change their behavior. Countercontrol requires access to
reinforcers, however. If a participant in a behavior-modification program
does not have control of reinforcers for the behavior-change agent, that
individual has lost a potent form of countercontrol.

Skinner (1971) pointed out that mental hospitals and institutions for the
retarded, for orphans, and for the senile "are noted for weak countercontrol,
because those who are concerned for the welfare of such people often do not
know what is happening. Prisons offer little opportunity for countercontrol
[p. 171]." In regard to the hospitals and institutions, those who are concerned for the welfare of the inmates often not only do not know what is
happening, but do not have control of the necessary reinforcers to change
the staff even if the outsiders were aware of institutional practices.

When participants in behavioral programs are not the client, they often
do not have access to many of the reinforcers that control the professional's
behavior, and thus have little opportunity for countercontrol. Prison inmates, for example, have little access to meaningful reinforcers for prison
employees, except through engaging in aggressive actions and prison riots.

One suggestion often made for compensating for participants' lack of
effective reinforcers for program personnel is to institute an advisory committee to cooperate with the professional in choosing the goals and methods
of the intervention. This committee is generally supposed to include representatives of those whose behavior is to be modified, their guardians, or
advocates. Establishing such an advisory committee does not resolve the
problem, however. Consider the sources of reinforcement for the individuals
on the committee. The official guardians of the participants in an intervention may, for example, have a vested interest in controlling them in a way
more convenient (and reinforcing) for the guardians than beneficial for their
wards (Friedman, P.R., 1975). Mental health professionals, receiving their
pay from the client institution, are still subject to its control.

At best, such an advisory committee provides a regularized opportunity
for conflicting points of view to be expressed, an opportunity generally not
otherwise available (Brown, B.S., et al., 1975). The group's discussions may
sensitize program administrators to the conflicting interests involved. The

reinforcement contingencies will still function, however, and subtle coercions may well be used to manipulate decisions.

Should the Behavior Be Modified?   Whether behavior should be modified involves the definition of deviance and individuals' roles in societal change. This is at the heart of the controversies over the ethics of interventions. Whenever an intervention is contemplated, a decision must be made about whether the target individual's behavior should be modified at all. The professional and any others involved in the decision-making process must determine whether the behavior of concern is deviant and whether some form of intervention is needed.

Some behavior is widely defined as deviant or inappropriate, i.e., it is positively reinforcing to no segment of society. Persons engaging in such behavior would presumably refer themselves for treatment. Examples of such behavior are severe self-injurious behavior or debilitating phobias. Other behavior is widely valued, and general agreement can be obtained that it is an appropriate goal of interventions. Examples include communication between marital partners and increased academic achievement (London, 1964; Shaw, 1972, Stolz, in press).

Conflicts about the appropriateness of intervening also tend to be minimal when the mental health professional and the target individual are similar in status and culture. When client and professional agree on values (London, 1964), when they have similar histories of reinforcement and are subject to similar cultural contingencies, their decisions about whether particular behavior should be modified are likely to agree.

The problems labeled as ethical dilemmas arise when the professional and the target individual are from different social classes or have different status (Stolz et al., 1975), or when the true client, professional, and target individual disagree among themselves on whether particular behavior should be modified. In such cases the decision-making process may be clarified if the definition of deviance is analyzed in behavioral terms.

Deviant or problem behavior can be described as that not positively reinforced by society as a whole, or not reinforcing to the agents of society. Krasner and Ullmann (1965), later in the passage quoted above, articulate this as follows: "The ultimate source of values is neither the patient's nor the therapist's wishes, but the requirements of the society in which both live [p. 363]." In other words, society, as the source of reinforcers, determines whether behavior should be changed.

If this definition were a comprehensive analysis of the long-range contingencies, so that all appropriate behavior was, in the final analysis, what society would consistently reinforce, one implication would be that values would not change. A definition of deviance as that behavior not reinforced by society as a whole or its agents includes no mechanism for changes in values. Yet we know that customs and values are constantly changing. What seems to happen is that different elements within society reinforce different behavior; society per se has few clear and consistent requirements. The conflicts referred to as ethical issues arise from disagreements among differing segments of society as to which behavior is best for the society in the long run.

Professionals' behavior is a product of their histories of reinforcement, including any long-range reinforcers that they have learned to value. Professionals may consider societal stability an important value, or change; they may value client self-determination or their own clinical judgment; they may consider society's institutions to be environments appropriate for the teaching of behavior useful for society in the long run, or environments designed to interfere with that behavior. The professionals' values and their behavior reflect what they have learned as a consequence of reinforcement from a larger or smaller part of the total society.

Contemporary critics of past interventions (Beit-Hallahmi, 1974; Halleck, 1971) argue that professionals have tended to be a conservative force, defining deviance in accord with majority values and adjusting people to existing conditions. In this view professional's values have been congruent with those who have power in society, and deviance has been defined in line with those values, i.e., in terms of what would reinforce the professionals and other people who have power in society. Behavior-change agents working for agencies and institutions are, unlike therapists working in private practice, under special pressure, these critics say, to define the goals of interventions in terms of society's accepted values (Halleck, 1971; Szasz, 1970) and to design programs to adapt individuals to the existing environment (Chapter 15).

In a climate in which many persons are questioning current values and advocating changes in society's values, these critics urge that the professional be an agent of social change, rather than social control (Halleck, 1971). Several writers have suggested, for example, that behavioral professionals should be less compliant when their client—whether agency, institution, or individual—defines a particular behavior as deviant and asks that it be changed. O'Leary (Chapter 6) says that behavioral clinicians should seriously question whether the behavior they are being asked to change should be changed (cf. O'Leary, K.D., 1972). Begelman (1975), Davison (1976), and Serber and Keith (1974) recommended that when homosexual clients ask for orgasmic retraining to become heterosexual, the behavioral clinician should first consider therapy that would aid the clients in dealing with the adverse reactions they receive from society because of their homosexuality. Only if the clients continue, after completing this program, to request sexual redirection do these writers suggest that the clinician provide such therapy.

The critics ask that behavioral professionals question the design of the existing environment (Martin, R., 1975), and they suggest that adjusting the individual to an inadequate environment may be a disservice to society (Chapter 15). In their view, professionals, rather than defining target individuals' behavior as deviant and teaching them the behavior needed to fit into society as presently constructed, should define the present structure of society as deviant and teach target individuals the behavior they will need to change society (cf. Halleck, 1971). Their recommendation thus calls for professionals who plan interventions to be responsive to a different set of reinforcers from those offered by society as a whole. They implicitly offer reinforcers contingent on the professionals changing society's values, but the professionals must reject the reinforcers of society at large to do so.

The recommendation that current practices and contingencies be changed for the long-range good of society implies that those making the recommendation know what the long-range good of society is, and what practices and contingencies are necessary to bring it about. However, although much behavior has been explained in terms of the extent to which it works for the survival of a culture (Skinner, 1971), the only way to discover which behavior has survival value and which reinforcers shape behavior good for society in the long run seems to be to wait and see. Even then, an analysis is not possible, because only correlational data are obtained. No empirical method that can be employed at any given time can indicate the long-range consequences of one practice relative to another with respect to societal survival.

Given this impasse, how can the decision be made about whether any given behavior should be modified? The critics of past interventions are correct that decisions have often been made without a balancing of differing value systems. The analysis of the possible outcomes of an intervention and their consequences should cover a broad range of possibilities. Persons involved in the decision-making process should attempt to specify what their values are, what reinforcers are controlling their behavior in the short and long run, and should be sensitive to potential conflicts among the value systems of the true client, the professional, and the target individual. They should attempt to identify the long-term consequences of the modification being considered. Because it is not likely that current practices will be either always beneficial or always harmful for the long-range good of society, intervention decisions should neither always follow current social values nor always target those values for change.

What Are Possible Alternative Goals? Once the decision is made to modify some behavior, once some behavior has been defined as a problem, the professional must decide in what direction modification should go.

Applied behavior analysis is identified with the study of socially significant behavior, behavior important to people and society, rather than behavior relevant only to theory, and with the production of changes of practical, rather than statistical importance (Baer, Wolf, & Risley, 1968; Chapter 3 in this book). No rules exist, however, for identifying which behavior is socially significant, although some steps have been made toward objective measures of whether the change obtained is large enough to be important. For the latter, the target individual's behavior can be compared with other individuals in the same environment, or consumers can be asked to evaluate their satisfaction with the behavior change obtained (Chapter 18).

No research has been done as yet on the goal-selection process (Kazdin, 1975a; Chapter 14 in this book). O'Leary (Chapter 6) called for empirical research to determine which goals are the most functional for particular groups in given settings. In order to plan research like that, however, a decision needs to be made first about what the desired long-range outcome is for those persons in that setting. A researcher cannot compare several alternative goals unless some external standard is available against which those goals can be measured. For example, before research can determine the amount of activity, noise, and rebellion consistent with optimum achievement in classrooms, a decision has to be made about what sort of achievement is desired and how much of it would be optimal. In short, conducting research on the problem does not resolve the value issue; it merely alters its form.

Regulations and recommendations concerning interventions suggest that the target individuals or their guardians be consulted about goals before behavior-change programs are introduced. Ideally, those directing interventions would offer target individuals or their guardians several alternative goals, explaining the potential benefits of each (Brown, B.S., et al., 1975). But how are those alternatives selected? The analysis suggests that the alternatives chosen reflect the short- and long-range contingencies on the professionals' behavior.

The target individuals, whether or not they are true clients, may also request some particular goals. As suggested earlier in this chapter, when the professional and the target individuals share values and are subject to the same reinforcement contingencies, it is likely that the professional will agree to the goals suggested by the target individuals. If they are not subject to the same contingencies, it is possible that the professional will reject the alternative offered, because of some long- or short-term consequences for the professional's behavior. When harsh parents ask for guidance in obtaining even firmer control over their children, behavioral professionals might refuse that request, even if the parents are paying them and hence are true clients. Similarly, therapists are not likely to acquiesce to a rapist's request for therapy to eliminate the anxiety associated with his crimes. In such cases, the professionals are responding to consequences other than the immediate reinforcement from their clients' fees. Possible reinforcers for their behavior would be verbal ones they give themselves or the approval of their peers, supervisors, and professional society, all of which presumably act to mediate some more long-range consequence. Mental-health professionals working for institutions such as mental hospitals and prisons have, in the past, tended to select target behavior that was conducive to good order in the ward or cell block, to passive, apathetic obedience on the part of the target individuals (Halleck, 1971; Holland, 1977; Shaw, 1972). The previous section of this chapter suggested that behavioral professionals should be more sensitive to the value implications of the selection of the goals of interventions. The process of environmental and behavioral change can act to strengthen existing societal practices or can help to engineer social change. Behavioral professionals should realize that their decisions can play a role in whether society's values remain stable or change. If professionals analyze the contingencies controlling their own behavior, then the decision among alternative goals for interventions can be made in the context of the reinforcers available for various classes of target behavior.

Operating as agents of social change, behavioral professionals can teach lower-class persons assertive skills needed for effective community action (Shaw, 1972); alternatively, they can teach them submissive behavior and middle-class values (Heldman, 1973). Educational interventions can teach school children to be still, quiet, and docile; alternatively, behavioral professionals can analyze the reinforcement contingencies of the classroom situation and design them so as to emphasize enhancing academic achievement (Winett & Winkler, 1972; Chapter 15 in this book). Behavior-modification programs can be used in prisons to control the rebellious and nonconformist behavior of the inmates (Dirks, 1974; Opton, 1974); behavioral professionals can also concentrate on developing programs to build social and occupational skills useful to the prisoners once they are released.

More generally, goals offered to target individuals can adjust their behavior to the existing contingencies or teach behavior that may be useful for changing the environment (Halleck, 1971). The decision between these alternative goals should be made after an analysis of the long- and short-term contingencies on the behavior of those involved in the intervention. Neither type of goal should be excluded without consideration of the effects of such a decision.

How Should the Behavior Be Modified!   In planning an intervention, decisions must be made about the means to be used, as well as about the goals of the intervention. The preceding chapters in this book provide many examples of how behavior modification is conducted. It typically involves redesigning the existing contingencies of reinforcement, shaping new behavior, and extinguishing or punishing the existing deviant (inappropriate) behavior.

In the selection of the alternative methods to be considered, the behavior of the professional and the target individuals is, like all other behavior, responsive to the contingencies of society. Although the technology of behavior modification may provide information on the efficacy of various interventions, it does not mandate any particular one for any particular problem. Rather, the behavioral professional chooses from among an array of possible methods. Reinforcers that may affect that choice include the approval of the professional's peers and supervisors, and consideration of the short- and long-range good of the target individuals.

Holland's (1978) analysis of the process of selection of treatment modalities identifies another contingency that appears to control the selection of the method of intervention in at least some cases—the professional's own ethical system. Holland points out that painful aversive stimuli are commonly restricted to use for behavior that is the object of severe sanction, retaliation, scorn, and retribution, such as alcoholism, sexual deviance, and substance abuse. For these classes of behavior, punishers such as electric (faradic) shock, emetic (nausea-inducing) drugs such as apomorphine, and paralytic drugs, chiefly succinylcholine chloride (Anectine) are used. The latter produces a brief but total paralysis, including paralysis of the respiratory muscles and consequently a temporary but terrifying sensation of death by drowning.

The use of aversive techniques for the treatment of substance abuse and certain sexual behavior is generally justified on the grounds that the immediate consequences of such behavior are naturally reinforcing, even though the long-term consequences may be detrimental to the individual (Stolz et al., 1975). Holland (1978) appears to be correct, however, in pointing out that strong aversive techniques are used only for behavior that society considers repugnant.

Painful aversive stimuli seem to be used seldom, if ever, as treatments for behavior that society values, even though it would be possible to design training programs incorporating aversive stimuli that might be effective in building such behavior. For example, alcoholics are administered electric shocks (Sobell & Sobell, 1973), given apomorphine (Rachman & Teasdale, 1969), or treated with Anectine (Farrar, Powell, & Martin, 1968) to decrease the future probability of the behavior society defines as inappropriate. Compare this to an intervention that is likely to be used with a comparable case in which the deviant behavior is not subject to strong negative social consequences: Nonassertive adults engage too frequently in submissive behavior, just as the alcoholic person's problem is an excess of drinking behavior. Nonassertive individuals are not, however, shocked when they emit submissive responses; rather, therapists generally ignore nonassertive behavior while modeling and reinforcing assertive responses.

Similarly, when homosexuals are receiving behavioral treatment intended to redirect their interests to heterosexual stimuli, shock (Serber & Keith, 1974), emetic drugs (Stolz, in press), or Anectine (Reimringer, Morgan, & Bramwell, 1970) is used to punish arousal to homosexual stimuli. Compare this to an analogous case: A preschool child may spend a large portion of the school day staying near the teachers, so much so that the child's interests need to be redirected to playing primarily with peers. The typical intervention for such a child would be withdrawal of the teachers' attention to the child's behavior when the child is playing with peers. The child would certainly not be given shocks when near the teachers.

In short, although behavioral professionals have justified the selection of particular types of interventions in terms of short-term contingencies, the professionals' values—the long-term contingencies—have been an unrecognized factor in the selection of at least some forms of intervention.

Can Informed Consent Be Obtained? Informed consent is "the cornerstone of all considerations of the welfare and protection of subjects [Wolfensberger, 1967]" and, more broadly, of patients and clients as well (Stolz, in press). *Informed consent* is a legal term, referring to clients' right to decide whether they want to participate in a proposed program after they have been told what will be involved. More specifically, informed consent is considered to have three components: knowledge, voluntariness, and competency (Friedman, P.R., 1975).

"Knowledge" is the "informed" part of informed consent, and refers to describing the nature of the program and its goals, explaining that target individuals may refuse to participate before the program begins or at any time during the program, describing the risks and benefits associated with the program, and offering alternative programs. "Voluntariness" refers to the absence of coercion or duress when the decision to consent is made; "competency" reflects an assessment that the target individuals can understand the information that has been given to them and can make a judgment about it (cf. Friedman, P.R., 1975; Martin, R., 1975).

These legal terms need to be considered in the context of the conceptual framework of applied behavior analysis. Whether the target population has been given the information necessary to meet the "knowledge" requirement can be assessed objectively. Whether target individuals are competent to make the necessary decisions is, in principle, subject to objective measurement, although no generally accepted procedures have been developed yet for doing this, and no operational rules exist specifying how the description of the goals and methods of a proposed program should be modified so that otherwise incompetent individuals might be able to understand the explanations (Stolz, in press).

The part of informed consent most difficult to deal with in behavioral terms is the component of voluntariness. Legally, voluntariness refers to an absence of coercion and threat at the time the decision is made, so that the individual can choose freely. If, however, behavior is considered to be a function of environmental contingencies, it can be argued that all behavior is "coerced" by either negative or positive controls. In this view, we may feel freer in the absence of aversive control (Skinner, 1971), but we are no less under the control of contingencies.

Goldiamond (1969) has offered one possible behavioral interpretation of voluntariness. He suggests that behavior can be called voluntary when a range of alternative responses is available, with a range of consequences contingent on them (cf. Krasner, 1965). Understanding voluntariness in behavioral terms requires also an analysis of coercion. Maley and Hayes' (1977) analysis is that coercion reflects intrusive contingencies, contrasting with the individual's history of reinforcement, where the control tends to be through punishment, threat of punishment, deprivation of positive reinforcement, or the use of positive reinforcement in a barren environment, and where the reinforcers are so strong that compliance is very likely.

Voluntariness is difficult to ensure when those participating in a program are prisoners (Shapiro, M.H., 1974), but it is a problem with any institutionalized group (Martin, R., 1975; Spece, 1972). Even when institutionalized persons can understand the information given them and are competent to make a decision about an intervention, the range of response alternatives and contingencies available to them is often limited, and they typically live in a relatively barren environment, even if no other coercions are present.

The people that tend to be involved in behavior-modification programs are children, prisoners, and institutionalized persons such as the senile, retarded, and mentally ill. With children and institutionalized persons, uncertainties about informed consent revolve chiefly around their knowledge and competency (Lasagna, 1969); with prisoners, the primary issue relates to voluntariness (Kassirer, 1974a; Spece, 1972).

Consideration of the difficulties in obtaining truly informed consent with many types of target individuals has led various writers (e.g., Davison & Stuart, 1975; Schwitzgebel, 1975; Wexler, 1975; Wolfensberger, 1967) to offer alternative formulations. The intent of these is to rectify the defects in informed consent so that the rights of participants in interventions might be protected. A problem with all these alternatives, however, is that they are no more behavioral than the legal definition of informed consent, and hence are difficult to apply and do not take adequate account of the contingencies operating on the behavior of the persons involved.

The problems in obtaining informed consent have led others to recommend the elimination of experimental therapy programs when truly informed consent cannot be obtained (see Footnote 5). This recommendation is meant to refer to all types of therapy, not just to behavior modification. It is, of course, abhorrent to consider abandoning all attempts to help others, simply because of defects inherent in the concept of informed consent. Rather, when seeking to obtain consent, professionals should attempt to include in their description of an intervention an explanation of the contingencies presumed to operate on their behavior and on their clients' (cf. Alumbaugh, 1972). In that way, whatever safeguards are possible may be built in.

How Are Alternatives Presented?   Once alternative goals and methods of the intervention have been selected, they must be presented to the target individuals or their representatives for a final decision. When the intervention is part of a research program, the alternatives are presented in the consent form. In therapy, alternatives are generally discussed with the target individual by the therapist without a formal, written presentation.

Whoever makes the selection, the alternatives should, of course, be presented in such a way that they can be understood. Further, the alternatives should be designed so as to make explicit the reinforcers that may be operating on the behavior of the persons involved (Day, 1977). The presentation of the relevant contingencies should include not only the contingencies that would be part of the intervention, but also other contingencies on the behavior of the target persons that may affect their decision (Stolz, 1975), as well as contingencies on the behavior of the person recommending the intervention and those on the true client's behavior, if that individual is someone different from the target person. Public identification of these contingencies facilitates countercontrol.

Reinforcers outside the intervention that might affect the behavior of the target person include that person's values and the approval of the professional. Reinforcers for the professionals, apart from a possible preference for one of the alternative interventions on the ground of convenience or predicted efficacy, include their values and approval from their peers or supervisors. When the intervention proposed is part of a research program, the need for subjects may well influence the researcher's description of available alternatives (Barber, Lally, Makarushka, & Sullivan, 1973; Beecher, 1966; Gray, 1975). In the absence of other controls the professional will design the presentation of alternative goals and intervention techniques so that the target individual will make the decision most reinforcing to the professional.

In addition to making explicit the contingencies on the behavior of the people involved at all levels in the intervention, alternative interventions could be described by individuals who are advocates of those methods (Stolz, in press), particularly in instances where the proposed intervention would be seriously intrusive and potentially irreversible. In the *Kaimowitz* case,[5] for example, although the patient had agreed to psychosurgery after hearing his friendly doctor explain its advantages and risks, he withdrew his consent after a doctor with a different viewpoint also befriended him and then described his view of the risks of the surgery. Having an advocate for each side of the issue—for and against a particular intervention—thus made a major difference in the final outcome in this case.

How Are Decisions about Means and Goals Made? At the end of this long sequence of decision-making behavior, decisions must be made about whether to modify behavior, which response to modify and with what expected outcome, and how to modify the behavior. Ideally, the target individuals themselves would select the goals and methods of the intervention. When the target individuals or their representatives are involved in these decisions, they become part of the control process and have an influence on the design of the intervention. This, together with full exposure of the relevant contingencies, maximizes the possibilities for countercontrol. When, for any reason, the target individuals are unable to make decisions about the goals and methods of the intervention, good practice

5. Kaimowitz v. Department of Mental Health for the State of Michigan, 42 U.S.L.W. 2063 (1973).

calls for the appointment of an advisory committee to cooperate with the mental health professional in choosing the program goals (Brown, B.S., et al., 1975).

Whether the decisions are made by the target individuals or a committee, however, the thesis of this chapter is that those decisions themselves are behavior responsive to social contingencies, so that the goals and methods chosen will reflect the contingencies functional on the individuals making the selections.

A recommendation often made (Brown, B.S., et al., 1975; Ulrich, 1967) is that public awareness of behavioral principles be increased by dissemination efforts, so that people will have a better understanding of how environmental events can control their behavior. As public awareness increases, the likelihood lessens of people's behavior being manipulated without their awareness. "Awareness alone, however, is a weak countervalence," as Bandura (1974, p. 868) has said. Rather, awareness of behavioral principles needs to be combined with effective countercontrol through clients' access to meaningful reinforcers for professionals' behavior.

SUMMARY AND CONCLUSIONS

The latter part of this chapter reviewed, step by step, the behavior involved in designing the goals and methods of interventions in an attempt to identify the contingencies operating on the behavior of the various persons concerned, and to consider ethical issues from the point of view of applied behavior analysis. The contingencies and controls are there; this chapter calls attention to them so that controls and countercontrols might be better designed, and so that further analysis might be directed at these aspects of the interaction between professionals and their clients.

If principles of ethics are to be consistent with the approach of applied behavior analysis, they will have to begin with the kind of specification attempted in this chapter. This approach is consistent with the caution expressed by Skinner (1971): "The misue of a technology of behavior is a serious matter, but we can guard against it best by looking . . . at the contingencies under which [controllers] control [p. 182]."

References
And
Citation Index

REFERENCE ABBREVIATIONS

The following abbreviations are used for standard journals.

AJP	American Journal of Psychology	JCPP	Journal of Comparative and Physiological Psychology
AP	American Psychologist	JEAB	Journal of the Experimental Analysis of Behavior
ARP	Annual Review of Psychology	JECP	Journal of Experimental Child Psychology
BRT	Behavior Research and Therapy	JEdP	Journal of Educational Psychology
BT	Behavior Therapy	JEP	Journal of Experimental Psychology
CD	Child Development		
Cog P	Cognitive Psychology		
DP	Developmental Psychology	JER	Journal of Educational Research
EC	Exceptional Children		
ET	Educational Technology	JP	Journal of Psychology
HD	Human Development	JPSP	Journal of Personality and Social Psychology
JABA	Journal of Applied Behavior Analysis	JVLVB	Journal of Verbal Learning and Verbal Behavior
JACP	Journal of Abnormal Child Psychology	MPQ	Merrill Palmer Quarterly
JAP	Journal of Abnormal Psychology	PB	Psychological Bulletin
		P Rec	Psychological Record
JASP	Journal of Abnormal and Social Psychology	P Rep	Psychological Reports
		P Rev	Psychological Review
JCCP	Journal of Consulting and Clinical Psychology	PS	Psychonomic Science
		RER	Review of Educational Research

677

[Bracketed numbers indicate pages on which references are cited]

ABT ASSOCIATES, INC. *Education as experimentation: Evaluation of a planned varia-tion model.* Report No. AAI-74-13. Cambridge, Mass., 1973.   [370, 556-557]
ABT ASSOCIATES, INC. *Education as experimentation: A planned variation model.* Vol. IV. Cambridge, Mass., 1977.   [369, 375]
ADDISON, R., & HOMME, L. E. The reinforcing event (RE) menu. *National Society for Programmed Instruction Journal,* 1966, **5**, 8-9.   [505]
AD HOC COMMITTEE ON ETHICAL STANDARDS IN PSYCHOLOGICAL RESEARCH. *Ethical principles in the conduct of research with human participants.* Washington, D.C.: American Psychological Association, 1973.   [656]
AINSWORTH, M. D. S. *Infancy in Uganda: Infant care and the growth of love.* Baltimore: Johns Hopkins University Press, 1967.   [131]
AINSWORTH, M. D. S. Attachment and dependency: A comparison. In J. L. Gewirtz (Ed.), *Attachment and dependency.* Washington D.C.: Winston, 1972.
                                                                       [123, 130-131]
AINSWORTH, M. D. S. The development of infant-mother attachment. In B. M. Caldwell & H. N. Ricciuti (Eds), *Review of child development research. Vol. 3.* Chicago: University of Chicago Press, 1973.   [123]
AINSWORTH, M. D. S., & WITTIG, B. A. Attachment and exploratory behavior of one-year-olds in a strange situation. In B. M. Foss (Ed.), *Determinants of infant behaviour. Vol. IV.* London: Methuen, 1969.   [132]
ALBA, E., & PENNYPACKER, H. S. A multiple change score comparison of traditional and behavioral college teaching procedures. *JABA,* 1972, **5**, 121-124.
                                                                       [491, 493-496, 506]
ALLEN, D. J. Some effects of advance organizers and level of question on the learning and retention of written social studies material. *JEdP,* 1960, **61**, 333-339. [469]
ALLEN, G. J. Case study: Implementation of behavior modification techniques in summer camp settings. *BT,* 1973, **4**, 570-575.   [86-88]
ALLEN, J. D., PHILLIPS, E. L., PHILLIPS, E. A., FIXSEN, D. L. & WOLF, M. J. *The Achievement Place novel.* Lawrence: University of Kansas Printing Service, 1972.   [625]
ALLEN, M. W., ROZIN, P., & GLEITMAN, L. R. *A test of the blending abilities of Kindergarten children using syllable and phoneme segments.* Unpublished man-uscript, University of Pennsylvania, 1972.   [441]
ALLPORT, F. H. *Social psychology.* Cambridge, Mass.: Houghton Mifflin, 1924.
                                                                       [144]
ALUMBAUGH, R. V. Another "Malleur Maleficarum"? *AP,* 1972, **27**, 897-889. [674]
AMERICAN PSYCHOLOGICAL ASSOCIATION. Revised ethical standards of psychologists. *APA Monitor,* March 1977, 22-23.   [656]
ANDERSON, R. C. Educational psychology. *ARP, 1967,* **18**, 103-164.   [459]
ANDERSON, R. C. Control of student mediating processes during verbal learning and instruction. *RER,* 1970, **40**, 349-369.   [468]
ANDERSON, R. C. & FAUST, G. W. *Educational psychology: The science of instruc-tion and learning.* New York: Dodd, Mead, 1973.   [484]
ANDERSON, R. C., KULHAVY, R. W., & ANDRE, T. Feedback procedures in pro-grammed instruction. *JEdP,* 1971, **62**, 148-156.   [462]
ANDERSON, R. C., KULHAVY, R. W. & ANDRE, T. Conditions under which feedback facilitates learning from programmed lessons. *JEdP,* 1972, **63**, 186-188. [462]
ANGELL, D., & LUMSDAINE, A. A. *The effects of prompting trials and partial correc-tion procedures on learning by anticipation.* (AFOSR 1343), Research Report air-C14-9/65-SR5. San Mateo, Calif.: American Institute for Research, 1961.
                                                                       [464]

ANTONITOS, J. J. Response variability in the white rat during conditioning, extinction, and reconditioning. *JEP*, 1951, **42**, 273-281. [36]

APPEL, L., COOPER, R., KNIGHT, J., MCCARROLL, N., YUSSEN, S. & FLAVELL, J. The development of the distinction between perceiving and memorizing. *CD*, 1972, **43**, 1365-1381. [163]

ARONFREED, J. *Imitation and identification: An analysis of some affective and cognitive mechanisms.* Paper presented at the biennial meeting of the Society for Research in Child Development, New York, March 1967. [139]

ARONFREED, J. The concept of internalization. In D. A. Goslin (Ed.), *Handbook of socialization theory and research.* Skokie, Ill.: Rand McNally, 1969. (a)
[139, 146]

ARONFREED, J. The problem of imitation. In L. P. Lipsett & H. W. Reese (Eds), *Advances in child development and behavior.* Vol. 4. New York: Academic Press, 1969. (b) [144, 146-147]

ATKINSON, R. C. Computerized instruction and the learning process. *AP*, 1968, **23**, 225-239. [475]

ATKINSON, R. C. (Ed.) *Contemporary psychology: Readings from Scientific American.* San Francisco: Freeman, 1971. [578]

AUSUBEL, D. P., & FITZGERALD, D. Meaningful learning and retention: Interpersonal cognitive variables. *RER*, 1961, **31**, 500-510. [469]

AUSUBEL, D. P., & ROBINSON, R. G. *School learning: An introduction to educational psychology.* New York: Holt, Rinehart and Winston, 1969. [482, 484]

AXELROD, S. Comparison of individual and group contingencies in two special classes. *BT*, 1973, **4**, 83-90. [194]

AXELROD, S., HALL, R. V., WEIS, L. & ROHRER, S. Use of self-imposed contingencies to reduce the frequency of smoking behavior. In M. J. Mahoney & C. E. Thoresen (Eds.), *Self-control: Power to the person.* Monterey, Calif.: Brooks/Cole, 1974. [93]

AYALA, H. E., MINKIN, N., PHILLIPS, E. L., FIXSEN, D. L., & WOLF, M. M. Achievement Place: The training and analysis of vocational behavior. *JABA*, 1978, **11**, in press. [617]

AYLLON, T., & AZRIN, N. H. Reinforcement and instructions with mental patients. *JEAB*, 1964, **7**, 327-331. [33]

AYLLON, T., & AZRIN, N. H. The measurement and reinforcement of behavior of psychotics. *JEAB*, 1965, **8**, 357-383. [2, 527]

AYLLON, T., & AZRIN, N. H. Punishment as a discriminative stimulus and conditioned reinforcer with humans. *JEAB*, 1966, **9**, 411-419. [46]

AYLLON, T. & AZRIN, N.H. *The token economy: A motivational system for therapy and rehabilitation.* New York: Appleton-Century-Crofts, 1968. [200, 562, 629]

AYLLON, T., LAYMAN, D. & BURKE, S. Disruptive behavior and reinforcement of academic performance. *P Rec*, 1972, **22**, 315-323. [188]

AYLLON, T., & ROBERTS, M. D. Eliminating discipline problems by strengthening academic performance. *JABA*, 1974, **7**, 71-76. [50, 183, 187, 188]

M. D. Eliminating discipline problems by strengthening academic performance. *JABA*, 1974, **7**, 71-76. [50, 183, 187, 188]

AZRIN, N. H. Some effects of two intermittent schedules of immediate and nonimmediate punishment. *JP*, 1956, **42**, 3-21. [46]

AZRIN, N. H. Time-out from positive reinforcement. *Science*, 1961, **133**, 382-383. [35]

AZRIN, N. H. Punishment of elicited aggression. *JEAB*, 1970, **14**, 7-10. [28]

AZRIN, N.H., & HAKE, D. F. Positive conditioned suppression: Conditioned suppression using positive reinforcers as the unconditioned stimuli. *JEAB*, 1969, **12**, 167-173. [52]

AZRIN, N.H., & HOLZ, W. C. Punishment. In W. K. Honig (Ed.), *Operant behavior: Areas of research and application*. New York: Appleton-Century-Crofts, 1966.
[46, 199]
AZRIN, N. H., HOLZ, W. C., HAKE, D. F., & AYLLON, T. Fixed-ratio escape reinforcement. *JEAB*, 1963, 6, 449-456.   [42]
AZRIN, N. H., HOLZ, W. C., ULRICH, R. & GOLDIAMOND, I. The control of the content of conversation through reinforcement. *JEAB*, 1961, 4, 25-30.   [75]
AZRIN, N. H., & HUTCHINSON, R. R. Conditioning of the aggressive behavior of pigeons by a fixed-interval schedule of reinforcement. *JEAB*, 1967, 10, 395-402.
[28]
AZRIN, N. H., HUTCHINSON, R. R., & HAKE, D. F. Pain-induced fighting in the squirrel monkey. *JEAB*, 1963, 6, 620.   [27]
AZRIN, N. H., HUTCHINSON, R. R., & HAKE, D. F. Extinction-induced aggression. *JEAB*, 1966, 9, 191-204.   [27]
AZRIN, N. H., HUTCHINSON, R. R., & MCLAUGHLIN, R. The opportunity for aggression as an operant reinforcer during aversive stimulation. *JEAB*, 1965, 8, 171-180.   [28]
AZRIN, N. H., & LINDSLEY, O. R. The reinforcement of cooperation between children. *JASP*, 1956, 52, 100-102.   [217]
AZRIN, N. H., NASTER, B. J., & JONES, R. Reciprocity counseling: A rapid learning-based procedure for marital counseling. *BRT*, 1973, 11, 365-382.   [651]
AZRIN, N. H., & POWELL, J. Behavioral engineering: The reduction of smoking behavior by a conditioning apparatus and procedure. *JABA*, 1968, 1, 193-200.
[271]
AZRIN, N.H., & WESOLOWSKI, M. D. Theft reversal: An overcorrection procedure for eliminating stealing by retarded persons. *JABA*, 1974, 7, 577-581. [64, 83]
BADDELEY, A. D. & HITCH, G. Working memory. In G. H. Bower (Ed.), *The psychology of learning and motivation. Vol. 8*. New York: Academic Press, 1974.   [389]
BAER, D. M. Escape and avoidance response of preschool children to two schedules of reinforcement withdrawal. *JEAB*, 1960, 3, 155-159.   [42]
BAER, D. M. Laboratory control of thumbsucking by withdrawal and representation of reinforcement. *JEAB*, 1962, 5, 525-528.   [47]
BAER, D. M. Some remedial uses of the reinforcement contingency. In J. Shlien (Ed.), *Research in psychotherapy. Vol. III*. Washington D.C.: American Psychological Association, 1968.   [82]
BAER, D. M. An age-irrelevant concept of development. *MPQ*, 1970, 16, 238-245.
[117, 170]
BAER, D. M. In the beginning, there was the response. In E. Ramp & G. Semb (Eds.), *Behavior analysis: Areas of research and application*. Englewood Cliffs, N.J.: Prentice-Hall, 1975.   [79, 608]
BAER, D. M., PETERSON, R. F., & SHERMAN, J. A. The development of imitation by reinforcing behavioral similarity to a model. *JEAB*, 1967, 10, 405-416.
[106, 163, 172, 174, 326, 342]
BAER, D. M., & SHERMAN, J. A. Reinforcement control of generalized imitation in young children. *JECP*, 1964, 1, 37-49.   [33, 149, 151, 159, 171, 175]
BAER, D. M., WOLF, M. M., & RISLEY, T. R. Some current dimensions of applied behavior analysis. *JABA*, 1968, 1, 91-97.
[2, 61, 63, 79, 100, 470-473, 483, 492, 497, 500, 526, 669]
BAILEY, J. S., TIMBERS, G. D., PHILLIPS, E. L., & WOLF, M. M. Modification of articulation errors of pre-delinquents by their peers. *JABA*, 1971, 4, 265-281.
[64, 613]

BAILEY, J. S., WOLF, M. M., & PHILLIPS, E. L. Home-based reinforcement and the modification of predelinquents' classroom behavior. *JABA*, 1970, **3**, 223-233.
[187, 615]
BAILEY, L. G. Contingency management in college foreign language instruction. In J. M. Johnson (Ed.), *Behavior research and technology in higher education.* Springfield, Ill.: Charles C Thomas, 1975.   [491, 492]
BAKWIN, H. Loneliness in infants. *American Journal of Diseases of Children*, 1942, **63**, 30-40.   [108]
BAKWIN, H. Emotional deprivation in infants. *Journal of Pediatrics, 1949*, **35**, 512-521.   [108]
BANDURA, A. Influence of model's reinforcement contingencies on the acquisition of imitative responses. *JPSP*, 1965, 1, 589-595. (a)   [147, 164]
BANDURA, A. Vicarious processes: A case of no-trial learning. In L. Berkowitz (Ed.), *Advances in experimental social psychology. Vol. 2.* New York: Academic Press, 1965. (b)   [148, 164, 167, 168]
BANDURA, A. *Principles of behavior modification.* New York: Holt, Rinehart & Winston, 1969. (a)   [167, 168, 172, 202]
BANDURA, A. Social-learning theory of identificatory processes. In D. A. Goslin (Ed.), *Handbook of socialization theory and research.* Skokie, Ill.: Rand Mc-Nally, 1969. (b)   [139]
BANDURA, A. Analysis of modeling processes. In A. Bandura (Ed.), *Psychological modeling: Conflicting theories.* Chicago: Aldine-Atherton, 1971. (a)
[144, 146-148, 159, 164, 165, 167, 168, 178]
BANDURA, A. Vicarious and self-reinforcement processes. In R. Glaser (Ed.), *The nature of reinforcement.* New York: Academic Press, 1971. (b)
[164, 253, 267]
BANDURA, A. Modeling theory: Some traditions, trends, and disputes. In R. D. Parke (Ed.), *Recent trends in social learning theory.* New York: Academic Press, 1972.
[165]
BANDURA, A. Behavior theory and the models of man. *AP*, 1974, **29**, 259-869.
[579, 676]
BANDURA, A., & BARAB, P. G. Conditions governing nonreinforced imitation. *DP*, 1971, **5**, 244-255.   [163, 172, 173]
BANDURA, A., GRUSEC, J. E., & MENLOVE, F. L. Observational learning as a function of symbolism and incentive set. *CD*, 1966, **37**, 499-506.   [148]
BANDURA, A., & HARRIS, M. B. Modification of syntactic style. *JECP*, 1966, 4, 341-352.   [147, 163]
BANDURA, A., & JEFFREY, R. W. Role of symbolic coding and rehearsal processes in observational learning. *JPSP*, 1973, **26**, 122-130.   [167, 170]
BANDURA, A., & PERLOFF, B. Relative efficacy of self-monitored and externally imposed reinforcement systems. *JPSP*, 1967, **7**, 111-116.   [147, 201, 253]
BANDURA, A., & ROSENTHAL, T. L. Vicarious classical conditioning as a function of arousal level. *JPSP*, 1966, **3**, 54-62.   [147, 177]
BANDURA, A., ROSS, D., & ROSS, S. A. A comparative test of the status envy, social power, and secondary reinforcement theories of identificatory learning. *JASP*, 1963, **67**, 527-534. (a)   [148, 151]
BANDURA, A., ROSS, D., & ROSS, S. A. Vicarious reinforcement and imitative learning. *JASP*, 1963, **67**, 601-607.(b)   [147, 151]
BANDURA, A., & WALTERS, R. H. *Social learning and personality development.* New York: Holt, Rinehart & Winston, 1963.   [147]
BARBER, B., LALLY, J. J., MAKARUSHKA, J. L., & SULLIVAN, D. *Research on human subjects.* New York: Russell Sage Foundation, 1973.   [675]

BARLOW, D. H., BECKER, R., LEITENBERG, H., & AGRAS, W. S. A mechanical strain gauge for recording penile circumference change. *JABA*, 1970, **3**, 73-76.
[68]
BARLOW, D. H., & HERSEN, M. Single-case experimental designs. *Archives of General Psychiatry*, 1973, **29**, 319-325.   [89]
BARLOW, J. A. Conversational chaining in teaching machine programs. *P Rep*, 1960, **7**, 187-193.   [462]
BARLOW, J. A. *Stimulus and response*. New York: Harper & Row, 1968.   [463]
BARON, J. The word superiority effect. In W. K. Estes (Ed.), *Handbook of learning and cognitive processes. Vol. 6.* Hillsdale, N.J.: Erlbaum Asociates, 1978.
[415, 436]
BARON, J. & STRAWSON, C. Use of orthographic and word-specific knowledge in reading words aloud. *JEP, Human Perception and Performance*, 1976, **2**, 386-393.   [416]
BARTON, E. S., GUESS, D., GARCIA, E., & BAER, D. M. Improvements of retardates' mealtime behaviors by timeout procedures using multiple baseline techniques. *JABA*, 1970, **3**, 77-84.   [65]
BAUER, D. Pupil behavior project a surprise to board. *Washington Star-News*, October 23, 1972, D-1.   [580]
BAUM, W. M. The correlation-based law of effect. *JEAB*, 1973, **20**, 137-153. [248]
BAYLEY, N. *The Bayley scales of infant development*. New York: The Psychological Corp., 1969.   [114]
BEARISON, D. J. The role of measurement operations in the acquisition of conservation. *DP*, 1969, **1**, 653-660.   [384, 399]
BECK, B. B. Cooperative tool use by captive Hamadryas baboons. *Science*, 1973, **182**, 594-597.   [279]
BECK, I. L. *Comprehension during the acquisition of decoding skills*. Pittsburgh: University of Pittsburgh, Learning Research and Development Center, 1977 (No. 4).   [390]
BECK, I. L., & MITROFF, D. D. *The rationale and design of a primary grades reading system for an individualized classroom*. (Publication No. 1972/4; ERIC Document Reproduction Service No. ED 063 100.) Pittsburth: University of Pittsburgh, Learning Research and Development Center, 1972.   [390]
BECKER, J., & JACKSON, D. A. *The behavior Analysis phonics primer: Teacher's manual*. Lawrence, Kansas: Student Behavior Laboratories, Inc., 1974.
[541]
BECKER, W. A., & SHUMWAY, L. K. Innovative methods of learning in a general genetics course. *Journal of Heredity*, 1972, **63**, 122-128.   [491, 496]
BECKER, W. C., & ENGELMANN, S. *Analysis of achievement data on six cohorts of low-income children from 20 school districts in the University of Oregon direct instruction Follow Through model*. (Technical Report No. 76-1.) Eugene: University of Oregon Follow Through Project, April 1976.   [369, 371]
BECKER, W. C., ENGELMANN, S., & THOMAS, D. R. *Teaching: A course in applied psychology*. Chicago: Science Research Associates, 1971.   [517]
BECKER, W. C., ENGELMANN, S., & THOMAS, D. R. *Teaching 1: Classroom management*. Palo Alto, Calif.: Science Research Associates, 1975. (a)   [364]
BECKER, W. C., ENGELMANN, S., & THOMAS, D. R. *Teaching 2: Cognitive learning and instruction*. Palo Alto, Calif.: Science Research Associates, 1975. (b)
[325, 334, 337-338, 346]
BEECHER, H. K. Ethics and clinical research. *New England Journal of Medicine*, 1966, **274**, 1354-1360.   [675]
BEGELMAN, D. A. Ethical and legal issues of behavior modification. In M. Hersen, R. *tal Disease*, 1973, **156**, 412-419.   [662]

BEGELMAN, D.A. Ethical and legal issues of behavior modification. In M. Hersen, R. M. Eisler, & P. M. Miller (Eds.), *Progress in behavior modification. Vol. 1.* New York: Academic Press, 1975.   [658, 662, 668]

BEIT-HALLAHMI, B. Salvation and its vicissitudes: Clinical psychology and political values. *AP*, 1974, **29**, 124-129.   [668]

BELL, R. Q. A reinterpretation of the direction of effect in studies of socialization. *P Rev*, 1968, **75**, 81-95.   [113]

BELL, S. M., & AINSWORTH, M. D. S. Infant crying and maternal responsiveness. *CD*, 1972, **43**, 1171-1190.   [123-126, 131]

BELLER, E. K. Dependency and independence in young children. *Journal of Genetic Psychology*, 1955, **87**, 25-35.   [130]

BELLER, E. K. Exploratory studies of dependency. *Transactions of the New York Academy of Sciences*, 1959, **21**, 114-426.   [130]

BENNETT, P. S., & MALEY, R. S. Modification of interactive behaviors in chronic mental patients. *JABA*, 1973, **6**, 609-620.   [90]

BERKO, J. The child's learning of English morphology. *Word*, 1958, **14**, 150-177.   [287]

BERLYNE, D. E. Curiosity and exploration. *Science*, 1966, **153**, 25-33.   [160]

BERMAN, M. L. Shaping performance on programmed materials. *P Rep*, 1967, **21**, 29-32.   [462]

BERNARD, H. W. *Psychology of learning and teaching.* New York: McGraw-Hill, 1972.   [484]

BERNSTEIN, B. A sociolinguistic approach to socialization: With some reference to educability. In F. Williams (Ed.), *Language and poverty.* Chicago: Markham Publishing, 1970.   [305, 306]

BERNSTEIN, B. A critique of the concept of compensatory education. In C. B. Cazden, V. P. John, & D. Hymes (Eds.), *Functions of language in the classroom.* New York: Teachers College Press, 1972.   [306]

BERNSTEIN, J. E. Ethical considerations in human experimentation. *Journal of Clinical Pharmacology*, 1975, **15**, 579-590.   [654]

BEVAN, W. Behavior in unusual environments. In H. Helson & W. Bevan (Eds.), *Contemporary approaches to psychology.* Princeton, N.J.: Van Nostrand, 1967.   [109]

BIJOU, S. W. A systematic approach to an experimental analysis of young children. *CD*, 1955, **26**, 161-168.   [106]

BIJOU, S. W. What psychology has to offer education—now. *JABA*, 1970, 3, 65-71.   [484]

BIJOU, S. W. *Development in the preschool years: A functional analysis.* Paper presented at the meeting of the American Psychological Association, New Orleans, September 1974. (a)   [124]

BIJOU, S. W. Focus. *JABA*, 1974, 7(1), inside back cover. (b)   [191]

BIJOU, S. W., & BAER, D. M. Some methodological contributions from a functional analysis of child development. In L. P. Lipsitt & C. C. Spiker (Eds.), *Advances in child development and behavior. Vol. 1.* New York: Academic Press, 1963.   [106, 118]

BIJOU, S. W., & BAER, D. M. *Child development. Vol. II. Universal stage of infancy.* New York: Appleton-Century-crofts, 1965.   [106, 124]

BIJOU, S. W., PETERSON, R. F., & AULT, M. H. A method to integrate descriptive and experimental field studies at the level of data and empirical concepts. *JABA*, 1968, 1, 175-191.   [62, 64, 71]

BIJOU, S. W., PETERSON, R. F., HARRIS, F. R., ALLEN, K. E., & JOHNSTON, M. S. Methodology for experimental studies of young children in natural settings. *P Rec*, 1969, **19**, 177-210.   [62, 79, 83]

BIJOU, S. W., & STURGES, P. T. Positive reinforcers for experimental studies with children—consumables and manipulables. *CD*, 1959, **30**, 151-170.   [106]

BILLINGS, D. B. *PSI versus the lecture course in the principles of economics: A quasi-controlled experiment.* Paper presented at the West Coast PSI Conference, Long Beach, Calif., 1972.   [494, 496]

BILODEAU, I. McD., & SCHLOSBERG, H. Similarity in stimulating conditions as a variable in retroactive inhibition. *JEP*, 1951, **4**, 199-204.   [302]

BIRK, L., STOLZ, S. B., BRADY, J. P., BRADY, J. V., LAZARUS, A. A., LYNCH, J. J., ROSENTHAL, A. J., SKELTON, W. D., STEVENS, J. B., & THOMAS, E. J. *Behavior therapy in psychiatry.* Washington, D.C.: American Psychiatric Association, 1973.   [657]

BIRNBAUM, P. *A treasury of Judaism.* New York: Hebrew Publishing Co., 1962.   [179]

BIRNBRAUER, J. S., WOLF, M. M., KIDDER, J. D., & TAGUE, C. E. Classroom behavior of retarded pupils with token reinforcement. *JECP*, 1965, **2**, 219-235.   [2, 189, 527]

BISESE, V. S. Imitation behavior as a function of direct and vicarious reinforcement. *Dissertation Abstracts*, 1966, **26**, 6155.   [165]

BITGOOD, S. C., & KUCH, D. O. *A contingency managed introductory psychology course with a graduated point system.* Report to the Council on Teaching, University of Iowa, 1971.   [505]

BITGOOD, S. C., & SEGRAVE, K. A comparison of graduated and fixed point systems of contingency managed instruction. In J. M. Johnston (Ed.), *Behavior research and technology in higher education.* Springfield, Ill.: Charles C Thomas, 1975.   [502]

BLANK, M. Cognitive processes in auditory discrimination in normal and retarded readers. *CD*, 1968, **39**, 1091-1101.   [433]

BLOCK, J. H. (Ed.) *Mastery learning: Theory and practice.* New York: Holt, Rinehart and Winston, 1971.   [491]

BLOOM, B. S. (Ed.) *Taxonomy of educational objectives. Handbook I. Cognitive domain.* New York: Longmans, Green, 1956.   [471]

BLOOM, D., HOOD, L., & LIGHTBOWN, P. Imitation in language development: If, when, and why. *Cog P*, 1974, **6**, 380-420.   [171]

BLOOM, L. *Language development.* Cambridge, Mass.: The M.I.T. Press, 1970.   [309, 313]

BLOOMFIELD, T. M. Reinforcement schedules: contingency or contiguity. In R. M. Gilbert & J. R. Millenson (Eds.) *Reinforcement: behavioral analysis.* New York: Academic Press, 1972.   [248]

BLOUGH, D. S. Delayed matching in the pigeon. *JEAB*, 1959, **2**, 151-160.   [59]

BOLLES, R. C. Reinforcement, expectancy, and learning, *P Rev*, 1972, **79**, 394-410.   [250]

BOREN, J. J. An experimental social relation between two monkeys. *JEAB*, 1966, **9**, 691-700.   [211, 223, 229]

BORN, D. G. Exam performance and study behavior as a function of study unit size. In J. M. Johnston (Ed.), *Behavior research and technology in higher education.* Springfield, Ill.: Charles C Thomas, 1975.   [505, 513, 514]

BORN, D. G., DAVIS, M., WHELAN, P., & JACKSON, D. College student study behavior in a personalized instruction course and in a lecture course. In G. Semb (Ed.), *Behavior analysis and education.* Lawrence: University of Kansas, 1972.   [493-497, 507]

BORN, D. G., GLEDHILL, S. M., & DAVIS, M. L. Examination performance in lecture-discussion and personalized instruction courses. *JABA*, 1972, **5**, 33-43.   [488-490, 492-497, 499, 500, 505, 506]

BORN, D. G., & HERBERT, E. W. A further study of personalized instruction for students in large university classes. *Journal of Experimental Education*, 1971, **40**, 6-11. [515, 518, 584]

BORN, D. G., & WHELAN, P. Some descriptive characteristics of student performance in PSI and lecture courses. *P Rec*, 1973, **23**, 145-152. [505, 506]

BORN, D. G., & ZLUTNICK, S. Personalized instruction, or what to do when they put a number on the back of your sport coat, issue you a bullhorn, and schedule your class in the football stadium. *ET*, September 1972. 30-34. [485]

BOSTOW, D. E., & BAILEY, J. B. Modification of severe disruptive and aggressive behavior using brief time-out and reinforcement procedures. *JABA*, 1969, **2**, 31-37. [80]

BOSTOW, D. E., & BLUMFELD, G. J. The effect of two test retest procedures on the classroom performance of undergraduate college students. In G. Semb, (Ed.), *Behavior analysis and education*. Lawrence: University of Kansas, 1972. [510, 512]

BOSTOW, D. E., & O'CONNOR, R. J. A comparison of two college classroom testing procedures: Required remediation versus no remediation. *JABA*, 1973, **6**, 599-607. [497, 502, 505, 510, 512]

BOUSFIELD, W. A., & BARCLAY, W. D. The relationship between order and frequency of occurrence of restricted associative responses. *JEP*, 1950, **40**, 643-647. [289]

BOWER, G., & KAUFMAN, R. Transfer across drives of the discriminative effect of a Pavlovian conditioned stimulus. *JEAB*, 1963, **6**, 445-448. [52]

BOWERMAN, M. *Early syntactic development*. London: Cambridge University Press, 1973. [313]

BOWERS, K. S. Situationism in psychology: An analysis and a critique. *P Rev*, 1973, **80**, 307-336. [187]

BOWLBY, J. The influence of early environment in the development of neurosis and neurotic character. *International Journal of Psychoanalysis*, 1940, **21**(2), 154-178. [108]

BOWLBY, J. Maternal care and mental health. *Bulletin of the World Health Organization*, 1951, **3**, 355-534. [108]

BOWLBY, J. Some pathological processes set in train by early mother-child separation. *Journal of Mental Science*, 1953, **99**, 265-272. [108]

BOWLBY, J. The nature of the child's tie to his mother, *International Journal of Psychoanalysis*, 1958, **39**, 1-34. [127, 128, 131]

BOWLBY, J. *Attachment and loss. Vol. 1. Attachment*. New York: Basic Books, 1969. [129, 130, 131]

BOWLBY, J. *Attachment and loss. Vol. 2. Separation: Anxiety and anger*. New York: Basic Books, 1973. [129]

BRACELAND, F. J. Historical perspectives of the ethical practice of psychiatry. *American Journal of Psychiatry*, 1969, **126**, 230-237. [653]

BRAINE, M. D. S. On learning the grammatical order of words. *P Rev*, 1963, **70**, 323-348. [278]

BRAUKMANN, C. J., FIXSEN, D. L., KIRIGIN, K. A., PHILLIPS, E. A., PHILLIPS, E. L., & WOLF, M. M. Achievement Place: the training and certification of teaching parents. In W. S. Wood (Ed.) *Issues in evaluating behavior modification*. Champaign, Ill.: Research Press, 1975. [625]

BRAUKMANN, C. J., MALONEY, D. M., FIXSEN, D. L., PHILLIPS, E. L., & WOLF, M. M. An analysis of selection interview instructional package for pre-delinquents at Achievement Place. *Criminal Justice and Behavior*, 1974, **1**, 30-42. [616]

BRIGHAM, T. A., GRAUBARD, P. S., & STANS, A. Analysis of the effects of sequential reinforcement contingencies on aspects of composition. *JABA*, 1972, **5**, 421-429. [183, 205, 318]

BRIGHAM, T. A., & STOERZINGER, A. An experimental analysis of children's preference for self-selected rewards. In T. A. Brigham, R. Hawkins, J. Scott, & T. F. McLaughlin (Eds.), *Behavior analysis in education: Self-control and reading.* Dubuque, Iowa: Kendall/Hunt, 1976. [265]

BRODEN, M., BRUCE, C., MITCHELL, M. A., CARTER, V., & HALL, R. V. Effects of teacher attention on attending behavior of two boys at adjacent desks. *JABA*, 1970, **3**, 199-203. [67, 90]

BROOKS, L. Visual pattern in fluent word identification. In A. S. Reber & D. Scarborough (Eds.), *Reading: The CUNY conference.* Hillsdale, N.J.: Erlbaum Associates, 1977. [415, 416, 436, 448]

BROOKS, R. B., & SNOW, D. L. Two case illustrations of behavior modification in school settings. *BT*, 1972, **3**, 100-103. [206]

BROTSKY, J. S., & THOMAS, K. Cooperative behavior in preschool children. *PS*, 1967, **9**, 337-338. [218]

BROUDY, H. S. Historic examples of teaching method. In N. L. Gage (Ed.), *Handbook of research on teaching.* Skokie, Ill.: Rand McNally, 1963. [514]

BROWN, B. S., WIENCKOWSKI, L. A., & BIVENS, L. W. *Psychosurgery: Perspective on a current issue.* (DHEW Publication No. (HSM) 73-9119.) Washington, D.C.: U.S. Government Printing Office, 1973. [658]

BROWN, B. S., WIENCKOWSKI, L. A., & STOLZ, S. B. *Behavior modification: Perspective on a current issue.* (DHEW Publication No. (ADM) 75-202.) Washington, D.C.: U.S. Government Printing Office, 1975. [660, 663, 666, 670, 676]

BROWN, D. L. Some linguistic dimensions in auditory blending. In F. Green (Ed.), *Reading: The right to participate. Yearbook of the National Reading Conference*, 1971, **20**, 227-236. [441, 446]

BROWN, P. L., & JENKINS, H. M. Auto-shaping of the pigeon's key peck. *JEAB*, 1968, **11**, 1-8. [28, 29]

BROWN, R. *A first language: The early stages.* Cambridge, Mass.: Harvard University Press, 1973. [279-280, 298, 309, 313]

BROWN, R., & HANLON, C. Derivational complexity and order of acquisition in child speech. In J. R. Hayes (Ed.), *Cognition and the development of language.* New York: Wiley, 1970. [310-312]

BROWNELL, W. R., & STRETCH, L. B. The effect of unfamiliar settings on problem solving. *Duke University Research Studies in Education*, 1931, No. 1. [382]

BRUNER, J. S. *The process of education.* Cambridge, Mass.: Harvard University Press, 1961. [486]

BRUNER, J. S. Some theorems of instruction illustrated with reference to mathematics. *Yearbook of the National Society for the Study of Education*, 1964, **63** (Pt. 1), 306-335. [398-399]

BRUNER, J. S. *Toward a theory of instruction.* Cambridge, Mass.: Belknap, 1966. [468]

BRUNSWIK, E. The conceptual focus of some psychological systems. *Journal of Unified Science*, 1939, **8**, 36-49. [135]

BUCHANAN, C. D. *Programmed reading.* (3rd ed.) St. Louis: McGraw-Hill (Webster), 1973. [536, 544]

BUCHER, B., & HAWKINS, J. Comparison of response cost and token reinforcement systems in a class for academic underachievers. In R. D. Rubin & J. P. Brady (Eds.), *Advances in behavior therapy. Vol. 4.* New York: Academic Press, 1973. [200]

BUDZYNSKI, T. H., & STOYVA, J. M. An instrument for producing deep muscle relaxation by means of analog information feedback. *JABA*, 1969, **2**, 231-237. [651]

BUELL, J., STODDARD, P., HARRIS, F., & BAER, D. M. Collateral social development accompanying reinforcement of outdoor play in a preschool child. *JABA*, 1968, **1**, 167-173. [89]

BUGELSKI, B. R. *The psychology of learning applied to teaching.* Indianapolis: Bobbs-Merrill, 1964. [483]

BULLOCK, D. H. Repeated conditioning-extinction sessions as a function of the reinforcement schedule. *JEAB*, 1960, 3, 241-243. [43]

BURCHARD, J. D. Systematic socialization: A programmed environment for the habilitation of antisocial retardates. *P Rec*, 1967, 17, 461-476. [200, 528, 566]

BURGESS, H., EPLING, E., LLOYD, K. E. & MORROW, J. E. *Performance under group and individual contingencies in a contingency management system.* Paper presented at the meeting of the Western Psychological Association, San Francisco, April 1971. [499, 501, 516]

BURGESS, R. L., CLARK, R. N., & HENDEE, J. C. An experimental analysis of anti-litter procedures. *JABA*, 1971, 4, 71-75. [68]

BURNSTEIN, D. Individualized instruction and minimal pacing procedures applied to introductory psychology. *The College Student Journal.* 1971, 5 (Nov-Dec), 17-21. [485]

BURT, D. W. Study and test performance of college students on concurrent assignment schedules. In J. M. Johnston (Ed.), *Behavior research and technology in higher education.* Springfield, Ill.: Charles C. Thomas, 1975. [500, 501, 502, 507, 510]

BURTON, R. V., & WHITING, J. W. M. The absent father and cross-sex identity. *MPQ*, 1961, 7, 85-95. [139]

BUSHELL, D., JR. *Classroom behavior: A little book for teachers.* Englewood Cliffs, N.J.: Prentice-Hall, 1973. [465, 535]

BUSHELL, D., JR. The design of classroom contingencies. In F. S. Keller & E. Ribes-Inesta (Eds.), *Behavior modification.* New York: Academic Press, 1974. (a) [185]

BUSHELL, D., JR. *Tokens for the behavior analysis classroom: A teaching guide.* Lawrence: University of Kansas Support and Development Center for Follow Through, 1974. (b) [541]

BUSHELL, D., JR., & BRIGHAM, T. A. Classroom token systems as technology. In M. C. Berman (Ed.), *Motivation and learning: Applying contingency management techniques.* Englewood Cliffs, N.J.: Educational Technology, 1971. [1, 483]

BUSHELL, D., JR., JACKSON, D. A., & WEISS, L. C. Quality control in the Behavior Analysis approach to Project Follow Through. In W. S. Wood (Ed.),, *Issues in evaluating behavior modification.* Champaign, Ill.: Research Press, 1975. [525, 541]

BUSHELL, D., JR., & RAMP, E. A. *The behavior analysis classroom.* Lawrence: University of Kansas Support and Development Center for Follow Through, 1974. [541]

BUSHELL, D., JR., WROBEL, P. A., & MICHAELIS, M. L. Applying "group" contingencies to the classroom study behavior of preschool children. *JABA*, 1968, 1, 55-63. [186, 189, 197]

BYRD, L. D. Responding in the pigeon under chained schedules of food presentation: The repetition of a stimulus during alternate components. *JEAB*, 1971, 16, 31-38. [31]

CALFEE, R., CHAPMAN, R., & VENEZKY, R. How a child needs to think to learn to read. In L. W. Gregg (Ed.), *Cognition and learning in memory.* New York: Wiley, 1972. [420, 425]

CALVIN, A. D. A psychologist looks at the "teaching" of economics at the undergraduate level. In K. G. Lumsden (Ed.), *Recent research in economics education.* Englewood Cliffs, N.J.: Prentice-Hall, 1970. [491]

CAMPBELL, D. T., & STANLEY, J. C. Experimental and quasi-experimental designs for research and training. In N. L. Gage (Ed.), *Handbook of research on teaching.* Skokie, Ill.: Rand McNally, 1963. [79, 96, 98]

CARNINE, D. W. Effects of two teacher presentation rates on off-task behavior, answering correctly, and participation. *JABA*, 1976, **9**, 199-206. [375]

CARON, A. J. Conceptual transfer in preconceptual children as a consequence of dimensional highlighting. *JECP*, 1968, **6**, 522-542. [115]

CARRERA, F., III & ADAMS, P. L. An ethical perspective on operant conditioning. *Journal of the American Academy of Child Psychiatry*, 1970, **9**, 607-623. [652]

CARROLL, J. B. Defining language comprehension: Some speculations. In J. B. Carroll & R. O. Freedle (Eds.), *Language comprehension and the acquisition of knowledge*. Washington D.C.: Winston, 1972. [291-292]

CARROLL, J. B., & FREEDLE, R. O. (Eds.) *Language comprehension and the acquisition of knowledge*. Washington, D.C.: Winston, 1972. [291]

CARUSO, J. L., & RESNICK, L. B. *Task sequence and overtraining in children's learning and transfer of double classification skills.* (Publication No. 1971/18; ERIC Document Reproduction Service No. ED 058 969.) Pittsburgh: University of Pittsburgh, Learning Research and Development Center, 1971. [387]

CATANIA, A. C. Concurrent operants. In W. K. Honig (Ed.), *Operant behavior: Areas of research and application.* New York: Appleton-Century-Crofts, 1966. [53, 54]

CATANIA, A. C. Chomsky's formal analysis of natural languages: A behavioral translation. *Behaviorism*, 1972, **1**, 1-15. [276]

CATANIA, A. C. The psychologies of structure, function, and development. *AP*, 1973, **28**, 434-442. [4, 411]

CATANIA, A. C. The myth of self-reinforcement. *Behaviorism*, 1975, **3**, 192-199. [253]

CATANIA, A. C., & CUTTS, D. Experimental control of superstitious responding in humans. *JEAB*, 1963, **6**, 203-208. [26]

CATANIA, A. C., & REYNOLDS, G. S. A quantitative analysis of the responding maintained by interval schedules of reinforcement. *JEAB*, 1968, **11**, 327-383. [39]

CAZDEN, C. B. The neglected situation in child language research and education. In F. Williams (Ed.), *Language and poverty.* Chicago: Markham, 1970. [306]

CHALL, J. *Learning to read: The great debate.* New York: McGraw-Hill, 1967. [426, 438]

CHARNIAK, E. *Toward a model of children's story comprehension* (A1-TR-266.) Cambridge, Mass.: Artificial Intelligence Laboratory, 1972. [406]

CHARTERS, W. W., JR. The social background of teaching. In N. L. Gage (Ed.), *Handbook of research on teaching.* Skokie, Ill.: Rand McNally, 1963. [530]

CHENEY, C. D., & POWERS, R. B. A programmed approach to teaching in the social sciences. *Improving College and University Teaching*, 1971, **19**, 164-166. [485, 501]

CHOMSKY, N. *Syntactic structures.* 'sGravenhage: Mouton, 1957. [287]

CHOMSKY, N. Review of B. F. Skinner's *Verbal behavior. Language*, 1959, **35**, 26-58. [308]

CHOMSKY, N. *Aspects of the theory of syntax.* Cambridge, Mass.: The M. I. T. Press, 1965. [275, 308, 310, 427]

CHOMSKY, N. *Language and mind. (Enlarged ed.)* New York: Harcourt Brace Jovanovich, 1972. [275, 279, 304]

CHOMSKY, N., & HALLÉ, M. *The sound pattern of English.* New York: Harper & Row, 1968. [427]

CHRISTY, P. R. Does use of tangible rewards with individualized children affect peer observers? *JABA*, 1975, **8**, 187-196. [68, 90]

CLARK, D. C. Teaching concepts in the classroom: A set of teaching prescriptions derived from experimental research. *JEdP*, 1971, **62**, 253-278. [349]

CLARK, H. B. A program of delayed consequences for the management of class attendance and disruptive classroom behavior of 124 special education children. In G. Semb (Ed.), *Behavior analysis and education–1972*. Lawrence: University of Kansas Press, 1972.   [566]

CLARK, H. B., BOYD, S. B., & MACRAE, J. W. A classroom program teaching disadvantaged youths to write biographic information. *JABA*, 1975, **8**, 67-75.   [89]

CLARK, M., LACHOWICZ, J., & WOLF, M. M. A pilot basic education program for school drouputs incorporating a token reinforcement system. *BRT*, 1968, **6**, 183-188.   [184]

CLARK, R. A., WILLIAMS, F., & TANNENBAUM, P. H. Effects of shared referential experience upon encoder-decoder agreement. *Language and Speech*, 1965, **8**, 253-262.   [303]

CLARK, R. N., BURGESS, R. L., & HENDEE, J. C. The development of antilitter behavior in a forest campground. *JABA*, 1972, **5**, 1-5.   [98]

CLARK, S. G. An innovation for introductory sociology: Personalized system of instruction. In J. M. Johnston (Ed.), *Behavior research and technology in higher education*. Springfield, Ill.: Charles C Thomas, 1975.   [496]

COATES, B., & HARTUP, W. W. Age and verbalization in observational learning. *DP*, 1969, **1**, 556-562.   [166]

COHEN, H. L., & FILIPCZAK, J. *A new learning environment*. San Francisco: Jossey-Bass, 1971.   [50, 184, 206]

COHEN, H. L., FILIPCZAK, J., & BIS, J. S. CASE project. In J. Schlien (Ed.), *Research in psychotherapy. Vol. 3*. Washington, D.C.: American Psychological Association, 1968.   [2, 566]

COHEN, H. L., FILIPCZAK, J., & BIS, J. CASE project: Contingencies applicable to special education. Silver Springs, Md.: Educational Facility Press, Institute for Behavioral Research, 1967. (Mimeo).   [527]

COHEN, H. L., FILIPCZAK, J., BOREN, J., GODING, I., STORM, R., BISHOP, R., & BREILING, J. *Academic and social behavior change in a public school setting*. Silver Springs, Md.: Educational Facility Press, Institute for Behavorial Research, 1974.   [567, 569]

COHEN, H. L., KEYWORTH, J. M., KLEINER, R. Y., & LIBERT, J. M. The support of school behaviors by home-based reinforcement via parent-child contingency contracts. In E. A. Ramp & B. L. Hopkins (Eds.), *A new direction for education: Behavior analysis 1971*. Lawrence: University of Kansas Press, 1971.   [566]

COHEN, H. L., KIBLER, R. J., & MILES, D. T. A preliminary report on a pilot study for educating low achievers. *The Superior Student*, 1964, **3**, 36-45.   [527]

COHEN, P. S. DRL escape: Effects of minimum duration and intensity of electric shock. *JEAB*, 1970, **13**, 41-50.   [42]

COLE, C., MARTIN, S., & VINCENT, J. A comparison of two teaching formats at the college level. In J. M. Johnston (Ed.), *Behavior research and technology in higher education* Springfield, Ill.: Charles C Thomas, 1975.   [495, 498, 506]

COLEMAN, J. S., et al. *Equality of educational opportunity*. Washington D.C.: U.S. Department of Health, Education, and Welfare, Office of Education, 1966.
                                                                      [438, 530]

COLLIER, K. L., & SMITH, R. V. A behavior-based laboratory course in educational psychology. *ET*, 1971, **11** (Nov), 24-28.   [485]

COLMAN, A. D., & BOREN, J. J. An information system for measuring patient behavior and its use by staff. *JABA*, 1969, **2**, 207-214.   [66]

CONANT, J. B. *Trial and error in the improvement of education*. Washington, D.C.: Association for Supervision and Curriculum Development, U.E.A., 1961. [473]

CONE, J. D. Assessing the effectiveness of programmed generalization. *JABA*, 1973, 6, 713-718. [191]

COOK, D., & MECHNER, F. Fundamentals of programmed instruction. In S. Margulies & L. D. Eigen (Eds.), *Applied programmed instruction*. New York: Wiley, 1961. [461]

COOK, J. O. Processes underlying learning a single paired-associate item. *JEP*, 1958, 56, 455. [464]

COOK, J. O., & KENDLER, T. S. A theoretical model to explain some paired-associate learning data. In G. Finch & F. Cameron (Eds.) *Symposium on Air Force human engineering, personnel and training research*. Washington, D.C.: NAS-NRC, 1956. [464]

COOPER, J. L. Learning theory and effective instruction, *Journal of Higher Education*, 1973, 44, 217-234. [485]

COOPER, J. L., and GREINER, J. M. Contingency management in an introductory psychology course produces better retention. *P Rec*, 1971, 21, 391-400.
[493-496, 498, 505, 506, 512, 518]

COREY, J. R., & SHAMOW, J. The effects of fading on the acquisition and retention of oral reading. *JABA*, 1972, 5, 311-315. [566]

COREY, J. R., VALENTE, R. G., & SHAMOW, M. K. The retention of material learned in a personalized introductory psychology course. In J. G. Sherman (Ed.), *Personalized system of instruction*. Menlo Park, Calif.: Benjamin, 1974.
[493-496, 498]

COSSAIRT, A., HALL, R. V., & HOPKINS, B. L. The effects of experimenter's instructions, feedback, and praise on teacher praise and student attending behavior. *JABA*, 1973, 6 89-100. [198]

CRADLER, J. D., & GOODWIN, D. L. Conditioning of verbal behavior as a function of age, social class, and type of reinforcement. *JEdP*, 1971, 62, 779-784. [470]

CRANBERG, L. Ethical code for scientists? *Science*, 1963, 141, 1242. [656]

CROWDER, N. A. Automatic tutoring by means of intrinsic programming. In E. H. Galanter (Ed.), *Automatic teaching. The state of the art*. New York: Wiley, 1959.
[456, 466]

CROWDER, N. A. Characteristics of branching programs. In O. M. Haugh (Ed.), *The University of Kansas Conference on Programmed Learning. Vol. II*. Lawrence: University of Kansas Publications, 1961. [460]

CROWDER, N. A. The rationale of intrinsic programming. *Programmed Instruction*, 1962, 1, 3-6. [457]

CUMMING, W. W., & BERRYMAN, R. The complex discriminated operant: Studies of matching-to-sample and related problems. In D. I. Mostofsky (Ed.), *Stimulus generalization*. Stanford: Stanford University Press, 1965. [59]

CURRAN, W. J. Governmental regulation of the use of human subjects in medical research: The approach of two federal agencies. In P. A. Freund (Ed.), *Experimentation with human subjects*. New York: Braziller, 1969. [655, 656]

DALLETT, K., & WILCOX, S. G. Contextual stimuli and proactive inhibition. *JEP*. 1968, 78, 475-480. [302]

DALTON, A. J., RUBINO, C. A., & HISLOP, M. W. Some effects of token rewards on school achievement of children with Down's syndrome. *JABA*, 1973, 6, 251-260.
[189]

D'AMATO, M. R. Derived motives, *ARP*, 1974, 25, 83-106. [463]

DANIEL, W. J. Cooperative problem solving in rats. *Journal of Comparative Psychology*. 1942, 34, 361-368. [229]

D'ARRUDA, J. A. self-paced program of instruction at a two year institution. *The Physics Teacher*, 1973, 11, 177-178. [491]

DAVIS, J., & BITTERMAN, M. E. Differential reinforcement of other behavior (DRO): A yoked-control comparison, *JEAB*, 1971, 15, 237-241. [49]

DAVIS, R. H., MARZOCCO, F. N., & DENNY, M. R. Interaction of individual differences with modes of presenting programmed instruction. *JEdP*, 1970, **61**, 198-204 [470]

DAVISON, G. C. *Homosexuality: The ethical challenge, JCCP*, 1976, **44**, 157-162. [668]

DAVISON, G. C., & STUART, R. B. Behavior therapy and civil liberties. *AP*, 1975, **30**, 755-763. [652, 674]

DAY, W. F. Radical behaviorism in reconciliation with phenomenology, *JEAB*, 1969, **12**, 315-328. [167]

DAY, W. F. Ethical philosophy and the thought of B. F. Skinner. In J. E. Krapfl & E. A. Vargas (Eds.) *Behaviorism and ethics*. Kalamazoo, Mich.: Behaviordelia, 1977. [675]

DeCASPER, A. J., & ZEILER, M. D. Steady-state behavior in children: A method and some data, *JECP*, 1972, **13**, 231-239. [39]

deCHARMS, R. *Personal causation*, New York: Academic Press, 1968. [194]

DECI, E. L. The effects of externally mediated rewards on intrinsic motivation. *JPSP*, 1971, **18**, 105-115. [194]

DECI, E. L. The effects of contingent and noncontingent rewards on intrinsic motivation. *Organizational Behavior and Human Performance*. 1972, **8**, 217-229. [194]

DEESE, J. On the structure of associative meaning. *P Rev*. 1962, **69**, 161-175. [290]

DEESE, J., & HULSE, S. H. *The psychology of learning (3rd ed.)* New York: McGraw-Hill, 1967. [474]

DEPARTMENT OF HEALTH, EDUCATION, AND WELFARE, PUBLIC HEALTH SERVICE, NATIONAL INSTITUTES OF HEALTH. *The institutional guide to DHEW policy on protection of human subjects*. (DHEW Publication No. (NIII) 72-102.) Washington, D.C.: U.S. Government Printing Office, 1971. [656]

DEUTSCH, M., LEVINSON, A., BROWN, B. R., & PEISACH, E. C. Communications of information in the elementary school classroom. In M. Deutsch (Ed.), *The disadvantaged child*. New York: Basic Books, 1967. [306]

DEWS, P. B. The theory of fixed-interval responding. In W. N. Schoenfeld (Ed.), *The theory of reinforcement schedules*. New York: Appleton-Century-Crofts, 1970. [40]

DIENES, Z. P. *Mathematics in the primary school*. New York: St. Martin's Press, 1966. [399]

DIENES, Z. P. *Building up mathematics*. London: Hutchinson Educational Press, 1967. [399]

DIETZ, S. M., & REPP, A. C. Decreasing classroom misbehavior through the use of DRL schedules of reinforcement. *JABA*, 1973, **6**, 457-463. [93-95, 181]

DINSMOOR, J. A., & WINOGRAD, E. Shock intensity in variable-interval escape schedules. *JEAB*, 1958, **1**, 145-148. [41]

DIRINGER, D. *Writing*. New York: Praeger, 1962. [440]

DIRKS, S. J. Aversion therapy: Its limited potential for use in the correctional setting. *Stanford Law Review*, 1974, **26**, 1327-1341. [671]

DIVER, W. The system of relevance of the homeric verb. *Acta Linguistica Hafniensia*, 1969, **12**, 45-68. [276-277]

DIXON, P. W., & HAMMOND, S. Operant conditioning of spoken phonemes /s/ and /z/ and awareness. *P Rep*, 1970, **26**, 87-92.

DOLLARD, J., DOOB, L. W., MILLER, N. E., MOWRER, O. H., & SEARS, R. R. *Frustration and aggression*. New Haven: Yale University Press, 1939. [106]

DOLLARD, J., & MILLER, N. E. *Personality and psychotherapy*. New York: McGraw-Hill, 1950. [106, 314]

DOTY, D. Infant speech perception. *HB*, 1974, **17**, 74-80.   [288]

DOWNING, J. A. Children's concepts of language in learning to read. *RER*, 1970, **12**, 106-112.   [421]

DOWNING, J. A. *The i.t.a. reading experiment*. London: Evans Brothers, 1964.
                                                                                       [303]

DRABMAN, R. S. Child-versus teacher-administered token programs in a psychiatric hospital school. *JACP*, 1973, **1**, 68-87.   [193]

DRABMAN, R. S., & LAHEY, B. B. Feedback in classroom behavior modification: Effects on the target and her classmates. *JABA*, 1974, **7**, 591-598.   [68, 90]

DRABMAN, R. S., SPITALNIK, R., & O'LEARY, K. D. Teaching self-control to disruptive children, *JAP*, 1973, **82**, 10-16.   [187, 202-203]

DRABMAN, R. S., SPITALNIK, R., & SPITALNIK. K. Sociometric and disruptive behavior as a function of four types of token reinforcement programs. *JABA*, 1974, **7**, 93-102.   [104, 186]

DUBANOSKI, R. A., & PARTON, D. A. The effect of the presence of a human model on imitative behavior in children, *DP*, 1971, **4**, 489. (a)   [152, 162]

DUBANOSKI, R. A., & PARTON, D. A. Imitative aggression in children as a function of observing a human model. *DP*, 1974, **4**, 463-468. (b)   [152, 162]

DUBIN, R., & TAVEGGIA. T. C. *The teaching-learning paradox*, Eugene: University of Oregon Press, 1968.   [492]

DUFORT, R. H., GUTTMAN, N., & KIMBLE, G. A. One-trial discrimination reversal in the white rat. *JCPP*, 1954, **32**, 150-155.   [43]

DURRELL, D. E., & WEISBERG, P. Imitative play behavior of children: The importance of model distinctiveness and prior imitative training. *JECP*, 1973, **16**, 23-31.   [160, 175]

DUSTIN, D. S. Some effects of exam frequency. *P Rec.* 1971, **21**, 409-414.   [514]

EBBINGHAUS, H. *Über das Gedächtnis*. Leipzig: Dunker and Humblot, 1885. [17]

EGBERT, R. L. *Planned variation in Follow Through*. Unpublished manuscript, University of Nebraska—Lincoln, 1973.   [353, 532]

EIMAS, P. D., SIQUELAND, E. R., JUSCZYK, P., & VIGORITO, J. Speech perception in infants, *Science*, 1971, **171**, 303-306.   [288, 433]

EITZEN, D. S. The effects of behavior modification on the attitudes of delinquents. *BRT*, 1975, **13**, 295-299.   [623]

EKSTRAND, B. R. Backward associations. *PB*, 1966, **66**, 50-64.   [474]

ELKINS, F. S. A description of a strategy for implementing a systems approach to instruction on a campus-wide basis. In J. M. Johnston (Ed.), *Behavior research and technology in higher education*. Springfield, Ill.: Charles C Thomas, 1975.
                                                                                       [584]

ELKONIN, D. B. USSR (Trans, by R. Raeder and J. Downing). In J. Downing (Ed.), *Comparative reading: Cross-national studies of behavior and processes in reading and writing*. New York: Macmillan, 1973.   [441, 451]

ELOVSON, A. C. Effect of penalty and information on errors. *Proceedings of the 79th Annual Convention of the American Psychological Association*, 1971, 549-550.
                                                                                       [461]

EMPEY, L. T. *Studies in delinquency: Alternatives to incarceration*. U.S. Department of Health, Education, and Welfare, Office of Juvenile Delinquency and Youth Development, Publication No. 9001, 1967.   [604]

ENGELMANN, S., & BRUNER, E. *Distar Reading Level I*, Chicago: Science Research Associates, 1968.   [359]

ENGELMANN, S., & BRUNER, E. *DISTAR reading level II*. Chicago: Science Research Associates, 1969.   [359]

ENGELMANN, S., & BRUNER, E. *Teacher's guide for DISTAR reading I*. Chicago: Science Research Associates, 1974   [359]

ENGELMANN, S., & CARNINE, D. W. *DISTAR arithmetic I.* Chicago: Science Research Associates, 1970.   [359]
ENGELMANN, S., & CARNINE, D. W. *DISTAR arithmetic level II.* Chicago: Science Research Associates, 1971.   [343, 360]
ENGELMANN, S., & CARNINE, D. W. *DISTAR arithmetic level III.* Chicago: Science Research Associates, 1972.   [361]
ENGELMANN, S., & OSBORN, J. *DISTAR language level II.* Chicago: Science Research Associates, 1971.   [362]
ENGELMANN, S., & OSBORN, J. *DISTAR language level III.* Chicago: Science Research Associates, 1973.   [362]
ENGELMANN, S., OSBORN, J., & ENGELMANN, T. *DISTAR language level I.* Chicago: Science Research Associates, 1969.   [344-345, 361]
ENGELMANN, S., & STEARNS, S. *DISTAR reading level III: Reading to learn.* Chicago: Science Research Associates, 1972.   [359]
EPSTEIN, L. H., DOKE, L. A., SAJWAJ, T. E., SORRELL, S., & RIMMER, B. Generality and side effects of overcorrection. *JABA*, 1974, **7**, 386-390.   [67]
ERIKSEN, C. Discrimination and learning without awareness: A methodological survey and evaluation. *P Rev*, 1960, **67**, 279-300.   [168]
ERVIN-TRIPP, S. M. Sociolinguistics. In L. Berkowitz (Ed.), *Advances in Experimental Social Psychology, Volume 4.* New York: Academic Press, 1968.   [304]
ERVIN-TRIPP, S. M. Children's sociolinguistic competence and dialect diversity. *Seventy-First Yearbook. Pt. II.* Chicago, Ill.: National Society for the Study of Education, 1972.   [304]
THE ERWIN CONSTITUTIONAL RIGHTS SUBCOMMITTEE REPORT. *Individual rights and the federal role in behavior modification.* Stock number 5270-02620. Washington, D.C.: U.S. Government Printing Office, 1974.   [265, 659]
ESON, M. E. *Psychological foundations of education.* New York: Holt, Rinehart and Winston, 1972.   [484]
ESTES, K. W. *Some effects of reinforcement upon verbal behavior of children.* Unpublished doctoral dissertation, University of Minnesota, 1945.   [284]
ESTES, W. K. Discriminative conditioning: I. A discriminative property of conditioned anticipation. *JEP*, 1943, **32**, 150-155.   [51]
ESTES, W. K. An experimental study of punishment. *Psychological Monographs*, 1944, **57** (Whole No. 263).   [45]
ESTES, W. K. Reinforcement in human behavior. *American Scientist*, 1972, **60**, 723-729.   [466]
ESTES, W. K., & SKINNER, B. F. Some quantitative properties of anxiety, *JEP*, 1941, **29**, 390-400.   [52]
ETTERS, E. M. Tutorial assistance in college core courses. *JER*, 1967, 60, 406-407.   [487]
ETZEL, B. C., & GEWIRTZ, J. L. Experimental modification of caretaker-maintained high-rate operant crying in a 6- and a 20-week-old infant *(Infans tyrannotearus)*: Extinction of crying with reinforcement of eye contact and smiling. *JECP*, 1967, 5, 303-317.   [106, 119, 123, 132]
EVERETT, P. B., HAYWARD, S. C., & MEYERS, A. W. The effects of a token reinforcement procedure on bus ridership. *JABA*, 1974, 7, 1-9.   [66, 98]
FANTINO, E. Immediate reward followed by extinction versus later reward without extinction. *PS*, 1966, **6**, 233-234.   [249]
FANTINO, E. Aversive control. In J. Nevin & G. S. Reynolds (Eds.), *The study of behavior.* Glenview, Ill.: Scott, Foresman, 1973.   [266]
FANTINO, E. Conditioned reinforcement: Choice and information. In W. K. Honig & J. E. R. Staddon (Eds.), *Handbook of operant behavior.* Englewood Cliffs, N.J.: Prentice-Hall, 1977.   [54]

FARMER, J., LACHTER, G. D., BLAUSTEIN, J. J., & COLE, B. K. The role of proctoring in personalized instruction. *JABA*, 1972, 5, 401-404.   [501, 516]

FARRAR, C. H., POWELL, B. J., & MARTIN, L. K. Punishment of alcohol consumption by apneic paralysis. *BRT*, 1968, 6, 13-16.   [672]

FARTHING, G. W., & OPUDA, M. J. Transfer of matching-to-sample in pigeons. *JEAB*, 1974, 21, 199-213.   [59]

FAWCETT, S. B., & MILLER, L. K. Training public speaking behavior: An experimental analysis and social validation. *JABA*, 1975, 8, 125-135.   [643]

FAWCETT, S. B., MILLER, L. K., & BRAUKMANN, C. J. The observation of community canvassing behaviors in scripted role-playing sessions. *JABA*, 1977, 10, 504.   [643]

FEALLOCK, R., & MILLER, L. K. The design and evaluation of a worksharing system for experimental group living. *JABA*, 1976, 9, 277-288.   [634]

FEATHER, B. W. Semantic generalization of classically conditioned responses: A review. *PB*, 1965, 63, 425-441.   [297]

FELDMAN, R. S. Some characteristics of sentences as response units. In K. Salzinger & R. S. Feldman (Eds.), *Studies in verbal behavior: An empirical approach.* New York: Pergamon, 1973.   [295]

FELIXBROD, J. J. *Effects of prior locus of control over reinforcement on current performance and resistance to extinction.* Unpublished doctoral dissertation, SUNY—Stony Brook, N.Y., 1974.   [183, 201]

FELIXBROD, J. J., & O'LEARY, K. D. Effects of reinforcement on children's academic behavior as a function of self-determined and externally imposed contingencies. *JABA*, 1973, 6, 241-250.   [183, 196, 201]

FELIXBROD, J. J., & O'LEARY, K. D. Self-determination of academic standards by children: Toward freedom from external control. *JEdP*, 1974, 66, 845-850.
                                                                                    [183, 196, 201]

FELTON, M., & LYON, D. O. The post-reinforcement pause. *JEAB*, 1966, 9, 131-134.
                                                                                                 [39]

FERGUSON, C. A. Contrasting patterns of literacy acquisition in a multilingual nation. In W. H. Whiteley (Ed.), *Language use and social change.* London: Oxford University Press, 1971.   [414]

FERNALD, C. D. Control of grammar in imitation, comprehension, and production: Problems of replication. *JVLVB*, 1972, 11, 606-613.   [298]

FERRITOR, D. E., BUCKHOLDT, D., HAMBLIN, R. L., & SMITH, L. The noneffects of contingent reinforcement for attending behavior on work accomplished. *JABA*, 1972, 5, 7-17.   [188]

FERSTER, C. B. Intermittent reinforcement of matching-to-sample in the pigeon. *JEAB*, 1960, 3, 259-272.   [59]

FERSTER, C. B. Positive reinforcement and behavioral deficits of autistic children. *CD*, 1961, 32, 437-456.   [106]

FERSTER, C. B. Essentials of a science of behavior. In J. I. Nurnberger, C. B. Ferster, & J. P. Brady (Eds.), *An introduction to the science of human behavior.* New York: Appleton-Century-Crofts, 1963.   [106]

FERSTER, C. B. Individualized instruction in a large introductory psychology course. *P Rec*, 1968, 18, 521-532.   [485, 488, 501, 515]

FERSTER, C. B., & HAMMER, C. F., JR. Synthesizing the components of arithmetic behavior. In W. K. Honig (Ed.), *Operant behavior: Areas of research and application.* New York: Appleton-Century-Crofts, 1966.   [329, 332]

FERSTER, C. B., & PERROTT, M. C. *Behavior principles.* New York: Appleton-Century-Crofts, 1968.   [489]

FERSTER, C. B., & SKINNER, B. F. *Schedules of reinforcement.* New York: Appleton-Century-Crofts, 1957.   [25, 38, 39, 126, 196, 197, 483, 502]

FESTINGER, L. A theory of social comparison processes. *Human Relations*, 1954, **7**, 117-140. [230]

FEURZIG, W. *Educational potential of computer technology*. Dayton, Ohio: Charles F. Kettering Foundation, 1968. [475]

FILIPCZAK, J. A. Programming for disruptive and low achieving students: An experimental in-school alternative. *Journal of the International Association of Pupil Personnel Workers*, 1973, **17**, 38-42. [569]

FILLENBAUM, S. On the use of memorial techniques to assess syntactic structures. *PB*, 1970, **73**, 231-237. [292]

FILLENBAUM, S., & RAPOPORT, A. *Structures in the subjective lexicon*. New York: Academic Press, 1971. [290]

FINDLEY, J. D. Preference and switching under concurrent scheduling. *JEAB*, 1958, **1**, 123-144. [53]

FINDLEY, J. D. An experimental outline for building and exploring multi-operant behavior repertoires. *JEAB*, 1962, **5**, 133-166. [31]

FINDLEY, J. D., & BRADY, J. V. Facilitation of large ratio performance by use of conditioned reinforcement. *JEAB*, 1965, **8**, 124-129. [30]

FIRTH, I. *Components of reading disability*. Unpublished doctoral dissertation, University of New South Wales, Kensington, N.S.W., Australia, 1972. [418, 426, 438]

FISCHER, J. The easy chair: Preface to the catalogue of Curmudgeon College. *Harper's Magazine*, June 1970. [514]

FISHMAN, J. A. *Sociolinguistics*. Rowley, Mass.: Newbury House, 1970. [304]

FIXSEN, D. L., PHILLIPS, E. L., & WOLF, M. M. Achievement Place: The reliability of self-reporting and peer-reporting and their effects on behavior. *JABA*, 1972, **5**, 19-30. [617]

FIXSEN, D. L., PHILLIPS, E. L., & WOLF, M. M. The Teaching-Family model of group home treatment. In Y. Bakal (Ed.), *The closing down of institutions: New strategies for youth services*. New York: Heath, 1973. (a) [625]

FIXSEN, D. L., PHILLIPS, E. L., & WOLF, M. M. Achievement Place: Experiments in self-government with pre-delinquents. *JABA*, 1973, **6**, 31-47. (b) [612]

FIXSEN, D. L., WOLF, M. M., & PHILLIPS, E. L. Achievement Place: A Teaching-Family model of community-based group homes for youths in trouble. In L. A. Hamerlynck, L. C. Handy, & E. J. Mash (Eds.), *Behavior change: Methodology, concepts, and practice*. Champaign, Ill.: Research Press, 1973. [625]

FLANDERS, J. P. A review of research on imitative behavior. *PB*, 1968, **69**, 316-337. [167]

FLAVELL, J. H. *The developmental psychology of Jean Piaget*. Princeton, N.J.: Van Nostrand, 1963. [435]

FODOR, J., BEVER, T., & GARRETT, M. *The psychology of language*. New York: McGraw-Hill, 1974. [427]

FORD FOUNDATION. *A foundation goes to school*. November 1972. [542]

FOULKE, E., & STICHT, T. G. Review of research on the intelligibility and compression of accelerated speech. *PB*, 1969, **72**, 50-62. [415]

FOUTS, G. T., & PARTON, D. A. Imitation: Effects of movement and static events. *JECP*, 1969, **8**, 118-126. [152, 162]

FOX, L. Effecting the use of efficient study habits. *Journal of Mathetics*, 1962, **1**, 75-86. [484]

FOXX, R. M., & AZRIN, N. H. Restitution: A method of eliminating aggressive-disruptive behavior of retarded and brain damaged patients. *BRT*, 1972, **10**, 15-27. [83]

FOXX, R. M., & AZRIN, N. H. The elimination of autistic self-stimulatory behavior by overcorrection. *JABA*, 1973, **6**, 1-14. (a) [47, 83]

FOXX, R. M., & AZRIN, N. H. *Toilet training the retarded.* Campaign, Ill.: Research Press, 1973. (b)   [34, 50]

FRANKS, C. J., & WILSON, G. T. *Annual review of behavior therapy, theory, and practice.* New York: Brunner/Mazel, 1973.   [629]

FRASE, L. T. Effect of question location, pacing, and mode upon retention of prose material. *JEdP*, 1968, **59**, 244-249.   [468]

FRASER, C., BELLUGI, U., & BROWN, R. Control of grammar in imitation, comprehension, and production. *JVLVB*, 1963, **2**, 121-135.   [297-298]

FREEDLE, R. O. Response bias and serial effects in a modified Shannon guessing game. In K. Salzinger & R. S. Feldman (Eds.), *Studies in verbal behavior: An empirical approach.* New York: Pergamon, 1973.   [292-293]

FREUD, S. *An outline of psychoanalysis.* New York: Norton, 1949.   [146]

FRIEDMAN, C. P. A model for improving "advanced" courses in physics. *American Journal of Physics*, 1972, **40**, 1602-1606.   [491]

FRIEDMAN, P. R. Legal regulation of applied behavior analysis in mental institutions and prisons. *Arizona Law Review*, 1975, **17**, 39-104.   [658, 659, 666, 673]

FRIES, C. C. *Linguistics and reading.* New York: Holt, Rinehart and Winston, 1963.   [438]

FURTH, H. G. *Piaget for teachers.* Englewood Cliffs, N.J.: Prentice-Hall, 1970.   [384]

FYGETAKIS, L., & GRAY, B. B. Programmed conditioning of linguistic competence. *BRT*, 1970, **8**, 153-163.   [321]

GAGNÉ, R. M. The acquisition of knowledge. *P Rev*, 1962, **69**, 355-365.   [381, 382]

GAGNÉ, R. M. Learning hierarchies. *Educational Psychologist*, 1968, **6**, 1-9.   [382]

GAGNÉ, R. M. Context, isolation, and interference effects on the retention of fact. *JEdP*, 1969, **60**, 408-414.   [469]

GAGNÉ, R. M. *The conditions of learning. (2nd ed.)* New York: Holt, Rinehart and Winston, 1970.   [472]

GALLUP, H. F. The introductory psychology course at Lafayette College. Paper presented at the meeting of the Midwestern Psychological Association, Vancouver, B.C. April 1969.   [485, 515]

GALLUP, H. F. Individualized instruction in an introductory psychology course. Paper presented at the meeting of the Eastern Psychological Association, Atlantic City, N.J., 1970.   [485, 517]

GALLUP, H. F. Problems in the implementation of a course in personalized instruction. In J. G. Sherman, *Personalized System of instruction.* Menlo Park, Calif.: Benjamin, 1974.   [485, 518]

GARCIA, E., BAER, D. M., & FIRESTONE, I. The development of generalized imitation within topographically determined boundaries. *JABA*, 1971, **4**, 101-112.   [163, 172, 174]

GARCIA, E., GUESS, D., & BYRNES, J. Development of syntax in a retarded girl using procedures of imitation, reinforcement, and modeling. *JABA*, 1973, **6**, 299-310.   [321, 326, 342]

GARCIA, E. C. *The role of theory in linguistic analysis: The Spanish Pronoun system.* Amsterdam: North-Holland Publishing Co., 1975.   [276]

GARDNER, B. T., & GARDNER, R. A. Two-way communication with an infant chimpanzee. In A. M. Schrier & F. Stollnitz (Eds.), *Behavior of nonhuman primates*, Vol. 4. New York: Academic Press, 1971.   [278, 279]

GARDNER, B. T., & GARDNER, R. A. Evidence for sentence constituents in the early utterances of child and chimpanzee. *Journal of Experimental Psychology: General*, 1975, **104**, 244-267.   [278, 279]

GARDNER, H. The carnival of communal styles. *Harpers*, March 1973, 5-12. [637]

GARDNER, R. A., & GARDNER, B. T. Teaching sign language to a chimpanzee. *Science*, 1969, **165**, 664-672. [278, 279]

GARRY, R., & KINGSLEY, H. L. *The nature and conditions of learning.* Englewood Cliffs, N.J.: Prentice-Hall, 1970. [484]

GAZZANIGA, M. S. *The bisected brain.* New York: Appleton-Century-Crofts, 1970. [433]

GELB, I. J. *A study of writing.* Chicago: University of Chicago Press, 1952. [421, 425, 440, 441]

GELFAND, D. M. The influence of self-esteem on rate of verbal conditioning and social matching behavior. *JASP*, 1962, **65**, 259-265. [176]

GELFAND, D. M. *Social learning in childhood: Readings in theory and application.* (*2nd ed.*) Monterey, Calif.: Brooks/Cole, 1975. [106]

GELFAND, D. M., & HARTMANN, D. P. Behavior therapy with children: A review and evaluation of research methodology. *PB*, 1968, **69**, 204-215. [79]

GELFAND, D. M., HARTMANN, D. P., LAMB, A. K., SMITH, C. L., MAHON, M. A., & PAUL, S. C. The effects of adult models and described alternatives on children's choice of behavior management techniques. *CD*, 1974, **45**, 585-593. [204]

GELMAN, R. Conservation acquisition: A problem of learning to attend to relevant attributes. *JECP*, 1969, **7**, 167-187. [384]

GENTRY, W. D. Fixed-ratio schedule-induced aggression. *JEAB*, 1968, **11**, 813-817. [28]

GESCHWIND, N., QUADFASEL, F. A., & SEGARRA, J. M. Isolation of the speech area. *Neuropsychologia*, 1968, **6**, 327-340. [433]

GESELL, A., & AMATRUDA, C. S. *Developmental diagnosis.* (*2nd ed.*) New York: Hoeber, 1947. [114]

GEWIRTZ, J. L. Three determinants of attention-seeking in young children. *Monographs of the Society for Research in Child Development*, 1954, **19**, (2, Whole No. 59). [130]

GEWIRTZ, J. L. A program of research on the dimensions and antecedents of emotional dependence. *CD*, 1956, **27**, 205-221. [106, 130]

GEWIRTZ, J. L. A learning analysis of the effects of affective privation in childhood. *Acta Psychologica*, 1961, **19**, 404-405. (a) [108]

GEWIRTZ, J. L. A learning analysis of the effects of normal stimulation, privation and deprivation on the acquisition of social motivation and attachment. In B. M. Foss (Ed.), *Determinants of infant behavior.* New York: Wiley, 1961. (b) [106, 108, 113, 119, 127, 129, 131, 133, 138]

GEWIRTZ, J. L. Deprivation and satiation of social stimuli as determinants of their reinforcing efficacy. In J. P. Hill (Ed.), *Minnesota symposia on child psychology. Vol. 1.* Minneapolis: University of Minnesota Press, 1967. [117]

GEWIRTZ, J. L. On designing the functional environment of the child to facilitate behavioral development. In L. L. Dittmann (Ed.), *Early child care: The new perspectives.* New York: Atherton Press, 1968. (a) [113, 127, 138]

GEWIRTZ, J. L. The role of stimulation in models for child development. In L. L. Dittman (Ed.), *Early child care: The new perspectives.* New York: Atherton Press, 1968. (b) [114, 138]

GEWIRTZ, J. L. Levels of conceptual analysis in environment-infant interaction research. *MPQ*, 1969, **15**, 7-47. (a) [116, 136]

GEWIRTZ, J. L. Mechanisms of social learning: Some roles of stimulation and behavior in early human development. In D. A. Goslin (Ed.), *Handbook of socialization theory and research.* Skokie, Ill.: Rand McNally, 1969. (b) [106, 114, 116, 124, 127, 138, 150, 174]

GEWIRTZ, J. L. Conditional responding as a paradigm for observational, imitative learning and vicarious reinforcement. In H. W. Reese (Ed.), *Advances in child development and behavior. Vol. 6.* New York: Academic Press, 1971. (a)
[124, 144, 148, 150, 164, 168, 174]

GEWIRTZ, J. L. The roles of overt responding and extrinsic reinforcement in "self-" and "vicarious-reinforcement" phenomena and in "observational learning" and imitation. In R. Glaser (Ed.), *The nature of reinforcement.* New York: Academic Press, 1971. (b)   [124, 148, 150, 164, 168, 174]

GEWIRTZ, J. L. Stimulation, learning, and motivation principles for day-care settings. In E. H. Grotbert (Ed.), *Day care: Resources for decisions.* (OEO Pamphlet 6106-1), Washington, D.C.: U.S. Office of Economic Opportunity, June 1971. (c)   [121]

GEWIRTZ, J. L. Attachment, dependence, and a distinction in terms of stimulus control. In J. L. Gewirtz (Ed.), *Attachment and dependency.* Washington, D.C.: Winston, 1972. (a)   [124, 129-131]

GEWIRTZ, J. L. (Ed.) *Attachment and dependency.* Washington, D.C.: Winston, 1972. (b)   [129, 130]

GEWIRTZ, J. L. Deficiency conditions of stimulation and the reversal of their effects via enrichment. In F. J. Monks, W. W. Hartup, & J. de Wit (Eds.), *Determinants of behavioral development.* New York: Academic Press, 1972. (c)[121, 124]

GEWIRTZ, J. L. On the selection and use of attachment and dependency indices. In J. L. Gewirtz (Ed.), *Attachment and dependency.* Washington, D.C.: Winston, 1972. (d)   [129, 131]

GEWIRTZ, J. L. Some contextual determinants of stimulus potency. In R. D. Parke (Ed.), *Recent trends in social learning theory.* New York: Academic Press, 1972. (e)   [106, 117]

GEWIRTZ, J. L. The attachment acquisition process as evidenced in the maternal conditioning of cued infant responding (particularly crying). *HD*, 1976, **19**, 143-155.   [123, 133]

GEWIRTZ, J. L. Maternal responding and the conditioning of infant crying: Directions of influence within the attachment-acquisition process. In B. C. Etzel, J. M. LeBlanc, & D. M. Baer (Eds.), *New Developments in behavioral research: Theories, methods, and applications.* Hillsdale, N.J.: Erlbaum Associates, 1977.
[106, 126, 129]

GEWIRTZ, J. L., & BOYD, E. F. Mother-infant interaction and its study. In H. W. Reese (Ed.), *Advances in child development and behavior. Vol. 11.* New York: Academic Press, 1976.   [140]

GEWIRTZ, J. L., & BOYD, E. F. Does maternal responding imply reduced infant crying?: A critique of the 1972 Bell and Ainsworth Report. *CD*, 1977, **48**, 1200-1207. (a)   [125]

GEWIRTZ, J. L., & BOYD, E. F. Experiments on mother-infant interaction underlying mutual attachment acquisition: The infant conditions the mother. In T. Alloway, P. Pliner & L. Krames, (Eds.), *Attachment behavior. Advances in the study of communication and affect. Vol. 3.* New York and London: Plenum Press, 1977. (b)   [106, 113, 128]

GEWIRTZ, J. L., & GEWIRTZ, H. B. Stimulus conditions, infant behaviors, and social learning in four Israeli child-rearing environments: A preliminary report illustrating differences in environment and behavior between the 'only' and the 'youngest' child. In B. M. Foss (Ed.), *Determinants of infant behavior III.* New York: Wiley, 1965.   [139]

GEWIRTZ, J. L., & STINGLE, K. The learning of generalized imitation as the basis for identification. *P Rev*, 1968, **75**, 374-397.   [144, 148, 149, 150, 173, 174]

GIBSON, E. J. Learning to read. *Science*, 1965, **148**, 1066-1072.   [336, 420]

GIBSON, E. J. The ontogeny of reading. *AP*, 1970, **25**, 136-143.   [420]

GIBSON, E. J., & LEVIN, H. *The psychology of reading*, Cambridge, Mass.: M.I.T. Press, 1975. [411]

GIGLIOLI, P. P. (Ed.), *Language and social context*. Middlesex, England: Penguin, 1972. [304]

GILBERT, T. F. Mathetics: The technology of education. *Journal of Mathetics*, 1962, 1, 7-73. [457]

GLASER, R. Educational psychology and education. *AP*, 1973, 28, 557-566. [481]

GLASER, R., HOMME, L. E., & EVANS, J. L. *An evaluation of textbooks in terms of learning principles*. Paper presented at the meeting of the American Education Research Association, Atlantic City, N.J. February, 1959. [456]

GLASER, R., & RESNICK, L. B. Instructional psychology. *ARP*, 1972, 23, 207-276. [384, 470]

GLASS, G. V., WILLSON, V. L., & GOTTMAN, J. M. *Design and analysis of time-series experiments*. Boulder, Colorado: Colorado Associated University Press, 1974. [100]

GLEITMAN, L. R., GLEITMAN, H., & SHIPLEY, E. The emergence of the child as grammarian. *Cognition*, 1973, 1, 137-164. [434, 435]

GLEITMAN, L. R., & ROZIN, P. Phoenician go home? A response to Goodman. *Reading Research Quarterly*, 1973, 8, 494-501. (a) [419]

GLEITMAN, L. R., & ROZIN, P. Teaching reading by use of a syllabary. *Reading Research Quarterly*, 1973, 8, 447-483. (b) [425, 432, 440, 445]

GLEITMAN, L. R., & ROZIN, P. The structure and acquisition of reading I: Relations between orthographies and the structure of language. In A. S. Reber & D. Scarborough (Eds.) *Toward a psychology of reading*. Hillsdale, N.J.: Erlbaum Associates, 1977. [411, 421, 427]

GLOCK, N. D. (Ed.) *Guiding learning*. New York: Wiley, 1971. [484]

GLYNN, E. L. Classroom applications of self-determined reinforcement. *JABA*, 1970, 3, 123-132. [201]

GLYNN, E. L., THOMAS, J. P., & SHEE, S. M. Behavioral self-control of on-task behavior in an elementary classroom. *JABA*, 1973, 6, 105-113. [267]

GOFFMAN, E. *Asylums: Essays on the social situation of mental patients and other inmates*. New York: Doubleday, 1961. [603]

GOLDFARB, W. Psychological privation in infancy and subsequent adjustment. lation. *American Journal of Psychiatry*, 1945, 102, 18-33. (a) [108]

COLDFARB, W. Psychological privation in infancy and subsequent adjustment. *American Journal of Orthopsychiatry*, 1945, 15, 247-255. (b) [108]

GOLDFARB, W. Emotional and intellectual consequences of psychologic deprivation in infancy: A re-evaluation. In P. H. Hoch & J. Zubin (Eds.), *Psychopathology of children*. New York: Grune & Stratton, 1955. [108]

GOLDIAMOND, I. Perception, language, and conceptualization rules. In B. Kleinmuntz (Ed.), *Problem solving: Research, method, and theory*. New York: Wiley, 1966. [154-156]

GOLDIAMOND, I. Justified and unjustified alarm over behavioral control. In O. Milton & R. G. Wahler (Eds.), *Behavior disorders: Perspectives and trends* (2nd ed.) New York: Lippincott, 1969. [564, 673]

GOLDIAMOND, I., & HAWKINS, W. F. Vexierversuch: The log relationship between word-frequency and recognition obtained in the absence of stimulus words. *JEP*, 1958, 56, 457-463. [300, 302]

GOLDMAN-EISLER, F. The relationship between temporal aspects of speech, the structure of language, and the state of the speaker. In K. Salzinger & S. Salzinger (Eds.), *Research in verbal behavior and some neurophysiological implications*. New York: Academic Press, 1967. [292, 295, 304]

GOLDMAN-EISLER, F. *Psycholinguistics*. New York: Academic Press, 1968. [292, 295, 304]

GOODMAN, K. Reading: A psycholinguistic guessing game. In K. S. Goodman & J. Fleming (Eds.), *Selected papers from the IRA Preconvention Institute, Boston, April 1968*. Newark, Del.: International Reading Association, 1969.   [414]

GOODMAN, K. Reading: A psycholinguistic guessing game. In H. Singer & R. B. Ruddell (Eds.), *Theoretical models and processes of reading*. Newark, Del.: International Reading Association, 1970.   [406]

GOODMAN, K. The 13th easy way to make learning to read difficult: A reaction to Gleitman and Rozin. *Reading Research Quarterly*. 1973, 8, 484-493. [417, 419]

GONZALEZ, F. A., & WALLER, M. B. Handwriting as an operant. *JEAB*, 1974, **21**, 165-175.   [39]

GOTTMAN, J. M. N-of-one and N-of-two research in psychotherapy. *PB*, 1973, **80**, 93-105.   [100]

GOTTMAN, J. M., McFALL, R. M., & BARNETT, J. T. Design and analysis of research using time series. *PB*, 1969, **72**, 299-306.   [100]

GRANT, D. A. A preliminary model for processing information conveyed by verbal conditioned stimuli in classical conditioning. In A. H. Black & W. F. Prokasy (Eds.), *Classical conditioning II*. New York: Appleton-Century-Crofts, 1972.   [297]

GRAUBARD, P. S., ROSENBERG, H., & MILLER, M. B. Student applications of behavior modification to teachers and environments or ecological approaches to social deviancy. In R. Ulrich, T. Stachnick, & J. Mabry (Eds.), *Control of human behavior. Vol. 3*. Glenview, Ill.: Scott, Foresman, 1974.   [266]

GRAY, B., & RYAN, B. *A language program for the nonlanguage child*. Champaign, Ill.: Research Press, 1973.   [320]

GRAY, B. H. *Human subjects in medical experimentation*. New York: Wiley, 1975.   [656, 675]

GREEN, B. A. *Is the Keller plan catching on too fast?* Cambridge, Mass.: Education Research Center, M.I.T., June 1971. (a)   [488, 491, 517]

GREEN, B. A. Physics teaching by the Keller plan at M.I.T. *American Journal of Physics*, 1971, **39**, 764-775. (b)   [491, 501]

GREEN, B. A. Comment on "Keller vs Lecture Method in General Physics Instruction." *American Journal of Physics*, 1973, **41**, 706-707.   [491]

GREENO, J. G. The structure of memory and the process of solving problems. In R. L. Solso (Ed.), *Contemporary issues in cognitive psychology*. Washington, D.C.: Winston, 1973.   [408]

GREENSPOON, J. The reinforcing effect of two spoken sounds on the frequency of two responses. *AJP*, 1955, **68**, 409-416.   [313]

GREENSPOON, J. Should an entire college curriculum be taught by the Keller method. In J. G. Sherman (Ed.), *Personalized system of instruction*. Menlo Park, Calif.: Benjamin, 1974.   [521]

GREENSPOON, J., & RANYARD, R. Stimulus conditions and retroactive inhibition. *JEP*, 1957, **53**, 55-59.   [302]

GREENWOOD, C. H., HOPPS, H., DELQUADRI, J., & GUILD, J. Group contingencies for group consequences in classroom management: A further analysis. *JABA*, 1974, **7**, 413-426.   [194]

GREENWOOD, C. R., SLOANE, H. N., & BASKIN, A. Training elementary aged peer behavior managers to control small group programmed mathematics. *JABA*, 1974, **7**, 103-114.   [193]

GROEN, G.J., & PARKMAN, J. M. A chronometric analysis of simple addition. *P. Rev*, 1972, **79**, 329-343.   [391]

GROEN, G. J., & POLL, M. Subtraction and the solution of open-sentence problems *JECP*, 1973, **16**, 292-302.   [391]

GROEN, G. J., & RESNICK, L. B. Can preschool children invent addition algorithms? *JEdP*, 1977, **69**, 645-652.   [391, 392, 397, 400]

GUESS, D., & BAER, D. M. An analysis of individual differences in generalization between receptive and productive language in retarded children. *JABA*, 1973, **6**, 311-329.   [320]

GUESS, D., SAILOR, W., RUTHERFORD, G., & BAER, D. M. An experimental analysis of linguistic development: The productive use of the plural morpheme. *JABA*, 1968, **1**, 297-306.   [162, 320, 342]

GUILFORD, J. P. Intellectual factors in productive thinking. In M. S. Aschnen & C. E. Bish (Eds.), *National Education Association*, 1965, 5-20.   [341]

GUTHRIE, E. R. *The psychology of learning*. New York: Harper & Row, 1935. [464]

GUTHRIE, E. R., & HORTON, G. P. *Cats in a puzzle box*. New York: Rinehart, 1946.   [36]

GUTTMAN, N., & KALISH, H. I. Discriminability and stimulus generalization. *JEP*, 1956, **51**, 79-88.   [57]

HAKE, D. F., & LAWS, D. R. Social facilitation of responses during a stimulus paired with electric shock. *JEAB*, 1967, **10**, 387-392.   [227]

HAKE, D. F., POWELL, J., & OLSEN, R. Conditioned suppression as a sensitive baseline for social facilitation. *JEAB*, 1969, **12**, 807-816.   [227]

HAKE, D. F., & VUKELICH, R. A classification and review of cooperation procedures. *JEAB*, 1972, **18**, 333-343.   [216, 220-229]

HAKE, D.F., & VUKELICH, R. Analysis of the control exerted by a complex cooperation procedure. *JEAB*, 1973, **19**, 3-16.
                                       [210-214, 217-219, 223, 224, 228, 230, 232]

HAKE, D. F., VUKELICH, R. & KAPLAN, S. J. Audit responses: responses maintained by access to existing self or coactor scores during nonsocial, parallel work, and cooperation procedures. *JEAB*, 1973, **19**, 409-423.   [227, 230]

HAKE, D. F., VUKELICH, F., & OLVERA, D. The measurement of sharing and cooperation as equity effects and some relationships between them. *JEAB*, 1975, **23**, 63-79.   [210, 211, 229, 231-241]

HALL, J. F. *Verbal learning and retention*. New York: Lippincott, 1971.   [287]

HALL, R. V., CRISTLER, C., CRANSTON, S. S., & TUCKER, B. Teachers and parents as researchers using multiple baseline designs. *JABA*, 1970, **3**, 247-255.
                                                                            [66, 84, 87]

HALL, R. V., FOX, R., WILLARD, D., GOLDSMITH, L., EMERSON, M, OWEN, M., DAVIS, F., & PORCIA, E. The teacher as observer and experimenter in the modification of disputing and talking-out behaviors. *JABA*, 1971, **4**, 141-149.
                                                                              [80-81]

HALL, R. V., LUND, D., & JACKSON, D. Effects of teacher attention on studying behavior. *JABA*, 1968, **1**, 1-12.   [81]

HALL, R. V., PANYON, M., RABON, D., & BRODEN, M. Instructing beginning teachers in reinforcement procedures which improve classroom control. *JABA*, 1968, **1**, 315-322.   [566]

HALLECK, S. L. *The politics of therapy*. New York: Science House, 1971.
                                                                      [665, 668-671]

HAMBLIN, R. E., HATHAWAY, C., & WODARSKI, J. Group contingencies, peer tutoring, and accelerating academic achievement. In E. A. Ramp & B. L. Hopkins (Eds.), *A new direction for education: Behavior analysis. Vol. 1*. Lawrence, Kansas: University of Kansas Support and Development Center for Follow Through, 1971.   [194]

HAMMER, M., & HENDERSON, C. O. Beat the "loaf-cram" cycle with computer tests. *College Management*, October 1972, 25-27. (a)   [491]

HAMMER, M., and HENDERSON, C. O. Improving large enrollment instruction with computer generated, repeatable tests. *Proceedings of the 1972 Conference on Computers in the Undergraduate Curricula*. Atlanta: Southern Regional Education Board, 1972, 209-216. (b)   [491]

HAMMER, M., HENDERSON, C. O., & JOHNSON, L. Some promising techniques for improving large enrollment instruction. *American Assembly of Collegiate Schools of Business Bulletin*, October 1972, 18-30. [491]

HAMMER, M., POLGAR, S., & SALZINGER, K. Speech predictability and social contact patterns in an informal group. *Human Organization*, 1969, **28**, 235-242. [308]

HANSON, H. M. Effects of discrimination training on stimulus generalization. *JEP*, 1959, **58**, 321-334. [57]

HAPKIEWICZ, W. G. *The application of contingency management techniques to the teaching of teachers.* Paper presented at the meeting of the Midwestern Psychological Association, Cleveland, 1972. [494-496, 514]

HARLOW, H. F. Learning set and error factor theory. In S. Koch (Ed.), *Psychology, A study of a science. Vol. 2.* New York: McGraw-Hill, 1959. [328-330, 343]

HARMON, R. E. Response elimination in concurrent and single operant situations with pigeons. *Learning and Motivation*, 1973, **4**, 417-431. [49]

HARRIS, A. J. *How to increase reading ability.* (5th ed.) New York: David McKay, 1970. [413, 426]

HARRIS, V. W., & SHERMAN, J. A. Use and analysis of the "Good Behavior Game" to reduce disruptive classroom behavior, *JABA*, 1973, **6**, 405-417.
[186, 188, 194]

HARRIS, V. W., & SHERMAN, J. A. Homework assignments, consequences, and classroom performance in social studies and mathematics. *JABA*, 1974, **7**, 505-519. [64, 66]

HART, B. M., REYNOLDS, N. J., BAER, D. M., BRAWLEY, E. R., & HARRIS, F. R. Effect of contingent and noncontingent social reinforcement on the cooperative play of a preschool child. *JABA*, 1968, **1**, 73-76. [65]

HARTLEY, J. New approaches in the teaching of psychology: An annotated bibliography. *Bulletin of the British Psychological Society*, 1972, **25**, 291-304. [485]

HARTMANN, D. P. Forcing square pegs into round holes: Some comments on "An analysis-of-variance model for the intrasubject replication design." *JABA*, 1974, **7**, 635-638. [104]

HARTUP, W. W., & COATES, B. Imitation: Arguments for a developmental approach. In R. D. Parke (Ed.), *Recent trends in social learning theory.* New York: Academic Press, 1972. [174, 175]

HARZEM, P., LEE, I., & MILES, T. R. The effects of pictures on learning to read. *British Journal of Educational Psychology*, 1976, **46**, 318-322. [5]

HAUGAN, G. M., & MCINTIRE, R. W. Comparisons of vocal imitation, tactile stimulation, and food as reinforcers for infant vocalization. *DP*, 1972, **6**, 201-209.
[316]

HAUSERMAN, N., WALEN, S. R., & BEHLING, M. Reinforced racial integration in the first grade: A study in generalization. *JABA*, 1973, **6**, 193-200. [205]

HAWKINS, R. P., & DOBES, R. W. Behavioral definitions in applied behavior analysis: Explicit or implicit. In B. C. Etzel, J. M. LeBlanc, & D. M. Baer (Eds.), *New developments in behavior research: Theory, methods, and applications.* Hillsdale, N.J.: Erlbaum Associates, 1976. [62, 63, 104]

HAWKINS, R. P., & DOTSON, V. A. Reliability scores that delude: An Alice in Wonderland trip through the misleading characteristics of interobserver agreement scores in interval recording. In E. Ramp & G. Semb (Eds.), *Behavior analysis: Areas of research and application.* Englewood Cliffs, N.J.: Prentice-Hall, 1975.
[63, 71, 72, 104]

HAWKINS, R. P., SLUYTER, D. J., & SMITH, C. D. Modification of achievement by a simple technique involving parents and teacher. In M. Harris (Ed.), *Classroom uses of behavior modification.* Columbus, Ohio: Charles Merrill, 1972. [187]

HAY, W., HAY, L. R., & NELSON, R. O. *The effects of behavioral versus performance contingencies on attending behavior and academic performance.* Unpublished manuscript, University of North Carolina—Greensboro, 1974. [188]

HAYES, J. R., & SIMON, H. A. Understanding written problem instructions. In L. W. Gregg (Ed.), *Knowledge and cognition.* Hillsdale, N.J.: Erlbaum Associates, 1974. [406]

HAYES, K. J., & NISSEN, C. H. Higher mental functions of a home-raised chimpanzee. In A. M. Schrier & F. Stollnitz (Eds.), *Behavior of nonhuman primates. Vol. 4.* New York: Academic Press, 1971. [278]

HEARST, E. Resistance-to-extinction functions in the single organism. *JEAB*, 1961, **4**, 133-144. [44]

HEARST, E. Concurrent generalization gradients for food-controlled and shock-controlled behavior. *JEAB*, 1962, **4**, 19-31. [56]

HEARST, E., BESLEY, S., & FARTHING, G. W. Inhibition and the stimulus control of operant behavior. *JEAB*, 1970, **14**, 373-409. [57]

HEARST, E., KORESKO, M. B., & POPPEN, R. Stimulus generalization and the response-reinforcement contingency. *JEAB*, 1964, **7**, 369-379. [56]

HEIDER, E. R. Style and accuracy of verbal communications within and between social classes. *JPSP*, 1971, **18**, 33-47. [307]

HEKMAT, H., & VANIAN, D. Behavior modification through covert semantic desensitization. *JCCP*, 1971, **36**, 248-251. [299]

HELDMAN, A. W. Social psychology versus the first amendment freedoms, due process liberty, and limited government. *Cumberland-Samford Law Review*, 1973, **4**, 1-40. [652, 665, 671]

HELLER, J., & KIRALY, J. Behavior modification: A Clockwork Orange? *Elementary School Journal*, 1974, **74**, (No. 4). [564]

HENDERSHOT, C. H. *Programmed learning: A bibliography of programs and presentation devices.* (4th ed.) Bay City, Mich.: Hendershot Programmed Learning Consultants, 1973. [474]

HERMAN, S. H., & TRAMONTANA, J. Instructions and group versus individual reinforcement in modifying disruptive group behavior. *JABA*, 1971, **4**, 113-119. [194]

HERMANN, J. A., DE MONTES, A. I., DOMINGUEZ, B., MONTES, F., & HOPKINS, B. L. Effects of bonuses for punctuality on the tardiness of industrial workers. *JABA*, 1973, **6**, 563-570. [68, 97]

HERRICK, R. M. The successive differentiation of a lever displacement response. *JEAB*, 1964, **7**, 211-215. [37]

HERRNSTEIN, R. J. Relative and absolute strength of response as a function of frequency of reinforcement. *JEAB*, 1961, **4**, 267-272. [53]

HERRNSTEIN, R. J. Superstition: A corollary of the principles of operant conditioning. In W. K. Honig (Ed.), *Operant behavior: Areas of research and application.* New York: Appleton-Century-Crofts, 1966. [26, 66]

HERRNSTEIN, R. J. Method and theory in the study of avoidance. *P Rev*, 1969, **76**, 46-69. [42, 250]

HERRNSTEIN, R. J. On the law of effect. *JEAB*, 1970, **13**, 243-266. [54, 254, 256]

HERRNSTEIN, R. J. Formal properties of the matching law. *JEAB*, 1974, **21**, 159-164. [54]

HERRNSTEIN, R. J., & HINELINE, P. N. Negative reinforcement as shock-frequency reduction. *JEAB*, 1966, **9**, 421-435. [248]

HERRNSTEIN, R. J., & LOVELAND, D. H. Complex visual concept in the pigeon. *Science*, 1964, **146**, 549-551. [60]

HERSEN, M., & BARLOW, D. H. *Single-case experimental designs: Strategies for studying behavior change.* New York: Pergamon, 1976. [79, 80, 82]

HETHERINGTON, E. M., & FRANKIE, G. Effects of parental dominance, warmth, and conflict on imitation in children. *JPSP*, 1967, **6**, 119-125. [164]

HEWETT, F. M. Educational programs for children with behavior disorders. In H. C. Quay & J. S. Werry (Eds.), *Psychopathological disorders of children.* New York: Wiley, 1972. [184]

HEWETT, F. M., TAYLOR, F. D., & ARTUSO, A. A. The Santa Monica Project: Evaluation of an engineered classroom design with emotionally disturbed children. *EC*, 1969, **35**, 523-529. [82, 183]

HILGARD, E. R. Issues within learning theory and programmed instruction. *Psychology in the Schools*, 1964, **1**, 129-139. [468]

HILGARD, E. R., & BOWER, G. H. *Theories of learing.* (3rd ed.) New York: Appleton-Century-Crofts, 1966. [469, 483]

HILL, J. H. On the evolutionary foundations of language. *American Anthropologist*, 1972, **74**, 308-317. [279]

HILTS, P. J. *Behavior modification.* New York: Harper's Magazine Press, 1974. [564]

HINDE, R. A. *Animal behaviour: A synthesis of ethology and comparative psychology.* New York: McGraw-Hill, 1966. [119]

HINELINE, P. N., & RACHLIN, H. Notes on fixed-ratio and fixed-interval escape responding in the pigeon. *JEAB*, 1969, **12**, 397-410. [41, 42]

HINGTGEN, J. N., SANDERS, B. J., & DeMYER, M. K. Shaping cooperative responses in early childhood schizophrenics. In L. P. Ullmann & L. Krasner (Eds.), *Case studies in behavior modification.* New York: Holt, Rinehart and Winston, 1965. [211]

HIVELY, W. *Terminal behavior in mathematics.* Mimeographed paper, Harvard University, 1961. [472]

HOBART, S., GOLDMAN, B., & FISHEL, J. Small-group peer-instruction: A design for the introductory course. *Community College Social Science Quarterly.* Summer 1973, **4**, 32-36. [491]

HOBEROCK, L. L. Personalized instruction in mechanical engineering. *Engineering Education*, March 1971, **61**, 506-507. [491, 492]

HOBEROCK, L. L. Personalized proctorial instruction for dynamic systems and control. *Journal of Dynamic Systems, Measurement and Control*, June 1972, 165-167. [491, 492]

HOBEROCK, L. L., KOEN, B. B., ROTH, C. H., & WAGNER, G. R. Theory of PSI evaluated for engineering education. *IEEE Transactions on Education.* Feb. 1972, **E-15**, 25-29. [491]

HOCHBERG, J. Components of literacy: Speculations and exploratory research. In H. Levin & J. P. Williams (Eds.), *Basic studies on reading.* New York: Basic Books, 1970. [414]

HOCKETT, C. F. The origin of speech. *Scientific American*, 1960, **203**, 89-98. [279]

HOLDEN, M. H., & MACGINITIE, W. H. Children's conceptions of word boundaries in speech and print. *JEdP*, 1972, **63**, 551-557. [421]

HOLLAND, J. G. Technique for behavioral analysis of human observing. *Science*, 1957, **125**, 348-350. [39]

HOLLAND, J. G. Teaching machines: An application of principles from the laboratory. *JEAB*, 1960, **3**, 275-287. [458]

HOLLAND, J. G. A quantitative measure for programmed instruction. *American Educational Research Journal*, 1967, **4**, 87-101. [459-460]

HOLLAND, J. G. Is institutional change necessary? In J. E. Krapfl & E. A. Vargas (Eds.), *Behaviorism and ethics.* Kalamazoo, Mich.: Behaviordelia, 1977. [665, 670]

HOLLAND, J. G. Behaviorism: Part of the problem or part of the solution? *JABA*, 1978, **11**, 163-174.   [671, 672]

HOLLAND, J. G., & KEMP, F. D. A measure of programming in teaching machine material. *JEdP*, 1965, **56**, 264-269.   [459]

HOLLIS, J. H. Communication within dyads of severely retarded children. *American Journal of Mental Deficiency*, 1966, **70**, 729-744.   [229]

HOLT, E. B. *Animal drive and the learning process. Vol. 1*. New York: Holt, 1931.   [144]

HOLZ, W. C., & AZRIN, N. H. Discriminative properties of punishment. *JEAB*, 1961, **4**, 225-232.   [45]

HOLZ, W. C., & AZRIN, N. H. Interactions between the discriminative and aversive properties of punishment. *JEAB*, 1962, **5**, 229-234.   [46]

HOLZ, W. C., & AZRIN, N. H. Conditioning human verbal behavior. In W. K. Honig (Ed.), *Operant behavior: Areas of research and application*. New York: Appleton-Century-Crofts, 1966.   [316]

HOLZMAN, T. G., GLASER, R., & PELLEGRINO, J. W. Process training as a test of computer simulation theory. *Memory and Cognition*, 1976, **4**, 349-356.   [402]

HOMANS, G. C. The sociological relevance of behaviorism. In R. L. Burgess and D. Bushell (Eds.), *Behavioral sociology*. New York: Columbia University Press, 1969.   [209]

HOMME, L. E., DEBACA, P. C., COTTINGHAM, L., & HOMME, A. What behavioral engineering is. *P Rec*, 1968, **18**, 425-434.   [303]

HOMME, L. E., DEBACA, P. C., DEVINE, J. V., STEINHORST, R., & RICKERT, E. J. Use of the Premack principle in controlling the behavior of nursery school children. *JEAB*, 1963, **6**, 544.   [24]

HONIG, W. K. Discrimination, generalization, and transfer on the basis of stimulus differences. In D. I. Mostofsky (Ed.), *Stimulus generalization*. Stanford, Calif.: Stanford University Press, 1965.   [60]

HONIG, W. K. (Ed.) *Operant behavior: Areas of research and application*. New York: Appleton-Century-Crofts, 1966.   [483]

HOPKINS, B. L., SCHUTTE, R. C., & GARTON, K. L. The effects of access to a playroom on the rate and quality of printing and writing of first and second grade students. *JABA*, 1971, **4**, 77-87.   [181]

HOPPS, H., & COBB, J. A. Survival behaviors in the educational setting: Their implications for research and intervention. In L. A. Hamerlynck, L. C. Handy, & E. J. Mash (Eds.), *Behavior change; Methodology, concepts, and practice*. Champaign, Ill.: Research Press, 1973.   [188]

HORNER, V. M., & GUSSOW, J. D. John and Mary: A pilot study in linguistic ecology. In C. B. Cazden, B. P. John, & D. Hymes (Eds.), *Functions of language in the classroom*. New York: Teachers College, 1972.   [284, 306, 312]

HORTON, L. E. Generalization of aggressive behavior in adolescent delinquent boys. *JABA*, 1970, **3**, 205-211.   [64, 90]

HOSHAW, R. W., KURTZ, E. B., & FERKO, F. A. Plant morphology . . . a process approach. *Commission on Undergraduate Education in the Biological Sciences*, 1969, **5**, 1-3.   [491]

HOWES, D. On the relation between the probability of a word as an association and in general linguistic usage. *JASP*, 1957, **54**, 75-85.   [289]

HOWES, D., & OSGOOD, C. E. On the combination of associative probabilities in linguistic contests. *AJP*, 1954, **67**, 241-258.   [289]

HUEY, E. B. *The psychology and pedagogy of reading (1908)*. Cambridge, Mass.: M.I.T. Press, 1968.   [415]

HUGHES, J. F., & HUGHES, A. O. *Equal education: A new national strategy*. Bloomington: Indiana University Press, 1972.   [530, 558]

HULL, C. L. Quantitative aspects of the evolution of concepts. *Psychological Monographs*, 1920, **28** (Whole No. 123). [172]

HULL, C. L. *Principles of behavior*. New York: Appleton-Century-Crofts, 1943. [23, 106, 145]

HULSEBUS, R. C. Operant conditioning of infant behavior: A review. In H. W. Reese (Ed.), *Advances in child development and behavior. Vol. 8*. New York: Academic Press, 1973. [131, 132]

HUMPHREYS, L. G. Imitation and the conditioned reflex. *Pedagogical Seminary*, 1921, **28**, 1-21. [144]

HUMPHREYS, L. G. The effect of random alternation of reinforcement on the acquisition and extinction of conditioned eyelid reactions. *JEP*, 1939, **25**, 141-158. [44]

HUNT, J. G., & ZIMMERMAN, J. Stimulating productivity in a stimulated sheltered workshop setting. *American Journal of Mental Deficiency*, 1969, **74**, 43-49.[90]

HURSH, D. E., & SHERMAN, J. A. The effects of parent-presented models and praise on the vocal behavior of their children. *JECP*, 1973, **15**, 328-339. [317]

HURSH, D. E., SHELDON, J., MINKIN, B., MINKIN, N., SHERMAN, J. A., & WOLF, M. M. Proctors' discussions of students' quiz performance with students. In J. M. Johnston (Ed.) *Behavior research and technology in higher education*. Springfield, Ill.: Charles C Thomas, 1975. [498, 501, 517, 519, 520]

HYDLE, L. L., & CLAPP, F. L. *Elements of difficulty in the interpretation of concrete problems in arithmetic*. Bulletin No. 9. Madison: University of Wisconsin, Bureau of Education Research, 1927. [382]

HYMES, D. *Foundations in sociolinguistics*. Philadelphia: University of Pennsylvania, 1974. [304]

ITARD, J. M. *The wild boy of Aveyron (1801)*. New York: Appleton-Century-Crofts, 1962. [170-171]

IWATA, B. A., & BAILEY, J. S. Reward versus cost token systems: An analysis of the effects on students and teacher. *JABA*, 1974, **7**, 567-576. [183, 188, 200]

JACKSON, D. A. (Ed.), *Curriculum procedures for the behavior analysis classroom: A teaching guide*. Lawrence: University of Kansas Support and Development Center for Follow Through, 1974. [541]

JACKSON, D. A., & MINNIS-HAZEL, M. *A guide to staff training*. Lawrence: University of Kansas Support and Development Center for Follow Through, 1974. [541]

JACOBSEN, E. *You must relax*. New York: McGraw-Hill, 1962. [651]

JAMES, H. *Children in trouble: The national scandal*. New York: Pocket Books, 1971. [603]

JENCKS, C., SMITH, M., ACLAND, H., BANE, M. J., COHEN, D., GINTIS, H., HEYNS, B., & MICHELSON, S. *Inequality: A reassessment of the effects of family and schooling in America*. New York: Basic Books, 1972. [557]

JENKINS, H. M., & HARRISON, R. H. Effect of discrimination training on auditory generalization. *JEP*, 1960, **59**, 246-253. [57]

JENKINS, H. M., & SAINSBURY, R. S. The development of stimulus control through differential reinforcement. In N. J. MacKintosh & W. K. Honig (Eds.), *Fundamental issues in associative learning*. Halifax: Dalhousie, 1969. [58]

JENKINS, J. J., & PALERMO, D. S. Mediation processes and the acquisition of linguistic structure. In U. Bellugi & R. Brown (Eds.), *The acquisition of language. Monographs of the Society for Research in Child Development*, 1964, **29**(1), 141-169. [278]

JERSILD, A. T. *Child psychology*. New York: Prentice-Hall, 1933. [144]

JOHNSON, D. M. Word association and word frequency. *AJP*, 1956, **69**, 125-127. [289]

JOHNSON, S. M. & BOLSTAD, O. D. Methodological issues in naturalistic observation: Some problems and solutions for field research. In L. A. Hamerlynck, L. C. Handy, & E. J. Mash (Eds.), *Behavior change: Methodology, concepts, and practice*. Champaign, Ill.: Research Press, 1973. [70]

JOHNSON-LAIRD, P. N. Experimental psycholinguistics. *ARP*, 1974, **25**, 135-160. [277]

JOHNSTON, J. M. (Ed.) *Behavior research and technology in higher education*. Springfield, Ill.: Charles C Thomas, 1974. [584]

JOHNSTON, J. M. (Ed.) *Proceedings of the 2nd National Conference on Research and Technology in College and University Teaching*. Society for Behavioral Technology and Engineering, Psychology Department, University of Florida, 1975, 287-294. [584]

JOHNSTON, J. M., & O'NEILL, G. W. The analysis of performance criteria defining course grades as a determinant of college student academic performance. *JABA*, 1973, **6**, 261-268. [490, 501, 510-512]

JOHNSTON, J. M., & PENNYPACKER, H. S. A behavioral approach to college teaching. *AP*, 1971, **26**, 219-244. [493-496, 499-501, 511, 584, 586]

JOHNSTON, J. M., ROBERTS, M. D., & O'NEILL, G. W. The measurement and analysis of college student study behavior. In G. Semb (Ed.) *Behavior analysis and education*. Lawrence: University of Kansas, 1972. [506]

JOHNSTON, J. M., WALTERS, W. M., & O'NEILL, G. W., RASHEED, J. A. The measurement and analysis of college student study behavior: Tactics for research. In J. M. Johnston (Ed.) *Behavior research and technology in higher education*. Springfield, Ill.: Charles C Thomas, 1975. [508]

JONES, R. J., & AZRIN, N. H. An experimental application of a social reinforcement approach to the problem of job-finding. *JABA*, 1973, **6**, 345-353. [98]

JONES, R. R., VAUGHT, R. S., & REID, J. B. Time series analysis as a substitute for single subject analysis of variance designs. In G. R. Patterson, I. M. Marks, J. D. Matarazzo, R. A. Myers, G. E. Schwartz, & H. H. Strupp (Eds.), *Behavior change 1974*. Chicago: Aldine, 1975. [100]

JONES, R. T., & KAZDIN, A. E. Programming response maintenance after withdrawing token reinforcement. *BT*, 1975, **6**, 153-164. [82]

JOURNAL OF THE EXPERIMENTAL ANALYSIS OF BEHAVIOR. Bloomington, Ind.: Society for the Experimental Analysis of Behavior, 1958. [483]

KAESS, W., & ZEAMAN, D. Positive and negative knowledge of results in a Pressey type punchboard. *JEP*, 1960, **60**, 12-17. [461]

KALE, R. J., KAYE, J. H., WHELAN, P. A., & HOPKINS, B. L. The effects of reinforcement on the modification, maintenance, and generalization of social responses of mental patients. *JABA*, 1968, **1**, 307-314. [64, 82]

KAMII, C. An application of Piaget's theory to the conceptualization of a preschool curriculum. In R. K. Parker (Ed.), *The preschool in action: Explaining early childhood programs*. Boston: Allyn & Bacon, 1972. [384]

KAMIN, L. J. Selective association and conditioning. In N. J. MacKintosh & W. K. Honig (Eds.), *Fundamental issues in associative learning*. Halifax: Dalhousie, 1969. [58]

KANFER, F. H. Verbal conditioning: A review of its current status. In T. R. Dixon & D. L. Horton (Eds.), *Verbal behavior and general behavior theory*. Englewood Cliffs, N.J.: Prentice-Hall, 1968. [316]

KANFER, F. H., COX, L. E., GREINER, J. M., & KAROLY, P. Contracts, demand characteristics, and self-control. *JPSP*, 1974, **30**, 605-619. [268]

KANFER, F. H., & KAROLY, P. Self-control: A behavioristic excursion into the lion's den. *BT*, 1972, **3**, 398-416. [267, 270]

KAPEL, S. Baby's cries denote needs. *Kansas City Star*, June 13, 1974. [124]

KARIS, C., KENT, A., & GILBERT, J. E. *The interactive effects of responses per frame, response mode, and response confirmation on intraframe S-R association strength.* Washington, D.C.: U.S. Department of Health, Education and Welfare, Office of Education, 1970, Project No. 5-0773.   [460, 462]

KASS, R. E., & O'LEARY, K. D. *The effects of observer bias in field-experimental settings.* Paper presented at symposium on Behavior Analysis in Education, University of Kansas, Lawrence, Kansas, April, 1970.   [75]

KASSIRER, L. B. Behavior modification for patients and prisoners: Constitutional ramifications of enforced therapy. *Journal of Psychiatry and Law*, 1974, **2**, 245-302. (a)   [658, 659, 674]

KASSIRER, L. B. The right to treatment and the right to refuse treatment. Recent case law. *Journal of Psychiatry and Law*, 1974, **2**, 455-470. (b)   [658, 659]

KATONA, G. *Organizing and memorizing.* New York: Columbia University Press, 1940.   [383]

KAUFMAN, K. F. *Reward and cost procedures for disruptive adolescents in a psychiatric hospital school.* Unpublished doctoral dissertation, SUNY—Stony Brook, N. Y., 1971.   [200]

KAUFMAN, K. F., & O'LEARY, K. D. Reward, cost, and self-evaluation procedures for disruptive adolescents in a psychiatric hospital school. *JABA*, 1972, **5**, 293-309.
                                                  [98, 183, 184, 189, 200, 202]

KAUSLER, D. H. (Ed.), *Readings in verbal learning.* New York: Wiley, 1966. [287]

KAVANAGH, J. F., & MATTINGLY, I. G. (Eds.), *Language by ear and by eye: The relationships between speech and reading.* Cambridge, Mass.: M.I.T. Press, 1972.   [411]

KAYE, H. Infant sucking behavior and its modification. In L. P. Lipsitt & C. C. Spiker (Eds.), *Advances in child development and behavior. Vol. 3.* New York: Academic Press, 1967.   [32]

KAYE, H. *Learning by imitation in infants and young children.* Paper presented at Society for Research in Child Development, Minneapolis, April 1971.   [175]

KAZDIN, A. E. The effect of response cost in suppressing behavior in a pre-psychotic retardate. *Journal of Behavior Therapy and Experimental Psychiatry*, 1971, **2**, 137-140.   [83]

KAZDIN, A. E. The effects of response cost and aversive stimulation in suppressing punished and nonpunished speech disfluencies. *BT*, 1973, **4**, 73-82. (a)   [90]

KAZDIN, A. E. The effects of vicarious reinforcement on attentive behavior in the classroom. *JABA*, 1973, **6**, 71-78. (b)   [68, 82, 90]

KAZDIN, A. E. Methodological and assessment considerations in evaluation reinforcement programs in applied settings. *JABA*, 1973, **6**, 517-531. (c)
                                                  [79, 97, 488, 492, 495, 497, 500]

KAZDIN, A. E. Role of instructions and reinforcement in behavior changes in token reinforcement programs. *JEdP*, 1973, **64**, 63-71. (d)   [78, 90]

KAZDIN, A. E. *Behavior modification in applied settings.* Homewood, Ill.: Dorsey, 1975. (a)   [61, 65, 79, 98, 564, 670]

KAZDIN, A. E. Characteristics and trends in applied behavior analysis. *JABA*, 1975, **8**, 332. (b)   [61, 80, 96, 98, 104]

KAZDIN, A. E. The impact of applied behavior analysis on diverse areas of research. *JABA*, 1975, **8**, 213-229. (c)   [61]

KAZDIN, A. E. Recent advances in token economy research. In M. Hersen, R. M. Eisler, & P. M. Miller (Eds.), *Progress in behavior modification.* New York: Academic Press, 1975 (d)   [96]

KAZDIN, A. E. Statistical analyses for single-case experimental designs. In M. Hersen & D. H. Barlow, *Single-case experimental designs: Strategies for studying behavior change.* New York: Pergamon, 1976.   [100, 104]

KAZDIN, A. E., & BOOTZIN, R. R. The token eeconomy: An evaluation review. *JABA*, 1972, **5**, 343-372.   [517, 537]
KAZDIN, A. E., & KOPEL, S. A. On resolving ambiguities of the multiple-baseline design: Problems and recommendations. *BT*, 1975, **6**, 601-608.   [89]
KAZDIN, A. E., & POLSTER, R. Intermittent token reinforcement and response maintenance in extinction. *BT*, 1973, 4, 386-391.   [82]
KAZDIN, A. E., SILVERMAN, N. A., & SITTLER, J. L. The use of prompts to enhance vicarious effects of nonverbal approval. *JABA*, 1975, **8**, 279-286.   [68, 90]
KEEHN, J. D. Is bar-holding with negative reinforcement preparatory or perseverative? *JEAB*, 1967, **10**, 461-465.   [41]
KELLEHER, R. T. Concept formation in chimpanzees. *Science*, 1958, **128**, 777-778, (a)   [60]
KELLEHER, R. T. Fixed-ratio schedules of conditioned reinforcement with chimpanzees. *JEAB*, 1958, **I**, 281-289. (b)   [31]
KELLEHER, R. T. Stimulus-producing responses in chimpanzees. *JEAB*, 1958, **I**, 87-102. (c)   [31]
KELLEHER, R. T. Schedules of conditioned reinforcement during experimental extinction. *JEAB*, 1961, 4, 1-5.   [30]
KELLEHER, R. T. Chaining and conditioned reinforcement. In W. K. Honig (Ed.), *Operant behavior: Areas of research and application*. New York: Appleton-Century-Crofts, 1966. (a)   [30, 505]
KELLEHER, R. T. Conditioned reinforcement in second-order schedules. *JEAB*, 1966, 9, 475-485. (b)   [30]
KELLEHER, R. T., & FRY, W. T. Stimulus functions in chained fixed-interval schedules. *JEAB*, 1962, 5, 167-173.   [31]
KELLER, F. S. Light aversion in the white rat. *P Rec*, 1941, 4, 235-250.   [41]
KELLER, F. S. New reinforcement contingencies in the classroom? *AP*, 1965, **20**, 542.   [485]
KELLER, F. S. A personal course in psychology. In R. Ulrich, T. Stachnik, & J. Mabry (Eds.), *Control of human behavior*. Glenview, Ill.: Scott, Foresman, 1966.   [485, 584]
KELLER, F. S. Neglected rewards in the educational process. *Proceedings of the 23rd American Conference of Academic Deans*, Los Angeles, January 1967, 9-22.   [485]
KELLER, F. S. Goodbye teacher . . . *JABA*, 1968, 1, 79-89.
                [7, 485, 487, 489, 492, 504, 505, 513, 514, 517, 520, 584, 587, 645]
KELLER, F. S. A programmed system of instruction. *Educational Technology Monographs*, 1969, **2**, 1-27.   [485]
KELLER, F. S., & SCHOENFELD, W. N. *Principles of psychology*. New York. Appleton-Century-Crofts, 1950.   [211]
KELLER, O. J., & ALPER, B. S. *Half-way houses: Community-centered correction and treatment*. Lexington, Mass.: Heath, 1970.   [604]
KELLEY, H. H., THIBAUT, J. W., RADLOFF, R., & MUNDY, D. The development of cooperation in the "minimal social situation." *Psychological Monographs*, 1962, **76** (19, Whole No. 538).   [227]
KELLOGG, W. N., & KELLOGG, L. A. *The ape and the child*. New York: Whittlesey House, 1933.   [278]
KELLY, J. F., & HAKE, D. F. An extinction-induced increase in an aggressive response with humans. *JEAB*, 1970, 14, 153-164.   [27]
KEMP, F. D., & HOLLAND, J. G. Blackout ratio and overt responses in programmed instruction. Resolution of disparate results. *JEdP*, 1966, **57**, 109-114. [459-460]
KENDLER, H. H., & KENDLER, T. S. *Basic psychology: Brief edition*. New York: Appleton-Century-Crofts, 1971.   [518]

KENT, G. H., & ROSANOFF, A. J. A study of association in insanity. *American Journal of Insanity*, 1910, **67**, 37-96, 317-390.   [289]

KENT, R. N., KANOWITZ, J., O'LEARY, K. D., & CHEIKEN, M. Observer reliability as a function of circumstances of assessment. *JABA*, 1977, **10**, 317-324.

[74, 75, 77]

KENT, R. N., & O'LEARY, K. D. A controlled evaluation of behavior modification with conduct problem children. *JCCP*, 1976, **44**, 586-596.   [189]

KENT, R. N., O'LEARY, K. D., DIAMENT, C., & DIETZ, A. Expectation biases in observational evaluation of therapeutic change. *JCCP*, 1974, **42**, 774-780.

[74-76]

KESELMAN, H. J., & LEVANTHAL, L. Concerning the statistical procedures enumerated by Gentile et al.: Another perspective. *JABA*, 1974, **7**, 643-645.   [104]

KEYS, N. The influence on learning and retention of weekly as opposed to monthly tests. *JEdP*, 1934, **25**, 427-436.   [514]

KIFER, R. E., LEWIS, M. A., GREEN, D. R., & PHILLIPS, E. L. Training predelinquent youths and their parents to negotiate conflict situations. *JABA*, 1974, **7**, 357-364.   [650]

KIRIGIN, K. A., AYALA, H. E., BRAUKMANN, C. J., BROWN, W. G., PHILLIPS, E. L., FIXSEN, D. L., & WOLF, M. M. Training teaching-parents: An evaluation and analysis of workshop training procedures. In E. Ramp & G. Semb (Eds.), *Behavior analysis: Areas of research and application*. Englewood Cliffs, N.J.: Prentice-Hall, 1975.   [627]

KIRIGIN, K. A., BAILEY, J. S., PHILLIPS, E. L., FIXSEN, D. L., & WOLF, M. M. *The effects of homebased reinforcement on the study behavior and academic performance of pre-delinquent boys*. Unpublished manuscript, University of Kansas, Lawrence, Kans., 1975.   [615]

KIRIGIN, K. A., PHILLIPS, E. L., TIMBERS, G. D., FOXSEM, D. L., & WOLF, M. M. Achievement Place: the modification of academic behavior problems of delinquent youths in a group home setting. In B. C. Etzel, J. M. LeBlanc, & D. M. Baer (Eds.), *New developments in behavioral research: Theory methods and application*. Hillsdale, N.J.: Erlbaum Associates, 1977.   [616]

KIRIGIN, K. A., TIMBERS, G. D., AYALA, H. E., FIXSEN, D. L., PHILLIPS, E. L., & WOLF, M. M. *The negative effects of "positive" tutoring on the independent reading behavior of delinquent adolescents*. Paper presented at the meeting of the American Psychological Asosciation, Montreal, 1973.   [616]

KISSLER, G. R., & LLOYD, K. E. Effect of sentence interrelation and scrambling on the recall of factual information. *JEdP*, 1973, **64**, 187-190.   [501]

KLAHR, D. Steps toward the simulation of intellectual development. In L. B. Resnick (Ed.), *The nature of intelligence*. Hillsdale, N.J.: Erlbaum Associates, 1976.

[384]

KLAUS, D. J. An analysis of programming techniques. In R. Glaser (Ed.), *Teaching machines and programmed learning. Vol. II. Data and directions*. Washington, D.C.: National Education Association, 1965.   [468]

KLAUS, M.H., JERAULD, R., KREGER, N. C., MCALPINE, W., STEFFA, M., & KENNELL, J. H. Maternal attachment: Importance of the first post-partum days. *New England Journal of Medicine*. 1972, **286**, 460-463.   [129]

KLEIN, R. H. The effects of length of delay interval and expectancy control on preferences for delayed rewards in children and normals and schizophrenic adults. *Dissertation Abstracts*, 1967, **28**, 1199.   [257]

KNIGHTLY, J. J., & SAYRE, J. L. Self-paced instruction for library science students. *Journal of Education for Librarianship*, 1972, **12**, 193-197.   [491]

KOEN, B. V. An evaluation of an introductory nuclear engineering course taught by a self-paced method. *Transactions of the American Nuclear Society*, June 1970, 24-25. (a)   [491, 492]

KOEN, B. V. Self-paced instruction for engineering students. *Engineering Education*, 1970, **60**, 735-736. (b)   [491]

KOEN, B. V. Self-paced instruction in engineering. A case study. *IEEE Transactions on Education*, February 1971, **E-14**, 24-31.   [491, 492, 517]

KOEN, B. V. Determining the unit structure in a PSI course. *Engineering Education*, March 1973, 432-434.   [491]

KOEN, B. V., & KELLER, F. S. Experiences with a proctoral system of instruction. *Engineering Education*, March 1971, 504-505.   [491]

KOHLBERG, L. A cognitive-developmental analysis of children's sex-role concepts and attitudes. In E. E. Maccoby (Ed.), *The development of sex differences.* Stanford, Calif.: Stanford University Press, 1966.   [139]

KOHLBERG, L. Early education: A cognitive-developmental view. *CD*, 1968, **39**, 1013-1062.   [384]

KOLESNIK, W. B. *Educational psychology.* New York: McGraw-Hill, 1970.   [484]

KONORSKI, J. *Integrative activity of the brain.* Chicago: University of Chicago Press, 1967.   [34]

KOPP, J., & UDIN, H. Identification and discrimination functions for pure tone auditory frequencies. *PS*, 1969, **16**, 95-96.   [288]

KOTOVSKY, K., & SIMON, H. A. Empirical tests of a theory of human acquisition of concepts for sequential patterns. *Cog P*, 1973, **4**, 399-424.   [402]

KOUNIN, J. S., & GUMP, P. V. The ripple effect in discipline. *Elementary School Journal*, 1958, **59**, 158-162.   [68, 90]

KRAMER, P. E. *Young children's responses to commands differing in length, structure, and meaning.* Unpublished doctoral dissertation, Yeshiva University, 1973.   [299]

KRASNER, L. Studies of the conditioning of verbal behavior. *PB*, 958, **55**, 148-170.   [316]

KRASNER, L. The behavioral scientist and social responsibility: No place to hide. *Journal of Social Issues*, 1965, **21**(2), 9-30.   [673]

KRASNER, L. Verbal operant conditioning and awareness. In K. Salzinger & S. Salzinger (Eds.), *Research in verbal behavior and some neurophysiological implications.* New York: Academic Press, 1967.   [314]

KRASNER, L., & KRASNER, M. Token economies and other planned environments. *Yearbook of the National Society for the Study of Education*, 1973, 351-384.
                                                                              [203]

KRASNER, L., & ULLMAN, L. P. *Research in behavior modification.* New York: Holt, Rinehart and Winston, 1965.   [665, 667]

KRATOCHWILL, T., ALDEN, K., DEMUTH, D., DAWSON, D., PANICUCCI, C., ARNSTON, P., MCMURRAY, N., HEMPSTEAD, J., & LEVIN, J. A further consideration in the application of an analysis-of-variance model for the intrasubject replication design. *JABA*, 1974, **7**, 629-633.   [104]

KRUMBOLTZ, J. D. A new learning environment: A case for learning. *Contemporary Psychology*, 1973, **18**, 472-473.   [184]

KRUMBOLTZ, J. D. & KEISLER, C. A. The partial reinforcement paradigm and programmed instruction. *The Journal of Programmed Instruction*, 1965, **3**(2), 9-14.
                                                                              [463]

KRUMBOLTZ, J. D., & WEISMAN, R. G. The effect of intermittent confirmation on programmed instruction. *JEdP*, 1962, **53**, 250-253.   [462]

KULIK, J. A., KULIK, C. L., & CARMICHAEL, K. The Keller plan in science teaching. *Science*, 1974, **183**, 379-383.   [492, 493, 497, 504, 505, 518]

KUTNER, B., WILKINS, C., & YARROW, P. R. Verbal attitudes and overt behavior involving racial prejudice. *JASP*, 1952, **47**, 649-652.   [519]

KUYPERS, D. S., BECKER, W. C., & O'LEARY, K. D. How to make a token system fail. *EC*, 1968, **35**, 101-109.   [187, 189]

LABOV, W. The logic of nonstandard English. In F. Williams (Ed.), *Language and poverty*. Chicago: Markham, 1970.   [306]

LABOV, W. *Sociolinguistic patterns*. Philadelphia: University of Pennsylvania, 1972.
                                                                              [304-305]

LAFFAL, J. Response faults in word association as a function of response entropy. *JASP*, 1955, **50**, 265-270.   [289]

LAGRECA, A., & SANTOGROSSI, D. A. *The effects of reinforcement on the original responses of elementary school children*. Unpublished manuscript, SUNY—Stony Brook, N.Y., 1975.   [205]

LAHEY, B. B. Modification of the frequency of descriptive adjectives in the speech of Head Start children through modeling without reinforcement. *JABA*, 1971, **4**, 19-22.   [321]

LAHEY, B. B. Minority group lanuages. In B. B. Lahey (Ed.) *The modification of language behavior*. Springfield, Ill.: Charles C Thomas, 1973. (a)   [317]

LAHEY, B. B. (Ed.), The modification of language behavior. Springfield, Ill.: Charles C Thomas, 1973. (b)   [317]

LAHEY, B. B., & DRABMAN, R. S. Facilitation of the acquisition and retention of sight word vocabulary through token reinforcement. *JABA*, 1974, **7**, 307-312.   [183]

LAKOFF, G. Presuppositions and relative grammaticality. *Studies in Philosophical Linguistics*, 1969, **1**, 103-116.   [276]

LAMB, M. E. A defense of the concept of attachment. *HD*, 1974, **17**, 376-385.
                                                                              [130]

LAMBERT, J. V., BERSH, P. J., HINELINE, P. M., & SMITH, G. D. Avoidance conditioning with shock contingent upon the avoidance response. *JEAB*, 1973, **19**, 361-367.   [249]

LANDER, D. G., & IRWIN, R. J. Multiple schedules: Effects of the distribution of reinforcements between components on the distribution of responses between components. *JEAB*, 1968, **11**, 517-524.   [54]

LANE, H. L. The motor theory of speech perception: A critical review. *P Rev*, 1965, **72**, 275-309.   [288]

LANE, H.L. A behavioral basis for the polarity principle in linguistics. In K. Salzinger & S. Salzinger (Eds.), *Research in verbal behavior and some neurophysiological implications*. New York: Academic Press, 1967.   [288]

LANES, S. G. Communes: A firsthand report on a controversial life-style. *Parents Magazine*, October 1971, 61-118.   [631]

LASAGNA, L. Special subjects in human experimentation. In P. A. Freund (Ed.), *Experimentation with human subjects*. New York: Braziller, 1969.   [674]

LASHLEY, K. S. The mechanism of vision: XV. Preliminary studies of the rat's capacity for detailed vision. *Journal of General Psychology*. 1938, **18**, 123-293.
                                                                              [327]

LAW ENFORCEMENT ASSISTANCE ADMINISTRATION, Publicity Release. Washington, D.C., February 1974.   [265, 658-660]

LEACOCK, E. B. Abstract versus concrete speech: A false dichotomy. In C. B. Cazden, V. P. John, & D. Hymes (Eds.), *Functions of language in the classroom*. New York: Teachers College Press, 1972.   [306]

LEE, J. K., & GOLLUB, L. R. Second-order schedules with fixed-ratio components: Variation of component size. *JEAB*, 1971, **15**, 303-310.   [30]

LEIFER, A. D., LEIDERMAN, P. H., BARNETT, C. R., & WILLIAMS, J. A. Effects of mother-infant separation on maternal attachment behavior. *CD*, 1972, **43**, 1203-1218.   [129]

LEITENBERG, H. The use of single case methodology in psychotherapy research. *JAP*, 1973, **82**, 87-101.   [79-82]

LENNEBERG, E. H. Speech as a motor skill with special reference in nonaphasic disorcers. *Monographs of the Society for Research in Child Development*, 1964, **29**(1), 115-127.   [153]

LENNEBERG, E. H. *Biological foundations of language.* New York: Wiley, 1967.
[313, 432]

LEPPER, M. R., & GREENE, D. How teachers turn play into work. *Psychology Today,* September 1974, 49-54. [195]

LEPPER, M. R., GREENE, D., & NISBETT, R. E. Undermining children's intrinsic interest with extrinsic rewards. *JPSP,* 1973, **28**, 129-137. [195]

LEPPER, M. R., SAGOTSKY, G., & MAILER, J. Generalization and persistence of effects of exposure to self-reinforcement models. *CD,* 1975, **46**, 618-630. [202]

LEVIN, G., & SIMMONS, J. Response to food and praise by emotionally disturbed boys. *P Rep,* 1962, **2**, 539-546. [89]

LEVIN, H., & WILLIAMS, J. P. (Eds.), *Basic studies on reading.* New York: Basic Books, 1970. [411]

LEVINE, F. M., & FASNACHT, G. Token rewards may lead to token learning. *AP,* 1974, **29**(11), 816-820. [195, 196]

LEVONKRON, J., SANTOGROSSI, D. A., & O'LEARY, K. D. Increasing academic performance through contingent access to tutoring. *Psychology in the Schools,* 1974, **11**, 201-207. [206]

LEVY, D. M. Primary affect hunger. *American Journal of Psychiatry.* 1937, **94**, 643-652. [108]

LIBERMAN, A. M. The grammars of speech and language. *Cog P,* 1970, **1**, 301-323. [429]

LIBERMAN, A. M., COOPER, F. S., SHANKWEILER, D. P., & STUDDERT-KENNEDY, J. Perception of the speech code. *P Rev,* 1967, **74**, 431-461.
[427-428, 431, 433, 441]

LIBERMAN, A. M., HARRIS, K. S., HOFFMAN, H. S., & GRIFFITH, B. C. The discrimination of speech sounds within and across phoneme boundaries. *JEP,* 1957, **54**, 358-368. [288]

LIEBERMAN, I. Y., SHANKWEILER, D., FISHER, F. W., & CARTER, B. Explicit syllable and phoneme segmentation in the young child. *JECP,* 1974, **18**, 201-212.
[425, 432, 441]

LIEBERMAN, P. On the evolution of language: A unified view. *Cognition,* 1973, **2**, 59-94. [279]

LIEBERMAN, P. *On the origins of language.* New York: Macmillan, 1975. [433]

LIEBERMAN, P. H., KLATT, D. H., & WILSON, W. H. Vocal tract limitations on the vowel repertoires of rhesus monkey and other nonhuman primates. *Science,* 1969, **164**, 1185-1187. [278]

LIEBERT, R. M., & FERNANDEZ, L. E. Effects of vicarious consequences on imitative performance. *CD,* 1970, **41**, 847-852. [165, 167]

LIEBERT, R. M., SOBOL, M. P., & COPEMAN, C. D. Effects of vicarious consequences and race of model upon imitative performance by black children. *DP,* 1972, **6**, 453-456. [143, 164]

LINDER, S., & WHITEHURST, C. Is there a novelty effect on student attitudes toward personalized instruction? *Journal of Experimental Education,* 1973, **42**, 42-44.
[518]

LINDSLEY, O. R. Characteristics of the behavior of chronic psychotics as revealed by free-operant conditioning methods. *Diseases of the Nervous System,* 1960, **21**, 66-78. [101]

LINDSLEY, O. R. Experimental analysis of social reinforcement: Terms and methods. *American Journal of Orthopsychiatry,* 1963, **33**, 624-633. [227]

LINDSLEY, O. R. Characteristics of the behavior of chronic psychotics as revealed by free-operant conditioning methods. In C. M. Franks (Ed.), *Conditioning techniques in clinical practice and research.* New York: Springer, 1964. [209]

LINDSLEY, O. R. Experimental analysis of cooperation and competition. In T. Verhave (Ed.), *The experimental analysis of behavior.* New York: Appleton-Century-Crofts, 1966. [209, 218, 224-232, 237]

LLOYD, K. E. Retention of responses to stimulus classes and to specific stimuli. *JEP*, 1960, **59**, 54-59. [498]

LLOYD, K. E. Contingency management systems in university courses. *ET*, 1971, **11**, 18-23. [489-490, 501-504, 520]

LLOYD, K. E., GARLINGTON, W. K., LOWRY, D., BURGESS, H., EULER, H. A., & KNOWLTON, W. R. A note on some reinforcing properties of university lectures. *JABA*, 1972, **5**, 151-155. [500, 515]

LLOYD, K. E., & KNUTZEN, N. J. A self-paced programmed undergraduate course in the experimental analysis of behavior. *JABA*, 1969, **2**, 125-133. [485, 488-490, 501, 502, 505, 518]

LLOYD, K. E., McMULLIN, W. E., & FOX, R. A. Student pacing and instructor pacing of assignments in a university contingency management system. In T. A. Brigham, R. Hawkins, J. Scott, & T. McLaughlin (Eds.), *Behavior analysis in education: Self-control and reading.* Dubuque, Iowa: Kendall/Hunt, 1976. [499, 501, 503]

LLOYD, K. E., McMULLIN, W. E., FOX, R. A., RINKE, C., & DUNCAN, C. *Comparisons of personalized systems of instruction with traditional university courses.* Paper read at the meeting of the American Psychological Association, New Orleans, 1974. [519]

LOCKHART, K. A., SEXTON, J., & LEA, C. The Findley procedure: A method for examining choice-making behavior in academic settings. In J. M. Johnston (Ed.), *Behavior research and technology in higher education.* Springfield, Ill.: Charles C Thomas, 1975. [519]

LOGAN, F. A. Decision making by rats: Delay versus amount of reward. *JCPP*, 1965, **59**, 246-251. [254]

LONDON, P. *The modes and morals of psychotherapy.* New York: Holt, Rinehart and Winston, 1964. [652, 667]

LONDON, P. Behavior technology and social control-turning the tables. *APA Monitor*, 1974, **5**(4), 2. [583]

LONG, E. R. Additional techniques for producing multiple-schedule control in children. *JEAB*, 1962, **5**, 443-455. [39]

LONG, E. R., HAMMACK, J. T., MAY, F., & CAMPBELL, B. J. Intermittent reinforcement of operant behavior in children. *JEAB*, 1958, **1**, 315-339. [38, 196]

LONG, J. D., & WILLIAMS, R. L. The comparative effectiveness of group and individually contingent free time with inner-city junior high school students. *JABA*, 1973, **6**, 465-474. [194]

LONGSTRETH, L. E. A cognitive interpretation of secondary reinforcement. In J. K. Cole (Ed.), *Nebraska symposium on motivation.* Lincoln: University of Nebraska Press, 1971. [463]

LOVASS, O. I. Interaction between verbal and nonverbal behavior. *CD*, 1961, **32**, 329-336. [299]

LOVASS, O. I. Control of food intake in children by reinforcement of relevant verbal behavior. *JASP*, 1964, **68**, 672-677. [299]

LOVAAS, O. I. A behavior therapy approach to the treatment of childhood schizophrenia. In J. P. Hill (Ed.), *Minnesota symposia on child psychology. Vol. I.* Minneapolis: University of Minnesota Press, 1967. [161, 174]

LOVAAS, O. I. *Behavioral treatment of autistic children.* Morristown, N.J.: General Learning Press, 1973. [264, 319]

LOVASS, O. I., FREITAG, G., KINDER, M. I., RUBENSTEIN, B. D., SHAEFFER, B., & SIMMONS, J. Q. Establishment of social reinforcers in two schizophrenic children on the basis of food. *JECP*, 1966, **4**, 109-125. [199]

LOVAAS, O. I., KOEGEL, R., SIMMONS, J. Q., & LONG, J. S. Some generalization and follow-up measures on autistic children in behavior therapy. *JABA*, 1973, **6**, 131-166. [629]

LOVAAS, O. I., & SIMMONS, J. Q. Manipulation of self-destruction in three retarded children. *JABA*, 1969, **2**, 143-157. [103]

LOVIBOND, S. H., & CADDY, S. Discriminated aversive control in the moderation of alcoholics drinking behavior. *BT*, 1970, **1**, 437-444. [273]

LOVITT, T. C., & CURTISS, K. A. Academic response rate as a function of teacher and self-imposed contingencies. *JABA*, 1969, **2**, 45-53. [202]

LOVITT, T. C., GUPPY, T. E., & BLATTNER, J. E. The use of a free-time contingency with fourth graders to increase spelling accuracy. *BRT*, 1969, **7**, 151-156. [181, 566]

LUCHINS, A. S., & LUCHINS, E. H. *Wertheimer's seminars revisited: Problem-solving and thinking.* Albany: State University of New York, Faculty-Student Association, 1970. [383]

LUMSDAINE, A. A. Some conclusions concerning student response and science of interaction. In A. A. Lumsdaine (Ed.), *Student responses in programmed instruction.* (Pub. No. 943.) Washington, D.C.: National Academy of Science, National Research Council, 1961. [464]

LUMSDAINE, A. A. Some research problems in automated instructions: Instructional programming and subject-matter structure. In J. E. Coulsen (Ed.), *Programmed learning and computer-based instruction.* New York: Wiley, 1962. [464, 465]

LUMSDAINE, A. A., & MAY, M. A. Mass communication and educational media. *ARP*, 1965, **16**, 475-534. [460, 469]

LURIA, A. R. The regulative function of speech in its development and dissolution. In K. Salzinger and S. Salzinger (Eds.), *Research in verbal behavior and some neurophysiological implications.* New York: Academic Press, 1967. [299]

LURIA, A. R. Speech development and the formation of mental processes. In M. Cole & I. Maltzman (Eds.), *A handbook of contemporary Soviet psychology.* New York: Basic Books, 1969. [299]

MACCOBY, E. E., & MASTERS, J. C. Attachment and dependency. In P. H. Mussen (Ed.), *Carmichael's manual of child psychology Vol. 2. (3rd ed.).* New York: Wiley, 1970. [30]

MACNEILAGE, P. F. Motor control of serial ordering of speech. *P Rev.* 1970, **77**, 182-196. [289]

MADSEN, C. H., BECKER, W. C., & THOMAS, D. R. Rules, praise and ignoring: Elements of elementary classroom control. *JABA*, 1968, **1**, 139-150. [65]

MADSEN, C. H., MADSEN, C. K., & THOMPSON, F. Increasing rural Head Start children's consumption of middle-class meals. *JABA*, 1974, **7**, 257-262. [68]

MADSEN, M. D. Cooperative and competitive motivation of children in three Mexican sub-cultures. *P Rep*, 1967, **20**, 1307-1320. [235]

MAGER, R. F. *Preparing objectives for programmed instruction.* San Francisco: Fearon, 1961. [471]

MAHONEY, M. J., & BANDURA, A. Self-reinforcement in the pigeon. *Learning and Motivation*, 1972, **3**, 293-303. [253]

MAHONEY, M. J., & THORESEN, C. E. *Self-control: Power to the person.* Monterey, Calif.: Brooks/Cole, 1974. [651]

MAIER, S. F., SELIGMAN, M. E. P., & SOLOMON, R. L. Pavlovian fear conditioning and learned helplessness. In B. A. Campbell & R. M. Church (Eds.), *Punishment and aversive behavior.* New York: Appleton-Century-Crofts, 1969. [248]

MAITLAND, S. Time perspective, frustration failure and delay of gratification in middle-class and lower-class children from organized and disorganized families. *Dissertation Abstracts*, 1967, **27(B)**, 3676-3777. [257]

MALEY, R. F., FELDMAN, G. L., & RUSKIN, R. S. Evaluation of patient improvement in a token economy treatment program. *JAP*, 1973, **82**, 141-144. [90]

MALEY, R. F., & HAYES, S. C. Coercion and control: Ethical and legal issues. In J. E. Krapfl & E. A. Vargas (Eds.) *Behaviorism and ethics.* Kalamazoo, Mich.: Behaviordelia, 1977. [673]

MALONEY, D. M., HARPER, T. M., BRAUKMANN, C. J., FIXSEN, D. L., PHILLIPS, E.
L., & WOLF, M. M. Teaching conversation-related skills to pre-delinquent girls.
JABA, 1976, **9**, 371.   [614]

MALONEY, K. B., & HOPKINS, B. L. The modification of sentence structure and its
relationship to subjective judgments of creativity in writing. *JABA*, 1973, **6**,
425-433.   [205]

MALOTT, R. W., & CUMMING, W. W. Schedules of interresponse time reinforcement. *P Rec*, 1964, **14**, 211-252.   [39]

MALOTT, R. W., & SVINICKI, J. G. Contingency management in an introductory
psychology course for one thousand students. *P Rec*, 1969, **19**, 545-556.
                                                                   [485, 502, 512, 584]

MALOUF, R. E., & DODD, D. II. Role of exposure, imitation, and expansion in the
acquisition of an artificial grammatical rule. *DP*, 1972, **7**, 195-203.   [162]

MANDELKER, A. V., BRIGHAM, T. A., & BUSHELL, D., JR. The effects of token
procedures on a teacher's social contacts with her students. *JABA*, 1970, **3**,
169-174.   [537]

MARKLE, S. M. *Words: A programmed course in vocabulary development*. Chicago:
Science Research Associates, 1962.   [477]

MARKLE, S. M. *Good frames and bad. A grammar of frame writing*. (2nd ed.) New
York: Wiley, 1969.   [458, 473, 477]

MARR, M. J. Second-order schedules. In D. P. Hendry (Ed.), *Conditioned reinforcement*. Homewood, Ill.: Dorsey, 1969.   [30]

MARR, M. J. Sequence schedules of reinforcement. *JEAB*, 1971, **15**, 41-48.   [30]

MARTIN, J. A. The control of imitative and nonimitative behaviors in severely retarded children through "generalized-instruction following." *JECP*, 1971, **11**,
390-400.   [173]

MARTIN, R. *Legal challenges to behavior modification*. Champaign, Ill.: Research
Press, 1975.   [658, 668, 673, 674]

MASH, E. J., HAMMERLYNCK, L. A., & HANDY, L. C. (Eds.), *Behavior modification
and families*. New York: Brunner/Mazel, 1976.   [651]

MATHIS, B. C., COTTON, J. W., & SECHREST, L. *Psychological foundations of education*. New York: Academic Press, 1970.   [484]

MATTINGLY, I. G. Reading, the linguistic process, and linguistic awareness. In J. F.
Kavanagh & I. G. Mattingly (Eds.), *Language by ear and by eye: The relationships between speech and reading*. Cambridge, Mass.: M.I.T. Press, 1972.
                                                                                          [432]

MAWHINNEY, V. T., BOSTOW, D. E., LAWS, D. R., BLUMENFELD, G. J., & HOPKINS,
B. L. A comparison of students studying-behavior produced in daily, weekly,
and three-week testing schedules. *JABA*, 1971, **4**, 257-264.
                                                              [500-502, 506, 507, 510]

MCCLELLAND, J. J. Preliminary letter identification in the perception of words and
non words. *Journal of Experimental Psychology: Human Perception and Performance*, 1977, **2**, 80-92.   [415, 436]

MCCULLOUGH, J. P., CORNELL, J. E., MCDANIEL, M. H., & MUELLER, R. K.
Utilization of the simultaneous treatment design to improve student behavior in
a first-grade classroom. *JCCP*, 1974, **42**, 288-292.   [91-92]

MCFALL, R. M., & TWENTYMEN, C. T. Four experiments on the relative contributions of rehearsal, modeling, and coaching to assertion training. *JAP*, 1973, **81**,
199-218.   [650]

MCGINNIES, E. M., & FERSTER, C. B. (Eds.) *The reinforcement of social behavior*.
Boston: Houghton Mifflin, 1971.   [192, 517]

MCGUIGAN, F. J., & SCHOONOVER, R. A. *The psychophysiology of thinking: Studies
of covert processes*. New York: Academic Press, 1973.   [166]

McKEACHIE, W. J. Research on teaching at the college and university level. In N. L. Gage (Ed.), *Handbook of research on teaching*. Chicago: Rand McNally, 1963. [484]

McKEAN, H. E., NEWMAN, F. L., & PURTLE, R. Personalized instruction in a three semester mathematics and statistics service sequence. In J. G. Sherman (Ed.), *Personalized system of instruction*. Menlo Park, Calif.: Benjamin, 1974. [521]

McKEE, J. M. The Draper experiment: A programmed learning project. In F. Ofiesh & W. Meierhenry (Eds.), *Trends in programmed instruction*. Washington, D.C.: National Education Association, 1964. [527]

McKENZIE, H. S., CLARK, M., WOLF, M. M., KOTHERA, R., & BENSON, C. Behavior modification of children with learning disabilities using grades as tokens and allowances as back-up reinforcers. *EC*, 1968, **34**, 745-752. [187]

McLAUGHLIN, T. F., & MALABY, J. E. Intrinsic reinforcers in a classroom token economy. *JABA*, 1972, **5**, 263-270. [183, 197]

McLAUGHLIN, T. F., & MALABY, J. E. *Maintenance of assignment completion and accuracy across time under fixed, variable and extended token exchange periods in a classroom token program*. Unpublished manuscript, University of Kansas— Lawrence, 1975. [197, 200]

McMICHAEL, J. S., & COREY, J. R. Contingency management in an introductory psychology course produces better learning. *JABA*, 1969, **2**, 79-83. [494-499, 506, 515, 584]

McMICHAEL, J. S., & COREY, J. R. *Unit instructor's manual for Kendler and Kendler's "Basic psychology: Brief edition."* New York: Appleton-Century-Crofts, 1971. (a) [500]

McMICHAEL, J. S., & COREY, J. R. *Unit workbook for Kendler and Kendler's "Basic psychology: Brief edition."* New York: Appleton-Century-Crofts, 1971. (b) [500]

McMILLAN, D. E. A comparison of the punishing effects of response-produced shock and response-produced time out. *JEAB*, 1967, **10**, 439-449. [47]

McNEILL, D. Developmental psycholinguistics. In F. Smith & G. A. Miller (Eds.), *The genesis of language*. Cambridge, Mass.: M.I.T. Press, 1966. [166, 309, 310]

MEDICAL RESEARCH COUNCIL. Responsibility in investigations on human subjects: Statement by Medical Research Council. *British Medical Journal*, 1964, **2**, 178-180. [654]

MEDLAND, M. B., & STACHNICK, T. J. Good-behavior game: A replication and systematic analysis, *JABA*, 1972, **5**, 45-51. [82]

MEEHL, P. E. On the circularity of the law of effect. *PB*, 1950, **47**, 52-75. [23]

MEICHENBAUM, D. H., BOWERS, K. S., & ROSS, R. R. Modification of classroom behavior of institutionalized female adolescent offenders. *BRT*, 1968, **6**, 343-353. [187]

MICHAEL, J. *A behavioral analysis of behavioral college teaching systems*. Paper presented at the meeting of the American Psychological Association, Washington, D.C.: September 1971. [485, 491]

MICHAEL, J. Statistical inference for individual organism research: Mixed blessing or curse? *JABA*, 1974, **7**, 647-653. [104]

MILBY, J. B. Modification of extreme social isolation by contingent social reinforcement. *JABA*, 1970, **3**, 149-152. [89]

MILLAR, W. S. A study of operant conditioning under delayed reinforcement in early infancy. *Monographs of the Society for Research in Child Development*, 1972, **37**(2, Whole No. 147). [126]

MILLER, A. G., & THOMAS, R. Cooperation and competition among Blackfoot Indian and urban Canadian children, *CD*, 1972, **43**, 1104-1110. [235]

MILLER, G. A. Some psychological studies of grammar. *AP*, 1962, **17**, 748-762.
[277]

MILLER, G. A. A psychological method to investigate verbal concepts. *Journal of Mathematical Psychology*, 1969, **6**, 169-191. [290]

MILLER, G. A., & SELFRIDGE, J. Verbal context and the recall of meaningful material. *AJP*, 1950, **63**, 176-185. [293]

MILLER, L. K. *Principles of everyday behavior analysis*. Monterey, Calif.: Brooks/ Cole, 1975. [645, 650]

MILLER, L. K. The design of better communities through the application of behavioral principles. In W. E. Craighead, A. E. Kazdin, & M. J. Mahoney (Eds.), *Behavior modification: Principles, issues, and applications*. Boston: Houghton Mifflin, 1976. [630]

MILLER, L. K., & FEALLOCK, R. A behavioral system for group living. In E. Ramp & G. Semb (Eds.), *Behavior Analysis: Areas of research and application*. Englewood Cliffs, N.J.: Prentice-Hall, 1975. [528, 648]

MILLER, L. K., & LIES, A. A. Everyday behavior analysis: A new direction for applied behavior analysis. *Behavior Voice*, 1974, **2**(1), 5-13. [651]

MILLER, L. K., LIES, A., PETERSEN, D. L., & FEALLOCK, R. The positive community: A strategy for applying behavioral engineering to the redesign of family and community. In E. J. Mash, L. A. Hamerlynck, & L. C. Handy (Eds.), *Behavior modification and families*. New York: Brunner/Mazel, 1976. [633]

MILLER, L. K., & MILLER, O. L. Reinforcing self-help group activities of welfare recipients. *JABA*, 1970, **3**, 57-64. [66]

MILLER, L. K., & WEAVER, F. H. A multiple baseline achievement test. In G. Semb (Ed.), *Behavior analysis and education—1972*. Lawrence: University of Kansas Support and Development Center for Fellow Through, 1972. [497, 512, 520]

MILLER, L. K., & WEAVER, F. H. The use of "concept programming" to teach behavioral concepts to university students. In J. M. Johnston (Ed.), *Behavior research and technology in higher education*. Springfield, Ill.: Charles C Thomas, 1975. [497, 501, 520]

MILLER, L. K., & WEAVER, F. H. A behavioral technology for producing concept formation in university students. *JABA*, 1976, **9**, 289-300. [645]

MILLER, L. K., WEAVER, F. H., & SEMB, G. A. Procedure for maintaining student progress in a personalized university course. *JABA*, 1974, **7**, 87-91. [503]

MILLER, N. E. Liberalization of basic S-R concepts: Extension to conflict behavior, motivation and social learning. In S. Koch (Ed.), *Psychology: A study of a science. Vol. 2*. New York: McGraw-Hill, 1959. [106]

MILLER, N. E. Some reflections on the law of effect produce a new alternative to drive reduction. In M. R. Jones (Ed.), *Nebraska symposium on Motivation. Vol. II*. Lincoln: University of Nebraska Press, 1963. [23]

MILLER, N. E., & DOLLARD, J. Social learning and imitation. New Haven: Yale University Press, 1941. [106, 144-146, 159, 164, 171]

MINKE, K. A., & CARLSON, J. G. *Psychology and life: Unit mastery system*. Glenview, Ill.: Scott, Foresman, 1972. [485, 502]

MINKIN, N., BRAUKMANN, C. J., MINKIN, B. L., TIMBERS, B. J., FIXSEN, D. L. PHILLIPS, E. L., & WOLF, M. M. The social validation and training of conversation skills in pre-delinquent youths. *JABA*, 1976, **9**, 127-140. [650]

MISCHEL, W. Preference for delayed reinforcement: An experimental study of a cultural observation. *JASP*, 1958, **56**, 57-61. [257]

MISCHEL, W. Theory and research on the antecedents of self-imposed delay of reward. In B. A. Maher (Ed.), *Progress in experimental personality research. Vol. 3*. New York: Academic Press, 1966. [246]

MISCHEL, W., & METZNER, R. Preference for delayed reward as a function of age, intelligence and length of delay interval. *JASP*, 1962, **64**, 425-431. [257]

MITHAUG, D. E. The development of cooperation in alternative task situations. *JECP*, 1969, **8**, 443-460. [229]

MOESER, S. D., & BREGMAN, A. S. The role of reference in the acquisition of a miniature artificial language. *JVLVB*, 1972, **11**, 759-769. [310]

MOESER, S. D., & BREGMAN, A. S. Imagery and language acquisition. *JVLVB*, 1973, **12**, 91-98. [310]

MOON, L. E., & HARLOW, H. F. Analysis of oddity learning by rhesus monkeys. *JCPP*, 1955, **48**, 188-194. [328]

MOORE, J. W., & GAGNÉ, E. D. *The effects of continuous progress instruction on acquisition, transfer, and attitudes in a college religion course.* Unpublished manuscript, 1973. [494-499, 506]

MOORE, J. W., HAUCK, W. E., & GAGNÉ, E. D. Acquisition retention and transfer in an individualized college physics course. *JEdP*, 1973, **64**, 335-340. [494, 496, 498, 506]

MOORE, J. W., MAHAN, J. M., & RITTS, C. A. Continuous progress concept with university students. *P Rep*, 1969, **25**, 887-892. [491, 494, 496, 499, 506]

MOORE, O. K. *The automated responsive environment.* New Haven, Conn.: Yale University Press, 1962. [462]

MORRIS, C. J., & KIMBRELL, G. M. Performance and attitudinal effects of the Keller method in an introductory psychology course. *P Rec*, 1972, **22**, 523-530. [493-496, 501, 506]

MORRIS, L. L. *An information processing examination of skill assembly in problem solving using Wertheimer's area of a parallelogram problem.* Unpublished doctoral dissertation, University of Pittsburgh, 1975. [404]

MORSE, W. H. *An analysis of responding in the presence of a stimulus correlated with periods of nonreinforcement.* Unpublished doctoral dissertation, Harvard University, 1955. [54]

MORSE, W. H., & KELLEHER, R. T. Schedules using noxious stimuli. I. Multiple fixed-ratio and fixed-interval termination of schedule complexes. *JEAB*, 1966, **9**, 267-290. [42]

MORSE, W. H., & KELLEHER, R. T. Schedules as fundamental determinants of behavior. In W. N. Schoenfeld (Ed.), *The theory of reinforcement schedules.* New York: Appleton-Century-Crofts, 1970. [23]

MORSE, W. H., & SKINNER, B. F. A second type of supersition in the pigeons. *AJP*, 1957, **70**, 308-311. [25]

MORSE, W. H., & SKINNER, B. F. Some factors involved in the stimulus control of operant behavior. *JEAB*, 1958, **1**, 103-107. [52]

MOSKOWITZ, A. I. The two-year-old stage in the acquisition of English phonology, *Language*, 1970, **46**, 426-441. [419]

MOSKOWITZ, A. I. *The acquisition of phonology.* Unpublished doctoral dissertation, University of California—Berkeley, 1971. [419]

MOSS, H. A. Communication in mother-infant interaction. In L. Krames, P. Pliner, & T. Alloway (Eds.), *Nonverbal communication: Comparative aspects.* New York: Plenum, 1974. [127]

MOWRER, O. H. *Learning theory and personality dynamics.* New York: Ronald Press, 1950. [106]

MOWRER, O. H. *Learning theory and behavior.* New York: Wiley, 1960. [146, 175]

MOWRER, O. H., & KLUCKHOHN, C. Dynamic theory of personality. In J. McV. Hunt (Ed.), *Personality and the behavior disorders. Vol. I.* New York: Ronald Press, 1944. [106]

MUIR, W. R. *A comparison of classes taught by a conventional procedure under normal conditions and by a PSI procedure under adverse procedures.* Paper presented at the West Coast PSI Conference, Long Beach, Calif., 1972. [493-495]

MULHOLLAND, T. M. *Availability versus accessibility of a subroutine in problem solving*. Unpublished master's thesis, University of Pittsburgh, 1974. [404]

MYERS, W. A. Operant learning principles applied to teaching introductory statistics. *JABA*, 1970, **3**, 191-197. [490]

NEALE, J. M., & LIEBERT, R. M. (Eds.), *Science and behavior: An introduction to methods of research*. Englewood Cliffs, N.J.: Prentice-Hall, 1973. [96]

NEISSER, U. *Cognitive psychology*. New York: Appleton-Century-Crofts, 1967. [275, 415]

NELSON, T. F., & SCOTT, D. W. Personalized instruction in educational psychology. *Michigan Academician*, 1972, **4**, 293-302. [496]

NEMETH, C. Bargaining and reciprocity. *PB*, 1970, **74**, 309-326. [221]

NERBONNE, G. P., & HIPSKIND, N. M. Vocabularies of oral and graphic language. *Language and Speech*, 1973, **16**, 57-66. [286]

NEURINGER, A. J. Superstitious key pecking after three peck-produced reinforcements. *JEAB*, 1970, **13**, 127-134. [43]

NEVIN, J. A. On form of the relation between response rates in a multiple schedule. *JEAB*, 1974, **21**, 237-248. (a) [54]

NEVIN, J. A. Response strength in multiple schedules. *JEAB*, 1974, **21**, 389-408. (b) [54]

NIELSON, K. V., LLOYD, M. E., & LLOYD, K. E. *The effect of a class-based point system on correspondence between planned and actual study time and on amount of study time for other university classes*. Paper presented at the meeting of the American Psychological Association, New Orleans, 1974. [520]

NOLEN, P. A., KUNZELMANN, H. P., & HARING, N. G. Behavioral modification in a junior high learning disabilities classroom. *EC*, 1967, **34**, 163-168. [566]

NORDQUIST, V. M. The modification of a child's enuresis: Some response-response relationships. *JABA*, 1971, **4**, 241-247. [67, 90]

NOTTEBOHM, F. Ontogeny of bird song. *Science*, 1970, **167**, 950-956. [278]

NOTTERMAN, J. M., & MINTZ, D. E. Exteroceptive cueing of response force. *Science*, 1962, **135**, 1070-1071. [37]

O'CONNOR, R. D. Modification of social withdrawal through symbolic modeling. *JABA*, 1969, **2**, 15-22. [65]

O'DAY, E. F. *Programmed instruction: Techniques and trends*. New York: Appleton-Century-Crofts, 1971. [461, 462, 464, 467]

OELSNER, L. U.S. ends project on jail inmates. *The New York Times*, February 7, 1974, B-1. [564]

OLDFIELD, R. C., & WINGFIELD, A. The time it takes to name an object. *Nature*, 1964, **212**, 1031-1032. [301]

O'LEARY, K. D. Behavior modification in the classroom: A rejoinder to Winett and Winkler. *JABA*, 1972, **5**, 505-511. [205, 526, 668]

O'LEARY, K. D., & BECKER, W. C. Behavior modification of an adjustment class: A token reinforcement program. *EC*, 1967, **33**, 639-642. [186]

O'LEARY, K. D., BECKER, W. C., EVANS, M. B., & SAUDARGAS, R. A. A token reinforcement program in a public school: A replication and systematic analysis. *JABA*, 1969, **2**, 3-13. [98, 187]

O'LEARY, K. D., & DRABMAN, R. S. Token reinforcement programs in the classroom: A review. *PB*, 1971, **75**, 379-398. [175, 183-186, 191, 206]

O'LEARY, K. D., & KENT, R. N. Behavior modification for social action: Research tactics and problems. In L. A. Hamerlynk, P. O. Davidson, & L. E. Acker (Eds.), *Critical issues in research and practice*. Champaign, Ill.: Research Press, 1973. [74-77]

O'LEARY, K. D., KENT, R. N., & KANOWITZ, J. Shaping data collection congruent with experimental hypotheses. *JABA*, 1975, **8**, 43-51. [76]

O'LEARY, K. D., & O'LEARY, S. G. (Eds.) *Classroom management: The successful use of behavior modification.* New York: Pergamon, 1972. [65, 181]

O'LEARY, K. D., PELHAM, W. E., ROSENBAUM, A., & PRICE, G. Behavioral treatment of hyperkinetic children: An experimental evaluation of its usefulness. *Clinical Pediatrics,* 1976, **15**(5), 274-279. [187]

O'LEARY, K. D., POULOS, R. W., & DEVINE, V. T. Tangible reinforcers: Bonuses or bribes? *JCCP,* 1972, **38**, 1-8. [204]

O'LEARY, K. D., & WILSON, G. T. *Behavior therapy: Application and outcome.* Englewood Cliffs, N.J.: Prentice-Hall, 1975. [61]

O'LEARY, S. G., & O'LEARY, K. D. Behavior modification in the school. In H. Leitenberg (Ed.), *Handbook of behavior modification and behavior therapy.* Englewood Cliffs, N.J.: Prentice-Hall, 1977. [191, 200, 206]

O'NEILL, G. W., JOHNSTON, J. M., WALTERS, W. M., & RASHEED, J. A. The effects of quantity of assigned material on college student academic performance and study behavior. In J. M. Johnston (Ed.), *Behavior research and technology in higher education.* Springfield, Ill.: Charles C Thomas, 1975. [508, 513]

OPTON, E. M., JR. Psychiatric violence against prisoners: When therapy is punishment. *Mississippi Law Journal,* 1974, **45**, 605-644. [659, 671]

ORLANDO, R., & BIJOU, S. W. Single and multiple schedules of reinforcement in developmentally retarded children. *JEAB,* 1960, **3**, 339-348. [196]

OSBORNE, J. G. Free-time as a reinforcer in the management of classroom behavior. *JABA,* 1969, **2**, 113-118. [82, 181]

OSGOOD, C. E. Toward a wedding of insufficiencies. In T. R. Dixon & D. L. Horton (Eds.), *Verbal behavior and general behavior theory.* Englewood Cliffs, N.J.: Prentice-Hall, 1968. [290, 297]

OSGOOD, C. E., SUCI, G. J., & TANNENBAUM, P. H. *The measurement of meaning.* Urbana: University of Illinois Press, 1957. [289]

OSSER, H., & ENDLER, N. S. Lexical choice and social class. *Language and Speech,* 1970, **13**, 254-261. [305]

OVERTON, W. F. The active organism in structuralism. *HD,* 1976, **19**, 71-86. [140]

PACKARD, R. G. The control of "classroom attention": a group contingency for complex behavior. *JABA,* 1970, **3**, 13-28. [516]

PAIVIO, A. *Imagery and verbal processes.* New York: Holt, Rinehart and Winston, 1971. [301]

PALMER, T. The youth authority's community treatment project. *Federal Probation,* 1974, 3-14. [619]

PANYAN, M. BOOZER, H., & MORRIS, N. Feedback to attendants as a reinforcer for applying operant techniques. *JABA,* 1970, **3**, 1-4. [542]

PARKER, H. C. Contingency management and concomitant changes in elementary-school student's self-concepts. *Journal of School Psychology,* 1974, **11**, 70-79. [188]

PARSONS, H. M. What happened at Hawthorne. *Science,* 1974, **183**, 922-932. [552]

PARTON, D. A., & FOUTS, G. T. Effects of stimulus-response similarity and dissimilarity on children's matching performance. *JECP,* 1969, **8**, 461-468. [172]

PARTON, D. A., & GESHURI, Y. Learning of aggression as a function of presence of a human model, response intensity, and target of the response. *JECP,* 1971, **11**, 491-504. [152, 162]

PARTON, D. A., & PRIEFERT, M. J. *Children's preference for stimuli associated with being imitated.* Paper presented at the meeting of the Society for Research in Child Development, Philadelphia, April 1973. [172, 175]

PATTERSON, G. R. An application of conditioning techniques to the control of a hyperactive child. In L. P. Ullmann & L. Krasner (Eds.), *Case studies in behavior modification.* New York: Holt, Rinehart & Winston, 1965. [193, 194]

PATTERSON, G. R. *Families: Applications of social learning to family life.* Champaign, Ill.: Research Press, 1971. [651]

PATTERSON, G. R. Interventions for boys with conduct problems: Multiple settings, treatments, and criteria. *JCCP*, 1974, **42**, 471-481. [181]

PATTERSON, G. R., MCNEAL, S., HAWKINS, N., & PHELPS, R. Reprogramming the social environment. *Journal of Child Psychology and Psychiatry*, 1967, **8**, 181-195. [566]

PATTERSON, R. L. & TEIGEN, J. R. Conditioning and post-hospital generalization of non-delusional responses in a chronic psychotic patient. *JABA*, 1973, **6**, 65-70. [629]

PAVLOV, I. P. *Conditioned Reflexes.* (G. V. Anrep, trans.) Oxford, England: Oxford University Press, 1927. [21]

PEISACH, E. C. Children's comprehension of teacher and peer speech. *CD*, 1965, **36**, 467-480. [306]

PELHAM, W. *A remedial reading program using undergraduates as behavioral tutors: A model and results.* Unpublished manuscript, SUNY—Stony Brook, N.Y., 1974. [184]

PELLEGRINO, J. W. & SCHADLER, M. *Maximizing performance in a problem solving task.* Unpublished manuscript, University of Pittsburgh, Learning Research and Development Center, 1974. [404-405]

PENNYPACKER, H. S., KOENIG, C. H., & LINDSLEY, O. R. *Handbook of the standard behavior chart.* Kansas City, Mo.: Precision Media, 1972. [588]

PENNYPACKER, H. S., KOENIG, C. H., & SEAVER, W. H. Cost efficiency and effectiveness in the early detection and improvement of learning abilities. In P. O. Davidson, R. W. Clark, & L. A. Hamerlynk (Eds.), *Evaluation of Behavioral Programs in community, residential, and school settings.* Champaign, Ill.: Research Press, 1974. [598]

Personalized System of Instruction Newsletter. Center for Personalized Instruction, Georgetown University (29 Loyola Hall, Washington, D.C. 20007). October 1971. [491]

PETERSEN, D. L. & MILLER, L. K. *Training indigenous staff through the use of instructional packages.* Unpublished master's thesis, University of Kansas—Lawrence, 1976. [642, 645]

PETERSON, R. F. & WHITEHURST, G. J. A variable influencing the performance of generalized imitative behavior. *JABA*, 1971, **4**, 1-9. [173, 174]

PETRINOVICH, L. F., & HARDYCK, C. D. Generalization of an instrumental response between words and pictures. *PS*, 1970, **18**, 239-244. [301]

PHILIPPAS, M. A., & SOMMERFELDT, R. W. Keller versus lecture method in general physics instruction. *American Journal of Physics*, 1972, **40**, 1300-1306. [491-496, 505-506]

PHILLIPS, E. A., PHILLIPS, E. L., FIXSEN, D. L., & WOLF, M. M. *Achievement Place: The training of social skills.* Unpublished manuscript. University of Kansas— Lawrence, 1974. [614]

PHILLIPS, E. L. Achievement Place: Token reinforcement procedures in a home-style rehabilitation setting for "pre-delinquent" boys. *JABA*, 1968, **1**, 213-223. [66, 200, 613-618]

PHILLIPS, E. L., BAILEY, J., & WOLF, M. M. *Achievement Place: A token economy in a home style rehabilitation program for juvenile offenders.* Paper presented at the meeting of the American Psychological Association. Washington, D. C., 1969. [193]

PHILLIPS E. L., PHILLIPS, E. A., BAILEY J. S., FIXSEN, D. L., & WOLF, M. M. *Achievement Place.* 16 mm film University of Kansas—Lawrence, 1970. [625]

PHILLIPS, E. L., PHILLIPS, E. A., FIXSEN, D. L., & WOLF, M. M. Achievement Place: Modification of the behaviors of pre-delinquent boys within a token economy. *JABA*, 1971, **4**, 45-49.   [613-618]

PHILLIPS, E. L., PHILLIPS, E. A., FIXSEN, D. L., & WOLF, M. M. Behavior shaping works with delinquents. *Psychology Today*, June 1973.   [614]

PHILLIPS, E. L., PHILLIPS, E. A., FIXSEN, D. L., & WOLF, M. M. *The teaching-family handbook.* 2nd ed. Lawrence: University of Kansas Printing Service, 1974.   [624]

PHILLIPS, E. L., PHILLIPS, E. A., WOLF, M. M., & FIXSEN, D. L. Achievement Place: development of the elected manager system. *JABA*, 1973, **6**, 541-561.
                                                                        [618]

PIAGET, J. *Play, dreams and imitation in childhood.* New York: Norton, 1951.
                                                                 [106, 134, 326]

PIAGET, J. Les stades du developpement intellectuel de l'enfant et de l'adolescent. In P. Osterrieth, et al. (Eds.), *Le probleme des stades en psychologie de l'enfant.* Paris: Presses Univ. France, 1955.   [435]

PIAGET, J. *Science of education and the psychology of the child.* New York: Grossman, 1970. (a)   [381, 383]

PIAGET, J. *Structuralism.* New York: Harper & Row (Torchbooks), 1970. (b)
                                                                        [383]

PIERCE, C. H. & RISLEY, T. R. Recreation as a reinforcer: Increasing membership and decreasing disruptions in an urban recreation center. *JABA*, 1974, **7**, 403-411.   [84-85, 98]

PISONI, D. B. *On the nature of categorical perception of speech sounds.* Unpublished doctoral dissertation, University of Michigan, 1971.   [288]

PITTENGER, O. E., & GOODING, C. T. *Learning theories in educational practice.* New York: Wiley, 1971.   [484]

PLISKOFF, S. S. Rate-change with equal potential reinforcements during the "warning" stimulus. *JEAB*, 1963, **6**, 557-562.   [52]

POPPEN, R. Effects of concurrent schedules on human fixed interval performance. *JEAB*, 1972, **18**, 119-127.   [197]

PORTNOY, S. A comparison of oral and written verbal behavior. In K. Salzinger & R. S. Feldman (Eds.), *Studies in verbal behavior: An empirical approach.* New York: Pergamon, 1973.   [286]

PORTNOY, S., & SALZINGER, K. The conditionability of different verbal response classes: Positive, negative and nonaffect statements. *Journal of General Psychology.* 1964, **70**, 311-323.   [290]

POSNER, M. I. Representational systems for storing information in memory. In G. A. Talland & N. Waugh (Eds.), *The pathology of memory.* New York: Academic Press, 1969.   [415]

POSNER, M. I. & ROSSMAN, E. Effect of size and location of informational transforms upon short-term retention. *JEP*, 1965, **70**, 496-505.   [389]

POSTLETHWAIT, S. N., NOVAK, J., & MURRAY, H. *The audiotutorial approach to learning.* Minneapolis: Burgess, 1969.   [491]

POSTLETHWAIT, S. N., & RUSSELL, J. D. "Minicourses" the style of the future? In J. G. Creager & D. L. Murray (Eds.), *The use of modules in college biology teaching.* Publication No. 31. Washington, D.C.: Commission on Undergraduate Education in the Biological Sciences, 1971.   [491]

POSTMAN, L. The history and present status of the Law of Effect. *PB*, 1947, **44**, 489-563.   [23]

POSTMAN, L., & KEPPEL, G. (Eds.) *Verbal learning and memory.* Middlesex, England: Penguin, 1969.   [287]

POWELL, J. & AZRIN, N. The effects of shock as a punisher for cigarette smoking. *JABA*, 1968, **1**, 63-71.   [68]

POWELL, M., & MAGNUM, R. E. *Introduction to educational psychology.* Indianapolis, Ind.: Bobbs-Merrill, 1971.   [484]

PREMACK, D. Reinforcement theory. In D. Levine (Ed.), *Nebraska Symposium on Motivation. Vol. 13.* Lincoln: University of Nebraska, 1965.   [23]

PREMACK, D. A functional analysis of language. *JEAB*, 1970, **14**, 107-125. (a)
                                                                                    [278-280]

PREMACK, D. Mechanisms of self-control. In W. Hunt (Ed.) *Learning and mechanisms of control in smoking.* Chicago: Aldine, 1970. (b)   [268, 270]

PREMACK, D. On the assessment of language competence in the chimpanzee. In A. M. Schrier & F. Stollnitz (Eds.), *Behavior of nonhuman primates. Vol. 4.* New York: Academic Press, 1971. (a)   [278-280]

PREMACK, D. Catching up with common sense or two sides of a generalization: Reinforcement and punishment. In R. Glaser (Ed.), *The nature of reinforcement.* New York: Academic Press, 1971. (b)   [48]

PREMACK, D., & BAHWELL, R. Operant-level lever pressing by a monkey as a function of inter-test interval. *JEAB*, 1959, **2**, 127-131.   [32]

PRESIDENT'S COMMISSION ON LAW ENFORCEMENT AND ADMINISTRATION OF JUSTICE. *Task force report: Juvenile delinquency and youth crime.* Washington, D.C.: U.S. Government Printing Office, 1967.   [603]

PRESSEY, S. L. A simple device for teaching, testing, and research in learning. *School and Society*, 1926, **23**, 372-376.   [455]

PRESSEY, S. L. A machine for automatic teaching of drill material. *School and Society*, 1927, **25**, 549-552.   [455]

PRESSEY, S. L. Autopresentation versus autoelucidation. *Programmed Instruction*, 1963, **2**, 6-7. (a)   [467]

PRESSEY, S. L. Teaching machines (and learning theory) crisis. *Journal of Applied Psychology*, 1963, **47**, 1-6. (b)   [461, 468]

PRESSEY, S. L. Autoinstruction: perspectives, problems and potentials. In E. R. Hilgard (Ed.), *Theories of learning and instruction.* Chicago: The National Society for the Study of Education, 1964.   [461]

PRESSEY, S. L., & KINZER, J. R. Autoelucidation without programming. *NSPI Journal*, 1964, **3**, 12-13.   [467]

PRICE, G. & O'LEARY, K. D. *Teaching children to develop high performance standards.* Unpublished manuscript. SUNY—Stony Brook, N.Y., 1974.   [202]

PROTOPAPPAS, P. A report on the use of the Keller plan in a general biology course at Lowell State College. In J. G. Sherman (Ed.), *Personalized system of instruction.* Menlo Park, Calif.: Benjamin, 1974.   [492]

QUIGLEY, P. A. An analysis of student manager-student interactions during performance sessions. In J. M. Johnston (Ed.), *Behavior research and technology in higher education.* Springfield, Ill.: Charles C Thomas, 1975.
                                                                              [500, 501]

RACHLIN, H. The effect of shock intensity on concurrent and single-key responding in concurrent-chain schedules. *JEAB*, 1967, **10**, 87-93.   [46]

RACHLIN, H. Autoshaping of key pecking in pigeons with negative reinforcement. *JEAB*, 1969, **12**, 521-531.   [28]

RACHLIN, H. *Introduction to modern behaviorism.* San Francisco: W. H. Freeman, 1970.   [254]

RACHLIN, H. Self-control. *Behaviorism*, 1974, **2**, 94-107.   [246, 268]

RACHLIN, H., & GREEN, L. Commitment, choice and self-control. *JEAB*, 1972, **17**, 15-22.   [254-256, 270-271]

RACHLIN, H., & HERRNSTEIN, R. J. Hedonism revisited: On the negative law of effect. In B. A. Campbell & R. M. Church (Eds.), *Punishment and aversive behavior.* New York: Appleton-Century-Crofts, 1969.   [46]

RACHMAN, S. & TEASDALE, J. *Aversion therapy and behaviour disorders.* London: Routledge & Kegan Paul, 1969. [672]

RAMEY, C. T., & OURTH, L. L. Delayed reinforcement and vocalization rates of infants. *CD,* 1971, **42**, 291-297. [126]

RAMP, E., & SEMB, G. (Eds.) Behavior analysis: Areas of research and application. Englewood Cliffs, N.J.: Prentice-Hall, 1975. [61]

RAVITCH, D. *The great school wars: New York City, 1805-1973.* New York: Basic Books, 1974. [180, 199]

RAZRAN, G. Salivating, and thinking in different languages. *JP,* 1936, **1**, 145-151. [297]

RAZRAN, G. The observable unconscious and the inferable conscious in current Soviet psychophysiology: Interoceptive conditioning, semantic conditioning, and the orienting reflex. *P Rev,* 1961, **68**, 81-147. [297]

RAZRAN, G. *Mind in evolution.* New York: Houghton Mifflin, 1971. [297]

REBER, A. S. Implicit learning of artificial grammars. *JVLVB,* 1967, **6**, 855-863. [416, 436]

REBER, A. S. On psycho-linguistic paradigms. *Journal of Psycholinguistic Research,* 1973, **2**, 289-319. [275, 283]

REBER, A. S., & SCARBOROUGH, D. (Eds.) *Toward a psychology of reading.* Hillsdale, N.J.: Erlbaum Associates, 1977. [411]

REDD, W. H. Effects of mixed reinforcement contingencies on adults' control of children's behavior. *JABA,* 1969, **2**, 249-254. [66, 101]

REDD, W. H. SIDMAN, M., & FLETCHER, F. G. Timeouts as a reinforcer for errors in a serial position task. *JEAB,* 1974, **21**, 3-17. [35]

REDD, W. H., & WINSTON, A. S. *The role of antecedent positive and negative comments in the control of children's behavior.* Paper presented at the meeting of the Society for Research in Child Development, Philadelphia, April 1973. [163]

REESE, H. W. *The perception of stimulus relations: Discrimination learning and transposition.* New York: Academic Press, 1968. [59]

REID, J. B. Reliability assessment of observation data: A possible methodological problem. *CD,* 1970, **41**, 1143-1150. [74]

REID, R. L. The role of the reinforcer as a stimulus. *British Journal of Psychology,* 1957, **49**, 202-209. [27]

REIMRINGER, M. J., MORGAN, S. W., & BRAMWELL, P. F. Succinylcholine as a modifier of acting-out behavior. *Clinical Medicine,* 1970, **77**(7), 28-29. [672]

REISS, S., & SUSHINSKY, L. W. Overjustification, competing responses, and the acquisition of intrinsic interest. *JPSP,* 1975, **31**, 1116-1125. [196]

REPPUCCI, N. D., & SAUNDERS, J. T. Social psychology of behavior modification: Problems of implementation in natural settings. *AP,* 1974, **29**, 649-660. [8, 192, 264, 565, 583]

RESCORLA, R. A., & WAGNER, A. R. A theory of Pavlovian conditioning: Variations in the effectiveness of reinforcement and nonreinforcement. In A. H. Black & W. F. Prokasy (Eds.), *Classical conditioning II.* New York: Appleton-Century-Crofts, 1972. [58]

RESNICK, L. B. Programmed instruction and the teaching of complex intellectual skills: Problems and prospects. *Harvard Educational Review,* 1963, **33**, 439-471. [472]

RESNICK, L. B. Task analysis in instructional design: Some cases from mathematics. In D. Klahr (Ed.), *Cognition and instruction.* Hillsdale, N.J.: Erlbaum Associates, 1978. [378, 396]

RESNICK, L. B., & BECK, I. L. Designing instruction on reading: Interaction of theory and practice. In J. T. Guthrie (Ed.), *Aspects of reading acquisition.* Baltimore, Md.: Johns Hopkins University Press, 1976. [378, 387-390, 396, 397, 406-407]

RESNICK, L. B., & GLASER, R. *Problem solving and intelligence.* In L. B. Resnick (Ed.) *The nature of intelligence.* Hillsdale, N.J.: Erlbaum Associates, 1977.
[387, 402-404]

RESNICK, L. B., SIEGEL, A. W., & KRESH, E. Transfer and sequence in learning double classification skills. *JECP*, 1971, **11**, 139-149. [387]

RESNICK, L. B., WANG, M. C., & KAPLAN, J. Task analysis in curriculum deesign: A hierarchically sequenced introductory mathematics curriculum. *JABA*, 1973, **6**, 679-710. [385-386, 396]

REYNOLDS, G. S. An analysis of interactions in a multiple schedule. *JEAB*, 1961, **4**, 107-117. (a) [54]

REYNOLDS, G. S. Attention in the pigeon. *JEAB*, 1961, **4**, 203-208. (b) [57, 327]

REYNOLDS, G. S. *A primer of operant conditioning.* Glenview, Ill.: Scott, Foresman, 1968. [198]

RHEINGOLD, H. L., GEWIRTZ, J. L., & ROSS, H. W. Social conditioning of vocalizations in the infact. *JCPP*, 1959, **52**, 68-73. [147, 316]

RICHARDS, R. W., & RILLING, M. Aversive aspects of a fixed-interval schedule of food reinforcement. *JEAB*, 1972, **17**, 405-411. [28]

RIPPLE, R. E. *A comparison of the effectiveness of a programmed text with three other methods of presentation.* Unpublished manuscript, Cornell University, 1962. [462]

RISLEY, T. R. Behavior modification: An experimental therapeutic endeavor. In L. A. Hamerlynck, P. O. Davidson, & L. E. Acker (Eds.), *Behavior modification and ideal mental health services.* Calgary, Alberta, Canada: University of Calgary Press, 1970. [61, 79, 102, 103]

RISLEY, T. R., CLARK, H. B., & CATALDO, M. F. Behavioral technology for the normal middle-class family. In E. J. Mash, L. A. Hamerlynck, & L. C. Handy (Eds.), *Behavior modification and families.* New York: Brunner-Mazel, 1976.
[629, 643]

RISLEY, T. R., & HART, B. Developing correspondence between the non-verbal and verbal behavior of preschool children. *JABA*, 1968, **1**, 267-281. [519]

RISLEY, T. R., & REYNOLDS, N. J. Emphasis as a prompt for verbal imitation. *JABA*, 1970, **3**, 185-190. [160]

ROBBINS, D. Partial reinforcement: A selective review of the alleyway literature since 1960. *PB*, 1971, **76**, 415-431. [44]

ROBERTS, R. E. *The new communes.* Englewood Cliffs, N.J.: Prentice-Hall, 1971.
[637]

ROBIN, A., O'LEARY, K. D., & ARMEL, S. The effects of self-instruction on writing deficiencies. *BT*, 1975, **6**, 178-187. [183]

ROBINSON, W. P. Cloze procedure as a technique for the investigation of social class difference in language usage. *Language and Speech*, 1965, **8**, 42-55. [307]

ROBINSON, W. P. *Language and social behavior.* Middlesex, England: Penguin, 1972. [304, 305]

ROGERS, D. *110 Livingston Street.* New York: Random House, 1968. [542]

ROHWER, W. D. Learning, race and school success. *RER*, 1971, **41**, 191-210. (a)
[470]

ROHWER, W. D. Prime time for education: Early childhood or adolescence? *Harvard Educational Review*, 1971, **41**, 316-341. (b) [384]

ROMANCZYK, R. G., KENT, R. N., DIAMENT, C., & O'LEARY, K. D. Measuring the reliability of observational data: A reactive process. *JABA*, 1973, **6**, 175-184.
[74, 75]

ROMANCZYK, R. G., TRACEY, D. A., WILSON, G. T., & THORPE, G. L. Behavioral techniques in the treatment of obesity: A comparative analysis. *BRT*, 1974, **11**, 629-640. [257]

ROOP, J. M. Contingency management in the teaching of economics: Some results from an intermediate microeconomics course. *Intermountain Economic Review*, 1973, 4, 53-71.   [491-495, 499, 505]

ROSATI, P. A. A comparison of the personalized system of instruction with the lecture method in teaching elementary dynamics. In J. M. Johnston (Ed.), *Behavior research and technology in higher education*. Springfield, Ill.: Charles C Thomas, 1975.   [494, 496, 506]

ROSEKRANS, M. A. Imitation in children as a function of perceived similarity to a social model and vicarious reinforcement. *JPSP*, 1967, 7, 307-315.   [159]

ROSENBAUM, A., O'LEARY, K. D., & JACOB, R. G. Behavioral intervention with hyperactive children: Group consequences as a supplement to individual contingencies. *BT*, 1975, 6, 315-323.   [190, 194]

ROSENBERG, S. ,The maintenance of a learned response in controlled interpersonal conditions. *Sociometry*, 1959, 22, 124-138.   [223]

ROSENBERG, S. Cooperative behavior in dyads as a function of reinforcement parameters. *JASP*, 1960, 60, 318-333.   [223, 229]

ROSENBERG, S., & HALL, R. L. The effects of different social feedback conditions upon performance in dyadic teams. *JASP*, 1958, 57, 271-277.   [223]

ROSENFELD, H. M., & BAER, D. M. Unnoticed verbal conditioning of an aware experimenter by a more aware subject: The double-agent effect. *P Rev*, 1969, 76, 425-432.   [315]

ROSENFELD, H. M., & BAER, D. M. Unbiased and unnoticed verbal conditioning: The double-agent robot procedure. *JEAB*, 1970, 14, 99-107.   [315]

ROSENTHAL, R., & JACOBSON, L. *Pygmalion in the classroom: Teacher's expectation of pupils' intellectual ability.* New York: Holt, Rinehart & Winston, 1968.   [137]

ROSNER, J. *The development and validation of an individualized perceptual skills curriculum.* Learning Research and Development Center, University of Pittsburgh, Publication 1972/7.   [421, 425, 451]

ROSNER, J. Auditory analysis training with prereaders. *The Reading Teacher*, 1974, 27, 379-384.   [421, 425, 451]

ROSNER, J., & SIMON, D. P. *The auditory analysis test: An initial report.* Learning Research and Development Center, University of Pittsburgh, Publication 1971/3.   [425, 441, 451]

ROTHKOPF, E. Z. Learning from written materials: An exploration of the control of inspection behavior by test-like events. *American Educational Research Journal*, 1966, 3, 214-249.   [468]

ROTHKOPF, E. Z. Textual constraints as a function of repeated inspection. *JEdP*, 1968, 59, 20-25.   [468]

ROTHKOPF, E. Z. The concept of mathemagenic activities. *RER*, 1970, 40, 325-336.   [468]

ROTTER, J. B. *Social learning and clinical psychology.* Englewood Cliffs, N.J.: Prentice-Hall, 1954.   [246]

ROUTH, D. K. Conditioning of vocal response differentiation in infants. *DP*, 1969, 1, 219-226.   [316]

ROZIN, P. The evolution of intelligence and access to the cognitive unconscious. In J. Sprague & A. N. Epstein (Eds.), *Progress in psychobiology and physiological psychology*. Vol. 6. New York: Academic Press, 1976.   [434, 435]

ROZIN, P., BRESSMAN, B., & TAFT, M. Do children understand the basic relationship between speech and writing? The mow-motorcycle text. *Journal of Reading Behavior*, 1974, 6, 327-334.   [424, 438, 440]

ROZIN, P., & GLEITMAN, L. R. *Syllabary: An Introductory Reading Curriculum.* (*Pilot ed.*) Washington, D.C.: Curriculum Development Associates, 1974.   [442-443, 446-447]

ROZIN, P., & GLEITMAN, L. R. The structure and acquisition of reading. II: The reading process and the acquisition of the alphabetic principle, In A. S. Reber & D. Scarborough (Eds.), *Toward a psychology of reading*. Hillsdale, N.J.: Erlbaum Associates, 1977. (a)   [411, 415, 425, 432, 434, 436, 441, 450]

ROZIN, P., & GLEITMAN, L. R. *Syllabary: An Introductory Reading Curriculum*. Washington, D.C.: Curriculum Development Associates, 1977. (b)   [442-443]

ROZIN, P., PORITSKY, S., & SOTSKY, R. American children with reading problems can easily learn to read English represented by Chinese characters. *Science*, 1971, **171**, 1264-1267.   [303, 423, 440]

RUBIN, B. K., & STOLZ, S. B. Generalization of self-referent speech established in a retarded adolescent by operant procedures. *BT*, 1974, **5**, 93-106.   [321]

RUMBAUGH, D. M., & GILL, T. V. Language and the acquisition of language-type skills by a chimpanzee (*Pan*). *Annals of the New York Academy of Sciences*, 1976, **270**, 90-123.   [278-280]

RUMBAUGH, D. M., GILL, T. V., & VON GLASERSFELD, E. C. Reading and sentence completion by a chimpanzee (*Pan*). *Science*, 1973, **182**, 731-733.   [278-280]

RUSCH, F. R., WALKER, H. M., & GREENWOOD, C. R. Experimenter calculation errors: A potential factor affecting interpretation of results. *JABA*, 1975, **8**, 460.
                                                                                       [77]

SAILOR, W. Reinforcement and generalization of productive plural allomorphs in two retarded children. *JABA*, 1971, **4**, 305-310.   [320, 342]

SAJWAJ, T., TWARDOSZ, S., & BURIE, M. Side effects of extinction procedures in a remedial preschool. *JABA*, 1972, **5**, 163-175.   [67]

SAKAMOTO, T., & MAKITA, K. Japan. In J. Downing (Ed.), *Comparative reading: Cross-national studies of behavior and processes in reading and writing*. New York: Macmillan, 1973.   [440, 441]

SALZBERG, C. L. Freedom and responsibility in an elementary school. In G. Semb (Ed.), *Behavior analysis and education*. Lawrence: University of Kansas Support and Development Center for Follow Through, 1972.   [528]

SALZINGER, K. A method of analysis of the process of verbal communication between a group of emotionally disturbed adolescents and their friends and relatives. *Journal of Social Psychology*, 1958, **47**, 39-53.   [307]

SALZINGER, K. Experimental manipulation of verbal behavior: A review. *Journal of General Psychology*, 1959, **61**, 65-94.   [316]

SALZINGER, K. The problem of response class in verbal behavior. In K. Salzinger & S. Salzinger (Eds.), *Research in verbal behavior and some neurophysiological implications*. New York: Academic Press, 1967.   [275, 281, 300, 314]

SALZINGER, K. On the operant conditioning of complex behavior. In J. M. Shlien & H. Hunt (Eds.), *Research in psychotherapy*. Washington, D.C.; American Psychological Association, 1968.   [321]

SALZINGER, K. The place of operant conditioning of verbal behavior in psychotherapy. In C. Franks (Ed.) *Behavior therapy: Appraisal and status*. New York: McGraw-Hill, 1969. (a)   [316]

SALZINGER, K. *Psychology: The science of behavior*. New York: Springer, 1969. (b)
                                                                                      [280]

SALZINGER, K. Pleasing linguists: A parable. *JVLVB*, 1970, **9**, 725-727.   [275]

SALZINGER, K. Animal communication. In D. A. Dewsbury & D. A. Rethlingshafer (Eds.), *Comparative psychology*, New York: McGraw-Hill, 1973. (a)
                                                                                 [278, 279]

SALZINGER, K. Inside the black box, with apologies to Pandora. A review of Ulric Neisser's *Cognitive Psychology*. *JEAB*, 1973, **19**, 369-378. (b)   [275, 289]

SALZINGER, K. Some problems of response measurement in verbal behavior: The response unit and intraresponse relations. In K. Salzinger & R. S. Feldman (Eds.) *Studies in verbal behavior: An empirical approach*. New York: Pergamon, 1973. (c)   [275, 277, 289, 300]

SALZINGER, K. Are theories of competence necessary? *Annals of the New York Academy of Sciences*, 1975, **263**, 178-196.   [275, 283]

SALZINGER, K., & ECKERMAN, C. Grammar and the recall of chains of verbal responses. *JVLVB*, 1967, **6**, 232-239.   [275, 287]

SALZINGER, K., & FELDMAN, R. S. *Studies in verbal behavior: An empirical approach*. New York: Pergamon, 1973.   [275, 296]

SALZINGER, K., FELDMAN, R. S., COWAN, J. E., & SALZINGER, S. Operant conditioning of verbal behavior of two young speech-deficient boys. In L. Krasner & L. P. Ullmann (Eds.), *Research in behavior modification*. New York: Holt, Rinehart & Winston, 1965.   [318]

SALZINGER, K., HAMMER, M., PORTNOY, S., & POLGAR, S. K. Verbal behavior and social distance. *Language and Speech*, 1970, **13**, 25-37.   [307, 308]

SALZINGER, K., & PISONI, S. Reinforcement of affect responses of schizophrenics during the clinical interview. *JASP*, 1958, **57**, 84-90.   [315]

SALZINGER, K., & PISONI, S. Reinforcement of verbal affect responses of normal subjects during the interview. *JASP*, 1960, **60**, 127-130.   [315]

SALZINGER, K., & PISONI, S. Some parameters of the conditioning of verbal affect responses in schizophrenic subjects. *JASP*, 1961, **63**, 511-516.   [315]

SALZINGER, K., PORTNOY, S., & FELDMAN, R. S. The effect of order of approximation to the statistical structure of English on the emission of verbal responses. *JEP*, 1962, **64**, 52-57.   [293-294]

SALZINGER, K., PORTNOY, S., & FELDMAN, R. S. Verbal behavior of schizophrenic and normal subjects. *Annals of the New York Academy of Sciences*, 1964, **105**, 845-860.   [286, 294]

SALZINGER, K., PORTNOY, S., & FELDMAN, R. S. Verbal behavior in schizophrenics and some comments toward a theory of schizophrenia. In P. Hoch & J. Zubin (Eds.), *Psychopathology of schizophrenia*. New York: Grune & Stratton, 1966.   [286, 294]

SALZINGER, K., PORTNOY, S., PISONI, D. B., & FELDMAN, R. S. The immediacy hypothesis and response-produced stimuli in schizophrenic speech. *JAP*, 1970, **76**, 258-264.   [286, 294-295]

SALZINGER, K., PORTNOY, S., ZLOTOGURA, P., & KEISNER, R. The effect of reinforcement on continuous speech and on plural nouns in grammatical context. *JVLVB*, 1963, **1**, 477-485.   [314, 320]

SALZINGER, S. Some stimulus properties of syntagmatic and paradigmatic word sequences. In K. Salzinger & R. S. Feldman (Eds.), *Studies in verbal behavior: An empirical approach*. New York: Pergamon, 1973.   [284, 289, 296]

SALZINGER, S., SALZINGER, K., & PATENAUDE, J. Effect of verbal response class on shift in the preschool child's judgment of length in response to an anchor stimulus. *DP*, 1970, **2**, 49-57.   [301]

SALZINGER, S., SALZINGER, K., PORTNOY, S., ECKMAN, J., BACON, P. M., DEUTSCH, M., & ZUBIN, J. Operant conditioning of continuous speech in young children. *CD*, 1962, **33**, 683-695.   [317]

SANTOGROSSI, D. A. *Self-reinforcement and external monitoring of performance on an academic task*. Unpublished doctoral dissertation, SUNY—Stony Brook, N.Y., 1974.   [193]

SANTOGROSSI, D. A., O'LEARY, K. D., ROMANCZYK, R. G., & KAUFMAN, K. F. Self-evaluation by adolescents in a psychiatric hospital school token program. *JABA*, 1973, **6**, 277-288.   [202, 203]

SAVIN, H. B. What the child knows about speech when he starts to read. In J. F. Kavanagh & I. G. Mattingly (Eds.), *Language by ear and by eye: The relationships between speech and reading*. Cambridge, Mass.: M.I.T. Press, 1972.   [432]

SAVIN, H. B., & BEVER, T. G. The nonperceptual reality of the phoneme. *JVLVB*, 1970, **9**, 295-302.   [441]

SAWIRIS, M. Y. A factorial study of some variables relevant to a programmed learning situation. *Programmed Learning*, 1966, **3**, 30-34.   [470]

SCHAEFER, H. H., SOBELL, M. B., & MILLS, K. C. Baseline drinking behavior in alcoholics and social drinkers, kinds of drinks and sip magnitude, *BRT*, 1971, **9**, 23-27.   [273]

SCHAFFER, H. R., & EMERSON, P. ED. The development of social attachments in infancy. *Monographs of the Society for Research in Child Development*, 1964, **29** (3, Whole No. 94).   [131, 132]

SCHLESINGER, I. M. Learned grammar: From pivot to realization rule. In R. Huxley & E. Ingram (Eds.), *Language acquisition: Models and methods.* New York: Academic Press, 1971.   [308, 309]

SCHLOSBERG, H., & HEINEMAN, C. The relationship between two measures of response strength. *JEP*, 1950, **40**, 235-247.   [289]

SCHMIDT, G. W., & ULRICH, R. E. Effects of group contingent events upon classroom noise. *JABA*, 1969, **2**, 171-179.   [68, 516]

SCHMITT, D. R., & MARWELL, G. Stimulus control in the experimental study of cooperation. *JEAB*, 1968, **11**, 571-574.   [218]

SCHMITT, D. R., & MARWELL, G. Avoidance of risk as a determinant of cooperation. *JEAB*, 1971, **16**, 367-374. (a)   [42]

SCHMITT, D. R., & MARWELL, G. Taking and the disruption of cooperation. *JEAB*, 1971, **15**, 405-412. (b)   [42]

SCHNELLE, J. F. A brief report on invalidity of parent evaluations of behavior change. *JABA*, 1974, **7**, 341-343.   [78]

SCHNELLE, J. F., & FRANK, L. J. A quasi-experimental retrospective evaluation of a prison policy change. *JABA*, 1974, **7**, 483-494.   [100]

SCHNELLE, J. F., KIRCHNER, R. E., MCNEES, P. M., & LAWLER, J. M. Social evaluation research: The evaluation of two police patrolling strategies. *JABA*, 1975, **8**, 353-365.   [100]

SCHOENFELD, W. N. *The theory of reinforcement schedules.* New York: Appleton-Century-Crofts, 1970.   [126]

SCHOENFELD, W. N., ANTONITIS, J. J., & BERSH, P. J. Unconditioned response rate of the white rat in a barpressing apparatus. *JCPP*, 1950, **43**, 41-48.   [32]

SCHOENFELD, W. N., & CUMMING, W. W. Verbal dependencies in the analysis of language behavior: Experiment 1. In K. Salzinger & R. S. Feldman (Eds.), *Studies in verbal behavior: An empirical approach.* New York: Pergamon, 1973. (a)   [292, 294]

SCHOENFELD, W. N., & CUMMING, W. W. Verbal dependencies in the analysis of language behavior: Experiments 2 and 3. In K. Salzinger & R. S. Feldman (Eds.), *Studies in verbal behavior: An empirical approach.* New York: Pergamon, 1973. (b)   [295]

SCHROEDER, G. L., & BAER, D. M. Effects of concurrent and serial training on generalized vocal imitation in retarded children. *DP*, 1972, **6**, 293-301.   [162]

SCHUMAKER, J., & SHERMAN, J. A. Training generative verb usage by imitation and reinforcement procedures. *JABA*, 1970, **3**, 273-287.   [321]

SCHWITZGEBEL, R. K. *Development and legal regulations of coercive behavior modification techniques with offenders.* Washington, D.C.: U.S. Government Printing Office, 1971.   [564]

SCHWITZGEBEL, R. K. A contractual model for the protection of the rights of institutionalized mental patients. *AP*, 1975, **30**, 815-820.   [674]

SCOTT, J. W., & BUSHELL, D., JR. The length of teacher contacts and students' off-task behavior. *JABA*, 1974, **7**, 39-44.   [70]

SCOTT, P., BURTON, R. V., & YARROW, M. Social reinforcement under natural conditions. *CD*, 1967, **38**, 53-63.   [75]

SEARS, R. R. *Survey of objective studies of psychoanalytic concepts.* (Bulletin No. 51.) New York: Social Science Research Council, 1943.   [128]

SEARS, R. R. A theoretical framework for personality and social behavior. *AP,* 1951, **6,** 476-483.   [106]

SEARS, R. R., MACCOBY, E. E., & LEVIN, H. *Patterns of child rearing.* Evanston, Ill.: Row, Peterson, 1957.   [136]

SEARS, R. R., WHITING, J. W. M., NOWLIS, V., & SEARS, P. S. in collaboration with E. K. BELLER, J. C. COHEN, E. H. CHASDI, H. FAIGIN, J. L. GEWIRTZ, M. S. LAWRENCE, & J. P. MCKEE. Some child-rearing antecedents of aggression and dependency in young children. *Genetic Psychology Monographs,* 1953, **47,** 135-234.   [130, 136]

SEGAL, E. F. Towards a coherent psychology of language. In W. K. Honig & J. E. R. Staddon (Eds.), *Handbook of operant behavior.* Englewood Cliffs, N.J.: Prentice-Hall, 1977.   [275]

SELFRIDGE, J. A. *Investigations into the structure of verbal context.* Unpublished honor's thesis, Harvard University, 1949.   [293-294]

SELIGMAN, M. E. P., & JOHNSTON, J. C. Does teleology have a place in conditioning. In F. J. McGuigan & D. B. Lumsden (Eds.), *Contemporary approaches to conditioning and learning.* New York: Halsted Press, 1973.   [250]

SEMB, G. (Ed.), *Behavior analysis and education—1972.* Lawrence: University of Kansas. Support and Development Center for Follow Through, 1972.
                                                                              [629, 651]

SEMB, G. *Research strategies in higher education.* Paper presented at the meeting of the American Psychological Association, Montreal 1973.   [491]

SEMB, G. The effects of mastery criteria and assignment length on college student test performance. *JABA,* 1974, **7,** 61-70.   [491, 500, 501, 510-514]

SEMB, G. An analysis of the effects of hour exams and student-answered study questions on test performance in a course taught by personalized instruction. In J. M. Johnston (Ed.), *Behavior research and technology in higher education.* Springfield, Ill.: Charles C Thomas, 1975.   [491, 500, 501, 509]

SEMB, G., CONYERS, D., SPENCER, R., & SOSA, J. J. S. An experimental comparison of four pacing contingencies. In J. M. Johnston (Ed.), *Behavior research and technology in higher education.* Springfield, Ill.: Charles C Thomas, 1975.
                                                                              [500-502]

SEMB, G., HOPKINS, B. L., & HURSH, D. E. The effects of study questions and grades on student test performance in a college course. *JABA,* 1973, 6, 631-642.
                                                                         [500-501, 509]

SERBER, M., & KEITH, C. G. The Atascadero project: Model of a sexual retraining program for incarcerated homosexual pedophiles. *Journal of Homosexuality,* 1974, 1, 87-97.   [668, 672]

SHAH, S. A., & LALLEY, T. *Information dissemination and research utilization efforts.* Paper presented at the Workshop on the Use of Research in Decision-Making sponsored by the United Nations Social Defense Research Institute (Rome), Nijmegen, Netherlands, December 1973.   [607, 628]

SHANKWEILER, D., & LIBERMAN, I. Y. Misreading: A search for causes. In J. F. Kavanagh & I. G. Mattingly (Eds.), *Language by ear and by eye: The relationships between speech and reading.* Cambridge, Mass.: M.I.T. Press, 1972.
                                                                              [426, 438]

SHANNON, C. E. Prediction and entropy of printed English. *Bell System Technical Journal,* 1951, **30,** 50-64.   [292-293]

SHAPIRO, M. H. Legislating the control of behavior control: Autonomy and the coercive use of organic therapies. *Southern California Law Review,* 1974, **47,** 237-356.   [652, 674]

SHAPIRO, M. M. Salivary conditioning in dogs during fixed-interval reinforcement contingent upon lever pressing. *JEAB*, 1961, **4**, 361-364. [27]

SHAW, M. Ethical implications of a behavioural approach. In D. Jehn, P. Hardiker, M. Yelloly, & M. Shaw, *Behaviour modification in social work*. London: Wiley, 1972. [667, 670, 671]

SHEPPARD, W. C. & MACDERMOTT, H. G. Design and evaluation of a programmed course in introductory psychology. *JABA*, 1970, **3**, 5-11.
[493-496, 502, 505, 506, 584]

SHERMAN, J. A., SAUNDERS, R. R., & BRIGHAM, T. A. Transfer of matching and mismatching behavior in preschool children. *JECP*, 1970, **9**, 489-498.
[172, 174, 326]

SHERMAN, J. G. (Ed.), *Personalized system of instruction*. Menlo Park, Calif.: Benjamin, 1974. (a) [485-488, 517]

SHERMAN, J. G. PSI: An historical perspective. In J. G. Sherman (Ed.), *Personalized system of instruction*. Menlo Park, Calif.: Benjamin, 1974. (b)
[485, 487, 517]

SHERMAN, J. G. Some permutations on an innovation. In J. G. Sherman (Ed.), *Personalized system of instruction*. Menlo Park, Calif.: Benjamin, 1974. (c)
[487]

SHERMAN, J. G. The theory behind PSI. In J. G. Sherman (Ed.), *Personalized system of instruction*. Menlo Park, Calif.: Benjamin, 1974. (d) [485]

SHIDELER, M., & O'LEARY, K. D. *The effect of periodic quizzes on exam performance and course attitude*. Unpublished manuscript. SUNY—Stony Brook, N.Y., 1974. [196]

SHIPLEY, E. F., SMITH, C. S., & GLEITMAN, L. R. A study in the acquisition of language: Free responses to commands. *Language*, 1969, **45**, 322-342.
[298-299]

SHOEMAKER, D. M. Evaluating the effectiveness of competing instruction programs. *Educational Researcher*, May 1972, 5-8. [492]

SIDMAN, M. Two temporal parameters of the maintenance of avoidance behavior by the white rat. *JCPP*, 1953, **46**, 253-261. [42]

SIDMAN, M. *Tactics of scientific research*. New York: Basic Books, 1960.
[14, 79, 96, 99, 262]

SIDMAN, M., & BOREN, J. J. The relative aversiveness of warning signal and shock in an avoidance situation. *JASP*, 1957, **55**, 339-344. [42]

SIDMAN, M., HERRNSTEIN, R. J., & CONRAD, D. G. Maintenance of avoidance behavior by unavoidable shocks. *JCPP*, 1957, **50**, 553-557. [52]

SIDMAN, M., & STODDARD, L. T. The effectiveness of fading in programming a simultaneous form discrimination for retarded children. *JEAB*, 1967, **10**, 3-15.
[55]

SIDOWSKI, J. B. Reward and punishment in a minimal social situation. *JEP*, 1957, **54**, 318-326. [226-229, 233]

SIDOWSKI, J. B., WYCKOFF, L. B., & TABORY, L. The influence of reinforcement and punishment in a minimal social situation. *JASP*, 1956, **52**, 115-119. [226]

SIEGLER, R. S., & LIEBERT, R. M. Effects of contiguity, regularity, and age on children's causal inferences. *DP*, 1974, **10**, 574-579. [160]

SILBERMAN, C. E. *Crisis in the classroom: The remaking of American education*. New York: Random House, 1970. [542]

SILBERMAN, H. F. Reading and related verbal learning. In R. Glaser (Ed.), *Teaching machines and programmed learning. II. Data and Directions*. Washington, D.C.: National Educational Association, 1965. [462]

SILVERMAN, R. E. *How to write a program*. Carlisle, Mass.: Carlisle, 1970. [473]

SILVERMAN, R. E., & SUMMERS, J. *The reinforcing effects of two types of confirmation in programmed instruction.* Washington, D.C.: U.S. Dept. of Health, Education, and Welfare, Cooperative Research Program of the Office of Education, 1964. [461]

SIQUELAND, E. R., & LIPSITT, L. P. Conditioned head-turning in human newborns. *JECP*, 1966, **3**, 356-376. [32]

SKINRUD, K. Field evaluation of observer bias under overt and covert monitoring. In L. A. Hamerlynck, L. C. Handy, & E. J. Mash (Eds.), *Behavior change: Methodology, concepts, and practice.* Champaign, Ill.: Research Press, 1973. [77]

SKINNER, B. F. *The behavior of organisms.* New York: Appleton-Century-Crofts, 1938. [36, 37, 43, 106, 149, 280, 326, 483, 586, 587]

SKINNER, B. F. "Superstition" in the pigeon. *JEP*, 1948, **38**, 168-172. (a) [25]

SKINNER, B. F. *Walden Two.* New York: Macmillan, 1948. (b) [106, 263, 527, 630]

SKINNER, B. F. Are theories of learning necessary? *P Rev*, 1950, **57**, 193-216. [587] [587]

SKINNER, B. F. *Science and human behavior.* New York: Macmillan, 1953. (a) [2, 36, 106, 199, 263, 268, 270, 280, 382, 587]

SKINNER, B. F. Some contributions of an experimental analysis of behavior to psychology as a whole. *AP*, 1953, **8**, 69-78. (b) [64]

SKINNER, B. F. The science of learning and the art of teaching. *Harvard Educational Review*, 1954, **24**, 86-97. [454-455, 584]

SKINNER, B. F. A case history in scientific method. *AP*, 1956, **11**, 221-233. (a) [262]

SKINNER, B. F. What is psychotic behavior? In F. Gildea (Ed.), *Theory and treatment of the psychoses: Some newer aspects.* Washington University Studies. Seattle: University of Washington Press, 1956. (b) [247]

SKINNER, B. F. *Verbal behavior.* New York: Appleton-Century-Crofts, 1957. [278-281, 284, 300, 301, 306, 308, 319, 519]

SKINNER, B. F. Teaching machines. *Science*, 1958, **128**, 969-977. [454-456, 465, 584]

SKINNER, B. F. Learning theory and future research. In J. P. Lysaught (Ed.), *Programmed learning: Evolving principles and industrial applications.* Ann Arbor, Mich.: Foundation for Research on Human Behavior, 1961. (a) [458, 584]

SKINNER, B. F. Why we need teaching machines. *Harvard Educational Review*, 1961, **31**, 377-398. (b) [458, 460, 469, 584]

SKINNER, B. F. Operant behavior. *AP*, 1963, **18**, 503-515. [61, 95]

SKINNER, B. F. Contingencies of reinforcement in the design of a culture. *Behavioral Science*, 1966, **11**(3), 159-166. (a) [180]

SKINNER, B. F. What is the experimental analysis of behavior? *JEAB*, 1966, **9**, 213-218. (b) [64]

SKINNER, B. F. *The technology of teaching.* New York: Knopf, 1968. [106, 465]

SKINNER, B. F. *Contingencies of reinforcement.* New York: Appleton-Century-Crofts, 1969. [484]

SKINNER, B. F. *Beyond freedom and dignity.* New York: Knopf, 1971. [661-666, 669, 673, 676]

SKINNER, B. F. *About behaviorism.* New York: Knopf, 1974. [263, 280, 282]

SKINNER, B. F. Walden Two revisited. In B. F. Skinner, *Walden Two (new edition).* New York: Macmillan, 1976. [630]

SLAMA-CAZACU, T. Quo vadis, psycholinguistics? Is a "socio-psycholinguistics" necessary? *International Journal of Psycholinguistics*, 1973, **2**, 93-104. [278]

SLAMECKA, N. J. (Ed.), *Human learning and memory.* New York: Oxford University Press, 1967. [287]

SLOANE, H. N., & MACAULAY, B. D. *Operant procedures in remedial speech and language training.* Boston: Houghton Mifflin, 1968.   [174, 317]

SMEDSLUND, J. Concrete reasoning: A study of intellectual development. *Monographs of the Society for Research in Child Development*, 1964, **29**,(2, whole No. 93) 1-39.   [384]

SMEDSLUND, J. Determinants of performance on double classification tasks. I. Effects of covered vs. uncovered materials, labeling vs. perceptual matching, and age. *Scandinavian Journal of Psychology*, 1967, **8**, 88-96. (a)   [384]

SMEDSLUND, J. Determinants of performance on double classification tasks. II. Effects of direct perception and of words with specific, general, and no reference. *Scandinavian Journal of Psychology*, 1967, **8**, 97-101. (b)   [384]

SMITH, F. *Understanding reading: A psycholinguistics analysis of reading and learning to read.* New York: Holt, Rinehart and Winston, 1971.   [414]

SMITH, F., LOTT, D., & CRONNELL, B. The effect of type size and case alternation on word identification. *AJP*, 1969, **82**, 248-253.   [415]

SMITH, J. A. *The relationship between phonemic sensitivity and the effectiveness of phonemic retrieval cues in preliterate children.* Unpublished doctoral dissertation, University of Pennsylvania, 1974.   [434]

SMITH, R. F., GUSTAVSON, C. R., & GREGOR, G. L. Incompatibility between the pigeon's unconditioned response to shock and the conditioned key-peck response. *JEAB*, 1972, **18**, 147-153.   [41]

SNIDER, J. G., & OSGOOD, C. E. (Eds.) *Semantic differential technique.* Chicago: Aldine, 1969.   [289]

SNODGRASS, J. G., VOLVOVITZ, R., & WALFISH, E. R. Recognition memory for words, pictures, and words & pictures. *PS*, 1972, **27**, 345-347.   [301]

SOBELL, M. B., SCHAEFER, H. H., & MILLS, K. C. Differences in baseline drinking behaviors between alcoholics and normal drinkers. *BRT*, 1972, **10**, 257-268.
                                                                                  [273]

SOBELL, M. B., & SOBELL, L. C. Individualized behavior therapy for alcoholics. *BT*, 1973, **4**, 49-72.   [273, 672]

SOLOMON, R. L. Punishment. *AP*, 1964, **19**, 239-253.   [199]

SPECE, R.G., JR. Note: Conditioning and other technologies used to "treat?" "rehabilitate?" "demolish?" prisoners and mental patients. *Southern California Law Review*, 1972, **45**, 616-684.   [653, 674]

SPENCE, K. W. The differential response in animals to stimuli varying within a single dimension. *P Rev*, 1937, **44**, 430-444.   [57]

SPENCE, K. W., MELTON, A. W., & UNDERWOOD, B. J. A symposium: Can the laws of learning be applied in the classroom? *Harvard Educational Review*, 1959, **29**, 83-117.   [482-483]

SPITZ, R. A. Anaclitic depression. In R. S. Eissler, A. Freud, H. Hartmann & M. Kris (Eds.), *The psychoanalytic study of the child.* Vol. 2. New York: International Universities Press, 1946. (a)   [108]

SPITZ, R. A. Hospitalism: A follow-up report. In R. S. Eissler, A. Freud, H. Hartmann & M. Kris (Eds.), *The psychoanalytic study of the child.* Vol. 2. New York: International University Press, 1946. (b)   [108]

SPITZ, R. A. The role of ecological factors in emotional development in infancy. *CD*, 1949, **20**, 145-156.   [108, 110]

SPITZ, R. A. Anxiety in infancy: A study of its manifestations in the first year of life. *International Journal of Psychoanalysis*, 1950, **31**, 138-143.   [117]

SPITZ, R. A. Unhappy and fatal outcomes of emotional deprivation and stress in infancy. In I. Galdston (Ed.), *Beyond the germ theory.* New York: Health Education Council, 1954.   [108]

SPRADLIN, J. E., GIRARDEAU, F. L., & HOM, G. L. Stimulus properties of reinforcement during extinction of a free operant response. *JECP*, 1966, **4**, 369-380.
                                                                                   [27]

STAATS, A. W. Emotions and images in language: A learning analysis of their acquisition and function. In K. Salzinger and S. Salzinger (Eds.), *Research in verbal behavior and some neurophysiological implications*. New York: Academic Press, 1967.   [280, 291]

STAATS, A. W. *Learning, language and cognition*. New York: Holt, Rinehart and Winston, 1968.   [280, 303]

STAATS, A. W., & BUTTERFIELD, W. H. Treatment of non-reading in a culturally deprived juvenile delinquent: An application of reinforcement principles. *CD*, 1965, 36, 925-942.   [535]

STAATS, A. W., & HAMMOND, O. W. Natural words as physiological conditioned stimuli: Food-word-elicited salivation and deprivation effects. *JEP*, 1972, 96, 206-208.   [297]

STAATS, A. W., & STAATS, C. K. *Complex human behavior*. New York: Holt, Rinehart & Winston, 1963.   [291]

STADDON, J. E. R. On the notion of cause, with application to behaviorism. *Behaviorism*, 1973, 1, 25-64.   [248]

STAHL, J. R., THOMSON, L. E., LEITENBERG, H., & HASAZI, J. E. Establishment of praise as a conditioned reinforcer in socially unresponsive psychiatric patients. *JAP*, 1974, 83, 488-496.   [199]

STALLING, R. B. A one-proctor programmed course procedure for introductory psychology. *P Rec*, 1971, 21, 501-505.   [493-496, 499, 505-506, 512]

STALLING, R. B., WARD, T. O., & DUNLOP, T. *Contingency management: Better learning?* Paper presented at the meeting of the American Psychological Association, Honolulu, Hawaii, September, 1972.   [493-496, 499, 505]

STEINER, I. D. Let there be order, please. A review of *The bases of social behavior*. *Contemporary Psychology*, 1973, 18, 14-15.   [208]

STEINMAN, W. M. Generalized imitation and the discrimination hypothesis. *JECP*, 1970, 10, 79-99. (a)   [163, 173]

STEINMAN, W. M. The social control of generalized imitation. *JABA*, 1970, 3, 159-168. (b)   [173]

STEINMAN, W. M., & BOYCE, K. D. Generalized imitation as a function of discrimination difficulty and choice. *JECP*, 1971, 11, 251-265.   [173]

STEVENS, K. N. Segments, features, and analysis by synthesis. In J. F. Kavanagh & I. G. Mattingly (Eds.), *Language by ear and by eye: The relationships between speech and reading*. Cambridge, Mass.: M.I.T. Press, 1972.   [427, 430]

STEVENSON, H. W. Social reinforcement of children's behavior. In L. P. Lipsitt & C. C. Spiker (Eds.), *Advances in child development and behavior. Vol. 2*. New York: Academic Press, 1965.   [106]

STEVENSON, H. W. *Children's learning*. New York: Appleton-Century-Crofts, 1972.   [146]

STODDARD, L. T., & SIDMAN, M. The effects of errors on children's performance on a circle-ellipse discrimination. *JEAB*, 1967, 10, 467-478.   [55]

STOLZ, S. B. Ethical issues in research on behavior therapy. In W. S. Wood (Ed.), *Issues in evaluating behavior modification*. Champaign, Ill.: Research Press, 1975.   [653, 662, 675]

STOLZ, S. B. Ethical issues in behavior modification. In G. Bermant, H. Kelman & D. P. Warwick (Eds.), *Ethics of social intervention*. Washington, D.C.: Hemisphere Publications. (in press)   [667, 672, 673, 675]

STOLZ, S. B. & ASSOCIATES. *Ethical issues in behavior modification: Report of the APA Commission on Behavior Modification*. San Francisco: Jossey-Bass, 1978.   [657]

STOLZ, S. B., WIENCKOWSKY, L. A., & BROWN, B. S. Behavior modification: A perspective on critical issues. *AP*, 1975, 30, 1027-1048.   [658, 667, 672]

STONE, L. J., & CHURCH, J. *Childhood and adolescence. (3rd ed.)* New York: Random House, 1973.   [124]

STUART, R. B. Operant-interpersonal treatment for marital discord. *JCCP*, 1969, **33**, 675-682.   [651]

STUART, R. B. *Trick or treatment*. Champaign, Ill.: Research Press, 1970.   [603]

STUART, R. B., & DAVIS, B. *Slim chance in a fat world: Behavioral control of obesity.* Champaign, Ill,: Research Press, 1972.   [273]

STUBBS, D. A. Second-order schedules and the problem of conditioned reinforcement. *JEAB*, 1971, **16**, 289-313.   [31]

STUDDERT-KENNEDY, M., LIBERMAN, A. M., HARRIS, K. S., & COOPER, F. S. The motor theory of speech perception: A reply to Lane's critical review. *P Rev*, 1970, **77**, 234-249.   [288]

SULLIVAN, A. M. A structured individualized approach to the teaching of introductory psychology. In I. K. Davies & J. Hartley, (Eds.), *Contributions to an educational technology*. London: Butterworths, 1972.   [485, 492]

SULZBACHER, S. I., & HOUSER, J. E. A tactic to eliminate disruptive behaviors in the classroom. *American Journal of Mental Deficiency*, 1968, **1**, 182-187.   [516]

SULZBACHER, S. I., & KIDDER, J. D. Following up on the behavior analysis model: Results after ten years of early intervention with institutionalized, mentally retarded children. In E. Ramp & G. Semb (Eds.), *Behavior analysis: Areas of research and application*. Englewood Cliffs, N.J.: Prentice-Hall, 1975.   [189]

SULZER, B., & MAYER, G. R. *Behavior modification procedures for school personnel.* Hinsdale, Ill.: Dryden, 1972.   [197]

SUPPES, P. The use of computers in education. *Scientific American*, 1966, **215**, 206-223.   [475]

SUPPES, P., & GROEN, G. J. Some counting models for first grade performances on simple addition facts. In J. Scandura (Ed.), *Research in mathematics education*. Washington, D.C.: National Council of Teachers of Mathematics, 1967.   [393]

SURRATT, P. R., ULRICH, R. E., & HAWKINS, R. P. An elementary student as a behavioral engineer. *JABA*, 1969, **2**, 85-92.   [66, 82]

SUTTERER, J. R., & HOLLOWAY, R. E. An analysis of student behavior with and without limiting contingencies. In J. M. Johnston (Ed.), *Behavior research and technology in higher education*. Springfield, Ill.: Charles C Thomas, 1975.
                                                                       [501, 502, 505, 506]

SUTTON-SMITH, B. *Child psychology*. New York: Appleton-Century-Crofts, 1973.
                                                                                   [123]

SZASZ, T. *The manufacture of madness*. New York: Harper & Row, 1970.   [665, 668]

TAFFEL, S. J., & O'LEARY, K. D. Reinforcing math with more math: choosing special academic activities as a reward for academic performance. *JEdP*, 1976, **68**, 579-587.   [206]

TANNER, B. A., & ZEILER, M. Punishment of self-injurious behavior using aromatic ammonia as the aversive stimulus. *JABA*, 1975, **8**, 53-57.   [64]

TARDE, G. *The laws of imitation*. New York: Holt, 1903.   [143]

TAYLOR, J., & ERSPAMER, R. A method for the measurement of cooperative behavior in Albino rats. *P Rec*, 1971, **21**, 121-124.   [216]

TAYLOR, W. L. "Cloze procedure": A new tool for measuring readability. *Journalism Quarterly*, 1953, **30**, 415-433.   [286]

TERMAN, L. W., & MERRILL, M. E. *Measuring intelligence: A guide to the administration of the new revised Stanford-Binet tests of intelligence*. Boston, Mass.: Houghton Mifflin, 1937.   [114]

TERRACE, H. S. Discrimination learning with and without "errors." *JEAB*, 1963, **6**, 1-27.   [55]

TERRACE, H. S. Stimulus control. In W. K. Honig (Ed.), *Operant behavior: Areas of research and application*. New York: Appleton-Century-Crofts, 1966. [57, 161]

THELEN, M. H., & RENNIE, D. L. The effect of vicarious reinforcement on imitation: A review of the literature. In B. A. Maher (Ed.), *Progress in experimental personality research. Vol. 6.* New York: Academic Press, 1972. [165]

THELEN, M. H., & SOLTZ, W. The effect of vicarious reinforcement on imitation in two social-racial groups. *CD,* 1969, **40,** 879-887. [153, 164]

THOMAS, D. L., & MILLER, L. K. *Training writers of instructional packages for the Experimental Living Project: A replication.* Paper presented at the meeting of the American Psychological Association, Chicago, September 1975. [645]

THOMPSON, D. M. Escape from SD associated with fixed-ratio reinforcement. *JEAB,* 1964, **7,** 1-8. [35]

THORESEN, C. E., & MAHONEY, M. H. *Behavioral self-control.* New York: Holt, Rinehart & Winston, 1974. [201]

THORNDIKE, E. L. *Animal intelligence.* New York: Macmillan, 1911.[22, 33, 46, 482]

THORNDIKE, E. L. *The original nature of man. Educational Psychology. Vol. I.* New York: Columbia University Press, 1913. [482-483]

THORNDIKE, E. L. *The psychology of arithmetic.* New York: Macmillan, 1922. [381]

THORNDIKE, E. L. *Education.* New York: Macmillan, 1923. [381, 482, 514]

THORNDIKE, E. L., & LORGE, I. *The teacher's word book of 30,000 words.* New York: Teacher's College Press, 1944. [301]

THURSTONE, L. L., & THURSTONE, T. G. *Factorial studies of intelligence.* Chicago: University of Chicago Press, 1941. [402]

TIMBERS, G. D., TIMBERS, B. J., FIXSEN, D. L., PHILLIPS, E. L., & WOLF, M. M. *Achievement Place for girls: Token reinforcement, social reinforcement, and instructional procedures in a family-style treatment setting for "pre-delinquent" girls.* Paper presented at the meeting of the American Psychological Association, Montreal, 1973. [612, 614]

TOBIAS, S. Effect of creativity, response mode, and subject matter familiarity on achievement from programmed instruction. *JEdP,* 1969, **60,** 453-460. [460]

TOBIAS, S. Review of the response mode issue. *RER,* 1973, **43,** 193-204. [459, 460]

TOBIAS, S., & ABRAMSON, T. Interaction among anxiety, stress, response mode, and familiarity of subject matter on achievement from programmed instruction. *JEdP,* 1971, **62,** 357-364. [460]

TODD, G. A., & PALMER, B. Social reinforcement of infant babbling. *CD,* 1968, **39,** 591-596. [316]

TOFT, R. J. College IV: A new approach. In J. M. Johnston (Ed.), *Behavior research and technology in higher education.* Springfield, Ill.: Charles C Thomas, 1975. [584]

TORREY, J. W. Learning to read without a teacher: A case study. *Elementary English,* 1969, **46,** 550-556. [302]

TOUCHETTE, P. E. The effects of a graduated stimulus change on the acquisition of a simple discrimination in severely retarded boys. *JEAB,* 1968, 11, 39-48. [55]

TRAPOLD, M. A., & OVERMIER, J. B. The second learning process in instrumental learning. In A. H. Black & W. F. Prokasy (Eds.), *Classical conditioning II.* New York: Appleton-Century-Crofts, 1972. [52]

TROTTER, S., & WARREN, J. Behavior modification under fire. *APA Monitor,* 1974, 5(4), 1. [564]

TURKEWITZ, H., O'LEARY, K. D., & IRONSMITH, M. Generalization and maintenance of appropriate behavior through self-control. *JCCP,* 1975, **43,** 557-583. [187, 189, 203]

TURNBOUGH, P. D., BROWN, W. G., FIXSEN, D. L., PHILLIPS, E. L., & WOLF, M. M. *Monitoring youths' and parents' behavior in the natural home.* Paper presented at meeting of the American Psychological Association, Montreal, 1973. [614]

TURNBOUGH, P. D., FIXSEN, D. L., PHILLIPS, E. L., & WOLF, M. M. *Dissemination research: Usefulness ratings of various types of Achievement Place materials.* Unpublished manuscript, University of Kansas—Lawrence, 1973.   [625]

TWARDOSZ, S., & BAER, D. M. Training two severely retarded adolescents to ask questions. *JABA*, 1973, **6**, 655-661.   [342]

UHL, C. H., & GARCIA, E. E. Comparison of omission with extinction in response elimination in rats. *JCPP*, 1969, **69**, 554-562.   [48]

UHL, C. H. & SHERMAN, W. O. Comparison of combinations of omission, punishment, and extinction methods in response elimination in rats. *JCPP*, 1971, **74**, 59-65.   [49]

ULLMANN, L. P., & KRASNER, L. (Eds.) *Case studies in behavior modification.* New York: Holt, Rinehart & Winston, 1965.   ]483, 629]

ULRICH, R. Behavior control and public concern. *P Rec*, 1967, **17**, 229-234.   [676]

ULRICH, R. Toward experimental living, phase II: "Have you ever heard of a man named Frazier, Sir?" In E. Ramp & G. Semb (Eds.), *Behavior analysis: Areas of research and application.* Englewood Cliffs, N.J.: Prentice-Hall, 1975.   [528]

ULRICH, R., & AZRIN, N. H. Reflexive fighting in response to aversive stimulation. *JEAB*, 1962, **5**, 511-520.   [27]

ULRICH, R., STACHNIK, T., & MABRY, J. *Control of human behavior. Vol. II.* Glenview, Ill.: Scott, Foresman, 1970.   [61]

ULRICH, R. WOLFE, M., & BLUHM, M. Operant conditioning in the public schools. In R. Ulrich, T. Stachnik, & J. Mabry (Eds.), *Control of human behavior. Vol. II.* Glenview, Ill.: Scott, Foresman, 1970.   [564]

UNDERWOOD, B. J. Interference and forgetting. *P REV*, 1957, **64**, 49-60. (a)   [302]

UNDERWOOD, B. J. *Psychological research.* New York: Appleton-Century-Crofts, 1957. (b)   [96]

UNDERWOOD, B. J., & SHAUGHNESSY, J. J. *Experimentation in psychology.* New York: Wiley, 1975.   [96]

U.S. CONGRESS, HOUSE COMMITTEE ON THE JUDICIARY, SUBCOMMITTEE ON COURTS, CIVIL LIBERTIES, AND THE ADMINISTRATION OF JUSTICE. *Oversight hearing: Behavior modification programs in the Federal Bureau of Prisons,* 93rd Cong., 2nd sess., February 27, 1974 (Serial No. 26), Washington, D.C.: U.S. Government Printing Office, 1974. (a)   [652, 659]

U.S. CONGRESS, SENATE COMMITTEE ON THE JUDICIARY, SUBCOMMITTEE ON CONSTITUTIONAL RIGHTS. *Individual rights and the Federal role in behavior modification,* 93rd Cong., 2nd sess., November 1974. Washington, D.C.: U.S. Government Printing Office, 1974. (b)   [652, 658-660]

UZGIRIS, I. C., & HUNT, J. McV. *Ordinal scales of infant psychological development.* Six reels: (1) Object permanence; (2) Development of means; (3) Imitation: Gestural and vocal; (4) Operational causality; (5) Object relations in space; (6) Development of schemas. Urbana: University of Illinois Motion Picture Service, 1967.   [114]

VARGAS, E. A., & FRALEY, L. E. Cybernetic instruction. In J. M. Johnston (Ed.), *Behavior research and technology in higher education,* Springfield Ill.: Charles C. Thomas, 1975.   [584, 597]

VERHAVE, T. The functional properties of a time out from an avoidance schedule. *JEAB*, 1962, **5**, 391-422.   [43]

VETTER, H. J., & HOWELL, R. W. Theories of language acquisition. *Journal of Psycholinguistic Research*, 1971, **1**, 31-64.   [313]

VINCE, M. A. Developmental changes in learning capacity. In W. H. Thorpe & O. L. Zangwill (Eds.), *Current problems in animal behaviour.* New York: Cambridge University Press, 1961.   [118]

VOGLER, R. E. Possibility of artifact in studies of cooperation. *P Rep*, 1968, **28**, 9-10.   [218]

VUKELICH, R., & HAKE, D. F. Reduction of dangerously aggressive behavior in a severely retarded resident through a combination of positive reinforcement procedures. *JABA*, 1971, **4**, 215-225. [49]

VUKELICH, R., & HAKE, D. F. Effects of the difference between self and coactor scores upon the audit responses that allow access to these scores. *JEAB*, 1974, **22**, 61-71. [231]

WAHLER, R. G. Infant social development: Some experimental analyses of an infant-mother interaction during the first year of life. *JECP*, 1969, **7**, 101-113. (a) [147]

WAHLER, R. G. Setting generality: Some specific and general effects of child behavior therapy. *JABA*, 1969, **2**, 239-246. (b) [65]

WAHLER, R. G. Some structural aspects of deviant child behavior. *JABA*, 1975, **8**, 27-42. [67, 90]

WAHLER, R. G., & NORDQUIST, V. M. Adult discipline as a factor in childhood imitation. *JACP*, 1973, **1**, 40-56. [177]

WAHLER, R. G., SPERLING, K. A., THOMAS, M. R., TEETER, N. C., & LUPER, H. L. The modification of childhood stuttering: Some response-response relationships. *JECP*, 1970, **9**, 411-428. [67, 90]

WALKER, H. M., & BUCKLEY, N. K. Programming generalization and maintenance of treatment effects across time and across settings. *JABA*, 1972, **5**, 209-224. [190]

WALKER, H. M., & BUCKLEY, N. K. *Token reinforcement techniques*. Eugene, Ore.: Engelmann-Becker Press, 1974. [181-182, 184]

WALKER, W. Notes on native writing systems and the design of native literacy programs. *Anthropological Linguistics*, 1969, **11**, 148-166. [441]

WALLACE, J. G. *The adaptation of instruction to individual differences: An information processing approach*. Paper presented at the meeting of the American Psychological Association, Honolulu, September 1972. [391, 394]

WALTHER, R. E., & CROWDER, N. *A guide to preparing intrinsically programmed instructional materials*. (AMRL-TR-65-43) Wright Patterson Air Force Base, Ohio: Aerospace Medical Research Laboratories, 1965. [466-467, 469]

WANG, M. C. Psychometric studies in the validation of an early learning curriculum. *CD*, 1973, **44**, 54-60. [386, 396]

WANG, M. C., RESNICK, L. B., & BOOZER, R. F. The sequence of development of some early mathematics behaviors. *CD*, 1971, **42**, 1767-1778. [386, 396]

WANG, W. S-Y. The Chinese Language. *Scientific American*, 1973, **228**, 51-60. [424]

WAPNER, S., & CIRILLO, L. Imitation of a model's hand movements: Age changes in transposition of left-right relations. *CD*, 1968, **39**, 887-894. [153]

WAXLER, C. Z., & YARROW, M. R. Factors influencing imitative learning in preschool children. *JECP*, 1970, **9**, 115-130. [173]

WEAVER, F. H., & MILLER, L. K. The effects of a proctor training package on university students' proctoring behaviors. In J. M. Johnston (Ed.), *Behavior research and technology in higher education*. Springfield, Ill.: Charles C Thomas, 1975. [643]

WECHSLER, D. *The measurement and appraisal of adult intelligence*. (4th ed.) Baltimore, Md.: Williams and Wilkins, 1958. [114]

WEINER, H. Some effects of response cost upon human operant behavior. *JEAB*, 1962, **5**, 201-208. [47, 217, 226]

WEINER, H. Controlling human fixed-interval performance. *JEAB*, 1969, **12**, 349-373. [39, 196]

WEINER, H. Instructional control of human operant responding during extinction following fixed-ratio conditioning. *JEAB*, 1970, **13**, 391-394. [44]

WEINER, H. Controlling human fixed interval performance with fixed ratio responding or differential reinforcement of low rate responding in mixed schedules. *PS*, 1972, **26**, 191-192. [197]

WEINGOLD, H. P. & WEBSTER, R. L. Effects of punishment on a cooperative be-
havior in children. *CD*, 1964, **35**, 1211-1216.   [211]
WEINSTOCK, S. Acquisition and extinction of a partially reinforced running response
at a 24-hour intertrial interval. *JEP*, 1958, **56**, 151-158.   [44]
WEIS, L. C. *The dilemma of education-intervention research*. Unpublished manuscript, University of Kansas—Lawrence, 1974.   [544]
WEISBERG, P. Social and nonsocial conditioning of infant vocalizations. *CD*, 1963, **34**,
377-388.   [316]
WEISS, R. F., LOMBARDO, J. P., WARREN, D. R., & KELLEY, K. A. Reinforcing effects
of speaking in reply. *JPSP*, 1971, **20**, 186-199.   [316]
WEPMAN, J. M. *Wepman auditory discrimination test*. Chicago: Language Research
Associates, 1958.   [433]
WERTHEIMER, M. *Productive thinking (1945)*. (Enlarged ed.) New York: Harper &
Row, 1959.   [381, 383, 398, 404]
WEXLER, D. B. Token and taboo: Behavior modification, token economies, and the
law. *California Law Review*, 1973, **61**, 81-109.   [652, 658]
WEXLER, D. B. Behavior modification and legal developments. *American Behavioral
Scientist*, 1975, **18**, 679-684.   [674]
WHEELER, A. J., & SULZER, B. Operant training and generalization of a verbal
response form in a speech-deficient child. *JABA*, 1970, **3**, 139-147.   [321]
WHITE, G. D., NIELSEN, G., & JOHNSON, S. M. Timeout duration and the suppres-
sion of deviant behavior in children. JABA, 1972, **5**, 11-120.   [92, 104]
WHITE, R. W. Learning hierarchies. *RER*, 1973, **43**, 361-375.   [382]
WHITEHURST, C., & WHITEHURST, G. J. Forced excellence versus "free choice" of
grades in undergraduate instruction. In J. M. Johnston (Ed.), *Behavior research
and technology in higher education*. Springfield, Ill.: Charles C Thomas, 1975.
                                                                                         [512-513]
WHITEHURST, G. J. Academic responses and attitudes engendered by a programmed
course in child development. *JABA*, 1972, **5**, 283-291.   [504, 510, 515, 519]
WHITEHURST, G. J. Imitation, response novelty, and language acquisition. In B. C.
Etzel, J. M. LeBlanc, & D. M. Baer (Eds.), *New developments in behavioral
research: Theory, methods, and applications*. Hillsdale, N.J.: Erlbaum As-
sociates, 1977.   [178]
WHITEHURST, G. J., & NOVAK, G. Modeling, imitation training, and the acquisition
of sentence phrases. *JECP*, 1973, **16**, 332-345.   [162, 169-170]
WHITEHURST, G. J., & VASTA, R. Is language acquired through imitation? *Journal of
Psycholinguistic Research*, 1975, **4**, 37-59.   [171]
WHITING, J. W. M. Resource mediation and learning by identification. In I. Iscoe &
H. W. Stevenson (Eds.), *Personality development in children*. Austin: Univer-
sity of Texas Press, 1960.   [139]
WHITMAN, T. L., MERCURIO, J. R., & CAPONIGRI, V. Development of social re-
sponses in two severely retarded children. *JABA*, 1970, **3**, 133-138.   [66]
WILLEMS, E. P. Behavioral technology and behavioral ecology. *JABA*, 1974, **7**, 151-
165.   [548]
WILLIAMS, D. R., & WILLIAMS, H. Automaintenance in the pigeon: Sustained pecking despite contingent nonreinforcement. *JEAB*, 1969, **12**, 511-520.   [29]
WILLIAMS, F. Some preliminaries and prospects. In F. Williams (Ed.), *Language and
poverty*. Chicago: Markham, 1970.   [305, 306]
WILLIAMS, R. L. The combined and differential effects of two types of preparatory
quizzes on college student behaviors. In J. M. Johnston (Ed.), *Behavior research
and technology in higher education*. Springfield, Ill.: Charles C Thomas, 1975.
                                                                                         [509, 515]
WILSON, C. W., & HOPKINS, B. L. The effects of contingent music on the intensity of
noise in junior home economics classes. *JABA*, 1973, **6**, 269-275.   [181]

WINETT, R. A., & WINKLER, R. C. Current behavior modification in the classroom:
    Be still, be quiet, be docile. *JABA*, 1972, **5**, 499-504.
                                          [205, 526-529, 564, 652, 671]
WINOGRAD, E. Escape behavior under different fixed ratios and shock intensities.
    JEAB, 1965, **8**, 117-124.   [41]
WINOGRAD, T. Understanding natural language. *Cog P*, 1972, **3**, 1-191.   [406]
WITTERS, D. R., & KENT, G. W. Teaching without lecturing: Evidence in the case for
    individualized instruction. *P Rec*, 1972, **22**, 169-175.
                                          [491-496, 499, 505, 514, 518]
WODARSKI, J. S., & BUCKHOLDT, D. Behavioral instruction in college classrooms: A
    review of methodological procedures. In J. M. Johnston (Ed.), *Behavior re-
    search and technology in higher education*. Springfield, Ill.: Charles C Thomas,
    1975.   [488, 493, 496]
WOLF, M. M., GILES, D. K., & HALL, R. V. Experiments with token reinforcement
    in a remedial classroom. *BRT*, 1968, **6**, 51-64.   [184, 187]
WOLF, M. M., PHILLIPS, E. L., & FIXSEN, D. L. The teaching-family: A new model
    for the treatment of deviant child behavior in the community. In S. W. Bijou &
    E. L. Ribes-Inesta (Eds.), *Behavior modification*. New York: Academic Press,
    1972.   [625]
WOLF, M. M., & RISLEY, T. R. Reinforcement: Applied research. In R. Glaser (Ed.),
    The nature of reinforcement. New York: Academic Press, 1971.   [89]
WOLFENSBERGER, W. Ethical issues in research with human subjects. *Science*, 1967,
    155, 47-51.   [656, 673, 674]
WOLFENSBERGER, W. The principle of normalization and its implications to psychiat-
    ric service. *American Journal of Psychiatry*, 1970, **3**, 291-296.   [603]
WOLFF, M., & STEIN, A. *Six months later. Study I. A comparison of children who had
    Head Start, Summer, 1965, with their classmates in kindergarten: A case study of
    the kindergartens in four public elementary schools*. A report on the U. S. Office
    of Child Development Project 141-61. New York: Yeshiva University Press,
    1966.   [531]
WOOD, W. S., & WYLIE, R. G. Individualized systems of instruction are better . . .
    for whom? In J. M. Johnston (Ed.), *Behavior research and technology in higher
    education*. Springfield, Ill.: Charles C Thomas, 1975.   [506]
WOODCOCK, R. W. Rebus as a medium in beginning reading instruction. *IMRID
    Papers and Reports*, 1968, **5**, 1-34.   [445]
WOODCOCK, R. W., CLARK, C. R., & DAVIES, C. O. *The Peabody Rebus Reading
    Program*. Circle Pines, Minn.: American Guidance Service, 1968.   [445]
WOODS, S. S., RESNICK, L. B., & GROEN, G. J. An experimental test of five process
    models for subtraction. *JEdP*, 1975, **67**, 17-21.   [391-393, 397]
WORLD MEDICAL ASSOCIATION. Human experimentation: Code of ethics of the
    World Medical Association. *British Medical Journal*, 1964, **2**, 177.   [654]
YALOM, I. D., FIDLER, J. W., FRANK, J., MANN, J., SATA, L., PARLOFF, M., &
    SEASHORE, C. *Encounter groups and psychiatry*. Washington, D.C.: American
    Psychiatric Association, 1970.   [657]
YARROW, L. J. Maternal deprivation: Toward an empirical and conceptual re-
    evaluation. *PB*, 1961, **58**, 459-490.   [108]
YARROW, L. J. The development of focused relationships during infancy. In J.
    Hellmuth (Ed.), *Exceptional infant: The normal infant. Vol. I*. Seattle: Special
    Child Publications, 1967.   [131]
YARROW, L. J. Attachment and dependency: A development perspective. In J. L.
    Gewirtz (Ed.), *Attachment and dependency*. Washington, D.C.: Winston, 1972.
                                          [131]
ZAJONC, R. B. *Social psychology: An experimental approach*. Belmont, Calif.:
    Wadsworth, 1966.   [208, 227]

ZEILER, M. D. Fixed and variable schedules of response-independent reinforcement. *JEAB*, 1968, 11, 405-414.   [25, 48]

ZEILER, M. D. Repeated measurements of reinforcement schedule effects on gradients of stimulus control. *JEAB*, 1969, 12, 451-461.   [56]

ZEILER, M. D. Other behavior: Consequences of reinforcing not responding. *JP*, 1970, 74, 149-155.   [25, 49]

ZEILER, M. D. Eliminating behavior with reinforcement. *JEAB*, 1971, 16, 401-405.
                                                                                    [49]

ZEILER, M. D. Superstitious behavior in children: An experimental analysis. In H. W. Reese (Ed.), *Advances in child development and behavior. Vol. 7.* New York: Academic Press, 1972.   [26]

ZEILER, M. D., & JERVEY, S. S. Development of behavior: Self-feeding. *JCCP*, 1968, 32, 164-168.   [34]

ZEILER, M. D., & KELLEY, C. A. Fixed-ratio and fixed-interval schedules of cartoon presentation. *JECP*, 1969, 8, 306-313.   [42]

ZEIGLER, E., & KANZER, P. The effectiveness of two classes of verbal reinforcers on the performance of middle- and lower-class children. *Journal of Personality*, 1962, 30, 157-163.   [470]

ZIMMERMAN, B. J., & ROSENTHAL, T. L. Observational learning of rule-governed behavior by children. *PB*, 1974, 81, 29-42.   [320]

ZOELLNER, R. A behavioral approach to writing. *College English*, 1969, 30, 267-320.
                                                                        [285-286, 317]

ZUBIN, D. A. *The German case system.* Unpublished Master's Essay, Columbia University, 1972.   [276]

Subject Index